Keenan and Riches'
BUSINESS LAW

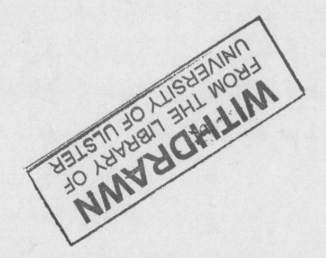

Also available:

Smith and Keenan's
LAW FOR BUSINESS

Smith and Keenan's
ENGLISH LAW
TEXT AND CASES

Smith and Keenan's
COMPANY LAW

Smith and Keenan's
COMPANY LAW
WITH SCOTTISH SUPPLEMENT

Tenth Edition

Keenan and Riches'
BUSINESS LAW

**Sarah Riches and
Vida Allen**

**Longman
is an imprint of**

Harlow, England • London • New York • Boston • San Francisco • Toronto
Sydney • Tokyo • Singapore • Hong Kong • Seoul • Taipei • New Delhi
Cape Town • Madrid • Mexico City • Amsterdam • Munich • Paris • Milan

Pearson Education Limited

Edinburgh Gate
Harlow
Essex CM20 2JE
England

and Associated Companies throughout the world

Visit us on the World Wide Web at:
www.pearsoned.co.uk

First published in Great Britain under the Pitman Publishing imprint in 1987
Second edition published 1990
Third edition published 1993
Fourth edition published 1995
Fifth edition published 1998
Sixth edition published under the Longman imprint in 2002
Seventh edition published 2005
Eighth edition published 2007
Ninth edition published 2009
Tenth edition published 2011

ISBN: 978-1-4082-5419-6

British Library Cataloguing-in-Publication Data
A catalogue record for this book is available from the British Library

Library of Congress Cataloging-in-Publication Data
A catalog record for this book is available from the Library of Congress

10 9 8 7 6 5 4 3 2 1
14 13 12 11

Typeset in 9.5/12pt Minion by 35
Printed by Ashford Colour Press Ltd., Gosport

Brief contents

Contents

Contents

Contents

premium
mylawchamber
unrivalled support for legal education

Your complete learning package

Visit **www.mylawchamber.co.uk/richesallen** to access a wealth of resources to support your studies and teaching.

All our premium sites provide access to **an interactive Pearson eText**, an electronic version of **Keenan and Riches' Business Law** which is fully **searchable**. You can **personalise** your Pearson eText with your own notes and bookmarks and extensive **links are provided to all of the resources** below. The eText page presentation mirrors that of your textbook.

Use the eText to link to **Case Navigator** for help and practise with **case reading and analysis** in **business law**.

In addition access:
- Answers to questions in the book to compare with your own responses
- Legal updates to help you stay up to date with the law and impress examiners

Use the access card at the back of the book to activate mylawchamber premium. Online purchase is also available at **www.mylawchamber.co.uk/register**.

Teaching support materials
- **Case Navigator** is easy to integrate into any course where case reading and analysis skills are required
- The **business law MyTest testbank** can be used to create print tests or to create tests to **download into your learning environment**. It gives you access to a wide variety of questions designed to be used in formal assessments or to check students' progress throughout the course and includes over **900** questions
- **Instructor's Manual** including ideas for seminars and assessment with handouts for use in class

Also: The regularly maintained mylawchamber premium site provides the following features:
- Search tool to help locate specific items of content.
- Online help and support to assist with website usage and troubleshooting.

Use the access card at the back of the book to activate mylawchamber premium. Online purchase is also available at **www.mylawchamber.co.uk/register**.

Case Navigator access is included with your mylawchamber premium registration. The LexisNexis element of Case Navigator is only available to those who currently subscribe to LexisNexis Butterworths online.

Guided tour

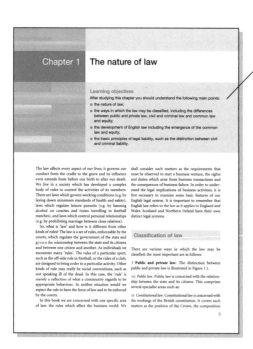

Learning objectives
Located at the start of each chapter the Learning objectives highlight the key points you should understand following your reading of the chapter

Case Summaries
Summaries and commentary of selected cases throughout highlight the key facts, legal principle, and context underlying important cases

Figures and diagrams
Illustrative figures and diagrams can be found throughout chapters as visual aids, strengthening your understanding of complex legal processes and areas in Business Law

Realia

Documents are reproduced throughout to give you a sense of how the law looks and feels in practice, offering you real examples encountered in the business world

Examples

Practical examples in each chapter illustrate the outcomes to possible scenarios, demonstrating how the law operates in the real world

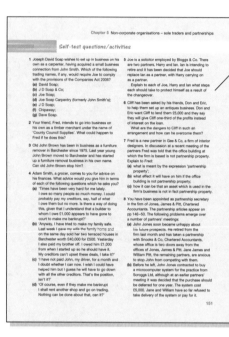

Self-test questions and activities

Located at the end of each chapter, self-test questions allow you to test your understanding of topics following your reading. Answers will be available on the companion website at http://www.mylawchamber.co.uk/richesallen

Specimen examination questions

Located at the end of each chapter, specimen examination questions provide useful examples of the sort of questions you could be faced with in your exams, and can be used to assist you in your exam preparation

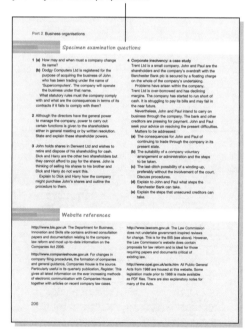

Website references

Annotated web references can be found at the end of each chapter, directing you to useful and relevant resources on the web

Part 2 Business organisations

company secretary, normally after public advertisement of the post. No special qualifications are required for secretaries of private companies where these are appointed but qualifications are laid down for secretaries of public companies. The relevant provisions are now contained in the Companies Act 2006. These are explained in Chapter 6 ⊙.

In the past, trading companies were incorporated by Royal Charter. However, incorporation by registration was set up in 1844 by the Joint Stock Companies Act of that year, and it is most unlikely that incorporation by Royal Charter would be used today to incorporate a commercial business. Charters are still used to incorporate certain organisations, such as professional bodies which control the professions, e.g. the Chartered Institute of Secretaries and Administrators, and for incorporating certain bodies in the public sector, such as the British Broadcasting Corporation.

As to how you get a charter, the organisation wanting one sends what is called a petition to the Privy Council. The Privy Council consists of members of the current Cabinet who become members of the Council when they first take office, former members of the Cabinet, and others appointed by the Queen on the recommendation of the Prime Minister as an honour for service in some branch of public affairs at home or overseas. There are also what are called *conventional members* who become members by reason of holding another office, e.g. the Speaker of the House of Commons. The petition asks for the grant of a charter and sets out the powers required. If the Privy Council considers that it is appropriate to grant a charter, the Crown will be advised to do so.

The public sector

At the end of the Second World War the then Labour government thought it right to bring into the public sector certain organisations providing goods or services to the public on a national basis with a complete or partial monopoly, e.g. the mining of coal. Public corporations were formed to manage these organisations. These organisations have now been returned to the private sector through the medium of public limited companies with shareholders. The commercial public corporations are for all practical purposes non-existent, though an example in the social services area is the Health and Safety Executive set up by the Health and Safety at Work etc. Act 1974 to supervise and enforce health and safety through inspectors (see further, Chapter 16 ⊙).

76

Natural and juristic persons

Natural persons

These are human beings who are known to the law as natural persons. An adult human being has in general terms the full range of legal rights and a full range of legal duties. Thus, if A makes a contract with B and B fails to perform it, A has a right, e.g. to damages, because B failed to perform a duty. A similar situation would occur if A failed in his duty to perform the contract, thus denying B his right to have it performed.

However, the law distinguishes between certain classes of human beings and gives them a status, which means that they have more limited rights and duties than are given to other persons. Examples are minors (persons under the age of 18) and persons who lack mental capacity.

Some contracts of minors are not binding on them and they cannot be sued for damages for breach of contract if they fail to perform them. As regards persons who allegedly lack mental capacity, the Mental Capacity Act 2005 provides that a person is assumed to have mental capacity, e.g. to make the contract in question, unless either party can prove to the contrary. If it is shown that there is insufficient mental capacity then the contract is not binding on either party. The Act contains provisions relating to payment for necessary goods, e.g. food and clothing and services, where these have been supplied and delivered to the person who lacks mental capacity. These matters are more fully dealt with in Chapter 7 ⊙.

Non-human creatures are not legal persons and do not have those rights and duties which a human being gets at birth. However, animals may be protected by the law for certain purposes, such as conservation. For example, s 9 of the Wildlife and Countryside Act 1981 protects certain wild animals by making it a criminal offence for a person intentionally to kill, injure or take any animal included in Sch 5 to that Act, e.g. bats.

The Animal Welfare Act 2006 is also relevant and is concerned, e.g. with trade in exotic animals where standards of animal care are often poor. It also has a wider impact on animal care in, e.g. pet shops and pet fairs where standards of care are too often wholly inadequate. There is also the Hunting Act 2004 which in general prohibits the use of dogs to hunt wild animals in England and Wales.

Chapter cross-references

Clear in-text cross-references come in handy to help you identify where to discover more information on key topics.

premium
mylawchamber
controlled support for legal education

Your complete learning package

Visit **www.mylawchamber.co.uk/richesallen** to access an **interactive Pearson eText**, an electronic version of **Keenan and Riches' Business Law** which is fully **searchable**. You can **personalise** your Pearson eText with your **own notes and bookmark** and extensive **links are provided to all of the self-study resources**:

- Case Navigator to help improve your case reading and analysis skills
- Answers to questions in the book to compare with your own responses
- Legal updates to help you stay up to date with the law and impress examiners

Preface

This book is designed for students studying Business Law at a variety of levels as part of a more general Business Studies course.

We have assumed that the reader has no previous knowledge of English law; our starting point is basic principles and, when specialist legal terms are used, we have given clear 'jargon free' explanations. The book is designed to give the reader an understanding of the changing legal framework within which modern business organisations must operate. The emphasis is on law in its business context. Thus a range of business documents has been included, enabling the reader to relate the principles of business law to the real world of business.

In this connection our thanks go to the Consumer Credit Trade Association, the Road Haulage Association and HMSO for giving us their kind permission to reproduce certain of these documents. The reader should appreciate that the versions of these documents and forms appearing in our text are reduced in size, and also that copyright in them must be respected. This extends also to any alterations or variations in them without the authorisation of the owner of the copyright.

The teaching and learning strategies for higher level courses stress the development of a variety of learning activities, with students increasingly taking greater responsibility for their own learning. At the end of each chapter we have provided a selection of self-test questions and activities related specifically to the material introduced in that chapter and a number of specimen examination questions. There is a companion website for the book at **www.mylawchamber.co.uk/richesallen**, which features regular updates on the law so that lecturers and students will remain up to date with new legislative and case developments. The website also provides selected outline answers to the self-test questions in the book. Lecturers who adopt the book can also access masters of diagrams and forms in the book and outline answers to the specimen examination questions.

The rate of legal change has continued apace since the last edition. The text has been thoroughly updated to incorporate changes in business law and in response to feedback from practitioners, especially the following:

- A new chapter devoted to agency.
- Expansion of the section on mistake.
- Changes to the Consumer Credit Act following implementation of the EU Consumer Credit Directive.
- Reorganisation of Part 3 on Business Transactions.

We have used the terminology introduced by Lord Woolf's civil justice reforms throughout the text. For example, we have used the term 'claimant' for all cases to describe the person with a complaint, even though the person was described as 'plaintiff' before the changes in civil procedure on 26 April 1999.

We wish to thank Mary Keenan for her continued support for *Business Law*. Sarah Riches extends her thanks to Ciaran and Brian McCaughey and Vida Allen would like to express sincere thanks to her family for their support.

Our thanks go to those who were closely involved with this edition, in particular Zoë Botterill, Owen Knight Gabriella Playford, Tim Parker and other members of staff at Pearson Education. Our thanks also go to those who set, printed and bound the book. For errors and omissions we are, of course, solely responsible.

Sarah Riches
Vida Allen

Legal study skills

Business Law is designed to provide a clear, easy to understand text for those who are new to the study of law or who may be studying law as part of a more general business course. We recognise that embarking on legal study for the first time may be a frightening prospect, but if you read this section before starting your studies you may find things a little easier. We have five useful study skills tips for success in law. Some of the tips covered in this section relate specifically to the study of law, but others can be applied to a range of subjects. We can't guarantee success if you follow the tips – that's largely up to the amount of effort you put into your studies – but we believe that if you adopt a few of our suggestions you will find studying law easier and possibly even enjoyable.

Study skills tips

1 Find out what is on the syllabus for your business law module or unit. A syllabus is a statement about a course of study. It usually includes an outline of the topics to be covered in the course, the learning objectives, the methods of assessment and an indicative reading list. Business law is a general title for a wide range of modules and units which cover the law relating to business. We have tried to cover many of the topics covered in 'Business Law' courses in our textbook but there are some topics which we cover in outline only (e.g. some torts such as defamation) or do not cover at all (e.g. the law of international trade). Our focus is on the introductory aspects of English law and the English legal system; the law relating to business organisations, namely sole traders, partnerships and companies; legal aspects of business transactions, covering contract, tort, sale and supply of goods and consumer law; the law relating to business resources, including an outline of the law governing the use of business property and employment law.

At the start of each chapter we have set out the learning objectives of that chapter. A learning objective is a statement of what you should understand when you have completed the chapter. You may find it useful to match the learning objectives of each chapter against the syllabus for your business law course. This will help you to identify and concentrate your efforts on the sections of *Business Law* which are directly relevant to your course of study.

2 Make the most of the contact time with your tutor. The learning time for a module or unit can be divided up into time where you have **direct contact with a tutor**, either in the form of lectures, seminars and tutorials, and **personal study time**, which can be used to prepare for classes, read more widely on a topic, complete assessments or prepare for exams. Although the balance between tutor-led and personal study may vary considerably depending on the level and method of delivery, it is important to understand that both kinds of learning are crucial for success.

Let's explore these different learning methods in more detail.

(a) *Tutor-led learning*: formal contact time with your tutor will probably be divided up into:

- *Lectures*: in which your tutor takes the lead in introducing a topic, outlining the main legal principles and their source, e.g. legislation, case law. You will be expected to take notes of what your tutor says and you should try to develop a system of abbreviating key words and phrases to save you time, e.g. cl for 'claimant' or def for 'defendant'.
- *Seminars*: although still tutor-led, you are expected to play a much more active role in proceedings. They are designed to increase your understanding of a topic by setting you tasks or questions which you must research in advance. The seminar may take the form of a group discussion led by your tutor on pre-prepared questions or you may be asked to present a topic and lead the resulting discussion. You will get the most out of this kind of learning if you prepare the topic thoroughly by reading over your lecture notes, reviewing the relevant chapter of your textbook and researching primary and secondary sources of information. (A primary source of information is

an Act of Parliament or a decided case; a secondary source of information is a textbook or journal articles.)

- *Tutorials*: you may get an opportunity for a one-to-one discussion with your tutor, either to discuss your general progress or perhaps to get feedback on assessed work. Make the most of any tutorial sessions offered, particularly if you are having difficulty understanding any aspects of a topic. Your tutor may be able to explain the concept or principle in a different way or may be able to direct you to other texts or sources of information.

(b) *Personal study time*: your tutor should advise you about the amount of time you need to spend outside class time for personal study. This time can be used for preparing for:

- lectures, by reading in advance the chapter in your textbook or other materials provided by your tutor on the topic in question;
- seminars, by reading about the topic in more depth or exploring related topics, or by preparing answers to problem questions;
- assessment, by researching primary and secondary sources of information, to help you develop your answer for an assignment, or by revising topics for examinations.

It is better to set aside a regular amount of time each week for personal study rather than trying to make up for lost time just before an assessment.

3 **Prepare for assessment.** Assessment of business law modules or units may either be in the form of in-course assignments or examinations. Whatever the method of assessment, there are some simple rules to remember.

- In the case of assessment by examination, get hold of copies of past papers to give you an idea of the format of the examination and the type of questions you will face. Check with your tutor that the past papers are a reasonable guide to the kind of examination that you will sit. Find out whether the examiners have published reports on the previous papers. ILEX, for example, publishes answers to their exams and examiners' reports. Using the past papers, practise answering questions under exam conditions.
- If you are sitting an exam, check in advance what materials you can bring into the exam room. You may be able to bring, for example, a copy of a statute book into the exam room. If this is the case it is best

to get hold of a copy in good time and become familiar with the content.

- Read the instructions very carefully. If in an exam you are asked to answer **three** questions including **one** from Section A and **one** from Section B, and you answer **four** questions from Section A, you will only receive marks for two of your answers. Similarly, if an assignment brief asks you to write no more than 2,000 words, and you submit a 'brilliant' answer but in 4,000 words, you should not be surprised if you are penalised. If you are asked to write a report or draft a letter, then it is likely that there will be marks allocated for setting your answer out in the requested format.
- Work out how much time you have to complete the assessment. If you are given a number of weeks to complete an in-course assessment, don't wait until the last minute to start work on your submission. You will need to do some background research and time to absorb the information and understand how to apply it to the assignment brief. You may need to work on several drafts of your answer before you hand it in. In an exam, you should work out how much time you can afford to spend on each question and leave some time at the end to read through your answer. Try to stick to the time you've allocated yourself otherwise you may find you've run out of time and cannot do justice to each of the questions.
- Read the question slowly and carefully. Identify the key elements of the question and make brief notes on what you know about the topic, e.g. main principles of law, legislation and cases. Prepare a plan for answering the question, marshalling your notes in a logical order. You should include an introduction, a paragraph for each main issue you intend to discuss, and finish with a conclusion.
- Find out the criteria by which you will be assessed. In other words, do you know what the person marking your work is looking for? Although it is difficult to generalise, the following criteria are likely to be included:
  - Identification of the main issues or problems raised by the question/task.
  - Description of the main principles of law which apply to the issue or problem, including the definition of key concepts.
  - Authority for the legal principles, e.g. legislation, case law, delegated legislation. (You should not recite the facts of the cases you are using as authority, unless the facts are directly relevant to the issue or problem you are analysing. The marker

is more interested in your understanding of the legal principles established by the case you have cited than your knowledge of the facts.)

- Analysis of the issue or the problem. This is your opportunity to show off the results of your research to demonstrate that you have acquired a thorough understanding of the topic. But make sure you do not stray off the point of the question.

- Application of the legal principles to the problem or issue, so as to reach a conclusion or recommendation. It is more important to explain to the person marking your work how you arrived at your conclusion rather than the conclusion itself.

■ Ensure you understand the academic rules and conventions which apply in particular to in-course assessments. You should always include a bibliography which records all the sources of information you used to complete your assignment. It is also good practice to list separately the Acts of Parliament, statutory instruments and cases you have referred to in your answer. The main body of your answer should include clear references to and acknowledgements of the sources of information you have used. There are two main systems of referencing: the numeric or footnote system and the Harvard or author/date system. You should check with your tutor which system they would prefer you to use.

■ Obtain feedback from your tutor after your work has been assessed. Your tutor may provide you with written or oral feedback on the strengths and weaknesses of your work. You should make use of your tutor's comments to help you improve your performance for the next assessment.

4 Make good use of the learning resources available to you. There will be a wide range of resources to assist your studies. They include:

■ Your tutor's lectures and notes.
■ Your recommended textbook.
■ Other textbooks, either on business law, or on specific aspects of business law such as contract or company law.
■ Journals, which may have articles on new developments in the law or an in-depth analysis of a particular issue.
■ Electronic resources, e.g. legal databases such as LexisNexis and LAWTEL, CD-ROMs and the World Wide Web. We have included references to helpful websites at the end of each chapter. You should be careful to confine your searches to English law, unless you have been specifically asked to research the international dimension of a topic.
■ Your own notes on the topics covered in lectures and seminars.

The volume of information now available especially since the advent of the World Wide Web can seem quite overwhelming. Seek advice from your tutor or from your librarian about how to make best use of the resources available for your module or unit.

5 Try to keep up to date. One of the themes of our book is that the law is always changing. There is a constant stream of legislation being enacted by Parliament and cases being decided by the courts. You can help keep yourself up to date by reading a quality newspaper, most of which have (weekly) law and (daily) business sections, and by listening to news features on the TV or radio. Our companion website for the book at **www.mylawchamber.co.uk/richesallen** features regular updates to the law so that you can remain up to date with new legislation and developments in case law.

Case names, citations and law report abbreviations

Case names

Every case which comes before a court is given a name, based on the names of the parties.

1 Civil cases. An example of a case name in a civil action would be *Carlill* (the claimant or plaintiff) **v** *Carbolic Smoke Ball Co* (the defendant). The 'v' is an abbreviation of 'versus' but if you are talking about the case (rather than writing about it), you would say 'Carlill and [the] Carbolic Smoke Ball Company' or, if it is a well-known case, 'Carlill's case'. If the case is appealed, then the name of the appellant (the person bringing the appeal) will come first. There are some variations from the general principle of naming civil cases. For example, in judicial review cases the interests of the state in the proceedings are reflected in the title, e.g. *R* **v** *Secretary of State for Employment, ex parte the Equal Opportunities Commission*. 'R' stands for Regina, Latin for the Queen (or Rex if there is a King on the throne) and 'ex parte' means 'by or for one party'. In family or probate cases the case name will usually consist of the family name: for example, *Re McArdle* or *In re McArdle*. 'Re' means 'in the matter of'. If the case involves a ship, then it is usually known by the name of the vessel: for example, *The Moorcock*.

2 Criminal cases. In criminal cases proceedings are brought in the name of the Crown and this is reflected in the name of the case: for example, *R* (the prosecutor) **v** *Brown* (the accused or defendant). 'R' stands for Regina, the Queen, or Rex, the King. If you were speaking about the case you would refer to it as 'The Crown against Brown' or simply 'Brown'. Sometimes the cases will be brought by the Law Officers (the Attorney-General and Solicitor General) or the Director of Public Prosecutions, and this will be reflected in the name of the case: for example, *A-G* **v** *Brown* or *DPP* **v** *Brown*.

When you are referring to cases in your written work you should make the case name stand out by using underlining, bold or, as we have done in this textbook, putting the name in **bold italics**.

Citations

When we have referred to cases in the main body of the text we have just used the case name and the date of the case. If you look at the Table of cases, you will see that in addition to the case name we have also given you a law report reference which will enable you to read the full report of the case. These references are known as case citations. The box below explains the different elements of the citation for *Lewis* **v** *Averay* [1971] 3 All ER 907.

Lewis	The family name of the claimant or plaintiff.
v	versus
Averay	The family name of the defendant.
[1971]	The year will be enclosed in square brackets if it is necessary for finding the case. So in this example the case is reported in the All England Law Reports for 1971. If the report series is not collected in years but is numbered sequentially, the year is given in round brackets as additional information.
3	The volume number. Some law reports may have two or more volumes each year.
All ER	This is the abbreviation for the All England Law Reports. Other abbreviations are given below.
907	The page number where the report of the case starts.

The increased availability of case reports via the Internet has led to the introduction of a neutral citation system for England and Wales and the United Kingdom.

The formats for neutral citations are:

- Court of Appeal – year, court, division, case number: e.g. [2006] EWCA Civ 13.

- High Court – year, court, case number, division: e.g. [2006] EWHC 13 (Ch). A unique case number is allocated to each case. There are no page numbers but paragraph numbers are used instead to help the reader locate a section of the judgment more precisely. A paragraph reference is cited as *Jones v Brown* [2006] EWCA Civ 13 at [45]. The abbreviations for neutral citation are as follows:

UKHL	House of Lords (from 2001–2009)
UKSC	Supreme Court (from 2009)
UKPC	Judicial Committee of the Privy Council
EWCA Civ	Court of Appeal Civil Division
EWCA Crim	Court of Appeal Criminal Division
EWHC (Admin)	High Court (Administrative Court)
EWHC (Admlty)	High Court (Admiralty Court)
EWHC (Ch)	High Court (Chancery Division)
EWHC (Comm)	High Court (Commercial Court)
EWHC (Fam)	High Court (Family Division)
EWHC (QB)	High Court (Queen's Bench Division)
EWHC (Pat)	High Court (Patents Court)
EWHC (TCC)	High Court (Technology and Construction Court)

Law report abbreviations

The following sets out the abbreviations used when citing the various series of certain law reports which are in common use, together with the periods over which they extend:

AC	Law Reports, Appeal Cases 1891–(current)
ATC	Annotated Tax Cases 1922–1975
All ER	All England Law Reports 1936–(current)
All ER Rep	All England Law Reports Reprint, 36 vols 1558–1935
App Cas	Law Reports, Appeal Cases, 15 vols 1875–1890
BCLC	Butterworths Company Law Cases 1983–(current)
B & CR	Reports of Bankruptcy and Companies Winding-up Cases 1918–(current)
CLY	Current Law Yearbook 1947–(current)
CMLR	Common Market Law Reports 1962–(current)
Ch	Law Reports Chancery Division 1891–(current)
Com Cas	Commercial Cases 1895–1941
Fam	Law Reports Family Division 1972–(current)
ICR	Industrial Court Reports 1972–1974; Industrial Cases Reports 1974–(current)
IRLB	Industrial Relations Law Bulletin 1993–(current)
IRLR	Industrial Relations Law Reports 1971–(current)
ITR	Reports of decisions of the Industrial Tribunals 1966–(current)
KB	Law Reports, King's Bench Division 1901–1952
LGR	Local Government Reports 1902–(current)

LRRP	Law Reports Restrictive Practices 1957–(current)
Lloyd LR *or*	Lloyd's List Law Reports 1919–(current)
Lloyd's Rep (from 1951)	
NLJ	New Law Journal
P	Law Reports, Probate, Divorce and Admiralty Division 1891–1971
P & CR	Planning and Compensation Reports 1949–(current)
PIQR	Personal Injuries and Quantum Reports
QB	Law Reports Queen's Bench Division 1891–1901; 1953–(current)
STC	Simon's Tax Cases 1973–(current)
Sol Jo	Solicitors' Journal 1856–(current)
Tax Cas (or TC)	Tax Cases 1875–(current)
WLR	Weekly Law Reports 1953–(current)

Acknowledgements

We are grateful to the following for permission to reproduce copyright material:

Figures

Figure 8.4 from the Road Haulage Association Ltd, by permission of the Road Haulage Association Ltd;

Figures 13.1, 13.3 and 13.4 from the Consumer Credit Trade Association, by kind permission of the Consumer Credit Trade Association.

In some instances we have been unable to trace the owners of copyright material, and we would appreciate any information that would enable us to do so.

Table of cases

Visit **www.mylawchamber.co.uk/richesallen** to access unique online support to improve your case reading and analysis skills.

Case Navigator cases are highlighted **with a symbol** in the margin

Case Navigator provides:
- **Direct deep links** to the core cases in **business law**.
- **Short introductions** provide guidance on what you should look out for while reading the case.
- **Questions** help you to test your understanding of the case, and provide feedback on what you should have grasped.
- **Summaries** contextualise the case and point you to further reading so that you are fully prepared for seminars and discussions.

Please note that access to Case Navigator is free with the purchase of this book, but you must register with us for access. Full registration instructions are available on the website. The LexisNexis element of Case Navigator is only available to those who currently subscribe to LexisNexis Butterworths online.

Table of cases

Table of statutes

Table of statutes

Table of statutory instruments

Table of statutory instruments

Table of European and other legislation

Part 1 INTRODUCTION TO LAW

Chapter 1   The nature of law

Learning objectives

After studying this chapter you should understand the following main points:

- the nature of law;
- the ways in which the law may be classified, including the differences between public and private law, civil and criminal law and common law and equity;
- the development of English law including the emergence of the common law and equity;
- the basic principles of legal liability, such as the distinction between civil and criminal liability.

The law affects every aspect of our lives; it governs our conduct from the cradle to the grave and its influence even extends from before our birth to after our death. We live in a society which has developed a complex body of rules to control the activities of its members. There are laws which govern working conditions (e.g. by laying down minimum standards of health and safety), laws which regulate leisure pursuits (e.g. by banning alcohol on coaches and trains travelling to football matches), and laws which control personal relationships (e.g. by prohibiting marriage between close relatives).

So, what is 'law' and how is it different from other kinds of rules? The law is a set of rules, enforceable by the courts, which regulate the government of the state and govern the relationship between the state and its citizens and between one citizen and another. As individuals we encounter many 'rules'. The rules of a particular sport, such as the off-side rule in football, or the rules of a club, are designed to bring order to a particular activity. Other kinds of rule may really be social conventions, such as not speaking ill of the dead. In this case, the 'rule' is merely a reflection of what a community regards to be appropriate behaviour. In neither situation would we expect the rule to have the force of law and to be enforced by the courts.

In this book we are concerned with one specific area of law: the rules which affect the business world. We shall consider such matters as the requirements that must be observed to start a business venture, the rights and duties which arise from business transactions and the consequences of business failure. In order to understand the legal implications of business activities, it is first necessary to examine some basic features of our English legal system. It is important to remember that English law refers to the law as it applies to England and Wales. Scotland and Northern Ireland have their own distinct legal systems.

Classification of law

There are various ways in which the law may be classified; the most important are as follows:

1 Public and private law. The distinction between public and private law is illustrated in Figure 1.1.

(a) *Public law.* Public law is concerned with the relationship between the state and its citizens. This comprises several specialist areas such as:

(i) *Constitutional law.* Constitutional law is concerned with the workings of the British constitution. It covers such matters as the position of the Crown, the composition

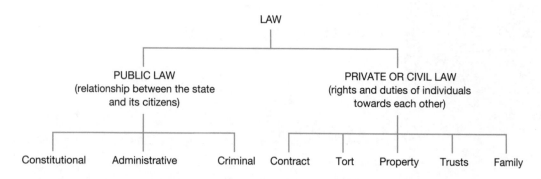

Figure 1.1 **The distinction between public and private law**

and procedures of Parliament, the functioning of central and local government, citizenship and the civil liberties of individual citizens.

(ii) *Administrative law.* There has been a dramatic increase in the activities of government during the last hundred years. Schemes have been introduced to help ensure a minimum standard of living for everybody. Government agencies are involved, for example, in the provision of a state retirement pension, income support and child benefit. A large number of disputes arise from the administration of these schemes and a body of law, administrative law, has developed to deal with the complaints of individuals against the decisions of the administering agency.

(iii) *Criminal law.* Certain kinds of wrongdoing pose such a serious threat to the good order of society that they are considered crimes against the whole community. The criminal law makes such anti-social behaviour an offence against the state and offenders are liable to punishment. The state accepts responsibility for the detection, prosecution and punishment of offenders.

(b) *Private law.* Private law is primarily concerned with the rights and duties of individuals towards each other. The state's involvement in this area of law is confined to providing a civilised method of resolving the dispute that has arisen. Thus, the legal process is begun by the aggrieved citizen and not by the state. Private law is also called civil law and is often contrasted with criminal law.

2 **Criminal and civil law.** Legal rules are generally divided into two categories: criminal and civil. It is important to understand the nature of the division because there are fundamental differences in the purpose, procedures and terminology of each branch of law.

(a) *Criminal law.* The criminal law is concerned with forbidding certain forms of wrongful conduct and punishing those who engage in the prohibited acts. Criminal proceedings are normally brought in the name of the Crown and are called prosecutions. In 1985 responsibility for the process of prosecution passed from the police to a newly created independent Crown Prosecution Service under the direction of the Director of Public Prosecutions (Prosecution of Offences Act 1985). It should be noted that prosecutions may also be undertaken by bodies, such as the trading standards department of the local authority, and by private individuals, e.g. a store detective prosecuting a shoplifter. In criminal cases you have a prosecutor who prosecutes a defendant in the criminal courts. The consequences of being found guilty are so serious that the standard of proof is higher than in civil cases: the allegations of criminal conduct must be proved beyond a reasonable doubt. If the prosecution is successful, the defendant is found guilty (convicted) and may be punished by the courts. The Criminal Justice Act 2003 sets out for the first time in legislation the purposes of sentencing adult offenders, which are punishment, crime reduction, the reform and rehabilitation of offenders, and reparation. Punishments available to the court include imprisonment, fines, or community orders such as an unpaid work requirement. If the prosecution is unsuccessful, the defendant is found not guilty (acquitted). A businessperson may find themselves in breach of the criminal law under such enactments as the Companies Act 2006, the Consumer Protection from Unfair Trading Regulations 2008 and the Health and Safety at Work etc. Act 1974.

(b) *Civil law.* The civil law deals with the private rights and obligations which arise between individuals. The

	Criminal law	Civil law
Concerns	Offences against the state	Disputes between private individuals
Purpose of the action	To preserve order in the community by punishing offenders and deterring others	To remedy the wrong which has been suffered
The parties	A prosecutor prosecutes a defendant Prosecutions are brought in the name of the Crown, signified by R for Rex (King) or Regina (Queen) Case title: *R v Smith*	A claimant sues a defendant Case title: *Jones v Patel*
Where the action is heard	The criminal courts, i.e. magistrates' court or Crown Court	The civil courts, i.e. county court or High Court
Standard and burden of proof	The prosecutor must prove his case beyond a reasonable doubt	The claimant must establish his case on the balance of probabilities
Decision	A defendant may be convicted if he is guilty and acquitted if he is innocent	A defendant may be found liable or not liable
Sanctions	Imprisonment, fine, community order	Damages, injunction, specific performance, rescission
Examples	Murder, theft, driving with excess alcohol, engaging in an unfair commercial practice	Contract, tort, trusts, property law

Figure 1.2 The differences between criminal and civil law

purpose of the action is to remedy the wrong that has been suffered. Enforcement of the civil law is the responsibility of the individual who has been wronged; the state's role is to provide the procedure and the courts necessary to resolve the dispute. In civil proceedings a claimant sues a defendant in the civil courts. The claimant will be successful if he can prove his case on the balance of probabilities, i.e. the evidence weighs more in favour of the claimant than the defendant. If the claimant wins his action, the defendant is said to be liable and the court will order an appropriate remedy, such as damages (financial compensation) or an injunction (an order to do or not do something). If the claimant is not successful, the defendant is found not liable. Many of the laws affecting the businessperson are part of the civil law, especially contract, tort and property law. The main differences between civil and criminal law are illustrated in Figure 1.2.

The distinction between the criminal and civil law does not depend on the nature of the wrongful act, because the same act may give rise to both civil and criminal proceedings. Consider the consequences of a typical motor accident. Julie is crossing the road at a zebra crossing when she is struck by a car driven by Gordon. An ambulance takes Julie to a local hospital where it is discovered that she has sustained a broken leg. Meanwhile, the police have arrived at the scene of the accident and they breathalyse Gordon. The result is positive and Gordon is charged with a criminal offence based on driving with excess alcohol. He appears before the local magistrates' court and is convicted. He is disqualified from driving for 18 months and fined £400. The fine is paid to the court: it does not go to compensate the victim of the criminal act. However, a criminal court now has a limited power to order an offender to pay compensation for any 'personal injury, loss or damage' caused to the victim of his offence (under s 130 of the Powers of Criminal Courts (Sentencing) Act 2000). Julie must pursue a separate civil action against Gordon to remedy the personal wrong she has suffered. She sues Gordon in the tort of negligence, seeking damages for the injuries she has sustained. The case is heard in the county court where Gordon is found liable. He is ordered to pay £6,000 in damages. Normally, the loser in a civil action pays the winner's costs. So Gordon is ordered to pay Julie's costs in bringing the action.

3 **Common law and equity.** Legal rules may also be classified according to whether they form part of the common law or equity. The distinction between these two systems of law is rooted in history and can only be understood properly by examining the origins of English law. English legal development can be traced back to 1066 when William of Normandy gained the crown of England by defeating King Harold at the Battle of Hastings. Before the arrival of the Normans in 1066 there really was no such thing as English law. The Anglo-Saxon legal system was based on the local community. Each area had its own courts in which local customs were applied. The Norman Conquest did not have an immediate effect on English law; indeed, William promised the English that they could keep their customary laws. The Normans were great administrators and they soon embarked on a process of centralisation, which created the right climate for the evolution of a uniform system of law for the whole country.

The common law

The Norman kings ruled with the help of the most important and powerful men in the land who formed a body known as the Curia Regis (King's Council). This assembly carried out a number of functions: it acted as a primitive legislature, performed administrative tasks and exercised certain judicial powers. The meetings of the Curia Regis came to be of two types: occasional assemblies attended by the barons and more frequent but smaller meetings of royal officials. These officials began to specialise in certain types of work and departments were formed. This trend eventually led to the development of courts to hear cases of a particular kind. The courts which had emerged by the end of the 13th century became known as the Courts of Common Law

and they sat at Westminster. The first to appear was the Court of Exchequer. It dealt with taxation disputes but later extended its jurisdiction to other civil cases. The Court of Common Pleas was the next court to be established. It heard disputes of a civil nature between one citizen and another. The Court of King's Bench, the last court to appear, became the most important of the three courts because of its close association with the king. Its jurisdiction included civil and criminal cases and it developed a supervisory function over the activities of inferior courts.

The Normans exercised central control by sending representatives of the king from Westminster to all parts of the country to check up on the local administration. At first these royal commissioners performed a number of tasks: they made records of land and wealth, collected taxes and adjudicated in disputes brought before them. Their judicial powers gradually became more important than their other functions. To begin with, these commissioners (or justices) applied local customary law at the hearings, but in time local customs were replaced by a body of rules applying to the whole country.

When they had completed their travels round the country, the justices returned to Westminster where they discussed the customs they had encountered. By a gradual process of sifting these customs, rejecting those which were unreasonable and accepting those which were not, they formed a uniform pattern of law throughout England. Thus, by selecting certain customs and applying them in all future similar cases, the common law of England was created.

A civil action at common law was begun with the issue of a writ which was purchased from the offices of the Chancery, a department of the Curia Regis under the control of the Chancellor. Different kinds of action were covered by different writs. The procedural rules and type of trial varied with the nature of the writ. It was essential that the correct writ was chosen, otherwise the claimant would not be allowed to proceed with his action.

Equity

Over a period of time the common law became a very rigid system of law and in many cases it was impossible to obtain justice from the courts. The main defects of the common law were as follows:

- The common law failed to keep pace with the needs of an increasingly complex society. The writ system was slow to respond to new types of action. If a suitable writ was not available, an injured party could not obtain a remedy, no matter how just his claim.
- The writ system was very complicated, but trivial mistakes could defeat a claim.
- The only remedy available in the common law courts was an award of damages. This was not always a suitable or adequate remedy.
- Men of wealth and power could overawe a court, and there were complaints of bribery and intimidation of jurors.

It became the practice of aggrieved citizens to petition the king for assistance. As the volume of petitions increased, the king passed them to the Curia Regis and a committee was set up to hear the petitions. The hearings were presided over by the Chancellor and in time petitions were addressed to him alone. By the 15th century the Chancellor had started to hear petitions on his own and the Court of Chancery was established. The body of rules applied by the court was called equity.

The early Chancellors were drawn from the ranks of the clergy and their decisions reflected their ecclesiastical background. They examined the consciences of the parties and then ordered what was fair and just. At first, each Chancellor acted as he thought best. Decisions varied from Chancellor to Chancellor and this resulted in a great deal of uncertainty for petitioners. Eventually, Chancellors began to follow previous decisions and a large body of fixed rules grew up. The decisions of the Court of Chancery were often at odds with those made in the common law courts. This proved a source of conflict until the start of the 17th century when James I ruled that, in cases of conflict, equity was to prevail. For several centuries the English legal system continued to develop with two distinct sets of rules administered in separate courts.

Equity is not a complete system of law. Equitable principles were formulated to remedy specific defects in the common law. They were designed to complement the common law rules and not to replace them. Equity has made an important contribution to the development of English law, particularly in the following areas:

1 **Recognition of new rights.** The common law did not recognise the concept of the trust. A trust arises where a settlor (S) conveys property to a trustee (T) to hold on trust for a beneficiary (B). The common law treated T as if he were the owner of the property and B's claims were ignored. The Court of Chancery, however, would require T to act according to his conscience and administer the trust on B's behalf. Thus, equity recognised and enforced the rights of a beneficiary under a trust. The Court of Chancery also came to the aid of borrowers who had mortgaged their property as security for a loan. If the loan was not repaid by the agreed date, the common law position was that the lender (mortgagee) became the owner of the property and the borrower (mortgagor) was still required to pay the outstanding balance. Equity gave the mortgagor the right to pay off the loan and recover his property even though the repayment date had passed. This equitable principle is known as the equity of redemption. It will be considered in more detail in Chapter 4 ●.

2 **Introduction of new remedies.** The new equitable rights were enforced by means of new equitable remedies. In the field of contract law, the Court of Chancery developed such remedies as the injunction, specific performance, rescission and rectification which will be examined in Chapters 7 and 9 ●. These remedies were not available as of right like common law remedies: they were discretionary. The Court of Chancery could refuse to grant an equitable remedy if, for example, the claimant had himself acted unfairly.

By the 19th century the administration of justice had reached an unhappy state of affairs and was heavily criticised. The existence of separate courts for the administration of common law and equity meant that someone who wanted help from both the common law and equity had to bring two separate cases in two separate courts. If a person started an action in the wrong court, he could not get a remedy until he brought his case to the right court. The proceedings in the Court of Chancery had become notorious for their length and expense. (Charles Dickens satirised the delays of Chancery in his novel *Bleak House*.) Comprehensive reform of the many deficiencies of the English legal system was effected by several statutes in the 19th century culminating in the Judicature Acts 1873–75. The separate common law courts and Court of Chancery were replaced by a Supreme Court of Judicature which comprised the Court of Appeal and High Court. Every judge was empowered thenceforth to administer both common law and equity in his court. Thus, a claimant seeking a common law and an equitable remedy need

Common law	Equity
Developed by circuit judges from English customary law applying the principle of *stare decisis*	Developed by Chancellors, in dealing with petitions addressed to the King from citizens complaining about the rigidity of the common law
Complete system of law	Complements the common law, but could not replace it
Does not recognise the existence of equity	Acknowledges the common law and tries to provide an alternative solution
Upholds rights irrespective of the motives or intentions of the parties	Originally, a court of conscience which ordered the parties to do what was just and fair. These principles are contained in equitable maxims, e.g. 'He who seeks equity must do equity' and 'Delay defeats equity'
Remedies available as of right	Discretionary remedies

Figure 1.3 Differences between the common law and equity

only pursue one action in one court. The Acts also confirmed that, where common law and equity conflict, equity should prevail. These reforms did not have the effect of removing the distinction between the two sets of rules: common law and equity are still two separate but complementary systems of law. A judge may draw upon both sets of rules to decide a case. See, for example, the decision of Denning J in the *High Trees Case* in Chapter 7 ○.

The differences between the common law and equity are summarised in Figure 1.3.

Some basic principles of legal liability

Before we consider the specific areas of law governing the activities of business organisations, we must first of all consider the branches of law which are most likely to affect those in business and certain basic principles of liability.

It is a basic function of the law to set out the circumstances in which a person may be required to answer for his actions. Legal liability describes a situation where a person is legally responsible for a breach of an obligation imposed by the law. Such obligations may arise from the operation of either the civil or criminal law. The activities of business organisations are subject to a wide

range of potential liability. So, before we consider the law governing the formation, operation and dissolution of business organisations, we must first examine in outline the nature and scope of legal liability for wrongful acts.

Civil liability

As we have already seen, the civil law is concerned with the rights and duties which arise between private individuals. The aim of taking legal action is to put right a wrong which has occurred, often by means of an award of compensation. The areas of civil liability which have the greatest impact on businesses are liability in contract and tort.

Contractual liability

Contractual liability arises when two or more persons enter into a legally enforceable agreement with each other. The law of contract is concerned with determining which agreements are binding, the nature and extent of the obligations freely undertaken by the parties and the legal consequences of breaking contractual promises.

Every type of business transaction, from buying and selling goods and services to employing staff, is governed by the law of contract. Contractual arrangements are so important to the conduct of business they are examined in more detail in later chapters. (See, in particular, Chapter 7, Forming business contracts ◐; Chapter 8, The terms of business contracts ◐; Chapter 9, Ending business contracts ◐; Chapter 10, Law of agency ◐; Chapter 11, Contracts for the supply of goods and services ◐; Chapter 16, Employing labour ◐.)

Tortious liability

A tort consists of the breach of a duty imposed by the law. The law of tort seeks to compensate the victims of certain forms of harmful conduct by an award of damages or to prevent harm occurring by granting an injunction. Examples of torts include negligence, nuisance, trespass, defamation (libel and slander) and conversion. These torts, along with others which are relevant to business, will be studied in more detail in Chapter 12 ◐.

Criminal liability

A crime is an offence against the state. The consequences of a criminal conviction are not confined to the punishment inflicted by the court. For example, if a person is convicted of theft, his name will probably appear in the local papers causing shame and embarrassment and he may even lose his job. The sanctions are so severe that the criminal law normally requires an element of moral fault on the part of the offender. Thus, the prosecution must establish two essential requirements: *actus reus* (prohibited act) and *mens rea* (guilty mind). For most criminal offences, both elements must be present to create criminal liability. If you pick someone's umbrella up thinking that it is your own, you cannot be guilty of theft, because of the absence of a guilty mind. There are, however, some statutory offences where Parliament has dispensed with the requirement of *mens rea*. Performance of the wrongful act alone makes the offender liable. These are known as crimes of strict liability. Selling food for human consumption which fails to comply with food safety requirements contrary to the Food Safety Act 1990 is an example of an offence of strict liability. The prosecutor is not required to show that the seller knew that the food did not comply with food safety requirements. He will secure a conviction by establishing that the food was unsafe and that it was sold. The seller may be able to defend himself by showing that he has taken all reasonable precautions and exercised due diligence to avoid commission of the offence.

Law of property

The law of property is concerned with the rights which may arise in relation to anything that can be owned. Thus, property covers land, goods and intangible rights such as debts, patents or the goodwill of a business. The legal implications of acquiring, using and disposing of business property will be studied in more depth in Chapter 15 ◐. In order fully to understand other principles of business law which you will encounter before then, it is necessary to consider the relationships which may arise between persons and property, namely, the rights of ownership and possession.

1 **Ownership.** Ownership describes the greatest rights that a person can have in relation to property. An owner enjoys the fullest powers of use and disposal over the property allowed by law. The owner of this book, for example, has the right to read it, lend it to a friend, hire it out, pledge it as security for a loan, or even tear it into shreds. An owner does not enjoy absolute rights; restrictions may be imposed to protect the rights of other members of the community. The ownership of a house does not entitle the occupants to hold frequent wild parties to the annoyance of neighbours.

2 **Possession.** Possession consists of two elements: physical control and the intention to exclude others. For example, you have possession of the watch you are wearing, the clothes in your wardrobe at home and your car which is parked while you are at work. Ownership and possession often go hand in hand, but may be divorced. The viewer of a hired TV enjoys possession of the set, but ownership remains with the TV rental firm. If your house is burgled, you remain the owner of the stolen property, but the burglar obtains (unlawful) possession.

Self-test questions/activities

1 What is law and why is it necessary?

2 Explain the difference between the following pairs:
   (a) public law and private law;
   (b) civil law and criminal law;
   (c) contract and tort;
   (d) common law and equity;
   (e) ownership and possession.

3 Consider the following legal actions and indicate whether civil or criminal proceedings would result:
   (a) Ann decides to divorce her husband, Barry, after 10 years of marriage;
   (b) Colin is given a parking ticket by a traffic warden for parking on double yellow lines;
   (c) Diane returns a faulty steam iron to the shop where she bought it, but the shop manager refuses to give her a refund;
   (d) Eamonn drives at 50 mph on a stretch of road where there is a 30 mph limit. He fails to see Fiona, who is crossing the road. She is knocked down and sustains severe injuries;
   (e) Graham takes a copy of *Business Law* from the reference section of the library, with the intention of returning it when he has finished his first assignment. He finds the book so valuable that he decides to keep it;
   (f) Hazel returns to England after working abroad for three years. While abroad, she rented her flat to Ian. She now gives him notice to quit, but he refuses to move out.

Specimen examination questions

1 Explain why equity developed and how it differs from the common law.
   What is the present relationship between the two systems?

2 David, a farmer, supplies organic free range eggs on a regular basis to the Peak Park Hotel and Country Club. David's hens, and the eggs they produce, have become infected with salmonella. The hotel uses the infected raw eggs to prepare a mayonnaise for Ian and Janet's wedding reception. Many of the guests are taken ill after the reception and Sybil, Janet's 90-year-old grandmother, dies.

   (a) Identify the different types of legal proceedings which might arise from these facts.
   (b) For each type of legal action you have identified in (a), discuss the nature of the legal liability and the purpose or objective of taking legal action.

3 'The prosecution in a criminal case must prove both *mens rea* and *actus reus* to establish the defendant's guilt, unless it is a crime of strict liability.'
   Explain and discuss.

Website references

http://www.kent.ac.uk/lawlinks This excellent site is basically an annotated set of links to legal information compiled by the Law Librarian at the University of Kent, Sarah Carter. It is a good starting point for legal research.

http://www.legalabbrevs.cardiff.ac.uk Cardiff index to legal abbreviations provides a searchable database of abbreviations of law publications, which can be searched either from abbreviation to title or title to abbreviation.

http://www.venables.co.uk A 'gateway' to legal resources in the UK and Ireland for the general browser, including free legal advice on the Internet. There is a section of the site especially for students: http://www.venables.co.uk/students.htm.

http://www.infolaw.co.uk Infolaw is the oldest established legal portal. It is an excellent starting point for anyone looking for legal information. Lawfinder provides free access to a wide range of legal resources, including key law sites.

Visit www.mylawchamber.co.uk/richesallen to access study support resources including answers to questions in this chapter and legal updates, all linked to the **Pearson eText** version of **Keenan and Riches' Business Law** which you can **search**, **highlight** and **personalise** with your **own notes** and **bookmarks**.

premium
mylawchamber
unrivalled support for legal education

Chapter 2 Law making

Learning objectives

After studying this chapter you should understand the following main points:

- the causes and sources of legal change and law reform;
- the characteristics of the main sources of law, including law made by Parliament (legislation), judge-made case law (judicial precedent), and law emanating from the European Union (EU);
- the nature of human rights legislation and its effect on other sources of law.

Over 900 years of history have helped shape the institutions, procedures and body of rules which make up our modern English legal system. The law is a living creation that reflects the needs of the society it serves, each generation leaving its mark on the law.

The rate of legal change has varied greatly down the centuries. English law developed at a relatively gentle pace until the end of the 18th century, but, as Britain moved into the industrial age, the pace of legal change quickened. Life at the start of the 21st century is fast moving and the rate of legal change is just as hectic. The law does not stand still for long today.

Ideally, business requires a stable environment within which to operate. Yet, the framework of law which governs business activities is subject to constant change. The burden of keeping up to date may be eased slightly by making use of professional people such as an accountant or solicitor to advise on the latest developments in such areas as tax or company law. Nevertheless, the businessperson will still need to keep himself informed of general legal changes which will affect his day-to-day running of the business. If he employs others in his business, he will need to keep up to date on such matters as health and safety at work, the rights of his employees and his duties as an employer. If he sells goods direct to the consumer, he must be aware of changes in consumer protection law. Almost every aspect of his business will be subject to legal regulation and the law could always change.

In this chapter we will explore why the law changes and the mechanism by which change takes place.

Causes of legal change

Legal changes can be divided into two broad categories according to their causes. The first type of legal change is caused by the law responding to changes taking place in society. Political, social and economic changes, technological advancements and changing moral beliefs all lead eventually to changes in the law. Indeed, the law must be responsive to new circumstances and attitudes if it is to enjoy continued respect. The second type of legal change arises from the need to keep the law in good working order. Like any piece of sophisticated machinery, the law machine must be kept in a neat and tidy condition, maintained on a regular basis, with essential repairs undertaken when necessary. We will now examine these two types of legal change in more detail.

Legal change and the changing world

Think about the changes that have taken place in our world over the past 100 years. The first to come to mind are probably the spectacular scientific and technological achievements of the past century – motor vehicles, aircraft, the telephone, radio and TV, computers and genetic engineering. Each new development creates its own demand for legal change. Consider, for example, the vast body of law which has grown up around the motor vehicle: there are regulations governing such matters as the construction and maintenance of motor vehicles, the conduct of drivers on the road and even where vehicles may be parked. Indeed, almost half of the criminal cases tried by magistrates' courts are directly related to the use of motor vehicles. The increasing volume of traffic on the roads and the resulting inexorable rise in traffic accidents have also led to developments in the civil law, especially in the areas of the law of tort and insurance. More dramatic changes to the system of compensating the victims of motor accidents have been canvassed over the years, principally by the Royal Commission on Civil Liability in 1978. Its recommendation of a 'no fault' system of compensation financed by a levy on petrol sales has never been implemented.

While science and technology have been taking great leaps forward over the last century, other less dramatic changes have been taking place. The role and functions of the elected government, for example, have altered quite considerably. Nineteenth-century government was characterised by the *laissez-faire* philosophy of minimum interference in the lives of individuals. The government's limited role was to defend the country from external threats, to promote Britain's interests abroad and maintain internal order. In the 20th century, governments took increasing responsibility for the social and economic well-being of citizens. Naturally, the political parties have their own conflicting ideas about how to cure the country's ills. New approaches are tried with each change of government. The law is used as a means of achieving the desired political, economic and social changes. The development of law on certain contentious issues can often resemble a swinging pendulum as successive governments pursue their opposing political objectives. The changes in the law relating to trade union rights and privileges over the past 40 years are a perfect illustration of the pendulum effect. In 1971 the Conservative government introduced the Industrial Relations Act in an attempt to curb what it saw as the damaging power of the unions by subjecting them to greater legal regulation. The changes were fiercely resisted by the trade union movement. The attempt to reform industrial relations law at a stroke was a dismal failure. One of the first tasks of the Labour government, which was elected in 1974, was to dismantle the Industrial Relations Act 1971 and restore the unions to their privileged legal position. When the Conservatives were returned to power in 1979, they did not repeat the mistakes of the previous Conservative government of 1970–74. Instead, they adopted a step-by-step approach to trade union reform and in a series of Acts implemented greater legal control over unions and their activities. Further adjustments to trade union law were made by the Employment Relations Act 1999, following the election of a Labour government in May 1997.

One of the more controversial changes of recent times was the United Kingdom's entry into the European Community (EC) in 1973. The government's motives were clearly directed at the economic and social benefits which it was expected would be derived from joining the EC. But membership also brought great legal changes in its wake: the traditional sovereignty of the Westminster Parliament has been called into question, our courts are now subject to the rulings of the European Court of Justice and parts of our substantive law have been remodelled to conform to European requirements, e.g. company, consumer and employment law.

Changing moral beliefs and social attitudes are potent causes of legal change. In the past 40 years or so, great changes have taken place in the laws governing personal morality: the laws against homosexuality have been relaxed, abortion has been legalised and divorce is more freely obtainable. Society's view of the role of women has altered greatly over the past century. The rights of women have been advanced, not only by Parliament in measures like the Sex Discrimination Act 1975, but also by the courts in their approach to such matters as rights to the matrimonial home when a marriage breaks down.

The law is an adaptable creature responsive to the complex changes taking place around it. But sometimes in the midst of all this change, the more technical parts of the law, sometimes known as 'lawyers' law', can be ignored. A programme of reform is necessary to ensure that these vitally important, if less glamorous, areas of law do not fall into a state of disrepair.

Law reform

'Lawyers' law' consists largely of the body of rules developed over many years by judges deciding cases according to principles laid down in past cases. One of the great strengths of the system of judge-made law is its flexibility; judges can adapt or rework the rules of common law or equity to meet changing circumstances. Although modern judges have shown themselves willing to take a bold approach to the task of keeping case law in tune with the times, there is a limit to what can be achieved. Judicial law reform is likely to lead to haphazard, unsystematic changes in the law. Legal change becomes dependent on the chance of an appropriate case cropping up in a court which can effect change. Furthermore, our adversarial trial system is not the best vehicle for investigating the likely consequences of changing the law. Judges cannot commission independent research or consult interested bodies to gauge the effect of the proposed change. The limitations of a system of judge-led law reform led to the setting up of an official law reform agency, which, along with other methods of effecting change in the law, will be considered below.

The sources of legal change

Ideas for changing the law flow from many sources:

Official law reform agencies

The main agent of law reform in England and Wales is the Law Commission, which was established by the Law Commission Act 1965. The Commission consists of a Chairman, a High Court judge, who may be appointed for up to three years, and four other Commissioners, who may be judges, solicitors, barristers or academic lawyers and may be appointed for up to five years. The Commission's job is to keep the law as a whole under review, with a view to its systematic development and reform. Its statutory duties include:

- codification of the law;
- elimination of anomalies;
- repeal of obsolete and unnecessary enactments;
- securing a reduction in the number of separate enactments;
- simplification and modernisation of the law.

A Law Commission project starts life by appearing as an item in its programme of work which is approved by the Lord Chancellor (who is also the Secretary of State for Justice). The Commission's full-time staff of lawyers then prepare a working paper containing alternative proposals for reform. Following consultations with the legal profession, government departments and other interested bodies, the Commission submits a final report on a firm proposal for reform accompanied by a draft Bill. The Law Commission's programme of work must be approved by the Lord Chancellor. A Ministerial Committee of the Law Commission advises the Lord Chancellor on the Law Commission's proposed programme, monitors the Law Commission's progress in delivering the programme and reviews actions taken by government departments in response to Law Commission Reports. The government is now required to account to Parliament for the way it has dealt with Law Commission proposals. The Law Commission Act 2009 places a requirement on the Lord Chancellor to prepare an annual report to be laid before Parliament on the implementation of Law Commission proposals. The Lord Chancellor must set out plans for dealing with any Law Commission proposals which have not yet been implemented and explain the reasoning for deciding not to implement a proposal. The Act allows the Lord Chancellor and the Law Commission to develop a protocol about the Commission's work to provide a framework for the relationship between the government and the Commission.

Another law reform agency is the Civil Justice Council which was set up under the Civil Procedure Act 1997, following recommendations by Lord Woolf in his 1996 report, *Access to Justice*. Membership of the Council must include members of the judiciary, members of the legal professions, civil servants concerned with the administration of the courts, people with experience and knowledge of consumer affairs and the lay advice sector, and people able to represent the interests of particular kinds of litigants, e.g. business or employees. The Council has a duty to keep the civil justice system under review; to consider how to make the civil justice system more accessible, fair and efficient; to advise the Lord Chancellor and the judiciary on the development of the civil justice system, referring proposals for change in the civil justice system to the Lord Chancellor and the Civil Procedure Rules Committee; and making proposals for research.

Government departments

Each government department is responsible for keeping the law in its own field of interest under constant review.

Where issues involving policy consideration rather than technical law reform arise, ministers may prefer to set up a **departmental committee** to investigate the subject, rather than leave it to the Law Commission. Particularly important or controversial matters may lead to the setting up of a **Royal Commission** by the Crown on the advice of a minister. The dozen or so members of a Royal Commission usually reflect a balance of expert, professional and lay opinion. They work on a part-time basis, often taking several years to investigate a problem thoroughly and make recommendations. Examples of Royal Commissions include the Benson Commission on Legal Services (1979) and the Philips Commission on Criminal Procedure (1981). Royal Commissions and departmental committees were notable by their absence during the 1980s. The appointment of a Royal Commission on Criminal Justice in 1991, following several well-publicised cases involving miscarriages of justice, marked a departure from the practice of the previous decade. Some Royal Commissions operate as standing advisory bodies. For example, the Royal Commission on Environmental Pollution, which was established in 1970, reported on special study topics for forty years until the coalition government announced its abolition in 2010.

Political parties and pressure groups

At election time, the political parties compete for our votes on the basis of a package of social and economic reforms which they promise to carry out if elected. The successful party is assumed to have a mandate to implement the proposals outlined in its election manifesto. Manifesto commitments, however, form only part of a government's legislative programme. Other competing claims to parliamentary time must be accommodated. For example, legislation may be required in connection with our membership of the EU, or to give effect to a proposal from the Law Commission or a Royal Commission, or simply to deal with an unforeseen emergency. Government claims on Parliament's time will alter during its period in office, as policy changes are made in response to pressures from within Westminster or in the country at large. One of the most significant extra-parliamentary influences on the formulation and execution of government policies is pressure-group activity. Pressure groups are organised groups of people seeking to influence or change government policy without themselves wishing to form a government.

Some pressure groups represent sectional interests in the community. The Confederation of British Industry (CBI), for example, represents business interests, while other pressure groups are formed to campaign on a single issue. The Campaign for Nuclear Disarmament (CND), for example, is concerned solely with the cause of nuclear disarmament. Pressure groups use a variety of techniques to promote their causes, from holding public demonstrations to more direct attempts to gain the support of MPs (known as 'lobbying'). Pressure-group activity may be negative in the sense of mobilising opposition to a proposed government measure, or positive, in seeking to persuade the government to adopt a specific proposal in its legislative programme or to win over a backbench MP, hoping that he will be successful in the ballot for private members' Bills.

Law-making processes

So far we have considered the main causes of legal change. We will now examine the mechanics of change. The expression 'sources of law' is often used to refer to the various ways in which law can come into being. The main sources of law today are legislation (Acts of Parliament), case law (judicial precedent) and EU law.

Legislation

Legislation is law enacted by the Queen in Parliament in the form of Acts of Parliament or statutes. Parliament is made up of two chambers: the House of Commons and the House of Lords. The Commons consists of 650 elected Members of Parliament (MPs) who represent an area of the country called a **constituency**. The political party which can command a majority of votes in the Commons forms the **government** and its leader becomes the **Prime Minister**. Ministers are appointed by the Prime Minister to take charge of the various government departments. The most important ministers form the **Cabinet**, which is responsible for formulating government policy. The UK is currently governed by a coalition government of Conservatives and Liberal Democrats following the May 2010 General Election, in which neither of the two main political parties won sufficient seats to command an overall majority in the Commons.

The coalition's programme for government includes a number of proposals for constitutional reform including:

- the introduction of five-year fixed-term parliaments;
- a referendum on introducing the alternative vote method of proportional representation;
- the introduction of a power of recall, to enable voters to force a by-election where an MP is found to have engaged in serious wrongdoing.

In July 2010 the government published the Parliamentary Voting System and Constituencies Bill. The Bill provides for:

- a referendum to be held on 5 May 2011 on whether to change the voting system for UK parliamentary elections from 'first past the post' to the 'alternative vote' (AV) system. In the AV system, voters rank candidates in order of preference. Candidates must achieve more than 50 per cent of the vote, either at an initial count, or after the second preference votes of the least popular candidate(s) are redistributed. Constituencies will continue to return a single member to Parliament;
- a reduction in the number of parliamentary constituencies from 650 to 600;
- the creation of constituencies based on equally-sized electorates.

Unlike the House of Commons, the House of Lords is not an elected body. In recent years it has been subject to reform involving changes to its membership and a review of its role, functions and powers. The first stage of reform involved the removal of the right of most hereditary peers to sit and vote in the House. Following the changes made by the House of Lords Act 1999, the House of Lords is composed of 638 life peers, 92 hereditary peers (75 were elected by their peers and 15 were royal or elected office holders), and 25 spiritual peers (the Archbishops of Canterbury and York, and 24 bishops of the Church of England). Law Lords who were in office at the time of the creation of the Supreme Court in October 2009 remain members of the House of Lords but are disqualified from participation until they retire.

The government published its proposals for the next stage of reform of the House of Lords in September 2003 but in March 2004 it announced that it did not intend to proceed with legislation to implement the changes proposed in its consultation paper. However, the government did proceed with its plans to reform the role of the Lord Chancellor and to establish a Supreme Court to replace the system of Law Lords hearing appeals as a Committee of the House of Lords. Under the Constitutional Reform Act 2005 the Lord Chancellor continues to be a government minister at Cabinet level with responsibility for the judiciary and the court system but his judicial functions have been transferred to the President of the Courts of England and Wales, an additional title for the Lord Chief Justice, and the Lord Chancellor's former role as Speaker in the House of Lords has been taken over by a Lord Speaker, elected for a five-year term by peers. The creation of the Supreme Court will be considered in more detail in Chapter 3 ◗.

In July 2008 the Labour government published a White Paper setting out its proposals for a reformed second chamber. In free parliamentary votes held in 2007, the Lords had voted for a wholly appointed House, while the Commons voted for a wholly or mainly (80 per cent) elected second chamber. The White Paper was based on the Commons votes and the outcome of subsequent cross-party talks. The key proposals were:

- The creation of a second chamber with directly elected members.
- The chamber might consist of 100 per cent elected members or 80 per cent elected and 20 per cent appointed members.
- Further consideration should be given to the voting system: the options included first past the post, alternative vote, single transferable vote or a list system.
- Members should serve a long term of office, e.g. a single non-renewable term of 12–15 years.
- New members would be elected in thirds coinciding with general elections.
- If there were an appointed element, appointments would be made by an Appointments Commission, which would seek applications and nominations. Individuals would be appointed on the basis of their ability, willingness and commitment to take part in the full range of work. Church of England bishops and retired Law Lords (and in the future Supreme Court judges) would continue to have seats if there was an appointed element. The main purpose of having an appointed element would be to ensure a significant independent (cross-bench) element.
- There would be a transition period of three electoral cycles during which the three new tranches of members would be phased in.

- Members would receive a salary.
- The link between a peerage and a seat in Parliament would be broken. Hereditary peers would no longer have a right to sit and vote in Parliament. Peerages would not be conferred on members of the second chamber.
- The new chamber would be significantly smaller than the current House of Lords.
- The new chamber would have the same powers as the current House of Lords. The primacy of the Commons in Parliament would be preserved although it is recognised that an elected chamber is likely to be more 'assertive'.
- Although the government did not express a view about what the second chamber should be called, it noted a consensus for 'Senate' among members of the cross-party group.

The new coalition government has established a committee to bring forward proposals for a wholly or mainly elected second chamber.

The history of the reform of the House of Lords since 1997 is set out in Figure 2.1.

Before leaving the subject of law making by Parliament, note should be made of the changes brought about by the devolution of the powers of the Westminster Parliament to Scotland, Wales and Northern Ireland since 1997. The Scotland Act 1998 created the first Scottish Parliament for almost 300 years. There are 129 Members of the Scottish Parliament (MSPs) who are elected by proportional representation every four years. The first elections took place in May 1999. The Parliament has power to pass legislation in all areas where it has 'legislative competence', which include education, health, transport, local government, the environment and non-statutory Scottish law. Certain matters are reserved for the UK Parliament: they include defence, the UK constitution, foreign affairs and economic policy. The Parliament also has the power to vary the basic rate of income tax in Scotland by 3p in the pound.

The Government of Wales Act 1998 provided for the establishment of a National Assembly for Wales. There are 60 members of the Welsh Assembly, who are elected every four years. Forty Assembly Members (AMs) are elected on a first past the post basis from constituencies and 20 AMs from electoral regions drawn from party regional lists. The first elections were held on 6 May 1999. The 1998 Act provided for the transfer of the powers and responsibilities from the Welsh Office to the Assembly. Unlike the arrangements for devolution in Scotland, the Government of Wales Act 1998 did not provide for a separation of the legislature from the executive and the Assembly was not empowered to pass primary legislation. Following a review of the operation of devolution by the Richard Commission in 2004, the government published a White Paper (*Better Governance for Wales*) in 2005, which proposed implementing a formal separation of powers between the executive and legislature within the Assembly; reforming the electoral arrangements; and extending the legislative powers of the Assembly. The Government of Wales Act 2006 gives effect to these proposals. The 2006 Act:

- establishes the Welsh Assembly Government as an entity which is separate from but accountable to the National Assembly;
- introduces a mechanism for conferring legislative competence on the Assembly in respect of specified matters, with the approval of the Westminster Parliament (these forms of secondary legislation are known as Assembly Measures);
- makes provision for a referendum to be held on whether the Assembly should be able to pass primary legislation on matters specified by the Westminster Parliament;
- makes provision for the election and remuneration of AMs and the establishment of an Assembly Commission to support the operation of the Assembly.

The coalition government has stated that it intends to hold a referendum on further devolution for Wales.

The Northern Ireland Assembly, which was created following a referendum supporting the 1998 'Good Friday Agreement', consists of 108 members elected by proportional representation. The Assembly has legislative and executive authority in respect of matters which were previously within the remit of Northern Ireland government departments, e.g. agriculture, education, the environment, health and social services, economic development and finance. The Northern Ireland Assembly was suspended and direct rule from Westminster restored in October 2002. An agreement to British and Irish government proposals for restoring devolved government was reached with the major political parties in Northern Ireland at talks held in St Andrews, Scotland, in October 2006. The Northern

1997	Labour Party manifesto	Commitment to remove the voting rights of hereditary peers.
January 1999	House of Lords Bill and White Paper *Modernising Parliament – Reforming the House of Lords*	First stage of reform – Bill to remove the right of hereditary peers to sit and vote, White Paper set out next stages including reformed arrangements for nominating life peers and appointment of a Royal Commission.
November 1999	House of Lords Act	Removed the right of most hereditary peers to sit and vote in the House of Lords. 92 hereditary peers were allowed to remain until the House was fully reformed.
2000	Royal Commission under the chairmanship of Lord Wakeham	Made recommendations about the composition, role and functions of a reformed second chamber. These included the creation of a 550-member House, with majority of members appointed (not elected) by an independent statutory Appointments Commission. It would have a revising and advisory role.
April 2001	Independent Appointments Commission	First round of appointments of non-party members of the House made by Independent Appointments Commission, reducing the Prime Minister's powers of patronage.
November 2001	Government White Paper *The House of Lords – Completing the Reform*	Broadly endorsed the Wakeham Report, agreeing that the second chamber should be largely nominated and there should be a statutory Independent Appointments Commission. However, it proposed a larger membership (600), a slightly higher proportion of elected members and no role for the Appointments Commission in the nomination of party political affiliated members.
February 2002	Public Administration Select Committee Report *The Second Chamber: Continuing the Reform*	Recommends a 60% elected House, statutory Appointments Commission responsible for 40% appointed members: 20% party political, 20% independent. Government's response proposes setting up a Joint Committee of both Houses to consider the role and function of the second chamber and to bring forward proposals on composition on which both Houses could vote.
December 2002	Joint Committee on House of Lords Reform *First Report*	Recommends little change to role and function of the House. Sets out seven options for composition ranging from 100% elected to 100% appointed. No clear majority for any of the options in the Commons' votes, Lords vote for wholly appointed House.
April 2003	Joint Committee on House of Lords Reform *Second Report*	Second Report sets out areas where progress may be possible, e.g. the status of the Appointments Commission, and asks guidance from the government and then Parliament on the future direction of their work.
July 2003	Department for Constitutional Affairs Consultation Paper *A Supreme Court for the United Kingdom*	Government proposes establishing a Supreme Court to replace the Law Lords sitting as a committee of the House of Lords. Members of the new court would cease to sit and vote in the House of Lords.
September 2003	Department for Constitutional Affairs Consultation Paper *Next Steps for the House of Lords*	Government proposes as next stage of reform to remove the remaining hereditaries from the Lords, to place the Appointments Commission on a statutory footing, to provide for disqualification of members convicted of offences, to allow the Prime Minister to make up to five ministerial appointments to the Lords and to allow life peers the right to renounce their peerage.
March 2004	Government Announcement	Government announces that it does not intend to proceed with legislation to enact proposals in the September 2003 Consultation Paper.
March 2005	Constitutional Reform Act	The Act receives the Royal Assent. It reforms the role of the Lord Chancellor, establishes an independent Supreme Court, creates a Judicial Appointments Commission and enshrines the concept of judicial independence in legislation.
April 2006	Implementation of the Act	From 3 April there are new roles for the Lord Chancellor and Lord Chief Justice and the new Judicial Appointments Commission starts work.
February 2007	Government White Paper: *The House of Lords: Reform*	The White Paper sets out the arguments for and against various aspects of reform to inform a free vote in both Houses.
March 2007	Free vote in the House of Commons and House of Lords	There is a majority in the Commons for 2 options: 80% elected and 100% elected second chamber. The Lords voted for a fully appointed second house.
July 2008	Government White Paper: *An Elected Second Chamber; Further Reform of the House of Lords*	The White Paper sets out the government's proposals for a reformed second chamber based on the Commons' vote for an 80% or 100% elected second chamber.
October 2009	Supreme Court	The new Supreme Court opened for business in the refurbished Middlesex Guildhall.
May 2010	Coalition Agreement	The coalition government commits to setting up a committee to bring forward proposals for a wholly or mainly elected second chamber.

Figure 2.1 Reform of the House of Lords since 1997

Ireland (St Andrews Agreement) Act 2006 provided for a Transitional Assembly whose purpose was to assist with preparations for the restoration of devolved government. Elections to a new Assembly took place on 7 March 2007 and on 26 March 2007 the leaders of the DUP and Sinn Fein agreed to enter into a power-sharing Executive from 8 May 2007.

Parliamentary sovereignty

The supremacy of Parliament in the legislative sphere is known as the doctrine of parliamentary sovereignty. It means that Parliament can make any laws it pleases, no matter how perverse or unfair. Parliament may repeal the enactments of an earlier Parliament; it may delegate its legislative powers to other bodies or individuals. The courts are bound to apply the law enacted by Parliament; the judiciary cannot challenge the validity of an Act of Parliament on the grounds that the legislation is absurd, unconstitutional or procured by fraud (*Pickin v British Railways Board* (1974)). However, the courts may challenge the validity of UK legislation if it is in conflict with EC law.

Factortame Ltd v Secretary of State for Transport (No 2) (1991)

The Merchant Shipping Act 1988 introduced a requirement that 75 per cent of the members of companies operating fishing vessels in UK waters must be resident and domiciled in the UK. The legislation was designed to stop the practice of 'quota hopping' whereby fishing quotas were 'plundered' by vessels flying the British flag but whose real owners had no connection with the UK. The appellants were companies registered in the UK but which were essentially owned or controlled by Spanish nationals. Their fishing vessels failed to meet the new requirements and they were barred from fishing. The appellants argued that the 1988 Act was incompatible with EC law. Since it would take several years to resolve the matter, the appellants asked the court to grant interim relief suspending the 1988 Act until a final ruling could be made. The House of Lords referred the case to the European Court of Justice which ruled that, if a rule of national law was the sole obstacle to the granting of interim relief in a case concerning EC law, that rule must be set aside. Applying this ruling, the House of Lords made an order suspending the operation of the disputed provisions of the Merchant Shipping Act 1988 pending final judgment of the issue.

Comment. In 1999 the House of Lords held that the UK's breach of EC law in passing the Merchant Shipping Act 1988 was sufficiently serious to entitle the appellants to compensation (*R v Secretary of State for Transport, ex parte Factortame Ltd (No 5)* (1999)).

R v Secretary of State for Employment, ex parte Equal Opportunities Commission (1994)

In this case the House of Lords upheld the right of a statutory body, the Equal Opportunities Commission, to challenge restrictions on part-time workers' rights to redundancy pay and unfair dismissal protection under UK law using the procedure of judicial review (see further, Chapter 3 ◯). Their Lordships held that the five-year qualifying period for protection in relation to redundancy and unfair dismissal for those working between 8 and 16 hours a week laid down in UK legislation was in breach of EC law (see further, Chapter 16 ◯).

Under the Human Rights Act 1998, certain courts may make a 'declaration of incompatibility' if legislation is incompatible with the European Convention on Human Rights. The Human Rights Act will be considered in more detail later in this chapter.

The making of an Act of Parliament

The procedure by which a legislative proposal is translated into an Act of Parliament is long and complicated. Until all the stages in the process have been completed, the embryonic Act is known as a Bill. There are different types of Bill:

1 **Public Bills** change general law or affect the whole of the country. It is assumed that the Bill extends to all of the United Kingdom unless there is a specific provision to the contrary. For example, the Supply of Goods and Services Act 1982 applies to England, Wales and Northern Ireland but not to Scotland.

2 **Private Bills** do not alter the law for the whole community but deal with matters of concern in a particular locality or to a private company or even individuals. Private Bills are mainly promoted by local authorities seeking additional powers to those granted by general legislation.

3 **Government Bills** are introduced by a minister with the backing of the government and are almost certain to

become law. Some of the Bills are designed to implement the government's political policies, but others may be introduced to deal with an emergency which has arisen or to amend or consolidate earlier legislation.

4 Private members' Bills are introduced by an individual MP or private peer (in the House of Lords) without guaranteed government backing. They usually deal with moral or legal questions rather than with purely party political matters. A private member's Bill is unlikely to become law unless the government lends its support. Some important law reform measures started life as a private member's Bill, including the Murder (Abolition of the Death Penalty) Act 1965 and the Abortion Act 1967.

A Bill must pass through several stages receiving the consent of the Commons and Lords before it is presented for the Royal Assent. A Bill may generally start life in either the Commons or the Lords and then pass to the other House, but in practice most public Bills start in the Commons and then proceed to the Lords; certain kinds of Bill, such as Money Bills, must originate in the Commons. The procedure for a Bill which is introduced in the Commons is illustrated in Figure 2.2.

All Bills go through both the House of Commons and the House or Lords before receiving the Royal Assent. Normally, the consent of both Houses is required but the Lords lost its right to reject legislation under the Parliament Act 1911, which was only passed by the Lords because of a threat by the King to create sufficient new peers to secure the passage of the Bill. This crisis had been precipitated by the refusal of the Lords to pass David Lloyd-George's 'people's budget' of 1909. The 1911 Act removed the Lords' right to veto legislation, except in relation to prolonging the life of Parliament, and introduced a power to delay a Bill by up to two years. The Parliament Act 1949 reduced the Lords' delaying powers to one year. Since 1949 four Acts have become law without the consent of the Lords:

- War Crimes Act 1991
- European Parliamentary Elections Act 1999
- Sexual Offences (Amendment) Act 2000
- Hunting Act 2004.

The validity of the Hunting Act 2004 was reviewed by the House of Lords in the following case.

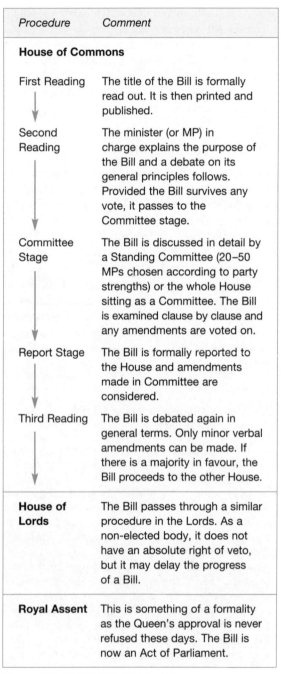

Procedure	Comment
House of Commons	
First Reading	The title of the Bill is formally read out. It is then printed and published.
Second Reading	The minister (or MP) in charge explains the purpose of the Bill and a debate on its general principles follows. Provided the Bill survives any vote, it passes to the Committee stage.
Committee Stage	The Bill is discussed in detail by a Standing Committee (20–50 MPs chosen according to party strengths) or the whole House sitting as a Committee. The Bill is examined clause by clause and any amendments are voted on.
Report Stage	The Bill is formally reported to the House and amendments made in Committee are considered.
Third Reading	The Bill is debated again in general terms. Only minor verbal amendments can be made. If there is a majority in favour, the Bill proceeds to the other House.
House of Lords	The Bill passes through a similar procedure in the Lords. As a non-elected body, it does not have an absolute right of veto, but it may delay the progress of a Bill.
Royal Assent	This is something of a formality as the Queen's approval is never refused these days. The Bill is now an Act of Parliament.

Figure 2.2 **The legislative process**

R (on the application of Jackson) v Attorney-General (2005)

The claimants in this case were challenging the validity of the Hunting Act 2004 which had made it an offence to hunt a wild mammal with a dog, i.e. foxhunting. The Hunting Act had been passed without the consent of the Lords using the Parliament Act 1911 as amended by the 1949 Act. The claimant's case revolved around the validity of the Parliament Act 1949, which had been passed under the provisions of the 1911 Act. They contended that the 1911 Act could only be amended with the consent of the Lords. The House of Lords rejected this argument. Both the Parliament Act 1949 and the Hunting Act 2004 were valid enactments. The 1949 Act had not changed the constitutional relationship between the Commons and Lords, but had simply reduced the Lords' delaying powers from two years to one year. The political realities were that both Houses had accepted that the 1949 Act was valid and had conducted their business on this basis for more than half a century.

Delegated legislation

The activities of modern government are so varied, and the problems it deals with are so complex and technical, that Parliament does not have sufficient time to deal personally with every piece of legislation required. This difficulty is overcome by passing an enabling Act of Parliament which sets out the basic structure of the legislation but allows other bodies or people to draw up the detailed rules necessary. Rules made in this way are known as delegated legislation. The main forms of delegated legislation are as follows:

1 Orders in Council. These are rules made under the authority of an Act by the Queen acting on the advice of the Privy Council (an honorary body descended from the old Curia Regis). In practice, the power to make orders is exercised by the Cabinet, whose members are all privy councillors. The Queen's assent is a pure formality.

2 Rules and regulations. These are made by a minister in respect of the area of government for which he is responsible, e.g. the power of the Secretary of State for Social Security to make detailed regulations about the income support scheme. (Most orders, rules and regulations are collectively referred to as statutory instruments.)

3 Byelaws. These are made by local authorities and certain other public and nationalised bodies to regulate their spheres of activity. This form of delegated legislation requires the consent of the appropriate minister.

Legislation and the judiciary

A Bill which successfully passes through the House of Commons and the House of Lords and has received the Royal Assent becomes an Act of Parliament. The sovereign law-making powers of the Queen in Parliament mean that the validity of a statute cannot be questioned by the courts. Nevertheless, the courts can exercise considerable influence over how the enacted law is applied to practical problems. Sooner or later, every Act of Parliament will be analysed by the judges in the course of cases which appear before them. It is the task of the judge to interpret and construe the words used by Parliament and thereby ascertain the intention of the legislature. The rules of interpretation followed by the judges may be classified according to their origin as either statutory rules or common law rules.

Statutory rules

1 Modern Acts usually contain an interpretation section which defines certain key words used in that Act, e.g. s 61(1) of the Sale of Goods Act 1979 contains definitions of words and phrases used throughout the Act.

2 The Interpretation Act 1978 lays down certain basic rules of interpretation for all Acts, e.g. unless the contrary intention is indicated 'words in the singular shall include the plural and words in the plural shall include the singular' (s 6 of the Interpretation Act 1978).

3 Certain elements of the Act itself may prove useful. These are known as internal or intrinsic aids. The courts may look at the long title of the Act and its preamble (only found in Private Acts and older Public Acts). Headings, side notes and punctuation may also be considered, but only to help clarify the meaning of ambiguous words.

Common law rules

Apart from the limited help provided by Parliament, the judges have been left to develop their own methods of statutory interpretation. A number of approaches to the task of interpretation have emerged, with the judges free to decide which approach is most appropriate to the case in hand. The most important rules of interpretation and various presumptions are explained below.

1 Literal rule. According to the literal rule, if the words of the statute are clear and unambiguous, the court must give them their ordinary plain meaning, regardless of the result. Where a literal interpretation produces an absurd or perverse decision, it is up to Parliament to put matters right, and is not the job of non-elected judges. For example, in the case of *Fisher* v *Bell* (1960) it was held that a shopkeeper who had flick knives in his shop window could not be guilty of the offence of offering for sale a flick knife contrary to the Restriction of Offensive Weapons Act 1959, even though it was precisely this kind of conduct that Parliament had intended to outlaw. It is an established principle of contract law that displaying goods in a shop window is not an offer to sell but merely an invitation to treat. The defendant had not offered to sell the flick knives and so could not be guilty of the offence. Parliament closed the loophole by passing amending legislation in 1961.

2 Golden rule. Under the golden rule, where the words of a statute are capable of two or more meanings, the judge must adopt the interpretation which produces the least absurd result. Some judges even argue that the golden rule can be applied where the words have only one meaning, but a literal interpretation would lead to an absurdity. For example, in *Re Sigsworth* (1935) it was held that a man who murdered his mother could not inherit her property even though he appeared to be entitled on a literal interpretation of the Administration of Estates Act 1925. There is a basic legal principle that a person should not profit from his own wrongdoing.

3 Mischief rule (rule in *Heydon's Case*). This rule, which derives from *Heydon's Case* (1584), lays down that the court must look at the Act to see what 'mischief' or defect in the common law the Act was passed to remedy, and then interpret the words of the Act in the light of this knowledge. In *Gardiner* v *Sevenoaks Rural District Council* (1950), for example, Gardiner claimed that he was not bound by an Act which laid down regulations about the storage of films in premises because he kept his film in a cave. It was held that the cave should be classed as premises because the purpose of the Act was to secure the safety of those working in the place of storage or living close by. The mischief rule is closely associated with the modern purposive approach to interpretation, which says that a judge should adopt the construction which will promote the general aims or purposes underlying the provision.

4 *Ejusdem generis* rule. Where general words follow particular words, the court should interpret the general words as meaning persons or things of the same class or genus, e.g. if the Act referred to 'cats, dogs or other animals', the general words, 'other animals', should be construed in the light of the particular words, 'cats' and 'dogs', as meaning other kinds of domesticated animals and not wild animals.

5 *Expressio unius est exclusio alterius* rule. Under this rule, the express mention of one or more things implies the exclusion of others, e.g. if the Act simply mentioned 'dogs and cats', other kinds of domesticated animals are excluded.

6 *Noscitur a sociis* rule. According to this rule, a word should take its meaning from the context in which it is found. In *Muir* v *Keay* (1875) it was held that a café which stayed open during the night should have been licensed under the provisions of the Refreshment Houses Act 1860. The Act required houses 'for public refreshment, resort and entertainment' to be licensed. The meaning of the word 'entertainment' was gathered from the context of the Act and held to refer to refreshment rooms for the public rather than involving musical or theatrical entertainment.

7 The presumptions. Unless there are clear words to the contrary, the court will make a number of assumptions. They include:

- the Act is not retrospective, i.e. it does not backdate the change in the law;
- the Act does not bind the Crown;
- the Act does not alter the common law;
- the Act does not restrict personal liberty;
- the Act does not create criminal liability unless *mens rea* is present.

8 Use of extrinsic material. Extrinsic materials are sources of information about a piece of legislation apart from the Act itself. The Act may have been prompted by a report of the Law Commission, a Royal Commission or other official committee. The government often sets out proposals for legislation in the form of a Green Paper (a discussion document) or a White Paper (firm proposals for legislation). In some cases the legislation is based on an international treaty. The Bill will have been debated in Parliament and the speeches reported in *Hansard* (the official report of proceedings in Parliament). The question arises whether a judge may refer to these materials to help him shed light on the meaning of a statutory provision. Historically, the use of extrinsic aids was severely restricted. In recent years, however, the rule has been relaxed, particularly where the court wishes to apply the 'mischief rule' and is seeking to discover the 'mischief' which the Act was intended to remedy. The rules at present are as follows:

(a) International conventions and treaties which form the basis of legislation may be consulted especially where the legislation is ambiguous. The court may also consider the preparatory material for such a convention or treaty (*travaux préparatoires*).

(b) Reports of the Law Commission, royal commissions and other similar bodies may be referred to but only to discover the 'mischief' the Act was designed to deal with.

(c) The previously strict rule that *Hansard* must not be consulted as an aid to statutory interpretation has now been relaxed. In *Pepper* v *Hart* (1993) the House of Lords held that, subject to any parliamentary privilege, the rule prohibiting courts from referring to parliamentary materials as an aid to statutory construction should be modified. Reference to parliamentary materials, i.e. *Hansard*, should be permitted where:

(i) the legislation is ambiguous or obscure or where a literal interpretation would lead to an absurdity;
(ii) the material referred to consists of statements by a minister or other promoter of the Bill, together with such other parliamentary material as is necessary to understand the statements and their effects;
(iii) the statements relied on are clear.

Their Lordships held that reference to parliamentary materials did not contravene Art 9 of the Bill of Rights (1688). No other claim to a defined parliamentary privilege was made by the Crown.

The decision of the House of Lords in *Pepper* v *Hart* marked a new approach to statutory interpretation by the English courts. The precise scope of the courts' new-found freedom has yet to be clearly and authoritatively established. It was not immediately clear, for example, whether a judge could only refer to *Hansard* where the legislation was ambiguous, obscure or would lead to an absurdity. Their Lordships have subsequently confirmed that the first threshold condition laid down in *Pepper* v *Hart* must be satisfied before reference is made to *Hansard* (*R* v *Secretary of State for the Environment, Transport and the Regions, ex parte Spath Holme Ltd*

(2001)). In a number of cases the House of Lords has referred to *Hansard* to confirm interpretations already made independently. There is also some doubt about whether the courts are confined to parliamentary material contained in *Hansard*. Can the courts also consider government press releases, briefing notes for ministers and so on? Lord Browne-Wilkinson in *Pepper* v *Hart* looked at a press release produced by the Inland Revenue (now known as HM Revenue and Customs). The House of Lords has confirmed that courts may have regard to matters stated in Parliament for background information when considering whether a statutory provision is compatible with the European Convention on Human Rights under the terms of the Human Rights Act 1998 (*Wilson* v *Secretary of State for Trade and Industry* (2003)). However, their Lordships felt that such occasions would seldom arise and the courts should remember that the intention of Parliament is expressed in the language used in its enactments.

Case law (judicial precedent)

Despite the enormous volume of legislation produced by parliaments down the ages, statute law remains an incomplete system of law. Large parts of our law still derive from the decisions of judges. This judge-made law is based on a rule known as the doctrine of binding judicial precedent. The principle underlying the doctrine is that a decision made by a court in a case involving a particular set of circumstances is binding on other courts in later cases, where the relevant facts are the same or similar. The idea of the judges making use of previously decided cases dates back to the formation of the common law by the royal justices out of English customary law. But it was not until the 19th century that the general principle of judicial consistency in decision-making developed into a more rigid system of binding precedents. The necessary conditions for such a system did not exist until the standard of law reporting was improved by the creation of the Council of Law Reporting in 1865 and a hierarchy of courts was established by the Judicature Acts 1873–75 and the Appellate Jurisdiction Act 1876.

Precedent in action

Whenever a judge decides a case, he or she makes a speech, which may last a few minutes in a simple matter but may run to many pages in the Law Reports in a complicated case before the House of Lords. Every judgment contains the following elements:

1 The judge records his or her findings as to the relevant facts of the case, established from evidence presented in court.
2 The judge discusses the law which relates to the facts as found; this may involve an examination of the provisions of an Act of Parliament and/or previous judicial decisions.
3 He explains the reasons for his decision; i.e. the rule of law on which his decision is based. This is known as the *ratio decidendi* of a case. It is this part of the judgment which forms a precedent for future similar cases. Other comments by the judge which do not form part of the reasoning necessary to make the decision are referred to as *obiter dicta* (things said by the way); they do not have binding force.
4 The judge concludes his speech by announcing the decision between the parties, e.g. 'I give judgment for the claimant for the amount claimed', or 'I would dismiss this appeal'.

Precedents may be either binding or persuasive. A binding precedent is one which a court must follow, while a persuasive precedent is one to which respect is paid but is not binding. Whether a court is bound by a particular precedent depends on its position in the hierarchy of courts relative to the court which established the precedent. The general rule is that the decisions of superior courts are binding on lower courts. The reader should refer to Chapter 3 ⊙ for an outline of the structure of the civil and criminal courts before considering the position of the principal courts which follows.

European Court of Justice

Since joining the EC in 1973, all English courts have been bound by the decisions of the European Court of Justice in matters of European law. The European Court tends to follow its own decisions but is not strictly bound to do so.

The Supreme Court (formerly the House of Lords)

The Supreme Court for the UK opened for business in Middlesex Guildhall on 1 October 2009. The judicial authority previously exercised by the House of Lords as the highest domestic court of appeal has been transferred now to the Supreme Court. The decisions of the Supreme Court and its predecessor, the House of Lords, are binding on all other English courts. The House of Lords used to be bound by its own previous decisions (**London Street Tramways** v **London County Council** (1898)). In 1966, however, the Lord Chancellor announced by way of a Practice Statement that the House would no longer regard itself absolutely bound by its own precedents. An example of the use of this freedom is **Miliangos** v **George Frank (Textiles) Ltd** (1976), in which the House overruled its own decision in **Re United Railways of Havana & Regla Warehouses Ltd** (1960) by holding that an English court may award damages in a foreign currency. It should be noted that the freedom to depart from previous precedents has not been exercised very often.

Court of Appeal

The Civil Division of the Court of Appeal is bound by the decisions of the Supreme Court or the House of Lords and its own previous decisions (**Young** v **Bristol Aeroplane Co** (1944)). There are three exceptions to this general rule:

1 the Court of Appeal must decide which of two conflicting decisions of its own it will follow;
2 the court must not follow one of its own decisions which is inconsistent with a later decision of the Supreme Court (or House of Lords);
3 the court is not bound to follow one of its own decisions which was given *per incuriam*, i.e. where the court has overlooked a relevant statute or case.

Court of Appeal decisions are binding on lower civil courts, such as the High Court and county court. The Criminal Division of the Court of Appeal is bound by the Supreme Court (or House of Lords') decisions and normally by its own decisions but, since it deals with questions of individual liberty, there appears to be greater freedom to depart from its own precedents. In a recent criminal case concerning provocation (**R v James** (2006)), the Court of Appeal had to decide whether to follow a decision of the House of Lords (**R v Smith (Morgan James)** (2000)) or a later decision of the Privy Council (**Attorney-General for Jersey** v **Holley** (2005)) which normally only has persuasive authority. The Court of Appeal decided to follow the Privy Council's ruling in **Holley**. The Judicial Committee of the Privy Council hearing **Holley** had been specially convened and comprised nine Law Lords. It concluded by a majority that **Smith (Morgan James)** was wrongly decided. The

Court of Appeal was justified in the circumstances in following the Privy Council decision in preference to the House of Lords.

Decisions of the Criminal Division of the Court of Appeal are binding on lower criminal courts, e.g. the Crown Court and magistrates' court.

Divisional courts

A divisional court is bound by the decisions of the Supreme Court (or House of Lords), the Court of Appeal and its own previous decisions, on the same lines as the Court of Appeal. Its decisions are binding on High Court judges sitting alone and lower courts such as the magistrates' court.

High Court

A High Court judge is bound by the decisions of the Supreme Court (or House of Lords), Court of Appeal and divisional courts, but is not bound by another High Court judge.

Other courts

Magistrates' courts and county courts are bound by the decisions of higher courts, but their own decisions have no binding force on other courts at the same level.

In a recent case, the House of Lords had to consider whether lower courts were bound to follow decisions of the House of Lords which were in conflict with later decisions of the European Court of Human Rights. In *Kay* v *London Borough of Lambeth; Leeds City Council* v *Price* (2006), Lord Bingham took the view that, unless there are exceptional circumstances, the courts should continue to follow binding precedent. If lower courts believe that they are bound by a precedent which is potentially inconsistent with a decision of the Court of Human Rights, they can give leave to appeal. 'Leap frog appeals' under the Administration of Justice Act 1969 (see Chapter 3 ◯) which allow fast track appeals direct from the High Court to the Supreme Court may be appropriate in these circumstances. Lord Bingham also referred to the nature of decisions emanating from the Court of Human Rights in Strasbourg:

> . . . in its decisions on particular cases the Strasbourg court accords a margin of appreciation, often generous, to the decisions of national authorities and attaches much importance to the peculiar facts of the case. Thus it is for national authorities, including national courts particularly, to decide in the first instance how the principles expounded in

Strasbourg should be applied in the special context of national legislation, law, practice and social and other conditions. It is by the decisions of national courts that the domestic standard must be initially set, and to those decisions the ordinary rules of precedent should apply.

At first sight, the system of precedent seems to consist of a very rigid set of rules, which have the effect of restricting possible growth in the law. It is certainly true that a court can find itself bound by a bad precedent, the application of which causes great injustice in the particular case before it. However, the system is more flexible in practice.

Since 1966, as we saw earlier, the House of Lords (now the Supreme Court) has not been bound by its own precedents, thus creating limited opportunities for the development of new legal principles. Moreover, any court can use a variety of techniques to avoid following an apparently binding precedent. There may be material differences between the facts of the case before the court and the facts of the case setting the precedent, and so the earlier case can be distinguished. It is by avoiding precedents in this way that the judges make law and contribute to the enormous wealth of detailed rules which characterises case law.

European Community law

On 1 January 1973 the United Kingdom became a member of the EC and thereby subject to a new source of law. Before we examine the nature of Community law and its impact on the English legal system, it is important to understand how the EC has developed and how it functions today.

Historical background

On 18 April 1951 ministers representing France, West Germany, Italy, Belgium, The Netherlands and Luxembourg took the first step towards the creation of the EC, which the United Kingdom finally joined in 1973. They signed the Treaty of Paris establishing the European Coal and Steel Community (ECSC) with the aim of placing coal and steel production under international control. The same six founding members came together again in March 1957 to sign the two Treaties of Rome which set up the European Economic Community

(EEC) and the European Atomic Energy Community (EURATOM).

The EEC was by far the most important of the three communities because its aim was the creation of a common market and harmonisation of the economic policies of member states. For these purposes, the EEC concerned itself with ensuring freedom of movement within the Community for persons, capital and services, devising common agricultural and transport policies and ensuring that competition within the EEC was not restricted or distorted. The constitution of each community is to be found in the Treaty which established it. Since the Merger Treaty of 1965, the three Communities have shared common institutions.

In January 1972 four more European countries agreed to join the EEC by signing the Treaty of Accession in Brussels. Only the United Kingdom, Republic of Ireland and Denmark took their places from 1 January 1973: Norway failed to ratify the Treaty following a negative vote by the Norwegian electorate in a national referendum. In 1981, the nine became ten with the accession of Greece, and membership was increased again when Spain and Portugal joined on 1 January 1986. The former territory of the German Democratic Republic became part of the Community in 1990 on the reunification of Germany.

In 1985 the heads of government of the member states committed themselves to removing all remaining barriers to the creation of a genuine 'common market' by the end of 1992. This commitment was contained in the Single European Act (SEA), which was approved by the European Council in December 1985 and signed in February 1986. The SEA had to be ratified by national Parliaments; this was achieved by the UK Parliament in the form of the European Communities (Amendment) Act 1986. The SEA, which came into force in the Community on 1 July 1987, contained the following elements:

- an agreement to establish an internal (or single) market by 31 December 1992 (the internal market was defined as 'an area without internal frontiers in which the free movement of goods, persons, services and capital is ensured');
- a declaration of the willingness of member states 'to transform relations as a whole among their States into a European Union';
- an acknowledgement of the objective of progressive realisation of economic and monetary union;

- an agreement to develop unrealised policies in the fields of economic and monetary convergence, social policy and the environment;
- a strengthening of the position of the European Parliament in the law-making process by means of a new 'co-operation procedure';
- an extension of the range of matters which could be decided by majority (rather than unanimous) voting by the Council of the European Union.

Further steps towards European integration were taken in December 1991 when the heads of government of the member states, meeting at Maastricht, agreed the details of a Treaty on European Union (TEU). The terms of the TEU include:

- the establishment of a European Union 'founded on the European Communities supplemented by the policies and forms of co-operation created by the TEU';
- the adoption of principles fundamental to the Union including respect for the national identities of the member states, respect for fundamental rights as a principle of Community law and respect for the principle of subsidiarity;
- a new agreement on economic and monetary union, accompanied by a strict timetable for its achievement;
- intergovernmental cooperation on a Common Foreign and Security Policy (CFSP);
- intergovernmental cooperation in the fields of Justice and Home Affairs (including asylum and immigration policies and police cooperation in combating terrorism and drug trafficking);
- expansion of Community powers in a number of economic and social fields, including health protection and overseas development cooperation;
- changes to the balance of power between EC institutions, in particular the strengthening of the role of the European Parliament in the law-making process;
- in a separate protocol all member states (except the UK) subscribed to the Social Chapter which incorporates the social policy objectives of the EC.

The Treaty had to be ratified by all member states before it could come into force. In order for the Treaty to take effect in the UK, Parliament passed the European Communities (Amendment) Act 1993.

On 1 January 1994 the Agreement on the European Economic Area (EEA) came into effect. Under this agreement, the principles and most of the rules of the single market were extended to five of the seven countries of the European Free Trade Association (EFTA) – Austria, Finland, Iceland, Norway and Sweden. Although these countries obtained the free-trade advantages of the single market, they did not become members and so had little say in the single market rules to which they were subject. To overcome this drawback, some of the countries sought EC membership – Austria, Finland and Sweden achieved full membership of the EC from 1 January 1995.

In June 1997, member states concluded negotiations on a new treaty at a European Council held in Amsterdam. The provisions of the Treaty of Amsterdam, which was signed by representatives of member states in October 1997, reflected not only the preoccupations of the Community in relation to, for example, unemployment and public health, but also paved the way for future enlargement of the Union.

The Treaty covers the following areas:

1 Freedom, security and justice

- Common action on asylum, visas, immigration and controls at external borders would be brought within Community rules and procedures, although the UK was permitted not to participate in any new measures adopted in relation to visas, asylum and immigration.
- Increased cooperation between police forces, customs and other law enforcement agencies in member states to assist the prevention, detection and investigation of criminal offences.

2 Union policies to benefit citizens

- Specifying the promotion of a high level of employment as a community objective, introducing a treaty-basis for developing a coordinated strategy for employment and establishing a coordination process for developing employment policies at Community level.
- Incorporation into the treaty of a strengthened Social Chapter applying to all member states, bringing to an end the UK's opt-out negotiated by the former Conservative Prime Minister John Major at Maastricht.
- In relation to environmental matters, the achievement of sustainable development became one of the objectives of the Community.
- Ensuring that Community policies and activities achieve a high level of human health protection.

- Measures to enhance the protection of consumers.
- A new treaty protocol setting out legally binding guidelines on the application of the principles of subsidiarity and proportionality. **Subsidiarity** means that the Community should have a subsidiary function and only take action in relation to matters which cannot be carried out effectively at local (member state) level. **Proportionality** means that in relation to Community matters, member states and European institutions should take action which is proportionate (i.e. not excessive) in order to achieve the intended object.

3 External policy

- Measures to improve the coherence and effectiveness of the Common Foreign and Security Policy.

4 Union's institutions and legislative procedures

- Introducing changes to the co-decision procedures and extending the areas where it may be used.
- Capping the number of members of the European Parliament at 700.
- Extending the areas where qualified majority voting may be used for adopting the acts of the Council.
- Introducing changes to the Commission, e.g. increasing the powers of the President to select Commissioners.
- Extending the powers of the Court of Justice in relation to, for example, safeguarding fundamental rights.
- Unofficial consolidation of all treaties, including the Treaty on European Union.

In December 2000 the EC heads of government concluded the Treaty of Nice which paved the way for the future enlargement of the Community from 15 to 27 member states. European states seeking membership included Poland, Romania, Czech Republic, Hungary, Bulgaria, Slovakia, Lithuania, Latvia, Slovenia, Estonia, Cyprus and Malta. The Treaty made a number of important changes to the organisation and operation of EC institutions to accommodate the expansion of the Community. They included:

- A new voting system for the Council of the European Union to come into effect on 1 January 2005.
- The European Parliament for 2004–09 to include representation from new member states which have

signed accession treaties by the beginning of 2004. The number of MEPs representing each member state would be scaled down. Similar arrangements would be made for the ECSC and the Committee of the Regions.

- The Commission to consist of one Commissioner for each member state from 1 January 2005. (The UK would have to lose one of its two Commissioners.) On accession, a new member state would be entitled to appoint its own Commissioner for one term.

In April 2003, 10 new member states signed the Treaty of Accession in Athens. Cyprus, the Czech Republic, Estonia, Hungary, Latvia, Lithuania, Malta, Poland, Slovenia and Slovakia joined the EC on 1 May 2004. Bulgaria and Romania joined the Community in January 2007. At the time of writing there are four candidate countries (Croatia, Iceland, the Former Yugoslav Republic of Macedonia and Turkey) and five potential candidates (Albania, Bosnia and Herzogovina, Montenegro, Serbia and Kosovo) A summary of the key dates in the enlargement of the EC is set out in Figure 2.3.

European Community or European Union?

It has become fashionable since the ratification of the TEU to refer to the European Union. Technically, the European Union consists of the European Community (the new formal title of what used to be known as the European Economic Community), the European Coal and Steel Community (ECSC), the European Atomic Energy Community (EURATOM), and the new areas of intergovernmental cooperation on foreign and security policy (CFSP), justice and home affairs. The European Community (EC) has not been replaced by the European Union. The EC, along with ECSC and EURATOM, is one 'pillar' of the European Union. The other two 'pillars' are CFSP, and justice and home affairs. Action in respect of these two pillars must be taken on the basis of intergovernmental cooperation: Community law does not apply and the European Court of Justice has no jurisdiction in these areas (although the Treaty of Amsterdam extends the powers of the Court of Justice in relation to action by the Union on asylum and immigration and cooperation on police and judicial matters).

Year	Member states joining the Community	Number of member states
1951	Belgium, France, West Germany, Italy, Luxembourg and The Netherlands form the European Coal and Steel Community	6
1957	Six founding members set up European Atomic Energy Authority and European Economic Community	6
1973	UK, Ireland and Denmark join the Community	9
1981	Greece accedes to EC membership	10
1986	Spain and Portugal join the EC	12
1990	German Democratic Republic (East Germany) becomes a member on reunification of Germany	12
1995	Austria, Finland and Sweden join the EC	15
2004	Cyprus, Czech Republic, Estonia, Hungary, Latvia, Lithuania, Malta, Poland, Slovenia and Slovakia accede to membership	25
2007	Bulgaria and Romania join the EC	27

Figure 2.3 **Enlargement of the European Union**

However, it should be noted that the Council (see below) now calls itself the Council of the European Union – even when it is enacting EC legislation.

Community institutions

The aims and objectives of the EC are put into effect by four main institutions: the Council of the European Union, the Commission, the European Parliament and the European Court of Justice.

The Council of the European Union

The Council is made up of heads of state or government of member states together with its President and the President of the Commission. Depending on the subject under discussion, the meetings may be attended by the relevant minister from each member state. Thus meetings of the Council may be attended by the foreign ministers of each country but if, say, the common transport policy is under discussion, the transport ministers of each state will attend. European Council meetings at head of state or government level take place twice every six months.

The Council is the supreme law maker for the EC, but this power is restricted by the fact that in most cases it can only legislate in respect of proposals put forward by the Commission. Although few decisions require the approval of all member states, under the Luxembourg Accords, the Council has adopted the practice of unanimity for decisions where vital national interests are at stake. Other decisions may be taken on a simple majority vote or on a qualified majority vote (QMV). In the latter case each country has a certain number of votes (France, Germany, Italy and the UK have 29 votes each; Spain and Poland have 27 each; Romania 14 votes; The Netherlands 13 votes; Belgium, Czech Republic, Greece, Hungary and Portugal have 12 votes apiece; Austria, Sweden and Bulgaria 10 votes; Denmark, Ireland, Lithuania, Slovakia and Finland 7 votes; Cyprus, Estonia, Latvia, Luxembourg and Slovenia have 4 votes each and Malta has 3). A qualified majority is achieved if a majority of member states (in some cases a two-thirds majority) agree and 255 votes are in favour. A member state may ask for confirmation that the votes in favour represent 62 per cent of the total population of the EC. The SEA extended the provisions for QMV to most single-market proposals to help the EC meet the 1992 target for the creation of the single (internal) market.

The Commission

The Commission, which is based in Brussels, comprises 27 members, one from each member state. Of the 27 Commission members, one is the President and five are Vice-Presidents. Commissioners are appointed for a period of five years by mutual agreement between the 27 member states. Once appointed, Commissioners must act with complete independence in the interests of the EC. Each Commissioner is assisted by a Cabinet consisting of six or more officials appointed by the Commissioner and responsible to him. Cabinet members have an important role to play in formulating proposals for approval by the Commission. The *Chefs de Cabinet* meet regularly to coordinate activities and prepare for Commission meetings. The Commission is divided into departments known as Directorates-General, headed by a Director-General who is responsible to a Commissioner. Each Directorate-General is divided into Directorates, which are further divided into Divisions. There are also various specialised services, e.g. a legal service.

The Commission plays an important part in the legislative process of the EC. It formulates Community policy, drafts proposed legislation to be laid before the Council, and it can exercise a limited legislative power of its own in some areas, e.g. competition policy and control of government subsidies. The Commission is also responsible for implementing Community legislation and ensuring that treaty obligations are being observed by member states.

The Parliament

Since 1979 MEPs have been directly elected by the citizens of member states. Elections are held every five years. There are currently 736 members of the European Parliament. The distribution of seats is set out in Figure 2.4. MEPs tend to sit and vote according to political rather than national allegiances. The European Parliament operates in two locations: plenary sessions are held in Strasbourg, while committee meetings take place in Brussels. Despite its name, the European Parliament is an advisory or consultative body rather than a legislative one. It is consulted by the Council and the Commission before certain decisions are taken: it can offer advice and opinions, it monitors the activities of the Commission and the Council and has the power to dismiss the full Commission. Its supervisory powers were extended under the TEU allowing it to set up Committees of Inquiry to investigate contraventions of, or maladministration

Member states	Number of seats from 1 January 2007
German Federal Republic	99
France	72
Italy	72
United Kingdom	72
Spain	50
Poland	50
Romania	33
Netherlands	25
Belgium	22
Greece	22
Portugal	22
Hungary	22
Czech Republic	22
Sweden	18
Austria	17
Bulgaria	17
Denmark	13
Finland	13
Slovakia	13
Ireland	12
Lithuania	12
Latvia	8
Slovenia	7
Cyprus	6
Estonia	6
Luxembourg	6
Malta	5
Total	736

Figure 2.4 Membership of the European Parliament

in, the implementation of Community law. It also has the power to appoint an ombudsman responsible for investigating complaints of maladministration. It plays an important part in drawing up the Community budget and can reject the entire budget. The SEA strengthened the role of the European Parliament in the legislative process and the TEU extends its powers by allowing it to veto certain proposals in areas such as the single market.

Court of Justice (ECJ)

The Court of Justice, which sits in Luxembourg, is composed of 27 judges, one from each member state. The court may sit as a Grand Chamber of 13 judges rather than requiring plenary sessions attended by all judges. The judges are assisted by several Advocates-General, whose function is to present an unbiased opinion of the case to the court. Judicial personnel are appointed by unanimous

agreement between the governments of member states for terms of six years, which may be renewed. The Court of Justice exercises judicial power within the EC. Its jurisdiction covers the following areas:

1 **Preliminary rulings.** Under Art 234 (previously Art 177) of the Treaty of Rome, any tribunal in a member state may ask the court to give a preliminary ruling concerning the interpretation of the treaties or Community legislation enacted under the treaties. If such a question is raised in a court against whose decision there is no further right of appeal, the ruling of the Court of Justice must be sought. References to the Court of Justice under Art 234 are not appeals as such. The proceedings of the national courts are suspended while the point of European law is determined by the European Court. The case then resumes in the national court, where the ruling is applied to the facts of the case.

2 **Actions against member states.** Proceedings may be taken against member states either by the Commission or by another member state in respect of violations of the treaties or Community legislation. If a case is established, the court will make an order requiring the member state to take the necessary measures to comply with the ECJ's judgment. In the past the ECJ has had to rely on political pressure to secure compliance, but the TEU gives the ECJ the power to impose financial sanctions.

3 **Actions against Community institutions.** Actions may be brought against Community institutions by other institutions, member states or, in certain circumstances, by corporate bodies and individuals. Such proceedings may be used to annul the acts of the Council and the Commission, to obtain a declaration that the Council or the Commission has failed to act as required by the treaties, to obtain compensation for damage caused by the unlawful actions of Community institutions and their servants and to review penalties imposed by the Commission.

4 **Community employment cases.** The court also deals with disputes between the EC and its employees.

The SEA provided for the creation of a Court of First Instance (CFI) to help relieve the Court of Justice of some of its workload. The CFI was inaugurated in 1989; its members are appointed for six-year terms by mutual agreement of the governments of the member states. It normally sits in divisions of three or five judges. Members of the court may be asked to perform the role of Advocates-General, in which case they must not participate in the deliberations of the court before judgment. The jurisdiction of the CFI is confined to disputes between the EC and its employees, appeals against implementation of EC competition rules and actions brought by undertakings against the Commission under the ECSC Treaty. Appeals against a decision of the CFI may be made to the Court of Justice, but on a point of law only.

Other institutions

The Court of Auditors

The Court of Auditors, which sits in Luxembourg, is the Community's financial watchdog. Its job is to scrutinise and report on the Community's financial management and oversee the implementation of the budget. It has 27 members from 1 January 2007, one from each member state, who are appointed every six years by the Council in consultation with the European Parliament. Since 1 May 2004 the Court has been able to set up 'chambers' of a few members in the interests of efficiency.

The Economic and Social Committee (ESC)

The ESC consists of representatives from all member states, drawn from various categories of economic and social activity, including employers, workers, professional bodies, consumers, environmentalists, farmers and so on. It is an advisory body whose opinion is sought by the Council and Commission on proposed legislation and other matters. The current membership of the ESC is 344.

The Committee of the Regions

This advisory Committee was established by the TEU. It consists of representatives from each member state, drawn from regional and local bodies. The Committee is consulted on proposed legislation in such areas as education, culture and public health to ensure that regional interests are considered. There are 344 members of the Committee.

The European Investment Bank (EIB)

The EIB, which is based in Luxembourg, is the Community's bank. It lends money to finance capital investment projects.

The EC Ombudsman

This position was created by the TEU. The EC Ombudsman, who is appointed by the European Parliament for a five-year term of office, has the task of receiving and dealing with complaints from citizens of member states concerning maladministration by any Community institution or body, except the European Court of Justice. The EC Ombudsman may receive complaints direct from aggrieved individuals and there is no limitation period on complaints. The EC Ombudsman may also receive complaints from MEPs or mount an investigation on his own initiative. Like his UK counterpart, the EC Ombudsman has no power to impose sanctions on institutions found guilty of maladministration. He or she must rely on adverse publicity and political pressure to secure an appropriate remedy. He or she must submit an annual report to the European Parliament and a report in each case where maladministration is found.

Sources of Community law

The nature and effect of Community law are summarised in Figure 2.5. The main sources of EC law are as follows:

1 The treaties

The treaties are the primary source of EC law. The foundations of the Community legal system were laid in the original Treaties of Paris and Rome and have been added to by further treaties, such as the Treaty of Accession and the TEU. These treaties have not been revised by the Amsterdam Treaty.

Under international law treaties are only binding on states at a government-to-government level and cannot normally be enforced by individuals in national courts. Although the treaties themselves make no reference to their effect and the rights of citizens to enforce treaty obligations, the European Court of Justice has developed the doctrine of 'direct effect' which enables an individual citizen to enforce Community rights derived from the treaties in domestic courts. The doctrine of direct effect was established in the following case.

Algemene Transport-en Expeditie Onderneming van Gend en Loos NV v Nederlandse Administratie der Belasting (1963)

This case concerned the payment of duty on chemicals being imported from Germany to the Netherlands. Van Gend en Loos, a Dutch transport company, brought an action before a Dutch tribunal claiming that an increase in the import duty being charged by the Dutch government infringed Art 12 of the EEC Treaty (now Art 25 of the EC Treaty). The tribunal referred the matter to the

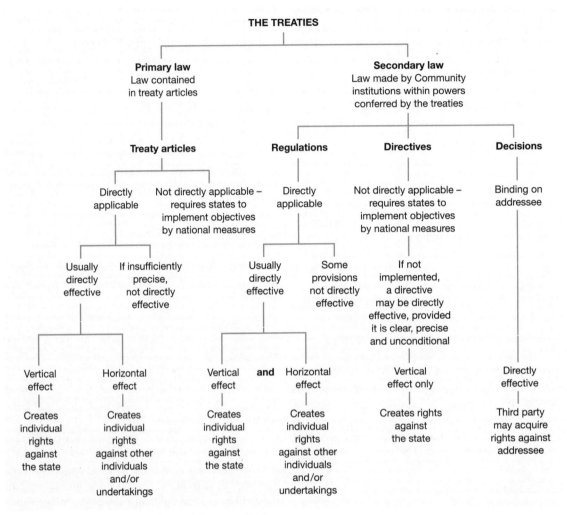

Figure 2.5 The nature and effect of Community law

ECJ for a preliminary ruling under Art 177 of the EEC Treaty (now Art 234 of the EC Treaty) as to 'whether Article 12 of the EEC Treaty has direct application within the territory of Member States, in other words whether nationals of such a state can, on the basis of the Article in question, lay claim to individual rights which the courts must protect'. The ECJ held that Art 12 was directly effective and could be relied on by Van Gend en Loos. The ECJ concluded that: 'the Community constitutes a new legal order of international law for the benefit of which the states have limited their sovereign rights, albeit within limited fields, and the subjects of which comprise not only Member States but also their nationals . . . Community law therefore not only imposes obligations on individuals but is also intended to confer upon

them rights which become part of their legal heritage. These rights arise not only when they are expressly granted by the Treaty but also by reason of obligations which the Treaty imposes in a clearly defined way upon individuals as well as upon the Member States and upon the institutions of the Community.'

Not all treaty provisions are directly effective. The criteria used to determine whether a provision is directly effective were developed by the ECJ in *Van Gend en Loos* and subsequent cases. The provision:

- must be clear and unconditional;
- must not be qualified by any reservation on the part of member states which would make its implementation

conditional on legislation being passed under national law;

- must contain an absolute prohibition; not an obligation to do something but an obligation to refrain from doing something (*Costa* v *ENEL* (1964));
- may be directly effective if the Community's institutions fail to fulfil treaty obligations, e.g. by issuing directives (*Reyners* v *Belgium* (1974)).

An example of a 'directly effective' provision is Art 141 (previously Art 119), which establishes the principle of 'equal pay for equal work' (*Defrenne* v *Sabena* (1976)). Any employee, irrespective of whether he or she works in the public or private sector, can rely on Art 141 against his or her employer in an action for equal pay in domestic courts. Article 141 is an example of a Community provision which gives an individual rights against other individuals or undertakings. Such a provision is said to have **horizontal direct effect**. (Provisions which create individual rights against a member state are said to have **vertical direct effect**.)

Some treaty provisions are insufficiently precise or, by their nature, are incapable of conferring rights on individuals. Member states are expected to give effect to these provisions by enacting specific legislation in their own parliaments.

2 Secondary law

The treaties empower the Council and Commission to make three types of legislation: regulations, directives and decisions.

(a) *Regulations* are designed to achieve uniformity of law among the member states. They are of general application and usually have direct force of law in all member states without the need for further legislation, i.e. they are directly effective (horizontally and vertically).

Consorzio del Prosciutto di Parma v Asda Stores Ltd (2003)

The Parma Ham Association brought a legal challenge against Asda in respect of the labelling of ham from Parma which had been sliced and packaged in the UK as 'Parma Ham'. The Association argued that this practice was unlawful under both Italian and European Law. The relevant European regulation provided a procedure for registering a 'protected designation of origin' (PDO). A PDO is the name of a place used to describe a product which originates in that place. The ECJ held that the regulation was directly effective and could be relied upon by individuals in member states. Although the regulation permitted the PDO to include the condition that slicing and packaging must take place in the region of production, the condition could not be enforced against businesses as it had not been brought to their attention by adequate publicity in Community legislation.

Although regulations are directly effective, some of the provisions may require implementation by member states. In this case, the provision will not have direct effect.

An example of a regulation is Regulation 1436/70, which requires tachographs to be fitted in commercial vehicles. The Commission brought enforcement proceedings against the UK for failure to implement Art 21 of the regulation (*EC Commission* v *United Kingdom (Re Tachographs)* (1979)).

(b) *Directives* seek to harmonise the law of member states. They are instructions to member states to bring their laws into line by a certain date. The states themselves are free to choose the methods by which the changes are implemented, e.g. by Act of Parliament or statutory instrument. Directives, unlike regulations, are therefore not directly applicable. However, provisions of a directive may take direct effect (vertically) if not duly implemented by a member state. The direct effect of directives was established in the following case.

Van Duyn v Home Office (1974)

Miss Van Duyn, a Dutch national, was refused entry to the UK by the Home Office. She wished to take up a job with the Church of Scientology. The British government regarded Scientology to be socially harmful and as a matter of policy it refused leave to enter the UK to all aliens who wanted to work on behalf of the Church of Scientology. Miss Van Duyn challenged the decision on the basis that it was contrary to treaty provisions guaranteeing freedom of movement within the Community. The UK government argued that the relevant article permitted exclusions on grounds of public policy. However, Miss Van Duyn relied on a later directive which provided that the public policy exclusion must be based on the personal conduct of the individual. Since she had done nothing wrong as an individual, the government could not justify its refusal to allow her to enter the UK. The

ECJ held that the directive laid down an obligation which was not subject to any exception or condition and which did not require further action either on the part of European institutions or member states. It conferred rights on individuals which they could enforce in their national courts and which the courts were bound to protect.

Comment. Member states are given a period of time within which to implement the provision of a directive and therefore they are only directly effective from the date set for implementation. In ***Pubblico Ministero* v *Ratti* (1979)**, R was prosecuted for breach of Italian law concerning the labelling of chemical solvents, even though he had observed the requirements of two EC directives. The Italian government had not implemented the relevant directives by the due date and as a result was prevented from relying on its own failure in order to take action against R under Italian law.

An example of a directive is Directive 93/13/EEC on unfair terms in consumer contracts (see further, Chapter 8 ○). The directive, which introduced a general requirement of fairness in consumer contracts, was implemented in the UK by means of delegated legislation (the Unfair Terms in Consumer Contracts Regulations (SI 1999/2083)).

If a directive is not implemented by the required date:

- The state in default may find itself subject to enforcement proceedings brought by the Commission. In 1982 the UK was found to be in breach of its Community obligations for failing to comply with the requirements of 'equal pay for work of equal value' set out in the Equal Pay Directive (*EC Commission* v *United Kingdom* (1982)).
- Public employees may be able to rely on the directive as against the state in its capacity as an employer (*Marshall* v *Southampton & SW Hampshire Area Health Authority (Teaching)* (1986) – see later). In *Foster* v *British Gas plc* (1991) the Court of Justice defined 'the state' in broad terms so that in certain circumstances it might include newly privatised industries.
- Individuals who have suffered loss as a result of failure to implement a directive may be able to sue the state for damages, provided that: (a) the result required by the directive involved conferring rights on individuals; (b) the content of the rights can be determined from the directive; and (c) there is a

causal link between the failure to implement the directive and the damage suffered by those affected (*Francovich and Bonifaci* v *Italy* (1991)).

The ECJ has also developed the concept of the **indirect effect** of directives by requiring national courts to interpret national law in light of the wording and purpose of a directive to achieve the result intended by the directive (***Von Colson and Kamann* v *Land Nordrhein-Westfalen* (1984)**). This principle was confirmed in the following case.

Marleasing SA v *La Comercial Internacional de Alimentacion SA* (1990)

Marleasing claimed that La Comercial, a Spanish company, had been established to defraud the creditors of Barvieso SA, a founding member of La Comercial. Marleasing was a creditor of Barvieso and it sought to have the formation of La Comercial declared void under the provision of Spanish national law. La Comercial argued that an EC directive did not allow the agreement establishing the company to be rendered void in these circumstances. The Spanish government should have implemented the directive on their accession to the EC but had not done so. The ECJ confirmed that it had consistently held that a directive does not of itself impose obligations on an individual and it cannot be relied on against an individual (i.e. it does not have horizontal direct effect). However, when applying national law, whether the domestic law was enacted before or after the directive, the national court is required to interpret the domestic legislation in light of the wording and purpose of the directive in order to achieve the result intended by the directive.

Comment. It is not entirely clear whether the obligation to interpret domestic law in accordance with a directive applies only where the domestic legislation is ambiguous or if it can apply where the legislation is clear and unambiguous but directly conflicts with a directive.

(c) *Decisions* may be addressed to a state, a company or an individual and are binding on the addressee. Some decisions may have direct effect in the sense that third parties may be able to rely on the decision in an action against the addressee. An example of a decision is Council Decision 89/469 'concerning certain protective measures relating to bovine spongiform encephalopathy in the United Kingdom', which was adopted in the wake of the discovery of 'mad cow' disease.

3 Decisions of the Court of Justice

Judgments of the Court of Justice on matters of European law are binding on courts within the member states.

The law-making process

Regulations, directives and decisions come into effect by a number of different procedures. The procedure to be followed in each case is determined by the relevant treaty article.

1 Consultation procedure. Before the amendment of the EEC Treaty by the SEA, this was the only procedure which operated. Under this procedure, the Commission formulates proposals which are submitted to the Council for consideration. The European Parliament has a right to be consulted and to give an opinion. A final decision is then taken by the Council on the proposal in accordance with the appropriate voting procedures. Although other procedures now predominate, the consultation procedure has been retained for some matters, e.g. the Common Agricultural Policy (CAP).

2 Cooperation procedure. This procedure, which was introduced by the SEA, involves the European Parliament more fully in the decision-making process. Parliament has the opportunity to give its opinion and propose amendments on two occasions: the first occasion is when the Commission proposal is submitted to the Council and the second is after the Council has considered Parliament's opinion and reached a 'Common Position'. Parliament has more opportunity to influence a proposal under this procedure but does not have a right of veto. This procedure now only applies to articles concerning Economic and Monetary Union (EMU), as a result of changes made at Amsterdam.

3 Co-decision procedure. This procedure was introduced by the TEU and will apply to most single-market proposals, consumer protection, culture and public health. The procedure follows the cooperation procedure up to the point where Parliament considers the Common Position adopted by the Council. If Parliament approves the proposal, the Council adopts the measure. If Parliament indicates its intention to reject the Common Position, a Conciliation Committee, consisting of 12 representatives of the Council and an equal number of MEPs, is convened with a view to reaching an agreement acceptable to both sides. If the Conciliation Committee is unable to reach an agreement or the agreement it does reach is unacceptable to Parliament,

the proposal lapses. If Parliament proposes amendments to the Common Position, then, following further consideration by the Commission and the Council, the Council may adopt the measure provided it approves all the amendments. If it does not, then the Conciliation Committee is convened. If a joint text is agreed by the two sides, the measure must be adopted within six weeks by the Council and Parliament. If the Committee fails to agree, the proposal will either lapse or it could be adopted unilaterally by the Council; but even then Parliament could reject it by an absolute majority. This complex procedure gives Parliament a power of veto.

4 Assent procedure. This procedure, which was introduced by the SEA, applies to applications for membership to the Community and agreements between the Community and other states or international organisations. The Council may only adopt a Commission proposal under this procedure by obtaining the formal approval of Parliament.

The Treaty of Amsterdam introduced a number of changes to the law-making processes within the EC. The co-decision procedure was simplified and the scope for using the new procedure was extended.

Impact of Community membership on English law

Britain's application to join the EC was formally accepted and signified on 22 January 1972 when ministers of the UK government signed the Treaty of Accession in Brussels. A treaty is an agreement between sovereign states, which is binding in international law only. Treaty obligations undertaken by the UK do not become law in this country unless and until they are embodied in legislation by Parliament. Membership of the EC involved the acceptance of Community law as part of English law. This could only be achieved by passing an Act of Parliament: the European Communities Act 1972.

Section 2(1) of the 1972 Act provides that Community law which is intended to take direct effect within member states (i.e. provisions of the treaties and regulations) shall automatically form part of the law of the UK. Under s 2(2), Community legislation which requires some act of implementation by member states (i.e. directives) may be brought into force by Orders in Council or ministerial regulations. Certain measures, such as the creation of major criminal offences, must be implemented by Act of Parliament. English courts are required to take note of the treaties and the decisions of the European Court of Justice. The supremacy of Community law over English law is illustrated by the following cases.

Macarthys Ltd v Smith (1979)

Mrs Smith was employed by Macarthys Ltd as a stock-room manager. She claimed that she was entitled to the same pay as her male predecessor in the job. The Court of Appeal held that the provisions of the Equal Pay Act 1970 applied only to comparisons between men and women employed by the same employer at the same time. However, Art 119 (now Art 141) of the Treaty of Rome provides that 'men and women should receive equal pay for equal work'. Mrs Smith's case was referred to the European Court of Justice, which ruled that Art 119 applied to cases of a woman following a man in a job. The provisions of Art 119 took priority over the Equal Pay Act 1970 by virtue of the European Communities Act 1972. Mrs Smith succeeded in her action for equal pay.

Comment. This case illustrates the direct applicability of treaty articles and their horizontal direct effect. Article 119 conferred rights on Mrs Smith which were enforceable against her private-sector employer in the UK courts.

Marshall v Southampton & SW Hampshire Area Health Authority (Teaching) (1986)

The Area Health Authority (AHA) had a policy that its employees should retire at the age at which social security pensions became payable, i.e. 60 for women and 65 for men. The AHA was prepared to waive the policy in respect of certain employees and in fact allowed Miss Marshall, a senior dietician, to work past the normal retiring age for female employees. When she was dismissed at the age of 62, Miss Marshall claimed she had been discriminated against on the grounds of her sex since if she had been a man she would have continued working until the age of 65. She based her claim on the Sex Discrimination Act 1975 and the EC Equal Treatment Directive. Both the industrial tribunal and the Employment Appeal Tribunal dismissed her claim under the Sex Discrimination Act because arrangements in relation to death and retirement are excluded from the Act's prohibition of discrimination. The Court of Appeal referred Miss Marshall's case to the European Court of Justice to determine whether her dismissal breached the Equal Treatment Directive and, if it did, whether she

could rely on the directive in the English courts. Miss Marshall succeeded on both points.

Comment.

(i) The European Court of Justice found that, as the UK had failed to implement fully the EC Equal Treatment Directive, Miss Marshall could rely on the directive against the state in its capacity as her employer, i.e. the directive had a vertical direct effect. Directives do not have a horizontal direct effect and do not create rights which individual workers can enforce against their private-sector employers.

(ii) The decision in the *Marshall* case prompted a change in the law. Employers are now required to set a common retirement age for their employees, irrespective of their sex. (The relevant statutory provision is now contained in the Equality Act 2010.)

(iii) Miss Marshall returned to the European Court of Justice to challenge the statutory limit on awards made under the Sex Discrimination Act 1975. The European Court agreed with her argument that such a limit was in breach of the Equal Treatment Directive (*Marshall v Southampton & SW Hampshire Area Health Authority (No 2)* (1993)). The statutory limits have now been removed in respect of claims made under both the Sex Discrimination Act 1975 and the Race Relations Act 1976.

By enacting the European Communities Act 1972, the UK Parliament has relinquished part of its sovereignty. Certain forms of Community law automatically take precedence over English law without reference to Parliament. Nevertheless, the 1972 Act is a statute like any other and could be repealed by a future Parliament and full sovereignty would be restored.

The future of the European Union – the European Constitution

At the Nice meeting of heads of state and government in December 2000, it was agreed that enlargement of the EC would necessitate constitutional reform. A year later, the European Council meeting in Laeken adopted a *Declaration on the Future of the European Union* which led to the setting up of a European Convention, chaired by the former French President Valéry Giscard D'Estaing, to develop a draft treaty establishing a Constitution for Europe.

Agreement on the Constitutional Treaty was reached in June 2004 and member states began the process of ratification in accordance with domestic arrangements.

The Treaty was ratified by 13 of the 25 member states but in 2005 the French and Dutch voted 'No' to the Constitution in national referenda. The leaders of member states agreed to a period of reflection before deciding what action to take next.

In December 2007 the European heads of government signed the European Reform Treaty (Treaty of Lisbon). The main features of the Lisbon Treaty are as follows:

■ The current system of a six-month rotating presidency would be replaced by the appointment by the Council of a permanent President of the Council for a term of two and a half years.

■ The creation of a new post of EU 'Foreign Minister' (and Vice-President of the Commission), combining the jobs of the High Representative of the Union for Foreign Affairs and Security Policy and the External Affairs Commissioner, with the aim of improving the effectiveness, consistency and coherence of the EU's foreign policy.

■ From 2014, two-thirds of the member states will have a Commissioner who will hold office for five years.

■ Qualified Majority Voting (QMV) will become the default voting method for the Council, except where the treaties require a different method. From 2014, QMV will be based on a 'double majority' requiring 55 per cent of member states and 65 per cent of the EU's population.

■ The number of MEPs will be capped at 751 (750 plus the president of the Parliament) and no member state will have more than 96 or less than six MEPs.

■ The introduction of a 'Citizen's Initiative', which requires the Commission to draft a proposal if 1 million citizens petition for reform.

■ National vetoes are removed in a number of areas including in relation to aspects of Justice and Home Affairs.

■ The European Union would acquire a single legal personality, enabling it to sign international treaties and join international organisations.

■ The provisions of the EU Charter of Fundamental Rights will be legally binding, although the UK government has entered into a protocol which ensures that no court can declare UK laws, regulations or administrative practices as inconsistent with the Charter.

Although the Lisbon Treaty contains many of the features of the Nice Treaty, it does not purport to be a Constitutional Treaty. The Lisbon Treaty amends current EU and EC treaties, whereas the Nice Con-stitutional Treaty aimed to create a single text for a European Constitution and replace all existing treaties.

The process of ratifying the Lisbon Treaty was thrown into doubt in June 2008, when Irish voters rejected the treaty in a referendum. Although the UK government had undertaken to hold a referendum on the Nice Constitutional Treaty in its 2005 election manifesto, it decided that the Lisbon Treaty should be ratified by Parliament and the European Union (Amendment) Act received the Royal Assent in June 2008.

An application for judicial review of the government's decision not to hold a referendum was unsuccessful (*R (on the application of Wheeler)* v *Office of the Prime Minister* (2008)). The High Court held that the 'promise' contained in the 2005 Labour Party Election Manifesto and various ministerial statements related to the Nice Constitutional Treaty and that treaty was materially different from the Lisbon Treaty; and even if ministerial statements could be regarded as a 'promise', that did not give rise to legitimate expectations enforce-able in public law. The subject matter, nature and con-text of the 'promise' placed it in the realm of politics rather than the courts. The Lisbon Treaty finally came into force on 1 December 2009, after the last member state (the Czech Republic) ratified the treaty in Novem-ber 2009. The main changes introduced by the treaty are:

■ The appointment of a permanent President of the Council for two and a half years, who will chair summits. The first President is Herman Van Rompuy, a former Prime Minister of Belgium.

■ The creation of a new post of High Representative of the Union for Foreign Affairs and Security Policy and Vice-President of the Commission. The first High Representative is Baroness Ashton from the UK.

■ Qualified majority voting (QMV) in the Council is extended, and from 2014 QMV will be based on a double majority of 55 per cent of member states and 65 per cent of the EU's population.

Human rights

European Convention on Human Rights and the Human Rights Act 1998

The UK is very unusual in having no written con-stitution which sets out the powers of the Crown, Parliament, the government and the judiciary, and the rights of citizens. In the UK, a person is free to do anything which is not specifically prohibited by the law. However, there is no statement of basic civil rights and no mechanism to prevent Parliament from passing legislation which restricts civil rights. Most other countries have written constitutions which incorporate a statement of fundamental civil rights guaranteed by the state and the courts.

In 1950 the Council of Europe adopted a European Convention on Human Rights (ECHR) which was based on the United Nations' Universal Declaration on Human Rights. The UK ratified the ECHR in 1951. The rights and freedoms protected by the ECHR and subsequent amendments (known as protocols) ratified by the UK are set out in Figure 2.6.

Rights under the Convention are not all the same. There are three types of Convention right:

- **absolute rights** (i.e. Arts 2 and 3) which cannot be restricted in any circumstances including times of war or other general emergency and which must not be balanced with any public interest;

- **limited rights** (i.e. Arts 5 and 6) which are rights that may be limited by provisions specified within the Article or where the government can enter a derogation, restricting the exercise of certain rights in times of war or other public emergency;

- **qualified rights** (i.e. Arts 8 and 9) which are those rights that may be limited or restricted provided the interference with rights is prescribed by law, is done to pursue a legitimate aim set out in the relevant Article (e.g. prevention of crime, interest of national security), the interference is necessary in a democratic society by fulfilling a pressing social need, pursuing a legitimate aim and is proportionate to the achievement of the aim.

Unlike the Universal Declaration on Human Rights, the ECHR established institutions and procedures for protecting the rights enshrined in the Convention. The European Court of Human Rights, which sits at Strasbourg, adjudicates on petitions brought by individual citizens against a state and cases brought by one state against another. Individual petitions may only be

Article	Rights and freedoms	Type of right
2	The right to life	Absolute
3	Freedom from torture or inhuman or degrading treatment	Absolute
4	Freedom from slavery and forced labour	Absolute
5	The right to liberty and security of the person	Limited
6	The right to a fair trial	Limited
7	Protection from any retrospective effect of the criminal law	Absolute
8	Right to respect for private and family life	Qualified
9	Freedom of thought, conscience and religion	Qualified
10	Freedom of expression	Qualified
11	Freedom of assembly and association	Qualified
12	The right to marry	Qualified
13	The right to an effective remedy	
14	The enjoyment of Convention rights without discrimination on the grounds of sex, race, colour, language, religion, political or other opinion, national or social origin, association with a national minority, property, birth or other status	
Protocol 1		
1	The right to peaceful enjoyment of one's possessions	Qualified
2	The right to education	Qualified
3	The right to free elections	Qualified
Protocol 6		
1	Abolition of the death penalty	Qualified by Art 2
2	Death penalty in times of war	

Figure 2.6 **The European Convention on Human Rights**

brought to the court if the relevant state has accepted the rights of its citizens to bring a petition and all domestic remedies have been exhausted. The European Commission on Human Rights is responsible for ensuring that the individual petition is admissible and in all cases trying to help the parties to resolve the dispute. If an out-of-court settlement cannot be reached, the case may be referred to the court. If the court decides that a state is in breach of the ECHR, it can award compensation or other 'just satisfaction' of the case. The court has no powers of enforcement and in practice it relies on the goodwill of states to implement its judgments.

Although the UK ratified the ECHR, and from 1966 allowed UK citizens to bring individual petitions to the court, the provisions of the ECHR were not incorporated into UK law. As with other treaties, UK judges in domestic courts could take the ECHR into account in interpreting UK legislation and in applying the rules of common law. However, if the legislation was clear but in conflict with the ECHR, judges had to apply the UK legislation. Individuals were forced to exhaust all rights of appeal in UK courts, at great expense, before being allowed to take the case to the European Court of Human Rights. About half of the other signatory states had incorporated the ECHR into their domestic law. Their citizens could rely on the ECHR in their domestic courts and any legislation in conflict with the ECHR could be declared invalid.

In 1997 the Labour government indicated its intention to incorporate the ECHR into UK law. The Human Rights Act 1998 (HRA 1998), which came fully into force on 2 October 2000, enables people to enforce their Convention rights in UK courts rather than having to exhaust all domestic remedies before bringing a case to the European Court of Human Rights in Strasbourg. UK legislation must now be interpreted as far as possible by the courts in a way which is compatible with Convention rights (s 3). If a provision of UK legislation is incompatible with Convention rights, specified courts are able under s 4 to make a 'declaration of incompatibility'. The courts specified include the House of Lords (now the Supreme Court), the Judicial Committee of the Privy Council, the Court of Appeal and the High Court. The incompatible provision remains in force until it is amended by ministerial order. Where the legislation emanates from the Scottish Parliament or the Assemblies in Wales and Northern Ireland, the courts have the power to overrule provisions which are incompatible with the ECHR. By July 2006, when the Lord Chancellor published a review of the implementation of the HRA 1998, there had been 11 declarations of incompatibility by superior courts and 12 occasions when the s 3 requirement to interpret UK legislation in a way which is compatible with Convention rights had been used. The following is an example of a case relevant to business where a declaration of incompatibility was upheld by the Court of Appeal.

International Transport Roth GmbH v Secretary of State for the Home Department (2002)

This case arose out of the government's attempts to reduce the number of people entering the UK illegally by imposing fixed penalties on those responsible. Under the scheme, established by Part II of the Immigration and Asylum Act 1999, owners, hirers and drivers of lorries were liable to pay a fixed penalty of £2,000 per clandestine entrant unless they could establish (i) that they were acting under duress, or (ii) that they had neither actual nor constructive knowledge of the clandestine entrant and that there was an effective system of preventing the carriage of illegal entrants which was operated properly on the occasion in question. Where a penalty notice had been issued, a senior immigration officer had the power to detain the vehicle if he believed that there was a serious risk that the penalty would not be paid. The six claimants, who were liable for penalties, sought judicial review of the statutory scheme on the grounds that it was incompatible with Art 6 and Protocol 1, Art 1 of the European Convention on Human Rights and that it was contrary to Arts 28 and 49 of the EC Treaty (the right to free movement of goods).

The Court of Appeal held by a majority that the scheme was incompatible with Art 6: the penalty was criminal rather than civil in character and therefore attracted the protection of Art 6. The fixed nature of the penalty offends the right of the person responsible to have the penalty determined by an independent tribunal. The scale and inflexibility of the penalty scheme had the effect of imposing an excessive burden on carriers in breach of Protocol 1, Art 1. The scheme was not inconsistent with Arts 28 and 49 of the EC Treaty. The declaration of incompatibility made by Sullivan J in the lower court was upheld. The scheme was amended by the Nationality, Immigration and Asylum Act 2002.

A minister in charge of a Bill is required to make a written statement that he believes the Bill is compatible with the ECHR or, if he is unable to make such a statement, that he nevertheless wishes the House to proceed with the legislation.

It is unlawful under s 6 for a public authority to act in a way which is incompatible with the ECHR. Although the HRA 1998 does not define the term 'public authority', s 6 states that it includes courts and tribunals and any person whose functions are of a public nature. Obvious examples of core public authorities include central and local government, the armed forces, the police, immigration and prison officers. However, there are hybrid organisations which exercise both public and non-public functions. Some examples of non-governmental organisations discharging public functions include the privatised utilities supplying gas, electricity and water, charities in receipt of public funds and commercial companies operating prisons. The House of Lords held that there was no single test which could be used to decide whether a function is public; a range of factors must be considered including whether 'the body is publicly funded, or is exercising statutory powers, or is taking the place of central government or local authorities, or is providing a public service' (*per* Lord Nichols, *Aston Cantlow and Wilmcote with Billesley Parochial Church Council* v *Wallbank* (2003)). A housing association has been held to be a public authority, as it had a close relationship with and was exercising similar functions to a local authority (*Poplar Housing and Regeneration Community Association Ltd* v *Donoghue* (2001)). In contrast, a parochial church council was found **not** to be a public authority (*Wallbank*, above), as was a charity providing residential care (*Heather* v *Leonard Cheshire Foundation* (2002)). In the following case the House of Lords had to decide whether a privately owned care home was a 'public authority'.

YL v Birmingham City Council (2007)

The claimant (YL) was aged 84 and suffering from Alzheimer's disease. The defendant local authority had placed the claimant in the care home under a three-way agreement between the care home, the local authority and the claimant's daughter (OL). The cost of YL's care at the home was met by the local authority and OL, who paid a top-up fee. The care home wrote to OL giving 28 days' notice to terminate YL's residence, claiming a breakdown in the relationship between OL and the managers of the care home. The Official Solicitor commenced proceedings on behalf of YL, claiming that the care home in providing accommodation and care for YL was exercising a public function. The House of Lords held (by a 3:2 majority) that the care home was not exercising functions of a public nature. Their Lordships drew a distinction between the actual provision of care and accommodation, which in this case was being provided by a private profit-earning company, and the local authority's involvement in making the arrangements for YL's care, which included part-funding the arrangement. The care home provided services for both privately and publicly funded residents, and although there were differences between them, they did not justify a differential application of the European Convention to privately and publicly funded residents in the same home. Apart from any contractual arrangements, the care home should treat all residents with equality.

Only individuals who are affected by the unlawful act, referred to as 'victims', are entitled to take proceedings. It should be noted that core public authorities do not enjoy Convention rights and cannot be 'victims' but non-governmental hybrid authorities acting in a private nature are not disabled from enjoying Convention rights and can be victims.

Under s 8 of the HRA 1998, a court may grant such relief or remedy as it considers just and appropriate and is within its powers. The remedies may include damages, in which case the court must take into account the principles established by the European Court of Human Rights in awarding damages. Other forms of relief include quashing an unlawful decision, releasing a defendant on a criminal charge or quashing the conviction, or preventing a public authority from taking an act which would be unlawful.

There is a time limit, known as a limitation period, of one year from the date when the act complained of took place in which proceedings must be commenced, although the period can be extended by the court if it deems it to be equitable. However, if there is a shorter time period for the type of proceeding in question, e.g. three months for judicial review, that limit will apply.

In November 2003 the Secretary of State for Constitutional Affairs announced the government's intention to establish a Commission for Equality and Human Rights, which would bring together the work undertaken at that time by the separate race, equal opportunities and disability commissions, and provide institutional support for promoting human rights. The Equality Act 2006 established the new Commission for Equality and Human Rights (CEHR) which commenced operations in October 2007.

The impact of the European Convention on Human Rights and its incorporation into English law by the HRA 1998 will be noted in the context of the specific area of business law under consideration later in the text.

European Union Charter of Fundamental Rights

The European Charter of Fundamental Rights was agreed by the Presidents of the Council, Commission and Parliament on behalf of their respective institutions in December 2000 in Nice. The European Charter extends beyond the scope of the Convention, covering, for example, economic and social rights. The contents of the Charter are set out in Figure 2.7.

The Lisbon Treaty guarantees the freedoms and principles enshrined in the Charter of Fundamental Rights and its provisions will have binding force in respect of European Union law.

Title I	Dignity	Title II	Freedoms	Title III	Equality
Art II-1	Human dignity must be respected and protected	Art II-6	Right to liberty and security	Art II-20	Equality before the law
Art II-2	Right to life	Art II-7	Respect for private and family life	Art II-21	Prohibition of discrimination on the grounds of sex, race, colour, ethnic or social origin, nationality, genetic features, language, religion or belief, political or other opinion, membership of a national minority, property, birth, disability, age or sexual orientation
Art II-3	Right to the integrity of the person	Art II-8	Protection of personal data		
Art II-4	Prohibition of torture or inhuman or degrading treatment or punishment	Art II-9	Right to marry and right to found a family		
Art II-5	Prohibition of slavery and forced labour	Art II-10	Freedom of thought, conscience and religion		
		Art II-11	Freedom of expression and information		
		Art II-12	Freedom of assembly and association	Art II-22	Respect for cultural, religious and linguistic diversity
		Art II-13	Freedom of the arts and sciences		
		Art II-14	Right to education	Art II-23	Equality between men and women
		Art II-15	Freedom to choose an occupation and right to engage in work	Art II-24	Rights of the child
				Art II-25	Rights of the elderly
		Art II-16	Freedom to conduct a business	Art II-26	Respect for rights of the disabled
		Art II-17	Right to property		
		Art II-18	Right to asylum		
		Art II-19	Protection in the event of removal, expulsion or extradition		

Figure 2.7 European Union Charter of Fundamental Rights

Title IV	Solidarity	Title V	Citizen's Rights	Title VI	Justice
Art II-27	Worker's right to information and consultation within the undertaking	Art II-39	Right to vote and to stand as a candidate at elections to the European Parliament	Art II-47	Right to an effective remedy and to a fair trial
Art II-28	Right of collective bargaining and action	Art II-40	Right to vote and stand as a candidate at municipal elections	Art II-48	Presumption of innocence and right of defence
Art II-29	Right of access to placement services	Art II-41	Right to good administration	Art II-49	Principles of legality and proportionality of criminal offences and penalties
Art II-30	Protection in the event of unjustified dismissal	Art II-42	Right of access to documents	Art II-50	Right not to be tried or punished twice for the same criminal offence
Art II-31	Fair and just working conditions	Art II-43	Right to refer maladministration to the European Ombudsman		
Art II-32	Prohibition of child labour and protection of young people at work	Art II-44	Right of petition to the European Parliament		
Art II-33	Protection for family and professional life	Art II-45	Freedom of movement and residence		
Art II-34	Entitlement to social security and social assistance	Art II-46	Entitlement to diplomatic and consular protection		
Art II-35	Right of access to health care				
Art II-36	Right of access to services of general economic interest				
Art II-37	Integration of environmental protection and improvements in the environment into policies of the union				
Art II-38	High level of consumer protection				

Figure 2.7 (*continued*)

Self-test questions/activities

1 Identify four sources of legal change and explain what objectives these organisations are seeking to achieve.

2 Describe the relationship between Parliament and the judiciary in respect of Acts of Parliament.

3 Explain the differences between the following pairs:
   (a) MP and MEP;
   (b) *ratio decidendi* and *obiter dicta*;
   (c) a Bill and a statute;
   (d) ECSC and EEC;
   (e) Orders in Council and byelaws;
   (f) a binding precedent and a persuasive precedent;
   (g) the golden rule and the mischief rule;
   (h) the Council of the European Union and the Commission;
   (i) a regulation and a directive;
   (j) the European Community and the European Union;
   (k) the European Convention on Human Rights and the European Union Charter of Fundamental Rights.

Specimen examination questions

1 (a) 'As I see it, that balance is this: Parliament enacts statute law and the judges interpret it. Statute law is necessarily expressed in words, Parliament decides upon these words. The judges say what those words mean.' Lord Denning, *The Closing Chapters* (1983)

Discuss critically the role of judges in the interpretation of statutes.

(b) Smoking (Prohibition) Act 2004

An Act to promote public health by prohibiting smoking in public buildings.
Section 1 It shall be an offence to smoke tobacco products in –

(a) an aircraft, train, ship or other vessel, or public service vehicle;
(b) a cinema, theatre, concert hall or other place normally used for public entertainment;
(c) all or part of a licensed premises, or place of work.

Section 2 There shall be displayed at all times at all premises to which members of the public have access, a sign indicating clearly that smoking is prohibited.

Discuss whether the Act has been breached in each of the following situations:

(i) Dylan is arrested while smoking a cigarette at an open air rock concert and charged with an offence under s 1(b). He claims that the Act is intended to deal with smoking in buildings and does not apply to smoking outside.

(ii) Charles is arrested while smoking a pipe in a pub. He claims that he is smoking a herbal mixture which does not contain tobacco and is not therefore covered by the Act.

(iii) Sharon and Tracey, who are students, are arrested while smoking cigarettes in the college café. They believe they should not be convicted because they were unaware that smoking was prohibited in the café because the college authorities had failed to display a 'no smoking' notice in accordance with s 2 of the Act.

2 How has Britain's membership of the European Community affected the English legal system?

3 What are the advantages and disadvantages of the doctrine of judicial precedent?

Website references

The following links are a useful resource for students to gain an appreciation of law making in the UK and Europe, the changing nature of statute-based law and the common law, including reform bodies. There are also links to many of the institutions and bodies in the field.

http://www.direct.gov.uk This is a first entry point to UK public sector information on the Internet. Key parts of this site relevant to the English legal system include:

http://www.justice.gov.uk One of the roles of the Ministry of Justice is to secure the efficient administration of justice in England and Wales. Broadly speaking, the Department is responsible for the effective management of the courts; the appointment of judges, magistrates and other judicial office holders; the administration of legal aid; overseeing a varied programme of government civil legislation and reform in such fields as family law, property law, defamation and legal aid; constitutional reform; the National Offender Management Service, including the operation of the prison and probation services. This site contains information about constitutional reform including the reform of the House of Lords, the abolition of the office of Lord Chancellor and the creation of a Supreme Court to replace the Judicial Committee of the House of Lords.

http://www.lawcom.gov.uk The Law Commission – an independent body that reviews and suggests reform of English law.

http://www.civiljusticecouncil.gov.uk The Civil Justice Council is charged with monitoring the civil justice system and ensuring that it is fair, efficient and accessible.

http://www.opsi.gov.uk/legislation This website provides access to UK Acts of Parliament and statutory instruments from 1988 onwards. Since 1999 explanatory notes have been produced for all General Public Acts to make legislation more accessible to ordinary readers.

http://www.parliament.uk The Houses of Parliament website – information on the Commons, Lords and Parliament, including daily business, publications, register of members' interests, etc.

Devolution

http://www.scottish.parliament.uk The Scottish Parliament, elected on 6 May 1999, sat for the first time the following week on 12 May 1999 and took up its full legislative powers on 1 July 1999. This website has information on the history and function of the Parliament as well as up-to-date information on current parliamentary business.

http://www.wales.gov.uk The website of the National Assembly for Wales. In July 1997, the government published its White Paper, *A Voice for Wales*, which outlined its proposals for devolution in Wales. These proposals were endorsed in the referendum of 18 September 1997. Subsequently, Parliament passed the Government of Wales Act 1998, which established the National Assembly for Wales, and the National Assembly for Wales (Transfer of Functions) Order 1999 (SI 1999/672), which enables the transfer of the devolved powers and responsibilities from the Secretary of State for Wales to the Assembly. Further devolution has taken place following the implementation of the recommendations of the Richards Commission by the Government of Wales Act 2006. This website has information on Welsh legislation, policy, current business and how the Assembly works.

http://www.niassembly.gov.uk The website for the Northern Ireland Assembly, which was established following the Good Friday Agreement. The Assembly met for the first time on 1 July 1998. It was suspended from midnight on 14 October 2002. Devolution was restored following elections to a new Assembly on 7 March 2007 which were held under the terms of the St Andrews Agreement. A power-sharing Executive was established and powers devolved on 8 May 2007.

EC law and institutions

http://europa.eu/index_en.htm Europa, the European Union's server. It hosts most of the sites set out below:

http://www.consilium.europa.eu The website of the European Council which brings together the heads of state or government of the member states of the European Union and the President of the European Commission.

http://ec.europa.eu/index_en.htm The website of the European Commission.

http://www.europarl.org.uk The website of the UK Office of the European Parliament. Its debates, opinions and resolutions are published in the *Official Journal of the European Union*.

http://curia.europa.eu The website of the European Court of Justice and the Court of First Instance.

http://europa.eu/lisbon_treaty/index_en.htm This official EU website provides information about the Lisbon Treaty.

Human Rights Act 1998

http://www.justice.gov.uk/whatwedo/humanrights.htm
This part of the Ministry of Justice website provides a range of resources on human rights and useful links to other sites such as the Commission for Equality and Human Rights (http://www.cehr.org.uk).

Visit www.mylawchamber.co.uk/richesallen to access study support resources including answers to questions in this chapter and legal updates, all linked to the **Pearson eText** version of **Keenan and Riches' Business Law** which you can **search**, **highlight** and **personalise** with your **own notes** and **bookmarks**.

Use **Case Navigator** to read in full some of the key cases referenced in this chapter with commentary and questions:

Wilson v *Secretary for Trade and Industry* [2003]

Chapter 3

Resolving disputes

Learning objectives

After studying this chapter you should understand the following main points:

- the sources of legal advice and assistance available to individuals and business;
- the civil and criminal justice systems, including the composition and jurisdiction of the main courts;
- the nature and distinctive features of tribunals;
- alternatives to litigation and the different forms of alternative dispute resolution (ADR).

Every facet of modern business life is governed by the law. Today's businessperson needs to be alert to the legal implications of his activities. He will require a basic understanding of the principles of business law so that legal considerations can be built into the planning and decision-making process. At some stage, however, professional legal advice and help are likely to be needed – to advise on the implications of a recent change in the law or to draft a legal document or to assist in resolving a dispute. In this chapter we will consider the sources of legal advice and information available to business and the various methods of resolving disputes.

Legal services

The question of who is allowed to provide particular types of legal service has undergone significant change as a result of reforms initiated by the Courts and Legal Services Act 1990 and continued by the Access to Justice Act 1999 and the Legal Services Act 2007.

The legal profession

The legal profession in England and Wales is divided into two distinct branches: barristers and solicitors. These

two types of lawyer fulfil different functions, although there is a certain amount of overlap in their activities.

Solicitors

Solicitors are the general practitioners of the legal profession, providing an all-round legal service. Solicitors may practise alone but usually they operate in partnership with other solicitors. Solicitors are often the first port of call for anyone with a legal problem; consequently, their work is enormously varied. The workload associated with personal or private clients includes drafting wills, conveyancing (the legal formalities of buying and selling a house), winding up a deceased person's estate, dealing with claims for compensation arising from accidents or matrimonial problems. Business clients generate a different kind of work: for example, forming companies or drafting partnership agreements, applying for licences, drawing up contracts, advising on tax changes or new legal obligations in respect of employees. When the legal problem involves court proceedings, the solicitor deals with the preparatory stages, such as gathering evidence and interviewing witnesses. A solicitor is entitled to appear in court on behalf of his client, although rights of audience used to be limited to the magistrates' court and the county court (if the case necessitated an appearance in a higher court, then the services of a barrister had to be obtained). The Courts and Legal Services Act 1990, however, introduced new arrangements for determining advocacy rights, which has led to suitably qualified solicitors enjoying more extensive rights of audience in the higher courts. Since 1996 solicitor advocates have been eligible for appointment as Queen's Counsel (QC) (see the section on barristers below). Solicitors **without** full rights of audience are now also allowed to appear in the higher courts in limited circumstances, e.g. in criminal appeals from the magistrates' court to the Crown Court and reading out formal unchallenged statements in the High Court.

The opportunity for a solicitor to become a judge used to be limited to appointment as a circuit judge. However, the introduction of increased rights of audience for some solicitors following the Courts and Legal Services Act 1990 has opened the way for solicitors to obtain higher judicial office, e.g. appointment as a High Court judge.

Solicitors in England and Wales are represented by the Law Society.

Barristers

If solicitors are the 'GPs' of the legal world, barristers are the consultant specialists. They specialise in advocacy (i.e. representing a client in court) and have a right to appear in any court or tribunal. They used to enjoy exclusive rights of audience in the higher courts, such as the House of Lords (now the Supreme Court), Court of Appeal and High Court. However, the Courts and Legal Services Act 1990 dismantled this monopoly and introduced new arrangements for deciding who may act as an advocate in the courts. A barrister's work is not confined to advocacy. Indeed, some barristers spend most of their time on paperwork – writing opinions on specialised and difficult areas of law for solicitors or drafting documents.

There are two types of barrister: QCs (Queen's Counsel) and juniors. After 15–20 years' practice, a barrister may apply to become a QC or to 'take silk'. Queen's Counsel (or 'silks') are appointed by the Queen on the advice of the Lord Chancellor. They represent the top 10 per cent of the barristers' profession (and 0.5 per cent of solicitor advocates). There are several advantages to taking silk: QCs enjoy a higher status, they command higher fees, they may specialise in particular types of legal work and may concentrate on advocacy and giving opinions rather than poorly remunerated 'paperwork'. They are known as 'leaders' because they manage the case, leading a team of barristers: they normally only appear in court accompanied by a junior barrister. In July 2003 the government published a consultation paper on the future of the system of QCs. In November 2004 the Bar Council and the Law Society reached agreement on new procedures for appointing QCs. The main features of the scheme are: creation of an independent selection panel which includes lay membership; self-assessment against competences required of an advocate; references from judges, professionals and clients; an interview with the candidate; and a complaints committee. The first appointments were made in 2006.

Barristers are not allowed to form partnerships; they must practise on their own account. Nevertheless, groups of barristers share chambers (rooms in an office) and collectively employ a barrister's clerk who acts as their office manager. The Courts and Legal Services Act 1990 abolished any common law rule which prevented barristers from forming multidisciplinary practices with other professions, but the Act preserved the right of the General Council of the Bar to make rules prohibiting such arrangements.

The General Council of the Bar, which was established in 1987, is the governing body of barristers. Admission to the Bar is controlled by the four Inns of Court (the Inner Temple, the Middle Temple, Gray's Inn and Lincoln's Inn). The education and examination of students for the Bar is the responsibility of the Bar Standards Board.

The relationship between solicitors and barristers

Together, solicitors and barristers provide a comprehensive legal service. A person with a legal problem starts by consulting a solicitor and in so doing will enter into a contract for legal services. The solicitor will be competent to deal with most of the matters brought to him but in some cases he will need to retain the services of a barrister. The barrister's brief may be to give an opinion on a difficult point of law or to represent the client in court. A solicitor may approach any barrister to undertake the brief and, according to the 'cab rank' principle, the barrister must accept the work subject to his availability and the negotiation of a proper fee. Traditionally, barristers have not stood in a contractual relationship with the solicitors who briefed them. The fee was regarded as an 'honorarium', and as a result barristers could not sue solicitors who were reluctant to pay, although the same solicitors could bring an action against recalcitrant clients. Section 61 of the Courts and Legal Services Act 1990 abolished any common law rule preventing a barrister from entering into a contract for the provision of his services, although the General Council may continue to make rules prohibiting barristers from entering into contracts.

Until recently, both solicitors and barristers were immune from actions in negligence arising from the conduct of a case in court or work immediately preparatory to such a case. However, in *Arthur Hall and Co v Simons* (2000) the House of Lords decided that the immunity could no longer be justified. Both branches of the legal profession can be liable in negligence now for all aspects of their work.

In the past, a barrister could only be instructed by a solicitor. Clients did not have direct access to the barrister's services. The rules have now been relaxed to allow certain organisations and individuals to instruct a barrister directly on their own behalf or on behalf of clients. The Bar Council has set up a Licensed Access scheme under which suitable organisations and individuals with expertise in particular legal matters (e.g. the Association of Building Engineers, Chartered Insurance Institute, Free Representation Unit) may apply to the Bar Council for a licence to instruct barristers directly for either advice or representation or both in those areas. In addition, members of some professional bodies such as the Institute of Chartered Accountants and Institution of Chemical Engineers, and ombudsmen, e.g. the Banking Ombudsman, may instruct barristers directly to obtain advice or representation for non-court litigation and in tribunals and magistrates' courts.

The Legal Services Act 2007, which received the Royal Assent on 30 October 2007, reforms the regulatory framework for legal services in England and Wales. In 2003 the government appointed Sir David Clementi to undertake an independent review of the regulation of legal services. He raised concerns about the regulatory framework, the systems for handling complaints and the restrictions on business structures. The government published a White Paper in 2005 (*The Future of Legal Services: Putting Consumers First*) in which it proposed a new regulatory framework in the form of a Legal Services Board and an Office for Legal Complaints, and taking steps to enable legal services to be provided by alternative business structures.

The main provisions of the Legal Services Act 2007 are as follows:

- The establishment of the Legal Services Board (LSB) to oversee the approved regulators of 'reserved legal activities', such as the Law Society and the Bar Council.

- Reserved legal activity includes the exercise of a right of audience; the conduct of litigation; reserved instrument activities (e.g. a contract for the sale or other disposition of land); probate activities; notarial activities; the administration of oaths. It is an offence for a person to carry on a reserved legal activity if they are not entitled to do so.

- The LSB has the duty to promote the regulatory objectives which include protecting and promoting the public interest; supporting the rule of law; improving access to justice; protecting and promoting the interests of consumers; promoting competition in the provision of legal services; encouraging an independent, strong, diverse and effective legal profession; increasing public understanding of their legal rights and duties; promoting and maintaining adherence to the professional principles by those providing legal services.

- The LSB has a number of powers and sanctions available to it, including making directions, public censure and financial penalties, to ensure that approved regulators are meeting these objectives.

- The LSB is required to establish a Consumer Panel.

- The LSB has established an independent Office for Legal Complaints (OLC), which operates an ombudsman scheme for complaints about legal services. This replaces the schemes previously operated by approved regulators.

- Provision has been made for licensing new Alternative Business Structures (ABS) to enable, e.g., lawyers and non-lawyers to work together to deliver services. The LSB will supervise licensing authorities and, in the absence of an appropriate licensing authority, can license ABS firms itself.

The LSB became operational on 1 January 2010; the OLC opened for business in October 2010.

Other legal personnel

Public notaries

A notary public is an officer of the law who is authorised, among other things, to draw up, attest and certify deeds and other documents, to prepare wills and probate documents, to administer oaths and take a statement of truth. Most notaries are also solicitors.

Legal executives

Most firms of solicitors employ staff who are not qualified as lawyers to deal with some of the more routine work of the legal office, such as conveyancing. Legal executives, as they are known, have achieved professional recognition with the establishment of the Institute of Legal Executives (ILEX) in 1963. Unadmitted clerks may now qualify for membership by combining practical experience with success in the Institute's examinations. In 1997, ILEX received approval from the Lord Chancellor and four designated senior judges for an application to grant limited rights of audience in the courts to suitably qualified Fellows of the Institute. Part 2 of the Tribunals, Courts and Enforcement Act 2007 enables the Lord Chancellor to extend the eligibility requirements for judicial office to include legal executives and to those who have gained experience in law through, for example, teaching or research.

Licensed conveyancers

Up until the mid-1980s, solicitors enjoyed a statutory monopoly over conveyancing work. (The monopoly extended to barristers as well, but, as a rule of practice, they do not carry out conveyancing work.) It was a criminal offence for an unqualified person to prepare documents relating to the transfer of title to property for gain. Many solicitors were heavily dependent on conveyancing work but there were growing criticisms of the level of charges and standard of service provided. A small measure of competition for conveyancing work was introduced with the creation of a new profession of 'licensed conveyancers' by Part II of the Administration of Justice Act 1985. The Council for Licensed Conveyancers is the regulatory body for licensed conveyancers and is responsible for the admission, training, professional standards and discipline of licensed conveyancers.

Lawyers in industry, commerce and public service

The vast majority of qualified lawyers work in private practice providing legal services to a wide range of clients. A growing number of organisations, however, have set up their own legal departments staffed by solicitors and barristers. The functions of these 'in-house' lawyers depend on the type of organisation they work for. Banks, insurance companies and building societies employ lawyers to fulfil their specialist legal requirements. Central government departments and local authorities employ their own lawyers to help them discharge their statutory functions. The legal department of a private company undertakes legal work of a general nature, i.e. conveyancing, drawing up contracts, providing advice on employment matters, company administration and so on.

Other sources of information and advice

Information and advice for business

The legal profession is not the only source of information and advice on legal matters which a businessperson can turn to. Accountants are well versed in the intricacies of tax laws and the complex requirements of company law. Some of the large firms of accountants have established business and management consultancy services. Government departments are a fruitful source of information for those in business: e.g. the Department for Business, Innovation and Skills on employment legislation; and HM Revenue and Customs on tax and VAT regulations. There is also a large number of government-sponsored organisations providing information and advice: the Commission for Equality and Human Rights (which merged the Equal Opportunities Commission, the Commission for Racial Equality and the Disability Rights Commission with effect from October 2007); the Health and Safety Commission, the Office of Fair Trading and Business Link, to name a few. A businessperson may also benefit from joining a trade association. The Consumer Credit Trade Association, for example, produces a quarterly journal which reports changes in the law. It also runs a Legal Advisory Bureau for its members. Professional associations (e.g. the Chartered Institute of Personnel and Development) perform a similar service for members employed in business.

Information and advice for citizens and consumers

Many people are deterred from seeking legal advice and taking legal action because of fear of what it will cost them. However, there are schemes and organisations which aim to provide low-cost legal help.

Community Legal Service Fund (Legal Aid)

Unlike businesspeople, private individuals may be able to obtain financial help in legal matters from the Community Legal Service Fund, which is administered by the Legal Services Commission, as established by the Access to Justice Act 1999. The help available includes:

1 Civil legal aid – available for individuals requiring help in relation to civil matters. A solicitor may provide **legal help** (previously referred to as 'advice and assistance') with problems which fall within the scope of the scheme, such as housing problems, clinical negligence, credit and debts, contract disputes, welfare benefits and financial claims arising from divorce. The scheme does not cover defamation and malicious falsehood, conveyancing, company or partnership law, neighbour or boundary disputes. Eligibility for immediate help is based on a means test carried out by the solicitor. Applicants will qualify for help if they are receiving certain state benefits or are on a low income. If the application is successful, the solicitor will be able to carry out two hours' worth of work (three hours in the case of divorce work). If more work is required, the solicitor must apply to the Legal Services Commission for permission to carry on. Permission will be granted only if the case satisfies a 'merits' test, i.e. the applicant has a good enough case to justify further support. If court proceedings become necessary, a Legal Representation Certificate must be obtained.

2 Criminal Defence Service. Under the Access to Justice Act 1999, the Criminal Defence Service has replaced the system of criminal legal aid. Advice, assistance and representation in criminal matters is available from private practice solicitors who have contracted with the Legal Services Commission to provide such services. The Legal Services Commission also directly employs a number of criminal defence lawyers, known as public defenders. The duty solicitor scheme ensures that solicitors are available in police stations and magistrates' courts to give free legal advice.

Conditional fees

The Courts and Legal Services Act 1990 introduced conditional fee arrangements. Advocates or litigators can enter into agreements with their clients whereby they receive their normal fee plus an uplift in the event of success (known as a success fee) but nothing if unsuccessful. The percentage of any uplift must be specified in the agreement and is subject to a maximum percentage determined by the Lord Chancellor in consultation with the designated judges, the Bar, the Law Society and other appropriate authorised bodies. The maximum uplift permitted is 100 per cent. The scheme, which became available in 1995, was originally limited to cases involving personal injury, insolvency and the European Court of Human Rights. However, in 1998 conditional fee arrangements were extended to all civil cases, other than family proceedings. The Access to Justice Act 1999 made a number of changes to the scheme. It allows the uplift payable in successful cases to be recovered from the losing side and for the cost of any insurance premiums to be similarly recoverable. Conditional fee arrangements are now an important method of funding civil actions, particularly as the Access to Justice Act 1999 removed personal injury cases (with the exception of clinical negligence) from eligibility for legal aid.

The Coroners and Justice Act 2009

In addition to some limited changes to the legal aid scheme, the 2009 Act also provides for regulation of damages-based agreements in employment matters. A damages-based agreement is an arrangement whereby a person representing a client in an employment matter receives a percentage of any compensation received by their client. The Damages-Based Agreements Regulations 2010 which came into force on 6 April 2010, set out the requirements which must be met for these agreement to be enforceable. These include:

- the agreement must specify the claim or proceedings to which it relates; the circumstances in which the representative will be paid; and the reason for setting the level of payment at the amount agreed (reg 3);
- the representative must provide certain information to the client before the agreement is made including alternative methods of pursuing the claim, an estimate of the amount likely to be spent on expenses and when expenses are payable (reg 4);
- the agreement must be in writing and signed by the client and the representative (reg 5);
- the amount of payment, including VAT, must not exceed 35 per cent of any damages recovered by the client.

Other organisations providing legal advice and help

There is a range of voluntary organisations which provide legal advice and assistance to private individuals. Citizens' Advice Bureaux provide free advice on many legal matters including housing, social security entitlement, consumer complaints and employment rights. Some inner-city areas are served by law centres. Law centres are staffed by lawyers and tend to provide more specialised advice and assistance on social welfare matters, including immigration, landlord and tenant, debt and social security benefits. There are also specialised advice centres available in the areas of housing and consumer problems. Over time the Community Legal Service will develop its role in coordinating the activities of these organisations with the aim of ensuring a comprehensive system of advice and other legal services to match local needs.

Trade unions often offer free legal advice and assistance on employment matters to their members. Legal advice and assistance may form part of a person's insurance cover. Motoring organisations, such as the AA and RAC, provide legal advice and help for their members.

Methods of dispute settlement: the courts

The courts are the focal point of our legal system. They provide a formal setting for the final settlement of many of the disputes that occur in our society. The conflict may be between individuals or, where a breach of the criminal law has been alleged, between the state and one of its citizens. It is the function of the court to establish the facts of the case, identify the legal rules to be applied and to formulate a solution. The decision of the court not only has an immediate impact on the parties concerned, but it also affects similar cases which may arise in the future as a result of the operation of the doctrine of judicial precedent. Our present-day system of courts and tribunals can be classified in a number of different ways:

1 Civil and criminal courts. Some courts deal exclusively with either civil or criminal matters, but the majority hear both civil and criminal cases, e.g. magistrates' courts.

2 First instance and appeal courts. A court which hears a case for the first time is known as a court of first instance or a court of original jurisdiction. These courts can make mistakes, so there is provision for cases to be reheard by an appeal court. Some courts hear cases both at first instance and on appeal, e.g. the High Court.

3 Courts and tribunals. In addition to the ordinary courts, Parliament has created a large number of special courts and tribunals to administer various aspects of social and welfare legislation. The Lands Tribunal (Lands Chamber of the Upper Tribunal), for example, has a wide jurisdiction in matters relating to land including the valuation of land, compensation for compulsory purchase and applications to discharge restrictive covenants.

In this part of the chapter we will consider an outline of the existing criminal and civil court systems and briefly explain the role of tribunals. We will also consider alternatives to going to court, such as arbitration, conciliation, mediation and ombudsmen as means of resolving disputes.

Classification of criminal offences

If a person is charged with a criminal offence, he or she will be tried by either the magistrates' court or the Crown Court. Cases are distributed between these two courts according to the seriousness of the offence. There are three types of criminal offence.

1 Summary offences. These are minor offences, for example most motoring offences, which are tried summarily in the magistrates' court.

2 Indictable offences. These are more serious offences, such as murder and robbery, which are tried on indictment in the Crown Court.

3 Either-way offences. These are offences which may be tried either in the Crown Court or in the magistrates' courts. Examples of either-way offences include theft and engaging in an unfair commercial practice. A person who is charged with an either-way offence may insist on being tried at the Crown Court. If the accused does not elect to go to the Crown Court, the magistrates decide the most appropriate venue for the trial, bearing in mind the seriousness of the offence and the limited sentencing powers available to them.

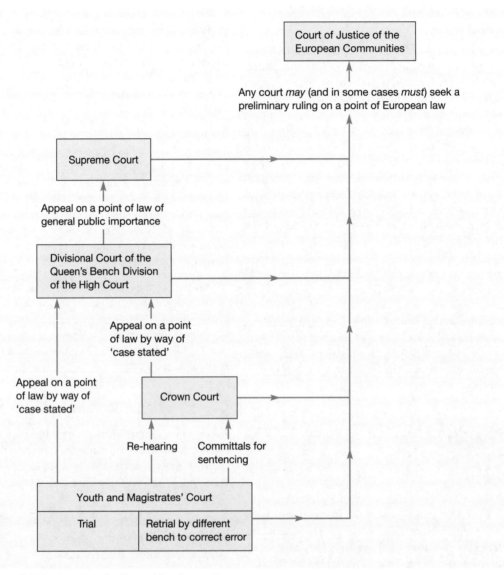

Figure 3.1 Criminal courts dealing with minor offences

The system of appeals from the decisions of these two courts is illustrated in Figure 3.1 (less serious offences) and Figure 3.2 (more serious offences).

Criminal courts

Criminal Courts Review

In December 1999, Sir Robin Auld, a senior Court of Appeal judge, was appointed to undertake a review of

the criminal courts. His report, which was published in 2001, contained the following recommendations:

- The criminal law should be codified with codes for offences, evidence, procedure and sentencing.
- A national Criminal Justice Board should be established to provide overall direction of the criminal justice system. Local Criminal Justice Boards would have responsibility for implementing the national board's plans and managing the system at local level.
- The Crown Court and magistrates' courts should be replaced by a unified criminal court organised into

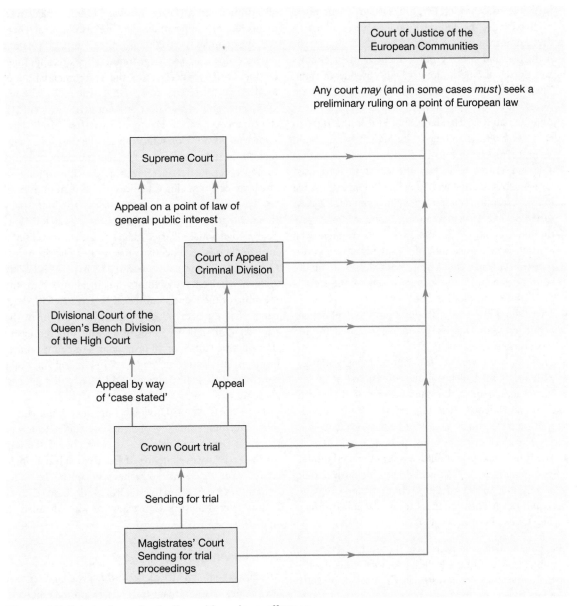

Figure 3.2 Criminal courts dealing with serious offences

three divisions: the Crown Division would deal with indictable and serious either-way offences, the District Division, consisting of a judge and two magistrates with sentencing powers of up to two years would deal with mid-range either-way offences, and the Magistrates Division would deal with summary offences and less serious either-way offences.

■ The defendant should lose the right to elect to be tried in any of the new divisions or, if the proposal

for a unified court was not accepted, the right to trial by jury for either-way offences under the existing arrangements.

■ A centrally funded executive agency should take over administrative arrangements for all courts except the House of Lords (now the Supreme Court).

■ Juries should be more representative of national and local communities. Although people with criminal convictions and mental disorder should remain ineligible to serve, other groups such as members of the clergy, the judiciary and those involved in the administration of justice should no longer be ineligible, and other groups, such as MPs, doctors and nurses, should no longer be excused as of right. There should be ethnic minority representation on juries where race is relevant to the case.

- As noted above, defendants should lose the right to elect trial by judge and jury. Although jury trial would continue to be the normal form of trial for indictable and serious either-way offences in the proposed Crown Division, trial without a jury would be possible in four exceptional cases: where the defendant agreed to a judge-only trial; in serious and complex fraud cases the judge could try the case with two lay members; a youth court, consisting of a judge and two youth panel magistrates could hear serious cases involving young defendants; and a judge sitting alone should decide fitness to plead issues.

- There should be greater flexibility in the deployment of judges, with High Court judges reserved for the most serious cases.

- There should be greater use of fixed penalty notices, with a right of challenge in the courts.

- There should be a thorough review of the law of criminal evidence, including reform of the rules in relation to the admissibility of hearsay evidence and the defendant's previous misconduct.

- The routes of appeal should be simplified and limited exceptions to the rule against double jeopardy should be permitted to allow the prosecution to appeal against acquittals where the offences are punishable by life or long terms of imprisonment.

The government's response to the Auld Review of Criminal Courts and the Halliday Report of the Review of the Sentencing Framework, also published in 2001, was set out in a White Paper, *Justice for All* (July 2002). The Criminal Justice Act 2003 implements the government's reforms in relation to court procedures and sentencing. Reference is made to the changes introduced by the 2003 Act in the following description of the criminal court structure.

Magistrates' courts

Magistrates' courts have been part of the legal scene for over 600 years. Today their importance lies in the fact that magistrates' courts handle over 95 per cent of all criminal cases. There are two kinds of magistrate, or justices of the peace, as they are also known. There are approximately 30,000 part-time, unpaid amateur judges, known as lay magistrates. They are appointed by the Lord Chancellor on the recommendation of local Advisory Committees. (In Greater Manchester, Lancashire and Merseyside, appointments are made by the Chancellor of the Duchy of Lancaster.) Since legal knowledge is not a qualification for the position, a new magistrate must undergo an initial course of training. In court, the justices are given guidance on points of law by a legally qualified justices' clerk. A minimum of two lay magistrates is required to try a case, but usually three sit together. There are approximately 130 full-time, paid, professional District Judges (Magistrates' Court), formerly known as stipendiary magistrates. District Judges (Magistrates' Court) are appointed from persons having a seven-year general advocacy qualification within the meaning of the Courts and Legal Services Act 1990. (A person has a general advocacy qualification if he or she has a right of audience in relation to any proceedings in the Supreme Court, or all proceedings in county courts or magistrates' courts.) They work in London and other big cities, such as Birmingham and Manchester, and sit alone to try a case.

The Courts Act 2003, which implements the court-related recommendations of Sir Robin Auld's Review of Criminal Courts in England and Wales, paved the way for the Secretary of State for Justice to establish a single centrally funded agency to manage all courts, including magistrates' courts, and to establish locally based Courts Boards. Her Majesty's Court Service was launched in April 2005.

Jurisdiction

As well as their civil jurisdiction, which will be discussed later in this chapter, magistrates deal with the following criminal matters.

1 **Trial of minor offences.** The magistrates are responsible for deciding both the verdict and the sentence. Their sentencing powers are limited to six months' imprisonment (or 12 months for consecutive offences) and a maximum fine of £5,000. Although magistrates exercise limited sentencing powers they have the power to send a convicted person to the Crown Court for sentencing, where a heavier sentence can be imposed.

Under the Magistrates' Courts Act 1980, as amended by the Criminal Appeals Act 1995, magistrates have the power to rectify an error by means of a retrial by a different bench.

2 Sending for trial and committal proceedings. Traditionally, a person could not be tried by the Crown Court unless the evidence had been examined by the magistrates' court to see whether the prosecution had a good enough case to justify a trial. Committal proceedings either took the form of a full hearing of the evidence, known as an 'old-style' committal, or without consideration of the evidence, a procedure known as a 'paper committal'. If there was a *prima facie* case, the accused was committed for trial in the Crown Court. One magistrate could sit alone for this purpose. The Criminal Justice and Public Order 1996 Act modified committal proceedings by excluding oral evidence at 'old-style' committal hearings. The evidence at contested old-style committals is now limited to documentary evidence, i.e. written statements and depositions, and exhibits presented by the prosecution.

A 'sending for trial procedure' was introduced by the Crime and Disorder Act 1998 for adults charged with indictable only offences. Under this new procedure, the accused appears before the magistrates' court in order to resolve issues relating to bail, legal aid, the taking of depositions and exhibits. The court provides the defendant with a statement of the offences with which he is charged and the evidence and the location of the trial. The defendant is then sent for trial at the Crown Court.

3 Youth courts. If a child (aged 10 to 13) or young person (aged 14 to 17) commits a criminal offence, he or she can be brought before a specially selected group of magistrates sitting as a youth court. The court has a wide range of sentences at its disposal, including custodial measures. Young people are protected from the potentially damaging effects of a court appearance in a number of ways. The less formal proceedings must be held separately from an adult court, the public is not admitted and there are strict controls on what the press can report.

4 Criminal administration. Magistrates issue summonses, warrants of arrest and search, and they can grant bail to people awaiting trial.

Crown Courts

Crown Courts were established in 1972 by the Courts Act 1971 to replace the long-established system of quarter sessions and assize courts. Trial on indictment in the Crown Court is by a judge normally assisted by a jury of 12. The most serious cases, such as murder, must be heard by a High Court judge, while less serious matters may be dealt with by either a circuit judge or a recorder (a part-time judge). The Criminal Justice Act 2003 introduced two circumstances in which trials on indictment may take place without a jury by a judge sitting alone. They are (i) the trial of serious or complex fraud cases, and (ii) where there is a danger of jury tampering or a jury has been discharged because of jury tampering. The first trial by judge alone because of alleged jury tampering was given the go-ahead in June 2009 by the Court of Appeal (Criminal Division) in a case involving four defendants accused of carrying out an armed robbery at a warehouse at Heathrow airport (*R v T & others* (2009)). The 'judge only' trial was the fourth in relation to the robbery. Juries at the first two trials were unable to reach a verdict and the jury in the third trial was discharged after reports that approaches had been made to two jurors. The judge in the third trial indicated that he had no difficulty in finding that a serious attempt at jury tampering had taken place. In the Court of Appeal, the Lord Chief Justice concluded that there was a very significant danger of jury tampering and that the package of protective measures proposed to protect jurors and their families would be unacceptable. The four defendants were subsequently convicted.

In 2007 the government sought to introduce trial of fraud cases by a judge alone without the need for an affirmative resolution in both Houses of Parliament which is required to trigger the commencement of the relevant section of the Criminal Justice Act 2003. The Fraud (Trials without a Jury) Bill completed its Commons stages but was defeated in the House of Lords at the second reading.

The jury comprises men and women between the ages of 18 and 70, drawn at random from the electoral roll. The main legislation governing jury service, the Juries Act 1974, has been amended by the Criminal Justice Act 2003 with the purpose of limiting the categories of people ineligible for jury service, curtailing opportunities to seek excusal from jury service and to redefine those disqualified from jury service because of their criminal convictions.

The functions of the judge and jury are quite distinct. The judge is responsible for the conduct of the trial. The judge rules on points of law and sums up the case for the jury. The jury must consider all the evidence to decide whether the accused is guilty or innocent. If the jury convicts, the judge plays the final part in the proceedings by passing sentence.

When the Crown Court is hearing an appeal, there is no jury: the judge sits with between two and four lay magistrates. Following changes made by the Access to Justice Act 1999, magistrates no longer sit on committals for sentencing.

Jurisdiction

The Crown Court has the power to deal with the following criminal matters:

1 Trial of serious offences.

2 Committals for sentencing from the magistrates' courts.

3 Appeals from magistrates' courts. The defendant (but not the prosecution) may appeal against conviction and/or sentence. The appeal takes the form of a complete rehearing of the case. The Crown Court can confirm or reverse or vary the decision of the magistrates or return the case to them with an expression of its opinion. The court can impose any sentence which the magistrates' court could have passed. This means that the defendant faces the danger that he may receive a more severe sentence on appeal.

High Court

The High Court is split into three divisions: Queen's Bench, Family and Chancery. In the past when the court was hearing an appeal or, in the case of the Queen's Bench Division, exercising its supervisory jurisdiction, a minimum of two High Court judges sat together and it became known as a 'Divisional Court'. Under the Access to Justice Act 1999, however, a single judge of the High Court is able to hear judicial review applications, appeals by way of case stated and applications for *habeas corpus* in criminal cases, which were previously only heard by a Divisional Court.

Jurisdiction

The jurisdiction of the High Court in criminal matters is as follows:

1 Appeals from magistrates' courts. An appeal may be made by way of 'case stated' by either the prosecution or the defence, but only on a point of law. This form of appeal requires the magistrates to provide a 'case' for the

opinion of the High Court. The 'case' consists of a statement containing the magistrates' findings of fact, the arguments put forward by the parties, the decision and the reasons for it. The Divisional Court has the power to confirm, reverse or amend the decision of the magistrates' court or it can send the case back with an expression of its opinion.

2 Appeals from Crown Court. The Divisional Court also hears appeals by way of case stated from the Crown Court, in respect of all criminal cases dealt with by that court.

3 Judicial review. The Divisional Court of the Queen's Bench plays an important role in monitoring abuse of power when it deals with applications for judicial review. As part of this general supervisory power, it can quash the decision of a magistrates' court which has exceeded its powers or failed to observe the rules of natural justice.

Court of Appeal (Criminal Division)

The Court of Appeal consists of two Divisions. The Criminal Division is composed of the Lord Chief Justice, and a maximum of 37 Lord or Lady Justices of Appeal and any High Court judge who is asked to sit. Normally, three judges sit to hear a case, but if a difficult or important point of law is involved, a court of five or seven may be convened.

Jurisdiction

The Court of Appeal deals with the following criminal cases:

1 Appeals from trials on indictment in the Crown Court. The defence (but not the prosecution) may appeal against the conviction and/or sentence. In an appeal against conviction, the court may confirm or quash the conviction or order a new trial. Where there is an appeal against the sentence, the court may confirm or reduce the sentence or substitute one form of sentence for another. The Criminal Justice Act 2003 introduces what is known as an 'interlocutory' right of appeal against the ruling of a judge in the Crown Court which is exercisable by the prosecution. ('Interlocutory' means in the course of the proceedings.) This right may be exercised in the case of two kinds of rulings: the first kind are rulings made during the proceedings up to the start of the judge's summing up which have the effect of terminating the trial and the second kind are evidentiary rulings made in trials for certain offences, up to the point of the opening of the defence case, which have the effect of significantly weakening the prosecution case.

2 References by the Attorney-General. There are two kinds of reference which may be made by the Attorney-General. The first is where a person has been acquitted following trial on indictment in the Crown Court. The Attorney-General may refer any point of law which has arisen in the case to the Court of Appeal for its opinion. The decision of the court does not affect the outcome of the original trial. The second kind of reference is where a person has been sentenced by the Crown Court but the Attorney-General considers the sentence to be unduly lenient. The Court of Appeal may impose any sentence which the Crown Court could have imposed. Thus, the defendant could be dealt with more severely by the Court of Appeal.

The Criminal Justice Act 2003 introduces a new right for the prosecution to apply to the Court of Appeal for an acquittal to be quashed and for a retrial to take place. This provision provides a limited exception to the law against 'double jeopardy', which prevents a person being tried twice for essentially the same offence. The prosecution's right to seek a retrial applies only in respect of acquittals for serious offences, i.e. specified offences which carry a maximum life sentence such as murder and rape, which are judged to have a particularly serious impact either on the victim or society generally. New and compelling evidence against the accused must have come to light since the trial. The prosecution must obtain the consent of the Director of Public Prosecutions (DPP) before taking significant steps in reopening investigations and in making an application to the Court of Appeal.

3 References by the Criminal Cases Review Commission. The Criminal Appeals Act 1995 established an independent body to investigate and, where appropriate, refer to the Court of Appeal cases involving possible wrongful conviction or sentence. The Criminal Cases Review Commission, which started work in April 1997, consists of 14 Commissioners. One-third of the commissioners must be legally qualified and the remaining two-thirds must have knowledge of some aspect of the criminal justice system. The Commission may only refer a case to the Court of Appeal if a new issue by way of argument or evidence is raised and there is a 'real possibility'

that the conviction, verdict, finding or sentence will not be upheld.

Supreme Court

The Constitutional Reform Act 2005 replaces the system of Law Lords sitting as an Appellate Committee of the House of Lords with a Supreme Court. The Supreme Court for the UK consists of 12 members. The Law Lords became the first Justices of the Supreme Court; they retain their membership of the House of Lords but are excluded from participation until their retirement. The Act provides for a new procedure for filling vacancies by a selection commission consisting of the President and Deputy President of the Supreme Court and members of the appointment bodies for England, Wales, Scotland and Northern Ireland. New judges do not become members of the House of Lords, and are known as Justices of the Supreme Court. The new Supreme Court, which is located in Middlesex Guildhall, opened for business on 1 October 2009.

The Supreme Court is the final court of appeal in both civil and criminal matters for both England and Northern Ireland, and in civil matters for Scotland. A minimum of three Justices is required, but in practice five normally sit to hear an appeal. Decisions are by majority judgment.

Jurisdiction

The Supreme Court hears the following criminal appeals:

1 Appeals from the Court of Appeal (Criminal Division).

2 Appeals from the Divisional Court of the Queen's Bench Division. In both cases, either the prosecution or defence may appeal, provided that a point of law of general public importance is involved. Permission must be obtained from the Supreme Court or the Court of Appeal or the Divisional Court, as appropriate.

Civil courts

Reform of civil litigation

In 1994 the then Lord Chancellor, Lord Mackay, invited Lord Woolf to undertake a review of the rules and procedures of the civil courts in England and Wales.

Lord Woolf produced an interim report in 1995 and his final report, *Access to Justice*, in July 1996. Lord Woolf identified the following problems with the civil justice system:

- a lack of equality between wealthy, powerful litigants and their under-resourced opponents;
- the system was too expensive, the costs of bringing a case often exceeding the value of the claim;
- it was difficult to estimate how long the litigation would last and how much it would cost;
- the system was very slow;
- civil procedure was too complicated;
- the system was fragmented; no one had overall responsibility for the administration of civil justice;
- the system was too adversarial; the parties set the pace of litigation, rather than the courts.

Some of the proposals in Lord Woolf's interim report were implemented before the publication of the final report. The financial limit for small claims cases was increased from £1,000 to £3,000 (except for personal injury cases) from January 1996 (since then the limit has been raised again to £5,000).

The main changes recommended in Lord Woolf's final report were given effect by the Civil Procedure Act 1997 and new Civil Procedure Rules 1998 (SI 1998/3132), which came into effect on 1 April 1999. The main changes are as follows:

1 New terminology. The new rules are expressed in more modern language. For example, 'plaintiffs' are now known as 'claimants', and 'writs' are called 'claim forms'. A summary of some of the more important changes to legal terminology is set out in Figure 3.3.

2 Encouraging settlement. The new rules contain a number of features which are designed to encourage the parties to settle their dispute.

(a) *Alternative dispute resolution (ADR)*. The parties are actively encouraged at various stages to use ADR (see later).

(b) *Pre-action protocols*. Cases are managed in accordance with pre-action protocols, which operate like codes of practice, with which the parties must comply at the pre-trial stage. The protocols include timetables for the exchange of information and use of expert witnesses, e.g. the parties are encouraged to instruct a single expert witness, rather than each side mustering their own expert witnesses. The effect of the protocols is that there

Civil justice reforms – a new language	
Old term	*New term*
Plaintiff	Claimant
Writ, originating summons, petition	Claim form
Pleading (the reason for the claim)	Statement of case
Minor/infant (person under the age of 18)	Child
Affidavit	Statement of truth
In chambers or in camera	In private
Ex parte	Without notice
Subpoena	Witness summons
Discovery (of documents)	Disclosure
Anton Piller orders (a pre-trial order empowering a plaintiff to enter the defendant's property to search for and seize documents and articles relating to the cause of action)	Search orders
Interlocutory injunction	Interim injunction
Mareva injunction (granted by a court to prevent the defendant transferring assets abroad)	Freezing injunction
Next friend (adult who acts on behalf of child in litigation)	Litigation friend

Figure 3.3 New terminology following the Woolf reforms

is more work, and therefore costs, which must be paid for up front.

(c) *Costs and payments into court*. The judge now has greater discretion about the award of costs. The criteria to be considered include the conduct of the parties at the pre-trial stage, whether it was reasonable to raise a particular issue and the way in which the parties have pursued their cases. It has always been the case that the defendant can make a payment into court so as to reduce costs if the claimant's award does not exceed the amount paid in. It is now possible for the claimant to make an offer to settle with a similar effect on the matter of costs.

3 A single jurisdiction. The High Court and county courts become a single jurisdiction operating to a common set of procedural rules. Proceedings are commenced in the same way in any court. Cases are then allocated to the most appropriate court.

4 Case management. Cases are allocated to one of three tracks, depending on their value and complexity.

(a) A *fast track* for claims between £5,000 and £25,000. These cases are heard by the county court within 30 weeks. The judge sets a timetable to ensure that the case can be tried on time. The normal hearing time should be three hours but with an absolute maximum of one day.

(b) A *small claims track* for all cases up to £5,000, except personal injury and housing cases, where the limit is £1,000. These cases are dealt with by the judge following any procedure he or she considers fair.

(c) A *multi-track* for all claims over £15,000 and for complex cases of less than £15,000. Judges manage these cases, setting and monitoring the timetable to be followed by the parties. Estimates of the costs are published by the court or agreed by the parties and approved by the court. The High Court deals with multi-track cases.

Appeals – Access to Justice Act 1999

The Access to Justice Act 1999 made provision for reform of the system of appeals in civil and family cases. The main changes in relation to civil appeals are as follows:

- Provision for permission to be required to exercise a right of appeal in civil cases at all levels.
- Limits to the right to bring a second appeal, unless the appeal would raise an important point of principle or practice, or there is some other compelling reason.
- The Lord Chancellor has the power to prescribe the routes of appeal within county courts, the High Court and the Civil Division of the Court of Appeal. The following appeal routes have now been prescribed:
  (a) appeals from county courts other than in family proceedings lie to the High Court;
  (b) appeals from the decisions of masters, registrars and district judges of the High Court lie to a judge of the High Court;
  (c) appeals from district judges in county courts lie to a judge of a county court;
  (d) in multi-track proceedings, appeals of final orders or where the decision itself was made on appeal, the appeal lies to the Court of Appeal irrespective of who heard the case in the first place.
- Provision for the Master of the Rolls or a lower court to direct that an appeal which would normally be heard by either the county court or the High Court should instead be heard by the Court of Appeal.

The structure of the civil courts is set out in Figure 3.4, overleaf.

County courts

County courts were established in 1846 to provide a cheap and speedy method for the settlement of small civil disputes. Today, the vast majority of civil proceedings are dealt with by these local courts.

The county courts are staffed by circuit judges. They usually sit alone to hear a case, but a jury of eight may be called where, for example, fraud has been alleged. The judge is assisted by a district judge, appointed from persons having a seven-year advocacy qualification within the meaning of the Courts and Legal Services Act 1990. He or she also has limited jurisdiction to try cases where the claim does not exceed £5,000 or, with the consent of both of the parties, any action within the general jurisdiction of the court.

Jurisdiction

The jurisdiction of the county courts is governed by the County Courts Act 1984, the Courts and Legal Services Act 1990, the Civil Procedure Act 1997 and the Civil Procedure Rules. The types of action which the court can deal with are as follows:

1 Actions in contract and tort (including defamation if the parties agree). The county court deals with all small claims track and fast track actions, and some multi-track cases.

2 Actions for the recovery of land or concerning title or rights over land.

3 Actions in equity where the amount involved does not exceed £30,000. This category includes proceedings involving mortgages and trusts.

4 Bankruptcies. The jurisdiction is unlimited in amount, but not all county courts have bankruptcy jurisdiction.

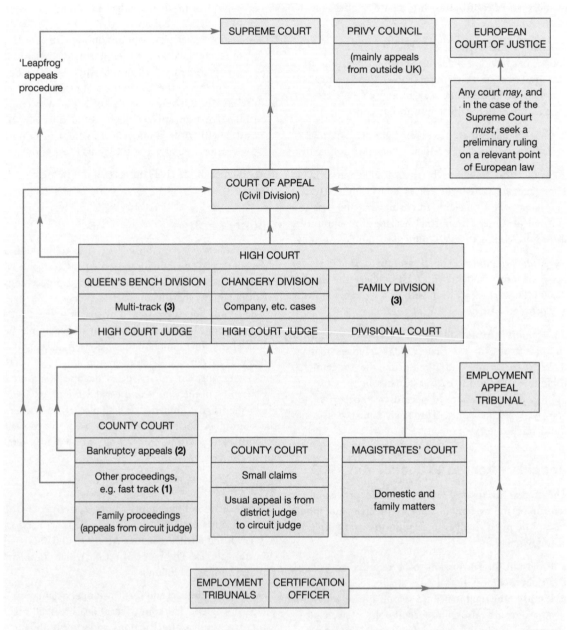

Routes of appeal
1 If heard by a circuit judge.
2 If heard by a district or circuit judge.
3 If heard by a High Court judge.

Figure 3.4 System of courts exercising civil jurisdiction

5 Company winding-ups where the paid-up share capital of the company does not exceed £120,000. The court must have a bankruptcy jurisdiction.

6 Contested probate proceedings where the amount of the deceased person's estate does not exceed £30,000.

7 Family matters, e.g. undefended divorce. The court must have divorce jurisdiction. Under the Civil Partnership Act 2004, a county court may be designated a civil partnership proceedings court and as such deal with the dissolution of civil partnerships (registered partnerships with homosexual and lesbian couples) and arrangements for the children of such partnerships. The jurisdiction of the courts in respect of the financial maintenance of children whose parents live apart is now the responsibility of the Child Support Agency.

8 Consumer credit, landlord and tenant, and racial discrimination cases.

9 Patents. Following the recommendation of the Oulton Committee, the Copyright, Designs and Patents Act 1988 made provision for the establishment of a patents county court with country-wide jurisdiction to deal with cases relating to patents and designs.

Actions which exceed the limits of the county court are normally heard by the High Court. However, the parties may agree to such an action being dealt with by the lower court.

Small claims

In 1973, the Lord Chancellor introduced a special scheme for small claims in the county court. This was a response to the criticism that people were discouraged from pursuing actions because county court justice was likely to cost more than the amount in dispute. At present, if the amount claimed does not exceed £5,000 (or £1,000 for personal injury), the case will be allocated to the small claims track. Small claims cases are usually heard by a district judge who will follow any procedure he or she considers fair. The parties are encouraged to do without legal representation: legal aid is not available and the costs of legal representation are not normally recoverable. The hearing can be held in private in an informal atmosphere and strict rules of procedure can be dispensed with. The procedure for making a small claim in the county court is considered in Chapter 14.

Magistrates' courts

The overwhelming majority of cases heard by the magistrates are criminal, but they also have a limited civil jurisdiction.

Jurisdiction

1 Family proceedings. The jurisdiction of the magistrates in family law matters includes:

(a) *Matrimonial proceedings*, such as separation orders where the parties to a marriage are not immediately seeking a divorce and orders for the financial maintenance of the parties and their children. (Under the Child Support Act 1991 responsibility for securing child maintenance payments from parents who live apart from their children has been transferred to the Child Support Agency. The Agency, operational from April 1993, is responsible for assessing, collecting and enforcing child maintenance. The amount of maintenance to be paid by absent parents is calculated according to a statutory formula. The jurisdiction of the courts in respect of child maintenance has been restricted accordingly.)

(b) *Child care proceedings*, including the power to make contact orders (replacing access orders) and residence orders (replacing custody orders).

(c) *Care proceedings*, whereby a child can be taken into the care of a local authority.

2 Recovery of certain civil debts, e.g. income tax, electricity and water charges.

3 Licensing. Magistrates used to have a role in liquor licensing. However, under the Licensing Act 2003, this responsibility has been transferred to local authorities who now operate a single system for licensing pubs, cinemas, theatres and other places of entertainment. The Gambling Act 2005 similarly transfers the responsibility formerly exercised by magistrates in relation to the licensing of gambling premises to local authorities.

High Court

The High Court has its headquarters in London at the Royal Courts of Justice in the Strand, but there are district registries in the larger cities in England and Wales. Each division of the High Court is presided over by a senior judge: the Lord Chief Justice is head of the Queen's Bench Division; from October 2005 the effective Head of the Chancery Division is the Chancellor of the High Court (formerly known as the Vice-Chancellor); and there is a President of the Family Division. They are assisted by a maximum of 106 High Court judges, who are distributed between the divisions, the largest number being attached to the Queen's Bench. When the High Court is operating as a court of first instance, trial is usually by judge alone. However, a jury of 12 may be called in cases involving defamation, malicious prosecution, false imprisonment or fraud. The Divisional Courts consist of two or three judges.

Jurisdiction

All three divisions are equally competent to hear any case, but in practice specific matters are allocated to each division.

1 Queen's Bench Division. The jurisdiction of this division covers civil and criminal matters, cases at first instance and on appeal. In addition, it exercises an extremely important supervisory function.

When sitting as an ordinary court, it hears the following cases:

(a) *Actions in contract and tort.* The High Court will normally deal with cases allocated to the multi-track procedure.

(b) *Judicial review.* Under the Access to Justice Act 1999, judicial review applications may now be heard by a single judge sitting alone.

(c) A *Commercial Court* deals with disputes concerning insurance, banking and the interpretation of commercial documents.

(d) An *Admiralty Court* deals with admiralty actions arising out of, for example, collisions at sea and salvage.

(e) A *Technology and Construction Court* (formerly known as the Official Referee's Court) deals with cases involving technical issues, such as construction and engineering disputes.

The Divisional Court of the Queen's Bench Division hears the following matters:

(a) *Civil appeals* (other than in matrimonial proceedings) by way of case stated from the magistrates' court and from the Crown Court.

(b) *Judicial review* of the actions of inferior courts, tribunals and administrative bodies. For this purpose, the court may make a mandatory order, a prohibiting order,

a quashing order or grant an injunction to restrain a person from acting in an office to which he or she is not entitled to act. If someone has been unlawfully detained, for example in a mental hospital, he or she may apply to the Divisional Court for a writ of *habeas corpus*.

2 Chancery Division. The Chancery Division hears the following actions:

(a) *Equity matters,* which were dealt with by the old Court of Chancery before 1875 and other cases allocated to it since then. These include actions involving trusts, mortgages, contentious probate, partnerships, specific performance of contracts, rectification of deeds, bankruptcies and taxation.

(b) A *Court of Protection* deals with actions involving the management of the property and affairs of mental patients.

(c) A *Companies Court* deals with applications relating to companies under legislation such as the Companies Act 2006.

(d) A *Patents Court* deals with patents and related matters outside the jurisdiction of the patents county court.

(e) Appeals from the Commissioners of Inland Revenue on income tax matters.

The Divisional Court of the Chancery Division hears appeals from the county courts in bankruptcy matters.

3 Family Division. The first-instance jurisdiction of the Family Division includes:

(a) *Matrimonial matters,* e.g. defended divorces.

(b) *Actions involving children,* e.g. adoption and legitimacy.

The Divisional Court of the Family Division hears appeals from magistrates' courts and county courts in matters relating to the family.

Crown Court

Like the magistrates' court, the Crown Court is mainly a criminal court, but it too has a civil jurisdiction, hearing appeals from the magistrates' court.

Court of Appeal (Civil Division)

The Civil Division of the Court of Appeal is headed by the Master of the Rolls, who is assisted by the Lord and

Lady Justices of Appeal. Normally, three judges sit to hear an appeal, although in important cases a full court of five may be assembled. The decisions are made by a simple majority. Since 1982, some cases have been heard by two judges, in an attempt to reduce the waiting time for hearings. Under the Access to Justice Act 1999, the Master of the Rolls, with the agreement of the Lord Chancellor, is allowed to give directions about the minimum number of judges required for various types of proceedings, and the Master of the Rolls will be able to decide how many judges should hear any particular appeal. The Civil Division of the Court of Appeal now has much greater flexibility in its operation by being able to operate in courts of one, two or more judges.

Jurisdiction

The court hears appeals from the High Court, county courts (except in bankruptcy cases) and various tribunals, such as the Lands Tribunal and the Employment Appeal Tribunal. It may uphold or reverse the decision of the lower court, or change the award of damages. In certain situations, it may order a new trial.

Supreme Court

The Supreme Court is the final court of appeal in civil matters. It also hears devolution references from courts in Scotland, Northern Ireland or England and Wales or Law Officers concerning the competence of devolved administrations under the devolution legislation. The composition of the Supreme Court was discussed earlier in this chapter.

Jurisdiction

The Justices of the Supreme Court hear civil appeals from the following sources:

1 The Court of Appeal, with the permission of the Court of Appeal or the Supreme Court.

2 The High Court, under the 'leapfrog' procedure introduced by the Administration of Justice Act 1969. This form of appeal goes straight to the Supreme Court, 'leapfrogging' the Court of Appeal. The trial judge must certify that the case is suitable for an appeal direct to the Supreme Court because it involves a point of law of general public importance relating wholly or mainly to a statute or statutory instrument (often concerned with taxation); the Supreme Court must grant leave to appeal and the parties must consent.

Other important courts

Court of Justice of the European Community

On joining the European Community in 1973, the United Kingdom agreed to accept the rulings of the European Court of Justice in matters of European law (see further Chapter 2 ○). The Supreme Court is the final court of appeal in respect of purely domestic law, but, where a dispute has a European element, any English court or tribunal may (and in some cases must) seek the opinion of the European Court in Luxembourg on the point of European law in question.

Judicial Committee of the Privy Council

The Judicial Committee of the Privy Council is not a formal part of our court structure, yet it has had a considerable influence on the development of English law. The jurisdiction of the Judicial Committee covers two main areas.

1 Final Court of Appeal for crown dependencies and certain Commonwealth countries. The Committee advises the Queen on criminal and civil appeals from the Isle of Man, the Channel Islands, British Colonies and Protectorates and from certain independent Commonwealth countries. The Committee's decisions are very influential because cases are usually heard by Supreme Court judges with the addition of senior Commonwealth judges, where appropriate.

2 Various domestic matters, e.g. pastoral schemes of the Church of England Commissioners, appeals from the Disciplinary Committee of the Royal College of Veterinary Surgeons.

European Court of Human Rights

The European Court of Human Rights, which sits at Strasbourg, deals with claims that the European Convention on Human Rights has been breached. Cases may be brought either by individuals, provided that the relevant state has accepted the right to bring an individual petition, or by one state against another.

The Court of Human Rights comprises 47 judges, a number equal to the number of states which have ratified the Convention. Cases are usually heard by seven judges sitting together.

The decisions of the court are binding on governments in international law but do not bind UK courts. However, UK courts must take the judgments of the Court of Human Rights into account when deciding a question in relation to a Convention right, following the incorporation of the European Convention on Human Rights into UK law by the Human Rights Act 1998.

Tribunals

The work of the ordinary courts is supplemented by a large number of tribunals set up by Act of Parliament to hear and decide upon disputes in specialised areas. As the lives of ordinary people have been affected more and more by the activities of government, particularly since the advent of the welfare state, so there has been a considerable growth in the number and jurisdiction of administrative tribunals.

In May 2000 the Lord Chancellor commissioned Sir Andrew Leggatt, a former Court of Appeal judge, to undertake a review of the tribunal system. The report, which was published in 2001, noted that there are 70 different administrative tribunals in England and Wales, dealing with nearly one million cases a year. Tribunals deal with a wide range of subjects, such as social security, employment, immigration and mental health. The attraction of tribunals is that they operate cheaply and quickly with a minimum of formalities. Although the chairman is usually legally qualified, other members are drawn from non-legal experts in the subject under consideration. Legal representation is discouraged as generally legal aid is not available and costs are not awarded. The work of tribunals is subject to scrutiny by the courts. An appeal from the decision of a tribunal can normally be made to the ordinary courts on a point of law but not on the facts. The Divisional Court of the Queen's Bench Division ensures that a tribunal acts fairly, according to its powers.

One of the best-known tribunals is the employment tribunal (formerly known as the industrial tribunal). When it was established in 1964, it had a very limited jurisdiction, but now it is one of the busiest tribunals. It sits locally to hear complaints by employees about contracts of employment; unfair dismissal; redundancy; sex, race, disability and age discrimination in employment; and equal pay. Since 1994 employment tribunals have also been able to hear claims for breach of a contract of employment where the amount claimed does not exceed £25,000. The breach must arise from or be outstanding at the termination of the employment. Previously these claims could only be heard in the ordinary courts. Personal injury claims and claims relating to living accommodation, intellectual property and restraint of trade are not included in the transfer of jurisdiction and will continue to be heard in the civil courts. The tribunal normally consists of a legally qualified chairman aided by two lay members, one representing employers and the other representing employees. However, changes introduced in 1993 enabled employment tribunal chairmen to sit alone to hear certain cases. The proceedings are relatively informal, especially as the strict rules of evidence are relaxed. Employees may receive 'legal help' from the Community Legal Service Fund to help them prepare for the hearing by, e.g., drafting documents. Financial help to cover the cost of representation at the tribunal hearing is not available, although applicants can be represented by a trade union official or a friend. Normally each side pays its own costs. The tribunal's powers include being able to make awards of compensation totalling thousands of pounds. An appeal lies to the Employment Appeal Tribunal and from there to the Court of Appeal. The Employment Rights (Dispute Resolution) Act 1998 introduced changes to the law relating to the resolution of individual employment rights disputes, which are discussed in more detail in Chapter 16 ○.

Reform of the tribunal system

As noted earlier, in August 2001, the government published Sir Andrew Leggatt's report on his review of the tribunal system, *Tribunals for Users: One System, One Service*. The report noted that, in the 44 years since tribunals were last reviewed, they had grown considerably in number and complexity. However, of the 70 tribunals identified, only 20 hear more than 500 cases a year. A consequence of having such a large number of disparate tribunals, many of which hear only a small number of cases, is that it has not been possible to achieve economies of scale. Resources have been wasted and training and IT have been under-resourced. Their procedures are often old-fashioned and are not accessible to users, who find the experience very daunting. Tribunals are often established and sponsored by a government department and, as a result, 'The tribunal neither appears to be independent, nor is independent in fact'. Sir Andrew stated that the objective of the report was to recommend a system that is independent, coherent, professional, cost-effective and user-friendly. The recommendations include:

- To establish a common, unified administrative service, known as the Tribunals Service, within the Lord Chancellor's Department.
- To establish a single Tribunal System, operating in divisions according to subject matter, e.g. education, financial, health and social services, immigration, land and valuation, social security and pensions, transport, regulatory and employment. Each division would have an appellate tribunal headed up by a President.
- The Tribunal System should be headed by a Senior President, who should be a High Court judge.
- There should be a right of appeal, but only by permission, on a point of law on the generic ground that the decision of the tribunal was unlawful. The appeal would lie from the first tier tribunal to the corresponding appellate tribunal and from there to the Court of Appeal.
- All appointments of chairmen and members of tribunals should be by the Lord Chancellor. Training, particularly in interpersonal skills, should be improved.
- There should be active case management, similar to the system used in the civil courts following the Woolf reforms.
- Tribunals should work with user groups to improve the accessibility of tribunals, for example, by ensuring that: (i) original decision-makers produce reasoned decisions; (ii) the Tribunal Service provides information about, for example, how to start a case, present it at a hearing and how to appeal; (iii) voluntary and other user groups are properly funded to assist users; and (iv) tribunal chairmen are appropriately trained to assist users to present their cases and make the proceedings intelligible.
- IT systems should be improved both to enhance administrative efficiency and also to improve public understanding of the work of tribunals.

The government's response was contained in a White Paper, *Transforming Public Services: Complaints, Redress and Tribunals* (2004). In April 2006 the Tribunals Service was established as an executive agency of the Department for Constitutional Affairs (now the Ministry for Justice) to provide a common administrative support to the main tribunals. Part 1 of the Tribunals, Courts and Enforcement Act 2007, which received the Royal Assent on 19 July 2007, introduces a new simplified statutory framework for tribunals. Existing tribunals have been brought into a unified structure, consisting of two new tribunals – the First Tier Tribunal and the Upper Tribunal, each organised into Chambers (groups of tribunals) headed by a Chamber President. The Chambers are:

First Tier Social entitlement, General Regulatory, Health, Education and Social Care, Taxation and Land, Property and Housing.

Upper Tier Administrative appeals, Finance and Tax, Lands.

The tribunal judiciary is overseen by a new judicial office, the Senior President of Tribunals. The Administrative Justice and Tribunals Council keeps the administrative system as a whole under review.

Alternative dispute resolution

So far in this chapter we have examined formal methods of settling disputes by means of legal action, known as litigation, in a court or tribunal. In practice, only a relatively small number of disputes are resolved in this way. The vast majority of disputes are settled by other means outside the formal court system. There are many good reasons why the parties themselves may prefer an 'out-of-court' compromise to courtroom conflict: e.g. fear of spoiling an otherwise satisfactory relationship; the cost of legal action, the amount of money at stake; difficulty in predicting the outcome of the case; or the likelihood of bad publicity. The drawbacks of pursuing a court action act as a powerful incentive for the parties to seek alternatives to litigation.

In its 1998 White Paper, *Modernising Justice*, the government stated that one of its objectives was to increase access to justice and to ensure that there were effective solutions available to people who needed help, which were proportionate to the issue at stake. In its view, litigation in courts and tribunals should only be used as a last resort. The different alternatives to litigation are usually referred to as alternative dispute resolution (ADR). In recent years, potential litigants have received strong encouragement to resolve their differences by using ADR. The new Civil Procedure Rules require courts to encourage the use of ADR in appropriate cases. So what is the position if one of the parties does not want to participate in ADR? The Court of Appeal cases of *Halsey v Milton Keynes General NHS Trust* and *Steel v Joy* (2004) both considered the circumstances in which a court should impose a costs sanction against a successful litigant on the grounds that he has refused to take part in ADR. The court's guidelines are as follows:

- A court cannot compel the parties to engage in mediation. ADR is a process which is entered into voluntarily and an order to engage in ADR may be a breach of Art 6 of the European Convention on Human Rights (right of access to the courts).
- The role of the court is to encourage ADR. The encouragement may be 'robust'.
- Costs may be awarded against the successful party if he has unreasonably refused to agree to ADR.
- The burden of showing that the refusal was unreasonable rests with the unsuccessful party.
- Factors which are relevant to deciding the question of reasonableness include the nature of the dispute, the merits of the case, the extent to which other settlement methods have been tried, whether the costs of ADR would be disproportionately high, whether any delay in establishing ADR would be prejudicial, and whether ADR has reasonable prospects of success.
- There is no presumption in favour of mediation.

The term ADR covers a wide range of techniques and processes for resolving disputes outside the courts. It is difficult to generalise about ADR as each type of ADR has different characteristics and therefore different benefits and drawbacks. Nevertheless, some of the disadvantages of litigation and the potential benefits of ADR are as follows:

- Litigation is adversarial and confrontational. The parties may wish to maintain a continuing relationship after the dispute has been resolved.
- In order to pursue litigation, you will usually need a lawyer to help prepare your case and to represent you, particularly in the higher courts. You may not be able to afford professional legal services or the amount at stake does not justify incurring significant costs.
- Despite the civil procedure reforms, litigation can still be very slow. You may need a speedy resolution to the problem.

- Litigation in the courts can be a daunting prospect for a lay person. ADR can be more user-friendly with simpler procedures.
- Litigation is very stressful and the fear of mounting costs can cause great anxiety. Some ADR techniques, e.g. conciliation, are specifically designed to overcome these problems.
- The remedies available to a court are quite limited, e.g. damages, injunction or a declaration of rights. A wider range of remedies may be available through ADR, e.g. securing a change in the way an organisation operates or securing an explanation of what happened.
- In most situations litigation is a public process. The case may be reported in the press and the judgment will be freely available to members of the public. Through ADR your case may be dealt with in privacy and you can avoid adverse or intrusive publicity.
- Although there is some degree of specialisation in the judiciary, most judges are generalists. The parties may wish to refer their dispute to someone with specialised or expert knowledge.
- Litigation takes place at a time and location specified by the courts and according to predetermined Civil Procedure Rules. ADR can operate more flexibly at a time and place convenient to the parties and sometimes by mutually agreed rules.

In this section we explain the main types of ADR.

Arbitration

Arbitration allows the parties to present their arguments to an independent arbitrator of their choice, in private and at their own convenience. The arbitrator may be legally qualified but usually he has special knowledge or experience of the subject matter. Sometimes an arbitration panel is used. Both sides agree to be bound by the decision of the arbitrator, which can be enforced as if it were the judgment of a court.

A court appearance can be a very costly and public way of resolving a dispute. Many in the commercial world seek to avoid the possibility by agreeing at the outset that any dispute will be referred to arbitration. Such clauses are often contained in contracts of insurance and partnership. Arbitration schemes have also been set up by trade bodies, such as the Association of British Travel Agents, to deal with complaints involving their members.

The Arbitration Act 1996 now provides a comprehensive statutory framework for the conduct of arbitration.

Early neutral evaluation

This is where a neutral person, who may be a lawyer or an expert in the field, looks at each side's case and gives an opinion on its merits. The opinion, which is not binding on the parties, can be used as a basis for further negotiation or reaching an agreement.

Expert determination

The parties agree to appoint an independent expert in the field to decide the dispute. The parties agree to be bound by the decision.

Mediation

Another alternative to litigation in the civil courts is mediation. This form of alternative dispute resolution consists of using a neutral third party (mediator) to help the parties to a legal dispute to reach a common position. Mediation can either be 'evaluative' in the sense that the mediator evaluates the strength of a case or 'facilitative' in that the mediator concentrates on helping the parties to reach agreement. The advantages of mediation compared to litigation include reduced costs and a reduction in conflict, making it particularly suitable for the following kinds of disputes:

- divorce, separation and other family problems;
- neighbours, e.g. about noise, boundaries;
- work, e.g. discrimination;
- education, e.g. exclusions from school.

If mediation is successful, the parties may record their agreement in the form of a binding contract, enforceable in the courts.

Conciliation

Conciliation is very similar to mediation, in that a third party helps the parties to reach a resolution. However, in conciliation the third party plays a more active role in bringing the parties together and suggesting solutions. In some cases the initiative for a settlement comes not from the parties themselves, but from an outside agency; for example, the Advisory, Conciliation and Arbitration Service (ACAS) tries to resolve both collective and individual disputes between employers and employees by means of conciliation. ACAS receives a copy of all employment tribunal applications. A conciliation officer will then offer his services to the parties to help them reach a settlement. Many claims are settled at this stage with the parties avoiding the ordeal of a tribunal hearing.

'Conciliation' is now regarded as a form of mediation.

Med-arb

This is a combination of mediation and arbitration. An independent person will first try mediation but, if it fails, the parties agree to refer the dispute to arbitration. The same person may act as both mediator and arbitrator.

Neutral fact finding

This is a process which is used in cases involving complex technical or factual issues. A neutral third party, who is usually an expert in the field, will review the facts in dispute and assess the merits of the case. The parties may use the outcome as a basis for further negotiations or to reach a settlement.

Ombudsmen

The Swedish term 'ombudsman' describes an official or commissioner who acts as an independent referee between a citizen and his government and its administration. The first ombudsman to be appointed in the UK was the Parliamentary Commissioner for Administration (PCA) in 1967. The job of the PCA is to investigate complaints of maladministration by government departments and various other public bodies, such as the Charity Commission and the English Tourist Board. Maladministration means poor or failed administration and can include unreasonable delay, bias or unfairness, failure to follow proper procedures, mistakes in handling claims and discourtesy. The PCA will not normally deal with matters which could be resolved through a court or tribunal. Complaints can only be brought by someone with a specific interest in the matter, i.e. it affects him or the organisation to which he belongs, and should not relate to events more than 12 months old.

Complaint about	Ombudsman	Comments
Estate agents	Property Ombudsman	Deals with disputes between members of the public who buy, sell or let property and the agents they deal with, i.e. estate agents and letting agents. Under the Consumers, Estate Agents and Redress Act 2007 all estate agents are required to be a member of an approved redress scheme. The Property Ombudsman can award compensation up to £25
Central government departments and other public bodies	Parliamentary Commissioner for Administration	Deals with complaints from the public about maladministration and obtaining access to official information. Complaints cannot be made direct and must be referred by an MP. The PCA can recommend a remedy but has no power to enforce his/her rulings.
Local government	Local Government Ombudsman	Deals with complaints about maladministration by local authorities. The ombudsman may make recommendations to resolve the complaint, including making suggestions about remedies.
Financial services, e.g. banks, building societies, insurance companies, financial advisers	Financial Ombudsman Service	Deals with complaints about most financial services. The ombudsman may make non-binding recommendations.
National Health Service (NHS)	Health Service Ombudsman	Covers complaints by or on behalf of patients about unsatisfactory treatment or service by the NHS. The ombudsman may ask the NHS to provide a suitable remedy but this would not normally include compensation.
Child Support Agency	Independent Case Examiner	Deals with complaints about the Child Support Agency.
Legal profession: including solicitors, barristers, licensed conveyancers, legal executives and patent agents	Office of the Legal Services Ombudsman (OLSO)	Deals with complaints about the way professional bodies have handled a complaint. The OLSO can recommend that the professional body reconsider its decision and/or pay compensation. The OLSO can also formally criticise the professional body and, in exceptional cases, make a binding order of compensation.
Housing	Housing Ombudsman Service	Deals with disputes between landlords and tenants. The ombudsman may recommend, e.g., that compensation be paid or that repairs be carried out.
Pensions	Pensions Ombudsman	Investigates and deals with complaints and disputes about the way occupational and personal pension schemes are run.
Judiciary	Judicial Appointments and Conduct Ombudsman	Created by the Constitutional Reform Act 2005, this ombudsman investigates complaints about the judicial appointments process and the handling of matters involving judicial conduct.

Figure 3.5 **Ombudsmen**

The PCA cannot investigate complaints received directly from the public; complaints about government organisations must be referred to the ombudsman by an MP. The powers of the PCA are confined to conducting an investigation into a complaint and, if the complaint is justified, recommending a remedy. The PCA has no power to order a specific remedy and there is no right of appeal from the decisions of the PCA. The ombudsman method of dealing with complaints has found favour in many areas of official and commercial activity. Examples of ombudsmen are set out in Figure 3.5.

Regulators

When public utilities were privatised in the 1980s and 1990s, the government established regulators to oversee the industries concerned. The main regulators are OFGEM (gas and electricity companies), OFCOM (telecommunications companies) and OFWAT (water companies). The regulators will not normally deal with complaints directly but they will investigate whether the company has dealt with a complaint properly.

Self-test questions/activities

1 For each of the actions listed below state:
  (a) Which court or tribunal would hear the case?
  (b) What type of lawyer could represent the parties?
  (c) Who would try the action?
  (d) To which court or tribunal would an appeal lie:
    (i) in a prosecution for murder;
    (ii) in an undefended divorce;
    (iii) in a claim for damages of £75,000 for negligence causing personal injury;
    (iv) in a claim by an employee that he has been unfairly dismissed;
    (v) in a bankruptcy petition where the debts are £20,000;
    (vi) in a claim by a resident that his local authority has failed to produce accounts for public inspection as required by law;
    (vii) in a claim for damages of £200 for breach of contract;
    (viii) in an application by a social services department to take a child into care?

2 What part do laypersons take in the administration of the legal system? Should they be replaced by professionals?

3 Our legal system often allows for two levels of appeal. Is this a wasteful use of resources?

4 What are the advantages and disadvantages of using tribunals rather than the ordinary courts to decide disputes?

Specimen examination questions

1 (a) Comment on the view that magistrates' courts are the workhorses of the criminal justice system.
  (b) Explain how criminal cases are allocated for trial between magistrates' courts and the Crown Court.

2 Critically evaluate the changes to civil justice procedure introduced by the Woolf reforms.

3 What alternatives to litigation in the ordinary courts are available? What are the advantages and disadvantages of these alternative methods of dispute resolution compared to litigation in the courts?

Website references

Legal profession

http://www.lawsociety.org.uk The Law Society is the representative body for solicitors in England and Wales. The Solicitors Regulation Authority deals with all regulatory and disciplinary matters relating to solicitors, while the Legal Complaints Service deals with complaints against solicitors.

http://www.lawscot.org.uk The Law Society of Scotland is the governing body for Scottish solicitors. In essence, the Society promotes the interests of solicitors in Scotland and provides services to the public in this field.

http://www.barcouncil.org.uk The Bar Council® is the regulatory and representative body for barristers in England and Wales. This site gives information on what barristers do, their history and how they are regulated, etc.

http://www.conveyancers.org.uk This is the website for the Council of Licensed Conveyancers, the professional body for those specialising in property law.

http://www.ilex.org.uk On this website you will find information about the Institute of Legal Executives (ILEX), the professional body which represents 22,000 legal executives.

Courts and tribunals

http://www.justice.gov.uk/ The website for the Ministry of Justice provides a broad range of legal information covering the legal system and there are links to the Courts Service, judgments and court procedure and a section dealing with tribunals.

Criminal justice and procedure, reform

http://www.direct.gov.uk/en/CrimeJusticeandtheLaw The Criminal Justice System website provides access to information about the operation of the Criminal Justice System in England and Wales.

http://www.criminal-courts-review.org.uk The site for the Auld Committee review of the criminal courts.

Civil justice and procedure, reform

http://www.dca.gov.uk/civil/cjustfr.htm On this part of the former Department for Constitutional Affairs' website you will find an archive of the Department's work on policy affecting the civil law, including the Woolf reforms.

http://www.dca.gov.uk/procedurerules/civilpr_background.htm This part of the former Department for Constitutional Affairs' website provides archived documents relating to the Civil Procedure Rules.

http://www.civiljusticecouncil.gov.uk The Civil Justice Council is charged with monitoring the civil justice system and ensuring that it is fair, efficient and accessible.

Alternative dispute resolution

http://www.adr.civiljusticecouncil.gov.uk This part of the Civil Justice Council's website deals with ADR.

http://www.legalservices.gov.uk/public/help/information_leaflets.asp The Community Legal Service (CLS) provides a range of leaflets on this site, including those dealing with debt, the Human Rights Act, and alternatives to court – which provides detailed guidance on ADR systems.

http://www.bioa.org.uk The website of the British and Irish Ombudsman Association provides links to the websites of UK ombudsmen and other complaint handling schemes.

Visit **www.mylawchamber.co.uk/richesallen** to access study support resources including answers to questions in this chapter and legal updates, all linked to the **Pearson eText** version of **Keenan and Riches' Business Law** which you can **search**, **highlight** and **personalise** with your **own notes** and **bookmarks**.

premium mylawchamber

Part 2 | BUSINESS ORGANISATIONS

Chapter 4

An introduction to types of business organisation

Learning objectives

After studying this chapter you should understand the following main points:

- the different types of business organisation, including advantages and disadvantages;
- the nature and consequences of the use of juristic personality in relevant organisations;
- methods of financing the organisations and the securities a lender may require;
- the publicity requirement placed on relevant organisations in terms of public disclosure;
- the nature of other criminal offences which may be relevant to business, such as fraud and insider dealing.

The importance of business to the UK economy cannot be underestimated. According to the World Bank, the UK is ranked fifth in the world and first place in Europe for ease of doing business (see Department for Business, Innovation and Skills (BIS) website). A business can be run in what is called the private sector of commerce and industry through any one of three types of business organisation:

- The sole trader.
- The partnership.
- The company.

It is important to be able to identify and understand the difference between types of businesses. An introduction is provided below. The nature of each type of businesses will be examined in Chapter 5 ○ (on sole traders and partnerships) and Chapter 6 ○ (on companies). Business law, as a policy area, falls under the remit of the Department for Business, Innovation and Skills (BIS). BIS replaced the Department for Business, Enterprise and Regulatory Reform (BERR), referred to extensively in the 9th edition, in June 2009. BIS is a creation after the merger between BERR and the Department for Innovation, Universities and Skills

(DIUS). The key role of BIS is 'to build Britain's capabilities to compete in the global economy'. It was hoped that the merger and reorganisation would create a regulatory environment that encourages 'enterprise, skilled people, innovation, and world-class science and research'.

Classification of business organisations and liability of the proprietors

The private sector

The sole trader

This means going it alone with a one-person business. A sole trader owns all the assets and takes all the profits out of the business. However, a sole trader is liable for the debts of the business to the extent of everything he owns. Even his private possessions may be ordered to be sold to pay the debts of the business. There is no such thing as limited liability. A sole trader can make a free transfer of personal assets to a husband or wife (spouse) or other relative, but the transfer can be set aside and the assets returned to the sole trader and then used to pay the business creditors if the court is satisfied the transfer was made to defeat creditors. Also, if property is transferred to a spouse, it is lost to the sole trader if the marriage ends in divorce and the spouse refuses to give it up.

The partnership – generally

There are three types of partnership that can be used as a business vehicle.

An unlimited partnership

The Partnership Act 1890 sets out the basic rules which apply to partnerships. You can share the losses (if any), the problems and worries with a partner or partners being in a business; the profits must also be shared. This is certainly the case with what are called full or equity partners; but liability for the debts of the firm can arise even where profits are not shared, as in the case of salaried partners and consultant partners who receive a salary or fees.

In the case of a partnership governed by the Partnership Act 1890, partners are jointly and severally liable for the debts and other liabilities of the firm, such as negligence liability, even though the negligence results from the work of only one of the partners. The problem is made more acute for these firms and the partners because there is unlikely to be full insurance cover on offer for professional liability claims.

They can be sued together by a creditor who has not been paid. They can also be sued individually (or severally). Thus, if A, B and C are partners and the firm owes X £3,000 but this cannot be paid from the partnership funds, then, for example, X may sue A for the whole £3,000 and A may then try to get a contribution of £1,000 from B and £1,000 from C. If they are insolvent, he will not get the contribution, or at least not all of it.

The liability extends to the private assets of the partners. Even the estate of a deceased partner is liable for the debts of the firm incurred while he was a partner if there is anything left in his estate after paying his private debts.

A ruling of the Court of Appeal in *M Young Legal Associates Ltd* v *Zahid Solicitors (A Firm)* (2006) is to the effect that it is not necessary to share profits before the legal status of partner, at least in the context of debt liability, can be established under the definition in s 1 of the Partnership Act 1890 which states that the partners

must be in business 'with a view of profit' but says nothing about sharing the profits. Becoming a partner by estoppel (see below) is a different way in which a person can come to be regarded as a partner (see further p 122 ◯). Others may be liable by estoppel or under the definition as in *M Young Legal Associates Ltd* v *Zahid Solicitors (A Firm)* (2006) (above).

The principle laid down in *M Young Legal Associates Ltd* v *Zahid (a firm)* was considered and applied in *Hodson* v *Hodson* (2009), where the principle as to whether sharing a profit was a prerequisite for a partnership. In this case, the claimant waived her entitlement to the appropriate share of the profits. The question was therefore to consider whether she remained as a partner. The point that sharing of profits was not a prerequisite for a partnership was reaffirmed.

While it is not legally required, it is normally sensible for the partners to make a contract called a partnership agreement which is often in writing because it then provides a good record of what was agreed about the business. However, writing is not necessary; a verbal agreement will do and, indeed, a partnership can in some cases be inferred from conduct. For example, if A acts as if he were the partner of B he may become one in law, at least to a creditor who has relied on the apparent situation, even though there is no contract, verbal or written, between them. Partnership by estoppel, as it is called, is more fully explained in Chapter 5 ◯.

The liability of the partners is unlimited, so if the firm cannot pay its debts, each general or equity partner is liable to pay them with a right to ask for a contribution from the others.

A limited partnership

The Limited Partnerships Act 1907 provides for the formation of limited partnerships in which one or more of the partners has only limited liability for the firm's debts. These partnerships are not commonly used in the generality of business organisations. They are used for collective investment schemes such as unit trusts. So long as one partner has full liability where the firm cannot pay a debt, the others may have limited liability. This means that if the business falls on hard times, they may lose the capital they invested in it but will have no further liability as the unlimited partner has. The firm manages the scheme and the investments. The limited partners cannot take part in management. If they do, they become personally liable for debts incurred by the firm during their period of management. This type of partnership is often seen as an useful vehicle 'for investors who do not wish to take an active role in the management of the investment to combine to create an investment fund under the control of a general partner who alone has unlimited liability for the partnership's obligations whilst the limited partners are only liable to the extent of their contributions (unless they take part in the management of the business)' (for further information, see the explanatory document published in June 2009 by BIS: http://www.berr.gov.uk/files/file51586. pdf). It should be noted that since 1987, the UK limited partnership has been recognised as one of the most important vehicles for venture capital investment across Europe.

The law on limited partnerships based on recommendations made in a joint report by the Law Commission and Scottish Law Commissions is in the process of reforming. It is envisaged that the Limited Partnerships Act 1907 would eventually be repealed and new provisions about limited partnerships would be inserted into the Partnership Act 1890. The proposed changes cover the following areas:

- Establishment, registration and de-registration of a limited partnership.
- The liability of limited partners to third parties.
- The rights and obligations of general and limited partners in a limited partnership.

See also Chapter 5 ⊙ for further information on this topic.

A limited liability partnership

This is the most recently created form of business ownership: the Limited Liability Partnerships Act 2000 made it possible for a business to be set as the limited liability partnership or LLP. It is registered with the Registrar of Companies and owns the assets of the business as a juristic person separate from the *members*, as they are called. The LLP is fully liable for its debts but there is no personal liability in the members as is the case with the unlimited partnership. If the LLP becomes insolvent, the members may well lose the capital they contributed but beyond this have no duty to contribute to the assets of the LLP if on winding-up there is a shortfall. They can agree to make such a contribution in the LLP agreement but are not forced by law to do so. However, the court has a discretion to order repayment of any withdrawals made by a member of an LLP within the two years prior to winding-up if the member knew

or ought to have concluded that the withdrawal would increase the risk of subsequent insolvency. Experience of the LLP shows that up to now the relevant legislation, i.e. the Limited Liability Partnerships Act 2000, has been used mainly by partnerships of solicitors and accountants and other professionals where personal liability, e.g. for negligence claims, can be high if the firm cannot meet the damages.

Detailed provisions contained in the Limited Liability Partnerships Act 2000 and regulations were made largely on the Companies Act 1985. The government consulted in November 2007 on the application of the Companies Act 2006 to Limited Liability Partnerships (LLPs). The intention was to ensure that LLPs remain an attractive business medium for businesses as it was envisaged that LLPs should remain distinct from companies. Accordingly, it is important to bring the LLP Regulations up to date with the 2006 Act. The provisions should achieve the right balance between the interests of those who want to become LLPs and those who are dealing with LLPs. Regulations on accounts and audits provisions were published ahead of other provisions and came into effect for LLPs in Great Britain and Northern Ireland on 1 October 2008, for financial years beginning on or after that date. The remaining provisions have been made based on the 2006 Act and came into effect in October 2009, i.e. in the main implementation stage of the CA 2006.

The company

A business may be incorporated as a **registered company**. This is created by following a registration procedure carried out through the Registrar of Companies in Cardiff. Companies House is an Executive Agency of the Department for Business, Innovation and Skills (BIS).

A registered company is commonly formed by one or more people who become its shareholders. Directors must be appointed to manage the company and act as its agents. Under the Companies Act 2006 a private company need not appoint a company secretary but may do so if it wishes. In a private company it is common for the appointment to be made either from the shareholders or from among those advising the business, such as an accountant (provided he is not also the company's auditor, who cannot hold an office of profit within the company) or solicitor. If the business is large enough and the company is a public limited company, it must under the Companies Act 2006 appoint a company secretary, normally after public advertisement of the post. No special qualifications are required for secretaries of private companies where these are appointed but qualifications are laid down for secretaries of public companies. The relevant provisions are now contained in the Companies Act 2006. These are explained in Chapter 6 ○.

In the past, trading companies were incorporated by Royal Charter. However, incorporation by registration was set up in 1844 by the Joint Stock Companies Act of that year, and it is most unlikely that incorporation by Royal Charter would be used today to incorporate a commercial business. Charters are still used to incorporate certain organisations, such as professional bodies which control the professions, e.g. the Chartered Institute of Secretaries and Administrators, and for incorporating certain bodies in the public sector, such as the British Broadcasting Corporation.

As to how you get a charter, the organisation wanting one sends what is called a petition to the Privy Council. The Privy Council consists of members of the current Cabinet who become members of the Council when they first take office, former members of the Cabinet, and others appointed by the Queen on the recommendation of the Prime Minister as an honour for service in some branch of public affairs at home or overseas. There are also what are called *convential members* who become members by reason of holding another office, e.g. the Speaker of the House of Commons. The petition asks for the grant of a charter and sets out the powers required. If the Privy Council considers that it is appropriate to grant a charter, the Crown will be advised to do so.

The public sector

At the end of the Second World War the then Labour government thought it right to bring into the public sector certain organisations providing goods or services to the public on a national basis with a complete or partial monopoly, e.g. the mining of coal. Public corporations were formed to manage these organisations. These organisations have now been returned to the private sector through the medium of public limited companies with shareholders. The commercial public corporations are for all practical purposes non-existent, though an example in the social services area is the Health and Safety Executive set up by the Health and Safety at Work etc. Act 1974 to supervise and enforce health and safety through inspectors (see further, Chapter 16 ○).

Natural and juristic persons

Natural persons

These are human beings who are known to the law as natural persons. An adult human being has in general terms the full range of legal rights and a full range of legal duties. Thus, if A makes a contract with B and B fails to perform it, A has a right, e.g. to damages, because B failed to perform a duty. A similar situation would occur if A failed in his duty to perform the contract, thus denying B his right to have it performed.

However, the law distinguishes between certain classes of human beings and gives them a status, which means that they have more limited rights and duties than are given to other persons. Examples are minors (persons under the age of 18), and persons who lack mental capacity.

Some contracts of minors are not binding on them and they cannot be sued for damages for breach of contract if they fail to perform them. As regards persons who allegedly lack mental capacity, the Mental Capacity Act 2005 provides that a person is assumed to have mental capacity, e.g. to make the contract in question, unless either party can prove to the contrary. If it is shown that there is insufficient mental capacity then the contract is not binding on either party. The Act contains provisions relating to payment for necessary goods, e.g. food and clothing and services, where these have been supplied and delivered to the person who lacks mental capacity. These matters are more fully dealt with in Chapter 7 ○.

Non-human creatures are not legal persons and do not have those rights and duties which a human being gets at birth. However, animals may be protected by the law for certain purposes, such as conservation. For example, s 9 of the Wildlife and Countryside Act 1981 protects certain wild animals by making it a criminal offence for a person intentionally to kill, injure or take any animal included in Sch 5 to that Act, e.g. bats.

The Animal Welfare Act 2006 is also relevant and is concerned, e.g., with trade in exotic animals where standards of animal care are often poor. It also has a wider impact on animal care in, e.g., pet shops and pet fairs where standards of care are too often wholly inadequate. There is also the Hunting Act 2004 which in general prohibits the use of dogs to hunt wild animals in England and Wales.

Juristic persons

Legal personality is not given only to human beings. Persons can form a corporation, that corporation having a legal personality with similar rights and duties to human beings. As we have seen, these corporations are formed by Royal Charter, Act of Parliament, or by registration under the Companies Act 2006 or previous Acts. There are also corporations sole, which were introduced by lawyers under common law.

Charter companies and those formed by Act of Parliament have their own legal personalities and act through human agents. This is also true of the registered company, which is allowed by law through the agency of its directors to make contracts, hold property, and carry on business on its own account, regardless of the particular persons who may happen at the particular time to hold its shares.

Thus, if A and B form a registered company, AB Ltd, the separate legal personality of AB Ltd is created on formation. A and B can now, if as is likely they have been appointed as directors of the company, make contracts on behalf of AB Ltd as its agents. The rights and duties under those contracts will belong to AB Ltd and not to A and B as individuals. The rule of corporate personality is illustrated by the following.

Salomon v Salomon & Co (1897)

Mr Salomon carried on business as a leather merchant and boot manufacturer. In 1892 he formed a limited company to take over the business. Mr Salomon was the major shareholder. His wife, daughter and four sons were also shareholders. They had only one share each. The subscribers to the company's memorandum met and appointed Mr Salomon and his two elder sons directors and, therefore, agents of the company (see further Chapter 6 ⃝). The company gave Mr Salomon 20,000 shares of £1 each in payment for the business and he said that a further £10,000 of the purchase price could be regarded as a loan to the company which it could repay later. Meanwhile, the loan was secured on the assets of the company. This charge on the assets made Mr Salomon a secured creditor who, under the rules of company law, would get his money before unsecured (or trade) creditors if the company was wound up. The company fell on hard times and a liquidator was appointed. The assets were sufficient to pay off the debentures but in that event the trade creditors would receive nothing. The unsecured creditors claimed all the remaining assets on the ground that Mr Salomon and the company were one. Thus he could not lend money to himself or give himself a security over his own assets. Eventually, the House of Lords held that the company was a separate and distinct person. The loan and the security were valid transactions between separate individuals, i.e. Mr Salomon and the company, and therefore Mr Salomon was entitled to the remaining assets in payment of the secured loan.

Comment. The creditors of Mr Salomon's original business had been paid off. The unsecured creditors were creditors of the company and the House of Lords said that they must be deemed to know that they were dealing with a limited company whose members, provided they had paid for their shares in full, could not be obliged to meet its debts.

Looking behind the corporate personality: lifting the corporate veil

While the corporate veil principle is fundamental to company law, the idea of corporate personality can also lead to abuse and it has been used to avoid legal obligations. One of the clear principles laid down in the *Salomon* case was that the court would not hesitate to ignore the separate personality of the company (or draw aside the corporate veil) if the company had been used for fraudulent purpose, and treat the business as if it was being run by its individual members; an illustration of this appears in the following case.

Gilford Motor Co Ltd v Horne (1933)

Mr Horne had been employed by Gilford. He had agreed to a restraint of trade in his contract under which he would not approach the company's customers to try to get them to transfer their custom to any similar business which Mr Horne might run himself.

Mr Horne left his job with Gilford and set up a similar business using a registered company structure. He then began to send out circulars to the customers of Gilford, inviting them to do business with his company.

Gilford asked the court for an injunction to stop Mr Horne's activities and Horne said that he was not competing but his company was and that the company had not agreed to a restraint of trade. An injunction was granted against both Mr Horne and his company to stop the circularisation of Gilford's customers. The corporate structure could not be used by Mr Horne to evade his legal contractual duties.

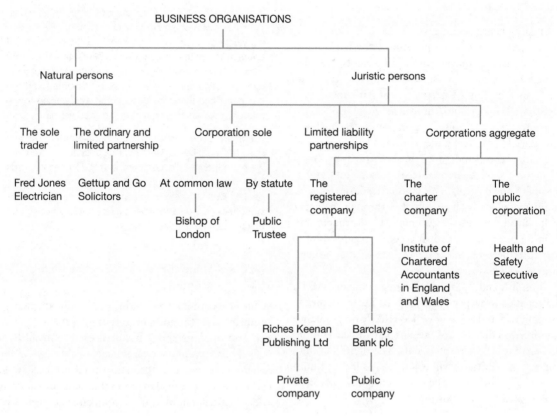

Figure 4.1 Business organisations in terms of natural and juristic persons

Corporations sole

All the forms of corporation which have been discussed so far have one feature in common, which is that they are corporations aggregate, having more than one member. However, English law also recognises the idea of the corporation sole, which is a corporation having only one member.

A number of such corporations were created by the common lawyers in early times because they were concerned that land did not always have an owner and that there could be a break, however slight, in ownership.

Church lands, for example, were vested in the vicar of the particular area and at higher levels in other church dignitaries, such as the bishop of the diocese. When such persons died, the land had no legal owner until a successor was appointed to the job so the common lawyers created the concept of the corporation sole under which the office of vicar or bishop was a corporation and the present vicar or bishop the sole member of

that corporation. The land was then transferred to the corporation and the death of the particular vicar or bishop had thereafter no effect on the landholding because the corporation did not die and continued to own the land. The Bishop of London is a corporation sole and the present holder of the office is the sole member of the corporation. The Crown is also a corporation sole.

It does not seem likely that any further corporations of this sort will be created by the common law but they can still be created by Act of Parliament. For example, the Public Trustee Act 1906 sets up the office of Public Trustee as a corporation sole. The Public Trustee will act as an executor to administer a person's estate when that person dies, or as a trustee, to look after property for beneficiaries such as young children, and a lot of property is put into his ownership for the benefit of others from time to time. It would be very difficult to transfer all this property to the new holder of the office on the death or retirement of the civil servant who is in fact the Public Trustee. So the person who holds the office of Public

Trustee is the sole member of a corporation called the Public Trustee and the property over which he has control is transferred to that corporation and not to the individual who is the holder of the office.

The Public Trust Office was abolished with effect from 1 April 2001. From that date, the work of the Public Trust Office was transferred to the Office of the Official Solicitor. The two posts of Official Solicitor and Public Trustee are now held by the same individual but the two posts have not been amalgamated and trust work can be undertaken in either capacity depending on administrative arrangements. The corporation sole principles still apply to the *individual* who holds the joint office. He is, in effect, a member of a corporation sole, either the Official Solicitor or Public Trustee.

Survey of types of business organisations: advantages and disadvantages

The major advantages and disadvantages of the various forms of business organisations in the private sector will now be looked at under the headings set out below.

Commencement of business

Sole traders, ordinary and limited partnerships

These organisations can commence business merely by opening the doors of the premises. It is usual to register for value added tax, though this is not compulsory unless the turnover of the business is at registration level (currently more than £70,000 as of August 2010), and of course the premises which are being used must, under planning and other regulations, be available for business purposes. Planning requirements are considered later in this chapter.

If the organisation is not using the name of its proprietor(s), but using a business name, as where Freda Green trades as 'London Fashions' (the business name), or Fred and Freda Brown trade as 'Paris Fashions' (the business name), then the organisation must comply with the requirements of the Companies Act 2006. This will be dealt with in more detail in later chapters, e.g.

Chapter 5 ⊙, but it contains provisions restricting the choice of the business name. For example, a name must not be chosen which suggests a connection with central and local government unless approval has been granted by BIS. This is to prevent the public getting a possibly false sense of security because these government authorities get a regular and safe income from taxes and council tax and business rates. There are also requirements regarding disclosure of the name during the lifetime of the business.

Limited liability partnerships

Those wishing to trade as a limited liability partnership (LLP) must send an incorporation document to the Registrar of Companies. If the Registrar is satisfied that the requirements for registration have been complied with the incorporation document will be registered and the Registrar will give a certificate that the LLP is incorporated. From the date of the certificate the members can trade through the medium of the LLP. Trading before that date could be construed as trading through an ordinary informal partnership governed by the Partnership Act 1890. An existing ordinary partnership converting to an LLP would until incorporation trade under its existing partnership articles and the 1890 Act. These matters apart, the above material relating to other partnerships applies.

Companies

A private company cannot trade until its application for registration has been dealt with by the Registrar of Companies and he has given the company a certificate of incorporation. The Companies Act 2006 requires public companies to have an authorised and issued share capital of at least £50,000 in nominal value, of which at least one-quarter has been paid plus the whole of any premium. This is essential so that the company can trade and/or borrow.

The choice of the corporate name and a business name, if the company uses one, is controlled by the Companies Act 2006, and this Act provides also for publicity to be given to the name. These matters will be dealt with in Chapter 6 ⊙.

Community interest companies

These companies are not involved in business as such and are included here for the sake of completeness. They are designed for use by social enterprises wishing to operate under a corporate structure.

They are intended for use by non-profit distributing enterprises providing benefit to the community. Organisations active in areas such as childcare, social housing, leisure and community transport may wish to make use of the corporate structure of a community interest company (CIC) given the relative freedom of a non-charitable company form but with a clear assurance of restricted profit distribution status.

A CIC is subject to the general framework of company law and to the Companies Act 2006. There are two forms of CIC: a company limited by guarantee (CIG); or a company limited by shares (CIS). CICs are registered with the Registrar of Companies and are subject to approval by the Regulator of Community Interest Companies. The Regulator is an independent public office holder appointed by the Secretary of State. The powers of the office are set out in the Act and the Community Interest Company Regulations 2005.

In addition to the requirement of 'community interest', 'asset lock' is another important feature of CICs. This is a general term used to cover all the provisions designed to ensure that the assets of the CIC are used for the benefit of the community. Although a non-profit distributing organisation may use the CIC form and carry on a policy of not paying dividends, a CIC limited by shares can pay a dividend on those shares if it wishes. There is a cap on the amount, which will be set from time to time by the Community Interest Company Regulator whose office is located in Companies House in Cardiff. The cap can be fixed by reference to a rate fixed by an outside body, e.g. the Bank of England's minimum lending rate, from time to time.

Raising business finance – generally

Sole traders and all partnerships

All businesses need money to begin trading: some kind of start-up finance. Sole traders must either put in enough of their own money if they have it or put in what they have and try to borrow the rest. Partners are in the same position.

It should be noted that most people use their own savings to start the business. Alternatively, it may be possible to try for a loan from one of the banks. Certainly, a bank will not lend 100 per cent of the finance. The bank will normally want some security for its money and this may mean giving the bank a mortgage on the house of the sole trader, or houses of the partners. This could be potentially very risky. It should be borne in mind that lenders such as banks will not advance the full market value of the property offered as a security. For example, a lender may lend up to, say, 70 per cent of the value of freehold land and buildings. The figures for borrowing are less than the asset value because of the impact on that value of the forced sale that takes place when a lender calls in the security, if the loan cannot be repaid.

Interest rates can differ according to the deal given by the bank. Interest may be variable and change with the base rate, as is the case where the bank allows the organisation to overdraw a bank account up to a certain amount. The alternative is a loan at a fixed rate of interest. These are usually more expensive but may be better than an overdraft facility if the loan is taken at a time of low interest rates.

A partnership can, of course, attract more capital by admitting new partners. There was a limit of 20 partners in a partnership. This was designed to force the larger partnership to become a registered company where there was greater statutory control of its business affairs. The Regulatory Reform (Removal of 20 Member Limit in Partnerships, etc.) Order 2002 (SI 2002/3203) removed the 20-partner limit from all unlimited and limited partnerships. Many of these partnerships including those of accountants and solicitors were already exempt under previous legislation. The restriction was never applied to the number of members in a limited liability partnership. These Regulatory Reform Orders can be used to reform any legislation, even a statute that imposes a burden on business. There is no need for primary legislation, i.e. an Act of Parliament.

Companies

Here the capital structure is more complicated. If two people wishing to form a private company and be its directors contribute £10,000 each to form the company, each of the two members taking 20,000 shares of £1 each, then:

1 all the company's current capital is issued;
2 the £20,000 cash received by the company is its paid-up capital.

Under previous legislation, a company had to be registered with a stated authorised capital and no capital could be issued beyond this limit unless the authorised capital was increased by a resolution of the members. The Companies Act 2006 abolished the concept of authorised capital and the company can issue further shares of an unlimited number provided that, after issue, it files with the Registrar of Companies a Statement of Share Capital which shows, among other things, the current number of shares in the company.

A company may also raise money by borrowing, often from a bank, either by way of a loan at fixed interest or, more commonly, by the granting of an overdraft facility.

The lender does not become a member of the company and if the company falls on hard times and is wound up the lender, being a creditor, is entitled to recover his loan before the shareholders get anything for their shares.

A lending bank will take a security (called a debenture) over the company's assets for its loan and will usually ask the directors to give another security by guaranteeing the loan so that if the company does not repay it they will have to. This takes away some of the advantages of limited liability.

Once again, the bank will not advance the full value of the property offered as a security by the company for the reasons stated above.

There is no limit on the number of shareholders which a company may have and so it can raise as much capital as it wishes if it can sell its shares to outsiders. A public company can offer its shares to the public, but a private company must negotiate personally with outsiders who might buy its shares.

Raising business finance – securities

We have already given some consideration to the methods of financing business organisations (see above). We have noted the advantage of forming a limited company because of the ability within the company structure to issue share capital. If required, share capital can be issued with a variety of different rights in terms, for example, of voting. It can be preference with a fixed dividend and/or ordinary on which dividend will be paid only if and when distributable profits are made.

However, in other forms of business organisation, for example the sole trader and the partnership, it is also necessary, as it is in the company structure, to consider in more detail the raising of loan capital and the method by which some sort of security, over and above the contractual promise of the borrower to repay the loan, can be given.

As regards loan capital, a company has a great advantage in that it can give a floating charge over its assets to a substantial lender, e.g. a bank. Partnerships and sole traders cannot do this because they are subject to bills of sale legislation which in effect stops it (see p 82). In 2000, the Law Commission issued a consultation paper prepared at the request of the then Department of Trade and Industry (now BIS) in which it invited views from business as to whether partnerships should be allowed to grant floating charges by making changes in the law. It should be noted that this area forms part of the wider reform on partnership law as the main proposal was to explore the possibility of allowing a 'registered unlimited partnership'. The issue was not taken any further (see *Partnership Law*, joint report by the Law Commission and Scottish Law Commission, Law Commission No. 283, November 2003).

Limited liability partnerships can give a floating charge over their assets in the same way as a company can. Bills of sale legislation does not apply.

A sole trader or a firm can only mortgage its business premises and fixed plant and give personal guarantees from the sole proprietor or the partners. Sole traders and partners can also mortgage their own private property. These forms of security are also quite common in the private limited company where directors will normally be asked to give guarantees of the company's major debts and mortgage their private property to secure, for example, bank lending to the company. All of this makes something of a mockery of limited liability so far as directors of private companies are concerned.

We shall now consider these securities in more detail.

Charges

A charge is a type of security by which a person who borrows money gives the lender rights over his (the borrower's) assets to support the duty of the borrower to repay what is owed under the contract of loan. The lender thus has two rights:

1 to sue the borrower on the contract of loan; and
2 to sell the assets which the borrower has charged in order to recover what is owed to him but no more. Any surplus on sale, less the costs of selling the property, must be returned to the borrower. The charge may be fixed or floating (see below).

A mortgage, which will be considered below, is a term most often used to mean a fixed charge over land. However, the term 'mortgage' may be used to describe any type of fixed (but not a floating) charge over any item of land or other property such as a mortgage by a shareholder who uses his shares, which are personal property, as security for a loan.

Fixed charges

A fixed legal charge can be given over identified property belonging to the borrower. This property may be either real property, e.g. land and buildings, or personal property, e.g. machinery and equipment.

If real property is being used, there is no need for the borrower to transfer his ownership in the land to the lender. The Law of Property Act 1925 allows the lender who has taken the fixed legal charge over, say, land and buildings to sell it on his own without any assistance from the borrower, even though the lender has not taken a transfer of the ownership from the borrower by what is called a conveyance.

If personal property, such as machinery and equipment, were to be used as security, the borrower would have to transfer, by a method called assignment, the ownership in the machinery and equipment to the lender. Unless this was done, the lender could not give a good title to a buyer of the machinery and equipment if he decided to sell it, which he would want to do if the borrower did not repay the loan.

The great benefit of the fixed legal charge is that once it has been given, the lender can sell the property charged by himself. The contract of loan will, of course, end his right to do this once the loan has been repaid.

Furthermore, if the company becomes insolvent the preferential creditors (e.g. those owed wages or salaries up to £800 for a period of four months) do *not count for payment before the fixed charge*. Therefore, a creditor, such as a bank with a fixed charge, will get more than it would under a floating charge, as preferential creditors do rank before a floating charge. Thus, if the directors have given a personal guarantee of the company's overdraft, they will have less to pay on the overdraft to the bank if the bank holds a fixed charge.

Floating charges

1 **Generally.** This is a charge which is not attached to any particular asset when the charge is made. Instead it applies to the assets of the borrower as they are at the time the charge crystallises, as it will, for example, if the borrower fails to make repayment of the loan as agreed. The borrower is in the meantime free to sell the assets he has and any new assets which his business acquires are available to be sold by the lender if they were in the ownership of the borrower when the charge crystallised. When the charge crystallises, it becomes, in effect, a fixed charge over the assets which the borrower then has. The lender can then sell them to recoup his loan.

2 **Floating charges restricted to companies and LLPs.** In theory, a floating charge could be used by a sole trader or other partnership but, because of legislation relating to bills of sale, such a charge is not viable except in the case where the borrower is a company.

A floating charge gives the lender an interest in the personal property, e.g. stock in trade, of the borrower, and yet those goods are left in the borrower's possession. This may make him appear more creditworthy to another trader who sees the borrower's assets but does not realise that these are already charged to secure a loan.

If such a charge is to be valid there must be the registration of a bill of sale listing the items charged, e.g. the stock, in the Bills of Sale Registry. The floating charge does not lend itself to the listing of the property charged in this way because its essential feature is that the assets charged are always changing. If the borrower sold a tin of beans from his stock, he would have to amend the bill of sale; if he bought four dozen jars of jam, it would also have to be amended. The Bills of Sale Acts 1878 and 1882 do not apply to charges given by companies and LLPs and so they do not have to follow this particular registration procedure. However, as we shall see in Chapter 6 ○, the registration procedures of the Companies Act 2006 must be carried out by *both* organisations.

Guarantees

Generally

If a bank lends money to a business it will normally want, in addition to a charge over the assets, a guarantee from the sole trader or partner, or the directors of the company. These persons promise to meet the business debt from their personal resources if the business cannot.

Partners' and directors' bank guarantees are usually joint and several. This means that any partner or director is obliged to pay the whole debt and may then sue his co-partners or co-directors for a contribution. The nature of this liability is explained in Chapter 5 ○ and the formalities necessary for a guarantee in Chapter 7 ○ .

Guarantees can be open, that is to cover whatever figure a loan or overdraft may reach, or be limited to a fixed amount.

Independent advice

A special problem has arisen in business law in relation to the giving of guarantees and other securities, e.g. charges over land, by third parties to support the business borrowing of another. The major examples relate to the giving of guarantees and other securities by a spouse or elderly parent to a bank to support the business borrowing of the other spouse or a son or daughter.

After much case law, often of an involved and less than definitive nature, those in business have now mainly to know the ruling of the House of Lords in *Royal Bank of Scotland* v *Etridge (No 2)* (2001). This ruling of the House of Lords simplifies at least for business lenders, such as banks, the law in relation to undue influence which is the contractual concept at the root of the lender's problems in these situations. The changes made by *Etridge* place significant burdens upon solicitors advising those entering into a security arrangement for the borrowing of another. These obligations are not of any real concern to the businessperson since if the lawyer does not give the kind of independent advice required of him or her by *Etridge*, it is the lawyer who will be sued in negligence and/or breach of contract. The security will be enforceable and this is really the only concern of the lender.

Little needs to be said about the facts of *Etridge* except that a wife in that case had charged her joint interest in the family home in favour of the bank as security for

Signed and delivered as a deed by the said Joseph Jones in my presence after the contents of this guarantee had been fully explained by me to him.

Signed

John Adams

Solicitor

Figure 4.2 An appropriate form of words for a guarantee

the debts of her husband and his business. She later wished to avoid the contract of charge and issues of undue influence and lack of proper advice were raised. The House of Lords dismissed Mrs Etridge's case finding on the facts that she had not established grounds to avoid the security. However, the House of Lords went on to lay down definitive guidelines for lenders and legal advisers. *So far as business lenders are concerned the position is as follows*:

- A transaction under which a wife guarantees her husband's debts does not call for an explanation of itself but it is clear that the lender is put on notice that undue influence is a possibility whenever a wife (or husband) offers to guarantee the other spouse's debts and or those of his or her company. This applies whether the couple are married, or, being homosexual, have registered a civil partnership under the Civil Partnership Act 2004, or are just living together in a heterosexual or homosexual relationship.

- However, the lender need go no further than taking reasonable steps to satisfy itself that the wife or other third party has brought home to her or him in a meaningful way the practical implications of the proposed transaction, e.g. that in the case of a joint interest in the family home that the home will be sold if the debt is not repaid and the joint interest will be lost.

- To achieve the above, the lender will ensure that the wife has independent legal advice and will provide that adviser with all the financial information needed to give appropriate advice. The wife should be contacted directly and the lender should ensure that it has the husband's authority to give the necessary information. If not, the transaction should not proceed.

- From then on, if the transaction does proceed and all permissions are given, the business lender can assume that the legal adviser has carried out his or her function as laid down in the *Etridge* case. The lender will have an enforceable transaction against the wife.
- Where the legal adviser has failed in his or her duties in terms of giving proper advice, the wife may make a claim against the adviser.

The problem, therefore, has been resolved by the *Etridge* case at the expense of the legal adviser, if that adviser does not understand or do what *Etridge* expects of him or her. The cost of advice in this type of transaction has, for obvious reasons, risen.

Mortgages

Generally

A mortgage is a type of loan. It is special because the borrower (called the mortgagor) has not just promised to repay the loan to the lender (called the mortgagee) but has given him also a charge on his (the borrower's) property. If the borrower fails, for example, to repay the loan, the lender can sell the property and pay himself from the sale price. Alternatively, if the lender thinks he can get his money back from the rents, if any, which the property is producing he can ask the court for the appointment of a receiver who will collect the rents until the loan is paid off.

A person when buying a house often gets a loan in the form of a mortgage from a bank or building society and charges the house as security.

Legal mortgages of land

If Alan Brown wishes to borrow money from the Barchester Bank by giving the bank a legal mortgage of his (Alan's) private house, he will normally create a charge by way of legal mortgage over the house. This is done by means of a short deed stating that a charge on the land is created.

An example of a suitable deed for Alan Brown to sign is given in the Law of Property Act 1925. The deed may be expanded to include other matters which the borrower agrees to do, e.g. to insure the property charged, but the basic provisions are set out below (Figure 4.3). Alan Brown will then sign the deed and his signature will be witnessed.

The mortgage deed usually provides that the money is to be repaid six months after the date of the deed. However, the borrower is not expected to repay the loan by this date. It is only put in so that the lender has all his remedies from that date since he can regard himself as being owed the principal sum. There is no particular reason to have six months as the repayment date and in fact it is not uncommon for mortgage deeds to be drafted to provide that the mortgage money is due immediately on the signing of the deed.

The contract of loan (or in some cases the mortgage itself) will state the time within which the loan must be

THIS LEGAL CHARGE, is made the first day of June 2004 between Alan Brown of 14 River Street, Barchester of the one part and the Barchester Bank of the other part.

WHEREAS Alan Brown is seised of the hereditaments hereby charged and described in the Schedule hereto for an estate in fee simple in possession free from encumbrances;

NOW IN CONSIDERATION, of the sum of £100 000 now paid by Barchester Bank to Alan Brown (the receipt whereof Alan Brown doth hereby acknowledge) this Deed witnesseth as follows;

1. Alan Brown hereby covenants with Barchester Bank to pay on the first day of December next the sum of £100 000 with interest thereon at the rate of 10 per cent per annum.

2. Alan Brown as beneficial owner hereby charges by way of legal mortgage All and Singular the property mentioned in the Schedule hereto with the payment to Barchester Bank of the principal money and interest hereby covenanted to be paid by Alan Brown.

Figure 4.3 A mortgage deed

repaid, but if the borrower is in breach of that arrangement the charge is fully effective for use by the lender after six months.

This form of charge could also be used by Alan Brown to give as security any leases which he had, as where he was only renting business premises under a 25-year lease and wished to give a legal mortgage of that lease.

Equitable mortgages of land

An equitable mortgage can arise where the lender and borrower do not follow the procedures set out in the section above. Where a customer wanted an overdraft from his bank, he could formerly just leave the title deeds of his house with the bank. This created an equitable mortgage. However, the law relating to equitable mortgages and charges has been changed by *United Bank of Kuwait plc* v *Sahib and others* (1995). The bank had obtained a charging order against the debtor's interest in his jointly owned home in Hampstead, London. Before the charging order was made an organisation called SoGenAl had made a loan to the debtor who orally agreed to hold his title deeds in the property to the order of SoGenAl. The court was asked whether there was an equitable charge or mortgage in favour of SoGenAl which took priority over the interest of the bank. The answer was no because the old rule that a mere deposit or oral agreement about title deeds created for the purpose of securing a debt operated, without more, as an equitable mortgage or charge had not survived s 2 of the Law of Property (Miscellaneous Provisions) Act 1989. This section requires that 'A contract for the sale *or other disposition* of an interest in land can only be made in writing and only by incorporating all the terms which the parties have expressly agreed in one document, or where contracts are exchanged in each' (emphasis is added). Therefore, such a written document must accompany the deposit of title deeds (see further, Chapter 7 ⊙).

The position of the lender is not so strong where the mortgage is equitable. The lender cannot sell the property but must first apply to the court for an order for sale or if he thinks he can get his money back from the rents, if any, which the property is producing, he can ask the court for an order appointing a receiver.

It is worth noting briefly at this point that when considering the words 'writing', 'signature' and 'deed' the passing of the Electronic Communications Act 2000 should be borne in mind. Section 7, which is already in force, allows electronic signatures to be adduced and acceptable as evidence of a signature. However, delegated legislation is required to make changes in legislation such as the Law of Property (Miscellaneous Provisions) Act 1989 to eliminate 'paper' requirements. The writing and signature requirements of the Act will come to cover electronic methods.

The borrower's right of redemption

Lawyers call this the 'equity of redemption' and, as we have seen, the mortgage deed provides when the money is to be repaid. It is usual to say 'after six months' in order that the lender's range of remedies is available after that period. Originally, at common law, the land used as a security became the property of the lender as soon as the date for repayment had passed unless the loan had been repaid by then, even if only a small amount was still owed. However, equity allowed and still allows the borrower the right to redeem the land and free it from its position as a security even though the contractual date for repayment has passed and even though it has not yet arrived.

If a person wants to repay a mortgage early, he will normally have to give notice, say, of six months, that he intends to do this or be prepared to pay interest for, say, six months ahead after he has repaid the loan, so that the lender can find another investment.

Thus, if A repays his loan on 30 June (ahead of time), he will probably, according to the agreement, have given notice not later than 31 December in the previous year. If not, he will, according to the agreement, pay off the capital plus the interest due to date on 30 June but also interest until 31 December next.

A mortgage is also subject to the rule of restraint of trade (see Chapter 7 ⊙). It may also sometimes happen that a mortgage may prevent repayment for a reasonable time as regards the rule as to equity of redemption and yet redemption may be allowed before that time because while the mortgage term lasts unreasonable restrictions are placed on the freedom of a person to pursue his trade or profession.

Thus, in *Esso Petroleum Co Ltd* v *Harper's Garage (Stourport) Ltd* (1967) (see also Chapter 7 ⊙) an agreement not to repay a mortgage on a garage for 21 years was probably not an unreasonable time in terms of the equity of redemption rule. However, during that time the garage owner had to sell only Esso fuels. It was decided that the restraint on fuel sales was unreasonable and that the mortgage could be repaid earlier, leaving the owner of the garage free to sell other fuels.

A further right of the borrower on repayment of the loan is that on redemption the property must be returned to him free of any conditions which applied while the loan was unpaid and the mortgage was in existence. Restrictions applicable before redemption are more likely to be upheld by the court than those which are stated to survive redemption.

Noakes and Co Ltd v *Rice* (1902)

Mr Rice wanted to buy a public house. He borrowed the money from Noakes and Co Ltd who were brewers and owners of the pub. The brewers lent Mr Rice the money but he had to agree to sell only Noakes' beer. After Mr Rice had repaid his mortgage, Noakes said he must still sell only their beer. The court decided that he was not bound to do so. During the mortgage Mr Rice was bound to sell only Noakes' beer but not after repayment of the loan.

Comment. Much depends upon the bargaining power of the parties. In mortgage arrangements between large companies what is called a collateral advantage may be allowed to continue after repayment of the loan. For example, in *Kreglinger* v *New Patagonia Meat and Cold Storage Co Ltd* (1914) Kreglinger had lent money to New Patagonia and New Patagonia gave Kreglinger a mortgage of its property. The mortgage said that for five years New Patagonia should not sell sheepskins to anyone without offering them first to Kreglinger. New Patagonia repaid the loan after two years but the House of Lords decided that New Patagonia was still bound to offer the sheepskins first to Kreglinger.

The possibility of using the rules of restraint of trade to attack restraints during the period of the mortgage is considered above (see *Esso Petroleum Co Ltd* v *Harper's Garage (Stourport) Ltd* (1967)).

Consumer Credit Act

By reason of sections inserted into the Consumer Credit Act 1974 by the Consumer Credit Act 2006, the court may make an order to regulate agreements arising out of a relationship that is 'unfair' as between the creditor and the debtor. The court has wide-ranging powers, e.g. to reduce or discharge any sum payable by the debtor. However, the unfair relationship test does not apply to credit agreements entered into by incorporated associations or partnerships of more than four members. It does apply to agreements made by individuals and so would apply to a sole trader (see further, Chapter 13 ⊙).

Mortgages of personal property

Just as land can be used as a means of securing debts, so also can personal goods. The main way in which this can be done is by mortgage.

In this case the person who borrows the money retains the business assets, e.g. office equipment, but transfers the ownership of them to the lender to secure the loan.

As we have seen, this raises a problem because, since the borrower keeps the assets, those who do business with him, perhaps on credit, may be misled as to his creditworthiness, because the assets displayed are owned by a lender and not by the borrower who has them.

To stop this happening the security is void and the lender cannot sell the goods mortgaged unless a bill of sale is made out and registered in the Central Office of the Supreme Court under the Bills of Sale Acts 1878–82. These bills must be re-registered every five years if they are still in operation. This Register is open to public examination and therefore those who do business with the borrower can find out whether he has mortgaged his goods.

Mortgages of choses in action

As we have seen, personal property (i.e. property other than land) is divided into two kinds known as choses in possession and choses in action. Choses in possession are goods such as jewellery and furniture which are tangible things and **can be physically used and enjoyed** by their owner. Choses in action are intangible forms of property which are **not really capable of physical use or enjoyment**. Their owner is normally compelled to bring an action at law if he wishes to enforce his rights over property of this sort. A contrast is provided by a fire extinguisher and a fire insurance policy. The extinguisher is a **chose in possession**. If you had a fire, **you could use the extinguisher** to put it out – the insurance policy would not be much use for this. However, it is a valuable piece of property because although, **as a chose in action, it has no physical use** it gives a right to require the insurance company to make good any loss caused by the fire. Other examples of choses in action are debts, patents, copyrights, trademarks, shares, negotiable instruments such as bearer bonds issued by some companies to those who lend them money, and the goodwill of a business.

It is possible to use a chose in action as security for a loan and lenders frequently take life assurance policies as security. A bank would do this in the case of an overdraft. However, shares in companies are perhaps the commonest chose in action to be used as security.

Shares can be made subject to a legal mortgage but the shares must actually be transferred to the lender and his name is in fact entered on the company's share register. An agreement is made out in which the lender agrees to retransfer the shares to the borrower when the loan is repaid.

You can also have an equitable mortgage of company shares and this is in fact often the method used. The share certificate is deposited with the lender, together with a blank transfer. This means that it is signed by the registered holder, i.e. the borrower, but the name of the person to whom the shares are to be transferred is left blank. The shares are not actually transferred, but the agreement which accompanies the loan allows the lender to sell the shares by completing the form of transfer and registering himself or someone else as the legal owner if the borrower fails to repay the loan. The shares can then be sold and transferred as required.

Publicity and external control of the undertaking

Sole traders and ordinary partnerships

Little, if any, publicity attaches by law to the affairs of these organisations. Their paperwork and administration is a matter for them to decide, subject, in a partnership, to anything that the partnership agreement may say about this. These organisations can keep their accounts on scraps of paper in a shoebox if they wish to, though obviously they should keep proper accounts. However, subject to satisfying the Revenue as to the genuineness of their accounts, usually through an independent

accountant, there are no legal formalities and no filing of documents or accounts for the public to see.

Limited liability partnerships

Section 15 of the Limited Liability Partnerships Act 2000 gives the Secretary of State power to make regulations that apply any law relating to companies to LLPs. These regulations, i.e. the Limited Liability Partnerships Regulations 2001 (SI 2001/1090), impose a disclosure and filing requirement in terms of accounts and reports similar to that of registered companies (see below). Thus, as is usual, the acquisition of limited liability will involve public disclosure of profits and the distribution among the partners.

Companies

A considerable amount of publicity attaches to companies – even small private ones.

Unless the members of the company have unlimited liability – which is a possible form of corporate organisation – the company must file its accounts annually together with the reports of its directors and auditors. These items are kept by the Registrar and are available for inspection by the public on request from Companies House.

In the past all companies whether public or private were required to appoint auditors, which was an expense forced on them but not upon sole traders and partnerships. However, there are now audit exemptions as described below.

For financial years starting on or after 6 April 2008, audit exemption is available provided the company is a *small* company with a turnover of not more than £6.5 million and a balance sheet total of not more than £3.26 million (i.e. asset value), and employees do not exceed 50 (see below). However, any member or members holding not less than one-tenth of the issued share capital can require the company to obtain an audit for its accounts for that year. A company is not entitled to the exemption if at any time during its financial year it was:

1 a public company;
2 a member of a group of companies if any of its members is a public company;
3 a banking or insurance company, or an organisation authorised to conduct investment business under the Financial Services and Market Act 2000.

In order to qualify for the exemption, the company must be an eligible company and the balance sheet must include a statement by the directors that:

1 in the year in question the company was entitled to the exemption;
2 no member or members have deposited with the company a notice requesting an audit;
3 the directors acknowledge their responsibility to ensure that the company keeps accounting records complying with s 392 of the Companies Act 2006 and for preparing accounts which give a true and fair view of the affairs of the company as at the end of the accounting reference period and of its profit and loss as required by s 399 of that Act and which in other respects comply with the Companies Act 2006 in relation to the accounts.

The Companies Act 2006 allows small companies to avoid certain publicity in regard to the accounts. A small company is one which has satisfied two of the following conditions for the current financial year and the one before:

1 **Turnover**, i.e. gross income before deducting the expenses of running the business, not exceeding £6.5 million.
2 **Balance sheet total**, which is in effect the total assets, not exceeding £3.26 million.
3 **Employees**, not exceeding 50 as a weekly or monthly average throughout the year.

A small company is allowed to file just an abbreviated version of its balance sheet with the Registrar instead of a copy of the full accounts required by the Companies Act 2006. The members of the company, however, are entitled to a copy of fuller accounts. In particular, the *abbreviated* accounts do not have to show details of the salaries of directors, nor is it necessary to file a directors' report or a profit and loss account.

As regards the fuller accounts to which members are entitled, these need not be full Companies Act 2006 accounts. The Companies Act 2006 provides that a small company will comply with the law if it provides what are called *shorter form financial statements* to the members. A number of items may be left out of the shorter form statements, e.g. details of any debentures issued in the course of the year.

The Companies Act 2006 also allows medium companies to avoid certain publicity in regard to the accounts but to a lesser degree. A medium company is one which has been within the limits of *two* of the following thresholds for the current year and the one before:

1 **Turnover**: not exceeding £25.9 million.
2 **Balance sheet total**: not exceeding £15.9 million.
3 **Employees**: not exceeding 250 as a weekly or monthly average throughout the year.

Shareholders are entitled to *full* Companies Act 2006 accounts. The modifications in regard to the filed accounts are:

1 the profit and loss account may commence with 'gross profit or loss' which combines 'turnover', 'cost of sales information' and 'other operating income' which would otherwise require separate disclosure;
2 there is no need to give, in the notes to the accounts, the analyses of turnover and profit according to the branches of the company's business in which they were made.

The directors' report and balance sheet are required in full. The reason for the modification is that details of turnover and profit were used, sometimes to the unreasonable disadvantage of medium companies, by competitors who could identify the most profitable and the most unprofitable areas of the medium company's business.

The directors must state in the accounts that the company satisfies the conditions for a small or medium company and this must be supported by a report by the auditors giving an opinion confirming this. The auditors' report on the full accounts must accompany the modified accounts, even though the full accounts are not sent to the Registrar. The references to reports of auditors do not apply where the company is exempt from the obligation to appoint auditors.

All companies must file with the Registrar of Companies an annual return showing, for example, who the company's directors and its secretary are and the interests of the directors as directors in other companies. The return also shows the changes in the company's membership over the year and a full list of members must be given every three years. However, the Companies Registration Office, i.e. Companies House, has a system under which it produces a document for the annual return listing all the relevant information which it has on the company. The company secretary merely confirms that it is correct or amends it as required. The 'shuttle system', as it is called, is designed to save a significant amount of form filling by company administrators. The form of the shuttle document appears at the end of Chapter 6 ⬡ but it is worth noting here that for companies with 20 or fewer members Companies House will give a list of members from previous records it holds so that the company will have only to correct the list if necessary. This will mean, in effect, that these companies, i.e. 98 per cent of the Register of Companies, will be able to submit a full list of members annually.

In addition, formal company meetings, called annual general meetings, must be held by a company at specified intervals so that shareholders are kept informed of corporate activities. However, private companies may opt out of this requirement by what is called an elective resolution (see further, Chapter 6 ⬡).

In conclusion, therefore, those who run companies and limited liability partnerships will have to spend some time in ensuring that the business is carried on in such a way as to comply with relevant legislation. The sole trader and ordinary partner have a much less complicated legal environment which can be to their advantage. However, the administrative burden on companies, particularly small companies, may be significantly reduced if deregulation proceeds.

In this connection, under regulations made under the Limited Liability Partnerships Act 2000 small LLPs will automatically qualify for audit exemption in the same way as companies limited by shares.

Small and medium-sized companies and international standards

The directors of companies have the option of preparing Companies Act accounts following the Companies Act 2006 and UK accounting standards or the Companies Act 2006 and international accounting standards (IAS). The only exception is charitable companies, which must follow UK standards.

This option applies also to small and medium-sized companies. However, it should be noted, if IAS accounts are produced, that the accounts exemptions available to small companies to prepare shorter form accounts and the option for both small and medium-sized companies to file abbreviated accounts apply only where UK standards are followed.

Taxation and national insurance

Once a business is running the question of taxation and national insurance (NIC) arises. The subject is one of extreme complexity and so only an outline of the system can be given.

Income tax – the system of Schedules

In the UK different types of income are taxed under what are known as Schedules. This dates back to the days when different departments of the HM Revenue & Customs dealt with the different kinds of income which a wealthy person might have. Its purpose was to achieve secrecy as to total income. These days one inspector of taxes deals with all parts of a taxpayer's income and the word 'Schedule' no longer has any significance. It simply means a 'type' of tax.

Income tax – generally

Income tax is the main tax which is paid by people who have earnings either from an occupation or from investment income. Employees pay income tax under Schedule E. They pay weekly or monthly by deduction from pay. The self-employed pay income tax under Schedule D and are responsible for making the relevant payment to the Collector of Taxes. For this reason the self-employed should keep full and accurate records of all transactions of the business.

Taxation and the self-employed sole trader

Sole traders should ideally draw up annual accounts, though it is not necessary to do so. The trader's annual tax return (see below) provides space for a return of business income and expenses in a standard format which may in some cases be regarded as enough and do away with the need for annual accounts. However, if accounts are drawn up, the question of what accounting date to use will arise. In other words, what is to be the year end for the relevant financial statements? Accounts can be made up to the end of the first year's trading or to the end of the calendar year, i.e. 31 December, or to the end of the tax year on 5 April. Where calendar year or tax year is chosen, the accounts may represent income for less than 12 months but the following year and subsequent years will cover a full 12 months' trading.

The method of taxation

Assessments of income tax are made for tax years which run from 6 April in each year. Thus, the tax year 2009/2010 runs from 6 April 2009 to 5 April 2010. In broad terms the assessment will be based on the profits of the business for the accounting year which ends in the same tax year. The tax will be paid according to the profits for that basis period. An accounting period is the period the accounts cover and the accounting date is the last day of the accounts. For example, if the accounting period for the 2009/2010 tax year is the 12-month period 1 January 2009 to 31 December 2009, the accounting date is 31 December 2009.

Payment of tax – method of assessment

This is based upon a tax return, which will be received by the sole trader in April of each year. The return requires the trader to give all the information required to calculate income tax and capital gains tax (see below) due for the year. Under the system of self-assessment, the trader can calculate what is due and there are explanatory notes on the return to assist in this. However, the trader may supply the relevant figures and ask Her Majesty's Revenue & Customs (HMRC) to calculate the tax bill or, alternatively, if the trader has an accountant, the accountant may do it. The method is entirely a matter for the trader. The tax return also explains how to calculate any national insurance contributions (see below) that may be due. These are paid to the Collector at the same time as the income tax.

The trader will then be required to make the two payments towards the tax bill: one on 31 January and the other on 31 July (but see below).

If the business makes a loss, this may be set against any other taxable income or may be carried forward to offset profits in subsequent years.

Payment of tax – timing

In an attempt to bring the self-employed more into line with the PAYE system for employed persons, HMRC has devised a system of payment that involves estimating the income of the self-employed. An illustration follows:

Example

John is a freelance journalist. His payment position is:

Tax year 2009/10: The year ends on 5 April 2010 and John's tax liability from earnings and, e.g., interest and income from investments is calculated as £10,000. His tax bill for 2009/10 must be paid by 31 January 2011. However, this is not the end of the matter. John may also be required to pay the first of two 'payments on account' (advance payments) for the current tax year. *HMRC will require one-half of the tax John will owe for the tax year 2010/11 that ends on 5 April 2011.* This is estimated on John's earnings during the 2009/10 tax year, i.e. a liability of £10,000. If John has been asked to make payments on account, the deadline for making his second payment on account will be 31 July 2011 – this will be the second payment on account for the tax year of 2010/11.

If when the *actual figures for the tax year 2010/11* are available John's income has gone down, he can ask for the tax to be reduced.

Where accounts are prepared

An accountant should normally be employed to draw up the business accounts. Nevertheless, the trader is still responsible for the accuracy of the records on which they are based and therefore for the accuracy of the accounts and for correctly declaring the amount of profit.

Under the rules of self-assessment it is not necessary to send the accounts with the tax return. The relevant information can instead be included as indicated in the tax return. However, it should be borne in mind that HMRC can ask to see the accounts (if any) and the business records in order to check the figures given in the return. These powers will be used more often and include random checks because where the trader or his accountant computes the tax payable there must be a more rigorous check on records and computation.

Employing labour

If the trader employs someone for the first time, the local office of HMRC must be informed. The employee's office may not be the same as the trader's but the trader's local office will send the information to the correct office. The office will send the trader a New Employer's Starter Pack which includes the necessary instructions, tables and forms.

The trader will then be responsible for deducting income tax and Class 1 national insurance contributions from the employee's pay in accordance with the 'Pay As You Earn' system (PAYE). The tax and NIC which the trader has deducted must be sent to the HMRC accounts office. All employees have the right to receive an itemised pay statement from their employer *every time they are paid*. The statement must show all the deductions which have been made including income tax and national insurance contributions. If the employer fails to comply, the employee may take the matter to an employment tribunal which can award the employee compensation if deductions have been made without the employee's knowledge. If the employer deducts national insurance contributions from earnings and fails to pay them over to HMRC, the employee is treated as though they had been paid over unless the employee is negligent or has consented to connive in the non-payment. The trader must also tell the tax office, at the end of each tax year, how much each employee has earned and the amount of deductions for tax and NIC together with any benefits paid, e.g. car allowance. The employees must also be given a statement showing their earnings for the year, the tax and NIC deductions paid, and any benefits provided.

National insurance

Most people who are in work pay national insurance contributions. The class of contribution paid depends upon whether the person concerned is employed or self-employed.

Class 1 contributions are paid by employed earners (primary contributors) and their employers (secondary contributors). The figures are for the year 2010/11 and change annually. They are therefore an illustration only:

The 2010/11 Class 1 national insurance rates are:

- if the earning is more than £110 a week and up to £844 a week, the rate is 11 per cent of the earned amount (between £110 and £844);
- if the earning is more than £844 a week, there is an extra 1 per cent of all the earnings over £844.

Those who are self-employed pay two kinds of NIC: Class 2 which all self-employed people pay and Class 4 which becomes payable if profits are above a certain limit.

Class 2 contributions must be paid by self-employed earners unless they have a certificate of exemption on the ground that their income is below a certain level,

e.g. £5,075 pa in 2010/11. Expenses are deducted when calculating earnings. Class 2 contributions are payable at a flat rate; this is £2.40 a week for 2010/11. Class 2 contributions can be paid by a bank direct debit or under other billing arrangements provided by HMRC national insurance contributions office, the old Contributions Agency having been merged with HMRC.

Class 2 contributions do not count for the payment of unemployment benefit, but they do count for incapacity benefit, basic retirement pension, widow's benefit and maternity allowance. Application can be made for repayment of Class 2 contributions if the earnings in the relevant year are low enough to entitle the earner to exemption.

Class 4 contributions are paid by self-employed earners. They are levied as a percentage of profits, i.e. for 2010/11 it is payable on earnings between £5,715 and £43,875 at the rate of 8 per cent. For profits above the band, i.e. profits in excess of £43,875, the rate is currently 1 per cent.

The profits are those chargeable to income tax under Schedule D, and Class 4 contributions are usually collected by HMRC with the income tax. Class 4 contributions do not give the trader any additional benefits.

Schedule D – advantages

A major advantage with Schedule D is the trader's ability to deduct expenses which would not be allowable to employed persons. For example, the trader may use a room in his home as a study from which to write and a partner may use another room as an office from which to help with the work. If so, a proportion of the heating and lighting and other costs of the home may be allowable against tax, whereas they would not be allowable to an employee who brought work home to complete in a study. There are also capital allowances available to the trader in regard, for example, to plant and machinery, such as a new computer which has been purchased during the year.

Partnerships

The trading and professional income of a partnership is charged to tax under Schedule D which applies the current year basis of assessment to this income as in the case of sole traders.

To a large extent a partnership is treated as a separate entity for tax purposes in that assessments are made jointly on the partnership. The profits assessed for the tax year in question are allocated among the partners according to the partnership agreement, e.g. in the profit-sharing ratio. The tax assessment for each partner is then calculated separately taking into account personal circumstances, e.g. whether they are married or single and whether they are entitled to mortgage relief and so on. The individual assessments are then aggregated and the total bill is a liability of the firm. Because partners are 'jointly and severally' liable for the debts of the firm (see further, Chapter 5 ⊙) any of the partners could be liable for the whole bill if the other partners were insolvent.

As to settling the bill, there are two main ways as follows:

- each partner pays his share of the liability into the partnership account and the partnership pays the bill; or
- the partnership pays the full amount and the current accounts of the individual partners are charged with each one's share.

Capital allowances are allowed as deductions from the profits of the firm for expenditure on, for example, plant and machinery and motor vehicles.

Salaried partners will normally be regarded as employees and pay income tax under Schedule E by the PAYE system.

The profits of a limited liability partnership will be taxed as if the business was carried on by individuals in an ordinary partnership and not as if the business was carried on by a company.

Companies

Companies pay what is called corporation tax. The tax is also levied on unincorporated associations but not partnerships. It is thus payable by companies which are limited or unlimited and extends to many clubs. The tax is payable on profits of a UK resident company whether these profits arise in the UK or abroad. The tax is therefore 'residence' based. Relief is given in respect of any foreign tax paid on profits earned abroad. The tax is charged on the profits of the company and this includes income from all sources including capital gains. The basis of assessment is the accounting period of the company. Rates of tax are settled for each financial year, i.e. the 12 months ended 31 March. If a company's accounting period straddles two 31 March periods, profits are apportioned and the tax is charged on each part of the year at the rate applicable to that part.

Capital allowances are deducted as part of adjustment of total business profits but appropriations of profit such as dividends and transfers to reserves are not allowable as deductions. Directors' emoluments are allowed so long as they appear reasonable.

Large companies pay their corporation tax by quarterly instalments. Broadly these are companies with profits of over £1.5 million. For other companies the whole of the tax is due on the date following the expiry of nine months from the end of the company's accounting period (or year end).

Traders who consider changing from a sole trader or partnership regime usually do so for tax purposes, but all the implications should be considered. Corporate status involves giving more publicity to the affairs of the business in terms of the need to file documents, such as the annual return with the Registrar of Companies, and to prepare statutory accounts under the Companies Act 2006. These must be filed, at least in an abbreviated version. A small company will not require an audit, as we have seen, but, since an accountant will normally prepare the business accounts, the trader will find that the charge will increase for statutory accounts.

The tax advantages depend on circumstances. Those who commonly draw all the profits from the business will find that the company faces higher national insurance since a charge of 12.8 per cent is levied on benefits paid to directors but not on sole traders' or partners' drawings. Dividends escape national insurance. However, dividend income like savings income is always treated as the highest part of income when deciding what tax rates apply to it. If it is intended to leave profits in the business, there may be an advantage. The main corporation tax rate is 28 per cent but there is a Small Profits Rate of 21 per cent that can be claimed by qualifying companies with profits at a rate not exceeding £300,000. This compares with the highest income tax of 40 per cent (or 50 per cent on the portion of income that is over £150,000). In addition, the transfer of assets from a sole trader's or partnership business can result in an assessment for capital gains tax, though it is possible to follow methods that allow some deferment of payment of this tax. These matters are beyond the scope of this book and are not considered further.

Capital gains tax

So far as 'business' is concerned, the taxation implications of this tax are likely to arise in a situation outside the scope of this book, i.e. business transfers. If we assume that a sole trader or a partnership is to transfer the business and its assets to a limited company with the sole trader or partners becoming the major shareholders in the new company, then in so far as certain of the assets may have been purchased some years ago, e.g. land and buildings, and are now valued at a higher price than when purchased, a charge to capital gains tax may arise on the transfer. There are somewhat complicated provisions called tapering under which account is taken of the fact that some of the gain may be merely inflation and this element is deducted from the gain.

Planning

One of the features of the operation of a business, no matter which vehicle is chosen, may be the need to obtain at some stage planning permission in connection with a business development.

Following the consolidation of the Planning Acts in 1990, the statute law governing town and country planning is now contained in the Town and Country Planning Act 1990 and the Planning and Compensation Act 1991. Further changes have been made by the Planning and Compulsory Purchase Act 2004.

In Wales the planning functions of the Secretary of State are assumed by the Welsh Assembly.

To obtain planning permission it is necessary to apply to the relevant local planning authority. Permission should be granted unless there are clear-cut reasons for refusal. The authority has in general to decide applications in accordance with the development plan for the area. Matters such as road safety and congestion, and adequacy of water supply and sewage disposal, are also relevant. It should also be borne in mind that most building work is subject to building regulations regarding health and safety, energy conservation and arrangements for the disabled.

A check should be made with the relevant authority to see whether planning permission is required. Internal alterations do not generally require it unless they in some way affect the exterior. Repair and maintenance of existing buildings does not normally require permission but you will need it if you are putting up a new building. Extensions to premises may require planning permission depending on the size of the extension intended. Permission is not normally required if the premises were previously used for broadly the same purpose, e.g. a shop, but it is if they are to be used for a different purpose.

The time taken

From the time of application, it can take anything from about four weeks to three months or more for a decision to be made, depending on the size and complexity of the scheme.

Outline planning permission

It is possible to make an application for outline planning permission to see whether permission will be given in principle. This has the advantage that detailed drawings are not required though as much information as possible should be given. This can then be followed with an application for full planning permission. There is a fee involved and the relevant authority will give the necessary information.

Statements of development principles

Under the Planning and Compulsory Purchase Act 2004 outline planning permission is supplemented and will eventually be replaced by statements of development principles (SDPs). Councils will be required to indicate whether they agree or disagree with the principles of the proposed development. The SDPs will not amount to consent. However, these SDPs may become outline planning permission in all but name, though at present it is difficult to see how an SDP will operate and what reliance a developer may place upon it.

Appeals

If the relevant authority refuses planning permission, an appeal can be made to the Secretary of State for the Environment. An appeal may also be made on the ground that the authority has imposed conditions which the applicant cannot or does not wish to accept. Failure to reach a decision within a time limit of eight weeks or such longer period agreed with the authority is also a ground for appeal. Appeals can be made at any time within six months of the authority's decision or six months from the date when it ought to have been made. There is no charge for the appeal itself, but there are bound to be some legal and other expenses. Most appeals are dealt with within 20 weeks.

How long does permission last?

Both outline and detailed planning permission will normally include a condition that the development must be begun within three years. How soon it is completed is a matter for the developer.

It is also worth remembering that planning permission runs with the land and is not personal to the owner or occupier. This means that land or buildings can usually be sold or let with the benefit of planning permission, which should encourage and assist a sale or letting and the price or rental.

Going ahead without permission

If the authority thinks the development is unacceptable, it may make an enforcement notice to put matters right. This may even involve the demolition of any building work carried out. It is possible to appeal against an enforcement notice to the Secretary of State, but if the appeal is dismissed and the enforcement notice becomes effective, it is an offence not to comply with it and could lead to a prosecution in a magistrates' court.

Planning and environmental considerations

In addition to problems of business development in terms of planning, a business may also fall foul of laws relating to the environment and the two may clash. In some cases the applicant must submit an Environmental Impact Assessment setting out likely environmental effects of the development together with proposals for remedying these effects. In addition, the business may ask the High Court for judicial review of the offending restriction as in *R v Kennet District Council, ex parte Somerfield Stores* (1999) where in terms of noise being emitted from refrigeration equipment the council planning authority placed a restriction of a lower number of decibels on the planning permission than the environment authorities had in an abatement order served under the Environmental Protection Act 1990. The High Court ruled in favour of the planning authority.

Crimes relevant to business

Of the considerable number of criminal offences, students of business law may find it useful to have knowledge of the following areas:

Theft

The Theft Act 1968 applies and s 1(1) of that Act provides: 'A person is guilty of theft if he dishonestly appropriates property belonging to another with the intention of permanently depriving the other of it.'

Actus reus

The prohibited act in theft is an act of appropriation of property in a situation where that property belongs to another. Appropriation occurs when a person other than the owner assumes the rights of that owner over the property (s 3(1)). The most usual form of assumption of rights is when the property is taken away but destruction of property is also included since this is in infringement of the owner's rights. In addition, a later assumption of rights, as where property is kept after it should have been returned, can also amount to theft. Some sort of conduct is required so that a mere intention to own is not enough.

Partial assumption of rights

It is not necessary to assume all of the rights of the owner; it is enough if one or more of those rights is assumed, as the following cases show.

R v Morris (1984)

Morris took some items from the shelves of a supermarket and replaced the correct labels with others showing a lower price. He went through the checkout paying the lower price.

Anderton v Burnside (1983)

The defendant took a label off a joint of meat and put it on a more expensive piece of meat. This was discovered before he reached the checkout.

Comment. In both cases the House of Lords held that theft had been committed. The defendants had assumed rights in the owner's labels and this was adverse interference. Furthermore, since the offence was committed when the appropriation took place, it was irrelevant that Burnside had not left the store. There is no appropriation after a contract of sale has been made because the property in the goods will normally have passed to the buyer and the goods will not 'belong to another'.

A person who buys property in good faith only to find out later that they were stolen is not guilty of theft if he or she assumes rights in the property which he or she believed they had acquired under the transaction (s 3(2)).

Authorised appropriation

If the appropriation is authorised, then theft is not committed as the following case illustrates:

Eddy v Niman (1981)

The defendant went to a supermarket with every intention of stealing. Accordingly, he put some goods in a basket but then decided not to go ahead with the theft and left the store. It was held that he had not appropriated the goods for the purpose of theft because he was only doing what the supermarket had by implication authorised him to do, i.e. put goods in the basket prior to going to the checkout.

However, in this connection the decision of the House of Lords in *R v Hinks* (2000) should be noted. There the defendant persuaded a man of limited intelligence to withdraw and give to her the sum of £60,000 from his savings over a period of eight months. The House of Lords agreed that she could be successfully charged with theft. There was an appropriation although the transfer was in the nature of a gift. Thus, a gift can amount to an appropriation if the jury decides, as here, that the recipient acted dishonestly in accepting it.

A further development occurred in *R v Gomez* (1993) where the House of Lords decided that a person could be guilty of theft by dishonestly appropriating goods belonging to another if the owner of the goods was induced by fraud, deception or a false representation to consent to or authorise the taking of the goods.

R v Gomez (1993)

Gomez, in order to assist a friend to dispose of stolen cheques which were undated and bore no payee's name, persuaded his boss, the manager of an electrical goods shop, to accept them for a quantity of goods which the manager authorised for delivery to the friend. The friend and Gomez were charged with theft. Gomez appealed on the issue of appropriation, their Lordships finding him guilty because there had been an appropriation.

Comment. The House of Lords followed one of its earlier cases, *Lawrence v Metropolitan Police Commissioner* (1971), where a tourist gave his wallet full of unfamiliar English money to a taxi driver so that the latter could take his fare. The driver 'appropriated' much more than was due and his act was regarded as an appropriation for the purposes of theft, even though the wallet and its contents had been handed over freely.

The line of cases cited above shows the ability of the court to distinguish cases on the facts, which is particularly common in the criminal law where the liberty of the subject is at stake. The degree of dishonesty in *Eddy* is clearly much less than in the other two cases.

It is worth noting, however, that where the victim makes the transfer on the basis of some deception by the defendant, a safer charge is obtaining by deception rather than theft. For example, in *R v Briggs* (2003) the defendant arranged the sale of the house of her elderly uncle and aunt. The uncle and aunt authorised the solicitors to transfer £49,950 to another firm of solicitors to complete the purchase of another house for the uncle and aunt and to transfer the balance of the purchase price into the bank account of the uncle and aunt. However, the defendant arranged for the new property to be registered in the name of herself and her uncle and not her uncle and aunt. Had she stolen her share in the new property? No, said the Court of Appeal. She had not appropriated her share of the £49,950 because it had been transferred to purchase the property by the consent of the victims, though obviously they were under a misapprehension as to who was to take the title.

The Court of Appeal said that obtaining by deception could have been charged, but the prosecution had stuck to a charge of theft throughout and no substitution of deception for theft would be made. The conviction of theft was quashed.

Property

There must be a theft of property. Section 4 defines property as including real and personal property, money and intangible property, e.g. a credit balance in a bank account or a software program. In general terms, and in spite of the inclusion in the definition of real property, a person cannot steal land or anything forming part of land, i.e. fixtures rather than fittings (see further, Chapter 15 ◯). However, things which can be severed from the land can be stolen so that a farmer who without authorisation grazes his cattle on another's land steals the grass which has been severed from the land. Wild plants, flowers and mushrooms can only be stolen if for commercial gain. Thus, picking mushrooms to sell in a local market would be theft if the owner of the land had not given permission. Wild animals cannot be stolen unless kept in captivity.

Belonging to another

Although the definition of theft states that the property must belong to another, a person can steal his own property from someone with an interest in it short of ownership as the following case illustrates.

R v Turner (1971)

The defendant left his car at a garage for repair. After the repairs were completed he removed the car from where it was parked with the intention of not paying for the repairs. The court held he was guilty of theft. For the purposes of the 1968 Act, the car belonged to the repairer when it was taken since the garage had control of it.

Property received on behalf of another

Section 5(3) provides: 'Where a person receives property from or on account of another and is under an obligation to the other to retain and deal with that property or its proceeds in a particular way the property or proceeds shall be regarded (as against him) as belonging to the other.' Examples under s 5(3) most commonly involve receiving money from others to retain and use in a certain way, e.g. travel agents taking deposits for holidays, solicitors holding funds for mortgages or managers of pension funds collecting pension contributions. However, it is essential that a particular obligation be imposed and this obligation must have been known to the accused. The following cases provide contrasting examples.

Davidge v Bunnett (1984)

The defendant had been given money by her flatmates through the medium of cheques in order that the proceeds would be used to pay gas bills. She spent the proceeds on other things and was found guilty of theft. A specific obligation had been imposed on her as to the use of the money.

R v Hall (1972)

The defendant was a travel agent who had received money from clients and did not arrange trips and could not repay the money. He was not guilty of theft since the money was handed over as part of a contractual obligation and not specifically for use in a particular way.

Comment. The decision seems to be rather a technical one. Perhaps the court should have construed a constructive trust in the agent to use the money for holiday purposes. However, although the law often construes such a trust in order to allow recovery of property at civil law, it has never been prepared to do so for the purposes of criminal liability.

Receiving property under a mistake

Section 5(4) provides:

Where a person gets property by another's mistake and is under an obligation to make restoration (in whole or in part) of the property or its proceeds or of the value thereof then as to the extent of that obligation the property or proceeds shall be regarded (as against him) as belonging to the person entitled to restoration . . .

The provision applies only where the ownership of the property has passed to the defendant so that it will not apply in a contractual mistake as to identity where the contract is void and no ownership passes (see further, Chapter 7 ◯). An illustration is provided by the following case.

A-G's Reference (No 1 of 1983) (1985)

A woman police constable was paid a sum of £74.74 by crediting her bank account. It was said to be a payment for overtime which she had not, in fact, worked. She realised she had been overpaid but did nothing. The Court of Appeal decided that there had been an appropriation and that the necessary ingredients for theft were present.

The obligation to make restoration is a legal one so that where a betting shop paid out winnings against the wrong horse, there was no recovery of it by the bookmaker in civil law, and the recipient was not under an obligation to return it in terms of the Theft Act 1968 and had committed no offence by retaining it (see *R* v *Gilks* (1972) and Chapter 7 ☉).

Mens rea

The *mens rea* of theft has two branches:

- dishonesty; and
- an intention permanently to deprive another of his property.

Dishonesty

Section 2(1) sets out situations in which as a matter of law an individual is not dishonest. They are:

- where the defendant believes he has a legal right to deprive the owner of the property;
- where the defendant believes that the victim would have consented if the victim had known of the circumstances;
- where the defendant finds property when the owner cannot be found by taking reasonable steps.

Examples are to be found in *R* v *Wootton* (1990) where the defendant took some of his employer's pottery in lieu of wages due. Further, in *R* v *Flynn* (1970) a cinema manager took £6 as an advance on his wages in the belief that his employer would have consented. It should be noted that as regards finding, there may be an appropriation for the purposes of theft if the finder does not initially know who the owner is but later finds out and does nothing. In cases not falling within s 2(1) it is necessary to prove dishonesty. The test for deciding dishonesty was laid down in *R* v *Ghosh* (1982). The defendant was a surgeon who claimed fees from a hospital for operations he had not carried out. Although the case was concerned with obtaining money by deception, the Court of Appeal laid down a test for dishonesty which applies also to cases of theft. The test has two branches as follows:

- The jury is to apply the ordinary standards of reasonable and honest people, and, if the behaviour of the defendant was dishonest by those standards, he may be guilty. If not, he is not guilty.
- However, even if the defendant is dishonest by the above ordinary and decent standards, he will still not be guilty unless he realised that ordinary people would regard him as dishonest. The test is, therefore, subjective.

However, in the usual case of theft the judge may consider that there is no evidence to show that the defendant believed that he was not dishonest and where this is so the judge need not give a direction to the jury in terms of *Ghosh*. The test is a difficult one to explain to a jury and can lead to inconsistent decisions according to the make-up of the jury and the part of the country in which it sits. As an example, we may take a trial for theft of some committed anti-vivisectionists who have stolen animals from a laboratory. Apply the test and see what you think. What do your fellow students think? Fred regularly robs the rich to give to the poor. How do you find on Fred's trial for theft?

Intention permanently to deprive

This is the second branch of the *mens rea* of theft. Its main purpose is to prevent most unauthorised borrowings from being theft. An intention to return the property sooner or later is not an intention permanently to deprive. However, if there is an intention permanently to deprive at the time of taking, giving the property back will not change the fact of theft and the charge of theft will be made out (see *R* v *McHugh* (1993)). The concept is dealt with by s 6(1); it does not often apply. In addition, s 6(2) applies and covers an even smaller number of cases. It applies where A being in possession of B's property pawns it. Despite A's intention to retrieve the property and return it, he is regarded as having treated it as his own for the purposes of theft.

Intention may be **conditional** as where A puts his hand into B's pocket intending to deprive him permanently of any money he may find there. However, there is no money so the crime of theft is not committed. In such a case a charge of attempted theft is appropriate.

Fraud and malpractice

Here we consider some common types of fraud and malpractice. The subject is a difficult one to grasp because the criminal fraternity is always developing new variations of existing crimes.

The following reforms to the law which are designed to make it easier to successfully prosecute fraud should be noted.

The Fraud Act 2006

This Act, which received the Royal Assent on 8 November 2006, follows from the government's Fraud Review set up in October 2005. It aims to protect consumers and business against fraud by giving prosecutors powers that are more effective to cope with fraud, particularly those forms which involve modern technology.

English criminal law did not contain a specific offence of fraud. Prosecutors have had to use offences of deception set out in the Theft Act 1968, putting forward these charges and trying to find an offence that matches the facts. This has encouraged technical defences and long and complex trials. The 2006 Act contains a new general offence of fraud. There are three ways of committing the offence, as follows:

1 **Fraud by false representation** as where emails are sent to a large number of people on the representation that they have been sent by a financial institution and seeking information such as a bank account or credit card number. A representation may be made in a number of ways, e.g. orally or through a website or by conduct, as where a fraudster uses a stolen credit card to pay for goods.

2 **Fraud by failing to disclose information** where there is a legal duty to do so, as where, e.g., there is a failure to disclose an existing medical condition in an application for life assurance or non-disclosure in a prospectus offering shares.

3 **Fraud by abuse of position.** This will arise, e.g., in the recognised fiduciary relationships such as trustee and beneficiary, director and the company, and agent and principal. Employer and employee will also be covered to catch, e.g., the dishonest employee who copies customers' details or software for sale or use in a competing business. It would also cover directors' secret profits made in conducting the company's business.

Dishonesty is an essential ingredient in each offence and the fact that the defendant intends a gain to himself or herself or another, or to cause another loss or expose another to loss, must be shown.

There is also a new offence of obtaining services dishonestly. Under existing law services cannot be stolen. This would cover, e.g., obtaining access to satellite or cable television without making payment.

Insider dealing

Persons may indulge in what is called insider dealing or trading, e.g. buying or selling shares on the basis of inside knowledge not available to others about matters likely to influence the price of the shares.

Part V of the Criminal Justice Act 1993 applies and Schedule 2 to that Act sets out the securities covered by its provisions. There are three offences provided under s 52: dealing, encouraging and disclosing. The 1993 Act covers any security which falls within Schedule 2 to the Act.

The securities must be listed on a regulated market, such as the London Stock Exchange, but dealing in differences is covered too. Those who deal in differences do not buy shares or even take an option on them. The deal consists of a forecast of the price of a particular security at a given future time, and those who enter into such deals with inside information which helps them to predict the price will commit an offence.

The Act does not apply to unlisted securities or face-to-face transactions as may be the case in the sale and purchase of private company shares.

Meaning of dealing

A person deals in securities if he acquires or disposes of the securities himself, whether for himself or as the agent of some other person, or procures an acquisition or a disposal of the securities by someone else. Therefore, A could acquire shares for himself, or acquire shares as a broker for his client or dispose of them in the same contexts. Alternatively, A may simply advise B to purchase or dispose of shares and still be potentially liable if he has inside information. B may also be liable in this situation if he is what is called a tippee (see below).

What is inside information?

Definition of inside information can be found under s 56. Basically this is information which relates to the securities themselves or to the state of the company which issued them. It must be specific and precise so that general information about a company, e.g. that it was desirous of moving into a new market, would not be enough. In addition, the information must not have been made public and must be the sort of information which, if it had been made public, would be likely to have had a significant effect on the price of those securities, e.g. falling or rising profits or decisions to pay a higher dividend than expected, or a lower one or no dividend at all.

Insiders

In order to be guilty of the offence of insider dealing, the individual concerned must be an insider. Definition of an insider can be found under s 57:

A person has information as an insider if:

- the information which he has is and he knows it is 'insider information';
- he has the information and he knows that he has it from an 'inside source'.

A person is in possession of information from an 'inside source' if:

- he has the information through being a director, employee or shareholder of a company or by having access to it by reason of his employment, e.g. as auditor; or
- the source of the information is a person within the above categories.

This can be seen in the 2006 case heard in the Southwark Crown Court in which, over a period of three years, the defendant entered into spread bets using inside information relating to certain companies gained through his employment. The transactions took place in his friends' names and the profits were shared between them.

Disclosure in the course of employment

Sometimes it is necessary for a person to pass on inside information as part of his employment, as may be the case with an audit manager who passes on inside information to a senior partner of the firm who is in charge of the audit. If the senior partner deals, he will be potentially liable, but the audit manager will not since the 1993 Act exempts such persons.

Necessity for intent

Since insider dealing is a crime, it requires, as most but not all crimes do, an intention to see a dealing take place to secure a profit or prevent a loss. It is unlikely that an examiner would go deeply into what is essentially the field of the criminal lawyer, but consider this example: A's son was at college and broke. He asked his father for a loan and his father said, 'Look son, you're not getting any more money from me – pity you cannot buy some shares in Boxo plc of which I am a director. Next month's profit announcement will be way up on last year's. You could make a killing.' If for some reason A's son was able to scrape up sufficient funds to buy shares in Boxo plc, it is unlikely that his father would be liable because he had no idea that his son would be in a position to buy the shares.

Penalty for insider dealing

The contract to buy or sell the shares is unaffected. The sanctions are criminal, the maximum sentence being seven years' imprisonment and/or a fine of unlimited amount. In order to be found guilty, the offence must in general terms be committed while the person concerned was in the UK or the trading market was.

Exemptions

Schedule 2 to the Criminal Justice Act 1993 sets out, in particular, an exemption for persons operating as dealers, so that, for example, those engaged in dealing for clients on the stock exchange are exempt because they would find it difficult to operate deals in shares if they had to stop dealing in them when in possession of what might be inside information about some of them. It should be noted, however, that the exemption covers only the offence of dealing. They are not exempt from the offence of encouraging another to deal.

Regarded as a difficult crime to secure indictment, the Financial Services Authority has in the recent years successfully prosecuted several cases. In *R* v *McQuoid* (2009), a solicitor and former general counsel of a public limited company passed insider information regarding a takeover by another public limited company to his father-in-law, who purchased 150,000 shares based on the information received. The takeover was then made public and the offer price for the shares was more than triple what was originally paid, generating a profit of almost £50,000. The profits were shared equally. It was said in the appeal case that insider dealing should not be treated as a victimless crime.

Market abuse – the civil powers of the Financial Services Authority (FSA)

The Financial Services Authority (FSA) is the regulator of the UK financial sector. It was given statutory powers by the Financial Services and Markets Act 2000 (FSMA). The FSA is, however, a company limited by guarantee and is funded through firms it regulates.

The regulation on market abuse in the UK can be found in the FSMA 2000, part VIII (ss 118 to 131). Section 119 of the FSMA requires the FSA to issue a code which contains provisions that will give appropriate guidance in determining whether certain behaviour amounts to market abuse according to the FSA. Accordingly, detailed rules can be found in the FSA's Market Abuse sourcebook and, in particular, in the Code of Market Conduct. The Code was updated to include the changes resulting from the EU Market Abuse Directive that came into force on 1 July 2005.

Under the FSMA 2000, market abuse is behaviour in relation to investments traded on recognised UK investment exchanges, e.g. the London Stock Exchange, which satisfies at least one of the following tests:

- *the misleading impression test*, being behaviour likely to give those participating in the market a mistaken impression as to supply, demand, price or value;
- *the distortion test*, being behaviour likely to distort the market;
- *the privileged information test*, being behaviour based on information which is not available to participants in the market who would regard that information as relevant when deciding whether or not to trade.

Proof of market abuse is on a balance of probabilities (the civil standard). However, under guidance from the Treasury, those dealt with for market abuse, such as insider dealing, will get additional protection given for criminal trials, and there is to be some support for legal costs. Thus, the FSA will not be allowed to use evidence which it has compelled someone to give as part of an investigation of market abuse. In other words, there is to be a rule against self-incrimination. The accusation that the FSA might act as 'prosecutor', judge and jury has been addressed. The investigation and disciplinary roles of the FSA will be kept separate and cases will be heard by an independent tribunal. The Criminal Justice Act 1993, which provides a criminal regime, remains in force.

The 'true and fair' aspect of the definition was regarded as too vague, so the government has now amended the relevant section and replaced it with a requirement that for behaviour to be abusive it must be regarded by a 'regular user' of the market as a failure on the part of the person concerned to observe the standards which the regular user would reasonably expect of a person 'in his . . . position in relation to the market'. A 'regular user' is defined as a reasonable person who regularly deals on the market concerned in relevant investments. Other changes introduced into the Act are:

- Before deciding whether or not to take action for market abuse, the FSA must have regard to the extent to which the person involved took care to avoid engaging in abuse or actually believed that his behaviour was not abusive. There is, however, no 'safe harbour'

provision for those who take reasonable steps to avoid engaging in market abuse. It is a matter for the FSA.

- A person will not be found to have engaged in abuse if he has complied with rules made by the FSA as where, for example, he acts in accordance with the FSA's rules regarding the stabilisation of investments.
- In determining the amount of any penalty to be imposed for market abuse, the FSA must take into account whether the behaviour has had an adverse effect on the market and how serious the effect has been, together with the extent to which the behaviour was deliberate or reckless and whether the person who is to be penalised is an individual as distinct from, e.g., a corporate organisation.
- As regards the possibility that the FSA would not accept conduct that was within the City Code as a defence to market abuse, the Act now allows the FSA to offer a safe harbour status in market abuse enforcement where there has been compliance with the Code, though the FSA is still required to keep itself informed about the way the Takeover Panel interprets and administers the Code.

The FSA has given some examples of what could constitute market abuse under the Code of Market Conduct that it has published. These include:

- persons using Internet bulletin boards to post misleading information; and
- financial journalists using inside knowledge to trade in shares.

It appears that the FSA will be able to identify persons hiding behind aliases on the bulletin boards. As we have seen, because the FSA operates under the civil regime, it will only have to prove 'on a balance of probabilities' that a market user behaved in a way that amounted to market abuse.

Currently the UK market abuse system has a wider scope than required by the European Union 2003 Market Abuse Directive. The HM Treasury Consultation Paper published in February 2008 was to review the scope of the UK market abuse scheme. A consultation into possible amendments to the Market Abuse Directive was published by the European Commission on 28 June 2010.

The Sarbanes-Oxley Act 2002 and UK fraud control

The above materials relate to particular types of abuses covering companies having a UK listing. However, it is worth noting that increasingly today UK companies have secondary listings on other financial markets and may be subject to the controls put in place by other countries. In particular, the US Sarbanes-Oxley Act of 2002 applies to UK companies with a secondary listing in the USA, and the need to comply with it affects, to some extent, the whole operation of the companies concerned. The aim of the Act (SOX) is to boost the confidence of investors in the US market and to deter and punish corporate and accounting fraud and corruption and bring the wrong-doers to justice. At the same time, it provides protection for employees who blow the whistle on corporate fraud. It requires an increase in financial disclosure, greater accountability of corporate executives, the greater independence of the audit process and punishment for improper conduct by senior executives of companies.

Relevant UK measures are as follows:

- the *Enterprise Act 2002*, the anti-cartel provisions of which are intended to build on those of the Competition Act 1998 (see Chapter 7 ●);
- the *Public Interest Disclosure Act 1998*, which provides protection for whistleblowing employees to encourage them to speak out about perceived acts of business fraud (see Chapter 16 ●);
- the *Companies Act 2006*, which places a legal obligation on directors to volunteer information to auditors and gives auditors increased rights to ask for company information from employees (see Chapter 6 ●);
- the *Proceeds of Crime Act 2002*, whose main functions include extending the scope of money-laundering offences, introducing reporting requirements by professionals and others in respect of money laundering (see below) and the setting up of an Assets Recovery Agency to relieve wrongdoers of their illegal funds. This is of real concern to professionals, such as accountants and solicitors, who fail to report suspicious transactions, as where Fred, an accountant, fails to report to the police the fact that one of his clients, who runs

a street-corner garage, has recently bought a private jet and seems to fly quite often to Central and South America. Prison sentences for such professionals are available and will be used in appropriate cases.

In addition to creating money laundering provisions, the Proceeds of Crime Act 2002 also deals with confiscation criminal proceedings. In *Serious Fraud Office and Lexi Holdings plc (In Administration) and M* (2008), the appeal concerned a claim raised by a third party which would reduce the amount of the restrained assets under the restraint orders made under the 2002 Act. This is presumably the first case to reach the Court of Appeal Criminal Division since the Proceeds of Crime Act 2002 came into effect. In this case, a restraint order was made prohibiting the second respondent, M, from removing, disposing of, dealing with or diminishing the value of any of his assets. There was provision in the order for up to £250 per week to be spent on M's ordinary living expenses. The order was made on an application by the Director of the Serious Fraud Office. The argument was that the restraint order was made on 20 April 2006 on the basis that a criminal investigation had been started and the terms of s 40(2) were satisfied but that no prosecution has been begun after two years. The respondent submits that a reasonable time has elapsed. Given the 'very complex' nature of the investigation, it was in no position to conclude that a reasonable time within which criminal proceedings should have begun has elapsed.

- **Money Laundering Regulations 2007** (SI 2007/3075) apply to a wide range of business types and are supervised by various supervisory authorities such as HMRC or FSA. Most UK financial institutions are covered and so are the legal and accounting professionals; the regulations also cover casinos, estate agents and other 'high value dealers' ('€15,000 or more in one single transaction').

Self-test questions/activities

1 Which of the following business organisations have been formed by registration?
   (a) Wilkinson-Brown & Co, Chartered Accountants;
   (b) Mammoth plc;
   (c) The United Kingdom Atomic Energy Authority;
   (d) Small Ltd.

2 'A registered company is a juristic or legal person and is therefore a legal entity distinct from its members.'
   Explain this statement and state two advantages of incorporation, showing how these advantages depend upon corporate personality.

3 The court will not allow the theory of corporate personality to be used as a means of fraud or sharp practice – the judge has the power to 'draw aside the corporate veil'.

Explain what happens when the court does draw aside the veil and describe a situation in which the court has exercised its power.

4 A and B are partners in an ordinary partnership. The firm is insolvent. Joe, a creditor, has successfully sued A for a debt of £2,000. What rights, if any, has A against B?

5 A, B, C and D wish to form a partnership in which all of them will be limited partners. Advise them.

6 What is the maximum number of employees allowed to a company which wishes to qualify as a 'small' company?

7 Outline the provisions under which companies can dispense with the audit requirement.

8 Explain the regime of taxation which applies to:
■ sole traders; and
■ companies.

9 Give a short account of ways in which mortgages of real and personal property may be created. Explain what is meant by the 'equity of redemption'.

10 Discuss the importance in securities transactions of the Bills of Sale Acts.

11 When is it important for a person giving a guarantee or other security to be advised by an independent solicitor? State with reasons whether or not the guarantee or other security will be unenforceable if independent advice is not received.

12 Fred Jones is a sole trader who wishes to expand his business premises. Explain the basic planning procedures to be followed.

Specimen examination questions

1 Explain the requirements that a company must comply with in order to be entitled to the maximum exemptions in terms of its financial statements.

2 Assume you are one of a number of entrepreneurs who are considering the form of business organisation that might be used to run a business. The other members of the group seek your advice as to whether they should form a partnership or a company – their only concern at this stage being the liability of themselves for the debts of the organisation.

Explain what forms of business vehicles are available in the partnership and corporate structures and then consider the position in terms of individual liability for the debts of each one.

3 You have been appointed to manage a branch of the National Knightsbridge Bank plc. A business customer, Mr Egon Toast, has asked for a business loan and is offering the family home, of which he is the joint owner with Mrs Toast, as security.

Explain why you should be concerned about making the loan and security transaction and what steps you would take to overcome those concerns.

Website references

http://www.companieshouse.gov.uk This chapter is of a general introductory nature but further information on partnerships, particularly LLPs and companies, including guidance notes on a wide variety of corporate topics, can be accessed on the website of Companies House.

Visit www.mylawchamber.co.uk/richesallen to access study support resources including answers to questions in this chapter and legal updates, all linked to the **Pearson eText** version of **Keenan and Riches' Business Law** which you can **search**, **highlight** and **personalise** with your **own notes** and **bookmarks**.

Use **Case Navigator** to read in full some of the key cases referenced in this chapter with commentary and questions:

Salomon v Salomon & Co (1897)

Chapter 5

Non-corporate organisations – sole traders and partnerships

Learning objectives

After studying this chapter you should understand the following main points:

- the rules that apply to the choice of a name for a business organisation;
- the law relating to the various kinds of partnership;
- the bankruptcy procedure that follows individual insolvency.

The sole trader

Having introduced the various business organisations, we will now consider, in more detail, the legal environment in which sole traders operate.

Formation of the business

Name of the organisation

Business names

1 Generally. The main formality facing the sole trader on commencement of business is the Companies Act 2006. The Companies Act 2006 replaced the Business Names Act 1985 and legislation from the 1985 Act has been incorporated into the CA 2006. However, its scope is wider than the Business Names Act 1985. The restrictions on the use of names in the course of business now apply to all persons carrying on business in the UK. This does not apply to certain individuals or partnerships though if individuals are trading alone, or in partnerships, under their surnames. If a business name is chosen, then the 2006 Act must be complied with.

For example, a business name occurs where the organisation is run in a name which does not consist only of the surname of the sole trader. Forenames or initials are allowed in addition (see s 1192). If Charlie Brown is in business as 'Brown', or 'C Brown', or 'Charlie Brown',

the name of the organisation is not affected by the Act. The names are not business names. Recognised abbreviations may also be used, such as 'Chas Brown', and still the name is not a business name.

However, if Charlie Brown is in business as 'High Road Garage', or 'Chas Brown & Co', 'C Brown & Co', 'Brown & Co', he is using a business name and the 2006 Act must be complied with as regards choice of the name and disclosure of the name of the true owner.

The rules regarding disclosure do not apply where the only addition to the name of the sole trader is an indication that the business is being carried on in succession to a former owner.

Often a sole trader will want to use the name of the previous owner of the business so that he can use the goodwill attached to it. Goodwill is the probability that customers will continue to use the old business for their requirements. It may also be a reputation for a certain class of article, such as a Rolex watch. If Charlie Brown bought a business called 'The Village Stores' from Harry Lime, the new business could be called 'Charlie ["Chas" or "C"] Brown (formerly Harry Lime's)' and would not be affected by the Act. However, if Charlie Brown went further than merely including his own name and that of the previous owner if he traded as 'Charlie ["Chas" or "C"] Brown Village Stores (formerly Harry Lime's)' or 'Village Stores', he would have a business name and would have to comply with the Act.

2 Restriction on choice of business name. As we have seen, the **main** controls are that a sole trader's business must not be carried on in Great Britain:

(a) Under a name which leads people to believe that it is connected with a central or local government authority unless the Secretary of State for BIS agrees. This is to prevent a possibly false sense of security in the public who deal with the business because these authorities get regular income from the enforced payment of taxes and council tax.

Also in this category, and requiring the consent of the Secretary of State for BIS, are names which imply a national or international connection, such as 'The International Metal Co', and names which imply that the organisation is in some way distinguished, e.g. 'Society' or 'Institute'. Words which imply the carrying on of a specific function also require BIS permission, e.g. 'Insurance' and 'Building Society'. This will not be obtained unless those functions are the ones which the organisation carries out.

(b) Under a sensitive name unless the relevant body agrees. A comprehensive list can be found on Companies House website.

The use of the word 'Charity' requires the permission of the Charity Commissioners. Regulations in 1992 have made it clear that plural or possessive forms of sensitive names are included. So 'Charities' and 'Charities'' are controlled.

(c) Under obscene names such as 'Hookers & Co' or names obtained by deception, as where a person is using the word 'charity' having got permission from the Charity Commissioners following the submission of false or misleading information about the functions of the organisation.

3 Disclosure of true owner's name: what must be disclosed? A user of a business name must disclose his or her name together with a business or other address in Great Britain. This is to enable documents, such as claim forms to commence a legal claim, to be served at that address.

However, the High Court ruled in *Department of Trade and Industry* v *Cedenio* (2001) that the address need not be pointed up specifically as the address for serving documents. Section 4 of the Business Names Act 1985 provides merely for the stating of an address as follows: 'an address in Great Britain at which the service of any document relating in any way to the business will be effective'. This wording is retained by s 1201 of the 2006 Act.

4 Where must the information be disclosed?

(a) In a clear and readable way on all business letters, written orders for the supply of goods or services, invoices and receipts issued by the business, and written demands for the payment of money owed to the business.

(b) Prominently, so that it can be easily seen and read in any premises where the business is carried on, but only if customers or suppliers of goods or services go on to those premises.

(c) Disclosure must also be made immediately and in writing to anybody with whom business is being done or discussed if the person concerned asks for the information. This would mean, for example, giving the information on, say, a business card, to a salesperson to whom an order was being given or discussed if the salesperson asks for the names of the owners of the business.

5 What happens if an owner does not comply with the law? A sole trader who does not obey the law commits a **criminal offence** and is liable to a fine. On the **civil side** he may not be able to enforce his contracts, for example to sue successfully for debts owed to him. This will be so where, for instance, the other party to the contract can show if he is sued that he has been unable to bring a claim against the business because of lack of knowledge of the name and address of the owner.

Suppose that Freda Green trades as 'Paris Fashions' in Lancashire and supplies Jane Brown with dresses for her boutique in Yorkshire, but without giving Jane Brown any idea that she, Freda Green, owns Paris Fashions. Suppose, further, that Freda moves her business to Kent and Jane Brown finds that the dresses are substandard and wants to return them, but cannot because she does not know where 'Paris Fashions' has gone. If Jane is sued for non-payment by Freda, the court may refuse Freda's claim, though the judge has discretion to enforce it if in the circumstances he thinks it is just and equitable to do so.

Protection of business names

The fact that there is no registration of business names places businesses that use them in a more difficult position in terms of protecting the name than companies that trade in their corporate names (see further, Chapter 6 ○). As we shall see, the Registrar keeps an index of company names and a company cannot be registered in a name that is the 'same' as a name already on the index. In addition, the Secretary of State can direct a company to change its name within 12 months of registration if it is 'too like' the name of a company on the index. The above provisions do not apply to business names and a passing off action would have to be brought (see below). This is a difficult and often expensive claim. However, if the name is in the nature of a trade mark it can be registered and protected more easily. The Trade Marks Act 1994 has extended this possibility particularly in allowing registration of geographical locations, e.g. 'The Barbican Tandoori'. Thus, persons trading in a name which includes a geographical location, as where J Singh does in fact trade under the name of 'The Barbican Tandoori', the name can be registered under the 1994 Act and will be easier to protect (see further, Chapter 15 ◯).

Passing off

A sole trader must not run his business under a name which is so like that of an existing concern that the public will confuse the two businesses. Similarity of name is not enough; usually the two concerns must also carry on the same or a similar business.

If this does happen, the sole trader will be liable to a civil action for the tort of passing off and the existing concern can ask the court for an injunction to stop the use of its name. If it is successful in getting the injunction and the new organisation still carries on business under the confusing name, its owner is in contempt of court and may be fined or imprisoned until he complies and changes the name of his business.

However, a sole trader may do business in his own name even if this does cause confusion, provided that he does not go further and advertise or manufacture his goods in such a way as to confuse his products with those of the existing concern or operate to deceive the public.

Thus in *Asprey & Garrard Ltd* v *WRA (Guns) Ltd* (2001) the claimants were a well-known and established trader in luxury goods in London. The defendants traded in the same line of business, also in London, under the business name of William R. Asprey Esq. William Asprey, who was formerly employed by the claimants, effectively controlled the defendant company. The High Court granted an injunction against passing off and infringement of the claimants' trade mark. The court dismissed the defence of own name on

the grounds that it is anyway an exception to the passing off rules and must not as in this case cause deception. Although the problems in the above case arose from the use of a business name, the same principles would apply if the defendant business had been run in the name of Asprey as a sole trader, partnership or company name.

Dissolution

Our sole trader, whom we shall call Fred Smith, may decide at any time to retire from the business and dissolve it by selling off the assets of the business to other tradespeople. Alternatively, the business may be sold as a going concern to another trader and continue under him.

Apart from the legal formalities involved in selling and transferring assets, for example conveying shop premises to a new owner, there are no special legal difficulties provided all the debts of the business are paid in full. However, if Fred cannot pay his debts, he may be forced to dissolve his business by his creditors under a process called bankruptcy.

Debt recovery

Before proceeding to look at insolvency procedures it is worth noting what is available to recover debts before taking the ultimate step which is to put insolvency procedures in train.

If Fred's creditors have tried all the usual ways of recovering their debts, e.g. statements, solicitor's letters and so on, they may think about suing Fred in the county court. The jurisdiction and procedure of that court have already been described in Chapter 3 ◯ .

Interest on debt – generally

As regards the payment of interest on debt that the court can award as part of the judgment, we must first look at the contract to see whether there is any provision for interest. If there is, the court will follow the provision in making its award.

Late payment of commercial debts legislation

The Late Payment of Commercial Debts (Interest) Act 1998, as amended and supplemented by the Late Payment Commercial Debts Regulations 2002, gives creditors a statutory right to claim interest from debtors on debts relating to commercial contracts for the supply of goods and services. The Act was brought into force by stages. On 7 August 2002 the final phase of the implementation was made and the Act now applies to all businesses and public sector bodies.

Application of the Act

The Act applies to contracts for the supply of goods or services where the purchaser and the supplier are acting in the course of a business. It does not apply to consumer credit agreements or to any contract that operates by way of a security, for instance a mortgage, pledge, or charge.

What is the rate of interest?

Interest is calculated at 8 per cent above the Bank of England base rate. To simplify matters and avoid an ever changing rate, interest is calculated at 8 per cent above the base rate in force on 30 June for interest that starts to run between 1 July and 31 December or the base rate in force on 31 December for interest that starts to run between 1 January and 30 June. Thus where the base rate is, say, 4 per cent on the applicable date, the late payment rate will be 12 per cent (the current rate as of 1 July 2010 is 8.5 per cent based on a reference rate of 0.5 per cent). The Act gives suppliers an entitlement to simple interest only and not compound interest, i.e. interest on interest.

From when does interest run?

Interest starts to run from the day after the due date for payment or, where no such date has been agreed, when 30 days have elapsed from the delivery of the goods or the carrying out of the services or notice being given to the purchaser of the amount of the debt, whichever is the later.

Recovering the costs

In addition to interest, a business can claim reasonable debt recovery costs.

Where the customer still does not pay

Let us assume that one of Fred's creditors has obtained a judgment against him and that he still will not pay.

The judgment itself orders Fred to pay direct to his creditor. The creditor will therefore know quite quickly whether he needs to consider further action (called enforcement) to try to get the money.

If Fred has not paid, the creditor can try to get the money by asking the county court for any of the following:

- a warrant of execution;
- a third-party debt claim (formerly a garnishee order); or
- a charging order.

The court can, in an appropriate case, make an attachment of earnings order under which an employer deducts money from wages or salary through the court until the judgment is paid. This is not available in Fred's case because he is self-employed and an earnings order is not available against Fred's profits. It is necessary to pay a fee for any of the above procedures but the amount paid by the creditor will be added to the money he is already owed. The fee is not refunded if the enforcement does not succeed. If Fred has no money or assets (which is unlikely), it will fail and there is nothing the court can do by way of enforcement.

Warrant of execution

This gives the bailiffs, who work out of the office of the sheriff of the county, the authority to visit Fred's home or business. The bailiff(s) will try either:

- to collect the money owed; or
- to take goods to sell at auction to pay the debt.

It is worth noting that there may be some activity in this area under the Human Rights Act 1998. Article 1 of the First Protocol of the Human Rights Convention deals with property rights and, since the bailiff service is an emanation of the state, the Convention applies. Property taken in execution is sold at very cheap prices at sheriffs' sales and makes less contribution than it might in paying off the debtor's debts. This provides an imbalance between the rights of the creditor and the debtor that may lead to cases and changes on the basis of a breach of the 'fair balance' test implicit in the Protocol.

Third-party debt claims (formerly garnishee orders)

If a creditor knows that Fred is owed money by a third party as where, for example, there is a credit balance on Fred's bank account or building society account, the creditor may wish to divert the payment away from Fred to himself. This can be done by the creditor applying to the court for an order for enforcement of a third-party debt claim. The order is addressed to the bank or building society forbidding it to pay the debt to the debtor, Fred, and requiring a representative of the bank or building society to attend before the court to show why the money in the account (or according to the order perhaps part of it) should not be paid to the creditor. The order is served at least seven days before the next court hearing on the matter and, if at that hearing no reason has been shown as to why the payment should not be made to the creditor, the court may make an order requiring payment by the bank or building society to the creditor. The creditor, in order to use these proceedings, must be a person who has obtained a judgment from the court that the relevant debt is owed to him.

Charging order

This order prevents Fred from selling property over which it is made, e.g. a house, land, business premises and any shares Fred may hold, until the creditor is paid. The creditor will have to wait for the money until the property is sold but can ask the court for an order to force Fred to sell.

Getting a third-party debt enforcement order or a charging order can be complicated and the creditor would normally require the help of a solicitor.

We will now consider the situation where for some reason or another the creditor has been unable to get his money and turns to the ultimate procedure – to make Fred bankrupt.

Debt enforcement: reform

The Tribunals, Courts and Enforcement Act 2007, published in draft in July 2006, received Royal Assent in July 2007. The aim of the Act is to improve the working of the system of tribunals by providing a new statutory framework, offices and bodies that will deliver improvements in services to those who use tribunals.

Of particular interest to business are the provisions relating to debt as follows:

Part 3 unifies existing bailiff law relating to enforcement by seizure and sale of goods and replaces the existing law of rent distress by seizure of the tenant's property with a modified regime for recovering rent arrears in the commercial property sector.

Part 4 contains measures to help creditors with claims in the civil courts to enforce their judgments, including a new court-based scheme to help the court gain access to information about the judgment debtor on behalf of the creditor.

Part 5 contains measures to provide debtors who are unable to pay their debts with relief from enforcement and discharge from their debts. There are also non-court based measures to help over-indebted persons and those with multiple debt situations to manage their indebtedness.

Bankruptcy procedure – generally

Bankruptcy procedure is set out in the Insolvency Act 1986 as amended by the Enterprise Act 2002. Bankruptcy proceedings, which involve asking the court for a bankruptcy order, may be taken against Fred by creditors. Fred may also take proceedings to make himself bankrupt if he cannot pay his debts. His affairs will then be taken over by an insolvency practitioner, who is usually an accountant.

This may be a great relief to Fred if, as is likely, he is being pressed and harassed to pay debts he cannot meet. On bankruptcy his creditors will have to press the insolvency practitioner to pay. He is, of course, an independent person and a lot of the nastiness goes out of the situation once he takes over from Fred.

In particular, those who supply services to Fred's home – such as electricity, gas, water and telephone – must treat him as a new customer from the date of the bankruptcy order and cannot demand settlement of outstanding bills as a condition of continuing supply. They can, however, require a deposit as security for payment of future supplies.

The petition

A petition to the court for a bankruptcy order may be presented by a creditor or creditors only if:

1 The creditor presenting it is owed £750 or more (called the bankruptcy level) by Fred. Two or more creditors (none of whom is individually owed £750) may present

a joint petition if together they are owed £750 or more by Fred, as where A is owed £280 and B £600.

2 The debt is defined as a debt now due which Fred appears to be unable to pay, or a future debt which Fred has no reasonable prospect of being able to pay.

3 The creditor, to show that this is so, and if the debt is now due, sends Fred a further demand asking for payment. If the demand is not complied with within three weeks, the court will accept that Fred cannot pay the debt.

4 The debt is a **future debt**, such as a loan repayable in the future. The creditor(s) must send Fred a demand asking him to give evidence that he will be able to pay it. If Fred does not provide satisfactory evidence within three weeks of the demand that he will be able to meet the debt when it is due, the court will accept that there is no reasonable prospect that it will be paid.

5 The debt is not secured, as by a charge on Fred's property. A secured creditor cannot present a petition unless he is, for example, prepared to give up his security. In any case, secured creditors, such as banks who have taken a security in return, say, for giving Fred an overdraft facility, will normally get their money by selling that property of Fred's over which they have a charge. Any surplus of the sale price, after payment of the debt to the bank and the cost to the bank of selling the property, is returned to Fred's estate for distribution among his other creditors. If there is a shortfall in the sale price, the bank will have to prove in the bankruptcy as an unsecured creditor for the balance but will only receive the same dividend, as it is called, as other unsecured creditors on this balance, e.g. 25p in the £.

it may petition the court within one month of it being made asking that Fred be made bankrupt. The fact that the deed has been entered into is the ground for the petition. A possible practical scenario appears below.

1 Fred may wish to put a proposal to his creditors under which he will hand over his business to a trustee for the benefit of his creditors. The trustee will be an independent person such as an accountant who may be able to deal more expertly with the sale of Fred's business or the running of it and so pay the creditors off. If the creditors are willing to go along with this, Fred will not be made bankrupt.

2 Alternatively, Fred may wish to put up a scheme of arrangement by way of compromise of his debts. This would involve the creditors accepting final payment of, say, 50p in the £, which they may feel will be a better deal than bankruptcy, particularly if the cost of the bankruptcy proceedings is likely to be high.

3 These schemes need the consent of a majority in number and value of the creditors. For example, if there are 100 creditors and A is owed £901 and the other 99 are owed £1 each, the rest cannot force a scheme on A because he has the majority in value, although the others have a majority in number. Equally, A plus 49 of the rest cannot force the scheme on the others. A plus 49 creditors have a majority in value but not in number. However, A plus 50 of the rest could force the scheme on the others; they have a majority in number of 51 per cent and a clear majority in value.

However, as we have seen, dissentients can petition the court for a bankruptcy order so really all of the creditors need to be happy with the scheme, or at least too apathetic to petition.

Schemes of arrangement under the Deeds of Arrangement Act 1914

This is an alternative procedure to bankruptcy under which Fred would not become bankrupt at all. Deeds of arrangement are unaffected by the Insolvency Act 1986. Such a deed has advantages in that no applications to the court are required **but** creditors who do not accept

The interim order and voluntary arrangement under the Insolvency Act 1986

This is another alternative to bankruptcy. It involves an application to the court but once accepted by 75 per cent in value of the creditors it is binding on the dissentients who cannot petition for a bankruptcy order. A possible practical scenario follows.

1 It would, of course, be difficult for Fred to make proposals for a scheme if a particular creditor (or creditors) had presented a petition to bankrupt him and was proceeding with it.

2 Therefore, if Fred wants breathing space to try a scheme to prevent his bankruptcy, he may, when a creditor presents a petition (or, indeed, if he thinks a scheme might be acceptable after he has presented a petition against himself), apply to the court to make what is called an interim order.

3 This protects his property and stops the proceedings for a bankruptcy order from carrying on. Also, secured creditors are prevented from selling that property of Fred's on which the security has been taken, though any scheme which is accepted cannot take away the rights of secured creditors to be paid before unsecured creditors. Still, an interim order will keep Fred's property together while a scheme is considered.

4 As part of obtaining an interim order, Fred must give the name of a qualified insolvency practitioner (called a 'nominee') who is willing to act as a supervisor for the proposed scheme. The court must be satisfied that:

(a) the nominee is properly qualified as an insolvency practitioner and has stated in his report that he considers that the arrangement has a reasonable prospect of success; and

(b) Fred has not made a previous application for an interim order in the last 12 months. Obviously, a debtor cannot keep asking for these orders so as, perhaps artificially, to put off bankruptcy proceedings. The nominee will report to the court on the proposals in Fred's voluntary arrangement and if the court thinks that they are reasonable it will direct the holding of a meeting of creditors which the nominee will call. If 75 per cent in value of the creditors entitled to vote attending the meeting in person or by proxy approve the proposals by voting for them, they will be binding on all creditors.

Under Sch 3 to the Insolvency Act 2000 an individual voluntary arrangement binds *all* the debtor's creditors *including unknown creditors* and they are only entitled to the dividends under the arrangement and cannot sue for the full debt or commence bankruptcy proceedings. They may, however, apply to the court for relief on the ground that their interests are unfairly prejudiced by the arrangement.

The nominee, or another practitioner chosen by the creditors, will supervise the arrangement. If it is honoured the debtor, Fred, avoids bankruptcy and all the restrictions and publicity which go with it.

Under Sch 3 to the Insolvency Act 2000 an individual may put a proposal for a voluntary arrangement to his creditors without having to obtain an interim order.

Fast-track voluntary arrangements (IVAs)

The Enterprise Act 2002 inserted ss 263A and 263G into the Insolvency Act 1986 to provide for fast-track IVAs **available only to undischarged bankrupts.** The Insolvency Act 1986 already allows post-bankruptcy IVAs but little use has been made of the provisions. The new procedure is designed to cut the costs of an ordinary IVA. It will be used most often by consumer bankrupts who have not properly considered the options pre-bankruptcy and by professionals who discover that a bankruptcy will affect their professional status and wish to have the bankruptcy order annulled. If a post-bankruptcy IVA comes into force, the bankruptcy will be annulled.

The fast-track procedure is as follows:

- The Official Receiver (a civil servant from the Official Receiver's Department (see below)) acts as nominee.
- He or she puts proposals to the creditors on a 'take it or leave it' basis.
- There is no meeting of creditors and no opportunity to propose amendments.
- When the Official Receiver as nominee communicates with the creditors, he or she will have to explain the circumstances in which the IVA will be regarded as approved and ways in which creditors can object. This will not be at a meeting, but will be done by correspondence.
- If the IVA is approved under the Official Receiver's criteria, he or she will report the approval to the court which will annul the bankruptcy order.

Following approval, the Official Receiver will act as the supervisor of the arrangement. His fees as nominee will be at a flat rate and may be cheaper than the fees charged by professionals in the private sector. As supervisor the fees will be a percentage of the value of the property sold or debts collected for distribution to creditors under the scheme.

The effect of a bankruptcy order – generally

1 If a scheme is either not put forward or, if put forward, not accepted, the bankruptcy proceedings will, if successful, end in the court making a bankruptcy order.

2 Once the order is made and Fred becomes bankrupt, his property is automatically transferred to the control of the Official Receiver. He is a civil servant dealing with bankruptcy with the aid of a staff of suitably qualified people. If Fred had put up a scheme of arrangement which had failed to get acceptance, the 'supervisor' of that scheme could have been appointed as trustee to Fred instead of the Official Receiver.

The office of the Official Receiver, being part of the insolvency service, is an emanation of the state and therefore subject to the direct application of the Human Rights Convention. Thus, in *Foxley* v *United Kingdom* (2000) the Official Receiver had obtained a court order under s 371 of the Insolvency Act 1986 directing F's post to the Official Receiver as trustee in F's bankruptcy. F was serving a prison sentence of four years for corruption. The trustee opened letters and copied them, some being the subject of legal professional privilege. He was held to be in breach of Art 8 of the Convention (right to respect for family life, home and correspondence). No compensation was awarded but there will no doubt be more claims against insolvency procedures now that these claims can be heard, under the Human Rights Act 1998, in UK courts.

3 The transfer of Fred's property to the control of the Official Receiver does not apply to such tools, books, vehicles, and other items of equipment as are necessary to Fred to be used personally by him in his job as in the case of a sole trader plumber. Nor does it apply to such clothing, bedding, furniture, household equipment and provisions as are necessary for the basic domestic needs of Fred and his family. These items are retained in Fred's ownership and control unless their individual value is more than the cost of a reasonable replacement. Thus, very expensive tools and/or household items may have to be sold to swell Fred's estate for his creditors and be replaced by viable but cheaper lines.

4 Fred is required to submit a statement of affairs to the Official Receiver within 21 days of becoming bankrupt,

i.e. 21 days from the day on which the bankruptcy order was made. This statement is the starting point of the taking over of Fred's affairs by someone else. The statement will help in this.

5 The main contents of the statement of affairs are:

(a) particulars of Fred's assets and liabilities;
(b) the names, residences, and occupations of his creditors;
(c) the securities, if any, held by them, plus the dates on which these securities were given.

The debtor's income

There is no reason why Fred should not continue to receive money from his trade or profession. However, the trustee may apply to the court for an income payments order under which a specified sum from Fred's earnings will be paid to the trustee either by the debtor or the person making the payment, e.g., in the case of an author, by the publisher paying a sum from annual royalties to the trustee. The court will not, however, make an income payments order if it reduces the debtor's income to below the sum regarded by the court as necessary to meet the reasonable needs of the debtor and his family. In this connection, it was held in *Kilvert* v *Flackett* (1998) that a tax-free lump sum of £50,504 paid to a bankrupt on retirement was to be regarded as income and could be made the subject of an income payments order for the benefit of the creditors of the estate of the undischarged bankrupt to whom it was paid.

The Enterprise Act 2002 inserts a new s 310A into the Insolvency Act 1986. This introduces what are called income payment agreements. An income payment agreement is a written agreement made between the bankrupt and the trustee in bankruptcy under which the trustee can recover from the bankrupt part of his or her post-bankruptcy earnings *without obtaining a court order*. The agreement must specify the amount to be contributed. This may be a specific sum or a proportion of the bankrupt's income. The time period must be stated. A maximum period of three years from the date of the agreement is allowed whether or not the bankrupt obtains his or her discharge in the meantime. Failure by the bankrupt to comply means that the bankrupt's automatic discharge will be suspended or the trustee may ask for an order requiring that the income be paid directly into the bankrupt's estate.

Credit and other disabilities

Under s 360 of the Insolvency Act 1986 an undischarged bankrupt is guilty of a criminal offence punishable by a maximum of two years' imprisonment or an unlimited fine if either alone or jointly with any other persons the bankrupt obtains credit to the extent of £500 or more without disclosing to the person from whom he obtains it information about his bankrupt status *or* if he engages directly or indirectly in a business, other than the one in which he was made bankrupt, without disclosing to all persons with whom he does business, whether they give him credit or not, the name in which he was made bankrupt. Under s 11 of the Company Directors Disqualification Act 1986 an undischarged bankrupt commits a criminal offence if he acts as a company director or takes part in the management of a company unless the court gives permission.

Before the enactment of the Enterprise Act 2002 undischarged bankrupts were automatically disqualified from sitting in Parliament or as a magistrate and from any elective office in local government. To minimise the stigma of such disqualifications, they are now applied under ss 265 to 267 of the Insolvency Act 1986 (as amended) only to those bankrupts who are subject to a *bankruptcy restrictions order* (BRO). These are made by the court and are intended for 'culpable' bankrupts, such as those who have not kept proper accounting and other business records. The restrictions also apply to those culpable bankrupts who have not waited for the court to make an order against them but have instead offered a *bankruptcy restrictions undertaking* (BRU) to the Secretary of State who has accepted the undertaking.

Pensions

The Welfare Reform and Pensions Act 1999 provides that where a bankruptcy order is made against any person, any rights that he or she has in a Revenue-approved pension scheme are to be excluded from the estate for the purposes of bankruptcy proceedings. The Act covers occupational schemes, personal pensions and the government's new stakeholder pensions.

Committee of creditors

1 If someone other than the Official Receiver is appointed as Fred's trustee, the creditors may at a general meeting set up a committee of creditors of at least three and not more than five creditors to keep an eye on the way in which the trustee deals with the assets. The trustee must take into account any directions given to him by the committee or of a general meeting of creditors. If there is a difference of view between the committee and the general meeting, the general meeting decision is followed.

2 The trustee is not bound to set up a committee of creditors unless a majority in value of creditors present and voting in person or by proxy resolve to do so. However, it can be helpful to the trustee because the creditors, or some of them, may well have experience in Fred's area of trade. Thus, if Fred's debts are £50,000, a creditor, or more likely creditors, owed at least £25,001 must want a committee of creditors.

The public examination

1 Once a bankruptcy order has been made against Fred, the Official Receiver (even if he is not the trustee) or the trustee may apply to the court for the public examination of Fred. One-half in value of Fred's creditors may require the Official Receiver to make the application to the court for a public examination. This is not a majority but literally one-half, i.e. in the example given above, £25,000.

2 At the public examination Fred can be questioned by the Official Receiver or the trustee (where this is a different person from the Official Receiver), or by any creditor on the subject of his business affairs and dealings in property and the causes of business failure.

3 The main purpose of the public examination is to help the Official Receiver to find out why Fred's business failed and whether he has been guilty of some misconduct which could lead to his prosecution for a criminal offence, e.g. fraud.

The family home

1 The family home is likely to be Fred's most valuable asset. If it is in Fred's name only, it vests in (is owned in law by) the trustee on his appointment. If it is in the joint names of Fred and another, e.g. his wife, then only Fred's half vests in the trustee.

2 In any event the trustee will be keen to sell the property so that Fred's creditors can have the benefit of what Fred owns in the property, usually after repayment of a mortgage.

3 However, the trustee must honour rights of occupation of the home. Fred will have rights of occupation only if persons under 18 (e.g. his children) reside with him at the commencement of his bankruptcy. His wife will have rights of occupation in her own right whether she is a joint owner or not. These rights arise under the Matrimonial Homes Act 1983. The trustee will therefore want an order for sale and Fred and his family will want to continue in occupation. If they do, the trustee cannot sell with vacant possession, which gives the best price.

4 Under the Insolvency Act 1986 the order for sale, if asked for, can be postponed for 12 months from the date of the bankruptcy order so that Fred and his family can find somewhere else to live. In the meantime the trustee can, if he wishes, ask the court for a charge on the proceeds of sale, if any, of the property. If the court grants this charge, the ownership of the property goes back to Fred who could sell it, but if he did so the proceeds of sale would belong to the trustee under his charge.

5 Finally, if the trustee applies for an order for sale after 12 months from the bankruptcy order, the rights of the creditors will become paramount and he will normally get the order, and Fred and his family will have to move out. The court may still delay the order for sale further if there are special circumstances, as where the property is specially adapted for the use of the bankrupt, or a member of his family who is disabled.

The family home: Enterprise Act 2002 amendments

Section 283A of the Enterprise Act 2002 deals with a problem that had affected a bankrupt's family home in times of increasing house prices. It will be recalled that the family home vests in the trustee in bankruptcy and that as a rule of thumb a sale can be postponed for 12 months so that the bankrupt and his family can find other accommodation. However, if the trustee does not ask for an order for sale, the family home nevertheless

continues to be vested in him even after discharge of the bankrupt.

The reason why an order for sale was not asked for has often been the state of the market in earlier times when house prices fell below the level of the sum borrowed on them – called negative equity. However, as house prices have risen much beyond the amount lent on them, the trustee has asked for an order to sell the property still vested in him and obtained for the creditors a disproportionate windfall as a result of waiting for sale beyond the normal period. However, under s 283A the family home will have to be dealt with within three years of the bankruptcy order or it will revest automatically in the bankrupt. Also, if the trustee asks for an order to sell the family home at any stage of the bankruptcy and the court refuses the application, the family home will also revest in the bankrupt unless the court otherwise orders. Thus, in times of rising prices the trustee cannot hang on indefinitely to the family home in the hope of an ever greater windfall for the creditors. It is a 'use it or lose it' approach. There is also a provision in s 313A of the Insolvency Act 1986 (inserted by the Enterprise Act 2002) under which when the trustee asks for an order for sale of what is called a 'low-value' property then the trustee's application will be dismissed. These low-value arrangements are set out in regulations.

Proof of debt

1 Fred's creditors will send details of their debts to Fred's trustee. These details may be unsworn claims or may be sworn claims, which means that the creditor has gone to a solicitor and said to him on oath that the debt is really due.

2 Both unsworn and sworn claims are called proofs of debt. The trustee will normally accept an unsworn claim unless he is doubtful about it and is going to challenge it, possibly before the court. If this is so, he would probably ask the creditor to submit a sworn claim.

Mutual dealings – set off

1 Any mutual dealings between Fred and any of his creditors are important. Say Fred is owed £20 by a

customer, Sid, but Fred owes Sid £10. The trustee will ask Sid to pay the £20 to him but Sid will be able to set off (as it is called) the £10 Fred owes him against the £20 he owes the trustee, and pay only £10 to Fred's trustee.

2 This way Sid gets in fact a dividend of £1 in the £1 on the debt Fred owes him. If there was no law allowing set off, Sid would have to pay £20 to Fred's trustee and then prove for his debt of £10 in Fred's bankruptcy. If Fred's trustee had only sufficient assets from Fred's business to pay Fred's creditors 50p in the £1, then Sid would have had to pay £20 but would have got only £5 back. As it is he has had the whole £10 in value.

Carrying on the business and disclaimer

1 Fred's trustee may, with the permission of the committee of creditors or the court, carry on Fred's business for a while (but not for too long) if it will bring more money in for the creditors.

2 As we have seen, when the court makes the bankruptcy order Fred's property comes into the ownership and control of his trustee for the benefit of his creditors. One result of this is that in the case of an interest in land, such as a lease, say, for 20 years, the trustee becomes in effect the owner of the lease and the landlord can ask the trustee, quite legally, to pay the rent. If, as is likely, the trustee is an accountant with a good practice, he will obviously be in a position to pay the rent and cannot really defend himself if he does not do so. The trustee may find, additionally, that the lease has repairing clauses which Fred has not carried out and the landlord may call upon the trustee to put the premises in good order.

3 The trustee will therefore write to the landlord disclaiming the property. He then has no personal liability, nor has Fred any personal liability. The landlord is left to prove for his lost rent and perhaps the fact that Fred has not kept the premises in good order as damages in the bankruptcy. The landlord will get such payment as Fred's assets will allow. He is therefore by disclaimer put in the same position as the other creditors in the bankruptcy and loses any personal claim he may have made against the trustee or Fred.

Transactions at an undervalue and preferences

1 Fred's trustee may swell the amount of assets available to the creditors by using those provisions of the Insolvency Act 1986 which deal with two problems:

(a) Cases where Fred might have decided to transfer his property to his wife receiving little or nothing in return. This is called a transaction at an undervalue. However, the matter is not simply one of money paid for property. In the case of *Agricultural Mortgage Corporation plc* v *Woodward and another* (1994) the Court of Appeal decided that a tenancy of a farm granted by an insolvent farmer to his wife (to ensure that his creditors did not get vacant possession of the property and to discourage its sale to repay a loan they had made to him) was a transaction at undervalue and could be set aside, even though the wife agreed to pay an annual rent of £37,250, which was a proper market rent. This was because the wife had received substantial benefits over and above the specific rights of the tenancy agreement. She had safeguarded the family home, enabling her to acquire and carry on the family farm, and acquired a surrender value for the tenancy. Even more significantly, she could hold the mortgage corporation to ransom since it would have to negotiate with her and pay a high price to get vacant possession before selling the farm and repaying the debt owed to it.

(b) Cases where Fred has decided to pay certain of his creditors in full and prefer them to others. He might, for example, have decided to pay in full a debt to a person who had been particularly helpful to him in business or a debt which he owed a relative. This is not a transaction at undervalue because the person concerned is paid in full but it is a preference.

2 Fred's trustee can recover property or money passing in a transaction at undervalue or as a preference as follows:

(a) if the bankrupt was a party to any transactions at undervalue in the five years before the presentation of the petition (this is before he was made bankrupt by the bankruptcy order), the trustee can apply to the court to have the transaction set aside, provided that the trustee can show that the debtor was insolvent at the time of the transaction or became insolvent as a result of it;

(b) if the transaction at an undervalue took place within two years before the bankruptcy, insolvency of the debtor (Fred) at the time or as a result is not a requirement and the transaction can be set aside;

(c) where the transaction at undervalue is in favour of an 'associate' (e.g. a close relative), there is a presumption of insolvency, though the debtor can bring proof to show that this was not so;

(d) the trustee can make an application to have set aside any preference made within six months before the petition or within two years if the preference is in respect of an associate, e.g. a spouse or children.

The trustee must prove that in our case Fred was insolvent at the time of the preference or became insolvent as a result of it, and where the preference is in favour of an associate, there is a presumption that our debtor Fred intended to prefer the associate, although this may be refuted by Fred providing evidence to the contrary.

Transactions defrauding creditors

Section 423 of the Insolvency Act 1986 applies. The section is designed to operate in conjunction with the above provisions regarding transactions at undervalue and preferences. The above, as will have been noted, have time limits after which the transaction cannot be set aside. The value of s 423 is that it is not subject to specific time limits. Although s 423 carries the heading 'Transactions Defrauding Creditors', the section itself does not seem to require any fraudulent or dishonest intention. Its main ingredients are:

■ putting assets beyond the reach of a person who is making or may make a claim or;
■ otherwise prejudicing the interests of such a person in relation to the claim.

There is no need for any formal insolvency procedure to be in place before s 423 can be activated and while an insolvency practitioner can be the claimant it can also be a 'victim' creditor and such a creditor may be a person who was not a creditor at the time of the transaction.

Enterprise Act amendments

Section 262 of the Enterprise Act 2002 inserts a new paragraph in Sch 5 to the Insolvency Act 1986 the effect of which is that a trustee in bankruptcy needs the permission of the court or a creditors' committee (if any) before bringing proceedings in regard to transactions at undervalue, preferences and transactions defrauding creditors. There is a similar provision for company liquidators in a corporate insolvency (see s 253 of the Enterprise Act 2002). The object is to institute a check on insolvency practitioner litigation. Court actions are costly and the court or creditors' committee will want to be satisfied that there is a good prospect for a return on the claim.

Protection of innocent third parties

It should be noted that a transaction cannot be set aside under any of the above provisions against a person who acquired property *from a person other than the bankrupt* for value and in good faith without knowledge of the undervalue or preference. Thus, if Fred disposes of his property at an undervalue to person A, the transaction can be set aside as against A. However, if A sells the property to B, who takes it in good faith for value and without knowledge of the nature of the transaction between Fred and A, B can retain the property.

Payment of the creditors – preferential payments

1 As the trustee gets in money from Fred's business, either as income or from the sale of assets, he will pay Fred's creditors in a set order of priority laid down in Sch 6 to the Insolvency Act 1986 after providing money for his own fees and expenses.

2 The preferential debts are:

(a) wages or salaries of employees due within four months before the bankruptcy up to a maximum of £800 for each employee;
(b) all accrued holiday pay of employees;
(c) any sums owed by the debtor as a contribution to an occupational pension scheme.

Formerly, debts due to HMRC and social security contributions were preferential but these categories were removed by s 251 of the Enterprise Act 2002. They are now ranked with ordinary trade creditors. In corporate insolvencies a certain amount of assets are ring-fenced for the payment of unsecured creditors and do not go to secured lenders such as banks. For the avoidance of doubt, it should be noted that these ring-fencing provisions do not apply in bankruptcy.

If the above debts come in total to £5,000 and Fred's assets raise only £2,500, each claimant will get half of what is claimed and other creditors will get nothing.

Protection of employees

1 Under ss 189–190 of the Employment Rights Act 1996 an employee who loses his job when his employer (in this case Fred) becomes bankrupt can claim through the Department for Business, Innovation and Skills (BIS) the arrears of wages, holiday pay and certain other payments which are owed to him rather than rely on the preferential payments procedure.

2 Any payments made must be authorised by the BIS and the right to recover the sums payable are transferred to the BIS so that it can try to recover from the assets of the bankrupt employer the costs of any payments made, but only up to the preferential rights the actual employees would have had. What can be recovered from the BIS may, in fact, be a higher sum than the preferential payments in bankruptcy allow.

3 Major debts covered are as follows:

(a) arrears of pay for a period not exceeding eight weeks up to a rate prescribed annually by statutory instrument and currently £310 per week. Persons who earn more than £310 per week can only claim up to £310;

(b) pay in respect of holidays which has not been paid in respect of holidays actually taken and holidays due but not taken up to a rate again of £310 per week with a limit of six weeks;

(c) payments promised to an employee instead of giving him notice but not paid at a rate not exceeding £310 per week;

(d) any payment which Fred may not have made in regard to an award by an employment tribunal of compensation to an employee for unfair dismissal.

4 Claims on the DTI will not normally be allowed if the trustee can satisfy the Department that the preferential payments will be paid from funds available in the bankruptcy and without undue delay.

Trade creditors

If all the preferential creditors have been paid in full, payments can then be made to the ordinary unsecured or trade creditors. If these claims come in total to, say, £12,000 and the trustee has only £4,000, each trade creditor will get one-third of what is claimed and the deferred creditors will get nothing.

Deferred creditors

If all the unsecured creditors can be paid, the deferred creditors come next. These are, for example, debts owed by Fred to, say, his wife. They are not paid until all other creditors have received payment in full.

Discharge of the bankrupt

The Enterprise Act 2002 is designed to promote enterprise by minimising the effects of business failure. In this connection the Act differentiates between 'culpable' bankrupts who set out to run a business in a way that would mislead the public and other businesses and the 'non-culpable' bankrupt who for reasons beyond his or her control and despite best efforts has suffered business failure. The position regarding discharge is now as follows:

- there is automatic discharge from bankruptcy on the 12-month anniversary of the bankruptcy order. For non-culpable bankrupts, this will be the end of the undischarged bankrupt's disabilities, e.g. there is no credit restriction;
- for the culpable bankrupt, there will normally be a bankruptcy restriction order in place that contains such restrictions as are contained in the order.

Bankruptcy restriction orders (BRO)

The Official Receiver may consider applying to court for a bankruptcy restriction order (BRO) to be made if the conduct of a bankrupt has been dishonest or blameworthy in some other way. The court will consider this report and any other evidence put before it, and decide whether it should make a BRO. If it does, the bankrupt will be subject to certain restrictions for the period stated in the order. This can be from 2 to 15 years. The application which is to the court can be made within 12 months of the bankruptcy order although an extension of time can be applied for if, e.g., new evidence of reprehensible business conduct emerges. It is necessary for the Official Receiver to show to the court that the bankrupt's conduct has been sufficiently reprehensible for the public interest to require that bankruptcy restrictions, e.g. in terms of credit, should continue to apply. Schedule 4A to the Insolvency Act 1986 (as inserted by the Enterprise Act 2002) sets out reprehensible behaviour, e.g. failure to keep proper accounting and other business records and entering into transactions at undervalue and making preferences and trading while insolvent.

Effects of a BRO

The effects are much the same as an extension of the period for automatic discharge so that for the currency of a BRO, which can be any period between 2 years and 15 years, the person subject to the BRO cannot, e.g.:

- act as a company director;
- obtain credit above a specified limit without disclosing the existence of the BRO;
- trade in a name other than the name under which he or she was made bankrupt.

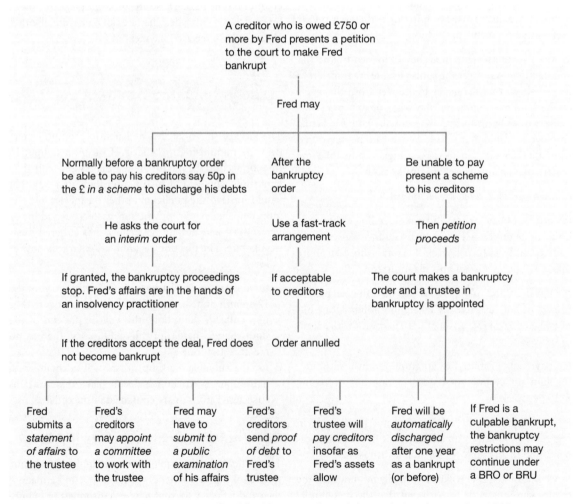

Figure 5.1 The personal insolvency of Fred Smith: an outline of the main Insolvency Act 1986 procedures

Interim BRO

Where the bankrupt is likely to obtain an automatic discharge before the hearing of an application for a BRO, the court may make an interim BRO pending a full hearing of the application.

Bankruptcy restriction undertakings (BRU)

Under this procedure a bankrupt can agree the terms of a bankruptcy restriction undertaking with the Official Receiver after offering the Official Receiver such an undertaking. The Official Receiver is not obliged to accept the undertaking in the terms offered. The rules and duration of a BRU are as for those of a BRO.

The 12-month rule: earlier discharge

It is worth noting that subject to experience with the current legislation the vast majority of bankrupts will be discharged even sooner than the 12-month period merely upon the Official Receiver conducting a small investigation and filing a certificate in court. This procedure presupposes that the bankrupt is not culpable.

The ordinary partnership

Having considered the legal position of sole traders, we now turn to the legal environment of the ordinary partnership. The provisions relating to limited and limited liability partnerships will be considered later in this chapter.

Definition and nature of a partnership

The Partnership Act 1890 sets out the basic rules which apply to this type of business organisation. All section references in this chapter are to that Act unless reference is given to some other Act.

In addition, the 1890 Act codified the case law on partnership which there had been up to 1890. Some of the cases we quote are earlier than the 1890 Act. We use them because the 1890 Act was based upon them and

they are, therefore, examples of what the Act was trying to achieve and presumably has achieved. The cases after 1890 are interpretations of the words used in the Act following its being passed by Parliament.

The legal environment of the ordinary partnership is much more complex than that of the sole trader and the two environments have little in common except that in both cases the corporate structure is not used. There are similar restrictions on the choice of name, but since a partnership is an association of persons and a sole trader regime is not, there are much wider rules to consider in partnership. For example, the ability of a sole trader to contract on behalf of the business, i.e. himself, is obvious, but in the partnership situation where there are two or more individuals involved questions such as to what extent one partner, particularly if not authorised by the others, can make a contract with an outsider which will bind the firm and himself and the other partners arise. Bearing this in mind, we can now proceed to consider the law of the ordinary partnership.

Definition

An **informal** partnership is defined as 'The relation which subsists between persons carrying on a business in common with a view of profit' (s 1).

It should be borne in mind that if the parties have agreed to be partners, then they will be. All the definition is saying is that any persons who carry on a business in common with a view of profit are partners, even if they have not expressly agreed to be. This is what we mean by an 'informal partnership'. The definition and what follows should be understood in that light – it is a definition of the facts required to make an informal partnership.

Explanation and consequences of the definition

1 **The relation which subsists is one of contract.** A partnership is a contract based on being in business together with **the intention to enter a joint venture as partners.**

It is not, according to the House of Lords in *Khan* v *Miah* (2001), necessary that the partnership has begun to trade. It is essential that the partners have taken some steps to evidence that the joint venture has been embarked upon. This may consist of preliminary steps taken to get ready to start business.

Khan v Miah (2001)

Three persons agreed to set up an Indian restaurant. The finance was provided almost entirely by one of them. Before the restaurant opened (i.e. began to trade) furniture and equipment were purchased and a laundry contract was entered into. Advertisements were placed and the freehold of premises was acquired by the person who supplied the money. The parties then fell out and the business did not proceed as planned. The question arose as to whether the parties were partners during the preliminary stages and who owned the assets acquired with one person's money. Were they partnership property, bearing in mind that in the absence of a contrary agreement partnership capital as represented by the firm's assets is owned equally by the partners regardless of capital actually put in? The House of Lords ruled that parties who agree on a joint venture to find, acquire and fit out premises for business purposes *which they intend to run as partners become partners in the business* from the time when they embark on those agreed activities and it is irrelevant whether or not the business has commenced trading. In other words, there must be evidence that the joint venture has commenced not necessarily traded.

Comment. The ruling of the House of Lords gives rise to some problems with the earlier case of *Keith Spicer Ltd v Mansell* (1970) where the Court of Appeal ruled that the taking of preliminary steps such as ordering goods and setting up a bank account for a restaurant business did not create a partnership because the restaurant never traded as a partnership. The distinction seems to be that the parties did all these acts while in the the process of forming a company to run the restaurant. Therefore, they did not take the preliminary steps with the intention of forming a partnership but as company promoters. In this sense *Spicer* can be reconciled with *Khan*. In fact, *Spicer* was not referred to in *Khan*, presumably because it was not in point, being a company promotion case.

2 A partnership is 'between persons', but a company, being a legal person, can be a partner with a human person, provided that its memorandum of association gives the necessary power. The members of the company may have limited liability while the human person has not. Two or more limited companies can be in partnership, forming a consortium as an alternative to merging one with the other. It should not be assumed that a limited company is a limited partner. The company

is liable for the partnership debts to the limit of its assets. It is the liability of the company's members which is limited – a very different thing.

3 Partners must be carrying on a joint business venture, and for this reason a group of people who run a social club would not be an informal partnership.

Under s 45 a business includes 'every trade, occupation, or profession', but this does not prevent a particular profession from having rules forbidding members to be in partnership, e.g. a barrister is not allowed to be in partnership with another barrister, at least for the purpose of practice at the Bar.

The importance of being in a joint business venture as partners is also shown by *Khan* v *Miah* (2001).

4 Partners must act in common, and the most important result of this is that, unless the agreement says something different, every general partner must be allowed to have a say in management, as s 24(5) also provides. A partner who is kept out of management has a ground to dissolve the firm unless there is something in the agreement which limits the right to manage.

The specimen ordinary partnership agreement which appears at the end of this chapter should be looked at to see how management rights have been dealt with.

5 There must be a view of profit, and so it is unlikely that those groups of persons who have got together to run railway preservation societies are informal partnerships.

In this connection the Court of Appeal has ruled that profit-sharing, i.e. actually taking a share of the profit, is not a prerequisite of partnership.

M Young Legal Associates Ltd v Zahid Solicitors (a firm) (2006)

Mr Bashir, a solicitor, wanted to set up his own practice. However, he had been qualified for less than three years and the Solicitors' Practice Rules require every practice to have at least one principal who has been qualified for three years or more. To get round this problem, Mr Bashir asked Robert Lees, who was a retired solicitor and a defendant also in this case, to set up in practice with him; and, from 2002, Zahid Solicitors (Z) began to do business.

Mr Lees was named as a partner on Z's letterhead and received a fixed salary of £18,000 per annum. This was not related to profits. However, Mr Lees was largely a figurehead and spent little time at the office. He had obtained from Z's bankers a letter saying that he would not be liable for the firm's debts to the bank and appeared to have agreed with Mr Bashir that he would not be liable for any of the debts of the firm.

The claimant, a claims handling company, made an agreement with Z in 2003 under which the claimant would arrange insurance or funding for Z's prospective clients. The claimant alleged that Z owed it money under this agreement that had not been paid.

When Z was dissolved in 2004, the claimant brought this action against the firm and Mr Lees on the basis that he was a partner at all relevant times. Mr Lees denied this, and whether he was a partner or not had to be decided as a preliminary issue before the claim could be taken forward. Mr Lees was held to be a partner at the initial hearing and made an appeal to the Court of Appeal. The defence which Mr Lees put forward was that he did not share in the profits of Z. He also contended that the sharing of profits had always been an essential requirement before the Partnership Act 1890 and pointed to s 46, which stated in effect that the former rules of equity and the common law were to be retained unless they were inconsistent with the Act.

The Court of Appeal ruled that the 1890 Act was clear. There was no reference in the s 1 definition to the sharing of profit so that the Act was inconsistent with previous law and the Act must be applied according to its words. Mr Lees was therefore a partner and the claim could proceed.

Comment. There was no liability in Mr Lees under s 14 of the 1890 Act (holding out as a partner) because there was no evidence that, although he had been held out as a partner, the claimant had relied on that in any way in deciding, e.g., to do business with Z, which is an essential ingredient of liability under s 14. The case is an important one and settles a major point of contention. Salaried partners across all professions should be aware of the potential liability that this ruling gives them, as should also consultants on fixed salaries.

6 The sharing of gross returns by A and B will not normally indicate a partnership between A and B. Partners share net profits, i.e. turnover less the outgoings of the business. Section 2 says that the sharing of gross returns does not, of itself, provide evidence of partnership, as the following case shows.

Cox v Coulson (1916)

Mr Coulson had a lease of a theatre. A Mr Mill was the employer/manager of a theatre company. Mr Coulson and Mr Mill agreed to present a play called *In Time of War*. Mr Coulson was to provide the theatre and pay for the lighting and advertising and get 60 per cent of the money which came in at the box office – the gross takings. Mr Mill paid those taking part in the play and provided the scenery and the play itself and got 40 per cent of the gross takings.

Mrs Cox paid to see the play. As part of the performance an actor had to fire a revolver with a blank round in it. Because of alleged negligence a defective cartridge was put in the revolver and when the actor fired it Mrs Cox, who was sitting in the dress circle, was shot and injured. She wanted to succeed in a claim for damages against Mr Coulson. He had more money than Mr Mill. However, the actor was employed by Mr Mill and he alone was liable vicariously for the actor's negligence unless Mrs Cox could convince the court that Mill and Coulson were partners. The court decided that they were not; they were merely sharing the gross returns. Only the actor and Mr Mill were liable.

Comment.
(i) The sharing of profits suggests a partnerlike concern with the expenses of the business and its general welfare. Sharing gross returns does not produce an implied agreement of partnership.
(ii) If there is an express agreement, oral or written, and in it the partners agree to share gross returns, then there would be a partnership.

7 Joint ownership, according to s 2, does not of itself make the co-owners partners. That means that there is no joint and several liability for debt between the co-owners, say, A and B. So if A and B are joint owners of 12 Acacia Avenue and A cannot pay a debt, say, for a carpet which he has had fitted in his bedroom, B cannot be made liable as a partner. Co-owners are not agents one of the other as partners are. It should not be thought from this that the joint owners of property can never be partners. If A and B are left a row of houses in a will and collect and spend the rents, their relationship will not be one of implied partnership because English law does not recognise joint ownership of property as a business and s 2 affirms this. However, if the joint owners enter into a partnership contract, written or oral, sharing the rents, say 50/50, and appear to **intend** a partnership, then a partnership there will be. But, if the only evidence of partnership is joint ownership of property, this is not enough to establish a partnership. This is the true meaning of s 2.

8 **Formalities**, that is, writing, are not required for a partnership agreement. In fact, there need not be a contract at all. If the definition in s 1 is complied with and the parties seem to intend a partnership, there will be one, and the Partnership Act 1890 will then set down the rules that will govern the arrangement if nothing else is agreed. These are only a fallback position imposed on the partners and most would-be partners would want to change some of them, hence the desirability of an agreement. In addition, and to make quite sure what has been agreed by the partners, there should be a written agreement.

A model form of partnership deed suitable for an ordinary partnership is provided later in this chapter. This shows what is normally dealt with by such agreements.

The sharing of profits as evidence of partnership

At one time the sharing of profits was almost conclusive evidence of informal partnership. During this period a number of everyday business transactions could give rise to a partnership, though the parties did not want this because of the possibility of incurring liability for another's debts (but see now *M Young Legal Associates Ltd* v *Zahid Solicitors (A Firm)* (2006): sharing of profits not essential). The position was eventually clarified in regard to certain business transactions, some of which are set out below, by s 2(3) of the Act of 1890. These statutory provisions are still valid, since *M Young Legal Associates Ltd* (2006) was not concerned specifically with them, but with the general definition in s 1.

1 **Partners can pay off a creditor by instalments out of the profits of the business.** This comes from the following case which was decided before the 1890 Act.

Cox v *Hickman* (1860)

A trader had got into debt and his creditors decided that instead of making him bankrupt and getting only a proportion of what he owed them, they would let him keep the business but supervise him in the running of it and take a share of the profits each year until their debts were paid in full.

An attempt was made in this case to make one of the supervising creditor/trustees liable for the trader's debts as a partner. But was he a partner? The court said he was not. He was a creditor being paid off by a share of profits.

Comment.

(i) There was, in addition, no mutual participation in trade here, but a mere supervision of the business. Of course, if creditors assume an active role in management they may well become informal partners.

(ii) The more modern approach would be for the creditors to ask the court for the appointment of a receiver to run the business. Obviously, he would not be regarded as a partner since that would hardly be his intention.

2 **Partners can pay their employees or agents by a share of profits.** It has long been the practice of some organisations to pay employees in part by some profit-sharing scheme. The Act makes this possible without putting the employees at risk of being regarded as partners and liable for the debts of the firm if the true partners run into money trouble.

The provision is also important to the true partners because the giving of labour is sufficient to form a partnership: the putting in of money by way of capital is not essential. So this provision makes sure that the employees themselves cannot claim to be partners just because they are sharing profits under an employees' scheme.

3 **Partners can pay interest on a loan by a share of net profits provided that the contract of loan is in writing and signed by all the parties to it.** This provision will protect a lender if a creditor tries to make him liable for the debts of the firm he has lent the money to, as where the creditor argues that the lender is really a dormant partner.

However, the lender must not take part in the running of the business. Remember also that the lender will not need the protection of this provision if he is paid a fixed rate of interest on his loan, e.g. 8 per cent per annum instead of 8 per cent per annum of the profit. If he is paid 8 per cent per annum interest, he is clearly a creditor and not a partner.

Do not think, because there is no written contract, that a lender will always be a partner. It is still a matter for the court to decide if it is argued that he is. Normally a properly drafted written contract should persuade the court that the lender is not a partner.

Deferred creditors

Under s 3 those receiving money from the firm under heading (c) above are deferred creditors if the partners go bankrupt during their lifetime or die insolvent.

Lenders will not get any of the money owed to them until all other creditors have been paid £1 in the £.

Thus, lenders of money do not get the best of both worlds. Section 2 provides that they do not become partners and liable for debts, but s 3 makes them deferred creditors if the partners are insolvent.

Types of partners

Partners are of different types in law as set out below.

The general partner

This is the usual type of partner who, under s 24, has the right to take part in the management of the business unless there is an agreement between himself and the other partner(s) that he should not. For example, the partnership agreement may say that some junior partners are not to order goods or sign cheques. We shall see, however, that in spite of restrictions of this kind, if a junior partner ordered goods on behalf of the firm, though he had no authority to do so, the contract would be good and the seller could sue the partners for the price if they did not pay.

However, by ignoring the partnership agreement and making unauthorised contracts in this way, the junior partner could give his co-partners grounds to dissolve the firm, on the grounds that he was in breach of the partnership agreement, and exclude him from their future business operations.

The dormant partner

The 1890 Act does not mention this type of partner but in fact he is a partner who puts money (capital) into the firm but takes no active part in the management of the business. If he does take part in management, he would cease to be a dormant partner and become a general partner.

The salaried partner

It is quite common today, at least in professional practices of, for example, solicitors and accountants, to offer a young assistant a salaried partnership without the assistant putting any money into the firm as the general (or equity) partners do.

Normally, these salaried partners are paid a salary just as an employee is with tax and national insurance being deducted from it. They are not partners for the purpose of dissolving the firm. If they want to leave they do so by serving out their notice or getting paid instead.

However, because they usually appear on the firm's letterheading as partners, or on the list of partners for inspection under the Business Names Act 1985 (see later), they could, according to the decision in *Stekel* v *Ellice* (1973), be liable to pay the debts of the firm as a partner if the outsider has **relied** on their status as such.

Because of this case a salaried partner should get a full indemnity, as it is called, from the general partners in case he is made to pay the firm's debts or meet its liability to its clients. In practice this will not happen unless the firm has not paid its debts or satisfied its liability to clients. Liability as a partner is joint and several so that if A is a full partner and B a salaried partner, and the debt £2,000, either A or B could be made to pay it all and then claim only a contribution, which would often be one half, from the other partner. Thus, if B pays the £2,000, he is entitled to £1,000 from A. However, if B gets an indemnity from A, then if B has to pay the £2,000, he can recover all of it from A.

There is no real problem for the salaried partner in the large firm which has insurance and extensive assets, but the practice has spread to medium and small firms of, e.g., accountants and solicitors where problems could arise in terms of partner liability.

An illustration involving a small law firm appears overleaf.

Nationwide Building Society v Lewis (1998)

Bryan Lewis & Co, a two-partner law firm, was sued by the building society for alleged negligence in connection with advice given to the society on a mortgage application. The second defendant was a Mr Williams who was a salaried partner described as a partner on the firm's letterhead. Mr Lewis wrote the relevant report which allegedly contained negligent advice but was bankrupt and the society pursued its claim for damages against Mr Williams. He was found initially by the High Court to be jointly and severally liable with Mr Lewis and required to pay any damages awarded without much hope of getting a contribution from Mr Lewis, and this even though Mr Williams did not write the relevant report and played no part in its preparation. On appeal he was held not liable. The society had not relied on him as a partner.

It appeared that the society had had no dealings with Mr Williams and only knew of him when it received the firm's letter which accompanied the report.

Comment. The Court of Appeal did not change the general principles of the law relating to the holding-out liabilities of salaried partners. It was merely that the judges did not feel that they applied to the facts of this case. In other circumstances a salaried partner may well find that there is liability as a 'held-out' equity partner.

Salaried partners: a comment

It will not often be the case that a salaried partner will be liable under s 14 of the 1890 Act (holding out) (see below) because s 14 liability depends on the fact that the outsider **relied** on the fact that the salaried partner was a fully liable partner. Reliance was not shown in *Lewis* (see above) and outsiders are unlikely to enter into business arrangements by relying on the full liability of salaried partners unless, perhaps, they have a special expertise or are known to be wealthy.

As was indicated in *M Young Legal Associates Ltd* (see above), a salaried partner will not be able to claim that the fact that he or she does not share profits means that there cannot be a partnership. Section 1 requires only that the partners have a view of profit, not that they must share it. This is not helpful to salaried partners or consultants who work for the firm but are not profit-sharing. If there is reliance by an outsider they could be liable under s 14 and the definition in s 1 will not prevent this liability.

Describing themselves as 'salaried partner' or 'consultant' on the firm's letterhead may help to avoid liability as a full partner, depending always on the facts of the case.

The partner by holding out (or by estoppel)

The usual way in which this happens in practice is where a person allows his or her name to appear on the firm's letterheading, or on the list of partners for inspection under the Companies Act 2006 whether that person is or is not a full partner. (See *Stekel v Ellice* (1973) and *Nationwide Building Society v Lewis* (1998).) It can also happen on the retirement of a partner if the partner retiring does not get his name off the letterheading or list.

Under s 14 everyone who by words, spoken or written, or by conduct, represents himself, or knowingly allows himself to be represented, as a partner in a particular firm, is liable as a partner to anyone who has, because of that, given credit to the firm or advanced money to it.

Thus, although such a person is not truly a partner, he may be sued by a client or creditor who has **relied** on the fact he was a partner.

However, to become a partner by holding out (or estoppel, as it is also called), the person held out must **know** that he is being held out as a partner and if he knows it must also be shown that he **consents**. The following case is an example.

Tower Cabinet Co Ltd v Ingram (1949)

In January 1946 Ingram and a person named Christmas began to carry on business in partnership as household furnishers under the name of 'Merry's' at Silver Street, Edmonton, London. The partnership lasted until April 1947 when it was brought to an end by mutual agreement. After the dissolution of the firm, Christmas continued to run 'Merry's' and had new notepaper printed on which Ingram's name did not appear. In January 1948 Christmas was approached by a representative of Tower Cabinet and eventually ordered some furniture from them. The order was confirmed on letterheading which had been in use before the original partnership was dissolved and Ingram's name was on it, as well as that of Christmas. Ingram had no knowledge of this and it was contrary to an agreement which had been made between him and Christmas that the old letterheading was not to be used.

Tower Cabinet obtained a judgment for the price of the goods against 'Merry's' and then tried to enforce that judgment against Ingram as a member of the firm. The court decided that since Ingram had not knowingly allowed himself to be represented as a partner in 'Merry's' within s 14 of the Partnership Act 1890, he was not liable as a partner by holding out (or estoppel).

Comment. As the case shows, a partner who has retired will not be liable if after retirement his name appears on the firm's letterheading if the other partners agree before he retires that the stock of old letterheading will be destroyed, or that his name will be crossed out. If old notepaper is used in spite of the agreement, the ex-partner is not liable: there is no duty in law to stop people telling lies! However, something should be done to show lack of consent if it is known that old letterheading is being used. This could be, for example, a recorded delivery letter to the continuing partners expressing dissent.

A partner who intends to work with the firm, perhaps part time, after retirement, can avoid the above problems by describing himself on the firm's letterheading as a 'consultant'.

The person who is held out is liable to a client or creditor who has relied on him being a partner. That is all s 14 says. However, in *Hudgell, Yeates & Co* v *Watson* (1978), the court said that the true or actual partners could also be liable to such a client or creditor if they themselves were responsible for the holding out or knowingly allowed holding out to take place.

Section 14 provides that the continued use of a deceased partner's name will not make his estate (that is, the property he has left on death) liable for the debts of the firm.

It is worth noting that the 'holding out' provisions of s 14 are applied by the court when making a salaried partner liable.

Membership of the firm

As we have seen, there is no limit on the number of persons who may be partners in an unlimited or limited partnership, nor is there any restriction on the number of members in a limited liability partnership. This applies to partnerships in all trades and professions though barristers cannot practise together as partners.

A barrister is a sole practitioner practising with others from chambers but not as partners.

Discrimination legislation is also applied to all partnerships regardless of size. The relevant areas are discrimination on the grounds of sex, race, sexual orientation, religion and belief, disability and age. There are exceptions for a genuine occupational requirement, as where a male partner is required because the work will be with a number of clients in countries that do not accept that women can or should take on business roles.

However, so far as disability is concerned, it may be that a disabled person can work successfully as a partner if adjustments are made in, e.g., the physical environment. There is a legal requirement to make these adjustments where necessary and possible and in the case of a partnership regulations provide that a person who is or becomes a partner can be required to bear such of the costs of adjustment as are reasonable. These matters are given further consideration in Chapter 16 ○.

A minor may become a member of a partnership (*Lovell and Christmas* v *Beauchamp* (1894)) but can avoid (get out of) the contract at any time while he is under 18 or for a reasonable period of time afterwards.

Insofar as a partnership is set up by a contract, express or implied, the Mental Capacity Act 2005 applies and under it a person is assumed to have capacity unless it is established that he or she lacks it. The court will make an assessment mainly under s 3 of the 2005 Act, which sets out circumstances of inability to make a decision, e.g., to understand information relating to the decision – in this case whether to become a partner. Failure to establish capacity will prevent a partnership with the person concerned from coming into force. The burden of proving lack of capacity is on the person who says that capacity is lacking and the burden is on a balance of probabilities, not beyond reasonable doubt. These capacity problems are also dealt with in Chapter 7 ○.

The firm and the firm name

Generally

In English law the unlimited and limited partnership firm is not an artificial person separate from the partners. In other words, it is not a person (or *persona*) at law as a company or LLP is.

If there are 10 partners in 'Snooks, Twitchett & Co', then the firm name, that is 'Snooks, Twitchett & Co', is only a convenient short form for (or a collective designation of) all the partners. It saves reeling off all their names when business is done. Thus, a contract can be made in the firm name.

If the firm wishes to sue, or if it is sued by a creditor, the Civil Procedure Rules (which are rules made by the judges to deal with procedure in court) do give a sort of personality to the firm in that they allow:

- actions by and against outsiders in the firm name; 'Snooks, Twitchett & Co' can sue or be sued in that name;
- enforcement of judgments and orders against the assets of the firm, as by taking and selling those assets to pay the judgment creditor;
- HMRC to make an assessment to taxation on the firm as such in respect of the profits (see further, Chapter 4 ○).

A judgment against the firm can also be enforced in the same way against the private property of any partner if the assets of the firm are not enough.

So, although in legal theory a partnership firm is not a *persona* at law, for some practical purposes, e.g. contracting, suing and being sued, and taxation, the firm is regarded as a sort of independent entity.

Choice of name

Restrictions on the name chosen for the firm are set out below.

Passing off at common law

As far as the common law is concerned, partners, say A and B, can trade in any name that suits them so long as the name does not suggest that their business is the same as that of a competitor. It must not deceive or confuse the customers of some other person or persons, say, C and D.

If it does, the court will, if asked, give an injunction and/or damages against A and B to protect the business of C and D.

However, people can carry on business in their **own names**, even if there is some confusion with another person's business, unless it is, for example, part of a scheme deliberately to deceive the public as the following case shows.

Croft v Day (1843)

A firm called Day & Martin were well-known makers of boot polish. The original Mr Day and Mr Martin had been dead for some time but Mr Croft had bought the business and carried it on in the 'Day & Martin' name. A real Mr Day and a real Mr Martin went into the manufacture of boot polish and adopted the Day & Martin name for the fraudulent purpose of representing to the public that they were the old and widely known firm of that name. Mr Croft went to court and was given an injunction to stop the real Mr Day and the real Mr Martin from trading in their own names in the circumstances of this case.

However, it must be borne in mind that despite the fact that the law will allow a firm to trade in the names of the partners, this law is exceptional and a passing-off action against an 'own-name' firm may well succeed where there is likely to be public confusion affecting the goodwill of the existing firm. It is not necessary for the claimants to prove a deliberate scheme of deceit (see *Asprey & Garrard Ltd* v *WRA (Guns) Ltd* (2001) at p 103).

Business names and company legislation

Under the Companies Act 2006 the names of all the members of a partnership and their addresses in Great Britain where documents can be served must be stated in a notice which must be prominently displayed so that it can be easily read at all the firm's business premises. The names must also be stated in readable form on all business letters and documents. However, this requirement is relaxed in the case of a firm which has more than 20 partners. If there are more than 20 partners, the firm may choose not to list the names of the partners on the relevant documents but have instead a statement on the business letters and documents of the firm's principal place of business with an indication that a list of partners' names can be obtained and inspected there. If this choice is made, no partner's name shall appear on the relevant documents except in the text of a letter or by way of signature. The Act also requires every partnership to provide to anyone with whom it is doing or discussing business a note of the partners' names and addresses on such information being asked for by that person.

In some cases official approval is required for the use of certain partnership names. For example, the use of the word 'Royal' in a firm's name requires the approval of the Home Office. These matters were more fully considered in Chapter 4 ●.

Under the Companies Act 2006 the use of the descriptions 'Company' or 'and Company' are allowed for partnerships even though they suggest that they are companies. However, the Companies Act 2006 makes it an offence to use a firm name which ends with the expression 'Public Limited Company' or 'plc' or 'Limited' or 'Ltd' for associations such as partnerships, whether unlimited partnerships, limited partnerships or LLPs. Failure to comply with this rule results in liability to a fine for every day it goes on.

The relationship between partners and outsiders

The power of a partner, including a salaried partner, to make himself and his other partners liable for transactions which he enters into **on behalf of the firm** (not on his own behalf) is based on the law of agency. Each partner is the agent of his co-partners.

Section 5 of the Partnership Act 1890 makes this clear. It says that every partner is the agent of the firm and of his co-partners for the purpose of the business of the partnership.

Partners' powers

A partner's authority to enter into transactions on behalf of the firm and his co-partners may be set out under the following headings.

Actual authority

If a partner is asked by his co-partners to buy a new van for the firm's use and makes a contract to purchase one, the firm is bound. Section 6 of the 1890 Act deals with authorised acts and says that the firm will be liable for the authorised acts of partners and also of employees of the firm.

Actual authority inferred

It may be possible in some circumstances to infer the consent of the other partners to a transaction entered

into by only some of them. If so, the firm will be bound by it as the following case shows.

Bank of Scotland v Henry Butcher & Co (2003)

In this case the Court of Appeal had to consider whether a guarantee given to the bank by four out of 13 partners bound the firm. It was held that it did. The other partners had not passed a resolution authorising the four to make the guarantee of overdraft arrangements but they were informed that it was being made and in the absence of an objection it was reasonable to infer that they consented to it. Furthermore, the four partners signed the guarantee for and on behalf of the firm, thus indicating that they were agents of the firm and were not giving the guarantee in a personal capacity. In addition, the bank had no intention of taking a guarantee from them but only from the firm.

Comment. The guarantee was of a bank overdraft granted to another organisation with which the defendant firm was involved in a joint business venture. It is also worth noting that the partnership agreement stated in clause 14(c) that 'no partner shall without the consent of the other partners . . . give any guarantee on behalf of the partnership'. However, the Court of Appeal affirmed the ruling of the High Court that it was reasonable in the circumstances for the bank to infer that the partners entering into the guarantee did so with the consent of all the partners.

Apparent or 'ostensible' authority

If a partner enters into a transaction on behalf of the firm without authority, the person he deals with may, if he does not know of the lack of authority, hold the firm bound under the provisions of s 5 of the Partnership Act 1890 which gives partners some apparent authority.

However, s 5 says that **the transaction must be connected with the business**. If there is a dispute about this, the court will decide what can be said to be 'connected', regardless of what the partnership agreement may say.

Mercantile Credit Co Ltd v Garrod (1962)

Mr Parkin and Mr Garrod had entered into an agreement as partners for the letting of garages and the carrying out of motor repairs, but the agreement expressly excluded the buying and selling of cars. Parkin, without Garrod's knowledge, sold a car to Mercantile for the sum of £700 but the owner of the car had not consented to the sale. The finance company did not, therefore, become the owner of the car and wanted its money back. The court held that the firm was liable and that Mr Garrod was liable as a partner to repay what the firm owed to Mercantile. The judge dismissed the argument that the transaction did not bind the firm because the agreement excluded the buying and selling of cars. He looked at the matter instead from 'what was apparent to the outside world in general'. Parkin was doing an act of a like kind to the business carried on by persons trading as a garage.

Comment. The point of the case is that although the buying and selling of cars was expressly forbidden by the partnership agreement, the firm was bound. This is a correct application of s 8, which provides that internal restrictions on the authority of partners will have effect only if the outsider deals with a partner, but with actual notice of the restrictions. In this case Mercantile had no such knowledge of the restrictions.

Also the transaction must be carried out **in the usual way of business**. In other words, it must be a **normal** transaction for the business.

An example can be seen in *Goldberg* v *Jenkins* (1889) where a partner borrowed money on behalf of the firm at 60 per cent interest per annum when money could be borrowed at between 6 per cent and 10 per cent per annum. He had no actual authority to enter into such a transaction and the court held that the firm was not bound to accept the loan. The firm did borrow money but it was not usual or normal to borrow at that high rate.

Finally, s 5 says that **the outsider must know or believe that he is dealing with a partner in the firm**. Because of the requirements of the Companies Act 2006 as regards the display of the names of the owners of the firm on various documents and in various places which we have already considered, a **dormant partner** is now more likely to be known as a partner to an outsider. So if a dormant partner makes an unauthorised contract in the ordinary course of business in the usual or normal way, the outsider should now be able to say that he knew or believed the dormant partner to be a partner. If so, a dormant partner can enter into an unauthorised transaction which will bind the firm under s 5. If the outsider does not know the dormant partner is a member of the firm, as where the 2006 Act is not being complied with, then

the firm will not be bound. The dormant partner would be liable to compensate the outsider for any loss following upon his failure to get a contract with the firm.

Examples of apparent authority as laid down by case law

Section 5 does not say what acts are 'in the usual course of business'. However, the courts have, over the years, and sometimes in cases heard before the 1890 Act was passed codifying the law, decided that there are a number of definite areas in which a partner has apparent authority. These are set out below.

1 **All partners in all businesses.** Here there is apparent authority to sell the goods (but not the land) of the firm, and to buy goods (but not land) on behalf of the firm; to receive money in payment of debts due to the firm and give valid receipts. So if A pays a debt due to the firm to B, a partner, who gives A a receipt and then fails to put the money into the firm's funds, A is nevertheless discharged from payment of the debt. There is also a power to pay debts owed by the firm including a power to draw cheques for this purpose. Partners can also employ workers, but once they are set on they are employees of **all** the partners so that one partner cannot discharge an employee without the consent of the others. Partners also have an insurable interest in the firm's property and can insure it. They may also employ a solicitor to defend the firm if an action is brought against it. The authority of an individual partner to employ a solicitor to bring an action on behalf of the firm seems to be restricted to actions to recover debts owing to the firm.

2 **All partners in trading partnerships.** Partners in trading firms have powers **which are additional** to those set out in 1 above. Thus partners in a firm of grocers have more powers than partners in a professional practice of, e.g., law or accountancy. There does not seem to be any good reason for this, but it has been confirmed by many cases in court and cannot be ignored.

In *Wheatley* v *Smithers* (1906) the judge said in regard to what was meant by the word 'trader': 'One important element in any definition of the term would be that trading implies buying or selling.' This was applied in *Higgins* v *Beauchamp* (1914) where it was decided that a partner in a business running a cinema had no implied power to borrow on behalf of the firm. The partnership agreement did not give power to borrow and, because the firm did not trade in the *Wheatley* v *Smithers* sense, there was no implied power to borrow. If a firm is engaged in trade, the main additional implied powers of the partners are:

■ to borrow money on the credit of the firm even beyond any limit agreed on by the partners unless this limit is known to the lender. Borrowing includes overdrawing a bank account;

■ to secure the loan, which means giving the lender a right to sell property belonging to the firm if the loan is not repaid.

Situations of no apparent authority

No partner, whether in a trading firm or not, has apparent authority in the following situations:

1 He cannot make the firm liable on a deed. He needs the authority of the other partners. This authority must be given by deed. In English law an agent who is to make contracts by deed must be appointed as an agent by a written document which states that it is a deed.

2 He cannot give a guarantee, e.g. of another person's debt, on which the firm will be liable unless there is a situation of inferred actual authority where the consent of the other partners is inferred or presumed as in *Bank of Scotland* v *Henry Butcher & Co* (2003) (see p 125).

3 He cannot accept payment of a debt at a discount by, e.g., accepting 75p instead of £1, nor can he take something for the debt which is not money. He cannot, therefore, take shares in a company in payment of a debt owed to the firm.

4 He cannot bind the firm by agreeing to go to arbitration with a dispute. Going to arbitration with a dispute and having it heard by, say, an engineer, if the dispute relates, for example, to the quality of engineering work done under a contract is a sort of compromise of the right to go first to a court of law and have the case heard by a judge. A partner cannot compromise the legal rights of the firm.

5 As we have seen, a partner has no apparent authority to convey or enter into a contract for the sale of partnership land.

A partner's liability for debt and breach of contract by the firm

If, because of actual or apparent authority, a partner (or for that matter another agent such as an employee)

makes the firm liable to pay a debt or carry out a contract, as where goods are ordered and the firm refuses to take delivery, the usual procedure will be to sue the firm in the firm name. If the court gives the claimant a judgment and the firm does not have sufficient assets to meet it, the partners are liable to pay it from their private assets. Under s 3 of the Civil Liability (Contribution) Act 1978 each partner is liable to pay the amount of the judgment in full. He will then have a right to what is called a contribution from his co-partners.

Before the 1978 Act contribution was equal. Thus, if A paid a partnership debt of £300, he could ask his partners, B and C, for a contribution of £100 each.

This rule of equal contribution was taken away by s 2 of the 1978 Act, which provides that the amount of any contribution which the court may give is to be what it thinks is 'just and equitable' so that it need not in all cases be equal, but most often will be.

The effect of the above rules is that a partner can be required to pay the firm's debts from his private assets. From this we can see that only if **all** the partners are unable to pay the firm's debts will the firm be truly insolvent (decided most recently in *Secretary of State for Trade and Industry* v *Forde* (1997)).

Under s 9 the estate of a deceased partner is also liable but **only** for the debts of the firm which were incurred while the deceased was a partner.

Torts

Under s 10 the firm is liable for the torts of partners which they commit in the ordinary course of business, but not where the partner acts outside the scope of the firm's usual activities.

Therefore, a partner in an accountancy practice who prepares the financial statements of a company negligently in the course of the firm's business will not only be liable to the client and possibly to others who he knows will rely on those statements, say, to invest in the company, but will also make his fellow partners liable.

This is not the case in a limited liability partnership under the Act of the same name passed in 2000. In such a case only the firm's assets and the private assets of the negligent partner are at risk. The Act of 2000 is further considered at the end of this chapter.

At common law the firm is also liable for the torts of its employees committed in the course of their employment. So if the firm's van driver injures a pedestrian by negligent driving, both he and the firm would be liable under the common law rule of vicarious liability.

The words of s 10 make it clear that there is no action by one partner against the firm's assets for injuries caused by torts in the course of business. Thus, in *Mair v Wood* (1948) fishermen operated a trawler in partnership. One partner was injured when he fell because another partner had failed to replace an engine hatch properly. The court held that the injured partner had no claim in negligence against the firm and its assets but only against the negligent partner in his personal capacity, a successful claim resulting in the payment of damages from the negligent partner's personal assets and not from those of the firm.

In a claim under s 10 the House of Lords has ruled that the firm and the other partners can be vicariously liable for the **fraud of a partner** (see *Dubai Aluminium Co Ltd v Salaam* (2003)). In that case a partner in a firm of solicitors was involved, while acting in the ordinary business of the firm, in the receipt of some £50 million for provision of consultancy services to Dubai that were in fact bogus. The House of Lords decided that the firm and the other partners, though personally blameless, were liable vicariously for the partner's fraud. It was perpetrated in the ordinary course of the business of the firm and closely connected with his authorised work for clients.

Misappropriation of property

Under s 11 the firm and partners are liable to make good loss incurred if a partner misapplies money or property received from a third person, such as a client. However, the partner receiving the money or property must have been acting within the scope of his or her actual or apparent authority, i.e. held out as being authorised to receive money or property at the time of receipt. Additionally, the firm is liable for the misapplication of the money or property of third persons *which is already in its possession*.

Liability of incoming and outgoing partners

Now we shall deal with the period during which the partner is liable for the firm's debts, or, to put it in another way, from what date do his co-partners become his agents and when does that agency come to an end?

There are four things to look at as set out below.

1 Admission as a partner. Under s 17 a person does not simply by becoming a partner take on liability for debts or torts incurred by the firm before he joined it. He can if he wishes take on this liability by a process called novation (see below).

The position of incoming partners, or joiners as they are sometimes called, was affirmed by the High Court in *HF Pension Scheme Trustees Ltd v Ellison* (1999) where it was decided that since the relationship of partners was based on agency, an incoming partner could not be liable as a principal in terms of his personal capacity for the negligence of a co-partner that took place before he joined the firm, because the negligent acts could not have been done on his behalf.

2 Retirement as a partner. Also under s 17 a person does not, by retiring, cease to be liable for the debts and obligations of the firm incurred before he retired. The law is not likely to allow a partner to avoid his liabilities simply by retiring from the firm.

A retiring partner is not liable for future debts or liabilities unless, as we have seen, he is held out under s 14 or under s 36 because he has not given proper notice of his retirement (see below).

The date on which the contract was made or order given decides the matter of liability. So in a contract for the sale of goods, A, a retired partner, will be liable if the contract or order was made or given when he was a partner, even if the goods were delivered after he had retired.

3 Novation and indemnity. Under s 17 a retiring partner may be discharged from liabilities incurred before retirement if an agreement to that effect, called a **novation**, is made with the following people as parties to it:

- the partners who are to continue the business;
- the creditor concerned; and
- the retiring partner.

The agreement releases the retiring partner from his liabilities and accepts in his place the liability of the continuing partners, either alone or with the addition of any new partners.

The use of a novation is rare except perhaps in the case of banks which may well release an outgoing partner if they have enough cover from the other partners including any new partner in terms of a guarantee of the firm's indebtedness.

Creditors are not forced to accept or take part in novation and may continue to regard the retiring partner as liable for debts incurred while he was a partner. If this is so, the retiring partner should get an indemnity from the continuing partners. This will not release him from liability to the creditors but if he does have to pay a pre-retirement debt, he can recover what he has paid in full under the indemnity, and not just a contribution which is all he could recover without the indemnity.

The indemnity approach is much more common than the novation approach. It is in any case impractical to use a novation where there are a considerable number of creditors. It would be a lengthy and difficult process to get, say, 100 trade creditors to join in a novation. In fact, the indemnity is often found in the partnership agreement which may have a clause such as 'In the event of retirement the remaining partners shall take over the liabilities of the firm'.

4 Notifying retirement. The law requires a retiring partner to notify his retirement. The reason for this is that people who deal with the firm are entitled, in all fairness, to assume when they do business with it that all the partners are the same unless there has been notice of a change.

The rules are set out in s 36 which states, in effect, that if X, who was a partner in Y & Co, leaves the firm and the firm contracts with Z who knew that X was a member of the firm but does not know that he has left, X will be liable to Z (along with other partners of course) if the firm does not meet its obligations. To avoid this liability there must have been adequate notice of X's retirement.

In order to indicate what adequate notice is, the law divides creditors into three classes as follows:

1 Creditors who have previously dealt with the firm and who knew X was a partner. In this case it is necessary to show that the creditor received actual notice of the retirement. This may be by a letter from the firm, or by receiving a letter from the firm on which X's name is deleted, or by seeing the notice of retirement in *The London Gazette* (see below), **but only if he actually reads the *Gazette*.**

2 Creditors who have not had previous dealings with the firm but who knew or believed X to be a partner before he retired. As far as these people go, X will not be liable for post-retirement debts:

■ if they had for some reason actual knowledge of X's retirement; or

■ X's retirement was published in *The London Gazette*, **whether it was seen or not.**

The London Gazette is published daily by the Stationery Office and contains all sorts of public announcements: for example, bankruptcies, company liquidations and partnership dissolutions.

3 Creditors who have not had previous dealings with the firm and do not know that X was ever a partner. These people cannot hold X liable for post-retirement debts even if no notice has been received by them and even though no notice has been put in the *Gazette*. X could only be liable to these people if he was knowingly held out as a partner under s 14.

In *Tower Cabinet Co Ltd* v *Ingram* (1949), which was dealt with earlier in this chapter (see p 122 ○), no notice of Mr Ingram's retirement was put in the *Gazette*, but he was not liable to Tower Cabinet under s 36 because they did not know or believe him to be a partner prior to his retirement. He was not liable either under s 14 (holding out) for reasons already given.

Section 36 states that the estate of a deceased or bankrupt partner is not liable for debts incurred after death or bankruptcy, as the case may be, even if no advertisement or notice of any kind has been given.

Just as a written partnership agreement is to be recommended at the beginning of the relationship, so it is very sensible to address the matters that arise when a partner leaves by retirement and record them in a binding deed of retirement.

Relationship of partners within the partnership

We shall now deal with the relation of partners to one another. It is governed by ss 19–31 of the 1890 Act, the provisions of which are set out below.

The ability to change the partnership agreement

Section 19 states that partners can change the business of the firm but because of the provisions of s 24 **all** the partners must be in agreement about this.

Partners can also change the provisions of the 1890 Act which the Act puts into partnership agreements unless the partners have dealt with the matter in the agreement themselves. For example, the Act provides in s 24 that profits and losses are to be shared equally but the partners may provide for a different share, e.g. one-third/two-thirds, in their agreement.

The provisions of the Act which deal with the relationship of the partners and outsiders cannot be changed in this way. Section 8 says that internal restrictions on the authority of partners, for example in the partnership agreement, have no effect on an outsider unless he has **actual** notice of the restriction.

This was illustrated by the case of ***Mercantile Credit Co Ltd v Garrod*** (1962) where the partnership agreement said that there was to be no buying or selling of cars. This did not prevent the sale of a car to Mercantile by a partner being good, since Mercantile had no knowledge of the restriction.

A written partnership agreement may be varied by attaching a written and signed indorsement to the original agreement. However, even where the original agreement is written (and obviously if it is oral) the partners may, either orally or by the way they deal with one another, vary the agreement. This is not surprising since the original agreement of partners does not have to be in writing.

The case which follows is an example of partners agreeing to one thing but sliding into a different way of going on. The books of the firm were kept and the accounts prepared from them in a way which was different from the original agreement.

Pilling v Pilling (1887)

A father took his two sons into partnership with him. The partnership agreement provided that the assets of the business were to remain the father's and that he and his sons should share profits and losses in thirds. Each son was to have, in addition to a one-third share of the profits, £150 a year out of the father's share of profit, and repairs and expenses were to be paid out of profits. It was also agreed that the father only should have 4 per cent on his capital per annum and that the depreciation of the mill and machinery, i.e. the major assets, was to be deducted before the profit was calculated.

The partnership lasted for 10 years and no depreciation was charged on the mill and machinery. The £150 per annum was paid to the sons but it was charged against the profits of the business and not against the father's share. Each partner was credited with interest

---

on capital, not merely the father, but, as it happens, the profit was divided into thirds. Later on the court was asked to decide whether the assets of the business still belonged to the father or whether they belonged to the firm as partnership property. The court decided that the way in which the partners had dealt with each other was evidence of a new agreement. The assets were therefore partnership property, even though the articles had said that they were to continue to belong to the father.

Comment. The major change here was to allow each partner interest on capital although only the father brought any in. From this the court presumed that the father's capital had become partnership property and had not remained his personal property, as was the original intention in the agreement.

Partnership property

Whether property becomes partnership property or remains in the separate ownership of a particular partner depends upon the intention of the partners. Ideally this intention should be made absolutely clear in the partnership agreement if there is one. If property is treated as partnership property, it becomes an asset of the firm and is transferred to all the partners as co-owners.

Under ss 20 and 21 of the 1890 Act, and in the absence of an express agreement to the contrary, property will be regarded as partnership property if:

- it is purchased with partnership money, as by a cheque drawn on the firm's account;
- it is brought into the firm by a partner who has the value of it credited to his capital account, which clearly indicates the intention to bring it in;
- it is treated as an essential part of the firm's property by the partners; but the mere fact that the property is used in the business is not enough to transfer that property to the firm. This statement is supported by the following case.

Miles v Clarke (1953)

Mr Clarke wished to start a photography business and he took a lease of premises for the purpose. He was not a skilled photographer and employed other people to do the photography work. The business made a loss but after some negotiations Mr Miles, who was a successful freelance photographer, decided to join in with Mr Clarke. Miles brought in his customers and there were a large number of these. The agreement made between Miles and Clarke provided that the profits were to be shared equally and that Miles was to draw £153 per month on account of his profits. The business did well but Miles and Clarke quarrelled and it had to be wound up. In this action the court was asked to decide the ownership of the assets and Miles was claiming a share in all the assets of the business. The court decided that there was no agreement except as to the way profits were to be divided and so the stock in trade of the firm and other consumable items, such as films, must be considered as part of the partnership assets, even though they were brought in by Clarke. However, the lease and other plant and equipment should be treated as belonging to the partner who brought them in – that was Clarke. The personal goodwill, i.e. customers, belonged to the person who brought them in, so Miles retained the value of his customers and Clarke retained the value of his.

In normal circumstances there is no doubt about the ownership at least of the major assets of the firm. For example, a lease of premises from which to conduct business would be bought with the firm's money and transferred into the names of some or all of the partners to hold as trustees for themselves and others as partners. The device of the trust is required because, as we know, an ordinary partnership is not a *persona* at law. The problems outlined above arise when, say, the lease is used as business premises but is held in the name of one partner who has allowed its use within the firm. Does he hold it on an implied trust for himself and the others or not? That is the question which a court may have to decide.

The commercial importance of identifying partnership property

The ability to identify partnership property is important in the business world:

1 To the partners themselves, because any increase in value of partnership property belongs to the firm (i.e. all the partners), but if the property belongs to only one partner the increased value belongs to him alone. Also, a decrease in value is suffered by the firm if it is partnership property but if it belongs to only one partner all the loss is his.

2 To the creditors of the firm and the creditors of the partners individually, since this affects what property is available to pay their debts if the business fails. If a firm goes out of business and all the partners are also insolvent, then the firm's creditors can have the firm's assets sold to pay their debts before the private creditors of the partners have access to those assets. Also, private creditors have first right to sell private assets before the firm's creditors have access to them.

3 Because dealings with partnership property must be only for partnership purposes in accordance with the partnership agreement. If the property is owned personally by a partner, he can do what he likes with it unless the firm has some contractual rights over it, as where the firm is renting it from the partner. Obviously, the contract must be complied with or an action for damages would be available to the firm against the partner.

Implied financial terms

These are set out below.

Profits and losses

Section 24 says that unless there is some other agreement between the partners, all the partners are to share equally in the capital and profits of the business and must contribute equally towards losses of capital or otherwise.

This is regardless of capital contributed. If those who have contributed more capital are to get more of the capital and profit, the partnership agreement must say so.

Interest on capital

Section 24 also says that, unless the partners agree, no partner is to get interest on the capital he puts into the firm. In practice, where partners do not make equal contributions of capital it is often agreed that those who contributed more are to get interest on capital at an agreed rate per annum. This interest is taken away from profits before they are distributed to the partners.

Interest on advances (loans)

If a partner helps to finance the firm by making it a loan on top of contributing capital, then s 24 provides that he is entitled to 5 per cent per annum on the advance (or loan) from the date when it was made. There is no rule that an advance by a partner to the firm carries any higher interest. This has to be specially provided for.

Indemnity

Section 24 also requires the firm to indemnify every partner who makes payments from his own funds in the ordinary conduct of the business. Thus, if while a partner is negotiating an insurance for the firm he is told by the broker that a premium on an existing policy is due that day and he pays it with his own private cheque, the firm must pay him back.

Implied management powers

Management powers are normally written out in the partnership agreement. If not, the following rules apply:

1 Under s 24(5) every partner may take part in the management of the business. This is not surprising because a partnership is defined as the carrying on of business 'in common'. The right is also a fair one because a partner may find himself saddled with the debts of a firm, and, if this is so, he should at least have the chance of managing it.

Any unjustified exclusion of a partner from the management of the firm will almost certainly enable him to petition to dissolve the firm on the just and equitable ground in s 35.

This right to manage concept has also been applied to small companies which are essentially partnerships in all but legal form. Cases illustrating this, such as *Ebrahimi* v *Westbourne Galleries* (1972) will be looked at in Chapter 6 .

2 Section 24(6) says that a partner is not entitled to a salary. Partners share profits, but if the firm has some partners who are more active in the business than others it is usual for the partnership agreement to provide for a salary for the active partners which is paid in addition to a share of profit. A further exception is, as we have seen, the salaried partner where there is an entitlement to salary to the exclusion of any share of profits.

Apart from that, a partner who has had to work harder than usual because his fellow partner has failed to work as he should in the business is not entitled to an extra amount from the firm's assets. In the absence of agreement, the court will not make an award of remuneration while the firm is a going concern. The partner who is failing to work properly in the business

is, however, in breach of a term which requires him to do so and this is a ground for the dissolution of the firm. The term may be found stated expressly in the partnership agreement but will in any case be implied.

3 Under s 24(7) and (8) no new partners can be brought in and no change may be made in the business of the firm unless all the partners consent. It should be noted, however, that a retiring partner's consent is not required.

This is a fair provision. New partners ought not to be thrust upon the old partners by a majority vote. Mutual confidence is essential.

As regards what are called 'ordinary matters', these are to be settled by a majority of the partners regardless of capital contributed, provided the decisions are made in good faith and after proper consultation with all of the partners. The Act makes no attempt to define 'ordinary matters'. There is no case law to help us. Much will depend upon the circumstances of the case.

4 Under s 24(9) every partner is entitled to access to, and may also inspect and copy, the firm's books. These books must be kept at the place where the business is run or, if there is more than one place, at the main place of business.

The court will make an order (an injunction) preventing a partner from exercising the above rights if he is, e.g., taking the names of customers from the books to try to get them to use his own separate business instead of that of the firm.

Inspection may be through an agent (*Bevan* v *Webb* (1901)), so that a partner who was not able himself to assess financial information could employ an accountant to inspect the books.

5 Although the 1890 Act says nothing about it, it is implied by law that every partner shall attend at, and work in, the business. If he does not, the other partners have a ground to dissolve the firm. However, there is normally no claim for damages for breach of contract, this being a common law remedy, and partnership, being based on equity, has no remedy of damages for breach of duty between partners.

Expulsion of a partner

Section 25 says that no majority of partners can expel any other partner unless a power to do so appears in the partnership agreement.

If an expulsion is challenged in the courts, the judge will be most concerned to see that a majority expulsion clause has not been abused.

It must be shown:

1 That the complaint which is said to allow expulsion is covered by the expulsion clause. For example, in *Snow v Milford* (1868) the court decided that the 'adultery of a banker all over Exeter' was not a ground for his expulsion because it was not within the wording of the expulsion clause. This dealt only with financial frauds which would discredit a banking business.

2 That the partner expelled was told what he had done wrong and given a chance to explain. An illustration is to be found in *Barnes v Youngs* (1898) where a partner who was living with a woman to whom he was not married continued to do so after becoming a partner. There was nothing to show that this was damaging to the firm's business. Even so, he was expelled by his fellow partners who refused to tell him why they were doing so. The court held that his expulsion was unlawful and ineffective.

3 That those who exercised the power of expulsion did so in all good faith. For example, in *Blisset v Daniel* (1853) a partner was expelled. He had done nothing wrong to hurt the firm, but the partnership agreement said that a majority of the partners could buy out another. The motive of the other partners was just to get a bigger share of the property and profits. The court said that the expulsion was not effective. It was done in bad faith.

However, if 1 to 3 above are satisfied, the court will regard the expulsion as valid. For example, in *Greenaway v Greenaway* (1940), the partnership agreement provided for expulsion in the event of conduct contrary to the good faith required of partners or prejudicial to their general interest. After several years of quarrelling, one partner assaulted another. The offender was given notice of expulsion. The court later said that although quarrelling by itself was not enough, the assault was inexcusable. Another reason for the expulsion was the fact that the offending partner had made disapproving remarks about a fellow partner to the firm's employees. This was not in line with the good faith rule. The expulsion was valid.

Of course, the expelled partner is entitled to his share of the firm's assets, as he would be if he retired.

However, provision is often made to pay him out over a period of time and not immediately so that he cannot demand his total share of the assets as soon as he is expelled.

Relationship of utmost good faith

It is a basic principle of partnership law that each partner must treat his co-partners with utmost fairness and good faith. An example of bad faith in this context is, as we have seen, *Blisset v Daniel* (1853), above.

The principle of utmost good faith is not set out as a general proposition in the 1890 Act. The Act does, however, set out certain areas to which the good faith principle is applied. They are as follows:

1 The duty to account. Section 28 requires every partner to give true accounts and full information regarding all things affecting the firm to any partner.

This is a **positive duty** to disclose facts. It is not merely a **negative duty** not to misrepresent facts.

As the following case shows, silence can amount to misrepresentation as between partner and partner.

Law v Law (1905)

Two brothers, William Law and James Law, were partners in a woollen manufacturers' business in Halifax. William lived in London and did not take a very active part in the business and James offered to buy William's share for £10,000. After the sale William discovered that certain partnership assets, that is money lent on mortgage, had not been disclosed to him by James. William brought an action against James for misrepresentation. The court decided that there was a duty of disclosure in this sort of case and the action was settled by the payment of £3,550 to William, which he accepted in discharge of all claims between him and his brother.

So far as s 28 is concerned, the 1890 Act makes clear that the duty arises once the parties are in fact partners but at **common law** the duty of disclosure arises also at the negotiation or pre-contract stage of the arrangements. This has never been made clear in partnership law but the following decision states quite clearly that the duties of disclosure are also pre-contractual.

Conlon v Simms (2006)

The case involved a partnership of City solicitors, Bower Cotton. Paul Simms, a senior partner, had been subject to investigation by the Office for the Supervision of Solicitors for alleged dishonesty involving his clients' bogus investments and money laundering schemes.

Mr Simms began negotiating a new partnership agreement with the claimant, Michael Conlon, after a number of partners left Bower Cotton. Mr Conlon knew that there was an investigation but he was assured by Mr Simms that he had not been dishonest. However, later the Solicitors Disciplinary Tribunal decided that he had been dishonest and he was struck off.

The claimant asked for damages on the basis that Mr Simms owed him a duty of good faith at common law and that he had breached that duty by failing to disclose matters which might affect his entitlement to practise. Mr Conlon said that he would not have entered into the partnership agreement if he had known about Mr Simms' dishonesty.

Mr Simms contended that he did not have a duty of good faith or disclosure before he and Mr Conlon became partners and, further, since he knew of the investigation there was nothing more to disclose.

The High Court did not accept these contentions. The duty of good faith and disclosure extended beyond actual partners to prospective partners. There was support for this view in *Bell v Lever Bros* (1932), where Lord Atkin had stated in his judgment that such a duty existed towards an intending partner. This did not settle matters at the time because the case did not concern a partnership but was dealing with the fiduciary duty of directors. The fact that Mr Conlon knew of the investigation was irrelevant. He did not know of its outcome. In addition, while mere nondisclosure leads only to the contract being avoided, where the failure to disclose is fraudulent, i.e. deliberate and dishonest or reckless, there is an action in deceit for which damages are also available as a remedy.

Comment. Lindley on Partnership, the standard practitioners' work, states that the duty of disclosure is pre-contractual also. The judge noted this but said that it did not settle the matter because the decisions quoted in *Lindley* did not support the conclusion. This decision does clear up the matter of pre-contractual disclosure.

Under s 29 each partner must also account to the firm for any benefit he has had without the consent of the other partners from any transaction concerning the firm or from any use by him of the partnership name or customer connection. An illustration is to be found in the following case.

Bentley v Craven (1853)

Mr Bentley carried on business in partnership with the defendants, Messrs Craven, Prest and Younge, as sugar refiners at Southampton. Craven was the firm's buyer and because of this he was able to buy sugar at a great advantage as to price. He bought supplies of sugar cheaply and sold it to the firm at the market price. The other partners did not realise that he was selling on his own account and Bentley, when he found out, brought this action, claiming for the firm a profit of some £853 made by Craven. The court decided that the firm was entitled to it.

Comment. Those who wish to make comparisons with other fiduciaries will note that a partner, like a trustee, may not make a private gain out of his membership of the firm. There is also a comparison with directors' secret profits and benefits, which will be dealt with in Chapter 6 ⬤.

2 Duty not to compete with the firm. Section 30 provides that if a partner without the consent of his co-partners carries on any business of the same kind as his firm so as to compete with it, he must account for and pay over to the firm all the profits he has made from that competing business.

Section 30 is in fact no more than an extension of the duty to account because a partner cannot be prevented from competing by the use of s 30. The section actually allows him to compete but requires him to hand over all the profits of the competing business.

A particular partnership agreement may expressly provide that there shall be no competing business. If this is so, the other partners can get an injunction from the court to stop the competing business from being carried on.

Dissolution

A partnership is usually dissolved without the help of the court, though sometimes the court is brought in.

Non-judicial dissolution

Any of the following events will normally bring about a dissolution of a partnership.

1 The ending of the period for which the partnership was to exist. Section 32(a) states that a partnership for a fixed term is dissolved when the term expires. A partnership for the joint lives of A, B and C ends on the death of A or B or C.

2 The achievement of the purpose for which the partnership was formed. By reason of s 32(b) a partnership for a single undertaking is dissolved at the end of it. In *Winsor* v *Schroeder* (1979), S and W put up equal amounts of cash to buy a house, improve it, and then sell it at a profit which was to be divided equally. The court decided that they were partners under s 32(b) and that the partnership would end when the land was sold and the profit, if any, divided.

If in partnerships of the types set out in 1 and 2 above, the firm continues in business after the period has expired, without any settlement of their affairs by the partners, an agreement not to dissolve will be implied. Unless there is a new agreement to cover the continuing partnership, it is a partnership at will. Section 27 applies to it so that the rights and duties of the partners are the same as before the original partnership ended. However, since it has now become a partnership at will, any partner can give notice to end it.

3 By the giving of notice. Under s 32(c) a partnership which is not entered into for a period of time or for a particular purpose can be dissolved by notice given by **any partner**, but not a limited partner.

The notice must be in writing if the partnership agreement is in the form of a deed (s 26(2)). If not, oral notice will do.

The notice takes effect when all the partners know of it or from any later date which the person giving the notice states as the date of dissolution (s 32(c)). No particular period of notice is required. Withdrawal of the notice requires the consent of all the partners (*Jones* v *Lloyd* (1874)), otherwise the dissolution goes ahead and the court will, if asked by a partner, order the other partners to wind up the firm with him. The court said in *Peyton* v *Mindham* (1971) that it could and would declare a dissolution notice to be of no effect if it was given in bad faith as where A and B dissolve a partnership with C by notice in order to exclude C from valuable future contracts.

Dissolution by notice depends on what the partnership agreement says. If, as in *Moss* v *Elphick* (1910), the partnership agreement says that dissolution is only to be by mutual consent of the partners, s 32(c) does not apply.

4 Death of a partner. Under s 33(1) the death of a partner (but not a limited partner) dissolves the firm. The share of the partner who has died goes to his personal representatives who are usually appointed by his will. They have the rights of a partner in a dissolution. Partnership agreements usually provide that the firm shall continue after the death of a partner so that the dissolution is only a technical one. A deceased partner's share is paid out to his personal representatives, although partnership agreements do sometimes provide for repayment of capital by instalments, or by annuities, e.g. to a spouse or other dependant. Of course, there is bound to be a true dissolution of a two-partner firm when one partner dies since if the other carries on business, it is as a sole trader.

5 Bankruptcy of a partner. By reason of s 33(1) the bankruptcy of a partner (not a limited partner) dissolves the firm. The partnership agreement usually provides that the business shall continue under the non-bankrupt partners, which means that the dissolution is again only a technical one, and the bankrupt partner's share is paid out to his trustee in bankruptcy. The agreement to continue the business must be made before the partner becomes bankrupt (*Whitmore* v *Mason* (1861)).

6 Illegality. Under s 34 a partnership is in every case dissolved by illegality. There can be no contracting-out in the partnership agreement.

There are two types of illegality:

(a) *Where the business is unlawful*; for example, where the objects are unlawful because, as in *Stevenson & Sons Ltd* v *AG für Cartonnagen Industrie* (1918) the English company, Stevenson, was in partnership with a German company as a sole agent to sell the German company's goods. This would obviously involve day-to-day trading with an enemy in wartime and the partnership was therefore dissolved on the grounds of illegality. The classic case is *Everet* v *Williams* (1725). This was a claim by one highwayman against another to recover his share of profits derived from a partnership covering activities as a highwayman. The claim was dismissed because the partnership was illegal, being to commit crime, and the 'partners' were sentenced to be hanged!

(b) *Where the partners cannot legally form a partnership to carry on what is otherwise a legal business,* as in **Hudgell, Yeates & Co v Watson** (1978) where a firm of solicitors was regarded as dissolved when one partner had made himself unqualified to practise as a solicitor by mistakenly failing to renew his annual practising certificate.

Judicial dissolution

Dissolution by the court (normally the Chancery Division of the High Court) is necessary if there is a partnership for a fixed time or purpose and a partner wants to dissolve a firm before the time has expired or the purpose has been achieved and there is nothing in the partnership agreement which allows this to be done.

There must be grounds for dissolution. These are set out below.

1 Partner's mental incapability. This a ground under the Mental Capacity Act 2005. The petition for dissolution is in this case heard by the Court of Protection which sits to look after the property of people who lack mental capacity. The partner concerned must be incapable, because of mental incapacity, of managing his property and affairs.

A petition may be presented on behalf of the partner who is incapacitated or by any of the other partners.

2 Partner's physical incapacity. This is a ground under s 35(b). The incapacity must be permanent. In **Whitwell v Arthur** (1865) a partner was paralysed for some months. He had recovered when the court heard the petition and it would not grant a dissolution.

Partnership agreements often contain express clauses which allow dissolution after a stated period of incapacity. In **Peyton v Mindham** (1971) a clause allowing a fixed-term partnership to be dissolved after nine months' incapacity was enforced. (See the model partnership deed, clause 16(g) on p 146.)

Section 35(b) states that the incapacitated partner cannot petition. It is up to his co-partners to do so, otherwise he continues as a partner.

3 Conduct prejudicial to the business. Section 35(c) provides for this. The conduct may relate to the business, as in **Essell v Hayward** (1860), where a solicitor/partner misappropriated £8,000 of trust money in the course of his duties as a partner. This was a ground for

dissolving a partnership for a fixed term, i.e. the joint lives of the partners.

It may, of course, be outside conduct. This will usually justify a dissolution if it results in a criminal conviction for fraud or dishonesty.

Moral misconduct is not enough unless, in the view of the court, it is likely to affect the business. In **Snow v Milford** (1868) where the matter of dissolution was also considered, as well as the matter of expulsion, 'massive adultery all over Exeter' was not regarded by the court as sufficient grounds for dissolution under s 35(c). There was no evidence that the adulterous conduct had affected the business of the bank.

Section 35(c) forbids a petition by the partner in default.

4 Wilful or persistent breach of the agreement or conduct affecting the relationship. This is covered by s 35(d). It includes, for example, refusal to meet on business or keep accounts, continued quarrelling and very serious internal disagreements. However, as the court said in **Loscombe v Russell** (1830), the conduct must be 'serious'. Thus, occasional rudeness or bad temper would not suffice.

'Wilful' means a serious breach inflicting damage on the firm. Less serious breaches are enough if 'persistent'. In **Cheesman v Price** (1865) a partner failed 17 times to enter small amounts of money he had received in the firm's books. The court ordered dissolution. The essential trust between the partners had gone.

Again, s 35(d) forbids a petition by the partner in default. No partner can force a dissolution by his own default.

As regards the application of s 35(d), the two cases that follow are of importance.

Hurst v Bryk (2000)

In this case the House of Lords ruled that a fundamental breach of the partnership agreement by one or more of the partners that leads to a dissolution of the firm does not discharge the innocent partner(s) from liability to contribute to the debts and obligations of the firm in that dissolution.

As regards the facts, it appeared that relations between the partners in a firm of solicitors had broken down. All the partners except the claimant, Mr Hurst (a salaried partner), made an agreement to dissolve the firm. The claimant would not sign it. He said that the other partners were guilty of a repudiatory breach of the partnership agreement. Since he had accepted the breach he was discharged he said from all his obligations to his former partners and therefore could not be required to make a contribution in the dissolution. There were significant obligations for continuing rent under a lease owned on trust for the firm by the equity (i.e. profit-sharing) partners. The lease was not easily saleable so the matter was one of some substance. The House of Lords ruled that there had been a repudiatory breach of the partnership agreement. However, that did not discharge the claimant from his liability to contribute in the winding-up. A repudiatory breach does not bring to an end rights and liabilities existing at the date of acceptance of the breach. These included the joint and several liability of partners for the debts and liabilities of the firm under s 9 of the Partnership Act 1890 and a right to a contribution between the partners under s 44 of the 1890 Act.

The precise effect of s 35(d) was raised again in the following case.

Mullins v Laughton (2003)

The claimant said that because of the conduct (undisclosed in the report) of the defendants, who were his partners, in a meeting with him and subsequently, they were in repudiatory breach of the partnership contract. He said he had accepted that repudiation so that the partnership had terminated and he should be paid his share in the firm under dissolution arrangements. The other partners did not accept that the firm was dissolved. In this case the High Court agreed with them. Wilful and persistent breach could dissolve a partnership under s 35(d) *but only at the discretion of the court to order that it had been dissolved.* The judge in the High Court did agree that the conduct was such as to entitle the claimant to a dissolution under s 35(d) (breach) or s 35(f) (just and equitable). Rather than winding up the partnership, the judge relying on statements made by the House of Lords in *Syers v Syers* (1876), ordered the other partners to buy the claimant out.

Comment. It is therefore the law that a repudiatory breach of the partnership contract will not, as is the case with other commercial contracts, discharge the agreement. The court must be involved before dissolution takes place and the dissolution rights of the partners can arise.

5 The business can only be carried on at a loss. This is provided for by s 35(e). It is hardly surprising as a ground for dissolution in view of the fact that partners are in business together with a view to profit, as s 1 states. Therefore, they must have a means to release themselves from loss.

Section 35(e) is not available if the losses are temporary. In *Handyside v Campbell* (1901) a sound business was losing money because a senior managing partner was ill. He asked the court for a dissolution. The court would not grant it. The other partners could manage the firm back to financial prosperity.

The court will not, however, expect the partners to put in more capital (*Jennings v Baddeley* (1856)).

Any partner may petition.

6 The just and equitable ground. Under s 35(f) the court may dissolve a partnership if it is just and equitable to do so. Although there is no direct authority on s 35(f), it appears to give the court wide powers to hear petitions which could not be made under the other five heads that we have considered.

In *Harrison v Tennant* (1856) a judicial dissolution was ordered where a partner was involved in long and messy litigation which he refused to settle. A similar order was made in *Baring v Dix* (1786) where the objects of the firm could not be achieved. The partnership was to further a patent device for spinning cotton which had wholly failed but Dix would not agree to dissolution. The court dissolved the firm.

It appears from *Re Yenidje Tobacco Co Ltd* (1916), a company dissolution based upon the fact that the company was in reality a partnership, that deadlock between the partners is enough for dissolution, even though the business is prospering.

Any partner may petition. The court is unlikely, however, to dissolve a firm on the petition of a partner committing misconduct unless the other partners are doing so as well.

The power of creditors to seek the dissolution of a partnership is considered under the heading 'The insolvent partnership' (see later in this chapter).

Effect of dissolution

Realisation and distribution of the assets

1 Realisation. If it is not intended to bring the business to an end (i.e. wind it up) following a dissolution by reason, e.g., of death or retirement, the partnership agreement usually provides that the deceased or retiring partner's share in the firm's assets shall go to the remaining partners and that they shall pay a price for it based on the last set of accounts.

If this is not to be done, the assets of the firm will be sold on dissolution.

Section 39 gives each partner on dissolution the right to insist that the assets of the firm be used to pay creditors in full and that any surplus be paid to the partners according to their entitlement. For this purpose each partner has what is called a lien over the assets. It becomes effective only on dissolution. It is enforceable by the partner concerned applying to the court for the appointment of a receiver under his lien who will make the appropriate distribution.

2 Sale of goodwill. If the assets are sold one of them may well be goodwill. It is unlikely these days that goodwill will appear on the balance sheet of the partnership accounts, but that does not mean that it does not exist. There are varying definitions of goodwill, e.g. 'the probability of the old customers resorting to the old place' (Lord Eldon, a famous Lord Chancellor); 'the public approbation which has been won by the business' (Sir Arthur Underhill – an authority on partnership law); and 'the benefit arising from connection and reputation' (Lord Lindley – one of our greatest equity lawyers, and later a judge who was the first author of the standard practitioners' work *Lindley on Partnership*).

Goodwill is in financial terms the excess of the price you pay for a business over the net tangible assets, such as plant and machinery, which you acquire.

When goodwill is sold, the seller and buyer usually agree by the contract of sale to restrictions to stop the seller from, for example, setting up in the same business again next door to the one he has just sold and taking back the goodwill of that business.

If there is no agreement as to restrictions on the seller, the position is as set out below:

- the purchaser may represent himself as continuing the business of the seller (*Churton* v *Douglas* (1859)), but he must not hold out the seller as still being in the business;
- the seller may, however, carry on a similar business and compete with the buyer (*Trego* v *Hunt* (1896)); this can decrease the value of partnership goodwill;
- the seller must not, however, compete under the name of the former firm or represent himself as continuing the same business;

- the seller may advertise his new business but may not actually circularise or otherwise canvass customers of his old firm.

3 Final account. When the firm is dissolved and the property sold there is a final account between the partners and then a distribution of the assets. This account is a record of transactions from the date of the last accounts to the date of the winding-up.

4 Distribution of assets. Section 44 applies and if the assets when realised are sufficient to satisfy all claims, payment is made first to outside creditors, both secured and unsecured. Then each partner is paid what is due to him as advances or loans, as distinct from capital. The costs of the winding-up are then paid (*Potter* v *Jackson* (1880)). Then each partner is paid the amount of capital due to him; any surplus is divided between the partners in the profit-sharing ratio.

If there are insufficient assets to pay outside creditors and the partners' entitlements, s 44(a) applies and the partners have to make good the deficiency in the profit and loss-sharing ratio.

The insolvent partnership

The Insolvent Partnerships Order 1994 (SI 1994/2421) came into force on 1 December 1994. It revokes and replaces the Insolvent Partnerships Order 1986 (SI 1986/2142). It provides a code for the winding-up of insolvent partnerships and introduces two new procedures, i.e. voluntary arrangements and administration orders for insolvent partnerships. The main provisions appear below. References to Articles and Schedules are references to Articles and Schedules in the Order.

Voluntary arrangements

Article 4 and Sch 1 introduce the rescue procedure of a voluntary arrangement into partnership insolvency. The members of an insolvent partnership make a proposal to the firm's creditors for the settlement of its debts by a binding voluntary arrangement. Part I of the Insolvency Act 1986 (company voluntary arrangements) is applied with appropriate modifications as set out in Sch 1.

Insolvent members of the firm may under Art 5 make use of the voluntary arrangement provisions of Part I of the 1986 Act (if corporate members of the firm) or Part VIII (if individuals).

Administration orders

Article 6 and Sch 2 provide for the appointment by the court of an administrator who can put proposals to creditors for the survival of the firm or a more advantageous realisation of its assets by applying Part II of the 1986 Act (Administration orders) with appropriate amendments for partnerships as set out in Sch 2. An application to the court must be presented by the members of the insolvent partnership or by a creditor or creditors or by all of those parties together or separately.

The partners may appoint an administrator without going to the court (see below).

A partnership may qualify for administration even though one of the partners is solvent. It is a requirement of administration that the partnership is unable or likely to become unable to pay its debts. If one of the partners is solvent then under the joint and several liability rule that partner is liable to pay the debts and liabilities of the firm. How does this affect administration? The matter was raised in the following case.

Re H S Smith and Sons (1999)

H S Smith and Sons was a family farming partnership comprising Harry Seabrook Smith, Frances Smith and their son Ivan Smith. The firm was unable to pay its debts and applied to the court for an administration order. The application stated that the appointment of an administrator would be likely to achieve the survival of the firm. However, the difficulty was that under the rule of joint and several liability of partners for the debts of the firm Harry Smith could comfortably afford to pay off the firm's debts. Did this prevent the court from making an administration order?

The court has a discretion whether or not to make such an order and the judge exercised that discretion by making the order. Although the creditors would have had full recourse against Harry Smith, the firm itself was unable to pay its debts. The making of the order would, said the judge, hold off creditors from petitioning the court to wind up the firm and give Harry Smith time to recapitalise the partnership. In this way the business would survive as a going concern.

As a result of amendments to the Insolvent Partnerships Order 1994, partnerships can use the out-of-court appointment of administrators procedure set out in amendments made to the Insolvency Act 1986 by the Enterprise Act 2002. The partners or a majority of them are able to use the out-of-court route into administration in addition to the route into administration by means of a petition to the court for an administration order. They also have the advantage of the revised purpose of administration which gives primary weight to rescuing the partnership as a going concern. The out-of-court procedure mirrors that for corporate appointments set out in Chapter 6 ○.

Winding-up by the court

Under Art 7 any insolvent partnership may be wound up by the court (there is no provision for voluntary winding-up) under Part V of the 1986 Act (as modified by Sch 3) where no concurrent petition is presented against the partners. They become contributories to the full amount of the firm's debts. Before the court has jurisdiction, the firm must have carried on business in England and Wales at some time within the period of three years ending with the day on which the winding-up petition was presented.

A petition against the firm may be presented by a creditor or creditors and also by the liquidator or administrator of a corporate member of the firm or former corporate member. Also included are the administrator of the firm, a trustee in bankruptcy of a partner or former partner and the supervisor of a relevant voluntary arrangement.

The grounds are set out in s 221 of the 1986 Act as modified and set out in Sch 3. Of these, inability to pay debts will be the usual creditor ground but there are others, e.g. cessation of business and just and equitable ground, but in all cases the firm must be insolvent. Inability may be proved under s 222 of the 1986 Act (as modified and set out in Sch 3) by serving a written demand on the firm requiring it to pay a debt or debts exceeding £750 then due and the firm does not pay, secure or compound the debt within three weeks of service.

Application of Company Directors Disqualification Act 1986

Where there is a winding-up of the firm by the court, each partner is deemed an officer and director of the firm. If the court is satisfied that they have not run the firm responsibly, the partners could be disqualified as unfit to act as a director or in the management of a company (registered or unregistered (i.e. a trading partnership)) for up to 15 years. Article 16 and Sch 8 apply.

Ordinary limited partnerships

Generally

The Limited Partnerships Act 1907 provides for the formation of limited partnerships in which one or more of the partners has only limited liability for the firm's debts. These partnerships are not common because in most cases the objective of limited liability can be better achieved by incorporation as a private company. However, they are increasingly used by institutional investors, such as insurance companies and pension funds, that are wholly or partially exempt from tax. These investors can, through the medium of the limited partnership, invest jointly with other investors who are liable to tax without losing their own tax status. Limited partnerships are also used extensively by venture capitalists.

A limited partnership is not a legal entity but can have an unlimited number of members. There must also be one general partner whose liability for the debts of the firm is unlimited. A body corporate may be a limited partner.

Registration

Every limited partnership must be registered with the Registrar of Companies. The following particulars must be registered by means of a statement signed by the partners:

- the firm name;
- the general nature of the business;
- the principal place of business;
- the full name of each partner;
- the date of commencement of the term of the partnership, if any;
- a statement that it is a limited partnership;
- the particulars of each limited partner and the amount contributed by him, whether in cash or otherwise.

Any change in the above particulars or the fact that a general partner becomes a limited partner must be notified to the Registrar within seven days. Failure to register means that the limited partner is fully liable as a general partner. When a general partner becomes a limited partner, the fact must be advertised in *The London Gazette* if the transaction is to be effective in law.

The Register of Limited Partnerships is open to inspection by the public who may also obtain certified copies of, or extracts from, any registered statement.

Rights and duties of a limited partner

A limited partner is not liable for the debts of the firm beyond his capital, but he may not withdraw any part of his capital and, even if he were to do so, he would still be liable to the firm's creditors for the amount he originally subscribed.

A limited partner has no power to bind the firm and may not take part in its management. If he does manage the firm, he becomes liable for all the liabilities incurred by the firm during that period. Nevertheless, he may give advice on management to the other partners and he may also inspect the books.

The death, bankruptcy or mental incapacity of a limited partner does not dissolve the partnership and a limited partner cannot dissolve the partnership by notice.

In addition, any question arising as to ordinary business matters may be decided by a majority of general partners, and a new partner can be introduced without the consent of the existing limited partners.

Limited liability partnerships

We have now completed our study of the ordinary partnership and the ordinary limited partnership. Quite a lot of material is involved and the reader may wonder whether in view of the changes to be introduced by the new limited liability partnership it is worth looking at the older forms of business organisation. The answer has to be yes because the newer limited liability arrangements are designed mainly for the professional firms of lawyers and accountants who have for so long been liable to the full extent of their capital in the firm and personal property in meeting claims for negligence even though full indemnity insurance is not normally available. There are in the field of UK business many other partnerships consisting of trading firms and some small professional firms which, of course, can use the limited liability regime. However, many may feel that registration and the filing of accounts for public inspection and other central controls are not worth a measure of limited liability. These trading partners are not really at risk of the major claims for damages faced by professional firms. This plus sheer inertia will mean that a large number of somewhat informal partnerships will continue to exist and that those embarking on a career in business will need to be familiar with all three structures, i.e. the unlimited partnership, the limited partnership, and the limited liability partnership which may be used mainly by the firms of those in professional practice of one sort or another.

The Limited Liability Partnerships Act

The Limited Liability Partnerships Act 2000 received the Royal Assent on 20 July 2000. It effects a radical change in the liability of the firm and its partners, for those who adopt this new form of business organisation. The Partnership Act 1890 and the Limited Partnerships Act 1907 remain in force and the law relating to them is unchanged.

The main purpose of the Act is to create a form of legal entity known as a limited liability partnership (LLP). An LLP combines the organisational flexibility and tax status of a partnership with limited liability for its members. The LLP and not its members will be liable to third parties, but a negligent member's personal assets may be at risk.

Section 1. This states that an LLP is a legal person with unlimited capacity. Its members may be liable to contribute to its assets on winding-up.

Section 2. This deals with incorporation and requires at least two people to subscribe to an incorporation document to be sent to the Registrar of Companies. The contents of the incorporation document are dealt with – in particular, the situation of the registered office and the members on incorporation and whether some or all of them are to be 'designated members' (see below).

Section 3. This deals with the issue of a certificate of incorporation by the Registrar and provides that it is conclusive evidence that all requirements have been complied with.

Section 4. This deals with membership and provides that the members are those who sign the incorporation document or who become members by agreement with the other members. Cessation of membership is also by agreement.

Section 5. This is concerned with the relationship of the members, which is to be governed by any agreement between them or, failing such agreement, is to be governed by any provision in regulations to be made by the Secretary of State.

Section 6 states that each member of the LLP is an agent of it, unless he has no authority to act in a particular matter, although there are ostensible authority provisions, in that the outsider must, for example, be aware that there is no authority to act.

Of particular importance in terms of liability is s 6(4), which provides that where a member of an LLP is liable to any person (other than another member of the LLP) as a result of a wrongful act or omission of his in the course of the business of the LLP or with its authority, the LLP is liable to the same extent as the member. *This provision does not make other members personally liable.*

Thus, if in a firm of accountants one partner negligently prepares accounts for a client that to the knowledge of the firm are to be relied on, for example, by a person intending to make a bid for the business, the firm's assets will be liable to pay damages for negligence, but only the negligent partner's assets may be liable if the firm's assets are insufficient. The other partners may, therefore, lose their capital in the firm but no more. They are, however, liable to contribute to the assets of the firm if it is wound up because of non-payment of business debts.

In practice, the negligent member or partner will not often be personally liable to the third party for loss caused by his or her negligence. This personal liability will only occur when it appears from the circumstances that the negligent member was undertaking a personal duty to the third party. Provided all correspondence and dealings with the third party are clearly made by the negligent partner in the capacity of agent of the firm, then only the LLP's assets will be at risk. None of the members will have personal liability.

Section 7 gives a member's representatives, e.g. executors or trustee in bankruptcy, a right to receive amounts due to the member (or former member) but with no power to interfere in management.

Section 8. This deals with designated members who achieve such status by being specified as such on the incorporation document or by agreement with members. These members are required for certain compliance functions under the Act, e.g. notification to the Registrar of a name change.

Section 9 provides for the registration of membership changes.

Sections 10 to 13 are concerned with taxation. These clauses are expressed in broad terms to apply in general existing rules for partnerships and partners.

Sections 14 to 17 are concerned with regulation-making powers, and *s 18* deals with interpretation.

The Schedule is concerned with names and situation of registered office. These provisions are similar to those applying to companies.

Limited liability partnerships: the regulations

The Limited Liability Partnerships Regulations 2001 (SI 2001/1090) came into force on 6 April 2001. They support the Limited Liability Partnerships Act 2000 and are vital to a more complete understanding of the law. They are quite detailed but broadly speaking they apply company law provisions to LLPs with appropriate and necessary changes of wording. The following provision heads are important.

Accounts and audit exemption

The requirements of company legislation relating to the keeping and retaining of accounting records and the preparation and publication of annual accounts, the form and content of annual accounts and the audit requirement are applied to LLPs in the same way as to companies with the members of the LLP taking on the duties of directors and their responsibilities. There is, however, no need to prepare the equivalent of a directors' report.

A period of 10 months is given for delivery of the annual accounts to the Registrar of Companies from the end of the financial year. Small LLPs and medium-sized LLPs can take advantage of the provisions of the Companies Act 2006 in terms of abbreviated and modified accounts and the qualifying thresholds in regard to turnover, balance sheet total and number of employees are the same as the corporate thresholds.

The usual company audit exemptions apply as do the dormant company rules apply to dormant LLPs.

The disadvantages of financial disclosure

One of the major disadvantages of the adoption of LLP status is the company-style financial disclosure. Even under the regime of abbreviated accounts, financial disclosure which is not required of other forms of partnership may make an LLP vulnerable to commercial pressure. Furthermore, where it is necessary to disclose the income of the highest paid member of the LLP (which is where the profit share of the member exceeds £200,000), there may be repercussions from clients, creditors and staff. The government is being pressed to remove the disclosure requirements and in general terms the company analogy is not perfectly made out because the disclosure, auditing and accounting rules in a company are largely to protect the shareholders against the directors. This is not the case with the members/managers of the LLP. United States LLPs do not have to disclose financial information at all, though some states do not permit the formation of LLPs.

Other provisions

- *Execution of documents.* Instead of the company rule of signature by a director and/or the secretary, it is provided that two members of an LLP are to be signatories for a valid document.
- *Register of debenture holders.* An LLP must keep a register of debenture holders (i.e. those who have lent it money) and the debenture holders have a right to inspect it.
- *Registered office.* The Registrar of Companies will receive notice of the address of the registered office and must be notified of changes.
- *Identification.* The name of the LLP must appear outside its place of business and on correspondence and on its common seal if it has one.
- *Annual return.* The regulations provide that an LLP must deliver an annual return to the Registrar of Companies and set out the requirements as to contents.
- *Auditors.* Subject to the applicability of the audit exemption rules, an LLP is, in general, required to appoint auditors. Provision is made for the Secretary of State to appoint auditors where an LLP is in default. The auditors have various rights including the right to have access to an LLP's books, accounts

and information as necessary, the right to attend meetings of the LLP and certain rights in the event of being removed from office or not being reappointed. Provision is also made for the resignation of auditors and the making of a statement by a person ceasing to hold office.

■ *Registration of charges.* An LLP is required to register charges with the Registrar of Companies. The relevant sections of the Companies Act 2006 apply.

■ *Arrangements and reconstructions.* An LLP has power to compromise with its members and creditors.

■ *Investigations.* An investigation of an LLP may be made following its own application or that of not less than one-fifth in number of its members.

■ *Fraudulent trading.* This is punished in the case of an LLP in the same way as a company trading fraudulently.

■ *Wrongful trading.* There are provisions relating to wrongful trading on the lines of the Insolvency Act 1986 provisions but with modifications to suit an LLP.

■ *Unfair prejudice.* Schedule 2 to the regulations applies the Companies Act 2006 so that in general there is a remedy for the members of an LLP who suffer unfair prejudice. The members of an LLP may, however, by unanimous agreement exclude the right set out in s 994(1) of the Companies Act 2006 for such period as may be agreed.

■ *Matters arising following winding-up.* There are provisions dealing with the power of the court to declare a dissolution void, the striking out by the Registrar of Companies of a defunct company and Crown disclaimer of property vesting as *bona vacantia*.

■ *Functions of the Registrar of Companies.* These are set out in Sch 2 and include the keeping of records of LLP's filed documents on the same lines as for registered companies.

■ *Miscellaneous provisions.* These include the form of registers, the use of computers for records, the service of documents, the powers of the court to grant relief and the punishment of offences.

■ *Disqualification.* Part III of the regulations applies the provisions of the Company Directors Disqualification Act 1986 to LLPs with appropriate modifications. Under the provisions members of an LLP will be subject to the same penalties that apply to company directors and may be disqualified from being a member of an LLP or a director of a company under those provisions.

■ *Insolvency.* Under Part IV of and Sch 3 to the regulations the insolvency provisions applied to LLPs include procedures for voluntary arrangements, administration orders, receivership and liquidation. There are two notable modifications to the company rules, i.e.:

– a new s 214A under which withdrawals made by members in the two years prior to winding-up will be subject to clawback if it is proved that, at the time of the relevant withdrawal, the member knew or had reasonable grounds to believe that the LLP was or would be made insolvent;

– a modified s 74 providing that in a winding-up both past and present members are liable to contribute to the assets of the LLP to the extent that they have agreed to do so with the other LLP members in the partnership agreement.

In effect, therefore, this gives members of an LLP protection in terms of limited liability. However, the matter is not straightforward. There is no obligation either in the 2000 Act or the regulations to have a written agreement and the default provisions in reg 7 do not deal with the extent of the liability of each member on liquidation. The position is therefore left ill-defined, there being no relation between capital contributed and liability to contribute to deficits as there is with companies. In these circumstances insolvency practitioners may find difficulty in determining the liability of members of an LLP on liquidation. This problem area underlines once again the need for a written agreement to be made in an LLP governing the maximum liability of each member on liquidation or stating that a member is to have no liability so that creditors would have to rely on the assets of the LLP alone. Unfortunately this situation would not necessarily be known to creditors since there is no requirement to file LLP agreements so that they are not open to public inspection.

It should be noted that the insolvency provisions relating to limited liability partnerships are subject to s 14 of the Insolvency Act 2000 since they follow corporate procedures. This means that if an LLP does business in other countries of the EU and becomes insolvent it may find that insolvency proceedings may be brought in regard to a place of operations in a particular EU territory.

■ *LLPs authorised under the financial services regime.* There are in corporate law special insolvency provisions for companies involved in the financial markets because of the special problems of corporate failure in that field. These provisions contained in Parts XV and XXIV of the Financial Services and Markets Act 2000 are applied to relevant LLPs.

- *Default provisions.* Part VI of the regulations contains 'fall-back' provisions that apply where there is no existing limited liability partnership agreement or where the agreement does not wholly deal with a particular issue. The provisions represent a modification of s 24 of the Partnership Act 1890. There are provisions relating, e.g., to profit share, remuneration, assignment of partnership share, inspection of books and records, expulsion and competition.

Need for membership agreement

The fall-back provisions of the regulations are not really a suitable basis on which to run a business. They are rigid and introduce a measure of inflexibility into the arrangement. There is nothing that is the equivalent of the detailed provisions of Table A that may be adopted by companies. The parties to the agreement and their professional advisers should therefore consider the construction of an agreement to cover:

- the matter of what business shall be conducted by the LLP and how it may be added to or changed (there is of course no *ultra vires* rule);
- the ownership of property;
- capital, e.g. interest on capital if any;
- profits and losses, e.g. division and drawings;
- banking arrangements;
- members' entitlements, e.g. pensions, salaries, cars and health insurance;
- authority of members;
- meetings and voting;
- admission of members;
- retirement of members;
- rights and obligations of retiring members;
- serving of notices;
- arbitration provisions;
- winding-up. This is of particular importance because neither the Act nor the regulations are specific about membership liability.

Membership agreement: confidentiality

It is worth noting that the contents of the membership agreement do not become known to the public. It is not registered with the Registrar of Companies either on incorporation or subsequently and there are no rights of inspection in terms of outsiders such as creditors.

Insolvency

The Limited Liability Partnerships Regulations 2001 apply and LLPs follow insolvency patterns in line with companies. Part III of the regulations applies the insolvency provisions of the Companies Act 2006 and the Company Directors Disqualification Act 1986 to LLPs. Part IV applies the provisions of the Insolvency Act 1986 to LLPs in terms of voluntary arrangements, administration and winding-up. Company procedures are followed.

Reform: a partnership with legal personality

The Law Commission has issued a *Consultation Paper on Partnership Law* in response to a request from the then DTI (now BIS). There are also proposals regarding partnerships in Scotland made by the Scottish Law Commission that are not considered here. The review is being conducted in respect of the provisions of the Partnership Act 1890, many but not all of which operate as default provisions in the absence of a contrary agreement of the partners, and the Limited Partnerships Act 1907. The Limited Liability Partnerships Act 2000 (see above) is not involved. The reforms would, however, if implemented, narrow the present distinction between ordinary partnerships and the new limited liability partnership.

The three main proposals were:

1 Proposals to introduce separate legal personality. There are two sub-proposals here:

(a) to confer legal personality on all partnerships without registration. There would be a transitional period to allow the parties to a partnership agreement to organise their affairs or to opt out of the continuing aspect of separate personality of the firm;

(b) to make legal personality depend on registration. Under this sub-proposal only a registered partnership would have legal personality capable of continuing regardless of changes in the membership of the firm. Under this option non-registered partnerships would not have legal personality.

The Commission feels that having a system of registration would create a more complex situation in which there would be a legal environment for registered partnerships and another for non-registered firms. The Commission also feels that many small firms would not register and so lose the benefits of legal personality.

On balance, therefore, the provisional view of the Commission is the first option, i.e. continuity of legal personality without registration, and views are invited on this. The creation of a registered partnership regime would bring partnership law in the UK closer to those legal systems in Europe in which legal personality is conferred by registration.

2 Proposals to avoid the unnecessary discontinuance of business caused by the dissolution of the firm under the 1890 Act default rules when one person ceases to be a partner.

3 Proposals to provide a more efficient and cheaper mechanism for the dissolution of a solvent partnership.

The first of these reforms, concerning registration of limited partnerships, were introduced by the Legislative Reform (Limited Partnerships) Order 2009 (SI 2009/1940) that came into force on 1 October 2009. This Order applies to limited partnerships for which registration applications are received on or after that day. Articles 4 to 7 of this Order form a series of new sections to be inserted in the 1907 Act in place of s 8 concerning registration.

Other reform proposals

The following suggestions for reform are, according to the Commission, intended to clarify some of the uncertainties in the 1890 Act, to update provisions which are outdated or spent, and to propose adaptations of existing provisions if in the event consultees support the separate and continuing legal personality of the firm.

1 Partnership and agency. With the concept of legal entity the partners would be agents of the firm but not of each other.

2 Ownership of property. With separate personality the firm would be able to hold property in its own name. It would not be necessary, as now, to use the device of the trust. Also, the firm and not the partners would have an insurable interest in partnership property.

3 Partners' liability for the obligations of the firm. As a result of separate personality, the firm would be primarily liable.

A partner's liability would be subsidiary but unlimited. Creditors would normally need to get a judgment against the firm before enforcing the claim against the assets of the firm or the partners. The liability of partners would be joint and several for the debts and obligations of the firm.

4 Partners' duties. Partners have a duty to act in good faith in equity already. The Commission proposes to include the duty in a reformed statute and possibly also a duty of skill and care in negligence.

There is a suggestion that partners be relieved of the duty of good faith when, on the break-up of a firm, they are competing for its client base, provided that they act honestly and reasonably.

5 Litigation. A partnership with a separate legal personality would be sued in its own name and the partners could be sued in the same action.

6 Information about the firm, including former partners who may have subsidiary liability at the time of a claim, would be available if the partnership was registered. If this is not so, the Commission proposes an extension to the Business Names Act 1985 requiring display of such information by the firm administratively.

7 Floating charges. Currently partnerships cannot grant floating charges over the firm's assets. See also p 81 ○.

Model form of ordinary (or unlimited) partnership deed

AN AGREEMENT made this **4th** day of **June** two thousand
and **Seven** between **John Jones**
of **Bleak House, Barchester; Chartered Accountant**
and **Jane James**
of **12 Acacia Avenue, Barchester; Chartered Accountant**
and **William Pitt**
of **55 Low Terrace, Barchester; Chartered Accountant**

IT IS HEREBY AGREED AND DECLARED AS FOLLOWS:

Duration and objects

1. The said **John Jones, Jane James and William Pitt** shall become and remain partners in the business of Chartered Accountants for a term of **five** years from the date of this deed if they shall so long live.

   Comment The period of five years ensures that it is not a partnership at will. We do not want a partnership at will because it can be terminated by notice at any time thus allowing a partner to leave the firm with ease so that years of work are brought to an end at the will of one partner.

2. Although the partnership constituted by this Deed is for a period of **five** years nevertheless it is the intention of the parties hereto to continue in partnership from **five**-year period to **five**-year period subject only to the incidence of death or retirement.

   Comment Since a fixed term has been agreed, there should be provision for it to be continued upon the same terms on the expiry of the fixed term. It is better to include this in the deed so that there is no doubt what will happen at the end of each term of five years. In any case, of course, s 27 would apply and the partnership would be at will but on the same terms as the fixed partnership which had just expired.

3. The death, retirement, expulsion or bankruptcy of a partner shall not determine the partnership between the partners but without prejudice to the generality of this clause the parties hereto shall review the provisions of this deed whenever the admission of a new profit-sharing partner into the partnership is being contemplated.

   Comment This clause is inserted to make sure, for example, that the death of a partner does not cause a dissolution as between those partners who remain and that the business continues under the remaining partners. If this clause was not included, there would be an automatic dissolution under s 33(1) on the death of a partner.

Firm name

4. The partners shall practise in partnership under the firm name of **Jones, James, Pitt & Co.** (or such other name as the partners may hereafter agree).

Location of practice

5. The business of the partnership shall be carried on at **10 Oak Buildings, Barchester** and/or such other place or places as the partners may from time to time decide.

Bankers and application of partnership money

6. (i) The bankers of the firm shall be the **Barchester** Bank plc or such other bankers as the partners shall agree upon both for the moneys of clients for the time being in the keeping of the partnership and for the moneys of the partnership.

   (ii) All partnership money shall be paid to the bankers of the partnership to the credit of the partnership and the partners shall make such regulations as they may from time to time see fit for opening, operating or closing the bank accounts of the partnership and for providing the money required for current expenses.

(iii) All outgoings incurred for or in carrying on the partnership business and all losses and damages which shall happen or be incurred in relation to the business are to be paid out of the moneys and profits of the partnership and if there is a deficiency shall be contributed by the partners in the shares in which they are for the time being respectively entitled to the profits of the partnership.

Comment Clause 6(ii) gives the partners power to make regulations as to who may draw cheques in the name of the firm. In many cases this will be each partner alone, though where there are more than two partners it is usual to provide that all cheques over a certain amount are to be signed by at least two of the partners.

Capital 7. (i) The initial capital of the partnership shall be a sum of *£30,000* to be contributed by the partners in equal shares together with such further cash capital (if any) as the partners may from time to time agree to be required (in addition to any loan capital) for the purposes of the partnership and which shall be provided (except as may from time to time be otherwise agreed by the partners) in the proportion in which the partners are for the time being entitled to share in the profits of the partnership.

(ii) *Five thousand pounds (£5,000)* being the agreed value of the goodwill of the business carried on at *10 Sandy Lane, Barchester* by the said *John Jones* which will be taken over by the said partnership and which shall be credited in the books of the firm as part of the capital brought in by the said *John Jones.*

(iii) The said sum of *£30,000* and any further capital provided by the partners shall carry interest at the rate of *ten (10)* per cent per annum to be payable *half-yearly in arrears on 30th June and 31st December* or at such other rate and payable at such other times as the partners shall from time to time decide.

Comment Unless there is a specific provision, such as the one in (iii) above, interest on capital is not payable.

Profits 8. The partners shall be entitled to the net profits arising from the business in *equal shares* or such other shares as may from time to time be agreed by the partners. Such net profits shall be divided among the partners immediately after the settlement of the annual accounts in the manner hereafter provided.

Comment Oddly enough, although the 1890 Act says that partners are in business with a view of profit, it says nothing about dividing profit. This special provision makes the matter of division clear.

Management and control of the partnership 9. The control and management of the partnership shall remain in the hands of the partners and salaried partners (if any) shall not be entitled to take part therein.

Circulation of agendas and other information 10. All agendas and minutes of partners' meetings and balance sheets and profit and loss accounts shall be circulated to all partners.

Partnership accounts and partners' drawings 11. At the close of business on the *31st May* in the year two thousand and eight and on the same day in each succeeding year the accounts of the partnership shall be made up.

Each partner may draw on account of his share of profit to such extent as may be decided by the partners from time to time.

Comment The partners may agree, for example, that £1,000 per month as a maximum be drawn. It is usually also provided that, if on taking the annual account the sums drawn out by any of the partners are found to exceed the sum to which that partner is entitled as his share of the year's profits, the excess shall be refunded immediately.

Conduct of the partnership business

12. Each partner shall diligently employ himself in the partnership business and carry on and conduct the same for the greatest advantage of the partnership.

Holidays

13. Each partner shall be entitled to *five* weeks holiday in aggregate in each year of the partnership.

Comment It may sometimes be found that the agreement states that some or all of this holiday must be taken between certain dates in the year.

Restrictions

14. No partner shall without the previous consent of the others:

(a) hire or dismiss any employee or take on any trainee;

(b) purchase goods in the name or on behalf of the firm to an amount exceeding *one thousand (£1,000) pounds*;

(c) compound release or discharge any debt owing to the partnership without receiving the full amount therefor;

(d) be engaged or interested whether directly or indirectly in any business or occupation other than the partnership business;

(e) advance the moneys of or deliver on credit any goods belonging to the partnership;

(f) make any assignment either absolutely or by way of charge of his share in the partnership;

(g) give any security or undertaking for the payment of any debt or liability out of the moneys or property of the partnership;

(h) introduce or attempt to introduce another person into the business of the partnership;

(i) enter into any bond or become surety for any persons or do or knowingly permit to be done anything whereby the capital or property of the partnership may be seized, attached or taken in execution.

Comment This clause can be extended as required. However, since partners have considerable apparent authority under s 5 of the 1890 Act and case law, the above prohibitions will in many cases not prevent an outsider who has no knowledge of them from claiming against the firm.

They do provide grounds for dissolution of the firm if a partner is in wilful or persistent breach of them or the partnership agreement in general.

It is generally unwise to have a very large number of prohibitions because this is likely to restrict the activities of the firm and its individual partners unduly.

Partners' debts and engagements

15. Every partner shall during the partnership pay his present and future separate debts and at all times indemnify the other partners and each of them and the capital and effects of the partnership against his said debts and engagements and against all actions, suits, claims and demands on account thereof.

Expulsion
of
partners

16. If any partner shall:

(a) by act or default commit any flagrant breach of his duties as a partner or of the agreements and stipulations herein contained; or

(b) fail to account and pay over or refund to the partnership any money for which he is accountable to the partnership within 14 days after being required so to do by a partner specifically so authorised by a decision of the partners; or

(c) act in any respect contrary to the good faith which ought to be observed between partners; or

(d) become subject to the bankruptcy laws; or

(e) enter into any composition or arrangement with or for the benefit of his creditors; or

(f) be or become permanently incapacitated by mental incapacity, ill-health, accident or otherwise from attending the partnership business; or

(g) except with the consent of the other partners absent himself from the said business for more than *six* calendar months in any one year or for more than *ninety* consecutive days (absence during the usual holidays or due to temporary illness or as agreed not being reckoned);

then and in any such case the other partners may by notice in writing given to him or (in the case of his being found incapable by reason of mental incapacity of managing and administering his property and affairs for the purposes of ss 2–8 of the Mental Capacity Act 2005) to his deputy or other appropriate person or left at the office of the partnership determine the partnership so far as he may be concerned and publish a notice of dissolution of the partnership in the name of and as against such partner whereupon the partnership will so far as regards such partner immediately cease and determine accordingly but without prejudice to the remedies of the other partners for any antecedent breach of any of the stipulations or agreements aforesaid and any question as to a case having arisen to authorise such notice shall be referred to arbitration.

Dissolution

17. Upon the dissolution of the partnership by the death of a partner or by a partner retiring, the other partners shall be entitled to purchase upon the terms hereinafter specified the share of the partner (including goodwill) so dying or retiring: provided that written notice of intention to purchase shall be given to the retiring partner or to the personal representatives of the deceased partner within *two* calendar months after the date of the dissolution.

18. The purchase money payable under clause 17 hereof shall be the net value of the share of the deceased or retiring partner as at the date of the dissolution after satisfying all outstanding liabilities of the partnership with interest at the rate of *ten (10)* per cent per annum as from the date of dissolution: provided that if the value of the said share cannot be agreed upon the same shall be submitted to arbitration in the manner hereinafter provided.

The purchase money shall be paid by *six equal* instalments the first instalment to be paid at the end of *three months* after the date of the dissolution and thereafter at the end of each succeeding period of *three months* with interest at the rate of *ten (10)* per cent per annum upon so much of the purchase money as shall remain unpaid for the time being and such purchase money shall if required be secured by the bond of the surviving partners with not fewer than two sureties.

Goodwill

19. For the purposes of the foregoing clauses the goodwill of the partnership shall be deemed to be valued at *three years'* purchase of the average net profits of the partnership for the preceding *five years* or the average of the whole period if the partnership shall have subsisted for less than five years.

Comment Any other basis of assessment which the partners may decide upon could, of course, have been included or the matter of goodwill could have been omitted entirely.

20. In the event of one of the partners retiring and the other partners purchasing his share the retiring partner shall not during the unexpired residue of the term of the partnership carry on or be interested either directly or indirectly in any business similar to that of the said partnership and competing therewith within a radius of *one mile* of *10 Oak Buildings, Barchester* or of any other place of business belonging to the partnership at the date of the notice of retirement.

21. Upon the determination of the partnership any partner or his personal representative shall have power to sign in the name of the firm notice of the dissolution for publication in the Gazette.

Arbitration 22. Should any doubt or difference arise at any time between the said partners or their personal representatives with regard to the interpretation or effect of this agreement or in respect of the rights, duties and liabilities of any partner or his personal representatives whether in connection with the conduct or winding-up of the affairs of the partnership, such doubt or difference shall be submitted to a single arbitrator to be appointed by the President for the time being of the Institute of Chartered Accountants in England and Wales.

Comment Without an arbitration clause it is open to any partner to pursue a dispute through the courts. Nothing injures a business more than an open dispute between partners. Arbitration, which may be quicker and sometimes cheaper than court litigation and certainly more private, should always be considered. Also, it should be less confrontational than legal proceedings and so do less damage to the relationship between the partners, though the fact that even an arbitration is necessary means that some damage has already been done.

IN WITNESS whereof the parties hereto have hereunto set their hands and seals the day and year first above-mentioned.

Signed as a deed by the
above-named John Jones in the
presence of,

George Blake,
42 Hill Top,
Barchester.

Signed as a deed by the
above-named Jane James in the
presence of,

George Blake.

Signed as a deed by the
above-named William Pitt in the
presence of,

George Blake.

Note Partnership deeds also usually contain complex provisions relating to life assurance for retirement, annuities for partners' dependants in the case of death, and annuities to partners in the event of permanent incapacity. There are often, also, much more complex provisions relating to payments to be made to any partner on death or retirement and the continuation of the partnership for tax purposes. However, these do not assist in the understanding of the Partnership Act 1890 and involve knowledge of matters not dealt with in this text. They have accordingly been omitted.

Self-test questions/activities

1 Joseph David Soap wishes to set up in business on his own as a carpenter, having acquired a small business connection from John Smith. Which of the following trading names, if any, would require Joe to comply with the provisions of the Companies Act 2006?
   (a) David Soap;
   (b) J D Soap & Co;
   (c) Joe Soap;
   (d) Joe Soap Carpentry (formerly John Smith's);
   (e) J D Soap;
   (f) Chipaway;
   (g) Dave Soap.

2 Your friend, Fred, intends to go into business on his own as a timber merchant under the name of 'County Council Supplies'. What could happen to Fred if he does this?

3 Old John Brown has been in business as a furniture remover in Barchester since 1975. Last year young John Brown moved to Barchester and has started up a furniture removal business in his own name. Can old John Brown stop him?

4 Adam Smith, a grocer, comes to you for advice on his finances. What advice would you give him in terms of each of the following questions which he asks you?
   (a) 'Times have been very hard for me lately. I owe so many people so much money. I could probably pay my creditors, say, half of what I owe them but no more. Is there a way of doing this, given that I understand that a builder to whom I owe £1,000 appears to have gone to court to make me bankrupt?'
   (b) 'Anyway, I have tried to make my family safe. Last week I gave my wife the family home and on the same day sold her two terraced houses in Barchester worth £40,000 for £500. Yesterday I also paid my brother off. I owed him £1,000 from when I started up so he should have it. My creditors can't upset these deals, I take it?'
   (c) 'I have not paid John, my driver, for a month and I doubt whether I can now. I wish I could have helped him but I guess he will have to go down with all the other creditors. That's the position, isn't it?'
   (d) 'Of course, even if they make me bankrupt I shall rent another shop and go on trading. Nothing can be done about that, can it?'

5 Joe is a solicitor employed by Bloggs & Co. There are two partners, Harry and Ian. Ian is intending to retire and it has been decided that Joe should replace Ian as a partner, with Harry carrying on as a partner.
   Explain to each of Joe, Harry and Ian what steps each should take to protect himself as a result of the changeover.

6 Cliff has been asked by his friends, Don and Eric, to help them set up an antiques business. Don and Eric want Cliff to lend them £5,000 and they say they will give Cliff one-third of the profits instead of interest on the loan.
   What are the dangers to Cliff in such an arrangement and how can he overcome them?

7 Fred is a new partner in Gee & Co, a firm of interior designers. In discussion at a recent meeting of the partners Fred was told that the office building at which the firm is based is not partnership property. Explain to Fred:
   (a) what is meant by the expression 'partnership property';
   (b) what effect it will have on him if the office building is not partnership property;
   (c) how it can be that an asset which is used in the firm's business is not in fact partnership property.

8 You have been appointed as partnership secretary in the firm of Jones, James & Pitt, Chartered Accountants. The partnership articles appear on pp 146–50. The following problems emerge over a number of partners' meetings:
   (a) John Jones soon became unhappy about his future prospects. He retired from the firm last month and has taken a partnership with Snooks & Co, Chartered Accountants, whose office is two doors away from the offices of Jones, James & Pitt. Jane James and William Pitt, the remaining partners, are anxious to stop John from competing with them.
   (b) Before he left, John Jones contracted to buy a microcomputer system for the practice from Scroggs Ltd, although at an earlier partners' meeting it was decided that the purchase should be deferred for one year. The system cost £5,000. Jane and William have so far refused to take delivery of the system or pay for it.

(c) Scroggs Ltd have written to the firm saying that unless the debt is paid they will petition the court to wind up the firm.

Having read the partnership articles thoroughly:

(i) Prepare as part of your answer a memorandum for the next partners' meeting outlining the legal position of the firm in the three cases described above.

(ii) If you think there is a claim under **(a)** above, draft as part of your answer a letter to the firm's solicitors, Weeks & Co, for the signature of the partners, stating what has happened and describing the relevant provisions of the partnership articles.

(iii) Draft as part of your answer a letter to Scroggs Ltd to deal with whatever you think the legal position is under **(b)** and **(c)** above.

Specimen examination questions

1 Tom, Dick and Harry are partners in an unlimited partnership called We Restore. In the course of the partnership business, Harry undertook to restore a valuable painting for a customer. Harry carried out the work negligently and the painting is irreparably damaged. The customer proposes to sue both for tort and for breach of contract.

Explain the potential liability of We Restore, and Tom, Dick and Harry on the basis that:

(a) the firm is an unlimited partnership; and

(b) the firm is an LLP.

2 Arnold, Bill and Cuthbert have carried on business as an unlimited partnership for several years. They have had many disagreements largely because, according to Arnold and Bill, Cuthbert has totally disregarded the terms of the partnership agreement. They have now written to Cuthbert in the following terms:

In consequence of your breaches of our partnership agreement we Arnold and Bill propose to exclude you Cuthbert from the partnership.

What is the legal effect of this notice?

3 Charles retired as a partner from Adam & Co two years ago. The firm has carried on business under the two remaining partners Adam and Bernard. Three months ago Adam and Bernard ordered new office equipment using old notepaper bearing the names of all three partners. The firm is unable to pay the supplier who is threatening to sue Charles for the amount owing.

Explain the legal position to Charles, bearing in mind that, as its name indicates, Adam & Co is an unlimited partnership.

Website references

http://www.companieshouse.gov.uk As regards guidance on limited liability partnerships, the best access is through the website of Companies House.

http://www.bis.gov.uk As regards new legislation on partnership including regulations, the Department for Business, Innovation and Skills website is a relevant source.

http://www.lawcom.gov.uk This site contains changes suggested by the Law Commission.

Visit **www.mylawchamber.co.uk/richesallen** to access study support resources including answers to questions in this chapter and legal updates, all linked to the **Pearson eText** version of **Keenan and Riches' Business Law** which you can **search**, **highlight** and **personalise** with your **own notes** and **bookmarks**.

Use **Case Navigator** to read in full some of the key cases referenced in this chapter with commentary and questions:

Ebrahimi v Westbourne Galleries [1972]

Chapter 6   Companies

Learning objectives

After studying this chapter you should understand the following main points:

- the types of registered companies and the process of formation;
- the constitution of a registered company, i.e. the memorandum and articles;
- the different types of share capital together with loan capital and the issue of these securities;
- membership rights and meetings together with the provisions to protect minority shareholders;
- the management of a company through its directors and their powers and duties;
- methods of corporate rescue and dissolution by winding-up.

In Chapter 4 we made a general survey of the different types of business organisation – the sole trader, the partnership, and the corporation. In particular, we considered the role of the corporation as a business organisation in the public and private sectors.

This chapter is concerned only with one type of corporation – the registered company – because this is the basic form of corporate business organisation. The law relating to registered companies is to be found mainly in the Companies Act 2006 and case law. All section references in this chapter are to the Companies Act (CA) 2006 unless otherwise indicated.

Types of registered companies

Registered companies may be limited or unlimited and public or private.

Limited companies

Most registered companies are limited by shares. This means that the liability of the members of the company is limited. The company's liability is not limited. It must pay its debts so long as it has any funds from which to do so.

Where the liability of the members of the company is limited by shares, it means that once the members have paid the full nominal value of their shares, plus any premium that may have been payable on them, they cannot be asked to pay any more even if the company is wound up and cannot pay its creditors in full from the funds that are left.

If, therefore, John Green owns 100 shares issued at £1 each by Boxo plc, then once he has paid £100 to Boxo plc for them neither he nor anyone else who buys them from him can be required to pay more. If the shares had been issued at a premium of 50p, then once John had paid £150 to Boxo, neither he nor anyone else who bought the shares from him could be required to pay more. If John transferred the shares before he had paid for them in full, then the person who bought them from him would have to pay the balance if called upon to do so by Boxo plc.

Companies may also be limited by guarantee (s 3). Only brief mention needs to be made of them in a book on business law since they are mostly formed for charitable, social, political or other *non-trading purposes*. However, the members are liable only to the amount they have agreed upon in the statement of guarantee filed on incorporation (s 11). There is a separate clause in the guarantee which might say, for example:

> Every member of the company undertakes to contribute such amount as may be required (not exceeding £100) to the company's assets if it should be wound up while he is a member or within one year after he ceased to be a member, for payment of the company's debts and liabilities contracted before he ceased to be a member and of the costs charges and expenses of winding-up.

Obviously, this liability arises only if the company is wound up. Guarantee companies cannot be registered with a share capital (see s 5) as well so they will normally get their income from members' subscriptions, as in the case of a club. It is no longer possible to form (or re-register) as a company limited by guarantee and with a share capital. Given that guarantee companies cannot have a share capital, they must be formed as private companies since the definition of a public company is in part based upon the state of its share capital.

Once incorporated as a guarantee company, there is no provision for re-registration as a company limited by shares or vice versa.

Unlimited companies

Companies may be registered in which the liability of members is unlimited. Not many of these exist because of the personal liability of their members, which is unpopular. However, some organisations are prepared to put up with the fact that the liability of their members is unlimited in view of certain privileges available (see below).

Also, there is some advantage over an ordinary partnership in that there is a separate company *persona* for making contracts and holding property plus perpetual succession so that, for example, the death of a member does not cause a dissolution. A limited liability partnership is, of course, a legal entity.

The main advantage over the limited company is that unlimited companies do not have to file accounts with the Registrar so that the public has no access to their financial statements. However, the price of financial secrecy is unlimited liability. The above provisions do not apply if the company concerned is a subsidiary or holding company of a limited company.

These companies may also have a share capital, in which case the members must pay for their shares in full

plus any premium, and even then they have personal liability for the company's debts if it is wound up and does not have sufficient funds to pay its debts. These companies are always private companies.

Public and private companies

Section 4 of the Companies Act 2006 defines a public company and leaves private companies largely undefined other than by the fact that they are companies which do not satisfy the public limited company (PLC) definition. Section 755 prohibits private limited companies from offering their shares or debentures to the public. This prohibition can also be found in the Financial Services and Markets Act 2000 (Official Listing of Securities) Regulations 2001 (SI 2001/2956) preventing private companies from offering their securities, i.e. shares or debentures (loan capital), to the public.

A public company is a company limited by shares, whose certificate of incorporation says it is (s 4).

Two directors are required for a public company (who may also be the members of the company). Also, a public company cannot start trading or borrow money until it has received a trading certificate from the Registrar of Companies under s 762. The certificate must include a statement that the nominal value of the company's share capital is not less than the authorised minimum which is £50,000 (see s 763).

If a company does trade or borrow without a s 762 certificate, the directors are jointly and severally liable for any loss or damage caused to the other party to the transaction as a result of the company failing to meet its obligation.

Formation

The relevant provisions are set out in Part 2 of the CA 2006 (ss 7–16). It is now possible to use an electronic filing facility to incorporate a company. The sections in Part 2 are designed to remove any obstacle to formation of a company online. One person is now able to form any type of company (s 7) and not, as before, only a private company limited by shares, and not for an unlawful purpose.

Memorandum of association

Those who wish to form a company must subscribe their names to the memorandum of association, the form of which will be prescribed. The memorandum, which was once a major constitutional document, is now merely an incorporation document. No amendments will be possible. Provisions in the memorandum of existing companies will be regarded as in the articles and can be altered as such by special resolution. Companies formed under the CA 2006 and existing companies may have unrestricted objects (see below).

Requirements for registration

Section 9 registration documents

While it is possible to form a company through a formation agent, companies can be incorporated directly with Companies House. To incorporate a private limited company by shares or by guarantee, or a public limited company, an application of registration (FN01) must be sent to the Companies House. The application for registration must state:

■ the name of the company;
■ the situation of the registered office, i.e. England and Wales, Wales, Scotland or Northern Ireland;
■ the consenting company secretary (if applicable) and director(s);
■ the subscriber details;
■ whether the liability of the company's members is to be limited and if so whether it is to be limited by shares or by guarantee;
■ for companies limited by shares, information concerning the share capital details and the prescribed particulars relating to each class of shares must also be provided;
■ whether the company is going to be a private or public company.

A copy of the memorandum of association (with share capital or without share capital) must also be submitted to Companies House. This contains the names and signatures of the subscribers who are forming the company. The purpose of the memorandum of association is to confirm the subscribers' intention to form a company and become members of that company on formation. In the case of a company that is to be limited by shares, the memorandum will also provide evidence of the members' agreement to take at least one share each in the company, see s 8(1)(b).

If the company does not intend to adopt the model articles, the application must also be accompanied by a copy of the proposed articles of association outlining details of how the internal management should be governed.

Where the company is to have a share capital, there must be a statement of initial shareholdings (see below) and a statement of capital (see below); and if the company is to be limited by guarantee, a statement of the guarantee (see below).

Section 1068 gives the Registrar power to say how documents are to be delivered.

Statement of initial shareholding and share capital

The application for registration must also contain a statement of share capital and initial shareholding (s 1).

The statement contains the following:

■ the total number of shares of the company;
■ the aggregate nominal value of them;
■ the class rights for each class of shares;
■ the total number of shares in each class and the aggregate nominal value of them;
■ the amount, if any, paid up on the shares.

This statement is required on formation and when any alterations are made.

Statement of guarantee

In the case of a company limited by guarantee, a statement of guarantee must be included which states:

■ the names and addresses of the subscribers to the memorandum;
■ that new members must agree to make some contribution;
■ that the guarantee is to contribute to the assets of the company on winding-up while still a member or within one year after ceasing to be a member.

Statement of proposed officers

This contains particulars of directors and secretary. These persons have the option of having their addresses kept on a separate record at Companies House to which there is only limited access, e.g. to persons such as the police. The public record can contain a service address, e.g. the company's registered office.

Private companies need not have a company secretary.

Certificate of incorporation

When the Registrar is satisfied that all the requirements of the CA 2006 have been complied with the documents will be registered and a certificate of incorporation issued. The certificate is conclusive evidence that the CA 2006 has been complied with and that the company is duly registered as a public or private company. This means that there can be no challenge to the validity of the company's formation in any legal claim by it or against it. The directors and the secretary, where there is one, are duly appointed.

The CA 2006, in Schs 4 and 5, allows the electronic filing of the above documents. Where this is done, the order removes the need for witnesses to electronic signatures and statutory declarations, the latter being replaced by an electronic statement by a solicitor engaged in the formation or a person named as a director or secretary.

Pre-incorporation contracts

Generally

A company cannot make contracts until it has been incorporated. This takes place on the first moment of the day of the date on its certificate of incorporation.

Transactions entered into by the company's promoters and others in connection with its business before that time are not binding on the company when it is incorporated and the company cannot adopt these contracts after its incorporation. Thus, if the company's directors, who are its agents, were to write to a seller of goods and say that the company was now formed and would take over a pre-incorporation contract, the company would not be bound by it.

However, the company's promoters or other persons who may act for it at the pre-incorporation stage do incur personal liability to the other party to the contract under CA 2006, s 51.

Phonogram Ltd v Lane (1981)

Phonogram lent £6,000 for the business of a company to be called Fragile Management Ltd. Mr Lane, who was not a promoter of Fragile, signed 'for and on behalf of' the company a letter promising repayment by Fragile. The company was never formed and Phonogram sued

Mr Lane personally for repayment of the sum of £6,000 under what is now s 51. The Court of Appeal decided that Mr Lane was personally liable.

Comment.

(i) The case shows that although what is now s 51 is usually discussed in the context of making promoters personally liable, anyone acting on the company's business at the pre-incorporation stage is covered by what is now s 51. Also, the section says that a person acting for the company can avoid personal liability by an express agreement in the pre-incorporation contract that he is not to be liable. This case decides that the words 'for and on behalf of' the company were not enough. They do not amount to a specific agreement to prevent personal liability.

(ii) The *Phonogram* case made it clear that what is now s 51 can apply to make a promoter or other purported agent liable even though the company has not actually begun the process of formation. However it was held in *Cotronic (UK) Ltd v Dezonie* (1991) that there must at least be a clear intention to form the company as there was in *Phonogram*. In the *Cotronic* case a contract was made by Mr Dezonie on behalf of a company which had been struck off the register at a time when nobody concerned with its business had even thought about re-registering it. The Court of Appeal held that the contract was a nullity and Mr Dezonie was not liable on it under what is now s 51.

(iii) The words used by what is now s 51 are that the person making a pre-incorporation contract is 'personally liable on it'. Some commentators have suggested that this means that the maker of the contract cannot sue on it but only be sued by the other party. This interpretation would produce a rather one-sided agreement and the Court of Appeal affirmed in *Braymist Ltd v Wise Finance Co Ltd* (2002) that a claim can be brought on a pre-incorporation contract by the person purporting to act for the company. In that case a solicitor signed a pre-incorporation contract for the sale of land on behalf of Braymist. Wise Finance, the other party, later refused to go on with it. Braymist and the solicitor joined in a claim for damages and it was held that the presence of the solicitor as a claimant resulted in the claim succeeding. The solicitor was not merely liable on the contract but could also sue for its breach. The solicitor would hold any damages received on behalf of the company and could be made to account to the company for them if he or she refused to account though that scenario did not arise in this case nor would it be likely to in practice.

Solutions to the problem of personal liability of promoters

A promoter or other person conducting the company's business prior to its incorporation can overcome the difficulties facing him as regards personal liability in the following ways.

1 By incorporating the company before any business is done so that there are no pre-incorporation transactions.

2 By agreeing a draft contract with the other party and making it an object of the company that the company shall enter into it on formation. Nevertheless, if the company does not in fact enter into it, through the agency of its directors, there is no binding agreement either on the promoter or on the other party or the company.

3 By making a binding contract between the promoter and the other party and a draft contract on the same terms with the company. The binding contract must provide that once the company is formed and signs the draft contract through its agents, the promoter is released from the first contract which was binding on him.

This is a simple solution for most promoters who, after all, are usually promoting their own businesses as companies. They are normally in charge of the company and the board following incorporation and can easily arrange that the company signs through its agents the draft contract, thus releasing the promoter from his first binding contract.

4 By making a pre-incorporation contract with a specific clause saying that the promoter is not liable on it, as s 51 allows. There would seem to be little point in a third party signing such a contract since neither the company nor the promoter would be bound.

It is possible to purchase from company registration agents a company which is already formed, sometimes called a 'off-the-shelf' company because the agent takes it off his shelf and hands it over in terms, at least, of its essential documents. In such a case problems relating to pre-incorporation contracts do not arise because the company is in existence when the contract is made. It should, however, be noted that it will be necessary to change the directors and secretary of the shelf company since these will be the agents who formed it; also, the name may not suit and may need to be changed.

The company's constitution

Section 17 sets out the definition. Under its provisions a company's constitution includes the articles of association and any resolutions and agreements affecting it as set out in s 29, e.g. special resolutions as set out in s 29(1). This also extends to any resolutions that must be forwarded to the Companies House for registration.

The definition under s 17 is not exhaustive. For instance, the certificate of incorporation is of constitutional relevance as it is, as provided under s 15, the conclusive evidence that the requirements of this Act as to registration have been complied with and that the company is duly registered under the Act.

As stated above under company registration, the memorandum of association is no longer part of a company's constitution. It is merely a 'historical' document for use on incorporation as described in the Companies House incorporation guidance. For existing companies, s 28 allows provisions in their memoranda, which are no longer required under the CA 2006, to be treated as if those provisions had been automatically transferred to their articles. There will therefore be no need for existing companies to amend their articles unless they wish to do so.

The company's name

A company is only a legal person but, like a human being, it must have a name. The CA 2006 contains a system for controlling the names and business names of companies. The main rules are set out below.

On registration

The following rules apply.

1 The final words of the name – generally. A private company, whether limited by shares or guarantee, must end its name with the word 'limited' (s 59). A public company must end its name with the words 'public limited company' (s 58). The short forms – 'Ltd' and 'plc' – are allowed by ss 58 and 59. These words, or their short forms, must not appear elsewhere in the name (ss 58 and 59). One of the new company names adjudicators can direct an offending company to change its name to comply.

2 The final words of the name – an exemption.
Sections 60–64 allow private companies limited by guarantee to apply for exemption in the sense of leaving off the word 'limited' from the name. The section gives automatic exemption if the conditions are satisfied. The company simply sends to the Registrar of Companies what is called a statutory declaration, which is a statement made before a commissioner for oaths that certain facts are true. The declaration is signed by a director and the secretary of the company. The facts that it declares to be true are the ones which the above sections require for exemption, that is that:

- the objects of the company are to promote commerce, art, science, education, religion, charity, or any profession, and anything that would help that;
- the company's profits or income will be applied to the promotion of those objects;
- the payment of dividends is prohibited;
- all surplus assets on a winding-up will be transferred to another body with similar or charitable objects.

If the company at any time does not satisfy the above requirements, the Registrar may direct it to include 'limited' in its name again.

The exemption is not fully effective because, although the company need not use the word limited in its name, s 82 says that, despite the exemption, all business letters and order forms of the company must include a statement that it is limited. However, the company at least avoids the need to use the word 'limited' **as part of its name**. The word 'limited' generally connotes a commercial profit-orientated organisation which a s 60 company is not.

The CA 2006 allows, in Schs 4 and 5, in place of the statutory declaration, an electronically communicated statement made *on formation of the company* by a solicitor engaged in the formation, or by a person named as a director or secretary or, *in the case of a company changing its name to omit the word 'limited'*, by a director or secretary of the company.

3 Same, similar, and offensive names. Under s 53 a name will not be accepted by the Registrar if it is the same as one already on the Index of Names which he is required to keep by s 1099. **Similar** names will be registered. So if there is a company called Widgets Ltd on the Index the Registrar would register a new company called Widgets (Holdings) Ltd.

However, a company may be required by the Trade Secretary to change its name within 12 months of registration if it is 'too like' that of a company already on the Index (s 77). It is up to other companies to ascertain this, e.g. by purchasing daily extracts from the Register of the names of companies which have gone on it. There are firms which will supply these.

If a period of 12 months has passed, the Trade Secretary can do nothing under s 77 but Widgets Ltd could bring an action at common law for passing off. For example, in *Société Anonyme des Anciens Etablissements Panhard et Lavassor v Levassor Motor Co Ltd* (1901) (the *Panhard* case) the claimant was a French company whose cars were sold in England. The French company wished to set up an English company to act as an agent in England to improve the sales of its cars here. To try to stop this, the defendant English company was registered, the hope being that the French company could not then register an English company in its name in England because a company with that name would already be on the Register. The court said that the name of the English company must be taken off the Register. The members of the English company were told that they must change the name of their company or wind it up.

Finally, a name will not be registered if it is in the opinion of the Trade Secretary offensive or if its publication would be a criminal offence. Offensive words will not often be met with in business but the Registrar of Companies turned down the names 'Prostitutes Ltd' and 'Hookers Ltd' when application was made for the registration of the business of a prostitute. The expression 'Personal Services' was eventually accepted but the registration was later cancelled because the company had been formed for an immoral purpose contrary to public policy (see *Attorney-General v Lindi St Clair (Personal Services) Ltd* (1981)).

4 Connection with the government. A name which is likely to suggest a connection with the government or a local authority, e.g. 'District Council Supplies Ltd', will be registered only if the Trade Secretary approves (s 53).

5 Sensitive names. A name which includes any word or expression which is to be found in regulations made by the Trade Secretary under s 55 will not be registered as a company or business name unless the Trade Secretary approves.

The list of these sensitive names (which all imply some connection of prestige) also states the name of a government department or other organisation which can object to the use of the name and which must be approached and say that it does not disapprove before the Trade Secretary can give his approval.

Examples under regulations already issued are that for the use of 'Prince', 'Princess', 'Queen', approval of the Home Office is required, and for 'Bank', 'Banking', approval of the Bank of England is necessary. For the use of 'Charity' or 'Charitable', the approval of the Charity Commission is required.

Change of name

A company can change its name and have one which is different from the name it was registered in.

1 Voluntary change. A company may by special resolution change its name at any time – see ss 77–78 of the Act.

A private company is allowed by s 288 to use a unanimous written resolution which is effective without a meeting of the members. Further details of these resolutions appear later in the chapter but wherever a special or ordinary resolution is referred to in this text a private company can use the written resolution procedure except, so far as this text is concerned, for an ordinary resolution to remove a director from office or removing an auditor before the expiration of his term of office (see s 288(2)).

The new name must comply with the same requirements as on first registration which are listed above. The Registrar issues a new certificate of incorporation and the change does not take effect until that has been done.

2 Compulsory change. The Trade Secretary may (as we have seen) within 12 months of registration direct a change if the name in which the company has been registered is too like (or the same as) one which appears on the Registrar's Index of Names (s 67).

The Trade Secretary may also within five years of the date of registration direct a company to change its name if he believes that misleading information was provided at the time of its registration (s 75). There is no appeal to the court in this case.

A company might, for example, have misled the Registrar as to the nature of its business in order to obtain registration in a particular name. This would cover the obtaining of a sensitive name by deception where false information has been given to the approving authority. Thus, the use of the word 'Charity' requires the approval of the Charity Commissioners and if

promoters gave false information to the Commissioners in order to get permission to use, say, 'Barchester Charities' which they intended to use for personal gain, the name would have been obtained by deception and be subject to s 75.

Furthermore, the Trade Secretary may direct a company to change its name **at any time** if the registered name gives so misleading an indication of its activities as to be likely to cause confusion and harm to the public (s 32).

In this case the company may appeal to the court against the direction. Section 76 can apply where a company called, say, 'Prosperous Investments Trust' went through a genuine form of registration but was later acquired and used for the making of cheap home computers. These companies are called 'shell' companies and what goes on behind the shell is deceptive in terms of the name of that shell.

Directions under s 76 are rare but such a direction was given by the Secretary of State in regard to the Association of Certified Public Accountants of Britain which the Secretary of State considered was a registered name that was likely to mislead the public. The direction was based on the use of the word 'certified' – it could lead to confusion with other accounting bodies such as the Association of Chartered Certified Accountants. An application to the court to set aside the direction was dismissed (see *Association of Certified Public Accountants of Britain v Secretary of State for Trade and Industry* (1998)).

Company names and symbols

The increasing use of symbols in company names, e.g. '@', has led Companies House to revise its policy on the registration of company names. There are two main possibilities as follows:

■ *On incorporation or change of name.* Here the use of a symbol may be sufficient to allow registration of a name which is not the same as an existing company. So if there was already on the register a company called 'Florists at City House Ltd', it would seem that a company called 'Florists @ City House Ltd' would be registered either on incorporation or on change of name.

■ *Challenge to a name said to be 'too like' an existing one.* It appears that the mere use of a symbol may not be enough to prevent a possibly successful challenge so that in the example given above the second registration could be challenged as 'too like'. This also applies to abbreviations such as 'UK' or 'GB' or 'com', the addition of which to a name will not prevent a 'too like' challenge. The Registrar will presumably adopt the above procedures when faced with the new domain names that have become available such as 'info' and 'biz'.

Objection to a company's registered name

Section 69 contains this new provision and under it any person, not only a company, can object to a company names adjudicator if the company's registered name is similar to a name in which the objector has goodwill. Goodwill includes reputation of any description. The section contains a list of circumstances in which the respondent will be held to have adopted the name legitimately. The circumstances are as follows:

1 that the name was registered by the respondent before the commencement of the activities on which the applicant relies to show goodwill; *or*
2 that the company:
   ■ is operating under the name, *or*
   ■ is proposing to operate under the name and has incurred substantial start-up costs in preparation, *or*
   ■ was formerly operating under the name and is now dormant; *or*
3 that the name was registered in the ordinary course of a company formation business and the company is available for sale to the applicant on the standard terms of that business; *or*
4 that the name was adopted in good faith; *or*
5 that the interests of the applicant are not adversely affected to any significant extent.

If none of the above are shown, the objection will be upheld.

However, if the circumstances set out in 1, 2 above 3 above are established the objection will nevertheless be upheld if the applicant shows that the main purpose of the respondents (or any of them) in registering the name was to obtain money or other consideration from the applicant or prevent him or her from registering the name.

Section 70 gives the Secretary of State power to appoint company names adjudicators. One of the adjudicators is the Chief Adjudicator.

If an objection under s 69 is upheld, the adjudicator will direct the company with the offending name to change

it to one which does not similarly offend. If the company does not change the name, the adjudicator will decide on a new name for the company.

Appeal from a ruling of the adjudicator lies to the court to uphold or dismiss an application under s 69.

Publication of name

Sections 82 and 84 provide that the company's full name must be shown in an obvious place and in readable form outside the registered office and all places of business, and on all business letters, notices, and official publications, and in all bills of exchange, cheques, promissory notes, orders for money or goods, receipts and invoices, signed or issued on its behalf; emails and websites are now included.

Fines can be imposed on the company and its officers for failure to comply with the sections and also the officers of the company may incur personal liability for any amount due unless it is paid by the company. Thus, in *Hendon* v *Adelman* (1973) a cheque signed on behalf of L & R Agencies Ltd omitted the ampersand (&) in the company's name, which appeared as L R Agencies Ltd. It was held that the directors who had signed the cheque had not complied with what is now s 84 and so they were personally liable on it.

However, according to a more recent decision, it seems that so long as the outsider knows that he is dealing with a company and that the liability of its members is limited, trifling errors in the name will not trigger the liability. Thus, in *Jenice Ltd and others* v *Dan* (1993) the defendant who was a director of Primekeen Ltd signed a cheque incorrectly printed by the bank in the name of 'Primkeen Ltd'. The company went into liquidation and did not meet the cheque. Nevertheless, Mr Dan was not liable on it. There was no doubt that outsiders would have known that they were dealing with a limited company and no mischief had been done. Some judges have interpreted the section strictly, as the *Hendon* case shows, and regarded it as requiring that every part of the name be correct. The interpretation used in *Jenice* seems more sensible.

Business names

If a company has a place of business in Great Britain and carries on business here in a name which is not the corporate name – for example, Boxo Ltd carrying on business as 'Paris Fashions' – then the business name (Paris Fashions) must not suggest a connection with government or a local authority or contain sensitive words without the approval of the Trade Secretary, and in the case of sensitive names, also the approval of the body listed in the Regulations referred to above (CA 2006, Part 41).

A company which is using a business name has to state its corporate name in readable form on all business letters, orders for goods and services, invoices, receipts, and written demands for payment of business debts, and must also give an address in Great Britain where the service of documents will be effective. This is normally the registered office. Given that an address such as the address of the registered office is stated, there is no need to specifically state that that address is the document serving address (see *Department of Trade and Industry v Cedenio* (2001) in Chapter 5 ⬤).

A notice giving the same information must be shown in a prominent place in any premises where the business is carried on and to which customers and suppliers have access. Furthermore, the corporate name and address for service of documents must be given straight away and in writing on request to anyone who is doing or negotiating business with the company.

The criminal sanction consists of default fines on the company if it does not comply and also on its directors and other officers such as a secretary. The civil sanction is that the company may not be able to enforce its contracts (CA 2006, s 83). The rules on this are the same as for partners and sole traders who are operating under a business name but have not followed the CA 2006.

This civil sanction is now available under s 83 of the CA 2006 in regard to all company names registered or business. A company may be formed in the personal names of the shareholders and directors. Those who form companies often have to do this because all the made up names they want, e.g. City Publishing Ltd, are already on the Index. If this is so, personal names will be registered even though a company with that name is already on the Register, provided that the names are at the time of registration those of directors of the business.

In some cases where it is intended to use a personal name, the Registrar may require some addition to it where it is felt that an own or personal name might cause public confusion, e.g. Bloggs and Snooks (Furnishings) Ltd. However, even if an own name has been registered, this will not necessarily prevent an action at common law for passing off which, if successful, may lead the court to award damages and/or an injunction to prevent the continued use of the name (see *Asprey & Garrard Ltd v WRA (Guns) Ltd* (2001)).

Abuse of names by Internet users

Persons can select any name for their Internet address, provided it has not already been registered with Nominet UK, the body responsible for allocating UK domain names. A decision of the High Court indicates that if, by error, the same Internet domain name is allocated to two or more organisations, the court is prepared to resolve a dispute. The case *Pitman Training Ltd v Nominet UK* (1997) decided that a genuine registration of a name to which the organisation applying is entitled will be protected. The case confirms that the rule of 'first come, first served' applies. In the case Pitman Publishing registered the name *Pitman.co.uk* and later when the publisher tried to use the name it discovered that the name had been allocated and was in use by Pitman Training. Nominet restored the domain name to the publisher and a claim by the training company to establish its right to the name failed.

An additional problem, which has arisen because of the rapid growth of the Internet and its use by business organisations for email and commerce generally, is the parallel growth of a breed of speculators who register domain names which form a crucial part of a particular business website and email address, in the hope, for example, of offering it for sale to the business concerned with the possibility of receiving a high price for exclusivity. In *British Telecommunications plc v One in a Million Ltd* [1998] 4 All ER 476, the High Court granted injunctions to restrain defendants who had registered company names and/or trade marks as domain names on the Internet on the basis of passing off and trade mark infringement. The court also said that, since the names were now of no use to the defendants, they should be assigned to the claimants. The decision was applied in the 2006 Court of Appeal case of *Phones 4U Ltd v Phones4U.co.uk Internet Ltd* (2006).

Registered office

As will be seen from the registration documents, there is a statement that the registered office is situated in England. The actual address is also given.

A major purpose of the registered office is to keep various statutory registers, such as the register of members and records, for the purpose of inspection. In addition, it is the company's address where legal documents, notices and other communications can be served.

Objects

Pre-Companies Act 2006

Under former companies legislation an objects clause was contained in the memorandum, which was a constitutional document. The clause listed the things which a company could do. If it entered into a transaction which was not included in the clause that transaction was *ultra vires* (beyond its powers) and void (of no effect).

Ashbury Railway Carriage & Iron Co v Riche (1875)

The company was formed for the purposes of making and selling railway waggons and other railway plant. It got a contract to build a railway system in Belgium and entered into an agreement under which Riche was to be a subcontractor in this exercise. The company later ran into difficulties and the directors told Riche that his contract was at an end. He sued for breach of that contract. The House of Lords decided that he had no claim because the contract which the company had made to construct the railway system and of which he was a subcontractor was *ultra vires* and void. On a proper reading of the objects, the company had power to supply things for railways but had no power actually to make them.

By way of explanation of the decision of the above case, it should be said that the *ultra vires* rule was brought in by the courts to protect shareholders. It was thought that if a shareholder, X, bought shares in a company which had as its main object publishing and allied activities, then X would not want the directors of that company to start up a different kind of business because he wanted his money in publishing.

Objects today

Having given the reader a flavour of the *ultra vires* rule it would seem pointless to consider the many cases brought in regard to it in earlier times. The objects clause, if there is one, is to be in the articles and if the articles do not restrict the objects (which is not a requirement) then the company's objects are unrestricted. Even where the company has objects in its articles, this will not affect its capacity to make valid and enforceable contracts. Where the articles do restrict the objects, then any alterations or additions:

- must be notified the Registrar who will register the notice;
- are not effective until the notice is registered;
- have no effect on the rights and obligations of the company or on legal proceedings by or against the company.

However, directors must observe the company's constitution and work within any object restriction. Failure to do so will not affect the company's capacity or the directors' power to bind the company.

A company's capacity

Section 39 provides that the acts of a company are not to be questioned on the ground of lack of capacity because of anything in the constitution of the company. Thus contracts beyond the company's powers (where the articles contain restrictions) are valid and enforceable by the company and the other party. The members have no right to restrain acts of the directors beyond the company's powers since, in general, companies will have unrestricted objects. There are provisions under which the company has civil remedies, e.g. to recoup any loss to the company by claiming damages against the directors involved.

Power of the directors to bind the company

For those who deal in good faith with the company the power of the directors to bind the company or authorise others to do so is deemed not to be constrained by the company's constitution. External parties need not enquire whether there are any limitations on the power of the directors, nor are they affected by actual knowledge that the directors have no power. External parties must, however, be dealing with the company, which will in general require involvement with a commercial transaction (s 40).

Constitutional limitations: directors and their associates

Insiders, such as directors, and their associated persons, e.g. spouse, will not have the protection of s 40 so that the relevant transaction will be voidable and not enforceable against the company.

Regardless of whether the company avoids the transaction, the insider and any authorising directors are liable to account to the company for any gain made and to indemnify the company for any loss or damage caused to it.

Insiders who are not directors may be able to avoid the above-mentioned liability if they did not know when entering into the transaction with the company that the directors were acting beyond their powers; and so a connected person such as a spouse may not be liable.

Transactions will not be voidable if restitution of the company's property is not possible (as where the company's money has been spent by a director on a cruise – there is no restitution against the cruise company unless it was in some way involved in the director's breach of duty) or the company has been indemnified or the company through its members has affirmed the transaction (s 41).

Companies that are charities

Section 42 provides that for companies that are charities the rules relating to the capacity of a company and the power of its directors to bind it shall not apply to an external party unless that party did not know that the company was a charity when the act was done or the charity receives full consideration in regard to the act done and the external party did not know that the act was beyond the capacity of the company and therefore beyond the powers of the directors to bind it.

Charitable companies cannot affirm so as to make valid acts infringing the above rules without the prior written consent of the Charity Commissioners.

Altering the objects

Since a company that has restrictive objects will now put them in the articles, or, if the objects were contained in an old-style memorandum they will be deemed under CA 2006 to have been transferred into the articles, they can be changed as general articles can be changed, i.e. by special resolution of the members.

Limitation of liability

The source of this knowledge is the capital documents filed on incorporation and changes notified since. The relevant document may simply state: 'The liability of the members is limited' – unless of course the company is unlimited, when this clause is not put in.

The clause cannot be altered so as to make the company an unlimited one. However, the company may be re-registered as unlimited under s 102. All unlimited companies must be private companies and public companies cannot apply for re-registration under s 102, but must convert to private companies first.

An unlimited company may re-register as a limited company under s 105. This does not apply to a company which was previously a limited company but re-registered as an unlimited one. In this case there is no going back.

It will be recalled that an unlimited company is in general not required to file accounts with the Registrar and so there can be no going backwards and forwards between limited and unlimited status because this could lead to selective filing of accounts: e.g. if the accounts are bad, re-register as unlimited; if they improve, re-register as limited and file them and so on. The CA 2006 prevents this.

Capital

The source of this information is now the statement of share capital filed on incorporation plus any changes noted since. Previously, a company was registered with an authorised capital which it could then issue. Once it had issued its authorised capital it had to have an ordinary resolution of the members to increase it so that more shares could be issued. This procedure is now abolished. The company may increase its capital by allotting more shares under proper authority.

Articles of association

The articles are now the company's main constitutional document containing all the company's key rules and powers including the allocation of powers between the members and the directors. The memorandum is now a formation document evidencing an intention to form a company which then becomes of historical significance only.

All companies must have and register articles unless they adopt model articles in full. The articles must be printed, divided into paragraphs numbered consecutively (s 18).

Power of Secretary of State to prescribe model articles

Section 19 gives the Secretary power to prescribe model articles for different types of companies. The version of model articles in force when an existing company was registered will continue to apply. Thus for many existing companies the model or default articles will be Table A to the Companies Act 1985. They can, however, adopt the new model articles instead of Table A. Provisions in the model articles can be incorporated or excluded where the company registers special articles much as before so that the company could file special articles incorporating by reference the model articles 'except for Arts 1, 4 and 6'.

One of the main criticisms for the model articles (Table A) under the Companies Act 1985 was that the articles were largely irrelevant and inapplicable for small and medium-sized companies. Given that one of its main objectives was to 'think small', the 2006 Act has sought to address the different needs of small/medium-sized companies and large public companies. The then BERR (now BIS), in its consultation document published in July 2007, suggested three main types of articles of associations for private companies limited by shares, private companies limited by guarantee and public companies. It was specifically mentioned in the government's consultation document that 'the draft Articles for private companies also continue to be written with small companies in mind.' This main point is therefore to make certain provisions, which are irrelevant to small companies, redundant. The Companies (Model Articles) Regulations 2008 (SI 2008/3229) were made on 16 December 2008. These Articles are to be used as default articles by companies formed and registered on or after 1 October 2009.

One of the notable points is that the limited liability provision has been inserted into each of the new model articles which limits the liability of the members in the company.

Default application of model articles

Under s 20, where special articles fail to provide for a particular matter the model articles are applied and the same is true where no articles at all are filed by the company.

Entrenched provisions in the articles

Under s 22, provisions in the articles may say that they are not alterable at all or alterable only subject to certain conditions. Such a provision may be in relation to the class rights of shareholders which may not be alterable or alterable only with the consent of a 75 per cent vote in agreement by the class concerned.

Provision for entrenchment may be made:

- on formation; or
- subsequently but only with the unanimous consent of all members.

Notice to the Registrar of entrenchment

The Registrar must be notified when a company entrenches a provision either on formation or subsequently. Entrenchment by subsequent alteration requires a notice of compliance (s 23).

Notice to Registrar of removal of entrenched provisions

The notice must be accompanied by a notice of compliance.

The purpose of the entrenched provisions rule is to put people searching the register on notice that there are entrenched provisions and as to whether they have been removed. The notice of compliance is to the effect that the alteration has been made in accordance with the company's articles. The Registrar may rely on this as evidence of procedural correctness.

Existing companies: provisions of memorandum transferred to articles

Under s 28, those provisions of existing companies not required in the new memorandum are to be regarded as in the articles and alterable as such, i.e. special or written special resolution.

Electronic communication

It should be noted that the CA 2006, in Schs 4 and 5, allows the electronic appointment of proxies and the sending of notices. Further detail as to method could be contained in the articles.

Legal effect of the articles

Section 33 provides that the provisions of the company's constitution constitute a special kind of contract whose terms bind the company and its members from time to time.

It follows from this that:

1 **The members are bound to the company by the provisions of the articles.** This is illustrated by the following case.

Hickman v Kent or Romney Marsh Sheep Breeders' Association (1915)

1 The articles of the association provided that any dispute between a member and the company must be taken first to arbitration. H, a shareholder, who was complaining that he had been wrongfully expelled from the company, took his case first to the High Court. The court decided that the action could not continue in the High Court. H was contractually bound by the articles to take the dispute to arbitration first.
2 The company is also bound to the members in respect of their rights as members.

Again, the following case is an illustration of this point.

Pender v Lushington (1877)

The articles of the Direct United States Cable Co gave its members voting rights but fixed a maximum amount of votes (100) which each member could cast no matter how many shares he held. The Globe Telegraph and Trust Co held a large number of shares in Direct United and to evade the 100 votes rule and increase its voting power it transferred some of its shares to P who agreed to be a nominee of Globe and vote with it. L, who was the chairman of Direct United, refused to allow P to cast his votes and a resolution supported by Globe and P was lost. P asked the court for an injunction to restrain the company and L from declaring that P's votes were bad. The court granted the injunction. P had a contractual right to vote given to him by the articles and he could enforce this right. His votes must be accepted.

3 Each member is bound to the other members.

This is illustrated by the following case.

Rayfield v Hands (1958)

A clause in the articles of a company provided that: 'Every member who intends to transfer shares shall inform the directors who will take the said shares equally between them at a fair value.' Rayfield, a member, told the defendant directors that he wanted to transfer his shares. The directors refused to take and pay for them, saying that they had no liability to do so.

The court decided that the word 'will' indicated an obligation to take the shares and that the clause imposed a contractual obligation on the directors to take them. This was in the nature of a collateral contract. When a member bought shares he made a contract with the company but also a collateral contract with the other members to observe the provisions of the articles. Thus, the members could sue each other and there was no need for the company, with whom the main contract was made, to be a party to the action.

Comment. Although the article placed the obligation to take shares on the directors, the judge construed this as an obligation falling upon the directors in their capacity as members. Otherwise the contractual aspect of the provision in the articles would not have applied. The articles are not a contract between the company and the directors who, in their capacity as directors, are outsiders for this purpose (see below).

4 Neither the company nor the members are bound to outsiders.

This is illustrated by the following case.

Eley v The Positive Government Security Life Assurance Co Ltd (1876)

The articles of the company appointed Mr Eley as solicitor of the company for life. During the course of this employment he became a member of the company. Later he was dismissed and brought an action against the company for damages for breach of the contract which he said was contained in the articles. The court decided that his action failed. There was no contract between the company and Mr Eley. He was an outsider in his capacity as a solicitor. The articles gave him rights only in his capacity as a member.

It should be noted that the Contracts (Rights of Third Parties) Act 1999 does not apply to the statutory contract set out in s 33. The 1999 Act specifically excludes it to prevent third-party rights from arising – see s 6(2) of the 1999 Act. Thus, the legal decisions set out above continue to apply and are not affected by the 1999 Act or the CA 2006.

Alteration of the articles

The company may alter or add to its articles by a special (or written) resolution (s 21), subject to certain restrictions of which the following are the most important.

1 The court will not allow an alteration to be enforced if it is not for the benefit of the members as a whole, as where the company takes a power of expulsion of members for no particular reason.

Brown v British Abrasive Wheel Co Ltd (1919)

The majority shareholders (98 per cent) in a company agreed to provide more capital for the company on condition that the 2 per cent minority (who were not prepared to put more money in) would sell their shares to the majority. Negotiations having failed, the articles were altered to include a clause under which a shareholder was forced to transfer his shares to the other members at a fair value if requested to do so in writing. The court decided that the alteration could not be allowed. The clause could be used to deprive any minority shareholder of his shares without any reason being given and it was not for the benefit of the company (i.e. the members) as a whole that any one or more of their number should be expelled for no good reason.

However, expulsion is allowed if it does benefit the members as a whole as where the member expelled is competing with the company.

Sidebottom v Kershaw Leese & Co Ltd (1920)

Mr Sidebottom, who was a minority shareholder in the company, carried on a business which competed with the company. Because of this the articles were altered to include a clause under which any shareholder who competed with the company had to transfer his shares at a fair value to persons nominated by the directors. The Court of Appeal decided that the alteration was valid. Although it only applied to a particular member at the time, it could be applied in the future to any member who competed with the company (but not, of course, to members who did not). This would always be for the benefit of the company in that its members would have power to exclude a competitor.

2 A company cannot justify breach of a contract outside the articles by showing that the breach resulted from an alteration of the articles.

Southern Foundries Ltd v Shirlaw (1940)

Mr Shirlaw, who was a director of Southern Foundries, was appointed managing director of that company for 10 years by a contract outside the articles. The company was taken over by Federated Industries. With their voting power they altered the articles to provide that Federated Industries had power to remove any director of Southern Foundries and that the managing director of Southern Foundries must also be a director. Mr Shirlaw was subsequently removed from his directorship and therefore could no longer qualify as managing director and his contract was terminated while it still had some years to run. The House of Lords decided that the company was liable in damages. Although a company always had a legal right to change its articles, if by doing so it caused a breach of an outside contract, then, while the alteration could not be prevented, the company was liable in damages if there was a breach of a contract outside the articles as a result of the alteration.

3 Shareholders' rights are contained in the articles. Obviously, these rights can be changed by a special resolution of the company in general meeting. There would seem to be no objection to the use of the written resolution by private companies because under the CA 2006 these resolutions no longer require unanimity. Instead, they need only be signed by the majority that would have been required to pass the resolution at a general meeting. However, if the company has more than one class of shares, e.g. A Ordinaries and B Ordinaries, then the special resolution is not enough.

Under s 630 a special resolution is not effective unless holders of three-quarters of the issued shares of each class consent in writing, e.g. by returning a tear-off slip on a letter to indicate their agreement or not, or by means of an extraordinary resolution at a class meeting. A private company cannot insist on unanimous objection by the unanimous written resolution approach because objection by only three-quarters is enough.

In addition, s 633 applies; under this 15 per cent of the class who did not vote for the variation may apply to the court within 21 days of the resolution which altered the articles. Once such an application has been made, the variation will not take effect unless and until it is confirmed by the court.

The point of this is that those holding the A Ordinary shares may well be able to get a special resolution in general meeting and so weaken the position of the B Ordinary shareholders, but they cannot do so without the necessary class consent of the B Ordinary shareholders. The changes do not need the consent of those holding A Ordinary shares because their rights have not been varied, each A Ordinary shareholder having one vote per share as before.

Alteration of the articles by the court

The articles are a contract and the court has power to rectify (alter) contracts where the parties have orally agreed something which they have written down incorrectly but where one party will not cooperate in making a change usually because the written contract is more favourable to him or her than the oral one. If the court is satisfied that what is written does not represent what was agreed, it will alter the contract by order to fit the genuine agreement of the parties.

The court, however, is reluctant to use this power on the articles preferring that the members make the alteration by the requisite resolution (see *Frank Scott* v *Frank Scott (London) Ltd* (1940)).

However, the court did make an alteration in the articles in *Folkes Group plc* v *Alexander* (2002) where because of bad drafting an alteration to the articles took away the voting control of the Folkes family in the group. The other shareholders were not prepared to cooperate in the necessary resolution and on the articles, as wrongly altered, the Folkes family shareholders could not get a special resolution without them. The High Court changed the articles to what had been intended and restored the control of the Folkes family. The judge said he had been faced with an absurd result consequent upon a serious drafting error in the original alteration. He felt able to make an order changing the articles to reflect what had been intended.

Financing the company

We shall now deal with the raising of money for the company.

Share capital

The capital of a company may be divided into preference and ordinary shares. In addition, both of these classes of shares may, under s 684, be issued as redeemable by the company at a future date.

Preference shares

These shares have the right to payment of a fixed dividend, e.g. 10 per cent of the nominal value, before any dividend is paid on the other shares. However, there is no right to such dividend unless the company has sufficient distributable profits to pay it. This is why preference shares differ from loan capital. Interest on loan capital must be paid whether the company has distributable profits or not. If it has no profits, it must be paid from capital as by a sale of assets or the raising of a further loan.

Once the preference dividend has been paid in full, the preference shareholders have no right to share in surplus profit with the ordinary shareholders unless, as is rare, the preference shares are participating preference shares. Preference shares may be cumulative or non-cumulative. If they are cumulative and in any one year there are insufficient profits to pay the preference dividend, it is carried forward and added to the dividend for the following year and is paid then if there are sufficient profits.

So if Eric is the holder of 100 preference shares of £1 each, carrying a preference dividend of 10 per cent, then if in year one the dividend cannot be paid, the £10 to which Eric is entitled is carried forward to year two and if there are sufficient profits in that year Eric will receive £20. If the shares are non-cumulative, Eric would not receive the £10 lost in year one, but only £10 for year two and subsequently.

Ordinary (or equity) shares

These rank for dividend after the preference shares and sometimes also the terms of issue provide that the preference shares shall have a right to claim repayment of capital before the ordinary shares if the company is wound up.

Ordinary shares, therefore, carry most risk. Generally they have most of the voting rights in general meetings and therefore control the company, it being common to provide that the preference shares shall not have a vote at all unless their dividend is in arrears. Ordinary shares receive a fluctuating dividend which depends upon distributable profits left after the preference dividend has been paid.

Redeemable shares

Under s 684 a public limited company with a share capital may, if authorised by its articles, issue redeemable shares, whether ordinary or preference. Private companies do not require prior authorisation in the articles. Redeemable shares may be made redeemable between certain dates at the option of the company's directors. The holder thus knows that his shares cannot be redeemed before the earlier of the two dates, which is usually a number of years after the issue of the shares in order to give him an investment which will last for a reasonable period. He also knows that the shares are bound to be redeemed by the later of the two dates mentioned. However, there are no legal provisions requiring a company to fix the time of redemption at the time of issue, and a company may wish to leave the date of redemption to be decided by the board when financially convenient.

Redeemable shares may be issued only if there are in issue other shares which cannot be redeemed. It is not therefore possible for a company to redeem all its share capital and end up under a board of directors with no members. The shares must be cancelled after redemption. The company cannot hold and trade in redeemed shares.

The power to issue redeemable equity shares is useful in the expansion of the small business. Outside investors often like ordinary share capital with its greater potential returns in the way of dividend and capital gain, but the smaller businessperson may wish to buy them out after the business has developed. He can do this by issuing redeemable ordinary shares. Redeemable preference shares are less attractive to the speculative investor. They are safe but carry only a fixed dividend no matter how high the profits.

Purchase of own shares

Sections 690–708 apply and any company may by following the procedures laid down in these sections purchase its own shares, including any redeemable shares – as where the date for redemption has not arrived. The shareholder(s) concerned must of course be willing to sell the shares and the company must want to buy them. The company cannot be forced to buy them, nor can a shareholder be forced to sell.

The important legal considerations are set out below.

1 Prior authorisation in the articles is not required.
2 The shares must be fully paid. The CA 2006 does not allow the purchase (or, for that matter, redemption) of partly paid shares.

3 A company cannot purchase its shares if as a result of the purchase there would no longer be any member of the company holding shares other than redeemable shares. There must be a member or members holding non-redeemable shares.
4 A public limited company must have allotted share capital of at least £50,000.
5 The shares must, in general terms, be cancelled following purchase (but see below).

Treasury shares

The CA 2006 in Chapter 6 allows *public companies* whose shares are listed on the Official List of the Stock Exchange or traded on the Alternative Investment Market or traded on equivalent markets in another European Economic Area member state to keep shares in what is called treasury after they have been purchased back by the company. The company is registered as the holder of the shares that have gone into treasury and not more than 10 per cent of the company's issued shares can be held in treasury or 10 per cent of any class of shares. This means that the whole of the treasury shares cannot be taken from one class where the company has different classes of shares. If the company therefore has A Ordinary, B Ordinary and C Ordinary shares and each class contains 100 shares, then 10 per cent of the issued capital is 30 shares but these cannot all come from one class since to take 30 shares from any one of the classes would be to take 30 per cent of the class which is not allowed. Therefore, the purchases must be spread across the classes 10 from each or, if only the A Ordinaries are purchased, then only 10 shares of that class may be kept in treasury. Any purchase in excess of this must be disposed of by the company within 12 months of the purchase or cancelled. The following additional provisions should be noted:

■ To make a purchase of its own shares for treasury, the company must have sufficient distributable profits. If the shares are purchased from the proceeds of a fresh issue of shares, the shares purchased must be cancelled.

■ When treasury shares are sold for a price equal to or less than the price the company paid for them, the proceeds of sale can under the Act be treated as realised profits, but if the sale price is more, the excess is treated as capital and must be transferred to a share premium account. The excess is not therefore distributable.

- Treasury shares must not receive dividends or give the company as holder any voting rights but on a bonus issue the company may receive bonus shares in respect of the treasury shares it holds.
- Pre-emption rights apply and so treasury shares must, on sale, be offered to existing shareholders first. In fact, listed companies can only issue 5 per cent of their securities to persons other than existing shareholders in any one year. This may remove some of the flexibility in the disposal of treasury shares outside the company.
- Under the UK Listing Rules treasury shares will continue to be quoted but are not to be sold at more than a 10 per cent discount to current market price.

Market purchase

Public companies may make a market purchase on, for example, the Stock Exchange or the Alternative Investment Market (AIM) (see below), or an off-market purchase from an individual shareholder.

Before a Stock Exchange or AIM purchase can be made by the directors the members must approve by ordinary resolution. The resolution must state the maximum number of shares which the directors can acquire and the maximum and minimum prices which they can pay. The minimum price is often specified, but the maximum price is usually according to a formula, for example one based upon the Daily Official List of the Stock Exchange on a day or days preceding the day on which the share is contracted to be purchased, e.g. an amount equal to 105 per cent of the average of the upper and lower prices shown in the quotation for ordinary shares of the company in the daily list of the Stock Exchange on the three business days immediately preceding the day on which the contract to purchase is made.

The duration of the authority to purchase must be stated in the resolution by stating the date on which it expires.

A copy of the resolution must be filed with the Registrar of Companies within 15 days after it is passed.

Off-market purchase

These provisions are mainly for private companies but can be used, as we have seen, by PLCs whose shares are not listed on the Stock Exchange or quoted on the AIM, which is regulated by the Stock Exchange for the smaller PLCs which cannot or who do not wish to comply with the conditions for a full listing on the Stock Exchange.

The procedure is as follows:

1 A special (or, in private companies, written) resolution of the members is required before the contract is entered into. The contract must therefore be approved in advance. So far as PLCs are concerned (but not private companies), the resolution must specify the duration of authority to make the contract being a period not longer than 18 months.

Section 694 allows the company to make a contract for an off-market purchase conditional upon its approval by the shareholders.

2 The special resolution is not effective unless the draft contract is made available for inspection by the members at the registered office or an alternative place to be specified in regulations during the 15 days immediately preceding the meeting and at the meeting. Where the written resolution procedure is used there will not, of course, be a meeting and so the draft contract will have to be circulated to the members with their copy of the resolution for signature. This applies wherever in this text it is stated that documents must be available at a meeting.

The special resolution is invalid if passed by the votes of the member whose shares are being purchased. Thus there must be sufficient other shareholders' votes to give the necessary majority of 75 per cent of those voting in person or by proxy. The member whose shares are being purchased can vote other shares he may have which are not being purchased on a poll but he cannot in any event vote on a show of hands.

Off-market contingent contracts

All companies may make contingent purchase contracts. These are contracts by the company to buy its own shares on the happening of a future event, for example a contract to buy the shares of an employee on retirement. This is permitted if the procedures for an off-market purchase set out above are followed.

It should be noted that the company cannot assign its right to buy the shares to someone else. This is to prevent a market developing in contingent purchase contracts.

The company cannot release, i.e. give up, its right to buy except by authorisation of a special resolution of the members.

Purchase of own shares: miscellaneous provisions

When a company has purchased its own shares it must within 28 days disclose the fact to the Registrar, giving the number and nominal value of the shares purchased and the date they were delivered to the company. Furthermore, the contract of purchase must be kept at the registered office for 10 years and can be inspected by members. In a PLC it can be inspected also by any other person without charge.

If a company fails to purchase the shares when it has agreed to do so there is no action by the member for damages. However, he can bring an action for specific performance but the court will not make such an order unless the company can pay for the shares from its distributable profits.

Payment for shares purchased by the company (or redeemed by it) must be made at the time of purchase (or redemption). A creditor cannot be created following the relevant transaction. Until case law came along it had been assumed that a payment in cash was required. However, the matter was considered in *BDG Roof-Bond Ltd* v *Douglas* (2000) where the court found it acceptable that a payment for shares by the company was made by some cash plus a piece of property and a car owned by the company.

Purchase (or redemption) partly from capital – private companies only

This provision is intended for private companies who have some distributable profits **but these are not enough** to purchase or redeem the shares and the company is either unwilling or unable to raise money from a fresh issue of shares. In such a case it can purchase or redeem its shares partly from capital.

It is in effect an easier procedure for private companies to reduce their share capital or to satisfy the claims of a retiring member or the estate of a deceased member in respect of shares in the company which might not be easily saleable elsewhere.

As regards the conditions, there is now no requirement for prior authorisation in the articles. The 'permissible capital payment' (PCP) is the shortfall after taking into account distributable profits or the proceeds of a fresh issue of shares, which the company must utilise first. If there are no distributable profits or proceeds of a fresh issue of shares, there can be no purchase or redemption wholly from capital. This restricts the advantages of the section to some extent.

There must be a statutory declaration of solvency by the directors. This says that the company will be solvent immediately after making the purchase (or redemption) and for one year afterwards. The statutory declaration states the PCP and the declaration itself is based on accounts prepared within three months before the statutory declaration, taking into account any distributions (e.g. dividends) which may have been made between the accounts and the statutory declaration.

A report by the auditors must be attached to the statutory declaration stating that the PCP has been properly calculated and that the directors' opinion as to solvency is reasonable in terms of the facts of which the auditors are aware.

A special (or written) resolution of the members is also required and the statutory declaration and auditors' report must be available for inspection at the meeting. The position regarding voting and circularisation of documents in the case of a unanimous written resolution has already been described. In spite of the audit exemption provisions, the requirement for an auditors' report when purchasing shares from capital is retained. This means that very small companies can exempt themselves from the requirement to appoint an auditor unless and until it becomes necessary for some purpose other than the audit of annual financial statements. If it becomes necessary, an auditor will have to be appointed unless the relevant regulations say otherwise. This is indicated as required throughout this chapter.

The resolution must be passed within one week of the date of the statutory declaration. It is invalid if passed with the votes of the shares of the person whose shares are being bought. Such persons may vote other shares on a poll but not on a show of hands. (The position in regard to written resolutions has already been explained.)

The capital payment must be made not earlier than five weeks (to allow for objections) and not later than seven weeks from the resolution. If an indefinite period was allowed for the capital payment the statutory declaration would be getting outdated, so seven weeks is the maximum time.

Publicity must be given in order to protect creditors. A notice in writing may be given to all the company's creditors stating the fact and the date of the special (or written) resolution, the amount of the PCP, that the statutory declaration and auditors' report can be inspected at the registered office and that any creditor may seek to restrain the payment by applying to the court to cancel the special resolution during the period of five weeks from the special resolution. The statutory declaration and auditors' report must be kept at the registered office for inspection by any member or creditor until the end of the fifth week following the special resolution.

Alternatively, an advertisement may be put in *The London Gazette* and one national newspaper giving the same information as listed above.

At the date of the notice or advertisement copies of the statutory declaration and auditors' report must have been sent to the Registrar so that they are available for inspection by a company search.

Dissentient shareholders or creditors may also apply to the court, within five weeks of the resolution, to cancel it, for example if available profits have not been utilised. The court may order the purchase of the dissentient shares or the payment of creditors. This provision is obviously inapplicable, so far as members are concerned, where there is a written resolution.

If the company goes into insolvent winding-up within 12 months of a payment from capital, then the seller of the shares and the directors giving the statutory declaration are each liable to repay the money in full with a right of contribution against the others involved.

Transfer of purchased shares

A transfer form is not required on completion of the purchase. The seller merely hands over his share certificate to the company for cancellation.

Where shares are to be held in treasury, they are transferred to the company so that it may hold them in treasury.

Loan capital

Trading companies have an implied power to borrow and charge their assets as security for a loan, i.e. to give the lender a right to appoint, for example, a receiver to sell the company's assets in order to repay the loan if the company does not otherwise repay it, or, where practicable, to run the business for a while in order to sell it as a going concern (see below).

Even so, the memorandum usually gives an express power to borrow and details of the extent to which the company can charge its assets as security.

Section 761 puts restrictions on borrowing by newly formed PLCs. Such companies cannot commence business or borrow until they have received a certificate allowing them to do this from the Registrar of Companies.

The certificate will not be issued until at least £50,000-worth of the company's capital has been allotted (sold) and at least one-quarter of the nominal value of each share and the whole of any premium has been received by the company.

Debenture and debenture stock

When a lender makes a loan to a company he will obviously require some evidence of that fact. This is usually a written document in the form of a deed which is called a debenture, a term which has its origin in the Latin word for 'owing'.

A **single debenture** evidences a loan from a person where the lender is in privity of contract with the company and is a creditor of it. Its modern use is to secure a loan or overdraft facility from a bank. In this context it is the document by which the company charges in favour of the bank all its assets and undertakings, thus giving the bank the right to appoint an administrator. The functions of an administrator are contained in the Insolvency Act 1986, Sch B1, para 3 (as inserted by the Enterprise Act 2002, Part 10). An administrator has the function of carrying out statutory purposes in the following order:

- to rescue the company as a going concern;
- if this is not reasonably practicable, to achieve a better result for the company's creditors as a whole than would be likely if the company were wound up without first being in administration. Thus, an administrator may manage the company for a period of time to allow it to complete an order which will provide income; or
- if neither of the above is reasonably practicable and the administrator does not harm the interests of the creditors as a whole, realising (selling) the company's property to make a distribution of the proceeds to one or more secured or preferential creditors.

The only other corporate insolvency practitioner likely to be met with in the generality of business is a liquidator whose function is to wind up the company. He is really an undertaker and his job is to sell what assets the company has to pay the creditors as far as he can and then see that the company is removed from the Register.

Debenture stock is found where the loan is to come from the public, those who subscribe for the debenture stock receiving a stock certificate rather like a share certificate. The company keeps a register of debenture holders and the stock certificates can be transferred from one person to another in a similar way to shares. However, unlike shares, which cannot be issued at a discount (s 100), debentures can be so issued. It would, for example, be unlawful to issue, say, a £1 share at 75p, but this would be legal in the case of a debenture.

When debentures are issued for public subscription, the company enters into a trust deed with trustees for the debenture holders. The trustees are often an insurance company. The insurance company has the charge over the assets and the power to appoint a receiver or an administrative receiver and the trustees are the creditors of the company on trust for the individual stock holders who are not in privity of contract with the company.

From a commercial point of view this is necessary because the holders of debenture stock are widely dispersed and need some central authority, such as the trustees, to look after their interests with the company.

Registration of charges

The much revised provisions relating to company charges contained in the Companies Act 1989 have been repealed by the CA 2006, which now applies.

Under s 860 particulars of a charge to secure a debenture or an issue of debentures must be registered with the Registrar of Companies. The object of this is to show those doing business with the company, who may inspect the Register, what charges there are affecting the company's property.

In addition, copies of the documents creating charges are to be kept at the company's registered office or other place as appropriate and be available for inspection by members and creditors without charge (s 876).

The company must also keep a register of charges affecting its property (s 876). This may also be inspected by members and creditors without charge (s 877).

Failure to register a charge

Failure to register particulars of a charge with the Registrar within 21 days of its creation means that the charge will be void if the company is wound up and a liquidator appointed, or if an administrator is appointed. The lender would then become an unsecured creditor and would have no rights over the property which the company had charged to secure his loan. Nevertheless, the money intended to be secured, if not on demand, becomes immediately repayable. In addition, an unregistered charge is not void while the company is a going concern.

It is because the security may be lost that the law allows a secured creditor to register the charge himself and to claim the costs from the company (s 860).

However, in practice, banks, which commonly lend money or give overdraft facilities to companies on a secured debenture, get the signatures of the appropriate officers of the company on the document registering the charge and then post it to the Registrar in Cardiff themselves. Thus, the company registers the charge but the bank ensures that this is done.

Failure to register the charge in the company's register leads to a default fine on the company's officers at fault; the debt for which the charge was given remains payable, but it will be as an unsecured loan.

There are also provisions allowing the court to approve the registration of particulars of a charge delivered after 21 days. The charge will be valid from the date of its registration but has no priority over persons who took charges over the company's property while it was not registered.

Releasing the charge

Under s 872 and on application being made by the company to the Registrar of Companies that the charge has been redeemed or released the Registrar will enter what is called a memorandum of satisfaction on the Companies House register of charges. It is in the company's interests to clear the register by an entry of satisfaction in case of further borrowing.

The issue of shares and debentures

Generally

Under s 549 the directors of public and private companies (in this case with more than one class of shares) cannot issue shares without the express authority of the members. Directors of private companies with only one class of shares are able to allot them without shareholder approval unless the articles forbid this.

Authority is usually given by the members by ordinary resolution at a general meeting of the company. The authority may be given for a particular allotment of shares or it may be a general power, though if it is it can be given only for a maximum period of five years and then it must be renewed. The authority once given may be taken away or varied by the members by ordinary resolution insofar as it has not been exercised.

Under s 549 private companies may elect by ordinary resolution that the authority given to the directors to allot shares can be given for an indefinite period or a fixed period of longer than five years (see s 551). The fixed period is renewable, and further renewable, by the company in general meeting. The authority may also be varied or revoked by the company in general meeting. The authority must in all cases state the maximum number of relevant securities that may be allotted, e.g. the whole of the company's unissued share capital.

Similar permission to allot debenture stock is not required unless the debentures can, by the terms of issue, be converted at some time in the future to shares.

Section 561 deals with existing shareholders' right of pre-emption. When public and private companies wish to offer shares where the members have given them power under s 549, they must offer them to existing members first in proportion to their present holdings, e.g. one new for three existing shares, or whatever formula covers the number of shares being issued.

This requirement to issue to existing members may be excluded. A private company with only one class of shares can add to its articles by a special resolution a clause stating that these pre-emption rights, as they are called, shall not apply to the company and this will last unless and until the articles are altered by special resolution or the company ceases to be a private company, see s 569. It may in fact be permanent.

A public company (and a private company to which the approach does apply) can disapply the pre-emption rights by special resolution of its members which may be for a particular issue or a general disapplication for a fixed period and then must be renewed (s 570).

The provisions of ss 549 and 561 prevent the directors from using the power of allotment to issue shares to persons favourable to themselves in order to keep their position on the board and thus their control of the company. This did happen in the past but now the consent of the members is required, with the exception just considered, both to allot the shares in the first place and then to issue them outside to persons other than existing members.

Even in a private company which has given the directors a power of allotment for an indefinite period, or where there is only one class of shares, the members must still approve the disapplication of pre-emption rights. This assumes that the private company has not opted out of the pre-emption provisions altogether (see above).

When considering pre-emption rights it should be noted that companies that have a full listing on the stock exchange are governed also by the Listing Rules. The following can be found under Rule 9.18 of the Listing Rules:

Pre-emption rights

9.18 (a) Unless shareholders otherwise permit, a company proposing to issue equity securities for cash or sell treasury shares that are equity securities for cash must first offer those securities to existing equity shareholders (other than the company itself by virtue of it holding treasury shares) and to holders of other equity securities of the company who are entitled to be offered them in proportion to their existing holding [. . .] Only to the extent that the securities are not taken up by such persons under the offer may they then be issued.

Procedures for issuing shares to the public

Before the introduction of pre-emption rights, public companies would often issue their shares to the public by a publicly advertised prospectus. An investment was employed to provide the necessary stock market specialism and some might agree to buy the shares and offer them on to the public retaining any not sold. This operated as an underwriting agreement and meant that the company sold all the shares. This method was and is for that matter referred to as an offer for sale.

There are now two main methods of issuing new shares as follows:

A rights issue

This is an issue to existing shareholders in proportion to their holding, e.g. one new share for every five held. The document that accompanies the rights issue must comply with the listing requirements under the aegis of the Financial Services Authority. These requirements and the penalties for not complying with them appear below.

A placing

Shares that are not taken up by shareholders in the rights issue are placed by the company's brokers with their clients and any of these that are not taken up will be taken by the merchant bank that has underwritten the issues or any sub-underwriters.

It is now necessary to consider the control on the contents of the listing particulars and the regime of control that surrounds the above procedures. These appear below.

Regulation of the securities market and of admission to it

European Union law requires each member state to nominate and create a Competent Authority to maintain an Official List (or market) of securities which is to regulate the admission of securities to the Official List and to monitor those who issue shares in terms of adherence to the Listing Rules (FSA Full Handbook – Listing, Prospectus and Disclosure). This function is carried out here by the Financial Services Authority (FSA) under the Financial Services and Markets Act 2000.

The FSA can refuse an application for listing where it considers that granting it would be detrimental to the interests of investors. It can also suspend a listing as where, for example, a company has failed to comply with reporting requirements in the Listing Rules so that investors and potential investors do not have sufficient information on which to make informed decisions about the company's securities in order to deal in them.

General duty of disclosure in Listing Rules particulars

The Financial Services and Markets Act (FSMA) 2000 in s 80 makes statutory only 'financial condition' information. This, according to the section, is information which investors and their professional advisers would reasonably require in order to make an informed assessment of the company's financial position, its assets and liabilities and prospects. Less information may be given to sophisticated investors, e.g. professional advisers (s 80(4)(c)).

Supplementary listing particulars

Section 81 of the FSMA 2000 provides that where there is any significant change following the submission of listing particulars to the Financial Services Authority, but before dealings in the securities have started, supplementary particulars must be approved and published.

Exemptions from disclosure

Section 82 of the FSMA 2000 gives the Financial Services Authority power to authorise the omission of material from the listing particulars which would otherwise be required. The discretion is limited to particular grounds, e.g. discretion is given for international securities which are only dealt in by those who understand the risks. This will, for example, preserve the informality and speed which is vital to the Eurobond market (s 82(1)(c)).

Prospectuses

The Prospectus Regulations 2005 (SI 2005/1433) substitute sections in the FSMA 2000 relating to offers of shares through a prospectus. The regulations implement the EU Prospectus Directive. The prospectus contents are under the supervision of the Financial Services Authority, which must approve the contents before the prospectus can be used in share offers to the public. Thus, in a placing by brokers, an approved prospectus must be available for consultation. The contents relate largely to financial information about the company.

Compensation for false or misleading particulars

Section 90 (as amended by the CA 2006) gives express liability to those responsible for the Part 6 particulars and prospectus for material misstatements, material omissions, and misleading opinions. The remedy given is for persons suffering loss to sue for a money compensation.

However, under s 90(6) any liability, civil or criminal, which a person may incur under the general law continues to exist. Thus, a claimant could still sue for fraud or misrepresentation under the Misrepresentation Act 1967, or for a negligent misstatement under the rule in *Hedley Byrne & Co v Heller & Partners* (1963) (see further, Chapter 11 ○).

As regards who can sue, s 90(1) states that 'any person responsible for the listing particulars is liable to pay compensation to a person who has – (a) acquired securities to which the particulars apply; and (b) suffered loss in respect of them . . .' This would seem to include all subscribers whether they have relied on the prospectus or not. Materiality in terms of loss appears to be the test and not reliance. It seems, therefore, that a subscriber need not be aware of the error or even have seen the listing particulars.

Section 90(1) would seem also to cover subsequent purchases in the market. However, such a purchaser could presumably only sue if he bought while the particulars were the only source of information affecting the price of the securities. Once the company issues new information, e.g. supplementary particulars, or other new material has been published, e.g. the loss of a major contract, then it would presumably be unreasonable to allow a claim.

The Prospectus Regulations 2005 add a new subsection, s 90(12), which provides that a person is not to be subject to civil liability solely on the basis of a summary in a prospectus unless the summary is misleading, inaccurate or inconsistent when read with the rest of the prospectus. In other words, a summary is not to be regarded as the source of a claim just because it is a summary.

Persons responsible

As regards civil claims, regulations made under s 79(3) set out those who can be regarded as responsible for all or some part of the Listing Rules. These include the issuing company and its directors and anyone who expressly takes responsibility for a part or parts of the particulars, e.g. an expert who authorised the contents of the particulars or part of them.

Exemption is given for those who merely give advice in a professional capacity but who do not give specific reports for inclusion as experts.

As regards criminal liability, there is, under s 397 of the Financial Services and Markets Act 2000, a sanction of up to seven years' imprisonment and/or a fine for those who make false statements in the particulars.

Section 91 of the FSMA 2000 gives the Financial Services Authority power to impose financial penalties on issuers who have breached the Listing Rules. In addition, the Authority may issue public or private censures and suspend or cancel the listing of the securities.

Defences

Section 151 provides that a person responsible for noncompliance with or a contravention of s 150 shall not be liable if he can prove:

(a) that he had a reasonable belief in the truth of the statement or that it was reasonable to allow the relevant omission;

(b) that the statement was by an expert and that he had reasonable belief in the expert's competence and consent to inclusion of his statement; and

(c) if (a) and (b) above cannot be proved, that he published a correction or took reasonable steps to see that one was published and he reasonably believed it had been.

There is also exemption if the relevant statement is from an official document and also if the person who acquired the securities knew of the defect in the particulars.

Offers of unlisted securities

Offers of securities on the Alternative Investment Market are governed by the Public Offers of Securities Regulations 1995 (SI 1995/1537). These are not considered in any detail in this text which is intended for students and not would-be specialists in the field of company flotation. In any case, there are no great differences between the form and contents of a prospectus under the regulations and under the Financial Services and Markets Act 2000. In addition, the main learning requirement in general business law – who is responsible for the prospectus and what happens if it is misleading? – is covered by provisions in the regulations which again show no great difference from the rules applying to a Stock Exchange prospectus or Part 6 particulars, which we have already described.

The remedy of rescission

The main remedy for loss resulting from a misstatement in a prospectus is, as we have seen, damages based either on breach of a statutory duty under the Financial Services and Markets Act 2000 (or the Public Offers of Securities Regulations 1995) or the Misrepresentation Act 1967, or at common law under the case of *Hedley Byrne* which laid down the principles of liability for negligent misstatements.

The remedy of rescission involves taking the name of the shareholder off the register of members and returning money paid to the company by him. This is against the modern trend because it goes contrary to the principle of protection of the creditors' buffer which is the major purpose of the many statutory rules relating to capital maintenance.

The modern trend is to leave the shareholder's capital in the company but allow him a remedy for money compensation if the shares are less valuable because of the misstatement against those who were responsible for the misstatement such as directors or experts.

The cases which are illustrative of the remedy of rescission are rather old and are not referred to here. Suffice it to say that in order to obtain rescission the shareholder must prove a material misstatement of fact, not opinion (the principles in the *Hedley Byrne* case cover actions for damages for opinions), and that the misstatement induced the subscription for the shares. The action can only be brought by the subscriber for the shares under the prospectus. It is thus less wide than the claim for money compensation under s 90(1) which, as we have seen, seems to extend to subsequent purchasers in the market.

The right to rescind is a fragile one, being lost unless the action is brought quickly; or if the contract is affirmed, as where the shareholder has attended a meeting and voted on the shares; or where the company is in liquidation or liquidation is imminent.

Membership

Becoming a member

A person may become a member of a company:

1 **By subscribing** to the memorandum of association. Membership commences from the moment of subscription. On registration of the company the names of the subscribers (or subscriber in the case of a one-person company) must be entered in the register of members (s 112). They are, however, members without such an entry.

2 **By agreeing** to become a member and having his name entered on the register of members. Actual entry on the register is essential for membership, which commences only from the date of entry. A person may show agreement to become a member:

(a) by obtaining shares from the company, by applying for them as a result of a prospectus (public company), or following private negotiation (private company);

(b) by taking a transfer from an existing member following a purchase or a gift of the shares.

Minors

A minor may be a member unless the articles forbid this. The contract is voidable, which means that the minor can repudiate his shares at any time while a minor and for a reasonable time after becoming 18. He cannot recover any money paid on the shares unless there has been total failure of consideration. Since being a member of a company appears in itself to be a benefit regardless of dividends, the minor is unlikely to be able to use this 'no consideration' rule.

Personal representatives

The personal representatives of a deceased member do not become members themselves unless they ask for and obtain registration. However, s 770 gives them the right to transfer the shares.

Bankrupts

A bankrupt member can still exercise the rights of a member. He may, for example, vote or appoint a proxy to vote for him. However, he must exercise his rights and deal with any dividends he receives in the way in which his trustee in bankruptcy directs. The trustee in bankruptcy has the same right as a personal representative to ask for registration as the holder of the shares.

Shareholders' rights

The main rights given by law to a shareholder are as follows:

1 **A right to transfer his shares.** This is subject to any restrictions which may be found in the articles. Private companies may restrict the right to transfer shares, for example by giving the directors in the articles a right to refuse registration of the person to whom they have been transferred. Public companies listed on the Stock Exchange or quoted on the AIM cannot have restrictions of this kind in their articles because the agreement with the relevant regulatory authority forbids it.

2 **Meetings.** A member is entitled to receive notice of meetings and to attend and vote or appoint a proxy to attend and vote for him.

The CA 2006, in Schs 4 and 5, enables notices of company meetings to be sent electronically to those entitled to receive them. It also enables a member to appoint a proxy electronically by communicating with an electronic address supplied by the company for the purpose.

3 Dividends. A shareholder's right to dividend depends on the company having sufficient distributable profits out of which to pay the dividend.

Although dividend is declared by the members in general meeting, the members cannot declare a dividend unless the directors recommend one. Furthermore, they can resolve to reduce the dividend recommended by the directors but cannot increase it.

4 Accounts. A shareholder is entitled to a copy of the company's accounts within six months of its accounting reference date (i.e. the end of its financial year) in the case of a public company and nine months in the case of a private company. The accounts must be filed with the Registrar of Companies at Companies House at or before the end of the above periods according to the type of company involved.

Part 6 companies can, however, provide their shareholders with a summary financial statement giving merely key information from the full accounts. Nevertheless, those shareholders who want a copy of the full accounts are entitled to one on request. This is designed to alleviate the problems faced by certain of the privatised industries such as British Telecom and British Gas which have large numbers of shareholders who, formerly, had all to receive very bulky and expensive copies of the full accounts. The full (or shorter form) accounts of private companies must be circulated to members but those members can, by unanimous agreement, called an elective resolution, dispense with the requirement to lay the accounts before a general meeting. A member and, where the company has one, the auditor can require them to be laid and can call a general meeting for the purpose if the directors will not do so.

The matter of the alteration of shareholders' rights has already been considered.

The CA 2006, in Schs 4 and 5, enables copies of the annual accounts and reports including the summary financial statements to be sent electronically to those entitled to receive them or to appear on the company's website provided the articles or a members' resolution permits this.

Shareholders' duties

A shareholder is under a duty to pay for his shares when called upon to do so but is not in general liable for the company's debts beyond the amount (if any) outstanding on his shares.

Cessation of membership

The most usual ways in practice that a person may cease to be a member of a company are by:

1 transfer of his shares to a purchaser or as a gift;
2 rescission of the contract under a misleading prospectus, though the more likely and acceptable remedy today would be to remain a member but receive monetary compensation;
3 redemption or purchase of shares by the company;
4 death or bankruptcy;
5 winding-up of the company.

Meetings, resolutions and annual return

Shareholders' meetings

There are two kinds of company general meeting: the annual general meeting and an extraordinary general meeting.

Annual general meeting

Section 336 states that an annual general meeting must be held within six months of a company's financial year end.

The notice of the meeting must say that it is the annual general meeting.

Private companies are no longer required to hold AGMs or table their accounts and reports or appoint auditors at a company meeting although they may do so if they choose. Private companies will need to amend their articles to take advantage of these deregulations, by removing any relevant restrictions.

Extraordinary general meetings

All general meetings other than the annual general meeting are extraordinary general meetings. They may be called by the directors at any time.

Section 303 gives holders of not less than one-tenth of the paid-up share capital on which all calls due have been paid the right to requisition an extraordinary general meeting. The requisition must state the objects of the meeting, be signed by the requisitionists, and deposited at the registered office of the company. If the directors do not call a meeting within 21 days of the date of depositing the requisition, the requisitionists, or the majority in value of them, may call the meeting within three months of the date of the deposit of the requisition.

To prevent the directors from convening (i.e. calling) the meeting to be held on a long distant date so that the members' desire to discuss urgent matters is defeated, s 303 provides that the directors are not deemed to have duly convened a meeting if they convene it for more than 28 days after the date of the notice convening the meeting. So if they called it to be held, say, six months after the date of the notice they would not have complied with the Act and the requisitionists could call it. It should be noted that the above provisions refer to 'holders' of shares and 'requisitionists'. One member with one-tenth or more of the paid-up share capital cannot therefore ask for an EGM to be held. Two members holding at least one-tenth of the paid-up share capital are required. This is to ensure that there will be a quorum at any meeting which is called and the provision of the Interpretation Act 1978 that the singular includes the plural and vice versa does not apply because of this (see *Morgan* v *Morgan Insurance Brokers Ltd* (1993).

The percentage required for a public company remains as above at 10 per cent. However, in private companies the percentage may be reduced to 5 per cent where no requisitioned meetings have been held in the last 12 months. Requests in electronic form are permitted.

Convening of meetings in deadlocked companies

In the smaller private company a problem that may arise if the shareholders have fallen out is that a majority shareholder is unable to exercise control of the company because a non-controlling member will not attend a meeting to put policies into effect. Where this situation exists it is important to note that the controlling shareholder can achieve an effective meeting as follows:

■ *Under s 306* the court can call extraordinary meetings and the AGM and direct that one member of the company present in person or by proxy shall constitute a quorum and validly conduct business. Application is by a director or member.

It should be noted that the above power is not intended to sort out problems between shareholders simply because they have equal shareholdings. Thus, if in a company with two members, A and B, the company is deadlocked because they have equal shareholdings and A votes one way and B votes in another, the powers would not be used to call a meeting and declare that one member, say A, could validly conduct business in the absence of B. Such deadlock will, unless it can be sorted out by the agreement of the shareholders concerned, generally result in the liquidation of the company.

Ross v *Telford* (1998)

In this case the members were husband and wife. The quorum at meetings of the company was two. During acrimonious divorce proceedings the parties would not cooperate in terms of convening company meetings. The husband asked the court for an order convening a meeting with himself as constituting a quorum to conduct business. A district judge ordered such a meeting but the Court of Appeal allowed the wife's appeal against the order. The court ruled that s 371 was not an appropriate vehicle to resolve deadlock between two equal shareholders.

Comment. Presumably, if either of the parties had been a majority shareholder, the court could and would have convened a meeting to allow the majority shareholder to rightfully exercise control.

Notice of general meetings

Section 307 retains the former minimum notice requirement of 21 days for public company AGMs, with 14 days' notice being required for all other general meetings, whether public or private company general meetings. The notice may be given in electronic form where a shareholder has provided such an address.

The articles usually provide that a meeting shall not be invalid because a particular member does not receive notice, unless of course this is deliberate as distinct from accidental.

Quorum at general meetings

Section 318 provides that in one-member companies one qualifying person shall constitute a quorum. In other cases two qualifying persons are required. Qualifying persons are individuals who are members, corporate representatives and proxies. The section excludes the possibility of two or more corporate representatives or proxies of the same member from comprising a quorum.

Quorum

Section 318 sets the quorum. It sets a quorum for a meeting of one 'qualifying person' in the case of a single member company and – as a default – two 'qualifying persons'.

Where an AGM or EGM is called by the court under s 306(4), the court may decide upon the quorum which may even be one person present in person or proxy (see *Ross* v *Telford* (1988)).

Voting

This may be by a show of hands, in which case, obviously, each member has one vote, regardless of the number of shares or proxies he holds. However, the articles usually lay down that the chairman or a certain number of members may demand a poll, e.g. two members. If a poll is successfully demanded, each member has one vote per share and proxies can be used.

Proxies

Section 324 sets out new provisions for the appointment of proxies. In future, members of both public and private companies will have the right to appoint proxies. The proxies will be able to attend and speak and vote at a meeting. Where a member holds different types of voting shares, that member may appoint two proxies, one in respect of each type of share. Proxies have one vote on a show of hands.

Minutes

A company must keep minutes of the proceedings at its general and board meetings. Members have a right to inspect the minutes of general meetings but not those of directors' meetings.

Resolutions – generally

There are four main kinds of resolution passed at company meetings as set out below.

1 An ordinary resolution, which may be defined as 'a resolution passed by a majority (over 50 per cent) of persons present and voting in person or by proxy at a general meeting' (CA 2006, s 282).

Any business may be validly done by this type of resolution unless the articles or the CA 2006 provide for a special or extraordinary resolution for that particular business.

An example of the use of an ordinary resolution is for the members to give their permission for the directors of public companies to allot the company's unissued share capital under s 549.

2 A special resolution, which is one passed by a 75 per cent majority. There is no longer a requirement for 21 days' notice.

It will be appreciated that if a special resolution is to be proposed at the annual general meeting, 21 days' notice will have to be given because that is the requirement for the AGM.

A special resolution is required, for example, to change the company's articles. Section 30 provides that within 15 days of the passing of a special resolution a copy of the resolution must be forwarded to the Registrar of Companies.

The copy sent to the Registrar may be printed or be in any form approved by the Registrar including electronic form (s 30).

3 Written resolutions of private companies. Under s 288, private companies can use a written resolution procedure in which the resolution is circulated for approval by members without a meeting. A major change here is that these resolutions will no longer be required to be unanimous. Instead, they will only need to be signed by the majority that would have been required to pass the resolution in general meeting: e.g. in the case of a written special resolution, 75 per cent.

4 Ordinary resolutions after special notice. Section 312 requires that for certain ordinary resolutions to be passed at a meeting, for example one removing a director before his period of office is ended, special notice must be given.

Where special notice is required it must be given to the company not less than 28 days before the meeting at which the resolution is to be proposed and by the company to the members not less than 21 days before that meeting.

This means that if, for example, a member wishes to propose the removal of a director by this procedure under s 168, then when he stands up at the meeting to propose that removal, the company, through its officers, must have been on notice of his intention to do so for 28 days at least and the members for 21 days at least.

The purpose of the notice of 28 days is so that the company can, as s 169 requires, alert the director concerned to the possibility of his removal so that the director can circulate members with his reasons why he should not be removed or, that failing, prepare an oral statement to be given at the meeting at which his removal is proposed.

Before leaving the topic of resolutions passed at meetings, it should be noted that resolutions can be passed by a small number of members. For example, if a company has 5,000 members but only 30 attend the meeting and 70 appoint proxies, a special or ordinary resolution can be validly passed by three-quarters or at least 51 per cent, as the case may be, taken from those present at the meeting and voting in person or by proxy.

Members' resolutions at the AGM

Under s 314, a member (or members) representing not less than one-twentieth of the total voting rights of all the members can by making a written requisition to the company compel the directors:

1 to give to members who are entitled to receive notice of the next AGM notice of any resolution which may be properly moved and which they intend to move at that meeting; and
2 to circulate to the members any statement of not more than 1,000 words with respect to the matter referred to in any proposed resolution or the business to be dealt with at the meeting.

The requisition must be made not later than six weeks before the AGM if a resolution is proposed and not less than one week before if no resolution is proposed.

It should be noted that since s 314 uses the expression 'member or members' the section can be used by one member with the required shareholding.

Requests in electronic form are permitted.

Written resolutions of private companies

Chapter 2 of Part 13 of the CA 2006 provides for written resolutions of private companies only. These need no longer be passed unanimously but require the same majority as the resolution they are covering would require if passed in general meeting. Thus, for a written special resolution the majority is 75 per cent. There are, as before, two exceptions where a written resolution cannot be used: a resolution to remove a director or an auditor before the expiration of his or her period of office.

This is because in both cases the person concerned can make representations to the members in general meeting regarding the removal.

Members' powers

Members having 5 per cent of the total voting rights of the membership can request the directors to circulate a written resolution (s 292). The directors must circulate it within 21 days of the request.

Other main points

There is a time limit of 28 days for the passing of a written resolution; otherwise it cannot be passed. Finally, the articles cannot remove the ability of a private company and its members to use the written resolution procedure.

Auditor's rights

Section 503 provides that, in relation to a written resolution proposed to be agreed by a private company, the company's auditor is entitled to receive all such communications relating to the resolution. This will not apply where the company has taken the audit exemption and has no auditors.

Records

The company is required to keep a record of written resolutions and the signatures of those members who signed them in a record book which is, in effect, a substitute for what would, in the case of a meeting, be the minutes.

Resolutions and the 'Duomatic principle' of unanimous consent

Some of the smaller private companies are not always meticulous at observing the legal formalities of decision-making within corporate law. It is therefore helpful to note in this regard that where all the shareholders of a company assent on a matter that should be brought into effect by a resolution in general meeting (or a written resolution) the unanimous consent of all the shareholders without a formal meeting or written resolution is enough to satisfy the law. This is called the *Duomatic* principle, from the case in which it was most famously canvassed, i.e. *Re Duomatic* (1969). A more recent example of the use of the principle appears below.

Deakin v Faulding (2001)

The case was brought to decide upon the validity of certain bonuses paid to a director of a company. The payment had not been approved by an ordinary resolution of the members either in a meeting or by written resolution as the articles required. The new owners of the company wanted to recover the bonuses. It appeared that all the shareholders had informally agreed to the payment which were declared by the High Court to be valid under the *Duomatic* principle.

Impact of Schs 4 and 5 to the CA 2006

- *Notices of meetings* can be sent electronically to those entitled to receive them. Either notices can be sent directly to an electronic address supplied for the purpose by the recipient or they can be published on a website and the recipient notified of their availability in a manner agreed with him. In the latter case, the notice must be published on the website for at least the period for which notice of the meeting must normally be given.
- *As regards proxies*, a member may appoint a proxy electronically by communicating with an electronic address supplied by the company for the purpose.
- *As regards the filing of resolutions* and other documents with the Registrar of Companies, the order enables the Registrar to direct that any document required to be delivered to him under the Companies Act 1985 and the Insolvency Act 1986 may be delivered electronically in a form and manner directed by him. In practice, Companies House gives guidance on these matters.
- Special articles are overriden and do not require amendment, but companies should do so in line with best practice.

The annual return

Under s 854 a company must file an annual return with the Registrar of Companies. It must be made up to a date of 12 months after the previous return or, in the case of the first return, 12 months after incorporation. The company may move the date of its next annual return by indicating the new date on the current annual return. The new date then governs future annual submissions. The return must be delivered to the Registrar within 28 days of the make-up date.

Under a procedure introduced by the Registrar of Companies, it was possible for companies to be issued with a shuttle document containing all the information relevant to the annual return which the Register already holds on the company's file. The company was merely required to confirm or amend the shuttle document and return it. The 'shuttle' concept has now been discontinued. This was no longer a prescribed form for annual returns after 1 October 2008.

Protection of minority interests

There are two major areas of minority protection as follows:

- Part 11, Chapter 1 (ss 260–264) of the CA 2006 (the derivative claim); and
- Part 30 (ss 994–999) of the CA 2006, to protect members against unfair prejudice.

Part 11, Chapter 1: the derivative claim against directors

This is a new statutory area of claim designed to allow a minority of members to bring a claim on behalf of the company for compensation from directors who, being in breach of duty, have caused it loss.

What is a derivative claim?

It occurs when A claims, say, damages which have been suffered by B (not A). Any damages awarded will go to B, though A can recover the costs of a successful claim from the defendant. Attempts to use such a form of claim were made by shareholders who wished to sue on behalf of their company for damages caused by the acts of its directors, those directors being also in voting control of the company. This type of claim was blocked by the rule in *Foss v Harbottle* (1843), which ruled that such claims were invalid. Then came a long history of case law providing exceptions to *Foss* and letting, now and again, a derivative claim through. The rule in *Foss* and the exceptions to it remain in the common law.

The new procedure

The CA 2006 introduces a new procedure under which a shareholder may bring proceedings on behalf of the company against a director for damage caused to it by negligence, default, breach of duty or breach of trust. If the claim is successful the compensation will go to the company; but the derivative claimant, the shareholder, will recover costs in a successful claim.

There are safeguards for directors:

- A claimant must obtain court permission to proceed with the claim. This is a two-stage process: a preliminary stage aimed at removing vexatious claims, followed by a full hearing to see whether permission should be granted.
- The court must refuse permission where the claim is in the view of the court not in accordance with the duty to promote the success of the company, or if it is satisfied that the act or omission has been authorised or ratified by the company, or where it is likely to be ratified by the company.

Despite the safeguards, more derivative claims are likely to be brought against wrongdoing directors. The claim should however be seen as 'a weapon of last resort' (see for example *Hansard*, HL, Vol. 679 (Official Report) cols GC4–5 (Lord Goldsmith) (27 February 2006) quoted by Keay and Loughrey in *Journal of Business Law*, 2010, page 151). Under the new procedure, as outlined above, the applicant is required to make a prima facie case for permission to continue a derivative claim; the court needs to be satisfied that the cause of the action arose from an act or omission involving negligence, default, breach of duty or breach of trust by a director. The application of the principles can be seen in *Iesini v Westrip Holdings Ltd* (2009), in which an application for permission to continue a derivative claim on behalf of Westrip was submitted. The application was to reverse the alleged stripping of the company's assets and claims about the company's ownership of assets. There was also the irregular process concerning issuance of shares when shares were issued without voting, dividend or winding-up rights when the company's articles of association did not permit the share issue. The court would have to form a provisional view on the strength of the claim to properly consider the requirements of s 263(2)(a) and s 263(3)(b). Section 263(2)(a) applied only where the court was satisfied that no director acting in accordance with s 172 would seek to continue the claim. If some directors would, and others would not, seek to continue the claim, s 263(3)(b) should be applied, when many of the same considerations would apply. As a matter of strict legal right, B and W had been

entitled to rescind or terminate the agreement when they had done so. Westrip's board had taken and followed counsel's advice on that matter.

Stainer v Lee (2010)

Stainer applied under s 261 of the Companies Act 2006 for permission to continue a derivative claim seeking relief on behalf of the company (Kerrington Ltd) against the company's two directors and Eldington Holdings Ltd. Stainer, who has a small shareholding of the company's issued share, argued that Lee and his fellow director had acted in breach of their duties to the company in allowing the company to lend money to Eldington Holdings Ltd on an interest-free basis and in lending sums to E for some purpose other than discharging or reducing the liability which Eldington had incurred for the acquisition of shares in the company, which purpose had not been approved by the company's members and was not in its interests. As stated in the judgment, 'something more than simply a prima facie case was required and that the court had to form a view on the strength of the claim'. The failure to obtain interest over a period of almost nine years on lending to E that rose from £4.6 million to £8.1 million was regarded as very strong grounds for a claim that the directors were in breach of their fiduciary duties. The application was granted.

Other statutory protection of the minority

In addition to the protection available to the minority by reason of the **exceptions** to *Foss*, various minority rights are given by statute.

The most far-reaching is the right of a minority shareholder to petition the court for relief where the shareholder believes that his interests are being 'unfairly prejudiced' by the way in which the company's affairs are being carried on. This section will be looked at separately.

Other main examples of statutory protection are:

- the right given to 15 per cent to object to the courts in regard to a proposed variation of class rights;
- the right of a member of a solvent company to petition the court for a compulsory winding-up on the just and equitable ground;
- the right given to one-tenth of the members to require the convening of a general meeting;

- the right given to a member or members with a one-twentieth interest to get an item up for discussion at the AGM.

Relief from unfair prejudice

Under s 994 any member may petition the court on the grounds that the affairs of the company are being conducted in a manner which is unfairly prejudicial to the interests of its members generally or of some part of its members (including the petitioner himself) or that any actual or proposed act is so unfairly prejudicial.

Note: the CA 2006, ss 994–998 *merely restate* the former rules in the Companies Act 1985.

A summary of the main points arising from case law and other sources appears below.

Unfair prejudice

The circumstances leading to 'unfair prejudice', according to the Jenkins Committee, which was set up to consider company law reform and reported in 1962, were as follows:

1 Directors paying themselves excessive salaries, thus depriving members who are not directors of any dividends or of adequate dividends.

This was the scenario in *Re Sam Weller* (1989) and the High Court decided that minority shareholders whose only income from the company was dividends could be regarded as unfairly prejudiced under what is now s 994 by low dividend payments.

2 Refusal of the board of a private company to put the personal representatives of a deceased shareholder on the register, thus preventing the shares from being voted and leading sometimes to the personal representatives selling the shares to the directors at an inadequate price.

3 The issue of shares to directors on advantageous terms.

4 The refusal by the board to recommend payment of dividends on non-cumulative preference shares held by a minority.

It may also be that negligent mismanagement by the directors causing loss to the company is unfairly prejudicial conduct, though this is as yet uncertain in view of the absence of definitive case law.

According to the court in *Re a Company* (1983), it is not unfairly prejudicial for the directors to refuse to purchase the company's shares under s 162. In that case the executors of a deceased shareholder in a private company wanted to cash in the shares to provide a trust fund for the education and maintenance of the deceased shareholder's minor children. This fund would have yielded more than the company was paying in dividends on the shares. In the event the directors would not buy the shares, though they were prepared to approve a sale to an outsider if one could be found. This conduct was not unfairly prejudicial, said the court.

However, it seems that removal from the board as in *Ebrahimi* v *Westbourne Galleries* (1972), or other exclusion from management, is covered. This has, in fact, been the basis of the majority of cases brought under the section since it came into law. The section talks about conduct unfairly prejudicial **to the interests** of some part of the members, and in a private company a substantial shareholder can expect to be a director: it is an interest of his membership.

The case was applied in *Shah* v *Shah* (2010), which involved two sets of proceedings. In a first action, S issued an unfair prejudice petition against his brothers. In a second action, D, as claimant, alleged that the transfer of shares in the company from him to one of his brothers was void or ineffective. The brothers had been involved in the running of the company together. Following a long-running feud which involved a separate claim of unfair dismissal, Shah issued his unfair prejudicial petition under the Companies Act 2006, s 944, submitting that the exclusion from the company management amounted to unfair prejudice – he submitted an order that the brothers be required to buy his shareholding in the company at a price to be determined by the court or, alternatively, that the company be wound up under s 122(1)(g) of the Insolvency Act 1986.

As demonstrated in *Ebrahimi* v *Westbourne Galleries Ltd* (1972), and applied by the judge 'a company with certain characteristics may, on principles of equity, engage obligations that were common to partnership relations. In such a company, which was a quasi-partnership, it might be unjust or unfair to exclude a member from participation in the management without an offer to buy the minority shareholder's shares or make some other fair arrangement'. While the claim did not justify the winding-up petition, it was held that the company had the character of a quasi-partnership, and that there was nothing to justify excluding Shah from the overall management of the company. A remedy in terms of a purchase of Shah's shares was made accordingly, pursuant to CA 2006 s 996.

The court said that this was the case in *Re London School of Electronics* (1985) where a director was excluded from management. The court made an order for the purchase of his shares by the majority shareholders. Thus he got his capital out and could go into another business. It will be seen that this is a better remedy than *Westbourne*, i.e. winding-up under the just and equitable ground. The person excluded from management gets his capital out without the need to wind up a solvent company when the directors have merely fallen out with each other.

Nevertheless, it was held in *Re a Company (No 001363 of 1988)* (1989) that a petition for winding-up on the just and equitable ground can still be made if that is the petitioner's choice.

Finally, it should be noted that the House of Lords ruled in *O'Neill v Phillips* (1999) that, provided a member of a company has not been excluded from management as a director, he cannot demand that his shares be purchased under s 994 simply because he feels that the company is not being managed properly. The decision makes clear that the new s 994 remedy is not a 'cure-all' for shareholders who, for a variety of reasons, are not satisfied with the way in which a company is being run. This is particularly true where they are also in management.

Relief available

Section 996 gives the court a power to make any order it sees fit to relieve the unfair prejudice, including in particular the following:

1 Order to regulate the future conduct of the company's affairs. This could include the making of a court order altering the articles as in the following case decided under earlier minority protection law.

Re H R Harmer (1959)

Mr H senior, formed a company through which to deal in stamps. He gave his two sons shares in the company but kept voting control himself. Mr H senior was 'governing director' and his sons were also directors. Mr H senior ignored resolutions of the board; he set up a branch abroad which the board had resolved should not be set up; he dismissed trusted employees, drew unauthorised expenses; and engaged a private detective to watch the staff, presumably because he thought they might steal valuable stamps (imagine the effect on industrial relations!). Eventually the sons petitioned the court.

The court found, in effect, unfair prejudice. In giving relief the court ordered Mr H senior to act in accordance with the decisions of the board and ordered that he should not interfere in the company's affairs otherwise than as the board decided. The company's articles were altered by the court order to this effect.

Comment. Once the articles have been altered by the court order, a special resolution is not enough to change the articles affected by the court order. The court itself must give permission for the change.

2 Order to restrain the doing or continuance of any act complained of by the petitioner. Under this the court could make an order directing the reduction of directors' remuneration found to be excessive and preventing the payment of dividends to the minority.

3 Order to authorise civil proceedings to be brought in the name of the company by such persons and on such terms as the court directs. This provision is of particular interest in that the court may authorise the bringing of civil proceedings by the company, seemingly without any of the restrictions of *Foss* on derivative claims. It should be noted that the claim would not be derivative. The company would be the claimant under the court order and there would be no need for the nominal defendant procedure.

4 Order to provide for the purchase of a member's shares by the company or its other members and, if the former is chosen, reduce the company's share capital as required. This provision was, of course, applied in *Re London School of Electronics* (1985) where the order was that the majority shareholders should buy the shares of the member/director who had been excluded from management. This has been the remedy most frequently asked for and obtained in these claims.

Directors and secretary

The management of a company is usually entrusted to a small group of people called directors. The main control of the shareholders lies in their power to appoint or remove directors. The company secretary is an important officer of the company in terms of its day-to-day administration.

Every public company must have at least two directors and every private company at least one (s 154). Public companies must have a secretary and a sole director cannot also be the secretary (s 271).

Company secretaries (CA 2006, Part 12)

Section 270 states that private companies may, at their discretion, have or not have a company secretary. The company's articles may contain the relevant provision following choice. Where no provision appears in the articles then the articles will be treated as providing that the company is permitted to have a secretary but not required to. The articles will not be deemed to provide that the company is not to have a secretary. Where articles are altered to state that the company is required to have a secretary, or is permitted to have one, or is not to have one, this change can be made once only.

If there is no secretary in post because of a temporary vacancy or because the company is not to have a secretary by the articles, then under s 274 the function will fall either to a director or to another person authorised generally or specifically to carry out the function(s). This is an interesting provision, because if a person is authorised generally to carry out the function a company whose articles provide that it is not to have a secretary would appear to have one in fact in all but name. If there is a failure to authorise a director or other person the function goes to the board of directors.

As regards the register of secretaries, s 275 requires a public company to keep such a register. As regards private companies, s 275 also provides that such a company whose articles require it to have a secretary, or whose articles permit it to have a secretary, and in this latter case it has one, may keep a register of secretaries. The register, if kept, is to be available at the registered office and available for inspection by members free and others on payment of such fee as may be prescribed.

Appointment

The documents sent to the Registrar seeking incorporation must state the company's proposed officers, i.e. directors and secretary. A private company need not have a secretary but may have if desired. On registration those officers are deemed appointed. In this way the appointment of the company's first directors is achieved.

Subsequently, directors are usually appointed by the members of the company in general meeting by ordinary resolution. The board of directors is normally allowed to fill casual vacancies, that is, vacancies which come about because, e.g., a director dies, or resigns his directorship before his term of office has come to an end, or to appoint additional directors up to the permitted maximum, say five, and so if we have only two directors the board could appoint up to three more. Directors approved as additional or to fill casual vacancies usually hold office until the next AGM when the members decide by ordinary resolution whether they are to continue in office.

There are a number of new provisions in the CA 2006 that are worth noting. Under s 155, companies are required to have at least one director who is a natural person, i.e. an individual, so that the board cannot consist of companies represented by corporate representatives. Section 156 allows the Secretary of State to direct the company to make appointments so that one director is in place for a private company and two for a public company. Section 157 introduces a minimum age of 16 for a natural person to be a director.

Generally, one or more full-time directors is appointed a managing director. The articles must provide for the appointment and articles normally enable the board to confer on the managing director any of the powers exercisable by the board and to vary these powers.

Many of the provisions of company law, e.g. the rules relating to directors' loans and the disclosure of those loans in the accounts, apply to 'shadow directors'. These are, under s 251, people in accordance with whose directions or instructions the board of the company is accustomed to act but excluding professional advisers such as lawyers and accountants who may give the board professional advice on which they usually act.

However, those who give advice other than purely in a professional capacity in the sense of legal and accounting advice may be included. The Court of Appeal ruled – in a case that appears to extend the definition of shadow director – that the concepts of direction and instruction in the definition did not exclude the giving of advice. The company concerned was in the travel business. It went into liquidation owing creditors an estimated £4.46 million. Disqualification proceedings were brought successfully against three of its directors and two of its advisers who were consultants with experience in the travel business (see *Secretary of State for Trade and Industry* v *Deverell* (2000)). It should be noted that such a disqualification also prevents the holding of directorships in other companies.

The above provisions are intended to stop the evasion of the law relating to directors by a major shareholder who can control the company without being on the board. Such a person cannot, for example, get around the law relating to directors' loans by resigning temporarily from the board in order to allow the company to make him a loan. He would be covered because he would be a 'shadow director'.

Remuneration – generally

If a director is to receive remuneration, his contract of service (if he is an employee, executive director (e.g. sales director)) or the articles (in the case of a fee-paid non-executive director) must provide for it. As regards an executive director's service contract, s 228 says that the company must keep a copy of it, for at least one year after it has expired, normally at the registered office, and that this copy is to be open to the inspection of members, who can now, under the 2006 Act, obtain copies as well. While this may be of general interest, it is vital where a member (or members) intends to try to remove a director from the board before his term of office has expired. A director who is removed in this way has a right to sue for damages if he has a contract which has still some time to run.

Members can look at the contract and see what their act in removing the director might cost the company.

The notes to the accounts of the company must disclose the salaries or fees of the directors and the chairman. This is not required in the 'abbreviated' accounts which small companies may file with Companies House.

Controlling directors' pay

One of the major difficulties arising in connection with directors' pay at least in more recent times has been the seemingly excessive payments made to directors in terms of remuneration while in office and compensation packages at the end of what has not always been a successful period of office in terms of the profitability of the company.

So far as UK corporate law is concerned, the board has a largely unsupervised freedom to fix the incomes of the board. This would not be the case if directors took their remuneration by way of fees because the articles normally provide the mechanism for dealing with this and it is usually necessary for directors' fees to be approved by an ordinary resolution of the members.

However, directors' remuneration is normally dealt with by the issue of a contract and articles normally provide that contracts may be made by the board with individual directors and no member vote is required.

There are now in place two main methods of controlling directors' pay but these apply only to companies listed on the Stock Exchange.

1 The Combined Code of Best Practice

This code of practice is the result of separate reports over a period of years by the Greenbury Committee and the Hampel Committee as amended to include certain of the recommendations of the Higgs Committee and a Committee chaired by Sir Robert Smith. It is enforced extra-legally as a code of best practice that is now part of the Part 6 Rules. It must therefore be complied with as part of obtaining and retaining a quotation for the company's shares on the Stock Exchange without which they would not be readily saleable. It requires listed companies to set up remuneration committees of independent non-executive directors to make recommendations to the board on the executive directors' remuneration packages. The remuneration of non-executive directors is envisaged as being set by the board or, if the articles require it, by shareholder approval. The company's annual report should contain a statement of remuneration policy. The code also states that the notice or contract period for directors should move towards one year. This is designed to cut down the compensation required where a director of a failing company has his contract withdrawn with, say, two years still to go.

2 The Directors' Remuneration Report Regulations for listed companies

The Directors' Remuneration Report Regulations 2002 (SI 2002/1986) apply to listed companies with financial years ending on or after 31 December 2002. Under the regulations, quoted companies must publish a report on directors' pay as part of their annual reporting cycle. The report must be approved by the board of directors and copies must be sent to the Registrar of Companies. Companies must hold a shareholder vote on the report at each AGM. The Report must include:

- details of individual directors' pay packages and justification for any compensation packages given in the preceding year;
- details of the board's consideration of directors' pay;
- membership of the remuneration committee;

- names of any remuneration consultants used, whether they were appointed independently, and whether they provide any other services to the company;
- a forward-looking statement of the company policy on directors' pay, including details of incentive and share option schemes, an explanation of how packages relate to performance, and details and explanations of policy on contract and notice periods;
- a performance graph providing information on the company's performance in comparison with an appropriate share market index.

Comment. **The shareholder vote is advisory only and the company is not legally bound to act upon it.** Nevertheless, the government takes the view that any company that defies such a vote will face considerable criticism and pressure for change. The regulations fly in the face of calls from investor groups, such as the Association of British Insurers and the National Association of Pension Funds, for the matter to be addressed only by means of corporate governance codes rather than what they regard as inflexible legislation.

Statutory requirements on disclosure of remuneration

New requirements for the disclosure of directors' remuneration were introduced by the Company Accounts (Disclosure of Directors' Emoluments) Regulations 1997 (SI 1997/570). They apply to all companies listed and unlisted for accounting periods ending on or after 31 March 1997.

The regulations amend provisions of companies legislation relating to the disclosure of directors' emoluments or other benefits in the notes to a company's annual accounts in respect of any financial year.

Under the regulations:

- companies will be required to show aggregate details of directors' remuneration under four headings – emoluments (i.e. basic salary and annual bonuses); gains made on the exercise of share options; gains made under long-term incentive schemes; and company contributions to money purchase pension schemes. Small companies' full and shorter form accounts can show merely the total of the aggregate amounts;
- where the aggregate remuneration exceeds or is equal to £200,000, companies will be required to show also the figures attributable to the highest paid director and the amount of his or her accrued retirement benefits if he or she is a member of a defined benefit

pension scheme, i.e. a pension scheme in which the rules specify the benefits to be paid, and the scheme must be financed accordingly;

- companies are no longer required to show the number of directors whose emoluments fell within each band of £5,000.

For listed companies, the regulations bring the Companies Act into line with Greenbury and the Part 6 Rules. For unlisted companies they streamline the former disclosure requirements.

Exceptions for unlisted companies

The above requirements apply to companies listed on the Stock Exchange and on the Alternative Investment Market. Unlisted companies must comply with the requirements, with two important exceptions:

- unlisted companies do not have to disclose the amount of gains made when directors exercise share options. They have merely to disclose the number of directors who have exercised their share options;
- unlisted companies do not have to disclose the net value of any assets that comprise shares which would otherwise be disclosed in respect of assets received under long-term incentive schemes. Instead they disclose the number of directors in respect of whose qualifying service shares were received or receivable under long-term incentive schemes.

Enforcement of fair dealing by directors

Duration of contracts of employment

Under ss 188 and 189 contracts of employment with directors which are for a period of more than two years and cannot be terminated by the company by notice must be approved by the members by ordinary resolution in general meeting. If this is not done the contract can be terminated by reasonable notice, which is not defined by the Act but which at common law would be at least three months (*James* v *Kent & Co Ltd* (1950)).

This provision is also useful to those who want to remove a director from office. In the past boards of directors have given themselves long contracts without consulting the members. This has made it difficult to remove them because the compensation payable under a long service contract which had been broken by removal of the director concerned was sometimes more than the company could afford. It can still be costly.

Substantial property transactions

Sections 190–196 require the approval of the members by ordinary resolution in general meeting (or written resolution) of any arrangement to transfer to, or receive from, a director (or connected person, see below) a non-cash asset, e.g. land, exceeding £100,000 or exceeding 10 per cent of the company's net assets, whichever is the lower. The section does not apply, however, to non-cash assets of less than £5,000 in value.

Thus, a company whose assets less its liabilities amounted to £200,000 would have to comply with the Act in respect of a transaction with a director for a non-cash asset worth more than £20,500.

The Act is designed to prevent directors (at least without member approval) from buying assets from the company at less than their true value or transferring their own property to the company at more than market value.

Transfers to and from connected persons are regarded as transfers to and from a director himself. The main category of connected persons is a director's wife or husband and children under 18, plus companies in which the director, together with his connected persons, holds one-fifth or more interest in the equity share capital. A director's partner is also included.

The rules apply to all companies and shadow directors are included.

It should be noted that the Act refers to 'arrangements' rather than contracts and this will catch transactions where they are not to be carried out under legally binding agreements.

A major change under the 2006 Act is to allow the company and the director to enter into a contract that is **conditional on member approval**. This is to cope with the case where the transacting company is a member of a group and allows that company to enter into the contract conditionally on the approval of members of its holding company.

Loans, quasi-loans and credit taken by directors

Sections 197–214 deal with the above matters. The major change in the CA 2006 is that it abolishes the prohibition on loans, quasi-loans, etc to directors and replaces this with a requirement for approval of the transaction by the members by ordinary resolution (or written resolution).

First, a description of loans, quasi-loans, and credit.

1 Loans and quasi-loans. Basically, a quasi-loan occurs when a director incurs personal expenditure but the company pays the bill. The director pays the company back later. In a loan the company would put the director in funds; he would buy, e.g. personal goods, and then repay the loan.

Examples of quasi-loans are:

- the company buys a yearly railway season ticket for a director to get to work; he repays the company over 12 months;
- a director uses a company credit card to pay for personal goods, e.g. a video. The company pays the credit card company and the director repays his company over an agreed period;
- the company purchases an airline ticket for a director's wife who is accompanying him on a business trip at the director's expense. The director repays the company over an agreed period.

It should be noted that the director's own expenses for the trip which would be paid by the company are not affected. It is only **personal** and not business transactions which are controlled.

2 Credit. Examples of credit are:

- a furniture company sells furniture to a director on terms that payment be deferred for 12 months;
- the company services a director's personal car in its workshops and the director is given time to pay;
- the company sells a Rolls-Royce to the wife of one of its directors under a hire-purchase agreement.

Loans, quasi-loans and credit

The position is as follows.

In the case of a private company which is not associated with a public company (as where the two companies are part of the same group), the Act requires member approval for loans and related guarantees or security made by a company for:

- a director of the company or a director of its holding company.

In the case of a public company or a private company associated with a public company, member approval is required for loans, quasi-loans and credit transactions and related guarantees or security made by the company for:

- a director of the company;
- a director of its holding company;

- a person connected with a director of the company, e.g. spouse; or
- a person connected with a director of its holding company.

Member approval is not required by the above provisions in the following circumstances:

- for loans, quasi-loans and credit transactions to meet expenditure in the company's business but total value of loans, etc. to those in the above list, including connected parties, must in the aggregate not exceed £50,000;
- money advanced to a director's defence costs in legal proceedings in connection with any alleged negligence, default, breach of duty or breach of trust in relation to the company or an associated company;
- small loans and quasi-loans, as long as the total value of such loans and quasi-loans to a director and connected persons does not exceed £10,000;
- small credit transactions provided the value aggregated across the director and connected persons does not exceed £15,000;
- credit transactions made in the ordinary course of the company's business, as where a director of a furniture retail company enters into a credit transaction for the purchase of a sofa for his or her own home;
- loans and quasi-loans made by a money-lending company in the ordinary course of its business and the loan is on commercial not favourable terms.

There is now no criminal penalty for breach of the above provisions. However, the loans, etc. would be unlawful and recoverable by the company.

Disclosure in accounts

Under s 413, all transactions involving loans, quasi-loans and credit to directors and their connected persons in all companies must be disclosed in notes to the company's accounts.

Material interests

Material interests of directors and their connected persons must also be disclosed in a note to the accounts. A material interest could be, for example, a contract to build a new office block which the company had entered into with a building firm run by a director, or by the spouse of a director.

It might also be a loan to the brother of a director. A brother is not a connected person but the loan might be a material interest.

The board of directors will decide whether a transaction is material, though the auditors must disclose it in their report if the directors fail to disclose it in the accounts as s 413 requires and the auditor thinks it is material.

Contracts with a sole member/director

Section 231 applies. This provides that the terms of a contract with a sole member/director must either be set out in a written memorandum or recorded in the minutes of the next board meeting. This does not apply if the contract is in writing or is entered into in the ordinary course of business as where the company buys raw materials from the sole member/director.

Disclosing interests in contracts

Section 182 provides that every director who has an interest whether direct or indirect (as through a connected person) in a contract or proposed contract with the company must disclose his interest either at the board meeting at which the contract is first discussed or if the interest has not arisen at that time then at the first board meeting after the interest arises. In *Guinness* v *Saunders* (1990) the House of Lords decided that disclosure had to be made at a full meeting of the board and not at a meeting of a committee of the board. The section provides for a general notice procedure under which a director may give notice that he is a member of a specified company or a partner in a specified firm and is to be regarded as interested in any contract which may, after the date of the notice, be made with that company or firm. This general notice procedure is not available unless the interest arises only because the director is a member of a company or partner in a firm. Thus, if the interest arises because the director is a director of the other company but not a member of it, disclosure should be made in relation to each transaction as it arises.

A director who fails to make disclosure as required is liable to a fine. In addition, the contract can in appropriate circumstances be regarded as cancelled (or rescinded) but this must be done quickly and preferably before any performance has taken place (see below). The company's articles may waive the right to rescind, or the members by ordinary or unanimous written resolution can do so.

There can be no waiver by the board. However, the director concerned can vote in favour of adopting it under the written resolution procedure or at a general meeting and even in the latter case if he controls the voting at the meeting. This is because the director is not in breach of duty in terms of the making of the contract but only in breach of the duty of disclosure.

Incidentally, a director is not required to declare any interest which is not likely to give rise to any conflict of interest.

The above disclosures should be made by new directors at the first board meeting in so far as they apply to then existing contracts.

Craven Textile Engineers Ltd v Batley Football Club Ltd (2001)

A director of the claimant company was also a former director of the football club. The claimant company did work for and supplied goods to the football club during the period of the dual directorship. The football club did not pay the relevant invoices and when sued tried to avoid the contract because it appeared that the director concerned had not disclosed his interest in the contracts to the company. The Court of Appeal noted that s 317 does not deal with the consequences of a breach but at common law the contracts could be avoided by the company. However, it must be possible to restore the parties to their pre-contractual positions before this could be done. In this case that was not possible as the goods and services had already been supplied. The company was therefore entitled to payment of the invoices.

The provisions of s 182 extend to any transaction or arrangement set out in s 330, i.e. loans, quasi-loans and credit to a director or connected persons such as a spouse or minor child of the director. The principle of disclosure also applies whether or not the arrangement is a valid and enforceable contract so that the disclosure provisions cannot be avoided by including in, e.g., a loan arrangement a clause to the effect that it is not intended to create legal relations (see s 185).

The principles of disclosure are also applied to shadow directors by s 182. But the interest of a shadow director must be declared by notice in writing to the directors and not at a meeting of the board. The notice may state a specific interest and be given before the date of the meeting at which the shadow director would have been required to declare his interest if he had been a director or it may be a general one (s 317(8)(a) and (b)).

In *Re Neptune (Vehicle Washing Equipment) Ltd* (1995) the High Court held that even a sole director

must declare and record his interest in a contract with the company at a board meeting. The sole director concerned had resolved to pay himself £100,000 as severance pay on the termination of his employment and the shareholders caused the company to sue to recover it on the grounds that he had not disclosed his interest in the contract at a board meeting under what is now the CA 2006, s 182. Therefore, the company claimed the contract could be avoided. In deciding preliminary matters prior to the trial, it was decided that he should have made disclosure at a board meeting, even though he was a sole director. The court said he could have a meeting on his own, or perhaps with the company secretary present, so that the declaration could be made and recorded in the minutes. However, the declaration need not be made aloud: the director could silently declare it while thinking about any conflicts of interest there might be. Obviously, to record it in the minutes is the important point.

Removal under statute

Under the provisions of s 168 every company has power to remove any director before the end of his period of office.

The provisions are, for practical purposes, the same as those they replace.

The removal is carried out by an ordinary resolution of the members in general meeting. A written resolution cannot be used. Special notice of 28 days must be given to the company secretary that the resolution will be moved. The meeting at which the removal of a director under s 168 is to be considered must be called by at least 21 days' notice.

The director is entitled to have a written statement in his defence, as it were, sent with the notice of the meeting. That failing, he can make an oral statement at the meeting.

As we have seen, the removal of a director does not affect any right he may have to claim money compensation for the dismissal.

Removal under the articles

The power to remove directors under s 168 is a somewhat drawn out procedure and company directors may wish to exercise the power of director removal themselves. A power in the articles of the company can achieve this, as in the case of a clause in the articles allowing a simple majority of the board to remove a director by written notice in writing. The director removed would not have the statutory right to make representations though he or she may, depending on the circumstances, have a claim against the company for wrongful dismissal.

The fact that the articles contain such a provision will not prevent members with a sufficient majority from using the s 168 route as where they have lost confidence in a director and the board remain inactive. Section 168 states that it applies even when other methods of removal also apply (s 168(5), (6)).

A quite common use of a removal power in the articles is a removal clause in the articles of a subsidiary company allowing the holding company to remove directors of the subsidiary, something that cannot be achieved under s 168.

Retirement

The company's articles generally provide that a certain number of directors shall retire annually. This is called retirement by rotation. Articles may provide for one-third to retire annually. Those retiring are usually eligible for re-election.

Resignation

The articles usually provide that a director vacates office when he notifies his resignation to the company.

Disqualification

The grounds for disqualification of directors may be set out in the articles.

In addition, the court may disqualify directors. For example, under s 3 of the Company Directors Disqualification Act 1986 (which is not repealed by the CA 2006 and continues 'stand alone' and unchanged), the court can disqualify a director following persistent default in filing returns, accounts and other documents with the Registrar. Persistent default is conclusively proved by the fact that the director has had three convictions in a period of five years for this kind of offence. The maximum period of disqualification in this case is five years.

Another ground for disqualification, which is increasingly coming before the courts, is to be found in s 10 of the 1986 Act. It occurs when a company goes into liquidation and the evidence shows that the directors have negligently struggled on for too long with an insolvent company in the hope that things would get better but which has in the end gone into insolvent liquidation. This is called wrongful trading and the maximum period of disqualification is 15 years. The directors are also jointly and severally liable for such of the company's debts as the court thinks fit. The court is not restricted to making an order relating only to debts incurred during the period of wrongful trading.

A director may also be disqualified if he or she is held by the court to be 'unfit' to hold the office of director. The company must be insolvent, generally as a result of serious management failures, and often involving failure to pay NIC and taxes. There is no personal liability for the debts of the company but disqualification can be for a period of up to 15 years and there is a minimum period of two years. Sections 6, 7 and 8 of the 1986 Act apply.

A register of disqualification orders made by the court is kept by the Registrar of Companies. The public can inspect that register and see the names of those currently disqualified from acting as directors. Obviously, the name is removed at the end of the period of disqualification.

Disqualification – some case law

The High Court decided in *Re Seagull Manufacturing Co (No 2)* (1994) that a disqualification order may be made against a director regardless of his or her nationality and current residence and domicile. Furthermore, the conduct leading to the disqualification need not have occurred within the jurisdiction. In other words, you can run an English company badly from abroad. The director concerned was a British subject but at all material times he was resident and domiciled in the Channel Islands. Nevertheless, he could be disqualified under s 6 for unfitness. The relevant legislation contained no express jurisdiction requirement or territorial distinction.

The High Court also decided in *Re Pamstock Ltd* (1994) that a director who was also the secretary of the company could be disqualified as much for failure to perform his duties as secretary as those of a director. The company had two directors and one was also the company secretary. It traded beyond the point at which it should have ceased to do so and went into insolvent liquidation. The judge said that as the company secretary one of the directors had failed to ensure that accounts and returns were filed on time and that an adequate system of management was put in place. These were serious defaults which must be taken into account when dealing with the period of disqualification. This implies that it was the director's failure to carry out his duties as secretary that were at the root of his disqualification for two years. There is, of course, no power to disqualify a company secretary from acting as such.

Powers of directors

The Act requires certain powers to be exercised by the members, e.g. alteration of the articles. Apart from this the distribution of powers between the board and the members depends entirely on the articles.

Duties of directors

Statutory framework

One of the major changes in the CA 2006 for directors is the setting out, for the first time, of a statutory framework for their legal duties. The statutory duties of directors can be found under Part 10, Chapter 2 of the CA 2006: ss 171–177. Before the CA 2006, duties of directors arose and developed mainly outside statute law. These duties of directors were based on common law principles from which, in case law, the judiciary carved out a series of duties that became well-established rules: a director was bound by the fiduciary duties established by case law to act for a proper purpose and a duty to act bona fide in the interest of the company, and by the common law duties to exercise care and skills.

As stated in the explanatory notes to the Act, these statutory duties form a 'code of conduct, which sets out how directors are expected to behave; it does not tell them in terms what to do'. Accordingly, the established case law remains important as it is envisaged that the judicial interpretation of the new provisions will draw heavily from the existing case law. Although the new duties are in some cases expressed in broader terms than the common law rules, arguably, it can be said that the court's approach has long departed from the two-tier test laid down in *Re City Equitable Fire Insurance Co Ltd* (1925), as demonstrated in *Lexi Holdings Plc (In Administration)* v *Luqman* (2007): the issue was not

whether the directors knew of their fellow directors' misconduct, but had they performed their duties as directors, they would have discovered it and either prevented it or brought it to an end. Accordingly, the judge commented that 'the defence that complete inactivity was a sufficient discharge of her fiduciary and common law duties fails the reality test'. Further, in *Foster Bryant Surveying Ltd* v *Bryant* (2007) the law on directors' duties was considered. This case concerned the alleged breach of a director's fiduciary duties during a period of notice after he had resigned as a director but when his resignation had not yet taken effect. It was said that:

[a director] has an obligation to deal towards it with loyalty, good faith and avoidance of the conflict of duty and self-interest . . . A requirement to avoid a conflict of duty and self-interest means that a director is precluded from obtaining for himself, either secretly or without the informed approval of the Company, any property or business advantage either belonging to the Company or for which it has been negotiating, especially where the director or officer is a participant in the negotiations.

It went further to provide 'directors, no less than employees, acquire a general fund of skill, knowledge and expertise in the course of their work, which is plainly in the public interest that they should be free to exploit it in a new position'.

The seven general statutory duties are:

Duties owed to the company

Section 170 makes clear that the duties are owed to the company and this gives directors a shield against claims by a wide variety of interest groups. The duty is to the company and not outsiders.

Duty to act within powers

This states that a director must act in accordance with the company's constitution and use those powers only for the purposes for which they were granted.

Note: the major constitutional document is the articles and not the memorandum.

Duty to promote the success of the company

Under s 172, a director of a company must act in a way that he or she considers to be in good faith and would be most likely to promote the success of the company for the benefit of its members as a whole.

The Act goes on to state that, in fulfilling the duty imposed by this section, a director must (so far as reasonably practicable) have regard to:

- the likely consequences of any decision in the long term;
- the interests of the company's employees;
- the need to foster the company's business relationships with suppliers, customers and others;
- the impact of the company's operation in the community and the environment;
- the desirability of the company maintaining a reputation for high standards of business conduct;
- the need to act fairly as between members of the company.

Note: the duty is owed to the company alone and not to any other stakeholder, e.g. the workforce. However, what is new is that stakeholder interests must be considered. This could lead to litigation in the sense that in reaching a particular decision the interests of one or more stakeholders were not considered fully or at all. Board meetings could become more difficult in terms of decisions taken. Has the board got a trail of evidence showing that relevant consideration was given?

Duty to exercise independent judgement

Section 173 provides that a director of a company must exercise independent judgement. This duty, the section states, is not infringed by acting:

- in accordance with an agreement made with the company that restricts the exercise of discretion by its directors; or
- in a way authorised by the company's constitution.

It is not certain whether delegation of duties, which is not dealt with by the duties expressly, is included. It probably neither permits nor restricts delegation. This matter should be dealt with in the articles.

Duty to exercise reasonable care, skill and diligence

This means, according to s 174, the care, skill and diligence that would be exercised by a reasonably diligent person with:

- the general knowledge, skill and experience that may reasonably be expected of a person carrying out the functions carried out by the director in relation to the company; and
- the general knowledge, skill and experience that the director has.

This test is not new but is relatively underdeveloped by the courts.

Duty to avoid conflicts of interest

Section 175 provides that a director must avoid a situation in which he or she has or can have a direct or indirect interest that conflicts or may conflict with the interests of the company. The duty is not infringed:

- if the situation cannot reasonably be regarded as likely to give rise to a conflict of interest; or
- where the matter has been authorised by the directors.

This could be problematic for those who hold directorships in different companies.

Duty not to accept benefits from third parties

Section 176 applies and provides that a director must not accept a benefit from a third party conferred by reason of:

- being a director; or
- doing or not doing anything as a director.

This deals with bribes and personal benefits. There may be board authorisation.

Duty to declare interest in proposed transaction or arrangement

Section 177 states that a director who is directly or indirectly interested in a proposed transaction with the company must declare the nature and extent of the interest. There is also, as we have noted, a separate regime for disclosure in s 182 (and subsequently) backed by criminal sanctions for non-compliance.

Shareholders' claim on behalf of the company

We have already described the effect of the new derivative claim on behalf of the company so that it is no longer necessary to find a gap in *Foss* v *Harbottle* (1843), where the wrongdoing directors had also to be the controlling shareholders in the company. The new claim does not require this.

Corporate indemnification of directors

New provisions relating to the indemnification of directors appeared in the Companies (Audit Investigation and Community Enterprises) Act 2004. They were brought into force on 6 April 2005. These provisions have now been transferred to the CA 2006 and appear in Chapter 7 of Part 10. They are as follows:

- For liabilities in connection with claims brought by third parties both legal costs as they are incurred and judgment costs can be paid by the company even if judgment goes against the director. The only exclusions will be criminal fines and fines by regulators, and the legal costs of unsucessful criminal proceedings. Thus a director could be indemnified against the costs of legal proceedings brought against him by the Financial Services Authority in regard to a breach of the Listing Rules (or Part 6 Rules, as they are also known) governing the listing of shares on the Stock Exchange. However, no indemnity could be given in regard to a civil fine imposed by the FSA if the director was found to have infringed the rules.
- Companies are allowed to pay a director's defence costs as they are incurred, even where the claim is brought by the company. However, if the director's defence is unsuccessful, he or she will have to pay the company its damages and repay to the company any defence costs paid by the company as the case proceeded.
- The prohibition on companies indemnifying their company secretaries and managers is removed totally.
- All indemnities must be disclosed in the directors' annual report and indemnity agreements must be available for inspection by members.

Relief from liability: effect of s 1157

The company cannot excuse a director from liability altogether, but the court can under s 1157 of the CA 2006. The director is required to show to the court the following:

- that he or she acted honestly and reasonably; and
- that, having regard to all the circumstances, he or she ought fairly to be excused.

Directors' meetings

Notice of board meetings must be given to all directors unless they are out of the UK. Unless the articles otherwise provide, any director can call a board meeting.

Quorum

This is a matter for the articles but a usual provision is that the quorum necessary for the valid transaction of business by the directors may be fixed by the directors themselves and unless it is so fixed then the quorum is two directors personally present.

Voting

Unless the articles say differently, each director has one vote and resolutions of the board require a majority of only one. If there is an equality of votes, the resolution is lost unless the chairman has and exercises a casting vote in favour of the resolution.

Minutes

Section 248 provides that every company must keep minutes of all proceedings at meetings of directors. The members of the company have no general right to inspect the minutes of board meetings but the directors have (*R* v *Merchant Tailors' Co* (1831)).

The minutes must now be kept for at least ten years. Failure to keep them is a criminal offence by those officers in default. Liability no longer falls upon the company, it rests solely with the officers.

The secretary

Part 12 of the 2006 Act applies. Main points to note are that a private company is not required to have a company secretary. Where a private company does in fact make an appointment, which it may choose to do, that person appointed has all the duties and powers of a company secretary (see below).

A public company must appoint a secretary. There is a new power for the Secretary of State to give the company concerned a direction to make an appointment. It is an offence to fail to comply with the direction. The new law requires a company with a secretary to keep a Register of Secretaries; not, as in the past, to include them in the Register of Directors and Secretaries.

Where no secretary is appointed, the duties can be carried out by any person nominated and authorised by the board. A corporation may be a secretary to a company, but a company, X, cannot have as secretary a company, Y, if the sole director of company Y is also the sole director or secretary of company X.

The CA 2006 provides that a provision requiring or authorising a thing to be done by or to a director and the secretary shall not be satisfied by its being done by or to the same person acting both as director and secretary. This means that the single-member company may have only one member but must have at least two officers since the sole member/director cannot also be the secretary.

It is usual for the secretary to be appointed by the directors, who may fix his term of office and the conditions upon which he is to hold office. The articles usually confer such a power upon the board. The secretary is an employee of the company. He is regarded as such for the purpose of preferential payments in a winding-up.

The secretary enjoys the power to make contracts on behalf of the company even without authority. This is, however, restricted to contracts in the administrative operations of the company, including the employment of office staff and the management of the office, together with the hiring of transport. Thus, in *Panorama Developments* v *Fidelis Furnishing Fabrics* (1971) the secretary of a company ordered cars from a hire firm, representing that they were required to meet the company's customers at Heathrow. In fact, he used the cars for his own purposes. When the company discovered this, it refused to pay the bill. The court, however, held that the company was liable to pay it. A company secretary was a well-known business appointment and such a person had usual authority, even if no actual authority, to bind the company to the contract of hire.

His authority is not unlimited. He cannot, without authority, borrow money on behalf of the company (*Re Cleadon Trust Ltd* (1939)). He cannot, without authority, commence an action in the courts on the company's behalf (*Daimler Co Ltd* v *Continental Tyre and Rubber Co Ltd* (1916)). He cannot summon a general meeting himself (*Re State of Wyoming Syndicate* (1901)), nor register a transfer of shares without the board's approval (*Chida Mines Ltd* v *Anderson* (1905)). These are powers which are vested in the directors.

Certain duties are directly imposed on the secretary by statute. The most important of these includes the submission of the annual return. The CA 2006 authorises the company secretary to sign forms prescribed under the Act.

Company insolvency and corporate rescue

Section references are to the Insolvency Act 1986 unless otherwise indicated.

In the event that a company becomes insolvent, the company's business and assets and its affairs generally will be controlled by an insolvency practitioner. The relevant practitioner will be a member of an accounting firm or a firm specialising in insolvency work or, in the case of a liquidation, a person from the Official Receiver's Office. The Official Receiver and those who act in that capacity are civil servants who take office in companies in liquidation and continue to wind them up unless there is an appointment of an insolvency practitioner from the private sector, e.g. from an accounting firm. Such an appointment would be made by the creditors if they so wished.

Some solicitors are authorised by the Law Society to act as insolvency practitioners but most practitioners are accountants authorised by their professional bodies or by the Insolvency Practitioners Association to act. Thus, the public interest in the proper procedures being applied is safeguarded by the need for authorisation and the monitoring functions of the authorising bodies.

Insolvency procedures

There are three main corporate insolvency procedures as follows:

- *liquidation*, in which the company is wound up and taken off the register of companies;
- *administration*, which is designed to rescue the company from insolvency; and
- *a company voluntary arrangement*, which is designed to allow the company to continue to trade under arrangements to make some payments to those who are its creditors at the time of the making of the arrangement.

The demise of the administrative receiver

An administrative receiver was the normal appointment of a bank where a company was in financial difficulties with a bank overdraft. The bank held a floating charge on the company's undertaking and the function of the administrative receiver was to undertake such procedures with the company as would pay off the bank. An administrative receiver was not primarily part of the company rescue procedure as an administrator is. What is more, the existence of the office of administrative receiver inhibited the rescue procedures of administration because when the company or its creditors sought to make the appointment of an administrator the bank, which had to be notified, would often immediately appoint an administrative receiver and veto the administration.

The Enterprise Act 2002 prevents the holder of a floating charge, such as a bank, from appointing an administrative receiver except in a restricted number of organisations, such as companies involved in the financial market. These are beyond the scope of this text and of courses in business law at our level. Banks which had taken floating charges before that date will still be able to appoint such practitioners. However, the office is, from a student point of view, redundant and no more will be said about it in this text.

It is worth noting that the practice of appointing receivers by those who have taken fixed charges over property will continue. These practitioners are in no sense managers being appointed to pay off the debt by a sale of the charged property or by collecting rents if it is let until the debt is paid. They do not have to be authorised insolvency practitioners and the practice is to appoint chartered surveyors to do this work.

Liquidation

Liquidation is a procedure by which the existence of a company is brought to an end and its property administered for the benefit of creditors and members. A liquidator takes control of the company, collects in its assets and pays its debts and liabilities and distributes any surplus between the members. The company is then dissolved and it is removed from the register of companies.

There are three types of liquidation (or winding-up) as follows:

- a compulsory liquidation;
- a members' voluntary liquidation;
- a creditors' voluntary liquidation.

These procedures are controlled in the main by the Insolvency Act 1986.

Compulsory liquidation

The petition

A compulsory liquidation begins with the presentation of a petition to the court. It is usually on the grounds that the company cannot pay its debts. A company is to be regarded in law as unable to pay its debts if:

- a statutory demand in a special form *for more than* £750 has been left at the registered office of the company and this has not been complied with to the satisfaction of the creditor(s) for a period of at least three weeks;
- the company has failed to satisfy a debt where the creditor has obtained a court judgment and there has been an unsuccessful attempt to levy execution, i.e. take property from the company for sale to pay the debt;
- the company's assets are worth less than its liabilities taking into account contingent and prospective liabilities, such as penalties under a contract that will fall due because the company cannot perform it;
- it is proved to the satisfaction of the court that the company is unable to pay its debts as they fall due.

The petitioners

The company itself can present the petition as where the directors see no hope of survival though such petitions are rare in compulsory liquidation. More commonly the petitioner is a creditor. There may also be a joint petition where it is necessary to combine the debts of two or more creditors to make up the debt exceeding £750 that is required. The court may in its discretion refuse to make a winding-up order and will normally do so where a majority of the creditors oppose the petition.

The usual ground for presentation of a petition is the unsatisfied statutory demand referred to above. However, where a company's assets are seriously at risk of diminution, three weeks may be too long a time to wait and other grounds have been used successfully. So in *Taylors Industrial Flooring Ltd* v *M & H Plant Hire (Manchester) Ltd* (1990) goods were supplied in December 1998 and in spite of subsequent billings nothing had been paid by the debtor company by April 1999 when the petition was presented and the court made a winding-up order. The petitioners did not therefore have to wait a further three weeks before presenting the petition.

Where a winding-up order is made

The Official Receiver becomes the liquidator on the making of an order for compulsory winding-up and will remain in office unless the creditors decide to appoint an insolvency practitioner of their choice. The Official Receiver proceeds as follows:

- to advertise the winding-up in *The London Gazette* which is an official journal for public announcements, and a local newspaper;
- to notify the Registrar of Companies and the company itself;
- to exercise the powers of the directors and administer the company's affairs until liquidation. The directors' powers are withdrawn on the making of the order;
- to arrange for the company's stationery to state that it is in liquidation;
- to receive from the directors a statement of affairs which they must prepare or have prepared within 14 days of the order. The statement gives the company's assets and liabilities, the names of its creditors and details of any security which they have;
- to prepare a report for the court setting out the financial position of the company and the reasons for its failure;
- to call separate meetings of the creditors and members. These meetings may nominate someone else as liquidator. Where the meetings do this and disagree, the person nominated by the creditors takes precedence.

Voluntary liquidation

A voluntary winding-up is commenced by a resolution of the members. This must be advertised in *The London Gazette* within 14 days of its passing.

Where the company is insolvent, the members must pass an extraordinary resolution stating that the company cannot by reason of its liabilities continue its business. In other cases a special resolution is used. As already noted, these resolutions need the same majority, i.e. 75 per cent of those present and voting in person or by proxy but the notice period is different, i.e. 14 days for the extraordinary resolution and 21 days for the special resolution. Unanimous written resolutions can be used in both cases.

The extraordinary resolution results in a creditors' voluntary winding-up and the special resolution in a members' voluntary winding-up.

Members' voluntary winding-up

The winding-up will proceed as a members' voluntary if the directors are able and willing to make a statutory declaration (a statement on oath) within five weeks before the resolution is passed stating that the company is solvent and will be able to pay all its debts in full

within a stated period not exceeding twelve months. If this can be done, the members appoint an insolvency practitioner as the liquidator.

Creditors' voluntary winding-up

Where the directors cannot or are not prepared to make the statutory declaration – and they can suffer penalties if it does not come true – then the liquidation is a creditors' voluntary. The creditors must be called to a meeting to be held not later than 14 days after the resolution to wind up is passed. An insolvency practitioner will be appointed as liquidator by the creditors.

It should be noted that a members' voluntary may become a creditors' voluntary if the statutory declaration of solvency is not complied with.

The creditors are then in charge of the winding-up in terms, for example, of the power to appoint a different liquidator.

The powers of the directors cease in both a members' and a creditors' winding-up and are taken over by the liquidator. The creditors can agree to the powers of the directors continuing but this is not likely particularly in a creditors' voluntary.

Actions against the company

- In a compulsory winding-up, no action can be brought against the company unless the court gives leave. Where a creditor has brought a claim and completed it before the order the creditor concerned may keep the proceeds of any company property realised (sold) as a result. If an action is brought against the company between the presentation of the petition and the making of the winding-up order, any creditor can apply to have it stayed (stopped).
- In a voluntary liquidation, application may similarly be made to have actions against the company stopped. The court has a discretion whether to stop claims or not.

The property of the company

The liquidator does not own the company's property but has a duty to take possession of it in order to realise it and use the proceeds to pay the debts and liabilities of the company in a prescribed order (see below). Any surplus is distributable among the members.

It is important to note that certain property is excluded and not available to the liquidator for realisation. Of significance in business is property held by the company that is subject to a retention clause (see further Chapter 10 ○). This property is not owned by the company if the property concerned has not been paid for by the company. A retention of title clause is often inserted into business contracts and is to the effect that the ownership of goods sold to a customer does not pass to the customer until they have been paid for.

Distribution of assets

The funds realised by the liquidator must be distributed in a given order. However, it should be noted that secured creditors with a fixed charge over specific property of the company such as land or buildings will usually enforce their security by a sale of the property. They are not subject to the preferential debts or expenses of the winding-up though they will have to pay some costs in order to sell the security. If the sale funds do not pay off the debt the secured creditor can try to recover the balance in the liquidation process but with the rank of an unsecured creditor. If the sale proceeds are more than sufficient to pay the debt and the costs of realisation, the balance must be paid to the liquidator for distribution.

Creditors other than holders of a fixed charge

The liquidator will distribute funds in the following order.

- *In meeting the expenses of winding-up.* This includes the cost of collecting and realising assets and the remuneration of the liquidator.
- *In paying preferential creditors.* The Enterprise Act 2002 abolished Crown preference and so debts owed to the Inland Revenue, Customs and Excise for VAT and Social Security debts such as national insurance contributions are no longer preferential. They join the ranks of the unsecured creditors for payment. Preferential status is retained for unpaid contributions to occupational pension schemes and employees' wages or salaries (see below).
- Wages or salaries owed to employees for the previous four months up to a current maximum of £800 per employee plus accrued holiday pay. These figures are taken as gross.
- Money that was lent, e.g. by a bank, to the company as employer before the liquidation to pay debts in the above category and which was used for that purpose.

This provision encourages banks to lend money for wages and salaries before liquidation to try to keep the company operating as a going concern. The bank knows that if the company does fail it will at least be a preferential creditor for the relevant sum of money.

Where the assets are insufficient to pay the preferential debts in full, they *abate equally*, i.e. each creditor is paid the same proportion of the debt. For example, if the preferential debts are £2,000 but the assets available amount only to £1,000, each preferential creditor would receive only half the debt.

Creditors having a floating charge

These rank as regards priority of payment in the order of their creation so that those created first are paid off first.

Unsecured creditors

When the above categories have been paid in full, a distribution may be made to ordinary unsecured creditors. Where funds are insufficient to make a full payment, those debts in the category abate equally (see the example above).

Members

If all the above debts have been paid in full, a distribution may be made to members. This is called a dividend and is expressed as a percentage in the pound of the sum owed. Obviously, there will not be a distribution to the members where the company is insolvent but such a distribution could be made in a members' voluntary liquidation.

Swelling the assets

The assets available to the liquidator or administrator (not an administrative receiver) can be increased where prior to the administration or liquidation there have been transactions at undervalue (s 238) and preferences (s 239) (as where a creditor has been preferred over the others). An example is to be found in *Re Kushler* (1943), a case decided under previous legislation. In that case ordinary creditors were ignored but the company paid some £700 into its bank account merely to clear the overdraft which the directors had personally guaranteed. Repayment by the bank was ordered.

A further and common example of a preference concerns the repayment of directors' loan accounts. In many smaller companies the directors may have lent money to the company and it will repay these loan accounts so as to avoid problems relating to repayment once an insolvency practitioner takes over. If the relevant repayment is made within two years of the insolvency practitioner's appointment, as is often the case, it is recoverable by him from the directors concerned and may be used to pay the company's debts in the prescribed order. A major authority for this is the ruling of the court in *Re Exchange Travel (Holdings) Ltd* (1996).

Under s 241 the court can set these transactions aside and allow the liquidator to recover money or property for the company. Preferences made in the six months prior to administration or liquidation can be recovered. If the preference is to a person connected or associated with the company, e.g. a director or a relative of a director (see s 435), the period is two years (see *Re Exchange Travel (Holdings) Ltd* (1996)). Transactions at undervalue made up to two years before can be set aside, whether the recipient was connected or associated with the company or not. The company must have been insolvent at the time of such transaction or have become insolvent as a result of it.

Alternatives to liquidation: company rescue procedures

The two main alternatives most commonly used in business as alternatives to liquidation and with a view to company rescue are:

- placing the company into administration; and
- making a company voluntary arrangement.

Administration

The Enterprise Act 2002 made significant changes in the administration procedure. This was achieved by inserting an additional Sch (B1) into the Insolvency Act 1986.

The nature of administration

An administrator of a company is a person appointed under Sch B1 to manage the company's affairs, business and property. The effect of the Schedule is as follows:

- Whether appointed by the court or not (under the Schedule appointment may be out of court), an administrator is an officer of the court and an agent of the company and can only be appointed if qualified to act as an insolvency practitioner.
- An administrator cannot be appointed if the company has already been put into administration. Thus, an appointment out of court cannot effectively be made if the court has already made an appointment and vice versa, although this does not affect provisions relating to the replacement of an administrator nor the appointment of additional administrators if required.
- A company cannot be put into administration if:
  - the members have passed a resolution for a voluntary winding-up; or
  - a compulsory winding-up order has been made by the court.

However, in both of the above situations the liquidator and/or the holder of a qualifying floating charge, i.e. a floating charge over the whole or substantially the whole of the company's property, such as a bank, would normally apply to the court for the appointment of an administrator if they can make a case that the company's interests would be better served by administration.

The purpose of administration

The Schedule clarifies the purpose of an administration and puts greater emphasis on company rescue. The prime objective is to rescue the company. Where this is not reasonably practicable, the objective becomes the realisation of the company's property in order to make a distribution to one or more preferential and secured creditors. Finally, where there are insufficient funds to pay off the unsecured creditors, the administrator must not harm their interests when making the above payments as by selling property too cheaply to conclude more quickly the payments that can be made to the priority categories.

The objectives are not alternatives but must be applied in sequence, if the primary objective of rescue is not reasonably possible. In the absence of bad faith, the viability of company rescue will be a matter for the administrator whose judgement the court will normally accept, should the matter be raised. An obvious reason for not pursuing rescue would be where this would need the support of the company's bankers that was not forthcoming and where no other means of financing the company was available. Where rescue is not possible the administrator in turning to the objective of seeking a better result for creditors than in a winding-up might try to sell one or more of the company's businesses as a going concern or sell the assets without a going concern basis. Where none of the company's businesses is viable, all that can be done is to sell the company's assets in order to make a distribution to those holding fixed charges (if these persons have not already sold the charged asset but have relied on the administration) and then preferential debts and then floating charge holders.

Appointment of an administrator

Formerly, an administrator could be appointed only by order of the court. This route into administration has been retained. To speed up administration the Schedule contains provisions under which those holding floating charges and companies or their directors can appoint an administrator without a court hearing.

Appointment by the court

Those holding floating charges can apply as can the company or its directors or one or more of its creditors. Before making an order the court must be satisfied that the company is or is likely to become unable to pay its debts and that the administration is likely to achieve the purposes of an administration according to its objective. Those applying for an order must notify anyone who has appointed or is entitled to appoint an administrative receiver or an administrator. There are still some restricted circumstances in which an administrative receiver can be appointed (see pp 195–6). The permission of the court is required before the application can be withdrawn. If the court does not make an administration order, it may make any other appropriate order, e.g. by treating the application as a petition for winding-up.

Appointment by the court: effect of presentation of petition

Following notification of presentation of a petition to holders of floating charges, those holders can, if they have enforceable qualifying charges, make an appointment of an alternative administrator under the procedure set out for appointments out of court (see below). They cannot appoint an administrative receiver unless they

are holders of a security granted to them as a holder of a capital market investment.

The administration order is an alternative to liquidation and cannot be made after any form of liquidation has started.

The order sets up a 'moratorium' which prevents the individual enforcement of claims against the company. A winding-up petition may be presented but will only be allowed to proceed if the application for an administrator is dismissed. All existing actions against the company are stayed and no new action may be started. Goods in the company's possession that are not owned by the company as where they are on hire purchase or on retention may not be repossessed.

Appointment out of court

1 By holders of a floating charge

Holders of an enforceable floating charge are able to appoint an administrator of their own choosing. Conditions are:

- that the charge is a qualifying charge, i.e. the charge (or charges) are over the whole or substantially the whole of the company's property;
- the charge is enforceable at the date of the appointment;
- the company must not have a provisional liquidator in office;
- there must not be an administrative receiver in office.

Comment. The court has power to appoint a provisional liquidator at any time after the presentation of a petition for compulsory winding-up of the company, e.g. to safeguard the company's property until a liquidator is appointed.

Method of appointment

Given that an insolvency practitioner is willing to act as administrator, the person making the appointment must give two business days' notice to holders of any qualifying floating charge operating in priority to his or her own stating the intention to appoint an administrator. Notice to appoint an administrator is filed at court together with a statutory declaration confirming that the appointor holds an enforceable floating charge. This is accompanied by a statement from the administrator consenting to the appointment and stating that in his or her opinion the particular purpose of the administration is reasonably likely to be achieved. When this is done the appointment commences.

2 By the company or its directors

A company or its directors will only be able to appoint an administrator if:

- the company has *not* been in administration on the instigation of the company or its directors in the previous 12 months;
- the company has *not* been subject to a moratorium in regard to a failed company voluntary arrangement in the previous 12 months;
- the company *is* or *is likely* to become unable to pay its debts;
- the company is *not* the subject of a winding-up petition or in liquidation;
- there is *not* an administrator or administrative receiver in office.

The procedure then depends upon whether there is or is not a floating charge holder

Where there is *not* a floating charge holder. Notice of the appointment of the administrator is filed with the court with a statutory declaration and statement from the administrator consenting to the appointment. *The moratorium takes effect at this point.* Under Sch B1 this means that an effective resolution cannot be passed or an order made to wind up the company. There are some exceptions, e.g. where an order for compulsory winding-up is made on a petition by the Financial Services Authority in regard to an organisation authorised for investment business. Also no steps to enforce their rights may be taken by creditors without the consent of the administrator or permission of the court.

Where there *is* a floating charge holder. Here a statutory declaration is filed with the court with a notice but only of an *intention* to appoint an administrator. This notice of intent is sent to all floating charge holders. *The moratorium takes effect at this point.* The two possibilities are then as follows:

1 The floating charge holder is content with the appointment. Consent of the floating charge holder is ascertained in two ways as follows:

- he or she responds within five days saying that he or she is content with the appointment; or
- he or she does not respond within five days in which case agreement is implied.

Notice of the appointment is then filed in court with a statement from the administrator consenting to the appointment and stating that in his or her opinion the purpose of the administration is likely to be achieved. *The administrator is then in office.*

2 The floating charge holder is not content with the appointment. Such a holder can appoint an administrator of his choice to act in the administration. Having identified an alternative administrator the charge holder must give two business days' notice to holders of qualifying floating charges with priority over his own charge (if any) stating his intention to appoint. The notice to appoint is filed in court with a statutory declaration confirming that he or she holds an enforceable qualifying floating charge. This is accompanied by a statement from the administrator consenting to the appointment and stating that in his or her opinion the purpose of the administration is likely to be achieved. *The administrator is then in office.*

Effect of appointment of an administrator: generally

The following are the main effects of the appointment of an administrator *by any of the available means*.

- All business stationery must state that an administration exists and the administrator's name must appear alongside the company's name.
- The administrator manages the company's affairs generally and takes charge of its business and property. This includes the trusteeship of any employees' pension funds where the company has previously been trustee. The administrator has power to carry on the company's business to deal with or dispose of its assets and to borrow money in the company's name.
- The administrator can apply to have transactions at undervalue and preferences set aside just as a liquidator can. Similarly, unregistered and late charges are void against claims by him or her.
- The directors must submit a statement of affairs to the administrator but they remain in office unless the administrator removes them. An administrator can also appoint new directors without reference to the members.
- The administrator has eight weeks in which to make proposals which may save the company from liquidation and then to implement these proposals. The recommendations must have been approved by a simple majority in value of the company's unsecured creditors.

The special case of employment contracts

An administrator will often wish to retain the services of the company's employees at least for a period of time. Ultimately they may be transferred to a new organisation that has taken over the company's business as a going concern or made redundant if the assets are sold off without an effective rescue. The law contains provisions to ensure that the administrator can pay the employees or make them redundant at an early date in the administration so that the employees are *not* left to work on for a period of time after the commencement of the administration only to be told that the company cannot pay them for the work they have done.

This is achieved by giving an administrator a window of 14 days after the commencement of the administration to decide what to do about the employment contracts and nothing done by the administrator during that time is to be taken as adoption. The administrator is free to consider the matter without being regarded as having taken action to adopt the contracts. **Failure to act** will not amount to adoption **either during or after** the period of 14 days. (See the decision of the High Court in *Re Antal International Ltd* (2003) where the administrator became aware of the existence of some workers in France some 16 days after taking office. He then dismissed them and had not adopted the contract because he had not taken any 'action' to adopt the contracts as Sch B1 requires.)

What happens then if the administrator does adopt the contracts of employment and in the end is unable to pay the employees concerned? The law provides that the amounts owing to employees are charged on the assets of the company in priority to the administrator's fees and expenses. This is what adoption means and its effect. The sums involved and owing to employees do not include any payments because of the administrator's failure to give the proper contractual notice to the employees. The amounts concerned are wages or salaries including sickness and holiday pay and any contributions to a pension fund that the company has not paid. Payments in lieu of notice are excluded because of the considerable problems that would otherwise be faced by administrators who because of the failure of a rescue attempt had to dismiss employees without proper notice. Some of these employees might be senior staff on long periods of notice and high salaries that could wipe out the administrator's remuneration and expenses payments. So much so that firms of accountants and insolvency practitioners would not have accepted appointments of their staff as administrators.

Ending the administration

Under Sch B1 the administrator will automatically vacate office after one year from the date on which the appointment took effect. This period may be extended by the court for a period it may specify and by the consent of each secured creditor and 50 per cent in value of the unsecured creditors for a maximum period of six months. There can be only one creditors' extension. The court can bring an administration to an end on the application of the administrator. In most cases this will be where the administrator thinks the purpose of the administration has been achieved. A meeting of creditors may require the administrator to make application to the court or he or she may do so on his or her own volition where the purposes of the administration cannot be achieved. The termination of the administrator's office where the objects have been achieved will be notified to the Registrar of Companies and to every creditor. Where the objects of the administration cannot be achieved, notification will normally be of the setting up of other insolvency proceedings such as winding-up.

Ring-fencing assets for unsecured creditors: all insolvencies

The preferential debts are paid before those holding floating charges. However, the preferential debts are now much less in amount since Crown debts such as sums owed to the Inland Revenue have been reduced to unsecured status. In order that holders of floating charges, typically banks, do not get all the benefit of this, the insolvency practitioner **in all corporate insolvencies,** i.e. liquidation, administration or administrative receivership, must set aside from the proceeds raised a certain amount of money for payment to the unsecured creditors and not to the floating chargeholders.

The Insolvency Act 1986 (Prescribed Part) Order 2003 (SI 2003/2097) applies and requires the insolvency practitioner to set up a fund of £10,000 before making any payments to holders of floating charges. Given that more money than this is available then the prescribed percentage from realisations after that is:

- 50 per cent of the first floating charge realisations to be added to the initial £10,000;
- 20 per cent of floating charge realisations after that;
- up to a maximum ring-fenced fund for unsecured creditors of £600,000 but no more.

Voluntary arrangements

Provision for company voluntary arrangements (CVA) exists on the lines of the rules relating to insolvent sole traders which were considered in Chapter 5 ⊙.

Once again, the aim of a voluntary arrangement is to avoid insolvency proceedings by substituting a satisfactory settlement of the company's financial difficulties. For example, a composition may be made between the company and its creditors under which the creditors accept, say, 60p in the £1 in full settlement of their debts.

The directors must draw up proposals assisted by an insolvency practitioner, called a nominee, who will give a professional assessment as to the feasibility of the composition and report to the court as to whether the members and creditors should meet to consider the proposals. If the court agrees, the nominee will call the relevant meetings.

The composition is approved if a simple majority of members are in favour and 75 per cent in value of the unsecured creditors agree. If the composition is approved as required that approval is reported to the court by the nominee who becomes the supervisor of the arrangement and implements it. Creditors cannot sue for payment or petition for winding-up. Under the Insolvency Act 2000 a CVA binds **all** of the company's creditors, including unknown creditors and those who did not for some reason receive notice of the relevant meeting or did not attend and vote. These creditors, like all the others who participated in the arrangement, can claim only such distributions as they are entitled to under the CVA.

They may, however, apply to the court on the grounds (if they have any) that their interests are unfairly prejudiced by the CVA that has been approved by the participating creditors.

The above provisions do not excuse deliberate exclusion of creditors. If this happens, the resulting CVA is invalid, because the meeting is. The rights of secured and preferential creditors are not affected. At any stage *any* creditor may challenge a decision of the supervisor in court.

Company voluntary arrangements – the disadvantages

The main disadvantages of company voluntary arrangements (CVA) are that they cannot be made binding on a secured or preferential creditor in terms of priority of payment without the creditor's consent, and that there is no provision for obtaining a moratorium to hold off actions by hostile creditors while the proposal for a CVA is being drawn up and considered, unless the CVA proposal is being combined with the appointment of an administrator when the law relating to administrations applies and provides protection. Administration is costly and time-consuming. Although the company moratorium was left out of the Insolvency Act 1986, it will have been noted that the 'interim order' is available in the insolvency of individuals under the 1986 Act (see further, Chapter 5 ⊙).

The following provisions are now in force but only for small companies.

A company voluntary arrangement with a moratorium option for small companies

The Insolvency Act 2000 makes provision for a company CVA with a moratorium. The provisions are restricted to small companies, i.e. companies that can satisfy two or more of the conditions for being a small company for reporting purposes under the Companies Act 1985. Companies involved in financial markets such as stockbrokers, where existing law is designed to ensure that financial markets continue to function in the event of the insolvency of one or more of the participants, are excluded. Also excluded are companies already subject to formal insolvency proceedings as where a winding-up is in progress or where a moratorium has been tried and failed in the previous 12 months. The main provisions are set out below:

1 Nominee's statement. Directors who want a moratorium must appoint a nominee, normally an insolvency practitioner, and provide the nominee with the following information:

- a document setting out the terms of the proposed CVA;
- a statement of affairs giving details of the company's assets, debts and other liabilities together with any other information that the nominee may request.

2 Documents to be submitted to the court. If the nominee considers that the proposal has a reasonable prospect of success in terms of being approved and implemented and that sufficient funding is available and that meetings of the company and creditors should be called, he must provide the directors with a statement to that effect. In order to obtain a moratorium, the directors must file certain documents with the court; mainly the terms of the proposed CVA, the statement of affairs and the nominee's statement.

3 Duration of the moratorium. The moratorium comes into effect when the documents referred to above are filed with the court. The initial period is 28 days. A meeting of the company and of the creditors held within the initial period may decide to extend the moratorium by up to a further two months. The moratorium may be brought to an end by a decision of the meetings of the company and of creditors to approve a CVA. Alternatively, it may be brought to an end:

- by the court;
- by the withdrawal of the nominee of his consent to act;
- by a decision of the meetings of members and of creditors that the CVA should not be approved;
- at the end of the 28-day minimum period if both of the first meetings of the company and of the creditors has not taken place;
- if there is no decision of the above meetings to extend it.

4 Members and creditors: conflicting decisions. In this situation the decision of the creditors prevails but a member may apply to the court for an order that the members' decision should prevail. This is a matter for the court's discretion and the court may make any order it thinks fit.

5 Notification of the moratorium. When the moratorium comes into force and when it ends the nominee is required by the Insolvency Rules 1986 (SI 1986/1925) to advertise that fact, to notify the Registrar of Companies and to give an official notice to the company. When the moratorium comes into force he must notify any creditor who has petitioned for a winding-up; and when it ends he must notify any creditor of whose claim he is aware.

6 Effect of the moratorium on creditors. Other than for an 'excepted petition', i.e. a petition by the Secretary of State that winding-up is in the public interest, no petition to wind the company up nor any other insolvency proceedings can be commenced. No steps may be taken to enforce any security over the company's property or repossess any goods in the company's possession under any hire-purchase agreement or on retention; nor can any other proceedings be commenced or continued. Existing winding-up petitions cannot proceed.

7 Obtaining credit. During the moratorium the company may not obtain credit to the value of £250 or more without first telling the person giving the credit that a moratorium is in force. This includes payments in advance for the supply of goods and services. The company's officers commit a criminal offence if they breach these rules.

8 Disposals and payments. While the moratorium is in force the company may only dispose of any of its property or pay a debt that existed at the start of the moratorium if there are reasonable grounds for believing that it will benefit the company and the moratorium committee (see below) gives approval. If there is no committee, approval must be given by the nominee. This does not prevent the sale of property in the ordinary course of business as where a farming supplies company sells feed as part of its trade. Officers of the company commit an offence on breach of the above rules.

9 Disposal of charged property. So as not to inhibit a company rescue where it may be necessary to sell the undertaking or part of it, the Insolvency Act 2000 allows the disposal by the company during the moratorium of charged property and any goods in its possession under a hire-purchase agreement provided the holder of the security or owner of the goods or the court agrees. The holder of a fixed charge and the owner of goods on hire-purchase are entitled to have the proceeds of sale applied to the repayment of the loan or debt but the holder of a floating charge is not but retains a charge of equal priority to his original charge over the proceeds of the sale or disposal of the charged property.

10 Moratorium committee. In a case where the moratorium is extended there is provision for the setting up of a moratorium committee to exercise functions conferred upon it by the meetings of members and of creditors. The meetings must approve an estimate of the committee's expenses.

11 Effect of CVA. The CVA when approved binds all creditors including unknown creditors, which includes those creditors who were not, having followed the procedures in the insolvency rules, served with notice of the relevant meetings. The provision would not cover deliberate exclusion of creditors, which would lead to the invalidity of the relevant meeting and any CVA approved at it. Creditors not receiving notice can apply to the court on the grounds of unfair prejudice and the court may revoke or suspend the approval of the CVA. Otherwise, these creditors are entitled to dividends payable under the arrangement only. On the approval of the CVA the nominee becomes the supervisor.

12 Offences by officers of the company. The Act provides that if during the 12 months prior to the start of the moratorium any officer of the company who has committed certain acts, e.g. fraudulently removed the company's property worth £500 or more or falsified the company's records in relation to its property, commits an offence, as does an officer who acts in a similar way during the moratorium.

It is also an offence for an officer of the company to try to obtain a moratorium or an extension of it by making false statements or fraudulently doing or not doing any act.

Self-test questions/activities

1 Able and Ben are the promoters of Wye Ltd and are the two subscribers to the memorandum. The documents required to be sent to the Registrar of Companies in order to obtain the incorporation of Wye Ltd are ready to go. One of Wye Ltd's objects is to acquire the business of John Wye. John is getting difficult and insists that a contract for the sale of his business shall be signed now or the deal is off.

Advise Able and Ben, who do not want to lose the opportunity to acquire John Wye's undertaking.

2 The articles of association of Trent Ltd state that Cyril and David are appointed until aged 60 as Company Secretary and Chief Accountant respectively at salaries of £30,000 per annum. Cyril and David took up their posts five years ago, when they were 35 and 40 respectively.
   (a) Cyril has received a letter from the Chairman of Trent Ltd discharging him from the post of Company Secretary. Cyril would like to retain the job.
   (b) David has given his resignation to the board of Trent Ltd but the board will not accept it.
   Advise Cyril and David.

3 Derwent Ltd has suffered declining profits for four years. The directors have not declared a dividend for three years and in order to avoid facing the shareholders did not call an AGM last year.

Eric, who holds shares in Derwent, has got together with some of his fellow shareholders to form a group to see what can be done to get the company better managed.

Write a letter to Eric advising him and telling him how the group should proceed in practical terms.

4 Severn Ltd runs a very successful business and makes a good profit. However, over the past few years the controlling directors have increased their remuneration so that it absorbs all the profits. Jane, who is a minority shareholder not on the board, gets no dividends and wishes to do something about this state of affairs.

Explain to Jane what action she should take.

5 As Secretary of Ouse Ltd write a memorandum for the board explaining the differences between raising finance:
   (a) by an issue of shares;
   (b) by an issue of unsecured loan stock;
   (c) by an issue of debentures secured by a floating charge over the company's asets; and
   (d) by an issue of preference shares.

6 (a) How is the voluntary winding-up of a company brought about?
   (b) What decides whether a voluntary winding-up is controlled:
      (i) by the members, or
      (ii) by the creditors?

7 In relation to corporate insolvency, distinguish between an administrator and a liquidator.

Specimen examination questions

1 (a) How may and when must a company change its name?

(b) Dodgy Computers Ltd is registered for the purpose of acquiring the business of John who has been trading under the name of 'Supercomputers'. The company will operate the business under that name.

What statutory rules must the company comply with and what are the consequences in terms of its contracts if it fails to comply with them?

2 Although the directors have the general power to manage the company, power to carry out certain functions is given to the shareholders either in general meeting or by written resolution. State and explain these shareholder powers.

3 John holds shares in Derwent Ltd and wishes to retire and dispose of his shareholding for cash. Dick and Harry are the other two shareholders but they cannot afford to pay for the shares. John is thinking of selling his shares to his brother and Dick and Harry do not want this.

Explain to Dick and Harry how the company might purchase John's shares and outline the procedure to them.

4 Corporate insolvency: a case study

Trent Ltd is a small company. John and Paul are the shareholders and the company's overdraft with the Barchester Bank plc is secured by a floating charge on the whole of the company's undertaking.

Problems have arisen within the company. Trent Ltd is over-borrowed and has declining margins. The company has started to run short of cash. It is struggling to pay its bills and may fail in the near future.

Nevertheless, John and Paul intend to carry on business through the company. The bank and other creditors are pressing for payment. John and Paul seek your advice on resolving the present difficulties.

Matters to be addressed:

(a) The consequences for John and Paul of continuing to trade through the company in its present state.

(b) The suitability of a company voluntary arrangement or administration and the steps to be taken.

(c) The last-ditch possibility of a winding-up, preferably without the involvement of the court. Discuss procedures.

(d) Explain to John and Paul what steps the Barchester Bank can take.

(e) Explain the steps that unsecured creditors can take.

Website references

http://www.bis.gov.uk The Department for Business, Innovation and Skills site contains archived consultation papers and documentation relating to the company law reform and most up-to-date information on the Companies Act 2006.

http://www.companieshouse.gov.uk For changes in company filing procedures, the formation of companies and general guidance, Companies House is the source. Particularly useful is its quarterly publication, *Register*. This gives all latest information on the ever increasing methods of electronic communication with Companies House together with articles on recent company law cases.

http://www.lawcom.gov.uk The Law Commission does not undertake government-inspired reviews for change. This is for the BIS (see above). However, the Law Commission's website does contain proposals for law reform and is ideal for those requiring papers and documents critical of existing law.

http://www.opsi.gov.uk/acts.htm All Public General Acts from 1988 are housed at this website. Some legislation made prior to 1988 is made available as PDF files. There are also explanatory notes for many of the Acts.

http://www.publications.parliament.uk/pa/ld/ldjudgmt.htm
Decisions before 31 July 2009 by House of Lords, now
the Supreme Court, can be accessed at this website.
After 31 July 2009, the judgments can be accessed at:
http://www.supremecourt.gov.uk/decided-cases/
index.html.

http://www.hmcourts-service.gov.uk/cms/judgments.htm
A library of full reports from selected High Court cases and
many reports of the Court of Appeal can be accessed at
this website. Company cases are normally first heard in
the Chancery Division of the High Court.

Visit **www.mylawchamber.co.uk/richesallen** to
access study support resources including answers to
questions in this chapter and legal updates, all linked
to the **Pearson eText** version of **Keenan and Riches'
Business Law** which you can **search**, **highlight** and
personalise with your **own notes** and **bookmarks**.

Use **Case Navigator** to read in full some of the key cases
referenced in this chapter with commentary and questions:

O'Neill v *Phillips* (1999)
Ebrahimi v *Westbourne Galleries* [1972]

Part 3 BUSINESS TRANSACTIONS

Chapter 7   Forming business contracts

Learning objectives

After studying this chapter you should understand the following main points:

- the distinction between a contract and other types of non-binding agreement;
- the essential elements of a binding contract;
- the factors which may affect the validity of a contract.

Business contracting – generally

Once the businessperson has decided on the particular form of business organisation that suits his needs, he can concentrate on his main purpose: establishing and building up the business. This will involve acquiring premises and equipment, taking on employees, buying raw materials and stock, marketing the product or service and meeting orders. Underpinning all these business transactions is the presence of a contract.

Most people think that a contract is a formal written document which has been signed by the parties in the presence of independent witnesses. If all contracts took this form, there would be little room for argument about whether the parties had entered into a legally binding agreement, the obligations they had undertaken or the consequences of failing to carry out the terms of the agreement. In practice, however, few contracts are like this. The vast majority of contracts are entered into without formalities. The parties may even be unaware of the legal significance of their actions. Think about the agreements you have made over the past week:

- buying a newspaper;
- taking the bus or train into work or college;
- agreeing to complete an assignment by a particular date;
- getting a cup of coffee at breaktime;
- arranging to meet a friend for lunch.

Can all these transactions be classed as contracts? You probably feel that some of them were never intended to have legal consequences. So, what then is a contract? When is a contract formed? What are the obligations of the parties to a contract? What happens if either party breaks the agreement? The answers to these questions are provided by the law of contract.

The foundations of the present-day law of contract were laid in the 19th century. This period in our history saw the rapid expansion of trade and industry, and, inevitably, an increase in the volume of commercial disputes. Businessmen turned to the courts for a solution. Gradually, the judges developed a body of settled rules which reflected both the commercial background of the disputes from which they arose and the prevailing beliefs of the time. The dominant economic philosophy of the 19th century was *laissez-faire* individualism – the view that the state should not meddle in the affairs of business and that individuals should be free to determine their own destinies. This philosophy was mirrored in the law of contract by two assumptions: freedom of contract and equality of bargaining power. The judges assumed that everyone was free to choose which contracts they entered into and the terms on which they did so. If negotiations could not produce an acceptable basis for agreement, the parties were, in theory, free to take their business elsewhere. The parties were deemed to be of equal bargaining strength. The judges' assumptions produced an acceptable legal framework for the regulation of business transactions. Parliament, too, played its part by codifying parts of the common law of particular relevance to the businessman; for example, the law relating to contracts for the sale of goods became the Sale of Goods Act 1893 (now the Sale of Goods Act 1979). However, the same basic rules were applied in situations where one of the parties was in a weak bargaining position. Employees, consumers and borrowers, for example, found themselves without adequate protection from the law. It has been necessary for Parliament to intervene to redress the balance between employers and employees, businessmen and consumers, lenders and borrowers. In these areas, the concept of freedom of contract has been modified.

This section is concerned with the legal framework governing the supply of goods and services. It explores the nature and extent of any liability which may be incurred as a consequence of a business transaction, whether between one businessperson and another, or between a business person and a consumer. In order to understand these specific areas of business law, it is necessary first to look at the basic ground rules of the law of contract.

Nature of a contract

A contract has been defined as a legally binding agreement or, in the words of Sir Frederick Pollock: 'A promise or set of promises which the law will enforce.' However, not all promises or agreements give rise to contracts. If you agreed to keep the house tidy while your parents were away on holiday, you would not expect to find yourself in the county court being sued for breach of contract if you failed to do so. So what kinds of agreements does the law recognise as creating enforceable rights and duties?

Types of contract

Contracts may be divided into two broad classes: speciality contracts and simple contracts.

1 Speciality contracts. These formal contracts are also known as deeds. Formerly, these contracts had to be in writing and 'signed, sealed and delivered'. However, the Law of Property (Miscellaneous Provisions) Act 1989 abolished the requirement for a seal on a deed executed

by an individual. Under the 1989 Act it must be clear on the face of the document that it is intended to be a deed. The formalities are that the signature of the person making the deed must be witnessed and attested. 'Attestation' involves making a statement to the effect that the deed has been signed in the presence of a witness. The Court of Appeal has held that the failure to sign in the presence of a witness will not necessarily invalidate a deed.

Shah v Shah (2001)

In 1998 the claimant was induced by the defendants to invest £1.5 million in a Kenyan bank in which the defendants were senior officers. Later the same year the bank was placed under statutory management by the Kenyan authorities and it was unable to repay any of the claimant's investment. In 1999 the defendants signed a document described as a deed, in which they agreed to accept personal liability for repaying the claimant's money. Although the document stated that it was executed as a 'deed . . . in the presence of' an attesting witness, it was in fact taken away by the defendants, signed by them and then passed on to an attesting witness, who did not see them sign the document. The defendants argued that they were not bound by the document because it did not comply with the formalities for a deed set out in s 1 of the Law of Property (Miscellaneous Provisions) Act 1989. The Court of Appeal held that the document was a valid deed and the defendants were bound by it. The document had been described as a deed, it had been signed and attested by a witness albeit shortly after the defendants signed. The Court of Appeal applied the doctrine of estoppel to prevent the defendants from denying the validity of the deed. (Estoppel is a rule of evidence which prevents a person from stating what is in fact true because he has in the past led others to believe the contrary.) Pill LJ stated that: 'there are policy reasons for not permitting a party to escape his obligations under the deed by reasons of a defect, however minor, in the way his signature was attested.'

The previous rule that a deed must be written on paper or parchment has been abolished by the 1989 Act. The use of seals by corporate bodies is unaffected. Certain contracts, such as conveyances of land, must be made in the form of a deed, but these are relatively few in number.

2 Simple contracts. Contracts which are not deeds are known as simple contracts. They are informal contracts and may be made in any way – orally, in writing, or they may be implied from conduct.

Essentials of a valid contract

The essential ingredients of a contract are:

1 Agreement. An agreement is formed when one party accepts the offer of another.

2 Consideration. The parties must show that their agreement is part of a bargain; each side must promise to give or do something for the other.

3 Intention. The law will not concern itself with purely domestic or social arrangements. The parties must have intended their agreement to have legal consequences.

4 Form. In some cases, certain formalities must be observed.

5 Capacity. The parties must be legally capable of entering into a contract.

6 Genuineness of consent. The agreement must have been entered into freely and involve a 'meeting of minds'.

7 Legality. The purpose of the agreement must not be illegal or contrary to public policy.

A contract which possesses all these requirements is said to be valid. If one of the parties fails to live up to his or her promises, that party may be sued for a breach of contract. The absence of an essential element will render the contract either void, voidable or unenforceable.

1 Void contracts. The term 'void contract' is a contradiction in terms since the whole transaction is regarded as a nullity. It means that at no time has there been a contract between the parties. Any goods or money obtained under the agreement must be returned. Where items have been resold to a third party, they may be recovered by the original owner. A contract may be rendered void, for example, by some forms of mistake.

2 Voidable contracts. Contracts founded on a misrepresentation and some agreements made by minors fall into this category. The contract may operate in every respect as a valid contract unless and until one of the parties takes steps to avoid it. Anything obtained under the contract must be returned, insofar as this is possible. If goods have been resold before the contract was avoided, the original owner will not be able to reclaim them.

3 Unenforceable contracts. An unenforceable contract is a valid contract but it cannot be enforced in the courts if one of the parties refuses to carry out its terms. Items received under the contract cannot be reclaimed. Contracts of guarantee are unenforceable unless evidenced in writing.

The essential elements of a valid contract will now be considered in more detail. Remember – just as a house must have sound foundations, walls and a roof, so must a contract have all its essentials to be valid.

Agreement

The first requisite of any contract is an agreement. At least two parties are required; one of them, the offeror, makes an offer which the other, the offeree, accepts.

Offer

An offer is a proposal made on certain terms by the offeror together with a promise to be bound by that proposal if the offeree accepts the stated terms. An offer may be made expressly – for example, when an employer writes to a prospective employee to offer that person a job – or impliedly, by conduct – for example, bidding at an auction.

The offer may be made to a specific person, in which case it can only be accepted by that person. If an offer is made to a group of people, it may be accepted by any member of the group. An offer can even be made to the whole world, such as where someone offers a reward for the return of a lost dog. The offer can be accepted by anyone who knows about the reward, and finds the dog.

Carlill v Carbolic Smoke Ball Co (1893)

The company inserted advertisements in a number of newspapers stating that it would pay £100 to anyone who caught 'flu after using its smoke balls as directed for 14 days. The company further stated that to show its sincerity in the matter it had deposited £1,000 at the Alliance Bank to meet possible claims. Mrs Carlill bought one of the smoke balls, used it as directed but still caught 'flu. She claimed the £100 reward but was refused, so she sued the company in contract. The company put forward a number of arguments in its defence: (a) It claimed that it had attempted to contract with the whole world, which was clearly impossible. The Court of Appeal held that the company had made an offer to the whole world and it would be liable to anyone who came forward and performed the required conditions. (b) The company further submitted that the advertisement was in the nature of a trade 'puff' and too vague to be a contract. The court dealt with this argument by asking what ordinary members of the public would understand by the advertisement. The court took the view that the details of use were sufficiently definite to constitute the terms of a contract and that the reference to the £1,000 deposited at a bank was evidence of an intention to be bound. (c) The company also argued that the claimant had not provided any consideration in return for its promise. The court held that the inconvenience of using the smoke ball as directed was sufficient consideration. (d) Finally, the company submitted that there was no notification of acceptance in accordance with the general rule. The court held that in this kind of contract, which is known as a unilateral contract, acceptance consists of performing the requested act and notification of acceptance is not necessary.

The court concluded that Mrs Carlill was entitled to recover the £100 reward.

It is important to identify when a true offer has been made because once it is accepted the parties are bound. If the words and actions of one party do not amount to an offer, however, the other person cannot, by saying 'I accept', create a contract. A genuine offer must, therefore, be distinguished from what is known as an 'invitation to treat'.

An invitation to treat

This is where a person holds himself out as ready to receive offers, which he may then either accept or reject. The following are examples of invitations to treat.

1 **The display of goods with a price ticket attached in a shop window or on a supermarket shelf.** This is not an offer to sell but an invitation for customers to make an offer to buy.

Fisher v Bell (1960)

A shopkeeper had a flick-knife on display in his shop window. He was charged with offering for sale an offensive weapon contrary to the provisions of the Restriction of Offensive Weapons Act 1959. His conviction was quashed on appeal. The Divisional Court of the Queen's Bench Division held that the display of goods with a price ticket attached in a shop window is an invitation to treat and not an offer to sell. (The Restriction of Offensive Weapons Act 1961 was passed soon after this case to close the loophole in the law.)

Pharmaceutical Society of Great Britain v Boots Cash Chemists (Southern) Ltd (1953)

Boots operated a self-service 'supermarket' system at its Edgware branch in which the merchandise, including drugs on the Poisons List, was laid out on open shelves around the shop. Customers selected their purchases from the shelves, placed them in a wire basket and paid for them at a cash desk which was supervised by a registered pharmacist. The Pharmaceutical Society claimed that by operating this system Boots had committed an offence contrary to s 18 of the Pharmacy and Poisons Act 1933, which states that the sale of drugs included on the Poisons List must take place in the presence of a qualified pharmacist. The Pharmaceutical Society argued that the sale took place when a customer placed his purchase in the basket, which was not supervised by a pharmacist. The Court of Appeal held that the display of drugs on the open shelf constituted an invitation to treat. The customer made the offer to buy at the cash desk and the sale was completed when the cashier accepted the offer. Since the cash desks were supervised by a registered pharmacist, the requirements of the Act had been fulfilled and, therefore, Boots had not committed an offence.

Thus, it is a clearly established principle of civil law that if goods are displayed for sale with an incorrect price ticket attached to them, the retailer is not obliged to sell at that price. Under the criminal law, however, the retailer may find himself facing a prosecution for an unfair commercial practice.

2 Advertisements, catalogues and brochures. Many businesses make use of the press, TV, commercial radio and, in more recent times, the Internet, to sell their products direct to the public. Even if the word 'offer' is used, the advertisement is still an invitation to treat.

Partridge v *Crittenden* (1968)

Partridge placed an advertisement in the *Cage and Aviary Birds* magazine, which read 'Bramblefinch cocks, bramblefinch hens, 25s each'. A Mr Thompson replied to the advertisement and was sent a bramblefinch hen. Partridge was charged with 'offering for sale' a wild bird contrary to the provisions of the Protection of Birds Act 1954 and was convicted at the magistrates' court. His conviction was quashed on appeal to the Divisional Court of the Queen's Bench Division. The court held that since the advertisement constituted an invitation to treat and not an offer to sell, Partridge was not guilty of the offence with which he had been charged.

Comment. It should be noted that the word 'offer' did not appear in the advertisement in this case. However, in *Spencer* v *Harding* (1870) a circular containing the word 'offer' was held to be an invitation to treat.

An advertisement placed in a newspaper or magazine by a mail order firm constitutes an invitation to treat: the customer makes the offer, which may be accepted or rejected by the mail order firm.

Similar principles apply to electronic trading via the Internet, otherwise known as e-commerce. Posting advertisements on a website amounts to an invitation to treat; by selecting the products and services required, the customer is making an offer to buy, which may be accepted or rejected by the seller. So if a company by mistake advertises on its website £200 video recorders for sale at £2, it could refuse to sell the goods at the advertised price.

Although most advertisements will be treated as invitations to treat, there are some situations where an advertisement may be regarded as a definite offer, e.g. as in *Carlill* v *Carbolic Smoke Ball Co* (1893).

3 Company prospectuses. When a company wishes to raise capital by selling shares to the public, it must issue a prospectus (an invitation to treat). Potential investors apply for shares (the offer) and the directors then decide to whom to allot shares (the acceptance).

4 Auctions. At an auction sale the call for bids by an auctioneer is an invitation to treat. The bids are offers. The auctioneer selects the highest bid and acceptance is completed by the fall of the hammer.

Payne v *Cave* (1789)

The defendant made the highest bid for the claimant's goods at an auction sale, but he withdrew his bid before the fall of the auctioneer's hammer. It was held that the defendant was not bound to purchase the goods. His bid amounted to an offer which he was entitled to withdraw at any time before the auctioneer signified acceptance by knocking down the hammer. The common law rule laid down in this case has now been codified in s 57(2) of the Sale of Goods Act 1979.

Advertising a forthcoming auction sale does not amount to an offer to hold it.

Harris v *Nickerson* (1873)

The defendant, an auctioneer, advertised in the London papers that a sale of various goods including office furniture would take place in Bury St Edmunds. The claimant travelled from London to attend the sale, but the items of furniture he had been commissioned to buy were withdrawn from the sale. It was held that the defendant auctioneer was not obliged to compensate the claimant for a wasted journey. Advertising that a sale of certain items will take place is a mere declaration of intention. It does not create a binding contract with anyone who acts on the advertisement by attending the sale.

However, advertising that an auction will be 'without reserve' amounts to an offer by the auctioneer that once the auction has commenced the lot will be sold to the highest bidder however low the bids might be (*Warlow* v *Harrison* (1859) and more recently *Barry* v *Heathcote Ball & Co (Commercial Auctions) Ltd* (2000)).

5 Tenders. Large undertakings, such as public authorities, often place contracts by inviting interested firms to tender (offer) for the business. An invitation to tender can give rise to a binding obligation on the part of the inviter to consider tenders submitted in accordance with the conditions of the tender.

Blackpool and Fylde Aero Club Ltd v Blackpool Borough Council (1990)

The defendant council invited the claimant club, together with six other parties, to tender for the concession to offer pleasure flights from the council-owned airport. The invitation to tender required tenders to be submitted in accordance with an elaborate procedure and stated that tenders received after 12 noon on 17 March 1983 would not be considered. The club's tender was delivered by hand and placed in the letterbox in the Town Hall at 11 am on 17 March. Unfortunately, the letterbox was not cleared until the next day. The club's tender was marked late and was not considered by the council. The concession was awarded to another tenderer. The club sued for breach of a contract to consider tenders which conformed with the requirements specified by the council. The Court of Appeal held that by adopting a formal tendering procedure the council impliedly undertook to consider all conforming tenders. The council's invitation to tender was an offer to consider all qualifying tenders and the submission by the club of a tender within the time limit was an acceptance. The club was entitled to damages for breach of contract.

The acceptance of a tender has different legal consequences, depending on the wording of the original invitation to tender. There are two possibilities, as follows.

Example 1

The Metropolitan Borough of Newtown invites tenders for the supply of 100 tons of potatoes for the use of the School Meals Service in the Borough from 1 January to 31 December. The acceptance of a tender creates a legally binding contract. The successful supplier must deliver 100 tons of potatoes which the Borough must pay for.

Example 2

The Metropolitan Borough of Newtown invites tenders for the supply of potatoes, not exceeding 100 tons, for the period 1 January to 31 December as and when required by the School Meals Service. The acceptance

of a tender in this situation has the effect of creating a standing offer on the part of the supplier to deliver potatoes if and when orders are placed by the School Meals Service. Each time an order is placed by the School Meals Service it constitutes an acceptance which creates an individual contract. If the supplier refuses to fulfil the order, he will be in breach of contract (**Great Northern Rly Co v Witham** (1873)). This form of tender does not prevent the supplier giving notice that he will not supply potatoes in the future or the School Meals Service from not placing orders, if they decide to cut potatoes from the school dinner menu.

The process of competitive tendering came under scrutiny in the following case.

Harvela Investments Ltd v Royal Trust Co of Canada Ltd (1985)

The first defendants decided to dispose of shares in a company by sealed competitive tender. They sent identical telexes to two prospective purchasers, the claimants and the second defendants, inviting tenders and promising to accept the highest offer. The claimants bid $2,175,000, while the second defendants bid '$2,100,000 or $101,000 in excess of any other offer'. The first defendants accepted the second defendants' offer. The House of Lords held that the second defendants' 'referential bid' was invalid. The decision was a practical one. The purpose of competitive tendering is to secure a sale at the best possible price. If both parties had submitted a referential bid, it would have been impossible to ascertain an offer and no sale would have resulted from the process.

6 Statements of price in negotiations for the sale of land. Where the subject matter of a proposed sale is land, the courts are reluctant to find a definite offer to sell unless very clearly stated.

Harvey v Facey (1893)

Harvey sent a telegram to Facey. 'Will you sell us Bumper Hall Pen? Telegraph lowest cash price . . .' Facey replied by telegram: 'Lowest cash price for Bumper Hall Pen, £900'. Harvey telegraphed his response: 'We agree to buy Bumper Hall Pen for £900 asked by you. Please send us your title deeds.' The Judicial Committee of the Privy

Council held that there was no contract. Facey's reply to Harvey's initial enquiry was not an offer to sell but merely a statement of the price he might be prepared to sell at if he wished to sell. As Facey had not made an offer, Harvey's second telegram could not amount to an acceptance.

Clifton v Palumbo (1944)

In the course of negotiations for the sale of a large estate, the claimant wrote to the defendant: 'I am prepared to offer my Lytham estate for £600,000. I also agree that sufficient time shall be given to you to complete a schedule of completion.' The Court of Appeal held that these words did not amount to a firm offer to sell, but rather a preliminary statement as to price.

Gibson v Manchester City Council (1979)

In 1970 the Council adopted a policy of selling its council houses to tenants. The City Treasurer wrote to Mr Gibson in February 1971 stating that the council 'may be prepared to sell' the freehold of his house to him at a discount price. The letter invited Mr Gibson to make a formal application which he duly did. In May 1971 control of the council passed from the Conservatives to Labour and the policy of selling council houses was reversed. Only legally binding transactions were allowed to proceed. The council did not proceed with Mr Gibson's application. The House of Lords held that the City Treasurer's letter was an invitation to treat and not an offer to sell. Mr Gibson's application was the offer and, as this had not been accepted by the council, a binding contract had not been formed.

Termination of the offer

An offer can end in a number of ways:

1 By acceptance. An offer which has been accepted constitutes a contract. That offer is no longer available for acceptance.

2 By rejection. An offer is rejected if:

- the offeree notifies the offeror that he does not wish to accept the offer;
- the offeree attempts to accept subject to certain conditions;
- the offeree makes a counter-offer.

Hyde v Wrench (1840)

Wrench offered to sell his farm to Hyde for £1,000. Hyde replied with a 'counter-offer' of £950, which was refused. Hyde then said that he was prepared to meet the original offer of £1,000. It was held that no contract had been formed. The 'counter-offer' of £950 had the effect of rejecting Wrench's original offer.

Sometimes it is difficult to decide whether the offeree is making a counter-offer or simply asking for more information about the offer. A request for more information will not reject the offer.

Stevenson v McLean (1880)

The defendant offered to sell a quantity of iron to the claimants for cash. The claimants asked whether they could have credit terms. When no reply to their enquiry was forthcoming, the claimants accepted the terms of the original offer. Meanwhile, the defendant had sold the iron elsewhere. It was held that the enquiry was a request for more information, not a rejection of the offer. The defendant was liable for breach of contract.

3 By revocation before acceptance. An offer may be revoked (withdrawn) at any time before acceptance but it will only be effective when the offeree learns about it.

Byrne v Van Tienhoven (1880)

The defendants posted a letter in Cardiff on 1 October to the claimants in New York, offering to sell them 1,000 boxes of tinplates. On 8 October the defendants posted a letter withdrawing the offer, which was received by the claimants on 20 October. However, on 11 October the claimants telegraphed their acceptance which they confirmed by letter posted on 15 October. It was held that a revocation takes effect only when communicated to the offeree. The contract in this case came into existence when the defendants' offer was accepted by the claimants on 11 October. The letter of revocation was ineffective as it was received after the acceptance was complete.

It is not necessary that the offeror himself should tell the offeree that the offer has been revoked; the information may be conveyed by a reliable third party.

Dickinson v Dodds (1876)

The defendant, on Wednesday, offered to sell some property to the claimant, the offer to be left open until 9 am, Friday. On Thursday, the claimant heard from a Mr Berry that the defendant had sold the property to someone else. Nevertheless, the claimant wrote a letter of acceptance which was handed to the defendant at 7 am on the Friday morning. The Court of Appeal held that as the claimant had heard about the revocation from Berry, who was a reliable source, the offer was no longer available for acceptance. No contract had been formed.

In *Dickinson v Dodds* the offer was expressed to be open until Friday at 9 am. Such an offer may be revoked before the end of the time limit, unless it has already been accepted.

Routledge v Grant (1828)

The defendant offered to buy the claimant's house, giving the claimant six weeks to consider the proposal. It was held that the defendant could withdraw the offer at any time before acceptance, even though the deadline had not yet expired. The claimant's attempt to accept the offer after it had been withdrawn was ineffective.

An offer may be revoked by a second, subsequent offer. However, the second offer must be sufficiently at odds with the first offer so that both cannot be accepted.

Pickfords Ltd v Celestica Ltd (2003)

As Dyson LJ stated in the opening remarks of his judgment in the Court of Appeal: 'it is as if the facts of this case have been devised for an examination question on the law of contract for first year law students.'

The claimant P, a removal company, had been approached by the defendant C, an IT company, concerning a proposed move of workshop and office equipment from Stoke-on-Trent to Telford. On 13 September 2001, P sent a fax to C, offering to carry out the work at a rate of £890 per load (excluding VAT) plus extras for

insurance etc. P calculated that it would take 96 loads to complete the move, giving rise to an estimated budget figure of £100,000. During the next fortnight P carried out a more detailed survey of the proposed move and on 27 September sent a further more detailed document to C in which it was stated that P would carry out the work for a fixed price quotation of £98,760. A copy of P's standard terms and conditions were enclosed. On 15 October 2001, C sent a fax to P headed 'Confirmation' which stated that an order had been raised to cover the quotation and that the cost was not to exceed £100,000. P carried out the work and claimed the fixed sum of £98,760. C paid only £33,000.

The Court of Appeal applied the following analysis to the sequence of events.

1 13 September fax from P to C was an offer to carry out the work for a fixed price per vehicle load (the first offer).
2 27 September proposal from P to C was an offer to carry out the work for a fixed overall price of £98,760 (the second offer). The court took the view that this second offer superseded the first offer and had the effect of revoking the first offer. Its reasons for reaching this conclusion were that the basis for calculating the price was quite different in the two offers; the second offer contained more detail than the first offer and included P's standard terms and conditions.
3 C's fax of 15 October purported to be an acceptance of the first offer. However, as this offer had been revoked, it could not be accepted. C's fax was a counter-offer, which P accepted by carrying out the removal. Even if the first offer had not been revoked C's fax would have been a counter-offer as it included a new term limiting the overall cost to £100,000.

A promise to keep an offer open will be binding if it can be enforced as a separate contract. A legally binding option will be created if the offeree provides some consideration in return for the offeror's promise to keep the offer open.

Mountford v Scott (1975)

The purchaser of a house paid the seller £1 for an option to buy, exercisable within six months. The Court of Appeal held that the seller could not withdraw the offer before the option expired.

The Law Revision Committee recommended in 1937 that a promise to keep an offer open for a definite period of time or until the happening of a specific event should be binding even if there is no consideration for the promise. In 1975 the Law Commission made a similar recommendation but limited to promises made 'in the course of a business'.

The effect of revocation in the case of a potentially 'unilateral' contract, such as in *Carlill*'s case, is not straightforward. Where the offer has been made to the whole world, as, for example, where a reward has been offered in a newspaper for the return of a lost dog, a revocation will probably be effective as against any-one who has yet to start looking for the dog, provided it is given the same publicity as the original offer of the reward. However, if someone has started to per-form the act requested in the offer, the offer cannot be revoked.

> 'Once the promisee acts on the promise by inhaling the smoke ball, by starting the walk to York or (as here) by not suing for the maintenance to which she was entitled, the promisor cannot revoke or withdraw his offer. But there is no obligation on the promisee to continue to inhale, to walk the whole way to York or to refrain from suing. It is just that if she inhales no more, gives up the walk to York or does sue for her maintenance, she is not entitled to claim the promised sum'.

4 If the offer lapses. The offeror may stipulate that the offer is only open for a limited period of time. Once the time limit has passed, any acceptance will be invalid. Even if no time limit is mentioned, the offer will not remain open indefinitely. It must be accepted within a reasonable time.

Errington v Errington (1952)

A father bought a house for his son and daughter-in-law to live in. The father paid a deposit of one-third of the purchase price and borrowed the balance from a build-ing society. He told his son and daughter-in-law that if they paid the mortgage he would convey the house to them when all the instalments had been paid. The Court of Appeal held that the father's offer could not be revoked provided the son and daughter-in-law con-tinued to make the mortgage payments.

Ramsgate Victoria Hotel Co v Montefiore (1866)

The defendant offered to buy shares in the claimant's company in June. The shares were eventually allotted in November. The defendant refused to take them up. The Court of Exchequer held that the defendant's offer to take the shares had lapsed through an unreasonable delay in acceptance.

What is a reasonable time will vary with the type of contract.

5 Death. If the offeror dies after having made an offer and the offeree is notified of the death, any acceptance will be invalid. However, where the offeree accepts in ignorance of what has happened, the fate of the offer seems to depend on the nature of the contract. An offer which involves the personal service of the offeror clearly cannot be enforced, but other offers may survive, be accepted and carried out by the deceased's personal representatives. If the offeree dies, there can be no acceptance. The offer was made to that person and no one else can accept.

6 Failure of a condition attached to the offer. An offer may be made subject to conditions. Such a condition may be stated expressly by the offeror or implied by the courts from the circumstances. If the condition is not satisfied, the offer is not capable of being accepted.

Soulsbury v Soulsbury (2007)

In this case the Court of Appeal had to consider whether an agreement between a divorced couple whereby the husband agreed to leave his former wife £100,000 in his will rather than paying maintenance of £12,000 a year could be enforced by the courts. The husband made a will in 1991 leaving his former wife £100,000 but shortly before his death in 2002 he married again, which had the effect of revoking the 1991 will. The Court of Appeal held that the agreement was binding on the husband's estate and his former wife was entitled to damages. Longmore LJ described the arrangement as a classic unilateral contract of the *Carlill* v *Carbolic Smoke Ball* or the 'walk to York' kind:

Financings Ltd v Stimson (1962)

The defendant saw a car at the premises of a dealer on 16 March. He wished to obtain the car on hire-purchase. He signed a form provided by the claimant finance company which stated that the agreement would be binding only when signed by the finance company. The defendant took possession of the car and paid the first instalment on 18 March. However, being dissatisfied with the car, he returned it to the dealer two days later. On the night of 24–25 March the car was stolen from the dealer's premises, but was recovered badly damaged. On 25 March the finance company signed the hire-purchase agreement, unaware of what had happened. The defendant refused to pay the instalments and was sued for breach of the hire-purchase agreement. The Court of Appeal held that the hire-purchase agreement was not binding because the defendant's offer to obtain the car on hire-purchase was subject to an implied condition that the car would remain in substantially the same state until acceptance. Since the implied condition had not been fulfilled at the time the finance company purported to accept, no contract had come into existence.

Acceptance

Once the presence of a valid offer has been established, the next stage in the formation of an agreement is to find an acceptance of that offer. The acceptance must be made while the offer is still open. It must be absolute and unqualified.

Unconditional acceptance

If the offeree attempts to vary the terms offered, this will be treated as a counter-offer. As we have already seen in *Hyde* v *Wrench*, this has the effect of rejecting the original offer. A similar problem exists in 'battle of forms' cases. A typical 'battle of forms' case is where a purchaser makes an offer to buy on his own pre-printed standard form containing his terms of business and the seller 'accepts' on his own standard form which contains conflicting terms. Delivery is then made, but a dispute subsequently arises. The question is whose terms should apply? A formal analysis of the transaction in offer and acceptance terms would suggest that the purchaser's offer to buy has been rejected by a counter-offer from the seller, and if the counter-offer is 'accepted' by the

purchaser, e.g. by an acknowledgement of the purchase, then the result is a contract on the seller's terms. This was the outcome in the *Butler Machine Tool* case.

Butler Machine Tool Co v Ex-Cell-O Corp (England) (1979)

The claimants offered to supply a machine tool to the defendants for £75,535. However, the quotation included a term which would entitle the sellers to increase this price (price-variation clause). The defendants accepted the offer on their own standard terms which did not provide for any variation of their quoted price. The claimants acknowledged the order. When the machine was delivered, the claimants claimed an extra £2,892 which the defendants refused to pay. The Court of Appeal held that the defendants had not unconditionally accepted the original offer. They had made a counter-offer which had been accepted by the claimants. The defendants' terms governed the contract. The claimants' action to recover the increase in price, therefore, failed.

The position is less clear where the seller's counter-offer is never formally accepted by the purchaser, but delivery nevertheless takes place. Assuming that there is a contract between the parties (the acceptance consisting of the conduct of the parties), whose terms prevail? It has been suggested that the terms of the party who fires the 'last shot' in the battle of forms should govern the contract, i.e. the contract will be based on the final document in the exchange of forms. The question facing the Court of Appeal in *Tekdata Interconnections Ltd* v *Amphenol Ltd* (2009) was whether the conduct of the parties in the course of a long relationship could displace the traditional analysis. The Court held that although this was a possibility, the circumstances in the *Tekdata* case were not sufficiently strong to displace the traditional offer and acceptance analysis. In another recent case, *GHSP Incorporated* v *AB Electronic Ltd* (2010) the High Court concluded that there might be some situations where neither set of standard terms had been accepted by the other party. Where this was the case terms implied by the Sale of Goods Act 1979 could be incorporated into the contract. The incorporation of statutory implied term will considered in Chapter 8 ⊙.

One form of conditional acceptance is the use of the phrase 'subject to contract' in negotiations involving the sale of land. These words usually mean that the parties do not intend to be bound at that stage. However, if there is clear evidence of a contrary intention, a court may be prepared to find that a contract has been concluded despite the use of the customary words 'subject to contract' (*Alpenstow Ltd* v *Regalian Properties plc* (1985)). The advantage of 'subject to contract' agreements is that they allow either party to withdraw from the agreement at any time and for any reason without facing an action for breach of contract. The problem is that the parties may incur considerable expense on negotiations which do not ultimately result in a contract being formed. Some legal systems overcome this problem by imposing a duty to negotiate in good faith. English law, however, does not recognise such a duty and an agreement to negotiate will not be binding.

Walford v *Miles* (1992)

The defendants owned a photographic processing business, which they wished to sell. In 1985 there were unsuccessful negotiations with a company. In 1986, the claimants heard that the business was for sale for about £2 million. The claimants were keen to buy at this price because they thought that the business had been considerably undervalued. In March 1987, the claimants and defendants reached a 'subject to contract' agreement for the sale of the business. The defendants asked for a letter, known as a 'comfort letter', from the claimants' bankers confirming that they would provide the finance for the deal and in return the defendants promised to terminate negotiations with any third parties. The comfort letter was provided as agreed but the defendants sold the business to the company which had made the unsuccessful offer in 1985. The claimants sued for breach of an implied term to negotiate in good faith. The House of Lords held that an agreement to negotiate is unenforceable because it lacks the requirement of certainty. In this case no time limit was given for exclusive negotiations. Their Lordships indicated, however, that it would be possible to enter into a binding 'lock-out' agreement, i.e. an agreement to deal exclusively with one party and not to consider other offers for a limited period. The Court of Appeal upheld such an agreement in *Pitt* v *PHH Asset Management Ltd* (1993) (discussed later in this chapter).

Method of acceptance

An acceptance may take any form. It can be given orally or in writing but silence cannot normally amount to an acceptance.

Felthouse v *Bindley* (1862)

The claimant had been negotiating to buy his nephew's horse. He eventually wrote to his nephew: 'If I hear no more about him, I shall consider the horse is mine at £30 15s.' The nephew did not reply to this letter but he did ask the auctioneer, who had been engaged to sell all his farming stock, to keep the horse out of the sale, as he had sold it to his uncle. The auctioneer by mistake included the horse in the sale and was sued by the uncle in the tort of conversion. The basis of the uncle's claim was that the auctioneer had sold his property. The court held that the uncle had no claim. Although the nephew had mentally accepted the offer, some form of positive action was required for a valid acceptance. Since there was no contract between the uncle and nephew, ownership of the horse had not passed to the uncle.

Comment. This case established the principle that the offeree's silence or failure to act cannot constitute a valid acceptance. The rule has a particularly useful application to the problem of 'inertia selling'. This is where a trader sends unsolicited goods to a person's home, stipulating that if he does not receive a reply within a specified time, he will assume that his offer to sell the goods has been accepted and the indicated price is payable. The *Felthouse* rule makes it clear that a recipient of goods in these circumstances is not obliged to pay, because his silence or inaction cannot amount to an acceptance. Many people, however, have paid up in ignorance of the law.

More effective control of 'inertia selling' was introduced in the form of the Unsolicited Goods and Services Act 1971, which has now been updated and extended by the Consumer Protection (Distance Selling) Regulations 2000 (SI 2000/2334). The regulations outlaw the supply of unsolicited goods and services to consumers. The recipient of unsolicited goods may treat them as an unconditional gift. It is also an offence to make a demand for payment from a consumer for unsolicited goods or services.

Felthouse v *Bindley* would seem to suggest that only an oral or written acceptance will be valid. However, acceptance may be implied from a person's conduct.

Brogden v Metropolitan Railway Co (1877)

Brogden had supplied the railway company with coal for many years without the benefit of a formal agreement. Eventually the parties decided to put their relationship on a firmer footing. A draft agreement was drawn up by the company's agent and sent to Brogden. Brogden filled in some blanks, including the name of an arbitrator, marked it as 'approved' and returned it to the company's agent who put it in his drawer. Coal was ordered and supplied in accordance with the terms of the 'agreement'. However, a dispute arose between the parties and Brogden refused to supply coal to the company, denying the existence of a binding contract between them. The House of Lords held that a contract had been concluded. Brogden's amendments to the draft agreement amounted to an offer which was accepted by the company either when the first order was placed under the terms of the agreement or at the latest when the coal was supplied. By their conduct the parties had indicated their approval of the agreement.

Examples of acceptance by conduct include returning a lost dog in a reward case, or using a smoke ball in the prescribed manner in *Carlill* v *Carbolic Smoke Ball Co.* Examples of more recent cases involving an offer being accepted by conduct include *Day Morris Associates* v *Voyce* (2003) in which the Court of Appeal held that the claimant estate agent's offer to market the defendant's house was accepted by the conduct of the defendant, which consisted of her acquiescence in the process of marketing the property. The defendant was liable to pay commission in relation to the subsequent sale. In *Confetti Records* v *Warner Music UK Ltd (t/a East West Records)* (2003), Confetti Records sent to Warner Music a copy of a track called 'Burnin' and an invoice for an advance payment (the offer) which Warner accepted by their conduct of including the track on a compilation album. Confetti's attempt to revoke the offer came too late as Warner's had already incurred the expense of producing the album.

An offeror may state that the acceptance must be in a particular form. It follows that the offeror's wishes should be respected. So if he asks for an acceptance in writing, a verbal acceptance by telephone will not be valid. Sometimes the offeror may say 'reply by return post', when he really means 'reply quickly' and a telephone call or email would be acceptable. Provided that the chosen method of acceptance fulfils the intentions of the offeror, it will be binding.

Yates Building Co Ltd v R J Pulleyn & Sons (York) Ltd (1975)

The vendors of a piece of land stated that an option to buy it should be exercised by 'notice in writing . . . to be sent registered or recorded delivery'. The acceptance was sent by ordinary post. The Court of Appeal held that the vendor's intention was to ensure that they received written notification of acceptance. The requirement to use registered or recorded delivery was more in the nature of a helpful suggestion than a condition of acceptance.

Communication of acceptance

The general rule is that an acceptance must be communicated to the offeror, either by the offeree himself or by someone authorised by the offeree. The contract is formed at the time and place the acceptance is received by the offeror. If the post, however, is the anticipated method of communication between the parties, then acceptance is effective immediately the letter of acceptance is posted. Provided the letter is properly stamped, addressed and posted, the contract is formed on posting, even if the letter is delayed or never reaches its destination. This special rule was established in 1818.

Adams v Lindsell (1818)

On 2 September 1817 the defendants who were wool traders based in Huntingdon wrote to the claimants, who were woollen manufacturers in Bromsgrove, offering to sell them some wool and asking for an answer 'in course of post'. This letter was wrongly addressed and as a result it did not reach the claimants until 5 September. The same day the claimants posted a letter of acceptance which reached the defendants on 9 September. The evidence was that if the offer letter had been correctly addressed a reply 'in course of post' could have been expected by 7 September. On 8 September the defendants sold the wool to someone else. It was held that the contract was formed when the claimants posted their letter of acceptance. In reaching this conclusion the court may have been influenced by the fact that it was the defendants' misdirection of the offer letter which led to the delayed acceptance.

Household Fire Insurance Co v Grant (1879)

Grant applied for shares in the claimant company. A letter of allotment was posted but Grant never received it. When the company went into liquidation, Grant was asked, as a shareholder, to contribute the amount still outstanding on the shares he held. The Court of Appeal held that Grant was a shareholder of the company. The contract to buy shares was formed when the letter of allotment (acceptance) was posted.

The 'postal rules' have been applied to acceptances by telegram but not to more instantaneous methods of communication such as telex and telephone.

Entores v Miles Far East Corp (1955)

The claimants, a London company, made an offer to the defendants' agents in Amsterdam by means of a telex message. The Dutch agents accepted the offer by the same method. The claimants later alleged that the defendants had broken their contract and wished to serve a writ (now claim form) on them, which they could do if the contract was made in England. The Court of Appeal held in favour of the claimants. The decision of the court was expressed by Parker LJ in the following terms: 'So far as Telex messages are concerned, though the despatch and receipt of a message is not completely instantaneous, the parties are to all intents and purposes in each other's presence just as if they were in telephonic communication, and I can see no reason for departing from the general rule that there is no binding contract until notice of the acceptance is received by the offeror. That being so, and since the offer . . . was made by the [claimants] in London and notification of the acceptance was received by them in London, the contract resulting therefrom was made in London.' The approach of the Court of Appeal was confirmed by the House of Lords in *Brinkibon v Stahag Stahl* (1982).

Comment. The decisions of the Court of Appeal and House of Lords in *Entores* and *Brinkibon* respectively were considered by Mann J in *Apple Corps Ltd v Apple Computers, Inc* (2004), a case which required the court to decide where a contract had been formed. The contract had been completed during the course of a transatlantic telephone conversation between parties in London and California, but the judge was unable to say precisely which party had made the offer and which accepted. He held that in principle it is possible for a contract to be made in two (or more) places at once.

Acceptances sent by electronic means are likely to be treated in the same way as telephone or telex acceptances; the seller's acceptance will only be effective when received by the customer. The problem of applying this approach to e-commerce is that if a seller is doing business with customers based in different countries, the contract will be formed in the country (and jurisdiction) where the customer is based. E-traders can avoid these difficulties by confirming customers' orders by email and asking the customer to confirm the purchase by clicking on a confirmation button. The effect of these precautions is that the contract will be concluded at the seller's place of business.

Clearly, the 'postal rules' are a potential problem for an offeror: if the letter of acceptance is lost in the post, the offeror may be unaware that a binding contract has been formed. An offeror can protect himself by specifically stating that the acceptance is only complete when received on or before a certain date.

Holwell Securities v Hughes (1974)

Dr Hughes had agreed to grant Holwell Securities Ltd an option to buy his premises. The option, which would constitute the acceptance, was exercisable 'by notice in writing' to the doctor within six months. The company posted a letter of acceptance but it was never delivered. The Court of Appeal held that no contract had been formed. Since Dr Hughes had stipulated actual 'notice' of the acceptance, the postal rules did not apply. The acceptance would only be effective when received by the doctor.

Note that the postal rules only apply to the communication of acceptances: offers and revocations of offers must be communicated to be effective.

The Electronic Commerce (EC Directive) Regulations 2002 (SI 2002/2013) provide a legal framework for the conclusion of contracts by electronic means. The regulations, which came into force in August 2002, apply to online trading and advertising using the Internet, email or mobile phones. This kind of business is referred to as 'information society services'. The regulations protect consumers but may apply to business customers unless they agree otherwise. Regulation 9 provides that where a contract is to be concluded by electronic means (but not by exchange of emails), the service provider must, prior to an order being placed, provide to the recipient (the consumer) the following information in a clear, comprehensible and unambiguous manner:

- the different technical steps to follow to conclude the contract;
- whether the concluded contract will be filed by the service provider and whether it will be accessible;
- the technical means for identifying and correcting input errors before the order is placed;
- the languages offered for conclusion of the contract.

In addition, the service provider must:

- indicate which relevant codes of conduct he subscribes to and how they can be accessed electronically;
- make available any terms and conditions, provided in a way which allows the recipient to store and reproduce them.

If the recipient places an order electronically the service provider must acknowledge receipt of the order without undue delay and by electronic means and make available appropriate, effective and accessible means to allow the recipient to identify and correct input errors before placing the order. Acknowledgement of the order is deemed to be received only when the recipient is able to access it. A consumer will be entitled to rescind a contract where the service provider has not made available the means of identifying and correcting input errors. Other breaches of the regulations may give rise to an action in damages for breach of statutory duty against the service provider.

Consideration

On the previous pages we have seen how an agreement is formed – the requirements of offer and acceptance – but the mere fact of an agreement alone does not make a contract. The law concerns itself with bargains. This means that each side must promise to give or do something for the other, although it does not appear to be a requirement that the parties must be conscious that they are providing a benefit or suffering a detriment (*Pitts* v *Jones* (2007)).

The element of exchange is known as 'consideration' and is an essential element of every valid simple contract. A promise of a gift will not be binding unless made in the form of a deed. Consideration can take two forms: executed or executory. What is the difference between them?

1 Executed consideration is where one party promises to do something in return for the act of another, e.g. reward cases.

Promise	Act
£10 reward offered for the return of 'Lucky' – black and white cat. Ring Mrs Smith (01308 215 8793).	David sees the advert in the local paper. He finds the cat, returns it to Mrs Smith and claims the reward.

'Cash with order' terms are an example of executed consideration.

2 Executory consideration is where the parties exchange promises to perform acts in the future, e.g. 'cash on delivery' terms.

Promise	Act
Jones & Co Ltd promises to pay £950 when a new computer is delivered.	Fastype Ltd promises to deliver the computer within six weeks.

Rules governing consideration

1 Consideration must not be in the past. If one party voluntarily performs an act, and the other party then makes a promise, the consideration for the promise is said to be in the past. Past consideration is regarded as no consideration at all.

Act	Promise
John gives Susan a lift home in his car after work.	On arrival, Susan offers John £1 towards the petrol but, finding that she has not got any change, she says she will give him the money the next day at work.

In this example, John cannot enforce Susan's promise to pay £1 because the consideration for the promise (giving the lift) is in the past. John would have given Susan the lift home without expecting payment and so there was no bargain between the parties.

Re McArdle (1951)

Mr McArdle died leaving a house to his wife for her lifetime and then to his children. While Mrs McArdle was still alive, one of the children and his wife moved into the house. The wife made a number of improvements to the house costing £488. After the work had been completed, all the children signed a document in which they promised to reimburse the wife when their father's estate was finally distributed. The Court of Appeal held that this was a case of past consideration. The promise to pay £488 to the wife was made after the improvements had been completed and was, therefore, not binding.

The rule about past consideration is not strictly followed. If, for example, a person is asked to perform a service, which he duly carries out, and later a promise to pay is made, the promise will be binding.

Re Casey's Patents, Stewart v Casey (1892)

Casey agreed to promote certain patents which had been granted to Stewart and another. (A patent gives the holder exclusive rights to profit from an invention.) Two years later Stewart wrote to Casey promising him a one-third share of the patents 'in consideration' of Casey's efforts. It was held that Stewart's original request raised an implication that Casey's work would be paid for. The later letter merely fixed the amount of the payment.

2 Consideration must move from the promisee. If A (the promisor) makes a promise to B (the promisee), the promise will only be enforceable (unless made in the form of a deed) if B can show that he has provided consideration in return for A's promise.

Tweddle v Atkinson (1861)

John Tweddle and William Guy agreed that they would pay a sum of money to Tweddle's son, William, who had married Guy's daughter. William Guy died without paying his share and William Tweddle sued his late father-in-law's executor (Atkinson). His claim failed because he had not provided any consideration for the promise to pay.

The rule that consideration must move from the promisee is closely related to the doctrine of privity of contract. This doctrine states that a person cannot be bound by or take advantage of a contract to which he was not a party. The doctrine of privity of contract and the exceptions to the rule, including the changes contained in the Contracts (Rights of Third Parties) Act 1999, will be examined in more detail later in this chapter. It should be noted at this point, however, that the 1999 Act does not change the requirement that the promisee must show consideration to enforce any promise not made in the form of a deed.

3 Consideration must not be illegal. The courts will not entertain an action where the consideration is contrary to a rule of law or is immoral. The question of legality will be considered in more detail later in this chapter.

4 Consideration must be sufficient but need not be adequate. It must be possible to attach some value to the consideration but there is no requirement for the bargain to be strictly commercial. If a man is prepared to sell his Bentley car for £1, the contract will not fail for lack of consideration. The courts will not help someone who complains of making a bad bargain.

The following are examples of cases where the consideration was of little value, but, nevertheless, it was held to be sufficient.

Thomas v Thomas (1842)

After the death of her husband, Mrs Thomas agreed to pay rent of £1 a year in order to continue living in the same house. It was held that the payment of £1 was valid consideration.

Chappell & Co Ltd v Nestlé Co Ltd (1959)

Nestlé was running a special offer whereby members of the public could obtain a copy of the record 'Rockin' Shoes' by sending off three wrappers from Nestlé's six-penny chocolate bars, plus 1s 6d. The records had been made by Hardy & Co but the copyright was owned by Chappell & Co Ltd, which claimed that there had been breaches of its copyright. The case turned on whether the three wrappers were part of the consideration. The House of Lords held that they were – even though they were thrown away when received. In the words of Lord Somervell, 'A peppercorn does not cease to be good consideration if it is established that the promisee does not like pepper and will throw away the corn.'

A person who promises to carry out a duty which he is already obliged to perform is in reality offering nothing of value. The 'consideration' will be insufficient. However, if a person does more than he is bound to do, there may be sufficient consideration. The promise may involve a public duty imposed by law.

Collins v Godefroy (1831)

Collins was subpoenaed to give evidence in a case in which Godefroy was a party. (A subpoena is a court order which compels a person's attendance at court.) Godefroy promised to pay 6 guineas for Collins' loss of time. Collins' action to recover this money failed because he was already under a legal duty to appear in court. He had not done anything extra.

Glasbrook Bros Ltd v Glamorgan County Council (1925)

Glasbrook Bros were the owners of a strike-hit mine. They asked for police protection for the safety of men whose presence was necessary to prevent the mine flooding. They were unhappy with the arrangements originally offered by the local police. Eventually it was agreed that 70 policemen would be stationed in the colliery and that Glasbrook Bros would pay for this extra security. The House of Lords held that, since the police had provided more protection than they thought necessary, this constituted consideration. They were entitled to payment.

Comment. Glasbrook v Glamorgan was considered by the Court of Appeal in upholding a claim by a police authority for £51,699 against Sheffield United Football Club for special police services provided at the club's home matches between August 1982 and November 1983 (*Harris v Sheffield United Football Club* (1987)).

Similar principles apply where a person is bound by a pre-existing contractual duty.

Stilk v Myrick (1809)

During the course of a voyage from London to the Baltic and back, two of a ship's crew deserted. The captain promised to share the wages of the deserters amongst the remaining crew. It was held that this promise was not binding as the sailors were already contractually bound to meet such emergencies of the voyage. They had not provided consideration.

The decision in *Stilk v Myrick* was reconsidered by the Court of Appeal in the following case.

Williams v Roffey Bros & Nicholls (Contractors) Ltd (1990)

The defendant building contractors had a contract to refurbish a block of 27 flats. They had subcontracted the carpentry work to Williams for £20,000. After the contract had been running some months, during which time Williams had completed nine flats and received some £16,200 on account, it became apparent that Williams had underestimated the cost of the work and was in financial difficulties. The defendants, concerned that the carpentry work would not be completed on time and that as a result they would fall foul of a penalty clause in their main contract, agreed to a further £575 per flat. Williams completed eight more flats but did not receive full payment. He stopped work and brought an action for damages. The defendants argued that they were not obliged to pay as they had promised Williams extra pay for something he was already contractually bound to do, i.e. complete the work. Williams in turn submitted that the defendants obtained a benefit in that they had avoided a penalty for late completion and did not have the expense of engaging another contractor. The Court of Appeal held that Williams was entitled to the extra payments. Where A promises additional payments to B in return for B's promise to complete work on time, and by giving this promise A obtains a benefit by avoiding a penalty clause, for example, then B's promise may constitute sufficient consideration to support A's promise of extra pay, provided A's promise has not been obtained as a result of fraud or economic duress (see p 250).

Comment. Doubt has been cast over the correctness of the decision in **Williams**. In *South Caribbean Trading Ltd v Trafigura Beeher BV* (2004) Colman J sitting in the Commercial Court noted that the decision in **Williams** is inconsistent with the long-standing rule that consideration must move from the promise. However, but for the fact that **Williams** is a Court of Appeal decision, which has not yet been held by the House of Lords to have been wrongly decided, the judge stated that he would not have followed it.

Hartley v Ponsonby (1857)

When almost half of the crew of a ship deserted, the captain offered those remaining £40 extra to complete the voyage. In this case, the ship was so seriously undermanned that the rest of the journey had become extremely hazardous. It was held that this fact discharged the sailors from their existing contract and left them free to enter into a new contract for the rest of the voyage.

A slightly different problem arises where a person agrees to accept a smaller sum of money as full payment under a contract to pay a larger amount. For example, what is the legal position if Derek owes Graham £100, but Graham says that he will accept £90 in full settlement? Can Graham change his mind and sue for the outstanding £10? The long-established common law rule, known as the rule in *Pinnel's Case* (1602), is that an agreement to accept a lesser sum is not binding unless supported by fresh consideration.

Foakes v Beer (1884)

Mrs Beer had obtained judgment for a debt against Dr Foakes. She agreed that she would take no further action in the matter, provided that Foakes paid £500 immediately and the rest by half-yearly instalments of £150. Foakes duly kept to his side of the agreement. Judgment debts, however, carry interest. The House of Lords held that Mrs Beer was entitled to the £360 interest which had accrued. Foakes had not 'bought' her promise to take no further action on the judgment. He had not provided any consideration.

The decision in *Foakes* v *Beer* was reconsidered by the Court of Appeal in the following case.

Re Selectmove Ltd (1995)

Selectmove owed the Inland Revenue large sums of tax and national insurance. In July 1991, Selectmove's managing director suggested to a collector of taxes that the company should pay future income tax and national insurance contributions as they became due and clear the arrears at £1,000 per month from 1 February 1992. The collector said that he would have to obtain approval for this proposal and that he would come back to the company if it was not acceptable. Selectmove heard no more from the Inland Revenue until 9 October 1991, when the Revenue demanded payment of the arrears in full and threatened to present a winding-up petition. The question was whether the proposal made by Selectmove's managing director in July had become a binding agreement. It was argued on behalf of Selectmove that the decision in *Williams* v *Roffey Bros* was authority for the proposition that a promise to perform an existing obligation can amount to good consideration provided that there are practical benefits to the promisee. The Court of Appeal held that the *Williams* principle, which related to a case involving the supply of services, should not be extended to a situation involving an obligation to make a payment which is clearly governed by the authority of the House of Lords in *Foakes* v *Beer*. The court concluded that, if there was an agreement between Selectmove and the Inland Revenue, it was unenforceable because of the absence of consideration.

There are some exceptions to the rule.

1 If the smaller payment is made, at the creditor's request, at an earlier time, at a different place, with an additional item or by a different method, consideration has been shown. It should be noted that payment by cheque rather than by cash does not necessarily release a debtor from his obligation to pay the full amount.

Stour Valley Builders v Stuart (1993)

The claimants were a small firm of builders. They carried out some work for Mr and Mrs Stuart. On completion of the work, the claimants submitted a bill which, after deductions for payments on account, came to £10,204. Following a query by Mr Stuart, the bill was revised to £10,163. Mr Stuart continued to dispute an amount of £3,000 but made an offer to settle of £8,471. He wrote to the claimants enclosing a cheque for £8,471 'in full and final settlement'. The claimants paid the cheque in to their bank account but, after seeking advice from their solicitor the following day, contacted Mr Stuart to say that they would not accept the cheque in full settlement. The Court of Appeal held that although cashing in of a cheque is strong evidence of agreement, if, as in this case, the banking of the cheque was closely followed by a rejection of the offer to settle, there could be no 'accord and satisfaction' so as to discharge the debt.

Comment. Another example of this principle can be found in the decision of the High Court in *Inland Revenue Commissioners* v *Fry* (2001). Mrs Fry owed the Inland Revenue £113,000. Her husband wrote to the Revenue enclosing a cheque for £10,000. He stated that if the

Revenue presented the cheque for payment it would be taken as acceptance of the offer of £10,000 in full and final settlement of Mrs Fry's liabilities. Unknown to Mr Fry, the procedure in the Revenue's post room was to send all cheques to the cashier's section for banking and to send any correspondence to the appropriate caseworker. As soon as Mr Fry's letter reached the caseworker, she telephoned Mr Fry to say that although the cheque had been banked his offer to settle had not been accepted. The High Court held that the encashment of the cheque by the Revenue had not discharged Mrs Fry from the obligation to pay the full amount. As Jacob J put it: the 'Cashing of a cheque gives rise to no more than a rebuttable presumption of acceptance of the accompanying letter. That presumption is fully rebutted here'.

2 The rule does not apply to a composition agreement. This is where a debtor agrees with all his creditors to pay so much in the £ of what he owes. Provided that the debtor honours the agreement, a creditor cannot sue for any outstanding sum.

3 A promise to accept a smaller sum in full satisfaction will be binding on a creditor where the part payment is made by a third party on condition that the debtor is released from the obligation to pay the full amount (*Hirachand Punamchand* v *Temple* (1911)).

4 The final exception is provided by equity. You will remember from Chapter 1 that equity is a system of law based on the idea of fairness and doing right according to conscience. The rule about part payment would seem an ideal candidate for intervention by equity. It seems very unfair that a court will support a person who has gone back on his word, especially where the agreement to accept a lesser amount has been relied upon. The equitable rule of promissory estoppel which was developed by Denning J in the *High Trees* case may provide some assistance.

Central London Property Trust Ltd v
High Trees House Ltd (1947)

In 1937 the claimants granted a 99-year lease on a block of flats in London to the defendants at an annual rent of £2,500. Owing to the outbreak of war in 1939, the defendants found it very difficult to get tenants for the flats and so in 1940 it was agreed that the rent should be reduced to £1,250. By 1945 the flats were full again and the claimants sued to recover the arrears of rent as

fixed by the 1937 agreement for the last two quarters of 1945. Denning J held that they were entitled to recover this money, but if they had sued for the arrears from 1940–45, the 1940 agreement would have defeated their claim. The defendants had relied upon the reduction in rent and equity would require the claimants to honour the promises contained in the 1940 agreement.

Thus, it seems that if a person promises that he will not insist on his strict legal rights, and the promise is acted upon, then the law will require the promise to be honoured even though it is not supported by consideration.

The following points should be noted about promissory estoppel:

1 The rule can only be used as a defence and not as a cause of action. In the words of Birkett LJ in *Combe* v *Combe* (1951), promissory estoppel must be 'used as a shield and not as a sword'. Consideration is still an essential requirement for the formation of a contract. The principle was confirmed in the following Court of Appeal case.

Baird Textile Holdings Ltd v *Marks and Spencer* (2002)

The claimant B had supplied garments to the defendants M & S for 30 years, when M & S terminated the agreement with effect from the end of the then current production season. B brought an action against M & S arguing that: (i) the termination was in breach of a contract, which could be implied from the long-standing relationship between the parties, that obliged M & S to continue to place orders unless and until the contract was ended by giving reasonable notice, and B contended that a notice period of at least three years was reasonable; and (ii) M & S were estopped from giving less than three years' notice. The Court of Appeal held that the alleged contract obliging M & S to continue to place orders with B failed for uncertainty. (The requirement of certainty will be discussed in more detail in Chapter 8 .) The court confirmed that estoppel did not create the type of enforceable right claimed by B. It could not be used to found a cause of action.

2 The rule will only operate if the promisee has relied upon the promise so that it would be inequitable to allow the promisor to insist on his strict legal rights. At first it was thought that the promisee must have acted to his detriment. However, Lord Denning argued that detrimental reliance is not essential and that it is sufficient that the promisee has altered his position by acting differently from what he otherwise would have done.

3 It is a principle of equity that whoever seeks the help of equity must himself have acted equitably or fairly. Thus, the promisee must have acted according to his conscience if he is to rely on promissory estoppel as a defence.

D & C Builders v Rees (1965)

D & C Builders, a small building company, had completed some work for Mr Rees for which he owed the company £482. For months the company, which was in severe financial difficulties, pressed for payment. Eventually, Mrs Rees, who had become aware of the company's problems, contacted the company and offered £300 in full settlement. She added that if the company refused this offer, it would get nothing. The company reluctantly accepted a cheque for £300 'in completion of the account'. The company later sued for the balance. The Court of Appeal held that the company was entitled to succeed. Mr Rees could not rely on promissory estoppel to resist the claim because his wife had held the company to ransom and could not be said to have acted equitably. Moreover, the different method of payment, i.e. by cheque rather than by cash, did not release Mr Rees from the obligation to pay the full amount owed.

4 The rule does not as yet extinguish rights: it only suspends the rights of the promisor. So if the promise refers to a particular period of time or a state of affairs (e.g. war conditions), the promisor can revert to the original position at the end of the stated time or when conditions change by giving notice to the promisee.

Tool Metal Manufacturing Co Ltd v Tungsten Electric Co Ltd (1955)

Tool Metal granted a licence to Tungsten Electric to deal in products protected by patents owned by Tool Metal. Tungsten Electric agreed to pay 'compensation' if it manufactured more than a specific amount. In 1942 Tool Metal indicated that it wished to prepare a new licence agreement and in the meantime would not claim compensation. Tool Metal later gave notice that it wished to resume its claim to compensation. The House of Lords held that Tool Metal was entitled to claim compensation after giving reasonable notice of its intention to do so.

The Court of Appeal had a recent opportunity to consider the rule in *Pinnel's* case and the doctrine of promissory estoppel in the following case.

Collier v P & M J Wright (Holdings) Ltd (2007)

C and his two partners B and F, had obtained a loan from W, for which the partners were jointly liable. W obtained a judgment against C, B and F for £46,800 in 1999. The partners were ordered to pay £600 a month and initially the payments were made from the partners' joint bank account. However, the partnership came to an end in 2000. At a meeting between C and W towards the end of 2000, W told C that B and F had not been paying their shares. C alleged that when he asked W what he should do, W said that it was his (W's) responsibility to pursue B and F and that C should carry on paying £200 per month. C continued making monthly payments for the next five years until he had paid one-third of the total judgment debt. In 2006, W served a statutory demand on C for the outstanding balance. Meanwhile, B and F had been declared bankrupt in 2002 and 2004 respectively. C applied to have the statutory demand set aside on the following grounds:

1 that the agreement he made in 2000 was binding, because by accepting sole responsibility for a one-third share of the debt, he gave consideration for W's promise to accept him as a debtor of one-third share of the judgment debt;
2 that W was estopped from proceeding against him for more than one-third of the judgment debt.

The Court of Appeal applied the rule in *Pinnel's* case to hold that the 2000 agreement between C and W was not binding. However, all three Lord Justices agreed that C had raised a triable issue as to promissory estoppel. In the words of Arden LJ:

> if (1) a debtor offers to pay part only of the amount he owes; (2) the creditor voluntary accepts that offer; and (3) in reliance of the creditor's acceptance the debtor pays that part of the amount he owes in full, the creditor will by virtue of the doctrine of promissory estoppel, be bound to accept that sum in full and final satisfaction of the whole debt. For him to resile will of itself be inequitable . . . in these circumstances, the promissory estoppel has the effect of extinguishing the creditor's right to the balance of the debt.

These comments are *obiter dicta* as the Appeal Court was not trying the substantive issue, only considering whether C had raised a triable issue.

Privity of contract

The common law doctrine of privity of contract states that a person cannot be bound by, or take advantage of, a contract to which he is not a party. The doctrine, which had been developed by the common law judges by the middle of the 19th century, was reaffirmed by the House of Lords in 1915.

Dunlop Pneumatic Tyre Co Ltd v Selfridge & Co Ltd (1915)

The claimants, Dunlop, sold a quantity of tyres to Dew and Co, dealers in motor accessories, on the basis that Dew and Co would not sell the tyres below the claimants' list price and they would obtain a similar undertaking from anyone they supplied with tyres. Dew and Co sold tyres to the defendants, Selfridge, which agreed to observe the restrictions and to pay Dunlop £5 for each tyre sold below the list price. Selfridge sold some of the tyres below list price and Dunlop sued for breach of contract. Selfridge argued that they were not a party to a contract with Dunlop. The House of Lords held that, as there was no contract between Dunlop and Selfridge, Dunlop could not enforce the penalty of £5 for every tyre sold below Dunlop's list price. Viscount Haldane based his decision on two principles: first, that only a person who is party to a contract can sue on it; and second, in order to enforce a simple contract, a person must provide consideration.

Comment. The agreement between Dunlop and Dew and Co is known as a resale price maintenance agreement. Such agreements are now outlawed by Art 81 of the EC Treaty and s 2 of the Competition Act 1998. UK and EC competition law will be considered in more detail later in this chapter.

If A enters into a contract with B for the benefit of C, the common law doctrine of privity prevents C from suing B on the contract. There is nothing to stop A from suing on behalf of C, but the question arises whether A is limited to recovering damages only for his own loss, or can he also recover for losses suffered by C?

Jackson v Horizon Holidays Ltd (1975)

Mr Jackson entered into a contract with Horizon for a four-week family holiday to Ceylon for £1,200. The holiday was a disaster. Mr Jackson was awarded £1,100 for breach of contract by the Court of Appeal. The damages covered not only his own distress and disappointment but also that suffered by his wife and children. Although the outcome in this case can be justified by saying that the damages were compensation for his own distress because his family's holiday had been ruined, Lord Denning made it clear that the award was designed to cover not only Mr Jackson's loss but also the loss suffered by his wife and children.

The House of Lords expressed disapproval of Lord Denning's reasoning in the *Jackson* case in **Woodar Investment Development Ltd v Wimpey Construction UK Ltd** (1980), but gave its support for the level of damages awarded. More recently the House of Lords has shown that it is prepared in limited circumstances to allow a party to a contract to recover damages which represent a third party's loss.

Linden Garden Trust Ltd v Lenesta Sludge Disposals Ltd (1993)

The owner of land entered into a building contract with a contractor to develop a site for shops, offices and flats. The parties envisaged that the site would subsequently be transferred to a third party. It was alleged that the third party had suffered financial loss as a result of the contractor's poor workmanship which amounted to a breach of contract. The owner of the site brought an action for breach of contract but was met by the defence that as the site had been transferred to a third party he had only suffered nominal loss. The House of Lords rejected this argument and upheld the right of the owner to recover full damages on behalf of the third party.

Although privity of contract has been regarded as a fundamental principle of English law, there are a large number of exceptions to the rule. Where an exception applies, a person who is not a party to a contract may be able to take legal action.

1 **Assignment of contractual rights.** It is possible for a party to a contract to transfer the benefit of a contract to another person. For example, A may agree to sell B his CD collection for £2,000. A may transfer his right to payment under the contract to a third party, C. This process is known as assignment. Provided the assignment is absolute, in writing and notice is given to the debtor, it will take effect as a statutory assignment under s 136 of the Law of Property Act 1925. This means that

the assignee (C in the example above) can sue the debtor (B) in his own name. The assignee gets the same rights as the assignor (A) had. The burden of a contract cannot be assigned unless the other party consents.

2 Agency. An agent is a person who is employed by a principal to make contracts on his behalf with third parties. A principal will be bound by contracts made by the agent with the third party even if the existence of the agency is not revealed. This is known as the doctrine of the undisclosed principal. The law of agency will be considered in more detail in Chapter 10 .

3 Land law. There are many situations in land law where the doctrine of privity of contract does not apply. For example, a lease of property often contains a number of covenants by the landlord and the tenant. If the tenant assigns the lease to a third party, either party, landlord or new tenant may enforce a covenant in the original lease against each other.

4 Trusts. The doctrine of privity does not apply to the law of trusts. If X and Y by contract create a trust for the benefit of B, B can enforce his rights under the trust even though he was not a party to the contract.

5 Collateral contract. A collateral contract may arise where one party makes a promise to another, the consideration for which is that the promisee will enter into a contract with a third party. The device of a collateral contract was often used to enforce a promise made by car dealers before a purchaser entered into a hire-purchase agreement with a finance company.

Andrews v Hopkinson (1956)

The defendant car dealer recommended a car to the claimant saying: 'It's a good little bus. I would stake my life on it.' The claimant entered into a hire-purchase agreement with a finance company and when the car was delivered he was asked to sign a delivery note which said that he was satisfied with its condition. This was the first opportunity the claimant had to examine the vehicle. The claimant was seriously injured when a week later the car suddenly swerved into a lorry. The car was completely wrecked. A subsequent examination revealed that the steering mechanism was faulty at the time of delivery. As the law then stood, the delivery note may have barred the claimant from suing the finance company. The claimant successfully sued the defendant for breach of the promise made before he entered into the hire-purchase agreement. The defendant was also liable in the tort of negligence.

6 Other causes of action. The doctrine of privity of contract means that a person who is not a party to a contract cannot bring an action in contract. He may have some other cause of action on which to base a claim. If a husband enters into a contract with a garage to have his wife's car serviced, she will not be able to sue the garage in contract if the service is carried out badly. However, if she is injured in an accident caused by a defective service to the car's brakes, she may be able to sue the garage in the tort of negligence (see Chapter 11).

Beswick v Beswick (1967)

Peter Beswick was a coal merchant. He agreed to sell the business to his nephew, John, provided that John paid him £6.50 per week for the rest of his life and if his wife survived him she would receive an annuity of £5 per week. John took over the business and paid the agreed sum to Peter until Peter died. John paid Peter's widow for one week but then refused to make any more payments. Peter's widow sued John for specific performance of the contract and arrears of the annuity. She sued in her personal capacity and as administratrix of her husband's estate. The House of Lords held that she was entitled to succeed in her capacity as administratrix but privity of contract would prevent her from succeeding in her personal capacity.

7 Contracts (Rights of Third Parties) Act 1999. In 1996 the Law Commission recommended that the doctrine of privity be relaxed to allow a person who is not a party to a contract to sue on it, provided that the contract contains an express term to that effect and it purports to confer a benefit on the third party. These recommendations have now been implemented by the Contracts (Rights of Third Parties) Act 1999.

The 1999 Act institutes reform of the doctrine of privity by recognising the right of third parties to enforce contracts which have been made for their benefit. It should be noted that the Act applies only to contracts for the **benefit** of third parties and does not affect the established principle that **burdens** cannot be imposed on a third party without his consent.

The main provisions of the Contracts (Rights of Third Parties) Act 1999 are set out below.

Right of a third party to enforce a term of a contract (s 1)

A third party will have the right to enforce a term of a contract:

- where the contract expressly so provides;
- where the term purports to confer a benefit on the third party, unless it appears that the contracting parties did not intend him to have the right to enforce the term.

The third party must be expressly identified in the contract either by **name**, e.g. Fred Smith; **class**, e.g. Fred Smith's employees; or **description**, e.g. Fred Smith's son. It is not necessary, however, for the third party to be in existence when the contract is made. This provision allows the contracting parties to confer enforceable rights on, for example, a company which, although in the process of formation, has not yet been incorporated.

Avraamides v *Colwill* (2006)

C had purchased a business from B Ltd. The transfer agreement provided that C undertook to complete outstanding customer orders and to pay any liabilities properly incurred by the company. A was a dissatisfied customer of B Ltd and brought a claim against C based on the contract between B Ltd and C, claiming that the transfer agreement had conferred an enforceable benefit on C. The Court of Appeal held that under s 1(3) of the Contracts (Rights of Third Parties) Act 1999, the contract must expressly identify third parties by name or class and no such identification had occurred in this case.

The right of a third party to enforce a contract is subject to the terms and conditions of the contract. It is, therefore, open to the contracting parties to limit or impose conditions on the rights of the third party to enforce the contract.

The third party is entitled to all the remedies for a breach of contract which would have been available to him if he had been a party to the contract. The rules relating to damages (including the duty to mitigate loss), injunctions, specific performance and other types of remedy will all apply.

Although the Act is primarily designed to enable third parties to enforce positive rights, it also allows third parties to take advantage of any exclusion or limitation clauses in the contract. The effect of the Act on exemption clauses will be examined further in Chapter 8 ○.

For the purposes of the Act, the 'promisor' is defined as the party to the contract against whom the contractual term is enforceable by the third party, while the 'promisee' is the party to the contract by whom the term is enforceable against the promisor. So if A makes a contract with B, by which B agrees to confer a benefit on C, B is the 'promisor', A is the 'promisee', and C is the 'third party'.

Applying the provisions of the Act to the facts of *Beswick* v *Beswick* (above), it is probable that if the case arose today Mrs Beswick would have the right to enforce John Beswick's promise to pay her an annuity. The contract between Peter Beswick and his nephew John purported to confer a benefit (the payment of an annuity) on Mrs Beswick, who was expressly named. Under s 1 of the 1999 Act, a presumed right of enforceability by Mrs Beswick would be created, which could only be rebutted if John Beswick could show 'on a proper construction of the contract that the parties did not intend the term to be enforceable by a third party'.

Variation and rescission of the contract (s 2)

The effect of this section is to restrict attempts by the contracting parties to alter (vary) the contract or cancel (rescind) it without the agreement of the third party. Where a third party has a right under s 1 to enforce a term of a contract, the contracting parties may not, by agreement, rescind or vary the contract in such a way as to extinguish or alter the third party's entitlement, without the third party's consent if:

- the third party has communicated to the promisor his/her acceptance of the term; or
- the promisor is aware that the third party has relied on the term;
- the promisor can reasonably be expected to have foreseen that the third party would rely on the term and the third party has in fact relied on the term.

Acceptance may be in the form of words or conduct, but if the acceptance is sent by post, the 'postal rules' will not apply and the acceptance will only be effective when received by the promisor.

The principle that variation or rescission of the contract can only be made with the third party's consent will not apply in the following circumstances:

- Where there is an express term in the contract allowing the contracting parties to vary or rescind without the third party's consent.
- Where, on the application of the contracting parties, a court dispenses with the requirement of consent because the third party's whereabouts are unknown or he is incapable of giving consent because of mental incapacity or it cannot be ascertained whether he has relied on the contractual term. This power is exercisable by either the High Court or county court.

Defences, set-offs or counterclaims available to the promisor (s 3)

This section applies where the third party is seeking to enforce a contractual term against the promisor. It sets out the defences, set-offs and counterclaims available to the promisor in any proceedings by the third party. The following principles apply:

1 The third party's claim will be subject to all the defences and set-offs which would have been available to the promisor in an action by the promisee arising from or in connection with the contract and relevant to the term the third party is seeking to enforce (s 3(2)).

Example 1

The contract is void because of mistake or illegality, or has been discharged because of frustration, or is unenforceable because of a failure to observe necessary formalities. In these circumstances the third party will not be able to enforce the term because the promisee would not have been able to enforce the contract.

Example 2

A and B enter into a contract for the sale of goods, whereby the purchase price is to be paid to C. B delivers goods which are not of satisfactory quality in breach of the statutory implied term contained in s 14 of the Sale of Goods Act 1979. In an action for the price of the goods brought by C, A will be entitled to reduce or extinguish the price because of B's breach of contract.

2 The contracting parties may include an express term in the contract to the effect that the promisor may have available to him any matter by way of defence or set-off in proceedings brought by the third party or the promisee (s 3(3)).

Example

A agrees to buy B's car for £3,000, with the purchase price to be paid to C. B owes A money under a completely unrelated contract. A and B agree to an express term in the contract for the sale of the car that allows A to raise in any claim brought by C any matter which would have given A a defence or set-off in a claim brought by B. So if C brought a claim for the purchase price, A would be able to set off the money owed by B.

3 The promisor will also have available to him any defence or set-off, or any counterclaim not arising from the contract, but which is specific to the third party (s 3(4)).

Example 1

A enters into a contract with B whereby A will pay C £1,000. C already owes A £400. A has a set-off to a claim by C and need only pay £600.

Example 2

C induces A to enter into a contract with B by misrepresentation, but B is unaware of the misrepresentation. A may have a defence (or a counterclaim for damages) if sued by C, which would not have been available if the action had been brought by B.

4 The contracting parties may include an express provision to the effect that the promisor cannot raise any defences, set-offs or counterclaims that would have been available to the promisor had the third party been party to the contract (s 3(5)).

Example

B agrees to buy a painting from A, an art dealer, for his daughter C's birthday. C is expressly given the right to enforce delivery of the painting. B already owes a considerable amount of money for other works of art he has purchased. B is concerned that C's right to enforce the contract is unaffected and so A and B agree that A cannot raise against C any defences or set-offs which would have been available to A in any action by B.

Enforcement by the promisee (s 4)

This section makes it clear the rights given to third parties under the Act are in addition to any rights that the promisee has to enforce the contract. This means that in a contract between A and B for the benefit of C, B can sue on behalf of C.

Protection against double liability (s 5)

This section provides that where the promisee has already recovered damages from the promisor in respect of the third party's loss, in a claim against the promisor by the third party, any award will be reduced to take into account sums already recovered. This section is designed to protect the promisor against double liability.

Exceptions (s 6)

This section excludes certain kinds of contracts from the operation of the Act. Third parties acquire no rights of enforcement in relation to the following contracts:

- contracts on a bill of exchange, promissory note or other negotiable instruments;
- contracts under s 33 of the Companies Act 2006, by which a company's constitution is deemed to constitute a contract between the company and its members;
- contracts of employment: without this provision, employees taking lawful industrial action would be at risk of being sued for breach of their contracts of employment by customers of any employer;
- contracts for the carriage of goods by sea; however, third parties will be able to take advantage of any exclusion or limitation clauses made for their benefit in such contracts.

The application of the Act to exemption clauses will be discussed in more detail in Chapter 8 ◯.

Supplementary provisions (s 7)

The section clarifies that any existing rights or remedies available to a third party are not affected by the Act.

It also prevents a third party from invoking s 2(2) of the Unfair Contract Terms Act 1977 to contest the validity of an exemption clause which purports to exclude or limit liability for negligently caused loss and damage (other than death or personal injury). The Unfair Contract Terms Act will be considered in more detail in Chapter 8 ◯.

234

Intention

So far we have established two requirements for a binding contract: agreement and consideration. The law demands, in addition, that the parties intended to enter into a legal relationship. After all, if you invite a friend round for a social evening at your house, you would not expect legal action to follow if the occasion has to be cancelled. So how does the law decide what the parties intended? For the purpose of establishing the intention of the parties, agreements are divided into two categories: business/commercial and social/domestic agreements.

Business/commercial agreements

In the case of a business agreement, it is automatically presumed that the parties intended to make a legally enforceable contract. It is possible, however, to remove the intention by the inclusion of an express statement to that effect in the agreement.

Rose and Frank Co v Crompton (J R) & Brothers Ltd (1923)

The defendants, English paper tissue manufacturers, entered into an agreement with the claimants, an American company, whereby the claimants were to act as sole agents for the sale of the defendants' tissues in the USA. The written agreement contained the following 'Honourable Pledge Clause':

> This arrangement is not entered into . . . as a formal or legal agreement and shall not be subject to legal jurisdiction in the law courts . . . but it is only a definite expression and record of the purpose and intention of the parties concerned to which they honourably pledge themselves that it will be carried through with mutual loyalty and friendly co-operation.

The claimants placed orders for tissues which were accepted by the defendants. Before the orders were sent, the defendants terminated the agency agreement and refused to send the tissues. The House of Lords held that the sole agency agreement was not binding owing to the inclusion of the 'honourable pledge clause'. Insofar as orders had been placed and accepted, however, contracts had been created and the defendants, in failing to execute them, were in breach of contract.

When the parties enter into an agreement subject to contract, they are expressly stating that they will not be bound unless and until a formal contract is drawn up.

There are situations where it would appear at first sight that the parties had entered into a commercial arrangement, but, nevertheless, a contract is not created.

1 Collective agreements. Employers and trade unions regularly enter into collective agreements about rates of pay and conditions of employment. Section 179 of the Trade Union and Labour Relations (Consolidation) Act 1992 states that such agreements are not intended to be legally enforceable unless they are in writing and expressly affirm that they are to be binding. It should be noted, however, that the Employment Relations Act 1999 inserted a new s 70A in the 1992 Act, which deals with recognition of trade unions. Under s 70A, agreements between an employer and a trade union about the method by which they will conduct collective bargaining (or if not agreed by the parties, specified by the Central Arbitration Committee) will take effect as if they were contained in a legally enforceable contract. The only remedy for breach is specific performance.

2 Advertisements. Generally speaking, vague promises or guarantees given in the course of promoting a product are not intended to be taken seriously. By contrast, more specific pledges such as, 'If you can find the same holiday at a lower price in a different brochure, we will refund you the difference', are likely to be binding. (See *Carlill* v *Carbolic Smoke Ball Co.*)

3 Public bodies. Where one of the parties is a public body which is bound by Act of Parliament to supply a particular service, there is no intention to enter into a contract with customers. For example, if you post a letter by ordinary first class mail and it is delayed or lost, you cannot sue the Post Office for breach of contract.

4 Letters of comfort. A comfort letter is a document supplied by a third party to a creditor, indicating a concern to ensure that a debtor meets his obligations to the creditor. Comfort letters are sometimes provided as an alternative to a formal guarantee in respect of a loan but are usually carefully worded so as to avoid the creation of any legal obligation. In *Kleinwort Benson Ltd* v *Malaysian Mining Corporation Bhd* (1989) the Court of Appeal held that, despite the commercial nature of the transaction which gave rise to a presumption of an intention to create legal relations, the comfort letter provided by Malaysian Mining merely stated its current policy and did not amount to a contractual promise to meet the liabilities of its subsidiary.

5 Letters of intent. A letter of intent is a device by which one person indicates to another that he is likely to place a contract with him, but is not yet ready to be contractually bound. A typical example of a situation where a letter of intent might be provided is where a main contractor is preparing a tender and he plans to subcontract some of the work. He would need to know the cost of the subcontracted work in order to calculate his own tender, but would not want to be committed to that subcontractor until he knows whether his tender has been successful. In these circumstances, the main contractor writes to tell the subcontractor that he has been chosen. Normally, the letter is carefully worded so as to avoid any legal obligations. However, if the letter of intent invites the subcontractor to begin preliminary work, an obligation to pay for the work will arise even though a formal contract may never be concluded (*British Steel Corporation* v *Cleveland Bridge and Engineering Co Ltd* (1984)).

Social/domestic arrangements

Social arrangements between friends do not usually amount to contracts because the parties never intend their agreement to be legally binding. You might agree to meet someone for lunch or accept an invitation to a party, but in neither case have you entered into a contract. If it can be shown, however, that the transaction had a commercial flavour, the court may be prepared to find the necessary intention for a contract.

Simpkins v *Pays* (1955)

The claimant, Simpkins, lodged with the defendant, Mrs Pays, and her granddaughter. Each week all three ladies jointly completed a competition run by a Sunday newspaper. The entries were sent off in the defendant's name. One entry won a prize of £750 which the defendant refused to share with the claimant. It was held that the parties had embarked on a joint enterprise, expecting to share any prize money. There was an intention to enter into a legal relationship and the claimant was entitled to one-third of the winnings.

Most domestic arrangements within families are not intended to be legally binding. An agreement between husband and wife or parent and child does not normally give rise to a contract. That is not to say that there can never be business contracts between members of a family. Many family businesses are run as partnerships; a wife can be employed by her husband.

If the husband and wife are living apart, they can make a binding separation agreement.

Merritt v Merritt (1970)

Mr Merritt had left his wife to live with another woman. He agreed that if his wife completed the mortgage repayments on the matrimonial home he would transfer the house to her. Mrs Merritt duly completed the repayments but her husband refused to convey the house to her. The Court of Appeal held that, as the parties were living apart, the agreement was enforceable.

The context in which a promise is made might indicate that it was not intended to be legally binding.

Judge v Crown Leisure Ltd (2005)

J was employed as an Operations Manager for CL. He was paid substantially less than a new office manager, who had been recruited from CL's sister company. (The reason for the differential was that the incoming manager had received assurances that his remuneration would not be reduced.) A senior manager at CL had informed all the operation managers that their remuneration would be brought into line. J claimed that the senior manager promised at CL's Christmas Party in 2001 that J would be put onto the same scale as the transferred manager within two years. When J was told subsequently that his remuneration would not be increased to match that of the transferred manager, he resigned, claiming constructive dismissal in that CL was in breach of contract by not fulfilling the promises made at the Christmas Party. The Court of Appeal upheld the decision of the EAT which held that, even if the alleged promise had been made at the Christmas Party, it had been made during the course of a casual conversation at a social event and, given the 'convivial spirit of the evening', there was no intention to create a legally binding contract.

Form

If you ask someone what a contract is, you will probably be told that it is a written document. Some contracts are indeed in writing but the majority are created much more informally either orally or implied from conduct.

Generally, the law does not require complex formalities to be observed to form a contract. There are, however, some types of contract which are exceptions to this rule.

1 Contracts which must be in the form of a deed. Certain transactions involving land require the execution of a deed, i.e. conveyances, legal mortgages and leases for more than three years. A promise of a gift is not binding unless in this form.

2 Contracts which must be in writing. The Law of Property (Miscellaneous Provisions) Act 1989 provides that a contract for the sale or other disposition of land can only be made in writing and by incorporating all the terms which the parties have expressly agreed in one document, or, where the contracts are exchanged, in each. The document must be signed by or on behalf of each party to the contract.

In the following case the Court of Appeal considered whether the formalities required for the sale of land under the 1989 Act applied to a so-called 'lock-out' agreement, i.e. an agreement to deal exclusively with one party and not to consider other offers for a limited period.

Pitt v PHH Asset Management Ltd (1993)

The claimant, Mr Pitt, and a Miss Buckle were both interested in purchasing a cottage in Suffolk from the defendant, PHH Asset Management. Every time Mr Pitt made an offer for the property, he was gazumped by Miss Buckle. On the occasion of Mr Pitt's third offer for the property, it was agreed orally that PHH would not consider any further offers, provided that Mr Pitt exchanged contracts within two weeks. PHH sold the cottage to Miss Buckle at a higher price before the two-week period had expired. Mr Pitt sued PHH for breach of the 'lock-out' agreement. PHH argued that the agreement was unenforceable on three grounds: (i) the agreement formed part of the continuing negotiations for the sale of the property and as such was 'subject to contract'; (ii) the agreement was a contract for the sale of an interest in land and was, therefore, only enforceable if the formalities required by the Law of Property (Miscellaneous Provisions) Act 1989 were observed; and (iii) Mr Pitt had given no consideration for the agreement. The Court of Appeal held that PHH was in breach of contract and was liable to pay damages. The court said that the lock-out agreement was capable of existing independently of any agreement to sell the cottage and was, therefore, not 'subject to contract'. The 1989 Act did not apply either, for the same reason. The court found that Mr Pitt had provided consideration in the form of removing a threat to make difficulties for Miss Buckle and in promising to exchange contracts within two weeks.

Under the Bills of Exchange Act 1882, bills of exchange, cheques and promissory notes must be in writing. Similarly, the transfer of shares in a limited company must be in writing. Regulations introduced under the Consumer Credit Act 1974 lay down requirements about the form and content of regulated consumer credit and hire agreements. The Employment Rights Act 1996 requires that employees be given a written statement of the terms and conditions of employment within two months of starting work. Failure to provide a written statement does not affect the validity of a contract of employment, although it does entitle an employee to refer the matter to an employment tribunal. The tribunal can decide on the particulars which should have been included in the written statement. An example of a possible form of written statement may be seen in Chapter 16 ○ .

3 Contracts which must be evidenced in writing. There is only one type of contract which must be evidenced in writing: s 4 of the Statute of Frauds 1677 requires a contract of guarantee to be evidenced in writing. If you borrow money or buy goods on credit, you may be asked to find someone who will guarantee the debt. This means that if you do not or cannot repay the money, the guarantor will pay your debt for you. The requirement of written evidence does not affect the formation of such contracts. The absence of writing does not make the agreement void, so, if any money or property has changed hands, it can be kept. However, if one of the parties wishes to enforce the contract in the courts, the necessary note or memorandum must be produced.

Actionstrength Ltd v International Glass Engineering & Saint-Gobain Glass UK Ltd (2003)

Saint-Gobain Glass (SGG) had retained International Glass Engineering (IGE) as the main contractor to build a new factory. IGE engaged Actionstrength (AS) to supply labour. The contract between IGE and AS entitled AS to terminate the contract with 30 days' notice if invoices were not paid. IGE fell behind on payments and AS threatened to withdraw from the contract. SGG allegedly then made an oral promise to AS that if IGE did not settle the invoices, SGG would pay them. AS continued working but, when IGE did not pay, AS sought to enforce SGG's promise to pay. SGG defended the claim by arguing that its oral guarantee could not be enforced because it had not been evidenced in writing. The House of Lords held that SGG's oral guarantee was unenforceable because it had not been evidenced in writing as required by s 4 of the Statute of Frauds 1677.

Formalities and electronic communications

At the start of the third millennium, we find ourselves in the midst of a new industrial revolution. It is widely predicted that the rapid development of electronic communication technology will revolutionise the way in which business is conducted in the future. Although e-commerce currently accounts for a small proportion of transactions in the UK, the government recognises the enormous potential for electronic trading and has set itself the ambitious target of making the UK the best place in the world to trade electronically. The Electronic Communications Act 2000 is designed to facilitate the development of electronic commerce by providing for:

■ a voluntary registration system for organisations providing cryptography support services, such as electronic signature and confidentiality services;
■ legal recognition of electronic signatures;
■ the removal of obstacles in other legislation to the use of electronic communication and electronic storage in place of paper. (It should be noted that the Law of Property (Miscellaneous Provisions) Act 1989 has already abolished the requirement that a deed must be written on paper.) The power to modify legislation to facilitate the use of electronic communications or electronic storage will be exercisable by ministerial order.

Capacity

If there is one thing which more than another public policy requires it is that men of full age and competent understanding shall have the utmost liberty of contracting and their contracts when entered into freely and voluntarily shall be held sacred and shall be enforced by courts of justice. (Sir George Jessel, 1875)

This classic statement of freedom of contract by a 19th-century Master of the Rolls still essentially holds good today – it is assumed that everyone is capable of entering into a contract. There are, however, some groups of people who are in need of the law's protection either because of their age or inability to appreciate their own actions. The groups which are covered by special rules are those under the age of 18 (minors), mental patients and drunks.

Minors

Before 1970 anyone under the age of 21 was known as an infant. The age of majority was lowered to 18 on 1 January 1970 and 'infants' were renamed 'minors'. The rules relating to contractual capacity are designed to protect the minor from exploitation by adults. A minor is free to enter into contracts and enforce his rights against an adult. The adult's rights will depend on the way in which the contract is classified.

1 Valid contracts. There are two types of contract which will bind a minor: contracts for necessary goods and services and beneficial contracts of service. A minor must pay a reasonable price for 'necessaries' sold and delivered to him or her. Section 3 of the Sale of Goods Act 1979 defines 'necessaries' as 'goods suitable to the condition in life of the minor and to his actual requirements at the time of sale and delivery'. Clearly, luxury goods are excluded. Expensive but useful items may be necessaries if they are appropriate to the social background and financial circumstances of the minor. If the minor is already adequately supplied, the goods will not be classed as necessaries.

Nash v Inman (1908)

A Saville Row tailor sued an infant Cambridge student for the price of clothes (including 11 fancy waistcoats) he had supplied. The tailor failed in his action because the student was already adequately supplied with clothes.

A minor is also bound by contracts of employment, apprenticeship and education, which, taken as a whole, are for his or her benefit.

Roberts v Gray (1913)

The infant defendant had agreed to go on a world tour with the claimant, a professional billiards player. After the claimant had spent much time and some money organising the tour, the infant changed his mind and refused to go. The claimant sued for breach of contract. The Court of Appeal held that this was essentially a contract to receive instruction. Since this was for the infant's benefit, the contract was valid. The claimant was awarded £1,500 damages.

Comment. A more recent application of these principles can be found in a case involving the footballer, Wayne Rooney. In *Proform Sports Management Ltd v Proactive Sports Management Ltd* (2006), Hodge J held that there was no real prospect that the claimant Proform would succeed in establishing that an agreement concluded in 2000 when Rooney was 15, whereby the claimant would act as the player's executive agent and personal representative, fell within the type of contracts analogous to contracts for necessaries, contracts of employment, apprenticeship or education. For the duration of the agreement, Rooney was playing for Everton and the claimants did not undertake any activities essential to his training. As the judge notes: 'Players' representatives do not undertake matters that are essential to the player's training or his livelihood. They do not enable the minor to earn a living or to advance his skills as a professional footballer.'

If the minor sets himself up in business, he will not be bound by his trading contracts, even though they are for his benefit. The minor can, none the less, sue on these contracts.

Cowern v Nield (1912)

Nield was an infant hay and straw dealer. He refused to deliver a quantity of hay which had been paid for by Cowern. It was held that, provided the infant had not acted fraudulently, he was not liable to repay Cowern.

2 Voidable contracts. There are three kinds of contract which are voidable: leases of land, partnerships and the purchase of shares. Voidable means that the contract is binding on the minor until he decides to reject it. He must repudiate the contract before becoming 18 or within a reasonable time of reaching 18. The main effect of repudiation is to relieve the minor of all future liabilities, but he can be sued for liabilities which have already accrued, such as arrears of rent.

3 Other contracts. Before looking at how the law deals with other contracts made by minors, we will consider the effect of changes introduced by the Minors' Contracts Act 1987 (MCA 1987). The law concerning contracts made by minors used to be governed mainly by the Infants Relief Act 1874. Section 1 of the 1874 Act provided that contracts for the repayment of money lent or to be lent, contracts for the supply of non-necessary goods and accounts stated were 'absolutely void'. Section 7 placed a bar on enforcement proceedings against a minor who ratified a contract on reaching 18 unless the ratification was contained in a new contract for which fresh consideration had been provided.

The MCA 1987 implements the recommendations of the Law Commission contained in its 1984 Report on Minors' Contracts. Section 1 disapplies the Infants Relief Act 1874 to contracts made in England and Wales after 9 June 1987 (and by a subsequent Order, to contracts in Northern Ireland from 26 July 1988). The result is to restore the application of the common law rules to such contracts. In particular, a contract made by a minor, which is later ratified by the minor on reaching 18, is now enforceable against the minor without the need for a fresh contract. Section 2 makes any guarantee supporting a loan to a minor enforceable against the adult guarantor, thus reversing the position established in *Coutts & Co v Browne-Lecky* (1946). Section 3 improves the remedies available to an adult who has contracted with a minor. We shall now examine in more detail the combined effect of the common law and the MCA 1987.

Contracts which are neither valid nor voidable do not bind the minor but are binding on the other party. As has been noted above, a minor may be bound by such a contract if he ratifies it, either expressly or impliedly, on reaching 18. Although the minor can enforce the contract against the other party, his remedies are limited since he will not be able to obtain an order of specific performance because of lack of mutuality.

Once the contract has been performed by the minor, he or she cannot recover money paid or property transferred under the contract except in the same circumstances in which such a remedy would be available to an adult, i.e. where there has been a total failure of consideration. The case of *Stocks* v *Wilson* (1913) and s 3(1) of the MCA 1987 support the view that a minor acquires title (rights of ownership) to any property transferred to

the minor under such a contract. Similarly, a minor can transfer title in property under a non-binding contract. A minor may be liable to restore certain benefits which he has received under a contract which does not bind him. Section 3(1) of the MCA 1987 provides that where a contract has been made with a minor which is unenforceable against him, or he has repudiated it, because he was a minor, the court may, if it thinks it just and equitable to do so, require him to return the property or any property representing that which he has acquired. The scope of the statutory remedy is as follows:

(a) The minor can be made to return the goods and money which he still has in his possession. So if Sebastian, age 17, acquires a case of champagne on credit and fails to pay he can be required to return the goods to the seller.

(b) If the minor has exchanged the original goods for other property, the court may require him to hand over the goods received in exchange. So if Sebastian, in the example above, has bartered a bottle of champagne for a dozen quail's eggs, the seller of the champagne may be able to recover the quail's eggs.

(c) If the minor has sold the original goods for cash, he can be ordered to hand over the sale proceeds. So if Sebastian sold the case of champagne for cash, he could be required to hand over the money to the seller.

(d) If the minor has consumed or disposed of the goods, or the proceeds of any sale of the goods, he cannot be made to compensate the other party. So if Sebastian drank the champagne or used the proceeds of any sale of the champagne to pay for an evening at a night club, he could not be required to compensate the unpaid seller.

Section 3(2) of the MCA 1987 expressly preserves the remedies which were available before the MCA was passed. The equitable doctrine of restitution allows an adult to recover money or property acquired by a minor as a result of fraud. The remedy is confined to restitution of the actual property acquired. Thus, if a minor has parted with the goods or the precise notes and coins, this remedy is not available. In practice, adults seeking restitution are likely to base their claims on the statutory remedy contained in s 3(1) since it is not subject to the same limitations which apply to the equitable remedy.

Drunks and mental patients

Section 3 of the Sale of Goods Act 1979 provides that they are required to pay a reasonable price for necessaries in the same way as minors. Other kinds of contract are governed by common law. If a person is suffering from mental disability or drunkenness at the time of making the contract, he will be able to avoid his liabilities if he can show that he did not understand what the agreement was about and the other person was aware of his disability.

The judges of the Court of Protection may exercise wide powers over the property and affairs of mental patients placed in their care under the Mental Health Act 1983. They can make contracts on behalf of the patient and carry out contracts already made by him.

The Mental Capacity Act 2005 establishes a new statutory framework to protect adults who lack mental capacity and are unable to make their own decisions. Section 7 of the 2005 Act provides that a person lacking capacity must pay for necessary goods and services. The Act came into force on 1 April 2007.

Genuineness of consent

The most basic requirement of a contract is the presence of an agreement. It must have been entered into voluntarily and involved 'a genuine meeting of minds'. The agreement may be invalidated by a number of factors – mistake, misrepresentation, duress and undue influence.

Mistake

Types of mistake

There are three possible types of mistake which may be made:

bilateral mistake

1 A common mistake is a situation where both parties make the same mistake. The parties have entered into an agreement on the assumption that a certain state of affairs exists but they subsequently discover that this is not the case. The parties may have agreed to the sale of certain goods but unknown to either of them, the goods have been destroyed (see *Couturier* v *Hastie* below).

2 A mutual mistake is where the parties are at cross purposes. For example, A offers to sell his car to B. B accepts thinking that A wishes to sell his Bentley, but A is referring to his other car, which is a Jaguar.

3 A **unilateral mistake** is a situation where only one of the parties is mistaken and the other party either knows, or is assumed to know, that a mistake has been made.

Although there are three types of mistake, if the situations are analysed in terms of whether an agreement has been reached, there are really only two types of mistake. In the case of **common mistake**, the parties are in agreement; there is *consensus ad idem*. They are agreed about the same thing, but both are mistaken about some fundamental aspect of the contract. The parties would accept that they have an agreement but would argue that it has been rendered a nullity because of the fundamental common mistake they have made. In the case of **mutual and unilateral mistake**, the argument is that there is no agreement at all, because the acceptance does not match the offer.

The effect of a mistake in common law

1 Common mistake

The general rule of common law is that a common mistake does not affect the validity of a contract.

Bell v *Lever Bros Ltd* (1932)

B and S had entered into five-year contracts to act as chairman and vice-chairman respectively of a company in which LB Ltd had a controlling interest. LB Ltd wished to dispense with their services and, because they still had some time to run on their contracts, it was agreed that B and S would receive £30,000 and £20,000 respectively for loss of office. Unknown to LB Ltd, B and S had been engaged in activities which would have entitled LB Ltd to terminate their contracts without compensation for breach of contract. LB Ltd sought to recover the money it had paid to B and S on the ground that the agreement to pay them compensation was void for mistake. The House of Lords held by a majority of three to two that this was a case of common mistake, i.e. both parties had made the same mistake. (B and S had managed to convince a jury that when they had agreed to compensation for loss of office, they had forgotten about their previous misconduct. Both parties thought B and S were entitled to compensation.) LB Ltd got what it bargained for – the termination of B's contract and S's contract. LB Ltd was mistaken about the qualities of B and S, but this kind of mistake does not invalidate a contract.

Comment. In 1949 in **Solle v Butcher** Denning LJ in the Court of Appeal argued that in cases of common mistake where the contract is valid at common law, a court may intervene and rescind the agreement on terms in exercise of its equitable jurisdiction. In a more recent case the Court of Appeal reviewed the apparent conflict between the decision of the House of Lords in **Bell** and the approach taken by the Court of Appeal in **Solle**. In **Great Peace Shipping Ltd v Tsavliris (International) Ltd** (2002), the defendants offered to provide salvage services to a ship called the *Cape Providence* which had got into difficulties in the South Indian Ocean. They asked hirers (H) to find a vessel which was close to the *Cape Providence* and willing to assist with the evacuation of the crew. H was advised that the *Great Peace* was the nearest vessel, and on this basis entered into a charter with the owners of the *Great Peace* for a minimum of five days while it diverted to help the *Cape Providence*. After the contract was concluded, the defendants discovered that the *Great Peace* was 400 miles away from the *Cape Providence* and there was another vessel much closer. The defendants refused to pay for the hire of the *Great Peace* on the grounds that the charter was void at common law for mistake and/or the charter was voidable for a 'common' mistake and could be rescinded in equity. The Court of Appeal held this was a case of common mistake as in **Bell**. The court took the view that it was not possible to reconcile **Solle** with **Bell** and the previous decision of the Court of Appeal in **Solle** should be disregarded. In the present case, the distance between the two vessels was not so great as to confound the common assumption of both parties that the vessels were sufficiently close to each other to allow the *Great Peace* to carry out the service for which she had been chartered. The contract for the hire of *Great Peace* was valid and the defendants were liable to pay the hire charges.

Leaf v International Galleries (1950)

Mr Leaf bought a painting of 'Salisbury Cathedral' from International Galleries for £85. The gallery attributed the painting to John Constable. When Leaf tried to sell the painting five years later, he was informed that it was not by Constable. Both the buyer and seller had made a common mistake about the quality and value of the painting but this did not affect the validity of the contract.

There are some kinds of common mistake which so undermine the agreement that the contract is void. If this is the case, no rights of ownership can pass and any goods which have changed hands can be recovered.

A common mistake will invalidate the contract in the following situations:

1 Mistakes of law. It used to be the case that a mistake of law would not invalidate a contract on the basis that everyone is presumed to know the law (a principle expressed in the Latin as *ignorantia juris non excusat*). However, in *Kleinwort Benson Ltd v Lincoln City Council* (1998), the House of Lords took the view that 'the rule precluding recovery of money paid under a mistake of law could no longer be maintained' (see p 304 ○ for a fuller discussion of the decision in *Kleinwort*).

2 Mistakes as to the existence of the subject matter of the contract. When the parties contract in the mistaken belief that a particular thing is in existence, but in fact it has ceased to exist, the contract is void. These situations are known as cases of *res extincta*.

Couturier v Hastie (1856)

A contract was made for the sale of Indian corn which the parties believed to be on board a ship bound for the UK. Unknown to the parties, the corn had overheated during the voyage and been landed at the nearest port and sold. The House of Lords held that the agreement was void.

The common law *res extincta* rules are reflected in the provisions of the Sale of Goods Act 1979. Section 6 provides: 'where there is a contract for the sale of specific goods and the goods without the knowledge of the seller have perished at the time when the contract is made, the contract is void'. In some situations, the non-existence of the subject matter will not render the contract void. A court may be prepared to place responsibility for non-existence on one of the parties.

McRae v Commonwealth Disposals Commission (1951)

The Commission contracted to sell to McRae the wreck of an oil tanker which was described as lying on Jourmand Reef off Papua. McRae incurred considerable expenditure in preparation for the salvage operation. In fact, there was no tanker anywhere near the specified location and no place known as Jourmand Reef. The High Court of Australia awarded damages to McRae for breach of contract. It was held that the contract contained an implied promise by the Commission that there was a tanker at the stated location.

3 Mistake as to title. This is where the parties are mistaken about the ownership of the subject matter of the contract. This is sometimes referred to as *res sua*.

Cooper v *Phibbs* (1867)

C agreed to lease a salmon fishery from P. Unknown to both C and P, C already owned the fishery. The House of Lords set the agreement aside. However, they did not apply common law principles to do so, but granted the equitable remedy of rescission. Lord Atkin in *Bell* v *Lever Bros* (see above), thought the contract in *Cooper* to be void at common law for *res sua*.

2 Mutual or unilateral mistakes

As we have noted earlier the issue with mutual or unilateral mistakes is whether an agreement has been reached at all.

1 A **mutual mistake** is where the parties are talking at cross-purposes. The approach taken by the courts is to consider objectively whether there is an agreement based on either party's understanding or whether there is such a level of misunderstanding that it is impossible to find any agreement at all. The following case provides an example of this approach.

Scriven Bros & Co v *Hindley & Co* (1913)

The defendants wished to purchase a quantity of hemp from the claimants at auction. There were two lots from the same ship in the auctioneer's catalogue: one of 47 bales and the other of 176 bales. The catalogue did not state that the larger lot consisted of tow not hemp. The defendants, thinking that both lots consisted of hemp, bid successfully for the larger lot (of tow) paying well above the market price (for tow). The auctioneer realised that the defendants had made a mistake but thought that they had misjudged the price of the tow. The defendants refused to pay, arguing that there had been a mutual mistake. The court held that the contract was void for mistake. Applying an objective test, a reasonable person would have been unclear about the content of each lot.

Another example is provided by the following case.

Raffles v *Wichelhaus* (1864)

The defendant agreed to buy cotton which was described as 'arriving on the *Peerless* from Bombay'. There were two ships called the *Peerless* sailing from Bombay, one in October and the other in December. It was held that there was no binding contract between the parties as the defendant meant one ship and the claimant the other.

2 A **unilateral mistake** is where one party is aware, or presumed to be aware, of the other party's mistake. In this situation, the test is a subjective one, as it is concerned with the awareness of the parties, rather than the objective views of a reasonable third party. As with other examples of mistake the general starting point is that a unilateral mistake does not invalidate a contract. However, if there is a fundamental mistake as to the nature of the promise being made, a court may conclude that the contract is void. There are two main situations where a unilateral mistake will invalidate a contract.

(a) Mistake as to the terms of the contract. This is where one party makes an offer to another party and he is aware that the other party is fundamentally mistaken about the terms.

Hartog v *Colin and Shields* (1939)

The defendants offered to sell a quantity of hareskins to the claimant at a certain price per pound. They actually meant to offer them at a price per piece. (The price of a piece was approximately one-third of a pound.) The preliminary negotiations had been conducted on the basis of the skins were being offered at a price per piece and there was a trade custom that prices were set by reference to pieces. The court held that the claimant must have realised that the defendant had made a mistake. The contract was void for mistake.

Comment. A more recent example of this principle is illustrated by the Singapore case of *Chwee Kin Keong* v *Digilandmall.com Pte Ltd* (2005). The defendants mistakenly advertised laser printers for sale on the internet for S$66. The correct price was S$3,854. Before the mistake was detected and corrected, the six claimants placed orders for a total of 1,606 printers.

The defendants sought to cancel the transactions as soon as they became aware of the error. The Singapore Court of Appeal held that there was no contract. The claimants had 'snapped up' the defendants' offer indicating that they were well aware that the defendants had made a mistake.

(b) Mistake as to the identity of one of the parties. If one party makes a mistake about the identity of the person he is contracting with, this may invalidate the contract on the basis of a unilateral mistake. A typical 'mistaken identity' case is where a crook (C) fraudulently represents to the owner of goods (O) that he is someone else (X), and on this basis O hands over his goods to C by way of a sale either on credit or in return for a (worthless) cheque. C sells the goods to an innocent buyer (B) and then disappears, pocketing the proceeds of his deception. When the fraud is discovered, O seeks to recover his goods from B by suing in the tort of conversion. This typical scenario is set out in Figure 7.1.

The courts have tended to take different approaches depending on whether the parties had face-to-face dealings or agreement was reached by written correspondence.

Where the parties have not met and the agreement has been concluded in writing, if the identity of the party contracted with is material to the contract, then a mistake as to identity will result in the contract being void.

Cundy v Lindsay (1878)

Lindsay & Co, Belfast linen manufacturers, received an order for a large quantity of handkerchiefs from a rogue called Blenkarn. The rogue had signed his name in such a way that it looked like 'Blenkiron & Co', a well-known, respectable firm. Lindsay & Co despatched the goods on credit to Blenkarn who resold 250 dozen to Cundy. Blenkarn did not pay for the goods and was later convicted of obtaining goods by false pretences. Lindsay & Co sued Cundy for conversion. The House of Lords held that the contract between Lindsay & Co and Blenkarn was void for mistake. Lindsay & Co intended to deal with Blenkiron & Co, not the rogue, Blenkarn. Cundy was liable in conversion.

Where the parties have face-to-face dealings, the courts are likely to assume that the identity of the other party is not material and that the mistaken party O intends to contract with the person in front of him. In this situation the contract will be valid until O realises that he has been misled and avoids the contract for a fraudulent misrepresentation.

Phillips v Brooks Ltd (1919)

A man entered the claimant's shop to buy some jewellery. He selected various items of jewellery and offered to pay by cheque. While writing the cheque the man said, 'You see who I am, I am Sir George Bullough.'

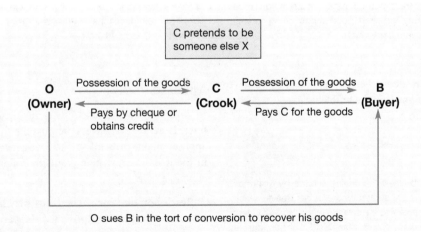

Figure 7.1 **A typical mistaken identity case**

He gave an address in St James's Square. The claimant knew of a Sir George Bullough and, after checking in a directory that Sir George had an address in St James's Square, he asked if the man would like to take the jewellery with him. The man replied that the jeweller had better let the cheque clear first but he would like to take the ring as it was his wife's birthday the following day. The cheque was dishonoured. The man, who was in fact a rogue called North, pledged the ring with the defendant pawnbrokers. The claimant sued the defendants for the return of the ring or its value. It was held that the contract between the claimant and the rogue North was not void for mistake but voidable for fraud. At the time the contract was made the claimant intended to deal with the person physically in his shop and his identity was immaterial. As the claimant had not rescinded the contract by the time North pledged the ring, the defendants obtained good title (rights of ownership).

Lewis v *Averay* (1971)

Lewis sold his car to a man who claimed he was Richard Greene, the star of the popular 1960s television series *Robin Hood*. The man paid by cheque, producing a pass to Pinewood Studios as proof of his identity. He resold the car to Averay. The cheque had been taken from a stolen cheque book and was later dishonoured. Lewis sued Averay in the tort of conversion. The Court of Appeal held that Lewis intended to deal with the man actually in front of him, despite his fraudulent claim to be Richard Greene. The contract between Lewis and the rogue was not void for mistake, but rather voidable for a fraudulent misrepresentation. Since Lewis had not avoided the contract by the time the rogue sold the car to Averay, Averay acquired good rights of ownership. He was not liable in conversion.

The 'mistaken identity' cases were recently reviewed by the House of Lords in the following case.

Shogun Finance Ltd v *Hudson* (2004)

A fraudster R obtained P's driving licence by dishonest means. R visited the showrooms of a car dealer, where he introduced himself to the sales manager as Mr Durlabh Patel. R agreed to buy a Mitsubishi Shogun car for £22,250, subject to obtaining hire-purchase finance. R completed a hire-purchase proposal form in the name of Mr Patel. The sales manager contacted Shogun Finance's sales support team, which ran a check on the details of Mr Patel provided by R. Shogun was satisfied with the information provided and it accepted the hire-purchase proposal. R paid a 10 per cent deposit, partly in cash and partly by cheque. The cheque was subsequently dishonoured. The sales manager handed over the car with full documentation. R sold the car to Mr Hudson for £17,000. Hudson bought the car for his own use and not as a dealer. R disappeared without trace. Shogun was claiming the return of the car or its value from Hudson. Hudson argued that he had obtained good title to the car by virtue of the provisions of s 27 of the Hire Purchase Act 1964. The House of Lords held (by a majority of three to two) that Shogun was entitled to recover the car. Lord Phillips concluded that:

> the correct approach in the present case is to treat the agreement as one concluded in writing and to approach the identification of the parties to that agreement as turning on its construction. The particulars in the agreement are only capable of applying to Mr Patel. It was the intention of the rogue that they should identify Mr Patel as the hirer. The hirer was so identified by Shogun. Before deciding to enter into the agreement they checked that Mr Patel existed and that he was worthy of credit. On that basis they decided to contract with him and with no-one else. Mr Patel was the hirer under the agreement. As the agreement was concluded without his authority, it was a nullity. The rogue took no title under it and was in no position to convey any title to Mr Hudson.

Lords Nicholls and Millett, dissenting, took the view that in cases of mistaken identity the distinction between face-to-face dealings and transactions concluded in writing should be removed and a person should be presumed to contract with the person with whom he or she was actually dealing. In their minority judgment their Lordships preferred the decisions of *Phillips* v *Brooks* and *Lewis* v *Averay* to *Cundy* v *Lindsay*.

Mistake in equity

At common law, mistake only rarely invalidates a contract. It may, nevertheless, be possible for the court to apply equitable principles to achieve a measure of justice in the case. A court may grant the following forms of equitable relief.

1 Rescission on terms. The court may be prepared to set aside an agreement, provided the parties accept the conditions imposed by the court for a fairer solution to the problem.

Grist v Bailey (1966)

Bailey agreed to sell a house to Grist for £850. The price was based on both parties' belief that the house had a sitting tenant. The value of the house with vacant possession would have been about £2,250. Unknown to the parties, the tenants had died and their son did not stay on in the property. The judge held that the contract was not void at common law but he was prepared to set the contract aside provided Bailey offered to sell the property to Grist for the proper market price of £2,250.

2 Rectification. If a mistake is made in reducing an oral agreement into writing, the court may rectify the document so that it expresses the true intention of the parties. In the following case the Court of Appeal was asked to consider a trial judge's decision to order rectification.

George Wimpey UK Ltd v VI Construction Ltd (2005)

Wimpey had entered into a contract to buy land from VI Construction for the development of residential flats. During the negotiations, it had been understood that Wimpey would pay an 'overage payment' if the overall sale prices of the flats exceeded a base amount and a formula was proposed which took into account the value of enhancements to each flat (referred to as '+ E'). How-ever, the contract omitted '+ E'. The omission benefited VI Construction by approximately £800,000. Wimpey brought an action against VI Construction for rectification of the contract based on mistake. The trial judge concluded that there had been a unilateral mistake and ordered rectification of the contract to include '+ E'. VI Construction successfully appealed. The Court of Appeal held that it was not open to the trial judge to infer dishonesty on the part of VI Construction's surveyor and director and Wimpey had not discharged the onus on it of providing convincing proof that VI Construction had actual know-ledge of Wimpey's mistake. The court noted that Wimpey was one of the country's largest construction and develop-ment enterprises and therefore very experienced in these matters whereas VI Construction had no relevant experi-ence. Peter Gibson LJ concluded: 'I recognise that the mistake has had serious consequences for Wimpey and brought a benefit to [VI Construction] which it did not foresee in putting forward the formula. But it is not deter-minative of whether Wimpey can successfully invoke the exceptional jurisdiction to rectify for mutual mistake.'

3 Specific performance. A court may refuse to grant an order of specific performance against a party who made a mistake, if it would be unfair to enforce the contract against him.

Documents mistakenly signed

There are a group of cases where typically a person is induced by a false statement to sign a document which is fundamentally different from what he thought he was signing. These situations form a separate category of mistake at common law.

As a general rule, a person who signs a document is assumed to have read, understood and agreed to its contents. Exceptionally, a person may be able to plead *non est factum* – 'it is not my deed'. Three elements must be present if the contract is to be avoided:

(i)   the signature must have been induced by fraud;
(ii) the document signed must be fundamentally dif-ferent from that thought to be signed; and
(iii) the signer must not have acted negligently.

Saunders v Anglia Building Society (1971)

Mrs Gallie was a 78-year-old widow. In June 1962 she was visited by her nephew, Walter Parkin, and a Mr Lee. Lee asked her to sign a document, which he told her was a deed of gift of her house to her nephew Walter. Mrs Gallie had broken her spectacles and, as she could not read without them, she signed the document with-out reading it through. The document which Mrs Gallie signed was in fact an assignment of her leasehold interest in the house to Lee. The Anglia Building Society advanced £2,000 to Lee on the strength of the deed. Mrs Gallie brought an action against Lee and the building society claiming that the deed was void. She pleaded *non est factum*. She succeeded at first instance against both Lee and the building society. However, the building society won on appeal to the Court of Appeal. Then Mrs Gallie died and an appeal to the House of Lords was brought by Mrs Saunders, the executrix of her estate. The House of Lords held that the plea of *non est factum* must fail. Although her signature had been induced by fraud, the document she signed was not fundamentally different from that which she thought she had signed. Moreover, persons wishing to plead *non est factum* must show that they exercised reasonable care in signing. Mrs Gallie had not taken the trouble to read the document.

The principles set out in *Saunders* will apply to a person who signs a blank form (*United Dominions Trust Ltd v Western* (1975)).

Misrepresentation

The formation of a contract is often preceded by a series of negotiations between the parties. Some of the statements made may later turn out to be false. The nature of the statement will determine whether a remedy is available and, if it is, the type of remedy (see Figure 7.2).

A false statement, which is not incorporated into the contract, is known as a misrepresentation. A misrepresentation is a false statement made by one party which induces the other to enter into a contract. As a general rule, a positive statement must be made; keeping quiet about something does not normally amount to misrepresentation. In a recent case the seller of a house failed to disclose that it been the scene of a gruesome murder of a young girl, with the possibility that parts of the victim's body might still be hidden in the house. The silence of the seller was held not to amount to a misrepresentation (*Sykes v Taylor-Rose* (2004)).

Gestures, smiles and nods can amount to a statement. A course of conduct can also amount to a representation.

Spice Girls Ltd v Aprilia World Service BV (2000)

The claimant, SGL, was a company formed to promote the Spice Girls pop group. At the beginning of May 1998, SGL entered into a contract with the defendant, AWS, an Italian company which manufactures motorcycles and scooters, to film a TV commercial to be shown until March 1999. When the contract was signed, the Spice Girls consisted of five members. However, a month earlier Geri Halliwell had announced to the other members of the group and its management that she intended to leave the group at the end of September 1998. It had been decided to keep this information confidential and AWS was not informed when the contract was signed. In an action by SGL for money allegedly due under the agreement, the High Court held that by participating in the 'shoot' of the TV commercial, SGL represented by conduct that it did not know or had no reasonable grounds to believe that any of the members of the group intended to leave. As the members of the group knew Ms Halliwell intended to leave during the period when the commercial was to be used, this amounted to a misrepresentation.

There are certain situations where a failure to speak will amount to an actionable misrepresentation:

- where there is a relationship of good faith between the parties, e.g. between partners;
- where the contract is one of utmost good faith, e.g. proposals for insurance cover;
- where a half-truth is offered. In one case a solicitor stated that he was not aware of any restrictive covenants on a piece of land, which was literally true, but, if he had bothered to read relevant documents, he would have discovered that there were indeed restrictive covenants (*Nottingham Patent Brick and Tile Co v Butler* (1886));
- where there has been a change in circumstances between the time of the negotiations and the conclusion of the contract.

With v O'Flanagan (1936)

The defendant was a doctor who wished to sell his medical practice. In January 1934, during the course of negotiations with the claimant, he stated (correctly) that the practice was worth £2,000 a year. Unfortunately, the

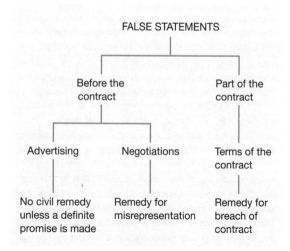

Figure 7.2 Remedies for false statements

defendant then fell ill and the practice was run by other doctors. By the time the contract of sale to the claimant was signed in May, receipts had fallen to £5 per week. It was held that the defendant's failure to inform the claimant of the change of circumstances between initial negotiations and the conclusion of the contract was a misrepresentation.

A failure to correct a representation may constitute an actionable misrepresentation.

Fitzroy Robinson Ltd v Mentmore Towers Ltd; Fitzoy Robinson Ltd v Good Start Ltd and another (2009)

The claimants (FRL), a firm of architects, were engaged by the defendants in connection with a scheme to develop buildings in London and Mentmore Towers. JB was a director of FRL. He had been responsible for putting together the bid documents and was involved in all the pre-contract meetings. The defendants were told by FRL's Chief Executive that JB would be the team leader for the project. FRL started work in March 2006 although the contracts were not finally executed until May 2006. The projects were due to be completed in March 2009. On 17 March JB resigned and was required to work out his notice of 12 months. The claimants did not inform the defendants of JB's resignation until November 2006. In June 2007 the defendants stopping making payments of fees payable under the contracts and in December the claimants were informed that the projects had been suspended. The claimants brought claims for unpaid fees. The High Court held that the claimants' failure to correct the representation that JB would be involved throughout the project was a misrepresentation. Moreover, it was a fraudulent misrepresentation; between the 21 March, when it was clear that JB could not be persuaded to stay at FRL, and the execution of the contracts in May, the Chief Executive knowingly and dishonestly failed to correct the representation as to JB's involvement in the project, because he feared that FRL might not be awarded the contract. However the defendants had failed to show that JB's departure had caused any delay to the project and so any loss would be modest.

The misrepresentation must involve a statement of fact, opinion or intention. A statement of law may amount to a misrepresentation.

Pankhania v London Borough of Hackney (2002)

The claimant (P) bought a property in London at auction from the defendants. The auction catalogue stated that the tenant of the property had a licence whereas in fact the tenant held a secure tenancy. The High Court held that the principle that no action could lay for a misrepresentation as to law had not survived the House of Lords decision in **Kleinwort Benson Ltd v Lincoln City Council** (1998) (see further, p 304 (see further, p 304)).

A statement of intention will not normally amount to a misrepresentation because a representation is a statement about existing facts or past events. However, if a person misrepresents what he intends to do in the future, he may be liable for misrepresentation.

Edgington v Fitzmaurice (1885)

The directors of a company invited members of the public to lend money to the company. The directors stated that the money would be used to improve the company's buildings and extend the business. The directors' real intention was to pay off the company's existing debts. It was held that the directors' statement was a fraudulent misrepresentation. As Bowen LJ put it: 'There must be a misstatement of an existing fact: but the state of a man's mind is as much a fact as the state of his digestion. It is true that it is very difficult to prove what the state of a man's mind at a particular time is, but if it can be ascertained it is as much a fact as anything else. A misrepresentation as to the state of a man's mind is, therefore, a misstatement of fact.'

A statement of opinion will not normally be actionable as a misrepresentation because an opinion is a statement of belief which is not capable of proof.

Bissett v Wilkinson (1927)

During the course of negotiations for the sale of a farm in New Zealand to Wilkinson, Bissett stated that the land would support 2,000 sheep. The farm had not previously been used for grazing sheep and Wilkinson knew this. It was held that Bissett was merely expressing his opinion. There was no misrepresentation.

There are occasions when a statement of opinion may amount to a representation of fact. If it can be established that the person making the statement did not hold that opinion or that he was in a position to know the facts on which his opinion was based, there may be an actionable misrepresentation.

Smith v Land and House Property Corporation (1884)

The vendors of a hotel stated that it was 'let to a Mr Frederick Fleck (a most desirable tenant)'. In fact, Mr Fleck was in arrears of rent. It was held that the description of Mr Fleck was not a mere expression of opinion. The vendors were in a position to know the facts about their tenant. Their opinion that he was a desirable tenant was not supported by facts within their knowledge.

It must be shown that the statement has induced the person to whom it was made to enter into the contract. If the person attempts to check the truth of what has been said, he clearly has not relied on the statement.

Attwood v Small (1838)

The seller of a mine made exaggerated claims about its earning capacity. The buyer appointed expert agents to investigate the mine. The agents reported that the seller's claims were true and the sale went ahead. The House of Lords held that an action by the buyer to rescind the contract must fail because the buyer had relied on his agents' report rather than the seller's statements.

Comment. If a person is given an opportunity to test the accuracy of a statement, but he does not take it, he can still bring a claim (*Redgrave v Hurd* (1881)).

Kinds of misrepresentation and their effects

There are three kinds of misrepresentation: fraudulent, negligent or innocent. In each case, the contract is voidable.

1 Fraudulent misrepresentation. A person will be liable for fraud if he makes a statement which he knows to be false, or he has no belief in its truth or he is reckless, careless whether it is true or false (*Derry v Peek* (1889)).

The injured party may rescind the contract and also sue for damages for the tort of deceit. The assessment of damages for a fraudulent misrepresentation was discussed by the House of Lords in the following case.

Smith New Court Securities Ltd v Scrimgeour Vickers (1996)

The claimant, Smith New Court, was induced by a fraudulent misrepresentation made by the defendants' employee to buy shares in Ferranti at 82.25p per share. At the time of purchase, the shares were trading at about 78p per share. Unknown to either party, the shares were grossly overvalued because Ferranti was the victim of a fraud totally unconnected with the current case. When the fraud became known, the price of the shares slumped. The question for the court was whether the claimant could recover the difference between the price it had paid (the contract price) and the market price (4.25p per share) or the difference between the contract price and the value of the shares had it known of the fraud (44p per share). The House of Lords held that the claimant was entitled to recover for all the damage resulting from the transaction. The loss suffered by the claimant was £10,764,005, which represented the difference between the contract price and the value of the shares with knowledge of the fraud.

The House of Lords has confirmed that a defendant who makes a fraudulent misrepresentation cannot raise a defence of contributory negligence (*Standard Chartered Bank* v *Pakistan National Shipping Corporation* (2003)).

2 Negligent misrepresentation. This is where the person making the false statement has no reasonable grounds for believing the statement to be true. Damages may be awarded in tort for a negligent misstatement under the principle established in *Hedley Byrne & Co Ltd* v *Heller and Partners Ltd* (1963) (discussed in Chapter 11 ○).

Esso Petroleum Co Ltd v Mardon (1976)

Mardon entered into a three-year tenancy agreement with Esso in respect of a newly developed petrol filling station. During the negotiations an experienced dealer representative employed by Esso told Mardon that the station would have an annual throughput of 200,000 gallons by the third year. Despite Mardon's best efforts, the throughput only reached 86,000 by the third year. Mardon lost a considerable sum of money and was unable to pay for petrol supplied by Esso. Esso sued for money owed and possession of the petrol station. Mardon counterclaimed for rescission of the tenancy agreement and damages for negligence. The Court of Appeal applied the principle established in *Hedley Byrne & Co Ltd* v *Heller and Partners Ltd*. When Esso's representative forecast the station's potential as part of the pre-contractual negotiations, a duty of care arose. Esso intended that its forecast would be relied upon by Mardon. Esso was in breach of the duty of care because of the error made by its representative. Esso was liable in damages for its negligence.

Comment. Although this case was decided in 1976, the events to which the decision relates took place in the early 1960s, before the introduction of the Misrepresentation Act 1967.

Damages may now also be awarded under s 2(1) of the Misrepresentation Act 1967.

Howard Marine and Dredging Co Ltd v *A Ogden & Sons (Excavations) Ltd* (1978)

The defendants won a contract to carry out excavation work for the Northumbrian Water Authority. The work involved dumping the spoil at sea, for which purpose the defendants needed to charter seagoing barges. The defendants approached the claimants who were the owners of two suitable barges. During the course of negotiations, the claimants' marine manager stated that the payload of the barges was 1,600 tonnes. This was based on the deadweight figure of 1,800 tonnes given in the Lloyd's Register. However, the Register was wrong. The shipping documents, which the marine manager had seen, gave the true deadweight as 1,195 tonnes, and this gave a payload of 1,055 tonnes. The contract to charter the barges did not mention these figures.

The defendants fell behind schedule because of the shortfall in the capacity of the barges. They ceased to pay the charter hire and were sued by the claimants. The defendants counterclaimed for damages under the Misrepresentation Act 1967 and in negligence at common law. The Court of Appeal held the claimants were liable under s 2(1) of the Misrepresentation Act 1967 for the misrepresentation of the barges' capacity. The claimants were unable to prove that their marine manager had reasonable grounds for relying on the capacity figures given in the Register in preference to the figures contained in the shipping documents. The court did not reach a firm conclusion about the claimants' liability for negligence at common law.

Comment.
(i) The Court of Appeal in this case was concerned only with the question of liability and not the measure of damages. There had been some uncertainty as to whether the basis of damages under s 2(1) of the Misrepresentation Act 1967 was contractual or tortious. However, in *Sharneyford Supplies Ltd* v *Edge* (1987) the Court of Appeal held that it should be tortious. The effect of this is that the representee can only recover loss which he has incurred through reliance on the misrepresentation. However, the damages will be assessed in the same way as for fraud so that the misrepresentee can recover for all losses flowing from the misrepresentation (*Royscot Trust Ltd* v *Rogerson* (1991)).

(ii) In *IFE Fund SA* v *Goldman Sachs International* (2007) the Court of Appeal considered (*obiter*) the relationship between an action under the Misrepresentation Act and in tort. Waller LJ commented that where there is a contract between the parties, the Misrepresentation Act would apply. If the Act did not provide a remedy, there would be no room for an action for negligent misstatement.

The injured party is more likely to be successful under the Act, because it reverses the normal burden of proof. Thus, the defendant will only escape liability if he or she can prove that the statement was made innocently. The judge may also award rescission as well as damages.

3 Innocent misrepresentation. An innocent misrepresentation is a false statement made by a person who had reasonable grounds to believe that it was true, not only when it was made, but also when the contract was entered into. The basic remedy is rescission of the contract: under s 2(2) of the Misrepresentation Act 1967, the court may in its discretion award damages instead. There was some uncertainty about whether damages could be awarded under s 2(2) if rescission was no longer available because, for example, a third party had acquired rights in the subject matter of the contract (see below). In *Thomas Witter Ltd* v *TBP Industries Ltd* (1996) the Court of Appeal decided that damages could be awarded under s 2(2), provided that the right to rescind had existed at some time, but it was not necessary for the right to rescind to exist at the time the court gave judgment.

Rescission

Rescission aims to restore the parties to their pre-contractual positions. Money or goods which have changed hands must be returned. Like all equitable remedies, it is not available as of right. In particular, the court may refuse to award rescission in the following circumstances:

■ where the injured party has received some benefit under the contract or has in some way affirmed it: a long delay in taking legal action is taken as evidence of affirmation (*Leaf* v *International Galleries* (1950): see above, p 241);
■ where the parties cannot be restored to their original positions because, for example, goods have been destroyed or they have been sold to a third party (*Lewis* v *Averay* (1971): see above, p 244 ⬤).

Duress and undue influence

The general rule of law is that a contract will be valid only if the parties entered into it freely and voluntarily. At common law, where a party to a contract or his or her family is subjected to violence or threats of violence, the contract may be avoided on the grounds of duress.

Barton v Armstrong (1975)

Armstrong was the chairman and Barton the managing director of an Australian company. Armstrong threatened to have Barton killed if he did not sign an agreement to buy out Armstrong's interest in the company on very favourable terms. The Privy Council held that the agreement was signed under duress and could be avoided by Barton.

Traditionally, the common law doctrine of duress was limited to violence and threats of violence to the person. However, in recent years the courts have recognised economic duress as a factor which may invalidate consent and render a contract voidable.

North Ocean Shipping Co Ltd v Hyundai Construction Co Ltd (1978)

The defendant shipbuilders agreed to build a tanker for the claimant shipowners. The price was payable in US dollars in five instalments. After the first instalment had been paid, there was a sharp fall in the value of the US dollar and the defendants threatened to break the contract unless the claimants paid an extra 10 per cent on each of the remaining instalments. The claimants had already entered into a lucrative contract to charter the tanker on its completion and, anxious to take delivery, they reluctantly paid the increased instalments. Eight months later they brought an action to recover the excess over the original contract price. It was held that the contract was voidable on the grounds of economic duress, but that the claimants could not recover the excess because they had affirmed the contract by failing to protest before they did.

Atlas Express Ltd v Kafco (Importers and Distributors) Ltd (1989)

Atlas, a road carrier, entered into a contract with Kafco, a small company importing and distributing basketware, to deliver cartons of basketware which Kafco had sold to Woolworths. Atlas's manager had quoted a price of £1.10 per carton based on an assumption that each load would contain between 400 and 600 cartons. However, the first load contained only 200 cartons. Atlas's manager refused to carry any more cartons unless Kafco agreed to pay a minimum of £440 per load. Kafco was anxious about maintaining a good relationship with Woolworths but was unable easily to find another carrier. Accordingly, Kafco agreed to the new terms but later refused to pay. The High Court held that Kafco was not liable as Kafco's agreement to the new terms had been obtained by economic duress.

Equity recognises a more subtle form of pressure: undue influence. The relationship between the parties may be such that one occupies a position of dominance and influence over the other. There are several relationships, such as doctor and patient, solicitor and client, parent and child, where it is automatically assumed that undue influence has been at work. The contract will be set aside unless the dominant person can show that the complainant had independent advice. Where there is no special relationship between the parties, the claimant must prove that pressure was applied.

A number of cases have raised the question whether a presumption of undue influence is created by the relationship between a banker and his customer.

Lloyds Bank Ltd v *Bundy* (1974)

An elderly farmer, inexperienced in business matters, mortgaged his home and only asset to the bank to guarantee his son's business overdraft. The Court of Appeal set aside the guarantee and charge. The farmer had placed himself in the hands of the bank and had looked to the assistant bank manager for advice. It was clearly in the bank's interest that the farmer provided the guarantee. The court held that the presumption of undue influence applied. The bank had failed to rebut the presumption since the farmer had not been advised to seek independent advice.

The *Bundy* case is exceptional and normally the presumption does not apply to the banker/customer relationship.

National Westminster Bank plc v *Morgan* (1985)

Mrs Morgan agreed to the family home being mortgaged to secure an advance to her husband by the bank. She signed the legal charge after receiving assurances from the bank manager that the mortgage only covered the house loan and not her husband's business liability. Mr Morgan died. His only liability to the bank was in respect of the house loan. Mrs Morgan appealed against a possession order obtained by the bank, on the ground that the mortgage transaction should be set aside because of undue influence on the part of the bank. The House of Lords held that Mrs Morgan's action should fail. Although Mrs Morgan had not had the benefit of independent advice, the bank manager had not taken advantage of her and the transaction was not to her disadvantage.

The legal considerations involved in giving guarantees to secure business loans, including the effect of the decision of the House of Lords in the *Royal Bank of Scotland* v *Etridge* (**No 2**) (2001) case, are discussed in detail in Chapter 4 ○.

Legality

The principle of freedom of contract is subject to a basic rule that the courts will not uphold an agreement which is illegal or contrary to public policy. Where the contract involves some kind of moral wrongdoing, it will be illegal. If, however, the conduct is neither immoral nor blameworthy, but simply undesirable, the contract will be void. A court may object to an agreement either because of a rule of common law or because it is contrary to statute.

Contracts illegal at common law

The following agreements come into this category:

1 Contracts to commit crimes or civil wrongs, e.g. a contract to assassinate someone or to defraud HM Revenue & Customs.

2 Contracts involving sexual immorality, e.g. an agreement to pay an allowance to a mistress or any contract with an immoral purpose.

Pearce v *Brooks* (1866)

Pearce let a coach out on hire to a prostitute (Brooks) knowing that it would be used by her to ply her trade. The coach was returned in a damaged state. Pearce was unable to recover the hire charges or money for the damage, as the court refused to help him to enforce a contract for an immoral purpose.

---

3 Contracts tending to promote corruption in public life, e.g. a contract to bribe an official or to procure a title.

4 Contracts of trading with an enemy in wartime.

5 Contracts directed against the welfare of a friendly foreign state, e.g. a partnership intending to import whisky into America during Prohibition (*Foster* v *Driscoll* (1929)).

6 Contracts prejudicial to the administration of justice, e.g. a contract not to prosecute a person for an offence concerning the public.

Consequences of illegality

A contract which is illegal from the start will be void and unenforceable. Money or property transferred under the contract is not usually recoverable. This general rule is subject to three exceptions:

1 a party can recover money or property if he can establish his case without relying on the illegal contract, e.g. by suing in tort;
2 if the parties are not equally at fault, the less guilty party may be allowed to recover;
3 a party may recover if he repents before the contract has been substantially performed.

Some contracts are quite innocent at the outset, but become illegal because of the intention of one of the parties, e.g. a landlord lets out a flat, unaware of the tenant's intention to install his mistress in it. In this situation, one of the parties is innocent. The guilty party cannot sue on the contract or succeed in any way against the innocent party. The innocent party will protect his rights if he repudiates the contract as soon as he is aware of the illegality.

Contracts void at common law

There are three types of contract in this category:

1 Contracts to oust the jurisdiction of the courts. A clause which seeks to prevent the courts trying an issue is void. This rule does not affect 'binding in honour only' clauses, by which the parties agree not to create a contract.

2 Contracts prejudicial to the status of marriage. This includes a contract to restrain a person from marrying at all or except for one person. Contracts not to marry a person of a particular religious faith or nationality may be upheld if they are reasonable.

A contract which provides for a possible future separation of husband and wife will be void, but, if the marriage is breaking up, they may make a contract to provide for their immediate separation. Contracts to introduce men and women with a view to their subsequent marriage are void. These are known as marriage-brokage contracts.

3 Contracts in restraint of trade. These are contracts which restrict the future liberty of a person to carry on his business, trade or profession in any way he chooses. A contract in restraint of trade is contrary to public policy and void unless it is shown to be reasonable as between the parties and from the point of view of the community. A restraint will be reasonable if it is designed to protect legitimate interests, such as trade secrets or business connections. A restraint which is excessive as regards its area, time of operation or the trades it forbids will be void.

There are four main types of restraint which we will consider.

(a) A term in a contract of employment which restricts an employee's freedom of conduct either during the period of employment or after the employment has terminated. Such a restraint will only be reasonable if it protects the employer's interests and is not excessive. The only matters in which an employer has a legitimate interest is the protection of trade secrets and his customer connections. The following case involves an employer seeking to protect his trade secrets.

Forster & Sons Ltd v *Suggett* (1918)

The claimants were manufacturers of glass and glass bottles. They had trained their works manager in the use of certain secret processes, including the correct mixture of gas and air in the furnaces. The works manager had agreed that for a period of five years after his employment with the claimants ended he would not carry on in the UK, or be interested in, glass bottle manufacture or any other business connected with glass-making as carried on by the claimants. It was held that the restraint was enforceable. Secret processes are a legitimate object of protection and in this case the restraint was reasonable.

A distinction must be drawn between protecting trade secrets, which is a protectable interest, and preventing an employee from making use of knowledge and skills which he has acquired in the course of his employment, which is not protectable.

Herbert Morris Ltd v *Saxelby* (1916)

A seven-year restraint on an engineer employed by a leading UK manufacturer of hoisting machinery was declared void. Although the engineer had access to confidential information, such as drawings, charts and company systems, all that he could take away with him was a very general knowledge of the company's methods and systems. The House of Lords did not regard such knowledge as a trade secret.

In the *Forster* case, the employee was bound by an **express** term in his contract. An express term was not really needed as there is an implied duty on the part of employees not to reveal their employers' trade secrets or other highly confidential information. The implied duty will not cover all commercially sensitive information.

Faccenda Chicken Ltd v Fowler **(1986)**

The defendant, Fowler, had been employed as the claimant company's sales manager until he resigned to set up a rival business selling chickens from refrigerated vans. Several of Faccenda's employees joined Fowler in his new business. Their contracts of employment with Faccenda did not include an express term restricting their activities if they left their jobs with Faccenda. Faccenda argued that Fowler and his colleagues had broken an implied term of the contract by making use of confidential sales information. The Court of Appeal confirmed the existence of an implied duty of confidentiality but held that the information which Faccenda was trying to protect was not confidential.

An alternative form of protection for an employer is to insert a so-called 'garden leave' clause in an employee's contract of employment (***Evening Standard Co Ltd v Henderson*** (1987)). Such a clause typically requires the employee to give a long period of notice, e.g. one year. During the notice period, the employee can be barred from the workplace to stop him from acquiring any further information, and he can also be prevented from working for a new employer until his notice period expires. Although the employee will continue to be paid, he or she is left with nothing to do but look after their garden.

An employer is also entitled to protect his customer connections by preventing employees from enticing his customers away from him. A restraint of this kind will only be valid if the nature of the employment is such that the employee has personal contact with customers and some influence over them. Restraints have been upheld in the case of a solicitor's clerk (***Fitch v Dewes*** (1921)), a milk roundsman (***Home Counties Dairies v Skilton*** (1970)) and an estate agent's clerk (***Scorer v Seymour Jones*** (1966)). However, an agreement by a manager of a bookmakers not to engage in a similar business to his employer within a 12-mile radius on the termination of his employment was not upheld as the manager did not have face-to-face contact with his customers (***S W Strange Ltd v Mann*** (1965)).

Once it is established that the restraint only protects a legitimate interest, the next step is to show that it is reasonable in the circumstances. The restraint must not be excessive as regards its area and time of operation. The two factors are complementary: the wider the area of the restraint, the shorter the duration which might be regarded as reasonable, and vice versa. There are no precise limits; each case is decided on its merits. In ***Fitch v Dewes*** (1921) an agreement by a solicitor's clerk never to practise within seven miles of Tamworth Town Hall was held to be reasonable, whereas in ***Commercial Plastics Ltd v Vincent*** (1964) one of the grounds for finding a one-year restraint to be unreasonable in the context of the plastics industry was that it was unlimited in its area of operation.

If a restraint is upheld by the courts, it can be enforced by an injunction (see later). However, if a court finds that a restraint within a contract is illegal and therefore void, the clause will be unenforceable. Whether the contract itself survives depends on whether it is possible to sever the illegal parts. A court may be prepared to 'blue pencil' the void sections and enforce the lawful main part of the contract.

Norbrook Laboratories (GB) Ltd v Adair **(2008)**

Ms Adair worked for a pharmaceutical company (N) as a Territory Manager. Her contract of employment included a confidentiality clause restricting any disclosure of confidential information obtained during the course of her employment while employed by N and after her contract terminated; and a clause which prevented her from obtaining employment with any rival business. Ms Adair left N to work for a rival company (P). N sought an injunction against Ms Adair and P to enforce the confidentiality clause and the post-termination restriction. Ms Adair accepted that the confidentiality clause was reasonable and consented to the injunction to protect N's confidential information. The Court also granted an injunction relating to the post-termination restriction but only after one clause was declared unenforceable because it was wider than necessary to protect N's interests, and another clause was subject to a 'blue pencil' deletion of certain words.

(b) A 'solus' agreement by which a trader agrees to restrict his orders from one supplier. Although such an agreement is subject to the doctrine of restraint of trade, it may be enforceable if it is reasonable and not contrary to the public interest. A number of cases have arisen from the operation of 'solus' agreements in the petrol industry.

Esso Petroleum Ltd v Harper's Garage (Stourport) Ltd (1967)

Harper's owned two garages. It entered into a 'solus' agreement with Esso by which it agreed to buy all its motor fuel from Esso, to keep the garages open all reasonable hours and not to sell the garages without ensuring that the purchaser entered into a similar agreement with Esso. In return, Esso allowed a rebate on all fuels bought. The agreement was to last for four and a half years in respect of one garage and 21 years for the other. The latter garage was mortgaged to Esso for a loan of £7,000 repayable over 21 years and not earlier. The House of Lords held that the agreements were in restraint of trade and, therefore, void, unless they could be justified as reasonable. The agreement which lasted for four and a half years was reasonable, but the other, which lasted 21 years, was not.

Although the length of the restraint was the deciding factor in the *Harper's* case, a long restraint may be reasonable in certain situations.

Alec Lobb (Garages) Ltd v Total Oil (GB) Ltd (1985)

The Court of Appeal upheld a 21-year restraint tied to a loan agreement as reasonable in the circumstances. The loan was part of a rescue package which greatly benefited the garage. There were also opportunities for the garage to break the arrangement after 7 and 14 years. Taking these facts into account, the restraint was not unreasonable.

(c) A contract for the sale of a business by which the seller agrees not to compete with the buyer. This kind of restraint is more likely to be upheld by the courts than a restraint on an employee because there is a greater likelihood of the parties bargaining as equals. Nevertheless, the parties must be careful to ensure that the restraint is no wider than is necessary to provide protection for the purchaser.

British Reinforced Concrete Engineering Co Ltd v Schelff (1921)

The claimants carried on a large business manufacturing and selling 'BRC' road reinforcements. The defendant had a small business selling 'Loop' road reinforcements. The defendant sold his business to the claimants and agreed not to compete with them in the manufacture or sale of road reinforcements. It was held that the restraint was void as it covered a wider area of business than the defendant had transferred to the claimants.

(d) Contracts between traders and businesspersons to regulate prices or output. This branch of the law is now largely covered by legislation and will be considered later.

Consequences

A clause which is in restraint of trade is void and unenforceable. It may be possible, however, to sever the void parts of the contract. The lawful main part can then be enforced by the court. Any money paid or property transferred is recoverable.

Contracts illegal by statute

Some statutes expressly prohibit a certain type of contract. For example, under Chapter 1 of the Competition Act 1998 agreements by two or more persons to fix the price at which goods may be resold are unlawful. The provision outlaws the practice of 'blacklisting' retailers who sell goods below a minimum resale price fixed by suppliers. Not all statutes are quite so specific. Some contracts may incidentally infringe the provisions of an Act of Parliament because, for example, one of the parties is trading without a licence, or statutory requirements have not been observed. It seems that the contract will be illegal if it was Parliament's intention in the passing of the Act to preserve public order or protect the public.

Cope v Rowlands (1836)

A court refused to enforce a contract on behalf of an unlicensed broker because the purpose of the licensing requirements was to protect the public.

The contract will be valid if it appears that the statutory provision was imposed for an administrative purpose.

Smith v Mawhood (1894)

A tobacconist was able to sue on a contract for the sale of tobacco even though he did not have a licence as required by statute. The sole aim of the statute was to raise revenue, not to prohibit contracts made by unlicensed tobacconists.

Consequences

The effects of the illegality on the contract are the same as for contracts which are illegal at common law.

Contracts void by statute

1 Gambling contracts. It used to be the case that gaming and wagering contracts were rendered null and void by legislation (the Gaming Act 1845). However, the Gambling Act 2005 repeals all statutory provisions preventing enforcement and provides that gambling contracts are as enforceable as other contracts. The Gambling Commission has the power to void a bet in specified circumstances, e.g. where one of the parties believes that the offence of cheating is likely to be committed in relation to the bet, and the Commission believes that the bet was substantially unfair. If the bet is declared void any money paid must be returned.

2 Anti-competitive agreements. Statutory control of anti-competitive agreements in the UK is set out in the Competition Act 1998 (CA 1998) and the Enterprise Act 2002 (EA 2002). The CA 1998 introduced a new regime for dealing with anti-competitive practices based on European Community competition law contained in Arts 81 and 82 of the EC Treaty. The EA 2002 builds on the changes made by the CA 1998 and introduces a number of new measures to strengthen the UK's competition law framework.

Competition policy

Competition is an essential requirement of a free-market economy. It encourages efficiency among producers and suppliers by providing consumers with a choice of goods and services at the best possible price. Paradoxically, however, unregulated competition in a free market leads inevitably to monopoly and other undesirable practices. A company which is aggressively competitive will seek to win as large a share of the market as is possible and in so doing reduce the competition it faces. If the company is too successful, it may in time completely eliminate any competition. Another problem which may arise is that companies may find it more profitable to cooperate with each other than to compete. Companies within a particular industry may form a cartel to fix minimum prices for their products or restrict production, denying consumers the benefits of a competitive market. Thus, it is necessary to regulate the competitive process in order to maintain a healthy free market which serves the interests of consumers. Statutory regulation of competition in the UK is relatively recent. Before the enactment of the Monopolies and Trade Practices Act 1948, the only control over anti-competitive practices was the common law doctrine of restraint of trade, but this was of limited application. Statutory intervention was confined initially to the establishment of an investigatory system but tough powers to ban anti-competitive practices soon followed. Competition law in the UK developed in a piecemeal fashion after 1948 in response to changing needs and circumstances.

By 1997 the law had become a complex mixture of UK and EC provisions with responsibility for the enforcement spread between a number of different agencies. In 1997 the government announced its intention of reforming UK competition law. The CA 1998 came into force on 1 March 2000.

The EA 2002 introduces a wide range of measures designed to enhance the UK's enterprise capability. They include modernising the insolvency laws, creating the Office of Fair Trading as a statutory authority, and strengthening consumer protection. The provisions which deal with the reform of competition law are designed to complement the changes introduced by the CA 1998 and largely replace the Fair Trading Act 1973. The competition law provisions of the EA 2002 came into effect in June 2003.

An outline of the new legal framework is set out below.

European Community competition law

Under Arts 81 and 82 of the Treaty of Rome all agreements between businesses which operate to prevent or restrict competition in the EC are void. Article 81 bans practices which distort competition between members of the EC. These include price fixing, restrictions in production and market sharing. The European Commission may grant exemptions in relation to individual agreements and block exemptions for certain categories of agreement.

Crehan v Inntrepreneur Pub Company and Brewman Group Ltd (2003)

The claimant C was the tenant of two tied public houses of which IPC, a property company, was the lessor and B was the nominated supplier of beer. C's pubs were not successful and he surrendered the leases. C was sued by B for unpaid deliveries of beer and C counter-claimed for damages arguing that his business had failed because of competition from untied pubs that could buy beer at a discount and retail it for less than C could as a tied tenant. C claimed that the beer-tie agreement infringed Art 81. IPC contended that the beer ties did not breach Art 81 and, even if they did, they were protected by a block exemption. The case was referred to the European Court of Justice (ECJ) which ruled that parties to an agreement that breaches Art 81 may bring a claim in domestic courts for breach of Art 81. The High Court held that, in order to establish a claim under Art 81, two conditions must be satisfied: first, having regard to the legal and economic context of the leases, it was difficult for businesses to enter the market or increase their market share; and, second, if there was a network of similar leases, this had contributed to sealing off the market. The court found that the first condition had not been breached. The enactment of the Supply of Beer (Tied Estates) Order 1989 (SI 1989/2390) had led to the break-up of the breweries' tied estates and a significant number of previously tied pubs had been sold. It was not difficult for newcomers to enter the market or for existing participants to increase their market share. The beer ties did not infringe Art 81 and C's claim therefore failed even though the court concluded that the failure of the business was caused by the beer ties. The court also decided that the block exemption was not available.

Comment. The trial judge's decision was overturned in the Court of Appeal on the grounds that he had not complied with the duty of 'sincere co-operation' required by Art 10 of the EC Treaty in that he had not accepted the Commission's view about the state of the UK beer market as expressed in a different case involving Whitbread. The House of Lords held that the trial judge's decision should be reinstated. The Commission's findings might constitute a highly persuasive part of the evidence which he should consider but he was entitled to consider additional evidence and form his own view.

Article 82 prohibits the abuse of a monopolistic position by an organisation within the EC. Practices which might be considered abuses include imposing unfair buying or selling prices. Responsibility for enforcing these provisions rests with the European Commission.

Publishers' Association v Commission of the European Communities (1992)

This European Court of Justice case involved the operation of the Net Book Agreement under which publishers enforced resale price maintenance in respect of books. The agreement had been approved by the Restrictive Practices Court under UK legislation (*Re Net Book Agreement* (1962)). However, in 1988 the European Commission found that the Agreement infringed Art 81 in respect of books sold from the UK to other EC states. The Commission turned down an application for exemption. The Publishers' Association applied to the European Court for an annulment of the Commission's decision. The European Court upheld the Commission's view that the Agreement infringed Art 81.

Comment. The European Court's judgment did not affect the operation of the Net Book Agreement within the UK: the Commission's challenge was confined to how it operated in other EC states. However, the Net Book Agreement only lasted for a few years after this judgment. The agreement collapsed in practice in 1995, and in March 1997 the Restrictive Practices Court discharged the orders which upheld the agreement.

The European Commission also has the power to control mergers with a Community dimension under an EC Merger Control Regulation which came into force in 1990. A merger will come within the terms of the EC Regulation if both:

(a) the aggregate worldwide turnover exceeds 5 billion euros; and

(b) at least two of the parties have a community turnover in excess of 250 million euros unless each of the undertakings makes more than two-thirds of its turnover in the same member state.

Mergers falling within the threshold must be notified to the Commission within a week of the conclusion of the agreement to acquire control. The Commission must decide within a month of notification whether to launch a full investigation, which must be completed within a further four months. If the Commission concludes that the merger will significantly impede effective competition in the whole or part of the EC, it must be blocked.

UK competition law

Competition Act 1998

The CA 1998 introduced two prohibitions which are largely based on the prohibitions operating at European level under Arts 81 and 82.

Chapter I prohibition

The first prohibition, the Chapter I prohibition, is based on Art 81. It prohibits agreements which have the object or effect of preventing, restricting or distorting competition in the UK. The anti-competitive nature of the agreement will be judged according to its effects or intended effects on competition. The Act sets out illustrative examples of agreements to which the prohibition applies:

- agreeing to fix purchase or selling prices or other trading conditions;
- agreeing to limit or control production, markets, technical development or investment;
- agreeing to share markets or supply sources;
- agreeing to apply different trading conditions to equivalent transactions, thereby placing some parties at a competitive disadvantage;
- agreeing to make contracts subject to unrelated conditions.

The agreement must have an 'appreciable effect' on competition. An agreement is unlikely to be considered as having an appreciable effect where the combined market share of the parties does not exceed 25 per cent. However, agreements to fix prices, impose minimum resale prices or share markets will be seen as capable of having an appreciable effect even where the market share falls below 25 per cent.

Certain types of agreement are excluded from the Chapter I prohibition, such as where there are overriding considerations of national policy. Some agreements are exempt from the prohibition. There are three types of exemption:

1 Individual exemption. The parties to an individual agreement may apply to the Office of Fair Trading (OFT) for exemption for their agreement, if it can be shown that the agreement contributes to improving production or distribution, or to promoting technical or economic progress and allows consumers a fair share of the resulting benefit. Any restrictions in the agreement must be indispensable to achieving these aims and the agreement must not eliminate competition.

2 Block exemptions. These exemptions apply automatically to certain types of agreement which meet the same exemption criteria as for individual exemption.

3 Parallel exemptions. These exemptions automatically apply where an agreement is covered by an EC individual or block exemption under Art 81(3) of the EC Treaty, or would be covered by an EC block exemption if the agreement had an effect on trade between member states of the EU. In certain circumstances, the OFT may impose conditions on the exemption or vary or cancel the exemption.

Chapter II prohibition

The second prohibition, the Chapter II prohibition, is based on Art 82. It prohibits the abuse by an undertaking of a dominant position in the UK or part of the UK, where this affects trade within the UK. The Act contains an illustrative list of the kinds of conduct which may be deemed an abuse:

- imposing unfair purchase or selling prices;
- limiting production, markets or technical developments to the prejudice of consumers;
- applying different trading conditions to equivalent transactions, thereby placing certain parties at a competitive disadvantage;
- attaching unrelated supplementary conditions to contracts.

There are two tests for determining whether the Chapter II prohibition applies:

- whether an undertaking is dominant; and
- if it is dominant, whether it is abusing its dominant position.

An undertaking will be regarded as dominant if it can behave 'to an appreciable extent independently of its competitors and customers and ultimately of consumers' when making decisions. The Act does not set any market share thresholds for a presumption of dominance but guidance from EC case law is relevant. The European Court of Justice has stated that dominance can be presumed if an undertaking has a market share persistently above 50 per cent. The OFT takes the view that an undertaking is unlikely to be considered dominant if its market share is less than 40 per cent.

Nevertheless, an undertaking with a lower market share may be considered dominant if, for example, the structure of the market enables it to act independently of its competitors. The OFT will consider the number and size of existing competitors as well as the potential for new competitors to enter the market.

The Chapter II prohibition is subject to similar exclusions to the Chapter I prohibition. There are, however, no exemptions from Chapter II.

Enforcement

Responsibility for enforcing the new legislation rests primarily with the OFT. It has the power to grant exemptions, investigate suspected breaches, make decisions enforceable by a court order and publish advice and information. The utility regulators enjoy equivalent powers within their own areas of responsibility.

If the OFT has reasonable grounds for suspecting an infringement of the Act, it may exercise the following powers:

- order the production of any relevant documents or information (it may take copies of any documents produced and require an explanation of the contents);
- enter premises without a warrant in order to obtain documents, take copies of them, obtain an explanation of the documents or obtain information held on a computer to be produced in a readable form (two working days' notice must be given to the occupier of the premises unless, for example, the undertaking is already under investigation);
- enter premises without notice on the authority of a High Court warrant, to search for documentary evidence.

Failure to cooperate with an investigation may amount to a criminal offence, punishable by a fine or imprisonment.

If the OFT concludes that infringement of either prohibition has occurred, it may give a direction to either party to bring the infringement to an end. This may include directions to modify or terminate the agreement or modify or cease the offending conduct. If a party fails to comply with a direction, the OFT can seek a court order to secure compliance. Any breach of a court order will be dealt with as a contempt of court.

Consequences of breach

The OFT has the power to impose civil fines of up to 10 per cent of an undertaking's turnover for infringement of either Chapter I or Chapter II prohibitions. Small businesses enjoy limited immunity from financial penalties in respect of small agreements (Chapter I prohibition) and conduct of minor significance (Chapter II prohibition).

An agreement which infringes the Chapter I prohibition is void and unenforceable. Third parties who believe that they have suffered loss as a result of an unlawful agreement or conduct may have a claim for damages in the courts under the terms of s 60, which requires the UK authorities to deal with cases in a way which is consistent with EC law.

Competition Commission

The CA 1998 established the Competition Commission (CC), which replaced the Monopolies and Mergers Commission. The CC is an independent administrative tribunal whose chairman and members are appointed by the Secretary of State. The CC carries out two functions:

1 It hears appeals against decisions made by the OFT in enforcing the prohibitions.
2 It investigates specific markets or the conduct of companies or mergers, decides what is in the public interest and reports to the Secretary of State with any recommendations for action. It has no power to initiate its own inquiries. Examples of investigations include the supply of groceries by supermarkets, the supply of new cars and the supply of airport services by BAA in the UK.

The Enterprise Act 2002

The EA 2002 made a number of significant changes to UK competition law.

1 Office of Fair Trading (OFT). The EA 2002 abolished the statutory position of the Director General of Fair Trading and transferred his functions to the OFT, which became a corporate body with effect from 1 April 2003. The OFT consists of a Chairman, Chief Executive and four other board members. One of the ways in which the OFT carries out its functions is by undertaking studies of markets which are not operating well for consumers. These market studies are carried out by the Markets and Policy Initiatives Division (MPI) and can result in a range of outcomes including OFT enforcement action, a market investigation reference to the CC, proposals for changes in the law or publishing better information for consumers.

2 Competition Appeal Tribunal. Part 2 of the EA 2002 established an independent Competition Appeal

Tribunal to replace the Competition Commission Appeal Tribunal.

3 Mergers. Part 3 of the EA 2002 reformed the UK's merger control framework by replacing most of the merger control provisions of the Fair Trading Act 1973. The main provisions are:

- Decisions on mergers have been de-politicised; they are now taken by the OFT and CC as independent competition authorities rather than by the Secretary of State for Business, Innovation and Skills (formerly Trade and Industry).

- Mergers are considered against a new 'competition test' rather than the wider 'public interest test' previously applied. Mergers will be prohibited if they would result in a substantial lessening of competition in a UK market. The competition authorities have discretion to allow a merger even if there is a substantial lessening of competition where they expect defined types of consumer benefit to result.

- The OFT may investigate mergers which meet either a 'turnover test' or a 'share of supply' test. The 'turnover test', which replaces the previous assets test, will be met if the target company has a UK turnover of at least £70 million. The 'share of supply test' will be met if the merged companies will together supply at least 25 per cent of the goods or services of a market, either in the UK as a whole or in a substantial part of it. If the merger meets the EC merger test, the OFT will not investigate and cannot refer the merger.

- The OFT can investigate changes in levels of control of companies. The provisions envisage three different levels of control: material influence over policy, control of policy (known as *de facto* control) and having a controlling interest (known as *de jure* control), which normally involves acquiring 50 per cent of voting rights.

- The OFT must refer a merger to the CC if it believes that the merger may substantially lessen competition. Alternatively, the OFT may seek undertakings from the merging companies to remedy the adverse effects of the merger. The duty to refer does not apply in three situations:
  (a) where the merger is insufficiently advanced;
  (b) if the market is of insufficient importance; or
  (c) the benefits to consumers outweigh the adverse effect on competition.

- If the merger is referred to the CC, it will conduct a full investigation. If the CC concludes that the merger has caused or will cause a substantial lessening of competition, the CC can stop the merger or impose remedies, such as undertakings from the parties or orders. The OFT will monitor compliance with any undertakings or orders.

- Mergers involving defence companies, newspapers and water companies will be treated as special cases and may be subject to different procedures.

- The Secretary of State will continue to decide mergers which raise public interest considerations, e.g. national security concerns.

Office of Fair Trading v IBA Health Ltd (2004)

In July 2003 iSoft Group plc offered to acquire the share capital of Torex Ltd. Both companies were engaged in the supply of software and systems to the healthcare applications market. The OFT was notified of the offer because, if it were accepted, there would be a relevant merger situation within the terms of the EA 2002, which had come into force on 20 June 2003. IBA, an Australian company in the same market, complained to the OFT in August about the proposed merger. The OFT investigated the proposed merger and in November 2003 decided not to refer the merger to the CC because, although the merged company would have a significant market power, it did not believe that the proposed merger would result in substantial lessening of competition in the UK. In reaching this view, the OFT had been influenced by forthcoming changes to the process of procuring IT systems in the NHS. IBA was unhappy with the outcome and applied to the Competition Appeal Tribunal (CAT) for a review of the decision. The CAT quashed the OFT's decision. The OFT, iSoft and Torex appealed against that decision. The Court of Appeal held that the test to be applied was that stated in s 33(1) of the EA 2002. The OFT had a duty to make a reference if it had a reasonable and objectively justified belief that the proposed merger may be expected to result in substantial lessening of competition. The Court of Appeal held that, although the CAT had not applied the proper test, its decision to quash the OFT's decision not to refer was correct. The court was not satisfied that the OFT had taken all material matters into account in reaching its decision.

4 Market investigation references. Part 4 of the EA 2002 established a new system of market investigations by the CC, which replaced the system of monopoly enquiries under the Fair Trading Act 1973. The OFT (and specified regulators such as the rail regulator) may make market investigation references to the CC where it appears that the structure of the market or the conduct of businesses is harming competition. The CC will carry out a detailed investigation to establish whether any aspects of the referred market prevents, restricts or distorts competition in relation to the supply or acquisition of goods or services in the UK as a whole or part of it. If the CC identifies an adverse effect, it must decide on action to remedy the effect, which may include seeking undertakings or making orders. The Secretary of State has the power to intervene in cases involving public interest considerations (currently only matters of national security). Parties affected may seek a review of the lawfulness and fairness of any decision by the OFT, the CC or the Secretary of State by the Competition Appeal Tribunal, which can ask for a reconsideration of the decision.

5 Criminalisation of cartels. Part 6 of the EA 2002 introduced a new offence for individuals who dishonestly engage in cartel agreements. The cartel offence operates alongside the provision of the CA 1998 which provides civil sanctions for undertakings that engage in anti-competitive agreements. A person will be guilty of an offence if he dishonestly agrees with another that undertakings will engage in one or more of the following cartel activities:

- price fixing;
- limitation of supply or production;
- market-sharing;
- bid-rigging.

The offence can only be committed in respect of horizontal agreements, i.e. between undertakings at the same level of the supply chain. It does not apply to vertical agreements. The offence will be committed irrespective of whether an agreement is reached or implemented. The offence is triable either in the magistrates' court or by the Crown Court. If convicted by magistrates, the offender may be sentenced to a maximum of six months' imprisonment or a fine up to the statutory maximum. If convicted by the Crown Court, an offender may be sentenced to a maximum of five years' imprisonment or an unlimited fine. Prosecutions will normally be brought by the Serious Fraud Office, although the OFT may also undertake prosecutions. If an individual provides information to investigatory authorities and cooperates with any investigation, the OFT may issue a 'no-action letter' confirming that an individual will not be prosecuted. The EA 2002 gives the OFT a range of powers

to investigate cartel offences including the power to compel individuals to answer questions or provide documents, to enter premises and carry out surveillance.

6 Super-complaints. The EA 2002 introduced a new procedure to allow certain designated consumer bodies to make super-complaints to the OFT and other specified regulators where 'any feature or combination of features of a market in the UK for goods or services is or appears to be significantly harming the interests of consumers'. The OFT and other regulators have up to 90 days to respond to a super-complaint. The response must state whether action is to be taken and, if so, what is proposed. Any of the powers of the OFT or regulators may be used. In the case of the OFT, actions could include an enforcement action under either competition or consumer regulation powers, launching a market study, market investigation reference to the CC for further investigation or recommendations for changes in legislation. Super-complaints will be considered in more detail in Chapter 14 ○.

7 Disqualification of directors. The EA 2002 amended the Company Directors Disqualification Act 1986 to allow the OFT (and specified regulators) to apply to the High Court for an order to disqualify directors of companies which have committed breaches of the following competition law provisions:

- Chapter I prohibition of the CA 1998;
- Art 81 of the EC Treaty;
- Chapter II prohibition of the CA 1998;
- Art 82 of the EC Treaty.

The maximum period of disqualification is 15 years.

8 Changes to the CA 1998. The following changes took effect from 1 April 2003:

- The exclusion of designated professional rules from the Chapter 1 prohibition of anti-competitive provisions is repealed.
- Where the OFT obtains a warrant to enter premises to undertake a CA 1998 investigation, the warrant may authorise certain individuals, e.g. IT experts, to accompany the OFT official. (A similar provision is enacted in relation to the power to enter premises to investigate the new cartel offence introduced by the EA 2002.)

In this chapter we have considered how a contract is formed, the ingredients for a valid contract and the factors which may affect its validity. In the next chapter will look at the terms of a contract.

Self-test questions/activities

1 Make a list of all the agreements you made (a) today, and (b) yesterday. Identify which agreements are contracts and explain why they are legally binding.

2 Are these statements true or false?
   (a) Most of the law of contract can be found in Acts of Parliament.
   (b) All contracts must be in writing.
   (c) Conveyances of land must be in the form of a speciality contract.
   (d) The absence of an essential element will always render a contract void.

3 Analyse the following transactions in terms of offer and acceptance:
   (a) filling a job vacancy;
   (b) parking a car in a multi-storey car park;
   (c) taking a bus ride;
   (d) buying a cup of coffee from an automatic vending machine;
   (e) buying a packet of soap powder from a supermarket;
   (f) buying an antique dresser at an auction;
   (g) acquiring shares in a privatisation issue;
   (h) buying a book via the Internet.

4 On 13 September, Fiona, a newly qualified dentist, receives the following note from her uncle:

> 10 Park Street
> LONDON
> WI A54
>
> Dear Fiona
> We talked some time ago about your buying some of my dental equipment when I retire from my London practice at the end of this month. I am prepared to let you have everything for £15,000. Let me know fairly quickly if you're interested because I've already had a very good offer from one of my colleagues.
>
> Your affectionate uncle
> Arnold

Fiona is keen to take advantage of her uncle's offer but is unsure whether she can raise such a large amount of money by the end of September. She phones her uncle to find out whether she can have until after Christmas to pay. Her uncle is away at a conference and so Fiona leaves a message with his secretary. Two weeks pass by and, as Fiona has not heard from her uncle, she arranges a loan with her bank. On 28 September she writes to her uncle accepting his offer and enclosing a cheque for £15,000. On 30 September, her uncle phones to say that he has already sold the equipment to someone else.
   Advise Fiona.

5 Lynx Cars Ltd, the manufacturer of a revolutionary fuel-efficient small car, enters into a five-year dealership agreement with Roadstar Ltd, a northern-based company of car dealers, in November 2010. A clause in the agreement states: 'This agreement is not intended to be legally binding but the parties honourably pledge that they will carry out its terms.' Roadstar Ltd places an initial order for 2,000 cars to be delivered by the end of 2011, which is accepted by the manufacturer. One month after the successful launch of the car at the Motor Show, Lynx Cars Ltd writes to Roadstar Ltd informing it that, owing to production difficulties, the company estimates that it will be able to deliver only 200 cars by the end of 2011. It further states that it will be withdrawing from the dealership agreement from the end of 2011 to be able to concentrate its resources on its south of England car dealers.
   Advise Roadstar Ltd.

6 Mrs Harris, the owner of three rented houses in Extown, asks her next-door neighbour, Ted, to collect rent from the tenants for her while she is abroad on business. Ted collects the rents and when Mrs Harris returns she says to him, 'I'll give you £50 for your work.'
   Can Ted enforce the promise?

7 John, a plumber, installs a new bathroom for Mr and Mrs Bolton for an agreed price of £500. Five weeks after sending the bill John still has not received payment. He rings the Boltons and speaks to Mrs Bolton. She says that she is unhappy about the quality of John's work, which she claims is only worth £350 at most. She also tells John that her husband has just lost his job and they can only afford to pay £100. John reluctantly agrees to accept a cheque for this amount 'in full settlement'.
   Three months later John hears that Mr Bolton is back in employment and he wonders whether he can recover the outstanding money.

8 What formalities, if any, must be completed for the following contracts?
   (a) a guarantee for a bank overdraft;
   (b) the sale of a second-hand car;
   (c) a contract of employment;
   (d) the lease of a house for 21 years;
   (e) a promise to pay £50 a year for the next five years to a charity.

9 Kathy, aged 17, decides to leave home because she does not get on with her parents. Over the next three weeks she enters into the following agreements:
   (a) She borrows £500 from her older brother to tide her over until she can find a job.
   (b) She takes a two-year lease on a bed-sit, paying three months' rent in advance.
   (c) By pretending to be 21, she orders a £700 suite of furniture from Palatial Pads Ltd on 12 months' interest-free credit.
   (d) She sets up a home catering business and immediately agrees to cater for 100 people attending a 21st birthday party for a price of £500. She insists on £100 deposit. As the day for the party approaches, she finds that she has taken on too much work for one person, so she rings her customers on the afternoon of the party to say that she will not be able to do the catering after all.
   Discuss the legal effects of these transactions.

10 Arthur, the manager of Lookout Cars Ltd, asks his young assistant, Terry, to look after the business while he is away on holiday. It is an eventful week for Terry.
   (a) Early Monday morning Terry sells a second-hand Escort to Doris. The car had been advertised in the local press as follows:

   93 (N) Ford Escort 45,000 miles. Blue £1,000

   Doris returns on Wednesday to tell Terry that the Escort's clock has been turned back and that it has actually done 90,000 miles.
   (b) On Tuesday, Terry finalises a part-exchange deal with Mr Walker. Unknown to either of them, Mrs Walker was involved, earlier in the day, in a serious car crash while driving the old car. The car is a 'write-off'.
   (c) On Wednesday, a man calls into the showrooms introducing himself, falsely, as James Dean MP. He agrees to buy a new Orion car, but when he pulls out a cheque book, Terry says that he is reluctant to accept a cheque. The man then produces a pass to the House of Commons as proof of his identity. Terry accepts the cheque and the man drives off in the car. Terry has just learned from the bank that the cheque has been dishonoured. The man sold the car to Pete, a university student.
   (d) On Thursday, Daisy, Lookout Ltd's secretary, puts a number of letters in front of Terry for his signature. Terry is busy talking to the workshop manager at the time and signs his name without reading each one. He has now discovered that one of the letters was an undertaking to act as a guarantor for a £5,000 loan to Daisy by the Midshires Bank plc.
   Explain to Terry the legal position in each situation.

11 George is the owner of a confectioner's shop in Chorley, which is world famous for its unique Chorley Chocolate Bar. The secret recipe for the chocolate bar has been handed down by four generations of George's family. George himself is a bachelor and, with no one to carry on the business, he decides to retire and sell the shop. After much careful vetting, George agrees to sell the shop, including the goodwill and the secret recipe, to Maria. As part of the contract George agrees that:
   (a) he will not engage in any form of sweet-making in the whole of the United Kingdom for the next 20 years; and
   (b) he will not reveal the secret formula for the chocolate bar to anyone else.
   Maria bought the business with the aid of a 20-year mortgage from Castletown Cocoa Co Ltd. Maria has further agreed to obtain all her supplies of cocoa from this company for the next 20 years. After three very successful years in Chorley, Maria hears that George is supplying Chorley Chocolate Bars to shops near to his retirement home in Bournemouth. About the same time, Maria is approached by Cocoa Suppliers Ltd which offers to supply all her cocoa needs at cheaper prices than she is currently paying Castletown Cocoa Co Ltd.
   Advise Maria.

Specimen examination questions

1 Explain the circumstances in which the courts will refuse to enforce agreements as contracts because of a lack of intention to create a legal relationship.

2 On 11 May Andrew wrote to Ben offering to sell him 200 bags of potatoes at £10 per bag. On 13 May, Ben posted a reply accepting Andrew's offer but adding that if he did not hear from Andrew, he would assume that the price included delivery to his (Ben's) house. The following morning, before Ben's letter arrived, Andrew heard a rumour that the price of potatoes was about to slump dramatically. Andrew immediately sent a fax to Ben, stating that 'the price includes delivery'.

Ben received Andrew's fax at 10 am on 14 May, whereupon he immediately posted a letter confirming his acceptance of Andrew's terms. Over lunch, however, Ben also heard the news about a slump in the price of potatoes, whereupon he sent Andrew a text message stating: 'decline yr offr of pots'.

The price of potatoes has now fallen to £7 per bag and Ben refuses to accept delivery of Andrew's pricey potatoes.

Advise Andrew.

3 Caroline's house was badly damaged by storms in March. She engaged David, a builder, to repair the damage. David told Caroline that the work would cost £10,000 and would be finished by 1 June. Caroline accepted David's terms because she wanted to be able to put the house up for sale in June.

David started work on the repairs to Caroline's house in April, but further storms delayed the work. Four weeks later David approached Caroline asking her to increase the contract price to £15,000 due to increased overtime costs David would face to meet the deadline of 1 June. Reluctantly Caroline agreed.

David completed the repair before the end of May and sent Caroline a bill for £15,000. However, Caroline informed David that she could only afford to pay £10,000 because she was in financial difficulties. David, fearing that he would otherwise receive no payment at all, reluctantly accepted £10,000 in full settlement.

David has now discovered that Caroline has made a substantial profit on the sale of her house and is about to depart on a round-the-world holiday.

Advise David on whether he can recover the rest of the money.

4 To what extent, if at all, is it possible to bind or benefit a person under the terms of a contract to which he or she is not a party?

Website references

http://www.lawcom.gov.uk The Law Commission's website contains copies of Law Commission Reports, including *Privity of Contract: Contracts for the Benefit of Third Parties*, prepared by the Commercial and Common Law team.

http://www.oft.gov.uk The Office of Fair Trading's website provides information about competition regulation, including the Competition Act 1998 and the Enterprise Act 2002.

http://www.competition-commission.org.uk The Competition Commission (CC) is an independent public body which undertakes inquiries into mergers, markets and the regulation of certain regulated industries. You can access CC reports from this website, such as the BAA Airports investigation.

Visit **www.mylawchamber.co.uk/richesallen** to access study support resources including answers to questions in this chapter and legal updates, all linked to the **Pearson eText** version of **Keenan and Riches' Business Law** which you can **search**, **highlight** and **personalise** with your **own notes** and **bookmarks**.

Use **Case Navigator** to read in full some of the key cases referenced in this chapter with commentary and questions:

Carlill v *Carbolic Smoke Ball Co* (1893)
Brinkibon v *Stahag Stahl* (1982)
Butler Machine Tool Co v *Ex-Cell-O Corp (England)* (1979)
Central London Property Trust Ltd v *High Trees House Ltd* [1947]
Williams v *Roffey Bros & Nicholls (Contractors) Ltd* (1990)

Learning objectives

After studying this chapter you should understand the following main points:

- the terms of an agreement must be certain or capable of being made certain for a contract to be formed;
- the distinction between puffs, representations and terms, and the remedies available for false and misleading statements;
- the distinction between express and implied terms, and the circumstances in which terms may be implied into a contract;
- the benefits and drawbacks of using standard form contracts in business;
- the ways in which the law regulates exemption clauses, and proposals for reform.

As we have already seen, a contract comprises a set of promises which the law will enforce. The obligations undertaken by the parties are known as the terms of the contract. If a dispute arises, the terms will become the object of intense scrutiny as the parties seek to justify their positions. The first task for any court is to establish exactly what was agreed by the parties. This may appear to be a relatively simple matter where the details of the agreement have been enshrined in a written contract, but even then problems can arise. The parties may have failed to express their intentions clearly; they may have omitted to mention a particular matter which later assumes great importance; or the written document may contradict what was said during the course of oral negotiations. Where the contract is made wholly by word of mouth, the job of ascertaining the contents of the contract becomes even more difficult.

The terms of a contract are essentially a matter of express agreement between the parties. It should be noted, however, that additional terms can be implied into an agreement, even against the wishes of the parties, and certain terms which have been clearly stated, such as exclusion clauses, can be rendered completely ineffective by operation of the law.

In this chapter we examine the basic requirement of certainty of terms for the creation of a contract, how the contents of a contract are determined and the relative importance that may be attached to the duties and obligations undertaken by the parties. Finally, we will consider the nature of standard form contracts and the effect of clauses which purport to exclude or limit the liability of one of the parties.

Certainty of terms

The terms of an agreement may be so vague and indefinite that in reality there is no contract in existence at all.

Scammell v Ouston (1941)

Ouston agreed to buy a new motor van from Scammell. When placing the order for a particular type of van, Ouston wrote: 'This order is given on the understanding that the balance of the purchase price can be had on hire-purchase terms over a period of two years.' Scammell accepted the order but no discussions subsequently took place about the details of the hire-purchase arrangement. Scammell later refused to deliver the van and Ouston sued for damages for non-delivery. Scammell defended the case by arguing that a contract had never been concluded. The House of Lords held that the phrase 'hire-purchase terms' was so vague and indefinite that there was no contract at all. The parties needed to complete the agreement by reaching a consensus about unresolved matters such as rates of interest and frequency of payments.

Comment.

(i) The decision might have been different in *Scammell* if there had been usual or standard hire-purchase terms to which the court could refer to <u>ascertain the</u> intention of the parties.

(ii) A phrase which sometimes appears in contracts is that one of the parties will use his or her 'best endeavours' or 'reasonable endeavours'. It would be a mistake to think that such clauses are unenforceable for lack of certainty. In *Lambert v HTV Cymru (Wales) Ltd* (1998) the Court of Appeal held that the defendant's promise to 'use all reasonable endeavours' to obtain rights of first negotiation for the claimant to write books in connection with a film was not uncertain and could be enforced.

Bushwall Properties Ltd v Vortex Properties Ltd (1976)

The parties concluded an agreement for the sale of $51\frac{1}{2}$ acres of land at £500,000 to be paid in three instalments. The first payment of £250,000 was to be followed in 12 months by a second payment of £125,000 with the balance to be paid after a further 12 months, and 'on the occasion of each completion a proportionate part of the land' should be released to the buyers. The Court of Appeal held that as the parties had failed to provide a mechanism for allocating the 'proportionate part of the land', the entire agreement failed for uncertainty.

The presence of a <u>vague</u> term will not <u>prove fatal</u> <u>in every case.</u> Various devices exist for <u>ascertaining the</u> <u>meaning of terms.</u>

1 The contract itself may provide the machinery whereby any disputes about the operation of the agreement can be resolved.

Foley v Classique Coaches Ltd (1934)

Foley sold part of his land to a coach company for use as a coach station, on condition that the company would buy all its petrol from him 'at a price to be agreed

between the parties'. It was also agreed that any dispute arising from the contract should be submitted to arbitration. The parties failed to agree a price and the company refused to buy petrol from Foley. The agreement to buy petrol was held to be binding despite the failure to agree a price because the parties had agreed a method by which the price could be ascertained, i.e. by arbitration.

Comment. The price is an essential term of a contract and, in the absence of a mechanism to ascertain the price, failure to agree on this core term is likely to render the contract unenforceable. In *Rafsanjan Pistachio Producers Co-operative v Kauffmans Ltd* (1998) the High Court held that a contract for the sale of raw pistachio nuts, which provided that the price was to be agreed before each delivery, was an agreement to agree and was not enforceable.

2 A court can <u>ascertain</u> the terms of a contract by reference to <u>a trade custom</u> or a <u>course of</u> previous dealings between the parties.

Hillas & Co Ltd v Arcos Ltd (1932)

The parties concluded a contract for the sale of a certain quantity of softwood timber 'of fair specification' over the 1930 season. The agreement also contained an option to buy further quantities in 1931, but no details were given as to the kind or size of the timber or the date of shipment. The 1930 agreement was carried out without difficulty but when the buyers tried to exercise the option for 1931, the sellers refused to supply the wood, claiming that they had only agreed to negotiate a further contract for 1931. The House of Lords held that the sellers were bound to carry out the 1931 option. The terms of the contract could be ascertained by reference to the previous course of dealings between the parties.

Comment. It should not be assumed that just because the parties have dealt with each other over a long period of time that a court will find an obligation to continue doing business with each other. In *Baird Textile Holdings Ltd v Marks & Spencer plc* (2002) (discussed in Chapter 7 ○), the Court of Appeal held that, although B had supplied M & S for 30 years, a continuing obligation to place orders after M & S terminated the relationship could not be implied because of lack of certainty.

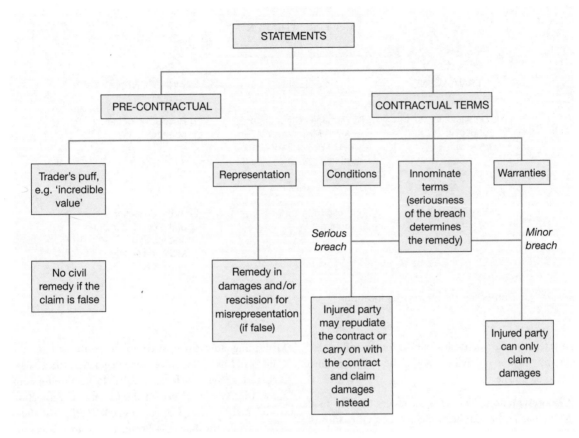

Figure 8.1 The nature of pre-contractual and contractual statements

3 A meaningless term which is subsidiary to the main agreement can be ignored and the rest of the contract enforced.

Nicolene Ltd v Simmonds (1953)

The claimants placed an order with the defendant for the supply of 3,000 tons of steel reinforcing bars. The defendant wrote to the claimants to accept the order adding that 'we are in agreement that the usual conditions of acceptance apply'. There were no usual conditions of acceptance, so the words were meaningless. The Court of Appeal held that, as the rest of the contract made sense, the meaningless clause could be ignored.

The House of Lords has recently confirmed that it was not prepared to depart from its long-standing rule that excludes evidence of pre-contractual negotiations

for the purposes of deciding what the terms of a contract mean (*Chartbrook Ltd v Persimmon Homes Ltd* (2009)).

Puffs, representations and terms

The first step in determining the terms of a contract is to establish what the parties said or wrote. That is not to say that all statements made during the course of negotiations will automatically be incorporated in the resulting contract. The statement may be a trader's puff, a representation or a term, and, if it turns out to be untrue, the claimant's remedy will depend on how the statement is classified. The differences are as follows:

1 Trader's puff. If a car is described as 'totally immaculate' and 'incredible value', this is nothing more than typical advertising exaggeration. We are not

267

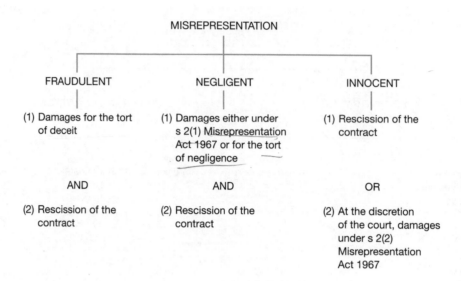

Figure 8.2 Remedies for misrepresentation

expected to take such sales talk seriously and, consequently, there is no civil remedy if the statement turns out to be untrue.

2 Representation. This is a statement of fact made by one party which induces the other to enter into the contract. As we have already seen in Chapter 7 ○, the remedy for a misrepresentation is determined by the type of misrepresentation. You can refresh your memory by referring to Figure 8.2.

3 Term. Breach of a term of the contract entitles the injured party to claim damages and, if he has been deprived of substantially what he bargained for, he will also be able to repudiate the contract. The distinction between a mere representation and a statement which becomes a term of the contract used to be very important. Before 1967 damages were not available for a misrepresentation unless it was made fraudulently, and the only remedy, rescission, could be easily lost. The injured party, therefore, would be keen to establish that the statement had been incorporated into the contract, so that he could claim damages for a breach of a contractual term. This generated a considerable body of complex case law. The Misrepresentation Act 1967, however, opened the way for an award of damages for non-fraudulent misrepresentation and, as a result, the distinction between terms and representations has become much less important.

Misleading advertising used to be controlled by the Control of Misleading Advertising Regulation 1988. These regulations have now been repealed. Protection for consumers is now contained in the Consumer Protection from Unfair Trading Regulations 2008 (CPRs) (SI 2008/1277), while the Business Protection from Misleading Marketing Regulations 2008 (BPRs) (SI 2008/1276) contain business to business protections in respect of misleading advertising and also controls comparative advertising whether to business or consumers. Breaches of the BPRs are enforced by the Office of Fair Trading or local trading standards departments by securing an injunction to prevent the breach. Misleading advertising in breach of the BPRs is also a criminal offence. The CPRs will be considered in more detail in Chapter 14 ○.

Types of contractual terms

The terms of a contract delineate the obligations of the parties and these may vary greatly in importance. Traditionally, terms have been divided into two categories: conditions and warranties.

1 Conditions. A condition is a major term which is vital to the main purpose of the contract. A breach of condition will entitle the injured party to repudiate the contract and claim damages. The breach does not automatically end the contract and the injured party may choose to go on with the relationship, despite the breach, and recover damages instead.

2 Warranties. A warranty is a less important term: it does not go to the root of the contract. A breach of warranty will only give the injured party the right to claim damages; he cannot repudiate the contract.

The difference between a condition and a warranty is illustrated by the following cases.

Poussard v Spiers (1876)

Madame Poussard was engaged to appear in an operetta from the start of its London run. Owing to illness, she was not available until a week after the show had opened and the producers were forced to engage a substitute. They now refused Madame Poussard's offer to take up her part. It was held that the obligation to perform from the first night was a condition of the contract. Failure to carry out this term entitled the producers to repudiate Madame Poussard's contract.

Bettini v Gye (1876)

Bettini, an opera singer, was engaged by Gye to appear in a season of concerts. He undertook to be in London at least six days before the first concert for the purpose of rehearsals. He arrived three days late and Gye refused to accept his services. It was held that the promise to appear for rehearsals was a less important term of the contract. Gye could claim compensation for a breach of warranty but he could not repudiate Bettini's contract.

The division of terms into conditions and warranties was included in the original Sale of Goods Act 1893 (now the Sale of Goods Act 1979, as amended). In s 11(3) a condition is described as a stipulation 'the breach of which may give rise to a right to treat the contract as repudiated', while a warranty is a stipulation 'the breach of which may give rise to a claim for damages but not a right to reject the goods and treat the contract as repudiated'. In recent years, the courts have recognised that it may be impossible to classify a term neatly in advance as either a condition or a warranty. Some undertakings may occupy an intermediate position, in that the term can be assessed only in the light of the consequences

of a breach. If a breach of the term results in severe loss and damage, the injured party will be entitled to repudiate the contract; where the breach involves only minor loss, the injured party's remedies will be restricted to damages. These intermediate terms have become known as innominate terms.

Cehave NV v Bremer Handelsgesellschaft mbH (The Hansa Nord) (1975)

A clause in a contract for the sale of citrus pulp pellets stipulated that shipment was 'to be made in good condition'. Part of one consignment arrived in Rotterdam in a damaged condition and the buyers rejected the whole cargo. The defects were not particularly serious because some time later the buyers bought the very same cargo at a considerably reduced price, which they then proceeded to use for their original purpose. The Court of Appeal held that the clause in question was an intermediate term. The breach was not so serious that it entitled the buyers to reject the whole cargo. It could be dealt with by an award of damages.

Express and implied terms

Another way in which the contents of a contract can be classified is according to whether the terms are express or implied.

Express terms

Express terms are the details of a contract which have been specifically agreed between the parties. They may be contained wholly in a written document or ascertained entirely from what the parties said to each other. In some cases, the terms may be partly written and partly verbal.

Harling v Eddy (1951)

A heifer was put up for sale by auction at Ashford Cattle Market. The sale was subject to the auctioneer's printed conditions of sale which stated that the auctioneer did not guarantee the condition of the animals sold. The appearance of this particular heifer was so poor when she entered the auction ring that no one was prepared to make a bid for her. The auctioneer then stated that there was nothing wrong with her and he would guarantee her in every respect. The heifer was sold to the claimant but was dead from tuberculosis within three months. The claimant successfully sued the auctioneer for damages. The Court of Appeal held that the auctioneer was bound by his oral guarantee despite the contents of the written conditions of sale.

Types of express term

The most common types of express term, which are often a particular feature of standard form contracts (see later), are exemption clauses, liquidated damages clauses and price variation clauses.

Exemption clause – generally

This term is used to describe an express term in a contract or a statement in a notice or sign which seeks to exclude or limit the responsibilities that might otherwise belong to a party.

Example 1 (sales brochure)

'We reserve the right to change component type, manufacturers, sources of supply and technical specifications at any time. Dimensions, weights and colours contained in this brochure are approximate. Products and prices may be altered without notice at any time.'

Example 2 (car park ticket)

'Entry to or use of this car park is subject to the current terms and conditions of the company. These conditions contain limited exemption clauses affecting all persons who enter or use the car park. Entry to and use of this car park is at your own risk.'

The legal effect of exemption clauses will be examined in detail later in this chapter.

Liquidated damages clause

This is a term in a contract which lays down the amount of damages that will be payable in the event of a breach of contract. Cancellation charges are an example of a liquidated damages clause.

Price variation clause

Calculating a contract price in a period of inflation can be a very hit-and-miss operation. A contractor may find himself bound by a fixed price which has failed to take sufficient account of increases in the cost of raw materials, wages or overheads, such as business rates. One solution to this problem is to insert a term in a contract which allows a variation in the contract price under certain circumstances.

Example 1 (holiday brochure)

'Our prices are based on known costs and projections at 1 March 2011 and we do not expect to make any changes. However, we reserve the right to increase prices at any time until 30 days before departure to allow for variations in: (a) exchange rates, (b) transportation costs, and (c) increases in tax rates imposed in any country including dues, taxes or fees chargeable for services such as landing taxes or embarkation or disembarkation fees at ports and airports. Even in these cases we will absorb an amount equivalent to 2 per cent of the price. Any increase will be calculated by reference to the total cost of the variation, to be divided by our best estimate of the number of passengers likely to be affected, so as to arrive at an increase for each passenger. If this means paying more than 10 per cent on the price, you will be entitled to cancel with a full refund of money paid. Should you decide to cancel because of this, you must exercise your right to do so within 14 days from the issue date printed on the invoice.'

Example 2 (building contract)

'Unless otherwise stated the contract price is based on the cost of labour, materials and all necessary services at the date of the quotation and increases or decreases in any such costs shall be a net addition to or deduction from the contract price.'

Implied terms

In general, the contents of a contract are determined by agreement between the parties. Nevertheless, there are various circumstances in which additional terms may be implied into the agreement.

1 By custom. A contract must always be examined in the light of its surrounding commercial context. The terms of a contract may have been negotiated against the background of the customs of a particular locality or trade. The parties automatically assume that their contract will be subject to such customs and so do not deal specifically with the matter in their contract.

Hutton v Warren (1836)

The tenant of a farm was given six months' notice to quit. His landlord insisted that he continue to cultivate the land during the notice period in keeping with custom. The tenant successfully argued that the same custom entitled him to a fair allowance for the seeds and labour he used on the land.

2 By the common law. The courts will be prepared to imply a term into a contract in order to give effect to the obvious intentions of the parties. Sometimes the point at issue has been overlooked or the parties have failed to express their intention clearly. In these circumstances, the court will supply a term in the interests of 'business efficacy' so that the contract makes commercial common sense.

The Moorcock (1889)

The owner of a wharf agreed to provide mooring facilities for *The Moorcock*. The ship was damaged when it hit a ridge of rock at low tide. The court implied an undertaking on the part of the wharf owner that it was a reasonably safe place to moor the ship. The wharf owner had broken his implied undertaking and was, therefore, liable in damages to the ship owner.

Certain standard terms have been implied by the common law in a number of business contracts. The courts will imply a term into a lease of a furnished house that it will be reasonably fit for habitation at the start of the tenancy. A contract of employment is subject to a number of implied terms. An employer is under a common law duty to provide a safe system of work for his employees, while an employee is under common law duties to obey legitimate orders and show good faith towards his employer.

By implying a term into the contract, the court is imposing reasonable obligations, which the parties would have no doubt included in their agreement if they had troubled to think about the matter. These implied

terms may be excluded by express agreement between the parties.

3 By statute. A term may be implied into a contract by Act of Parliament. In many cases, these implied terms began life among the customs of merchants, were recognised by the courts and then included in the statute which codified the common law rules. The best example of this process is provided by the law relating to the sale of goods. The original Sale of Goods Act 1893 was a codification of the common law rules which had been developed by the courts during the 19th century. The present Sale of Goods Act 1979 re-enacts the 1893 Act, incorporating the changes made in the intervening years. The Sale and Supply of Goods Act 1994, Sale of Goods (Amendment) Acts 1994 and 1995 and the Sale and Supply of Goods to Consumers Regulations 2002 (SI 2002/3045) make a number of changes to the 1979 Act.

Some terms are implied into a contract for the sale of goods under the Sale of Goods Act 1979. The best known are contained in ss 12–15.

(a) *Section 12 (title).* There is an implied condition in every contract for the sale of goods that the seller has the right to sell the goods and that he will transfer good title to the buyer. The seller will break this term, for example, if it transpires that the goods were stolen.

(b) *Section 13 (description).* Where there is a sale of goods by description, there is an implied condition that the goods will correspond with the description. A shirt described as 100 per cent cotton, for example, should not contain man-made fibres.

(c) *Section 14 (quality and suitability).* Although this section preserves the well-established principle of *caveat emptor* (let the buyer beware), it does impose two duties on a seller who sells in the course of a business. First, there is an implied condition that the goods are of satisfactory quality. This means that if you buy a washing machine, it should actually work when you get it home. Second, where the buyer expressly or impliedly makes known any particular purpose for which the goods are required, there is an implied condition that the goods will be fit for that purpose. If you ask the salesperson to recommend a heavy-duty carpet which would be suitable for a lounge, it should not be threadbare after a couple of months.

(d) *Section 15 (sample).* In sales by sample, there is an implied condition that the bulk will correspond with

		Goods supplied by way of:				
		Sale of goods	Hire-purchase	Barter, work and materials	Hire	Redemption of trading stamps
		Sale of Goods Act 1979	Supply of Goods (Implied Terms) Act 1973*	Supply of Goods and Services Act 1982	Supply of Goods and Services Act 1982	Trading Stamps Act 1964**
Implied Terms	Title	s 12	s 8	s 2	s 7	s 4
	Description	s 13	s 9	s 3	s 8	–
	Quality and suitability***	s 14	s 10	s 4	s 9	s 4
	Sample	s 15	s 11	s 5	s 10	–

* As amended by the Consumer Credit Act 1974

** As amended by the Supply of Goods (Implied Terms) Act 1973

*** The implied term as to quality has been amended by the Sale and Supply of Goods Act 1994 and the Sale and Supply of Goods to Consumers Regulations 2002

Figure 8.3 The sources of statutory implied terms in contracts for the supply of goods

the sample. This means that if you have curtains made up for you, the quality of the material should match the sample that you examined in the shop.

Similar terms are implied into contracts for the supply of goods by way of hire-purchase, hire, barter, and under work and materials contracts. Warranties relating to title and quality are implied on the redemption of trading stamps for goods. The sources of these implied terms are summarised in Figure 8.3.

Standard form contracts

One way of avoiding being bound by terms you have not specifically agreed is to ensure that all the terms are contained in a written contract. It has long been the case that businesses contract on the basis of standard terms contained in a pre-printed document known as a **standard form contract**. The terms are not usually open to negotiation: the customer must either accept them in their entirety as part and parcel of the deal or take his business elsewhere.

The use of standard form contracts has several clear advantages for business:

1 If the terms of the contract are contained in a written document, the parties will be quite clear about what they have agreed to and this is likely to minimise the possibility of disputes at a later stage.

2 It would be very time-consuming to negotiate individual terms with every customer, especially where a fairly standard service is offered to a large number of people. For example, train services would soon come to a standstill if every intending passenger had to negotiate an individual contract before setting out on a journey.

3 Once an organisation has adopted standard terms of business, the formation of a contract becomes a relatively routine matter which can be delegated to junior staff.

4 Businesspeople are constantly seeking ways to minimise their potential risks. A standard form contract can be used to 'dictate' terms which will be favourable to the businessperson. He may include, for example, limitation or exclusion clauses which seek to limit or exempt him completely from liabilities which might otherwise be his responsibility.

The use of standard form contracts may be convenient and economical for the businessperson, but it puts his customers at a considerable disadvantage.

The drawbacks are as follows:

1 Standard terms of business are often expressed in language which is virtually unintelligible to most people. A consumer may find himself bound by a contract even though he did not properly understand what had been 'agreed'. In some cases, the document may be so awe-inspiring that it is not read at all.

2 The concept of freedom of contract, on which the law of contract is founded, would seem to suggest that if the terms contained in a standard form contract are unacceptable, the customer can simply shop around for a better deal. This may well happen in a competitive market where the parties possess equal bargaining powers, but, in practice, the parties rarely contract as equals. Consumers, in particular, have found themselves in a weak bargaining position, victims of very one-sided contracts.

An example of a standard form contract appears in Figure 8.4.

Exemption clauses

Exemption clauses are a common feature of business contracts. They are express terms which seek to exclude or limit the liability that might belong to one party in the event of a breach of contract. Such clauses are perfectly fair where they are the result of free negotiations between equals, but all too often they are imposed on a weaker party by a stronger party. This abuse of freedom of contract was most commonly practised against consumers. The courts attempted to deal with the problem, but the common law ultimately proved unequal to the ingenuity of those who sought the protection of the exemption. Over the years, Parliament stepped in to control the use of unfair exemption clauses in particular kinds of contracts and now the overwhelming majority of these clauses are covered by the provisions of the Unfair Contract Terms Act 1977, as supplemented by the Unfair Terms in Consumer Contracts Regulations 1999 (SI 1999/2083). Statutory control of exemption clauses has been grafted on to the pre-existing common law rules. It is still necessary, therefore, to examine the attitude of the courts to these clauses. After we have done this, we will consider how Parliament has dealt with the problem.

Judicial control

The judges based their attack on exemption clauses on two main fronts: incorporation and interpretation.

Incorporation

The person wishing to rely on the exclusion clause must show that it formed part of the contract. In this connection note the following rules.

1 **Signed documents.** Where the exemption clause is contained in a document which has been signed, it will automatically form part of the contract. The signer is presumed to have read and understood the significance of all the terms contained in the document.

L'Estrange v Graucob (1934)

Miss L'Estrange bought an automatic cigarette vending machine for use in her café. She signed a 'sales agreement' which provided that: 'Any express or implied condition, statement or warranty statutory or otherwise, not stated herein is hereby excluded.' She did not read this document and was completely unaware of the sweeping exclusion clause hidden in the small print. The machine did not work properly but it was held that she was still bound to pay for it because by signing the agreement she had effectively signed her rights away.

This general rule will not apply where the signer can plead *non est factum* (see p 245 ◯) or if the other party has misrepresented the terms of the agreement.

Curtis v Chemical Cleaning and Dyeing Co (1951)

Mrs Curtis took a wedding dress to be cleaned by the defendants. She signed a piece of paper headed 'Receipt', after being told by the assistant that it exempted the cleaners from liability for damage to beads and sequins. The 'Receipt', however, contained a clause excluding liability 'for any damage howsoever arising'. When the dress was returned, it was badly stained. It was held that the cleaners could not escape liability for damage to the material of the dress by relying on the exemption clause because its scope had been misrepresented by the defendant's assistant.

2 **Unsigned documents.** The exemption clause may be contained in an unsigned document such as a ticket or a notice. The clause will form part of the contract only if two conditions are met. First, the document must be regarded by a reasonable person as contractual in nature and, as such, likely to contain exemption clauses.

Road Haulage Association Limited
CONDITIONS OF CARRIAGE 1998 - Effective 1 September 1998

PLEASE NOTE THAT THE CUSTOMER WILL NOT IN ALL CIRCUMSTANCES BE ENTITLED TO COMPENSATION, OR TO FULL COMPENSATION, FOR ANY LOSS AND IS THEREFORE RECOMMENDED TO SEEK PROFESSIONAL ADVICE AS TO APPROPRIATE INSURANCE COVER TO BE MAINTAINED WHILE CONSIGNMENTS ARE IN TRANSIT.

RHA membership number

(hereinafter referred to as *"the Carrier"*) is not a common carrier and accepts goods for carriage only upon that condition and the Conditions set out below. No servant or agent of the Carrier is permitted to alter or vary these Conditions in any way unless expressly authorised in writing to do so by a Director, Principal, Partner or other authorised person. If any legislation is compulsorily applicable to the Contract and any part of these Conditions is incompatible with such legislation, such part shall, as regards the Contract, be overridden to that extent and no further.

1. Definitions

In these Conditions:

"Customer" means the person or company who contracts for the services of the Carrier including any other carrier who gives a Consignment to the Carrier for carriage.

"Contract" means the contract of carriage between the Customer and the Carrier.

"Consignee" means the person or company to whom the Carrier contracts to deliver the Consignment.

"Consignment" means goods, whether a single item or in bulk or contained in one parcel, package or container, as the case may be, or any number of separate items, parcels, packages or containers sent at one time in one load by or for the Customer from one address to one address.

"Dangerous Goods" means goods named individually in the Approved Carriage List issued from time to time by the Health and Safety Commission, explosives, radioactive material, and any other goods presenting a similar hazard.

2. Parties and Sub-Contracting

(1) The Customer warrants that he is either the owner of the Consignment or is authorised by such owner to accept these Conditions on such owner's behalf.

(2) The Carrier and any other carrier employed by the Carrier may employ the services of any other carrier for the purpose of fulfilling the Contract in whole or in part and the name of every other such carrier shall be provided to the Customer upon request.

(3) The Carrier contracts for itself and as agent of and trustee for its servants and agents and all other carriers referred to in (2) above and such other carriers' servants and agents and every reference in these Conditions to "the Carrier" shall be deemed to include every other such carrier, servant and agent with the intention that they shall have the benefit of the Contract and collectively and together with the Carrier be under no greater liability to the Customer or any other party than is the Carrier hereunder.

(4) Notwithstanding Condition 2(3) the carriage of any Consignment by rail, sea, inland waterway or air is arranged by the Carrier as agent of the Customer and shall be subject to the Conditions of the rail, shipping, inland waterway or air carrier contracted to carry the Consignment. The Carrier shall be under no liability whatever to whomsoever and howsoever arising in respect of such carriage: Provided that where the Consignment is carried partly by road and partly by such other means of transport any loss, damage or delay shall be deemed to have occurred while the Consignment was being carried by road unless the contrary is proved by the Carrier.

3. Dangerous Goods

Dangerous Goods must be disclosed by the Customer and if the Carrier agrees to accept them for carriage they must be classified, packed and labelled in accordance with the statutory regulations for the carriage by road of the substance declared. Transport Emergency Cards (Tremcards) or information in writing in the manner required by the relevant statutory provisions must be provided by the Customer in respect of each substance and must accompany the Consignment.

4. Loading and Unloading

(1) Unless the Carrier has agreed in writing to the contrary with the Customer:

(a) The Carrier shall not be under any obligation to provide any plant, power or labour, other than that carried by the vehicle, required for loading or unloading the Consignment.

(b) The Customer warrants that any special appliances required for loading or unloading the Consignment which are not carried by the vehicle will be provided by the Customer or on the Customer's behalf.

(c) The Carrier shall be under no liability whatever to the Customer for any damage whatever, however caused, if the Carrier is instructed to load or unload any Consignment requiring special appliances which, in breach of the warranty in (b) above, have not been provided by the Customer or on the Customer's behalf.

(d) The Carrier shall not be required to provide service beyond the usual place of collection or delivery but if any such service is given by the Carrier it shall be at the sole risk of the Customer.

(2) The Customer shall indemnify the Carrier against all claims and demands whatever which could not have been made if such instructions as are referred to in (1)(c) of this Condition and such service as is referred to in (1)(d) of this Condition had not been given.

5. Signed Receipts

The Carrier shall, if so required, sign a document prepared by the sender acknowledging the receipt of the Consignment but no such document shall be evidence of the condition or of the correctness of the declared nature, quantity, or weight of the Consignment at the time it is received by the Carrier and the burden of proving the condition of the Consignment on receipt by the Carrier and that the Consignment was of the nature, quantity or weight declared in the relevant document shall rest with the Customer.

6. Transit

(1) Transit shall commence when the Carrier takes possession of the Consignment whether at the point of collection or at the Carrier's premises.

(2) Transit shall (unless otherwise previously determined) end when the Consignment is tendered at the usual place of delivery at the Consignee's address within the customary cartage hours of the district: Provided that;

(a) if no safe and adequate access or no adequate unloading facilities there exist then transit shall be deemed to end at the expiry of one clear day after notice in writing (or by telephone if so previously agreed in writing) of the arrival of the Consignment at the Carrier's premises has been sent to the Consignee; and

(b) when for any other reason whatever a Consignment cannot be delivered or when a Consignment is held by the Carrier 'to await order' or 'to be kept till called for' or upon any like instructions and such instructions are not given or the Consignment is not called for and removed within a reasonable time, then transit shall be deemed to end.

7. Undelivered or Unclaimed Consignments

Where the Carrier is unable for any reason to deliver a Consignment to the Consignee or as he may order, or where by virtue of the proviso to Condition 6(2) hereof transit is deemed to be at an end, the Carrier may sell the Consignment, and payment or tender of the proceeds after deduction of all proper charges and expenses in relation thereto and of all outstanding charges in relation to the carriage and storage of the Consignment shall (without prejudice to any claim or right which the Customer may have against the Carrier otherwise arising under these Conditions) discharge the Carrier from all liability in respect of such Consignment, its carriage and storage:

Provided that:

(1) the Carrier shall do what is reasonable to obtain the value of the Consignment; and

(2) the power of sale shall not be exercised where the name and address of the sender or of the Consignee is known unless the Carrier shall have done what is reasonable in the circumstances to give notice to the sender or, if the name and address of the sender is not known, to the Consignee that the Consignment will be sold unless within the time specified in such notice, being a reasonable time in the circumstances from the giving of such notice, the Consignment is taken away or instructions are given for its disposal.

8. Carrier's Charges

(1) The Carrier's charges shall be payable by the Customer without prejudice to the Carrier's rights against the Consignee or any other person: Provided that when any Consignment is consigned 'carriage forward' the Customer shall not be required to pay such charges unless the Consignee fails to pay after a reasonable demand has been made by the Carrier for payment thereof.

(2) Charges shall be payable when due without reduction or deferment on account of any claim, counterclaim or set-off. The Carrier shall be entitled to interest at 8 per cent above the Bank of England Base Rate prevailing at the date of the Carrier's invoice or account, calculated on a daily basis on all amounts overdue to the Carrier.

Figure 8.4 A standard form contract

9. **Liability for Loss and Damage**

    (1) The Customer shall be deemed to have elected to accept the terms set out in (2) of this Condition unless, before the transit commences, the Customer has agreed in writing that the Carrier shall not be liable for any loss or mis-delivery of or damage to or in connection with the Consignment however or whenever caused and whether or not caused or contributed to directly or indirectly by any act, omission, neglect, default or other wrongdoing on the part of the Carrier, its servants, agents or sub-contractors.

    (2) Subject to these Conditions the Carrier shall be liable for:

    (a) physical loss, mis-delivery of or damage to living creatures, bullion, money, securities, stamps, precious metals or precious stones comprising the Consignment only if:

    (i) the Carrier has specifically agreed in writing to carry any such items; and

    (ii) the Customer has agreed in writing to reimburse the Carrier in respect of all additional costs which result from the carriage of the said items; and

    (iii) the loss, mis-delivery or damage is occasioned during transit and is proved to be due to the negligence of the Carrier, its servants, agents or sub-contractors.

    (b) physical loss, mis-delivery of or damage to any other goods comprising the Consignment unless the same has arisen from, and the Carrier has used reasonable care to minimise the effects of:

    (i) Act of God;

    (ii) any consequences of war, invasion, act of foreign enemy, hostilities (whether war or not), civil war, rebellion, insurrection, terrorist act, military or usurped power or confiscation, requisition, or destruction or damage by or under the order of any government or public or local authority;

    (iii) seizure or forfeiture under legal process;

    (iv) error, act, omission, mis-statement or misrepresentation by the Customer or other owner of the Consignment or by servants or agents of either of them;

    (v) inherent liability to wastage in bulk or weight, faulty design, latent defect or inherent defect, vice or natural deterioration of the Consignment;

    (vi) insufficient or improper packing;

    (vii) insufficient or improper labelling or addressing;

    (viii) riot, civil commotion, strike, lockout, general or partial stoppage or restraint of labour from whatever cause;

    (ix) Consignee not taking or accepting delivery within a reasonable time after the Consignment has been tendered.

    (3) The Carrier shall not in any circumstances be liable for loss or damage arising after transit is deemed to have ended within the meaning of Condition 6(2) hereof, whether or not caused or contributed to directly or indirectly by any act, omission, neglect, default or other wrongdoing on the part of the Carrier, its servants, agents or sub-contractors.

10. **Fraud**

    The Carrier shall not in any circumstances be liable in respect of a Consignment where there has been fraud on the part of the Customer or the owner, or the servants or agents of either, in respect of that Consignment, unless the fraud has been contributed to by the complicity of the Carrier or of any servant of the Carrier acting in the course of his employment.

11. **Limitation of Liability**

    (1) Except as otherwise provided in these Conditions, the liability of the Carrier in respect of claims for physical loss, mis-delivery of or damage to goods comprising the Consignment, howsoever arising, shall in all circumstances be limited to the lesser of

    (a) the value of the goods actually lost, mis-delivered or damaged; or

    (b) the cost of repairing any damage or of reconditioning the goods; or

    (c) a sum calculated at the rate of £1,300 Sterling per tonne on the gross weight of the goods actually lost, mis-delivered or damaged;

    and the value of the goods actually lost, mis-delivered or damaged shall be taken to be their invoice value if they have been sold and shall otherwise be taken to be the replacement cost thereof to the owner at the commencement of transit, but in all cases shall be taken to include any Customs and Excise duties or taxes payable in respect of those goods: Provided that:

    (i) in the case of loss, mis-delivery of or damage to a part of the Consignment the weight to be taken into consideration in determining the amount to which the Carrier's liability is limited shall be only the gross weight of that part regardless of whether the loss, mis-delivery or damage affects the value of other parts of the Consignment;

    (ii) nothing in this Condition shall limit the liability of the Carrier to less than the sum of £10;

    (iii) the Carrier shall be entitled to proof of the weight and value of the whole of the Consignment and of any part thereof lost, mis-delivered or damaged;

    (iv) the Customer shall be entitled to give to the Carrier written notice to be delivered at least 7 days prior to commencement of transit requiring that the £1,300 per tonne limit in 11 (1)(c) above be increased, but not so as to exceed the value of the Consignment, and in the event of such notice being given the Customer shall be required to agree with the Carrier an increase in the carriage charges in consideration of the increased limit, but if no such agreement can be reached the aforementioned £1,300 per tonne limit shall continue to apply.

    (2) The liability of the Carrier in respect of claims for any other loss whatsoever (including indirect or consequential loss or damage and loss of market), and howsoever arising in connection with the Consignment, shall not exceed the amount of the carriage charges in respect of the Consignment or the amount of the claimant's proved loss, whichever is the lesser, unless;

    (a) at the time of entering into the Contract with the Carrier the Customer declares to the Carrier a special interest in delivery in the event of physical loss mis-delivery or damage or of an agreed time limit being exceeded and agrees to pay a surcharge calculated on the amount of that interest, and

    (b) at least 7 days prior to the commencement of transit the Customer has delivered to the Carrier written confirmation of the special interest, agreed time limit and amount of the interest.

12. **Indemnity to the Carrier**

    The Customer shall indemnify the Carrier against:

    (1) all liabilities and costs incurred by the Carrier (including but not limited to claims, demands, proceedings, fines, penalties, damages, expenses and loss of or damage to the carrying vehicle and to other goods carried) by reason of any error, omission, mis-statement or misrepresentation by the Customer or other owner of the Consignment or by any servant or agent of either of them, insufficient or improper packing, labelling or addressing of the Consignment or fraud as in Condition 10;

    (2) all claims and demands whatsoever (including for the avoidance of doubt claims alleging negligence), by whomsoever made and howsoever arising (including but not limited to claims caused by or arising out of the carriage of Dangerous Goods and claims made upon the Carrier by HM Customs and Excise in respect of dutiable goods consigned in bond) in excess of the liability of the Carrier under these Conditions in respect of any loss or damage whatsoever to, or in connection with, the Consignment whether or not caused or contributed to directly or indirectly by any act, omission, neglect, default or other wrongdoing on the part of the Carrier, its servants, agents or sub-contractors.

13. **Time Limits for Claims**

    (1) The Carrier shall not be liable for:

    (a) damage to the whole or any part of the Consignment, or physical loss, mis-delivery or non-delivery of part of the Consignment unless advised thereof in writing within seven days, and the claim is made in writing within fourteen days, after the termination of transit;

    (b) any other loss unless advised thereof in writing within twenty-eight days, and the claim is made in writing within forty-two days, after the commencement of transit.

    Provided that if the Customer proves that,

    (i) it was not reasonably possible for the Customer to advise the Carrier or make a claim in writing within the time limit applicable, and

    (ii) such advice or claim was given or made within a reasonable time,

    the Carrier shall not have the benefit of the exclusion of liability afforded by this Condition.

    (2) The Carrier shall in any event be discharged from all liability whatsoever and howsoever arising in respect of the Consignment unless suit is brought within one year of the date when transit commenced.

    (3) In the computation of time where any period provided by these Conditions is seven days or less, Saturdays, Sundays and all statutory public holidays shall be excluded.

14. **Lien**

    (1) The Carrier shall have a general lien against the Customer, where the Customer is the owner of the Consignment, for any monies whatever due from the Customer to the Carrier. If such a lien is not satisfied within a reasonable time, the Carrier may, at its absolute discretion sell the Consignment, or part thereof, as agent for the Customer and apply the proceeds towards the monies due and the expenses of the retention, insurance and sale of the Consignment and shall, upon accounting to the Customer for any balance remaining, be discharged from all liability whatever in respect of the Consignment.

    (2) Where the Customer is not the owner of the Consignment, the Carrier shall have a particular lien against the said owner, allowing the Carrier to retain possession, but not to dispose of, the Consignment against monies due from the Customer in respect of the Consignment.

15. **Unreasonable Detention**

    The Customer shall be liable to pay demurrage for unreasonable detention of any vehicle, trailer, container or other equipment but the rights of the Carrier against any other person in respect thereof shall remain unaffected.

16. **Law and Jurisdiction**

    The Contract shall be governed by English law and United Kingdom courts alone shall have jurisdiction in any dispute between the Carrier and the Customer.

Figure 8.4 (*continued*)

Road Haulage Association Limited
CONDITIONS OF CARRIAGE 1998
Explanatory Notes

STATUS OF THE CONDITIONS

The RHA Conditions of Carriage 1998 result from a review of the RHA Conditions of Carriage 1991. They take effect from 1st September 1998 and include amendments reflecting changes in Law and Members' use of the RHA Conditions of Carriage 1991. The opportunity has also been taken to bring other Specialist Group Conditions into line with the new RHA Conditions of Carriage and these will be introduced as self-standing Conditions of Carriage for Specialist Trades.

The 1998 Conditions have been registered with the Office of Fair Trading as an update of the 1991 Conditions. The use of the Conditions by Members is not compulsory but Members are recommended to use them as they are designed to enable a contractual balance to be struck between the interests of Members as carriers and those of their customers. It is recommended that Members seek professional advice before making or agreeing any variation in the Conditions to meet special circumstances.

The Conditions are the copyright of the RHA and may not be used by non-members. It is most important that Members should arrange to have the printed forms stamped with their details in the box provided at the top and with their Membership number in the space provided as this will deter the use of the form by non-members.

TO USE THE CONDITIONS

A Member who intends to trade under these Conditions, or any of the Specialist Group Conditions, should take the following action:

1. Refer the Conditions to his insurers or brokers and secure any necessary adjustments to existing insurance covers.

2. Inform existing customers in writing, by Recorded Delivery, of the intention to trade subject to the new Conditions saying for example: 'Please note that as from the ... day of ... 1998 goods will be accepted for carriage only subject to the RHA Conditions of Carriage 1998 a copy of which is attached'. If it is intended to use the Specialist Group Conditions reference should instead be made to the relevant specialist conditions.

3. Inform existing sub-contractors in writing, by Recorded Delivery, that as from the ... day of ... 1998 goods will be accepted for carriage and sub-contracted only subject to the RHA Conditions of Carriage 1998. If it is intended to use the Specialist Group Conditions reference should instead be made to the relevant Specialist Group Conditions. You should confirm that any previously agreed amendment in the financial limit per tonne continues to apply.

4. Retain Recorded Delivery receipts or, if the above letters are not sent by Recorded Delivery, maintain a permanent record of customers and sub-contractors and the dates on which letters were dispatched.

5. Print (or overprint) at the foot of all letter heads, quotation forms, fax forms, confirmation forms and notes, Consignment Notes and invoices etc: 'Goods are accepted for carriage (and sub-contracted) only subject to the RHA Conditions of Carriage 1998 a copy of which is available on request'. If it is intended to use the Specialist Group Conditions, reference should instead be made to the relevant Specialist Conditions. If present letter heads etc refer to the 'current RHA Conditions of Carriage' this will probably suffice provided that all existing customers and sub-contractors have been informed in accordance with 2-4 above that you are now operating under the 1998 Conditions.

6. Maintain a stock of the printed Conditions for issue to customers or sub-contractors as and when requested.

7. Specifically mention that the Conditions will apply during any telephone call in which the terms of the Contract are first agreed verbally, and confirm this immediately afterwards to the customer by fax, e-mail, letter, note or memo. Clear, simple, contemporary, dated and timed documents provide better proof than later conflicting oral evidence of recollections of conversations.

EFFECT OF THE CONDITIONS

The intention in revising the RHA Conditions is to retain their distinctive style and layout. The order of Clauses found in the 1998 Conditions will also be used in Specialist Group Conditions which will make them more user friendly. The principal amendments are set out below:

PREAMBLE: It now includes a notice to the customer making it clear that the carrier does not 'insure' the goods. This should help prevent later allegations by customers that they did not know that the liability of the carrier was limited under the Conditions and that the carrier insured its liabilities under the Conditions but did not cover the goods on an 'All Risks' basis. The preamble also clarifies who can agree variations to the Conditions and that the Conditions will not override Statute such as CMR, where applicable.

CONDITION 1: The Definitions have been up-dated taking account of changes in Law since 1991 but are not substantively altered.

CONDITION 2: There are no substantive changes.

CONDITION 3: There are no substantive changes.

CONDITION 4: There are no substantive changes.

CONDITION 5: The wording has been amended in order better to protect the carrier against 'hollow pallet syndrome' type claims where the 'missing' goods were never loaded in the first place.

CONDITION 6: There are no substantive changes.

CONDITION 7: There are no substantive changes.

CONDITION 8: The 'volumetric' or 'size' based method of calculation of charges has been dropped. This was originally introduced with containerisation in the 1967 Conditions to enable carriers to charge other than on a tonnage basis. Charging techniques have become considerably more sophisticated since then and carriers now maintain a variety of different charging methods with individual customers. This aspect of charging is more appropriately left to individual negotiation than dealt with in the Conditions. Also, as the result of a recent Court decision the existence of the 'volumetric' Clause opened up the possibility of some substantially larger claims by customers, whether or not charges had been calculated or quoted on a volumetric basis. The opportunity has been taken to remove this distortion in the interpretation of the Conditions by deleting all reference to the basis of charging in Condition 8.

CONDITION 9: This is little altered but additional exceptions from liability in the case of a terrorist act or faulty design are introduced to deal with some commonly occurring problems which are outside the control of the carrier and for which the carrier should not be liable. Reference is now made to 'living creatures' rather than 'livestock' in Condition 9(2)(a) to include non-commercial consignments such as pigeons.

CONDITION 10: There are no substantive changes.

CONDITION 11: Clause 11(1) has been up-dated stylistically to reflect the fact that most goods are carried under the standard limit and not under specially uplifted compensation limits. 11(1)(b) also now refers specifically to repair costs. A modified version of the previous Clause 18 from the 1991 Conditions has been incorporated into the main text of Condition 11(1) to bring those details concerning calculation of compensation into a more appropriate place in the Conditions. All other relevant elements of the previous Clause 11(1) have been brought together as a set of provisos to Clause 11(1) with clarification of the way in which compensation is calculated in the event of partial losses being given in proviso (i).

In the light of the Court case mentioned in relation to Clause 8, the volumetric calculation is also deleted for the purposes of defining compensation payable under Clause 11. Carriers can continue to charge on whatever basis they agree with their customers, but liability will be calculated solely on the basis of gross weight, as is done under CMR and all other commonly encountered Trading Conditions. Some existing customers may wish to discuss revised arrangements for the carriage of particularly light bulky goods. It will be open to customer and carrier, after discussion with respective insurers, to agree an uplift in the tonnage financial limitation under Clause 11(1)(c). In this way an agreed and appropriate level of compensation will apply, rather than the arbitrary formula which applied with the 'volumetric' calculation. The opportunity has also been taken to abandon the obscure proviso for 'proportional loss', which could in practice create quite arbitrary limits of liability quite different from those for loss of the whole consignment.

Note that, under general Law, a contract of carriage need only be completed within a reasonable time unless the contract makes time of the essence of the contract by, for example, stipulating a specific delivery time or date, in which case failure to deliver on time could result in a claim. As in previous RHA Conditions, the 1998 Conditions provide for this situation in Clause 11(2) and limit the amount of compensation recoverable where a carrier is in breach of contract to a maximum of the haulage charges paid by the customer, unless special uplifts in liability have been agreed in writing, in advance of the transit commencing.

CONDITION 12: The former Clause 13 becomes Clause 12, as it used to be in the 1982 Conditions. The indemnities to which the carrier is entitled from the customer remain broadly the same but the former 1982 and 1991 sub-clauses (2), (3) and (4) have now been combined in one sub-clause.

CONDITION 13: The provisions on time limits have been simplified to make them clearer and the notice provision for damage or partial loss brought in line with some other commonly encountered Trading Conditions, with 7 and not 3 days being available for notification of loss by the customer. A time period of one year is introduced within which legal proceedings must be brought against the carrier. This should prevent Writs appearing unexpectedly several years after events and when the carrier no longer has any recollection of those events.

CONDITION 14: There are no substantive changes.

CONDITION 15: This now refers specifically to the right to demurrage and the right extends to any equipment of the carrier which is detained. Carriers must establish their own scales for demurrage based on operating costs as Restrictive Trade Practices Law prevents the RHA from making specific recommendations.

CONDITION 16: A new Clause states that English Law applies to the contract and proceedings should be brought only in the United Kingdom. Carriers and their customers can of course vary the Clause to apply whatever Law and Jurisdiction they wish, for example, Scots Law.

Figure 8.4 (*continued*)

Chapelton v Barry Urban District Council (1940)

Mr Chapelton hired two deck chairs for three hours from the defendant council. He received two tickets which he put into his pocket unread. Each ticket contained a clause exempting the defendant from liability for 'any accident or damage arising from the hire of the chair'. Mr Chapelton was injured when the chair he sat on collapsed. He successfully sued the council. The Court of Appeal held that a reasonable man would assume that the ticket was a mere receipt and not a contractual document which might contain conditions. The defendant had not succeeded in incorporating the exemption into its contract with Mr Chapelton.

Notice of the exemption clause must have been given before the contract was made or at the time the contract was made. Attempts to give notice after the contract has been concluded will be ineffective.

Olley v Marlborough Court Ltd (1949)

Mr and Mrs Olley booked in for a week's stay at the defendants' hotel. There was a notice in the bedroom which stated that 'the proprietors will not hold themselves responsible for articles lost or stolen unless handed to the manageress for safe custody'. A stranger gained access to the Olleys' room and stole Mrs Olley's furs. The Court of Appeal held that the defendants were liable. The Olleys saw the notice only after the contract had been concluded at the reception desk. The exclusion clause could not protect the defendants because it had not been incorporated into the contract with the Olleys.

Thornton v Shoe Lane Parking Ltd (1971)

Mr Thornton decided to park his car in the defendant's car park. There was a notice at the entrance which stated: 'All cars parked at owner's risk.' As Mr Thornton drove into the car park, a light changed from red to green and he took a ticket from an automatic machine. He noticed that there was some writing on the ticket but he did not read it. The ticket stated that it was 'issued subject to the conditions of issue as displayed on the premises'. The conditions which were displayed inside the car park purported to exempt the defendant for not only damage to vehicles but also injury to customers. When Mr Thornton returned to the car park to collect his car, he was involved in an accident and he suffered personal injury partly as a result of the defendant's negligence. The Court of Appeal held that the defendant could not rely on the exemption clause displayed inside the car park because it had been introduced after the contract was formed. The contract was concluded when the lights changed from red to green and the machine dispensed a ticket. It is important to note that Mr Thornton was using the car park for the first time. If he had visited the car park before, the defendant may have been able to argue that the notice inside the car park had been incorporated into the contract by a previous source of dealings (see later).

The person seeking to rely on the exemption clause must show that reasonable steps have been taken to give notice of the clause to the other contracting party. What amounts to reasonably sufficient notice will vary according to the nature of the clause. As Denning LJ commented in *Spurling* v *Bradshaw* (1956) (see later):

> The more unreasonable a clause is the greater the notice which must be given of it. Some clauses would need to be printed in red ink with a red hand pointing to it before the notice could be held to be sufficient.

The 'red hand rule' was applied by the Court of Appeal in the following case.

Interfoto Picture Library v Stiletto Visual Programmes Ltd (1989)

Stiletto, an advertising agency, ordered 47 photographic transparencies from Interfoto, which operated a photo library. The transparencies were accompanied by a delivery note which contained a number of conditions. Condition 2 provided that a holding fee of £5 per day was payable in respect of each transparency retained after 14 days. Stiletto did not return the transparencies on time and Interfoto sued for the holding fee payable under Condition 2, which amounted to £3,785. The Court of Appeal held that Condition 2 had not been incorporated into the contract. Interfoto had not taken reasonable steps to bring such an unusual, unreasonable and onerous term to Stiletto's attention. Interfoto was awarded £3.50 per transparency per week on a *quantum meruit* basis.

3 Previous course of dealings. An exclusion clause may be binding even though it has not been included in the contract in question, if a previous course of dealings between the parties on the basis of such terms can be established. This principle has been accepted more readily in commercial contracts than in consumer transactions.

J Spurling v Bradshaw (1956)

The defendant delivered eight barrels of orange juice to the claimants who were warehousemen. A few days later the defendant received a document from the claimants which acknowledged receipt of the barrels. It also contained a clause exempting the claimants from liability for loss or damage 'occasioned by the negligence, wrongful act or default' caused by themselves, their employees or agents. When the defendant collected the barrels, some were empty and some contained dirty water. He refused to pay the storage charges and was sued by the claimants. Although the defendant did not receive the document containing the exclusion clause until after the conclusion of the contract, the clause had been incorporated into the contract as a result of a regular course of dealings between the parties over the years. The defendant had received similar documents on previous occasions and he was now bound by the terms contained in them.

Hollier v Rambler Motors (AMC) Ltd (1972)

Mr Hollier entered into an oral contract with the defendant garage to have his car repaired. While the car was in the garage, it was damaged in a fire caused by the defendant's negligence. Mr Hollier had had his car repaired by the defendant on three or four occasions in the previous five years. In the past he had been asked to sign a form which stated: 'The company is not responsible for damage caused by fire to customers' cars on the premises', but he did not sign such a form on this occasion. The defendant argued that the exemption clause had been incorporated into the oral contract by a previous course of dealings. The Court of Appeal rejected this argument and held that the defendant was liable. Three or four transactions over five years did not constitute a regular course of dealings.

---

4 Privity of contract. According to the doctrine of privity of contract, a person who is not a party to a contract can neither benefit from the contract nor be made liable under it. So while a duly incorporated exemption clause may protect a party to a contract, it will not protect his servants or agents. They are strangers to the contract and so cannot take advantage of an exclusion or limitation clause.

Scruttons Ltd v Midland Silicones Ltd (1962)

A shipping company (the carrier) agreed to ship a drum of chemicals belonging to the claimants from New York to London. The contract of carriage limited the liability of the carrier for damage to $500 (£179) per package. The drum was damaged by the negligence of the defendants, a firm of stevedores, who had been engaged by the carriers to unload the ship. The claimants sued the defendants in tort for the full extent of the damage, which amounted to £593. The defendants claimed the protection of the limitation clause. The House of Lords held in favour of the claimants. The defendants were not parties to the contract of carriage and so they could not take advantage of the limitation clause.

Comment. During the course of his speech in the House of Lords, Lord Reid suggested a way in which the benefit of an exemption clause could be made available to a third party, such as the firm of stevedores in this case. He said that four conditions must be fulfilled: (1) a contract of carriage must specifically state that the stevedore is intended to be protected by the exemption clause; (2) the carrier must make it clear that he is contracting both on his own behalf and as agent for the stevedores; (3) the carrier has authority from the stevedore to act in this way; and (4) there is some consideration moving from the stevedores. Legal draftsmen duly took notice of the formula and it received the approval of the Privy Council in *New Zealand Shipping Co Ltd v A M Satterthwaite & Co Ltd (The Eurymedon)* (1974).

This common law position is now subject to the provisions of the Contracts (Rights of Third Parties) Act 1999, which was discussed in detail in Chapter 7 ⊙. The Act allows contracting parties to confer third-party rights in relation to exclusion clauses in contracts such as those dealt with in the *Satterthwaite* case. (You should note, however, the effect of s 7(2) of the 1999 Act in relation to s 2(2) of the Unfair Contract Terms Act 1977, which is discussed later.)

Interpretation

Where a clause is duly incorporated into a contract, the courts will proceed to examine the words used to see if the clause covers the breach and loss which has actually occurred. The main rules of interpretation used by the courts are as follows:

1 Strict interpretation. An exemption clause will be effective only if it expressly covers the kind of liability which has in fact arisen. A clause, for example, which excludes liability for a breach of warranty will not provide protection against liability for a breach of condition.

Baldry v *Marshall* (1925)

The claimant asked the defendants, who were motor dealers, to supply a car that would be suitable for touring purposes. The defendants recommended a Bugatti, which the claimant bought. The written contract excluded the defendants' liability for any 'guarantee or warranty, statutory or otherwise'. The car turned out to be unsuitable for the claimant's purposes, so he rejected it and sued to recover what he had paid. The Court of Appeal held that the requirement that the car be suitable for touring was a condition. Since the clause did not exclude liability for breach of a condition, the claimant was not bound by it.

Andrews Bros Ltd v *Singer & Co Ltd* (1934)

The claimants agreed to buy some new Singer cars from the defendants. A clause in the contract provided that 'all conditions, warranties and liabilities implied by common law, statute or otherwise are excluded'. One of the cars supplied was not new and the claimants were seeking damages for breach of contract. The defendants argued that they were protected by the exclusion clause. The Court of Appeal held that the promise to supply new cars was an express term of the contract. As the exclusion clause covered only implied terms, the defendants could not rely on the exclusion.

2 *Contra proferentem.* If there is any ambiguity or doubt as to the meaning of an exemption clause the court will construe it *contra proferentem,* i.e. against the party who inserted it in the contract. Very clear words must be used before a party will be held exempt from liability in negligence.

White v *John Warwick & Co Ltd* (1953)

The claimant hired a tradesman's cycle from the defendants. The written hire agreement stated: 'Nothing in this agreement shall render the owners liable for any personal injury.' While the claimant was riding the cycle, the saddle tilted forward and he was injured. The defendants might have been liable in tort (for negligence) as well as in contract. The Court of Appeal held that the ambiguous wording of the exclusion clause would effectively protect the defendants from their strict contractual liability, but it would not exempt them from liability in negligence.

3 Repugnancy. Under this rule, a court can strike out an exemption clause which is inconsistent with or repugnant to the main purpose of the contract.

J Evans & Sons (Portsmouth) Ltd v *Andrea Merzario Ltd* (1976)

The claimants had imported machines from Italy for many years and for this purpose they used the services of the defendant forwarding agents. When the defendants changed over to containers, the claimants were orally promised by the defendants that their goods would continue to be stowed below deck. On one occasion, the claimants' container was stored on deck and it was lost when it slid overboard. The Court of Appeal held that the defendants could not rely on an exemption clause contained in the standard conditions of the forwarding trade, on which the parties had contracted, because it was repugnant to the oral promise that had been given.

The doctrine of fundamental breach

The doctrine of fundamental breach was developed particularly by Lord Denning MR in the Court of Appeal as an additional weapon in the judiciary's fight against exclusion clauses which had been properly incorporated into a contract. According to the doctrine, no exemption clause, however clear and unambiguous, could, as a matter of law, protect a party from liability for a serious or fundamental breach of contract. This line of argument was rejected by the House of Lords in the *Suisse* case (1966) but was then revived by the Court of Appeal. The House of Lords re-established its authority and finally demolished the doctrine in *Photo Production Ltd* v *Securicor Transport Ltd* (1980).

Photo Production Ltd v Securicor Transport Ltd (1980)

The defendant security company agreed to provide a visiting patrol service at nights and weekends for the claimants' factory. One night, the defendant's patrolman lit a fire inside the factory. The fire got out of control and the factory and its contents, worth a total of £615,000, were completely destroyed. The defendant relied on an exclusion clause in its contract which stated that it would not be responsible 'for any injurious act or default by any employee . . . unless such act or default could have been foreseen and avoided by the exercise of due diligence' by the defendant. The claimants did not allege that the defendant had been negligent in employing the man who lit the fire. The House of Lords held that the defendant was protected by the exemption clause. Although a breach of contract with serious consequences had taken place, the exclusion clause, as a matter of construction, was clear and unambiguous and it covered even the 'fundamental' breach that had taken place.

The contract in the *Photo Production* case was entered into before 1 February 1978 and so the House of Lords could not apply the provisions of the Unfair Contract Terms Act 1977. Nevertheless, their Lordships' decision was greatly influenced by the principles contained in the Act. In the words of Lord Wilberforce:

> After this Act, in commercial matters generally, when the parties are not of unequal bargaining power, and when risks are normally borne by insurance, there is everything to be said for leaving the parties free to apportion the risks as they think fit and for respecting their decision.

In this case the parties had contracted as equals and were clearly in the best position to decide how to allocate the risk of the factory being damaged or destroyed.

Statutory control

At first, Parliament intervened on a piecemeal basis to control the use of exemption clauses in specific types of contract. Section 43(7) of the Transport Act 1962 (repealed in 1977), for example, declared that any clause which purports to exclude or limit the liability of the British Railways Board in respect of injury or death to a passenger 'shall be void and of no effect'. Other examples of statutory control of exemption clauses include the Occupiers' Liability Act 1957, the Carriage of Goods by Sea Act 1971 and the Defective Premises Act 1972.

Parliamentary interest in exemption clauses culminated in the enactment of the Unfair Contract Terms Act 1977, which lays down rules of general application to most contracts. The 1977 Act is now supplemented by the Unfair Terms in Consumer Contracts Regulations 1999.

Unfair Contract Terms Act 1977

Preliminary matters

1 The Act came into force on 1 February 1978. It does not apply to contracts made before that date.

2 The title of the Act is misleading in two respects. First, it affects the law of tort as well as contract law because it covers non-contractual notices and signs. Second, it does not deal with all unfair terms in contracts, only unfair exemption clauses.

3 Most of the provisions of the Act apply only to 'business liability', i.e. liability for things done in the course of business or from the occupation of premises used for business purposes. A business includes a profession, the activities of government departments and those of a local or public authority.

4 The Act does not apply to international supply contracts, and ss 2–4 do not apply to certain contracts listed in Sch 1, which include:

(a) contracts of insurance;
(b) contracts in relation to land.

5 The Act affords the greatest protection to consumers: under s 12(1) a person 'deals as a consumer' if:

(a) he neither makes the contract in the course of a business nor holds himself out as doing so; and
(b) the other party does make the contract in the course of a business; and
(c) where it involves a contract for the sale or supply of goods, they are of a type ordinarily supplied for private use or consumption. This requirement has been amended by the Sale and Supply of Goods to Consumers Regulations 2002, which came into force on 31 March 2003. If the consumer is an individual it is no longer necessary to show that the goods are of a type ordinarily supplied for private use or consumption.

The possibilities are summarised in Figure 8.5.

The parties	Types of transaction
Business person/ private person	Consumer transaction*
Business person/ business person	Non-consumer transaction
Private person/ private person	Non-consumer transaction

* If goods are supplied, they must be of a type ordinarily supplied for private use or consumption for the contract to be classed as a consumer transaction, unless the consumer is an individual, in which case, it is not necessary to show that the goods are of a type ordinarily supplied for private use or consumption.

Figure 8.5 Consumer and non-consumer transactions under the Unfair Contract Terms Act 1977

The courts have interpreted s 12 so as to confine the impact of the more limited protection afforded to non-consumer transactions only to those business contracts which form an integral part of the business.

R & B Customs Brokers Co Ltd v United Dominions Trust Ltd (1988)

The claimant company, which was a freight forwarding and shipping agency, bought a second-hand car for the use of a director. The sale was arranged through the defendant finance company under a conditional sale agreement which contained exclusion clauses. The car was defective. The Court of Appeal held that the car was not fit for the purpose as required by s 14(3) of the Sale of Goods Act 1979 and that, as the claimant company was dealing as a consumer, this implied term could not be excluded by virtue of s 6 of the Unfair Contract Terms Act 1977. The court decided that there was not a sufficient degree of regularity to make the transaction an integral part of the company's business and, therefore, a contract made in the course of a business.

Comment. The Court of Appeal applied the same principle in *Feldaroll Foundry plc v Hermes Leasing (London) Ltd* (2004). Feldaroll entered into a hire-purchase agreement with Hermes for a Lamborghini car to be used by their managing director. The car was defective and Feldaroll sought to rely on the statutory implied conditions of satisfactory quality and fitness for purpose. Hermes argued that these terms had been excluded by a clause in the finance agreement. The Court of Appeal held that Feldaroll were entitled to reject the car. The court was bound by the decision in *R & B Custom Brokers*.

6 Exemption clauses are regulated by the Act in two ways. They are either rendered void and completely ineffective or they are made subject to a test of reasonableness. Although the application of the 'reasonableness test' is a matter for the court to decide in the light of all the circumstances of a particular case, the Act lays down some guiding principles for the judges.

(a) Reasonableness must be judged in the case of a contractual term in the light of circumstances at the time when the contract was made and, in the case of a non-contractual notice or sign, when the liability arose.

(b) It is up to the person who claims that a term or notice is reasonable to show that it is.

(c) Where the clause seeks to limit liability rather than exclude it completely, the court must have regard to two factors: the resources available to meet the liability and the extent to which insurance cover was available.

(d) Where the exemption clause appears in any kind of contract under which goods are supplied, its reasonableness may be judged according to the criteria contained in Sch 2, which are as follows:

- *The bargaining strengths of the parties relative to each other and the availability of alternative supplies.* A monopoly supplier, for example, will find it difficult to justify a wide exclusion clause.
- *Whether the customer received an inducement to agree to the term.* The supplier may have offered the customer a choice: a lower price, but subject to an exemption clause, or a higher price without the exemption. Where a real choice is available, the supplier will probably be able to show that the exemption clause was reasonable.
- *Whether the customer knew or ought reasonably to have known of the existence and extent of the term.* If the customer goes into the contract with his eyes wide open, he may have to accept the exemption clause.
- *Where the term excludes or restricts any relevant liability if some condition is not complied with, whether it was reasonable at the time of the contract to expect that compliance with that condition would be practicable.* A supplier, for example, may limit his liability to defects which are brought to his attention within a certain time, e.g. three days. The court will consider whether compliance with such a time limit is practicable.

- *Whether the goods were manufactured, processed or adapted to the special order of the customer.* An exemption clause may well be reasonable if the customer has insisted on the supplier complying with detailed specifications.

The reasonableness of exemption clauses in contracts other than for the sale or supply of goods must be judged without the benefit of these criteria. The leading case on unreasonableness is a decision of the House of Lords in which the reasonableness test contained in the sale of goods legislation, which preceded s 6 of the Unfair Contract Terms Act 1977, was considered.

George Mitchell (Chesterhall) Ltd v Finney Lock Seeds Ltd (1983)

The defendant seed merchants supplied the claimant farmers with 30 lb of Dutch winter cabbage seed for a price of £192. The claimants planted the seed on 63 acres but the seed was defective and the crop was a total failure. When the claimants claimed compensation for loss of the crop (over £60,000), the defendants sought to rely on a clause in the contract which purported to limit their liability to replacing the seed or refunding the purchase price. The House of Lords held that the defendants could not rely on the clause since it did not satisfy the reasonableness test. The House referred to the following factors as indicating that the clause was unreasonable: (a) the defendants had made ex gratia payments in similar cases in the past; (b) the breach had occurred as a result of the defendants' negligence; and (c) the defendants could have insured against the risk of crop failure without significantly increasing the price of the seed. In an attempt to discourage appeals on the question of reasonableness, Lord Bridge indicated that the decision of the trial judge should be treated with the utmost respect and should not be interfered with on appeal unless it was plainly and obviously wrong.

The following cases provide further examples of the application of the reasonableness test.

St Albans City and District Council v International Computers Ltd (1996)

The defendant company supplied the claimant local authority with a computer software system for administering the collection of the Community Charge. The software was defective with the result that the local authority collected far less than it expected. The supply

contract contained a clause limiting the liability for the defendant company to £100,000. The trial judge held that the limitation clause was not reasonable. The parties did not enjoy equal bargaining power; the defendant was a multinational company with large resources. The company was insured for £50 million and was, therefore, clearly better able to bear the loss than the local authority's Community Charge payers. The defendant appealed. Although the discussions in the Court of Appeal focused on the amount of damages recoverable, the court also considered whether the contract had been made on the company's written standard terms of business (see below). Although some negotiations had taken place between the parties, the company's conditions were accepted with a few changes. The contract, therefore, had been made on the company's written standard terms of business.

Britvic Soft Drinks Ltd v Messer UK Ltd (2002)

The defendants agreed to supply bulk liquid carbon dioxide (CO_2) to the claimants for use in the manufacture of carbonated soft and alcoholic drinks. The contract stated that the CO_2 complied with BS 4105. The CO_2 was in fact contaminated with benzene and the claimants decided to recall all drinks above a certain level of contamination. The defendants sought to rely on limitation of liability clauses in the contract. The Court of Appeal upheld the trial judge's conclusion that the limitation clause was unreasonable. It was accepted that the parties should be regarded as having equality of bargaining power as there were other suppliers of CO_2 to which the claimants could have gone for supplies. However, the parties did not discuss or negotiate about the clause; it was simply incorporated as part of the defendants' standard provisions. The court did not accept that it was reasonable for a supplier (as opposed to a manufacturer) to limit its liability for breach of the implied conditions under s 14 of the Sale of Goods Act 1979.

Exemption of liability for negligence (s 2)

Under s 2(1) no one acting in the course of a business can exclude or restrict his or her liability in negligence for death or personal injury by means of a term in a contract or by way of a notice. Liability for negligence for any other kind of loss or damage can be excluded if the term or notice satisfies the 'reasonableness test' (s 2(2)).

Phillips Products Ltd v Hyland (1987)

The claimant company hired an excavator and driver from the defendant plant hire company. A term in the standard form hire contract provided that the hirer was responsible for all claims arising in connection with the operation of the plant by the driver. The driver negligently drove the excavator into the claimant's building, causing damage. The trial judge held that the term was covered by s 2(2) of the Unfair Contract Terms Act 1977 and was, therefore, subject to the reasonableness test. The exclusion of liability was unreasonable because the hire was for a short period, arranged at short notice and on the defendant's standard terms. The claimant had little experience of such hiring agreements and virtually no opportunity to arrange insurance cover. Moreover, the claimant did not have the power to select the driver or to control the way in which he did his job. As the defendant was unable to satisfy the judge that the term was fair and reasonable, the exclusion of liability was invalid. The defendant was held liable for the damage caused to the claimant's building. The Court of Appeal dismissed the defendant's appeal.

Section 2(2) will not apply where the negligence consists of a breach of an obligation arising from a contract and the person seeking to enforce the obligation is a third party (s 7(2) of the Contracts (Rights of Third Parties) Act 1999). The effect of this provision is best explained by the following example.

Example

Alan enters into a contract with Brian, a builder, to build a detached double garage for his mother, Cynthia. The contract contains an exemption clause which seeks to exclude Brian's liability for negligent construction work. Brian carries out the work defectively and, as a result, the roof of the garage collapses. If Alan and Cynthia were in the garage at the time and were injured, the exemption clause would be void under s 2(1) of the Unfair Contract Terms Act 1977, and both Alan and Cynthia would be able to bring a claim against Brian: in Alan's case as party to the contract, and in Cynthia's case under the provisions of s 1 of the Contracts (Rights of Third Parties) Act 1999. If, however, the roof collapse only caused damage to Alan's and Cynthia's cars, the position would be different. Alan would be able to sue Brian as a party to the contract unless Brian were able to show that the exemption clause was reasonable under s 2(2) of the Unfair Contract

Terms Act 1977. If Cynthia sues Brian as a third party to the contract, the effect of s 7(2) of the Contracts (Rights of Third Parties) Act 1999 is that Brian will be able to rely on the exemption clause no matter how unreasonable.

Exemption of liability for breach of contract (s 3)

Section 3 applies to two types of contract made in the course of a business:

- where the other party deals as a consumer; and
- where the businessperson contracts on his own written standard terms of business.

In both cases, the businessperson cannot exclude or limit his liability for breach of contract, non-performance of the contract or different performance of the contract unless the exemption clause satisfies the requirement of reasonableness.

Unreasonable indemnity clauses (s 4)

An indemnity clause is a term in a contract between two parties (A and B) in which B agrees to indemnify A for any liability that A may be under. A may incur liability in respect of a third party (C), in which case B must compensate A for any claim which is made by C against A. A builder, for example, may get the owner of a house to agree to indemnify him for any injury or damage that his work on the house might cause to third parties. So if the builder negligently demolishes a wall and injures a next-door neighbour, the builder can call on the house owner to make good any award of damages. In some cases, B is required to indemnify A in respect of a liability that A may be under to B himself. Such an indemnity clause has the same effect as an exclusion clause.

Under s 4, indemnity clauses in contracts where one of the parties deals as a consumer are unenforceable unless they satisfy the requirement of reasonableness.

Guarantees of consumer goods (s 5)

At one time, it was common practice for guarantees given with goods to contain a clause exempting the manufacturer from liability in negligence if the product proved defective. Under s 5 a manufacturer or distributor cannot exclude or restrict his liability in negligence for loss arising from defects in goods ordinarily supplied for private use or consumption by means of a term or notice contained in a guarantee. (Manufacturers' guarantees will be examined in Chapter 11 ⊙.)

Exemption of implied terms in contracts of sale and hire-purchase (s 6)

The original Sale of Goods Act 1893 gave the parties complete freedom to exclude the implied terms contained in ss 12–15. Retailers often used the opportunity to deprive consumers of their rights by getting customers to sign an order form, which included an exemption clause hidden in the small print, or by displaying suitably worded notices at the point of sale. The Molony Committee on Consumer Protection, which reported in 1962, identified the ease with which the implied terms could be excluded as a major defect in the Act, and in 1969 the Law Commission made proposals for reform. The changes were effected by the Supply of Goods (Implied Terms) Act 1973 and incorporated into the revised Sale of Goods Act 1979. The implied obligations as to title contained in s 12 of the Sale of Goods Act 1979 (sale of goods) and s 8 of the Supply of Goods (Implied Terms) Act 1973 (hire-purchase) cannot be excluded or restricted by any contract term. The implied terms as to description, quality, etc. contained in ss 13–15 of the Sale of Goods Act 1979 (sale of goods) and ss 9–11 of the Supply of Goods (Implied Terms) Act 1973 (hire-purchase) cannot be excluded or restricted by any contract term against a person dealing as a consumer. Where the person is not dealing as a consumer, the exemption clause is subject to the 'reasonableness test'.

Exemption of implied terms in other contracts for the supply of goods (s 7)

Terms as to title, description, satisfactory quality, fitness for purpose and sample are now included in contracts for the supply of goods by way of hire, exchange or work and materials contracts by virtue of the Supply of Goods and Services Act 1982. The implied obligation as to title contained in s 2 of the 1982 Act (contracts of exchange or work and materials) cannot be excluded or restricted. Exclusion clauses relating to title in contracts of hire, contained in s 7, are subject to the reasonableness test. The other implied terms cannot be excluded or restricted at all in consumer contracts but in other transactions the exemption clause is subject to the reasonableness test. The complicated provisions of the Unfair Contract

Terms Act 1977 in relation to the exclusion of statutory implied terms are summarised in Figure 8.6.

Exemption of liability for misrepresentation (s 8)

Section 3 of the Misrepresentation Act 1967, as amended by s 8 of the Unfair Contract Terms Act 1977, provides that any clause which excludes or restricts liability for misrepresentation is ineffective unless it satisfies the requirement of reasonableness.

Cases decided under the Unfair Contract Terms Act 1977

Lally and Weller v *George Bird* (1980)

The defendant agreed to undertake a house removal for the claimants for £100.80. The contract contained exemption clauses which limited the defendant's liability for losses or breakages to £10 per article and excluded all liability unless claims were made within three days. It was held that these clauses were unreasonable.

Waldron-Kelly v *British Railways Board* (1981)

The claimant placed a suitcase in the care of BR at Stockport railway station for delivery to Haverford West railway station. BR's General Conditions of Carriage limited its liability for non-delivery to an amount assessed by reference to the weight of the goods. The suitcase disappeared and the claimant claimed £320.32 as the full value of the suitcase. BR sought to rely on its conditions, which limited BR's liability to £27. It was held that BR could not rely on the exemption clause because it did not satisfy the requirement of reasonableness. The claimant was awarded £320.32.

Woodman v *Photo Trade Processing Ltd* (1981)

Mr Woodman deposited a reel of film containing pictures of a friend's wedding with the defendants for processing. Unfortunately, most of the pictures were lost, and when sued the defendants relied on the following exclusion clause: 'All photographic materials are accepted on the basis that their value does not exceed the cost of the material itself. Responsibility is limited to the replacement

		Exemption clauses in contracts for the supply of goods by way of:			
		Sale, HP, exchange and work + materials		Hire	
		Consumer transaction	Non-consumer transaction	Consumer transaction	Non-consumer transaction
Implied Terms	Title	Void	Void	Subject to reasonableness test	Subject to reasonableness test
	Description	Void	Subject to reasonableness test	Void	Subject to reasonableness test
	Quality and Suitability	Void	Subject to reasonableness test	Void	Subject to reasonableness test
	Sample	Void	Subject to reasonableness test	Void	Subject to reasonableness test

Figure 8.6 Exemption of statutory implied terms in contract for the supply of goods

of the films. No liability will be accepted consequential or otherwise, however caused.' The county court judge held that the clause was unreasonable for the following reasons: (a) the clause was in standard use throughout the trade and so Mr Woodman had no real alternative but to have his film processed on these terms; and (b) the code of practice for the photographic industry envisaged the possibility of processors offering a two-tier service, either a lower price but with full exclusion of liability or a higher price with the processor accepting fuller liability. Mr Woodman was not offered such a choice. He was awarded £75 in compensation.

Comment. The **Woodman** case indicates that failure to provide customers with an alternative is likely to lead to any exemption clause being declared unreasonable. However, it is not enough merely to inform customers that an alternative exists: sufficient detail must be provided for customers to be able to exercise a genuine choice. In **Warren v Truprint Ltd** (1986), another county court case involving lost film, the defendant film processors had made the following addition to their limitation clause: '. . . we will undertake further liability at a supplementary charge. Written details on request.' The judge held that this did not pass the reasonableness test since the defendants had failed to 'plainly and clearly set out the alternative' and the cost to the customer.

Unfair Terms in Consumer Contracts Regulations 1999

The statutory restrictions on the use of exemption clauses contained in the Unfair Contract Terms Act 1977 have been supplemented by the Unfair Terms in Consumer Contracts Regulations 1999 (SI 1999/2083). The regulations implement Directive 93/13/EEC on Unfair Terms in Consumer Contracts. The 1999 regulations replace, with amendment, the 1994 regulations of the same name (SI 1994/3159) which came into force on 1 July 1995.

Although there is a certain amount of overlap between the 1977 Act and the regulations as well as points of similarity (i.e. the test of reasonableness in the Act and the tests of fairness in the regulations), there are some important differences, as illustrated in Figure 8.7, overleaf.

The above regulations apply, with certain exceptions, to unfair terms in contracts between a business seller or supplier and a consumer (reg 4(1)). A consumer is defined as a natural person who is acting for purposes outside his trade, business or profession. A business includes a trade or profession, any government department and local and public authorities. The regulations do not cover terms in non-consumer contracts such as:

Unfair Contract Terms Act 1977	Unfair Terms in Consumer Contracts Regulations 1999
Mainly exemption clauses	All unfair terms
Business and consumer contracts	Only consumer contracts
Negotiated and non-negotiated contracts	Only non-negotiated contracts
Exemptions in contracts and notices	Only terms in consumer contracts
Exemptions are either automatically void or rendered void if unreasonable	Unfair terms are rendered voidable
Individual right of civil action	Individual right of civil action and administrative control by the Office of Fair Trading and other qualifying bodies, which may seek an injunction to prevent the continued general use of an unfair term

Figure 8.7 A comparison of the Unfair Contract Terms Act 1977 and the Unfair Terms in Consumer Contracts Regulations 1999

- employment contracts;
- agreements dealing with succession rights;
- family law rights;
- the incorporation or organisation of companies or partnerships.

Also excluded are terms which have been incorporated to comply with or reflect statutory or regulatory provisions of the UK or the provisions or principles of international conventions to which either the UK or the EC is party.

Terms in consumer contracts, which have not been individually negotiated, will be regarded as unfair if, contrary to the requirement of good faith, they cause a significant imbalance in the parties' rights and obligations under the contract, to the detriment of the consumer (reg 5(1)). A term will always be regarded as not having been individually negotiated where it has

been drafted in advance and the consumer has not been able to influence the substance of the term. The burden of proof is placed on the trader to show that the term has been individually negotiated.

Schedule 2 to the regulations sets out an indicative, non-exhaustive list of terms which may be regarded as unfair. It should not be assumed that terms covered by the list are automatically unfair; they may be unfair in some circumstances but fair in different circumstances. It is also the case that certain terms not covered by the list may be regarded as unfair. There are 17 examples set out in Sch 2, including the following terms:

- excluding or limiting the legal liability of a seller or supplier for the death of or personal injury to a consumer arising from an act or omission of the seller or supplier, e.g. 'products are used at customers' own risk';
- allowing the seller or supplier to keep sums paid by the consumer in case the consumer decides to cancel without providing for the consumer to receive compensation of an equivalent amount if the seller or supplier cancels, e.g. 'no refunds of deposits if orders are cancelled';
- enabling the seller or supplier unilaterally to change the terms of a contract without a valid reason which is set out in the contract, e.g. 'products supplied may vary in specification from those ordered';
- providing that the price of goods can be varied without giving the consumer the right to cancel if the price is too high, e.g. 'the price of goods may be increased where there is an increase in costs prior to delivery';
- restricting the consumer's right to take legal action, for example by requiring disputes to be resolved by arbitration, or by restricting the evidence available or by changing the usual burden of proof, e.g. 'all disputes concerning this agreement will be resolved by arbitration'.

'Core terms' which define the main subject matter of the contract or concern the adequacy of the price of the goods or services are not subject to an assessment of fairness provided they are in plain and intelligible language. Any written term of a consumer contract must be 'expressed in plain intelligible language'. Where there is any doubt about the meaning of a term, the interpretation which is most favourable to the consumer must prevail.

Two different types of remedy are available under the regulations. First, unfair terms are deemed voidable as against the consumer, although the contract itself will still be binding if it can continue in existence without the unfair term. Second, the Office of Fair Trading (OFT) is under a duty to receive and consider complaints that a contract term drawn up for general use is unfair. Having considered such a complaint and any undertakings given about the continued use of such unfair terms, the OFT may apply for an injunction from the High Court to prevent the continued use of the particular unfair term and any similar terms by any party to the proceedings. The 1999 Regulations provide for the first time that certain qualifying bodies (e.g. statutory regulators, such as the Rail Regulator and the Director General of Gas Supply, trading standards departments and the Consumers' Association) can also apply for an injunction to prevent the continued use of an unfair term.

The following cases provide interesting examples of the application of the regulations.

Director General of Fair Trading v First National Bank plc (2001)

The Director General of Fair Trading applied to the High Court for an injunction to restrain the defendant bank from using a term in its standard form loan agreement. The term in question provided for the accrual of interest on any judgments obtained by the bank under the loan agreement. The Director General was concerned that customers who agreed to judgment on terms involving payment of the balance by instalments would find themselves faced with further payments of interest once the balance had been cleared. The Director General argued that the term was unfair in that 'contrary to the requirement of good faith, [it caused] a significant imbalance in the parties' rights and obligations . . . to the detriment of the consumer'. The bank argued that the provision concerning interest on judgments was a 'core term' as it related to the adequacy of the price or remuneration, and so was not subject to the requirement of fairness. The Court of Appeal held that the term in question could not be classed as a 'core term' as it did not define the main subject matter of the contract, nor did it relate to the adequacy of the remuneration as it applied only where a consumer was in default. The court took the view that the term was unfair. It did not satisfy the requirement of good faith and caused a significant imbalance in the rights and obligations of the parties. The House of Lords agreed with the Court of Appeal that the provision about interest was not a core term, and it was,

therefore, subject to a requirement of reasonableness. Their Lordships held that the interest provision was not unfair. Borrowers could easily understand the essential elements of the bargain, which was that the bank would lend money in return for the borrower agreeing to repay the loan with interest. The interest provision in question was designed to ensure that this remained the position if the bank obtained judgment against a borrower in default. The term itself was not detrimental to borrowers. What was detrimental was the fact that the Consumer Credit Act 1974 did not contain a procedure to require courts to consider using their powers under the Act, e.g. to vary interest rates, when borrowers defaulted.

Munkenbeck & Marshall v Harold (2005)

The defendant H engaged the claimant firm of architects M under the RIBA SFA/99 standard terms after negotiating a reduction in fees. The terms of the contract provided that the defendant should indemnify the claimant in respect of any legal and other costs in any proceedings and that interest would be payable on unpaid sums at 8 per cent over the Bank of England base rate. There was no provision for the architect to pay his client. The High Court held that: (i) the rate of interest was a genuine pre-estimate of the loss likely to be suffered by the claimant and it did not amount to a penalty; (ii) the terms of the standard form contract were unfair under reg 5 of the 1999 Regulations and consequently were unenforceable. Even though the terms formed part of profession-wide standard terms, they were, in the words of Havery J, 'unusual and onerous'. They had not been drawn to the defendant's attention, and, although the defendant was not without bargaining power (he had negotiated a reduction in fees), there was an imbalance between the parties to the detriment of the consumer.

Office of Fair Trading v Abbey National plc (2009)

This was a test case brought by the Office of Fair Trading (OFT) with the agreement of eight high street banks concerning the application of the Unfair Terms in Consumer Contracts Regulations to charges for unarranged overdrafts. At first instance the High Court ruled that: (i) the terms used for current accounts were in, or largely in, plain and intelligible language; (ii) the terms were not exempt from an assessment for fairness under the regulations. The banks had argued that the relevant terms related to the adequacy of the price, which is expressly excluded from an assessment of fairness if the terms were in plain and intelligible language. The Court of Appeal confirmed the decision of the High Court, but these ruling were overturned by the Supreme Court. The Justices concluded the charges for unarranged overdrafts, which amount to about one-third of the revenues from personal current account holders, form part of the price for banking services and, in so far as t he relevant terms are in plain and intelligible language, no assessment of the fairness of the terms relating to the adequacy of the price for the services could be made under the Regulations. In December 2009 the OFT announced that it would be exploring a number of options in relation to the operation of personal current accounts, ranging from voluntary action on the part of the banks to legislation.

Reform

In 2001 the DTI asked the Law Commission and the Scottish Law Commission to review the statutory regulation of unfair contract terms contained in the Unfair Contract Terms Act 1977 and the Unfair Terms in Consumer Contracts Regulations 1999 with a view to creating a single piece of legislation which was clearer and more accessible. In 2002 the Law Commission and the Scottish Law Commission issued a joint consultation paper on Unfair Terms in Contracts and their Final Report and Draft Bill was published in 2005. The main proposals are as follows:

- There should be a single piece of legislation for the whole UK that preserves the existing level of consumer protection.
- Where there is currently a difference in the level of protection afforded by the Act and the regulations, the protection should be rounded up to the higher level.
- Terms which are automatically void under UCTA should continue to be of no effect.
- The definition of a 'consumer' should refer to a person acting for purposes unrelated to his or her business and only natural persons should be considered consumers.

- In respect of consumer contracts:
  - the legislation should extend to all terms covered by the regulations (not just exclusion clauses);
  - terms which exclude liability for the quality and fitness of goods should continue to be ineffective;
  - the legislation should cover negotiated clauses as well as standard contract terms;
  - where claims are brought by consumers the burden of proof is placed on the business to show that the term is fair. (Where the OFT and other qualifying bodies are exercising preventive powers, they must show the term is unfair.)
- The OFT and other qualifying bodies will acquire additional powers, e.g. to require that 'No liability' or 'No refund' notices which are legally ineffective should be taken down.
- Small 'micro' businesses, with nine or fewer staff, would acquire special protection. Small businesses will be able to challenge any standard term of a contract which has not been individually negotiated provided it does not concern the main subject matter of the contract or the price. However, there are exceptions to the small business protection, namely:
  - contracts for financial services;
  - contracts over £500,000;
  - contracts for land, intellectual property, security interests;
  - where the business is associated with other businesses, so that overall there are more than nine employees.
- Businesses should be able to negotiate to exclude or limit liability for the implied terms relating to description, quality and fitness in the supply of goods legislation.

Meanwhile, the European Commission is undertaking a review of eight key directives that comprise the 'Consumer Acquis'. The Unfair Contract Terms Directive is included in the scope of the review. In February 2007 the Commission adopted a Green Paper setting out options for reform of a number of consumer directives, including the Directive on Unfair Terms in Consumer Contracts. In 2008 the Commission published a proposal for a Directive on Consumer Rights, which will if implemented replace four separate Directives, including the Unfair Contract Terms Directive.

Fair Trading Act 1973

Parliament chose to focus the fight against exemption clauses by changing the civil law. The most offensive exemptions from liability, though void, were not illegal. Retailers continued to display notices such as 'No Refunds', and to include exclusion clauses in sales agreements. In many cases, the consumer was 'conned' into believing that he had been deprived of his rights. The Fair Trading Act 1973, however, opened the way for such unfair consumer trade practices to be made illegal. The Consumer Transactions (Restrictions on Statements) Order 1976 (SI 1976/1813) (as amended) makes it a criminal offence for a trader to continue to use exclusion clauses rendered void by ss 6 and 7 of the Unfair Contract Terms Act 1977. This outlaws the use of 'No money refunded' notices.

Self-test questions/activities

1 (a) Explain what is meant by the following saying: 'The terms of a contract must be certain or capable of being made certain.'

(b) Consider the legal position in each of the situations given below:

(i) Sally, an actress, accepts an offer to play Ophelia in a new London production of *Hamlet* 'at a West End salary to be mutually agreed'. Sally and the producers cannot agree on an appropriate salary.

(ii) Gary agrees to buy a motorcycle from Speedy Garages Ltd 'on usual HP terms'. Gary has now learnt that he will be required to pay a 50 per cent deposit. He has not saved up enough money.

(iii) After lengthy negotiations for the sale of a flat, Anne, the purchaser, writes to the vendors, 'I accept your offer to sell 12A Sea Terrace, Sandy Bar, for £150,000, subject to the usual conditions of acceptance appropriate to this kind of sale.' Anne has been offered a job 100 miles away and now wishes to withdraw from the purchase.

(iv) Mercurial Property Co Ltd grants a five-year lease on shop premises to Frosted Foods Ltd at a rent of £10,000 a year. It is agreed that Frosted Foods Ltd will be able to extend the lease by a further three years 'at such rent as may be agreed between the parties', and that any dispute should be referred to arbitration. The parties have failed to agree the rent for the extension of the lease.

2 Paul is looking for a second-hand car when he sees an advertisement in his local evening paper which reads:

> SLICK CAR SALES LTD
> Hundreds of used car bargains. Lowest prices you've ever seen
> Definitely the lowest prices in Britain
> All cars purchased this month will include Vehicle Tax, Radio, Stereo and a full tank of petrol

Paul visits the showrooms of Slick Cars and selects a car priced £1,995 which the salesperson tells him is a 2004 Mondeo which has done 30,000 miles and has had only one owner. Paul signs a sales agreement which describes the car as '2004 Ford Mondeo. Cayman Blue. Registration Number LT04XYZ'.

(a) From the facts given above, identify an example of each of the following: trader's puff, a representation, a condition and a warranty.

(b) What remedies will be available to Paul if any of the statements you identified in your answer to (a) turns out to be false?

(c) Identify three terms which will be implied into the contract.

3 While on holiday at the seaside, Jim agrees to take his family to 'Fun Park'. He pays £1 to park his car on a car park run by the Strand Council. A notice at the entrance of the car park, which has been partly obscured by overgrown shrubs, states: 'Cars parked entirely at owner's risk'. Jim pays £7 for a family admission ticket to

'Fun Park', which is managed by Leisure Ltd. The back of the ticket contains the following clause: 'The company does not accept liability for death or personal injury to visitors, howsoever caused.' Jim and his wife are watching their children on the 'waltzer' when a metal bar flies off, injuring Jim and his wife. After receiving hospital treatment, Jim returns to his car to discover that it has been damaged by a Strand Council refuse van.

Advise Jim and his wife.

4 Angela buys an 'Onion' personal computer from Future Computers Ltd. She signs a sales note in the shop which states: 'Any express or implied condition, statement or warranty, statutory or otherwise is hereby excluded'. After a week's satisfactory use, the 'Onion' refuses to work.

What is the legal position if:

(a) Angela bought the 'Onion' for her own personal use?

(b) Angela bought the 'Onion' to help in her work as an accountant?

Specimen examination questions

1 'It is indisputable that unless all the material terms of the contract are agreed there is no binding contract. An agreement to agree in the future is not a contract; nor is there a contract if a material term is neither settled nor implied by law and the document contains no machinery for ascertaining it' (Maughan LJ, *Foley* v *Classique Coaches Ltd* (1934)).

Explain this statement.

2 Tony, the owner of a London-based manufacturing company, has to attend an important business meeting in Edinburgh on Monday. He is virtually certain to be awarded a lucrative contract for his company if he keeps the appointment. He books a flight online with PlanesRus. The booking conditions include the following statement: 'The company gives no guarantee that a seat will be available on a particular flight and reserves the right to transfer customers to later or earlier flights and will not in such circumstances be liable to pay compensation.' Tony books a taxi to take him to the airport in London and overnight accommodation in Edinburgh for the Monday night. On arrival at the airport for his flight, he is informed that the morning flight to Edinburgh is full but he is allocated a seat on the Tuesday morning flight. He fails to keep his appointment and as a result loses the contract for his company.

Advise Tony who wishes to claim damages for the lost business deal, the cost of his taxi fare and the hotel booking.

3 Explain what is meant by the term 'standard form contract'. What are the advantages and

disadvantages of using standard form contracts in business?

4 Critically evaluate the similarities and differences between the protection provided by the Unfair Contract Terms Act 1977 and the Unfair Terms in Consumer Contracts Regulations 1999.

5 Fred is a newsagent in Fordsworth. A salesman from Tills Ltd calls and attempts to persuade him to take out a hire agreement on a new electronic till with stock-control facilities. The agreement is for a period of three years. Knowing that the machine is likely to become dated fairly quickly, Fred asks what will happen in such a case. The salesman replies that his company will update the machine every 12 months at a nominal charge; Fred signs the hire agreement, which does not contain this term. Fifteen months later Fred learns that Tills has launched a new electronic till which is much more reliable and easier to use than the model he has hired. He contacts Tills Ltd which tells him he is not entitled to the new model but that as a gesture of goodwill the company will replace his current till for £500 and a 20 per cent increase in his rental. Fred cannot afford this and finds he can get a new electronic till with the features he requires from another company much more cheaply than his current rental. He wishes to withdraw from his agreement with Tills Ltd.

(a) Advise Fred.

(b) What difference, if any, would it make to your answer if the salesman's statement had been included in the hire agreement?

Website references

http://www.oft.gov.uk The Office of Fair Trading website contains information and guidance on unfair terms.

http://www.bis.gov.uk/policies/consumer-issues/buying-and-selling The Department for Business, Innovation and Skills' website provides information about consumer law issues including unfair terms.

http://www.lawcom.gov.uk The Law Commission and Scottish Law Commission's final report and draft bill on Unfair Contract Terms can be found on the Law Commission's website in the Commercial and Common Law section.

Visit www.mylawchamber.co.uk/richesallen to access study support resources including answers to questions in this chapter and legal updates, all linked to the **Pearson eText** version of **Keenan and Riches' Business Law** which you can **search**, **highlight** and **personalise** with your **own notes** and **bookmarks**.

Use **Case Navigator** to read in full some of the key cases referenced in this chapter with commentary and questions:

Director General of Fair Trading v *First National Bank plc* (2001)
Interfoto Picture Library v *Stiletto Visual Programmes Ltd* (1989)

Chapter 9

Ending business contracts

Learning objectives

After studying this chapter you should understand the following main points:

■ the ways in which the obligations under a contract may be discharged;

■ the remedies available for breach of contract;

■ time limits for commencing legal action.

In the last two chapters we have considered how contracts are formed, the factors which may affect the validity of the contract and the terms of a contract. We will now look at the ways in which a contract can come to an end and the remedies available to an injured party when a contract is broken. The termination of a contract is often referred to as the discharge of a contract, as it explains the ways the parties can be discharged from their contractual obligations.

Discharge of contracts

The contract may come to an end and the parties discharged from their contractual obligations in four ways: by performance, agreement, frustration and breach.

Performance

The general rule is that the parties must carry out precisely what they agreed under their contract. If one of the parties does something less than or different from that which he agreed to do, he is not discharged from the contract and, moreover, cannot sue on the contract.

Cutter v Powell (1795)

Cutter agreed to serve on a ship sailing from Jamaica to Liverpool. He was to be paid 30 guineas on arrival at Liverpool. The ship sailed on 2 August, arriving in Liverpool

on 9 October, but Cutter died at sea on 20 September. It was held that his widow could not recover anything for the work he had done before he died. Cutter was obliged to complete the voyage before he was entitled to payment.

Comment. This old case is often presented as a classic illustration of the law's insistence on complete performance as a prerequisite of the right to sue in respect of an entire contract. Although the point being made is still valid, the case itself would not be decided in the same way today. Cutter's widow would now be able to argue that her husband's untimely death had frustrated the contract and that she should recover in respect of the valuable benefit her husband conferred on his employer before his death under s 1(3) of the Law Reform (Frustrated Contracts) Act 1943.

Bolton v Mahadeva (1972)

Bolton installed a central heating system in Mahadeva's house for an agreed price of £560. The work was carried out defectively and it was estimated that it would cost £179 to put matters right. The Court of Appeal held that since Bolton had not performed his side of the contract, he could recover nothing for the work he had done.

In each of these cases, one party has profited from the failure of the other to provide complete performance. A strict application of the rule about precise performance would frequently lead to injustice. It is not surprising, therefore, that certain exceptions to the rule have developed.

1 Doctrine of substantial performance. If the court decides that the claimant has substantially carried out the terms of the contract, the claimant may recover for the work he or she has done. The defendant can counter-claim for any defects in performance.

Hoenig v *Isaacs* (1952)

The claimant agreed to decorate the defendant's flat and fit a bookcase and wardrobe for £750. On completion of the work, the defendant paid £400 but he complained about faulty workmanship and refused to pay the balance of £350. The Court of Appeal held that the contract had been substantially performed. The claimant was entitled to the outstanding £350, less the cost of remedying the defects, which was estimated at £55 18s 2d.

2 Acceptance of partial performance. If one of the parties only partially carries out his side of the contract, but the other party, exercising a genuine choice, accepts the benefit of the partial performance, the court will infer a promise to pay for the benefit received.

3 Performance prevented by the promise. A person who is prevented from carrying out his side of the bargain by the other party can bring an action to recover for the work he has done.

Planché v *Colburn* (1831)

The claimant agreed to write a book on 'Costume and Ancient Armour', on completion of which he was to receive £100. After he had done the necessary research and written part of the book, the publishers abandoned the project. He recovered 50 guineas for the work he had done. The claimant's claim was based on quasi-contract. He could not sue on the contract because the obligation to pay him did not arise until he had completed and delivered the work to the publishers, which he had not done. He was able to sue on a *quantum meruit* (see later in this chapter) for the work he had done.

4 Divisible contracts. Some contracts are said to be 'entire'. This means that a party is not entitled to

payment until he has completely performed his part of the contract, e.g. *Cutter* v *Powell* (1795). Other contracts may be divisible, i.e. the obligations can be split up into stages or parts. Payment can be claimed for each completed stage. A contract to build a house usually provides for payment to be made in three stages: after the foundations have been laid, when the roof goes on, and on completion of the house.

Agreement

The parties may have agreed in their original contract that it should end automatically with the happening of some event or after a fixed period of time. The agreement may have included a term allowing either party to terminate the contract by giving notice. A contract of employment, for example, can be brought to an end by either the employer or employee giving reasonable notice to the other. The Employment Rights Act 1996 lays down statutory minimum periods of notice. Employers must also consider the rules about unfair dismissal and redundancy. A contract may be discharged by the execution of a separate agreement. The new agreement will only discharge the old contract if it possesses all the characteristics of a valid contract; in particular, consideration must be present. When neither party has yet performed his side of the contract, there is no difficulty. Both sides, by waiving their rights, are providing something of value which constitutes consideration. The situation is different where one side has already completely performed his obligations and the other party wishes to be released. The person seeking release must either provide fresh consideration or the agreement must be drawn up in the form of a deed.

Frustration

An agreement which is impossible of performance from the outset will be void for mistake, as in *Couturier* v *Hastie* (1856). But what is the legal position where initially it is perfectly possible to carry out the contract, and then a change in circumstances occurs making it impossible to carry out the agreement?

Until the 19th century, the rule was that the parties were under an absolute duty to perform their contractual obligations. A person was not excused simply because outside events had made performance impossible.

Paradine v *Jane* (1647)

During the course of the English Civil War a tenant was evicted from certain property by Prince Rupert and his army. In an action by the landlord to recover three years' arrears of rent, it was held that the tenant was not relieved from the obligation to pay rent simply because he had been unable to enjoy the property.

Starting with the case of *Taylor* v *Caldwell* (1863), the courts recognised an exception to the rule about absolute contracts under the doctrine of frustration: if further performance of the contract is prevented because of events beyond the control of the parties, the contract is terminated and the parties discharged from their obligations. The doctrine will apply in the circumstances described below.

1 Physical impossibility. This is where something or someone necessary to carry out the contract ceases to be available.

Taylor v *Caldwell* (1863)

The claimant had hired the Surrey Gardens and Music Hall for a series of concerts. However, after making the agreement and before the date of the first performance, the hall was destroyed by fire. It was held that the contract was discharged and the parties were released from their obligations.

If the presence of a particular person is necessary for the execution of the contract, the death of that person will clearly discharge the contract. Frustration may also apply if a party is unavailable because of illness, internment or imprisonment.

Hare v *Murphy Bros* (1974)

Hare was sentenced to 12 months' imprisonment for unlawful wounding and was, therefore, unavailable to carry out his responsibilities as a foreman. It was held that this frustrated his contract of employment.

Comment. An employee who loses his job as a result of long-term illness or, as in Hare's case, a substantial term

of imprisonment, may find that his contract of employment has been frustrated. The significance of such a finding is that there will not have been a 'dismissal' according to the statutory provisions relating to unfair dismissal (and redundancy). If there has been no 'dismissal', the employee cannot bring a claim for unfair dismissal (or redundancy) against his employer. Unfair dismissal and redundancy will be discussed in more detail in Chapter 16 ◐ .

2 Supervening illegality. A subsequent change in the law or in circumstances may make performance of the contract illegal. An export contract will be discharged if war breaks out with the country of destination.

Denny, Mott & Dickson Ltd v *James B Fraser & Co Ltd* (1944)

The House of Lords refused to enforce an option to purchase a timber yard which was part of a contract involving the sale of timber because subsequent government regulations had made performance of the main part of the contract, trading in timber, illegal.

3 Foundation of the contract destroyed. The parties may have made their contract on the basis of some forthcoming event. If the event fails to take place and, as a result, the main purpose of the contract cannot be achieved, the doctrine of frustration will apply.

Krell v *Henry* (1903)

Henry hired a room overlooking the route of Edward VII's coronation procession. The procession was cancelled owing to the King's serious illness. Although it would have been possible to come and sit in the room, the main purpose of the contract, to view the procession, had been destroyed. The Court of Appeal held that the contract had been frustrated.

A contract will only be frustrated if the change in circumstances has had a substantial effect on the main purpose of the contract.

Herne Bay Steam Boat Company v Hutton (1903)

The claimant agreed to hire a steamboat, the *Cynthia*, to the defendant for two days so that the defendant could take paying passengers to see the naval review at Spithead on the occasion of Edward VII's coronation. An official announcement was made cancelling the review, but the fleet still gathered and the *Cynthia* could have been used for a cruise around the fleet. The defendant did not make use of the boat and the claimant used her for ordinary sailings. The claimant sued for £200, which was the outstanding balance on the contract to hire the boat. A Court of Appeal held that the contract was not discharged through frustration. The happening of the naval review was not the foundation of the contract. The claimant was entitled, therefore, to recover the £200 he was owed under the contract.

The fact that the contract has become more difficult and more expensive to carry out will not excuse the parties.

Tsakiroglou & Co Ltd v Noblee and Thorl GmbH (1961)

In October 1956 sellers agreed to deliver ground nuts from Port Sudan to buyers in Hamburg, shipment to take place during November/December 1956. On 2 November the Suez Canal was closed to traffic. The sellers failed to deliver and, when sued for breach of contract, argued that the contract had been frustrated. Clearly, it had not become impossible to carry out the contract: shipment could have been made via the Cape of Good Hope – a longer and much more expensive journey. The House of Lords held that this was not sufficient to discharge the contract for frustration.

Davis Contractors Ltd v Fareham Urban District Council (1956)

The claimant contractors agreed to build 78 houses in eight months for the defendant council. Owing to post-war shortages of skilled labour and building materials, it took the contractors 22 months to complete the houses at an additional cost of £17,651. The claimants argued that the contract was frustrated because of the long delay caused by circumstances beyond their control and they should be able to recover the full cost incurred on a *quantum meruit* basis. The House of Lords held that the contract was not discharged by frustration. The contractors could have foreseen the possibility of shortages and taken it into account when tendering for the work.

The doctrine of frustration will not apply in the following situations:

- Where the parties have foreseen the likelihood of such an event occurring and have made express provision for it in the contract.
- Where one of the parties is responsible for the frustrating event. This is known as 'self-induced frustration'.

Maritime National Fish Ltd v Ocean Trawlers Ltd (1938)

The appellants chartered a trawler from the respondents which needed to be fitted with an otter trawl. It was illegal to operate with an otter trawl unless a licence had been obtained. The appellants applied for five licences to cover four trawlers of their own and the trawler on charter; however, they were granted only three licences. They decided to nominate their own trawlers for licences rather than the chartered trawler. The Judicial Committee of the Privy Council held that the contract was not frustrated as the appellants had decided quite deliberately not to nominate the respondents' trawler and were, therefore, responsible for the frustrating event.

The doctrine of frustration was considered recently by the Court of Appeal in *Edwinton Commercial Corporation v Tsavliris (Worldwide Salvage and Towage) Ltd, The Sea Angel* (2007), a case which required the court to decide whether a charterparty had been frustrated. Rix LJ stated that the application of the doctrine required a multifactorial approach. The factors to be considered included the terms of the contract, its context, the parties' knowledge, expectations, assumptions and contemplations, in particular as to risk, as at the time the contract was concluded, the nature of the supervening event, and the parties' calculations as to the possibilities of future performance in the new circumstances. The test of 'radically different' is important: it means that the doctrine should not be invoked lightly. The mere incidence of expense or delay or onerousness is not sufficient. There has to be a break in the identity between the contract as provided for and contemplated and its performance in new circumstances. As Rix LJ put it 'the doctrine is one of justice'.

The consequences of frustration

At common law, a frustrating event has the effect of bringing the contract to an immediate end. The rights and liabilities of the parties are frozen at the moment of frustration. The rule was that money payable before frustration remained payable and money paid before frustration could not be recovered. Any money which did not become payable until after frustration ceased to be payable. The harsh consequences of this rule were modified by the House of Lords in the *Fibrosa* case (1943) and wider changes were introduced under the Law Reform (Frustrated Contracts) Act 1943. The Act made two important changes:

1 money payable before frustration ceases to be payable and money paid before frustration can be recovered (the court may in its discretion allow the payee to recover or retain all or part of the sums to cover any expenses incurred);

2 a party who has carried out acts of part performance can recover compensation for any valuable benefit (other than a payment of money) conferred on the other party.

The Act does not apply to (a) contracts for the carriage of goods by sea, (b) insurance contracts, or (c) contracts for the sale of specific goods, which are covered by s 7 of the Sale of Goods Act 1979 (see Chapter 11 ⊙). The parties may exclude the effect of the Act by express agreement.

Breach

A breach of contract may occur in a number of ways. It may be an anticipatory or an actual breach.

Anticipatory breach

This is where a party states in advance that he does not intend to carry out his side of the contract or puts himself in a position whereby he will be unable to perform his contractual obligations. The injured party may sue immediately for breach of contract or, alternatively, wait for the time for performance to arrive to see whether the other party is prepared to carry out the contract.

Hochster v *De la Tour* (1853)

The claimant was engaged by the defendant in April 1852 to act as a courier for travel in Europe from 1 June 1852. On 11 May the defendant wrote to the claimant to inform him that his services were no longer required. The claimant started an action for breach of contract on 22 May. Although the date for performance had not yet arrived, it was held that the defendant's letter constituted an actionable breach of contract.

It can be dangerous to wait for the time for performance. The injured party may lose the right to sue for breach of contract if in the meantime the contract is discharged for frustration or illegality.

Avery v *Bowden* (1855)

The defendant chartered the claimant's ship, the *Lebanon*, and agreed to load her with a cargo at Odessa within 45 days. During this period, the defendant told the claimant on a number of occasions to sail the ship away as it would not be possible to provide a cargo. The claimant kept the ship at Odessa hoping that the defendant would carry out his side of the contract. Before the 45 days had expired, the Crimean War broke out. Odessa became an enemy port and it would have been illegal to carry out the contract. Assuming that the defendant's repeated statements amounted to an anticipatory breach, the claimant could have accepted the breach and sued at once. However, by choosing to keep the contract alive he lost his right to sue because of the illegality.

Actual breach

One party may fail completely to perform his side of the bargain or he may fail to carry out one or more of his obligations. Not every breach of contract has the effect of discharging the parties from their contractual obligations. The terms of a contract may be divided into those terms which are important (**conditions**) and the less important terms (**warranties**). The distinction was considered in Chapter 8 ⊙ . A breach of condition does not automatically terminate the contract. The injured party has a choice: he may wish to be discharged from the contract or he may prefer to carry on with the contract and claim damages for the breach. A breach of warranty only entitles the injured party to sue for damages.

Remedies

So far we have looked at the essential elements of a valid contract, the factors which may affect the validity of an agreement and the ways in which a contract may come to an end. We now turn to the remedies available to the injured party when a term of the contract has been broken. Every breach of contract will give the injured party the common law right to recover damages (financial compensation). Other remedies, such as specific performance and injunction, may be granted at the discretion of the court as part of its equitable jurisdiction.

Damages

In the business world it is quite common for the parties to agree in advance the damages that will be payable in the event of a breach of contract. These are known as liquidated damages. If there is no prior agreement as to the sum to be paid, the amount of damages is said to be unliquidated.

Liquidated damages

It makes commercial common sense for the parties to establish at the outset of their relationship the financial consequences of failing to live up to their bargain. Provided the parties have made a genuine attempt to estimate the likely loss, the courts will accept the relevant figure as the damages payable. In practice, knowing the likely outcome of any legal action, the party at fault will simply pay up without argument. An example of liquidated damages are the charges imposed for cancelling a holiday (see Figure 9.1).

Of course, there is a temptation for a party with stronger bargaining power to try to impose a penalty clause, which is really designed as a threat to secure performance. The distinction between liquidated damages and penalty clauses is illustrated by the following cases.

Sunkist Tours – Cancellation charges	
Cancellation notified	*Charges*
Over 6 weeks prior to departure	Loss of deposit
Within 4 to 6 weeks of departure	30% of holiday cost
Within 2 to 4 weeks of departure	45% of holiday cost
Within 1 day to 2 weeks of departure	60% of holiday cost
On or after the day of departure	100% of holiday cost

Figure 9.1 An example of a cancellation charges notice

More recent examples of the distinction between liquidated damages and penalty clauses are provided by the following cases.

Murray v LeisurePlay Ltd (2005)

Murray, a director of LeisurePlay, had a clause in his service contract which entitled him to payment of a year's gross salary if his contract was terminated without one year's notice. Murray was given seven and a half weeks' notice and he brought a claim for liquidated damages. LeisurePlay argued that the clause was a penalty clause and therefore unenforceable. The Court of Appeal held that it was not a penalty clause. In deciding such cases courts should consider:

(a) to what breaches of contract the clause applies;
(b) what amount is payable on breach;
(c) what amount would be payable if the claim was brought under common law;
(d) what were the parties' reasons for agreeing the clause;
(e) whether the party that claims the clause is a penalty can show that it was imposed as a deterrent and that it does not constitute a genuine pre-estimate of loss.

Dunlop Pneumatic Tyre Co Ltd v New Garage & Motor Co Ltd (1915)

Dunlop supplied tyres to New Garage under an agreement by which, in return for a trade discount, New Garage agreed to pay £5 by way of 'liquidated damages' for every item sold below list prices. The House of Lords held that since the sum was not extravagant, it was a genuine attempt by the parties to estimate the damage which price undercutting would cause Dunlop. The £5 was liquidated damages.

Ford Motor Co v Armstrong (1915)

Armstrong, a retailer, agreed to pay £250 for each Ford car sold below the manufacturer's list price. The Court of Appeal held that the clause was void as a penalty.

M & J Polymers Ltd v Imerys Minerals Ltd (2008)

The Commercial Court had to decide whether a 'take or pay' clause in a contract for the supply of chemical dispersants amounted to a penalty. A 'take or pay' clause is a provision which obliges a buyer to pay for a minimum quantity of products, irrespective of whether that quantity is ordered. Burton J held that the clause in question was not a penalty, although as a matter of principle the rule against penalties could apply to 'take and pay' clauses. Based on the facts of the case, he was satisfied that the clause was commercially justifiable, was not oppressive, was entered into freely by parties of comparable bargaining power, and did not have the predominant purpose of deterring a breach of contract or amount to a provision '*in terrorem*'.

If the court holds that the sum is liquidated damages, it will be enforced irrespective of whether the actual loss is greater or smaller.

Cellulose Acetate Silk Co Ltd v Widnes Foundry Ltd (1933)

Widnes Foundry agreed to pay £20 for every week of delay in completing a plant for the Silk Co. The work was completed 30 weeks late. The Silk Co claimed that its actual losses amounted to nearly £6,000. It was held that Widnes Foundry was only liable to pay £20 a week (i.e. £600) as agreed.

Unliquidated damages

The aim of unliquidated damages is to put the injured party in the position he would have been in if the contract had been carried out properly. Damages are designed to compensate for loss. If no loss has been suffered, the court will only award nominal damages, which is a small sum to mark the fact that there had been a breach of contract. The courts observe the following guidelines when awarding damages:

1 The damage can include sums for financial loss, damage to property, personal injury and distress, disappointment and upset caused to the claimant.

Jarvis v Swans Tours (1973)

Jarvis, a solicitor, paid £63.45 for a two-week winter sports holiday in Switzerland. The Swans Tours brochure promised a 'house party' atmosphere at the hotel, a bar which would be open several evenings a week and a host who spoke English. The holiday was a considerable

disappointment: in the second week, he was the only guest in the hotel and no one else could speak English. The bar was only open one evening and the skiing was disappointing. The Court of Appeal awarded him £125 to compensate for 'the loss of entertainment and enjoyment which he was promised'.

Exemplary or punitive damages designed to punish the party in breach are not normally awarded in contract.

2 The injured party cannot necessarily recover damages for every kind of loss which he has suffered. The breach might have caused a chain reaction of events to occur. Clearly, there is a point beyond which the damage becomes too remote from the original breach. The rules relating to remoteness of damage were laid down in *Hadley v Baxendale* (1854). The injured party may recover damages for:

- loss which has resulted naturally and in the ordinary course of events from the defendant's breach; and
- the loss which, although not a natural consequence of the defendant's breach, was in the minds of the parties when the contract was made.

The application of these rules is illustrated by the following cases.

Victoria Laundry (Windsor) Ltd v Newman Industries Ltd (1949)

The claimant company of launderers and dyers wished to expand its business and, for this purpose, had ordered a new boiler from the defendants. The boiler was damaged during the course of its removal and, as a result, there was a five-month delay in delivery. The claimant claimed:

(a) damages of £16 per week for the loss of profits it would have made on the planned expansion of the laundry business; and

(b) damages of £262 a week for loss of profits it would have made on extremely lucrative dyeing contracts.

The Court of Appeal held that the claimant was entitled to recover for the normal loss of profits on both cleaning and dyeing contracts, but it could not recover for the especially profitable dyeing contracts of which the defendants were unaware.

Simpson v London and North Western Rail Co (1876)

Simpson entrusted samples of his products to the defendants for delivery to Newcastle, for exhibition at an agricultural show. The goods were marked 'must be at Newcastle on Monday certain'. They failed to arrive in time. The defendants were held liable for Simpson's prospective loss of profit arising from his inability to exhibit at Newcastle. They had agreed to carry the goods knowing of the special instructions of the customer.

Transfield Shipping Inc v Mercator Shipping Inc, The Achilleas (2008)

This case is probably the most important decision on damages in contract since *Hadley v Baxendale*. The case involved the charter of a bulk carrier, the *Achilleas*. In January 2003 the owners chartered the vessel to charterers for five to seven months at a daily rate of US$13,500. In September 2003 the charter was extended for a further five to seven months at a daily rate of US$16,750. The last date for re-delivery to the owners was 2 May 2004. By April 2004 the market rate had increased significantly and, having received notice of the re-delivery between 30 April and 2 May, the owners agreed a follow-on charter for four to six months with another charterer, Cargill, at daily rate of US$39,500. When it became clear that the *Achilleas* would not be available before the cancellation date, the owners negotiated an extension to the cancellation date but in return had to agree a reduced daily rate of US$31,500 for the follow-on charter. The *Achilleas* was delivered nine days late on 9 May and the owners immediately delivered the vessel to Cargill. It was agreed that the charterers had broken the contract. The owners claimed damages for the difference between the original follow-on charter rate agreed with Cargill and the reduced rate subsequently agreed i.e. US$8,000 per day for the follow-on charter. This amounted to US$1,364,584. The charterers claimed that they were only liable to pay the difference between the market rate and the charter rate for nine days delay in re-delivery, which amounted to US$158,301. The claim was referred to arbitration and by a majority of 2:1 the arbitrators upheld the owners' claim. The majority arbitrators stated that the loss fell within the first rule in *Hadley v Baxendale* as arising 'naturally, i.e. according to the usual course of things, from such breach of contract itself'. The decision was upheld by the Commercial Court and the Court of Appeal. The House of Lords unanimously reversed the decision of the Court of Appeal. The charterers were only liable for the difference between the market rate and the contract rate for the nine days of delay. Lords Hoffmann and Hope based their decision on similar grounds, holding that the charterers could not reasonably be regarded as having assumed the risk of the owner's loss of profit on the follow-on charter. This was based on the general understanding in the shipping market that liability was restricted to the difference between the market rate and the charter rate for the overrun period. Lord Rodger based his decision on narrower grounds: that the type of loss claimed by the owners caused by extreme volatility in charter rates could not have been foreseen as being likely to occur as a result of the delay. He stated: '. . . neither party would reasonably have contemplated that an overrun of nine days would, in the ordinary course of things, cause the owners the kind of loss for which they claim damages'. Baroness Hale preferred the narrower ground given by Lord Rodger than the wider ground stated by Lords Hoffmann and Hope. The distinction between the two positions was set out by Baroness Hale. For Lords Hoffmann and Hope the question to be considered is whether the parties must be taken to have *liability* for this type of loss within their contemplation: 'If that is the question, then it becomes relevant to ask what has been the normal expectations of the parties to such contracts in this particular market.' For Lord Rodger the question is whether the parties must be taken to have had this particular type of loss within their contemplation: 'It was only because of the unusual volatility of the market at that particular time that this particular loss was suffered.'

3 Provided the loss is not too remote, the next matter to consider is how much is payable by way of damages. As we have already seen, the object is to put the injured party in the same position as if the contract had been performed. This is sometimes described as providing compensation for loss of expectation. Expectation losses may include loss of profit which would have been made but for the breach or the cost of achieving agreed performance. In some situations the claimant may prefer to recover the losses he has incurred in reliance on the contract. Reliance loss includes wasted expenditure. It seems that the claimant may claim for reliance losses rather than expectation losses if he so chooses.

Anglia Television Ltd v Reed (1971)

The claimants engaged the defendant, a well-known American actor, to play the lead in a film they were making for television. At the last moment the defendant repudiated the contract and, as the claimants were unable to find a suitable replacement, the film was abandoned. The claimants did not attempt to claim for loss of profits as it was not possible to say whether the film would have been a success. However, they were successful in recovering their wasted expenditure (on employing a director, scriptwriter and other actors, researching locations and so on), even though some of the expenses had been incurred before the defendant entered into the contract. Lord Denning explained the decision as follows: 'it is plain that, when Mr Reed entered into this contract, he must have known perfectly well that much expenditure had already been incurred on director's fees and the like. He must have contemplated – or at any rate, it is reasonably to be imputed to him – that if he broke his contract, all that expenditure would be wasted, whether or not it was incurred before or after the contract.'

Comment. This unanimous decision of the Court of Appeal has been criticised for allowing recovery of pre-contractual expenditure which has not been incurred in reliance on the defendant's promise.

If the claimant has not suffered a loss as a result of the breach, the court will only award nominal damages.

C & P Haulage v Middleton (1983)

C & P had granted Mr Middleton a six-month renewable licence to occupy a garage which he used to carry on his business. Mr Middleton spent some money equipping the premises, but the terms of his agreement prevented him from removing such equipment at the end of the licence. The parties quarrelled and, as a result, Mr Middleton was unlawfully evicted from the garage ten weeks before the end of a six-month period. Fortunately, Mr Middleton's local council allowed him to use his own garage for more than ten weeks, which meant that he did not have to pay rent. He sued C & P for the cost of equipping the premises. The Court of Appeal held that he was entitled to nominal damages only. The cost of equipping the garage would have been lost even if the contract had been carried out as agreed. It is not the function of the courts to put the injured party in a better financial position than if the contract had been properly performed.

Where the breach of contract consists of defective performance of a building contract, the courts have sometimes based the award of damages on the difference between the value of the building contracted for and the defective building, and sometimes on the cost of curing the defect.

Ruxley Electronics and Construction Ltd v Forsyth (1995)

The claimant company agreed to build a swimming pool for Mr Forsyth. It was a term of the contract that the pool should be 7ft 6in at the deep end, to allow for safe diving. When the pool was built, however, it had a maximum depth of 6ft 9in and was only 6ft under the diving board. The trial judge held that, even though the pool was not as deep as specified in the contract, it was still safe for diving. There was no evidence that the value of the pool had decreased because of the shortfall in depth. The only way of curing the defect would be to demolish the pool and build a new one at a cost of £21,560. The judge doubted whether Mr Forsyth would build a new pool as it would not be reasonable to do so. The judge awarded £2,500 for loss of amenity. The Court of Appeal reversed the decision of the trial judge and awarded Mr Forsyth the full cost of achieving a cure, i.e. £21,560. The House of Lords reversed the decision of the Court of Appeal and reinstated the trial judge's original decision. Their Lordships took the view that if the cost of cure was unreasonable, the measure of damages should be the difference in value. Although the pool was probably no less valuable, Mr Forsyth was entitled to some compensation for his loss of satisfaction.

Breaches of contract for the sale of goods are subject to the rules laid down in the Sale of Goods Act 1979. They will be considered in more detail in Chapter 11 ⊙.

Although as a general rule damages for breach of contract should be assessed as at the date of the breach, there are exceptions, as can be illustrated by this recent case.

Golden Strait Corporation v Nippon Yusen Kubishka Kaisha (The Golden Victory) (2007)

In 1998 GSC chartered a tanker (*The Golden Victory*) to NYKK for a period of seven years. The charterparty contained a clause which entitled either party to terminate the contract if war broke out between any two or more countries which included the United States, the United Kingdom and Iraq. In 2001 NYKK repudiated the charter by re-delivering the tanker to the owners GSC. There were nearly four years left to run on the charter and GSC claimed damages for the remaining term of the contract. NYKK argued that they would have been entitled to terminate the contract in March 2003 when the second Gulf War broke out and therefore damages should only be assessed up to this (earlier) date. The House of Lords held (by 3:2) that (i) damages for breach of contract are designed to compensate the injured party for the loss of his contractual bargain and he should be placed in the position he would have been in had the contract been performed. However, if the contract would have terminated earlier (because of the occurrence of an event anticipated in the contract), then this should be taken into account. (ii) Although, as a general rule, damages should be assessed as at the date of the breach, the rule was subject to exceptions and should not be applied mechanistically, and there may be another date which might be used as the basis for compensating the injured party.

4 Once a breach of contract has occurred, the innocent party is under a duty to mitigate (minimise) his loss. He cannot stand back and allow the loss to get worse. A seller whose goods have been rejected, for example, must attempt to get the best possible price for them elsewhere. The claimant will not be able to recover for that part of the loss which has resulted from his failure to mitigate.

Brace v *Calder* (1895)

The claimant was dismissed by his employers but offered immediate re-engagement on the same terms and conditions as before. He refused the offer and instead sued to recover the salary he would have received for the remaining 19 months of his two-year contract. It was held that the claimant should have mitigated the loss by accepting the employer's reasonable offer of re-employment. He was entitled to nominal damages only.

The duty to mitigate any loss does not arise until there has been a breach of contract which the injured party has accepted as a breach.

White and Carter (Councils) Ltd v *McGregor* (1961)

The claimants were advertising agents who supplied local authorities with litter bins on which they displayed advertisements. The defendant entered into a contract with the claimants to advertise his garage in this way for a three-year period. Later the same day, however, the defendant cancelled the contract. The claimants refused to accept the cancellation and proceeded to carry out the contract by preparing advertising plates and attaching them to litter bins. The claimants sued for the full amount due under the contract. The House of Lords upheld their claim. The claimants were under no duty to mitigate their loss because they had not accepted the defendant's breach.

Comment. Although the reasoning in this case is logical, the result, as Lord Keith put it, is 'startling'. However, a limitation to the principle was suggested by Lord Reid when he said that the rule would not apply if the injured party has no legitimate interest in performing the contract rather than claiming damages. This approach has been accepted in subsequent cases (*Clea Shipping Corpn* v *Bulk Oil International Ltd (The Alaskan Trader) (No 2)* (1984)).

Debt recovery

So far we have considered the basis on which **damages** can be recovered for a **breach of contract**. It is worth noting at this point that where one party performs his part of the contract, e.g. by delivering goods, and the other party refuses to pay, the claim is for payment of the **debt** rather than an action for damages.

Late payment of bills has been a persistent problem for UK businesses, often causing serious cash flow difficulties, particularly for small businesses. It is, of course, possible to include a clause in a supply contract providing for the payment of interest if payment is not made by the due date. Alternatively, debts can be pursued through the courts and the courts can award interest. Neither course of action is appropriate for small businesses. The relatively weak bargaining position of small businesses means that they are, in practice, unable to insist on default clauses, while pursuing a debt through the courts can be a costly and lengthy process, which a small business can ill afford.

The Late Payment of Commercial Debts (Interest) Act 1998 introduced a statutory right for businesses to claim interest on the late payment of commercial debts.

Businesses are encouraged to agree their own contractual terms providing for contractual interest to be payable if bills are paid late. However, the Act prevents abuse of contractual interest, by requiring any contractual remedy to be 'substantial'. A remedy for late payment will be 'substantial' if it is enough to compensate the supplier for the cost of late payment and it deters late payment and it is fair and reasonable, in all the circumstances, to allow the contractual remedy to replace the statutory right. In deciding whether a contractual remedy is reasonable, the courts will consider all the circumstances, including the rate of interest applying to late payments and the length of credit periods. If the credit period is found to be excessive, the court can strike it down and replace it with the 30-day statutory default period.

If the parties do not agree to contractual interest for late payment, the Act will apply. Payment will be classed as late if it is made after the expiry of:

- the credit period agreed by the parties;
- the credit period determined by trade custom or practice or a course of dealings between the parties;
- the statutory default credit period of 30 days from delivery of the invoice or the goods or the service.

The Court of Appeal has held a mistake in an invoice does not enable a paying party to avoid paying statutory interest for late payment of a commercial debt under the Act (*Ruttle Plant Hire* v *Secretary of State for the Environment, Food and Rural Affairs* (2009)).

The rate of statutory interest is set by the Secretary of State and is currently the UK base rate (as announced by the Monetary Policy Committee of the Bank of England) plus 8 per cent.

A Directive on Late Payment of Commercial Debts (Directive 2000/35/EC), implemented by member states by 8 August 2002, ensures a common approach to the problem of late payment across the EU.

In a recent case the House of Lords held that at common law the loss suffered as a result of late payment is recoverable, subject to the usual rules relating to proof of loss, remoteness and the duty to mitigate (*Sempra Metals Ltd* v *Inland Revenue Commissioners* (2007)). Both simple and compound interest can be awarded.

Equitable remedies

The normal remedy for a breach of contract is an award of damages at common law. There are some situations, however, where damages would be neither adequate nor appropriate. Equity developed other forms of relief to ensure that justice is done. The more important of these equitable remedies are specific performance and injunction.

Specific performance

A decree of specific performance is an order of the court requiring the party in breach to carry out his contractual obligations. Failure to comply with the directions of the court lays the defendant open to the imposition of penalties for contempt of court. Like all equitable remedies, the grant of specific performance is discretionary. It may be withheld in the following circumstances:

1 **Damages adequate.** An order for specific performance will not be made if damages would be an adequate remedy. Most breaches of contract can be remedied by an award of monetary compensation. If it is a contract for the sale of a unique item, however, no sum of money can compensate the disappointed buyer for his lost opportunity, and specific performance will be granted. Each piece of land is regarded as being unique and thus the remedy is available for contracts for the sale of land.

2 **Mutuality.** Equity requires mutuality as regards its remedies. This means that both parties must potentially be able to seek an order of specific performance. An adult cannot obtain such an order against a minor, so a minor will not be awarded specific performance either.

3 **Supervision.** An order will not be made unless the court can adequately supervise its enforcement. It is for this reason that specific performance will not be awarded to enforce building contracts, because the court cannot supervise on the day-to-day basis which would be necessary. Similar principles apply to employment contracts.

Ryan v *Mutual Tontine Westminster Chambers Association* (1893)

The landlord of a flat agreed to provide a resident porter who would undertake certain duties for residents. A porter was appointed but he had another job as a chef in a nearby club, which meant he was absent from the building for several hours each day. While he was away, his duties were performed by various non-resident cleaners and boys. It was held that the only remedy for the breach of contract was an action in damages. Specific performance would not be granted.

Comment. In a more recent similar case, the court had no difficulty in awarding specific performance of a contract to provide a resident porter. It was held that damages would not be an adequate remedy. It was relatively easy to define what was required under the contract and it did not involve constant supervision (*Posner v Scott-Lewis* (1986)).

4 Discretion. The court may refuse specific performance where it is felt that it would not be just and equitable to grant it.

Injunction

This is an order of the court requiring the party at fault not to break the contract. Its main use is to enforce the negative promises that can occasionally be found in employment contracts. The employee may agree, for example, not to work in a similar capacity for a rival employer during the period of his contract.

Warner Brothers v Nelson (1936)

The film actress Bette Davis had agreed not to work as an actress for anyone else during the period of her contract with Warner Bros. In breach of this agreement, she left the USA and entered into a contract with a third party in the UK. The court held that Warner Bros were entitled to an injunction to prevent the star from breaking the negative provision in the contract.

It should be noted that an injunction cannot be used as a back-door method of enforcing a contract of employment for which specific performance is not available. Warner Bros could prevent Miss Davis from working as an actress for anyone else. They could not have obtained a decree of specific performance to force her to return to their studio.

Claims for restitution: quasi-contract

The law of restitution may provide a claimant with a remedy in situations where the defendant has obtained an unjust benefit. The requirement to repay money does not arise because of a breach of a legal duty, such as a breach of contract or a tort, but because the defendant has been unjustly enriched. The liability is said to be quasi-contractual – *as if* from a contract – although in reality there is no liability in contract.

An action for restitution may arise in the circumstances summarised below.

Claims on a *quantum meruit*

Instead of claiming a precise sum, the claimant may be able to sue on a *quantum meruit* for payment for work he has actually done. A *quantum meruit* claim can arise either contractually or quasi-contractually in the following situations:

1 Contractually: where the contract is for the supply of goods and services but the parties have not fixed a sum to be paid. The common law position is supported now by statutory provisions. Section 8 of the Sale of Goods Act 1979 provides that if the price of goods cannot be fixed by the contract or in a way agreed under the contract or by trade custom, the buyer must pay a reasonable price. There is similar obligation to pay a reasonable sum for services under s 15 of the Supply of Goods and Services Act 1982 (see also Chapter 11 ○).

2 Quasi-contractually:

■ Where the defendant has abandoned or refused to perform his part of the contract, as was the case in *Planché v Colburn* (1831).
■ Where work has been performed by the claimant and accepted by the defendant under a void contract. In *Craven-Ellis v Canons Ltd* (1936) a managing director of a company was able to recover a reasonable sum by way of remuneration for work he had done until it was discovered that his appointment was invalid under the company's articles.
■ Where one party confers a benefit on the other with the intention on both sides that the benefit is to be paid for even though a contract is not finally concluded (*British Steel Corporation v Cleveland Bridge & Engineering Co Ltd* (1984)).

Total failure of consideration

If the claimant has paid money to the defendant in respect of a valid contract, and the defendant completely fails to honour his part of the bargain, the claimant has a choice of remedy. He can bring a claim for breach of contract and claim damages for breach or he can terminate the contract and sue in quasi-contract to recover the money he has paid over on the basis that there has been a total failure of consideration. *Rowland v Divall* (1923), which will be considered in detail in Chapter 11 ⊙, is an example of a claim based on a total failure of consideration.

Money paid under a mistake

A claimant may recover money which has been paid over under a **mistake of fact**. A mistake of fact would include, for example, errors in a restaurant bill because the waiter had made a mistake when adding up all the items, or at the supermarket check-out when a cashier inadvertently scans an item twice. In *Admiralty Comrs* v *National Provincial and Union Bank Ltd* (1922), money paid into a bank account of a customer, on the basis that he was alive, was held to be recoverable under a mistake of fact, when he turned out to be dead.

Until recently it was settled law that moneys paid under a **mistake of law** could not be recovered. However, this rule has now been overturned by the House of Lords in the following case.

Kleinwort Benson Ltd v *Lincoln City Council* (1998)

The case involved the use of 'interest rate swap' transactions by local authorities. Following a case brought by an auditor appointed by the Audit Commission, such contracts were held to be *ultra vires* for local authorities and, therefore, void. Kleinwort Benson (KB) claimed restitution of the money it had paid to four local authorities under these transactions. KB claimed that the money had been paid under a mistake so as to avoid the six-year time limit laid down in the Limitation Act 1980. The House of Lords held that the 'mistake of law rule', under which money was not recoverable in restitution because it had been paid under a mistake of law, should no longer form part of English law.

Comment. This case is an interesting example of judicial law-making. The 'mistake of law rule' had been the subject of much criticism over the years and had been referred to the Law Commission. The Law Commission concluded that the rule should be changed by legislation. Their Lordships decided to press ahead with the reform themselves, rather than wait for Parliament to legislate, even though considerable difficulties have been created because of the retrospective effect of the judgment. These problems could have been avoided if the change had been made by legislation.

Limitation of actions

The right to sue does not last indefinitely. The parties may include a provision in their contract which limits the time within which a claim must be made. Where such an agreement is made between businesses and the parties are of equal bargaining strength, it is likely to be upheld by the courts.

Granville Oil and Chemicals Ltd v *Davis Turner & Co Ltd* (2003)

DT, an international freight forwarder, agreed to carry a consignment of paint from Kuwait to GOC's warehouse in the UK. The contract was subject to the British International Freight Association (BIFA) standard terms and conditions which required any legal action to be brought within nine months. GOC claimed that the paint had been damaged in transit and brought proceedings for breach of contract more than a year after the nine-month time limit expired. GOC argued that the time bar was void for unreasonableness under the Unfair Contract Terms Act 1977. The Court of Appeal held that the clause was not void under the Act. The parties were both in business, they were of equal bargaining strength and GOC might have been able to contract on different terms. Moreover, the clause had been brought to GOC's attention. It was reasonably practicable for GOC to comply with the nine-month time limit as the goods could have been checked on delivery. The clause was effective to bar GOC's claim.

Where no time limit is agreed between the parties, the Limitation Act 1980 will apply. The Act imposes statutory time limits within which an action for breach of contract must be brought. They are:

1 an action on a simple contract must be brought within six years of the date when the cause of action accrued;
2 an action on a contract made in the form of a deed will be statute barred after 12 years from the date when the cause of action accrued.

These time limits may be extended as follows:

(a) where fraud or mistake is alleged, time does not start to run until 'the claimant has discovered the fraud, concealment or mistake or could with reasonable diligence have discovered it';
(b) if the claimant is under a disability, such as minority or mental incapacity, the time limits do not start

to operate until the disability is removed, e.g. in the case of a minor on reaching 18;

(c) where the claim is for a debt or a liquidated sum, and the defendant acknowledges the claim or makes part-payment, time will run from the date of acknowledgement or part-payment.

The rules about limitation of actions do not apply to the equitable remedies. Nevertheless, the equitable maxim of 'delay defeats equity' will apply to defeat a claimant who waits too long before taking legal action.

Self-test questions/activities

1 Jeremy, a prosperous City trader, decides to pay for his parents, Bill and Irene, to go on holiday to celebrate their silver wedding anniversary. Jeremy enters into a contract with Sunset Cruises, to provide his parents with a deluxe cabin for a two-week cruise round the Caribbean. Bill and Irene are very disappointed with their holiday. As a result of a booking error by Sunset Cruises, they are not allocated a deluxe cabin. The ship's engines suffer a mechanical failure on the third day and, as a result, the ship does not visit all the islands on its scheduled itinerary. Bill and Irene wish to take action against Sunset Cruises.

Advise them.

How would your advice differ if Jeremy took action on behalf of his parents?

2 Kevin is the owner of a small Hull-based firm, which specialises in office removals. He operates with two vans and three employees. He contracts to remove two partners in a firm of accountants, who are moving from their main office in Hull to establish a branch office in Scunthorpe. To minimise the disruption to office routine, the move is to take place on a Sunday. What is the legal position in the following situations?

(a) The Humber Bridge is closed because of high winds (the only alternative route is a much longer and more expensive journey via Goole).

(b) As an environmental measure, the government imposes regulations banning business traffic from the roads on Sundays.

(c) Kevin takes on a house removal for the same day. One of the vans fails its MOT on the Friday and Kevin decides to use the only one available for the house removal.

(d) Kevin and his three employees are taken ill with influenza and are not well enough to carry out the move.

(e) Kevin completes the removal except for one filing cabinet which he did not have room for.

He refuses to make a special journey for it because 'it would cost too much in petrol'.

3 Wholesome Foods Ltd decided to build an extension to its Newtown bakery to cope with increased demand for its wholemeal bread. The contract is awarded to Bettabuilders Co Ltd, which agrees to complete the work by 1 May. On the strength of the planned increased capacity at the bakery, Wholesome Foods Ltd concludes an extremely profitable contract with the Newtown Council to supply all the bread to local schools from 4 May. Owing to extreme bad weather in February and March, Bettabuilders Co Ltd completes the extension 10 weeks late. Wholesome Foods Ltd estimates its losses as:

- £100 a week for the profits it would have made on the expected general increase in bread sales; and
- £400 a week for the profits it would have made on the schools contract.

What damages will Wholesome Foods Ltd recover?

How would your answer differ if Bettabuilders Co Ltd had agreed to pay £50 for every week of delay in completing the extension?

4 Wreckless Eric, a rock concert promoter, pulls off one of the sensations of the rock world by getting the American rock star, Tex Toucan, to come to Britain to give a six-concert tour to coincide with the release of his latest album. Tex agrees to give his exclusive services to Eric and promises that he 'will not sing, perform as a musician or act as an entertainer' for anyone else during the period of his stay. After completing the first sell-out concert in Dagenham, Tex is approached by Crispin Green, a rival promoter, who persuades Tex to break his contract with Eric and appear instead at alternative venues arranged by Crispin.

Eric, who has made a considerable investment in this tour, wants to know what remedies are available to him.

Specimen examination questions

1 Limited Horizons Holiday plc engaged Mandy, a modern languages undergraduate, to act as its representative for its Majorcan Culture holidays for a summer season for a lump sum of £3,000 and all accommodation, food and travelling expenses. A term of the contract requires Mandy to attend a total of five training days before commencing the job. Some of the training days are held during Mandy's examinations and, as a result, she only attends on three days. On 5 June, only 10 days before she was due to fly out to Majorca, Limited Horizons informs her that her services will not be required. Mandy is furious and, although she has been offered alternative employment in the local corner shop working part-time for £7 per hour, she decides to go to Majorca anyway. She spends the entire summer holiday in Majorca, living in the same three-star hotel she would have been based at under the terms of her contract with Limited Horizons. Her total expenses are £4,000. On her return to the UK she writes to Limited Horizons demanding payment of the £3,000 lump sum and reimbursement of her expenses of £4,000.

Advise Limited Horizons.

Website references

http://www.ucc.ie/law/restitution A site hosted by Steve Hedley of University College Cork which provides links and resources on the subject of quasi-contract, restitution and unjust enrichment.

http://www.payontime.co.uk The Better Payment Practice Group operates this site. It provides information and advice for businesses about the implementation of the Late Payment of Commercial Debts (Interest) Act 1998.

Visit www.mylawchamber.co.uk/richesallen to access study support resources including answers to questions in this chapter and legal updates, all linked to the **Pearson eText** version of **Keenan and Riches' Business Law** which you can **search**, **highlight** and **personalise** with your **own notes** and **bookmarks**.

Use **Case Navigator** to read in full some of the key cases referenced in this chapter with commentary and questions:

Ruxley Electronics and Construction Ltd v *Forsyth* (1995)

Chapter 10

Law of agency

Contracts of agency

As noted by Munday, 'law of agency first emerged as a largely unitary body of common law [. . .], particular customs, many of which later hardened into rules, came to be recognized to apply to particular classes of intermediary' (see *Law of Agency*). Over the years, such 'particular classes of intermediary' have become indispensible to businesses. In essence, agency is a consensual and fiduciary relationship between a principal and an agent. The relationship has been created when one person, a principal, grants authority to another person to act on his or her behalf thereby appointing the person as his or her agent. An employee who makes contracts on behalf of his employer is acting as an agent. As examined in Chapter 6 ⬤, directors are agents of the company and have the authority to act on behalf of the company. For example, the authority to allot shares is granted by shareholders at a general meeting (see p 177 ⬤) and the authority can be either renewed or revoked. A shop assistant, for example, is also in this category. Alternatively, an agent may be an independent contractor who is engaged for his specialist skills and knowledge. A person who wishes to sell his or her shares will usually employ the services of a stockbroker to arrange the sale. Travel agents, estate agents, auctioneers and insurance brokers are all examples of agents.

Through the creation of an agency, the principal grants authority to the agent to enter, modify or terminate a contract with third parties on the principal's behalf. There are therefore two main issues that need to be considered in every agency: the first one is the granting of authority and the second one is the scope of authority as either factor could affect the enforceability of the underlying contract with the third party. This may lead to further questions: has the authority been granted? Does the authority granted cover the underlying contract or has the agent acted outside his or her authority? If the agent's act exceeded the authority granted, what is the consequence? Is the principal bound by the contract? These issues are examined in the chapter.

It should, however, be noted that the term of agency can be used in various contexts: some types of agency created in a business context might not be strictly governed by the law of agency. Furthermore, different types of agent might be governed by different sets of rules.

Types of agent

An agent may fall into one or more of the following categories:

1 **A general agent** has the power to act for his principal in relation to particular kinds of transaction, e.g. an estate agent.

2 **A special agent** is limited to acting for the principal in respect of one specific transaction.

3 **A mercantile agent** or factor – factor was defined as 'an agent, but an agent of a particular kind. He is an agent entrusted with the possession of goods for the purpose of sale' in *Stevens* v *Biller* (1883). The statutory definition of a factor can be found under s 1(1) of the Factors Act 1889 as a 'mercantile agent having in the customary course of his business as such agent authority either to sell goods or to consign goods for the purpose of sale, or to buy goods, or to raise money on the security of goods'. As Lord Justice Robert Walker commented in the 2000 case of *Triffitt Nurseries (a Firm) and others v Salads Etcetera Ltd and others* (2000), 'it is a curiosity that the word "factor" occurs in the Act only in its long and short titles'. The 1889 Act gives a mercantile agent wide powers to pass title to goods of his principal which are in the agent's possession, but s 12 contains savings for the rights of the true owner, i.e. the principal. The right to collect outstanding payment from customers following the appointment of receivers and the cessation of trading of the factor was discussed in the *Triffitt* case.

4 A *del credere* **agent** is an agent who, in return for extra commission, guarantees that if the third party he has introduced fails to pay for goods received, the agent will indemnify the principal. This can be seen in *Clyde Marine Insurance Co v Renwick & Co* (1924) concerning a marine insurance policy that 'a broker may charge his client a *del credere* commission and guarantee that the under-writer will pay the loss'. This can also be seen in *Blything v Bv V/H FA Dekker First Wright-Manley (a firm)* (1999):

> a *del credere* agent is an agent who for a special commis-sion undertakes in effect the liability of a surety to his principal for the due performance, by the persons with whom he deals, of contracts made by him with them on his principal's behalf . . . A *del credere* agency may in prin-ciple be inferred from the course of conduct between the parties, though such inference would nowadays be rare.

The nature of a 'sole agency' arrangement between a seller of property and an estate agent was considered in the following case.

Foxtons Ltd v Pelkey Bicknell (2008)

Foxtons, a firm of estate agents, claimed £20,000 commis-sion when a buyer they had introduced to the defendant while appointed as 'sole agents', but who decided not to buy the property at that time, subsequently bought the house through another estate agent. The Court of Appeal held that estate agents cannot claim their commission under a 'sole agency' agreement unless they can show that they introduced the buyer to the purchase and not just to the property.

Actual express, actual implied and apparent (ostensible) authority

Even the most straightforward agency creates complicated legal rights between three parties: the principal, the agent and a third party. As an agent is granted authority by the principal to enter into contracts on his or her behalf, the existence and the scope of the authority is not only essential to the legal relationship between the principal and the agent, but it may also determine the rights of the third party. In most cases, the existence and the scope of the authority have been granted expressly but it is also possible for the authority to be 'implied when it is inferred from the conduct of the parties and the circumstances of the case', as defined by Lord Denning MR in the following case.

Hely-Hutchinson v Brayhead Ltd (1968)

The chairman of the company (B) acted as its de facto managing director. He was the chief executive who made the final decision on any matters concerning finance. He often committed B to contracts without the knowledge of the board and reported the matter afterwards. The board knew of and acquiesced in that. A guarantee was provided by B to another company that eventually went into liquidation. B denied the liability arising under the guarantee and argued that the chairman had no authority to provide such guarantee.

It was held that, on the facts, the chairman had actual authority – to be implied from the conduct of the parties and the circumstances of the case – to enter into the contracts. As Lord Denning further expanded in the judgment:

> The actual authority may be express or implied [. . .] It is *implied* when it is inferred from the conduct of the parties and the circumstances of the case, such as when the board of directors appoint one of their number to be managing director. They thereby impliedly authorise him to do all such things as fall within the usual scope of that office. Actual authority, express or implied, is binding as between the company and the agent, and also as between the company and others, whether they are within the company or outside it.

Sometimes an agent will act without authority or he may exceed his actual or implied authority. The principal will be bound by the agent's action if he or she chooses to ratify the contract or if the agency arises through necessity. Both will be explained later in this chapter. However, the principal will also be bound by the agent's action if the agent is acting within the scope of his or her apparent (ostensible) authority. The nature of apparent or ostensible authority, as put by Lord Denning, is 'the authority of an agent as it *appears* to others' whereas the agent may not actually have the authority, or when ostensible authority exceeds actual authority. This can be seen in *Royal British Bank Turquand* (1856), that the directors 'appeared to have authority' (see page 327 of the judgment) when in actual fact the necessary resolution had not been obtained from the shareholders. In *Freeman & Lockyer v Buckhurst Park Properties* (1964), at page 503, Lord Diplock LJ described apparent or ostensible authority as 'warranty of authority'; the judgment also provides a useful and interesting explanation of 'actual authority' and 'apparent authority' (see page 502 of the judgment):

> It is necessary at the outset to distinguish between an 'actual' authority of an agent on the one hand, and an 'apparent' or 'ostensible' authority on the other. Actual authority and apparent authority are quite independent of one another. Generally they co-exist and coincide, but either may exist without the other and their respective scopes may be different [. . .], it is upon the apparent authority of the agent that the contractor normally relies in the ordinary course of business when entering into contracts.
>
> An 'actual' authority is a legal relationship between principal and agent created by a consensual agreement to which they alone are parties. Its scope is to be ascertained by applying ordinary principles of construction of contracts, including any proper implications from the express words used, the usages of the trade, or the course of business between the parties. To this agreement the contractor is a stranger; he may be totally ignorant of the existence of any authority on the part of the agent. Nevertheless, if the agent does enter into a contract pursuant to the 'actual' authority, it does create contractual rights and liabilities between the principal and the contractor.
>
> . . . [a]n 'apparent' or 'ostensible' authority is a legal relationship between the principal and the contractor created by a representation, made by the principal to the contractor, intended to be and in fact acted upon by the contractor, that the agent has authority to enter on behalf of the principal into a contract of a kind within the scope of the 'apparent' authority.

Rights of the third parties

The existence and the scope of authority determine if the third party has the right to sue the principal. Further, the rights of the third party depend largely on whether the third party is aware that he is dealing with an agent. If the agent discloses that he is an agent, he will drop out of the picture and the third party can only sue and be sued by the principal. As we have already seen in Chapter 7, the common law rules relating to privity of contract do not apply in agency situations. If the agent does not reveal that he is an agent, either the agent or the principal can sue on the contract. When the third party discovers the agency, he can choose whether to sue the agent or the now-revealed principal. Once he has made his choice of whom to sue, the election is binding and he cannot change his mind if, for example, the person he has chosen to sue cannot or will not pay.

Formation of agency

As can be seen from the above discussion concerning authority of an agent, an agency is usually created by agreement between the principal and agent, but in some situations an agency can be created without such an agreement. The main ways in which an agency can be formed are as follows:

1 Express appointment. This is the main way in which an agency is created. A principal will expressly appoint an agent either to carry out a particular job or to undertake a range of transactions. The relationship between the principal and agent will usually be contractual. The agreement will also determine the scope of an agent's authority.

2 By implication. This form of agency usually arises where there is a pre-existing agency relationship and it is assumed by a third party that the principal has given the agent authority to act as an agent in matters not covered by the express appointment. This implied or ostensible authority may arise from the position held by the agent. Sometimes, the difficulty is to determine the nature of the duty as there is long-accepted opinion that there is an overlap between implied authority and apparent authority, as observed by Lord Diplock, that the duties 'co-exist and coincide but either may exist without the other'. As can be seen in the *Panorama* case (see also Chapter 6), the question was whether a company secretary had apparent authority to enter into contracts on behalf of a company. As commented by Lord Denning:

> he regularly makes representations on behalf of the company and enters into contracts on its behalf which come within the day-to-day running of the company's business. So much so that he may be regarded as held out as having authority to do such things on behalf of the company.

In *Waugh v HB Clifford & Sons Ltd* (1982), the difference between the implied authority and the apparent authority was again considered. The question was whether a solicitor had ostensible authority to compromise a suit for his client. Brightman LJ drew a distinction between:

> on the one hand the *implied* authority of a solicitor to compromise an action without prior reference to his client for consent: and on the other hand the *ostensible or apparent* authority of a solicitor to compromise an action on behalf of his client without the opposing litigant being required for his own protection either (1) to scrutinise the authority of the solicitor of the other party, or (2) to demand that the other party (if an individual) himself signs the terms of compromise or (if a corporation) affixes its seal or signs by a director or other agent possessing the requisite power under the articles of association or other constitution of the corporation.

He went on to quote from *Matthews v Munster* (1887) in that:

> when the client has requested counsel to act as his advocate . . . he thereby represents to the other side that counsel is to act for him in the usual course, and he must be bound by that representation so long as it continues . . . The request does not mean that counsel is to act in any other character than that of advocate or to do any other act than such as an advocate usually does.

It is probably safe to conclude that, in some cases, the distinction between implied authority and apparent authority may well depend on the circumstances of the case as to what would be regarded as 'day-to-day' operation of the business. Moreover, as Munday suggested:

> the purpose underlying the two concepts may also be rather different. Whereas actual implied authority has particular relevance to legal relations as between

principal and agent, an agent's apparent authority is more directed at protecting the expectations of third parties who have been induced to assume that the agent was acting within his actual authority.

This will be further explained under estoppel.

3 By ratification. This arises where a principal retrospectively adopts a contract made on his behalf by an agent who has either no authority or acted outside his or her authority. The effect of ratification, as commented by Treitel, is 'to put principal, agent and third party into the position in which they would have been, if the agent's acts had been authorised from the start: his authority is said to relate back to the time of the unauthorised act' (see *Treitel's Law of Contract*). This can be seen in *Bolton Partners v Lambert* (1889), where Kekewich J stated:

> the doctrine of ratification is this, that when a principal on whose behalf a contract has been made, though it may be made in the first instance without his authority, adopts it and ratifies it, then, whether the contract is one which is for his benefit and which he is enforcing, or which is sought to be enforced against him, the ratification is referred to the date of the original contract, and the contract becomes as from its inception as binding on him as if he had been originally a party.

Ratification will, however, only be effective if strict conditions are met:

- the agent must have disclosed that he was acting for a principal;
- the principal must have been in existence when the agent entered into the contract, e.g. if the principal is a company, the certificate of incorporation must have been issued;
- the principal must have had the capacity to enter into the contract not only when the contract was made but also at the time of ratification;
- the principal must ratify the whole contract;
- ratification must take place within a reasonable time.

Another important aspect to the doctrine is that the ratification will not be effective where unfair prejudice would be caused to the third party.

4 By necessity. This type of agency arises where a person takes urgent action on behalf of another in the event of an emergency. There will normally be some kind of pre-existing contractual relationship between the parties, e.g. a contract to transport perishable goods. The person who purports to act as an agent of necessity must show that he acted in the best interests of the 'principal', his actions were reasonably necessary in the circumstances, and that it was impossible to contact the 'principal' to obtain instructions.

The event of an emergency is therefore an essential factor. As Brown has pointed out (see 'Authority and Necessity in the Law of Agency' (1992) 55 MLR 414):

> the origins of this agency are found in the authority of the shipmaster to act in emergencies as agent of the shipowner in order to preserve the ship and her cargo, and the acceptor of a bill of exchange for the honour of the drawer who has an entitlement to be reimbursed by the person for whom he pays.

The doctrine is fragmented and depends on 'practical conditions which render it operative'.

Sachs v Miklos (1948)

In 1940 the owner of certain furniture was allowed by the defendant to store it free of charge in their house. Thereafter those defendants lost touch with the claimant through the latter's failure to keep them informed of his whereabouts. The defendant sought to contact the claimant but no reply was received. The furniture was later sold through an auction house. The question was whether the defendant was therefore entitled as agents of necessity to sell the goods. On appeal, it was held that the facts gave rise to no agency of necessity since there was 'no emergency compelling' the defendant to sell the furniture.

In *Industrie Chimiche Italia Centrale and Cerealfin SA v Alexander G Tsavliris & Sons Maritime Co The Choko Star*, (1990) the issue concerned was a salvage agreement to refloat the vessel that was grounded in Argentina; the question was if the law would imply a term conferring on the shipowners and master authority to enter into salvage contracts on behalf of cargo owners when the circumstances give rise to an agency of necessity. Slade LJ set out the following in his judgment:

> [. . .] the criteria of an agency of necessity will be satisfied if in all the circumstances
> (1) it is necessary to take salvage assistance; and
> (2) it is not reasonably practicable to communicate with the cargo owners or to obtain their instructions; and
> (3) the master or shipowners act bona fide in the interests of the cargo; and
> (4) it is reasonable for the master or shipowner to enter into the particular contract.

5 By estoppel. This arises where a principal represents that a person is acting as his agent. The principal will be prevented (estopped) from later denying that the person had authority to act as his agent. Apparent (ostensible) authority is often seen as a form of estoppel, as can be seen in *Rama Corporation Ltd* v *Proved Tin and General Investment Ltd* (1952). Moreover, it can be seen in the judgment to *Freeman & Lockyer* v *Buckhurst Park Properties* (1964) (see page 503 of the judgment):

> The representation, when acted upon by the contractor by entering into a contract with the agent, operates as an estoppel, preventing the principal from asserting that he is not bound by the contract. It is irrelevant whether the agent had actual authority to enter into the contract.

Four conditions must be fulfilled to entitle a contractor to enforce against a company a contract entered into on behalf of the company by an agent who had no actual authority to do so. It must be shown:

(1) that a representation that the agent had authority to enter on behalf of the company into a contract of the kind sought to be enforced was made to the contractor;

(2) that such representation was made by a person or persons who had 'actual' authority to manage the business of the company either generally or in respect of those matters to which the contract relates;

(3) that he (the contractor) was induced by such representation to enter into the contract, that is, that he in fact relied upon it; and

(4) that under its memorandum or articles of association the company was not deprived of the capacity either to enter into a contract of the kind sought to be enforced or to delegate authority to enter into a contract of that kind to the agent.

The principle laid down in *Freeman & Lockyer* was applied in the following case.

Racing UK Ltd v *Doncaster Racecourse Ltd* (2004)

The company sought to enforce a purported agreement with the racecourse management company and the racecourse owner concerning television picture rights in respect of a racecourse. The racecourse owner argued that the chief executive of the management company did not have authority, whether actual, apparent or ostensible to enter into the agreement on its behalf, and the agreement was not binding upon it. It was held that while, on the evidence presented, there was no actual implied authority for the management company to enter into the agreement nor had the agreement been ratified by the owner, the owner presented by conduct that the chief executive had authority to enter into the contract on the owner's behalf and there was a representation made to the company; the relevant section from *Freeman & Lockyer* concerning estoppels was discussed in the judgment: 'the company is estopped from denying to anyone who has entered into a contract with the agent in reliance upon such "apparent" authority that the agent had authority to contract on behalf of the company.'

Prudential Assurance Co Ltd v *Exel UK Ltd* (2009)

A notice served on a landlord with a view to exercising the tenant's right to break a commercial lease was not a valid notice as it had been given in the name of only one of the two companies that formed the tenant, and the landlord was not estopped from denying its validity.

Commercial Agents (Council Directive) Regulations 1993

The Commercial Agents (Council Directive) Regulations 1993 (SI 1993/3053) implement the European Directive relating to Self Employed Commercial Agents into UK law. The purpose was to harmonise European legislation governing contracts between agents and their principals, and in general to strengthen the position of agents.

Under reg 2(1), commercial agents are defined as self-employed intermediaries who have continuing authority to negotiate the sale or purchase of goods on behalf of a principal, or to negotiate and conclude the sale or purchase of goods on behalf of and in the name of a principal. The regulations lay down the minimum requirements of a contract between an agent and principal, for example, minimum periods of notice, when commission is due and the right to claim compensation on the termination of the contract.

Tamarind International Ltd v *Eastern Natural Gas (Retail) Ltd* (2000)

T, a company appointed by E to market 'Eastern Natural Gas' following the deregulation of the gas industry, brought an action against E, alleging wrongful termination of its agency contract. T applied for determination of a preliminary issue, as to whether the Commercial Agents (Council Directive) Regulations 1993, implementing the Commercial Agents Directive, applied to its activities as commercial agents for E. E submitted that T's activities were 'secondary', thus falling outside the provisions of the Regulations by virtue of reg 2(4). T argued that since it worked exclusively for E its activities must be described as primary and not secondary.

It was held that the marketing activities of T amounted to the activities of a commercial agent since those activities had been contemplated by both parties as involving referral techniques from which E would derive long-term benefits. The correct test was for the court to enquire into the primary purpose of the agency agreement to determine whether the agent had been appointed to develop goodwill in the principal's business, giving the principal a commercial advantage. Such activities were not 'secondary' under reg 2(4). Accordingly, in the event of wrongful termination of a contract, T would be entitled to an indemnity or compensation.

The duties of the principal and agent

The agent owes a number of duties to his or her principal. These include the following.

To carry out the wishes of the principal in accordance with the agency agreement

As the essence of an agency is a contract, the agent must perform his side of the contractual obligations as agreed under the contract. This can be seen in *Bertram, Armstrong & Co* v *Hugh Godfray* (1830) in which it was stated that:

> when an agent acts under a general authority he is bound to act for his principal as he would act for himself; when he acts under a particular authority, and for a special purpose, he has no discretion.

The above principle can also be seen under reg 3, the Commercial Agents (Council Directive) Regulations 1993:

3. – Duties of a commercial agent to his principal

(1) In performing his activities a commercial agent must look after the interests of his principal and act dutifully and in good faith.

(2) In particular, a commercial agent must –

(a) make proper efforts to negotiate and, where appropriate, conclude the transactions he is instructed to take care of;

(b) communicate to his principal all the necessary information available to him;

(c) comply with reasonable instructions given by his principal.

In *Cureton* v *Mark Insulations Ltd* (2006), C claimed for commission following the termination of his agreement with M (a company). However, a conflict of interest arose by C's practice of going to M's customers to sell insulation and it was deemed that C was in firm breach of his duty towards M, under reg 3(1) and reg 3(2)(b) of the 1993 Regulations.

To exercise reasonable care and skill

In *Solomon* v *Barker* (1862) when considering the price of the goods, it was stated by Blackburn J that the question as to whether the agent performed their duty would depend on:

> the terms on which they were employed [. . .] If nothing was specially stipulated or directed, then it must be taken that they were employed to sell upon the ordinary terms. In that view, they were bound to employ due care and diligence, but would not be liable for mere mistake without negligence. [. . .] but it is part of the ordinary duty of brokers to fix a price before a sale, as they did not do so, they would be liable. But even in that case the defendants would be bound, as brokers, to use ordinary care and diligence. And they would be liable if they sold the goods at a sacrifice, and threw them (so to speak) away. Hence they were bound to make some estimate of the price or value for their own guidance in the sale. And if they did not do so, and thus sold under the fair value, they are liable. The question is, whether they used due care and diligence when they sold the goods for the price they took. It is not a question merely of price or value, but whether they were guilty of negligence in not getting a better price, and in not using the ordinary care to do so.

This applies even if the agent was a gratuitous agent as can be seen in *Chaudhry* v *Prabhakar* (1989) in which a friend agreed to find a car for the claimant for no payment. A car was found and the claimant relied on the advice provided by the friend to purchase the car.

Moreover, when the claimant asked if the car had been in an accident, she was given the assurance that the car had not and that she need not have it examined by a mechanic. Relying on those assurances the claimant bought the car but realised soon after that the car had been involved in an accident and was not roadworthy and worthless. A duty of care arose where the agent knew the principal to be relying on his skill and judgement. The standard of care imposed upon a gratuitous agent is the same. This can be seen at page 35 of Stuart-Smith LJ's judgment:

> [. . .] logically the standard of care, or the nature and extent of the duty, should be the same as that required of an unpaid agent. And [. . .] to take such care as is reasonably to be expected of him in all the circumstances'.

To carry out his duties personally unless there is express or implied authority for him to delegate his duties

As Lord Denning stated in the judgment to *John McCann & Co* v *Pow* (1975), 'the general rule is that an agent has no authority to appoint a subagent except with the express or implied authority of the principal'. The facts of the case can be found below.

John McCann & Co v Pow (1975)

P, the vendor, the owner of a leasehold flat, asked J (an estate agent) to put his flat on the market and agreed to pay the estate agents a reasonable commission if they introduced a purchaser, but without prejudice to a privately negotiated sale. On the same date J sent particulars of the flat to another firm of estate agents, D, with whom they had regular contact. P knew nothing about D. D advertised the flat and sent R to view the flat. When asked by P if he had come from the appointed agents, R said 'no' and they entered into a negotiation privately concerning the flat and agreed on a sale. The question was whether P would need to pay J any commission on the ground that R had been introduced by D. P denied knowledge of any subagency at the material time and denied liability for commission. It was held at appeal that P was not liable to pay commission to an estate agent who, while claiming to be 'sole agent', had delegated his personal functions and duties to a subagent without the express authority of his principal, the vendor, and that no authority could be implied where the delegated responsibilities went beyond merely ministerial acts.

Moreover, an agent is under fiduciary duties to the principal. Fiduciary duty is a concept that was examined in Chapter 6 ⊙. It might be useful to start with Milett LJ's judgment to *Bristol and West Building Society* v *Mothew* (1996) (at page 18):

a fiduciary is someone who has undertaken to act for or on behalf of another in a particular matter in circumstances which give rise to a relationship of trust and confidence. The distinguishing obligation of a fiduciary is the obligation of loyalty. The principal is entitled to the single-minded loyalty of his fiduciary. This core liability has several facets. A fiduciary must act in good faith; he must not make a profit out of his trust; he must not place himself in a position where his duty and his interest may conflict; he may not act for his own benefit or the benefit of a third person without the informed consent of his principal. This is not intended to be an exhaustive list, but it is sufficient to indicate the nature of fiduciary obligations. They are the defining characteristics of the fiduciary [. . .] he is not subject to fiduciary obligations because he is a fiduciary; it is because he is subject to them that he is a fiduciary. The nature of the obligation determines the nature of the breach. The various obligations of a fiduciary merely reflect different aspects of his core duties of loyalty and fidelity. Breach of fiduciary obligation, therefore, connotes disloyalty or infidelity. Mere incompetence is not enough. A servant who loyally does his incompetent best for his master is not unfaithful and is not guilty of a breach of fiduciary duty.

To account for all money and property received on behalf of the principal and to keep proper accounts

As can be seen in *Gray* v *Haig* (1855), where it was stated that:

the Court deals severely with any irregularities on the part of an agent, and requires him to act strictly, in all matters relating to such agency, for the benefit of his principal. It is imperative upon an agent to preserve correct accounts of all his dealings and transactions; and the loss [. . .]

To avoid a conflict of interest

In *Boardman* v *Phipps* (1967) a solicitor, acting for a trust, was concerned about a company in which the trust had a substantial holding of shares when the company's business appeared to be on the decline. He, and a beneficiary of the trust, decided to purchase shares in a company. They put ocnsiderable efforts into the

business of the company and subsequently made substantial profits. While they acted in a manner highly beneficial to the trust, it was held that they were placed in a special position, of a fiduciary character. The opportunity to make a profit was only obtained because it was related to the trust shares. Accordingly, they were accountable for the profit made.

See also *Kingsley IT Consulting Ltd* v *McIntosh* (2006) and *Imageview Management Ltd* v *Jack* (2009), where a football agent had acted in breach of its fiduciary duty to the footballer who required a work permit to work in the UK. The footballer had consequently to pay no more fees to the agent and was entitled to repayment of commission already paid as well as the fee received by the agent for the secret deal. As per Jacob LJ:

the law imposes on agents high standards [. . .] An agent's own personal interests come entirely second to the interest of his client. If you undertake to act for a man you must act 100 per cent body and soul for him. You must act as if you were him. You must not allow your own interest to get in the way without telling him. An undisclosed but realistic possibility of a conflict of interest is a breach of your duty of good faith to your client.

Not to take bribes or make a secret profit

In *Industries and General Mortgage Co Ltd* v *Lewis* (1949), it was stated that 'once the bribe is established, there is an irrebuttable presumption that it was given with an intention to induce the agent to act favourably to the payer, and, thereafter, unfavourably to the principal'. It was stated, as can be seen in *Attorney-General for Hong Kong* v *Reid* (1994), that where a fiduciary accepted a bribe in breach of duty, the fiduciary who acts in breach of his duties cannot be allowed to retain any gain, or any further gain of profits, that he has made.

The agent has the following rights against the principal:

To be paid the agreed amount or, if no fee is agreed, a reasonable amount

Given the nature of the agency, invariably, the agent will be entitled to remuneration for the work that he has performed on behalf of the principal. This will usually be dealt with by the contract between a principal and an agent. This could cover situations when the contract itself was void, as can be seen in the following case.

Craven Ellis v Canons Ltd **(1936)**

The claimant was appointed managing director of a company. By the articles of association of the company each director was required to obtain his qualification shares within two months after his appointment. The claimant did not do so. However, the claimant had done work for the company and claimed to recover the remuneration provided for in the agreement. As commented by Greer LJ, 'the obligation to pay reasonable remuneration for work done when there is no binding contract between the parties is imposed by a rule of law and not by an inference of fact from acceptance of the services'.

Regulation 6(1) of Commercial Agents (Council Directive) Regulations 1993 deals with remuneration concerning commercial agents.

To be indemnified for any expenses incurred in performing his duties

Again, this will usually be dealt with under the contract. However, there could be charges or expenses that arose outside the agreement. This can be seen in *PSA Transport Ltd* v *Newton, Landsdowne & Co Ltd* (1956) where the claimants were employed by the defendants to inspect and tranship certain goods at the London docks. As the goods had been landed, the Port of London Authority had demanded payment of certain port dues and wharfage charges before releasing the goods and the claimants had paid them. While the payments were not included in the claimants' agreed charges, it was held that they were entitled to be reimbursed by the defendants.

Where commercial agents are concerned, this is dealt with under reg 17 of the Commercial Agents (Council Directive) Regulations 1993, that a commercial agent shall be entitled to an indemnity if a commercial agent:

(a) [. . .] has brought the principal new customers or has significantly increased the volume of business with existing customers and the principal continues to derive substantial benefits from the business with such customers; and

(b) the payment of this indemnity is equitable having regard to all the circumstances and, in particular, the commission lost by the commercial agent on the business transacted with such customers.

(4) The amount of the indemnity shall not exceed a figure equivalent to an indemnity for one year calculated from the commercial agent's average annual remuneration over the preceding five years and if the contract goes back less than five years the indemnity shall be calculated on the average for the period in question.

It should be noted that under reg 17(5) that the grant of an indemnity would not prevent the commercial agent from seeking damages as the issue of compensation is dealt with separately under the regulation. This covers compensation for the damage a commercial agent 'suffers as a result of the termination of his relations with his principal' and, in particular, circumstances which (see reg 17(7)):

(a) deprive the commercial agent of the commission which proper performance of the agency contract would have procured for him whilst providing his principal with substantial benefits linked to the activities of the commercial agent; or

(b) have not enabled the commercial agent to amortize the costs and expenses that he had incurred in the performance of the agency contract on the advice of his principal.

To exercise a lien over the principal's goods and to stop them in transit where payment is outstanding

The lien of an agent only permits the agent to retain possession of goods until the principal has settled the debts. Munday provided a useful explanation:

English law has traditionally drawn a distinction between general liens and particular liens. A general lien confers on the agent the right to retain the principal's goods until the general balance of the account between principal and agent is settled. A particular lien, however, only entitles the agent to retain possession of his principal's goods until money owed to him by the principal on those particular goods has been paid over. (page 213)

It should be noted that there may also be the issue of vicarious liability to be considered if the agent is an employee of the principal. For discussion on vicarious liability, see Chapter 16 .

Termination of agency

The agency may come to an end either by the actions of the parties or by operation of the law.

1 Termination by the parties. The principal and agent may terminate their relationship by mutual agreement or the agency contract may allow either party to terminate by giving notice. Even if the contract does not provide for termination by notice, either party can end the contract unilaterally by giving reasonable notice.

In terms of commercial agent, the relevant regulation is reg 15 under which the minimum periods of notice for termination of a commercial agency contract have been set out (see reg 15(2)):

The period of notice shall be –
(a) 1 month for the first year of the contract;
(b) 2 months for the second year commenced;
(c) 3 months for the third year commenced and for the subsequent years.

No shorter periods of notice should be agreed and the regulation indicates that any earlier fixed period must be taken into account in the calculation of the period of notice where a commercial agency contract for a fixed period has been converted into an agency contract for an indefinite period.

2 Termination by operation of the law. The relationship will come to an end automatically with the death or insanity of either party or by the bankruptcy of the principal. The agency can also come to an end because of frustration or illegality.

Self-test questions/activities

1 Explain the differences between the following:
   (a) a general agent and a special agent;
   (b) a mercantile agent and a *del credere* agent;
   (c) agency by ratification and agency by necessity.

2 Explain the differences between actual and ostensible authority.

Website references

http://www.businesslink.gov.uk See Business Link website for further information on commercial agents.

http://webarchive.nationalarchives.gov.uk/+/ http://www.berr.gov.uk/whatwedo/consumers/ business/commercial-agents/index.html Information available on the Department for Business, Innovation and Skills on Commercial Agents Regulations 1993.

Visit **www.mylawchamber.co.uk/richesallen** to access study support resources including answers to questions in this chapter and legal updates, all linked to the **Pearson eText** version of **Keenan and Riches' Business Law** which you can **search**, **highlight** and **personalise** with your **own notes** and **bookmarks**.

Use **Case Navigator** to read in full some of the key cases referenced in this chapter with commentary and questions:
Freeman & Lockyer v *Buckhurst Park Properties* [1964]
Hely-Hutchinson v *Brayhead Ltd* (1968)

Chapter 11 — Contracts for the supply of goods and services

Learning objectives

After studying this chapter you should understand the following main points:

- the distinction between different types of business contract for the supply of goods and services;
- the legislative framework governing contracts for sale and supply of goods and services;
- the ways in which a manufacturer may be liable in contract for defective goods.

In this chapter we move away from studying basic principles of general application to all contracts to look at specific types of contract in use in the business world; namely, contracts for the supply of goods and services. It is important that you can distinguish between different kinds of transaction for the supply of goods and services because different statutory provisions apply. The rights and responsibilities of the parties to a contract for the supply of goods or services are determined primarily by agreement. However, Parliament has intervened increasingly in this area of law to provide a statutory framework for such transactions. We will examine the statutory framework in detail. The key pieces of legislation are set out in Figure 11.1. The chapter concludes by considering the effectiveness of the law of contract as a means of providing redress in respect of defective goods and services, and the responsibility in contract of a manufacturer for his products.

Type of contract	Sale of goods	Supply of goods and services
Main Act	Sale of Goods Act 1979	Supply of Goods and Services Act 1982
Amended by	Sale and Supply of Goods Act 1994 Sale of Goods (Amendment) Act 1994 Sale of Goods (Amendment) Act 1995 Sale and Supply of Goods to Consumers Regulations 2002	Sale and Supply of Goods Act 1994 Sale and Supply of Goods to Consumers Regulations 2002

Figure 11.1 Legislation governing contracts for the sale and supply of goods and services

Contracts for the supply of goods

Sale of goods

A contract for the sale of goods is probably the most common form of transaction in the business world. Whenever you buy goods, whether from a supermarket, market stall, doorstep salesman, by mail order or using the Internet, you have entered into a contract for the sale of goods. The rights and duties of the parties to this type of contract are set out in the Sale of Goods Act 1979 (as amended). The Act applies to all contracts for the sale of goods, from buying a sandwich at lunchtime to a multi-million pound deal to supply new aircraft to an airline company. A contract for the sale of goods is defined in s 2(1) of the Sale of Goods Act 1979 as:

> A contract by which the seller transfers or agrees to transfer the property in goods to the buyer for a money consideration called the price.

This definition is extremely important because only those contracts which fall within it will be covered by the provisions of the 1979 Act. A closer look at the definition will help you distinguish a contract for the sale of goods from other similar kinds of contracts in which goods change hands.

Section 2(1) covers two possibilities: an actual sale and an agreement to sell at some future time. The essence of the transaction is the transfer of property in goods from the seller to the buyer. ('Property' in this context means ownership of the goods.) Goods include all tangible items of personal property such as food, clothes and furniture: land and money are excluded from the definition. The consideration for the goods must be money, although a part-exchange deal in which goods are exchanged for other goods plus money will be covered by the Act because some money has changed hands.

Exchange or barter

No money changes hands in this type of contract. Instead there is a straight exchange of goods between the parties. The absence of money from the consideration means that the Sale of Goods Act 1979 does not apply to these contracts. Previously the obligations of the parties were governed by the common law, but now the Supply of Goods and Services Act 1982 (as amended by the Sale and Supply of Goods Act 1994) imposes certain statutory duties on the supplier of goods under a contract of exchange.

Work and materials

Another way in which you can acquire goods is in consequence of a contract whose main purpose is the provision of services. If you take your car to be serviced by a garage, the main substance of the contract is the skill and labour of the mechanic in checking the car. The supply of such items as brake fluid and the renewal of spark plugs is an ancillary part of the contract.

The distinction between a contract of sale and a contract of work and materials is often a fine one.

Robinson v Graves (1935)

Robinson, an artist, was commissioned to paint a portrait for 250 guineas. The Court of Appeal held that this was a contract for Robinson's skill as an artist and not a contract for the sale of goods, i.e. the finished portrait.

However, a contract to buy a painting from an art gallery would be a sale of goods contract. Contracts for work and materials are now subject to the Supply of Goods and Services Act 1982 (as amended by the Sale and Supply of Goods Act 1994 and the Sale and Supply of Goods to Consumers Regulations 2002).

Sale of goods

The law relating to contracts for the sale of goods is contained in the Sale of Goods Act 1979. This Act replaced the original Sale of Goods Act 1893 and includes all the amendments that had been made in the intervening years. The 1979 Act has been amended by four pieces of legislation: the Sale and Supply of Goods Act 1994, and the Sale of Goods (Amendment) Acts 1994 and 1995 and the Sale and Supply of Goods to Consumers Regulations 2002. The Sale of Goods Act 1979 provides a framework for the relationship between the buyer and seller and covers such matters as the rights and duties of the parties and their remedies in the event of a breach.

It would be wrong to think that the Act governs every aspect of a sale of goods contract. Many of the general principles of contract law which we studied in previous chapters still apply. A valid contract for the sale of goods, just like any other contract, must possess all the essential elements. The rules relating to the requirements of offer and acceptance, intention, consideration, etc. are largely untouched by the Act. The other important thing to remember is that the Act, in general, does not stop the parties from making their own tailor-made agreement. In many situations, the rules contained in the Act only apply where the parties have failed to make express arrangements as to their obligations. We will now look at some of the more important provisions of the Sale of Goods Act 1979. Section references are to the 1979 Act, unless otherwise indicated.

Definition

A contract of sale of goods is defined by s 2(1) as: 'a contract by which the seller transfers or agrees to transfer the property in goods to the buyer for a money consideration called the price'.

Formation

It is not necessary to observe complex formalities to create a contract for the sale of goods; it may be in writing or by word of mouth, or partly in writing and partly by word of mouth, or even implied from the conduct of the parties. Capacity to enter into a binding sale of goods contract is governed by the general law of contract, which we have already considered in Chapter 7 ⊙.

The implied terms

The parties are generally free to agree between themselves the details of their contract. However, the Act also automatically includes a number of conditions and warranties in every contract for the sale of goods. These are known as the implied terms and they can be found in ss 12–15.

Title (s 12)

There is an implied condition on the part of the seller that in the case of a sale he has a right to sell the goods, and in the case of an agreement to sell he will have the right to sell when the property is to pass (s 12(1)). If the seller cannot pass good title (rights of ownership) to the buyer, he will be liable for breach of a condition.

Rowland v Divall (1923)

Rowland bought a car from Divall for £334 and used it for four months. It later transpired that Divall had bought the car from someone who had stolen it, and it had to be returned to the true owner. Rowland sued Divall to recover the full purchase price that he had paid. The Court of Appeal held that Divall was in breach of

s 12. Rowland had paid £334 to become the owner of the car. Since he had not received what he had contracted for, there was a total failure of consideration entitling him to a full refund.

Section 12(2) implies two warranties into sale of goods contracts:

1 that the goods are free from any charges or encumbrances (third-party rights) not made known to the buyer before the contract; and

2 that the buyer will enjoy quiet possession of the goods.

Microbeads v Vinhurst Road Markings Ltd (1975)

The buyers purchased road marking machines from the sellers. Shortly after the sale, another company obtained a patent in respect of the machines and this company was seeking to enforce the patent against the buyers. The sellers brought an action against the buyers for the purchase price, and the buyers wished to include in their defence a breach of s 12(2). The Court of Appeal held that the buyers' quiet possession of the machines had been disturbed and, therefore, it would be appropriate to raise a breach of s 12(2) as a defence to an action for the price when the case came to full trial.

Section 12(3)–(5) provides for a situation where the seller is unsure about his title to goods. He can sell them on the basis that he is transferring only such rights of ownership as he may have. If he does this, there is no implied condition that he has the right to sell the goods, but the sale is subject to implied warranties relating to freedom from third-party rights and quiet possession.

Description (s 13)

Where there is a contract for the sale of goods by description, there is an implied condition that the goods will correspond with the description (s 13(1)). If the buyer does not see the goods before he buys them (e.g. from a mail order catalogue or through the Internet), there has clearly been a sale by description. Even where the buyer has seen the goods and, perhaps, selected them himself, it may still be a sale by description, if he has relied to some extent on a description.

Beale v *Taylor* (1967)

The defendant advertised a car for sale as a 1961 Triumph Herald. The claimant inspected the car before he bought it. He later discovered that the vehicle consisted of a rear half of a 1961 Herald, which had been welded to the front half of an earlier model. The Court of Appeal held that the claimant was entitled to damages for breach of s 13, even though he had seen and inspected the car. He had relied to some extent on the description contained in the advertisement.

If the buyer has forgotten about the description by the time he buys the goods or does not believe what he has been told and checks the details for himself, he may lose the protection of s 13 because he has not relied on the description.

Harlingdon & Leinster Enterprises Ltd v *Christopher Hull Fine Art Ltd* (1990)

The defendant sold a painting to the claimant which turned out to be a fake. The defendant believed that the painting was by Munter, an artist of the German Expressionist School, because he had seen it attributed to Munter in an auction catalogue. He described the painting as a Munter during negotiations with the claimant, although he made it clear that he knew nothing about Munter's work and lacked expertise in German Expressionist painting. The claimant, who was also lacking in relevant expertise, inspected the painting and decided that it was authentic. He agreed to buy it. The painting was described in the defendant's invoice as a Munter. When the claimant discovered that the painting was a fake, he sued under s 13(1) to recover the purchase price. The Court of Appeal held that the defendant had made it clear that his attribution could not be relied upon and that the claimant should have exercised his own judgement. A contract will not be a sale by description merely because the seller has issued some statement about the goods. The buyer must show that the description influenced the decision to buy. Since the claimant was unable to show this, his action failed.

Comment. The claimant also argued that the painting was not of merchantable quality under s 14 of the Sale of Goods Act 1979 (see later). The court held that the misattribution did not detract from the quality of the painting so as to make it unmerchantable. In the words of Nourse LJ: 'It could still have been hung on a wall somewhere and been enjoyed for what it was . . .'

The description of the goods may cover such matters as size, quantity, weight, ingredients, origin or even how they are to be packed. The slightest departure from the specifications will entitle the buyer to reject the goods for breach of a condition of the contract.

Re Moore & Co and Landauer & Co (1921)

The claimants agreed to supply 3,000 tins of Australian canned fruit, packed in cases containing 30 tins each. When the goods were delivered, it was discovered that about half of the consignment was packed in cases containing 24 tins. Although the correct quantity had been delivered, the defendants decided to reject the whole consignment. It was held that this was a sale by description under s 13 and since the goods did not correspond with that description, the defendants were entitled to repudiate the contract.

Comment. This decision seems to be at odds with a well-established principle that the law does not concern itself with trifling matters. Lord Wilberforce in *Reardon Smith Line* v *Yngvar Hanson-Tangen* (1976) cast doubt on the correctness of the *Moore and Landauer* decision and suggested that it should be re-examined by the House of Lords.

A seller may ensure that the transaction is not a sale by description by including such phrases as 'Bought as seen' or 'Sold as seen' in the contract (*Cavendish-Woodhouse Ltd* v *Manley* (1984)).

Quality and suitability (s 14)

Section 14 of the original 1893 Sale of Goods Act incorporated two implied terms into every sale of goods contract by a trader: that the goods were of merchantable quality, and that they were fit for a particular purpose. The implied term relating to quality attracted sustained criticism over the years. The failure to define what was meant by 'merchantable quality' in the original 1893 Act was remedied in 1973 with the introduction of a statutory definition. Goods were of merchantable quality, according to the new definition, if they were 'as fit for the purpose(s) for which goods of that kind are commonly bought as it is reasonable to expect having regard to any description applied to them, the price (if relevant) and all other relevant circumstances'. However, the inclusion of a statutory definition of 'merchantable quality' did not completely remove the uncertainty about the scope of the implied term. A report by the Law Commission highlighted a number of criticisms of the implied term of merchantable quality. The Sale and Supply of Goods Act 1994, which came into force on 3 January 1995, implemented the recommendations of the Law Commission contained in its *Report on the Sale and Supply of Goods* (1987). The new definition of quality applies to all contracts for the sale and supply of goods, including all agreements for the transfer of property in goods such as barter, work and materials, hire-purchase, hire and the exchange of goods for trading stamps.

Caveat emptor

Section 14 starts by stating that there is no implied condition or warranty as to quality or fitness for a particular purpose, except as provided by ss 14 and 15. This preserves the principle of *caveat emptor*: let the buyer beware. Both of the conditions implied by s 14 apply 'where the seller sells goods in the course of a business'. In the following case the Court of Appeal confirmed that the implied terms in s 14 apply to every sale by a business, even though the goods sold may not be part of the 'stock in trade'.

Stevenson v Rogers (1999)

A fisherman sold his only fishing boat in order to replace it. The purchaser claimed that the boat was not of merchantable (satisfactory) quality. At first instance the High Court decided that the contract of sale did not contain an implied term as to merchantable quality because the sale was not 'in the course of business'. The High Court arrived at this conclusion by reference to the interpretation of 'in the course of a business' in the context of the Unfair Contract Terms Act 1977 in *R & B Customs Brokers Co Ltd* v *United Dominion Trust Ltd* (1988) (see Chapter 8) and cases decided under the Trade Descriptions Act 1968 such as *Havering LBC* v *Stevenson* (1970) and *Davies* v *Sumner* (1984). In these earlier cases, some degree of 'regularity' had been required for the transaction to be 'in the course of a business'. Only those sales which were integral to the business (i.e. stock in trade) would come within the scope of business sales. The Court of Appeal held that the sale of the fishing boat was in the course of a business for the purposes of s 14 and that the implied term as to merchantable quality did apply. The court was greatly influenced by the fact that the wording of s 14 of the Sale

of Goods Act had been deliberately changed in 1973 so as to broaden the scope of its protection by covering all sales by traders, even those which may be incidental to the main business. The earlier authorities in relation to the Unfair Contract Terms Act 1977 (*R & B Customs Brokers*) and the Trade Descriptions Act 1968 (*Havering LBC* and *Davies*) were distinguished.

Section 14 implies two conditions into every sale by a trader: that the goods are of satisfactory quality and that they are fit for a particular purpose. The requirement of s 14, that the sale must be 'in the course of a business', means that the implied terms of quality and fitness cannot apply to sales by private individuals. So, if you buy something privately and it is defective or unsuitable, you cannot complain under s 14.

Satisfactory quality

Section 14(2), as amended by the Sale and Supply of Goods Act 1994, provides that where a seller sells goods in the course of a business there is an implied condition that the goods supplied are of satisfactory quality, except to the extent of defects which are brought specifically to the buyer's attention before the contract is made or ought to have been noticed by the buyer if he has examined the goods. Goods are of satisfactory quality according to s 14(2A) 'if they meet the standard that a reasonable person would regard as satisfactory, taking into account any description of the goods, the price (if relevant) and all other relevant circumstances'. Section 14(2B) explains that the quality of goods includes their state and condition and the following non-exhaustive aspects of quality:

(a) fitness for all purposes for which goods of the kind in question are commonly supplied;
(b) appearance and finish;
(c) freedom from minor defects;
(d) safety; and
(e) durability.

Under s 14(2D) the 'relevant circumstances' referred to in s 14(2A) include any public statements about the specific characteristics of the goods made by the seller, the producer or his representative particularly in advertising or labelling but only where the buyer deals as a consumer. A person is a consumer if he is a natural person acting for purposes outside his trade, business or profession. The seller will not be responsible for a public statement in the following situations:

- if at the time the contract was made he was not and could not have been aware of the statement, e.g. a retailer based in one part of the country may not be liable for an advertising campaign run by the manufacturer in a different part of the country;
- where, before the contract was made, the statement had been withdrawn or, if it was misleading or incorrect, it had been corrected in public;
- the consumer could not have been influenced by the statement.

It is likely to be some time before many cases are reported on the new definition of quality. The following explanation of the new implied term as to quality, of necessity, is illustrated by some cases decided according to the old definition of 'merchantable quality'.

The requirement that goods must be of satisfactory quality means that a brand new washing machine should wash your clothes properly; new shoes should not fall apart on their first outing; and a meat pie bought for your lunch should not make you ill. Section 14(2) does not impose absolute standards of quality with which all goods must comply. However, the goods must be satisfactory to a reasonable person. A reasonable person is unlikely, for example, to find the quality of new goods satisfactory if they have minor or cosmetic defects.

Rogers v Parish (Scarborough) Ltd (1987)

The claimants bought a new Range Rover for £16,000. After a few weeks of unsatisfactory use, the vehicle was returned to the dealers and the claimants accepted another Range Rover as a substitute. Unfortunately, the second vehicle proved no better than the first. Six months after delivery, the engine was misfiring at all road speeds and excessive noise was coming from the gearbox. There were also substantial defects in the bodywork. The claimants notified the dealers that they were rejecting the vehicle. The Court of Appeal held that the suppliers were in breach of the implied term as to quality. The court held that the definition of merchantability involved considering not only if the car was capable of getting from A to B safely, but also the buyer's reasonable expectations of being able to do so with the appropriate degree of comfort, ease of handling and reliability, and with appropriate pride in the vehicle's appearance. The court found that the buyers' reasonable expectations of a £16,000 new Range Rover had not been met in this case. The claimants had not received value for money.

Comment. In an earlier case, ***Millars of Falkirk Ltd v Turpie*** (1976), the Inner House of the Scottish Court of Session held that a car with a slight oil leak in the power-assisted steering (which could be repaired for about £25) was of merchantable quality. Factors relevant to the decision were: (i) the minor nature of the defect; (ii) the ease with which the defect could be cured; (iii) the willingness of the dealers to effect a repair; (iv) the obvious nature of the defect; (v) the absence of serious risk; and (vi) many new cars have minor defects on delivery. This case raised doubts whether a car which could be driven safely but with minor repairable defects could be said to be unmerchantable. The *Rogers* case resolved some of those doubts by deciding that merchantable quality should not be tested by usability alone. The Law Commission cited the decision in the *Rogers* case with approval. The Commissioners also took the view that the car in the *Millars* case would fail the new test of quality proposed in their report.

Shine v General Guarantee Corp Ltd (1988)

Mr Shine purchased an enthusiast's car. When he inquired subsequently whether there was a manufacturer's rust warranty, he discovered that the car had been written off after having been submerged in water for 24 hours. Mr Shine terminated the agreement. The Court of Appeal held that the car was unmerchantable. Mr Shine thought he was buying a second-hand enthusiast's car in good condition for a fair price when in fact he was buying, in the words of Bush J, 'one which no member of the public would touch with a barge pole unless they could get it at a substantially reduced price to reflect the risk they were taking'.

The test applied by the court is whether a reasonable person would regard the goods as being unsatisfactory.

Bramhill v Edwards (2004)

The claimants, Mr and Mrs Bramhill, bought a second-hand 'Dolphin' motor home from Mr and Mrs Edwards, which Mr Edwards had imported from the United States. The legal width for motor homes in the UK is 100 inches but the Dolphin was 102 inches wide. The Bramhills had used the Dolphin for six or seven months when they measured its width and found it was 102 inches. They spoke to Mrs Edwards about it and she wrote back to say that they had been allowed to import the vehicle into the UK and the width would have been checked as part of the process. The Bramhills continued to use the vehicle for another four months when Mr Bramhill wrote to complain about the width, and over the next three months he tried unsuccessfully to get Mr Edwards to take the Dolphin in part-exchange for another motor home. During this time he received an opinion from the Vehicle Inspectorate that the Dolphin did not comply with UK regulations and its use could lead to prosecution. The court had to consider: (i) whether the Edwards had misrepresented that the Dolphin complied with UK regulations as regards its width; (ii) whether the Dolphin was of satisfactory quality under s 14(2A); (iii) if the Dolphin was in breach of the implied term in s 14(2A), whether the Bramhills had lost their rights under s 14(2C) because they had inspected the vehicle before buying but they had not noticed that its width was unlawful; and (iv) what the measure of damages should be. The Court of Appeal held that the judge's decision that there was no misrepresentation was not perverse. It found that there was no breach of the implied term as to satisfactory quality. A reasonable buyer would be aware that there were a significant number of over-size vehicles on the roads and the authorities were turning a 'Nelsonian' blind eye to breaches of the width regulations. There was also evidence that it would be possible to insure the vehicle. Even if the vehicle had been in breach of s 14(2A), Mr Edwards would have had a defence under s 14(2C) as the examination of the vehicle should have revealed that it was over-size. Furthermore, even if there had been a breach of the implied term, the Bramhills would not have been entitled to damages because they were aware of the breach of the regulations long before they took any action to rescind the contract in reliance on it.

If you buy goods second-hand or very cheaply, you cannot reasonably expect the highest standards of quality.

Bartlett v Sidney Marcus Ltd (1965)

The claimant bought a second-hand car from the defendants who were car dealers. The claimant was warned that the clutch was defective and he agreed to a reduction in the price of the car to take account of this. The defect turned out to be more serious and, therefore, more costly to repair than he expected. He claimed that the defendants were in breach of the implied term as to quality. The Court of Appeal held that in the circumstances the car was of merchantable quality. As Lord Denning MR pointed out: 'A buyer should realise that when he buys a second-hand car defects may appear sooner or later.'

There had been some doubt under the old standard of merchantable quality whether goods commonly used for a number of purposes had to be fit for all such purposes. In *M/S Aswan Engineering Establishment Co v Lupdine Ltd* (1987) the Court of Appeal held that the definition of merchantable quality required goods to be suitable for one or more (but not all) purposes for which they were commonly bought. The Law Commission recommended that goods of a particular description and price should be fit for all common purposes. This recommendation is given effect by s 14(2B), which requires goods to be fit for 'all the purposes for which goods of the kind in question are commonly supplied'. A buyer is not obliged to examine goods before he buys them and, if he chooses not to do so, he will still be entitled to full protection under s 14(2). The buyer can lose his right to complain in two situations: first, where the seller specifically points out that the goods are faulty; second, where he decides to check the goods, but fails to spot an obvious defect (s 14(2C)).

Fitness for a particular purpose

Section 14(3) provides that where the seller sells goods in the course of a business and the buyer, expressly or by implication, makes known to the seller any particular purpose for which the goods are being bought, there is an implied condition that the goods supplied are reasonably fit for that purpose, except where it can be shown that the buyer has not relied – or that it would be unreasonable for him to rely – on the seller's skill and judgement. If the buyer specifies the particular purpose for which he requires the goods (e.g. shoes suitable for running in a marathon), the goods must be suitable for the stated purpose. Where the buyer purchases goods with only one normal purpose, he makes his purpose known by implication. Food must be fit for eating and clothes fit for wearing.

Grant v Australian Knitting Mills Ltd (1936)

Dr Grant bought a pair of woollen underpants from a shop. The manufacturers neglected to remove properly a chemical which was used in the manufacturing process. Dr Grant developed a skin rash which turned into dermatitis. It was held that the underpants were not of merchantable quality or reasonably fit for the purpose. Although Dr Grant had not specifically stated the purpose for which he required the underpants, it was clear by implication that he intended to wear them.

If the buyer has any special requirements, these must be made known to the seller.

Griffiths v *Peter Conway Ltd* (1939)

The claimant purchased a Harris tweed coat from the defendants. After wearing the coat for a short period of time, she contracted dermatitis. She failed in her claim for damages under s 14(3). It was shown that the coat would not have affected someone with a normal skin. The claimant had not made known to the defendants the fact that she had an abnormally sensitive skin.

In order to be successful under s 14(3), the buyer must show that he relied on the seller's skill and judgement. Reliance will normally be assumed from the fact that the buyer has taken his custom to that particular shop. However, if a buyer asks for an item under its brand name or lays down detailed specifications as to what he wants, he will find it difficult to show that he has relied on the seller's skill and judgement.

The relationship between s 14(2) and s 14(3) was explored by the Court of Appeal in the following case.

Jewson Ltd v *Kelly* (2003)

Kelly had acquired a former school building which he was converting into flats. He bought 12 electric boilers from Jewson Ltd but failed to pay for them. Jewson brought proceedings and Kelly counter-claimed for damages for breach of s 14(2) and (3) of the Sale of Goods Act 1979. Kelly's case was that the boilers were not of satisfactory quality nor fit for the purpose because the boilers relied on peak-rate electricity, they reduced the Standard Assessment Procedure (SAP) energy ratings of the flats and, as a result, Kelly had found it difficult to market the flats. He had been unable to keep up repayments on the loan he had taken out to finance the flat conversion and the lender had repossessed the building. The Court of Appeal held that it is the function of s 14(3), not s 14(2), to impose an obligation tailored to the particular circumstances of the buyer. The buyer had not argued that there was anything unsatisfactory about the intrinsic qualities of the boilers. The issue was whether their impact on the energy ratings for the flats rendered them unsatisfactory, and this depended on a number of factors relating to the boilers and the nature of the flat conversion. Although Kelly made it clear to

Jewson that he wanted to buy the boilers to install in flats for sale, he did not provide information about the particular characteristics of the building being converted. Kelly could not be said to have relied on Jewson's skill and judgement with respect to the suitability of the boilers for installation in the building in question because he did not give Jewson the relevant information nor did he ask specific questions about energy ratings. This was a case of partial reliance on the seller's skill and judgement; Kelly could reasonably rely on the seller's skill and judgement in respect of the boilers' intrinsic qualities but in this respect the boilers were reasonably fit for their purpose. Jewson Ltd was not in breach of s 14(3) and there was equally no breach of s 14(2); a reasonable man would not conclude that the boilers were not of satisfactory quality.

Sample (s 15)

Section 15 provides that in a contract of sale by sample there is an implied condition:

- that the bulk will correspond with the sample in quality;
- that the buyer will have a reasonable opportunity of comparing the bulk with the sample;
- that the goods will be free from any defect making their quality unsatisfactory which would not be apparent on reasonable examination of the sample.

This section, like s 13, applies to both business and private sales. The application of s 15 can be illustrated by the following case.

Godley v *Perry* (1960)

The claimant, a six-year-old boy, bought a plastic toy catapult for 6d from a newsagent's shop run by Perry, the first defendant. The catapult broke while in use and the claimant lost an eye. He sued Perry for breach of the implied conditions in s 14(2) and (3). Perry had bought the catapults by sample from a wholesaler. He had tested the sample catapult by pulling back the elastic, but no defect had been revealed. Perry now brought the wholesaler into the action claiming a breach of the conditions in s 15. The wholesaler had bought his supply of catapults by sample from another wholesaler, who had obtained the catapults from Hong Kong. The first wholesaler brought the second wholesaler into the action alleging a similar breach of s 15.

It was held that: (1) the claimant could recover damages from the first defendant for breach of s 14: the catapult was not of merchantable quality or fit for the purpose for which it had been bought; and (2) the first defendant could recover damages from the first wholesaler, who in turn could recover damages from the second wholesaler, in both cases because there had been a breach of s 15, which was implied in the relevant contract.

Transfer of property in the goods

The essence of a contract for the sale of goods is the transfer of property (ownership) in goods from the seller to the buyer. It is important to ascertain exactly when the property in goods passes from the seller to the buyer for the following reasons:

1 If the goods are accidentally destroyed, it is necessary to know who bears the loss. Section 20 provides that risk normally passes with ownership.
2 If either the seller or the buyer becomes bankrupt or, in the case of a company, goes into liquidation, it is necessary to discover who owns the goods.
3 The remedy of an unpaid seller against a buyer will depend on whether ownership has been transferred. If property has passed to the buyer, he can be sued for the price of the goods. If property has not passed to the buyer, the seller can only sue for non-acceptance. (Remedies under the Sale of Goods Act 1979 will be discussed later in this chapter.)

The rules relating to the transfer of ownership depend on whether the goods are classified as specific goods or unascertained goods. Specific goods are 'goods identified and agreed on at the time a contract of sale is made'. This includes contracts such as purchasing groceries from a supermarket or buying a sheepskin coat from a market trader. Unascertained goods are those goods which are not identified and agreed on when the contract is made. An order for 10 cwt of coal to be delivered in three days' time involves unascertained goods, because it is impossible to identify which specific lumps of coal lying in the coal merchant's yard will make up the order. As soon as the 10 cwt of coal is set aside to fulfil this order, the goods are said to be ascertained.

Specific goods

Section 17 provides that the property in specific goods passes when the parties intend it to pass and, to ascertain the intention of the parties, 'regard shall be had to the terms of the contract, the conduct of the parties and the circumstances of the case'. If the parties do not indicate, expressly or impliedly, when they want ownership to pass, s 18 sets out various rules to ascertain their presumed intention.

Rule 1 – where there is an unconditional contract for the sale of specific goods in a deliverable state, the property in the goods passes to the buyer when the contract is made, and it is immaterial whether the time of payment or the time of delivery, or both, be postponed.

This means that a buyer can become the owner of goods even though he has not paid for them yet and they are still in the seller's possession.

Tarling v Baxter (1827)

A haystack was sold, but before the buyer had taken it away it was burned down. It was held that the buyer was still liable to pay the price because he became the owner of the haystack when the contract was made. It was immaterial that he had not yet taken delivery of the goods.

Rule 2 – where there is a contract for the sale of specific goods and the seller is bound to do something to the goods for the purpose of putting them into a deliverable state, the property does not pass until the thing is done and the buyer has notice that it has been done.

Where the seller agrees to alter the goods in some way for the buyer, ownership will pass when the alterations are completed and the buyer has been informed.

Rule 3 – where there is a contract for the sale of specific goods in a deliverable state but the seller is bound to weigh, measure, test or do some other act or thing with reference to the goods for the purpose of ascertaining the price, the property does not pass until the act or thing is done and the buyer has notice that it has been done.

If, for example, you agree to buy a particular bag of potatoes, at a price of 80p per kg, you will not become the owner of the potatoes until the seller has weighed the bag and informed you of the price payable. If, however, it is agreed that the buyer will do the weighing, measuring or testing, ownership of the goods will pass in accordance with rule 1, i.e. when the contract is made.

Rule 4 – when goods are delivered to the buyer on approval or on sale or return . . . the property in the goods passes to the buyer:

(a) when he signifies his approval or acceptance to the seller or does any other act adopting the transaction;

(b) if he does not signify his approval or acceptance to the seller but retains the goods without giving notice of rejection, then, if a time has been fixed for the return of the goods, on the expiration of that time, and, if no time has been fixed, on the expiration of a reasonable time.

Property in goods delivered on approval will pass under part (a) of this rule either when the buyer informs the seller that he wishes to buy them or he 'adopts' the transaction, for example by reselling the goods. Part (b) of the rule is illustrated by the following case.

Elphick v *Barnes* (1880)

The seller handed a horse over to a prospective buyer on approval for eight days. Unfortunately, the horse died on the third day. It was held that ownership of the horse had not passed to the buyer and, therefore, the seller would have to bear the loss.

Unascertained goods

In a sale of unascertained goods, the property passes to the buyer only when the goods have been ascertained (s 16). If the parties then fail to mention when they intend ownership to pass, s 18, rule 5 will apply.

Rule 5 – (1) where there is a contract for the sale of unascertained or future goods by description, and goods of that description and in a deliverable state are unconditionally appropriated to the contract, either by the seller with the assent of the buyer or by the buyer with the assent of the seller, the property in the goods then passes to the buyer; and the assent may be express or implied and may be given either before or after the appropriation is made.

Goods are unconditionally appropriated to the contract when they are separated from the bulk and earmarked for a particular buyer. Delivery to a carrier will amount to an 'appropriation' if the buyer's goods can be clearly identified.

Healy v *Howlett & Sons* (1917)

The claimant agreed to sell 20 boxes of mackerel to the defendant. He despatched 190 boxes of mackerel by rail for delivery to various customers, but the boxes were not labelled for particular customers. Employees of the railway company were entrusted with the task of allocating the correct number of boxes to each destination. The train was delayed and the fish deteriorated before 20 boxes could be set aside for the defendant. It was held that the property in the goods had not passed to the buyer because the defendant's boxes had not been appropriated to the contract.

The Sale of Goods (Amendment) Act 1995, which came into force on 19 September 1995, contains two provisions in respect of the transfer of property in unascertained goods. The first provision, which becomes s 18, rule 5(3), gives statutory effect to the principle of 'ascertainment by exhaustion'. This is a situation where goods are successively drawn from a bulk until all that remains are the goods which fulfil the contract in question. For example, if restaurant A buys 10 bottles of whisky from a bulk of 200 bottles stored in a distillery and the distiller sells 190 bottles to other customers, the remaining 10 bottles belong to restaurant A. The property in the goods passes to the buyer when the bulk is so reduced as to match the buyer's contract. The buyer need not have made any payment but the goods must be in a deliverable state.

The second provision introduces a new concept of co-ownership of a bulk. Section 16 must now be considered subject to a new s 20A. Section 20A deals with the following type of situation: a buyer agrees to buy 500 tonnes of coal out of a cargo of coal in the holds of the ship *Icebreaker*. In the past, if 500 tonnes were not ascertained for a particular buyer, property in the goods did not pass to the buyer. If the seller became insolvent, the buyer would have no claim on the goods, even though he may have made some payment for them. He could usually only make a claim as an unsecured creditor in the insolvency proceedings. Under the new provisions, if the buyer has made whole or partial prepayment, he will become a co-owner with any other buyers who might have a claim on the goods. The legal consequences of co-ownership are modified in a new s 20B to allow trading in the bulk goods in the normal way.

Reserving a right of disposal

The seller's overriding concern is to ensure that he receives payment in full for his goods. Clearly, this presents no problem to a retailer: he can insist on payment in cash or near cash (i.e. by a cheque guaranteed with a cheque card, or by a recognised credit card) before he releases the goods. In the business world, however, sellers are expected to do business on credit terms. If ownership of the goods passes to the buyer before he pays for them and he subsequently becomes bankrupt or, in the case of a company, goes into liquidation, the seller will be treated as an ordinary trade creditor. As such, the seller is unlikely to recover what he is owed. He can protect himself from these considerable risks, by stating that the property in the goods shall not pass to the buyer until the contract price has been paid. Section 19 provides that where the seller has reserved the right of disposal of the goods until some condition is fulfilled, ownership of the goods will not pass to the buyer until that condition is met. The inclusion of such a reservation of title clause in the contract of sale will enable a seller to retrieve his goods and resell them if the buyer becomes bankrupt or goes into receivership or liquidation before paying for them.

The position becomes much more complicated in the following situations:

■ where the buyer has resold the goods; and
■ where the buyer has mixed them with other goods during a manufacturing process and then sold the manufactured product.

Clearly, the seller cannot simply reclaim 'his' goods. However, he may be able to protect himself in relation to point 1 by including a carefully worded clause in the contract, allowing him to trace the goods and claim the proceeds of sale. These terms are known as *Romalpa* clauses, after the name of the case in which they achieved prominence.

Aluminium Industrie Vaassan BV v Romalpa Aluminium Ltd (1976)

AIV, a Dutch company, sold aluminium foil to RA, an English company. A clause in the contract provided that: (1) ownership of the foil would not pass to RA until it was paid for; (2) if the foil became mixed with other items during a manufacturing process, AIV would become the owner of the finished product and property would not

pass until RA had paid for the foil; (3) unmixed foil and finished products should be stored separately; (4) RA was authorised to sell the finished product on condition that AIV was entitled to the proceeds of the sale. RA became insolvent and a receiver was appointed. The Court of Appeal held that AIV was entitled to recover a quantity of unmixed foil and the proceeds of resale of some unmixed foil.

The seller in the *Romalpa* case limited its claim to unmixed goods and so the Court of Appeal did not give a decision as to the position in relation to mixed goods. Later cases suggest that a *Romalpa* clause will be effective in respect of mixed goods only if it is registered with the Registrar of Companies as a charge over the assets of the buying company. The effect on retention clauses of the appointment of an administrator to an insolvent company was examined in Chapter 6 ⬤.

Transfer of risk

The general rule is that risk of accidental loss or destruction passes with ownership. Thus, s 20 provides that, unless otherwise agreed, the goods remain at the seller's risk until the property in them is transferred to the buyer, but when the property in them is transferred to the buyer the goods are at the buyer's risk whether delivery has been made or not. Suppose you buy a painting from an art gallery during an exhibition and it is agreed that you will take delivery at the end of the exhibition. If the gallery is destroyed by fire before the end of the exhibition, you must bear the risk of loss.

Where delivery has been delayed through the fault of either the seller or buyer, the goods are at the risk of the party at fault in respect of any loss which might not have occurred but for the fault (s 20(2)).

Demby, Hamilton & Co Ltd v Barden (1949)

The buyer neglected to take delivery of consignments of apple juice which the seller had prepared and stored in casks. As a result of the delay, the juice went off and had to be thrown away. The seller sued for the price of the goods sold and delivered. The buyer was liable. Under s 20(2) the goods were at the buyer's risk because he was responsible for the delay.

The Sale and Supply of Goods to Consumers Regulations 2002 amends s 20 of the Sale of Goods Act 1979 where the buyer deals as a consumer, to the effect that the goods remain at the seller's risk until delivered to the consumer. This means that if the seller employs a carrier to deliver the goods to the consumer, and the goods are accidentally damaged in transit, the seller bears the risk and not the consumer.

Sale by a person who is not the owner

As a general rule, a buyer cannot acquire ownership from someone who himself has neither ownership nor the owner's authority to sell. This rule, which is known as the *nemo dat* rule from the phrase *nemo dat quod non habet* – no one can give what he has not got – is embodied in s 21:

> Where goods are sold by a person who is not their owner, and who does not sell them under the authority or with the consent of the owner, the buyer acquires no better title to the goods than the seller had . . .

In these circumstances, the buyer will be required to return the goods to their true owner. The buyer's only remedy is to sue the person who sold him the item for breach of s 12. In most of these cases, however, the seller is a rogue who disappears before the buyer can take action against him. The unsuspecting buyer is left to bear the full brunt of the rogue's misdeeds. It is not surprising, therefore, that exceptions to the *nemo dat* rule have developed. The exceptions are outlined below.

Estoppel (s 21)

If the true owner by his conduct allows the innocent buyer to believe that the seller has the right to sell the goods, ownership of the goods will pass to the buyer because the true owner will be prevented (estopped) from denying that the seller had the right to sell.

Eastern Distributors Ltd v Goldring (1957)

Murphy was the owner of a van. He wanted to buy a car from Coker, a dealer, but he could not raise enough money for a deposit. Murphy and Coker then devised a scheme to generate the necessary finance. Coker would pretend that he owned the van: he would then sell the van and the car to a finance company, which would let both vehicles out on HP to Murphy. The proceeds of the sale of the van would raise sufficient money to finance the required HP deposits. Unfortunately, the finance company accepted the proposal for the van but turned the car down. Unknown to Murphy, Coker proceeded to sell the van to the finance company. It was held that the finance company had become the owner of the van, because the original owner (Murphy) by his conduct had allowed the buyer (the finance company) to believe that the seller (Coker) had a right to sell the goods.

Section 21(1) applies where goods are 'sold' by a person who is not their owner; it has no application to an agreement to sell.

Shaw v Commissioner of the Police of the Metropolis (1987)

The claimant agreed to buy a Porsche from a rogue. The rogue had obtained the car from its owner by saying that he wanted to show it to a prospective buyer. The rogue also acquired a document from the owner stating that he had bought the car, but this was untrue. The rogue left the car with the claimant and disappeared before being paid. The claimant argued that he had acquired good title under s 21(1) since the document signed by the owner raised an estoppel against him. The Court of Appeal held that the original owner was entitled to recover his car. Section 21(1) did not apply where the buyer had only agreed to buy.

Agency (s 21(2))

The law of agency applies to contracts for the sale of goods. An agent who sells his principal's goods in accordance with the principal's instructions passes a good title to the buyer because he is selling the goods with the authority and consent of the owner. The buyer may even acquire a good title to the goods where the agent has exceeded his actual authority, if the agent was acting within the scope of his apparent or ostensible authority and the buyer was unaware of the agent's lack of authority.

Section 21(2) expressly preserves the rules contained in the Factors Act 1889 which enables the apparent owner of goods to dispose of them as if he were their true owner. A factor is an independent mercantile agent who buys and sells goods on behalf of other people, but does so in his own name. A factor can pass good title to a buyer if the following conditions are met:

- the goods being sold were in the possession of the factor with the consent of the true owner;
- the factor, in selling the goods, was acting in the ordinary course of business; and
- the buyer was unaware of any lack of authority on the part of the factor.

Sale under a common law or statutory power (s 21(2))

Certain persons have the power under common law or statute to sell goods that belong to another. A pawnbroker, for example, has the right to sell goods which have been pledged with him, where the loan has not been repaid. The purchaser will acquire a good title to the goods.

Sale by a person with a voidable title (s 23)

A person may obtain possession of goods under a contract which is void (e.g. for mistake). A void contract is, in fact, no contract at all. A purchaser in these circumstances does not acquire title to the goods and, therefore, cannot pass good title on to anyone else. The original owner will be able to maintain an action in the tort of conversion to recover the goods or their value from a third party who bought them in good faith. This is what happened in *Cundy v Lindsay* (1878). A person may also acquire goods under a contract which is voidable (e.g. for misrepresentation). In this case, the contract is valid unless and until it is avoided. Section 23 provides that where goods are resold before the contract has been avoided, the buyer acquires a good title to them provided he buys them in good faith and without notice of the seller's defect of title (see *Lewis v Averay* (1971)). If the original owner acts quickly to rescind the contract and then the goods are resold, the seller may be prevented from passing a good title to a purchaser (but see *Newtons of Wembley Ltd v Williams* (1964) below).

Sale by a seller in possession of the goods (s 24)

Where a seller sells goods but remains in possession of them, or any documents of title relating to them, any resale to a second buyer who actually takes physical delivery of the goods or the documents of title will pass a good title to the second buyer. The disappointed first buyer may sue the seller for non-delivery of the goods. The remedies of a buyer will be considered later in this chapter.

Resale by a buyer in possession of the goods with the consent of the seller (s 25)

Section 25 provides:

> where a person who has bought or agreed to buy goods obtains possession of the goods with the consent of the seller, any resale to a person who takes the goods in good faith and without notice of the rights of the original seller, has the same effect as if the person making the delivery or transfer were a mercantile agent in possession of the goods ... with the consent of the owner.

This exception to the *nemo dat* rule can be illustrated by the following case.

Newtons of Wembley Ltd v Williams (1964)

The claimants sold a car to a rogue, who paid for it by a cheque which was later dishonoured. The claimants took immediate steps to rescind their contract with the rogue (by informing the police). Some time later, the rogue resold the car in Warren Street in London, a well-established street market in used cars. The buyer then sold the car to the defendant. The Court of Appeal held that the defendant acquired a good title to the car. When the rogue sold the car in Warren Street, he was a buyer in possession with the owner's consent, and he acted in the same way as a mercantile agent (or dealer) would have done. He passed a good title to the purchaser, who in turn passed title to the defendant.

Section 25 does not operate so as to make good a defective title, i.e. where the goods are stolen.

National Employers Mutual Insurance Association Ltd v Jones (1987)

Thieves stole H's car. H successfully claimed for her loss under her car insurance policy. The thieves sold the car to L, who sold it to T, who sold it to A (a dealer), who sold it to M (a dealer), who finally sold it to Jones. The insurer sought to recover the car from Jones. The Court of Appeal held that Jones had not acquired a good title to the car by virtue of s 25. If a person buys a car from a thief and then resells it, he is not a seller within the terms of the section because the transaction with the thief was not a contract of sale. A resale to a third party in these circumstances cannot cure a defective title.

Sale of motor vehicles on hire-purchase (Hire Purchase Act 1964, Part III)

If a vehicle which is subject to a hire-purchase (HP) agreement is sold by the hirer to a private person who buys in good faith and without notice of the HP agreement, the buyer acquires a good title to the vehicle, even as against the owner. Motor dealers and finance companies cannot claim the benefit of this provision, so they will not acquire good title to a vehicle which is already subject to an HP agreement. It also appears that business purchasers unconnected with the motor trade may be prevented from taking advantage of the exception to the *nemo dat* rule.

G E Capital Bank Ltd v Rushton and Jenking (2005)

The Bank was a finance house whose business included providing finance to motor dealers. The Bank entered into an agreement with T & T Motors under which the Bank advanced £100,000 to T & T to enable it to buy cars for its business. The agreement provided that the Bank retained title in any vehicle until the whole amount advanced by the Bank in respect of it had been repaid. T & T's owner ran short of cash and he approached Rushton for a loan. Rushton was not willing to lend money to T & T but he introduced Jenking to T & T's owner and, through Jenking's company, a short-term loan of £40,000 was agreed secured by a debenture and repayable on demand. After a few weeks Jenking called in the loan. It was agreed that T & T would have a short time to sell its stock and Rushton would buy any cars remaining. In the event Rushton bought 13 vehicles, one of which he sold to Jenking. When the Bank realised what had happened

it terminated its agreement with T & T and became entitled to recover seven vehicles of the cars sold to Rushton. Shortly afterwards T & T went into liquidation. The Court of Appeal held that Rushton had bought the cars as a business venture and with a view to selling them at a profit. Although he was not in business as a motor dealer and had no intention of becoming a dealer, he was a trade purchaser and not a private buyer. He could not claim the protection of Part III of the Hire Purchase Act and was therefore liable in conversion to the Bank. Jenking acquired good title to the car he bought as he was a bona fide purchaser without notice of the defect in title.

The majority of finance companies are members of Hire Purchase Information Ltd (HPI). This organisation maintains a register where finance companies can register their HP agreements. When a car dealer is offered a car for sale, he can check with HPI to see if it is already subject to an HP agreement.

The provisions of Part III of the Hire Purchase Act 1964 do not apply in circumstances where a rogue has obtained possession of a car on HP by providing a false identity and then subsequently sells the car to a private purchaser for value (see *Shogun Finance Ltd v Hudson* (2004), which was discussed in Chapter 7 ⊙).

Reform of the law relating to transfer of title contained in ss 21–26 of the Sale of Goods Act 1979

The rules relating to transfer of title contained in ss 21–26 have been the subject of considerable scrutiny over the years. In 1966 the Law Reform Committee made a number of recommendations for reform aimed at simplifying the rules in favour of the innocent purchaser. The Committee also recommended that the decision in *Rowland v Divall* (1923) should be modified so that the purchaser's right of recovery should take into account any benefit he may have had from the goods while in his possession. A further recommendation was that a purchaser of goods by normal retail sale or at a public auction should acquire good title to the goods irrespective of the seller's title. The Law Reform Committee's proposals were not implemented.

The issue was considered again in 1989 by Professor A L Diamond in his review of security interests in property (*A Review of Security Interests in Property* (DTI, 1989)). He considered that innocent purchasers were inadequately protected by the law. He recommended strengthening the rights of the innocent purchaser by providing that where the owner of goods has entrusted those goods to, or acquiesced in their possession by, another person, then an innocent purchaser of those goods should acquire good title. In 1994 the government initiated consultations on whether reform of the law was required. Views were sought on the following proposals:

- simplification of the law and increased protection for innocent purchasers based on Professor Diamond's recommendations;
- abolition of the rule of market overt (see below);
- extension of the principle in Part III, Hire Purchase Act 1964 to all goods subject to HP or conditional sale agreements and goods held on lease or covered by a bill of sale.

While the consultations were taking place, a private member's Bill to abolish the rule of market overt was enacted with government support.

Repeal of s 22 (sale in market overt)

The principle of *nemo dat* used not to apply to sales in market overt. The rule of market overt was established in the Middle Ages. It provided that if a purchaser bought goods according to the usages of the market in good faith and without notice of any defect in the title of the seller, he acquired good title. The term 'market overt' applied to every shop in the City of London and every public market legally constituted by Royal Charter, statute or custom. The common law rules of market overt were included in the statutory exceptions to *nemo dat* by s 22 of the Sale of Goods Act 1979. The rule of market overt led to some curious decisions. For example, in **Reid v Commissioner of Police of the Metropolis** (1973) title to a pair of stolen Adam candelabra depended on whether the purchase from a stall at the New Caledonian Market in Southwark had taken place before or after sunrise. (The rules of market overt only applied to sales which took place between sunrise and sunset.) The innocent purchaser did not acquire good title because the sale took place early in the morning before the sun had risen. Although the government was in the process of seeking views about the rule of sale in market overt, it allowed the rule to be abolished by the Sale of Goods (Amendment) Act 1994. The Act came into force on 3 January 1995. From that date, the purchaser of goods in market overt obtains no better title to them than the seller had.

Performance of the contract

It is the duty of the seller to deliver the goods and the buyer's duty to accept and pay for them. The parties are free to make their own arrangements about the time and place of delivery and payment. The Act sets out the obligations of the seller and buyer when they have not dealt with these matters specifically in their agreement. Section 28 provides:

> Unless otherwise agreed, delivery of the goods and payment of the price are concurrent conditions . . .

This means that the seller can hold on to the goods until the buyer has paid for them.

Delivery (s 29)

Delivery in the context of the Act means the voluntary transfer of possession from one person to another. The delivery may consist of:

- physically handing over the goods;
- handing over the means of control of the goods, e.g. the keys to the premises where they are stored;
- transferring documents of title; or
- where the goods are in the possession of a third party, an acknowledgement by the third party that he is holding the goods on behalf of the buyer.

Place of delivery (s 29)

In the absence of any agreement to the contrary, the place of delivery is the seller's place of business; it is up to the buyer to come and collect the goods (s 29(1)).

Delivery to a carrier (s 32)

If the seller agrees to send the goods and engages a carrier for this purpose, s 32 provides that delivery to the carrier is deemed to be delivery to the buyer. The seller must make the best possible contract with the carrier on behalf of the buyer to ensure the safe arrival of the goods. The Sale and Supply of Goods to Consumers Regulations 2002 amend s 32 of the Sale of Goods Act 1979 by providing that, where the buyer deals as a consumer, if the seller is authorised or required to send the goods to the buyer, delivery of goods to a carrier is not delivery to the buyer.

Time of delivery (ss 29(3) and 37)

The parties may have fixed a delivery date. Failure to make delivery by that date is a breach of condition, which entitles the buyer to repudiate the contract and sue for non-delivery (see later). Where the seller agrees to send the goods and no time for sending them has been agreed, he must despatch them within a reasonable time (s 29(3)). A demand for delivery by the buyer or an offer of delivery by the seller will not be valid unless made at a reasonable hour (s 29(3)). What is reasonable is a question of fact. If the seller is ready and willing to deliver the goods and he requests the buyer to take delivery, but the buyer does not comply with the request within a reasonable time, the buyer will be liable for any resulting loss and a reasonable charge for the care and custody of the goods (s 37).

Delivery of the wrong quantity (s 30)

If the seller delivers a smaller quantity than ordered, the buyer may reject the consignment, but, if he decides to accept the goods, he must pay for them at the contract rate. If the seller sends a larger quantity than agreed, the buyer has the following choices:

- he may accept the goods he ordered and reject the rest;
- he may reject the lot;
- he may accept the whole consignment, paying for the extra goods at the contract rate.

If the seller delivered the wrong quantity, the buyer used to be entitled under s 30 to reject the whole consignment no matter how slight the excess or shortfall. The buyer's rights were only qualified by the application of the legal maxim *de minimis non curat lex* – the law does not concern itself with trifling matters. Thus, in *Shipton, Anderson & Co Ltd* v *Weil Bros & Co Ltd* (1912) an excess of 55 lb in relation to a contract for 4,950 tons of wheat was held to be such a microscopic deviation from the contract specifications that it did not entitle the buyers to reject the whole consignment. The Law Commission considered the buyer's right to reject when the wrong quantity is delivered in its *Report on the Sale and Supply of Goods* (1987). It recommended that in non-consumer contracts the buyer should not be entitled to reject where the shortfall or excess delivered is so slight that rejection would be unreasonable. This

recommendation is given effect by the Sale and Supply of Goods Act 1994. Section 30(2A) of the Sale of Goods Act 1979 now provides that a commercial buyer may not reject goods for delivery of the wrong quantity where the seller can show that the excess or shortfall is so slight that it would be unreasonable for the buyer to reject the goods.

Delivery by instalments (s 31)

Unless otherwise agreed, the buyer is not bound to accept delivery by instalments (s 31(1)). The parties may, of course, agree that the goods are to be delivered in stated instalments. A breach of contract may occur in respect of one or more instalments (e.g. the seller may deliver goods which are unsatisfactory or the buyer may refuse to take delivery of an instalment). Clearly, the injured party will be able to sue for damages, but the question then arises whether he is also entitled to repudiate the contract. The answer depends on whether the contract is indivisible or severable. A contract is usually treated as being severable if each instalment is to be separately paid for.

1 **Indivisible contracts (ss 11(4) and 35(A)).** The general rule used to be that if the buyer accepted some of the goods he was deemed to have accepted all of them and had no right to reject part of the goods. In practice, this meant that where delivery was by instalments a buyer could repudiate the whole contract where the breach was in respect of the first instalment, but where the breach occurred in the second and subsequent instalments his rights were limited to an action for damages. The only exception to this rule was where the seller delivered unwanted goods of a different description to those in the contract. In this case the buyer could accept the contract goods and reject the unwanted goods or reject all the goods (s 30(4)). This right of partial rejection did not apply where part of the goods were defective.

The Law Commission in its *Report on the Sale and Supply of Goods* (1987) recommended that there should be a right of partial rejection where the goods are not in conformity with the contract. This recommendation is implemented by the Sale and Supply of Goods Act 1994. A new s 35A of the Sale of Goods Act 1979, which also applies to instalment contracts, provides that where a buyer has accepted some of the goods, he will not lose his right to reject the goods because of his acceptance where there is a breach in respect of some or all of the goods. Section 30(4) is repealed.

2 Severable contracts (s 31(2)). Whether a breach in relation to one or more instalments will entitle the injured party to repudiate the whole contract depends 'on the terms of the contract and the circumstances of the case'. If the contract is silent on the matter, the courts apply two main tests:

- the size of the breach in relation to the whole contract; and
- the likelihood that the breach will be repeated.

Maple Flock Co Ltd v Universal Furniture Products (Wembley) Ltd (1934)

The sellers agreed to deliver 100 tons of flock by instalments. The first 15 instalments were satisfactory but the 16th was not up to the required standard. The buyers then took delivery of four more satisfactory loads before refusing further deliveries. The court held that the buyers were not entitled to repudiate the contract. The defective flock constituted a small proportion of the total quantity delivered and there was little likelihood of the breach being repeated.

Acceptance (s 35)

The buyer is bound to accept the goods which the seller delivers in accordance with the contract. If the goods do not meet the requirements of the contract, the buyer will have a claim against the seller. The remedies for breach of a condition depend on whether the goods have been 'accepted'. If the goods have not been accepted, the buyer is entitled to reject the goods and claim his money back. He may also bring a claim for damages. However, if the goods have been accepted, the buyer loses his right to reject the goods, although he can still claim damages. What constituted 'acceptance' was set out in ss 34 and 35(1). Under these sections there were three ways in which a buyer could accept the goods:

1 he could expressly tell the seller that he had accepted the goods (s 35(1)(a)); or
2 he could do something to the goods which was inconsistent with the seller's ownership (s 35(1)(b)); or
3 he could retain the goods for a reasonable time without telling the seller that he had rejected them (s 35(4)).

A buyer was not deemed to have accepted the goods until he had had a reasonable opportunity to examine them to check that they were in accordance with the terms of the contract. The Law Commission's *Report on the Sale and Supply of Goods* (1987) identified a number of problems relating to the rules on acceptance:

1 the rules of acceptance applied to contracts of sale only and not to other contracts for the supply of goods;
2 the right to reject could be easily lost before defects became apparent, e.g. in *Bernstein v Pamsons Motors (Golders Green) Ltd* (1987) the purchaser of a new car lost the right to reject it after three weeks' use;
3 buyers have lost the right to reject the goods before they have had a chance to examine them because they have signed an 'acceptance note';
4 it was unclear whether a buyer would lose his right to reject if he asked the seller to repair defective goods;
5 it was unclear what amounted to an act inconsistent with the seller's ownership for the purpose of acceptance.

The Law Commission made a number of recommendations in relation to rules on acceptance, which have been implemented by the Sale and Supply of Goods Act 1994. An amended s 35 retains the three ways of accepting the goods (set out above), but adds the following qualifications:

1 a consumer cannot lose his right to reject the goods by agreement unless he has had a reasonable opportunity to examine them (s 35(3)), i.e. a consumer cannot be deprived of his right to examine the goods by means of an acceptance note;
2 a material factor in deciding whether goods have been accepted after the lapse of a reasonable time is whether the buyer has been given a reasonable opportunity to examine the goods (s 35(5));
3 a buyer is not deemed to have accepted the goods because he has asked for or agreed to a repair or where the goods have been sold or given to a third party (s 35(6));
4 where a buyer accepts goods which are part of a larger commercial unit, he is deemed to have accepted all the goods which make up the commercial unit, e.g. if you buy a pair of shoes and accept one shoe, you will be deemed to have accepted the pair.

The effect of some of the changes to the rules relating to acceptance contained in s 35 brought about by the Sale and Supply of Goods Act 1994 were considered in the following cases.

Clegg v Olle Andersson (t/a Nordic Marine) (2003)

Clegg agreed to buy a new yacht with a shoal draught keel 'in accordance with the manufacturer's standard specifications' from Andersson. The manufacturer delivered the yacht to Andersson on 25 July 2000 and Andersson in turn delivered it to Clegg on 12 August 2000. Andersson realised that the keel was heavier than the manufacturer's specifications and informed Clegg when the yacht was delivered. The parties then entered into negotiations but then on 6 March 2001 Clegg's solicitors wrote to Andersson stating that Clegg was rejecting the yacht and claiming a refund of the purchase price. The Court of Appeal held that the yacht was not of satisfactory quality because the keel was overweight. Andersson was in breach of condition under s 14(2) of the Sale of Goods Act. Clegg had not indicated to Andersson that he had accepted the contract nor had he done anything in relation to the yacht which would be deemed inconsistent with Andersson's ownership. In deciding whether acceptance had taken place after the lapse of a reasonable period of time, account could be taken of the time required to modify or repair goods. Clegg had requested information in August and September 2000 but did not receive a response until 15 February 2001. The three-week period which then elapsed before Clegg rejected the yacht on 6 March 2001 did not exceed a reasonable time under s 35(4) and Clegg was therefore entitled to reject the yacht. The court stated that *Bernstein v Pamsons Motors (Golders Green) Ltd* (1986) no longer represented the law after the enactment of the Sale and Supply of Goods Act 1994.

J & H Ritchie Ltd v Lloyd Ltd (2007)

The appellant farmers purchased a combination seed drill and power harrow from the respondent suppliers of agricultural machinery. After a few days' use, one of the appellants' directors noticed that the harrow was vibrating badly. By agreement the harrow was taken back to the suppliers, where on inspection it was found to be missing two bearings. The suppliers repaired the harrow and informed the appellants that it had been repaired to 'factory gate specification' and was ready for collection. Despite requests by the appellants, the suppliers refused to say what had been done to the harrow or to provide an engineer's report. The appellants decided to reject the equipment and brought an action to recover the purchase price of the harrow. The House of Lords held that the appellants were entitled to reject the harrow.

Under s 35 a buyer has the right to reject goods up to the point when the goods are accepted. A buyer is not deemed to accept goods merely because he has agreed to a repair. The harrow was a complex piece of machinery and the appellants were entitled to the information they requested so they could make an informed choice about whether to accept or reject the repaired equipment. The majority of the House of Lords based their decision not on the original contract of sale but on the agreement that the suppliers would try to effect a repair of the harrow. Depending on the circumstances, this agreement might be subject to an implied term that if asked the suppliers would tell the appellants what was wrong with the harrow and what they had done to put it right. As the suppliers had refused to provide this information, they were in breach of contract.

Payment

The price is such a fundamental part of the transaction that it will normally be fixed by the contract. However, it may be ascertained by the course of dealing between the parties or the contract may provide a mechanism for determining the price, such as by arbitration. The parties may make their own agreement as to the time of payment. The seller may insist on payment in advance of delivery or he may be prepared to extend a period of credit. In the absence of such express agreement, payment is due when the goods are delivered.

Remedies

Seller's remedies

Two sets of remedies are open to the seller. He can pursue personal remedies against the buyer himself and real remedies against the goods.

Personal remedies

The seller can sue the buyer for the contract price or for damages for non-acceptance.

1 Action for the price (s 49). The seller can bring an action for the contract price in two situations: where the property in the goods has passed to the buyer or where the buyer has failed to pay by a specified date, irrespective of whether ownership has passed to the buyer.

2 Damages for non-acceptance (s 50). If the property in the goods has not passed and the buyer will not accept the goods, the seller can sue for non-acceptance. The measure of damages is the estimated loss directly and naturally resulting in the ordinary course of events from the buyer's breach of contract (s 50(2)). If the buyer wrongfully refuses to accept and pay for the goods, the seller is expected to mitigate his loss and sell them elsewhere for the best possible price. Section 50(3) provides guidance as to the measure of damages where there is an available market for the goods. If the market price is less than the contract price, the seller can recover the difference by way of damages. Where the market price is the same or even higher than the contract price, the seller will be entitled to nominal damages only. (The market price is calculated at the time when the goods ought to have been accepted.)

The following cases illustrate how s 50 is applied by the courts.

W L Thompson Ltd v Robinson (Gunmakers) Ltd **(1955)**

The defendants ordered a new Vanguard car from the claimant car dealers, but then refused to accept it. The defendants argued that they were only liable to pay nominal damages, since the contract price and the market price were the same. It was held that there was no 'available market' for Vanguard cars because supply exceeded demand and, therefore, s 50(3) did not apply. The dealers had sold one car less and under s 50(2) they were entitled to their loss of profit on the sale.

Charter v Sullivan **(1957)**

A buyer refused to accept a new Hillman Minx car that he had ordered from a dealer. In contrast to the previous case, the demand for Hillman Minx cars exceeded supply and the dealer would have had no difficulty in finding another buyer. It was held that the dealer was entitled to nominal damages only. The buyer's breach would not have affected the total number of cars sold over a period of time.

Real remedies

The unpaid seller has three possible remedies in respect of the goods, even though the property in the goods has passed to the buyer. They are lien, stoppage in transit and resale.

1 Lien (ss 41–43). A lien is the right to retain possession of goods (but not to resell them) until the contract price has been paid. It is available in any of the following circumstances:

- where the goods have been sold without any mention of credit;
- where the goods have been sold on credit but the period of credit has expired;
- where the buyer becomes insolvent.

The seller will lose his right of lien if the price is paid or tendered or the buyer obtains possession of the goods. The seller cannot exercise this right to retain the goods if he has handed the goods to a carrier for transportation to the buyer without reserving the right of disposal of the goods or where he has given up the right.

2 Stoppage in transit (ss 44–46). This is the right of the seller to stop goods in transit to the buyer, regain possession of them and retain them until payment has been received. The seller can exercise his right to stoppage in transit in only one situation – where the buyer has become insolvent.

3 Right of resale (ss 47 and 48). The rights of lien and stoppage in transit by themselves do not give the seller any right to resell the goods. He is allowed, however, to resell the goods in the following circumstances:

- where the goods are of a perishable nature;
- where the seller gives notice to the buyer of his intention to resell and the buyer does not pay or tender the price within a reasonable time;
- where the seller expressly reserves the right of resale in the event of the buyer defaulting.

The seller can exercise the right of resale and also recover damages for any loss sustained by the buyer's breach of contract. The original contract of sale is rescinded and the new buyer acquires a good title to the goods as against the original buyer.

Buyer's remedies

Various remedies are available to the buyer where the seller is in breach of contract. Since 31 March 2003 consumer buyers have become entitled to a wider range of remedies as a result of the changes brought about by the Sale and Supply of Goods to Consumers Regulations 2002.

Rejection of the goods (ss 11 and 15A)

The buyer is entitled to repudiate the contract and reject the goods where the seller is in breach of a condition of the contract. Most of the implied terms contained in ss 12–15 are designated conditions, so, if the goods do not correspond with their description or are not of satisfactory quality or fit for a particular purpose, the buyer is entitled to reject them. The right to reject is lost as soon as the goods have been accepted under the rules set out in s 35. The rules relating to acceptance have already been considered. If the buyer is deemed to have accepted the goods, he must treat the breach of condition as a breach of warranty, thus limiting his remedy to a claim for damages.

The Law Commission in its *Report on the Sale and Supply of Goods* (1987) explored the possibility of laying down fixed periods during which the buyer would retain his right to reject. The suggestion was rejected on the ground that a single time limit would be inappropriate to the very different kinds of goods covered by the Act, while different time limits for different types of goods would require very complex legislation. The Law Commission felt that the 'reasonable time' provision in s 35 provided the appropriate flexibility and, in practice, gave rise to few disputes.

If the goods have not been accepted, the buyer has a right to reject for any breach of the implied promises as to title, description, quality and suitability set out in ss 12–15, no matter how slight the breach. This is because the Act classifies these promises as 'conditions'. (Any breach of a condition entitles the injured party to terminate the contract and claim damages.) However, not all breaches of the implied terms in ss 13–15 will be so serious as to justify the buyer's right to reject. It would seem unfair to the seller that a buyer should be able to reject goods for a very slight breach. There is also the danger that, where a buyer is trying to reject goods because of a very minor breach, the court may conclude that the claim is so unreasonable that there was really no breach at all.

The Law Commission considered the issue in its *Report on the Sale and Supply of Goods* (1987). It concluded that a distinction should be drawn between consumers and commercial buyers in relation to remedies. It recommended that a consumer's right to reject for breach of

the implied terms in ss 13–15 should be retained but that a non-consumer buyer should be prevented from rejecting goods where the breach is so slight that it would be unreasonable to reject. This recommendation is implemented by the Sale and Supply of Goods Act 1994, which introduces a new s 15A to the 1979 Act. Section 15A provides that where a seller can show that the breach of ss 13–15 is so slight that it would be unreasonable for a non-consumer buyer to reject, the breach is to be treated as a breach of warranty and not as a breach of condition. The modification of the buyer's rights does not apply where the contract indicates a contrary intention.

An action for damages

1 Non-delivery (s 51). The buyer can sue for non-delivery when the seller wrongfully neglects or refuses to deliver the goods. The measure of damages is the estimated loss directly and naturally resulting in the ordinary course of events from the seller's breach of contract. Where there is an available market for the goods, the measure of damages is usually the difference between the contract price and the higher price of obtaining similar goods elsewhere. If the buyer has paid in advance and the goods are not delivered, he can recover the amount paid (s 54) because there has been a total failure of consideration.

2 Breach of warranty (s 53). The buyer can sue for damages under s 53 in the following circumstances:

- where the seller is in breach of a warranty;
- where the seller is in breach of a condition, but the buyer has chosen to carry on with the contract and claim damages instead;
- where the seller is in breach of a condition, but the buyer has lost the right to reject the goods (because he has accepted them).

The measure of damages is the estimated loss directly and naturally resulting from the breach. This is usually the difference in value between the goods actually delivered and goods fulfilling the warranty.

Specific performance (s 52)

The buyer may sue for specific performance, but only in cases where the goods are specific or ascertained and where monetary damages would not be an adequate remedy. A court is unlikely to make such an order if similar goods are available elsewhere.

Additional rights of buyers in consumer cases (ss 48A–48F)

The Sale and Supply of Goods to Consumers Regulations 2002 introduce a range of additional rights for consumer buyers. The rights apply where the buyer deals as a consumer and the goods do not conform to the contract of sale at the time of delivery. A 'consumer' is a natural person who is acting for purposes outside of his or her trade, business or profession. Goods will not conform with the contract if there is a breach of an express term of the contract or an implied term under ss 13, 14 and 15 of the Sale of Goods Act 1979. Where defects emerge within six months of delivery, it is assumed that the goods did not conform at the time of delivery. This provision has the effect of reversing the burden of proof so that if the seller wishes to defend a claim he or she must prove that the goods were satisfactory at the time of delivery.

The additional rights are as follows:

1 Repair or replacement (s 48B). The buyer has the right to require the seller to repair or replace the goods within a reasonable time and without causing significant inconvenience to the buyer. The seller must bear any necessary cost associated with the repair or replacement, e.g. cost of labour, materials or postage. The seller is not required to undertake a repair or replacement if such a remedy is impossible, disproportionate in relation to other remedies or is disproportionate in comparison to a reduction in the price or to rescission of the contract. A remedy will be disproportionate to another if it imposes unreasonable costs taking into account the value the goods would have if they conformed with the contract, the significance of the lack of conformity and whether a different remedy could be used without causing significant inconvenience to the buyer. The nature of the goods and the purposes for which they were acquired are relevant factors in determining what is a reasonable time or significant inconvenience.

2 Reduction of the purchase price or rescission of the contract (s 48C). If repair or replacement are not practicable remedies or the seller has not fulfilled the requirement to repair or replace within a reasonable time and without significant inconvenience, the buyer is entitled to a partial or full reduction of the purchase price or to rescind the contract. If the buyer decides to rescind the contract, any refund may take into account the use that the buyer has had of the goods since they were delivered.

Auction sales

The Sale and Supply of Goods to Consumers Regulations 2002 also make some important changes to the rights of consumers who buy goods through auctions, including Internet auctions. The changes have been brought about by amending s 12(2) of the Unfair Contract Terms Act 1977. It was the case under s 12(2) that buyers at an auction sale or by competitive tender were not to be regarded as dealing as consumers. This meant that the implied terms under ss 12–15 of the Sale of Goods Act 1979 could be excluded or limited provided the reasonableness test was satisfied. The position now is that the implied terms in the Sale of Goods Act 1979 cannot be excluded or restricted in the following situations:

- where a consumer buys new goods at an auction;
- where a consumer buys second-hand goods at an auction which he or she cannot attend (this would include an Internet auction).

The new remedies of repair, replacement, full or partial refund will be available to consumers buying new goods at auction or second-hand goods at auctions which the consumer cannot attend.

The effect of the Sale and Supply of Goods to Consumers Regulations 2002 on the remedies available is set out in Figure 11.2, overleaf.

Supply of goods and services

The provisions of the Sale of Goods Act 1979, including the protection afforded to the buyer by the implied terms contained in ss 12–15, apply only to contracts where goods are sold for a money consideration. The sale of goods legislation did not cover other methods of obtaining goods (e.g. by hire purchase (HP), hire, barter or contracts for work and materials), although the need for protection was just as great, nor did it have anything to say about the provision of services.

Implied terms as to title, description, quality, fitness for purpose and correspondence with sample, similar to those in the Sale of Goods Act, were put on a statutory basis first in respect of goods supplied on HP and later in relation to goods acquired using trading stamps. In 1979, the Law Commission recommended that the protection of statutory implied terms should be extended to all contracts for the supply of goods. This was achieved

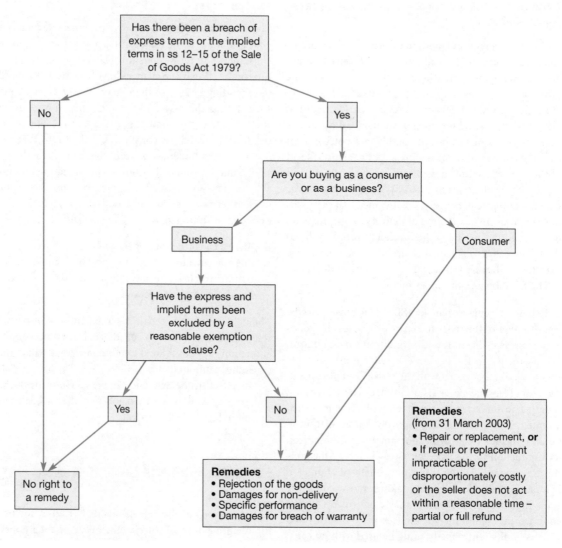

Figure 11.2 **Remedies under the Sale of Goods Act 1979 after 31 March 2003**

by the Supply of Goods and Services Act 1982. The Act also places on a statutory footing certain terms which had hitherto been implied by the common law in contracts for services.

The Supply of Goods and Services Act 1982 is divided into two main parts: Part I deals with implied terms in contracts for the supply of goods, while Part II covers implied terms in contracts for services. Section references are to the 1982 Act, as amended by the Sale and Supply of Goods Act 1994, unless otherwise indicated. We will now examine the provisions of the Act in more detail.

Implied terms in contracts for the supply of goods (Part I)

Part I of the Act was based on the recommendations of the Law Commission contained in its *Report on Implied Terms in Contracts for the Supply of Goods* (Law Com No 95), published in 1979. The provisions of Part I, which came into force in January 1983, consist of two sets of implied terms. The first set applies to contracts for the transfer of property in goods, the second set to contracts for hire.

Contracts for the transfer of property in goods

The first set of terms, detailed in ss 2–5 (see below), are implied into contracts for work and materials and barter, under which a person acquires ownership of goods. The terms, which were previously implied into these contracts by the common law, follow the pattern established by ss 12–15 of the Sale of Goods Act 1979 as amended, in relation to contracts for the sale of goods.

Section 2 contains an implied condition that the transferor has the right to transfer the property in the goods, and implied warranties that the goods are free from undisclosed third-party rights and that the buyer will enjoy quiet possession of the goods. Where there is a contract for the transfer of goods by description, under s 3 there is an implied condition that the goods will correspond to the description. Section 4 provides that where goods are transferred in the course of a business, there are implied conditions that the goods are of satisfactory quality, and reasonably fit for the purpose. According to s 5, where there is a transfer of goods by reference to a sample, there is an implied condition that the bulk will correspond with the sample.

These implied terms apply in exactly the same way as the terms implied by ss 12–15 of the Sale of Goods Act 1979 as amended. Similarly, attempts to exclude the obligations contained in ss 2–5 of the 1982 Act are subject to control on the 'Sale of Goods' model. The implied terms as to title (s 2) cannot be excluded or restricted by any contract term. Sections 3–5 cannot be excluded or restricted where the transferee is dealing as a consumer; if the transferee is not dealing as a consumer, the exemption is subject to the reasonableness test, as laid down in the Unfair Contract Terms Act 1977.

Contracts for the hire of goods

The second set of implied terms in Part I can be found in ss 7–10. They apply to contracts under which 'one person bails or agrees to bail goods to another by way of hire' (s 6). This includes both consumer and commercial hire agreements, but HP agreements are expressly excluded. The terms implied in hire contracts by ss 7–10 match, as far as is possible, the implied terms in contracts for the sale of goods. Section 7 provides that there is an implied condition that the bailor has a right to transfer possession of the goods to the bailee and that the bailee will enjoy quiet possession of the goods during the period of hire. By s 8, where there is a contract for the hire of goods by description, there is an implied condition that the goods will correspond with the description. Section 9 provides that, where goods are hired in the course of a business, there are implied conditions that the goods are of satisfactory quality and reasonably fit for the purpose. Section 10 covers implied conditions in relation to contracts for the hire of goods by reference to a sample.

The implied terms contained in s 7 (right to transfer and quiet possession) can be excluded or restricted if the exemption satisfies the reasonableness test. The implied terms as to description, quality and sample cannot be excluded or restricted as against a person dealing as a consumer; in a non-consumer transaction, these implied terms can be excluded subject to the requirement of reasonableness.

Additional rights and remedies of consumers under the Sale and Supply of Goods to Consumers Regulations 2002

The Sale and Supply of Goods to Consumers Regulations 2002 make amendments to the Supply of Goods and Services Act 1982 to ensure that the additional rights and remedies made available to consumers under the Sale of Goods Act 1979 are also extended to consumers who obtain goods other than by way of a contract for the sale of goods, e.g. by hire, HP or exchange. From 31 March 2003, the transferor of goods acquires liability for public statements made by himself, the producer of the goods or his representative. The new remedies for consumers are for repair or replacement or, if repair or replacement is impossible or disproportionate or the transferor fails to repair or replace the goods within a reasonable time and without significant inconvenience, the transferee may claim a full or partial refund.

Implied terms in contracts for the supply of services (Part II)

Recent years have witnessed a dramatic growth in the service industry, which has been matched by a corresponding increase in customer dissatisfaction. The National Consumer Council (NCC) highlighted the problems in its report, *Services Please*, published in 1981. Part II of the Supply of Goods and Services Act 1982, which deals with contracts for services, is based largely on the recommendations put forward by the

NCC. Part II of the Act came into force on 4 July 1983. A contract for the supply of services is one 'under which a person ("the supplier") agrees to carry out a service' (s 12). This covers agreements where the supplier simply provides a service and nothing more, such as dry-cleaning or hairdressing. It also includes contracts where the provision of a service also involves the transfer of goods (e.g. installing central heating or repairing a car). The Act does not apply to contracts of service (employment) or apprenticeship. The terms implied into a contract for services by this part of the Act are as follows.

Care and skill (s 13)

Section 13 provides that where the supplier is acting in the course of a business there is an implied term that the supplier will carry out the service with reasonable care and skill. So, if you take your raincoat to be dry-cleaned and it is returned with a large tear in the fabric, clearly the cleaning process will not have been carried out with reasonable care and skill. The duty to exercise reasonable care and skill was considered in the following case.

Wilson v Best Travel Ltd (1993)

The claimant sustained serious injuries when he tripped and fell through glass patio doors at the Greek hotel he was staying in while on a package holiday organised by the defendant tour operator. The doors had been fitted with 5mm glass which complied with Greek, but not British, safety standards. The claimant sought damages against the defendant, arguing that the defendant was in breach of the duty of care which arose from s 13 of the Supply of Goods and Services Act 1982. It was held that the defendant tour operator was not liable: its liability was to check that local safety standards had been complied with, provided that the absence of a safety feature was not such that a reasonable holidaymaker would decline to take a holiday at the hotel. A tour operator might be in breach of duty if, for example, it used a hotel where there were no fire precautions at all. In this case, the doors met Greek safety standards and the absence of thicker safety glass in doors was unlikely to cause the claimant to decline the holiday.

Time for performance (s 14)

Under s 14, where the supplier is acting in the course of a business and the time for performance cannot

be determined from the contract or ascertained by a course of dealing between the parties, there is an implied term that the supplier will carry out the service within a reasonable time. What is a reasonable time is a matter of fact. If you take your car into a garage for minor repairs, it is reasonable to allow a few days and, if spare parts have to be ordered, possibly a couple of weeks for the repairs to be completed. If the car is still in the garage six months later, the repairer will be in breach of s 14.

Consideration (s 15)

Section 15 provides that where the consideration cannot be determined from the contract or by a course of dealing between the parties, there is an implied term that the customer will pay a reasonable charge for the service. If you call a plumber out to mend a burst pipe and no reference is made to his charges, he is entitled to a reasonable amount for his services on completion of the job.

You should note the following points about Part II of the Act:

1 Sections 13–15 imply 'terms' into contracts for services. This means that the remedy available to the injured party will depend on the circumstances of the breach. If the breach goes to the root of the contract, it will be treated as a breach of a condition and the customer can repudiate the contract and claim damages – where the breach is slight, it will be regarded as a breach of a warranty and the customer can recover damages only.

2 The Secretary of State has the power to exempt certain contracts for services from one or more of the sections in Part II. An order has been made, for example, excluding s 13 from applying to:

- the services of an advocate in a court or tribunal, e.g. a solicitor appearing in a magistrates' court; and
- the services of a company director.

3 Under s 16 the rights, duties and liabilities imposed by ss 13–15 may be excluded or limited subject to the provisions of the Unfair Contract Terms Act 1977. The implied term contained in s 13 (care and skill) is, therefore, subject to s 2 of the 1977 Act, while the implied terms in ss 14 and 15 (time for performance and consideration) seem to be covered by s 3 of the 1977 Act.

Manufacturer's liability in contract

Generally

So far in this chapter we have examined the rights and responsibilities of the parties to a contract, concentrating especially on the duties of a supplier of goods and services. We now turn our attention to the person who produces the goods. What exactly are the responsibilities of a manufacturer who puts defective products into circulation? A striking feature of modern life is the constant bombardment we receive from expensive advertising or promotions conducted by manufacturers who are trying to persuade us to buy their products. It is hardly surprising, therefore, that if anything goes wrong with the product, the majority of people think that the manufacturer is responsible in law to put matters right. Certainly, most retailers do little to dispel this belief. It is true that if the manufacturer supplies goods directly to the customer, the customer is entitled to sue him in contract for breach of the terms which are implied now in all contracts for the supply of goods. Very often, however, goods are not sold straight to the customer, but are distributed through a wholesaler, who sells them to a retailer, who in turn supplies them to the ultimate consumer. If the goods are faulty, the consumer's rights lie against the retailer, not against the person who created the problem in the first place.

The primary responsibility for compensating the consumer in respect of defective products is placed by the law of contract on the person who sold or supplied the goods; he or she is liable irrespective of whether he or she was at fault. Thus, the law imposes what is known as 'strict liability' on retailers in respect of faulty goods. A good example of this principle is the case of *Godley* v *Perry* (1960), which was discussed earlier in this chapter. The action involved a young boy who lost an eye when his toy catapult broke. The boy had purchased the catapult three days earlier from a newsagent's shop. The newsagent had taken reasonable care to ensure that the catapults he sold were safe. Nevertheless, under the Sale of Goods Act, he was held strictly liable for injuries caused to the boy.

The law of contract provides the main avenue for redress in respect of faulty goods. However, a contractual solution to the problem of defective goods has its limitations.

1 The traditional doctrine of privity of contract meant that the rights and duties created by a contract were confined to the parties. Only the purchaser could take action in contract in respect of a defective product.

For example, if in *Godley* v *Perry* the boy had received the catapult as a Christmas present from his parents, he would not have been able to sue the newsagent for compensation for his injuries under the Sale of Goods Act because of the absence of a contract between himself and the newsagent.

However, under s 1 of the Contracts (Rights of Third Parties) Act 1999, a third party may have the right to enforce a term in the contract, such as the implied term contained in s 14 of the Sale of Goods Act 1979, where either the contract contains an express term to this effect or a term of the contract purports to confer a benefit on the third party. So, if a doting aunt buys a wedding present for her nephew and delivery is to be made to the nephew's house, it can be argued that the contract purports to confer a benefit on the nephew, and he will be able to sue if the present is defective.

2 The common law doctrine of privity also means that the consumer's rights in contract are restricted to an action against the person who sold or supplied him with the goods. Such 'rights' may prove illusory. The retailer may not have the means to pay compensation or he may have ceased trading because of insolvency.

3 The retailer is required to bear the brunt of claims for compensation from aggrieved customers, even though he may be completely blameless. Of course, the retailer can sue his immediate supplier in contract for breach of the implied terms in the Sale of Goods Act 1979. The supplier can sue the next person in the chain of contracts which ultimately ends with the manufacturer. This chain of responsibility is illustrated in Figure 11.3.

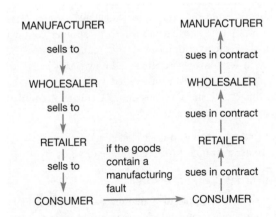

Figure 11.3 The chain of responsibility in contract for a defective product

Thus, the manufacturer is required, albeit in a roundabout way, to accept responsibility for his defective products. However, the chain of responsibility may be broken where, for example, there are reasonable exemption clauses in the contract between the retailer and the wholesaler. If this is the case, the manufacturer will escape liability and the innocent retailer must absorb the cost of compensation. There is a case for a consumer, irrespective of whether he purchased the defective item, being able to take direct action against the manufacturer, but there are limited circumstances in which the manufacturer can be sued. These are:

■ under a collateral contract between the manufacturer and the consumer;
■ in tort;
■ under Part I of the Consumer Protection Act 1987;
■ under the Sale and Supply of Goods to Consumers Regulations 2002.

Collateral contract

A manufacturer would soon go out of business if he directed all his energies to producing his goods as cheaply as possible. He must develop a marketing strategy to ensure that potential customers know about his products and are encouraged to buy them. This can be achieved, for example, by an advertising campaign, special promotions, personal visits by sales reps, or the inclusion of a 'guarantee' or 'warranty' with the goods. Such activities may result in the manufacturer being directly liable in contract to the consumer, even though the consumer buys the goods from the retailer. In this situation there is clearly a contract of sale between the consumer and the retailer to which the manufacturer is not a party, but there may also be another contract between the consumer and the manufacturer. The second less obvious contract is known as a collateral contract: it is, in effect, an implied contract between the manufacturer and the consumer. A collateral contract may arise in two situations:

■ from advertising and sales talk; and
■ under a manufacturer's guarantee or warranty.

Advertising and sales talk

The classic example of a manufacturer being held to account for extravagant claims in an advertising campaign is the case of *Carlill v Carbolic Smoke Ball Co* (1893). You will recall that the company promised in an advertisement to pay £100 to anyone who contracted' flu after using the smoke ball three times daily for two weeks. Mrs Carlill saw this advertisement, bought a smoke ball from a chemist and used it as directed but still caught flu. Even though Mrs Carlill had not bought the smoke ball directly from the company, there was a contract between them. The essential requirements of offer and acceptance and consideration were all present. The company had made Mrs Carlill an offer in its advertisement, which she had accepted by purchasing the smoke ball. The company's promise was supported by consideration from Mrs Carlill because she had bought the smoke ball from a retail chemist.

The same principle applies where the manufacturer's salesperson calls on the consumer and makes promises about the performance of a product. If the consumer acts on the sales talk by obtaining the product from his supplier and not directly from the manufacturer, the consumer will be able to hold the manufacturer to his promises under a collateral contract.

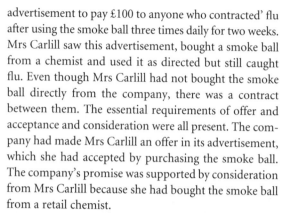

Shanklin Pier Ltd v Detel Products Ltd (1951)

Shanklin Pier Ltd engaged a firm of painting contractors to paint its pier at Shanklin on the Isle of Wight, specifying that they should use a paint called DMU, which was manufactured by Detel Products Ltd. A director of Detel Products had previously called on the managing director of the pier company and recommended DMU for the job, saying that it would last seven to ten years. In fact, the paint lasted only three months. The pier company could not sue the manufacturer for breach of a condition implied under the Sale of Goods Act (that the paint would be reasonably fit for the stated purpose) because it had not bought the paint itself. Nor could it sue the painters, who, after all, had only followed the instructions they were given. So the pier company sued Detel Products Ltd for breach of its promise that the paint would last seven to ten years.

It was held that, in addition to the contract for the sale of the paint (between the manufacturer and the painters) and the contract to paint the pier (between the painters and the pier owner), there was also a collateral contract between the pier company and the manufacturer. The bargain was that the manufacturer guaranteed the suitability of DMU and in return the pier company specified in its contract with the painters that DMU paint should be used.

Manufacturer's guarantees and warranties

Sometimes the manufacturer's confidence in his product is expressed formally in the shape of a written guarantee or warranty which accompanies the goods. A manufacturer's guarantee has become an expected standard feature of the sale of 'consumer durables'. The guarantee usually consists of an undertaking by the manufacturer to repair or replace faulty goods within a certain period of time.

The question arises of whether a manufacturer is bound to honour the promises contained in his guarantee. In other words, can the guarantee form the basis of a contract between the consumer and the manufacturer? Unfortunately, the legal position was far from clear. If the consumer could show that he knew about the guarantee before he bought the goods, he would be able to establish the existence of a collateral contract with the manufacturer by applying the reasoning employed in the *Carlill* case. The liability of the manufacturer of defective goods which are under guarantee could be established in another way. The guarantee often takes the form of a postcard, which the consumer must complete and send off to the manufacturer within a certain period of time. The inconvenience that this entails may be sufficient consideration to support the manufacturer's promise. In the past, guarantees often contained an exemption clause, which deprived the consumer of the rights he might otherwise have had against the manufacturer. Section 5 of the Unfair Contract Terms Act 1977 now prevents this practice by providing that any clause in the manufacturer's or distributor's guarantee purporting to exclude or restrict liability in negligence for loss or damage will be unenforceable against a consumer if the following conditions are met:

- the goods are of a type ordinarily supplied for private use and consumption;
- the goods have proved defective while in consumer use;
- the manufacturer or distributor did not sell the goods directly to the consumer.

Since 1 November 1978, manufacturers have been required to include a statement in their guarantees to the effect that the consumer's statutory rights are unaffected by the terms of the guarantee. Failure to make such a statement is a criminal offence by virtue of orders made under the Fair Trading Act 1973.

Reform and guarantees

The problems relating to guarantees were highlighted in an Office of Fair Trading (OFT) Report (*Consumer Guarantees*) published in 1984:

- the consumer may buy an extended guarantee, which may become worthless if the guarantor goes out of business;
- delays in dealing with complaints or authorising repair;
- consumers have expectations of 'peace of mind', which often disappear when they come to enforce the guarantee;
- the guarantee may not be transferable to a subsequent purchaser.

Over the years proposals for reform have been made variously by the OFT, the National Consumer Council and the DTI (now the Department of Business, Innovation and Skills). A private member's Consumer Guarantees Bill was introduced in 1990, but was lost because of a lack of parliamentary time and government opposition.

The European Directive on the Sale of Consumer Goods and Associated Guarantees, adopted on 7 July 1999, introduces the notion of a legally enforceable guarantee. The UK has implemented the requirements of the Directive by the Sale and Supply of Goods to Consumers Regulations 2002 which came into force on 31 March 2003. Where goods are sold or supplied to a consumer and a consumer guarantee is offered, then the guarantee will be legally binding as a contractual obligation. The guarantee must:

- be in writing, and, if the goods are offered in the UK, it must be in English;
- set out in plain and intelligible language the contents of the guarantee and the information necessary to make a claim, including the name and address of the guarantor and the duration and territorial scope of the guarantee;
- be made available within a reasonable time in writing or some other durable and accessible medium.

Enforcement authorities may apply for an injunction against the guarantor or other person offering the guarantee in the event of non-compliance.

Self-test questions/activities

1 Consider whether the following statements are true or false:
   (a) If a manufacturer gives a guarantee with his goods, he will be bound to the end-user to meet the terms of the guarantee – True/False?
   (b) The statutory implied conditions of satisfactory quality and fitness for purpose only apply to sales to consumers – True/False?
   (c) If a seller is unsure about his title to goods, he can transfer limited title to the buyer and will not be in breach of s 12 of the Sale of Goods Act 1979 – True/False?
   (d) The implied terms in ss 12–15, Sale of Goods Act cannot be excluded in any business or consumer contract – True/False?

2 Greenacres, a firm of estate agents, decides to give its image a face-lift by refurbishing its reception area. Greenacres places the contract with a local company, Office Style Ltd, which agrees to supply the following items:
   (a) six easy chairs and matching coffee table selected from Office Style's existing stock by Greenacres' senior partner;
   (b) a new carpet which has to be ordered direct from the manufacturer;
   (c) a set of free-standing display units, already in stock, which Office Style agrees to adapt to hold the particulars of houses for sale.
   The night before the refitting is due to take place, Office Style's warehouse, containing all the items for the Greenacres job, is completely destroyed by fire.
      Advise Greenacres.

3 Luigi owns an Italian restaurant. He has experienced a few problems with recent deliveries from his suppliers and he seeks your advice.
   (a) He orders 500 tins of Italian tomatoes. The supplier delivers 400 tins of Italian tomatoes and 100 tins of Greek tomatoes.
   (b) He orders 10 kg of parmesan cheese, but the supplier delivers only 2 kg.
   (c) He orders 50 kg of spaghetti. The supplier delivers 100 kg.
   (d) He has a regular order with a local baker for 100 bread rolls to be delivered by 11 am every day. On one occasion the rolls do not arrive until 2 pm.

4 Jim agrees to supply 300 turkeys to a London butcher's shop during a three-week period prior to Christmas. What are Jim's remedies in each of the following situations?
   (a) The butcher rings up at the end of November to cancel the order because he has found a cheaper supplier.
   (b) While the second consignment of 100 turkeys is being transported by rail to London, Jim hears from a neighbouring farmer that the butcher is having difficulty paying his debts.

5 Fred recently obtained a 24-inch remote control colour TV set. What are Fred's rights and the source of these rights in the following circumstances?
   (a) Just as he is sitting down to watch *Match of the Day*, there is a flash and a puff of smoke from the back of the TV and the screen goes blank. Fred bought the set new from a local department store. He paid for it in cash.
   (b) Fred obtained the TV from his brother-in-law, Tom, by swapping his music centre. Fred was assured by Tom that it was a colour TV, but so far he has only got a black-and-white picture.
   (c) Fred is an American football enthusiast. He told the salesperson at TV World Ltd, a local electrical shop, that he wanted a TV that would receive Channel 4 broadcasts because of his interest in American football. Fred, who is buying the TV on HP, has now discovered that he cannot get Channel 4 with this particular model.
   (d) The remote control unit refuses to work. Fred acquired the TV on hire from a local TV rental firm.

6 Mr and Mrs Carter decide to install double-glazing in their house. They get three firms to provide 'estimates' for the job, the cheapest (£4,000) being submitted by Kozee Ltd, which they ask to do the work. The Carters sign a contract, but the document does not mention the price payable for the work or how long it will take to complete. The workmen start the job in July, but the work proceeds in fits and starts and is finished finally in December. The Carters are very unhappy with the workmanship; the house is still very draughty and there has been no noticeable saving in their fuel bills. They have now received a bill from Kozee Ltd for £9,000 and they seek your advice.

Specimen examination questions

1 Sandra, who runs a flourishing florist's shop, decides to replace the van which she uses for making deliveries. She attends a long-established street market in used cars, where she sees a van with a notice in the front window which reads: 'For Sale. 1999 Bedford van'. After a thorough inspection and a test drive, she enters into a contract to buy the van from Mark. What is her legal position in the following circumstances?

(a) Sandra discovers that the vehicle is made up of two Bedford vans. The front half of a 1996 model has been welded to the rear half of a 1999 model and, as a result, the van is in a dangerous condition.

(b) During the test drive, Sandra noticed that the clutch was defective. Mark said that he was prepared to do the repairs himself or he would drop the price by £75. Sandra agreed to the reduction in price, but her local garage has now told her that it will cost £150 to put the defect right.

(c) She has now been informed by the police that the van was stolen six months previously and that it must be returned to its true owner.

2 Explain what remedies are available to a buyer of defective goods under sale of goods legislation.

Website references

http://www.bis.gov.uk/policies/consumer-issues The section of the Department of Business, Innovation and Skills' website which provides information on consumer policy and legislation such as the Sale of Goods Act 1979.

http://www.legalmax.info This site, written by Max Young, provides useful help in understanding basic concepts in contract law and the sale of goods. The tutorials and help are free, requiring simple registration only.

Visit **www.mylawchamber.co.uk/richesallen** to access study support resources including answers to questions in this chapter and legal updates, all linked to the **Pearson eText** version of **Keenan and Riches' Business Law** which you can **search**, **highlight** and **personalise** with your **own notes** and **bookmarks**.

Use **Case Navigator** to read in full some of the key cases referenced in this chapter with commentary and questions:

Carlill v *Carbolic Smoke Ball Co* [1893]
Harlingdon & Leinster Enterprises Ltd v *Christopher Hull Fine Art Ltd* [1990]
Jewson Ltd v *Kelly* (2003)
Stevenson v *Rogers* (1999)

Chapter 12

Business and the law of tort

In the last chapter we examined the scope of business liability in contract for the sale and supply of goods and services. In this chapter we will consider how the activities of business organisations may give rise to liability in tort.

Tortious liability

A tort is a civil wrong. Unlike the obligations voluntarily accepted by the parties to a contract, a tort consists of the breach of a duty imposed by the law. The law of tort seeks to provide a legal remedy for the victims of certain forms of harmful conduct. Tort duties are owed to a wide range of persons and are not dependent on the existence of a contractual relationship. Although this area of law is often referred to as the law of tort, in reality a number of distinct areas of tortious liability have been developed to protect people from the many forms of wrongful conduct which may occur in modern society. So it is probably more accurate to refer to a law of torts. Examples of the kinds of harmful conduct which the law provides protection against include:

■ interference with a person's ownership or possession of land or personal property, e.g. the torts of trespass to land and trespass to goods;

■ injury to business or personal reputations, e.g. tort of defamation;

■ interference with a person's use and enjoyment of land, e.g. tort of nuisance;

■ damage to land, e.g. tort of negligence, the rule in *Rylands* v *Fletcher*;

■ personal injury and death, e.g. torts of negligence and trespass to the person;

■ damage to commercial interests, e.g. torts of deceit, passing-off, inducement of breach of contract, conspiracy.

Each tort is governed by its own special rules covering such matters as the basis of liability, defences and remedies. General principles relating to these issues are set out below.

Basis of tortious liability

Liability in tort is essentially 'fault-based'. This means that a claimant must prove that the defendant acted intentionally or negligently and was, therefore, blameworthy. The defendant's reasons or motive for committing a wrongful act are generally not relevant to liability in tort. However, the presence of malice is relevant to some torts: malice is an essential ingredient of some torts, e.g. conspiracy requires proof of an intention to injure the claimant rather than to promote the defendant's legitimate interests; proof of malice can defeat certain defences to defamation, e.g. qualified privilege will not protect a defendant who acted maliciously; malice may make an otherwise reasonable act unreasonable so as to establish liability, e.g. in the tort of nuisance.

There are two situations where tortious liability may be imposed despite the defendant not being at fault.

1 Torts of strict liability. These are torts where the claimant can recover compensation for loss or damage without having to prove fault or intention on the part of the defendant. Part I of the Consumer Protection Act 1987, for example, provides that a manufacturer is strictly liable for injuries caused by his defective products. The rule in *Rylands* v *Fletcher*, breach of statutory duty and conversion are further examples of torts imposing strict liability.

2 Vicarious liability. In certain situations one person may be held liable for the torts of another. This type of liability is known as vicarious liability. An employer, for example, is vicariously liable for the torts of his employees committed during the course of their employment. Vicarious liability may also arise between partners and between a principal and agent. There are various justifications for the principles of vicarious liability:

- liability is incurred by the person best able financially to meet any award of damages (usually because the risk is covered by insurance);
- the claimant is given an additional defendant to sue, who is more likely to be able to satisfy any judgment;
- harm may be prevented by imposing liability on the person in control of the activity;
- the claimant is provided with a defendant in cases where it is impossible to establish precisely who was responsible within a particular organisation for the wrongful conduct.

The vicarious liability of an employer for the acts of his employees will be studied in more detail in Chapter 16 ⊙.

Proof of damage

The law of tort is concerned with providing a remedy for certain forms of wrongful conduct. In most torts, the claimant must prove that he has suffered some damage, e.g. personal injury or damage to his property, in order to establish liability. However, the fact that the claimant has suffered damage is not sufficient on its own to establish liability. The claimant must also prove that the damage was caused by the defendant's infringement of a right vested in the claimant which is recognised by the law. For example, the construction of an out-of-town shopping centre may result in a loss of trade for town centre shops, but since the law does not provide a right to protection from competition, affected shopkeepers will not have a remedy, no matter how severe their losses. The following case is an example of a situation where the claimants' business was ruined by the actions of others but no remedy was available.

Trent Strategic Health Authority v *Jain and another* (2009)

The claimants owned a nursing home which was registered under the requirements of the Registered Homes Act 1984 with the Nottingham Health Authority (subsequently succeeded by the Trent Strategic Health Authority). In 1998 the Authority made an *ex parte* and without notice application to a magistrate to cancel the registration. The application was granted by the stipendiary magistrate, with the result that all the residents were removed from the home. The claimants were not given prior notice of the application or the grounds on which it was being sought; they therefore did not have an opportunity to contest the application. The claimants appealed immediately to the Registered Homes Tribunal and some four months later they succeeded in overturning the magistrate's decision. However, by this time irrevocable damage had been done to the claimants' business. They brought an action in tort for the economic damage caused to them by the Authority's unjustified application. As there was no allegation of bad faith or of misfeasance in public office by officers of the Authority, the claimants framed their action in negligence. The House of Lords held that the Authority did not owe the claimants a duty of care and therefore no liability in negligence could arise. The events in this case took place before the implementation of the Human Rights Act 1998. Lords Scott and Neuberger and Baroness Hale expressed the view that the claimants would have had a claim under the 1998 Act for a breach of their convention rights.

Although proof of damage is an essential component of most torts, some rights are regarded as so important that the law will provide a remedy even though the claimant has not suffered any damage. These torts are said to be 'actionable *per se*' (actionable in itself) and the most important examples are libel and trespass. Nominal damages can be recovered in respect of these torts even though no loss has occurred.

Causation

Liability in tort is dependent on making a connection between the defendant's wrongful conduct and the damage suffered by the claimant. If the damage was caused by some other factor, the defendant will escape liability. The factual cause of the damage is established by applying the 'but for' test, i.e. would the damage have occurred 'but for' the defendant's tortious conduct? An example of the application of this test in the context of a claim in negligence is given below.

Barnett v *Chelsea & Kensington Hospital Management Committee* (1968)

Mr Barnett, a nightwatchman, attended the defendant's hospital in the early hours of the morning complaining of vomiting. The casualty doctor failed to examine him but instead sent a message that Mr Barnett should see his own GP in the morning if he was still unwell. Mr Barnett died five hours later from arsenic poisoning. The court held that, although the hospital doctor was negligent in failing to examine Mr Barnett, the failure to take reasonable care was not the cause of his death. The evidence was that, even if Mr Barnett had been examined, correctly diagnosed and treated, he would have died anyway.

Even if a claimant can establish a causal connection between the defendant's tortious conduct and the damage he has suffered using the 'but for' test, he cannot necessarily recover his loss. The damage may be too remote a consequence of the defendant's actions and, therefore, not the cause in law. The test for remoteness in tort derives from the decision of the Privy Council in a case known as the *Wagon Mound (No 1)* (1961).

Overseas Tankship (UK) Ltd v *Morts Dock and Engineering Co Ltd, The Wagon Mound* (1961)

The defendants were the charterers of a ship called the *Wagon Mound*. As a result of the carelessness of the defendant's servants, a quantity of furnace oil was spilled in Sydney harbour. The oil was carried towards the claimant's wharf where welding operations were being carried out. After receiving expert advice that the oil would not ignite on water, welding continued. However, a few days later the oil ignited when hot metal fell on a piece of cotton waste floating in the oil. The resulting fire caused extensive damage to the claimant's wharf. The Judicial Committee of the Privy Council held that reasonable foreseeability was the proper test of remoteness of damage in tort. The court would have awarded damages for oil damage to slipways had this been claimed since such damage was a reasonably foreseeable consequence of the defendant's negligence. However, it was not reasonably foreseeable that the oil would ignite in the circumstances which occurred and, therefore, damage caused by the fire was not recoverable.

Damage may be too remote if the chain of causation is broken by a new unforeseen act of a third person. Such an event is referred to as a *novus actus interveniens* – a new act intervening – and its effect is to relieve the defendant of the liability for the claimant's loss.

Cobb v *Great Western Railway* (1894)

The defendant railway had allowed a railway carriage to become overcrowded. The claimant was jostled and robbed of £89. The claimant sued the defendant to recover his loss. The court held that the loss was too remote as the actions of the thief were a *novus actus interveniens*, which broke the chain of causation.

Specific torts relevant to business

Negligence

The tort of negligence is concerned with certain kinds of careless conduct which cause damage or loss to others. The foundations of the modern law of negligence were laid down in one of the best-known cases in English law – *Donoghue* v *Stevenson* (1932).

Donoghue v Stevenson (1932)

Mrs Donoghue and a friend visited a café in Paisley run by Mr Minchella. The friend bought a bottle of ginger beer for Mrs Donoghue. Mr Minchella opened the bottle, which was made of dark opaque glass, and poured some of the ginger beer into a tumbler. Unsuspecting, Mrs Donoghue drank the contents, but, when her friend refilled the tumbler, the remains of a decomposing snail floated out. Mrs Donoghue suffered shock and severe gastroenteritis as a result. She could not sue Mr Minchella for compensation in contract for her injuries because she had not bought the ginger beer herself. So she brought an action against the manufacturer of the ginger beer, Stevenson, arguing that he had been negligent. The House of Lords held that, provided Mrs Donoghue could prove her allegations, she would be entitled to succeed. We shall never know whether there was, in fact, a snail in the bottle because the case was settled out of court for £100.

In order to establish negligence a claimant must prove that:

1 the defendant owed him a legal duty of care;
2 the defendant was in breach of this duty; and
3 the claimant suffered injury or loss as a result of the breach.

All three elements are essential to a successful negligence claim. We shall consider each of the requirements in turn.

Duty of care

It is important to know in what circumstances one person will owe a duty of care to another. In *Donoghue v Stevenson* (1932), Lord Atkin formulated a general test for determining the existence of a duty of care which could be applied to most situations. His statement of general principle, which was to become known as the 'neighbour' principle, is as follows:

You must take reasonable care to avoid acts or omissions which you can reasonably foresee would be likely to injure your neighbour. Who, then, in law, is my neighbour? The answer seems to be – persons who are so closely and directly affected by my act that I ought reasonably to have them in contemplation as being so affected when I am directing my mind to the acts or omissions which are called in question.

Lord Atkin's statement of the requirements for a duty of care to exist involved two main elements: reasonable foresight and proximity. A duty of care would be imposed if the damage was reasonably foreseeable and the relationship between the parties was sufficiently close (proximate).

The flexible nature of the 'neighbour' principle enabled the courts to recognise the existence of a duty of care in a variety of fact situations unless there were policy reasons for excluding it. This approach culminated in Lord Wilberforce's now discredited two-stage test for establishing the existence of a duty of care which he propounded in *Anns v Merton London Borough Council* (1977). Stage one required courts to apply the neighbour principle by asking whether there was sufficient proximity between the parties that the harm suffered by the claimant was reasonably foreseeable. Stage two involved the courts in considering whether the duty should be restricted or limited for reasons of economic, social or public policy.

In recent years the courts have sought to place limits on the expansion of the duty of care to new situations by adopting a so-called 'incremental' approach. The three-stage approach to establishing a duty of care recommended in *Caparo Industries plc v Dickman* (1990) requires consideration of the following questions:

- Was the harm suffered reasonably foreseeable?
- Was there a relationship of proximity between the parties?
- Is it fair, just and reasonable in all the circumstances to impose a duty of care?

An example of the application of this approach is provided by the following case.

John Munroe (Acrylics) Ltd v London Fire Brigade & Civil Defence Authority (1997)

Four fire engines were called out to a fire on wasteland. When they arrived, it appeared that the fire had been extinguished and, as there were no signs of fire, they left. Unfortunately, some of the debris was still smouldering. It later set alight and destroyed the claimant's premises, which were adjacent to the wasteland. The Court of Appeal held that a fire brigade is not under a duty to answer a call nor is it under a duty to take care when it is at the scene of a fire. There was not a sufficient proximity between a fire brigade and the owners of property for a duty of care to be imposed. It was not fair, just or reasonable to impose a personal duty of care to individual occupiers in addition to the statutory duty which was designed to benefit the public in general.

Comment. Although the courts have been reluctant to find that the emergency services, such as the fire brigade and coastguard, owe a duty of care to members of the public, in **Kent v Griffiths (No 3)** (2000) the Court of Appeal took the view that the ambulance service may owe a duty of care to individuals to provide a prompt service and to provide appropriate treatment during the journey to hospital.

Another interesting example of how the courts have approached the question of whether a duty of care should be imposed in any given situation is the development of liability for psychiatric illness caused by someone's negligence. These cases are sometimes known as 'nervous shock' cases. The following case marks the starting point in the development of the law.

Dulieu v White & Sons (1901)

A woman suffered extreme shock when a horse-drawn carriage was negligently driven into the public house where she was working. The shock caused her to miscarry her baby. The Court of Appeal held that she was entitled to recover damages. Although she was not physically harmed in the accident, she had been put in fear for her safety. Kennedy LJ took the view that there was a limitation to the right to recover: the shock must arise from a reasonable fear of immediate personal injury to oneself.

The limitation enunciated by Kennedy LJ in **Dulieu** was removed in the following case.

Hambrook v Stokes Bros (1925)

The claimant was the husband of a woman who died as a result of nervous shock caused by the defendant's negligence. The claimant's wife had witnessed a lorry careering downhill and she had reasonable cause to believe that her children may have been in the path of the lorry. The Court of Appeal held that it would not be fair to draw a distinction between a mother who feared for the safety of her children and a mother who only feared for her own safety. The claimant would be entitled

to recover if he could show that: (a) his wife's death was caused by the shock occasioned by the runaway lorry; (b) the shock resulted from what she saw or realised by her own unaided senses; and (c) the shock was due to a reasonable fear of immediate personal injury to herself or her children.

The next significant case was the decision of the House of Lords in the following case.

Bourhill v Young (1942)

The claimant was an Edinburgh fishwife who, after alighting from a tram, heard the impact of a traffic accident and later saw blood on the road. The accident was caused by the defendant motorcyclist who was killed. The claimant, who was eight months pregnant at the time of the accident, suffered severe shock and later gave birth to a stillborn child. The House of Lords held that she was not entitled to recover damages for her injuries. The defendant did not owe a duty of care to the claimant because he could not have reasonably foreseen the likelihood that she could be affected by his negligent act. She did not witness the accident; she was never in fear for her own physical safety nor was there any familial relationship between herself and those involved in the accident.

Although the claimant in **Bourhill** did not witness the accident, it is unlikely that she would have been successful had she done so. Lord Porter took the view that car drivers, even if careless, are entitled to expect to assume that 'the ordinary frequenter of the streets has sufficient fortitude to endure such incidents as may from time to time be expected to occur in them' without incurring liability for negligence.

The next important case was the decision of the House of Lords in **McLoughlin v O'Brian** (1982).

McLoughlin v O'Brian (1982)

The claimant's husband and children were involved in a serious accident. The claimant went to the hospital two hours after the accident, where she saw the serious injuries sustained by her husband and children. She was also informed that one of her children had been killed. She suffered psychiatric injury. The House of Lords held that the claimant was entitled to recover damages. The injury which brought on her nervous shock was caused to a near relative and although she was not at or near the scene of the accident she did witness the 'immediate aftermath' in the hospital. The shock that she suffered was a reasonably foreseeable consequence of the defendant's negligence. The sole test of liability is reasonable foreseeability, which should only be limited in terms of proximity by three elements: (a) the closeness of the relationship between the injured person and the claimant; (b) the proximity of the claimant to the accident in terms of place and time; and (c) proximity of communication about the accident to the claimant in terms of seeing the accident, hearing about it or coming across its immediate aftermath.

that a person can only recover for nervous shock which causes psychiatric illness as a result of apprehending the infliction of physical injury (or the risk of physical injury) to another person (the primary victim) if he can satisfy the test of reasonable foreseeability that he would be affected by psychiatric illness as a result of the accident because of the close relationship of love and affection with the primary victim and the test of proximity in terms of the claimant's connection in place and time with the accident. The three requirements for a successful claim are: (i) the claimant must have a close tie of love or affection with the person killed; (ii) he was close to the accident in terms of time and space; and (iii) he witnessed the incident or its immediate aftermath, rather than hearing about it from a third person.

The decision in *McLoughlin* marked a considerable expansion of liability for psychiatric injury but their Lordships assumed that it would not open the floodgates of litigation. In the following ten years, however, there was a growth of claims for psychiatric injury in areas such as workplace stress (e.g. *Walker v Northumberland County Council* (1994) – see Chapter 16) and against medical practitioners and health authorities. The House of Lords started to take greater account of policy considerations and began to take a more restrictive view of the scope of liability for psychiatric injury.

The next important case was the following decision of the House of Lords.

Page v Smith (1996)

The claimant (Page) was involved in a car accident caused by the defendant's negligence. Although the claimant was not physically injured in the accident, it did cause a reoccurrence of ME (chronic fatigue syndrome) from which he had previously suffered. The House of Lords held that the defendant was liable. A distinction should be drawn between primary victims, who were within the range of foreseeable physical injury, and all other victims (secondary victims) who must satisfy the tests set out in *Alcock*'s case. Page was a primary victim. The defendant could reasonably foresee that his conduct would expose Page to a risk of personal injury. Page did not have to show that nervous shock was reasonably foreseeable or that Page was particularly susceptible. (This is an application of the principle known as the 'thin skull' rule, which means that you must take your victim as you find him.)

Alcock v Chief Constable of the South Yorkshire Police (1991)

This case arose from the Hillsborough football stadium disaster in 1989, in which 95 spectators were crushed to death and over 400 injured. The immediate cause of the disaster was the decision of a senior police officer to open an outer gate to the Leppings Lane end of the stadium without cutting off access to pens which were already full. Scenes from the ground were broadcast live on television and news of the disaster was broadcast on the radio. Claims for psychiatric injury were brought by 16 claimants who were related to those killed. The claimants included, for example, those present in the ground who saw the horrific scenes unfold and were later informed that close relatives (two brothers) had been killed, and those who watched the scenes on television and were later informed that relatives had died. The Chief Constable admitted liability in negligence in respect of those who were killed or injured but argued that he did not owe a duty of care to the claimants. The House of Lords dismissed all the claims. Their Lordships held

The principles established in *Alcock* and *Page* were applied in the following case which also related to the Hillsborough disaster.

White v Chief Constable of South Yorkshire (1999)

A number of police officers sued the defendant Chief Constable for damages for post-traumatic stress disorder which they suffered as a result of being on duty at Hillsborough Stadium and being involved in the aftermath

of the disaster. They sued as employees and as rescuers. The House of Lords held that they were not entitled to claim. As employees they were secondary victims and they did not have a sufficiently close relationship with those who were killed or injured to meet the test laid down in *Alcock*. In order to recover compensation as rescuers, the claimants would have to show objectively that they had exposed themselves to danger or reasonably believed that they were doing so. There were strong public policy reasons which prevented them from recovering when the relatives of those killed had been denied compensation in the earlier case of *Alcock*.

Breach of duty

After establishing the existence of a duty of care, the claimant must show that this duty has been broken by the defendant. The test for deciding whether there has been a breach of duty is whether the defendant has failed to do what a reasonable person would have done or has done what a reasonable person would not have done. Whether the defendant's conduct amounts to a breach of duty depends on all the circumstances of the case. The court will consider a range of factors including:

- the likelihood that damage or injury will be incurred;
- the seriousness of any damage or injury;
- the cost and ease of taking precautions;
- the social need for the activity.

Bolton v Stone (1951)

Miss Stone was hit by a cricket ball while standing on the highway outside a cricket ground occupied by the defendant cricket club. The evidence was that in the last 30 years balls had been hit into the highway on only six occasions, no one had been hurt and at the point where the ball left the ground there was a 17-foot protective fence. The House of Lords held that for negligence to be established there must be a reasonable likelihood of the event occurring and injury being caused as a result. The risk of injury to those on the highway was so small and the cost of ensuring that balls could not be hit outside the ground so high, that a reasonable person would not have taken the precautions. The cricket club was not liable for Miss Stone's injuries.

In **Bolton v Stone**, their Lordships struck a balance between the magnitude of the risk of injury to passers-by

and the precautions required to prevent injury. As Lord Radcliffe stated:

> It seems to me that a reasonable man, taking account of the chances against an accident happening, would not have felt himself called on either to abandon the use of the ground for cricket or to increase the height of his surrounding fences. He would have done what the appellants did. In other words, he would have done nothing.

In more recent times, there has been growing concern about the development of a 'compensation culture' fuelled by 'no win, no fee' arrangements for legal services, the perception that most risks will be covered by insurance and a general increase in compensation payments. It is said that this has led to a much more risk-averse approach particularly by public authorities, who fear the financial and reputational impact of legal claims. The issues were aired in the following case.

Tomlinson v Congleton Borough Council and Cheshire County Council (2004)

The claimant, John Tomlinson, was severely injured when he made a shallow dive into a lake in a country park owned by the Borough Council and managed by the County Council. The County Council pursued a policy of prohibiting swimming in the lake: notices were placed near the lake stating 'Dangerous Water. No swimming' and the park rangers would try to get swimmers out of the water. However, the lake was a popular place to swim. The claimant based his claim on a breach of the Occupiers' Liability Act 1984 (see below, pp 439–40 ○). It was accepted that he was a trespasser as he had seen and ignored the warning notices but he claimed that the Council had not discharged the duty that it owed to him because they should have taken more drastic action to prevent him going swimming. The House of Lords held that the defendants were not liable. Although the defendants owed a duty of care to both visitors and trespassers, such as Mr Tomlinson, it was not reasonable to expect the defendants to protect him from dangers which were perfectly obvious. Their Lordships expressed concern that to hold otherwise might lead to the defendants curtailing the activities of responsible users of the park. As Lord Hoffmann put it:

> . . . I think that there is an important question of freedom at stake. It is unjust that the harmless recreation of responsible parents and children with buckets and spades on the beaches should be prohibited in order to comply with what is thought to be a legal duty to safeguard irresponsible visitors against dangers which are perfectly obvious. The fact that such people take no notice of warnings cannot create a duty to take other steps to protect them.

In a number of recent cases the courts have demonstrated their reluctance to award compensation for accidents where people should have taken responsibility for their actions. For example, in **Simonds v Isle of Wight** (2003) the defendant Council was not liable when a five-year-old child fell off a swing and broke his arm. A swing presents an inherent and obvious risk which a parent should appreciate if they allow their child to use the swing. There is further evidence of the courts' reluctance to award compensation when people are injured participating voluntarily in hazardous activities.

Poppleton v Trustees of the Portsmouth Youth Activities Committee (2008)

The claimant was paralysed when he fell from a climbing wall on to 12 inch absorbent matting. He had seen other climbers jumping from the walls to grab hold of metal bars which crossed the room, but when he tried to copy them, he did not complete the leap successfully and instead somersaulted in the air and landed on his head. At first instance, he was judged to be 75 per cent to blame for his injuries, and he was awarded 25 per cent of his loss against the defendants. The Court of Appeal held that he was wholly to blame. The risk of falling was plainly obvious. It was clear that no amount of matting could provide complete protection against an awkward fall. There were inherent and obvious risks to the activity which the claimant had undertaken. In these circumstances, the law did not require the defendants to prevent him from undertaking it, nor to train him or supervise him. It made no difference that the claimant had paid to use the climbing wall or that the rules could have been displayed more prominently.

In 2006 the government brought forward legislation to deal with the 'compensation culture' which it believed was leading to overly cautious behaviour. The Compensation Act 2006 puts on a statutory footing the principles already enunciated in recent cases, such as **Tomlinson**. When considering whether a particular standard of care is reasonable, the courts can take into account whether requiring particular steps to be taken to meet the standard of care would prevent or impede a desirable activity from taking place.

Res ipsa loquitur

It is normally the responsibility of the claimant to show that the defendant did not act reasonably, i.e. the burden of proof lies with the claimant. If the claimant is unable to present appropriate evidence, his case will fail. However, there are some situations where the only or most likely explanation of an accident is that the defendant was negligent. If this is the case, the claimant may claim *res ipsa loquitur* – the facts speak for themselves. This has the effect of placing the burden of proof on the defendant who must show either how the accident occurred or that he has not been negligent. Two conditions must be satisfied for *res ipsa* to come into play:

- the event which caused the accident must have been within the defendant's control; and
- the accident must be of such a nature that it would not have occurred if proper care had been taken by the defendant.

Cassidy v Ministry of Health (1951)

The claimant went into hospital for treatment with two stiff fingers. When he left hospital he had four stiff fingers and a useless hand. The Court of Appeal held that the defendant hospital was liable for the injuries. *Res ipsa loquitur* could be applied to assist the claimant in establishing his case. Lord Denning took the view that the claimant was entitled to say:

> I went into hospital to be cured of two stiff fingers. I have come out with four stiff fingers and my hand is useless. That should not have happened if due care had been used. Explain it, if you can.

Damage

Finally, the claimant must show he has suffered some damage, that it has been caused by the defendant's breach of duty and is not too remote a consequence of it. The kinds of damage which will give rise to an action in negligence are: death, personal injury, nervous shock, damage to property and, in limited circumstances, financial loss.

Defences

The defendant may raise a number of defences to an action in negligence. Consent, for example, is a complete defence and negates any liability. Contributory negligence is a partial defence and has the effect of reducing any award of damages. Contributory negligence will be considered in more detail later in this chapter (see p 369 ◯).

We will now examine in more detail the potential business liability by considering the extent of liability in tort for defective goods and services.

Defective goods

There are three circumstances when the person responsible for putting defective goods into circulation will incur liability in tort for his products. These are:

1 in the tort of negligence;
2 strict liability under Part I of the Consumer Protection Act 1987; and
3 for breach of statutory duty under Part II of the Consumer Protection Act 1987.

Negligence

A manufacturer may be liable to a consumer for loss and damage caused by his defective product under the tort of negligence.

A consumer must establish first of all that the manufacturer owed him a duty of care. In *Donoghue* v *Stevenson* the House of Lords established the principle that a manufacturer owes a duty of care to all persons who are likely to come into contact with his goods:

> ... [A] manufacturer of products which he sells in such a form as to show that he intends them to reach the ultimate consumer in the form in which they left him with no reasonable possibility of intermediate examination and with the knowledge that the absence of reasonable care in the preparation or putting up of the products will result in an injury to the consumer's life or property, owes a duty to the consumer to take that reasonable care.

There is no limit to the type of goods covered by the principle established in *Donoghue*: cases have involved goods as diverse as cars (*Herschtal* v *Stewart & Arden Ltd* (1940)), underpants (*Grant* v *Australian Knitting Mills* (1936)) and hair dyes (*Holmes* v *Ashford* (1950)). Since 1932, the pool of potential defendants has been extended from manufacturers to cover anyone who does some work on the goods, for example a repairer. The word 'consumer' has been given a wide interpretation to cover anyone who is likely to be injured by the lack of care.

Stennet v Hancock and Peters (1939)

Mrs Stennet was walking along a pavement when she was struck and injured by a piece of wheel which had come off a passing lorry. She received damages from the owner of the garage where the wheel had been negligently repaired shortly before the accident.

Probably the most difficult problem for a consumer to overcome is to establish a breach of the duty of care. This means that the consumer must be able to prove that the manufacturer failed to act reasonably in all the circumstances. In determining whether the defendant has acted reasonably the courts engage in a cost–benefit analysis in which they consider a number of factors. These include the likelihood and seriousness of injury or harm, the cost and ease of instituting precautions to eliminate or reduce the risk and the social need for the product. The following case is a good illustration of how the courts decide whether a manufacturer has exercised reasonable care.

Walton v British Leyland (UK) Ltd (1978)

The claimants were injured in a collision caused by a wheel coming off the Austin Allegro car they were travelling in at 60 mph on the M1. Although the accident happened in 1976, the manufacturer of the car, Leyland, had been aware since 1973 that there was a problem with wheels coming adrift on the Allegro. Leyland considered recalling all cars affected by the fault and even made an estimate of what it would cost (£300,000 in 1974). However, Leyland decided not to follow this course of action for commercial reasons. Instead it issued a product bulletin to all service managers of its accredited dealers advising them of a change in the method of adjusting the rear hub bearings. The court held that the failure to recall all Allegro cars was a breach of Leyland's duty to care for the safety of those put at risk by the fault, i.e. occupants of the Allegro and other road users.

Liability in negligence is fault-based and the onus of proving that the manufacturer was at fault is upon the consumer. This can be a very difficult task as usually the consumer has no means of knowing exactly what went wrong in the manufacturing process. Sometimes, however, the only reasonable explanation for the defect is that someone acted negligently; for example, buns do not usually have stones in the middle of them. In this kind of situation the consumer may be able to plead *res ipsa loquitur*, the facts speak for themselves. This has the effect of reversing the normal burden of proof; the manufacturer is presumed to have acted negligently unless he can prove that he took all reasonable care.

Steer v Durable Rubber Manufacturing Co Ltd (1958)

A girl aged six was scalded when her three-month-old hot water bottle burst. She could not prove exactly how the defect occurred, but she did establish that hot water bottles are expected to last three years. The Court of Appeal held that in the circumstances it was up to the manufacturing company to show that it had not been negligent. Since the company could not do this, it was liable.

Finally, the consumer must be able to prove that he has suffered loss or damage as a result of the manufacturer's breach of duty. If the damage is caused by some other factor, the manufacturer will not be liable.

Evans v Triplex Safety Glass Co Ltd (1936)

The manufacturer of a car windscreen was not liable in negligence when the windscreen shattered causing injury and shock to the occupants of the car because there were a number of possible causes of the accident. The claimants were unable to prove that the disintegration of the windscreen had been caused by the glass manufacturer's failure to take reasonable care.

Even if the consumer can establish a causal link between the breach of duty and the damage, he cannot necessarily recover damages for all the consequences of the manufacturer's negligence. A manufacturer is liable only for loss and damage which is reasonably foreseeable. It is well established that a consumer can recover damages if the defective product causes personal injury or damage to property. However, the position is far from clear where the defect does not result in physical injury or damage to other property. Until fairly recently it was a settled point of law that a consumer

could not recover damages for pure economic (financial) loss, unless:

- it was caused by a negligent misstatement (see later *Hedley Byrne & Co Ltd v Heller and Partners Ltd* (1963)); or
- it was consequent upon foreseeable physical injury or damage to property.

So, if a product simply ceased to work because of a manufacturing defect, the consumer could not sue the manufacturer in negligence for the cost of repair or replacement. The decision of the House of Lords in the *Junior Books* case suggested that in limited circumstances it may be possible to recover damages for economic or financial loss.

Junior Books Ltd v Veitchi Co Ltd (1982)

Junior Books entered into a contract with a building firm for the construction of a new factory. Under this contract, the architects acting for Junior Books were entitled to nominate which subcontractor was to be employed by the building firm to lay the flooring. The architects nominated Veitchi. The floor proved defective and Junior Books brought an action in negligence against Veitchi. Even though there was no suggestion that the floor was dangerous, Junior Books claimed damages for the cost of relaying the floor and the consequential financial loss that this would involve (i.e. the factory would have to be closed down to enable the floor to be replaced). The House of Lords held that Junior Books Ltd was entitled to recover damages from Veitchi. The relationship between the parties was so close that it gave rise to a duty to avoid careless work which would inevitably cause financial loss.

This decision raised expectations of a significant extension of the general principle laid down by Lord Atkin in *Donoghue v Stevenson* by imposing liability for pure economic loss. However, their Lordships stressed that their decision was based on the very close proximity between the parties which fell just short of a direct contractual relationship. A manufacturer does not normally have such a close relationship with the consumers of his products. Subsequent cases have demonstrated the limited application of *Junior Books*.

Muirhead v Industrial Tank Specialities Ltd (1985)

Muirhead, a wholesale fish merchant, wished to expand his lobster trade by buying lobsters cheaply in the summer, storing them in a tank and reselling them at Christmas when the prices are high. The scheme required sea water to be pumped continuously through the tank to oxygenate the water and thereby keep the lobsters alive. The tank and pumps were installed by ITS. The pumps were supplied to ITS by ITT. They were powered by electric motors made by a French company and supplied through its English subsidiary of Leroy Somer Electric Motors Ltd. Within a few days of installation, the pumps started to cut out and on one occasion Muirhead lost his entire stock of lobsters. The cause of the problem was that the motors were unsuitable for the English voltage system. Muirhead obtained judgment against ITS but, since it had gone into liquidation, the judgment was not satisfied. Muirhead, therefore, brought an action in negligence against ITT and Leroy Somer claiming compensation for the cost of the pumps, the cost of electrical engineers called out to deal with the pumps, the loss of lobsters and the loss of profit on intended sales of the lobsters. The Court of Appeal held that a manufacturer could be liable in negligence for economic loss suffered by a consumer if there was a very close relationship between the parties and the consumer had placed reliance on the manufacturer rather than on the retailer as was the case in *Junior Books*. However, there was no evidence in this case of such a close relationship or reliance. Therefore, Muirhead could not recover his economic loss, i.e. the loss of profit on the intended sales of lobsters (£127,375), although he could recover for loss of his lobster stock (£11,000) as this amounted to reasonably foreseeable physical damage.

Even if the consumer manages to overcome all the difficulties involved in proving negligence, the manufacturer may still be able to defeat the claim or secure a reduction in damages by showing that the accident was caused wholly or partly by the consumer's own negligence. The defence of contributory negligence may apply where, for example, the consumer has ignored operating instructions or continued to use a product knowing that it was defective. Under the Law Reform (Contributory Negligence) Act 1945, contributory negligence on the part of the consumer has the effect of reducing the damages awarded to the extent that the claimant was to blame for the accident. For example, if a court assesses the claimant's damages at £10,000, but finds that he was 50 per cent to blame for what happened, his damages will be reduced by 50 per cent and he will receive £5,000.

Part I of the Consumer Protection Act 1987

The difficulties of bringing an action and establishing liability in negligence against a manufacturer led to a growing interest in the subject of 'product liability'. This term is used to describe a system of strict liability for manufacturers in respect of injury or loss caused by their defective products.

The question of product liability was considered by no fewer than four bodies in the 1970s: the Law Commission, the Council of Europe, the Royal Commission on Civil Liability (chaired by Lord Pearson) and the EC. In every single case, the recommendations of these bodies involved imposing strict liability on the manufacturer of defective products. In 1985 the EC Council of Ministers adopted a directive on product liability and, consequently, the British government was committed to implementing changes to UK law within three years. Part I of the Consumer Protection Act 1987 (CPA 1987) implements the EC Directive.

Liability under Part I of the CPA 1987

Part I of the CPA 1987, which came into force on 1 March 1988, introduces a regime of strict liability for personal injury and damage to property caused by defective products. This means that a producer will be liable for harm caused by his products unless he can establish one of the defences provided by the CPA 1987. It is no longer necessary for a claimant to prove negligence. Nevertheless, to establish liability under the CPA 1987 the claimant must prove that:

- he has suffered damage;
- the product was defective; and
- the damage was caused by the defective product.

A 'producer' is defined in s 1(2) as:

- the manufacturer of a product;
- in the case of a substance which has been won or abstracted, the person who won or abstracted it, e.g. a mining company producing iron ore; and
- in the case of a product neither manufactured nor won or abstracted, but essential characteristics of which are attributable to an industrial or other process having been carried out, the person who carried out that process, e.g. the producer of canned vegetables.

Section 2 identifies those who are liable for injury or damage arising from a defective product. They are:

- the producer of the product (as defined in s 1(2));
- any person who by putting his name on the product or using a trade mark or other distinguishing mark in relation to the product has held himself out to be the producer of the product, e.g. 'own-branders' who market goods under their own label, even though manufactured by someone else;
- any person who imports the product into the EC in the course of a business; and
- where the producer cannot be identified within a reasonable time, any person who supplied the product, e.g. retailers or wholesalers who cannot identify the manufacturer of the product.

The net of strict liability under the CPA 1987 is cast fairly widely over the chain of supply with the objective of ensuring that an injured consumer will have someone in the EC against whom he can bring an action. However, there are some groups of people involved in the supply of products who are not specifically caught in the net. They include designers, retailers, repairers and installers. (These people will be liable, however, if they also fall into one of the categories of persons liable set out in points 1–4 above, i.e. a designer may be liable as a producer.)

'Product' is defined by s 1(2) as any goods or electricity. The definition covers not just finished goods but also components and raw materials. Game and agricultural produce which had not undergone an industrial process were specifically excluded from the scope of the CPA 1987, as originally enacted. The CPA 1987 did not define what was meant by an industrial process, and this had given rise to some uncertainty. It was not clear, for example, whether spraying crops amounted to an industrial process. In 1999 the EC adopted an amending Directive extending the scope of product liability to primary agricultural products and game. The UK implemented the amendment with effect from 4 December 2000.

Defect (s 3)

Section 3(1) provides that there is a defect in a product if the safety of the product is not such as persons are generally entitled to expect. Section 3(2) specifies a number of factors which should be taken into account when deciding what persons are entitled to expect. They include:

- the manner and purposes for which the product has been marketed;
- the use of any mark, instruction or warning;
- what might reasonably be expected to be done with the product; and
- the time when the product was supplied by the producer to another.

There have been relatively few reported cases of liability under the CPA 1987 being established. The following cases are examples of where the courts have imposed liability.

Abouzaid v Mothercare (UK) (2000)

The claimant was a 12-year-old boy who was injured while helping his mother to attach a product called a 'Cosytoes' to his younger brother's pushchair. The 'Cosytoes' supplied by the defendants consisted of a fleece-lined sleeping bag which was attached to the pushchair by means of elasticated straps joined by a metal buckle. The boy was trying to join the straps when one of the straps slipped from his grasp and the buckle hit his eye. He was left with no useful central vision in his left eye. The Court of Appeal held as follows: (i) The manufacturer was not liable in negligence. The absence of comparable accidents was a relevant factor. Elasticated tape was a commonly used fabric and there was no evidence that its use was likely to cause injury. Although there was the potential for a serious injury, the likelihood of injury occurring was assessed as very small. So while there was an identifiable risk, it was not such that a manufacturer in 1990 could be held liable for supplying the 'Cosytoes' product. (ii) The product was defective under the CPA 1987 in that the design permitted a risk to arise without warning that the user should position himself so as to avoid the risk of injury. The public were entitled to expect better. (iii) The defendants could not rely on the absence of recordable accidents as meeting the requirements of the 'state of scientific and technical knowledge' contained in s 4(1) (see below).

A v National Blood Authority (2001)

The High Court held that the defendant, the National Blood Authority (NBA), was liable to the recipients of blood infected with the Hepatitis C virus as a result of blood transfusions which took place after March 1988. Hepatitis C was identified in 1988 but the NBA did not introduce screening tests until September 1991. Blood and blood products contaminated with the virus were 'defective products' under Art 6 of the Product Liability Directive and s 3 of the CPA 1987, and the NBA, as a producer of the product, was liable to the recipients of the infected blood.

Damage (s 5)

The damage for which compensation is recoverable under the CPA 1987 is defined as death, personal injury or damage to any property (including land). The right of recovery in respect of property damage is restricted. There is no liability for damage to the product itself or to any product in which it was comprised. No claim can be brought for property damage if the amount claimed is less than £275. Furthermore, a claim for damage to property can only be made in respect of property ordinarily intended for private use, occupation or consumption and intended by the claimant mainly for his own private use, occupation or consumption.

Defences (s 4)

The following defences are available to an action under the CPA 1987:

1 The defect is attributable to compliance with UK legislation or EC obligations. The defence does not extend to compliance with, for example, British standards.
2 The person proceeded against did not at any time supply the product to another, e.g. where the product is an experimental prototype which is stolen by a rival.
3 The product was not supplied in the course of a business or for profit, e.g. a home-made product given as a birthday present.
4 The defect did not exist in the product at the relevant time.
5 The state of scientific and technical knowledge at the relevant time was not such that a producer of products of the same description as the product in question might be expected to have discovered the defect if it had existed in his products while they were under his control. This is the controversial 'development risks' defence. Under the EC Directive the adoption of such a defence was optional. The British government justified inclusion of the defence on the ground that to impose liability would stifle

innovation and make British industry less competitive. Opponents of the defence argue that it seriously weakens the principle of strict liability, so that the victims of another Thalidomide-type disaster would still have great difficulty establishing liability. Doubts about whether the defence, as it is worded in the CPA 1987, complied with the requirements of the EC Directive were resolved in 1997 when the European Court of Justice dismissed an application by the European Commission that the UK had failed to properly implement the provisions of the Directive in relation to this defence (*Commission of the European Communities* v *UK* (1997)).
6 In the case of a component or raw material, it was comprised in another product and the defect is wholly attributable to the design of the other product or to compliance with instructions given by the producer of the other product.

In addition to the defences provided by s 4, the person proceeded against can raise contributory negligence on the part of the injured party with a view to reducing any award of damages (s 6(4)).

Exclusion or limitation of liability (s 7)

Section 7 provides that liability under the CPA 1987 cannot be limited or excluded by any contract term, notice or any other provision.

Limitation of actions (Sch 1)

Schedule 1 to the CPA 1987 adds a new s 11A to the Limitation Act 1980. Actions in respect of personal injury and loss or damage to property must be brought within three years from the date of the cause of action accruing or the date of the claimant having knowledge of the cause of action or of any previous owner having such knowledge. The three-year limit may be extended in the case of legal disability, fraud, concealment or mistake. All claims are subject to a maximum limitation period of ten years from the date of supply. A person injured nine years after a product was supplied must bring an action before the expiration of ten years and cannot claim three years from the date of injury. The ten-year time limit operates as an absolute bar to proceedings.

Breach of statutory duty

The legal framework of protection for the public from the hazards of unsafe goods is contained in the General

Product Safety Regulations 2005 (SI 2005/1803) and Part II of the CPA 1987 (see Chapter 14 ○). This aim is achieved in the following ways:

1 Creation of a criminal offence of supplying consumer goods which fail to comply with the general safety requirement.
2 Empowering the Secretary of State to make safety regulations in respect of specific types of goods (failure to comply with the regulations is a criminal offence).
3 Enabling the Secretary of State to take action in respect of unsafe goods already on the market by issuing prohibition notices, notices to warn and suspension notices (it is a criminal offence to contravene these instructions).
4 Providing a civil remedy for an individual consumer who has suffered loss or damage as a result of a trader's failure to comply with safety regulations. For example, a child who is injured by a toy which contravenes the safety regulations will be able to sue the manufacturer for breach of statutory duty. There are two advantages to this kind of action: the child can claim compensation even if he received the toy as a gift, and he does not have to prove that the manufacturer acted negligently.

The criminal liability imposed by the General Product Safety Regulations 2005 will be examined in more detail in Chapter 14 ○.

Defective services – generally

The law of negligence has an important application to the provision of services. It opens up a remedy to those who are strangers to the contract for services but nevertheless have suffered a loss as a result of the contractor's negligence. Thus, the principle established in *Donoghue v Stevenson* (1932) applies not just to manufacturers but also to repairers who carry out their work carelessly. If a person is contracted to maintain and repair a lift, for example, he owes a legal duty, quite separate from his contractual obligations, to those using the lift to exercise reasonable care in his work.

Liability for physical injury or damage caused by a negligent act is well established. But what is the position of a person whose job involves giving professional advice? Clearly, he owes a duty to the person who has engaged

his services, but does it extend to others who may have acted on his statements? In the last 40 years or so, the courts have developed the *Donoghue v Stevenson* principle to encompass negligent statements which cause financial loss. Professional groups, such as solicitors, accountants, bankers and surveyors, have felt the full impact of the change in judicial attitudes in this area of negligence liability. In this section, we will consider the fast-developing area of law referred to as professional negligence. Prior to 1963, it was generally accepted that, in the absence of fraud, liability for making careless statements which caused financial loss depended on the existence of a contractual or fiduciary relationship between the parties. If the statement was made fraudulently, the injured party could recover damages for the tort of deceit. This view of the limited scope of a professional person's liability for careless statements is illustrated by the following case.

Candler v Crane, Christmas & Co (1951)

The defendants, a firm of accountants, prepared a company's balance sheet and accounts, knowing that they were going to be used by the managing director to persuade the claimant, Candler, to invest money in the company. Relying on the accounts, the claimant invested £2,000, which he lost when the company was wound up a year later. The claimant sued the defendants in negligence, alleging that the accounts had been prepared carelessly and did not accurately represent the true state of the company's affairs. The Court of Appeal held (Denning LJ dissenting) that the defendants were not liable to the claimant because, in the absence of any contractual or fiduciary relationship, they did not owe him a duty of care. In a powerful dissenting judgment, Denning LJ argued that the defendants did owe the claimant a duty of care. In his opinion:

Accountants owe a duty of care not only to their own clients but also to all those whom they know will rely on their accounts in the transactions for which those accounts are prepared.

The duty of care arose from the close relationship between the parties and it followed, therefore, that no duty would be owed to complete strangers. Denning LJ had to wait 12 years for his arguments to be accepted.

The new judicial approach to negligent statements was heralded in a case involving bankers' references.

Hedley Byrne & Co Ltd v Heller and Partners Ltd (1963)

Hedley Byrne was a firm of advertising agents and Easipower Ltd was one of its clients. Before placing advertising contracts on behalf of Easipower in circumstances which involved giving credit, Hedley Byrne instituted enquiries about Easipower's creditworthiness. Hedley Byrne asked its own bank, the National Provincial Bank Ltd, to obtain a reference from Easipower's bankers, Heller and Partners. Heller's reference, which was headed 'without responsibility on the part of the bank or its officials', stated that Easipower was 'a respectably constituted company considered good for its ordinary business engagements'. Relying on this satisfactory reply, Hedley Byrne executed advertising contracts for Easipower, but lost £17,000 when Easipower went into liquidation. Hedley Byrne sued Heller for the amount of the financial loss suffered as a result of the negligent preparation of the banker's reference. The House of Lords held that Heller and Partners were protected by the disclaimer of liability. Their Lordships then considered (*obiter dicta*) what the legal position would have been if the disclaimer had not been used. They all agreed that there could be liability for negligent misstatement causing financial loss, even in the absence of a contractual or fiduciary relationship (the majority decision in *Candler v Crane, Christmas & Co* was disapproved and the dissenting judgment of Denning LJ approved).

Comment. The disclaimer which so successfully protected Heller from liability would now be subject to the test of reasonableness set out in s 2(2) of the Unfair Contract Terms Act 1977. It is unlikely that such a disclaimer could be justified as reasonable.

In the *Hedley Byrne* case, their Lordships recognised a new type of liability: they indicated that damages could be received for careless statements. However, they were careful to avoid unleashing a Pandora's box of litigation. They ruled that the existence of a duty of care in respect of negligent misstatements was dependent on a 'special relationship' between the parties. Lord Morris described the relationship in the following terms:

> If someone possessed of a special skill undertakes, quite irrespective of contract, to apply that skill for the assistance of another person who relies on such skill, a duty of care will arise. Furthermore, if, in a sphere in which a person is so placed that others could reasonably rely on his judgment or his skill, or on his ability to make careful inquiry, a person takes it on himself to give

information or advice to, or allows his information or advice to be passed on to, another person who, as he knows or should know, will place reliance on it, then a duty of care will arise.

Their Lordships made it clear that a duty of care in respect of a negligent statement would only be owed to persons who the maker of the statement knows will rely on it and where the maker of the statement knows of the use to which it will be put (knowledge test). The duty of care would not extend to those who the maker of the statement might foresee would rely on the statement (foresight test). Although the *Hedley Byrne* case involved a banker, it is clear that the rule applies equally to the advice given by other professionals. We shall examine how the *Hedley Byrne* rule has been developed in relation to three particular professional groups: lawyers, accountants, and valuers and surveyors.

Lawyers

The liability of a legal adviser used to depend on the nature of the work he was engaged on. The decision of the House of Lords in *Rondel v Worsley* (1967) established that a barrister owed no duty of care to clients for whom he acted as advocate. In *Saif Ali v Sydney Mitchell & Co* (1978) the House extended the immunity from legal action to protect solicitors acting as advocates, but limited it so as to protect only pretrial work closely associated with the conduct of a trial. When it came to work outside of court, however, both branches of the legal profession could be held accountable in the tort of negligence. However, in *Arthur Hall and Co v Simons* (2000) the House of Lords decided that the immunity from liability for the negligent conduct of a case in court, as set out in *Rondel v Worsley* and explained in *Saif Ali v Sydney Mitchell & Co*, could no longer be justified. The immunity has now been removed in respect of both civil and criminal proceedings.

The duties owed by a solicitor to third parties are illustrated by the following cases.

Ross v Caunters (1979)

Mrs Ross was an intended beneficiary under a will drawn up on the testator's behalf by Caunters, a firm of solicitors. Caunters failed to advise the testator that attestation by a beneficiary or a beneficiary's spouse invalidates the gift. Mr Ross witnessed the will, and when the testator died the legacy to Mrs Ross was declared invalid. The court held that a solicitor owes a duty of care not just to his client, in this case the testator, but also to third parties, such as Mrs Ross, who were intended to be benefited by his work. Mrs Ross succeeded in her action.

White v Jones (1995)

A father quarrelled with his two daughters and cut them out of his will. A few months later the father changed his mind and instructed his solicitor to change his will and to give each of the daughters £9,000. The father died two months later before the solicitor had completed the changes to the will. The daughters did not receive the intended legacy because of their solicitor's delay in carrying out their father's instructions. The daughters succeeded in their action against the solicitor, even though they had not relied on the solicitor's skill. Lord Goff in the House of Lords took the view that a duty of care should be owed to beneficiaries under a will for reasons of 'practical justice'. 'If such a duty is not recognised, the only persons who might have a valid claim (i.e. the testator and his estate) have suffered no loss, and the only person who has suffered a loss (i.e. the disappointed beneficiary) has no claim.'

Accountants and auditors

The extent of an accountant's liability to non-clients was the subject of Lord Denning's influential judgment in *Candler v Crane, Christmas & Co* (1951). He expressed the opinion that a duty of care was owed only to third parties of whom they had knowledge; it did not extend to strangers. This view is echoed in the 'special relationship' restriction on liability laid down in the *Hedley Byrne* case. But in a subsequent case involving accountants, Woolf J broadened the scope of liability to include persons of whom the accountants had no prior knowledge.

JEB Fasteners Ltd v Marks, Bloom & Co (1983)

The defendants, a firm of accountants, prepared the accounts of a client company called JEB Fasteners. The audit report inflated the value of the company's stock and, as a result, a misleading picture of the company's financial health was given. The accounts were shown to the claimants who later took over the company. The claimants sued the defendants to recover the money they had spent in keeping the ailing company afloat. Woolf J found that the claimants had taken over the company in order to secure the services of its directors. They would have bought the company even if they had been aware of its true financial position. The defendants were not liable because their negligence was not the cause of the claimants' loss.

Comment. This case is significant because the judge accepted that an accountant could owe a duty of care to a person of whom he had no actual knowledge but where it was reasonably foreseeable that such a person would see the accounts and rely on them. The Court of Appeal upheld Woolf J's decision that the defendants were not liable because of the lack of a causal connection between the defendants' alleged carelessness and the claimants' loss. It was, therefore, unnecessary to consider Woolf J's views on the scope of an accountant's liability when auditing company accounts.

More recently, the courts have retreated from the foresight test advocated by Woolf J in *JEB Fasteners* and reaffirmed the requirement of knowledge of the user of the statement and the purpose to which it will be put to establish liability.

Caparo Industries plc v Dickman (1990)

Caparo, which already held shares in Fidelity plc, acquired more shares in the company and later made a take-over bid on the strength of accounts prepared by the defendant auditors. Caparo alleged that the accounts were inaccurate in that they showed a pre-tax profit of £1.3 million when there had been a loss of £400,000. Caparo claimed that, if they had known the true situation, they would not have made a bid at the price they did, and may not have made a bid at all. They argued that they were owed a duty of care as new investors and as existing shareholders, who in reliance on the accounts had bought more shares. The House of Lords held that no duty was owed by auditors to members of the public in general who might invest in a company in reliance on published accounts. Although it was fore-seeable that the accounts might be used by members of the public contemplating investing in the company, foreseeability alone was not sufficient to create liability. If it were otherwise, auditors might face almost unlimited liability. The purpose of preparing audited accounts under the Companies Act 1985 is to provide shareholders with certain information so that they can exercise their rights in respect of the company, i.e. voting at company meetings. The auditors did not owe a duty of care to individual shareholders, such as Caparo (which used the informa-tion for a quite different purpose), but to shareholders as a body. The auditors were, therefore, not liable.

Comment. This judgment confirms that liability for a negligent statement causing economic loss is based on knowledge of the persons relying on the statement and the likely purpose to which it will be put. If during a con-tested takeover bid the directors and financial advisers of a victim company make express statements to an identifiable bidder intending them to be relied upon, there will be sufficient proximity to establish a duty of care (*Morgan Crucible Co plc v Hill Samuel Bank Ltd* (1991)).

The law relating to the duty of care owed by profes-sionals, such as accountants and auditors, is still being developed. The following cases are examples of how the extent of liability is being tested.

Coulthard v Neville Russell (1998)

A firm of accountants sought to have a statement of claim in negligence against them struck out. It was alleged that they had failed to advise the directors of a company that a transaction that they intended to carry out might be in breach of the financial assistance provi-sions of the Companies Act 1985. The Court of Appeal refused to strike out the claim as there was an arguable case. The courts may be prepared to extend liability to omissions as well as positive statements.

Yorkshire Enterprise Ltd v Robson Rhodes (1998)

The claimants, who were providers of venture capital, invested £250,000 in a shopfitting company, which 18 months later went into liquidation. The claimants,

having lost most of their investment, brought an action for damages against the shopfitters' auditors, claiming that they had relied on negligent misstatements con-tained in the audited accounts and in letters sent to the claimants. The main problem with the accounts was that the provision for bad debts was inadequate with the result that the shopfitting company appeared to be pro-fitable when, in fact, it was not. The High Court held that the defendant auditors were liable. They were aware of the claimants as potential investors and the use to which the accounts would be put. The claimants were not contributory negligent in relying on the information contained in the accounts and subsequent letters, without instituting their own enquiries. They were entitled to take the information they received at face value.

Royal Bank of Scotland plc v Bannerman Johnstone Maclay (a firm) (2003)

RBS lent over £33 million to APC Ltd, most of which it lost when APC went into administrative receivership. RBS claimed to have made its lending decisions on the basis of accounts which had been audited by the defendant accountants, BJM. BJM had prepared APC's accounts in their capacity as the company's auditors but they had been provided to RBS in compliance with obligations set out in overdraft facility letters. In defend-ing RBS's claim, BJM argued that they did not owe a duty of care to RBS as RBS could not prove that BJM had intended that RBS should rely on the accounts to make further loans. The Scottish Court of Session (Outer House) held that it was not necessary to prove that the auditor intended the financial institution to rely on the financial statements prepared by that auditor for a duty of care to exist. It was enough to show that the person making the information or advice available knew that it would be passed to a third party for a specific purpose and was likely to be relied upon. The test is whether the person has knowledge of user and use. The fact that BJM had prepared the accounts for a statutory purpose did not mean that they could not assume responsibility for the accounts in relation to the use made of them by RBS. BJM could have included a disclaimer in relation to RBS but they had not done so.

Comment. As a response to the *Bannerman* case, the Institute of Chartered Accountants in England and Wales (ICAEW) has provided guidance to its members about the purpose of audit reports and the potential liability to third parties. The Guidance (Audit 01/03 as amended) makes it clear that auditors assume responsibility for their audit report to shareholders under the Companies

Act 2006 and that, in the absence of a disclaimer, courts may take the view that the auditor has also assumed responsibility to third parties. The ICAEW recommends the inclusion of the following disclaimer in audit reports:

> This report is made solely to the company's members, as a body, in accordance with [Sections 495 and 496/ Sections 495, 496 and 497*] of the Companies Act 2006. Our audit work has been undertaken so that we might state to the company's members those matters we are required to state to them in an auditor's report and for no other purpose. To the fullest extent permitted by law, we do not accept or assume responsibility to anyone other than the company and the company's members as a body, for our audit work, for this report, or for the opinions we have formed.
>
> *Include reference to Section 497 if the company is quoted.

Sayers v Clarke-Walker (a firm) (2002)

The claimant (S) alleged that the defendant firm of accountants (CW) had acted negligently in that they did not give him proper advice about the tax implications of buying a substantial shareholding in a company. The trial judge held that CW had been negligent in failing to structure the purchase in such a way that S's liability for tax would be minimised. The defendants based their appeal in part on S's failure to act on CW's (and his solicitor's) advice to obtain specialist independent financial advice. The Court of Appeal rejected the defence. This kind of advice was within the competence of a general firm of accountants. S was entitled to expect that CW would act as ordinarily competent accountants would have acted, i.e. to have advised S to structure the purchase in such a way as to minimise tax liabilities.

Valuers and surveyors

The scope of liability for negligent statements by valuers and surveyors was considered in the following cases.

Yianni v Edwin Evans & Sons (1981)

The claimants agreed to buy a house for £15,000 with the aid of a £12,000 mortgage from the Halifax Building Society. The building society instructed the defendants, a firm of surveyors and valuers, to value the house for

them. Although the claimants had to pay for the valuation, the contract was actually between the building society and the valuers. The building society made it clear that it did not accept responsibility for the valuers' report and that prospective purchasers were advised to have an independent survey carried out. The defendants' valuation report indicated that the house was satisfactory security for a £12,000 mortgage. After the claimants had purchased the property, they discovered structural defects which would cost £18,000 to put right. The claimants successfully sued the defendants in negligence. Despite the standard building society warning, at the time only 10–15 per cent of purchasers had independent surveys carried out. It was reasonable, therefore, that the defendants should have the claimants in contemplation as persons who were likely to rely on their valuation. The relationship between the parties gave rise to a duty of care. Accordingly, the valuers were held liable.

Smith v Eric S Bush and Harris v Wyre Forest District Council (1989)

In a twin appeal, the House of Lords had to consider the scope of valuers' and surveyors' liability for negligence and the effectiveness of any disclaimer of liability. The facts of the two cases were similar. The details of the *Harris* case are as follows. The claimants, Mr and Mrs Harris, were a young couple buying their first house. They applied to the council for a mortgage. They filled in an application and paid £22 for a valuation to be carried out. The application form contained a disclaimer which stated that the valuation was confidential and intended solely for the benefit of the council and no responsibility was accepted for the value and condition of the house. Applicants were advised to obtain their own survey. The council instructed its own in-house surveyor to inspect the property. He valued the house at the asking price and recommended a mortgage, subject to minor conditions. When the claimants tried to sell the house three years later, they discovered that it was subject to settlement and, as a result, the property was unsaleable. The House of Lords found in favour of the claimants and awarded them £12,000. Their Lordships held that a valuer owes a duty to purchasers to exercise reasonable care in carrying out a valuation. Furthermore, the disclaimer contained in the application form was ineffective under the Unfair Contract Terms Act 1977 since it did not satisfy the requirement of reasonableness. It was not fair and reasonable for valuers to impose on purchasers the risk of loss arising as a result of their incompetence or carelessness for the following reasons:

1 the parties were not of equal bargaining strength (the disclaimer was imposed on the claimants and they had no real power to object);

2 it was not reasonably practicable for the claimants to have obtained their own survey report (they were first-time buyers who could not easily afford to pay twice for the same service);

3 the task undertaken by the surveyor was not particularly difficult and it was not unreasonable to expect a valuer to take responsibility for the fairly elementary degree of skill and care involved; and

4 surveyors will carry insurance. If they are denied the opportunity of excluding their liability, insurance premiums will rise and the increased costs will be passed on to house purchasers in higher fees. It was fairer that the risk be distributed among all house purchasers by a modest increase in fees rather than the whole risk falling on one unlucky purchaser.

Other torts relevant to business

Trespass

The tort of trespass is one of the oldest torts. It takes three forms: trespass to the person, trespass to land and trespass to goods. Trespass to the person comprises three separate actions: battery, assault and false imprisonment. Battery is a direct and intentional application of force against the person. The slightest touch can amount to a battery. Assault involves putting a person in fear of a battery. Examples include swinging a punch, even if it does not connect, or pointing a gun at somebody. False imprisonment consists of unlawfully restraining a person from going wherever he or she wants, e.g. unlawful detention by a store detective who mistakenly believes that a customer has been shoplifting. Trespass to land can be defined as unlawful interference with the possession of someone's land. Straying off a footpath is an example of trespass to land. Trespass to goods is the wrongful interference with a person's possession of goods. This tort may be committed by destroying another's goods, stealing or simply moving them from one place to another.

Conversion

The tort of conversion involves doing some act in relation to another's goods which is inconsistent with the other's right to the goods. The wrongful act must constitute a challenge to, or a denial of, the claimant's title to the goods. Examples of conversion include stealing goods and reselling them, wrongfully refusing to return goods or destroying them. Conversion is one aspect of the tort of trespass to goods: both are examples of wrongful interference with goods which is now subject to legislation in the shape of the Torts (Interference with Goods) Act 1977.

Nuisance

There are two kinds of nuisance: public and private. Public nuisance (an act or omission which causes discomfort or inconvenience to a class of Her Majesty's subjects) is essentially a crime. However, individuals who have been particularly affected by the nuisance may bring an action in tort. Polluting a river could amount to a public nuisance. In two recent cases the House of Lords has signalled the death knell of the common law crime of public nuisance (*R* v *Rimmington*, *R* v *Goldstein* (2006)). Although their Lordships did not believe that it was open to them to abolish the common law crime of public nuisance (only Parliament could do this), they recognised that most kinds of conduct covered by the common law were now subject to statutory provisions, such as the Environmental Protection Act 1990 (noise, smoke, fumes) (see further below) and the Water Resources Act 1991 (water pollution).

Private nuisance consists of unreasonable interference with a person's use or enjoyment of land. The following requirements must be present to establish liability for a private nuisance:

■ an indirect interference with the use or enjoyment of land, e.g. by smoke, smells, noise;

■ either physical damage to land or interference with the land causing loss of enjoyment or discomfort; and

■ interference which is unreasonable.

In order to determine the question of unreasonableness, the court will consider both the conduct of the defendant and the effect of that conduct on the claimant. Factors which may be considered include:

■ *The character of the locality in which the interference occurs.* In the words of Thesinger LJ in **Sturges v Bridgman** (1879): 'What would be a nuisance in Belgrave Square would not necessarily be so in Bermondsey.'

- *The duration of the interference.* A single occurrence will not normally amount to a nuisance; a certain degree of continuity is required. However, if the interference is of only a short duration, it is less likely to constitute a nuisance.
- *Malice on the part of the defendant.* Although malice is not an essential ingredient of nuisance, it may be relevant to ascertaining whether the defendant's conduct was reasonable.

A person who is in occupation of land may sue in nuisance the creator of the nuisance, the occupier of the land from which the nuisance came or, in limited circumstances, the landlord of the person in occupation. The following defences are available to the defendant:

- consent to the nuisance, but consent will not be implied because the claimant came to the nuisance;
- prescription, e.g. carrying out the acts complained of for 20 years;
- statutory authority.

A successful claimant is entitled to compensation for damage caused by the nuisance, e.g. physical damage to land or loss in value of the property. It is also usual for a claimant to seek an injunction to prevent any continuance of the nuisance. The following case provides an illustration of how the law of nuisance tries to reconcile conflicting interests over the use of land.

Bringing a civil action in the tort of nuisance is a cumbersome and very expensive way of protecting people's enjoyment of their property from pollutants such as noise. The law of statutory nuisance contained in legislation such as the Environmental Protection Act 1990, the Noise and Statutory Nuisance Act 1993, the Noise Act 1996, the Anti-Social Behaviour Act 2003 and the Clean Neighbourhoods and Environment Act 2005 provides an alternative avenue for redress in respect of activities which are either prejudicial to health or a nuisance, e.g. smoke, fumes, dust, smells and noise. Local authority environmental health officers have the power to serve abatement notices requiring the person responsible for a statutory nuisance to abate, prohibit or restrict its occurrence or recurrence. Failure to comply with such a notice is a criminal offence and could lead to a fine, in the case of an offence on industrial, trade or business premises, not exceeding £20,000. It should be noted that the Environmental Protection Act 1990 also enables a private individual who is aggrieved by a statutory nuisance to initiate proceedings in a magistrates' court to obtain a court order to abate the nuisance.

Rule in *Rylands* v *Fletcher*

The rule in *Rylands* v *Fletcher* is an example of a tort of strict liability. The rule derives from the case of *Rylands* v *Fletcher*, which was decided by the House of Lords in 1868.

Kennaway v *Thompson* (1980)

In 1972 the claimant had a house built on land next to a lake which she knew was used for power-boat racing and waterskiing. Not long after the claimant moved into her house, the club became an international centre for power-boat racing and, as a result, there was an increase in the number of days on which racing took place and larger and much noisier boats took part. The claimant sought damages for the nuisance and an injunction. The trial judge found that the interference with the claimant's enjoyment of her land had gone beyond what was reasonable and awarded damages. However, he refused to grant an injunction on the ground that it was in the public interest to allow the club to continue to provide sports facilities. The Court of Appeal allowed the claimant's appeal against the refusal to grant an injunction. An injunction was granted restricting the number of occasions on which the club could hold noisy power-boat race meetings.

Rylands v *Fletcher* (1868)

A mill owner engaged competent contractors to construct a reservoir on his land to provide water for his mill. In the course of their work, the contractors came across disused mine shafts which appeared to be blocked by earth. These old mine workings, in fact, communicated with a neighbour's coal mine. So, when the reservoir was filled up, the water escaped and flooded the coal mine. The House of Lords held that the mill owner was liable for the damage caused to his neighbour's mine, even though he had not been negligent. Blackburn J, who heard the case in the Court of Exchequer Chamber, stated the rule in the following terms: '. . . the person who for his own purposes brings on his land and collects and keeps there anything likely to do mischief if it escapes, must keep it at his peril, and if he does not do so, is *prima facie* answerable for all the damage which is a natural consequence of its escape.' Lord Cairns added in the House of Lords that the defendant must be making a non-natural use of his land.

The rule has been applied to the escape of such things as fire, electricity, gas and vibrations. The rule was subsequently considered by the House of Lords in the following case.

Cambridge Water Co Ltd v Eastern Counties Leather plc (1994)

The defendants used a solvent in their tanning business. The solvent escaped from containers and seeped into the ground beneath the works. The solvent eventually percolated into the water supply, polluting the claimant's borehole. The claimants were forced to abandon the borehole and develop new water supplies. Their claim for compensation under the rule in *Rylands v Fletcher* failed in the House of Lords on the ground that the defendants could not reasonably have foreseen that the spillage of solvent over time would contaminate the water supply. Their Lordships held that foreseeability was an essential requirement of liability under the rule in *Rylands v Fletcher*. Although this requirement limits the availability of a claim under the rule of *Rylands v Fletcher*, Lord Goff possibly expanded the scope of the rule when he stated that the storage of chemicals was a classic example of a non-natural use of land.

In a more recent case the House of Lords reviewed the scope and application of the rule in *Rylands v Fletcher* and considered whether there was still a place for the rule in English law.

Transco plc v Stockport Metropolitan Borough Council (2004)

The claimant, Transco, brought an action against the defendant council to recover the cost of remedial action to its gas main, which had been left exposed and unsupported by the collapse of an embankment. The cause of the embankment collapse was a leak of water from a service pipe from the mains supply to tanks in the basement of a block of flats owned by the defendant council. The fracture in the service pipe was undetected for a prolonged period of time and a considerable amount of water escaped from the pipe inside the block of flats and found its way to the embankment. The embankment became saturated and eventually collapsed, leaving the claimant's gas pipe exposed and at risk of cracking. The claimant did not claim that the fracture of the pipe and the escape of water was caused by lack of care by the defendant but rather based its claim on the defendant's

strict liability under the rule in *Rylands v Fletcher*. The House of Lords held that the defendant council was not liable for two reasons: the council had not brought on to its land anything likely to cause danger or mischief if it escaped, and, in piping water to the flats, it was acting as an ordinary user of land.

Comment. Their Lordships gave four main reasons for retaining the strict liability rule of *Rylands v Fletcher*: (1) there is a small category of cases in which it is just to impose liability even in the absence of fault; (2) common law rules do not exist in a vacuum, especially those which have stood for over a century, during which time Parliament had legislated on the assumption that strict liability under *Rylands v Fletcher* applied in particular circumstances; (3) the House of Lords had not accepted a departure from *Rylands v Fletcher* in the *Cambridge Water* case. 'Stop-go' was a bad approach to legal development; (4) while replacement of the strict liability rule of *Rylands v Fletcher* by fault-based liability would assimilate the laws of England and Wales with the law in Scotland, it would increase the disparity with the laws of France and Germany. Their Lordships agreed that the rule should be retained but restated with certainty and clarity. The main points are:

(i) The rule is a sub-species of nuisance, which itself is a tort based on interference by one occupier of land with the right in or enjoyment of the land of another occupier. It follows that there is no liability if the events take place on the land of a single occupier. There must be an 'escape' from one person's land to another's (*Read v J Lyons & Co Ltd* (1946)). As the rule provides a remedy for damage to land or interests in land, no claim can be brought for death or personal injury.

(ii) The rule does not apply to works constructed or conducted under statutory authority.

(iii) Unusual natural events (acts of God) and the actions of third parties, e.g. vandals, will exclude strict liability.

(iv) The rule did not apply to 'natural' uses of land. What is a non-natural use of land should be judged by contemporary standards, and a relevant guide is whether the risk was something that the occupier would be likely to have insured himself against.

Defamation

Defamation is the publication of a false statement which damages a person's reputation and tends to lower him in the estimation of right-thinking members of society or tends to make them shun or avoid that person. It takes two forms: libel and slander. Libel is defamation in a permanent form, such as writing, pictures, a film or a play. Slander is defamation in a transitory form, for example speech or gestures. Examples of defamation include a bank mistakenly 'bouncing' a customer's cheque for lack of funds, when there is plenty of money in the account, or an employer writing a damaging character reference for an employee. An important difference between libel and slander is that in the case of libel the claimant does not have to prove that he suffered damage, i.e. libel is actionable *per se*. In contrast, most slanders are actionable only on proof of damage. The exceptional situations where slander is actionable *per se* are as follows:

■ an imputation that the claimant is guilty of a criminal offence for which he could be sent to prison;

■ an imputation of unchastity made against any woman or girl;

■ an imputation that the claimant has an infectious or contagious disease so that people would avoid him; and

■ any words that suggest that the claimant is unfit to carry on his trade, business or profession.

In order to establish a case in defamation, the claimant must establish the following requirements in relation to the statement:

■ it must be false;

■ the statement must be defamatory in the sense that it lowers the claimant's reputation;

■ it must refer to the claimant; and

■ it must be published, i.e. it must be communicated to someone other than the claimant.

The law tries to strike a balance between the right of an individual to protect his reputation and society's interest in freedom of speech by providing a number of defences to an action in defamation.

1 Justification or truth. A person cannot complain about a true statement, since the effect is to reduce an inflated reputation to its proper level.

2 Fair comment on a matter of public interest. Those who place themselves in the public eye must expect honest criticism of what they do. The defence is not available where the defendant acted out of malice or spite.

3 Privilege. Statements made on some occasions, for example in Parliament or in court, are absolutely privileged

and the person whose reputation has been injured is deprived of legal redress. Some statements attract qualified privilege – for example, job references. This means that the defence is available only to the extent that the defendant acted honestly and without malice.

4 Unintentional defamation under the Defamation Act 1996. The publisher of an innocent defamation may escape liability by making an offer of amends (the publication of a correction and apology), with damages assessed by a judge.

5 Consent to publication. If the claimant has consented to the publication of the defamatory material, this will be a defence.

A successful claimant may be awarded damages or granted an injunction. Defamation is one of the few areas of the civil law where juries are still commonly used. There has been considerable criticism in recent years of high awards made by juries in defamation cases, especially when compared with awards in personal injury cases. Under the Courts and Legal Services Act 1990, the Court of Appeal may now substitute its own award for that of a jury award which it deems inadequate or excessive. The Defamation Act 1996 provides for a new summary procedure for defamation cases, with judges assessing the damages rather than a jury.

An injunction may be granted, in addition to an award of damages, to prevent either initial or further publication of the defamatory material.

The limitation period for defamation claims was reduced from three years to one year by the Defamation Act 1996. In *Loutchansky* v *Times Newspapers (No 2)* (2002), the Court of Appeal held that where defamatory material is published on the Internet and is not removed, there is a continuing publication. The court rejected the rule applied in the USA that time runs from first publication.

Injurious or malicious falsehood is a separate tort which is related to defamation. It consists of maliciously making a false statement about a person or his property, which is calculated to cause damage, and damage is suffered as a result (see further, Chapter 15 ○).

Economic torts

The term 'economic torts' is often used to describe a number of torts which seek to protect business interests. Some of these torts are considered in outline below.

Inducement of breach of contract

This tort consists of one person (A) inducing another (B) to break his contract with a third person (C). C can sue B for breach of contract, but C can also sue A in tort.

Lumley v Gye (1853)

Gye persuaded a singer to break her exclusive contract to sing at Lumley's theatre and to sing for him instead. It was held that Lumley was entitled to sue Gye in tort for inducing a breach of the singer's contract.

A modern example of the tort is where trade union officials instruct their members to take industrial action. If the union officials act within limits contained in recent legislation, e.g. holding a secret postal ballot of its members, any liability in tort will be covered by a statutory immunity.

Conspiracy

This tort consists of an agreement between two or more persons to do an act which is intended to injure another person and does result in damage. There are two forms of tortious conspiracy: conspiracy where the means used are lawful, and agreements where the means used are unlawful.

1 Conspiracy using lawful means. It is not necessary to show that the conspirators used unlawful means; the tort encompasses conduct which would be perfectly lawful if committed by an individual acting alone. However, the claimant must be able to prove that the conspirators intended to injure him. If the conspirators intended to further or protect their own interests, there can be no liability.

Crofter Hand Woven Harris Tweed Co Ltd v Veitch (1942)

The defendants, officials of the Transport and General Workers Union, imposed a ban on cheap imports of yarn on to the island of Lewis by the claimant company and any subsequent export of Harris tweed made from the yarn. The union's instructions were carried out by docker members of the union without any breach of contract on their part, so the claimant company sued instead for conspiracy. The House of Lords held that, as the union's action was intended to protect the legitimate interests of its members rather than to inflict injury on the claimants, the union officials were not liable in conspiracy.

2 Conspiracy using unlawful means. If the conspirators intentionally injure a person and use means which are unlawful, i.e. a tort or a crime, they will not escape liability by showing that their purpose was to protect their own interests (*Lonrho plc v Fayed* (1991)).

The development of 'economic torts' was considered recently by the House of Lords in *OBG Ltd v Allan* (2007). The House considered three appeals which were concerned with claims in tort for economic loss caused by intentional acts, including breach of contract, causing loss by unlawful means, interference with contractual relations, breach of confidence and conversion. Their Lordships rejected the notion of a unified theory of economic torts, which treated procuring a breach of contract as one aspect of a more general tort of interference with contractual rights. The tort of causing loss by unlawful means differed from the tort of inducing breach of contract in a number of ways. Any attempt to create a union between them should be dissolved and the independence of the two causes of action should be recognised. With respect to the tort of causing economic loss by unlawful means, the unlawful means consists of acts intended to cause loss to the claimant by interfering with the freedom of a third party in a way which is unlawful as against that third party and which is intended to cause loss to the claimant. Acts against the third party would only constitute unlawful means if they were actionable by the third party or would be if he had suffered loss.

Deceit

This tort, which is also known as fraud, consists of knowingly or recklessly making a false statement to another person who acts on it to his detriment.

Passing-off

This tort protects a trader whose competitors pass off their goods as the trader's. Examples of passing-off include using another's trade name and imitating another's goods, for example by using similar wrappings or containers. Passing-off will be considered in more detail in Chapter 15 ○.

Defences

There are several defences which are available generally to a defendant facing an action in tort. These **general defences** are:

- consent;
- contributory negligence;
- statutory or common law justification;
- necessity;
- illegality.

Consent

Consent – or assumption of risk, as it is sometimes known – is a complete defence to an action in tort. Consent may arise either from an express agreement to run the risk of injury or may be implied from the claimant's conduct. An example of express agreement is where a patient signs a consent form before an operation. If this formality were not carried out, the surgeon could be sued for trespass to the person (battery). Implied consent is often referred to as *volenti non fit injuria* (no harm is done to one who is willing). Participants in a boxing match, for example, are deemed to have consented to the intentional infliction of harm which would otherwise amount to a trespass. The defence of consent was of greater importance in the 19th century when it was used by employers to defeat claims by their employees for injuries suffered during the course of employment caused by the employer's negligence. However, the significance of the defence in employment cases diminished greatly as a result of the decision of the House of Lords in *Smith v Baker & Sons* (1891). Their Lordships held that an employee who continued working despite knowing that he ran the risk of injury from stones falling from an overhead crane was not *volenti*. Consent cannot be inferred from knowledge of the risk: it must also be shown that the claimant freely and voluntarily accepted the risk. So, to establish the defence today, the defendant must prove that the claimant not only had full knowledge of the risk but also freely consented to running the risk.

Morris v *Murray* (1990)

The claimant and defendant had engaged in a prolonged drinking session before taking a flight in a light aircraft piloted by the defendant. The plane crashed, the defendant pilot was killed and the claimant was seriously injured. The Court of Appeal held that the claimant's action against the deceased pilot's estate was barred by *volenti*.

Conduct which might give rise to the defence of consent is also likely to involve contributory negligence (see further below). These days the courts are more likely to make a finding of contributory negligence which has the effect of apportioning fault between the parties, rather than consent which is a complete defence.

The defence of consent is not normally available in what are known as 'rescue cases'. These are situations where a claimant is injured while attempting to rescue someone or something from a dangerous situation caused by the defendant's negligence. Provided that the claimant's actions are reasonable in the circumstances, the defences of consent and contributory negligence will not apply.

Haynes v *Harwood* (1935)

The claimant policeman was injured trying to stop runaway horses pulling a van along a crowded street. The defendant had left the horses and van alone and a boy had caused them to bolt. It was held that the claimant could recover damages for his injuries. The defences of *volenti* and contributory negligence (below) did not apply.

Contributory negligence

Before 1945 contributory negligence was a complete defence to liability in tort. However, the Law Reform (Contributory Negligence) Act 1945 modified this harsh rule by providing for apportionment of blame between the claimant and defendant. Section 1(1) provides as follows:

> Where any person suffers damage as the result partly of his own fault and partly of the fault of any other person or persons, a claim in respect of that damage shall not be defeated by reason of the fault of the person suffering the damage, but the damages recoverable in respect thereof shall be reduced to such an extent as the court thinks just and equitable having regard to the claimant's share in the responsibility for the damage.

The effect of the provision is that any award of damages may be reduced to the extent that the claimant was to blame for the injury or loss. For example, if the court assesses the claimant's loss as £100,000, but finds that he was 25 per cent to blame for what happened, his damages will be reduced by 25 per cent and he will receive £75,000 damages. Failure to wear a seat belt is contributory negligence and can result in a 25 per cent deduction if wearing the belt would have prevented the injury, and a 15 per cent deduction if the belt would have reduced the injury (*Froom v Butcher* (1975)). Another illustration of the application of contributory negligence principles is provided by the following Court of Appeal case.

Eagle (by her litigation friend) v Chambers (2003)

The claimant (E), who was 17, sustained serious injuries when she was struck by a car driven by the defendant (C). E was walking down a dual carriageway late at night in light clothes. The road was straight and the street lighting good. E was in an emotional state and was not walking in a straight line. Bystanders and other motorists had noticed her and, being concerned for her safety, had tried to persuade her to stop. At the time of the accident C was driving at about the speed limit of 30 mph. He failed a roadside breath test but when tested later at the police station he was under the limit. The trial judge found that, had C exercised the standards expected of a reasonable driver, he would have seen E earlier and been able to avoid her. C had been negligent. The judge also found that E was partly to blame for the accident; she had drunk too much, was emotional and had placed herself in a dangerous position. She was 60 per cent to blame for the accident and her damages would be reduced by 60 per cent. E appealed against the judge's finding of 60 per cent contribution. C accepted that E was not drunk and the most that could be said from the evidence was that she had probably had a drink or two. The Court of Appeal reduced the level of E's contribution from 60 per cent to 40 per cent for the following reasons:

- A car is a potentially dangerous weapon and as a result a heavy burden of responsibility should be placed on drivers to take care. Drivers should look out for pedestrians. The road in question was in the middle of a busy seaside resort where you would expect to find pedestrians at that time of night. The trial judge had concluded that C would have failed to see and avoid any pedestrian, including one whose conduct could not be criticised.
- E had been careless for her own safety, justifying a finding of contributory negligence. However, it could not be said that she had been more to blame than the driver. She had not staggered or changed direction suddenly. C's conduct was much more causatively potent than E's behaviour.

In a recent case the High Court has considered whether continuing to smoke may constitute contributory negligence in respect of a claim relating to a death from lung cancer attributable to another cause.

Badger v Ministry of Defence (2006)

Mr Badger died of lung cancer in 2002 at the age 63. He had been employed by the Ministry of Defence as a boiler maker from 1954 to 1987 and in the course of his work he had been exposed to asbestos which was causative of the lung cancer. The Ministry of Defence accepted primary liability for Mr Badger's death but claimed that the award of damages should be reduced by 25 per cent because Mr Badger had not given up smoking. The High Court held that Mr Badger's failure to stop smoking after receiving specific advice about the effect of smoking on his health amounted to contributory negligence and that his damages should be reduced by 20 per cent. There was no contributory negligence when he started to smoke in 1955 because at the time the connection between smoking and ill health was not widely accepted. However, the government began to place health warnings on cigarette packets from the early 1970s and a reasonably prudent person would have given up smoking. Mr Badger's failure to do so amounted to contributory negligence: the reduction in damages should be calculated from the time when he should have stopped smoking.

Comment. Although the *Badger* case did not involve a situation where the exposure to asbestos had occurred while being employed by a number of different employers, it is worth noting here the provisions of the Compensation Act 2006. The Act provides for joint and several liability in cases where a claimant has contracted mesothelioma as a result of negligent exposure to asbestos. Claimants will be able to sue any of the responsible persons and receive full compensation from that person, who will be able to claim contributions from others who were also responsible for causing the mesothelioma.

Contributory negligence does not just apply to actions based in the tort of negligence. Section 4 of the 1945 Act defined 'fault' very broadly so as to include most forms of liability in tort. The only major torts for which the defence is not available are deceit and conversion.

Statutory or common law justification

A person may have a good defence to an action in tort if he can show that his acts are covered by statutory authority. The Police and Criminal Evidence Act 1984, for example, sets out police powers of arrest, entry and search. If these powers are exercised lawfully, the Act will provide a good defence to an action in tort. There may also be justification at common law for tortious acts. Self-defence and chastisement of a child by a parent are both defences to the tort of trespass to the person, provided that the force used is reasonable.

Necessity

If a person commits a tort but only in order to prevent a greater harm from occurring, he may be able to raise the defence of necessity. The defendant must be able to show that there is an imminent threat of danger to person or property and that his actions were a reasonable response to the circumstances. Necessity was successfully raised by prison officers who forcibly fed a suffragette who was on hunger strike (**Leigh v Gladstone** (1909)) and by an oil company facing an action for nuisance in respect of a discharge of oil from one of its ships into an estuary (**Esso Petroleum Co Ltd v Southport Corporation** (1955)).

Illegality

It is a general principle of law that a person will not be able to maintain a cause of action if he has to rely on conduct which is illegal or contrary to public policy. This principle is expressed in the Latin phrase of *ex turpi causa non oritur actio*. The following case is an example of how the defence of illegality applies in the law of tort.

Thackwell v Barclays Bank (1986)

Thackwell brought an action against the bank for conversion of a cheque to which he claimed to be entitled. The cheque represented the proceeds of fraud against a finance company in which Thackwell had been a party. The court held that Thackwell's claim was barred by illegality. It was contrary to public policy to allow him to enjoy the proceeds of his fraud.

Remedies

The remedies which are generally available in respect of tortious conduct are damages and an injunction. Damages consist of a payment of money by the defendant to the claimant. Tort damages are intended to be compensatory, i.e. the aim is to put the injured party in the position he would have been in had he not sustained the wrong. In some situations the courts will award non-compensatory damages. Nominal damages, for example, will be awarded in respect of torts which are actionable *per se*, e.g. trespass to land, where the claimant cannot show that he has suffered any loss. Exemplary damages, which are designed to punish the defendant, are available only in certain special cases, e.g. where there is arbitrary, unconstitutional or oppressive action by government servants such as false imprisonment by the police.

An injunction is a discretionary order of the court requiring the person to cease committing a tort. There are different kinds of injunction. An interim injunction is a temporary order which can be granted pending a full trial of the action. A *quia timet* injunction may be ordered before any damage is done as a preventative measure. A prohibitory injunction will stop the defendant from committing a tort, while a mandatory injunction requires the defendant to take positive steps to stop a tort from being committed. If the defendant fails to obey the injunction, he or she will be in contempt of court and may be dealt with by way of fine or imprisonment.

Limitation of actions

The right to bring legal action does not last indefinitely. The time limits within which action must be brought are covered by the Limitation Act 1980 and are as follows:

1 An action in tort must normally be brought within six years of the date when the cause of action accrued (s 2). The period of limitation normally runs from the date when the tort was committed or when the damage occurred. The Latent Damage Act 1986 amended the Limitation Act 1980 to provide for an extended period of limitation in 'latent damage' negligence cases (not involving personal injury). Under s 14A of the 1980 Act, the period of limitation may be extended by three years, with the three-year period starting from when the claimant had the knowledge required to bring an action for damages in respect of the relevant damage and a right to bring an action. A recent House of Lords case considered what constitutes the relevant 'knowledge' under s 14.

Haward v Fawcetts (A Firm) (2006)

Haward acquired a controlling interest in a company in 1994. He was aware from the outset that the company would require the injection of further capital, but further significant investments in 1995, 1996, 1997 and 1998 did not improve matters and the company failed in 1998. Fawcetts, a firm of accountants, had advised Haward throughout. Haward then sought the advice of a specialist in corporate rescue and in May 1999 he began to question the soundness of the financial advice he had received from Fawcetts. The claim for negligence was launched in December 2001. Applying the basic six-year rule, the claims for losses arising in 1994 and 1995 were time-barred. Haward sought to rely on s 14A to extend the limitation period to cover these losses. He claimed that he did not have the requisite knowledge until December 1998 and therefore he had commenced his claim within the three-year period. The House of Lords held that Haward did have the required knowledge before December 1998. The requisite knowledge was knowledge of facts constituting the essence of the complaint, not when Haward first realised that he might have a claim in negligence against Fawcetts. Time started to run from the point at which Haward knew enough to justify investigating the possibility that Fawcetts' advice had been defective and he had this knowledge much earlier than December 1998. The scale of the company's losses which necessitated much more substantial injections of cash than had been expected should have alerted Haward to the possibility that Fawcetts had been negligent.

2 An action in negligence, nuisance or breach of statutory duty for damages for personal injury must be brought within three years (s 11). The period of limitation runs from the date when the cause of the action accrued (i.e. the date of injury) or the date of the claimant's knowledge that the injury was significant and that it was attributable in whole or in part to the acts or omissions which are alleged to constitute the negligence, nuisance or breach of duty. These time limits may be extended as follows:

■ where fraud, concealment or mistake is alleged, time does not run until the claimant has discovered the fraud, concealment or mistake or could with reasonable diligence have discovered it;

■ if the claimant is under a disability, such as minority or mental incapacity, the time limits do not start to operate until the disability is removed, i.e. in the case of a minor, on reaching the age of 18.

The application of s 11 was considered in the following case.

A v Hoare (2008)

In this case, which involved six appeals, the House of Lords had to decide whether claims for sexual assault and abuse which had taken place many years before proceedings were started were barred under the Limitation Act 1980. The claimants were seeking to bring themselves within s 11 of the Act by arguing that their knowledge had not arisen within the three-year time limit laid down for claims for personal injury caused by negligence, nuisance or breach of statutory duty, or that the court should exercise its discretion under s 33 in their favour. The difficulty was that in an earlier case, *Stubbings* v *Webb* (1993), the House had decided that s 11 did not apply to cases involving deliberate assault. Their Lordships held (overruling *Stubbings* v *Webb*) that actions for personal injury for an intentional trespass to the person fell within s 11 and therefore the court had a discretion under s 33 to extend the time limit.

The Defamation Act 1996 reduced the limitation period for actions in defamation and malicious falsehood from three years to one year. The court can exercise its discretion to allow a later claim if this is reasonable.

Self-test questions/activities

1 In what circumstances does the law impose liability on a person who is not at fault? How can liability without fault be justified?

2 'Death, injury and loss from manufacture is a commonplace in our society, but compensation for it is pure roulette . . .' *Sunday Times*, 27 June 1976.

 Discuss with reference to the law as it stands at present. How did implementation of the Consumer Protection Act 1987 improve the rights of consumers in respect of faulty goods?

3 Steven, an accountant, returning home from his office, calls into a pub for a relaxing drink. He bumps into Paul, an old school friend, whom he has not seen for many years. During the course of the conversation over a number of pints, it emerges that Paul has recently inherited a substantial sum of money and is interested in investing in local businesses. Steven mentions that one of his clients, Precarious Ltd, is seeking financial backing and would make an attractive investment. By chance, he has a copy of the company's accounts in his briefcase which he gives to Paul. Relying on these accounts, Paul invests £10,000 in Precarious Ltd, but loses everything when Precarious goes into liquidation six months later. In fact, the accounts had been prepared negligently and did not reflect the parlous state of the company's affairs.

 Advise Paul.

4 Devise practical steps that might be taken by a person wishing to avoid liability for professional negligence.

5 Ian and John, employees of Oldtown Council, carelessly erect a temporary grandstand overlooking the finishing line at the council-owned sports arena. The grandstand collapses during an athletics event, fatally injuring several spectators.

 Discuss the civil liability of Ian and John and their employer for the accident.

6 Percy Brown's grandchildren club together to buy him a 'fully guaranteed' Warmglo Deluxe electric blanket for his 80th birthday. As the winter evenings draw in, Percy decides that he would be warmer in bed with his new electric blanket than in his draughty sitting room. He establishes a routine – he puts the blanket on for 30 minutes before he goes to bed and, despite warnings in the operating instructions, he keeps the blanket switched on at the highest setting while he reads in bed. One particularly cold January night, the electric blanket catches fire (as a result of faulty wiring), just as Percy is about to go to sleep. He suffers slight burns to his leg, but the fire causes extensive damage to his bed.

 Advise Percy.

Specimen examination questions

1 Dilip lives in a quiet residential area. Next door, Kwickbuild Ltd is carrying out extensive building work to a dilapidated old house. The builders, who are working from dawn to dusk, seven days a week, use a crane which passes over Dilip's house. Dilip and his family are annoyed by the dust, dirt and noise caused by the building work.

 Advise Dilip as to his legal position and any legal remedies he may have.

2 Mr and Mrs Sharp decide to buy a holiday cottage at Cliffville-on-Sea. They approach the Beach Building Society for a mortgage. The building society instructs

ABC Valuers and Surveyors to carry out a mortgage valuation. ABC send their staff valuer, Sandy, to carry out the survey. Despite evidence of subsidence, Sandy's valuation report is favourable. The report clearly states that it has been prepared for mortgage purposes only and is not a structural survey. Mr and Mrs Sharp, who are sent a copy of the report, decide to proceed with the purchase without undertaking their own survey, having secured the required loan. Shortly after completing the purchase, they discover that the cottage requires underpinning.

 Advise Mr and Mrs Sharp of any causes of action that may be available to them.

3 Brenda runs a small guesthouse in Morecambe and buys a new Cindy Microwave Oven from Electrical Superstores Ltd, a thriving electrical warehouse dealing in new and reconditioned goods. She pays the price of £350 by using her credit card. At the time of purchase, Brenda signs a form which includes the following statement:

'The seller shall be under no liability for any injury, loss or damage whatsoever and howsoever caused.'

Brenda did not read the form before signing it, but she did ask the sales assistant what it said. She is not sure whether she was told that it was a receipt or that it was a contract which included an exclusion clause, but she says that she paid no attention to it and signed it regardless of what she was told.

The microwave is delivered by Electrical Superstores Ltd. After a few weeks' use, Brenda notices that there is a faint burning smell when the microwave is in use. Nevertheless, she continues to use it both for her guests and for family cooking. One day her teenage student son, Roy, a talented drummer in an up-and-coming rock band, puts a ready-cooked meal in the microwave to warm up but leaves the kitchen to answer a telephone call from one of his friends. When he returns to the kitchen 20 minutes later, he discovers the microwave on fire and the fire is spreading to some of the fitted kitchen units. Roy tries to turn off the power to the microwave at the socket but he receives a severe electric shock and burns to his hands.

Roy spends a week in hospital recovering from his injuries. His hands will be scarred for life and it is unclear whether he will be able to drum at the top level in the future. Brenda's kitchen is gutted by the fire and she has to close the guesthouse for six weeks during the busy summer season. It will cost £4,000 to repair the kitchen.

The fire officer's report on the fire indicates that the microwave was not new when purchased and the cause of the fire was faulty wiring which probably occurred when the microwave was reconditioned. Electrical Superstores Ltd admits that the microwave which Brenda bought was reconditioned, but a new cleaner had inadvertently placed a 'new model' sign on top of the appliance when she was cleaning the warehouse.

Advise Brenda and Roy.

Website references

http://www.dca.gov.uk/legist/compensation.htm This archived section of the former Department for Constitutional Affairs' website provides information about the Compensation Act 2006 which contains provisions relating to negligence and breach of statutory duty and regulates claims management services. The Department

for Constitutional Affairs became part of the Ministry of Justice in May 2007.

http://www.defra.gov.uk/environment/quality The website of the Department of the Environment, Food and Rural Affairs (DEFRA) provides guidance on how to deal with noise and other forms of nuisance.

Visit **www.mylawchamber.co.uk/richesallen** to access study support resources including answers to questions in this chapter and legal updates, all linked to the **Pearson eText** version of **Keenan and Riches' Business Law** which you can **search**, **highlight** and **personalise** with your **own notes** and **bookmarks**.

Use **Case Navigator** to read in full some of the key cases referenced in this chapter with commentary and questions:

Caparo Industries plc v *Dickman* [1990]
Cambridge Water Co Ltd v *Eastern Counties Leather plc* [1994]
Tomlinson v *Congleton Borough Council and Cheshire County Council* (2004)
Transco plc v *Stockport Metropolitan Borough Council* (2004)
White v *Chief Constable of South Yorkshire Police* [1999]

Credit

At some time or another everyone makes use of credit. It may be a mortgage from a building society to buy your own home, or hire-purchase arranged by a car dealer to help you afford the latest model. When the monthly finances do not work out right, you will probably run up an overdraft at the bank. Even if it is just paying the milkman at the end of the week, you have made use of credit. People in business also rely on credit. A loan may be needed to translate a good idea into a marketable product. Established companies often have to look outside their own resources to finance expansion. Most businesses give and expect to receive a period of time in which to pay their trade bills.

Credit consists of either buying something and being given time to pay for it or borrowing money and paying it back later. The person giving the credit (the creditor) is providing service, which the borrower (the debtor) is usually required to pay for, the price being a certain rate of interest.

Credit is not a new idea. Moneylenders have been around for centuries. However, the last 30 years have witnessed a dramatic increase in the use of credit, particularly to finance private-home purchase and consumer spending on such items as cars, electrical goods and furniture. Despite the cautionary proverb, 'Neither a borrower nor a lender be', credit has several clear advantages. Most people lack the self-discipline to save up for expensive items. Credit allows them to enjoy the benefit of goods and services sooner than they otherwise would. In a period of inflation there is even the prospect

of getting them more cheaply. But the easy availability of credit can bring dangers to both sides. The problems facing the consumer are neatly summarised in a comment attributed to a county court judge: 'being persuaded by a man you don't know to sign an agreement you haven't read to buy furniture you don't need with money you haven't got'. Since creditors face the risk that they may not be repaid, they channel their energies into finding effective ways of securing their financial interests. Occasionally this has led to the imposition of unreasonably severe terms on borrowers. At first, it was left to the judges to intervene to redress the balance; thus, from medieval times equity and the Court of Chancery came to the aid of mortgagors of land. With the passing of time, Parliament felt it necessary to impose piecemeal controls on credit agreements.

In the 1960s, concern about the inadequacies of our credit laws led the Labour government to set up a Committee on Consumer Credit under the chairmanship of Lord Crowther. The Committee reported in 1971 and some of its recommendations were enacted by the Consumer Credit Act 1974. The provisions of the Act were brought into force by means of statutory instrument supplemented by ministerial regulation. The outstanding sections came into force on 19 May 1985 – 11 years after the Act was passed by Parliament. In December 2003 the Department of Trade and Industry published a White Paper – *Fair, Clear and Competitive – The Consumer Credit Market in the 21st Century* – setting out proposals for reforming the legal framework governing the consumer credit industry. Proposals in relation to pre-contractual disclosure, advertising and early settlement were enacted through a number of regulations in 2004. The remaining proposals for reform are contained in the Consumer Credit Act 2006, which amends the 1974 Act. The 2006 Act was implemented fully on 1 October 2008. In 2008 the EU adopted a new Consumer Credit Directive. The Directive has been implemented in the UK by six sets of regulations:

- the Consumer Credit (EU Directive) Regulations 2010 (SI 2010/1010) (the EU Directive Regulations);
- the Consumer Credit (Total Charge for Credit) Regulations 2010 (SI 2010/1011) (the TCC Regulations);
- the Consumer Credit (Disclosure of Information) Regulations 2010 (SI 2010/1013) (the Disclosure Regulations);
- the Consumer Credit (Agreements) Regulations 2010 (SI 2010/1014) (the Agreements Regulations);
- the Consumer Credit (Amendment) Regulations 2010 (SI 2010/1969) (the Amendment Regulations);
- the Consumer Credit (Advertisements) Regulations 2010 (SI 2010/1970) (the Advertisements Regulations).

The regulations came into force on 1 February 2011.

This chapter will examine the various types of credit available and how they are regulated by the law, particularly the Consumer Credit Act 1974 (as amended).

Types of credit

Hire-purchase

Hire-purchase (HP) is probably the best-known method of buying on the 'never-never'. From the legal point of view, it is something of an 'odd man out' since the customer pays regular amounts for the hire of goods, only becoming the owner if he exercises an option to buy. HP developed in the latter half of the 19th century. The traders of that time were looking for a form of credit to boost their sales which combined security for the creditor with a minimum of legal regulation. The chattel mortgage might have been a possibility, but the Bills of Sale Acts 1878 and 1882 provided for strict controls on mortgages of goods. Other ideas were tried and finally the right formula was found and judicially approved in *Helby* v *Matthews* (1895).

Helby v *Matthews* (1895)

Helby, a dealer, agreed to let a piano on HP to Brewster in return for 36 instalments of 10s/6d per month. The agreement stated that Brewster would become the owner of the piano on payment of the final instalment. However, he could end the agreement at any time and return the piano to Helby, his only liability being to pay any arrears of rent. Four months after the start of the agreement, Brewster pledged the piano with a pawnbroker (Matthews). The House of Lords held that Helby was entitled to recover the piano from the pawnbroker. Brewster was merely the hirer of the piano and, as such, he could not pass title to the pawnbroker under s 9 of the Factors Act 1889.

Comment. This is an application of the *nemo dat* rule, which we examined in Chapter 11.

The popularity of HP was guaranteed after this case. The advantages of this form of credit to traders were twofold: if the hirer failed to pay an instalment the owner could repossess the goods and if the goods fell into the hands of an innocent third party, the owner could recover them.

A modern HP agreement usually requires the customer to pay an initial deposit followed by equal weekly/monthly instalments for the hire of the goods. At the end of the agreement, the hirer may exercise an option to buy for a relatively small sum. A specimen HP agreement is reproduced in Figure 13.1. The owner may be the supplier of the goods but today it is more likely to be a specialist finance company introduced by the supplier. If this is the case, the HP arrangements will involve two transactions, as explained in Figure 13.2.

Conditional sale

Like HP, conditional sale gives the customer immediate possession of the goods, payment is by regular instalments and ownership only passes to the buyer when all the payments have been made. The important difference is that with HP the hirer may choose whether he wishes to buy the goods, while under a conditional sale agreement the customer is under an obligation to buy. The transfer of ownership is delayed until the buyer meets the condition specified in the agreement (usually payment of the final instalment).

Agreement no _____

HIRE-PURCHASE AGREEMENT REGULATED BY THE CONSUMER CREDIT ACT 1974
Between us (the Owner) and you (the Customer), on the terms set out below and over the page

Name (the Owner)

Address   Postcode

Name (the Customer)

Address

Postcode

KEY FINANCIAL INFORMATION

| 1 Amount of Credit (3-4) | £ | | Term | months |

| 2 Total Amount Payable (3+8) | £ | | APR | % |

Total Amount Payable (less Deposit) is payable by: £
a first instalment(incl Document Fee, if charged) of:
followed by   instalments, each in the sum of: £
followed by a final instalment
(incl Option to Purchase Fee, if payable) in the sum of £

Each instalment is due and payable on the same day of each consecutive month commencing one month from the date of this Agreement or, if a date is inserted opposite, on that date.

OTHER FINANCIAL INFORMATION

Description of the goods	Cash price (incl VAT)
	£
	£
	£
	£
3 Total Cash Price (incl VAT)	£
4 Deposit: Cash £ Trade- in £	£

5 Interest	£	Interest is charged at an equivalent rate of
6 Document Fee	£	% p.a. on the Amount of Credit,
7 Option to Purchase Fee	£	calculated and applied at the date, and for the
8 Total Charge For Credit (5+6+7)	£	Term, of this Agreement

KEY INFORMATION

Cancellation rights
You have no right to cancel this agreement under the Consumer Credit Act 1974,the Timeshare Act 1992 or the Financial Services (Distance Marketing) Regulations 2004.
Charges
We may charge you default interest in accordance with clause 9 over the page .We may also require payment of our reasonable charges for (a) sending arrears letters, reminders or documents to which you are not entitled; (b) tracing you if you move address without notifying us; (c) finding the goods if they are not at the address given by you; or (d) cheques, standing orders or direct debits which are dishonoured, stopped or not paid by you. Where known at the date of this agreement, our costs for the above are, for (a)   , for (b)   , for (c)   and for (d)   and otherwise as notified to you. See also clause 9 (b) - costs for enforcing this agreement.
Amount payable on early settlement under s94 Consumer Credit Act 1974
You can settle this agreement at any time by paying off the amount you owe, which may be reduced by a rebate. Appearing below are examples indicating the amount payable if you wanted to settle on the date when a ¼, ½ or ¾ of the term (shown in periods of months) has passed or, on the first repayment date after each of those dates.

months	months	months
£	£	£

The examples are illustrative only and are based on the assumption that all instalments are up to date. No account has been taken of any variation to this agreement.
IMPORTANT-READ THIS CAREFULLY TO FIND OUT ABOUT YOUR RIGHTS
The Consumer Credit Act 1974 lays down certain requirements for your protection which should have been complied with when this agreement was made. If they were not, we cannot enforce this agreement without getting a court order.
The Act also gives you a number of rights You can settle this agreement at any time by giving notice in writing and paying off the amount you owe under the agreement which may be reduced by a rebate. Examples indicating the amount you might have to pay appear in the agreement.
If you would like to know more about your rights under the Act, contact either your local Trading Standards Department or your nearest Citizens' Advice Bureau.
MISSING PAYMENTS
Missing payments could have severe consequences and make obtaining credit more difficult.

KEY INFORMATION (cont)

TERMINATION: YOUR RIGHTS
You have a right to end this agreement. To do so, you should write to the person you make your payments to. They will then be entitled to the return of the goods and to half the total amount payable under this agreement, that is £   . If you have already paid at least this amount plus any overdue instalments and have taken reasonable care of the goods, you will not have to pay any more.
REPOSSESSION: YOUR RIGHTS
If you do not keep your side of this agreement but you have paid at least one third of the total amount payable under this agreement, that is £   we may not take back the goods against your wishes unless we get a court order. (In Scotland, we may need to get a court order at any time.) If we do take the goods without your consent or a court order, you have the right to get back any money you have paid under this agreement.

This is a Hire-Purchase Agreement regulated by the Consumer Credit Act 1974.Sign it only if you want to be legally bound by its terms.
Signature(s)
of Customer(s)
The goods will not become your property until you have made all the payments. You must not sell them before then.

INSURANCE OF THE GOODS   See Clause 6 over the page
Comprehensive Cover Required
Name of Insurers/Brokers

Policy/Cover Note No   Expiry date

CUSTOMER'S CONTACT DETAILS

Tel   Fax

E-mail

OWNERS' CONTACT DETAILS AND SIGNATURE

Correspondence address

Regt'd in   Reg No

Tel

HPA 05/05 Original-White
First copy-Pink
Second copy-Yellow

Signed _____ for and on behalf of the Owner

Date_____ which is the date of this Agreement

Before you sign this Agreement please read the following:
This Agreement is entered into on the understanding that you are over the age of 18 and the information you have provided is true and accurate.
Read the column to the left first, then this column and then the terms over the page.
Note clause 11 over the page
If you settle this Agreement early as set out in the section headed **Key Information** opposite you will own the goods. However, if you terminate this Agreement and make the payment set out above under the heading **Termination: Your Rights,** you will have to return the goods to the Owners.

IMPORTANT: USE OF YOUR INFORMATION   Please read "Use of Your Information" over the page before you sign as by signing you are agreeing to this use and disclosure of your information. We may:
• send you information about our products and services and those of other businesses;
• pass your details to other selected businesses and to anyone who introduced you to us, to send you information about their products and services.
To stop us doing this, write to us or tick this box ☐
To stop us or other businesses contacting you by telephone
to offer you other products or services, write to us or tick this box ☐
If you are willing to be contacted by email, automated calling
system or personal fax, tick this box ☐

Information held about you by credit reference agencies may be linked to records relating to any person with whom you are linked financially. Please read "Use of Associated Records" over the page before you sign.

Figure 13.1 **A typical hire-purchase agreement form**

TERMS OF AGREEMENT

1 Payment by you

a) You must pay the Deposit (if any) shown over the page when, or before, you sign this agreement.

b) You agree to pay us the Total Amount Payable (less any Deposit paid) as shown over the page, for the hire of the goods, by the instalments and at the times shown over the page. Any Option to Purchase Fee, included in the final instalment, need only be paid if you want to become the owner of the goods, as set out in Clause 7.

c) It is essential that you make all payments in full and on time. If you pay by post, you will be responsible for any payment lost in the post.

2 Selling or disposing of the goods

You must keep the goods safely at your address shown over the page. You may not sell or dispose of the goods or transfer your rights under this agreement. You may only part with the goods to have them repaired. You may not use the goods as security for your outstanding debts or responsibilities. If the goods are a motor vehicle, you must keep it at your address shown over the page when it is not in use.

3 Caring for the goods

a) You must keep the goods in good working order and condition at your expense. You are responsible for all loss of, or damage to, the goods even if caused by events beyond your control. However, you are not responsible for loss or damage due to fair wear and tear.

b) You must not let a repairer, or any other person to whom you owe money, keep the goods as a result of your not paying the money you owe.

c) You must make sure that any tests or inspections needed by law or by the insurers are carried out.

d) Unless we have given you permission in writing, you may not make any alterations or additions to the goods (including fixing a personalised or non-original number plate). Any alterations or additions made without our permission will become our property.

e) You must allow our representative to inspect and test the goods at all reasonable times.

4 Change of address

You must let us know, in writing, within seven days about any change of your address.

5 Inspection

You must allow us or our representative to inspect and test the goods at all reasonable times.

6 Insuring the goods

At all times, you must insure the goods and keep them insured under a fully comprehensive policy with a reputable insurer at your own expense. You must tell us and your insurer about any loss or damage to the goods within 48 hours of the loss or damage happening, and whether you or anybody else will be making a claim under the policy. You agree to hold in trust for us any insurance money you receive. You authorise us to:

- negotiate and settle any claim with your insurer; and

- receive any money from your insurer under the policy. You may not withdraw this authority, and you agree to accept any settlement we may reach with the insurer. You must pay us any outstanding balance under this agreement. Unless any of the events referred to in clause 10 happens, this agreement will continue even if the goods are lost or damaged.

If you enter into this agreement for business purposes, you must get adequate insurance cover for employer's liability, liability to third parties and liability for negligence and loss, damage or injury arising out of you using and possessing the goods.

7 Ownership of the goods

We hire the goods to you for the Term shown over the page (subject to clause 10)

You will become the owner of the goods only when you have paid us all the instalments shown over the page, together with all other amounts you owe us under this agreement and you exercise the option to purchase by paying the Option to Purchase Fee shown over the page or, if none is shown, by notifying us in writing of your decision to retain the goods. Until then your rights are only those of a hirer.

8 Your right to end the agreement

You may end this agreement by taking the steps set out in the notice 'Termination: your rights' shown over the page. You must then (at your own expense) return the goods to us and, in the case of a motor vehicle, the registration document, tax disc and MOT test certificate. You must also pay us any further amount mentioned in the notice.

9 Default interest and other enforcement rights

a) If you fail to pay us any amount you owe under this agreement by the date it is due, we may charge you interest on that amount until you pay it. We will charge interest for each day you still owe the payment, at the rate shown in the section 'Other Financial Information' over the page. We can charge this interest even after we have received a court judgment against you.

b) You agree to pay us any charges or costs shown in 'Key Information' over the page which may become payable by you, including our reasonable legal costs for enforcing this agreement.

10 Our right to end the agreement

10.1 We will assume that you refuse to comply with the terms and conditions of this agreement, and we will be entitled to end this agreement after giving you a 'default notice', if:

a) you break any of clauses 1, 2 or 6 of this agreement;

b) you provided false information to enter into this agreement;

c) the goods are destroyed or treated as a total loss under any insurance claim;

d) you are a business and you stop trading, or you are a partnership and the partnership is ended or court action has begun to end it;

e) you have done something which would allow any of your belongings, property, income or savings to be legally removed to pay off any of your debts; or

f) any of the following happens:

- A statutory demand (that is, a written demand for paying a debt of at least £750, which, if not paid in full, may result in bankruptcy proceedings being brought against you) is not paid for 21 days, or any steps are taken by you or anyone else to declare you bankrupt.

- You take steps to enter into any arrangement or debt management plan with your creditors.

- A bailiff or other officer controls or seizes the goods or any of your goods following a court order.

- The landlord of the premises where the goods are situated threatens, or takes steps, to seize or in any other way control the goods or any of your goods.

10.2 If we end this agreement, we may take back the goods from you and you must pay us:

a) all payments you still owe us;

b) the balance of the Total Amount Payable; less

- any rebate (reduction) of charges you may be entitled to and;

- any money we receive from selling the goods after we have taken off the costs of recovery, insurance and storage.

However, your rights in the notice 'Repossession: your rights' over the page apply.

11 Exclusion

a) If you are dealing as a consumer, as described in the Unfair Contract Terms Act 1977, nothing in this agreement will take away your rights under the Supply of Goods (Implied Terms) Act 1973.

b) In all other cases:

- you must inspect the goods and use your own skill and judgement to decide whether the goods are of satisfactory quality and fit for their intended purpose; and

- we will not be responsible for the quality of the goods or whether they are fit for their intended purpose, or whether they match any description or specification.

12 General conditions

a) 'Goods' means the goods described over the page and includes any replacements, renewals and additions we or any insurers have agreed to.

b) References to any Act or regulation includes any amendments to that Act or regulation.

c) If at any time we allow you to do something which is against any of the terms and conditions of this agreement, this will not prevent us from insisting that you strictly follow the terms and conditions at any later time.

d) If two or more of you have signed this agreement as the Customer, you are liable jointly and severally, that is together as well as separately under this agreement. This means that either of you can be held fully responsible for the responsibilities of the Customer under this agreement.

e) We may transfer our rights and responsibilities under this agreement to another person. This will not take away any of your rights or responsibilities under this agreement. You may not transfer any of your rights or responsibilities under this agreement to another person.

f) English law will apply to this agreement. If you entered into this agreement in Scotland, words that are not in current use in Scotland will have their nearest equivalent meanings.

13 When this agreement comes into force

This agreement will only come into force when we or our authorised representative have signed it.

14 Rights of other people

Nothing in this agreement will give any person, other than you or us (or anyone who takes over from us or any person we have transferred our rights to under this agreement), any rights under this agreement.

USE OF YOUR INFORMATION

In considering whether to enter into this agreement we will search your record at credit reference agencies. They will add, to their record about you, details of our search and your application and this will be seen by other organisations that make searches. This and other information about you and those with whom you are linked financially may be used to make credit decisions about you and those with whom you are financially linked.

We may use a credit scoring or other automated decision making system.

We will also add to your record with the credit reference agencies details of your agreement with us, any payments you make under it and any default or failure to keep to its terms. These records will be shared with other organisations and may be used and searched by us and them to:

- consider applications for credit and credit related services, such as insurance, for you and any associated person;

- trace debtors, recover debts, prevent or detect money laundering and fraud, and to manage your account(s).

It is important that you provide us with accurate information. We may check your details with fraud prevention agencies and if you provide false or inaccurate information or we suspect fraud, this information may be recorded.

Fraud prevention agency records will be shared with other organisations to help make decisions on credit, motor, household, life and other insurance proposals or claims for you and members of your household.

We will use personal information about you which we acquire in connection with any application you make to us, or any agreement you enter into with us, to manage your agreement and for statistical or market research purposes. If we transfer, charge or assign your agreement to a third party or if we employ a third party to manage any aspect of your account, we will pass relevant information about you to them.

Please telephone or write to us at the telephone number/address stated overleaf if you want to have details of the credit reference agencies or any other agencies from whom we obtain, and to whom we pass, information about you. You have a legal right to these details. You have a right to receive a copy of the information we hold about you. A fee may be payable.

USE OF ASSOCIATED RECORDS

Before entering into this agreement we may search records at credit reference agencies, which may be linked to your spouse/partner, or other persons with whom you are linked financially. For the purposes of any application or this agreement you may be treated as financially linked and you will be assessed with reference to "associated records".

Where any search or application is completed or agreement entered into involving joint parties, you both consent to us recording details at credit reference agencies. As a result an 'association' will be created which will link your financial records and your associate's information may be taken into account when a future search is made by us or another lender unless you file a "disassociation" at the credit reference agency.

Figure 13.1 *(continued)*

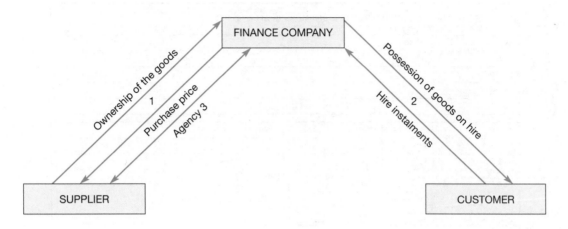

Notes

(1) Contract for the sale of goods between the supplier and the finance company covered by the Sale of Goods Act 1979.

(2) HP contract between the finance company and the customer. The agreement will be regulated by the Consumer Credit Act 1974, if the debtor is an individual, a sole trader or a partner in a partnership of two or three

partners. If the Act does not cover the agreement, the common law applies.

(3) If the HP agreement is a regulated agreement under the Consumer Credit Act 1974, the dealer is regarded as an agent of the finance company. The finance company is equally responsible with the supplier for any misrepresentation or breach of contract.

Figure 13.2 **A typical hire-purchase arrangement**

Conditional sale has never been popular in this country and today its use is mainly confined to the purchase of industrial plant and equipment. It was one of the formulas considered by Victorian traders prior to the case of *Helby* v *Matthews* (1895). However, the decision of the Court of Appeal in *Lee* v *Butler* (1893) showed that since the customer had agreed to buy the goods he could pass good title to a third party under the Factors Act 1889, leaving the creditor without the security he required. Conditional sale was treated as a contract for the sale of goods, although in reality it has more in common with HP. The Hire Purchase Act 1964 (followed by the Consumer Credit Act 1974) resolved this difficulty by equating conditional sale with HP for most purposes.

Credit sale

This is a contract for the sale of goods whereby ownership and possession of the goods pass immediately to the buyer, but he is given time to pay. Since the purchaser becomes the owner of the goods straight away, he can resell them before the end of the agreement, provided that he pays off what he owes, and if he defaults on his repayments, the seller cannot repossess the goods.

This is in marked contrast to the position under an HP agreement. A specimen credit sale agreement is reproduced in Figure 13.3. This form of credit is used, for example, in purchases from mail order catalogues.

Bank loans

There are various ways of borrowing from a bank.

1 Overdraft. An overdraft may arise in one of two ways: either the customer makes an arrangement with the bank to overdraw his current account up to an agreed amount or, without prior agreement, he simply writes cheques for an amount greater than in his account. A variable rate of interest is charged on the amount drawn by the customer, calculated on a daily basis, and bank charges usually become payable. Security may be needed for large sums. The bank can insist on repayment in full at any time. An overdraft is usually the cheapest way of borrowing from a bank.

2 Ordinary loan. This type of loan is extended to bank customers and for a particular purpose – to buy a car, for example. A specific sum of money is borrowed for an agreed period of time. A separate loan account is opened by the bank into which the instalments are paid, usually

Agreement No _____

CREDIT AGREEMENT REGULATED BY THE CONSUMER CREDIT ACT 1974
Between us (the Supplier) and you (the Customer), on the terms set out below and over the page

Name (the Supplier)

Address   Postcode

Name (the Customer)

Address

                                                                           Postcode

KEY FINANCIAL INFORMATION				CUSTOMER'S DETAILS		

KEY FINANCIAL INFORMATION

1 Amount of Credit (3-4)	£		Term	months
2 Total Amount Payable (3+5)	£		APR	%

Total Amount Payable (less Deposit) is payable by:
instalments, each in the sum of: £

Each instalment is due and payable on the same day of
each consecutive month commencing:
one month from the date of this Agreement or,
if a date is inserted opposite, on that date.

OTHER FINANCIAL INFORMATION

Description of the Goods or Services	Cash price (incl VAT)	
	£	
	£	
	£	
3 Total Cash Price (incl VAT)	£	
4 Deposit: *Cash/debit card/credit card/cheque £	£	
Trade-in £		
5 Total Charge For Credit (interest)	£	

Interest is charged at an equivalent rate of   % p.a. on the Amount of Credit,
calculated and applied at the date, and for the Term, of this Agreement

KEY INFORMATION

Charges
We may charge you default interest in accordance with clause 6 over the page .We may
also require payment of our reasonable charges for (a) sending arrears letters, reminders or
documents to which you are not entitled; (b) tracing you if you move address without
notifying us; (c) if you cancel the agreement and the goods are not held at the premises in
the agreement or (d) cheques, standing orders or direct debits which are dishonoured,
stopped or not paid by you. Where known at the date of this agreement, our costs for the
above are for (a)   , for (b)   , for (c)   and for (d)   and
otherwise as notified to you. See also clause 6(b) – costs for enforcing this agreement.
Amount payable on early settlement under s94 Consumer Credit Act 1974
You can settle this agreement at any time by paying off the amount you owe, which may
be reduced by a rebate. Appearing below are examples indicating the amount payable if
you wanted to settle on the date when a ¼, ½ or ¾ of the term (shown in periods of
months) has passed or, on the first repayment date after each of those dates.

	months		months		months
£		£		£	

The examples are illustrative only and are based on the assumption that all instalments are
up to date. No account has been taken of any variation to this agreement.
IMPORTANT-READ THIS CAREFULLY TO FIND OUT ABOUT YOUR RIGHTS
The Consumer Credit Act 1974 lays down certain requirements for your protection which
should have been complied with when this agreement was made. If they were not, we
cannot enforce this agreement without getting a court order.
The Act also gives you a number of rights You can settle this agreement at any time by
giving notice in writing and paying off the amount you owe under the agreement which
may be reduced by a rebate. Examples indicating the amount you might have to pay
appear in the agreement.
If you would like to know more about your rights under the Act, contact either your local
Trading Standards Department or your nearest Citizens' Advice Bureau.
MISSING PAYMENTS
Missing payments could have severe consequences and make obtaining credit more difficult.

YOUR RIGHT TO CANCEL
Once you have signed this agreement, you will have a short time in which you can cancel
it .We will send you exact details of how and when you can do this.

This is a Credit Agreement regulated by the Consumer Credit Act 1974.Sign it only if you
want to be legally bound by its terms.
Signature(s)
of Customer(s)
Date(s) of signature(s)

CUSTOMER'S DETAILS

Mr ☐	Mrs ☐	Miss ☐	Other (please state)
Married ☐	Single ☐	Divorced ☐	Other (please state)
Owner ☐	Tenant ☐	Lodger ☐	Other (please state)

Tel   Fax

E-mail

Date of birth   Years at address shown above

Previous address (if less than 3 yrs at address shown above)

                                 Postcode

Occupation   Employer's name

Address

SUPPLIER'S CONTACT DETAILS AND SIGNATURE

Correspondence address

                                 Postcode

Reg'd in   Reg No

Tel	CSC 05/05 Original

Signed _____for and on behalf of the Supplier

Date_____which is the date of this Agreement

Before you sign this Agreement please read the following.

This Agreement is entered into on the understanding that you are over the age of 18 and
the information you have provided is true and accurate.

Read this page and the Terms of Agreement over the page.

🔒 IMPORTANT: USE OF YOUR INFORMATION

Please read "Use of Your Information" below before you sign as by signing you are
agreeing to this use and disclosure of your information. We may:

• send you information about our products and services and those of other businesses;

• pass your details to other selected businesses and to anyone who introduced you to us, to
send you information about their products and services.

To stop us doing this, write to us or tick this box   ☐

To stop us or other businesses contacting you by telephone to offer
you other products or services, write to us or tick this box   ☐

If you are willing to be contacted by email, automated calling system
or personal fax, tick this box   ☐

Information held about you by credit reference agencies may be linked to records relating
to any person with whom you are linked financially. Please read "Use of Associated
Records" over the page before you sign.

* Delete nature of Deposit if inapplicable

Figure 13.3 A typical credit agreement form

Copyright © Consumer Credit Trade Association (original size A4)

TERMS OF AGREEMENT

1 Credit sale
We agree to sell to you, and you agree to buy from us, on credit, the goods or services shown over the page on the terms set out below and over the page.

2 Payment by you
a) You must pay the deposit (if any) shown over the page when, or before, you sign this agreement
b) You agree to pay us the Total Amount Payable (less any Deposit paid), as shown over the page, by the instalments and at the times shown over the page.
c) It is essential that you make all payments in full and on time. If you pay by post, you will be responsible for any payment lost in the post.

3 Earlier payment
If you pay the outstanding balance under this agreement early, you will usually be entitled to a rebate (reduction) of part of the interest.

4 Change of address
You must let us know, in writing, within seven days about any change of your address.

5 Right to demand earlier payment
We will assume that you refuse to comply with the terms and conditions of this agreement if any of the events set out below happens. We will then be entitled to demand that you pay us the outstanding balance under this agreement (together with interest) by sending you a 'default notice'. The events are:
a) If you do not pay us any amount you owe us within 14 days of its due date.
b) If you provided false information when entering into this agreement.
c) If you have done something which would allow any of your belongings, property, income or savings to be legally removed to pay off any of your debts.
d) If any of the following happens:
- A statutory demand (that is, a written demand for paying a debt of at least £750, which, if not paid in full, may result in bankruptcy proceedings being brought against you) is not paid for 21 days or any steps are taken by you or anyone else to declare you bankrupt.
- You take steps to enter into any arrangement or debt management plan with your creditors.
- A bailiff or other officer controls or seizes any of your goods following a court order.
- The landlord of the premises at your address threatens, or takes steps, to seize or in any other way control any of your goods.

6 Default interest and other enforcement rights
a) If you fail to pay us any amount you owe under this agreement by the date it is due, we may charge you interest on that amount until you pay it. We will charge interest for each day you still owe the payment, at the rate shown in the section 'Other Financial Information' over the page. We can charge this interest even after we have received a court judgment against you.
b) You agree to pay us any charges or costs shown in 'Key Information' over the page which may become payable by you, including our reasonable legal costs for enforcing this agreement.

7 General conditions
a) References to any Act or regulation include any amendments to that Act or regulation.
b) If at any time we allow you to do something which is against any of the terms and conditions of this agreement, this will not prevent us from insisting that you strictly follow the terms and conditions at any later time.
c) If two or more of you have signed this agreement as the Customer, you are liable jointly and severally, that is together as well as separately, under this agreement. This means that either of you can be held fully responsible for the responsibilities of the Customer under this agreement.
d) We may transfer our rights and responsibilities under this agreement to another person. This will not take away any of your rights or responsibilities under this agreement. You may not transfer any of your rights or responsibilities under this agreement to another person.
e) English law will apply to this agreement. If you entered into this agreement in Scotland, words that are not in current use in Scotland will have their nearest equivalent meanings.

8 When this agreement comes into force
This agreement will only come into force when we or our authorised representative have signed it.

9 Rights of other people
Nothing in this agreement will give any person, other than you or us (or anyone who takes over from us or any person we have transferred our rights to under this agreement), any rights under this agreement.

USE OF YOUR INFORMATION
In considering whether to enter into this agreement we will search your record at credit reference agencies. They will add, to their record about you, details of our search and your application and this will be seen by other organisations that make searches. This and other information about you and those with whom you are linked financially may be used to make credit decisions about you and those with whom you are financially linked.
We may use a credit scoring or other automated decision making system.
We will also add to your record with the credit reference agencies details of your agreement with us, any payments you make under it and any default or failure to keep to its terms. These records will be shared with other organisations and may be used and searched by us and them to:
- consider applications for credit and credit related services, such as insurance, for you and any associated person;
- trace debtors, recover debts, prevent or detect money laundering and fraud, and to manage your account(s).
It is important that you provide us with accurate information. We may check your details with fraud prevention agencies and if you provide false or inaccurate information or we suspect fraud, this information may be recorded.
Fraud prevention agency records will be shared with other organisations to help make decisions on credit, motor, household, life and other insurance proposals or claims for you and members of your household.
We will use personal information about you which we acquire in connection with any application you make to us, or any agreement you enter into with us, to manage your agreement and for statistical or market research purposes. If we transfer, charge or assign your agreement to a third party or if we employ a third party to manage any aspect of your account, we will pass relevant information about you to them.
Please telephone or write to us at the telephone number/address stated overleaf if you want to have details of the credit reference agencies or any other agencies from whom we obtain, and to whom we pass, information about you. You have a legal right to these details. You have a right to receive a copy of the information we hold about you. A fee may be payable.
USE OF ASSOCIATED RECORDS
Before entering into this agreement we may search records at credit reference agencies, which may be linked to your spouse/partner, or other persons with whom you are linked financially. For the purposes of any application or this agreement you may be treated as financially linked and you will be assessed with reference to "associated records".
Where any search or application is completed or agreement entered into involving joint parties, you both consent to us recording details at credit reference agencies. As a result an 'association' will be created which will link your financial records and your associate's information may be taken into account when a future search is made by us or another lender unless you file a "disassociation" at the credit reference agency.

Figure 13.3 (*continued*)

by means of a standing order from the customer's current account. Variable interest is charged and security may be required.

3 Personal loan. The loan is available to anyone, customer and non-customer alike, usually for a particular purpose. The period of the loan and interest are fixed when the credit is arranged. Again, security may be asked for. It is usually a more expensive way of borrowing than either the overdraft or ordinary loan.

4 Budget account. A budget account is used to help spread the payment of bills over the year. The customer calculates his annual outgoings on such items as gas, electricity, water and council tax. The bank adds to this its service charge for operating the account. The total is divided by 12 and a standing order for this amount is placed to the credit of the budget account. The bills can then be paid with confidence as and when they arrive.

Credit cards

A credit card allows the holder to pay (usually up to a limit) for goods and services or to obtain a cash advance by producing a plastic personalised card. There are three main kinds of credit card.

1 Bank credit cards (e.g. Mastercard, Visa). Although these cards are linked to particular banks, an application may be made to any bank for its card. The holder is given a personal credit limit and he can use the card to buy goods and services or obtain a cash advance wherever the card is accepted, up to this limit. Traders involved in the scheme send details of purchases to the credit card company and are then reimbursed after a charge of between 1 per cent and 4 per cent has been deducted. At the end of each month, the holder receives an account of his spending and details of the minimum amount that must be paid that month (£5 or 5 per cent, whichever is the greater). If the holder pays the account in full by the stipulated date, he is not charged interest on the credit obtained. (This does not apply to cash advances, for which a service charge is made.) Alternatively, part-payment may be sent, in which case interest is charged. Most banks now charge an annual fee for use of their credit cards.

2 Charge cards (e.g. American Express, Diners' Club). These cards work in much the same way as bank credit cards, allowing the holder to pay for goods and services at home and abroad by producing his card. The main differences are:

- the card-holder pays an initial joining fee plus an annual membership fee;
- there is no pre-set credit limit; and
- the companies insist that the account is paid in full each month.

3 Retailers' credit cards (e.g. M & S credit card). Many chain stores, supermarkets and garages issue their own credit cards. The period of credit is usually a few weeks between making the purchases and the presentation of the account.

The relationship between suppliers, credit or charge card-issuers and card-holders was examined by the Court of Appeal in *Re Charge Card Services Ltd* (1988). A company operating a charge card service had gone into liquidation and the question arose whether unpaid suppliers could recover payment direct from card-holders. The court held that when a card-holder uses his card to acquire goods and services, this operates as an unconditional discharge of his obligation to the supplier. An unpaid supplier can, therefore, take action only against the card-issuer to recover what he is owed.

Shop budget account

This form of credit is operated by many large stores. The customer decides how much he can afford to pay each month. He is then allowed a spending limit of, for example, 12 times the £15 agreed. This allows the customer to spend up to £180 but never more than this. As regular repayments are made, he can make more purchases if he does not exceed the £180 limit. This is known as 'revolving credit' or 'running account credit'. Interest is usually charged on the amount owing at the end of a specified period (usually a month).

Trading checks and vouchers

The check trader issues a check or voucher for a specified amount to his customer. The checks can be spent in any shop which has already agreed to accept them. The shop receives payment from the check trader, less a discount. The customer repays the check trader by small regular instalments including interest. Check trading is more common in the north of England. It is a fairly expensive way to borrow.

Credit unions

These are a form of self-help organisation which are particularly popular in North America and are now catching on in this country. Credit unions are formed by people with something in common; they may belong to the same club or work together. They agree to make regular savings to form a pool of money. If any of the members need money unexpectedly, they can borrow from the pool. They are governed by the Credit Unions Act 1979.

Insurance policy loan

This is a loan obtained from an insurance company based on the security of an insurance policy with a 'cash-in' value.

Finance company personal loan

Big stores, car dealers, gas and electricity companies often arrange these loans to finance large purchases. They are also advertised in local newspapers.

Moneylenders

Moneylenders are often used by people who cannot get credit from more traditional sources. They are usually prepared to lend without security and, as a result, their interest charges can be very high.

Pawnbroking

This is one of the oldest ways of lending money. A pawnbroker will advance money for a short period of time, and in return will take possession of goods (for example, jewellery) as security. If the loan and interest are repaid, the goods are returned to the borrower; if the pawn is not redeemed, the goods may be sold by the pawnbroker.

Mortgage

Building societies, banks and local authorities are willing to lend money to help people buy their own homes. The mortgage is the interest taken by the lender in the property which acts as security for the loan.

Hire

Although a hire contract does not involve credit, it is covered by the consumer credit legislation. Under a hire agreement, the owner of goods allows someone else (the hirer) to make use of them in return for regular rental payments. The hirer obtains possession of the goods but ownership never passes to him and at the end of the agreement the goods must be returned to the owner. Most people are familiar with hire contracts in the context of TV and DVD rentals. A typical rental agreement can be seen in Figure 13.4, overleaf. Businesses also take advantage of hire as a method of obtaining the use of equipment which they require. (Hire in this context is usually referred to as 'leasing', the owner being known as the 'lessor' and the hirer as the 'lessee'.) The leasing agreement often includes an undertaking by the lessor to service the equipment regularly and effect repairs when necessary. Equipment leasing has allowed businesses to take advantage of the opportunities created by the rapidly changing new technology in the field of information technology. Consumer hire agreements are covered by the provisions of the Consumer Credit Act 1974.

Consumer Credit Act 1974

Background to the Act

The Crowther Committee, which had been set up in 1965 to investigate consumer credit, found that our credit laws were in a mess. The rules, having developed in a piecemeal way, were to be found in a large number of statutes and in the common law. Different rules had been created for different kinds of credit, and in some areas the consumer was inadequately protected.

The Committee recommended the passing of two pieces of legislation. The government rejected the need for a Lending and Security Act, which would have set up, amongst other things, a security register. However, it accepted the argument for a Consumer Sale and Loan Act to extend and improve the protective rules, which already existed in relation to HP. This proposal became the Consumer Credit Act 1974. It replaces most of the earlier credit legislation with the exception of the Bills of Sale Acts 1878 and 1882 and the Hire Purchase Act 1964, Part III. The Consumer Credit Act 1974 has been

Agreement No _____

HIRE AGREEMENT REGULATED BY THE CONSUMER CREDIT ACT 1974

Between us (the Owner) and you (the Hirer), on the terms set out below and over the page.

Name (the Owner)

Address   Postcode

Name (the Hirer)

Address

                                                                        Postcode

KEY FINANCIAL INFORMATION

Description of Goods

Makers name

Model no

Serial no

Accessories

Hiring is payable by:	Rentals (incl VAT)	
an advance rental payment for the first_____month/s of the hiring, payable on your signing, of	£	
followed by _____ monthly rentals, each in the sum of	£	
followed by_____ monthly rentals, each in the sum of	£	
followed by _____ monthly rentals, each in the sum of	£	
followed by monthly rentals thereafter, each in the sum of	£	

Each monthly rental is due and payable on the same day of each consecutive month commencing:

The minimum period of hire of the goods under this Agreement is [   ] months*

We have the right, after the end of the minimum period of hire, to vary the amount of each rental payable by you by giving you one month's written notice of the variation, if there is a change in the Bank of England Base Rate, the Finance House Base Rate, interest rates generally or any other actual or expected change in market conditions generally. We shall not issue any such notice to expire before the end of the minimum period of hire except if the rate of VAT changes, when we may vary the rentals at any time.

KEY INFORMATION

Cancellation rights
This agreement is not cancellable.

Charges
We may charge you default interest in accordance with clause 10 over the page. We may also require payment of our reasonable charges for (a) sending arrears letters, reminders or documents to which you are not entitled; (b) tracing you if you move address without notifying us; (c) finding the goods if they are not at the address given by you; or (d) cheques, standing orders or direct debits which are dishonoured, stopped or not paid by you. Where known at the date of this agreement, our costs for the above are for
(a)   , for (b)   , for (c)   and for (d)   and otherwise as notified to you. See also clause 10 (b) - costs for enforcing this Agreement.

IMPORTANT-READ THIS CAREFULLY TO FIND OUT ABOUT YOUR RIGHTS
The Consumer Credit Act 1974 covers this agreement and lays down certain requirements for your protection which should have been complied with when this agreement was made. If they were not, we cannot enforce this agreement without getting a court order. If you would like to know more about your rights under the Act, contact either your local Trading Standards Department or your nearest Citizens' Advice Bureau.

MISSING PAYMENTS
Missing payments could have severe consequences and may make obtaining credit more difficult.

This is a Hire Agreement regulated by the Consumer Credit Act 1974. Sign it only if you want to be legally bound by its terms.
Signature(s)
of Hirers(s)
Under this agreement the goods do not become your property and you must not sell them

* Not to exceed 17 months

MAINTENANCE OF THE GOODS (see clause 8 over the page)

The Owner provides maintenance of the goods* [   ]

The Owner does not provide maintenance of the goods * [   ]

* Please place a tick in the appropriate box.

HIRER'S CONTACT DETAILS

Tel

Fax

E-mail

OWNER'S CONTACT DETAILS AND SIGNATURE

Correspondence address

Reg'd in	Reg No

Tel

Fax	RA 05/05 Original-White First copy-Pink Second copy-Yellow

Signed _____for and on behalf of the Owner

Date_____which is the date of this Agreement

Before you sign this Agreement please read the following.

This Agreement is entered into on the understanding that you are over the age of 18 and the information you have provided is true and accurate.

Read this page and the Terms of the Agreement over the page.

🔓 **IMPORTANT: USE OF YOUR INFORMATION**

You have a right to know how we will use your personal information.
It is important that you read "Use of Your Information" over the page before you sign since by signing you are agreeing to this use and disclosure of your information. We may:
• send you information about our products and services and those of other businesses;

• pass your details to other selected businesses and to anyone who introduced you to us, to send you information about their products and services.

To stop us doing this, write to us or tick this box [ ]

To stop us or other businesses contacting you by telephone to offer you other products or services, write to us or tick this box [ ]

If you are willing to be contacted by email, automated calling system or personal fax, tick this box [ ]

Information held about you by credit reference agencies may be linked to records relating to any person with whom you are linked financially. Please read "Use of Associated Records" over the page before you sign.

Figure 13.4 A typical hire agreement form

TERMS OF AGREEMENT

1 Hire of the goods
We agree to hire to you, and you agree to take on hire, the goods for the period (subject to clause 12) from the date of this agreement until the expiry of the period of the notice under clause 11.

2 Payment by you
a) You must pay the advance rental shown over the page when, or before, you sign this agreement.
b) You agree to pay us the monthly rentals in the amounts and at the times shown over the page.
c) It is essential that you make all payments in full and on time. If you pay by post, you will be responsible for any payment lost in the post

3 Change of address
You must let us know, in writing, within seven days about any change of your address.

4 Where the goods are to be kept
You must keep the goods safely at your address shown over the page. You may not move them elsewhere without first getting our permission in writing.

5 Caring for the goods
You must use the goods carefully and properly. Apart from any arrangements for maintenance under clause 8, you must keep the goods in good working order and condition at your expense. You must replace batteries in remote-control units at your expense. You may not tamper with the internal working parts of the goods.

6 Ownership of the goods
The goods will be our property at all times, and you must not sell or dispose of them

7 Insuring the goods
You must insure the goods and keep them insured with a reputable insurer against any and all loss of, or damage to, the goods (however it is caused).

8 Maintenance
If under this agreement we must maintain the goods, you must tell us when any maintenance or adjustment is needed. We, or our authorised representative, will then carry this out.
If we decide that the goods are no longer worth repairing or, in the case of a radio or television receiver, that the transmission is unsatisfactory, we may either:
a) replace the goods by other goods as similar as possible to those replaced; or
b) end this agreement by giving you seven days' notice in writing.
If we end this agreement under (b) above, you must let us collect the goods. We will repay you any rentals you have already paid and which relate to the period after this agreement has ended. This clause will not affect your legal rights, which you can find out about by contacting your nearest Citizens' Advice Bureau.

9 Licences
If the goods need a licence by law, you must keep them licensed at all times. You must, when we ask, make the licence or payment receipt available for us to inspect.

10 Default interest and other enforcement rights
a) If you fail to pay us any amount you owe us under this agreement by the date it is due, we may charge interest on that amount until you pay it. We will charge interest at the daily rate of 5% above the rate set at any time by the Finance and Leasing Association as the finance house base rate. We may charge this interest even after we have received a court judgment against you.
b) You agree to pay us any charges or costs shown in 'Key Information' over the page which may become payable by you, including our reasonable legal costs for enforcing this agreement.

11 Right to end the agreement
You or we may end this agreement by giving the other one month's notice in writing to expire on, or after, the last day of the minimum period of hire. You must then return the goods to us or make them available for us to collect.

12 Our further right to end the agreement
We will assume that you refuse to comply with the terms and conditions of this agreement, and we will be entitled to end this agreement and take back the goods after giving you a 'default notice', if:
a) you break any of clauses 2,6 or 7 of this agreement or commit any other material breach of your obligations under this agreement;
b) you provided false information to enter into this agreement;
c) the goods are destroyed or treated as a total loss under any insurance claim;

d) you are a business and you stop trading, or you are a partnership and the partnership is ended or court action has begun to end it;
e) you have done something which would allow any of your belongings, property, income or savings to be legally removed to pay off any of your debts; or
f) any of the following happens:
• A statutory demand (that is, a written demand for paying a debt of at least £750, which, if not paid in full, may result in bankruptcy proceedings being brought against you) is not paid for 21 days, or any steps are taken by you or anyone else to declare you bankrupt.
• You take steps to enter into any arrangement or debt management plan with your creditors.
• A bailiff or other officer controls or seizes the goods or any of your goods following a court order.
• The landlord of the premises where the goods are situated threatens, or takes steps, to seize or in any other way control the goods or any of your goods.

13 Your liability if we end the agreement
a) If we end this agreement under clause 11 or 12, you must pay us all rentals due up to the date this agreement ends.
b) If we end this agreement under clause 12 before the end of the minimum period of hire, you must pay us all rentals due up to the date this agreement ends:
• plus the total of the remaining rentals which would have become due up to the end of the minimum period of hire had we not ended this agreement;
• less any rentals we may receive by re-letting the goods for the remainder of the minimum period of hire, and less any other deduction we may consider reasonable.

14 Varying the rentals
If there is a change in the Bank of England Base Rate, the Finance House Base Rate, or interest rates generally or any other actual or expected change in market conditions generally, we will be entitled to vary the rentals you owe us after the minimum period of hire has ended. We may also vary the rentals at any time if the rate of VAT is changed. We will give you at least one month's notice, in writing, of any varied rentals.

15 TV transmissions
If the goods are a television receiver, we guarantee that it will receive those stations it receives on the installation date. We are not responsible for poor or no reception, or any failure caused by faulty equipment we have not supplied under this agreement.

16 General conditions
a) 'Goods' means the goods described over the page and includes any replacements, renewals and additions we or any insurers have agreed to.
b) References to any Act or regulation includes any amendments to that Act or regulation.
c) If at any time we allow you to do something which is against any of the terms and conditions of this agreement, this will not prevent us from insisting that you strictly follow the terms and conditions at any later time.
d) If two or more of you have signed this agreement as the Hirer, you are liable jointly and separately under this agreement. This means that either of you can be held fully responsible for the responsibilities of the Hirer under this agreement.
e) We may transfer our rights and responsibilities under this agreement to another person. This will not take away any of your rights or responsibilities under this agreement. You may not transfer any of your rights or responsibilities under this agreement to another person.
f) English law will apply to this agreement. If you entered into this agreement in Scotland, words that are not in current use in Scotland will have their nearest equivalent meanings.

17 When this agreement comes into force
This agreement will only come into force when we or our authorised representative have signed it.

18 Rights of other people
Nothing in this agreement will give any person, other than you or us (or anyone who takes over from us or any person we have transferred our rights to under this agreement), any rights under this agreement.

USE OF YOUR INFORMATION
In considering whether to enter into this agreement we will search your record at credit reference agencies. They will add, to their record about you, details of our search and your application and this will be seen by other organisations that make searches. This and other information about you and those with whom you are linked financially may be used to make credit decisions about you and those with whom you are financially linked.
We may use a credit scoring or other automated decision making system.
We will also add to your record with the credit reference agencies details of your agreement with us, any payments you make under it and any default or failure to keep to its terms. These records will be shared with other organisations and may be used and searched by us and them to:
• consider applications for credit and credit related services, such as insurance, for you and any associated person;
• trace debtors, recover debts, prevent or detect money laundering and fraud, and to manage your account(s).
It is important that you provide us with accurate information. We may check your details with fraud prevention agencies and if you provide false or inaccurate information or we suspect fraud, this information may be recorded.
Fraud prevention agency records will be shared with other organisations to help make decisions on credit, motor, household, life and other insurance proposals or claims for you and members of your household.
We will use personal information about you which we acquire in connection with any application you make to us, or any agreement you enter into with us, to manage your agreement and for statistical or market research purposes. If we transfer, charge or assign your agreement to a third party or if we employ a third party to manage any aspect of your account, we will pass relevant information about you to them.
Please telephone or write to us at the telephone number/address stated overleaf if you want to have details of the credit reference agencies or any other agencies from whom we obtain, and to whom we pass, information about you. You have a legal right to receive these details. You have a right to receive a copy of the information we hold about you. A fee may be payable.
USE OF ASSOCIATED RECORDS
Before entering into this agreement we may search records at credit reference agencies, which may be linked to your spouse/partner, or other persons with whom you are linked financially. For the purposes of any application or this agreement you may be treated as financially linked and you will be assessed with reference to "associated records".
Where any search or application is completed or agreement entered into involving joint parties, you both consent to us recording details at credit reference agencies. As a result an 'association' will be created which will link your financial records and your associate's information may be taken into account when a future search is made by us or another lender unless you file a "disassociation" at the credit reference agency.

Figure 13.4 *(continued)*

overhauled by the Consumer Credit Act 2006. Further changes have been made by the six regulations implementing the 2008 EU Consumer Credit Directive.

For the rest of this chapter, section references are to the 1974 Act unless otherwise indicated.

Terminology

The Act introduced a new set of terms, the most important of which are explained below.

1 Debtor-creditor-supplier agreement (DCSA) (s 12) and debtor-creditor agreement (DCA) (s 13). A DCSA arises where there is a connection between the creditor and the transaction for which the finance is being provided. The creditor and supplier of the goods or services for which the credit is being made available may be the same person. Where they are different people, it will be a DCSA if there is an arrangement between the supplier and creditor. Examples include HP, credit cards and trading checks. If there is no connection between the creditor and any supplier, it will be a DCA. An overdraft from a bank to be spent as the customer wishes is an example of a DCA.

2 Restricted-use credit agreement and unrestricted-use credit agreement (s 11). If the debtor is free to use the credit as he or she pleases, e.g. overdraft, it will be an unrestricted-use credit agreement. Where the credit is tied to a particular transaction, it will be restricted-use credit. Examples include HP, credit sale, shop's budget account, check trading and the use of credit cards to obtain goods and services.

3 Fixed-sum credit and running-account credit (s 10). Fixed-sum credit is where the agreement is made for a specific sum of credit (e.g. HP, bank loan). Running-account credit is sometimes referred to as revolving credit. It is where the debtor can receive cash, goods or services from time to time to an amount which does not exceed his credit limit (e.g. overdraft, shop's budget account).

4 Credit tokens (s 14). The definition of a credit token covers credit cards, trading checks and vouchers, but not cheque guarantee cards.

5 APR. The Act promotes its primary objective of 'truth in lending' by creating a standard measure of the true cost of borrowing, which is the annual percentage rate of charge (APR). This is intended to allow the consumer to make a fair comparison between different credit deals.

The TCC Regulations set out what must be included in the total charge for credit and how this is expressed as an APR. The total charge for credit includes all the costs known to the creditor and which are required to be paid by or on behalf of the borrower (or a relative) in connection with the credit agreement. It includes interest, commission, taxes and any other kind of fees. The total is then expressed as an annual percentage rate (APR), calculated according a statutory formula set out in the TCC Regulations. The method of calculating APR is very technical and involves the use of complex concepts and mathematical methods. The Office of Fair Trading publishes a booklet which explains how the APR is calculated, with illustrative examples of calculations based on typical credit agreements.

Agreements covered by the Act

Most of the Act only applies to 'regulated agreements'. Some agreements are 'partially regulated' while other agreements are said to be 'exempt'.

Regulated agreements

Two types of agreement are regulated by the Act – consumer credit agreements and consumer hire agreements.

1 Regulated consumer credit agreement. With effect from 6 April 2008 this is a consumer credit agreement between an individual (the debtor) and any other person (the creditor) by which the creditor provides the debtor with credit of any amount (s 8). Individuals include sole traders and partnerships of two or three partners. (If the agreement was made before 6 April 2008, it will be regulated if it is a personal credit agreement, where the credit does not exceed £25,000. It will be personal credit if the borrower is an individual or partnership (of any size), but not a company.) Credit is defined in s 9 as a 'cash loan or any other form of financial accommodation'. This covers HP, conditional sale, credit sale, loans, overdrafts, credit cards, shop budget accounts and trading checks.

The monetary limit which applies to agreements concluded before 6 April 2008 refers to the credit given. It does not include any deposit or interest charges. The total price paid, therefore, may exceed the limit but the agreement could still be regulated, as explained in the example below.

Example

Cash price of the goods = £27,000 paid for by:
> £2,500 deposit
> £24,500 credit
> £750 interest
> Total credit price = £27,750

Although the debtor pays a total of £27,750, the credit obtained is only £24,500, and so if the agreement was made before 6 April 2008 it will be regulated.

2 Regulated consumer hire agreement. This is an agreement under which goods are hired, leased, rented or bailed to an individual, which is capable of lasting more than three months (s 15). Consumer hire agreements entered into before 6 April 2008 will be regulated if the amount does not exceed £25,000.

A House of Lords case provides an interesting illustration of how the framework of regulation applies in practice.

Dimond v Lovell (2000)

The case arose out of a car accident in which Mr Lovell drove into the back of Mrs Dimond's car. While Mrs Dimond's car was being repaired, she hired a replacement car from 1st Automotive Ltd. 1st Automotive specialises in hiring cars to drivers whose cars have been damaged by the negligence of other drivers and are off the road being repaired. 1st Automotive does not ask drivers, like Mrs Dimond, to pay anything until the claim for damages against the negligent driver is settled. Mr Lovell's insurer, the Co-operative Insurance Society (CIS), paid Mrs Dimond's repair bills promptly, but it refused to pay 1st Automotive's hire charges, which amounted to £346.63. The CIS put forward two defences. The first was that the agreement between Mrs Dimond and 1st Automotive was a regulated consumer credit agreement but it was unenforceable because it did not comply with the requirements of the Consumer Credit Act. If it was unenforceable, Mrs Dimond did not owe 1st Automotive £346.63 and, therefore, she could not recover that amount from Mr Lovell as she had not suffered any loss. The second line of defence was that Mrs Dimond had not mitigated her loss. The 'spot rate' for car hire was considerably lower than 1st Automotive's charges. The House of Lords held that the agreement entered into by Mrs Dimond with 1st Automotive was a regulated consumer credit agreement. The agreement

was unenforceable because it did not contain all the terms 'prescribed' in regulations made under the Consumer Credit Act 1974. Lord Hoffmann noted that 1st Automotive could obtain exemption from the 1974 Act by including a clause in its agreement requiring that the hire charges be paid within 12 months. (For details of 'exempt agreements' see below.) Their Lordships also considered what the position would have been if the agreement had been exempt and, as a result, enforceable. They took the view that although Mrs Dimond acted reasonably in engaging the services of 1st Automotive, it did not mean she was entitled to recover the full amount of the charges. She had obtained additional services (e.g. not having to pay over the cost of the hire car, relief from the trouble and anxiety of pursuing a claim against Mr Lovell). These additional services are not recoverable in English law. Mrs Dimond's claim, therefore, would have been limited to the 'spot rate' for hire cars.

Comment. In the Court of Appeal, the Vice-Chancellor found that the 1st Automotive agreement was a personal credit agreement, a consumer credit agreement, an agreement for a fixed-sum credit facility, a restricted-use credit agreement and a debtor-creditor-supplier agreement. It would also have been a consumer hire agreement if it had been capable of lasting for more than three months.

Partially regulated agreements

Two kinds of agreements are only partially regulated by the Act.

1 Small agreement. A small agreement is either a regulated consumer credit agreement (other than an HP or conditional sale agreement) where the credit does not exceed £50, or a regulated consumer hire agreement which does not require the hirer to pay more than £50 in rentals (s 17).

2 Non-commercial agreement. This is a consumer credit agreement or consumer hire agreement which is not made by the creditor or owner in the course of a business carried on by him (s 189(1)).

Exempt agreements (s 16)

1 Exempt consumer credit agreements. The exemptions are as follows:

(a) *Agreements secured on land* – various agreements to finance the purchase of land secured by a mortgage.

(b) *Low-cost credit* – e.g. DCAs where the APR does not exceed the highest of the London and Scottish clearing banks' base rates plus 1 per cent.

(c) *Finance of foreign trade* – credit agreements made in connection with the export of goods and services outside the UK or their import into this country.

(d) *Normal trade credit* – the exemption covers two situations: first, where traders advance credit to sell goods and services and require the bill to be paid in one instalment (e.g. the milk and paper bill). Second, a DCSA for fixed-sum credit where the number of payments does not exceed four, within a year of the start of the agreement and the credit is provided without interest or any other charges; or, where it is for running-account credit, the credit has to be repaid in full by a single repayment in respect of a period not exceeding three months and there are either no charges or only insignificant charges payable for the credit. The agreement will not qualify for exemption if it is an HP or conditional sale or secured by an article taken in pawn.

(e) *Land transaction lending* – certain DCSAs and DCAs to finance the purchase of land or buildings.

(f) *Certain insurance policy loans* – the exemption is confined to loans made by building societies and other bodies whose lending is already exempt (see (a) above) to cover the payment of insurance premiums related to the mortgage, i.e. mortgage protection insurance premiums, and the credit is provided without interest and any other charges.

(g) *Credit union agreements* – where the APR does not exceed 26.9 per cent.

2 Exempt consumer hire agreements. The only exempt consumer hire agreements are those for the hire of meters or metering equipment for electricity, gas and water, where the owner is an organisation authorised by statute to supply electricity, water or gas.

3 New categories introduced by the 2006 Act (as amended) – which apply to both consumer credit and consumer hire agreements.

(a) *High net worth individuals* – the individual must be a natural person, they must agree to forgo the protection contained in the Act and they must provide a statement of high net worth by a specified person, e.g. a solicitor or accountant. 'High net worth' means that

the individual has a net income in excess of £150,000 or net assets exceeding £500,000. The exemption only applies to agreements above £60,260.

(b) *Business agreements* – where the creditor provides credit exceeding £25,000 or the hirer is required to make payments in excess of £25,000, and the agreement is wholly or predominantly for business purposes.

(c) *'Buy to let' agreements* – the lending must be secured by a mortgage and less than 40 per cent of the property is to be used as a dwelling by the debtor, their spouse or a close relative.

General provisions with wider application

Some parts of the Act apply to otherwise exempt agreements. For example, the safeguards on extortionate credit affect all credit irrespective of the amount, and certain credit advertisements are exempt, e.g. if the advertisement indicates that the credit is only available to corporate bodies.

Licensing of credit and hire businesses

The Act set up a comprehensive licensing system to control the activities of those in the credit and hire business. The following categories of business require a consumer credit licence:

1 consumer credit business, e.g. banks, moneylenders, finance companies;
2 consumer hire business, e.g. TV and car rental companies;
3 credit brokerage, e.g. car dealers, estate agents;
4 debt adjusting;
5 non-commercial debt adjusting;
6 debt counselling;
7 non-commercial debt counselling;
8 debt collecting;
9 debt administration (from October 2008);
10 provision of credit information services – including credit repair (from October 2008);
11 provision of credit information services – excluding credit repair (from October 2008);
12 provision of non-commercial credit information services – including non-commercial credit repair;
13 credit reference agencies.

The Act also applies to brokers who, for example, arrange credit for their customers with a finance company.

The OFT is charged with determining the fitness of applicants to hold a licence and to have regard to the skills, knowledge and experience of the licence holder and his employees, and the practices and procedures that will be implemented by the business. Matters which the OFT should take into account include whether the applicant or an associate:

(i)   has committed an offence involving fraud, dishonesty or violence;
(ii) has contravened provisions of relevant legislation, e.g. the 1974 Act;
(iii) has practised discrimination;
(iv) has engaged in business practices which appear to the OFT to be deceitful, unfair or improper, which may include irresponsible lending.

The OFT must publish guidance on the way it determines the fitness of a person to hold a licence.

Anyone who carries on any of the activities listed above without a licence commits a criminal offence. Moreover, an agreement made by an unlicensed trader is enforceable only at the discretion of the OFT.

The OFT has the power to vary, suspend and revoke licences and to issue indefinite licences. It also acquires powers to impose requirements on existing and new licensees where it is dissatisfied with the conduct of the business.

The OFT may require applicants for a licence to provide additional information and a duty is imposed on applicants to inform it of any changes in the information supplied within 28 days. The OFT can enter the licensee's premises on reasonable notice to observe how the business is being carried on or to inspect relevant documents; it can obtain a warrant to enter premises. The OFT has the power to impose a civil penalty of up to £50,000 on 'defaulters' for every breach of an OFT requirement. It must publish a statement of policy in regard to the exercise of its powers in relation to civil penalties.

A Consumer Credit Appeals Tribunal has been established to deal with appeals from decisions of the OFT. There will be a right of appeal to the Court of Appeal and from there to the House of Lords. The jurisdiction of the Financial Services Ombudsman is extended to cover consumer credit licensees.

Seeking business

The Act controls three ways of attracting business: advertising, giving quotations and canvassing.

Advertising (ss 43–47)

The Act requires the Secretary of State to make regulations about the form and content of advertisements to ensure that they convey a fair and reasonably comprehensive indication of the nature of the credit facilities offered and their true cost. The aim is to promote 'truth in lending' and so encourage consumers to shop around for the best credit bargain. The specific regulations relating to credit advertising contained in the 2010 Advertisements Regulations are supplemented by the more general rules contained in the Consumer Protection from Unfair Trading Regulations 2008 (see Chapter 14 ○).

The Advertisements Regulations replace the 2004 Advertisement Regulations except in relation to agreements secured on land. Certain credit advertisements are exempt, e.g. if the advertisement states that the credit is only for business purposes. The regulations apply to all forms of advertising including TV, radio, on the Internet and teletext, and by telephone. If the advertisement includes an interest rate or any amount relating to the cost of the credit, a representative example of the credit must be included in the advertisement. The representative example must include standard information (see Figure 13.5, overleaf).

It is a criminal offence to cause an advertisement to be published which breaches the regulations. Offences can be committed by an advertiser, the publisher, and anyone who devised the advert or arranged for its publication. It is a defence if a person can show that he did not know and had no reason to suspect that the publication would be an offence.

It is also an offence to advertise goods or services on credit where the advertiser does not hold himself out as prepared to sell for cash.

Quotations (s 52)

Traders used to be under an obligation to give a written quotation if one was requested. The relevant regulations were revoked in 1997. However, the Consumer Credit (Content of Quotations) and Consumer Credit (Advertisements) (Amendment) Regulations 1999 (SI

Standard information to be included in a representative sample
The rate of interest
Fees or charges to be included in the total credit charge
Total amount of credit
Representative APR
The cash price and amount of any advance payment
Duration of the agreement
Total amount payable
Amount of each repayment of credit

Figure 13.5 Information to be provided in credit advertising

1999/2725), which came into force on 28 February 2000, require the inclusion of certain prescribed information where a quotation is provided by the trader. Quotations must include a statement, if applicable, that security is or may be required and the warning: 'Your home is at risk if you do not keep up repayments on a mortgage or other loan secured on it.'

Canvassing (ss 48–51)

It is an offence to canvass a DCA off trade premises. This outlaws the practice of stopping people in the street or calling uninvited at their houses to persuade them to take a loan. Traders need a special licence to canvass off trade premises credit agreements linked to the supply of goods and services or the hire of goods. It is an offence to send any documents to a minor inviting him to borrow money, obtain goods or services on credit, or to apply for information or advice on borrowing. It is also an offence to give or send a person a credit token if he has not asked for it. This rule does not apply to the renewal of credit cards.

Creditworthiness checks (s 55B)

The EU Directive Regulations introduces a new provision requiring creditors to assess a borrower's creditworthiness

before entering into a credit agreement or before increasing significantly the amount of credit to be provided. The requirement applies to all regulated consumer credit agreements except those secured on land and pawnbroking. The Regulations do not specify exactly how creditors should assess creditworthiness; however, the assessment must be based on information from the borrower, where this appropriate, and from a credit reference agency, where this is necessary. The OFT has produced guidance in *Irresponsible Lending* and creditors will be expected to take this into account in assessing creditworthiness.

Adequate explanations (s 55A)

The 2008 EU Directive introduces a new s 55A which applies to all regulated consumer credit agreements except:

- agreements secured on land;
- agreements for credit in excess of £60,260;
- non-business overdrafts repayable within three months or on demand; and
- business overdrafts

A creditor is required to:

- provide borrowers with an adequate explanation of certain matters;
- advise the borrower to consider pre-contractual information and where this has been provided in person, to allow the borrower to take the information away;
- give the borrower the opportunity to ask questions about the agreement;
- advise the debtor how to ask for further information, e.g. by providing contact details.

The matters which must be explained to the borrower are:

(a) *the features of the agreement which may make the credit to be provided under the agreement unsuitable for particular types of use*, e.g. a creditor must explain why a particular kind of credit would not be suitable for long-term borrowing, if this was the case;

(b) *how much the borrower will have to pay periodically and, where the amount can be determined, in total under the agreement*, e.g. an explanation of how the cost of credit card use varies depending on the amount of monthly repayments and the effect of only paying the minimum amount;

(c) *the features of the agreement which may operate in a manner which would have a significant effect on the borrower in a way which the borrower is unlikely to foresee*, e.g. the complex arrangements relating to 0% balance transfers for credit cards;

(d) *the principal consequences for the borrower arising from a failure to make payments under the agreement at the times required by the agreement including legal proceedings and, where this is a possibility, repossession of the borrower's home*, e.g. any additional charges for late payments;

(e) *the effects of the exercise of any right to withdraw from the agreement and how and when this right may be exercised*, e.g. details of the interest that will be charged until the credit is repaid.

The explanations must be adequate to enable the borrower to assess whether the proposed credit agreement is suitable. A borrower cannot waive the requirement to be given adequate explanations. A creditor can decide how to give the explanation; this could be orally or in writing, or both.

Pre-contractual information and agreements (the Disclosure Regulations)

The Disclosure Regulations apply to all regulated consumer credit agreements from 1 February 2011, with the following exceptions:

■ agreements secured on land;
■ agreements for credit exceeding £60,260;
■ any agreement entered into wholly or predominantly for business purposes.

The Regulations require certain information to be provided to the borrower before the agreement is entered into. (There are separate rules in relation to telephone contracts, non-telephone distance contracts, excluded pawn agreements or overdraft agreements.) The information must be provided in good time and the borrower must be given an adequate opportunity to consider the information before concluding the agreement. In most cases the information must be provided in a standard format, known as the Pre-contract Credit Information (PCI) form. In addition to providing the PCI, the creditor must inform the borrower about the following:

■ if a decision not to enter into the agreement is based on information provided by a credit reference agency, and the particulars of the credit reference agency;
■ the right to request a copy of the draft agreement;
■ the period of time during which the creditor is bound by the information in the PCI.

Signing credit agreements (the Agreements Regulations)

The Agreements Regulations apply to all regulated consumer credit agreements including all authorised overdrafts, with the following exceptions:

■ an agreement secured on land;
■ an agreement for credit exceeding £60,260; and
■ agreements entered into wholly or predominantly for business purposes.

The agreement must contain the information specified in the Regulations in a clear and concise manner. The relevant headings are as follows: the nature of the agreement, the parties to the agreement, the provision of credit, the rate of interest, the total amount payable, repayments, statements of account, statement where no credit reduction, charges, notarial fees, the right of withdrawal, linked credit agreements, early settlement, termination by the borrower, ombudsman scheme, supervisory authority.

Certain terms are 'prescribed terms' for the purposes of the Consumer Credit Act. If these terms are not included the agreement will not be executed properly and the creditor cannot enforce the agreement without a court order. The 'prescribed terms' are;

■ the amount of credit or credit limit;
■ the rate of interest; and
■ the timing of repayments.

The agreement must be signed by the borrower (or on behalf of the borrower in the case of an unincorporated association) in the space indicated for the purpose in the agreement; and by or on behalf of the creditor.

Copies of the agreement (s 61A)

The creditor must give a copy of the executed agreement to the borrower once the agreement has been made. If the creditor has already given the borrower a copy of the unexecuted agreement, which is identical to the executed agreement, the creditor must inform the borrower that the agreement has been executed and the date of execution, the fact that the executed agreement is identical and the borrower's right to a copy before the end of the 14-day withdrawal period.

Failure to comply with the requirements as to formalities renders the agreement improperly executed. This means that it can be enforced against the debtor only by order of a court (s 127).

Wilson v First County Trust Ltd (2003)

W borrowed £5,000 from First County Trust (FCT) by pawning her car. She was charged a £250 'document fee', which, because she was unable or unwilling to pay it immediately, was added to her loan. W and FCT entered into an agreement which stated the amount of the loan and the fee, i.e. £5,250. W later brought proceedings against FCT under s 127 of the Consumer Credit Act, arguing that the agreement was unenforceable because it did not correctly state the amount of the loan. The judge at first instance rejected W's claim, holding that the fee was part of the credit and therefore the agreement contained the prescribed terms including the amount of the credit. The Court of Appeal overturned this decision, finding that the 'document fee' was not credit and, as a result, one of the prescribed terms was incorrect rendering the agreement unenforceable. The House of Lords upheld the Appeal Court's decision on this point. W was entitled to keep her car, the amount she had been lent and was relieved of paying interest on the loan.

Comment. The Court of Appeal declared that s 127 of the Consumer Credit Act 1974 was incompatible with Art 6 of the European Convention on Human Rights because the section excludes all judicial remedies and disproportionately affects the rights of the lender. The House of Lords did not uphold the declaration of incompatibility. The human rights aspect of this case is discussed in Chapter 3 ◯.

Cancellation (ss 66A and 67)

There is a new right to withdraw from a credit agreement which applies to all consumer credit agreements except for the following:

- agreements for credit exceeding £60,260;
- agreements secured on land;
- restricted-use credit agreements to finance the purchase of land;
- agreements for bridging loans in connection with the purchase of land.

Borrowers have a right to withdraw from a credit agreement within 14 days from when the agreement was made. Notice of withdrawal can be given in writing or orally. If the withdrawal is faxed, emailed or using other electronic means, it is effective at the time of transmission. If the withdrawal notice is posted it is effective at the time of posting. The right to withdraw only applies to the credit agreement and does not give any right to return goods or cancel services which have been purchased using the credit. The borrower must still pay for the goods or services. The borrower must repay the credit provided and any interest that has accrued within 30 days. Any ancillary contracts, for example for insurance, will also terminate with the cancellation. Section 66A makes special provision for the statutory passing of title in goods under HP, conditional sale and credit-sale agreements where the borrower has exercised the right to withdraw. Section 66A(11) provides that title will pass to the borrower on the same terms as would have applied had the borrower not withdrawn from the agreement. This provision is designed to ensure that the borrower benefits from relevant consumer protection measures that apply to the goods.

The new right to withdraw replaces any cancellation rights previously provided under s 67. Section 67 still applies to agreements where the credit exceeds £60,260 and cancellable hire agreements. The cooling-off period applies to agreements signed off trade premises where there has been some personal contact between the debtor or hirer and the salesperson. The debtor or hirer may serve notice of cancellation at any time between signing the agreement and five clear days after receiving the second copy of the agreement. If the s 67 right is exercised, the parties are returned to the position they were in before the agreement was signed. Any money received must be repaid, and if the debtor or hirer has acquired goods, they must be made available for return.

Post-contract information

The 1974 Act included requirements in relation to the provision of information after the contract had been concluded. These included periodic statements for running-account credit, notices of variation in the agreement, default, enforcement and termination notices (see later), and information to be provided on request. The 2006 Act introduces new rights to post-contract information. Creditors in regulated fixed-sum credit agreements must provide debtors with an annual statement of their position. The first statement is due within one year of the day after the agreement was made. If the creditor fails to provide a statement he will not be able to enforce the agreement, nor charge interest during the period in which he is in default. The debtor will not be liable for any default sum that would have become payable for breach of the agreement during the period of non-compliance. Annual statements must also be provided to debtors in relation to running-account credit. There are also new requirements in relation to notices of arrears, default notices and notices relating to post-judgment interest. The OFT is also required to produce information sheets, explaining the consumer's rights and responsibilities and sources of information and advice, to be in included in arrears and default notices.

The EU Directive Regulations introduce a new right (s 77B) for borrowers to request a statement of account showing instalment payments in respect of fixed sum credit agreements of fixed duration where the credit is repayable in instalments. The request can be made at any time during the operation of the agreement and the statement must be provided as soon as reasonably practicable.

The EU Directive also introduces a new requirement (s 78A) that obliges creditors to inform borrowers in writing prior to any changes in the rate of interest. There are some limited exceptions to the notification requirement, e.g. if the agreement provides for the information about interest rates to be provided in writing periodically.

Credit reference agencies

These organisations collect information about people's creditworthiness. It is normal practice for traders in the credit business to use the services of such an agency to vet the suitability of applicants for credit. Sections 157–159 give consumers the right to obtain the name and address of any agency used and, for a £2 fee, a copy of any files held. If the information is wrong, the consumer can add a correction to the file.

Credit intermediaries (s 160A)

The EU Directive Regulations introduces a new s 160A imposing requirements on credit intermediaries to disclose the extent to which they are acting independently or working for one or more creditors. Breach of the requirements is an offence punishable by a fine.

Liability of the supplier and creditor

A supplier of goods and services will be liable for any false statements he makes which persuade a customer to enter into an agreement. In addition, certain terms are implied into contracts for the supply of goods and services. If the supplier does not live up to his obligations, he may be sued by the customer for breach of contract.

If credit is involved, the situation may be complicated by the fact that the creditor and supplier are not the same person. For example, a credit card may have been used to buy goods. The Act contains two provisions which have the effect of making the credit grantor equally liable for any misrepresentations or breach of contract by the supplier.

1 Section 56. In the case of regulated agreements, the dealer is deemed to be acting as the creditor's agent. The creditor is, therefore, responsible for the negotiations conducted on his behalf by the supplier including, for example, any misrepresentations.

2 Section 75. This makes the creditor equally responsible with the supplier for any misrepresentation or breach of contract. However, the section only applies if the agreement meets the following conditions:

(a) it is a regulated credit agreement;
(b) the cash price of the item is between £100 and £30,000;
(c) the credit is granted under an agreement between the creditor and supplier.

Equal liability does not apply to non-commercial agreements or where the customer has arranged his own credit, such as a bank overdraft or a cash advance from a credit card company.

The EU Directive introduces a new s 75A which applies to agreements not covered by s 75. Section 75A only applies if the following conditions are met:

- the cash price of the goods or services is more than £30,000;
- the amount of credit agreement does not exceed £60,260;
- the goods or services are purchased under a 'linked credit agreement' where the credit exclusively finances a contract for the supply of specific goods or services; or where the creditor uses the supplier in connection with the preparation or making of the credit agreement; or the goods or services are explicitly specified in the credit agreement;
- there has been a breach of contract, and the borrower is unable to get satisfaction from the supplier.

The following differences between s 75 and the new s 75A should be noted.

1 Section 75A applies only where the credit has been used to purchase specific goods and services, rather than for more general purposes. As a result it will not usually apply to credit cards, although s 75 may apply.
2 Under s 75 the borrower can choose to pursue the creditor rather than the supplier. The new s 75A requires the borrower to pursue the supplier first. The borrower will only be able to take action against the creditor if:

- the supplier cannot be traced;
- the borrower has contacted the supplier but has not received a response;
- the supplier is insolvent;
- the borrower has taken reasonable steps to pursue his claim against the supplier but has not obtained satisfaction. This does not mean that the borrower must take legal action.

The scope of the equal liability provisions

The precise effect of s 75, particularly in relation to transactions paid for by credit card, has been the subject of ongoing discussions between the Director General of Fair Trading and the credit card companies. The problem areas are as follows:

- Section 75 came into effect on 1 July 1977 and applies to regulated agreements made on or after that date. It is unclear whether s 75 applies to card-holders who first obtained their cards before 1 July 1977. Following discussions with the Director General of Fair Trading, Barclaycard and Access voluntarily agreed to accept liability to card-holders who first obtained their cards before 1977. However, this voluntary liability is limited to the amount of the transaction charged to the credit card account.
- It is unclear whether the equal liability provisions apply to second card-holders or just to the account holder.
- The credit card companies have argued that card-holders should be required to exhaust all remedies against the supplier of the goods and services before taking action against the credit card company. In particular, it has been argued that where a holiday tour operator goes into liquidation, holidaymakers who have paid by credit card should have recourse to the special fund set up by tour operators to deal with this situation. The Director General rejected the idea that card-holders should look first to the supplier, but he did propose that liability be limited to the amount of the transaction.
- There is some doubt about whether card-holders who book a package tour with a tour operator through a travel agent can claim the protection of s 75. Although the Office of Fair Trading takes the view that s 75 does apply if the travel agent is acting as the agent of the tour operator, card-holders are advised to pay the tour operator directly to avoid potential problems.
- It has been argued that the liability of a credit card company ceases once the credit has been repaid. If this were the case, card-holders who paid their credit card bills in full each month would enjoy greatly reduced protection.
- It has been argued that the equal liability provisions do not apply to overseas transactions by UK card-holders. However, in *Jarrett* v *Barclays Bank plc* (1997), the Court of Appeal held that English courts had jurisdiction over a transaction in which a Barclaycard had been used to pay for a timeshare in a Portuguese property and in the *Office of Fair Trading v Lloyds TSB Bank plc* (2008) the House of Lords confirmed that purchases made abroad using a credit card attract the same protection as those made in the UK under s 75 of the 1974 Act.

Loss or misuse of credit tokens

Sections 66 and 84 set out the extent of a debtor's liability if his credit token (i.e. credit card) is misused. Under s 66 the debtor is not liable at all for another person's use of the credit token unless the debtor has previously accepted the credit token or the use by the other person constituted an acceptance by him. The debtor accepts the credit token when (a) he signs it; (b) he signs a receipt for it; or (c) it is first used, either by the debtor himself or a person authorised to use it.

Section 84 deals with the debtor's liability for misuse which occurs after acceptance. The debtor should give notice as soon as possible to the creditor (card-issuer) that the credit token has been lost, stolen or liable to misuse because he will not be liable for any loss arising after notice has been received by the creditor. Notice can be given orally but the agreement can provide that it will not be effective unless written confirmation is received within seven days. The extent of any liability for misuse in the period before notice takes effect depends on the circumstances. If the person who misuses the token obtained possession of it with the debtor's consent, the debtor is liable without limit. If the debtor did not consent (i.e. the token was lost or stolen), the debtor's liability is limited to £50 or the credit limit if lower.

The Consumer Protection (Distance Selling) Regulations 2000 (SI 2000/2334) introduce increased protection for consumers who use credit cards in connection with 'distance selling' contracts, such as purchases made via the Internet or by mail order. If a credit card is used fraudulently in connection with the distance contract, the consumer is entitled to cancel the payment, or, if the payment has already been made, the consumer will be entitled to a re-credit or to have all sums returned by the card-issuer. The regulations also amend the Consumer Credit Act 1974 so as to remove the potential liability of a card-holder for the first £50 of any loss arising from misuse in connection with a distance contract.

Extortionate terms (ss 137–140)

Sections 137–140 contain powers for the courts to reopen extortionate credit bargains so as to do justice between the parties. The provisions apply to all credit, irrespective of the amount involved. They allow an individual debtor or surety (a person who has given security for credit) to bring the credit bargain to the attention of the court either in a specific action or during the course of proceedings relating to the agreement. A credit bargain is extortionate if it requires the debtor or his relatives to make payments which are grossly exorbitant or which otherwise contravene the ordinary principles of fair dealing.

The Act is not precise about what should be regarded as an extortionate rate of interest. Instead, it mentions general factors which should be taken into account by the court such as:

1 prevailing interest rates;
2 the age, experience, business capacity and state of health of the debtor;
3 the degree of financial pressure put on the debtor and the nature of that pressure;
4 the degree of risk accepted by the creditor;
5 the creditor's relationship with the debtor;
6 whether the cash price quoted for the goods was true or 'colourable', i.e. inflated to make the credit charges appear more reasonable.

In *Barcabe* v *Edwards* (1983) the court held that a loan with an APR of 319 per cent was, prima facie, extortionate. It reopened the agreement and substituted a flat rate of interest of 40 per cent which is equivalent to an APR of 92 per cent! In *A Ketley Ltd* v *Scott* (1981), a bridging loan with an estimated APR of 57.35 per cent was held not to be extortionate. The court took into account the high degree of risk taken by the creditors and the business experience of the debtor.

If the court finds that the credit bargain is extortionate, it may:

1 direct a state of account between the two parties to be taken to establish, for example, how much money has been paid by the debtor and the amount still outstanding;
2 set aside any obligation under the agreement;
3 require the creditor to repay all or part of any sum paid under the agreement;
4 direct the return of any property provided as security; or
5 alter the terms of the credit agreement.

Paragon Finance plc v Nash and Staunton (2002)

The defendants, the Nashes and the Stauntons, had taken out variable rate mortgages with the claimant, Paragon, secured on their homes. The defendants had fallen into arrears and the claimant was seeking possession of their homes. The defendants were seeking to have the agreements reopened under s 139 of the Consumer Credit Act 1974, arguing that the mortgage agreement was an extortionate credit bargain because the claimant had not reduced the interest rate in line with the Bank of England's prevailing rate. The Court of Appeal held that a mortgage lender was under a limited duty not to vary interest rates dishonestly, improperly, arbitrarily or unreasonably. The claimant was not in breach of this duty simply because its rates were higher than high street lenders. In deciding whether a loan agreement amounted to an extortionate credit bargain, the transaction must be looked at when it was entered into rather than in the light of subsequent interest rate rises.

Reform of the extortionate credit provisions

Background

The 2003 White Paper (*Fair, Clear and Competitive – The Consumer Credit Market in the 21st Century*) identified a number of reasons why the extortionate credit provisions were in need of reform:

- very few cases had reached the courts because the Act's requirements were too high, and the courts have applied a restrictive interpretation;
- the courts had concentrated on interest rates rather than considering all the elements of the agreement, e.g. the security required;
- the legislation did not deal with unfair practices, such as high pressure sales and 'churning' of agreements;
- as we have seen in the *Paragon* case, the courts tended to focus on the agreement when it was entered into, rather than considering subsequent events which may have made the agreement unfair;
- those who were most at risk of entering into an unfair credit bargain were least likely, either financially or culturally, to be able to pursue legal action.

The White Paper proposed replacing the existing extortionate credit provisions with a much wider 'unfairness' test, which would be able to take into account all aspects of the transaction both at the outset of the agreement and in the light of subsequent events.

The 2006 Act

The 2006 Act repeals the extortionate credit provisions contained in ss 137–140 of the 1974 Act and replaces them with new provisions in ss 140A and 140B which provide the power for a court to consider whether the relationship between the creditor and debtor is unfair to the debtor because of:

(i) any of the terms of the agreement or any related agreement;
(ii) the way in which the creditor has exercised or enforced any of his rights under the agreement or any related agreement;
(iii) any other thing done (or not done) by or on behalf of the creditor before or after the agreement or any related agreement was made.

The court can take into account all matters which it thinks relevant, including matters relevant to the debtor and creditor in deciding whether the relationship is unfair.

The orders which may be made by the court where it finds an unfair relationship are set out in the new s 140B. They include:

(i) requiring the creditor to repay in whole or part any sums paid by the debtor;
(ii) reducing or discharging any sum payable by the debtor;
(iii) altering the terms of the agreement;
(iv) requiring the creditor to do or not to do anything specified in the court order;
(v) setting aside in whole or part any duty imposed on the debtor by virtue of the agreement;
(vi) directing the return to a surety of any property provided as security;
(vii) directing accounts to be taken between parties.

The new 'unfair relationship' rules apply to new agreements with effect from 6 April 2007 and to pre-existing agreements from 6 April 2008. The old extortionate credit provisions will continue to apply to agreements completed before the new provisions came into force. 'Completed' means that there are no sums which are or may become payable.

Termination and default

Both debtor and creditor may have reasons why they want their relationship to end. The debtor may have come into some money and wishes to pay off his debt. Alternatively, he may have lost his job and is no longer able to afford the repayments. The creditor will want to take action against people who have not lived up to the agreements they have made.

Early settlement (ss 94–97)

The debtor under a regulated consumer credit agreement is entitled to pay off what he owes at any time on giving notice to the creditor of his intention to do this. This may entitle him to a rebate of interest.

The 2003 Consumer Credit White Paper noted that the formula contained in the Act, known as the 'Rule of 78', can result in substantial benefits to the lender, and may not reflect the real cost to the lender of repaying early. Some lenders do not apply the rule and charge lower amounts or nothing at all. The government stated its intention to abolish the Rule of 78 and to introduce a new method to calculate maximum early settlement charges. Credit agreements would be required to state clearly the right to early settlement and to give three examples of repayment charges calculated at different points in the lifetime of the agreement. The Consumer Credit (Early Settlement) Regulations 2004 (SI 2004/1483) gave effect to these proposals. They also limit the deferral of any settlement by the debtor to one month for agreements of more than a year.

The EU Directive Regulations amend s 94 of the Act to give borrowers the right to make partial early repayment of a credit agreement. The new provisions operate the same way as those for full early settlement.

Termination (ss 98–101)

1 By the debtor. The debtor under a regulated HP or conditional sale agreement may give notice to terminate the agreement at any time before the final instalment is due. The debtor must return the goods and pay off any arrears. In addition, he or she must pay the smaller of the following:

- a minimum amount specified in the agreement;
- half of the total purchase price;
- an amount ordered by the court to compensate the creditor for his loss.

If the debtor has failed to take reasonable care of the goods, he or she must pay damages to the creditor.

2 By the creditor. Usually the creditor will wish to terminate the agreement because the debtor has broken the agreement in some way (this is dealt with below). However, it should be noted that some agreements allow the creditor to terminate where there has been no default by the debtor. The agreement may specify that it can be terminated at any time or if, for example, the creditor becomes unemployed or is convicted of a crime of dishonesty. If it is an agreement for a specified period, which has time to run, the creditor must give seven days' notice of his intention. The debtor may apply to the court for a 'time order'.

The EU Directive Regulations introduce a new s 98A which introduces new provisions relating to the termination of open-ended agreements and the termination or suspension of the right to draw down credit under such agreements.

Default (ss 87–89)

If the debtor has committed a breach of the agreement, the creditor must serve a 'default notice' before taking any of the following actions:

- to terminate the agreement;
- to demand earlier payment;
- to recover the possession of any goods or land;
- to regard rights conferred on the debtor by agreement as terminated, restricted or deferred;
- to enforce any security.

The default notice must explain to the debtor the nature of his alleged breach, what he must do to put it right and by when, or, if the breach cannot be remedied, what must be paid by way of compensation.

Woodchester Lease Management Services Ltd v Swain & Co (1999)

The defendants, a firm of solicitors, had entered into an agreement with the claimants for the hire of a photocopier. Payments were made regularly by the defendants for more than two years when they suddenly stopped. The claimants sent a default notice to the defendants, but a mistake was made in calculating the amount which should be paid to remedy the default, with the result that the amount was overstated by more than £240. The Court of Appeal held that the default notice must specify accurately the sum of money to be paid to remedy the default. Although a court might be prepared to overlook a minor discrepancy, the overstatement in this case was substantial. The notice was, therefore, invalid.

The time allowed for the debtor to remedy the breach must be at least seven days from the service of the default notice. It must contain certain information about the consequences of failing to comply with the notice.

If the debtor carries out the requirements of the notice, the breach is treated as if it had never happened. Where the notice is not heeded, the creditor may pursue any remedies contained in the agreement, subject to the provisions of the Act. At this point the debtor may seek the help of the court by applying for a time order.

Under changes introduced by the 2006 Act, creditors must give debtors or hirers notices of sums in arrears within 14 days after a default event has occurred and at six-month intervals thereafter. Failure to serve a sums in arrears notice prevents the creditor from enforcing the agreement during the period of non-compliance and the debtor is not liable to pay interest.

Time orders (ss 129–130)

A debtor may apply to the court for a time order where he has been served with either a default or a non-default notice or in the course of an action by the creditor to enforce a regulated agreement. The court can allow the debtor time to remedy a breach or, where the breach consists of non-payment, time in which to pay the arrears. In the case of an HP or conditional sale agreement, the court may rearrange the pattern of future instalments. A debtor can also apply for a time order after receiving a sums in arrears notice. In this case the debtor or hirer can make an application for a time order only if he has given notice to the creditor or owner and a period of 14 days has passed since he gave notice. The debtor must indicate that he wants to make a proposal in relation to making payments under the agreement and provide details of his proposal.

Information sheets (s 86A)

The 2006 Act creates a new s 86A which requires the OFT to prepare and publish information sheets for debtors and hirers about arrears and default. The information sheet must be given to a debtor or hirer at the same time as a notice of sums in arrears or at the same time as a default notice. The information sheets are designed to help the debtor and contain, for example, information about debt management options and contact details for providers of advice.

Repossession of the goods (ss 90–92)

One of the attractions of HP to Victorian traders was that, if the hirer defaulted at any stage, the owner could recover the goods. Many HP agreements even gave creditors the right to enter the hirer's home for this purpose.

Debtors under regulated HP and conditional sale agreements now enjoy protection against the so-called 'snatch back':

■ A creditor must obtain a court order before he enters any premises to repossess goods.
■ If the debtor has paid at least one-third of the total price and he has not terminated the agreement, the goods are protected. The creditor cannot recover possession of protected goods unless he obtains a court order. If a creditor ignores this requirement, he faces severe penalties. The agreement terminates immediately; the debtor is released from all liabilities under the agreement and, in addition, can recover money already paid.

Capital Finance Co Ltd v Bray (1964)

Bray had paid over a third of the HP price of a car when he fell into arrears. A representative of the finance company took the car back without either Bray's consent or a court order. The company realised its mistake and returned the car to Bray. When the repayments were still not forthcoming, the company sued for possession of the car. This was granted by the court, which further held that Bray was entitled to recover everything that he had previously paid to the finance company.

Self-test questions/activities

1 What kinds of credit are likely to be used by:
   (a) a typical family;
   (b) a sole trader;
   (c) a limited company?

2 What forms of credit would be available for the following purchases:
   (a) furniture;
   (b) clothes;
   (c) a car;
   (d) a house?
   What kinds of institutions would provide the credit?

3 What are the points of similarity between HP and credit sale? What are the differences?

4 Using the terminology of the Consumer Credit Act 1974 contained in List A below, describe the credit transactions in List B below.

   List A:
   (a) DCSA;
   (b) DCA;
   (c) restricted-use credit;
   (d) unrestricted-use credit;
   (e) fixed-sum credit;
   (f) running-account credit;
   (g) credit token agreement;
   (h) regulated consumer credit agreement;
   (i) regulated consumer hire agreement;
   (j) small agreement;
   (k) non-commercial agreement;
   (l) exempt agreement.

   List B:
   (a) Arthur buys a suite of furniture from Matchstick Furniture plc, paying 12 monthly instalments of £50 each. Ownership of the furniture passes to Arthur immediately.
   (b) The Portland Bank plc allows Beryl to overdraw her current account up to a limit of £1,000.
   (c) Colin sees a new car that he wishes to buy in the showrooms of Rattle Cars Co Ltd. The company introduces him to Shady Finance Co Ltd, which agrees to let Colin have the car on HP. Colin pays a deposit of £1,500 and 24 monthly instalments of £20 each.
   (d) Doris uses her credit card (on which she has a personal limit of £800) to buy a camera from Snapshot Ltd.
   (e) Evan has the *Financial Times* delivered to his home every day. He pays the bill at the end of each month.
   (f) Freda buys and obtains possession of a coat and dress from Bondsman Mail Order Co Ltd for £90. She pays this in 20 instalments of £4.50 each.

5 Gerald buys a new DVD player. After two weeks' use, the player stops working. What are his rights, and against whom, if the purchase was financed in the following ways:
   (a) cash payment direct to the retailers, Viewscene Ltd;
   (b) bank credit card;
   (c) HP arranged by Viewscene Ltd with Eazimoney Finance Co Ltd;
   (d) bank overdraft?

Specimen examination questions

1 'Consumers need clear, consistent information to be able to make informed comparisons between the plethora of [credit] products currently available to them' DTI (2003), *Fair, Clear and Competitive – The Consumer Credit Market in the 21st Century* p 5.

   Evaluate the adequacy of the provisions of the Consumer Credit Act 1974 (as amended) which are designed to address the informational needs of consumers *before* they enter into a credit agreement.

2 Sections 56 and 75 of the Consumer Credit Act 1974 together provide a powerful remedy for consumers who have bought defective goods on credit.

   Outline the scope of these provisions and assess their effectiveness in protecting consumers.

3 Wesley agrees to take a car on HP from Tite Finance
Co Ltd for a total HP price of £6,500, made up of a
deposit of £1,700 plus 24 monthly payments of £200.

(a) The company receives a letter from Wesley
terminating the agreement because he has lost
his job. What will Wesley have to pay if he
terminates in the following situations:

   (i) after he has paid three instalments but
before the fourth is due;

   (ii) after he has paid four instalments and the
fifth and sixth are still owing;

   (iii) after he has paid 12 instalments and before
the 13th is due, but the car was badly
damaged in an accident?

(b) Wesley does not terminate the agreement
but fails to pay any instalments after the
seventh instalment. What action can Tite
Finance Co Ltd take?

Website references

http://www.bis.gov.uk/policies/consumer-issues/
consumer-credit-and-debt The Department for Business
Innovation and Skills is responsible for consumer policy
including regulation of consumer credit.

http://www.oft.gov.uk The OFT website provides
detailed information for both consumers and

credit businesses about the Consumer Credit
Act 1974.

http://www.ccta.co.uk The website of the Consumer
Credit Trade Association provides information, products
and services for credit-related businesses.

Visit www.mylawchamber.co.uk/richesallen to
access study support resources including answers to
questions in this chapter and legal updates, all linked
to the **Pearson eText** version of **Keenan and Riches'
Business Law** which you can **search**, **highlight** and
personalise with your **own notes** and **bookmarks**.

premium
mylawchamber
unrivalled support for legal education

Use **Case Navigator** to read in full some of the key cases
referenced in this chapter with commentary and questions:

Wilson v First County Trust Ltd (2003)

POWERED BY LexisNexis

Consumer protection

So far in Part 3 of this book we have examined the law governing the supply of goods and services and the liability of a supplier of goods and services in contract and tort. In this chapter, we turn our attention to the consumer of the product or service. We will consider the nature and scope of the law of consumer protection, the role of the criminal law in protecting consumers, the rights of consumers and the role of various organisations which protect and represent consumers. First, we will explore the questions of who is a consumer and why do consumers need protecting?

Who is a consumer?

At the outset it is important to establish who is intended to be benefited by the law of consumer protection. Dictionary definitions of the word 'consumer' are either so broad that they cover anyone who consumes goods or services, including even those who are acting in a commercial capacity, or so narrow that they cover only

purchasers, rather than all users, or just goods, rather than both goods and services.

A 'consumer transaction' generally has three essential elements: an individual who purchases or uses goods and services for his own private purposes; a supplier who is acting in a business capacity; and goods or services which must be intended for private use or consumption. Despite this consensus, Parliament and the courts have had considerable difficulty in deciding precisely who is worthy of special protection, as an examination of each of the elements will show.

1 Individual purchaser or user acting in a private capacity. The net of protection has often been cast so wide that even businesses have benefited from protective measures. Although the provisions of the Consumer Credit Act 1974 apply only where the debtor is an individual, the definition of an 'individual' is so broad that it encompasses borrowing by sole traders and small partnerships. The Unfair Contract Terms Act 1977 also purports to extend the greatest protection in respect of exclusion clauses to those who 'deal as a consumer' (s 12(1)). However, the courts have interpreted the requirements of s 12(1) so generously that even occasional purchases by a company, provided they are not an integral part of the business, may be classed as consumer transactions (*R & B Customs Brokers Ltd* v *United Dominions Trust Ltd* (1988), see Chapter 8 ○).

2 Supplier acting in the course of a business. The requirement that the supplier must be acting in a business capacity has not always been consistently applied. The implied terms in s 14 of the Sale of Goods Act 1979 apply to all sales by a business, not just to those which form a regular part of the business (see *Stevenson* **v** *Rogers* (1999) in Chapter 11 ○). In contrast, the offence of knowingly or recklessly engaging in an unfair commercial practice under reg 8 of the Consumer Protection from Unfair Trading Regulations 2008 (CPRs) can only be committed by a trader who is acting for the purposes relating to his business. Although we do not know yet how the courts will approach the question of whether a trader is acting for business purposes, case law relating to the Trade Descriptions Act 1968, which the CPRs replace, indicates that the courts are likely to take a restrictive approach. The principles are set out in the following cases.

Havering LBC v *Stevenson* (1970)

The Divisional Court of the Queen's Bench held that the purchase and sale of cars used in a car hire business formed an integral part of the business and were covered by s 1 of the Trade Descriptions Act 1968 which provided that anyone who in the course of a trade or business applied a false trade description to goods or supplied or offered to supply any goods to which a false trade description was applied was guilty of an offence.

Davies v *Sumner* (1984)

The House of Lords held that the sale of a car which had been used by the defendant in his business as a self-employed courier was not 'in the course of trade or business' since the transaction lacked the degree of regularity which was present in the *Havering* case.

The more exacting requirements developed by the courts in relation to trade description can be justified because the Trade Descriptions Act 1968 imposed criminal penalties, while the Sale of Goods Act 1979 merely establishes civil liability.

3 Goods and services intended for private use or consumption. Section 12 of the Unfair Contract Terms Act 1977, for example, stipulates that a person only deals as a consumer where there is a contract for the supply of goods if the goods are of a type ordinarily supplied for private use or consumption. There are problems with such an approach. Is a person dealing as a consumer if the goods are used for both business and private purposes? What is the position in relation to goods which are ordinarily supplied for business purposes but then put to private use, or vice versa? Some of these uncertainties have been resolved by amendments to s 12 made by the Sale and Supply of Goods to Consumers Regulations 2002 (SI 2002/3045), which came into force on 31 March 2003. If the consumer is an individual (rather than a business as in the *R & B Customs Brokers* case) it is no longer necessary to show that the goods are of a type ordinarily supplied for private use or consumption.

Consumers do not have to have a contract with the business supplier in order to attract protection. Many consumers will have purchased the goods and services and have a contractual relationship with the supplier, but there are also other consumers who make use of goods and services without having entered into a contract. In recent years, there has been growing recognition of the need to protect non-contractual consumers.

Why do consumers need protection?

The idea that consumers need protecting has been around since the Middle Ages, yet most of the consumer protection measures which exist today have been developed over the past 40 or so years. The earliest forms of consumer protection were designed to discourage fraudulent trading practices and to protect the consumer from danger. The main justification for intervening on behalf of consumers today is that the nature of modern markets is such that consumers can no longer make prudent shopping decisions. Enormous changes in the way we acquire goods and services have taken place since the Second World War. Consumers now have access to a much wider range of more technologically complex goods.

Whereas in the past retailers were expected to use their skill and judgement to select good quality products, today's retailer often has limited technical knowledge of the products he sells. There has been a move towards large-scale retail businesses, e.g. supermarkets and, more recently, the development of large out-of-town shopping complexes. At the same time, advertising and marketing techniques have become much more sophisticated. Today's consumers enjoy far greater spending power than their grandparents did; disposable incomes are higher and credit is more easily available. Expensive and highly complex goods can be purchased relatively easily, but there is less time for consumers to spend on shopping. Changes in working patterns and, in particular, the increased participation of women in the labour market mean that shopping often has to be fitted around work. The overall effect of these changes has been to increase the power of suppliers at the expense of consumers. The underlying aim of most modern consumer protection law is to redress the balance of power.

Consumer protection institutions

A large number of organisations have a role in protecting consumers.

European institutions

The UK became a member of the European Community (EC) in 1973 and since that time has been subject to a new source of law emanating from the Council and Commission in the form of regulations, directives and decisions. The UK is also bound by the decisions of the European Court of Justice. The Treaty of Rome, which established the European Economic Community in 1957, provides that the main aim of the EC is the establishment of a common market. Although the original Treaty of Rome did not contain a specific provision in relation to consumer protection, it was recognised that the creation of a genuine common market would entail harmonisation of the consumer protection laws of member states. A Consumer Protection Programme was approved in 1972 and a Consumers' Consultative Committee was set up by the Commission in the following year. A second Consumer Protection Programme followed in 1981. Unfortunately, progress was very slow because of the requirement that any directives must be adopted unanimously by all member states. The Single European Act, which took effect in 1987, amended the relevant treaty Article (Art 94, previously Art 100) to allow proposals in relation to consumer protection to be adopted by qualified majority voting. The 1991 Maastricht Treaty makes a specific reference to the role of the EC in contributing to 'the attainment of a high level of consumer protection'. EC Directives on consumer protection already adopted include:

- Directive on Liability for Defective Products, implemented in the UK as Part I of the Consumer Protection Act 1987 (see Chapter 12 ○).
- Directive on Misleading Advertisements, implemented by the Control of Misleading Advertisements Regulations 1988 (SI 1988/915), which have been revoked by the Consumer Protection from Unfair Trading Regulations 2008 (discussed later in this chapter).
- Directive on Doorstep Selling, implemented by the Consumer Protection (Cancellation of Contracts Concluded away from Business Premises) Regulations 1987 (SI 1987/2117), now replaced by the Cancellation of Contracts made in a Consumer's Home or Place of Work etc. Regulations 2008 (SI 2008/1816). Under the regulations consumers have a seven-day cooling-off period within which they can exercise a right to cancel if they conclude a contract for goods and services away from the trader's business premises. The new regulations cover both solicited and unsolicited visits by traders and will include contracts concluded at the consumer's home, work place, at another individual's home or on an excursion organised by the trader away from business premises. The seven-day cooling-off period will apply to all contracts with total payments of more than £35. Any consumer credit agreement which is entered at the same time as a contract for goods and services is automatically cancelled if the contract for goods and services is cancelled. Traders are required to include details of the cancellation rights in any written contract or provide written details if there is no written contract. It is an offence, punishable by a maximum fine of £5,000, for a trader to enter into a contract to which the regulations apply without complying with the requirements as to notification of cancellation rights.
- Directive on Package Travel, Package Holidays and Package Tours, implemented by the Package Travel, Package Holidays and Package Tours Regulations 1992 (SI 1992/3288) (discussed later in this chapter).

- Directive on General Product Safety, implemented by the General Product Safety Regulations 2005 (SI 2005/1803) (discussed later in this chapter).
- Directive on Unfair Terms in Consumer Contracts, implemented by the Unfair Terms in Consumer Contracts Regulations 1999 (SI 1999/2083) (see Chapter 8 ○).
- Directive on Timeshare, implemented by the Timeshare Regulations 1997 (SI 1997/1081).
- Directive on Distance Selling, implemented by the Consumer Protection (Distance Selling) Regulations 2000 (SI 2000/2334).
- Directive on Injunctions for the Protection of Consumers' Interests, implemented by the Stop Now Orders (EC Directives) Regulations 2001 (SI 2001/1422), and subsequently superseded by Part 8 of the Enterprise Act 2002.
- Directive on Sale of Consumer Goods and Associated Guarantees, implemented by the Sale and Supply of Goods to Consumers Regulations 2002 (SI 2002/3045).
- Directive on Unfair Commercial Practices (UCP) 2005, implemented by the Consumer Protection from Unfair Trading Regulations 2008 (SI 2008/1277) (discussed later in this chapter).

In March 2007 the European Commission set out its six-year strategy for consumer policy. The Consumer Strategy Policy 2007–2013 sets out the following objectives:

1 to empower EU citizens who need 'real choices, accurate information, market transparency and the confidence that comes from effective protection and solid rights';
2 to enhance EU consumers' welfare in terms of price, choice, quality, diversity, affordability and safety;
3 to protect consumers from the serious risks and threats that they cannot tackle as individuals.

The interests of UK consumers in relation to EU policy are represented by the European Consumer Consultative Group (ECCG).

Central government institutions

Department for Business, Innovation and Skills

The Department for Business, Innovation and Skills (BIS) is responsible for developing policy and promoting legislation in the fields of trading standards, fair trading, weights and measures, shops legislation, consumer credit and consumer safety. It also has functions in relation to competition policy, i.e. monopolies, mergers and restrictive practices. In addition, BIS has responsibility for a number of agencies, e.g. Office of Fair Trading, Competition Commission, British Hallmarking Council, Consumer Focus, utility regulators such as OFWAT and OFCOM, and it sponsors the British Standards Institute.

In 2009 the Labour Government published a White Paper on consumer matters: *A Better Deal for Consumers: Delivering Real Help Now and Change for the Future*. The White Paper covered the following themes:

- Providing real help now for vulnerable consumers.
- Taking a new approach to consumer credit.
- Empowering consumers through better enforcement and information.
- Modernising consumer law.

The Home Office

The Home Office is responsible for supervision of the control of explosives, firearms, dangerous drugs and poisons. Responsibility for liquor licensing has been transferred to the Department for Culture, Media and Sport.

The Department of Health

The Department of Health and the former Ministry of Agriculture, Fisheries and Food were both partly responsible for matters of food hygiene and safety and used to share responsibility for the enforcement of the Food Safety Act 1990 and the Medicines Act 1968. Food issues are now the responsibility of the Food Standards Agency. The Department of Health offers medical advice on contamination of consumer goods and is involved in the control of drugs.

The Department for Environment, Food and Rural Affairs (DEFRA)

DEFRA has taken over the responsibilities of the Ministry of Agriculture, Fisheries and Food (MAFF). One of DEFRA's objectives is 'to promote a sustainable, competitive and safe food supply chain which meets consumers' requirements'.

The Department for Culture, Media and Sport

This department has taken over responsibility from the Home Office for liquor licensing.

The Office of Fair Trading (OFT)

The Office of the Director General of Fair Trading (DGFT) was established in 1973 under the terms of the Fair Trading Act 1973. The organisation, known as the OFT, was the administrative support which developed to enable the DGFT to carry out his statutory responsibilities. The Enterprise Act 2002 abolished the office of DGFT and established a new corporate authority to be known as the OFT. The DGFT's functions and responsibilities were transferred to the OFT. The Enterprise Act 2002 sets out the general functions of the OFT as:

- obtaining and reviewing information relating to its functions in respect of competition and consumer matters so that it can take informed decisions and carry out its other functions effectively;
- promoting to the public the benefits that competition may have for consumers and the economy in general and giving information and advice about its functions in relation to competition, including publishing educational literature or participating in educational activities;
- promoting good consumer practice, e.g. by encouragement for the development of consumer codes of practice and approving such duties.

In October 2010 the Government proposed merging the OFT with the Competition Commission and transferring its consumer and enforcement duties.

Food Standards Agency (FSA)

Concerns about the quality of our food in recent times (BSE, salmonella, E. coli, etc.) led to the establishment of the Food Standards Agency by the Food Standards Act 1999. The Food Standards Agency became operational on 3 April 2000. The main objective of the Agency is to protect public health in relation to food, and also to protect the wider food standards interests of consumers, such as labelling.

The Agency's functions are to:

- provide advice and information to the public and to the government on food safety from 'farm to fork', nutrition and diet;
- protect consumers through effective enforcement and monitoring;
- support consumer choice through promoting accurate and meaningful labelling.

Local government

Local authorities have two main roles in respect of consumer protection: enforcement of regulatory statutes and the provision of consumer advice and information.

1 Enforcement. Local government has the day-to-day responsibility for enforcing many of the statutory consumer protection measures. Most local authorities have consumer protection or trading standards departments which have responsibility for enforcing the provisions of the Consumer Credit Act 1974, the Weights and Measures Act 1985, the Food Safety Act 1990 and various regulations and orders made under consumer protection legislation, e.g. the Consumer Protection from Unfair Trading Regulations 2008. Local authorities also have responsibility for testing equipment used by traders and sampling products put on the market by manufacturers and retailers.

2 Consumer advice. Many local authorities have set up consumer advice centres to provide pre-shopping advice and to give advice on complaints. Sometimes they will take up individual complaints.

Government-sponsored bodies

Consumer Protection Advisory Committee (CPAC)

The Committee was established under Part II of the Fair Trading Act 1973 to consider references on the question of whether a consumer trade practice adversely affected the economic interests of UK consumers. The CPAC reported to the Secretary of State, who could give effect to any proposals by means of an order made by statutory instrument. The orders are enforced by criminal sanction only.

Membership of the Committee was suspended in 1983 and has now been formally abolished by s 10 of the Enterprise Act 2002. By 2002 there were only two orders still in force and therefore the repeal of Part II of the Fair Trading Act 1973 is partial until such time as the orders are revoked. The orders are the Consumer Transactions (Restrictions on Statements) Order 1976 (SI 1976/1813) and the Business Advertisements (Disclosure) Order 1977 (SI 1977/1918).

1 Consumer Transactions (Restrictions on Statements) Order 1976. Article 3 of the order makes it an offence to display at any place where consumer transactions are effected a notice containing a term invalidated by s 6 of the Unfair Contract Terms Act 1977. It is also an offence under Art 4 to supply goods, their container or a document to a consumer with a statement about his rights against the supplier with regard to defects, fitness for purpose or correspondence with description unless there is in close proximity to the statement another clear and conspicuous statement to the effect that the statutory rights of the consumer are not affected. Article 5 is similar to Art 4 except that it applies, although there is no direct consumer transaction between the business supplier and the consumer, where the supplier intended or reasonably expected his goods to become the subject of a subsequent consumer transaction.

2 The Business Advertisements (Disclosure) Order 1977. This order requires business sellers of goods to make it clear in their advertisements directed at consumers that they are traders. The fact can be made apparent by the content of the advertisement, its format or size.

Consumer Focus (formerly the National Consumer Council)

The National Consumer Council was set up in 1975 to represent consumer interests in dealings with the government, local authorities, the Office of Fair Trading and trade bodies. It also advised on consumer-protection policy through the publication of reports and making representations to relevant bodies. Following the Consumers, Estate Agents and Redress Act 2007, the Welsh, Scottish and National Consumer Councils merged with Postwatch and Energywatch to create Consumer Focus.

Consumer Focus was established on 1 October 2008. It is sponsored by the government. In October 2010 the Government signalled its intention to abolish Consumer Focus and transfer its functions to Citizens Advice.

Public services and privatised industries

Newly privatised, large-scale suppliers of goods and services, such as British Gas, BT, the water and electricity supply companies, have found themselves in a position of having a monopoly or near-monopoly of supply. It has, therefore, been thought necessary to regulate their operations by appointing statutory 'regulators', and, in some cases, formalising consumer representation in the industry (see Figure 14.1). The duties of the regulators may include promoting competition and protecting the consumer in relation to pricing and terms of supply.

In 1991 the government launched its Citizens' Charter initiative for public services. The aim of the initiative is to raise standards in public services such as health, education and the courts, by producing charters which set out what kind of services consumers are entitled to expect and how they can complain if things go wrong. The Charter Mark standards are being replaced by Customer Service Excellence awards.

Voluntary organisations

Consumers' Association

The Consumers' Association was established in 1957. The inspiration for its creation came from the USA. It has five main aims:

Industry	Regulator	Office	Consumer representation
Communications	Office of Communications	OFCOM	Ofcom Consumer Panel
Gas and electricity	Chairman of Gas and Electricity Markets Authority	OFGEM	Gas and Electricity Consumer Council (Consumer Focus)
Water	Director General of Water Services	OFWAT	Consumer Council for Water and local customer service committees
Rail transport	Rail Regulator	ORR	Rail Passengers Council and rail passengers committees
Air traffic	Civil Aviation Authority	CAA	–

Figure 14.1 Regulators

1 to encourage people to spend their money wisely;

2 to reduce the inequality between the shopper and the manufacturer or supplier;

3 to improve the quality of British goods, creating more discriminating purchasers;

4 to tackle the growing complaints about unsatisfactory goods;

5 to combat the power of advertising by providing information so the consumer can choose goods on more rational grounds.

The main aim of the Consumers' Association is to provide information to the consumer about products and services by testing them thoroughly and giving the subscriber an independent appraisal through the medium of its magazine *Which?* In addition, the Consumers' Association seeks to influence consumer protection policy by lobbying Parliament or by representation on other bodies in the UK and Europe.

Citizens' Advice Bureaux (CABx)

These were first established in 1939 by the National Council of Social Service. They deal with a wide range of problems: employment rights, social security, landlord and tenant disputes, etc. Approximately 20 per cent of the enquiries they deal with are consumer problems. The Citizens Advice Service is a charity but is funded through government grants.

National Consumer Federation (NCF)

The NCF was established in 2001 following the amalgamation of the Consumer Congress and the National Federation of Consumer Groups. It encourages and coordinates the activities of the local consumer groups.

British Standards Institute (BSI)

The BSI was established in 1929. It sets standards, dimensions and specifications for manufactured goods. A 'British Standard' is a document which stipulates the specifications, requirements for testing or measurements with which a product must comply in order to be suited for its intended purpose and work efficiently. Compliance with such a standard is a matter of choice on the part of the producer. However, in some cases compliance is compulsory, e.g. crash helmets. A producer may apply to the BSI for certification of his products, in which case he may display a BSI kitemark on the product.

Other organisations

Trade associations

An important aspect of consumer protection is the extent to which laws are supplemented by codes of practice drawn up by trade associations in consultation with the Office of Fair Trading (discussed in more detail later in this chapter).

Advertising Standards Authority (ASA)

The ASA was established in 1962 to provide independent supervision of the advertising industry's system of self-regulation through a monitoring programme and investigation of complaints. The main instrument of control is the British Code of Advertising Practice (BCAP) which was published in 1961. It is kept under continuous review and amendment by the Committee of Advertising Practice (CAP). The code applies to all advertisements in newspapers, magazines, posters, brochures and leaflets for the public, cinema, commercial and viewdata services. The ASA and CAP also administer the British Code of Sales Promotion Practice. Separate systems operate in relation to broadcasting and cable operations.

Professional bodies

The Law Society, for example, operates a compensation fund for the victims of dishonest or insolvent solicitors and requires compulsory insurance against negligence.

Ombudsmen

The financial sector has appointed a number of 'ombudsmen' to deal with complaints, e.g. insurance, building societies, pensions, banking. The powers of these ombudsmen vary from scheme to scheme, but, as a minimum, they provide a channel for complaints and, at best, they can require an organisation to pay compensation.

Different approaches to consumer protection

The law on consumer protection has been developed on a piecemeal basis over many years and has a variety of sources: EU regulations and directives, statutes, ministerial regulations and case law. Over the years different approaches have been taken, causing problems of overlap and complexity. The four main approaches are: providing civil remedies, imposing criminal liability, administrative controls, and business self-regulation.

Providing civil remedies

An individual consumer may be able to bring a civil action against a trader for a breach of contract or for liability in tort, e.g. negligence. The liability of a supplier of goods and services for breach of contract was examined in Chapter 11 ○, and his liability in tort was considered in Chapter 12 ○.

Imposing criminal liability

Since the earliest times, the criminal law has been used to protect consumers and restrain dishonest and unfair trading practices. This approach has clear advantages. The maintenance of high standards in business and protection of the public are not dependent on isolated individuals taking civil actions in contract or tort. Instead, since crimes are regarded as offences against the community as a whole, responsibility for enforcement is entrusted to public officials who bring proceedings against rogue traders at public expense. Traders who ignore the rules run the substantial risk of prosecution and criminal conviction, especially as most of the crimes against consumers are strict liability offences which do not require proof of fault. This is a powerful incentive to businesses to ensure their compliance. Suppliers today are subject to extensive criminal controls over their activities. In this chapter we shall concentrate on some of the more significant provisions of the criminal law as they affect the supplier of goods and services, namely in relation to:

- unfair commercial practices;
- safety of consumer goods;
- safety and quality of food.

Other areas of business activity relating to the supply of goods and services which are subject to the criminal law are also noted.

Unfair commercial practices

Prior to May 2008, the main pieces of UK legislation dealing with unfair trading practices were the Trade Descriptions Act 1968, which prohibited the use of certain false trade descriptions by a person acting in the course of a trade or business, and Part III of the Consumer Protection Act 1987, which contained controls over false and misleading statements as to prices. The majority of the provisions of the Trade Descriptions Act and all of Part III of the Consumers Protection Act have been repealed by the Consumer Protection from Unfair Trading Regulations 2008 (SI 2008/1277), which implement the EC Directive on Unfair Commercial Practices (UCP).

The UCP Directive is designed to harmonise the unfair trading laws of member states and its scope is very broad. The government decided to use the opportunity, when implementing the Directive, to rationalise the UK's consumer protection legislation. The new Consumer Protection from Unfair Trading Regulations 2008 (CPRs) which came into force on 26 May 2008, repeal in whole or in part 23 legislative provisions, including all of Part III of the Consumer Protection Act 1987 covering misleading price indications, and most of the Trade Descriptions Act 1968.

The CPRs consist of three main elements:

- a general prohibition of **unfair commercial practices**;
- prohibition of **misleading and aggressive practices**; and
- **banned practices**, which are prohibited in all circumstances.

Definitions

The CPRs introduce a number of new concepts, which include the following:

- The **average consumer**. A consumer is defined as 'any individual who in relation to a commercial practice is acting for purposes which are outside his business'. The CPRs recognise three kinds of average consumer: (a) the 'average' consumer, whose characteristics include being reasonably well informed, reasonably observant and circumspect; (b) the 'average member' of a targeted group of consumers; and (c) 'average member' of a vulnerable group of consumers. The concept of the average consumer does not refer to actual consumers and therefore it is not necessary to show how actual consumers have been affected by the unfair practice.
- **Commercial practices**, defined as 'any act, omission, course of conduct, representation or commercial

communication (including advertising and marketing) by a trader, which is directly connected with the promotion, sale or supply of a product to or from consumers, whether occurring before, during or after a commercial transaction (if any) in relation to a product'.

- **Materially distorting the economic behaviour** of the average consumer means 'appreciably to impair the average consumer's ability to make an informed decision thereby causing him to take a transactional decision that he would not have taken otherwise'.
- **Products.** This word is given a wide meaning so as to include products and services, and immovable property, rights and obligations.
- **Professional diligence** is defined as 'the standard of special skill and care which a trader may reasonably be expected to exercise towards consumers which is commensurate with either (a) honest market practice in the trader's field of activity, or (b) the general principle of good faith in the trader's field of activity'.
- **Transactional decision** is 'any decision taken by a consumer whether it is to act or refrain from acting concerning (a) whether, how or on what terms to purchase, make payment in whole or in part for, retain or dispose of a product, or (b) whether, how or on what terms to exercise a contractual right in relation to a product'.

Scope of the CPRs

In general terms the CPRs apply to 'business to consumer' transactions and 'business to business' transactions with the potential to affect consumers. The CPRs do not apply to 'consumer to consumer' transactions and 'business to business' transactions which do not have the potential to affect consumers. So if a trader sells only to business customers, he is not required to comply with the CPRs, but if his customers include both businesses and consumers he must comply with the CPRs. Similarly, a transaction between businesses, e.g. between a manufacturer and wholesaler higher up the supply chain, may be covered by the CPRs if the goods are intended for the consumer market. The CPRs will apply where the trader is selling to a consumer and also when he is buying from a consumer.

The CPRs also apply to practices which occur before, during and after the transaction. This includes advertising and marketing, and after-sales service and debt collection.

The general prohibition (reg 3)

The general prohibition against unfair commercial practices is set out in reg 3. There are two strands to the prohibition.

1 A commercial practice is unfair if it contravenes the requirements of professional diligence, and it materially distorts or is likely to distort the economic behaviour of the average consumer with regard to the product (reg 3(3)).

2 A commercial practice is also unfair if it is:

(i) a misleading action;
(ii) a misleading omission;
(iii) an aggressive commercial practice;
(iv) listed in Sch 1 as a practice which is in all circumstances unfair (reg 3(4)).

Misleading and aggressive practices (regs 5–7)

The CPRs prohibit misleading actions and omissions.

Misleading actions (reg 5)

A commercial practice is a misleading action if it satisfies the condition in reg 5(2) or (3).

Giving false information to, or deceiving, consumers (reg 5(2))

A commercial practice will be misleading if it contains false information and is untruthful in relation to certain specified matters contained in reg 5(4) or if its overall presentation deceives or is likely to deceive the average consumer in relation to the matters in reg 5(4) even if the information is factually correct **and** it causes or is likely to cause the average consumer to take a transactional decision he would not have taken otherwise.

Creating confusion and failing to honour commitments made in a code of practice (reg 5(3))

A commercial practice will be misleading if it concerns any marketing of a product which creates confusion with any products, trade marks, trade names or other distinguishing marks of a competitor, or it concerns the failure of a trader to comply with a commitment contained in a code of conduct where the trader has indicated that he is bound by the code **and** the commitment is firm and capable of being verified (and is not aspirational) and it causes or is likely to cause the average consumer to take a transactional decision he would not have taken otherwise.

Specified matters (reg 5(4))

The matters referred to in reg 5(2) include the main factors which a consumer is likely to take into account in making decisions about a product. The list includes:

(a) the existence or nature of the product;
(b) the main characteristics of the product, e.g. availability, delivery, after-sales assistance;
(c) the extent of the trader's commitments;
(d) the motives for the commercial practice;
(e) the nature of the sales process;
(f) any statement or symbol relating to direct or indirect sponsorship or approval of the trader or the product;
(g) the price or the manner in which it is calculated;
(h) the existence of a specific price advantage;
(i) the need for a service, part, replacement or repair;
(j) the nature, attributes and rights of the trader, e.g. qualifications, status, assets;
(k) the consumer's rights or the risks he may face.

Misleading omissions (reg 6)

A commercial practice is a misleading omission if in its factual context the practice omits or hides material information or provides it in an unclear, unintelligible, ambiguous or untimely manner and as a result it causes or is likely to cause the average consumer to take a different transactional decision. An assessment of the factual context includes all the features and circumstances of the commercial practice, the limitations of the medium of communication used (i.e. in space or time) and steps taken by the trader to make the information available to consumers by other means. Material information is the information the consumer needs to have in order to make an informed decision and includes any information required by EC law.

Where the commercial practice is an invitation to purchase then the following information is automatically regarded as material:

- the main characteristics of the product;
- the identity of the trader;
- the geographical address of the trader;
- the price (including taxes) or the manner in which the price is calculated;

- where appropriate, all additional freight, delivery or postal charges, or, if they cannot be calculated in advance, the fact that charges may be payable;
- arrangements for payment, delivery, performance and complaint handling if they vary from the requirements of professional diligence;
- cancellation rights.

Aggressive commercial practices (reg 7)

A commercial practice is aggressive if it significantly impairs or is likely significantly to impair the average consumer's freedom of choice or conduct through the use of harassment, coercion or undue influence **and** it causes or is likely to cause him to take a different transactional decision. In determining whether a commercial practice uses harassment, coercion or undue influence, account must be taken of:

- its timing, location or persistence;
- the use of threatening or abusive language or behaviour;
- the exploitation of any misfortune or circumstance impairing the consumer's judgement, which the trader is aware of, to influence the consumer's decision in relation to the product;
- any onerous or disproportionate non-contractual barrier imposed by the trader where a consumer wishes to exercise rights under the contract, including, for example, the right to terminate the contract or to switch to another trader or product;
- any threat to take any action which cannot legally be taken.

Banned practices (reg 3(4)(d) and Sch 1)

Schedule 1 to the CPRs contains a list of 31 commercial practices which are regarded as unfair in all circumstances and are banned outright, without the need to consider the likely effect on consumers. The list includes the following:

- claiming to be a signatory to a code of conduct when the trader is not;
- displaying a trust mark, quality mark or equivalent without having obtained the necessary authorisation;
- claiming that a trader or a product has been approved, endorsed or authorised by a public or private body when they have not, or making such a claim without complying with the terms of approval, endorsement or authorisation;

- making an invitation to purchase products at a specified price without disclosing the existence of any reasonable grounds the trader may have for believing that he will not be able to offer for supply, or to procure another trader to supply, those products or equivalent products at that price for a period that is, and in quantities that are, reasonable having regard to the product, the scale of advertising of the product and the price offered (known as bait advertising);
- making an invitation to purchase products at a specified price and then (a) refusing to show the advertised item to consumers, (b) refusing to take orders for it or deliver it within a reasonable time, or (c) demonstrating a defective sample of it, with the intention of promoting a different product (known as bait and switch);
- falsely stating that a product will only be available for a very limited time, or that it will only be available on particular terms for a very limited time, in order to elicit an immediate decision and deprive consumers of sufficient opportunity or time to make an informed choice;
- presenting rights given to consumers in law as a distinctive feature of the trader's offer;
- claiming that the trader is about to cease trading or move premises when he is not;
- establishing, operating or promoting a pyramid promotional scheme;
- falsely claiming that a product is able to cure illnesses, dysfunction or malformations;
- describing a product as 'gratis', 'free', 'without charge' or similar if the consumer has to pay anything other than the unavoidable cost of responding to the commercial practice and collecting or paying for delivery of the item;
- including in marketing material an invoice or similar document seeking payment which gives the consumer the impression that he has already ordered the marketed product when he has not;
- falsely claiming or creating the impression that the trader is not acting for purposes relating to his trade, business, craft or profession, or falsely representing oneself as a consumer;
- creating the impression that the consumer cannot leave the premises until a contract is formed;
- making persistent and unwarranted solicitations by telephone, fax, email or other remote media except in circumstances and to the extent justified to enforce a contractual obligation;
- including in an advertisement a direct exhortation to children to buy advertised products or persuade their parents or other adults to buy advertised products for them;
- explicitly informing a consumer that if he does not buy the product or service the trader's job or livelihood will be in jeopardy.

Offences (regs 8–12)

It is a criminal offence under reg 8(1) if a trader (a) knowingly or recklessly engages in a commercial practice which contravenes the requirements of professional diligence **and** (b) the practice materially distorts or is likely to materially distort the economic behaviour of the average consumer. For the purposes of reg 8(1)(a) a trader who engages in a commercial practice without regard to whether the practice contravenes the requirements of due diligence will be deemed to have acted recklessly, whether or not he has reason for believing that the practice might contravene the requirements. A reg 8 offence requires proof of *mens rea*.

The CPRs also create a number of strict liability offences in relation to: misleading actions (with the exception of code of practice commitments) (reg 9); misleading omissions (reg 10); aggressive practices (reg 11); and specific unfair practices listed in Sch 1 (subject to some exceptions relating to advertorials and advertising to children) (reg 12).

The penalties on conviction are, in the magistrates' court, a fine up to the maximum of £5,000, and, in the Crown Court, an unlimited fine or two years' imprisonment.

Defences (regs 16–18)

In respect of the strict liability offences, the CPRs provide defences of due diligence and innocent publication of advertisements and there is a 'by-pass' provision. To rely on the defence of due diligence, the accused must prove: that the commission of the offence was due to a mistake, reliance on information given by another person, the act or default of another, an accident, or another cause beyond his reasonable control; and that he took all reasonable precautions and exercised due diligence to avoid the commission of an offence by himself or anyone under his control (reg 17). A person who publishes, or arranges the publication of advertisements, has a defence if he can show that he received the advertisement in the ordinary course of business and that he did not know and had no reason to suspect that its publication would amount to an offence (reg 18). A by-pass provision allows the prosecution to take action against a person who is really responsible for an unfair trade practice, who could not otherwise be charged with an offence, e.g. a private (consumer) seller (reg 16).

Enforcement (regs 19–27)

Responsibility for enforcement rests with the Office of Fair Trading and local authority Trading Standards Services in England and Wales. Enforcement authorities are given the power to investigate whether a breach of the regulations has occurred, and can make test purchases, enter premises, copy documents, and seize and detain goods.

Product safety

The legal framework for dealing with the problem of unsafe general products is contained in the General Product Safety Regulations 2005 (SI 2005/1803) and Part II of the Consumer Protection Act 1987. It should be noted that food is also covered by the Food Safety Act 1990.

The General Product Safety Regulations (GPS) 2005

The 2005 GPS Regulations implement the provisions of a 2001 EC Directive on GPS. The 2001 Directive and the 2005 Regulations supersede an earlier 1992 Directive on GPS and 1994 GPS Regulations respectively. The 2005 Regulations also repeal s 10 of the CPA 1987. The GPS Regulations impose requirements concerning the safety of products intended for consumers or likely to be used by consumers where such products are placed on the market by producers or supplied by distributors. The new regulations came into force on 1 October 2005.

1 Scope of the regulations. The regulations apply to products intended or likely to be used for consumer use which have been supplied in the course of a commercial activity. A 'consumer' is a person who is not acting in the course of a commercial activity. A commercial activity is defined as any business or trade. The regulations apply

whether the products are new, used or reconditioned. Products used exclusively in the context of a commercial activity, even if for or by a consumer, are not subject to the regulations.

The regulations do not apply to the following types of products:

(a) second-hand products which are antiques;
(b) products supplied for repair or reconditioning before use, but the supplier must inform the customer to that effect;
(c) products that are subject to specific provisions of EC law covering aspects of their safety.

2 General safety requirement. Regulation 5 provides that a producer may not place a product on the market unless it is a safe product. It is an offence to fail to comply with the general safety requirement. It is also an offence for a producer or distributor to offer or agree to place (or supply) a dangerous product or expose or possess such a product for placing on the market (or for supply) (reg 20).

3 Safe product. Regulation 2 sets out what is meant by a 'safe product'. A product will be safe if, under normal or reasonably foreseeable conditions of use (including duration), there is no risk or the risk has been reduced to a minimum. Any risk must be compatible with the product's use, considered acceptable and consistent with a high level of health and safety protection. In this respect, account should be taken of the following matters:

(a) the characteristics of the product, including its composition, packaging, instructions for assembly and maintenance;
(b) the effect on other products, if it is likely to be used with other products;
(c) the presentation of the product, the labelling, any instructions for use and disposal, and any other instructions or information regarding the producer;
(d) the categories of consumer at serious risk in using the product, particularly children and the elderly.

The fact that higher levels of safety can be achieved or that there are less risky products available will not of itself render a product unsafe.

Products which comply with UK legal requirements concerning health and safety are presumed to be safe products (reg 6). If no specific rules exist, the safety of a product will be assessed according to:

(a) voluntary UK standards which give effect to a European standard; or

(b) other national standards drawn up in the UK;

(c) EC recommendations setting guidelines on product safety;

(d) sector-based product safety codes of good practice;

(e) the state of the art and technology; and

(f) reasonable consumer expectations concerning safety.

4 Producer. A 'producer' is defined in reg 2 as:

(a) a manufacturer established in the EC;

(b) where the manufacturer is not established in the EC, his representative or the importer of the product;

(c) other professionals in the supply chain, but only to the extent that their activities might affect the safety of the product.

5 Information requirements. A producer is required under reg 7 to provide consumers with information so that they can assess inherent risks and take precautions. The duty only arises where the risks are not immediately obvious without adequate warnings. A producer must also adopt measures to keep himself informed of any risks which his products may present. This may include:

(a) marking the products (or product batches) so they can be identified;

(b) sample testing of marketed products;

(c) investigating complaints;

(d) keeping distributors informed of monitoring arrangements.

The producer must also take appropriate action to avoid risks which may include withdrawing the product from the market.

6 Duty of distributors. A distributor must act with due care to help producers comply with the general safety requirement. In particular, a distributor will commit an offence if he supplies dangerous products. He must also, within the limits of his activities, participate in monitoring the safety of products, including passing on information about product risks and cooperating in action to avoid the risks (reg 8(b)).

7 Defence of due diligence. It is a defence for a person accused of an offence under the regulations to show that he took all reasonable steps and exercised all due diligence to avoid committing the offence (reg 29). The defence cannot be relied on in the following situations:

(a) where the defendant has failed to serve a notice at least seven days before the hearing that his defence involves an allegation that the commission of the offence was due to either the act or default of another or reliance on information given by another;

(b) where it was unreasonable for the defendant to have relied on information supplied by another (the court will have regard to the steps which were taken – or might reasonably have been taken – to verify the information and whether the defendant had any reason to disbelieve the information);

8 By-pass provision. Regulation 31 provides a by-pass provision to enable the prosecution of the person, in the course of a commercial activity of his, whose act or default causes another to commit an offence.

9 Enforcement, notices and penalties. The regulations are enforced by a variety of authorities depending on the type of products and their location. Enforcement authorities include local trading standards authorities (in England, Wales and Scotland), Environmental Health Officers (in Northern Ireland, and for certain kinds of products in England, Wales and Scotland), the Vehicle Operator Services Agency (vehicles), and the Medicines and Healthcare Products Regulatory Agency (medicines and medical devices). Enforcement authorities may issue a range of notices:

(a) a *suspension notice* which requires a trader to suspend temporarily the supply of a product while tests are carried out (reg 11);

(b) a *requirement to mark* products with suitable warnings where it could pose a risk in certain conditions (reg 12);

(c) a *requirement to warn* those who have already been supplied with a product, e.g. for those who are particularly at risk, such as children (reg 13);

(d) a *withdrawal notice* requiring a product not to be placed on the market or supplied if already on the market (reg 14);

(e) a *recall notice* requiring the recall from consumers of a product that has been supplied to them (reg 15). A recall notice can only be issued as a last resort where voluntary action has not been sufficient to remove the risk.

The penalties for offences under the regulations are, in the case of serious offences, a maximum prison sentence of 12 months or a £20,000 fine, or, in the case of more minor offences, three months or a £5,000 fine, if convicted in the magistrates' court.

Part II of the Consumer Protection Act 1987 (CPA 1987)

Until the GPS Regulations were introduced in 1994, the legal framework for dealing with the problem of unsafe goods was contained in Part II of the CPA 1987. At the heart of the legislation was a general statutory offence, contained in s 10, of supplying consumer goods which fail to comply with the general safety requirement. The General Product Safety Regulations 1994 disapplied the general safety requirement set out in s 10 and the 2005 Regulations have now repealed s 10 of the CPA 1987.

The remaining provisions of Part II of the CPA 1987 concerning the power to make safety regulations and issue various notices continue to apply.

Safety regulations

Section 11 empowers the Secretary of State to make safety regulations for other purposes, such as ensuring that appropriate information is provided with goods or that goods which are unsafe in the hands of certain people are not made available to these persons. Section 11(2) sets out a list of matters which may be dealt with by such safety regulations. They include:

- composition, content, design, construction, finish or packaging of goods;
- approvals of the goods;
- requirements as to testing or inspection;
- warnings, instructions or other information about the goods;
- prohibitions on the supply of such goods or component parts or raw materials;
- requiring information to be given to officials.

Section 12 sets out a number of offences relating to contravention of the safety regulations including:

- contravening a prohibition on the supply of goods in breach of the regulations;
- failing to comply with tests or procedures required by the regulations;
- failing to provide information as required by the regulations.

Notices

Unsafe goods can be dealt with by means of various notices. The Secretary of State can issue two kinds of notice: a prohibition notice requiring a trader to cease supplying unsafe goods, and a notice to warn requiring a manufacturer or distributor to warn the public about the dangers of a product in circulation. Any enforcement authority, such as the local authority trading standards department, may issue a suspension notice, which requires a trader to cease supplying goods suspected of breaching any safety provisions for a period of six months. It is a criminal offence to contravene these notices.

Enforcement and penalties

The provisions of Part II of the CPA 1987 are enforced by trading standards officers. In addition to the power to obtain a suspension notice already mentioned, they may apply for a court order for the forfeiture of any goods which contravene any safety provision.

The penalties for offences are a maximum fine of £5,000 and six months' imprisonment on conviction in the magistrates' court.

Safety and quality of food

Food has been the subject of protective legislation since the Middle Ages. Modern food law is contained in the Food Safety Act 1990 (FSA 1990) as amended by the Food Safety Act 1990 (Amendment) Regulations 2004 (SI 2004/2990) and the General Food Regulations 2004 (SI 2004/3279). The scope of the FSA 1990 is not confined to food safety; it also covers matters such as composition, labelling and advertising.

Food Safety Act 1990

Before we consider the main offences created by the FSA 1990, it is necessary to establish what is meant by the word 'food'. Following amendment in 2004, the FSA 1990 now uses the definition of 'food' contained in the EC General Food Law Regulations (EC 178/2002). Food means 'any substance or product, whether processed, partially processed, or unprocessed, intended to be or reasonably expected to be ingested by humans'. It includes drink, chewing gum and any substances (including water) intentionally incorporated into food during its manufacture, preparation or treatment. Anything supplied to a customer which purports to be food will be treated as such. For example, if a customer in a restaurant orders lemonade but by mistake is supplied with caustic soda, the owner of the restaurant cannot argue that caustic soda is not 'food' because he purported to supply lemonade, which is within the definition of food (*Meah v Roberts* (1978)). Live animals, feeding stuffs for animals, tobacco and tobacco products, narcotics and psychotropic substances, cosmetics, controlled drugs and medicine are all excluded from the definition of 'food'.

The main offences under the Food Safety Act

Rendering food injurious to health (s 7)

It is an offence under s 7(1) for a person to render food injurious to health with the intent that it shall be sold for human consumption. To be guilty of an offence under s 7, the defendant must have done some positive act, which has resulted in the food becoming injurious to health. Such acts include:

(a) adding an article to the food (s 7(1)(a));
(b) using an article or substance as an ingredient in the preparation of food (s 7(1)(b)) (preparation includes any form of processing and treatment, such as subjecting food to heat or cold);
(c) abstracting any constituent from the food (s 7(1)(c));
(d) subjecting the food to any other process or treatment (s 7(1)(d)) (processing and treatment may cover the early stages in the production of food, e.g. crop spraying).

Defects in food arising from inaction (i.e. natural growth of mould) and failure to remove natural features of food, e.g. naturally occurring toxins in red kidney beans, are not covered by s 7.

Article 14(4) of Regulation EC 178/2002 states that, in deciding whether food is injurious to health, regard should be had:

(a) to not only the probable immediate and/or short-term and/or long-term effects of that food on the health of a person consuming it, but also on subsequent generations;
(b) to the probable cumulative toxic effects;

(c) to the particular health sensitivities of specific categories of consumers where food is intended for that category of consumer.

Selling food not of the nature, substance or quality demanded (s 14)

Section 14 provides that it is an offence for a person to sell to the purchaser's prejudice any food which is not of the nature or substance or quality demanded by the purchaser (s 14(1)). The food must be intended for human consumption (s 14(2)).

Note the following features of the offence created by s 14:

1 **Sale.** An offence will be committed only where there is a sale. Sale is defined broadly to include all supplies of food in the course of a business (s 2(1)), giving food away as a prize at a place of public entertainment (s 2(2)(a)) or as part of a promotional exercise (s 2(2)(b)).

2 **Nature or substance or quality.** Section 14 is worded in such a way as to create three separate offences; the characteristics listed are alternatives. So far as 'nature' is concerned, an offence will be committed if the customer does not get what he asked for, e.g. where the customer asks for butter but is supplied with margarine. With respect to 'substance', an offence will be committed if the food contains unwanted additives or where the food fails to comply with a statutory standard, e.g. a fish cake which contained less fish than required by regulations. So far as 'quality' is concerned, an offence will be committed if the food fails to comply with the standard of quality demanded. The standard of quality expected will depend on factors such as price paid or any description which has been applied, e.g. extra lean mince should not contain an excessive amount of fat.

3 **Sale to the purchaser's prejudice.** The seller must have supplied food which is inferior to that which could be reasonably expected. It is not necessary to show actual damage. A seller may avoid liability by use of a very clear notice: a consumer who knows exactly what he is getting cannot claim to have been prejudiced.

Falsely describing or presenting food (s 15)

Section 15 creates an offence of giving with any food sold or displaying with any food exposed for sale or in possession for the purposes of sale, a label whether or not attached to or printed on the wrapper or container which (a) falsely describes the food, or (b) is likely to mislead as to the nature, substance or quality of the food. It is also an offence to publish or be a party to the publication of an advertisement which is false or calculated to mislead. Section 15 is supplemented by regulations as to the labelling and description of food.

Defences

A number of defences are available to a person charged with an offence under the FSA 1990.

- In the case of ss 14 and 15 offences, that the defendant has taken all reasonable precautions and has exercised due diligence to avoid the commission of an offence by himself or a person under his control (s 21).
- The innocent publication of an advertisement which contravenes the FSA 1990 by a publisher or advertising agency (s 22).

By-pass provisions

Under s 20, where the commission by any person of the relevant offence is due to the act or default of some other person, that other person shall be guilty of the offence.

Enforcement and penalties

Enforcement authorities enjoy powers of inspection and seizure, the powers to apply to the court for a prohibition order, emergency prohibition order or an emergency control order to deal with suspected offenders. Enforcement has been assisted by the requirement since 1 May 1992 that all food premises register with local environmental health departments. Failure to comply is an offence.

The penalties for contravening the FSA 1990 are a prison sentence not exceeding two years and/or an unlimited fine in respect of a Crown Court conviction, and, on summary conviction in the magistrates' court, a prison sentence not exceeding six months and/or a £20,000 fine in respect of ss 7 and 14 offences and the statutory fine of £5,000 in respect of other offences.

The General Food Regulations 2004

It is an offence under the General Food Regulations, which came into force on 1 January 2005, to fail to comply with the following provisions of Regulation EC 178/2002:

- art 12 (food and feed exported from the EC) insofar as it relates to food;
- art 14(1) (food safety requirement);
- art 16 (presentation) as it relates to food;
- art 18(2) and (3) (traceability) as it relates to food business operators;
- art 19 (responsibilities for food and food business operators).

Regulation EC 178/2002

In addition to the provisions of the Regulation EC 178/2002, noted above, the additional requirements for businesses include:

(a) to ensure that the labelling, advertising and presentation of food does not mislead consumers (art 16);
(b) to keep records of suppliers and businesses they supply to and to make the records available to competent authorities (art 18);
(c) to recall or withdraw food from the market if it is not in compliance with food safety requirements (art 19).

Other criminal liability for the supply of goods and services

The range of criminal controls over the supply of goods and services is extensive and not confined solely to the provisions examined in this chapter. Other examples include:

1 **Weights and Measures Act 1985,** under which it is an offence to sell short weight, measure or number.

2 **Consumer Credit Act 1974 (as amended),** which makes it an offence to carry on a consumer credit business without a licence (see Chapter 13 ○).

3 **Property Misdescriptions Act 1991,** which makes it a criminal offence to make a false or misleading statement about property matters in the course of an estate agency or property development business.

Administrative controls

An alternative to using the civil or criminal law as a means of consumer protection is to place responsibility for the regulation of traders in the hands of an administrative body which is given powers to deal with unfair trade practices. The advantages of administrative controls compared to legal controls are as follows:

1 Individual consumers are often ignorant of their rights or reluctant to enforce them in the courts. The creation of administrative controls allows action to be taken on behalf of all consumers.

2 Depending on the powers vested in the administrative agency, it may be able to act more quickly than Parliament to deal with new forms of unfair trading.

3 The administrative agency may be able to achieve the desired effect by persuasion rather than using the threat of legal action, and it may be able to use its influence to raise standards above the minimum acceptable by encouraging self-regulation.

4 Dishonest traders may not be deterred by the threat of legal action. Some forms of control, such as licensing, may stop undesirable traders from operating in the market.

The main forms of administrative control are to be found in the Enterprise Act 2002.

Administrative controls under the Enterprise Act 2002 (EA 2002)

1 Super-complaints. The EA 2002 introduces a new procedure to allow certain designated consumer bodies to make super-complaints to the OFT and other specified regulators where 'any feature or combination of features of a market in the UK for goods or services is or appears to be significantly harming the interests of consumers'. Features of a market which could give rise to a complaint are the structure of the market, the conduct of those supplying or acquiring goods and services in the market and the conduct of any customers. The market can be regional, national or international although the OFT and regulators can only act in the UK. The OFT and other regulators have up to 90 days to respond to a super-complaint. The response must state whether action is to be taken and, if so, what is proposed. Any of the powers of the OFT or regulators may be used. In the case of the OFT, actions could include:

- bringing enforcement action under either competition or consumer regulation powers;
- launching a market study;
- making a market investigation reference to the Competition Commission (CC) for further investigation;
- making recommendations for changes in legislation.

Super-complaints can be made to the OFT and the following regulators: Civil Aviation Authority (CAA), Office of Gas and Energy Markets (OFGEM), Office of Communications (OFCOM), Northern Ireland Authority for Energy Regulation (OFREG-NI), Office of the Rail Regulator (ORR) and the Office of Water Services (OFWAT). The following have been granted designated consumer body status: the Consumers' Association; Consumer Focus; Citizens Advice; Consumer Council for Water (formerly known as Watervoice); CAMRA and General Consumer Council of Northern Ireland. The OFT has received super-complaints in relation to private dentistry, door-step selling, mail consolidation, care homes, home-collected credit, Northern Ireland banking, credit card interest calculation methods, payment protection insurance and the Scottish legal profession.

2 Enforcement orders (Part 8 of EA 2002). Part 8 of the EA 2002 introduces a new procedure for the enforcement of specified consumer legislation by means of court orders, known as enforcement orders, taken against businesses in breach of the legislation which harms the collective interests of consumers. This new procedure replaces Part III of the Fair Trading Act 1973 and the Stop Now Orders (EC Directive) Regulations 2001, which had been implemented by the 1998 EC Directive on injunctions for the protection of consumers' interests (the 'Injunctions Directive').

Enforcement orders can be obtained for two types of infringement:

- *Community infringements* – these are breaches of UK laws which give effect to specific EC Directives, e.g. Package Travel, Package Holidays and Package Tours Regulations 1992 and Unfair Terms in Consumer Contracts Regulations 1999.

- *Domestic infringements* – these are breaches of specified UK law, listed in delegated legislation, which are committed in the course of a business and which harm the collective interests of consumers, e.g. Consumer Credit Act 1974 and Sale of Goods Act 1979.

The EA 2002 identifies three kinds of enforcers:

- general enforcers, e.g. the OFT, Trading Standards Service and the Department of Enterprise, Trade and Investment in Northern Ireland;
- enforcers designated by the Secretary of State, e.g. regulators, such the CAA, ORR, FSA; the Information Commissioner, Consumers' Association;
- Community enforcers, which are limited to enforcers from other EEA states.

The OFT has responsibility for leading enforcement activity and coordinating action by enforcers, to ensure that only the most appropriate body takes action.

Before seeking an enforcement order, the enforcer must first consult the OFT (if it is not the enforcer) and the trader against whom the order may be made with a view to giving the trader an opportunity to stop the infringement and avoid the need for court action. At this stage the enforcer may accept an undertaking from the trader about his future conduct. After 14 days the enforcer may apply to the High Court or county court for an enforcement order. (This period is reduced to seven days for an interim order where urgent action is required.) Where proceedings are brought against a trader the court may:

- Accept an undertaking from a trader about his conduct instead of making an enforcement order.
- Make an enforcement order, requiring the trader to stop and not continue the infringing conduct. The order also stops the trader from pursuing similar infringing conduct through other businesses with which he or she might have a connection, e.g. as a director.

If a trader breaches an enforcement order or an undertaking given to the court (but not to an enforcer), the trader will be in contempt of court and can be fined or imprisoned for a maximum of two years.

The OFT and other general and designated enforcers which are public bodies with statutory powers have the right to require information, including documents, from traders by issuing a written notice. If a trader fails to comply with a notice, an enforcer can seek a court order requiring the trader to produce the information.

Licensing of traders under the Consumer Credit Act 1974

The OFT is responsible for administering the system of licensing for consumer credit and hire businesses (see Chapter 13 ⬤). Undesirable traders may be refused a licence or have their licences withdrawn.

Business self-regulation

The OFT is under a statutory duty to encourage relevant trade associations to prepare and disseminate to their members codes of practice for guidance in safeguarding and promoting the interests of consumers in the UK. The aim of such codes is to enable a particular industry to try to regulate the practices of its members. The advantages of voluntary codes of practice are as follows:

- codes can deal with matters which it would be difficult to deal with by means of legislation, e.g. availability of spare parts;
- codes may be able to go further than the existing law or improve upon legal remedies, e.g. the Code of Practice for the Motor Industry provides that copies of information provided by previous owners of a car concerning its history should be passed on to the new owner;
- any change in trading practices can be dealt with quickly by the association, whereas changing the law to deal with an undesirable trade practice may take a long time;
- codes encourage an industry to put its own house in order; complaints may be dealt with within the spirit of the code rather than according to the letter of the law; and the code may even explain legal requirements to its members;
- codes are developed for a particular trade or industry and can, therefore, deal with the problems which are specific to the industry;
- disputes can be dealt with in a less formal way, e.g. by conciliation;
- most codes provide for arbitration in the event of a dispute; arbitration may be preferable to bringing a case through the courts.

Although codes of practice have a number of advantages, there are some significant drawbacks to self-regulation. They are:

- not all traders are members of the trade associations and subject to their rules and codes of practice;
- members of the public are often not aware of the existence of codes of practice and their rights under those codes;

- the sanctions which a trade association can impose against a member for failing to comply with the code are often very weak;
- codes are drawn up by a trade or industry and may not adequately address the interests of consumers.

The EA 2002 requires the OFT to establish criteria for approving codes and to allow a symbol to be used to show which codes have been approved by the OFT.

A summary of the different approaches to consumer protection is set out in Figure 14.2, overleaf.

In the next part of this chapter we will examine how the law is applied to protect consumers by considering a consumer transaction which gives rise to a large number of complaints: the package holiday.

Consumer protection case study – package holidays

Over the past 30 years there has been an enormous growth in the package holiday market. As the volume of trade has increased, the real cost of taking a package holiday has fallen. A package holiday to popular European destinations such as Spain, Greece and Turkey is now well within the financial resources of most people. Intense price competition between the main tour operators has led to UK holidaymakers enjoying the lowest prices in Europe, but at the expense of standards. There is a high level of dissatisfaction with package holidays. In 2009/10 the Association of British Travel Agents (ABTA) received 12,504 complaints about holidays and in 2009/10 Consumer Direct received 14,851 complaints about holidays.

The problems with package holidays

1 A package holiday involves a complex set of legal relationships between the travel agent, tour operator, hotelier, carrier and local suppliers of services. In most cases, the tour operator does not own the airlines or hotels but contracts with independent suppliers to make up the package. Although the contract is usually made in this country, most of the components of the package are delivered abroad. The consumer may be unsure who, exactly, is responsible if something goes wrong and which country's law applies.

2 The holiday is often arranged by one individual on behalf of himself and his family or a group of friends. The rights of holidaymakers who did not personally make a booking may not be clear.

3 Holiday selections are made on the basis of advertising, descriptions in a brochure and advice by travel agents. Customers need adequate and accurate information to make an appropriate choice, but brochures are usually prepared a long time in advance of the holidays to which they relate.

4 The holiday may be disrupted by events beyond the control of the tour operator: flights may be delayed by bad weather or industrial action by airport staff, or independent hoteliers may have overbooked their hotels. To what extent should the operator be held responsible for the holidaymakers' loss of enjoyment when such things happen?

5 Competitive pricing policies have led to low profit margins and the need to reduce financial risk to a minimum by restricting consumers' rights through the use of standard terms and conditions.

Legal controls over package holidays

Before 1993 there were few legal rules designed specifically to control the package holiday industry. By and large, general consumer protection measures were used.

1 Civil law remedies. Individual holidaymakers could bring actions in contract or tort against the tour operator if the holiday failed to live up to expectations (see, e.g. *Jarvis* v *Swans Tours* (1973)). Although the travel agent acts on behalf of the tour operator, the agent may incur liability to the consumer in tort if, for example, he or she makes untrue statements about a holiday. Consumers' civil remedies were enhanced by general consumer protection legislation, such as:

- the Misrepresentation Act 1967, which provided a remedy for a negligent misrepresentation;
- the Consumer Credit Act 1974, which by s 75 imposed equal liability on credit card companies;
- the Unfair Contract Terms Act 1977, which controlled the use of unfair exemption clauses;
- the Supply of Goods and Services Act 1982, which provided that the supplier of services should exercise reasonable care and skill.

2 Criminal penalties. Travel agents and tour operators are vulnerable to prosecution under the Consumer

	Civil law	Criminal law	Administrative controls	Business self-regulation
Aims	To remedy a wrong suffered by an individual consumer	To protect all consumers by punishing traders who fail to meet minimum standards To protect honest traders from unfair competition by unscrupulous traders	To ban dishonest traders To persuade traders to improve upon minimum legal standards To promote competition between traders by regulation of anti-competitive practices	To encourage traders to observe high standards To tailor standards to particular industries To allow traders to police themselves
False/misleading statements **Advertisements**	No civil liability for inaccurate 'trader's puff' unless specific promise made as in *Carlill*'s case Directors/experts are liable for false/misleading descriptions in company prospectuses (Financial Services and Markets Act 2000) Package holiday providers are liable for misleading descriptions of package holidays (Package Travel etc. Regulations 1992)	Various offences under the Consumer Protection from Unfair Trading Regulations 2008 in respect of unfair trading practices Offence to fail to disclose specified information to package holiday customers (Package Travel etc. Regulations 1992) Offence for estate agents to give false/misleading statements about property (Property Misdescriptions Act 1991)	Office of Fair Trading may apply for an injunction to stop publication of misleading advertisements (Control of Misleading Advertisements Regulations 1988) Enforcement orders to stop breaches of consumer legislation under the EA 2002 Super-complaints under the EA 2002	The British Code of Advertising Practice requires advertisements to be legal, decent, honest and truthful Breaches of the code are publicised and offenders warned. OFCOM has powers to deal with misleading TV advertising Trade association codes of practice
Representations	Civil liability for misrepresentation Rescission of the contract and/or damages (i) at common law (tort of deceit or tort of negligence) (ii) under the Misrepresentation Act 1967	Offences under the Consumer Protection from Unfair Trading Regulations 2008 and Property Misdescriptions Act 1991 (see above) Deception offences under the Fraud Act 2006 Offence to apply false descriptions to food (Food Safety Act 1990)	Enforcement orders to stop breaches of consumer legislation under the EA 2002 Super-complaints under the EA 2002	Trade association codes of practice
Terms	Damages for breach of express or implied terms of contract and repudiation of the contract for breach of condition or serious breach of innominate term	Offences under the Consumer Protection from Unfair Trading Regulations 2008 (see above)	Enforcement orders to stop breaches of consumer legislation under the EA 2002 Super-complaints under the EA 2002	Trade association codes of practice
Unsolicited goods/services	No contractual obligation to pay for unsolicited goods. They are treated as unconditional gift (Consumer Protection (Distance Selling) Regulations 2000)	Offence to demand payment for or threaten proceedings in respect of unsolicited goods and services (Unsolicited Goods and Services Act 1971 and Consumer Protection (Distance Selling) Regulations 2000)	Enforcement orders to stop breaches of consumer legislation under the EA 2002 Super-complaints under the EA 2002	Trade association codes of practice

Figure 14.2 Consumer protection – a summary

Civil law	Criminal law	Administrative controls	Business self-regulation
Cancellation rights Credit agreements signed away from business premises are cancellable (Consumer Credit Act 1974) Non-credit agreements involving payments over £35 signed away from business premises are cancellable (Cancellation of Contracts made in a Consumer's Home or Place of Work etc. Regulations 2008) Timeshare agreements made in the UK are cancellable (Timeshare Act 1992) Distance contracts are cancellable (Consumer Protection (Distance Selling) Regulations 2000)	Offence not to inform timeshare customer of cancellation rights (Timeshare Act 1992)	Enforcement orders to stop breaches of consumer legislation under the EA 2002 Super-complaints under the EA 2002 Licence required to carry on consumer credit business (Consumer Credit Act 1974)	Trade association codes of practice Timeshare Council Code of Practice
Defective goods Strict liability for breach of implied contractual terms as to quality and suitability (Trading Stamps Act 1964, Supply of Goods (Implied Terms) Act 1973, Sale of Goods Act 1979, Supply of Goods and Services Act 1982, Sale and Supply of Goods to Consumers Regulations 2002) Fault-based liability in the tort of negligence Strict liability for breach of statutory duty under Part II, Consumer Protection Act 1987 Strict liability under Part I, Consumer Protection Act 1987	Offence to supply unsafe consumer goods (General Product Safety Regulations 2005) Various offences related to the sale of food (Food Safety Act 1990) Offences under the Consumer Protection from Unfair Trading Regulations 2008	Secretary of State can issue prohibition notices and notices to warn; trading standards officers can issue suspension notices and apply for forfeiture orders in respect of unsafe goods (Part II, Consumer Protection Act 1987) Food authorities can apply for e.g. improvement notices, prohibition orders or emergency orders to deal with unsafe food. Food premises must be registered (Food Safety Act 1990) Enforcement orders to stop breaches of consumer legislation under the EA 2002 Super-complaints under the EA 2002	Trade association codes of practice
Defective services Liability for breach of implied contractual terms as to use of reasonable care and skill, time of performance and consideration (Supply of Goods and Services Act 1982) Fault-based liability in the tort of negligence Liability for breach of implied contractual terms in package holidays (Package Travel etc. Regulations 1992)	Offences under the Consumer Protection from Unfair Trading Regulations 2008 and Package Travel etc. Regulations 1992 (see above)	Enforcement orders to stop breaches of consumer legislation under the EA 2002 Super-complaints under the EA 2002 Licence required to carry on consumer credit business (Consumer Credit Act 1974) Bonding requirement for package travel organisers and retailers (Package Travel etc. Regulations 1992)	Trade association codes of practice Professional bodies' codes of practice Citizens' Charter standards for public services
Exclusion of liability Exclusion clauses may be ineffective under the common law or rendered void by statute (Unfair Contract Terms Act 1977, Unfair Terms in Consumer Contracts Regulations 1999)	Offence to display 'no refunds' notices (Consumer Transactions (Restriction on Statements) Order 1976)	Enforcement orders to stop breaches of consumer legislation under the EA 2002 Super-complaints under the EA 2002 Office of Fair Trading and other qualifying bodies can challenge unfair contract terms (Unfair Terms in Consumer Contracts Regulations 1999)	Trade association codes of practice

Figure 14.2 (*continued*)

Protection from Unfair Trading Regulations 2008 for false and misleading statements.

3 Administrative controls. One of the consequences of cut-throat price competition in the travel industry has been a high rate of company failures because of insolvency. The problem for the consumer is that they may find themselves stranded abroad. Administrative controls have, therefore, tended to concentrate on putting in place arrangements to safeguard holidaymakers in the event of the tour operator becoming insolvent. The Civil Aviation Authority (CAA), for example, required anyone organising inclusive holidays involving air travel to obtain an Air Travel Organiser's Licence (ATOL). Such operators were required to satisfy financial requirements and to provide a bond to cover liabilities, which may arise from insolvency. An Air Travel Reserve Fund was set up as an additional precaution.

4 Business self-regulation. The Association of British Travel Agents (ABTA) was set up in 1951 and, despite its name, represents the interests of both travel agents and tour operators. All ABTA members are bound by the codes of practice: the Tour Operator's Code of Conduct and the Travel Agent's Code of Conduct.

The fragmented nature of the controls over the package holiday industry, the high level of consumer dissatisfaction and the obvious European dimension to the industry made this form of consumer transaction a natural target for EC legislation. The EC Directive on Package Travel, Package Holidays and Package Tours was adopted by the EC Council in 1990. Member states were required to implement the measure by 31 December 1992. The directive was given effect in the UK by the Package Travel, Package Holidays and Package Tours Regulations 1992, which came into force on 23 December 1992.

The Package Travel, Package Holidays and Package Tours Regulations 1992

The main provisions of the regulations (SI 1992/3288) as they affect consumers are as follows:

1 Package. The regulations do not apply to travel or accommodation, which are separately arranged. The regulations apply only to 'packages' which are sold or offered for sale in the UK. The definition of a 'package' requires the existence of the following elements:

■ a pre-arranged combination of at least two or more specified components which are: (i) transport;

(ii) accommodation; (iii) other tourist services not ancillary to transport or accommodation, but which account for a significant proportion of the package;

■ the combination is sold or offered for sale at an inclusive price;

■ the service covers a period of 24 hours or more or includes overnight accommodation.

2 The parties. The regulations use the terms 'organiser' and 'retailer' to describe the tour operator and travel agent respectively. The 'consumer' is given a broad definition so as to include not only the person who makes the contract for the package but also anyone else on whose behalf he has contracted, i.e. members of a family or someone to whom the contracting person has transferred the package.

3 Misleading information. Regulation 4 provides that a consumer is entitled to be compensated by the organiser or retailer for any loss arising from misleading information about the package, its price or any other conditions applying to the contract.

Mawdsley v Cosmosair Plc **(2002)**

Mr and Mrs Mawdsley booked a full board package holiday in Turkey with Cosmos for themselves and their two young children, J and C, aged three-and-a-half and six months respectively. The Cosmos brochure included the following entry for the hotel chosen by the Mawdsleys under the heading 'Facilities': 'Lift (in main building)'. There was a lift in the main building but it did not stop at the floor where the restaurant was located. Mrs Mawdsley was injured while trying with her husband to carry their daughter C in her pushchair down the stairs to the restaurant. Mrs Mawdsley lost her footing, slipped and fell. The Court of Appeal upheld the decision of the trial judge that the statement 'Lift (in main building)' amounted to a misrepresentation that all levels of the hotel were accessible by lift and that it was reasonable to assume that the restaurant was in the main building and therefore also accessible by lift. The misrepresentation constituted 'misleading information' under reg 4 of the Package Travel Regulations. In the absence of a *novus actus interveniens*, Cosmos was liable for Mrs Mawdsley's injuries.

4 Provision of information. The regulations set out what information must be given to consumers in brochures and before the package starts:

(a) *Brochures*. Regulation 5 provides that brochures must contain certain specified information, e.g. the destination, the means of transport, the type of accommodation, its location, main features and category, inclusive meals and the itinerary. It is an offence for an organiser to make available a brochure which does not comply with the requirements. It is also an offence for a retailer to make a brochure available to a possible consumer which he knows or has reasonable cause to believe does not comply with the requirements. The penalties are a maximum fine of £5,000 in the magistrates' court or an unlimited fine in respect of a Crown Court conviction.

Inspirations East Ltd v Dudley Metropolitan Borough Council (1997)

Inspirations, an organiser of package holidays, included a statement in its 'Inspirations Cyprus' brochure that a certain hotel in Limassol was very suitable for people who use a wheelchair. A customer booked a holiday at the hotel but discovered on arrival that there was no access to the swimming pool for people in wheelchairs. Inspirations' conviction was upheld. The magistrates were entitled to find that the indication that the hotel was suitable for the disabled was a misdescription about a main feature of the package in breach of reg 5.

Regulation 6 provides that particulars in the brochure have the status of implied warranties, unless the parties agree otherwise. If the brochure contains an express statement that particulars are subject to change and any changes are clearly communicated to the consumer before the contract is concluded, then no liability for breach of warranty will arise.

(b) *Before the package starts*. Regulation 7 requires the organiser and retailer to provide the consumer with information about matters such as passport and visa requirements, health formalities and arrangements for security of money paid and arrangements for repatriation. Regulation 8 requires the organiser and retailer to provide the consumer in good time before the journey starts with information about transport arrangements and local representatives. Both regulations create criminal offences with maximum penalties of £5,000 on conviction in the magistrates' court and an unlimited fine in the Crown Court.

5 Content of the contract. It is an implied condition of the contract that the organiser or retailer supplies a written copy of the terms of the contract to the consumer before the contract is made and that the contract contains specified elements, e.g. travel destination(s), travel dates, accommodation, the itinerary, inclusive meals and excursions, the price and payment schedule and time limits for complaints (reg 9).

6 Transfer of bookings. If the consumer is prevented from going ahead with the package, he has the right under reg 10 to transfer the package to a third party if he gives reasonable notice. However, a transfer may involve extra costs and the transferor and transferee are jointly and severally liable for the price of the package.

7 Surcharges. Price variation clauses will be void under reg 11 unless they comply with the following requirements:

- the clauses provide for both upward and downward revision; and
- the contract states precisely how the revised price is to be calculated; and
- the variation is solely due to changes in the cost of transportation; or dues, taxes or fees for services, such as landing taxes; or exchange rates.

A price increase cannot be made within 30 days of departure or where the increase is less than 2 per cent of the price.

8 Alteration of the terms. Regulation 12 incorporates an implied term into every contract that the organiser will inform the consumer of a significant alteration of any of the essential terms of the contract, e.g. price, so the consumer can decide whether to cancel, or accept the alteration. If the consumer decides to cancel, he or she is entitled to a substitute package of the same or superior quality, or a lower quality package with an adjustment of price, or a full refund (reg 13).

9 Significant proportion of services not provided. Regulation 14 provides that there is an implied term that where after a departure a significant proportion of the services contracted for are not provided, the organiser must make suitable alternative arrangements for the consumer to continue the package, at no extra cost. If there is a difference in the services supplied under the alternative arrangements, the consumer must be compensated. If it is impossible to make alternative arrangements or the consumer reasonably refuses to accept the alternative offered, the consumer must be provided with equivalent transport back to the departure point or another place agreed by the consumer.

10 Liability for proper performance of the contract. Under reg 15 the organiser and retailer are liable to the consumer for the proper performance of the contract, irrespective of whether the obligations are to be performed by the organiser or retailer or by other suppliers. Liability will not arise where the failures in performance are attributable:

- to the consumer himself; or
- to a third party unconnected with the services contracted for; or
- to unusual or unforeseeable circumstances beyond the control of the organiser or retailer (known as *force majeure*).

Where the second and third points occur, the organiser and retailer must give prompt assistance to any consumer in difficulty. The contract can include a reasonable term which limits the amount of compensation payable for non-performance or improper performance of the contract. However, liability for death or personal injury cannot be excluded. If the consumer complains, the organiser or retailer or his local representative must take prompt action to find a solution. For their part, consumers are under an obligation to make their complaints known to the supplier of the service at the place where the service is supplied. If, for example, the consumer is unhappy with the standard of his hotel room, he must make his complaint known to the hotel management.

11 Protection against insolvency. The regulations provide that the organiser and retailer must provide evidence of security for the refund of money paid over and for the repatriation of a consumer in the event of insolvency. The protection against insolvency is further strengthened by compulsory bonding arrangements.

12 Offences and enforcement. As we have seen already, the regulations create a number of offences. It is a defence for a defendant to show that he took all reasonable steps and exercised due diligence to avoid committing a crime (reg 24). The regulations are enforced by local trading standards departments.

Enforcing consumer rights

There has been a considerable improvement in consumers' rights over the past 30 years, which is set to continue as the EU pursues its aim of a high level of protection for consumers. However, creating more and better rights will count for little if consumers do not have a cheap and simple way of enforcing those rights. There are currently three main ways in which a consumer may obtain redress: compensation orders, conciliation or arbitration under a code of practice, and arbitration under the county court small claims procedure.

Compensation orders

If a trader is convicted of a criminal offence, e.g. under the Consumer Protection from Unfair Trading Regulations 2008, the court may make a compensation order requiring the trader to pay compensation for 'any personal injury, loss or damage' resulting from the offence under the Powers of Criminal Courts (Sentencing) Act 2000. Magistrates' courts are limited to £5,000 in respect of each offence for which the trader is convicted. There is no limit to the amount of compensation which can be awarded by the Crown Court. Compensation orders are beneficial to the consumer in the following situations:

- where the amount of loss suffered by the consumer is so small that it is not worth bringing a civil action to try to recover it;
- where the consumer has no remedy in civil law, e.g. there is no civil remedy for misleading advertising but an offence under the Consumer Protection from Unfair Trading Regulations 2008 may have been committed.

Conciliation or arbitration under a code of practice

The trader may be a member of a trade association which operates a conciliation or arbitration scheme to deal with complaints against members. The aim of conciliation is to get the parties to resolve their differences in an informal way. If conciliation does not result in agreement, the consumer is still free to take the matter to arbitration or to the courts. Arbitration consists of an independent person hearing both sides of the dispute and then making a decision which is binding on the parties. Arbitration is usually very informal and is often done in writing. It is usually inexpensive but in some cases can be more expensive than going to court. One of the problems with some arbitration schemes was that an agreement to refer the dispute to arbitration precluded the consumer from bringing an action in the ordinary courts. The Consumer Arbitration Agreements Act 1988 was designed to deal with this problem by providing that a consumer was not bound by a clause in a contract which said that any dispute must be referred to arbitration where the amount claimed fell within the small claims limit for county court arbitrations (see below). It has now been decided that consumer arbitration agreements should be dealt with as potentially unfair terms in a consumer contract and therefore subject to the protections contained in the Unfair Terms in Consumer Contracts Regulations 1999 (SI 1999/2083). The Arbitration Act 1996 repealed the Consumer Arbitration Agreements Act 1988 and extended the application of the Unfair Terms in Consumer Contracts Regulations to consumer arbitration agreements. A term which constitutes an arbitration agreement is unfair if it relates to a claim for a pecuniary remedy which does not exceed an amount specified by an order made under the Act.

The small claims track

Since 1973 the county court has operated a special scheme for 'small claims'. If a claim for £5,000 or less (or £1,000 or less in the case of a personal injury claim) is defended the case will be allocated to the small claims track. Small claims cases are usually heard by a district judge but complex cases can be referred to a circuit judge. The judge can adopt any procedure he considers fair. The court has the power to use an external arbitrator if the parties agree. The procedure for bringing a claim is relatively straightforward so that it should not be necessary to have legal assistance. There are a number of leaflets available from the county court which provide a step-by-step guide to making a small claim. The parties are discouraged from using lawyers by the 'no-costs' rule which means that each side must pay its own legal costs whatever the outcome. The only exception is where one of the parties has incurred unnecessary cost because of the unreasonable behaviour of the other, e.g. failing to turn up to a hearing. The procedure for bringing a small claim in the county court is summarised in Figure 14.3, overleaf.

Although the small claims procedure is a more user-friendly method of obtaining redress for consumer problems than normal civil court procedure, it is not particularly well used by consumers. It is often used by businesses to recover money owed by consumers! The reluctance to use the procedure suggests that consumers are generally unaware of the small claims system or daunted by the prospect of taking DIY legal action. Even where a consumer pursues a claim and obtains a judgment, it may be more difficult to then enforce it and get payment. A further problem is that an appeal can be made against the judge's decision only on very limited grounds. Moreover, if a consumer appeals and is unsuccessful, he or she may have to pay costs.

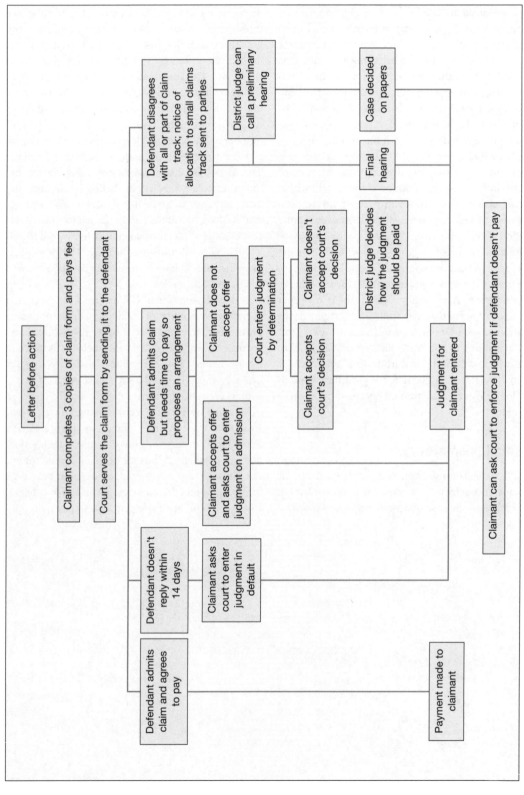

Figure 14.3 Small claims track

Self-test questions/activities

1 How would you define a consumer for the purposes of framing protective legislation?

2 What justification could you give for providing special protection for consumers?

3 What contribution has the EC made to the law of consumer protection?

4 If you had a consumer problem, where could you go to obtain advice and assistance? How, if at all, would you justify the use of the criminal law to control unfair trading practices?

5 What are the advantages and disadvantages of imposing strict liability for criminal offences in the field of consumer protection?

6 How have the Package Travel etc. Regulations 1992 improved the rights of consumers in relation to package holidays?

7 What matters should you consider before deciding to sue a trader?

8 What are the advantages and disadvantages of arbitration as a mechanism for resolving consumer complaints?

9 David is the author of a guide to British cafés and snack bars. During the course of a year he travels considerable distances in his car pursuing his researches and consequently he changes his car regularly every 12 months. After three months' use David's current car develops a fault with the odometer which necessitates its replacement. When David trades the car in at the end of the year, he forgets to tell Newtown Motor Co Ltd that the car has done 10,000 more miles than appear on the odometer. Newtown Motor Co Ltd sells the car to June, who discovers a few weeks later that the mileage displayed on the odometer is incorrect.

She reports the matter to the local trading standards department.

(a) Discuss the criminal liability of David and Newtown Motor Co Ltd.

(b) What defences may be available to David and Newtown Motor Co Ltd if they are prosecuted?

(c) What advice would you give Newtown Motor Co Ltd to help it avoid prosecution in the future?

10 Skaters Ltd, a manufacturer of skateboards, supplies several hundred skateboards to retailers throughout the country in preparation for the Christmas market. It soon becomes apparent that the design of the skateboard is defective. Several children are injured attempting to execute 180-degree turns when the back pair of wheels shear off from their mountings on the skateboard. Despite these problems, Skaters Ltd continues to supply the skateboard to retailers and takes no steps to warn the public.

What action may be taken to protect the public from the potential dangers of the skateboard?

11 Margaret visits her local butcher, Chops Ltd, and buys 1 kg of Chops Ltd's own sausages, a pork pie bought in by Chops Ltd from a local pie manufacturer and 500 g of extra-lean minced beef, which is 25 per cent more expensive than ordinary minced beef. When Margaret and her family eat the food over the next few days they discover a piece of glass in one of the sausages, penicillin mould growing on the crust of the pork pie, and that there appears to be an excessive amount of fat in the minced beef.

(a) Discuss the criminal liability of Chops Ltd and the local pie manufacturer.

(b) What defences may be available to Chops Ltd and the pie manufacturer if they are prosecuted?

(c) Advise Margaret about any civil action she may be able to bring against Chops Ltd and/or the pie manufacturer.

Specimen examination questions

1 Outline the powers available to protect consumers.

2 Vera runs a small bed and breakfast establishment in the ferry port of Heysham. At the end of another wet summer season she places the following advert in several south of England newspapers: 'Small, friendly family hotel, a stone's throw from Blackpool's famous beaches, jacuzzi and swimming pool available. Winter Weekend Breaks; Dinner, Bed and Breakfast £30 per person per night.'

   Latisha, who lives in Bournemouth, books a room for a Saturday night in February. The weekend proves to be a great disappointment. She finds that Heysham is an hour's drive away from Blackpool. The jacuzzi and sauna are still under construction and the swimming pool referred to is the municipal pool located half a mile away from Vera's B & B. Latisha is charged £40 for her night's stay. When she complains, she is informed by Vera that the advertised rate applies only to stays of more than two nights where two people share a room. On her return home, Latisha complains to the local trading standards department.

Discuss the criminal liability of Vera, bearing in mind any defences that may be available to her.

3 Your friends have just returned from a holiday in Spain complaining bitterly about a catalogue of disasters which occurred, namely:
- 24 hours before departure your friends received a telephone call from the tour operator to say that the hotel was overbooked and it would be necessary to transfer surplus holidaymakers to another hotel in a different, less attractive resort;
- the flight to Spain was delayed by 18 hours because of industrial action by British air traffic controllers;
- the hotel to which your friends were transferred had a lower star rating than the hotel originally booked; it was further away from the sea and there was no swimming pool;
- the free excursions advertised in the brochure were not available.

   One of your friends paid by credit card. The others paid by cheque.

   Advise your friends of any rights they may have and against whom they may be able to exercise them.

Website references

http://ec.europa.eu/dgs/health_consumer/index_en.htm The website of the European Commission Directorate of Health and Consumer Protection.

http://www.which.co.uk This part of the *Which?* site contains some useful information for consumers, including some real-life 'case studies'.

http://www.oft.gov.uk The OFT website provides guidance on its responsibilities under the EA 2002, including super-complaints and enforcement of consumer legislation under Part 8.

http://www.consumerfocus.org.uk Consumer Focus is the new champion for consumer interests in England, Wales and Scotland and for post in Northern Ireland. It was previously known as the National Consumer Council.

http://www.consumerdirect.gov.uk Consumer Direct is a government-funded service providing information and advice to consumers.

http://www.ncf.info This is the website for the National Consumer Federation which coordinates the work of local consumer groups.

http://www.courtservice.gov.uk/ The Court Service site provides information about the small claims track.

http://www.berr.gov.uk/whatwedo/consumers/buying-selling/ucp/index.html This archived website provides information on the implementation of Unfair Commercial Practices Directive 2005 by the Consumer Protection from Unfair Trading Regulations 2008.

Visit **www.mylawchamber.co.uk/richesallen** to access study support resources including answers to questions in this chapter and legal updates, all linked to the **Pearson eText** version of **Keenan and Riches' Business Law** which you can **search**, **highlight** and **personalise** with your **own notes** and **bookmarks**.

Use **Case Navigator** to read in full some of the key cases referenced in this chapter with commentary and questions:
Stevenson v Rogers (1999)

Part 4 | # BUSINESS RESOURCES

Chapter 15 Business property

Learning objectives

After studying this chapter you should understand the following main points:

■ the various legal classifications of property;

■ property rights and liabilities such as easements and restrictive covenants;

■ the legal estates in land including the commonhold;

■ the tort liability of occupiers of land;

■ intellectual property rights such as patents and copyright;

■ the legal framework governing data protection, the misuse of computers and freedom of information.

Generally

English law divides property into real property and personal property. The assets of a business are usually made up of both sorts of property.

The distinction between the two sorts of property is mainly that real property cannot be moved but personal property can.

However, this is not the only test because some things which can be moved are regarded as real property and called fixtures, while other moveables are regarded as fittings which do not become part of the real property to which they are attached. A diagram showing the broad classification of property in English law appears at Figure 15.1.

Fixtures and fittings

As we have seen, fixtures become part of the land itself; fittings do not. If a piece of personal property is securely attached to the ground it is probably a fixture, but a second test needs to be applied in order to finally decide. If the piece of personal property was

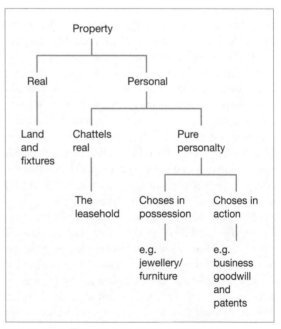

Figure 15.1 The classification of property

put on the land so that it could be better enjoyed for itself, it is not a fixture. However, if it was put on the land so that the land can be better enjoyed, then it is a fixture.

Leigh v *Taylor* (1902)

A person put some valuable tapestries on the wall of his house, the house being real property. He used tacks to fit them on a framework of wood and canvas which he then nailed to the wall. Upon his death the court had to decide whether the tapestries were real or personal property and it was decided that they were still personal property. They had been fixed to the wall so that they could be better enjoyed for themselves.

Comment. A contrast is provided by *D'Eyncourt* v *Gregory* (1866) where certain statues, vases and stone garden furniture standing on their own weight were decided to be real property because they formed part of the design of a landscaped garden. They were there for the better enjoyment of the land.

The importance of the idea of fixtures and fittings is that if you buy land and buildings, say as a business asset, then, in the absence of a special provision in the conveyance to the contrary, the conveyance will pass the fixtures to the buyer and they cannot be removed by the seller. They are also regarded as included in the price. Fittings are not and can be removed by the seller in the absence of an agreement to the contrary.

The distinction is also important to lenders on mortgages since if they take possession of a property because of the borrower's default, the mortgage will give the lender a charge over fixtures but not fittings in the premises. The matter came before the High Court in *TSB Bank plc* v *Botham* (1995) when the lending bank, which had taken possession of the borrower's flat, claimed that certain items were fixtures and as a result were subject to its mortgage and could be sold to the new flat buyer.

The judge said that whether a chattel had become a fixture depended first on the object and purpose for which it had been fixed. If the object and purpose was to make a permanent and substantial improvement to the land or buildings, the chattel would be regarded as a fixture. If it was attached so that it could be better enjoyed for itself, it would be a fitting, on the lines of the tapestry in *Leigh*. The judges also thought that if significant damage would be done to the premises on removal the chattel would be more likely to be a fixture. He then applied the principles to the items in dispute as follows:

- fitted carpets – fixtures;
- light fittings attached to the property – fixtures;
- mock coal gas fire piped in – fixture;
- curtains, blinds and pelmets specifically designed for the particular windows – fixtures;
- towel rails, soap fittings, tap fittings and shower heads – all fixtures;
- white goods fitted into standard-sized holes and piped or wired in and aligned with and abutted on to each other so as to be part of the overall fitted kitchen – all fixtures.

In practice, to avoid misunderstanding, the Law Society's National Protocol 'Transaction' for the sale of residential property requires a seller to complete a fixtures form detailing those fixtures that are included in the sale and those which are excluded. It is equally sensible and usual in sales of commercial property to follow a similar course in order to avoid disputes.

The lease

A lease of land, e.g. office premises, is obviously an interest in land (or realty) but for historical reasons it is regarded as personal property and not real property.

This distinction has lost much of its importance in law, though still today if a person, T, were to leave by his will 'all my personal property to P and all my real property to R', P would get any leases which T had when he died.

Pure personalty and chattels real

The word personalty is another name for personal property. The word chattel is also used to describe personal property.

Although leaseholds are regarded as personalty, they are over land and result in a person having use of land, and so they are referred to as chattels real to distinguish them from pure personalty, such as a watch or a fountain pen.

Pure personalty – choses in possession and choses in action

Things such as jewellery and furniture which are tangible objects and have not only a money value but can also be enjoyed by the person who owns them **in a physical way** through the senses are called choses (or things) in possession.

Things which cannot be enjoyed by the person who owns them in a physical way, but which, nevertheless, are worth money, are called choses (or things) in action. Examples are patents, copyrights, trade marks, shares and cheques and the goodwill of a business. The value lies not in the thing itself but the legal right to money which it represents and the right to bring an action at law to enforce or protect that right should this become necessary.

Thus, if you have a fire in your business premises, you will no doubt value your fire extinguisher (a chose in possession), but you will find your insurance policy (a chose in action) to be of greater value!

Easements and profits

We have already dealt with a property right called a lease. This is a right to use another person's land for a period of time (usually) in return for the payment of rent. It is, however, also possible to have ownership of other rights over someone else's property. These are typically known as third party rights.

Easements

A may have what is called an easement over B's land. This might be a right of way so that, for example, A could get goods and services into his business premises by bringing them across land belonging to another business.

An easement may also be a right to light which would prevent the owner of a neighbouring business from building on his own land but so close to A's premises that A was unable to use them without constant artificial light. A could stop such a building from being put up by asking the court for an injunction to protect his right of light.

The position as stated above was thought to be the law on rights to light. However, in *Midtown Ltd* v *City of London Real Property Co Ltd; Joseph* v *City of London Real Property Co Ltd* (2005) the High Court dealt a severe blow to those trying to protect the right of light to their property. Although the court accepted that the activities of a developer would have a significant effect on the claimant's right of light to his property, the court refused an injunction on the basis of the existence of artificial light. The court did not say that the existence of

artificial light should *always* prevent a claim for infringement of a right to light but the case will no doubt be put forward by defendants in future claims.

An easement may also be a right to support from other buildings. Where a house or business premises are attached to other property, as with a semi-detached house, one property needs the support of the other.

Thus, if B decides to pull down his semi-detached premises which will leave A's premises in danger of collapsing, A can, once again, ask the court for an injunction to prevent B from doing this.

The case of *Batchelor* v *Marlow* (2000) is also of interest in a modern context. In that case it was decided by the High Court that the right to park cars on another's property could exist as an easement.

However, the Court of Appeal in 2001 reversed the above decision of the High Court. The Court of Appeal did concede that an easement of vehicle parking could exist at law but not on the facts of the case. The right claimed was to park such a large number of vehicles that the owner of the land was virtually excluded from his property. As the Court of Appeal said, if the adjacent owner wanted such an extensive right, he would have to buy the land or lease it for a period of time. Only in such circumstances could he enjoy what amounted to exclusive possession.

The High Court reached the same conclusion in *Central Midlands Estates Ltd* v *Leicester Dyers Ltd* (2003) where the High Court accepted that there could be an easement of car parking. However, since the claim was to park an unlimited number of vehicles anywhere on the piece of land concerned being restricted only by the space available, there could be no easement on the facts because this would make the actual owner's right illusory.

It appears, however, that so long as the easement claimed will not *prevent* its use by the owner, the easement will be allowed, even if a *particular use* to which the owner wished to put the land *is restricted*. Thus, in *Mulvaney* v *Gough* (2003) the claimant, who owned a group of cottages, claimed an easement in regard to a communal garden at the back of the cottages over land owned by the defendants. The defendants intended to gravel the surface of the garden and use it as vehicular access to the adjoining land which they owned. They had already started to remove a flower bed. The Court of Appeal ruled that the right to use the land as a communal garden had been established by long use and was a valid easement for those who lived in the cottages. This was not to say that the defendants could not carry out works on the land but they would have to do so in a way that would substantially maintain its character as a communal garden and after prior consultation.

The focus on the servient tenement owner's ability to use his or her land was challenged by the House of Lords in *Moncrieff* v *Jamieson* (2007). It is important to note that, in *Moncrieff,* the House of Lords was acting as the final appellate court for the Scottish Court of Session. Accordingly, it was concerned with the application of Scottish law rather than English law. However, the House of Lords noted that the Scottish law on servitudes was very similar to the English law governing easements and so its decision has persuasive authority for English courts on this issue.

M claimed an entitlement to park one or two cars on J's land but the alleged right did not exclude J from any particular part of his land. The House of Lords considered the 'reasonable use' test that had been developed in cases such as *Batchelor* v *Marlow* (above) to be unreliable. In particular, the Law Lords drew a distinction between a situation where the owner of the dominant tenement had acquired the 'sole use' of part of the servient tenement for a limited purpose and one in which the owner of the servient tenement is excluded from his or her land in a way that deprives him or her of the ability to control his or her land.

As Lord Scott explained in *Moncrieff*, the proper test: 'asks whether the servient owner retains possession and, to subject to the reasonable exercise of the right in question, control of the servient land'. Evidently, there is a difference between 'exclusive use' (sometimes called 'exclusive occupation') and 'exclusive possession' of the land in this respect. The latter results in the total exclusion of the servient owner from his or her land and therefore such a claim cannot attract the status of an easement. The former is permissible and therefore it can give rise to a valid easement.

It should be noted that the distinction between exclusive occupation and exclusive possession is one that is made in relation to the lease/licence distinction. A tenant (or lessee) must have 'exclusive possession' of the property subject to the lease for a valid lease to exist whereas a licensee only needs to have exclusive occupation for the creation of a valid licence.

Comment. Although the decision of the House of Lords in *Moncrieff* v *Jameison* does not exclude the owner from the land as a matter of law. However, in practice, it is does restrict his or her use of the land significantly. The extent to which the presence of an easement restricts

the owner's use of the land will depend on the circumstances of the case . According to the test propounded in *Moncrieff* v *Jameison*, it could be argued that, on the facts, Batchelor v Marlow almost amounted to a claim for exclusive possession of the servient tenement.

The Acquisition of Easements

The entries relevant to the property in the Land Registry of the concerned properties will usually reveal what easements exist between the landowners. Easements can be acquired by express grant/reservation, implied grant/reservation, prescription (long use) or by statute. If a parcel of land has already had its title registered (the vast majority of land in England and Wales is already subject to the registration system created by the Land Registration Act 1925) any *expressly* created easement must be entered on the register for it to have binding effect under the Land Registration Act 2002. Nevertheless, if the easement was acquired through prescription (by open use for a period of at least 20 years) or it was implied into the conveyance that transferred the land to the registered proprietor then this unregistered interest may constitute an 'overriding interest' that will bind an owner despite the absence of registration. In relation to prescriptive claims, an unregistered interest will be overriding when it would not have been obvious on a reasonably careful inspection of the land.

This is a major change from the position adopted by the Land Registration Act 1925 which provided, under s 70(1), that all legal easements were overriding interests, which therefore did not have to be registered. This change was introduced to ensure that the register is a more accurate mirror of the totality of rights and interests over land in preparation for the forthcoming introduction of a system of electronic conveyancing. While not all land in England and Wales is subject to the registration system at present, since 1990 title registration has been compulsory for all land in the event of the sale. The Land Registration Act 2002 increased the number of situations ('trigger events') in which title registration is compulsory with the aim of ensuring that all land in England and Wales is subject to the registration system in the near future.

It is important to note that **an easement** is a **private** right (a public right of way is a different matter with which we shall not deal), enjoyed by owners or occupiers of **land** over **neighbouring** land. You cannot by owning land in Essex have an easement over land in Yorkshire.

Finally, it is not uncommon in business for a purchaser to take out indemnity insurance which will pay compensation if vital easements, e.g. of access, are later successfully challenged or easements are established that might prove a nuisance to the business.

Profits

Sometimes the right which exists over someone else's land is to take something from the land. It may, for example, be a right to fish or cut wood.

These rights can be acquired over any land. Unlike an easement, they are **not** restricted to rights over neighbouring land. You can, therefore, buy fishing rights over a river in Surrey even though you live in Lancashire and do not own any land at all in Surrey. The Land Registration Act 2002 added profits to the list of interests that are capable of being overriding interests.

Securities

A person may raise a loan on the security of his property, whether real (say, his house) or personal (say, his shareholding in a company), and the lender has certain rights over the property so used as a security if the loan is not repaid.

The use of mortgages on their own assets, such as the family home, by sole traders, partners and directors of companies together with the use of personal guarantees of business debt and fixed and floating charges over the assets of a company were considered in Chapter 4 as part of the topic of raising finance ◑.

A licence

Legislation giving business tenants (but not licensees) security of occupation has encouraged property owners to attempt to create licences rather than leases. A licence can be ended on reasonable notice; the rights of a business tenant may under the Landlord and Tenant Act 1954, Part II, survive the end of the period of the lease. In particular, the tenant is able to apply to the court for a new lease and the landlord can only oppose the application on one of the grounds set out in the Act, e.g. poor state of repair of the premises owing to a breach of the tenant's repair obligations in the lease.

If the agreement is to be a licence, the main test must be satisfied, which is that a licence will exist if the tenant does not have *exclusive possession* of the premises. Thus, in **Dresden Estates Ltd v Collinson** (1987) the landlord's right to relocate the licensee of an industrial unit to different premises deprived the licensee of exclusive possession and confirmed the agreement as a licence and not a lease.

Those in business should therefore ensure, through legal advice, that their tenancy agreement is indeed a lease covered by the 1954 Act.

Commercial uses of the licence

A main reason in business for the use of a licence rather than a tenancy is for short-term trading, for example, during the Christmas period or during the summer holiday period, either for retailing or storage purposes. The licence is also useful where a prospective tenant wants early access to the premises before a lease is granted or an existing tenant wishes to remain in occupation for a short period of time after the end of a lease. In these situations the landlord will want to retain rental income but will not want the tenant to acquire security of tenure under the Landlord and Tenant Act 1954.

Access to land

Access to Neighbouring Land Act 1992

The Access to Neighbouring Land Act 1992 deals with a situation in which a person who owns a building which is badly in need of repair cannot carry out necessary work on that building without entering on to his neighbour's property, and he cannot do this without committing a trespass because the neighbour will not consent to access. Under the Act the owner of the building can apply to the court for what is called an 'access order', under which he may enter the neighbouring property and carry out the necessary work on his own property. The applicant for an access order must show that the work is reasonably necessary to preserve the whole or part of his land including buildings, and that the work cannot be done at all, or that it would be substantially more difficult to do it, if entry to neighbouring land was not granted. The order will be made against the person who could otherwise sue for trespass, and so if the neighbouring property is let it will be made against the tenant.

The order may restrict entry to a specified area and provide for compensation to be made to the neighbouring owner if this is appropriate. It may also require the person given access to make a payment to the neighbouring owner, reflecting the financial benefit which the person given access has received. This does not apply where the property subject to the access order is residential land.

An order will not be granted if access would cause interference with or disturbance to the servient land or to anyone in occupation. Finally, all agreements, whether made before or after the Act came into force, which prevent a person applying for an access order or restricting rights to do so are void and of no effect.

Countryside and Rights of Way Act 2000

This Act also provides for access to land by non-owners. The main provisions are as follows:

- a right of access on foot for open air recreation to mountain, moor, heath, down and registered common land (or open country);
- land over 600 metres above sea level is automatically covered;
- open land will be shown on maps that will be available to the public (there is an appeal to the Secretary of State where land is included by mistake);
- there are exceptions for land that is cultivated, land covered by buildings, parks and gardens, mineral workings, railway land and golf courses, aerodromes, race courses and development land where planning permission has been granted, though it is unclear whether development must have been implemented;
- landowners must not erect false or misleading signs likely to deter people from using their statutory right of access, though signs indicating boundaries are acceptable so long as they do not deter walkers by giving them false information;
- landowners may need to provide for new access to open country where public rights of way do not exist or are insufficient;
- open country access may be closed for up to 28 days each year, but not over bank holidays or weekends.

Limitation on access rights

Even where access rights are granted, these rights are limited by Sch 2 to the 2000 Act so that, for example, no vehicle can be used (including bicycles), no craft can be sailed on waters and no organised games played – so no paintball games. Camping is also prohibited. If these activities are undertaken, the persons concerned become trespassers and can be removed by the use of reasonable force. Countryside bodies have power to further restrict access during a specified period in the event, for example, of a fire risk, and indefinitely for nature conservation, heritage preservation and national defence. The owner of the land is under a duty only to warn of dangers known to him or her or which are reasonably believed to exist.

Restrictive covenants

These covenants control the way in which a person uses his land. There is **public** control of the use of land through Town and Country Planning Acts (see further, Chapter 4 ◑) and there are also building regulations to cover the way in which buildings are constructed. As well as **public** control, however, there is also **private** control by means of restrictive covenants. If these are put into a lease of land the landlord can enforce them against the tenant because they are parties to the contract; in other words, there is a privity of estate or contract between them.

However, it is often desirable that covenants (or agreements) restricting the use of land should be enforceable between those who own freehold properties. For example, when estates of private houses are built, it is desirable in order to preserve the residential nature of the estate that covenants, e.g. to use the premises for residential purposes only, should be complied with by the purchasers of the individual houses and also by those who buy from them and so on, and that these covenants should be enforceable by the house owners as between themselves.

Covenants can be created by a common seller of the property, e.g. the builder or developer (whoever owns the land), and then they can be enforced by the purchasers of the houses as between themselves. The builder or developer will not normally be able to enforce them because he will not usually own any land on the estate, having sold it all off for housing plots. These are commonly known as building schemes.

These covenants can be enforced between subsequent owners of the houses as an exception to the rule of privity of contract (see also Chapter 7 ◑). They are, however, void unless registered as a land charge at the Land Registry.

When a person buys a house a solicitor acting in the matter will get a search of the Land Register done and will find the restrictive covenants which exist over the property. If he does not find any, because they are not registered, then they are void.

As far as business premises are concerned, these covenants can be a nuisance, in that they may restrict the development of the business. A person who wishes to get rid of a covenant is able to pursue an application to the Lands Tribunal, which deals with certain disputes over land, for modification or discharge.

However, the expense and delay which are unfortunately typical of so many legal procedures apply to Lands Tribunal applications so that developers of land who are faced with the possible enforcement of a covenant making development more expensive may insure against that possible loss. A Lands Tribunal application may be considered for a major development where insurance is expensive and not an economic option. It can also be used to sound out the strength and identity of possible objectors.

The method of enforcement is by a claim for damages or an injunction. The right to an injunction may be lost by delay and/or acquiescence (see further Chapter 7 on the remedy of injunction ●). Thus, it was held in *Gafford* v *Graham* (1998) that a landowner enjoying the benefit of a restrictive covenant over adjoining land who, with full knowledge of his rights, failed to seek relief to restrain the unlawful erection of an indoor riding school in breach of covenant could have damages only when he eventually brought a claim. Delay and acquiescence, which is assumed from delay, had barred his claim to injunctive relief.

Legal estates in land

There are three legal estates in land – the fee simple absolute in possession (usually called a freehold), the term of years absolute (usually called a leasehold) and the commonhold.

The word 'estate' is used because in theory at least the Queen owns all our land and we can only hold an estate, as it is called, from her; in other words, part of what she owns. However, the Queen has now no right to take back these estates from their owners.

The freehold

If we have an estate from the Queen, we want to know how long it will last. The fee simple absolute in possession (or freehold) lasts indefinitely and the word 'fee'

means that the land can be inherited, as where it is left by the owner to another person by a will. 'Simple' means that it can be passed on to anyone. The word 'absolute' means that it must not be what is called a modified fee, such as a life interest, which can only be an equitable interest behind a trust (see below).

There must also be possession of the land, though the freehold owner need not be living on the property; it is enough if he receives rent for it, as where he has let it on a lease to a tenant and is himself a landlord.

So, if freehold land is sold or left by will to X, the freehold will belong to X and he can pass it on to another.

If, however, land is left 'to X for life and after his death to Y', X does not take a legal estate of freehold, nor does Y. Y's interest is absolute but not yet in possession until X dies. X's interest is in possession but is not absolute because it is only for his life.

The above interests are equitable interests and can only be held on a trust. The trustees would have the freehold and when X died they would transfer the freehold to Y who would then be the absolute owner and the trust would come to an end.

The leasehold

A term of years absolute, usually called a lease, is an estate which lasts for a fixed time. It is usually given by a freehold owner to a tenant. It will normally be for a fixed period, e.g. 21 years.

A lease for a fixed term comes to an end when the term finishes, though in the case of business leases there may be statutory protection, in terms, e.g. of security of tenure under the Landlord and Tenant Act 1954, Part II, which was considered earlier in this chapter.

The commonhold

The Commonhold and Leasehold Reform Act 2002 (CLRA 2002) sets up the commonhold.

Generally

A commonhold is defined as a freehold with special characteristics – mainly that it is not necessary for the property to have foundations in the land, which is a requirement for the ordinary freehold. This is why it is often referred to colloquially as a 'flying freehold'.

The owners of commonhold units such as commonhold flats will be members automatically of the commonhold association that will own the common parts such as lifts, entrance halls, stairs, refuse areas, gardens and driveways. The association will be a company limited by guarantee governed by the Companies Act 1985. The use and maintenance of the units will be governed by the commonhold community statement (CCS): the CCS is the constitution of the commonhold land and must be registered at HM Land Registry, and a commonhold assessment will fix the percentage payable for each unit. This in other situations, e.g. leasehold flats, would be a service charge.

Most commonholds will be a block of flats but they could be shop units in an arcade or units on a business park. Therefore, property capable of becoming a commonhold unit is residential or commercial property. A unit-holder will have a registered freehold title to it.

The usual provisions for company winding-up will apply where a commonhold association becomes insolvent and it will be necessary to dissolve an association where the unit-holders wish to sell the block for redevelopment.

Three major points about commonhold from a commercial aspect are:

(a) Although it will be possible to convert from leasehold to commonhold, it will be necessary to obtain the consent of all the existing leaseholders, which indicates that the legislation is aimed mainly at new developments.
(b) In the case of a residential commonhold, there will be a restriction on the commonholder letting the premises. A maximum of only seven years will be permitted. This provision will be most unattractive to the property industry because it means in effect that investors will not want to invest in commonhold property. The object of the restriction is to develop a community and not encourage the absentee landlord syndrome which has often blighted leasehold developments. Business leases, e.g. shops within the development, will be subject to the terms of the commonhold statement that is filed at the Land Registry when the commonhold arrangement is set up, e.g. by the developer.
(c) It is anticipated that commonhold residential developments will become, in time, more desirable than leasehold properties and will trade at a premium compared with such properties.

Commonhold should not be confused with leasehold enfranchisement under which flat owners in blocks of flats collectively buy out the freehold owner of the property and so obtain control of the freehold of the block but not their individual flats in the sense that they are still tenants.

Comment. It is the responsibility of the association to enforce any breaches of the CCS. In effect, this gives the association a role similar to that of a landlord in a landlord and tenant relationship. In common with most leases, the CCS will restrict the granting of leases in the commonhold unit. In general, a unit-holder will not be able to grant a leasehold interest of the unit unless the commonhold association is a party to the lease or gives its consent (CLRA 2002, s 20(3)).

Advantages over leasehold

The commonhold legislation is concerned to overcome certain weaknesses in leasehold arrangements as follows:

- A lease is granted for a fixed term and admittedly the term may sometimes be lengthy. However, the issue of renewal will arise and this may require troublesome negotiation that can also be costly. A commonhold is a type of freehold and therefore permanent.
- Leasehold properties have no standard management structure as the commonhold has and the structures offered can vary greatly in their quality.
- Mistakes may occur in the documentation so that the terms of the various leases in, say, a block do not match. This can cause difficulty in enforcing conditions that do not occur in a commonhold development where one document, i.e. the CCS, sets out the obligations and terms of ownership for all units. There is thus no chance of mismatching provisions.
- Premature termination of a leasehold development can cause problems in terms of dividing assets. However, commonhold arrangements have documentation laying down the terms in advance of termination but the court has a power to vary these in a termination situation.
- A leasehold is a wasting asset. A leasehold is a term of years absolute that will eventually come to an end even where there is a long term, e.g. 99 years. A freehold is a *perpetual estate.*
- A lease is subject to forfeiture if there is a breach of covenant, e.g. assigning or sub-letting by the tenant.

A *main business application* is, therefore, that a freehold title in commonhold land is a better security than a lease in terms of lending and borrowing.

Setting up a commonhold

A commonhold may be established in two ways:

- It can be registered at the Land Registry *with unit-holders* where the identity of the unit-holders is known. The freehold of the units vests in them and the commonhold arrangements come into force on registration; this will occur where there is a conversion from a leasehold arrangement but will otherwise be uncommon.

■ A person developing by building afresh or converting an empty building with the intention of selling off the units will register a commonhold *without unit-holders*. The developer retains ownership after registration for an interim period until the first unit is sold. The developer has complete control during the interim period and can, if he wishes, abandon the development and cancel the registration. Even after the initial sale the developer's business is protected in the sense that the CCS can give him rights to prevent early purchasers from interfering with the process of marketing the units.

Comment. The cost of establishing commonhold arrangements will not always justify conversion of an existing leasehold arrangement unless the leases are near to termination. However, since commonhold arrangements will put a premium on sale of the units, this might prove an incentive to conversion from leasehold.

The nature of the property

Agricultural land cannot be registered as commonhold but an existing freehold or leasehold can be converted. An existing freehold can be divided into parcels or plots and held under commonhold arrangements.

Termination of commonhold

A commonhold arrangement is brought to an end by winding-up the commonhold association. Since the units are not owned by the association, they are not available to pay its debts. However, the court may make what is called a 'succession order' under which a new commonhold association is substituted, the members being those who have met their liabilities to the full. This has been called a 'Phoenix association' that takes over the management so that the unit-holders can continue to hold and enjoy their properties. If no succession order is made, the commonhold arrangement ceases to exist and the properties will be dealt with in accordance with the directions of the liquidator.

Joint owners

A commonhold unit can be held by joint owners.

The rights and duties of an occupier of land

The main right of an occupier of land is to seek an injunction against persons who trespass on his land or, alternatively, sue the trespasser for damages. These matters were considered in Chapter 11 ○. However, in addition to the general rules which apply to trespass to land, there are aspects specific to occupiers of land which are considered below. In addition, the question of the liability of occupiers of land and premises to persons suffering injury arising from that occupation may be regarded as an aspect of negligence (which has also been considered in general terms in Chapter 11 ○). However, specific aspects of liability applying to occupiers and arising from legislation are covered in the material which follows.

Duties to those who are not on the premises

We must look separately at liability to persons on the road (or highway), if any, which is next to the premises. We must also consider liability to persons on premises which are next to the property.

1 Liability to persons on the highway. The occupier has a duty not to injure persons on the highway by allowing a harmful situation to develop on his land.

Holling v Yorkshire Traction Co Ltd (1948)

Steam and smoke from the Traction Company's factory went across a road next to it and made it difficult to see. As a result, two vehicles collided and this caused the death of Holling. The court said that the Traction Company was liable. It was negligent of the company not to post a man at each end of the affected area to warn of the danger.

2 Liability to persons on adjoining premises. An occupier has a duty not to injure persons on adjoining premises by allowing a harmful situation to develop on the land.

Taylor v Liverpool Corporation (1939)

The claimant was the daughter of the tenant of some flats owned by the Corporation. She was injured when a chimney stack from adjoining premises, also owned by the Corporation, fell into a yard. The Corporation had been negligent in that it had not maintained the chimney properly. The Corporation was liable in negligence and the claimant won her case.

Duties to persons on the premises

Under the Occupiers' Liability Act 1957 an occupier of premises must take reasonable care to see that a visitor to his premises will be reasonably safe in using the premises for the purposes for which he is invited or permitted by the occupier to be on them.

The House of Lords has ruled that there is no duty to warn people of obvious dangers or to protect them from their own foolish acts.

Tomlinson v Congleton BC (2003)

The claimant was an 18-year-old who on a hot bank holiday and while in a country park owned and occupied by the defendant waded into a lake to cool off and when only up to his knees in water executed a dive and struck his head on the uneven bottom of the lake. He broke his neck and became tetraplegic. He claimed damages from the defendant council for what he alleged was a breach of duty by it under the 1957 Act. There were warning notices prohibiting swimming in the lake but, as the defendant knew, these were often ignored. The House of Lords turned down the claim because, in the view of their Lordships, the defendant council was not in breach of its duty. The claimant must have realised the dangers involved in diving into shallow water. He, therefore, was responsible for his own actions and the defendant was not under a duty to protect against foolishness. The result would appear to have been the same even if no notices had been placed by the council. As Lord Hoffmann said, 'A duty to protect against obvious risks or self-inflicted harm exists only in cases where there is no informed choice . . . such as the inability of children to recognise danger.'

This decision was reinforced by *Lewis v Six Continents plc* (2005), where the Court of Appeal dismissed Mr Lewis's claim for damages for personal injury caused when he fell out of a second floor window at the defendant's hotel. He had no explanation as to how this happened. The Court of Appeal ruled that, since Mr Lewis did not suffer from any disability, the test was

whether the windows were unsafe for *anyone*. The windows were quite safe for ordinary use. There was no need, for example, to restrict access to hotel windows.

Visitors – generally

The above duty is owed to all lawful visitors. These are individuals who enter the premises with the **express** permission of the occupier, as where A (an occupier) invites B (a plumber) to enter his home to repair a leaking pipe.

However, permission to enter premises is also **implied** by the law. So, for example, persons who enter premises to read, for example, gas and/or electricity meters are there by the implied permission of the occupier, as would also be a policeman with a search warrant, though in the last case it is unlikely that the occupier would expressly invite him on to the premises! The term 'visitor' does not apply to trespassers.

Children

The 1957 Act provides that persons who occupy premises must take into account the fact that children may be less careful than adults and therefore the duty of care owed to children is higher.

An example of this is that things which constitute a trap or are especially alluring to children must be given special attention by an occupier, because he may be liable for any damage which such things cause, even if the child involved is a trespasser.

Glasgow Corporation v Taylor (1922)

A boy aged seven years died after he had eaten some poisonous berries which he picked from a tree in a park owned by the Corporation.

There was a notice in the park but the court decided that this was not adequate as a means of communicating the danger to young children. Also, the berries were within easy reach and were attractive to children. The Corporation was liable.

Visitors who are experts

The 1957 Act provides that persons who enter premises as part of their job, e.g. plumbers and electricians, ought to have a better appreciation of the risks which may arise while they are doing their work.

Roles v Nathan (1963)

N employed two chimney sweeps to clean out the flues of a heating system fuelled by coke. Although N warned the sweeps against it, they blocked off a ventilation hole while the coke fire was still alight. They were later killed by the escape of carbon monoxide fumes. This action, which was brought by the dependants of the sweeps, failed. The court decided that an occupier is entitled to assume that a chimney sweep will guard against such dangers.

Warnings

The 1957 Act states that if the occupier gives a warning of the danger, it will free him from liability, but only if the warning makes the visitor safe.

It would not be enough, for example, for a cinema to give warning of a dangerous roof over what was the only approach to the ticket office. However, if customers in a shop are told not to go to the far end of it because builders have opened up a dangerous hole, the shopkeeper might well have no duty to a customer who defied his instruction and fell down the hole.

Exclusion of liability

The 1957 Act provides that an occupier may 'restrict or exclude his duty by agreement or otherwise'. However, because of the Unfair Contract Terms Act 1977 (see Chapter 9 ◯) there can be no exclusion of liability for death or personal injury on business premises. In regard to other loss, e.g. damage to the goods of a visitor, liability can be excluded only if it is reasonable to do so.

Faulty work of outside contractors

The 1957 Act allows an occupier to escape liability if the damage results from the faulty work of an outside contractor (called also an independent contractor) whose expertise is necessary to get the job done, provided the occupier behaved reasonably in the selection of the contractor.

Cook v Broderip (1968)

The owner of a flat, Major Broderip, employed an apparently competent electrical contractor to fix a new socket. Mrs Cook, who was a cleaner, received an electric shock from the socket while she was working in the flat. This was because the contractor had failed to test it properly.

The court decided that Major Broderip was not liable to Mrs Cook but the contractor was.

Comment. In a more recent case the Court of Appeal has ruled that it can be part of the occupier's duty to employ a competent contractor to see that the contractor has unexpired insurance so that if he or she is negligent and sued successfully by an injured claimant there is the backing of insurance to pay the damages. Failure to make such a check may result in the occupier being liable for the damage on the ground that the contractor was not competent. (See *Gwilliam v West Hertfordshire Hospital NHS Trust* (2003) where a fair was set up on the defendant's property and the claimant was injured by the fairground equipment arising from the fair contractor's negligence. His insurance had expired and because the trust did not check this it was held liable for the claimant's injuries.)

Trespassers

The position of trespassers is covered by the Occupiers' Liability Act 1984. The Act deals with the duty of an occupier to persons other than his visitors and this includes trespassers and persons entering land without the consent of the owner, but in the exercise of a private right of way or public access. In these cases the occupier owes a duty, if he is aware of the danger which exists, or has reasonable grounds to believe that it exists.

He must also know, or have reasonable grounds to believe, that the non-visitor concerned is in the vicinity of the danger – whether he has lawful authority to be in that vicinity or not.

Furthermore, the risk must be one which in all the circumstances of the case it is reasonable to expect the occupier to offer the non-visitor protection against. It was held, for example, in *Proffit v British Railways Board* (1984) that British Rail (as it then was) had no general duty to erect or maintain fences sufficient to keep trespassers out. The case applies to Network Rail, which is the successor to British Rail.

The duty is to take such care as is reasonable in all the circumstances of the case to see that the non-visitor does not suffer injury because of the danger concerned. The duty may be discharged by giving a warning of the danger or taking steps to discourage persons from incurring risk. Thus, the defence of assumption of risk is preserved.

A case in point is *Ratcliff v McConnell* (1999) where the claimant sued for tetraplegic injuries sustained by diving into the shallow end of a college swimming pool when the pool was closed for the winter. He had climbed over a locked gate in the early hours of the morning. There were warning notices and notices prohibiting use. The claimant, who was an adult, did not recover any damages against the college (represented by the defendant who was a governor). He willingly accepted the risk, said the Court of Appeal.

Intellectual property and its protection

Generally

Intellectual property is a term used to refer to a product or a process which is marketable and profitable because it is unique.

This uniqueness is protected by patent law, which gives protection to technological inventions. The law relating to registered designs protects articles which are mass produced but distinguished from others by a registered design which appears upon them. The law of copyright protects, for example, rights in literary, artistic, and musical works. The law of trade marks and service marks protects the use of a particular mark if it is used in trade.

The law also protects those in business from competitors who maliciously disparage their products or who pass off their own products as those of another business. There is also some protection in regard to the commercial use, e.g. by employees without permission, of confidential information.

The current main legislation is to be found in the Patents Act 1977 (as amended by the Patents Act 2004), the Copyright, Designs and Patents Act 1988 and the Trade Marks Act 1994.

Patents

Application

An application for a patent can be made by or on behalf of the inventor of a new process or device and the grant of a patent will be made to the inventor himself or to any person who is entitled to it, as where the inventor has sold the idea before patenting it.

What can be patented?

It should not be assumed that every bright idea can be the subject of a patent. When application is made for a patent certain essential criteria must be met. It must be shown that the applicant has an invention; the invention must not be excluded (see below); it must be new and not something that would be obvious to lots of people. The 1977 and 1988 Acts do not define an invention, but do require that it be made or used in industry. However, a product, article, material apparatus or process will generally come within the term 'invention' and the method of its operation or manufacture should be patentable. Thus, a toothbrush with an integral toothpaste tube, and the method of making a particular type of chocolate bar, should be patentable, as was the bagless vacuum cleaner invented by Dyson. As a matter of interest, the High Court has ruled that a bagless cleaner subsequently made by Hoover was an infringement of Dyson's patent for its bagless cyclonic vacuum cleaner (see *Dyson Appliances Ltd* v *Hoover Ltd* (2000)).

Exclusions

Under the Patents Act 1977 certain items cannot be protected by a patent. Among these are discoveries, so that if you had been the first person to develop the theory of gravity (actually it was Newton), you could not have patented the principle of gravity. However, the inventor of a pendulum clock which utilised gravity could seek to protect the device.

Computer programs (software) are generally protected by copyright, but exceptionally, if a program was invented which enabled the computer to work faster, patent protection would be available for the programmed computer and the method of operating it.

Registration

An application for a patent can be made by or on behalf of the inventor of a new process or device, and the grant of a patent will be made to the inventor himself or to any person who is entitled to it, as where the inventor has sold the idea before patenting it. Application is made to the Patent Office in London or in Newport, Gwent, South Wales. The Patent Office is part of the Department for Innovation, Universities & Skills and it deals with the granting of patents, registered trade marks and registered designs.

The Comptroller-General maintains at the Patent Office a register of patents and the date of entry gives priority over later inventions. A patent lasts for 20 years but must in effect be renewed annually by payment of a fee to the Patent Office. These fees are payable on the anniversary of the filing date and increase with the age of the patent. A patent cannot be extended beyond 20 years.

Using patents

It should be noted that a patent does not necessarily give the patent holder a right **to use** his invention. For example, a patented drug may have to be withdrawn from the market if it does not comply with government regulations. The right given by a patent is the right of the holder **to control** his invention, in the sense of having a total monopoly in the market or allowing others to market the invention subject to conditions imposed upon them by the patent holder.

Infringement

A UK patent will, in general, be infringed by making, using or selling something in the UK which is subject to the patent without the owner's consent. However, a UK patent applies only within the UK so that a German competitor could legally make the invention in Germany, unless of course there was also a German patent. The German goods could also quite legally be exported to any other country where there was no patent, though not of course to the UK.

Infringement of a patent is a matter for the civil rather than the criminal law and actions for an injunction, damages, or an account of profits, are brought in the Patents Court which is part of the Chancery Division of the High Court. However, the 1988 Act sets up the Patents County Court (see Chapter 3 ⊙) where the cost of actions against infringement are lower.

The Civil Procedure Rules now provide a streamlined procedure for patent claims in English courts. The aim is for the case to be completed within six months of being commenced. The procedure can be used if both sides agree to it or if the court agrees with one party that it is appropriate.

Further improvements that will assist particularly small businesses to enforce patent rights are contained in the Patents Act 2004. The Act, among other things, enables the Patent Office to provide an independent non-binding opinion on patent validity or alleged infringement to settle disputes over patent rights without the parties having to resort to litigation in the Patents Courts. Out-of-court settlement of disputes is encouraged and there are provisions to deter patent owners from making unreasonable allegations of infringement.

The European Patent Convention 1973, along with provisions in the Patents Act 2004, allows the issue of a Community patent protected in European states. Application is to the European Patent Office and a centralised Community Patent Court of first instance situated in Luxembourg has exclusive jurisdiction over invalidity and infringement proceedings.

Patents: effect of repair

The matter of infringement of patented goods by repair was raised in *United Wire Ltd* v *Screen Repair Services (Scotland) Ltd* (2000) where the Court of Appeal decided that, while in the normal way a repair would not amount to an infringement of the patent, much would depend on the extent of the repair. If, for example, it amounted to manufacture of a large part of the product, it might do so. In this instance repairs to filtering screens used in the oil industry were sufficiently extensive to infringe the patent in the screens held by United Wire.

Employees' inventions

Under the Patents Act 1977 an invention of an employee belongs to the employer if the employee arrives at it during his normal employment or during a specific job outside his normal duties. Other inventions, e.g. those made during the employee's spare time, belong to the employee.

Under the 1977 Act, where the invention turns out to be of outstanding benefit to the employer the employee may be awarded compensation by the Comptroller-General or the court so as to ensure that the employee gets a fair share of the benefit. The court will come in where the Comptroller-General will not deal with the matter because it is felt that the issues in a particular case would be better dealt with by the court. Terms of a contract of service which cut down an employee's rights in inventions where these exist are unenforceable.

Designs: the UK regime

What is meant by a design?

A design refers only to the features of shape, pattern or ornament applied to an article by an industrial process which appeals to, and is judged solely by, looking at the article, e.g. the shape of a Coca-Cola bottle.

For example, a firm making a special design of fabric for use in curtains or chair covers might register the design.

It is now possible to register the Coca-Cola bottle as a trade mark under the Trade Marks Act 1994 (see further, later in this chapter).

Registration

Designs may be registered at the Patent Office (Designs Registry) under the Registered Designs Act 1949 (as amended by the 1988 Act), and there is an appeal to the

Registered Designs Appeal Tribunal if the Registrar refuses to register a particular design. Registration gives the owner of the design protection for five years and this can be extended for four further periods of five years on payment of four further fees every five years, making 25 years in all. The Register of Designs can be inspected on payment of a fee.

Infringement

The registered or unregistered design right owner's remedies for infringement are to sue the person responsible for damages and/or an injunction, or an account of profits made from the wrongful use of the design or an order for the delivery-up of the infringing copies.

Unregistered design right

The Copyright Act 1956 gave protection against the reproduction of articles from drawings of them. The provisions were primarily intended to give protection against unauthorised use of drawings of cartoon characters, as by making dolls from them. Also, while the protection offered to an article under a registered design was limited to 15 years (now 25 years, see above), the copyright protection lasted for 50 years (now 70 years).

The law of copyright was therefore increasingly used to protect articles in effect by copyright law, by protecting a drawing from which they were made. This approach was used, in particular, by motor manufacturers to protect their exclusive production of spare parts for their vehicles.

The 1988 Act abolishes copyright protection for drawings but gives instead a new design right which is automatically acquired and does not require registration. It lasts for 10 years from the end of the year when the article is first marketed or 15 years after it was first designed, whichever period is the first to expire. During the last five years of its life anyone will be able to get a licence to make the article by paying a royalty to the owner at a rate to be determined by the Patent Office in the absence of agreement.

The Act excludes from the new right items which 'must fit' or 'must match', e.g. an exhaust system which 'must fit' a particular car or a body panel which 'must match' a particular car body. The exclusions are therefore those features of a design which are made to ensure that it fits or matches with another part. These exclusions will, in the main, deny protection to car manufacturers in regard to spare parts for their vehicles and

prevent what many regarded as the use of intellectual property law to sustain a restrictive practice.

Nevertheless, other aspects of a design are covered.

Example

Suppose that the open end of a replacement bag for a 'Hover' vacuum cleaner needs to be of a particular shape to fit the end of the hose of the 'Hover'. Anyone can copy this part of the 'Hover' bag but it would be an infringement of the 'Hover' bag design to copy other aspects of its shape which were not essential to the fitting of the 'Hover' bag.

The shape of the 'Hover' bag should now also be registrable as a trade mark under the Trade Marks Act 1994.

Infringement

The owner's remedies for infringement are to apply to the court for damages, an injunction and for delivery-up of infringing materials.

Designs: the Community regime

1 Community Registered Designs. Regulation 6/2002 on Community Designs came into force on 6 March 2002. It provides for a registrable design right that applies across all EU states. It lasts for renewable periods of between 5 and 25 years as does UK design law.

Application is made to the Office for Harmonisation of the Internal Market in Alicante. After registration the design is published in the *Community Designs Bulletin*. However, applicants can ask for publication to be deferred for 30 months where it is felt that publication might otherwise adversely affect the commercial success of the article. Organisations that have applied for design rights on a national, e.g. UK, basis have priority when they apply for a new registered Community Design Right for the same design. It is six months' priority from the date of first filing.

United Kingdom applicants may file community design rights applications through the UK Patent Office.

2 Unregistered Community Design Right. Regulation 6/2002 also brought in a new unregistered design right from March 2002. The UK now has two separate design rights.

The EU right lasts for only three years from when the design was first made available to the public in the EU. This contrasts with the UK right which lasts for 10 years. It protects designs that are new and of individual character. A design is deemed new if when it becomes available to the public it is not identical to an already existing design. The right is applicable to the whole of the product and includes its ornamentation. A design on a product will not be protected unless it remains visible during the normal use of the product. The EU right differs from the UK right since the latter lasts for 10 years and does not protect surface ornamentation.

Copyright

The 1988 Act does not require the owner of a copyright to register it or to follow any formalities in respect of it. The protection is given by the Act to every original literary, dramatic, musical and artistic work which was previously unpublished.

Copyright does not protect ideas. Anyone is entitled to incorporate those ideas in a new work provided that substantially the same words and examples are not used.

Ownership and duration

The author of the work is the owner of the copyright. However, it may be a term of the contract between, say, a newspaper company and its journalists that the entire copyright in the journalist's work is to belong to the newspaper company.

Under the Act, protection of copyright existed in a work during the lifetime of the author of it and until the end of the period of 50 years from the end of the calendar year in which the author of the work died. The copyright then came to an end.

The relevant rules are now contained in a statutory instrument, the Duration of Copyright and Rights in Performance Regulations 1995 (SI 1995/3297), passed in order to harmonise UK law with that of the EU. The regulations increase the basic term of copyright in literary, dramatic, musical and artistic works. This raises the former provision of the present life of the author plus 50 years after his death to life plus 70 years. Copyright in film now lasts for 70 years from the last to die of the principal director, the authors of the screenplay and dialogue, and the composer of any music specifically for the film. The regulations came into force on 1 January 1996 and apply to existing works. Copyrights that were due to expire on 31 December 1995 are continued in force and will be extended.

Infringement – generally

The person infringing the copyright will usually have copied from the work and an action can be brought for an injunction and/or damages or for an account of profits made from the wrongful use of the copyright work.

It was held in *Redrow Homes Ltd* v *Bett Brothers plc* (1997) that a claimant owner who asks the court to order the wrongful user of a copyright to hand over the profits made from the wrongful use cannot have, in addition, an award of damages. The case involved the infringement of copyright in drawings containing the designs of houses. The decision will presumably have application in other areas of intellectual property where there is an alternative remedy of damages and an account of profits.

Infringement – press-cuttings

Many companies institute a press-cuttings service for circulation among staff to alert them and inform them as to developments in relevant areas of business.

A property right subsists in the typographical arrangement of published editions (s 1 of the Copyright, Designs and Patents Act 1988). The term 'published edition', so far as a newspaper is concerned, means the whole newspaper, and questions as to the infringement of this property right by copying parts of a newspaper must focus on whether the infringement related to a *substantial part* of the whole newspaper (s 16(2) and (3)(a)).

In this connection, the Court of Appeal ruled that Marks & Spencer plc did not infringe the copyright in a newspaper's typographical arrangement when it photocopied an article for its internal press-cuttings service (see *Newspaper Licensing Agency* v *Marks & Spencer plc* (2000), particularly the *Comment*, below).

The Newspaper Licensing Agency (NLA) is a company formed to protect the intellectual property rights of national and provincial newspapers relating to press-cuttings. It operates a collective licensing scheme for making copies of press-cuttings. Marks & Spencer plc (the defendant) needs no introduction. Its involvement in these proceedings arose from its use of a press-cuttings agency (duly licensed by the NLA) to make copies of cuttings from newspapers; the defendant copied certain articles for circulation within the company.

Newspaper Licensing Agency v *Marks & Spencer plc* (2000)

The NLA sued the defendant for breach of copyright and Lightman J held in the High Court that the distribution of copies of such cuttings to 70 persons within the defendant company infringed copyright. The defendant appealed to the Court of Appeal, wherein Peter Gibson LJ (with whom Mance LJ agreed, Chadwick LJ dissenting) said that the first issue was to determine what was meant by the 'typographical arrangement of published editions' in s 1. One possible interpretation of this phrase was the typographical arrangement of each article published in a newspaper, but he preferred the view that the phrase referred to the typographical arrangement of the whole newspaper. The latter view was supported by an Australian decision, *Nationwide New Pty Ltd* v *Copyright Agency Ltd* (1996).

He turned next to the question of whether the defendant's copying of some articles constituted a copying of a substantial part of the copyright work. Although the court had been shown samples of cuttings and of the complete pages from which they had been extracted, the issue of whether substantial parts had been copied could be determined by judicial knowledge of the form of newspapers. The compiler of the cuttings had rearranged the format of the original article and accordingly the articles appeared in a different image from that in which they had appeared in the newspaper. Nevertheless, there was a facsimile copy of each part of any article which was cut up and pasted. Each such part was a separate part of the image on the page, and the 'substantiality' of each part had to be considered.

However, the court had not been shown any cutting which could properly be regarded as a 'substantial part' of the published edition from which it had been taken. That was decisive in the appeal, and was supported by the *Nationwide* case. The court had heard argument whether the copying constituted fair dealing in reporting current events in accordance with s 30(2). Peter Gibson LJ felt that, if what the defendant had done had been a prima facie breach of copyright, s 30(2) would have afforded no defence, but a decision on the point was not necessary in view of the decision which the court had reached.

Comment. The above case is retained as an example of copying for commercial research. However, the Copyright, Designs and Patents Act 1988 has been significantly changed by the Copyright and Related Rights Regulations 2003 (SI 2003/2498), which implement the EU Copyright Directive 2000/29/EC from October 2003. The regulations abolish the fair dealing exception for commercial research and businesses wishing to conduct research through press-cuttings, as in the above case, will need a licence.

For more on the regulations, see p 447 ○.

Exceptions

There are no statutory defences to copyright infringement. However, there are common law defences, the principal being known as 'non-derogation from grant'. This defence was developed from the decision of the House of Lords in *British Leyland* v *Armstrong Patents*

Co (1986). In this case the House of Lords refused to allow British Leyland (as it was then) to enforce its copyright in drawings relating to replacement exhaust pipes so as to prevent car owners from obtaining replacement exhausts from independent makers. The House of Lords said this would derogate from British Leyland's implied grant of rights to buyers of British Leyland cars, allowing them to repair their cars by the most economical method during the normal working life of the vehicle.

However, in *Canon Kabushiki* v *Green Cartridge Co (Hong Kong) Ltd* (1997) the Privy Council approved a decision of the court of trial granting an injunction to the claimants, thus prohibiting the defendants from infringing copyright in the claimants' drawings of replacement toner cartridges for photocopiers and laser printers.

The Privy Council said that the cost of a replacement exhaust was relatively small in relation to the capital and running costs of a car. In contrast, the cost of replacement cartridges for a laser printer substantially exceeded the cost of the printer itself. There was also competition for the claimants, as suppliers of replacement cartridges, from those who refilled exhausted toner cartridges. It could not, therefore, be said that the claimants were unfairly using their intellectual property rights to abuse their monopoly in replacement toner supplies.

Moral rights

Under the 1988 Act authors are given certain moral rights in their work which exist quite independently of copyright. They provide protection alongside a copyright and would be especially useful and necessary to an author who had sold the copyright to someone else.

The right of paternity

This is a right to be identified as the author of a literary, dramatic, musical or artistic work. In general terms this right operates whenever the work is performed in public, or issued to the public or commercially exploited. It includes the right to be identified as the author of a work from which any adaptation is made. The right extends to copies of the piece and to signs on buildings such as theatres, where the sign can be seen by people entering or approaching the building. This right of paternity must be specifically claimed by the author.

The *exceptions* to the right of paternity are quite extensive and include what are called fair dealing exceptions that also apply to copyright. These include the use of extracts of works for the purpose of reporting current events, incidental inclusion in a broadcast or cable television programme and extracts for use in examination papers. If the author consents to the publication of the work in collective works, such as encyclopedias and/or dictionaries, he or she forgoes the right to be credited in the work.

The right of integrity

Under this right the author may object to changes in his or her work by way of additions, deletions, alterations or adaption which amount to a distortion or mutilation of the work, or in some way harm the author's honour or reputation. Film directors are included in the expression 'authors' for this purpose.

As regards *exceptions*, an author may not exercise the right of integrity in translations of the underlying literary or dramatic work. So, authors may have to put up with poor translations of their work with no remedy.

False attribution

This gives the author a right against false attribution which mirrors the right of paternity referred to above. Under the paternity right an author is entitled to be recognised as the creator of the work. The right of attribution gives a person such as an author the right to prevent a work which he has *not produced* being attributed to him, or a film falsely attributed to him as a director.

Private or domestic commissions

There are special rights given to those who commission photographs or films for their own private or domestic purposes. Where there is copyright in the resulting work, the person who commissioned it has the right not to have the work issued, exhibited or shown to the public, or broadcast or included in a cable programme service.

Infringement

An author whose moral rights have been infringed is entitled to an injunction and damages. These moral rights continue for the same length of time as copyright, i.e. the life of the author plus 70 years except for false attribution which continues for only 20 years after the person's death. Moral rights can be left by will or separately from any copyright and the beneficiary would then be able to enforce them in the same way as the original author. So a son or daughter made the beneficiary of an author/parent's moral rights could protect those rights after the death of the parent, even though the parent had sold the copyright during his lifetime.

The Copyright etc. and Trade Marks (Offences and Enforcement) Act 2002 should also be noted. It will help enforcement against those who infringe copyright and trade mark rights. The Act gives the police power to obtain warrants to search and seize property from any business that they believe is using unlicensed software. Under previous law only traders and importers could be prosecuted.

Semiconductor product topographies

This is a new form of intellectual property protection introduced into the UK by statutory instrument under an EC Directive. It protects integrated circuit layout designs found in computers, and in home equipment such as hi-fi, compact disc players and food processors, in a similar way to literary copyright.

Computer software

The 1988 Act continues the previous position under which computer software is protected in the same way as that of literary copyright.

Copyright and the Internet

Advances in technology have resulted in the 1988 Act being applied in novel fact situations. Thus, in **Shetland Times Ltd v Jonathan Wills** (1997) the court decided that it would be appropriate to issue an injunction to prevent the defendants placing their newspaper headlines on the claimant's website.

The Copyright and Related Rights Regulations 2003

These regulations (SI 2003/2498) came into force on 31 October 2003. They make changes in the law by adding new provisions to the Copyright, Designs and Patents Act 1988. The main changes appear below.

Performers now have the right to consent or prohibit a recording of their performance being made available to the public by electronic transmission, including the Internet. There is a new criminal offence for those who make infringing copies and communicate them to the public or have reason to believe this will happen. Those making illicit recordings also commit an offence. If the 'making available' is not in the course of a business, there will only be an offence if the infringement is to such an extent as to be prejudicial to the holder of the right.

These new rights are designed to assist the music and film industries, in particular, in the fight against widespread and unauthorised downloading of their works on the Internet. Other areas of change that have impact on business generally are set out below.

1 Copying for commercial research. The most important change that the regulations make to the 1988 Act and the one that will have the most immediate effect on business is the abolition of the fair dealing exception for commercial research. Under previous law those in business could lawfully take copies of copyright works as a basis for commercial research so long as the copying was fair. There was no definition of what could be regarded as fair but the general understanding was copying that was not prejudicial to the rights of the holder of the copyright. In consequence, much of the copying by those in business arguably fell within the fair dealing exception. Under the regulations businesses including accounting and law firms will have to review their procedures to see whether a licence may be required.

2 Criticism, review and news reporting. The provisions of the 1988 Act have been amended but continue to allow fair dealing with acknowledgement provided that the work has been made available to the public. Making available to the public includes Internet publication.

3 Library copying. Copying works in libraries will be permitted only if required for non-commercial purposes or private study. Any other copying will require a licence, and some libraries are considering the taking up of licences.

Other matters of general interest are that it becomes an offence to supply a person with the means to get round anti-copying protection on CDs: and injunctions can be obtained against an Internet service provider if he or she has actual knowledge that another person is using the service to infringe copyright.

Trade marks

Types of trade marks

There are two types of trade marks:

- common law or unregistered trade marks; and
- registered trade marks.

A common law trade mark is any mark which has been so widely used on or in connection with a certain class of goods that it can be shown that the public recognised goods with such a mark as coming from the owner

of the mark. The remedy to restrict improper use is a passing-off action. In this category would come 'Persil' and 'Polaroid', which are household names in regard to the products concerned.

Registered trade marks

The law of registered trade marks in the UK was reformed by the Trade Marks Act 1994 which came into force on 31 October 1994. The impetus for the Act was the implementation of the EC Trade Marks Directive (89/104) which harmonised the law of trade marks throughout the EC. The distinction between trade marks on goods and on services, e.g. the black horse of Lloyds Bank, has gone. These are now under the same law. Also abolished was the system of registration as a Part A mark or a Part B mark. The main provisions which affect UK law appear below.

Definition

Section 1 of the Act states that a trade mark is any sign capable of being represented graphically which is capable of distinguishing goods or services of one undertaking from those of others. It can include words (including personal names), designs, letters, numerals or the shape of goods or their packaging. It is also expected to include sounds, smells and colours. The first application for registration of a smell was the scent of roses impregnated into Sumitomo tyres.

However, the registration of smells may now have become harder since the German Patent and Trade Mark Office (supported by the European Court of Justice) turned down a trade mark application for the smell of a scent described as 'balsamically fruity with a slight hint of cinnamon'. It appears that non-visual trade marks can be registered if they are capable of being represented graphically. Thus, in *Shield Mark BV* v *Kist* (2004) the European Court ruled that a mark consisting of the first five notes of Beethoven's composition 'Für Elise' could be the subject of a trade mark. The claimant used the sound in advertising its wares on radio commercials that commenced with the notes and on stands at bookshops and newspaper kiosks where removal of its news sheets from the stand caused the tune to play. It is, of course, possible to represent the notes graphically on a musical stave. The sound of a cockcrow was turned down in the same case.

Although personal names are allowed, they must comply with s 3 which allows the refusal of registration where the so-called mark is not distinctive. Thus, if Mr Brown trades in a business name of Brown & Co, this cannot be registered as a mark since it is not distinctive. In this connection it is of interest to note that the Court of Appeal held in *Elvis Presley Enterprises Inc* v *Sid Shaw Elvisly Yours* (1999) that the name Elvis Presley was too well known to have the inherent distinctiveness which is required for a registered trade mark for goods such as perfumes, soaps and other toiletries. The Trade Mark Registrar had therefore been in error when he registered the name in favour of Elvis Presley Enterprises Inc. The court decided in favour of a London businessman, Sid Shaw, who had been trading in Elvis products since 1979 and could continue to do so.

Mr Shaw also complained that the Elvis Presley Enterprises registration was an infringement of his own registration of the expression 'Elvisly Yours' as a trade mark, which is, of course, registrable since it is not merely a name. The court quoted from the judgment in *Du Boulay* v *Du Boulay* (1896) where it was said:

. . . in this country we do not recognise the absolute right of a person to a particular name to the extent of entitling him to prevent the assumption of that name by a stranger . . . [this] is a grievance for which our law affords no redress.

It would therefore be impossible, in the UK at least, to copyright as a trade mark the name 'Diana', though 'Diana Queen of Hearts' should be acceptable as should 'Diana Princess of Wales'.

However, if, say, a geographical location is added then it may be that a business name can be registered as a trade mark, e.g. Mr Ahmed trading as 'Ahmed's Barbican Tandoori'. This is an important change and since such geographical marks are registrable under the 1994 Act registration, where possible, should give better protection to a business name than the tort of passing-off (see later in this chapter). All that needs to be established once the mark has been registered is whether the marks are confusingly similar and they are in respect of goods or services covered by the registration. The case for infringement is then established. Passing-off is a much more difficult matter to prove. Deception is the essence of an action for passing-off. In the absence of any patent or trade mark infringement it is only unlawful for a trader to copy and market a rival's product if the rival can show that purchasers are being or will be deceived into buying the copy instead of the real thing (*Hodgkinson & Corby* v *Wards Mobility Services* (1994)).

Since the shape of goods is now covered, the decision of the House of Lords in *Coca-Cola Trade Marks* (1986), in which their Lordships held that the shape of a Coca-Cola bottle could not be registered as a trade mark under previous legislation, is now reversed. The change has produced a major revival of interest in trade marks as a cheap and effective way of protecting brands. In fact, Coca-Cola became the first company to register a three-dimensional shape as a trade mark in 1995.

In this regard, the Trade Marks Registry has granted trade mark status to Heinz for the shade of turquoise used on its tins of baked beans.

Registration: the mark must be distinctive

A mark that is not distinctive can be excluded from registration under the Trade Marks Act 1994, as the following case shows.

Société des Produits Nestlé v Mars UK Ltd (2003)

Nestlé attempted to register part of a familiar catchphrase 'Have a Break' in regard to its chocolate, chocolate products, confectionery, candy and biscuits. Its rival company, Mars, objected. The High Court ruled that registration for the first three words would not be granted because the shortened phrase was not distinctive. It was a slogan used in a number of contexts.

Comment. Mars' objection can be appreciated. Many companies might wish to tell us to take a break with their products and to give one company exclusive trade mark rights would be an unwarranted protection. In a separate case, *Beckham* v *Peterborough United Football Club* (2003), Victoria Beckham failed to get an injunction to restrain the football club from using the word 'Posh', a term the club had been using for some 50 years, even though Ms Beckham had registered 'Posh' as a trade mark. The case points up the fact that having a trade mark will not necessarily allow the owner totally to exclude its use in the absence of some evidence of public confusion. 'Posh' would not seem to have the distinctiveness required for registration but it had been accepted, though there were no objections, when Ms Beckham registered it during her time with the Spice Girls band.

Procedure for registration

Any person who claims to be the proprietor of a registrable trade mark and who wishes to register it must apply to the Registrar of Trade Marks giving a statement of the goods or services and a representation of the mark. The Registrar may accept the mark absolutely or approve registration subject to conditions or refuse to register the mark. The applicant is entitled to be heard before refusal. Where registration is acceptable, the Registrar must advertise the application in the *Trade Marks Journal*. Persons aggrieved by the application may then object to the Registrar giving grounds for their objection. The period for objection is three months from the advertisement with no provision for extension. If no application is made within that period or is made but fails, the mark will be registered and will be valid for 10 years from the date of application renewable every 10 years. Even after registration, application can be made to the Registrar or the court to rectify any error or omission in the Register, but not in respect of matters affecting the validity of the registration.

Collective and certification marks

The Act allows the registration of collective marks, e.g. the Wool Mark on clothing, and certification marks such as the mark of the British Standards Institute (the Kitemark).

Enforcement

The effect of a registered trade mark is to give rights of exclusive use to the owner. The general remedy is an injunction to prevent wrongful use. In this connection, use of a mark in a different business is no defence. Thus, in *Discovery Communications Inc v Discovery FM Ltd* (2000) the court granted an injunction to prevent the use of the claimants' registered mark 'Discovery Channel' by the defendants who were trading under 'Discovery 102'. The fact that the claimants were engaged in cable and satellite television, whereas the defendants were in radio, was no defence.

A more recent and high-profile case of infringement of a trade mark appears below.

***Arsenal Football Club plc v Reed* (2003)**

The case arose because Arsenal had registered the words 'Arsenal' and 'Arsenal Gunners' as trade marks along with its cannon and shield emblems. The marks were used on a wide variety of goods. Registration took place in 1989. Mr Reed had since 1970 sold unofficial Arsenal souvenirs outside the club's ground Highbury. The club contended that this was an infringement of their trade mark.

The High Court ruled against the club because it was known that the goods sold by Mr Reed were not official club merchandise. Mr Reed had a notice of disclaimer by his stall indicating that his products were not official club merchandise. However, the High Court asked the

---

European Court to consider the application of the law. Under Article 226 of the Treaty of Rome the ECJ can only pass judgment on the law and not on the facts of the case. The ECJ ruled that the function of a trade mark is to avoid confusion as to the origin of goods but went on to rule on the facts that Mr Reed had infringed the Arsenal trade mark.

The case came back to the High Court where the judge refused to apply the ECJ ruling because it was of mixed law and fact. The matter then went to the Court of Appeal. The High Court felt that the fact of the disclaimer avoided confusion. The ECJ did not think the disclaimer necessarily removed all confusion – a different view of the facts. The Court of Appeal accepted the ECJ's view of the facts and ruled that Mr Reed was infringing the Arsenal trade mark in spite of his disclaimer.

Comment. The case provides a singular illustration of a UK judge refusing to apply an ECJ ruling.

Section 92 of the Trade Marks Act 1994 contains the criminal offence of unauthorised use of trade mark materials and goods. The maximum penalty is an unlimited fine and/or imprisonment for up to 10 years. The section is used by trading standards in regard to the control of counterfeit goods. This produces the rather bizarre result of prosecutions being brought by trading standards to protect the consumer, but incidentally to protect the interests of enormously wealthy organisations, e.g. Microsoft, *at the UK taxpayers' expense*. The cost of these prosecutions awarded out of public funds may in some cases exceed £100,000!

The Community Trade Mark

The Community Trade Mark (CTM) is a single trade mark right which extends throughout the EU. The system is available to any country which is a member of the EU or person who is domiciled in a country in the EU or has a commercial establishment in the EU.

A CTM may consist of any distinctive sign capable of being represented graphically.

Applications are filed at any National Trade Marks Registry such as the UK Registry in London or directly at the CTM office in Alicante, Spain. The CTM office is known as the Office for Harmonisation in the Internal Market.

Enforcement

A CTM is enforced by what is called 'an infringement action' in a national court. It is possible to ask for a pan-European injunction covering the whole community and damages.

Advantages and disadvantages of the CTM system

A main advantage is that a single application allows a trade mark to be registered throughout the EU at less cost and administrative effort than individual applications to each country, making enforcement easier.

However, since CTM gives rights to so many countries it is likely that large numbers of conflicts will arise so that it will be difficult to select a CTM which will not be opposed at registration stage. The registry is required to publish applications, and oppositions must be lodged with the Registrar within three months.

Trade marks and comparative advertising

The law on comparative advertising (which is advertising by reference to a competitor's name or product) has been relaxed by the provisions of the Trade Marks Act 1994. It appears from the following case that the court felt that in considering the new provisions for the first time the main object of those provisions was to allow comparative advertising and that they should not be read in such a way as to effectively prohibit it.

Barclays Bank plc v RBS Advanta (1996)

RBS wished to promote its new credit card. It published a leaflet listing 15 ways in which its card was superior to others and in a brochure it included a comparative table listing six other credit cards including Barclaycard and Standard Visa, setting out their annual fees, annualised rates of interest on purchases and on cash advances, and their monthly interest rates. Barclays Bank, the owner of Barclaycard, claimed that in setting down details RBS had not been comparing like with like and had implied that its own card was superior on all 15 points. The bank asked for an injunction to prevent RBS from referring to its mark (Barclaycard) in literature promoting the RBS card.

Section 10(6) of the 1994 Act was at the root of the case. It provides as follows: 'Nothing in the preceding provisions of this section shall be construed as preventing the use of a registered trade mark by any person for the purpose of identifying goods or services as those of the proprietor or a licensee. But any such use otherwise than in accordance with honest practices in industrial or commercial matters shall be treated as infringing the registered trade mark if the use without due cause takes

---

unfair advantage of, or is detrimental to, the distinctive nature or repute of the trade mark.' The court decided that the literature conveyed the honest belief of RBS that its card, taken as a whole, offered customers a better deal, and refused the application by Barclays for an injunction.

Internet domain names

The Trade Mark Registry has issued guidelines on the treatment of Internet domain names. Signs including **http://, www., .co, .gov, .org** do not have any distinctive character as trade marks for goods and services sold via the Internet. Instead, trade mark examiners and hearing officers will look at the rest of the domain name. If it has a distinctive element, it will be considered for acceptance as a trade mark in the electronic information services class or in the software class.

Domain names containing the words 'web' and 'net' tacked on to descriptive or non-distinctive words will probably not be registrable as they are considered generic terms for discussing the Internet.

Injurious falsehood

In our present context a person is liable for injurious (or malicious) falsehood if he makes a statement about the goods of another which is malicious and is intended to cause and does cause damage to the business of the other person.

Injurious falsehood is an aspect of defamation and where the false statement is made about another's goods it is sometimes called 'slander of goods'.

De Beers Abrasive Products Ltd v International General Electric Company of New York Ltd (1975)

De Beers made a diamond abrasive known as and marketed under the trade mark 'Debdust'. It was used for cutting concrete. International made and marketed a competing product under the trade name 'MBS-70'.

International stated in a trade pamphlet that laboratory experiments had shown that MBS-70 was superior to Debdust. De Beers alleged that the contents of the pamphlet were false and misleading. The court said that the pamphlet would amount to an actionable slander of goods if De Beers could prove the allegations and show malice on the part of International.

Passing-off

Any person, company or other organisation which carries on or proposes to carry on business under a name calculated to deceive the public by confusion with the name of an existing concern, commits the civil wrong of passing-off and will be restrained by injunction from doing so. Other examples more important in our context of passing-off are the use of similar wrappings, identification marks and descriptions. Thus, in *Bollinger v Costa Brava Wine Co Ltd* (1959) the champagne producers of France objected to the use of the name 'Spanish Champagne' to describe a sparkling wine which was made in Spain and they were granted an injunction to prevent the use of that term. The remedies other than an injunction are an action for damages or for an account of profits made from wrongful use of the wrapping, mark or description.

The use of the passing-off rules in the context of branded products is illustrated by the following case.

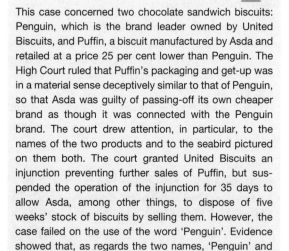

United Biscuits (UK) Ltd v Asda Stores Ltd (1997)

This case concerned two chocolate sandwich biscuits: Penguin, which is the brand leader owned by United Biscuits, and Puffin, a biscuit manufactured by Asda and retailed at a price 25 per cent lower than Penguin. The High Court ruled that Puffin's packaging and get-up was in a material sense deceptively similar to that of Penguin, so that Asda was guilty of passing-off its own cheaper brand as though it was connected with the Penguin brand. The court drew attention, in particular, to the names of the two products and to the seabird pictured on them both. The court granted United Biscuits an injunction preventing further sales of Puffin, but suspended the operation of the injunction for 35 days to allow Asda, among other things, to dispose of five weeks' stock of biscuits by selling them. However, the case failed on the use of the word 'Penguin'. Evidence showed that, as regards the two names, 'Penguin' and 'Puffin' taken alone did not cause significant confusion to consumers. Asda could therefore continue to use the 'Puffin' brand name.

The advantage of registration as a trade mark where possible has already been considered, as has the protection of Internet domain names (see *Pitman Training Ltd v Nominet UK* (1997)).

The High Court has also ruled that the fact that a company may find it harder to achieve brand recognition when another company is actively promoting a similar brand is not enough in itself to allow the aggrieved company to claim an injunction, particularly if there is no serious confusion. Thus, in *HFC Bank plc v Midland Bank plc* (2000) Midland Bank rebranded its business and associated businesses as HSBC. HFC Bank tried for an injunction to restrain the use of the HSBC brand name and failed. The High Court judge did not feel there was a serious likelihood of confusion and felt that the matter could in any case be solved by proper marketing. Interestingly, therefore, the judge was putting forward a commercial rather than a legal solution.

However, the High Court held in *Pfizer Ltd v Eurofood Link (UK) Ltd* (1999) that giving the name 'Viagrene' to a beverage that was to be marketed as an aphrodisiac was a passing-off of the name 'Viagra', the anti-impotence drug, as well as an infringement of UK and Community trade marks.

Confidentiality: employment

Certain activities by employees are regarded by the law as breaches of the duty of faithful service which an employee owes to his employer. Breaches of this duty of fidelity will sometimes be prevented by the court, so that a person who retains secret processes in his memory can be restrained from using them to his employer's disadvantage **without any contract in restraint of trade.**

An employer who copies names and addresses of his employer's customers for use after leaving his employment can be restrained from using the lists **without any express restrictions in his contract.**

Robb v Green (1895)

The claimant was a dealer in live game and eggs. The major part of his business consisted of procuring the eggs and the hatching, rearing and sale of gamebirds. His customers were numerous and for the most part were country gentlemen and their gamekeepers. The claimant kept a list of these customers in his order book. The defendant, who was for three years the claimant's manager, copied these names and addresses, and after leaving the claimant's employment set up in a similar business on his own and sent circulars, both to the claimant's customers and to their gamekeepers, inviting them to do business with him. The claimant asked for damages and an injunction and the Court of Appeal decided that, although there was no express term in the defendant's contract to restrain him from such activities, it was an implied term of the contract of service that the defendant would observe good faith towards his employer during the existence of the confidential relationship between them. The defendant's conduct was a breach of that duty of good faith in respect of which his employer was entitled to damages and an injunction.

Comment. In connection with the duty of fidelity, it should be noted that it does not matter who initiates the infidelity; although in most cases the employee approaches the customer, the rule still applies even where the customers approach the employee.

Although cases such as *Robb* can still be relied upon on their own facts, where the employer relies on the implied term of good faith to protect trade secrets or business connections that have simply been learned as part of doing the job, the implied-term theory is much less secure, and today a commercial lawyer would recommend an express contractual term setting out clearly what it is intended to protect. The complexity of some modern products is such that the court needs guidelines through the contractual term as to what is to be protected. Thus, in *Pocton Industries Ltd* v *Michael Ikem Horton* (2000) the Court of Appeal ruled that, although an electro-plating apparatus was a trade secret, it was not protectable under an implied duty of good faith and non-disclosure. There was no contractual provision regarding which part of the employee's knowledge was to be regarded as confidential and the plating process was only part of a number of pieces of information that the employee could not help but acquire from his duties. The implied term was too vague: more specific guidance was needed.

Confidentiality: other business applications

The defendant's breach of the law of confidentiality is an accepted head of liability in the common law for which there is a remedy of damages. Such a breach was the basis of the following high-profile case.

Douglas v *Hello! Ltd* (2003)

The first two claimants are well-known film stars. They married in November 2000. Before the ceremony they made a contract with the third claimant *OK!* magazine under which that magazine acquired exclusive photographic rights to the event. Unauthorised photographs were taken at the event and sold to *OK!*'s rival magazine *Hello!* which published them on the same day as *OK!* magazine. The claimants asked for damages for breach of confidence and the film stars additionally claimed damages for breach of the law of privacy.

The High Court ruled that there was no existing tort of privacy and refused to extend the common law into this area. Furthermore, there was no need to introduce Art 8 of the Convention on Human Rights (respect for private and family life) because English law was not inadequate in this case which could be dealt with as a branch of commercial confidence, i.e. a recognised head of law. The judge also awarded the Douglases compensation for damage and distress under the Data Protection Act 1998. The unauthorised pictures were to be regarded as personal data and the *Hello!* magazine was a data controller. Thus, publication of the pictures in England was processing by *Hello!* which was bound by the requirements of the Act.

Comment. The High Court took the view that if a general law of invasion of privacy was to be created it should be done by legislation through Parliament and not by the judiciary since the latter did not have adequate consultation powers with those interests that might be affected.

The Court of Appeal decided that the unauthorised photographs of the wedding reception plainly portrayed aspects of private life and fell within the protection of the law of confidentiality as extended to cover private or personal information. Thus, individuals have an enforceable right to privacy (in this case in the photographs) which was redressable in damages. See *Douglas* v *Hello! Ltd* (2005).

Data protection

One of the most important resources a business makes use of is information. Increasingly, the information collected is stored on computer and processed automatically. Some organisations, however, still keep a substantial amount of information in the form of paper records which are processed manually. The collection and processing of all forms of information about people is now subject to the provisions of the Data Protection Act 1998 (DPA 1998). The DPA 1998 replaces the Data Protection Act 1984, which was limited in its scope to data processed automatically, i.e. by computer.

We will examine the main provisions of the DPA 1998 and consider its implications for business. But first, why has it been necessary to legislate on data protection?

Background to the 1984 Act

There are two main reasons why the government decided in 1984 to take action to regulate the use of computers to process personal information: first, concern had been growing since the 1960s that the widespread use of increasingly sophisticated computers posed a considerable threat to the right to privacy. Computers not only had the ability to process large quantities of information at high speed, but could also transfer data quickly from one system to another, and combine information from different systems in ways which had not been possible before. Existing laws were inadequate to deal with this new threat to our civil liberties.

The second and main reason why the government introduced legislation was to avoid commercial isolation. In 1981 the UK had become a signatory to the Council of Europe Convention on Data Protection. The Convention permits ratifying countries to prohibit the transfer of personal data to countries without comparable data protection legislation. Failure to introduce such legislation in this country would have led some British businesses with international interests to face a boycott.

The government's response to these developments was the enactment of the Data Protection Act 1984, which became fully operational from 11 November 1987.

The background to the 1998 Act

We have noted how the 1984 Act was enacted to implement the Council of Europe Convention 'for the protection of individuals with regard to automatic processing of personal data'. Both the Convention and the 1984 Act were limited in scope to data which are processed automatically, i.e. by computer. In October 1995, the EC adopted a Data Protection Directive, which

had to be implemented by member states by October 1998. Although the 1984 Act met many of the requirements of the directive, there were some important differences which necessitated changes in the UK legislation. The DPA 1998, which came into force on 1 March 2000, introduces a new framework for the protection of data.

The 1998 Act itself

The DPA 1998 establishes a legal framework to regulate the storage and processing of personal information. Most persons who process, or have processed for them, personal information are affected by the legislation. At the centre of the scheme of regulation is the Information Commissioner (previously known as the Data Protection Registrar). The Commissioner is responsible for maintaining a public register of those involved in processing personal information, promoting good practice by data controllers and observance of the requirements of the DPA 1998, and disseminating information about the DPA 1998.

The DPA 1998 gives rights to individuals, including the right to obtain details of information held about them and a right to obtain compensation for damage suffered as the result of any contravention of the requirements of the DPA 1998 by a data controller. The DPA 1998 does not establish blanket regulation of all personal data: there are exemptions from some or all of its provisions.

Terminology

The terms used in the DPA 1998 are described below.

Data. This term refers to:

- information which can be processed automatically, i.e. by computer; or
- information which is recorded as part of a 'relevant filing system', that is a set of information in which the records are structured either by reference to individuals or by criteria relating to individuals; or
- information which does not fall within the two points above but which forms part of an 'accessible record', e.g. school pupil, housing, social services and health records.

The definition of data in the 1998 Act broadens the scope of regulation and protection to include not only information held on computers but also some manual information, i.e. paper records. It is important to note that not all manual information is covered by the DPA 1998; only manual information which falls within the definition of 'data' set out above is subject to regulation. It should also be noted that transitional arrangements exempt manual information kept in a relevant filing system before 24 October 1998 from full compliance with the DPA 1998 until 2007. However, individuals have the right to gain access to information held in paper records from 24 October 2001 irrespective of the date from which the information was held.

Personal data. These are items of information about a living individual who can be identified. 'Personal data' include factual information about the person, expressions of opinion about him and any indications of the intentions of the data controller in respect of that individual.

Data controller. This is a person who (either alone or jointly or in common with other persons) determines the purposes for which and the manner in which any personal data are, or are to be, processed.

Data processor. This refers to a person (other than an employee of the data controller) who processes personal data on behalf of the data controller.

Data subject. A data subject is an individual who is the subject of personal data. Information about corporate bodies is not covered.

Processing. In relation to information or data, this means obtaining, recording or holding the information or data or carrying out any operation on the data including:

- organisation, adaptation or alteration of the data;
- retrieval, consultation or use of the data;
- disclosure of the data;
- alignment, combination, blocking, erasure or destruction of the data.

The data protection principles

As under the 1984 Act, the DPA 1998 sets out eight data protection principles, which must be complied with by data controllers, subject to any exemption. The principles are as follows:

1 Personal data shall be processed fairly and lawfully, and, in particular, shall not be processed unless –

(a) **at least one of the conditions in Sch 2 is met, and**

(b) **in the case of sensitive personal data, at least one of the conditions in Sch 3 is also met.**

At least one of the following Sch 2 conditions for processing must be met:

- the data subject has given his consent to processing;
- the processing is necessary in relation to a contract to which the data subject is party;
- the processing is necessary to comply with a legal obligation to which the data controller is subject;
- the processing is necessary to protect the vital interests of the data subject (i.e. matters of life or death);
- the processing is necessary for the administration of justice, for the exercise of any statutory functions, or any functions of the Crown, ministers or government departments or other public functions carried out in the public interest;
- the processing is necessary for the legitimate interests of the data controller, except where the processing is unwarranted because of the prejudice to the rights, freedoms and legitimate interests of the data subject.

The DPA 1998 introduces special rules prohibiting the processing of sensitive personal data revealing, for example, racial or ethnic origin, political opinions, religious or philosophical beliefs, trade union membership, criminal proceedings or convictions and data concerning health or sexual life.

At least one of the Sch 3 conditions relating to processing sensitive data must be satisfied, in addition to one of the conditions applying to all personal data. The conditions include:

- the data subject has given his explicit consent;
- the processing is necessary for the purposes of fulfilling legal obligations in relation to employment;
- the processing is necessary to protect the vital interests of the data subject or another person and the data subject cannot give consent or the data controller cannot reasonably be expected to gain consent, or the data subject has unreasonably withheld consent and the processing is necessary to protect the vital interests of another person;
- the processing is carried out by not-for-profit organisations which exist for political, philosophical, religious and trade union purposes, subject to certain requirements;
- the personal data have been deliberately made public by the data subject;

- the processing is necessary in connection with legal proceedings, obtaining legal advice, or establishing, exercising or defending legal rights;
- the processing is necessary for medical purposes;
- the processing relates to racial or ethnic origins and the processing is necessary for equal opportunities monitoring.

As well as fulfilling one of the conditions for processing personal data, data controllers must also ensure that the processing is carried out fairly in accordance with the fair processing code. The code requires that data is obtained fairly (i.e. the provider of data must not be misled or deceived) and that certain information is provided to the data subject.

2 Personal data shall be obtained only for one or more specified and lawful purposes, and shall not be further processed in any manner incompatible with that purpose or those purposes. There are two methods by which a data controller can specify the purposes for which the data is obtained. First, by giving notice to the data subject in accordance with the fair processing code, and, secondly, by notifying the Information Commissioner under the notification procedures.

3 Personal data shall be adequate, relevant and not excessive in relation to the purpose or purposes for which they are processed. Data users must be selective about the data held; it must relate directly to the purposes for which it is obtained.

4 Personal data shall be accurate and, where necessary, kept up to date. Data controllers should take steps to check the accuracy of information. Data subjects have the right to compensation for damage caused by inaccurate data. Files should be reviewed from time to time to update the information.

5 Personal data processed for any purpose or purposes shall not be kept for longer than is necessary for that purpose or purposes. Once the specific purpose for which the data was collected has been achieved, the data should be destroyed.

6 Personal data shall be processed in accordance with the rights of data subjects under this Act. A data controller will contravene this principle if he or she fails to supply information following a subject access request or fails to comply with certain other notices under the DPA 1998.

7 Appropriate technical and organisational measures shall be taken against unauthorised or unlawful processing of personal data and against accidental loss or destruction of, or damage to, personal data. Data controllers and data processors must take steps to secure the personal data they hold. The level of security will depend on the nature of the personal data and the damage likely to be caused by a breach of the principle and the measures necessary to ensure security.

8 Personal data shall not be transferred to a country or territory outside the European Economic Area, unless that country or territory ensures an adequate level of protection for the rights and freedoms of data subjects in relation to the processing of personal data. This principle will not apply in certain circumstances, for example where the data subject consents to the transfer or the transfer is necessary for reasons of public interest or in connection with legal proceedings.

Notification

The 1984 Act established a Data Protection Register, which was open to public inspection. The DPA 1998 introduces a new simpler notification system. A data controller will be required to provide the following information:

- the data controller's name and address;
- the name and address of any representative;
- a description of the personal data being processed and the category of data subject to which they relate;
- a description of the purpose(s) for which the data are being processed;
- a description of any recipients of the data;
- a name or description of countries outside the European Economic Area to which the data may be transferred;
- a statement that the personal data are exempt and notification does not extend to that data;
- a general description of security measures to protect the data (this information will not appear on the register).

The notification requirements do not apply to manual data contained within a relevant filing system or data within non-automated accessible records.

The period of notification lasts for one year. In October 2009 the Information Commissioner introduced a two-tier notification fee structure. The Tier 1 fee for organisations with fewer than 250 staff remains at £35, while a Tier 2 higher fee of £500 is payable for larger organisations. Organisations are in Tier 2 if they:

- have a turnover of £25.9 million or more, and
- 250 or more employees.

The turnover criteria does not apply to public authorities. Charities are in Tier 1 irrespective of turnover or the number of employees.

It is an offence to process personal data without notification, unless it can be shown that a person exercised all due diligence to comply with the requirements. Offences are triable either by magistrates or in the Crown Court. If convicted, the offender is liable to a fine of £5,000 in the magistrates' court or an unlimited fine in the Crown Court.

Business organisations should decide who will take responsibility for ensuring that the organisation complies with the requirements of the DPA 1998. The duties of such a data protection officer must be defined and lines of responsibility established. The data protection officer should ensure that the notification requirements are complied with and the entry in the register kept up to date. This includes devising a system to monitor any changes taking place so that they can be recorded on the register.

Information Commissioner

In addition to maintaining the Register, the Commissioner is charged with promoting good practice by data controllers and in particular promoting observance of the data protection principles. The Commissioner is under a duty to make an assessment of whether processing of personal data is being carried out in compliance with the DPA 1998, if so requested.

The Commissioner has the power to issue the following notices:

1 An enforcement notice requires a data controller to observe the data protection principles.

2 An information notice requires a data controller to provide information relating to a request for assessment or to compliance with the data protection principles within a specified time.

3 A special information notice may be served to ascertain whether personal data are being processed only for special purposes or with a view to the publication of any journalistic, literary or artistic material not previously published by the data controller.

There is a right of appeal against the issue of any notice to the Information Tribunal.

The Commissioner can apply to a circuit judge for a warrant to enter and search premises if there are reasonable grounds for suspecting that an offence has been committed or that the data protection principles are being contravened.

Rights of data subjects

The DPA 1998 gives a number of rights to data subjects in respect of the personal data held about them. The corresponding duties of data controllers may give rise to claims for compensation. Business organisations should consider the possibility of obtaining insurance cover against such risks. The rights are as follows:

1 Access to personal data. A data subject is entitled to be informed of whether a data controller holds any data about him or her and to be supplied with a copy of such data in an intelligible form. The data controller may insist on receiving a written request, checking the data subject's identity and the payment of a fee (subject to a maximum fee of £10 in 2010). The information must be available within 40 days. Obviously, business organisations must establish a clear procedure for dealing with requests for access to data.

The Court of Appeal has provided useful guidance on the scope of the right to obtain access to personal data in the following case.

Durant v *Financial Services Authority* (2003)

Durant had been involved in unsuccessful litigation against his bank. Subsequently, he sought disclosure of documents which he believed might help him to reopen the dispute. He had asked the Financial Services Authority (FSA) to help him to obtain disclosure and he also wanted to know what information the FSA had obtained from the bank in its supervisory capacity. The FSA completed its investigations but, for reasons of confidentiality, did not inform Durant of the outcome. Durant complained to the FSA Complaints Commissioner but the complaints were dismissed. Durant then made two subject access requests under the DPA 1998, covering both electronic and manual information. The

FSA provided documents about Durant held in computerised form but refused access to manual files on the grounds that the information was not personal and, if it was, it did not form part of a relevant filing system. The Court of Appeal upheld the trial judge's refusal to order the FSA to make further disclosure. The mere mention of the data subject in a document did not necessarily amount to 'personal data' under the DPA 1998. Whether it did so in any particular case depended on where it falls in a 'continuum of relevance or proximity to the data subject as distinct, say, from transaction or matters in which he may have been involved to a greater or lesser degree'. Two factors may assist in judging relevance or proximity: whether the information was significantly biographical, and whether the data subject was the focus of the information. Moreover, the information must affect a person's privacy whether in his personal or family life, or his business or professional capacity. On the question of the meaning of a 'relevant filing system', the court concluded that the DPA 1998, and the EC Directive on which it was based, supported a restrictive interpretation. The protection is provided for personal data not documents. A relevant filing system is a system 'in which the files forming part of it are structured or referenced in such a way as to clearly indicate at the outset of the search whether specific information capable of amounting to personal data of an individual requesting it . . . is held within the system and, if so, in which file or files it is held; and which has as part of its own structure or referencing mechanism, a sufficiently sophisticated and detailed means of readily indicating whether or where an individual file or files and specific criteria or information about the applicant can be readily located.'

Comment. The Information Commissioner's view is that, following the *Durant* judgment, 'very few manual files will be covered by the provisions of the DPA'.

2 Right to prevent processing likely to cause damage or distress. A data subject can ask a data controller to stop, or not to begin, processing personal data relating to him where it is causing or is likely to cause substantial unwarranted damage or substantial distress to him or to another person. There are situations where this right is not available (e.g. where the data subject has previously consented) and data controllers do not always have to comply with the request.

3 The right to prevent processing for direct marketing. A data subject can ask a data controller to stop, or not to begin, processing data relating to him for the purposes of direct marketing. If the data controller does

not comply with such notice, the data subject can apply for a court order to that effect.

4 Rights in relation to automatic decision-taking. An individual can ask a data controller to ensure that no decision which significantly affects him is based solely on the processing of his personal data by automatic means. Examples of the purposes for which automatic decision-taking might be used include establishing creditworthiness or reliability. There are some exemptions to these rights.

5 Right to compensation. The data subject can claim compensation from a data controller for damage or damage and distress caused by a breach of the DPA 1998, where the data controller is unable to show that he or she has taken such care as is reasonable to ensure compliance. Damages for distress alone can be claimed only where the breach of the DPA 1998 relates to processing personal data for special purposes.

6 The right of rectification, blocking, erasure and destruction. Individuals can apply to the court for an order requiring a data controller to rectify, block, erase or destroy personal data which are inaccurate or contain expressions of opinion based on inaccurate data.

7 The right to request an assessment. Any individual may ask the Commissioner to assess whether the processing of personal data is being carried out in compliance with the DPA 1998. Depending on the outcome of the Commissioner's assessment, this may lead to enforcement action.

Exemptions

The nature and extent of each exemption is a complex matter and the guidance produced by the Information Commissioner should be consulted.

Exemptions are referred to as either 'primary' exemptions, meaning that they are more likely to be claimed or more wide ranging in scope, or 'miscellaneous' exemptions. 'Primary' exemptions include personal data related to:

- safeguarding national security;
- prevention and detection of crime;
- assessment and collection of taxation;
- health, education and social work;
- regulatory activity of certain bodies;
- special purposes covering journalism, artistic and literary purposes;

- historical or statistical research;
- information made available to the public by statute;
- disclosures required by law or in connection with any legal proceedings;
- domestic purposes, i.e. household matters.

The 'miscellaneous' exemptions include:

- confidential references given in connection with, for example, employment;
- information which would prejudice the combat effectiveness of the armed forces;
- processing personal data in connection with judicial appointments and honours;
- processing personal data in connection with assessing suitability for Crown employment and Crown or ministerial appointments;
- personal data used by businesses in connection with management forecasting and planning;
- personal data consisting of the intentions of the data controller in relation to any negotiations with the data subject;
- personal data processed in connection with a corporate finance service, where there may be concerns in relation to price sensitivity;
- personal data recorded by candidates in examinations;
- in the case of examination marks, a candidate's right of access can be delayed for up to five months or 40 days from the announcement of the results;
- personal data subject to professional legal privilege;
- self-incrimination by complying with a subject access request.

Offences under the DPA 1998

The DPA 1998 creates a number of criminal offences. These include processing personal data without complying with the notification requirements, unlawfully obtaining or disclosing personal data without the consent of the data controller and unlawfully selling personal data. The Criminal Justice and Immigration Act 2008 makes two changes to the DPA to strengthen enforcement:

1 The Secretary of State acquires the power to increase the maximum penalty for an offence under s 55 (knowingly or recklessly, without the consent of the data controller, obtaining or disclosing personal data or procuring the disclosure of personal data to another person). The penalties may be increased to six months' imprisonment on summary conviction (increasing to 12

months when the sentencing powers of the magistrates' court are increased) or two years' imprisonment if convicted on indictment in the Crown Court. A new defence against the s 55 offence is provided where a person acts for journalistic, literary or artistic purposes with a view to the publication of any journalistic, literary or artistic material and in the reasonable belief that their actions were justified as being in the public interest.

2 From 6 April 2010 the Information Commissioner acquires new powers to impose monetary penalties up to £500,000 on data controllers for serious breaches of the Data Protection Act. The data controller must either deliberately or recklessly breach the data protection principles and the contravention must be of a kind likely to cause substantial damage or distress.

Computer misuse

The Computer Misuse Act 1990, which came into force on 29 August 1990, creates three criminal offences to deal with the misuse of computers. The offences are as follows:

1 Unauthorised access to computer material. It is an offence knowingly to cause a computer to perform any function with intent to secure unauthorised access to programs or data held in a computer. This basic offence is designed to criminalise the activities of both outside 'hackers' who obtain access to computers using the public telecommunications system and insiders who knowingly exceed the limits of their authority. The offence is triable summarily and is punishable by a maximum of six months' imprisonment or a fine of £5,000.

2 Unauthorised access with intent to commit or facilitate commission of further offences. It is an offence triable either by magistrates or in the Crown Court to commit the basic unauthorised access offence with intent to commit or facilitate the commission of any serious offence for which the sentence is fixed by law or where the maximum sentence could be five years or more. These serious crimes would include theft and blackmail. This offence would cover a 'hacker' who obtains unauthorised access to a computer in order to hijack funds in the course of an electronic funds transfer. The maximum penalty for this offence if convicted on indictment is five years' imprisonment or an unlimited fine.

3 Unauthorised modification of computer material. It is an offence intentionally to cause the unauthorised modification of the contents of any computer with intent to impair a computer's operation, or to prevent or hinder access to any program or data held in any computer, or impair the operation of any such program or the reliability of any such data. This offence is designed to cover interference with computer programs and data such as the deletion or alteration of material or the introduction of computer viruses. The offence is triable either by magistrates or in the Crown Court where the maximum penalty is five years' imprisonment or an unlimited fine.

The Act also takes into account the international dimension of computer crime by giving UK courts wide jurisdiction to hear cases, provided that there is some connection between the offender's activities and the UK, and by making provision for extradition for these offences.

Freedom of information

The Freedom of Information Act 2000 requires every public authority to put in place a publication scheme to be approved by the Information Commissioner which identifies the information available from the authority and how it can be obtained. From 1 January 2005 individuals have had the right to make a request for information held by a public authority, subject to certain exemptions, e.g. information relating to national security or information given in confidence. Authorities must supply the requested information within 20 days, unless the information is exempt. The authority may make a charge for providing the information, subject to a maximum fee which is set by regulation. If an individual does not pay the fee within three months, the request for information lapses. Public authorities include central and local government, police and prosecution services, the health service and education organisations, e.g. colleges and universities. The Information Commissioner may issue the following notices:

1 A decision notice: a person who has made a request for information may apply for a decision as to whether his request has been dealt with by the public authority in accordance with Part I of the Act.

2 An information notice: requires a public authority to provide specified information.

3 An enforcement notice: requires a public authority to comply with the requirement to provide information.

Complainants and public authorities can appeal to the Information Tribunal against a decision notice and a public authority can appeal to the Information Tribunal against an enforcement notice.

Self-test questions/activities

1 Explain the difference between real property and personal property. What kinds of personal property are there?

2 John wants to buy a house. He tells you that he has seen some advertised as 'freehold' and some as 'leasehold'.

  Write a note explaining these terms stating how he would be affected as a buyer in each case.

3 Explain what is meant by an easement. How does an easement differ from a profit? Give two examples of each.

4 Anton is the owner of the Napoli restaurant. He engaged Edgar, a builder who was made redundant by Bodge Builders Ltd but has recently started up his own business, to renovate the restaurant.

  On Monday, the day before Anton reopened the restaurant to the public, he invited the mayor and his wife, Mr and Mrs Snooks, to take a meal at the restaurant.

  During the meal a large piece of plaster fell from the false ceiling which Edgar had installed. It fell on the mayor's table, injuring both him and Mrs Snooks.

  Several pieces of plaster hit and injured a local press photographer, Archie, who had got into the restaurant uninvited through a side door. Archie was hiding behind a rubber plant in the hope of getting some exclusive pictures of the new restaurant.

  Advise Mr and Mrs Snooks and Archie.

5 If you had registered a patent and a design, for how long would registration protect you, and what remedies would you have if someone infringed your rights?

6 Jane's father has died. He left her by his will the copyright in a very successful novel which he wrote five years before his death.

For how long will the publishers pay royalties to Jane?

7 Distinguish a trade mark from a service mark. How are trade and service marks protected?

8 Bob and Jane run a newsagents' shop. They have just acquired a computer to help them run the business more efficiently. They anticipate that they will use the computer for the following purposes: stock control, calculating the wages of their paper-boys and girls and customer records.

Will Bob and Jane need to register under the DPA 1998?

If they are required to register, what will their obligations be under the DPA 1998?

Specimen examination questions

1 Wharf Ltd occupies office premises in the High Street. Next to the office premises is a parking space for ten cars. The parking space is on land owned by Canary Ltd, which has office premises adjacent to it. For some 30 years the managing director and finance director of Wharf Ltd and their predecessors have used two parking spaces reserved for them. Now Canary Ltd, whose staff have used the other eight spaces, has increased its staff and proposes to take over the two spaces used by Wharf staff.

As company secretary to Wharf Ltd you have looked at the documents of title Wharf has to its premises and discover that there is no specific mention of the car parking right on Canary's land.

Advise the board of Wharf Ltd as to the company's position in law and, in particular, whether it is likely to be able to retain this right to park for the future.

2 Last week James, aged 21, was walking home from a party. It would be fair to describe his condition as drunk. When James was passing by the local park he vaguely remembered that the Barchester Council which owned the park ran an open-air swimming pool and, although it was mid-December and freezing cold, James decided that he would like a swim to clear his head. The park was closed and the gates locked but James climbed over them and went to the pool. It too was locked and there were notices saying it was closed for the winter season. James ignored these notices and climbed over the gates to the pool and dived in. The pool had been drained for the winter and James was severely injured. Two

nights after this incident Jane, a six-year-old child, climbed the gates of the park in the early evening after the park was closed and was injured when she fell off a swing.

James and Jane are bringing claims against Barchester Council for their injuries as occupiers of the park and its facilities.

Advise the council as to its potential liability to James and Jane.

3 Jane Smith is in her final year at Southtown High School where she is studying for eight GCSEs. During her time at the High School Jane has been mistaken for another pupil, Jayne Smith. Jayne Smith is a troublesome pupil who has been suspended on a number of occasions for poor behaviour. Jane Smith is a 'model' student and is predicted to achieve good grades in her GCSEs. Jane applies to her local FE college to study A-levels and is interviewed for a place. She is very disappointed when she receives a letter to say she has been rejected. She believes that the head teacher of the High School may have provided a reference for Jayne Smith rather than for herself and this has adversely affected her chances of obtaining a place. Jane would like to obtain the following information:

(a) a copy of her personal reference provided by the head teacher of the High School;

(b) the reasons for the Sixth Form College's rejection of her application;

(c) the Sixth Form College's admissions policy.

Advise Jane.

Website references

http://www.justice.gov.uk/about/civillawreform.htm The Ministry of Justice is responsible for changes in property law. It is one of the best websites for a great many types of interest: consultation papers, White Papers, Green Papers, etc., in connection with reforms such as commonhold and leasehold reform.

http://www.lawcom.gov.uk The Law Commission is also a useful site in regard to its proposals for property law reform.

http://www.ipo.gov.uk The Patent Office website provides information about intellectual property rights and current developments in this area.

http://oami.europa.eu/ows/rw/pages/index.en.do This is the website for the EU's Office for Harmonisation in the Internal Market in respect of Trade Marks and Designs.

http://www.ico.gov.uk The Information Commissioner's website provides information about the Data Protection Act 1998 and the Freedom of Information Act 2000.

Visit **www.mylawchamber.co.uk/richesallen** to access study support resources including answers to questions in this chapter and legal updates, all linked to the **Pearson eText** version of **Keenan and Riches' Business Law** which you can **search**, **highlight** and **personalise** with your **own notes** and **bookmarks**.

Use **Case Navigator** to read in full some of the key cases referenced in this chapter with commentary and questions:

Tomlinson v *Congleton BC* (2003)

Employing labour

In this chapter we are concerned with employment law. This is based upon and deals with the relationship of employer and employee. Employment law is made up of common law and, more and more these days, of statute law passed by Parliament.

Employer and employee

Generally

It is important to know how this relationship comes into being and to distinguish it from the relationship between a person who buys the services of someone who is self-employed (often called an independent contractor).

Usually it is not difficult to decide whether A is employed by B so that the relationship of employee and employer exists between them. If A is an employee, he or she will have been **selected** by B; A will usually work **full-time** for B under a degree of **supervision** for a **wage** or salary. Of course, A may still be an employee though working **part time**.

Also, if A is an employee, B will deduct **income tax** from A's pay (if it exceeds A's allowances) under PAYE (pay as you earn) arrangements. B will also make **social security contributions** for A and will often provide a **pension scheme** which A can join. In addition, although a contract of employment (or service) need not be in writing, if A is an employee, then B must, under the Employment Rights Act 1996, give A within two months after the beginning of the employment **written particulars** of the major terms of the contract.

The control test

In earlier times the above tests would not all have been available, particularly the deduction of income tax which, after some earlier experiments beginning in 1799, was finally brought in for good in 1842. Social security legislation and the modern deductions from pay, together with contributions from the employer, have only come in on the present scale since the Second World War.

In times past, therefore, a person, whether employed or self-employed, would simply receive money from the employer and it was less easy to distinguish one from the other.

There was, even so, a need to do so, because an employer was liable to pay damages to those injured by his employee if those injuries took place during the course of the employee's work. This is called an employer's vicarious liability and it is dealt with in greater detail later in this chapter.

A person was not vicariously liable for injury caused to others by a self-employed (or independent) contractor who was doing work for him. Obviously, then it was necessary to find a test to decide whether A was, or was not, an employee of B.

The earliest test was called 'the control test'. Since it is not normally necessary to use this test today in order to decide whether A is the employee of B because we have much more evidence of the relationship now, why should we bother with it?

The answer is that it is sometimes necessary to decide whether B, who is truly employed by A, has been temporarily transferred to another person, C, so that C (the temporary employer) and not A (the general employer) is liable vicariously for the injuries caused to a person or persons by B.

Mersey Docks and Harbour Board v Coggins & Griffiths (Liverpool) Ltd (1946)

The Board owned and hired out mobile cranes driven by skilled operators who were employees of the Board. Coggins & Griffiths, who were stevedores, hired one of the Board's cranes and an operator, Mr Newell, to unload a ship.

In the course of unloading the ship, a person was injured because of Mr Newell's negligence and the court had to decide whether the Board or Coggins & Griffiths were vicariously liable along with Mr Newell for the latter's negligence. The matter was one of control because the Board was quite clearly the general employer. Actually, the answers given by Mr Newell to questions put to him by counsel in court were highly important. At one point he said: 'I take no orders from anybody.' Since he was not truly employed by Coggins & Griffiths and since he did not, so he said, take orders from them, there was no way in which he could be regarded as under their

control. Therefore, his true employer, the Board, was vicariously liable for Mr Newell's negligence.

Comment. It is presumed in these cases that the general employer continues to be liable and it is up to him to satisfy the court that control has passed to a temporary employer. This is a very difficult thing to do and the temporary employer will not be liable very often, though it is a possibility.

Joint vicarious liability

In situations such as *Mersey Docks*, the possibility of joint liability between employing parties had never been considered.

The Court of Appeal did so in the following case and any principled objection to joint liability has been removed.

Viasystems Ltd v Thermal Transfer (Northern) Ltd (2005)

The claimant was having air conditioning installed in a factory. The main contractor, Thermal, subcontracted the ducting work to company A which used company B to supply a fitter and his mate. While working under the fitter and a supervisor from company A, the fitter's mate, C, by what the Court of Appeal described as foolish negligence, managed to flood the claimant's factory.

In a claim against Thermal and A and B, the High Court found that B was liable. In this appeal company B contended that company A was liable because they had control of C who was working within the environment of company A.

The Court of Appeal decided it was time to reassess existing law and ruled that company A and company B were liable for the negligence of C, each bearing 50 per cent of the damage, thus introducing joint vicarious liability, a concept hitherto unknown in this country.

Shareholders and directors

In spite of the fact that a majority shareholder and/or a director of a company are not, strictly speaking, under the control of the company which, of course, they in large measure control, it seems from the decision of the Court of Appeal in *Secretary of State for Trade and Industry* v *Bottrill* (1999) and of the Employment Appeal Tribunal in *Connolly* v *Sellers Arenascene Ltd* (2000) that majority shareholders and directors will be regarded as employees of the company where there is a written contract of employment and all the usual hallmarks of employment are present. Certainly, the almost blanket ban introduced by earlier cases such as *Buchan v Secretary of State for Employment* (1997) has been considerably eroded. The cases have generally arisen where the company has gone into an insolvency procedure and cannot pay wages and salaries.

Recent case law gives employed controlling shareholders and directors a better chance of doing that. Fee-paid directors could not claim. In any case, controlling shareholders and directors would seem to satisfy the organisation test set out below and come in as employees under that.

The organisation test

Later on a test called the 'organisation or integration' test was brought in because the control test was not really suitable for employees who were highly skilled.

There was a possibility that, even though there was a lot of general evidence of employment, such as PAYE deductions from pay, an employer would not be vicariously liable for the acts of a highly skilled employee, such as a doctor, or, really, anyone qualified and experienced and acting in a professional field, if that employer could convince the court in his defence that he did not have the necessary control of the skilled person.

This has not been possible because of the organisation test put forward by Lord Denning in *Stevenson, Jordan & Harrison Ltd v Macdonald & Evans Ltd* (1952). He decided in that case, in effect, that an employee is a person who is integrated with others in the workplace or business, even though the employer does not have a detailed control of what he does.

Independent contractors – self-employment

The main feature here is the absence of control or meaningful supervision which can be exercised by those who buy the services of an independent contractor by means of what is called a contract for services.

Particular cases examined

In the majority of cases there is no difficulty in deciding whether a person is employed or self-employed.

For example, factory employees, office clerical staff and agricultural workers are clearly employees. Garage proprietors, house-builders and dry cleaners are contractors independent of the members of the public who use them.

A particularly compelling example comes from a comparison between a chauffeur and a person who owns and drives his own taxi. The chauffeur is an employee; the taxi-driver is an independent contractor. Suppose, then, that Fred is employed as my chauffeur: I would have enough control over him to ask him to drive more slowly in a built-up area. In the case of the taxi-driver, I would not have (or even feel I had) the necessary control to insist on a change of speed.

Contract of service or for services – why distinguish?

First of all, because of the existence of vicarious liability, an employer is liable, for example, for damage caused to another by his employee's negligent acts while that employee is acting in the course of his employment, that is, doing his job, but not otherwise.

Second, the **rights and remedies provided by employment legislation**, such as the Employment Rights Act 1996, are available to an employee, but not all of them are available (but see below) to the self-employed. We shall be looking at these rights and remedies more closely later in this chapter.

Rights of non-employees

Certain statutory rights are given to persons who are not employees in any sense of the word. Rights in respect of racial and sex discrimination are enjoyed by job applicants, contract workers and partners. Job applicants also have the right not to be refused a job on the grounds of trade union membership or because they do not belong to a union.

An employer may also be liable for sex discrimination **after** employment has ceased. The Employment Appeal Tribunal (EAT) has ruled that the Sex Discrimination Act 1975 covers acts of discrimination, e.g. by failure to give a reference, even though the relevant acts took place after the claimant ceased to be employed (see *Coote v Granada Hospitality Ltd* (1999)).

Failure to give a post-employment reference ranks also as a detriment under s 47B of the Employment Rights Act 1996 where it is in regard to a person who has blown the whistle about some aspects of the employer's organisation, in what is called a public interest disclosure (*Woodward* v *Abbey National plc* (2006)).

A contract worker is one who is employed by a third party, such as an agency, and whose services are supplied under a contract with that third party. A claim against an employer could be made, for example, by a temporary secretary who is turned away or treated in a hostile manner on grounds of colour or disability or who is subjected to sexual harassment.

The same would be true of a salesperson without a contract of service who was paid by commission only, who was not given work because of his race (see *Hill Samuel Services Group Ltd* v *Nwauzu* (1994)).

In this connection, it is worth noting s 23 of the Employment Relations Act 1999, which gives the government power to extend employee status and rights to all workers other than the genuinely self-employed and so ensure that none are excluded merely because of technicalities relating to their working arrangements, which are often designed by less scrupulous employers to produce a virtually rightless and bogus self-employment.

The contract of employment

Generally

The ordinary principles of the law of contract apply. So, in a contract of employment there must be an offer and an acceptance, which is in effect the agreement. There must also be an intention to create legal relations, consideration, and capacity, together with proper consent by the parties, that is, no mistake, misrepresentation, duress or undue influence. In addition, the contract must not be illegal.

However, since we have already looked at these general principles of the law of contract, it is only necessary to highlight certain matters which are of importance in the context of employment law.

Fraud and illegality

The general rule is that the courts and employment tribunals will not do anything to enforce either party's rights under a contract which is illegal. The general rule does not apply, however, if the party seeking to enforce the contract was not aware of the illegality or, possibly, if his or her involvement is minimal compared to that of the other party.

If any employer and employee agree that the latter be treated as non-existent for tax and national insurance purposes, with all payments being unrecorded cash payments, neither party will be able to enforce the contract. The employee would have rights, however, if the employer deducted tax and national insurance contributions (NICs) and, without the employee's knowledge, failed to account for the payments or submit any records.

Legitimate tax avoidance schemes do not render a contract of employment illegal. Thus, in *Lightfoot* v *D & J Sporting Ltd* (1996), L was employed as a head gamekeeper and was assisted by his wife who initially received no remuneration from his employer. Later the employer entered into an agreement to pay one-third of L's income to his wife to save some liability on L's tax and NICs. This did not make the arrangement illegal and the husband and wife could claim unfair dismissal when they were later dismissed.

A party to a contract may also be unable to enforce the contract if it has been entered into as a result of that party's fraud. Suppose, therefore, that an accountancy firm employs a person purporting to be a qualified accountant. In fact, he has failed his examinations. Even if he carries out his work in an exemplary fashion, the employer will be entitled to terminate his employment forthwith when his fraud is discovered.

However, it is worth noting that in *Hall* v *Woolston Hall Leisure* (2000) the Court of Appeal allowed a claim for unfair dismissal based on sex discrimination to succeed where a chef was dismissed when she became pregnant, even though to her knowledge no tax or national insurance contributions were being deducted from her pay with her agreement. The court said that equal treatment was a requirement that transcended the usual rules of contract law.

Subsequently, however, the Court of Appeal decided in *Vakante* v *Addey & Stanhope School* (2004) that illegal and criminal conduct in connection with his employment did prevent the claimant from pursuing a race discrimination claim. His case was very different from *Hall* in that he concealed the fact that he had no work permit and did not reveal that he was an asylum applicant from Croatia. Although the claim in these cases is for discrimination, what has happened under any contract between the parties is clearly relevant to the court.

Written particulars

A contract of employment does not require any written formalities and can be made orally. However, certain written particulars of it are required to be given to the employee by the Employment Rights Act 1996 (s 1, ERA 1996). These particulars must be given to all employees within two months of starting work but not if the job is to last and does in fact last for less than one month. In addition, the statement of particulars need not be given if the employee has entered into a written contract with the employer containing all the relevant terms.

Furthermore, it was held by the House of Lords in *Carmichael* v *National Power plc* (2000) that casual workers operating under 'zero hours' contracts are not entitled to written particulars. In these contracts there are no fixed requirements to attend for work. Those involved may attend if called upon to do so. In this case the claimants were, when at work, engaged in showing visitors round a nuclear power station.

As a comment on the *Carmichael* case it can be said that some employers do try to avoid the application of expensive employment rights by using 'zero-hours' arrangements. *Carmichael* reinforces this right. Cases such as *Carmichael* may lead the government to exercise its powers under s 23 of the Employment Relations Act 1999 to extend employee rights to all workers other than the genuinely self-employed, such as practising accountants, solicitors and barristers. There is currently no government attempt to do this and *Carmichael* stands.

Contents – generally

The statement must contain the following information:

1 The names of the employer and the employee
A letter of engagement will usually be sent to the employee at his address. This will identify him and the letterheading will identify the employer.

2 The date when the employment began
This is important if it becomes necessary to decide what period of notice is to be given. The 1996 Act provides for certain minimum periods of notice to be given by employers. For example, they must give one week's notice after one month's continuous service, two weeks' after two years' service, and so on up to 12 weeks' after 12 years' service (see s 86). The date when the job began obviously settles this point.

In addition, the length of the employment affects the period necessary to make certain claims. For example, redundancy claims require two years' continuous service but by reason of the Employment Equality (Age) Regulations 2006 (SI 2006/1031) there is no lower age limit to commence the calculation of entitlement and the upper age limit of 65 is removed. Unfair dismissal requires one year of continuous service with some exceptions which will be noted, usually with a particular employer (but see below), regardless of the age at which the service began, unless the dismissal is automatically unfair, as where it was because the employee was (or proposed to become) a member of a trade union or it was in connection with pregnancy.

3 Whether the employment counts as a period of continuous employment with a previous employment, and the date of commencement of the previous employment where this is so
This is important because the rights of an employee to complain of unfair dismissal or to claim a redundancy payment, depend upon whether that employee has served the necessary period of continuous employment. This may be with one employer, but, if it is with more than one employer, it must be possible to regard the employments with the various employers as continuous. Situations of continuous employment, despite a change of employer, taken from the Employment Rights Act 1996, are:

(a) *A transfer between associated employers.* For example, if A is employed by B Ltd and is transferred to work for C Ltd, and B Ltd and C Ltd are subsidiaries of X plc, then A's employment with B Ltd and C Ltd is regarded as continuous.

(b) *A sale of the business in which the employee was employed to another person.* (See also below under TUPE 2006.) If a business is sold the general rule is that the employees automatically become employed by the owner of the business with full continuity of employment.

(c) *A change in the partners where a person is employed by a partnership.* A general partnership is not a separate person at law as a company is. Employees of a general partnership are employed by the partners as people. So, if A works for a partnership of C and D, and D retires and is replaced by E, then A's employers have changed but his employment with C and D and C and E is regarded as continuous. Therefore, if C and E unfairly dismiss A, he can make up his one year of continuous service to be able to claim by adding together his service with C and D and C and E in order to make a claim against C and E.

The legal context shown above would not apply to a limited liability partnership, which is a legal person, so that change of partners would not operate to change the employer.

(d) *A succession of contracts between the same parties is regarded as continuous.* So, if A works for B as a clerk and is then promoted to a manager under a new contract, the two contract periods can be added together to make a period of continuous employment.

On a general note, it is worth mentioning that the Employment Appeal Tribunal ruled in *Colley* v *Corkingdale (t/a Corker's Lounge Bar)* (1995) that the requirements of continuous service (or employment) necessary to make a claim for unfair dismissal could be established by a contract under which Ms Colley worked only alternate weeks.

However, the EAT ruled in *Booth* v *United States* (1999) that persons employed at a UK base of the US military on fixed-term contracts that were not end on but had short breaks between them did not satisfy the requirement of continuous service for an unfair dismissal claim. The Fixed-Term Employees (Prevention of Less Favourable Treatment) Regulations 2002 (SI 2002/2034) are unlikely to affect this decision because of the clear breaks between the fixed-term contracts. (See further p 479.)

Contents – terms of the employment

The written particulars then go on to set out the terms of the employment. The terms which must be given are:

1 The scale or rate of pay and the method of calculating pay where the employee is paid by commission or bonus (the employer must here have regard to the national minimum wage – see later in this chapter).

2 When the payment is made – that is weekly or monthly, and the day or date of payment.

3 Hours to be worked, e.g. 'The normal working hours are . . .' Compulsory overtime, if any, should be recorded to avoid disputes with employees who may sometimes not want to work it.

4 Holiday entitlement and provisions relating to holiday pay if the employee leaves in a particular year without taking holiday (if holiday entitlement is set out clearly, it can help to avoid disputes regarding a requirement to work in what is a normal holiday period in the area or during the school holidays).

(The terms and conditions to be specified at **3** and **4** above must, of course, be considered in the light of the Working Time Regulations 1998 (SI 1998/1833) (see later in this chapter).)

5 Sick pay and injury arrangements.

6 Whether or not there is a pension scheme.

7 The length of notice which the employee must give and the length of notice the employee is entitled to receive (we have already said that there are minimum periods of notice required to end contracts of employment and full details of these appear later in this chapter; the contract can, of course, provide for a longer period of notice but not a shorter one).

8 The job title, which is important in dealing with redundancy cases where to justify that a dismissal is because of redundancy and is not an unfair dismissal, the employer may show that there has been a reduction in 'work of a particular type' (the job title indicates what type of work the employee does; in equal pay claims also, it may show that a man or woman is employed on 'like work').

Under changes made by the ERA, the employer can give a brief job description instead of a job title.

9 The ERA also adds the following items to the required particulars:

- The duration of temporary contracts.
- Work location or locations.
- Collective agreements affecting the job.
- Where the job requires work outside the UK for more than one month the period of such work, the currency in which the employee will be paid and any other pay or benefits provided by reason of working outside the UK. Employees who begin work outside the UK within two months of starting must have the statement before leaving the UK.
- Particulars can be given in instalments, provided all are given within two months, but there must be a 'principal statement' in one document giving the following information:
  - The identities of the parties.
  - The date when the employment began.
  - Where the employment counts as a period of continuous employment with a previous one, a statement that this is so and the date when it began.

– The amount and frequency of pay, e.g. weekly or monthly.
– The hours of work.
– Holiday entitlement.
– Job title (or description).
– Work location.

Certain particulars can be given by reference to a document, e.g. a collective agreement with a trade union or a staff handbook, but any such document must be readily accessible to the employee. These particulars are pension arrangements, sickness provisions, notice entitlement and details of disciplinary matters and grievance procedures.

Disciplinary procedures deal, for example, with the number of warnings that will be given before suspension or dismissal and appeal proceedings. **Grievance procedures** relate to complaints in regard to any aspect of the employment with which the employee is not satisfied. As provided under s 3 ERA 1996 (amended by Employment Act 2002), all employers must inform their employees regarding disciplinary and grievance procedures. The statutory procedures set out in Schedule 2 to the Employment Act 2002 have been repealed by the Employment Act 2008. As reported in the 2007 Gibbons Review: 'the statutory procedures, whilst right in principle, have as a result of their mandatory nature led to unforeseen consequences. In particular, they have tended to lead to disputes becoming formalised, and lawyers getting involved, at an earlier stage than had previously been the case.'

Changes in the particulars

Changes must be given to the employee in writing as soon as possible and in any case not later than one month after the change. They may be given by reference to a document, e.g. a collective agreement, which is readily accessible provided a similar document was used to give the original information.

Terms of employment – collective agreements

If the terms of the employment can be changed by a collective agreement with a trade union, the particulars should say so because if this is the case, the terms of the job can be changed **without** the employees' consent. The results of the employer's negotiations with the unions are incorporated into the contracts of the employees and become binding as between employer and employee even though the agreement between the employer and the trade union is, as is usual, binding in honour only (*Marley* v *Forward Trust Group Ltd* (1986)). In other cases, the terms of the employment cannot be changed unless the employee has agreed and if the employer introduces a variation in the contract as by, say, lowering pay, then the employer is in breach of the contract.

It was held in *Rigby* v *Ferodo Ltd* (1987) that an employer cannot impose a pay cut on employees without breaking their contracts of employment.

Employees who have had a pay cut imposed on them may take proceedings in the ordinary courts for breach of contract or make an application to an employment tribunal under the ERA 1996 for money wrongfully deducted from pay (see further later in this chapter).

Alternatively, they can regard themselves as constructively dismissed and make a claim to an employment tribunal on that basis.

A valid reduction in pay can be achieved by negotiating a new contract with employees and under the original contract if this allows the employer to vary its terms without the employees' consent.

Failure to comply with the obligation to give written particulars

Section 11 of the Employment Rights Act 1996 provides that if an employer fails to give written particulars in the time scale required or fails to notify changes in the terms of the contract (agreed bilaterally or made unilaterally by the employer under contract provisions) the employee can go to an employment tribunal. If a statement is given but the employee thinks it is not complete, then either the employee or the employer can go to a tribunal to decide which of them is right.

The tribunal may make a declaratory judgment, e.g. declaring that the employee has a right to a statement, and may also say what should be in it. The statement as approved by the tribunal is then assumed in law to have been given by the employer to the employee and forms the basis of the contract of employment. Failure to give written particulars does not make the contract of employment unenforceable by the parties.

The Court of Appeal ruled in *Eagland* v *British Telecommunications plc* (1992) that a tribunal could not merely invent terms. Section 2(1) of the ERA 1996 allows the employer to give no details if none exist, provided that the statement says so at least under such headings as sick pay and pensions where provision of these benefits is not compulsory. It would be wrong of a tribunal to invent terms in these areas and force them as implied terms of the contract upon an employer who had not agreed to them and where there was no inference of agreement from the conduct of the parties.

However, in the case of mandatory terms which s 1 of the ERA 1996 requires to be stated in the written particulars such as remuneration and hours of work the Court of Appeal said that it would be exceptional if the evidence before a tribunal about these matters did not allow a tribunal to make an inference of agreement or to identify an agreement from the evidence. However, if this was not possible, the tribunal might have to imply one. This seems a fair approach. It must be rare indeed to find a contract of employment in which there is no intention to pay and receive wages!

Written particulars are a right of the employee and therefore they must be given whether the employee asks for them or not (*Coales v John Wood (Solicitors)* (1986)). Even so, an employee need not wait to be given them and if the employer is not complying with its obligations, an employee can request one if he or she has never had one or it is out of date. Dismissal for asserting this right is automatically unfair and there is no service requirement by reason of s 104 of the ERA 1996.

Under the Employment Act 2002 money compensation can be awarded where there is a claim, e.g., for unfair dismissal and the written particulars are incomplete, inaccurate or non-existent. (See further p 473. ◯)

TUPE 2006

The Transfer of Undertakings (Protection of Employment) Regulations 2006 (SI 2006/246) came into force on 6 April 2006. They replace the 1981 regulations of the same name (SI 1981/1794) in relation to transfers which take place on or after that date.

A relevant transfer

Regulation 3 applies and provides that a business transfer which will be affected by the regulations is a transfer of an undertaking, business or part of an undertaking or business situated immediately before the transfer in the UK to another person where there is a transfer of an economic entity which retains its identity. This is the conventional provision. However, reg 3 goes on to clarify that employees will be protected in a situation of service provision changes as where, e.g., a cleaning service is outsourced or passed from one contractor to another or is brought back in-house.

This is subject to there being, prior to the transfer, an organised grouping of employees, the grouping having as its principal purpose the carrying out of the activities that are contracted out on behalf of the client. There is an exception where services are bought in for a specific task or event of short duration and where the activity that is outsourced consists of making goods for the client's use.

Comment

- TUPE 2006 does not apply where there is no identifiable group of employees. Thus, if an organisation grants a contract for courier services but prior to this the services were carried out by a number of different couriers on an *ad hoc* basis as opposed to a permanent dedicated team, then the regulations would not apply.

  Even where there is an identifiable group of workers, the regulations will not apply if the purpose of the identifiable group is to carry out activities for a number of clients, as would be the case with a firm of solicitors or a travel agent, as opposed to working exclusively for a single client (but see below). Contracts for single specific tasks are not included, as in organising a conference or supplying sandwiches to a works canteen to sell on as distinct from running the canteen.

- In the view of the Department of Trade and Industry (now BIS), TUPE 2006 could apply and lead to the transfer of employees even though the transferee intends to carry out the service in a different way, e.g. by computerisation. If the transferred staff do not have the necessary skills, the transferee may choose to retrain them or make them redundant.

- It is also worth noting that TUPE 2006 does not specifically exclude professional business services. Could this have implications for the larger accountancy and law firms where employees are largely dedicated to providing services for one client organisation? If the client moves his instructions to another firm are the dedicated employees transferred to the new firm?

Effect of a relevant transfer on contracts of employment

The transfer of employees

Regulation 4 provides that employees, who are employed by the former operator of the business and assigned to the organised grouping of resources or employees that is subject to the relevant transfer, will be transferred to the new operator of the business.

Regulation 7 provides that employees who are dismissed before the transfer for a reason connected with it will transfer to the new operator of the business. Taken together, regs 4 and 7 reflect case law on the 1981 Regulations and close a loophole in TUPE 1981. There were cases where the former operator of the business retained employees at the actual time of the relevant transfer and then dismissed them soon after the transfer. TUPE 1981 did not protect employees against this tactic because it protected only workers whose contracts were terminated by the transfer and in the example given the contracts were not terminated by the transfer but after it.

This procedure is now contrary to the 2006 regulations and could result in an unfair dismissal unless the dismissals are for economic, technical or organisational reasons under reg 7(1)(b). This could occur, for example, where on transfer it is a condition of the contract that a new contractor reduces the contract price by reducing staff and this is done: what is the reason for the dismissals of the redundant staff? Is it merely a cost saving relating to the conduct of the business which would have happened anyway whether or not there had been a transfer or is it just a way to reduce the cost of running the contract to those who might wish to carry it on? If the former, the dismissals would not be unfair under reg 7(1)(b). If the other motive is behind the dismissals, they may be unfair.

Regulation 3(6) provides that a transfer may be effected by a series of two or more transactions. Thus in *Astley* v *Celtec Ltd* (2006) the House of Lords ruled that for the purposes of determining their continuous service for redundancy a number of civil servants whose department was privatised in 1990 were to be deemed to have been transferred to the new undertaking Newtec (now known as Celtec Ltd) at that time, even though in fact they were initially on secondment to Newtec and did not resign from the Civil Service until 1993.

Variation of contracts of employment

Regulation 4 of TUPE 2006 allows employees to agree to variations in their terms of employment. However, this is only where the variation is not connected with the transfer or is for an economic, technical or organisational reason connected with the transfer entailing changes in the workforce.

Obviously, employees could agree to changes in their terms of employment not made in the above context but such agreements would not bind them. It is also worth noting that, once again, these variations cannot be effectively made merely to make the business being transferred more attractive to the buyer, and that the consent of the workers must be freely given even where there are economic, technical or organisational reasons.

Changes in the terms of employees' contracts are allowed where the old employer's business is insolvent (see below). Further, employees can enforce a variation if they wish to do so (*Power* v *Regent Security Services* (2007)).

Workers abroad

TUPE 1981 excluded workers abroad from its provisions. TUPE 2006 has no such provision. Its extra-territorial application was confirmed in *Hollis Metal Industries* v *GMB* (2007), which concerned the transfer of part of the business to an employer in Israel.

Giving information to the new employer

Regulations 11 and 12 apply, the former imposing a new obligation on the transferor. Where a transfer takes place after 19 April 2006, the transferor must give information to the new operator in written or readily accessible form in regard to the identities of those employees who are transferring and their employment rights and liabilities. This information must be provided at least two weeks before the transfer is completed. If special circumstances make this impractical the information must be supplied as soon as reasonably practicable before the transfer. This is to ensure that the transferee is well placed to honour obligations towards the transferred employees.

Specifically the information to be supplied is:

- the identities and ages of all employees;
- the statement of terms and conditions of employees;
- details of any disciplinary proceedings against or grievances issued by any employee during the last two years;
- details of any court or tribunal cases that any employee has brought in the last two years, and of any which the transferor has reasonable grounds to believe may be brought by any employee;
- details of any collective agreement which will have effect after the transfer.

Where this information is not supplied, the transferee will be able to bring a tribunal claim against the transferor for such compensation as may be just and equitable in the circumstances and having regard to loss suffered by the transferee because of the failure to supply the information required. There is a minimum award of £500 for every employee in respect of whom the duty to supply the information was not properly carried out. A tribunal may, however, think it is just and equitable to award less (reg 12).

Duty to inform and consult representatives

Regulation 13 applies. An additional paragraph will be inserted in this regulation by virtue of Agency Workers Regulations 2010/93 to cover agency worker (to commence on 1 October 2011).

Long enough before a relevant transfer to allow appropriate representatives to be consulted by employees the employer must inform those representatives of:

- the fact that a transfer is to take place;
- the legal, economic and social implications of it for employees affected;
- the measures he or she will take in relation to any affected employee or if no measures will be taken;
- where the employer is the transferor, the measures, if any, that the transferee will take in regard to any employee affected. The transferee is obliged to give the transferor the necessary information.

Where an independent trade union is recognised by the employer, 'appropriate representatives' are representatives of the union; otherwise they are either:

- employee representatives appointed or elected by the workers affected for general consultation; or
- employee representatives appointed or elected for the TUPE 2006 consultation.

Each individual representative must be given the information by delivery or post and the representatives must be supplied with accommodation and facilities to consult with employees affected.

Failure to inform and consult

Regulation 15 applies. Failure to inform and consult properly can lead to a claim against the transferor *and* transferee of the business. Where one only of these parties is made the subject of a claim, that party can join the other in the claim. Where this is done, both the transferor and transferee are liable to pay compensation to each employee affected. The tribunal will rule on apportionment of payment. The award is set at a maximum of 13 weeks' actual pay per employee.

Insolvent employers

Transfer of debts. Some of the transferor's debts will not be transferred to the transferee. Under reg 8 these include statutory redundancy pay, any arrears of pay, payments in lieu of notice, holiday pay and basic award of compensation for unfair dismissal. In practice, these debts will often be met by the National Insurance Fund.

Other debts, including full notice pay and amounts in excess of the £330 per week cap, e.g. as in the case of a compensatory award for unfair dismissal, will transfer to the transferee.

The above provisions apply only where the insolvency practitioner is intending the survival of the company and not where the intention is only to liquidate the assets.

Variation of employment contracts. Regulation 9 applies and gives scope to change the terms and conditions of employment where the transferor is insolvent. The changes must be agreed either by the transferor or transferee with appropriate employee representatives.

Variations can be agreed even if they are the result of the transfer. However, strict rules are laid down as to how agreement should be reached.

Before any agreement is reached with appropriate representatives, every employee affected must be given a copy of the suggested agreement and receive any guidance that may be required to enable understanding. Although the variation of terms may leave the employees with inferior terms of employment, it cannot contravene statutory entitlement such as the national minimum wage.

In broad terms, under reg 9(7), the agreement must be designed to safeguard employment opportunities by ensuring the survival of the undertaking and the sole and principal reason for it must be the transfer itself or a reason connected with it that is not an economic, technical or organisational reason entailing changes in the workforce.

Pensions

Introduced under the Pensions Act 2004, these provisions provide for the first time a minimum standard of protection for the occupational pension rights of private sector employees on a TUPE transfer. The regulations provide that where an employee had access to an occupational pension scheme with employer contributions they will be entitled to the benefit of a new pension scheme post-transfer. The transferee employer must offer the employee a prescribed minimum level of membership as set out in the regulations, which came into force on 6 April 2005.

Health and safety

Section 2(3) of the Health and Safety at Work etc. Act 1974 states that an employer must prepare, and revise when necessary, a statement of his policy in regard to the health and safety at work of his employees and arrangements for carrying out the policy. This must be contained in a separate document but it is often given out with the written particulars which we are now looking at. Employers with fewer than five employees are not required to give this statement (Employers' Health and Safety Policy Statements (Exception) Regulations 1975 (SI 1975/1584); see reg 2).

Exemptions from the written particulars requirements

There are some situations under the 1996 Act where an employer does not have to give the written particulars. Those which may be found in the average business are:

1 Employees with fully written contracts containing all the necessary terms need not be given also the written particulars.
2 It is not necessary to give an employee written particulars if he is employed for a specific job, e.g. to clear a backlog of office work, which is not expected to last more than one month. If it does last for more than one month, the worker is entitled to written particulars.

It should be noted that certain of the former exceptions, e.g. that there was no need to give particulars where the employee was the husband or wife of the employer, have been repealed so that particulars are required, for instance, in the husband/wife situation.

Legal status of the statutory particulars

In this connection the decision of the EAT in *Lovett* v *Wigan Metropolitan Borough Council* (2000) is worth noting. The claimant in this case was told at his interview and in a subsequent letter of appointment that his promotion would depend on his 'gaining the appropriate qualifications and experience'. When he received his written particulars there was a document attached that added another requirement, i.e. 'the needs of the department'. The EAT held that the terms of the document also applied since they amplified and explained the letter of appointment. The EAT was applying *Robertson and Jackson* v *British Gas Corporation* (1983), where the Court of Appeal ruled that the statutory statement of particulars is neither the contract itself nor conclusive evidence of it.

Employment particulars: changes effected by the Employment Act 2002

The following sections of the 2002 Act make amendments to relevant sections of the Employment Rights Act 1996.

Section 35 provides that all stages of the new minimum disciplinary and dismissal procedures (see below) must be set out in the written statement.

Section 36 removes the exemption for employers that have fewer than 20 employees in terms of giving details of disciplinary rules and procedures. All employers have now to state these in the written particulars.

Section 37 allows particulars included in a contract of employment or letter of engagement to form all or part of the written particulars. It also enables such documents to be given to the employee before the employment begins.

Section 38 provides for tribunals to award monetary compensation to an employee where, on a claim being made, e.g. for unfair dismissal, it appears that the particulars received are incomplete or inaccurate. Where this is so, the tribunal may increase any award made against the employer by between two and four weeks' pay, according to whether the statement is merely inaccurate or has never been issued at all. One or two weeks' pay is also to be awarded where compensation is not a remedy for the particular complaint or is a remedy not chosen by the tribunal, as where it awards reinstatement in the job. Formerly there was no monetary penalty on the employer where particulars were incomplete, inaccurate or non-existent. (See Figure 16.1, overleaf.)

To: Ms Jane Doe
　　350 Elton Road
　　Manchester M62 10AS

The following particulars are given to you pursuant to the Employment Rights Act 1996 (as amended).

1. The parties are as follows:

　　Name and address of Employer:　Michael Snooks Ltd
　　　　　　　　　　　　　　　　　　520 London Square
　　　　　　　　　　　　　　　　　　Manchester M42 14SA

　　Name and address of Employee:　Jane Doe
　　　　　　　　　　　　　　　　　　350 Elton Road
　　　　　　　　　　　　　　　　　　Manchester M62 10AS

2. The date when your employment began was 2 February 2007.
　　Your employment with John Bloggs Ltd from whom Michael Snooks Ltd purchased the business and which began on 3 February 2004 counts as part of your period of continuous employment with Michael Snooks Ltd. No employment with a previous employer counts as part of your period of continuous employment.

3. The following are the particulars of the terms of your employment as at 8 March 2007.
　　(a) You are employed at 520 London Square, Manchester, M42 14SA, as a secretary/PA in the Educational Publishing Department. Our offices are a non-smoking environment.
　　(b) The rate of your remuneration is £420 per week.
　　(c) Your remuneration is paid at weekly intervals in arrears.
　　(d) Your normal working hours are from 9.30 am to 5 pm, Mondays to Fridays inclusive.
　　(e) (i)　You are entitled to 20 days' paid holiday per year, plus authorised bank holidays, which accrues on a pro rata basis. The holiday year runs from 1 January to 31 December. Up to five days' holiday may be carried over into the next holiday year. All holiday entitlements shall be taken at our discretion, but we will not unreasonably refuse your requests for a holiday.
　　　　(ii)　Regulations as to payment while absent during sickness or injury are available for inspection during normal working hours in the office of the secretary/PA to the Personnel Manager.
　　　　(iii)　The company offers a stakeholder pension scheme should you wish to join it. Details are available from the company secretary.
　　(f) The length of notice which you are obliged to give to end your contract of employment is one week and the length of notice you are entitled to receive unless your conduct is such that you may be summarily dismissed is as follows:
　　　　(i)　One week if your period of continuous employment is less than two years;
　　　　(ii)　One week for each year of continuous employment if your period of continuous employment is two years or more but less than 12 years; and
　　　　(iii)　Twelve weeks if your period of continuous employment is 12 years or more.
　　(g) There are no collective agreements which affect the terms and conditions of the employment.
　　(h) There is no requirement for work outside the United Kingdom.

4. Disciplinary procedure
　　(a) The employer must set out in writing the employee's alleged conduct or characteristics or other circumstances which lead him to contemplate dismissing or taking disciplinary action against the employee.
　　(b) The employer must send the statement, or a copy of it, to the employee and invite the employee to attend a meeting to discuss the matter.

　　Meeting
　　(c) The meeting will take place before action is taken except in the case where the disciplinary action consists of suspension.

Figure 16.1 Sample statement of written particulars of terms of employment

NB: Business Link provides a tool that will create a written statement of employment which covers all the employment terms and conditions an employer has to give employee. It must be issued not later than two months after the beginning of employment. For more information see Business Link website under 'Employment & Skills'.

(d) The meeting must not take place unless –
    (i) the employer has informed the employee what the basis was for including in the statement referred to above the ground or grounds that he has given in it, and
    (ii) the employee has had a reasonable opportunity to consider his response to that information.
(e) The employee must take all reasonable steps to attend the meeting.
(f) After the meeting the employer must inform the employee of his decision and notify him of the right to appeal against the decision if he is not satisfied with it.

Appeal
(g) If the employee does not wish to appeal, he must inform the employer.
(h) If the employee informs the employer of his wish to appeal, the employer must invite him to attend a further meeting.
(i) The employee must take all reasonable steps to attend the meeting.
(j) The appeal meeting need *not* take place before the dismissal or disciplinary action takes effect.
(k) After the appeal meeting the employer must inform the employee of his final decision.

5. Grievance procedure
  (a) The employee must set out in writing his grievance and send the statement or copy of it to the employer.

Meeting
  (b) The employer must invite the employee to attend a meeting to discuss the grievance.
  (c) The meeting must not take place unless –
    (i) the employee has informed the employer what the basis for the grievance was when he made the above statement, and
    (ii) the employer has had a reasonable opportunity to consider his response to that information.
  (d) The employee must take all reasonable steps to attend the meeting.
  (e) After the meeting the employer must inform the employee of his decision as to his response to the grievance and notify him of the right to appeal against the decision if he is not satisfied with it.

Appeal
  (f) If the employee does not wish to appeal, he must inform the employer.
  (g) If the employee informs the employer of his wish to appeal, the employer must invite him to attend a further meeting.
  (h) The employee must take all reasonable steps to attend the meeting.
    (i) After the appeal meeting the employer must inform the employee of his final decision.

Date eighth day of March 2007.

Signed
Sarah Snooks
Company Secretary

Comment
The employee should be required to sign the employer's copy in the following way:

'I have received and read a copy of the above particulars which are correct in all respects.'

Signed _____

Date _____

Note: The employer is required to offer a stakeholder pension from 1 October 2001 if there are more than four employees.

Figure 16.1 (*continued*)

The contract of employment: special situations

Part-timers and those on fixed-term contracts

It should be noted that the full range of employment rights are available to part-time workers not employed on 'zero-hours' arrangements. Furthermore, equality of treatment is assured by the Part-time Workers (Prevention of Less Favourable Treatment) Regulations 2000 (SI 2000/1551).

Part-timers: main effects of the regulations

1 Pay. Part-time employees should receive the same hourly rate of pay as a comparable full-time worker. A lower rate may be justified on objective grounds as where, e.g., there is performance-related pay.

2 Overtime. Part-time employees should receive the same hourly rate for overtime once they have worked more than full-time hours.

3 Contractual sick pay and maternity pay. Part-time employees should not be treated less favourably as regards these benefits but pro rata to their pay.

4 Occupational pensions and other benefits. Employers must not discriminate against part-time employees in terms of access to pension schemes. Benefits, of course, would be pro rata to their lower earnings.

There should also be pro rata equality in terms of annual leave, career breaks and parental leave. Access to training should also be on an equal basis.

5 Redundancy. Part-time employees must not be treated less favourably in regard to selection for redundancy.

Fixed-term workers: main effects of the regulations

The Fixed-term Employees (Prevention of Less Favourable Treatment) Regulations 2002 (SI 2002/2034) apply. The main points are set out below.

1 Definition. A fixed-term contract will generally be a contract of employment that terminates at the end of a specified term, fixed in advance, or automatically on completion of a particular task.

2 Comparators. Both individuals must be employed by the same employer and be engaged in the same or broadly similar work, having regard to whether they have a similar level of qualifications and skills.

3 Less favourable treatment. This can be in regard to levels of pay, pension and other benefits such as bonuses. Admission to a pension scheme may not be viable in the case of a short fixed-term contract.

4 Written statements. A fixed-term employee who feels that he has been treated less favourably has a right to ask the employer for a written statement of reasons. This must be provided within 21 days.

5 A tribunal claim. A fixed-term employee who thinks that he has been treated less favourably may present a claim to an employment tribunal normally after having exhausted all internal procedures.

6 Vacancies for permanent employment. The regulations give fixed-term employees a right to be informed of available vacancies for permanent employment.

7 Transfer to permanent employment. The regulations provide that where an employee is on a fixed-term contract that has been renewed or where there is a re-engagement on a new fixed-term contract, and where the employee has been employed for at least four years (excluding any period before 10 July 2002), the renewal of the contract will take effect as a permanent contract. The period of four years must be an unbroken one as where one fixed-term contract has immediately followed the previous one. The regulations, therefore, may not correct the abuse seen in *Booth* v *United States* (1999) where the USA employed men on fixed-term contracts at its UK base. There were intervals of two weeks between each one. They were not entitled to claim unfair dismissal or redundancy because their service was not continuous, nor would they have had four years of continuous service to trigger the permanent contract arrangements in the regulation. However, the employer's conduct in *Booth* may be actionable under the regulations as a 'detriment'.

It should be noted that the first fixed-term workers can become full time from 10 July 2006 unless keeping a particular employee on a fixed-term contract can be objectively justified.

8 Dismissal and detriment. Dismissal where the regulations have been infringed is automatically unfair so that there is no service requirement for a claim. Fixed-term workers are also protected against a detriment for trying to enforce the regulations.

9 Remedies. A tribunal may order compensation or recommend that reasonable action be taken to remove or reduce the effect of an employer's practice where less favourable treatment is found.

Rights and duties of the parties to the contract

The duties of an employer and an employee come from common law and Acts of Parliament. They will be dealt with under the headings which follow.

Before proceeding to them it could be said that one of the major duties of an employer is to comply with the Working Time Regulations. In this text, however, the regulations are considered as part of health and safety law and appear later in this chapter.

Duties of an employer

To provide remuneration

In business organisations the duty of the employer to pay his employees and the rate or amount of pay are decided as follows:

1 by the contract of employment; or
2 by the terms of what is called a collective agreement made between a trade union and the employer. The terms of this agreement, including the part on pay, are then assumed to be part of the individual contracts of employment of the members. The employer must comply with the national minimum wage provisions (see below).

The pay which the worker is to get should nearly always be definite because it is included in the written particulars which we have just dealt with and also because the ERA requires itemised pay statements.

If there is no provision for payment in the contract – which is highly unlikely – then if the worker sued for payment, the court would fix a fair rate of pay for the job by taking evidence as to what rates of pay were usual in the type of work being done.

Unless the employment contract allows an employer to reduce an employee's pay during short-time working, or the employee agrees to the reduction, the employer must continue to pay full wages during a period of short-time working (*Miller* v *Hamworthy Engineering Ltd*

(1986)). However, if an employee refuses to perform his contractual duties because he is taking industrial action his employer can, understandably, lawfully withhold wages for the relevant period (*Miles* v *Wakefield Metropolitan District Council* (1987)).

Where a worker returns to work after a strike but refuses to work normally, the employer is not bound to accept part performance and can terminate the contract. However, if he does not but decides to accept the part performance, he can withhold wages for the hours lost (see *British Telecommunications* v *Ticehurst* (1992)).

Cashless pay. As a general rule, wages can now be paid by cheque or credit transfer. However, employees who have been continuously employed since before the beginning of 1987 and who have always been paid in cash may have a contractual right to continue to be paid in that way. If an employer wishes to start paying such employees by cheque or by credit transfer, he should either obtain their consent or take the necessary steps to vary the contract.

National minimum wage (NMW)

The National Minimum Wage Act 1998 (NMWA 1998) was brought into force by regulations over the period of 1998/9. The Act was amended recently by the Employment Act 2008 to provide a clearer framework in terms of NMW enforcement. The Act and connected regulations provide workers with a floor below which their wages will not fall, regardless of the size of the employer's business. Those who work part time have benefited most. Section references are to the 1998 Act.

1 Entitlement. Those entitled must be 'workers' who work or ordinarily work in the UK under a contract of employment and are over compulsory school leaving age (ss 1(2) and 54(3)). Casual workers are included as are agency workers (s 34) and home-workers (s 35).

The self-employed are excluded, as are voluntary workers. These include charity workers who are either totally unpaid but receive only reasonable travel and out-of-pocket expenses. Regulations also exempt from the provisions those working and living as part of a family, e.g. au pairs. Those under 16 years of age are also excluded.

2 Owner-managed businesses. The 1998 Act applies to directors of owner-managed businesses. Thus, a person who works as a director of his company but takes no salary (or very little), relying on dividends as income, falls foul of the Act and must receive the minimum wage or adjust the hours worked to comply. The company must also pay employer's NIC. If the business is dis-incorporated, the former director would come under the exemption for the self-employed. Those who are starting up a business as a company and cannot initially pay themselves also fall foul of the Act though they could notionally pay themselves the minimum wage but remain as a creditor until the company can pay them. As an alternative, they could set up in partnership because partners are excluded from the minimum wage pro-visions, unless they are salaried employees as distinct from profit-sharing partners. A spouse employed in a family business is excluded from the provisions under the 'family business' exception as are other members of the employer's family who live at home, but not if the employer is incorporated, i.e. a family company.

A further solution for those directors who wish or have to work for less than the minimum wage is not to have a contract of employment, so that they are not employees. This appears to be accepted by the relevant authorities. Furthermore, the BIS has indicated that it will not try to show that the director has an *implied* contract.

3 Level. The National Minimum Wage rates (from 1 October 2010):

Workers aged 22 and over – £5.93 per hour
Workers aged 18–21 – £4.92 per hour
Workers aged 16–17 – £3.64 per hour

There is a new minimum wage of £2.50 per hour for apprentices who are either under 19 or in the first year of their apprenticeship.

4 Increases in level. This will depend upon the advice of the Low Pay Commission (LPC) and the economic situation and is not automatic.

5 Extensions. There is power to apply the Act to those who do not fit the current definition of a 'worker' (s 41). This could be used to deal with changes in working practices and to close loopholes which bad employers may exploit.

6 Calculation. The regulations set out the averaging period to be used in calculating whether a worker has been paid the NMW: the pay reference period. It is normally set at a month (i.e. 'calendar month') except where workers are currently paid by reference to periods of shorter than one month, e.g. a week, a fortnight or

four weeks. In the latter cases the pay reference period for NMW purposes will be the worker's existing pay period. In addition, the hourly rate for those who are paid an annual salary will be calculated on an average basis.

7 What counts as remuneration? The regulations deal with a number of instances of what does and does not count towards discharging an employer's obligation to pay the NMW. Examples of things which do not count are advances of wages, pensions, redundancy payments and benefits in kind with the exclusion of living accommodation at a fairly low limit.

Payments during absences from work such as sick pay, holiday pay, maternity pay and guarantee payments are not included and neither are service charges, tips, gratuities or cover charges *not paid through the payroll*. Thus, discretionary tips left for a worker by a customer and pocketed by the worker do not count nor would tips pooled under an employees' informal scheme and dis-tributed, but where tips are pooled by the employer and paid through the payroll they do count as remuneration.

Allowable deductions: a checklist

- Penalties imposed upon an employee for misconduct, provided that the employer is allowed under the terms of the contract of service to make the deduction.
- Deductions to repay loans, wages advances or purchase of shares.
- Deductions to repay any accidental overpayment of wages.
- Deductions or payments made by the employer or to the employer for goods or services purchased freely and without obligation.
- Deductions for accommodation: the maximum amount that an employer can deduct from the NMW rate. From 1 October 2010, the rate is £4.61 per day (reg 36, National Minimun Wage Regulations 1999 (SI 1999/584) (as amended by National Minimun Wage Regulations 1999 (Amendment) Regulations 2006 SI 2006/2001).

Deductions for the cost of items related to the worker's employment, e.g. tools and uniform, are not allowable.

Enforcement

The Secretary of State appoints enforcement officers (s 13) and HMRC is responsible for enforcement by checking employers' records to ensure compliance. Complaints by employees will be investigated and spot checks will be made on employers. Advice can also be sought from Pay and Work Rights Helpline.

Important provisions relating to the enforcement of the NMW are contained in the Employment Relations Act 2004, which inserts additional sections into the National Minimum Wage Act 1998. These provisions which are now in force are as follows:

1 Information supplied by worker and employer. The NMWA 1998 carried provisions relating to the supply and use of information obtained by enforcement officers. In general terms this information could not be supplied to any other person or body and even when this was allowed the Secretary of State had to authorise it. It was felt that, because of these restrictions, enforcement officers were unable to inform the worker what the employer's records revealed about the worker's claim. Similarly, the officers were unable to inform the employer about the ingredients of the worker's case. Section 16A enables an enforcement officer to disclose information obtained from the employer to the worker where it relates to his or her case and similarly to disclose information obtained from the worker to the employer.

2 Withdrawal and replacement of enforcement and penalty notices. Sections 22A–22F modify the former procedure (whereby following issue of an enforcement or penalty notice any change could come about as a result of an appeal to an employment tribunal) by the introduction of provisions under which enforcement officers may withdraw and replace enforcement notices. Similar provisions apply to the withdrawal and replacement by officers of penalty notices. An ultimate right of appeal still lies to an employment tribunal.

3 Penalties. Organisations that refuse to pay the NMW face fines of twice the NMW, a day for each employee (s 21). If defiance continues, the fine goes up to a maximum of £5,000 for each offence (s 31). Workers have the right to recover the difference between what they have been paid and the NMW before a tribunal as an unlawful deduction from wages (s 17). There is no limit of time on back claims.

As well as individuals bringing claims, HMRC officers have power to issue enforcement notices if they find underpayment. If the notice is not complied with, an officer can sue in an employment tribunal to recover what is due on behalf of the worker. In this connection, mention should be made of the National Minimum Wage (Enforcement Notices) Act 2003.

This Act ensures that HMRC can issue enforcement notices to require the payment of the NMW to *former* employees as well as current employees. The Act closes a loophole that was revealed by the decision of the EAT in *IRC* v *Bebb Travel plc* (2002). In the *Bebb* case the EAT ruled that under s 19(2) of the NMWA 1998 an enforcement notice could be issued in regard to a previous failure to pay the NMW if the notice also contained a requirement that the employer pay the NMW *in the future*. Thus, former employees could not claim merely for past failures to pay. The 2003 Act adds s 19(2A) to the 1998 Act which allows the service of an enforcement notice where it is of opinion that a worker who qualifies has 'at any time' not received the minimum wage. The 2003 Act is retrospective. Workers may bring claims under it to an employment tribunal, a county court or through HMRC's enforcement unit.

4 Action by employees. A worker who is dismissed for asking for the NMW can claim unfair dismissal. In *Butt* v *Euro Fashion (MCLR) Ltd* (ET Case No 240341499) B was paid £2.60 per hour. He asked for £3.60 (the then rate) and was told to get another job if he wanted the NMW. He resigned and subsequently a tribunal held that he had been constructively dismissed and that the dismissal was unfair.

5 Records. The record-keeping obligations were eased following consultation and it is now merely provided that an employer has to keep records 'sufficient to establish that he is remunerating the worker at a rate at least equal to the national minimum wage'. The records may be in a format and with a content of the employer's choosing and must be capable of being produced as a single document when requested either by an employee or HMRC.

Records can be kept on a computer, but the employer must be able to produce them in a single document which can be of any length on request.

6 Access to tax records. A government amendment made to the Employment Relations Act 1999 allows information obtained by a tax inspector to be supplied:

- by HMRC to the BIS for any purpose relating to the National Minimum Wage Act 1998; and
- by the BIS with the authority of HMRC to inspectors required to enforce the NMW or minimum agricultural wages.

7 Corporate offences. Where a relevant offence is committed by a company, its directors and other officers are jointly responsible with the company where they have consented to or connived at the offence or been neglectful in regard to it (s 32).

8 Contracting out. Section 29 makes void any agreement to exclude or limit the Act's provisions or prevent a complaint being made to a tribunal unless there has been conciliation by a conciliation officer or a valid compromise agreement.

9 Victimisation and unfair dismissal. Section 23 gives workers the right not to be subject to any detriment, e.g. failure to promote, because they have asserted rights under the 1998 Act. Under s 25 employees who are dismissed or selected for redundancy for similarly asserting rights will be regarded as unfairly dismissed.

10 Capability and the minimum wage. A Birmingham employment tribunal has ruled that a textile company was entitled to dismiss a worker who, though entitled to the minimum wage, did not in the employer's view have productivity to match.

Gurdev Kaur v *Ambertex Clothing* (2000)

Mrs Kaur, aged 54, was dismissed by Ambertex in July 1999, three months after the national minimum wage was introduced. It appeared that the company had been quite willing to employ Mrs Kaur during the previous two and a half years while she was being paid on a piece-work arrangement for sewing buttons on shirts. She was then paid about £2 per hour based on the speed with which she worked.

All Ambertex's employees were paid the minimum wage of £3.60 an hour when the legislation was brought into force, but employees were told that payment of the wage required a set level of productivity. Mrs Kaur failed to meet the required level and was dismissed. She claimed damages for unfair dismissal because of the introduction of the minimum wage. The tribunal rejected that argument. The principal reason for dismissal was in effect 'incapability' (or underperformance) which can be an acceptable reason for dismissal under s 98(2)(a) of the Employment Rights Act 1996. The tribunal did, however, decide that Mrs Kaur had been unfairly dismissed by reason of the *procedure* adopted. She had only been given one, rather than two, written warnings. Her compensation due to underpayment in some weeks because of clerical errors was £412.95.

Comment. This does appear to have been a capability dismissal rather than a minimum wage dismissal which would have been unfair. It does not appear on its own facts to suggest that there is a loophole in the minimum wage law.

Impact of NMW on employment awards

The EAT has ruled that an employment tribunal has a duty to consider and apply the NMW when determining a week's pay under the Employment Rights Act 1996 and calculating the net rate of pay for the loss of earnings element of the compensatory award under the same Act. In *Paggetti* v *Cobb* (2002). P succeeded in his claim for unfair dismissal against C. P appealed in regard to the assessment of his basic and compensatory awards. P had indicated to the employment tribunal hearing that he worked a 63-hour week for £120. He claimed that the NMW should impact on the calculation of his pay for the two awards. The EAT allowed the appeal and ruled that wages calculations prepared under the Employment Rights Act 1996 were automatically subject to the statutory minimum wage during the period of work, and that this was so even though the applicant did not make a specific claim in this regard under the NMW legislation.

Low Pay Commission

The Low Pay Commission was put on to a statutory footing when ss 5–8 of the NMWA 1998 came into force on 1 November 1998. In addition to continuing its role of monitoring and evaluating the impact of the NMW, the Commission considers whether there is a case for increasing the NMW and includes earnings growth in its assessment as well as inflation and the effect on employment. The inclusion of earnings growth has led to a higher minimum wage.

To give holidays and holiday pay

The rights and duties of the parties here depend upon what the contract of employment says or what the terms of a collective agreement with a union are. Again, there should be no doubt about holidays and holiday pay because the 1996 Act states that this information is to be given to the employee in the written particulars.

The employer must also bear in mind the Working Time Regulations 1998, under which the employee is entitled to four weeks of paid holiday. These regulations, which are part of the health and safety provisions, are considered later in this chapter.

To provide sick pay

Entitlement to sick pay must be dealt with by the written particulars. An employer has **no general duty to provide sick pay from his own funds**. There is no implied term in the contract of service that an employee is entitled to sick pay (*Mears v Safecar Security* (1982)). There is a **statutory duty** under the 1996 Act to pay an employee who goes sick during the statutory period of notice and is not able to work out all or part of the notice.

Employers were required to provide what is called **statutory sick pay** (SSP) on behalf of the government to employees who are aged 16 or over but not over 65. These upper and lower limits are removed from 1 October 2006 by the Age Regulations 2006. The law is to be found, in the main, in the Social Security Contributions and Benefits Act 1992. The Social Security Administration Act 1992 deals with the administration of statutory sick pay and statutory maternity pay. It is not necessary in a book of this nature to go into details in regard to the statutory sick pay scheme but the main principles are that when an employee falls sick he or she gets a weekly amount from the employer and not from the Department of Social Security.

The Statutory Sick Pay Act 1994 removed (from 6 April 1994) an employer's right to recover sums paid by way of SSP from the total amount of employers' and employees' national insurance contributions due to HMRC. However, this led to protests from employers, and the government introduced regulations under which all employers recover SSP under the 'percentage threshold scheme'. Under this scheme the employer takes the figure of NIC (employers and employees) due in any given tax month. The employer then ascertains the SSP paid in the same month. If this is more than 13 per cent of the NIC figure, the employer recovers the excess.

There is no other change to entitlement to SSP except that s 7 of the Social Security (Incapacity for Work) Act 1994 abolished the lower rate of SSP. There is now only one standard rate, this being currently £79.15 per week.

The provisions relating to SSP are notoriously difficult if taken in full detail, but in broad terms SSP is paid by an employer (or a series of employers) for up to 28 weeks of incapacity for work during a three-year period. The first three days of sickness are waiting days and no SSP is payable. However, as regards the second and subsequent periods of sickness, if the employee has not been back at work following the first period of sickness for eight weeks or more the periods are linked and there are no waiting days, SSP beginning on the first day of sickness in the second or subsequent period. We can illustrate what happens (see below).

In Norma's case, since she has not returned to work for the requisite period of more than eight weeks, her periods of incapacity are linked and no waiting days are applied to the second period of incapacity because it is not a new one. Both John and Norma have now exhausted their entitlement to SSP against their employer. An employer's liability to pay SSP ends when he has paid the employee SSP for 28 weeks during a three-year period commencing with the first incapacity. During the remainder of the three years John and Norma cannot have SSP but will be able to resume that right when a new period of three years begins three years after the first incapacity.

Employees who are still incapacitated after their entitlement has run out are entitled to state benefits (Incapacity Benefit). It is not possible to avoid the statutory sick pay provisions and any clause in a contract of employment which sets out to do this is void.

John's pattern of sickness

Norma's pattern of sickness

Exceptions

The person claiming for SSP must be an employee and in all cases the claimant must have earned the qualifying level, currently £97 a week.

Enforcement

If an employee is dissatisfied with an employer's decision in regard to entitlement to SSP or the employer has failed to make a decision, the employee can write to

HMRC asking for a decision on entitlement. Employer and employee have a right of appeal to a commissioner. HMRC has power to pay SSP itself and should also pay SSP if the employer is liable but insolvent.

To provide pay during suspension

1 On medical grounds. Under the ERA 1996 an employee who has had at least one month's continuous service with his employer and who is suspended from work, for example under the Health and Safety at Work etc. Act 1974, normally on the advice of an Employment Medical Adviser, not because he is ill but because he might become ill if he continues at work, since he is currently engaged on an industrial process which involves a potential hazard to his health, is entitled to be paid his normal wages while he is suspended for up to 26 weeks. This could occur, for example, where there was a leak of radioactivity at the workplace.

An employee may complain to an employment tribunal under the ERA if his employer has not paid him what he is entitled to during a period of suspension and the tribunal may order the employer to pay the employee the money which he should have had.

2 On disciplinary grounds. Suppose an employee takes a day off without permission, in order to go to a football match. His employer decides to suspend him for a further day without pay: is this legal? Well, there is no implied right to suspend an employee for disciplinary reasons without pay. In practice, if the employer wants a power to suspend it must be made an express term of the contract which is agreed to by the employee and be in the written particulars of the job. If so, it will be justified and the employee will have to accept it.

It should be noted also that there is no implied contractual term allowing an employer to suspend or fine a worker for poor quality work. An express term is required.

3 On maternity grounds. The ERA 1996 provides for suspension on maternity grounds. Formerly, a pregnant woman could be fairly dismissed if because of her condition she could not do her work, e.g. because of health and safety regulations and either there was no suitable alternative work or she had refused it. The ERA substitutes suspension on the grounds of pregnancy, recent childbirth or breastfeeding while the health hazard continues. The employee may complain to a tribunal if she is not offered available and suitable alternative work. Suspension continues even if such an offer is refused but pay ceases. For those who have not refused an offer,

as where it was not possible for the employer to make one, pay continues during suspension but only to a maximum of 'a week's pay' (currently £290) or normal remuneration if her contract so provides. Those whose employer does not make the payment can claim compensation before a tribunal.

If an employer dismisses an employee who tries to assert his or her rights in these various suspension matters, the dismissal is automatically unfair whatever the employee's length of service. A claim to an employment tribunal must be made within three months of the employment ending.

Employment Act 2008

First introduced in the House of Lords on 6 December 2007, having been announced in July 2007 in the government's Draft Legislative Programme following the Gibbons Review, the Employment Bill seeks to 'strengthen and clarify key aspects of employment law' (BIS, previously, BERR, 2008). The Act received Royal Assent in November 2008.

The Act repealed the Employment Act 2002 (Dispute Resolution) Regulations 2004 which were intended to reduce employment litigation. The key proposals of the Employment Act intended to:

- Improve the effectiveness of employment law to the benefit of employers, trade unions, individuals and the public sector.
- Bring together both elements of the government's employment relations strategy: increasing protection for vulnerable workers and lightening the load for law-abiding business.
- Promote compliance and help to ensure a level playing field for law-abiding businesses.

It also seeks to clarify and strengthen the enforcement framework for the National Minimum Wage and employment agency standards which cover voluntary workers who receive no monetary payment or benefit in kind. Voluntary workers are excluded from qualifying for the National Minimum Wage by s 44 of the 1998 Act.

Family-friendly provisions

There are now enshrined in law a number of employee rights that can be described as family-friendly laws. These follow.

Antenatal care

A pregnant employee who has, on the advice of her doctor, midwife or health visitor, made an appointment to get antenatal care must have time off to keep it and she must also be paid. Except for the first appointment, the employer can ask for proof of the appointment in the form, for example, of an appointment card. An employer who, acting unreasonably, does not give the employee these rights can be taken to a tribunal by the employee but this must normally be during the three months following the employer's refusal. Compensation may be given to the employee, both where the employer has failed to give time off and also where he has given time off but has failed to pay the employee. In either case the compensation will be the amount of pay to which she would have been entitled if time off with pay had been given as the law requires. All female employees are entitled to this time off and it does not make any difference how many hours they work each week; there is no service requirement.

Statutory maternity and adoption leave

The Maternity and Parental Leave etc. and the Paternity and Adoption Leave (Amendment) Regulations 2006 (SI 2006/2014) apply. They came into force on 1 October 2006. They follow on from the changes to statutory maternity and adoption leave sanctioned by the Work and Families Act 2006 which received the Royal Assent on 21 June 2006.

Who do the changes affect?
They have effect in relation to an employee whose expected week of childbirth is on or after 1 April 2007 and an employee whose child is expected to be placed with the employee for adoption by that date, or, in the case of an overseas adoption, an adopter whose child enters Great Britain on or after that date.

What are the changes?
Regulations 5 to 7 remove the additional length of service required to qualify for additional maternity (or adoption) leave (AML). An employee who qualifies for ordinary maternity (or adoption) leave (no length of service requirement) will qualify also for additional maternity (or adoption) leave. Previously, the right to AML was available only to employees who had been employed for 26 weeks.

Statutory maternity and adoption leave entitlement for all employees regardless of length of service is 12 months.

Notice to the employer
Regulation 8 extends the period of notice which an employee is required to give the employer of the intention to return to work earlier than the end of AML from 28 days to eight weeks. If the employee fails to give this notice the employer can postpone return for up to eight weeks. The same extension applies to return from adoption leave (reg 15).

Keeping in touch
Regulation 9 enables an employee on maternity leave to agree with the employer to work (which includes training) for up to ten days during the maternity leave period without bringing the period to an end. These are referred to as 'keeping in touch' days.

Removal of small employers' exemption
Regulations 11 and 17 remove the small employers' exemption in order to clarify that the employee has the right to return to the same or similar job regardless of the size of the organisation. If the employee is prevented from doing so in these circumstances a dismissal will be automatically unfair. Previously this protection did not apply where the total number of employees employed by the employer (and associated employers, e.g. group companies) did not exceed five.

Maternity leave and pay

Compulsory maternity leave

This leave is provided for by s 72 of the ERA 1996. The Work and Families Act 2006 extended the leave to 52 weeks. The employer of a woman is prohibited from allowing her to return to work during the two weeks from the day on which the child is born (s 72, Chapter 1, Part VIII, ERA 1996). An employer who contravenes this requirement commits a criminal offence and is liable to a fine currently not exceeding £500 (level 2 of the standard scale). It is accepted that the woman will be most unlikely to want to return to work. The provision is basically designed to prevent the employer from pressurising her to do so.

Statutory Maternity Pay administration

Employers can recover 92 per cent of the amount paid out by way of Statutory Maternity Pay (SMP) and small employers (broadly those whose national insurance contributions payments for the qualifying tax year do not exceed £45,000) can recover 100 per cent plus an additional 4.5 per cent of each payment of SMP which is designed to recoup the NI contributions payable on such payments.

The Equality Act 2010 has also introduced a maternity equality pay clause (see s 74 of the Equality Act 2010).

Paternity leave

Male and female employees have a right to be away from work on **paid** paternity leave. Most of the provisions outlined in the box below do not apply to paternity leave except as indicated in the notes. The qualifying conditions are set out below.

The right is available to employees who:

■ have continuous service with the employer of 26 weeks by the end of the 15th week before the expected week of confinement (EWC);
■ have or expect to have responsibility for bringing up the child;

Maternity and other statutory family-friendly payments

Maternity payments
The following statutory instrument is a consequence of provisions in the Work and Families Act 2006. It applies to women according to an expected week of childbirth and not the date on which the baby is born. The Statutory Maternity Pay, Social Security (Maternity Allowance) and Social Security (Overlapping Benefits) (Amendment) Regulations 2006 (SI 2006/2379) introduce the following provisions for women with an expected week of childbirth on or after 1 April 2008.

Length of maternity pay
This is extended to a maximum of 39 consecutive weeks. The pay for the first six weeks is 90 per cent of average weekly earnings and then the standard flat weekly rate (currently £124.88) for the remaining period of 33 weeks or 90 per cent of average earnings, whichever is lower.

Start of maternity pay
Maternity pay can begin on any day of the week as specified by the employee in the notification given to her employer as to when she wishes to finish work. This allows statutory maternity pay to align with the commencement of the woman's maternity leave in all cases. A pay week is a period of seven consecutive days.

Weekly rate of statutory maternity pay may be divided
Statutory maternity pay can be divided by seven to enable employers at their discretion to align weekly maternity pay with the pay practice in the job. Thus if an employer commences pay calculation from, say, Wednesday then the woman's maternity pay can be aligned with this as the commencement of her first seven-day period of pay. This does not mean that a woman can have one day's pay. It is not like statutory sick pay where an employee can be entitled to one day's pay.

Keeping in touch days
A woman retains the right to receive statutory maternity pay for the week in which any such work is carried out and the period is not terminated by this return to work. The relevant days need not be worked consecutively and will be agreed between employee and employer. Any additional pay for being at work is determined by the employment contract but the employee must receive as a minimum the statutory maternity rate for the week in question. Any work even for just one hour will count as a whole day for the 'keeping in touch' purposes. When the ten days are exhausted the woman will lose a week's statutory maternity pay for any week in which she does any work under her employment contract.

Notes
Other issues include:
Adoption pay. The extension of the pay period from 26 weeks to 39 weeks, allowing limited work during the pay period and the division by seven of the weekly rate of pay applies also to statutory adoption pay where the expected date of placement for adoption is on or after 1 April 2007.
Paternity pay. The division of the weekly rate by seven also applies where children are born on or after 1 April 2007.
Lower age limits. The lower age limit is removed from SMP and paternity pay so that employees under 16 gain entitlement. It is also removed from statutory adoption pay but this has little practical effect, as the minimum age to adopt remains at 21. The Work and Families Act 2006 provision to allow leave and pay to be transferred in part from mother to father took effect on 6 April 2010, but this would only apply where mother is due to give birth on or after 3 April 2011.

- are either the biological father of the child or are married to or are the partner of the child's mother;
- leave is for two weeks and whether taken in single weeks or a block of two consecutive weeks, it must be taken within a period of 56 days from the child's birth or the first day of the EWC. The second alternative is to deal with a very premature birth where the child might be kept in hospital for more than 56 days after the birth. The EWC will of course have been set to fit a normal term pregnancy and will obviously be later than in fact the birth was, giving the opportunity to take leave after the child comes home;
- statutory paternity pay is at the weekly rate of the lesser of £124.88 (currently) or 90 per cent of normal earnings;
- as in the case of SMP, employers can recover 92 per cent of the NI payments. The small employers' provision is as for SMP;
- employees can take paternity leave in addition to unpaid parental leave of 13 weeks (see below).

Maternity allowance

Those who do not qualify for statutory maternity pay may be able to get maternity allowance. The provisions are broadly as follows:

Amount of benefit

A successful claimant will receive weekly the lesser of £124.88 or 90 per cent of average earnings.

Payment period

Maternity allowance is paid for up to 39 weeks. The earliest the period can start is the 11th week before the EWC unless the child is born before this and the latest is the Sunday after the child is born.

Service requirement

In order to qualify for maternity allowance, the claimant must have worked as an employee and/or been self-employed for at least 26 weeks in the 66 weeks immediately before the EWC. The weeks do not need to be consecutive or for the same employer and a part-week of work counts as a full week.

Earnings requirement

To qualify for maternity allowance the claimant's average weekly earnings must be at least equal to the maternity allowance threshold which is £30 a week. There are a number of ways of calculating average earnings but, for example, the highest earnings for 13 weeks out of the 66 weeks referred to above may be taken and divided by 13 to produce the average.

Pregnancy dismissals

It might be useful at this stage to consider the effect of discrimination law in dismissal cases. A summary of the position appears below.

Under s 99 of the Employment Rights Act 1996 it is automatically unfair, so that no service requirement is necessary to dismiss a woman for a reason related to her pregnancy, maternity or maternity leave. It is also unlawful to take any action short of dismissal for any of those reasons.

Women may also claim that dismissal in the above circumstances is unlawful sex discrimination contrary to the Sex Discrimination Act 1975, as amended by the Employment Equality (Sex Discrimination) Regulations 2005 (SI 2005/2467), which makes discrimination while a woman is pregnant or on maternity leave expressly unlawful. There is thus no need to refer to the EC Equal Treatment Directive and its case law, such as *Webb v EMO Air Cargo (UK) Ltd* (1995), except perhaps where there is a suggestion that UK law has not properly implemented the directive. Such case law is beyond the scope of this text.

Where possible, a claim should be made for sex discrimination because a successful claim could lead to uncapped compensation whereas unfair dismissal claims are capped (currently at £63,000).

Constructive dismissals are also covered, as where the woman is not dismissed by the employer but resigns because of the unlawful conduct.

Adoption leave – generally

Male and female employees are entitled to take adoption leave. Where there is a joint adoption by married couples they will be able to choose who takes the adoption leave. Where the adoption is by one of them only then that person will be entitled to the adoption leave though the other spouse will be entitled to paternity leave if the criteria are met. It should be noted that in current law couples in a long-term relationship but who are not married cannot adopt. Only married couples or one person in an unmarried relationship can adopt. As we have seen, a married couple who adopt can choose which of them takes adoption leave and which takes paternity leave. The partner of a single person who adopts can take only paternity leave.

The main general points on adoption leave and pay appear in the boxes at pp 483–84.

Unpaid parental leave

Sections 76–78 of the ERA 1996 apply. These sections together with the regulations provide for collective agreements to be made with trade unions and workforce agreements to be made with employees in regard to parental leave. Nevertheless, employees retain their rights under what is called the statutory fallback scheme unless the collective or workforce scheme is more generous, in which case such schemes can replace the fallback scheme. This book considers only the fallback scheme as follows.

The fallback scheme. An employee who has been continuously employed for a period of not less than one year has a right to 13 weeks of unpaid parental leave in respect of each child born on or after 15 December 1999 and each child under 18 who is adopted by the employee on or after that date. Women who qualify for parental leave can take it immediately after taking maternity leave. A week means seven days' absence from work, even though the employee would not have been required to work on every one of the working days. *Leave must be taken in one-week blocks* (or the part-time equivalent) up to a maximum of four weeks' leave in respect of an individual child during a particular year calculated from the first time the employee became entitled to take parental leave. The Court of Appeal refused a different interpretation in *Rodway v New Southern Railways Ltd* (2005) and accepted as valid the employer's refusal to give Mr Rodway one day of parental leave to care for his two-year-old child while the mother visited her disabled sister. Leave may be taken in blocks of one day or multiples of one day where the child is disabled. The leave must be taken during the period of five years from the date of birth or adoption or until the child turns 18 years if disabled. As regards the adoption of older children, the leave period ends when they reach 18 even if five years from placement for adoption has not by then elapsed. Entitlement to leave after the child's fifth birthday occurs if the employer has previously postponed leave.

Notice

The employer must receive notice (not necessarily written notice) of 21 days specifying the dates on which leave is to begin and end. Where the leave is to be taken on birth, the notice must specify the EWC and the duration of leave to be taken and be given 21 days before the beginning of EWC. The same with adoption, except that notice must be given 21 days before the expected week of placement.

Evidence

The employer is entitled to require evidence of the employee's legal responsibility for the child as well as evidence of the child's age.

Postponement of leave

The employer may postpone a period of leave where he considers that the operation of the business would be affected in terms that it would be 'unduly disrupted'. He has only seven days to make his mind up about postponement which may be for a maximum period of six months. No postponement is allowed if leave is taken on the birth or adoption of a child.

The employment contract during leave

While on parental leave, employees remain bound by their obligation of good faith towards their employer and any express undertakings in the contract in regard to non-disclosure of confidential information and competition. The employer must continue to abide by the implied obligations of trust and confidence and offer the right to return to the same job but if that is not possible to another job which is suitable and appropriate in the circumstances. There is also protection in regard to salary, continuity of employment and pension rights on return.

Making a claim

The relevant provision is the new s 80 of the ERA 1996. It gives employees a right to complain to an employment tribunal within three months from the date when any of the rights under the parental leave arrangements are denied, in the sense that these have been unreasonably postponed or prevented. Any related dismissal is automatically unfair and there is no cap on the compensation that may be awarded.

Records

The regulations do not require the keeping of records, but it will be impossible for employers to avoid keeping them for accounting purposes to show that leave has been unpaid and that the rights are not being abused. Bearing in mind also that time off for domestic emergencies (also unpaid) exists (see below), employers must consider the need to set up systems and procedures to cope with the new rights and look at how they can run along with any existing contractual rights to paid parental leave that employees already have within a particular organisation.

Time off for dependants

Section 57A of the ERA 1996 applies. It entitles every employee, regardless of length of service, to take a reasonable amount of time off work 'to take action that is necessary':

- to help when a dependant gives birth, falls ill or is assaulted;
- to make longer term arrangements for the care of a sick or injured dependant;
- as a result of a dependant's death;
- to cope when the arrangements for caring for a dependant break down unexpectedly; or
- to deal with an unexpected incident that involves a dependant child during school hours, or on a school trip or in other situations when the school has responsibility for the child.

1 Dependants. This means a husband or wife or a child or parent of the employee whether they live with him or her or not or any member of the employee's household who is not employed by him or her and is not a tenant, lodger or boarder.

2 Amount of time off. There is no set limit. In every case the right is limited to the amount of time that is reasonable in the circumstances. Employment tribunals will be the ultimate arbitrators if a claim is brought by an employee.

It is automatically unfair dismissal if an employee is dismissed for asserting the right to dependant time off. It is in connection with dismissals for absence that cases have come before tribunals who have had to consider how much time can be taken. In two important cases the EAT has ruled that the amount of time taken must be reasonable and will depend upon the circumstances. However, it is clear that it is not intended to allow the employee to do more than *make arrangements to deal with the problem*. It is not intended to be an extended period to allow the employee to provide the care himself or herself. If this is necessary other arrangements for longer term absence must be made with the employer. Employers would seem to be within their rights to dismiss an employee for taking longer term absence under the guise of taking time off for dependants (see *Qua* v *John Ford Morrison Solicitors* (2003) and *Maculloch & Wallis Ltd* v *Moore* (2003)). It is time off for dependants and *not strictly speaking dependants' leave*.

More recently, the Employment Appeal Tribunal has ruled that leave to recover from bereavement, i.e. the death of a father, is not covered by the dependants' leave provisions (see *Forster* v *Cartwright Black* (2004)).

3 Payment for time off. The employer is under no obligation to pay the employee for time taken off.

4 Notification. The right only applies if the employee 'as soon as is reasonably practicable' tells the employer why he or she is absent and, unless the employee is already back at work, for how long the absence is likely to last.

5 Enforcing the right. The new s 57B of the ERA 1996 entitles an employee to complain to an employment tribunal that the employer has unreasonably refused to allow time off as required by s 57A. The period for application is three months from the employer's refusal, and compensation may be an uncapped award such as is just and equitable.

6 Victimisation and dismissal. There is protection in terms of a tribunal complaint for any victimisation, detriment or dismissal resulting from the exercise or purported exercise of the right in a proper way and dismissal is automatically unfair. Selection for redundancy for the same reason will be automatically an unfair dismissal.

Flexible working

Under Part 8A of the ERA 1996 (as inserted by s 47 of the Employment Act 2002) employers are under a duty to consider applications for flexible working from employees who are parents of children under age six or disabled children under 17. Changes in hours and times of work may be applied for.

Qualifying conditions for employees are:

- Continuous employment with the employer for not less than 26 weeks. The purpose must be to care for a child.

  The employee must be:
  (i) the biological parent, guardian or foster carer of the child;
  (ii) married to a person within (i) above and lives with the child; or
  (iii) the partner of a person within (i) above and lives with the child.

  The employee must also have, or expect to have, responsibility for the upbringing of the child.
- The employee must apply well in advance and the request must be in writing.

- The employer is then required to meet with the employee within 28 days of the application and the employer's decision must be notified to the employee within 14 days of the meeting. The employee must have a right of appeal. The employee also has the right to be accompanied by a fellow worker or a trade union representative at any meeting.
- The employee's application may be refused where the employer considers that one or more of the following grounds apply:
  - burden of additional costs;
  - detrimental effect on the ability to meet consumer demand;
  - inability to reorganise work among remaining staff;
  - detrimental effect on quality;
  - insufficiency of work during the periods the employee proposes to work, as where the employee proposes to be away at peak times and return at slack times when there might be a need for fewer staff;
  - structural changes would be involved and require planning.

The right to request flexible working was extended to carers of adults from 6 April 2007. An employee will be able to request flexible working in order to care for someone who is the spouse, civil partner or partner of the employee, a relative or someone who lives at the same address as the employee.

Where the employer fails to comply with his or her duties in regard to the application or bases his or her decision on incorrect facts, the employee may apply to an employment tribunal. If the employee's complaint is well founded, the tribunal may make an order to that effect and may order the employer to reconsider the matter and/or award compensation to the employee of up to eight weeks' pay (currently capped at £330 per week). A tribunal *may not order* the employer to implement the employee's request for flexible working.

There is also a formal binding arbitration scheme under ACAS.

What is flexible working?

Government's guidance gives the following examples:

- annualised hours;
- compressed hours;
- term-time working;
- flexitime;
- working from home;
- job sharing;

- self-rostering;
- shift working;
- staggered hours.

Employment Relations Act 2004: additional flexible working rights

Section 41 of the 2004 Act inserts sections into existing legislation to provide that dismissal of an employee for exercising flexible working rights will be automatically unfair despite that employee's participation in, or any connection with, industrial action. There is also a provision that a redundancy will be unfair if the reason or principal reason for selecting the employee for redundancy was that he or she was exercising flexible working rights. Furthermore, exercising flexible working rights becomes one of the exceptions to the requirement that an employee must have one year's continuous service to make a claim for unfair dismissal.

Flexible working and discrimination

Employers should ensure that, in refusing a request, including one made informally, for flexible hours they are not discriminating on grounds of sex, race, disability, sexual orientation, religion or belief or age either directly or indirectly, nor breaching their duty to make reasonable adjustments in regard to disabled employees.

In addition, the fact that the employer has complied with the statutory procedure does not mean that a discrimination claim will necessarily be successfully defended and fail.

To make payments during lay-off – guarantee payments

1 Lay-off. To avoid difficulty the right of the employer to lay off employees without pay because of lack of work should be made an express term of the contract of employment. However, even if the employer has given himself that right in the contract he must still comply with the provisions of the ERA 1996 in the matter and cannot have clauses in the contract which are worse for the employee than the basic statutory rights which provide for guarantee payments.

2 Guarantee payments. The ERA 1996 provides that employees with four weeks or more of continuous service are entitled to a guarantee payment up to a maximum sum, which is currently £21.20 per day (from February 2010), if they are not provided with work on a normal working day, e.g. because of a threatened power cut (*Miller* v *Harry Thornton (Lollies) Ltd* (1978)).

The precise formula is the average daily wage or £21.20, whichever is the smaller. This does not apply if the failure of the employer to provide work is because of industrial action by his employees or if the employee has been offered suitable alternative work but has refused it. In order to qualify for a guarantee payment, an employee must have been continuously employed for one month ending with the day before the workless day.

An employee can only receive a payment for five workless days during any period of three months. The effect of this is that in order to get payment for a day of lay-off the three months before that day of lay-off must be looked at to see whether the employee has already received the maximum five days' guarantee pay. If the lay-off was, for example, on 20 June and the worker had been paid for lay-offs on 5 June, 27 May, 21 May, 4 April, and 2 April, he would not be entitled to a payment, but he would for a lay-off on 3 July.

An employee can go to a tribunal if the employer fails to pay all or part of a guarantee payment which the employee should have had. The tribunal can order the employer to pay it. The employee must apply to a tribunal within three months of the workless day or within such longer period as the tribunal thinks reasonable if it is satisfied that it was not reasonable or practicable for the employee to present the claim in three months.

To pay during statutory time off

The ERA 1996 gives employees certain rights to time off work. In **two** cases the employee is also entitled to be paid during the time off. These situations are dealt with here as part of the law relating to the right to be paid. They are:

1 Time off with pay for carrying out union duties. Sections 168 to 173 of the Trade Union and Labour Relations (Consolidation) Act 1992 apply and provide that officials, e.g. branch officers and shop stewards, of a recognised and independent trade union must be given paid time off in order to carry out their duties as union officials. These include negotiation with the employer and representing members in disciplinary matters but not, perhaps obviously, lobbying Parliament in regard to unwanted legislation as in *Luce* v *Bexley London Borough Council* (1990). Paid time off must also be given to union officials to take training in aspects of industrial relations **which are relevant to matters for which the union is recognised by the employer.** An independent trade union is a union which is not dominated or controlled by the employer and is not liable to interference by the employer as some staff associations are.

It will be noted therefore that trade union officials will be allowed paid time off for core union activities, such as collective bargaining with management. The employee is entitled to be paid his normal hourly rate.

If there is a breach by the employer of this duty, the employee may complain to a tribunal which may declare the employee's rights in its order, so that the employer may carry them out, and may also award money compensation.

One of the most recent significant cases in the area of trade union law is *Aslef* v *the United Kingdom* (2007). The ECJ case concerns the freedom of trade unions under the UK law to expel or exclude individuals on the grounds of their political party membership, and the Court concluded that the relevant part of the UK law violated Article 11 of the European Convention on Human Rights (peaceful assembly and to freedom of association with others, including the right to form and to join trade unions for the protection of his interests). The government reaffirmed that the Trade Union and Labour Relations (Consolidation) Act 1992 needs to be amended. The amendment was introduced through the passing of the Employment Act 2008.

Trade union learning representatives

These workers have a right to take unpaid time off under s 168A of the Trade Union and Labour Relations (Consolidation) Act 1992 (inserted by the Employment Act 2002). The learning representatives' main function is to advise union members about their training and educational and development needs. The advice is usually given at the place of work, sometimes through face-to-face meetings with individuals.

Union members are entitled to unpaid time off to consult their learning representatives and are protected against victimisation for taking advantage of the right to consult.

2 Redundant employees. An employee who has been continuously employed by his employer for at least two years and who is given notice of dismissal because of redundancy has a right before the period of his notice expires to reasonable time off during working hours so that he can look for another job or make arrangements for training for future employment.

While absent, the employee is entitled to be paid but not more than two-fifths of a weeks' pay in respect of the time taken off. If the employer fails to pay at least this sum, the employee can complain to a tribunal within three months. The compensation awarded by the tribunal is limited to two-fifths of a weeks' pay. Anything the employer has paid is set off against the compensation.

Other cases

There are other circumstances in which employees are entitled to paid time off. Some of these are set out below:

- pregnant employees who require time off for antenatal care;
- employee/pension fund trustees under the Pensions Act 1995 who are allowed paid time off so that they may perform their duties and undergo relevant training;
- where, in a redundancy situation, the employer is to consult with worker representatives instead of, or as well as, a trade union representative the elected worker representatives are entitled to reasonable time off with pay during normal working hours to carry out their duties as representatives and to seek election;
- similar provisions apply also to employee safety representatives;
- the ERA 1996 (as amended by the Teaching and Higher Education Act 1998) gives employees aged 16 to 18 the right to take reasonable paid time off work in order to study or train for a designated qualification by a specified awarding body. These rights are enforceable by way of complaint to an employment tribunal and dismissal for asserting these rights is automatically unfair, so that no minimum period of service is required.

In all cases the right is to 'reasonable' time off in all the circumstances of the case.

Itemised pay statements

Under the ERA 1996 itemised pay statements must be provided for employees regardless of service, and whether they ask for them or not. It is an absolute right, said the EAT in *Coales* v *John Woods and Co* (*Solicitors*) (1986). All workers are entitled to a statement, including part-timers.

Under the Act the employee must receive a statement at the time of or before receiving pay, showing gross pay and take-home pay and the variable deductions, e.g. income tax, which make up the difference between the two figures. Details of how it is paid must also be given, e.g. is it contained in the pay packet or has it been credited to a bank account?

Fixed deductions, e.g. savings or repayment of a season ticket loan, need not be itemised every pay day. If the employer gives the employee a separate statement setting out the fixed deductions, this may simply be shown as a lump sum in the weekly/monthly pay statement. This fixed deduction statement must be updated in writing if it is changed and in any case it must be reissued every 12 months.

If the employer does not comply with the pay statement requirements, the employee can complain to a tribunal which will make a declaration of the law that a statement should have been given and as to what it should have included. The employer must comply with this declaration. In addition, the tribunal may order the employer to give back to the employee any deductions which were made from the employee's pay and which were not notified to him during the 13 weeks before the date of the application by the employee to the tribunal.

It is worth noting that the section is penal, i.e. in the nature of a penalty, and so where, for example, an employer has deducted tax and paid it over to HMRC but has not given the employee a written statement, he can be made to pay the employee the deductions made up to 13 weeks, *even though this means he has paid twice* (see *Cambiero* v *Aldo Zilli* (1998)).

If the particulars are complete but the employee wishes to question the accuracy of what has been deducted, then this is a contractual matter which can be dealt with by an employment tribunal:

- if the employment has ended; or
- if the employer's action amounts to an unlawful deduction from pay, as where the employee has not consented to a deduction for alleged shortages in cash received for sales.

Otherwise, the matter must be taken before a civil court, e.g. the county court.

Method of payment and deductions from pay

Under the ERA 1996 employees no longer have a right to be paid in cash. The Truck Acts 1831–1940, which used to give this right, are repealed. Payment may still, of course, be made in cash, but an employer can if he wishes pay the employee, for example, by cheque or by crediting the employee's bank account by credit transfer. It should be noted, however, that if a worker was paid in cash before 1987 when the repeal came into force the method of payment may only be changed if the worker agrees to a variation of the contract of service.

Deductions from pay are unlawful unless they are:

1 authorised by Act of Parliament, such as income tax and national insurance deductions; or

2 contained in a written contract of employment or the worker has previously signified in writing his agreement or consent to the making of them. In *Discount Tobacco and Confectionery Ltd* v *Williamson* (1993) the Employment Appeal Tribunal (EAT) held that deductions from an employee's pay in regard to stock shortages will be legal only if they relate to losses that occurred *after* the employee gave written consent. If not, the deductions are invalid and must be repaid to the employee. Deductions from the wages of workers in the retail trade, e.g. petrol station cashiers, for stock and cash shortages are limited to 10 per cent of the gross wages and deductions may be made only within the period of 12 months from the date when the employer knew or ought to have known of the shortage. Outstanding amounts may be recovered from a final pay packet when the employee leaves even though the deduction exceeds 10 per cent.

These provisions are enforceable by the employee against the employer in employment tribunals.

Low pay

Reference has already been made to the National Minimum Wage Act 1998 and to the functions of the Low Pay Commission.

Employer's duty to provide work

There is, *in general*, no duty at common law for an employer to provide work. If the employer still pays the agreed wages or salary, the employee cannot regard the employer as in breach of contract. The employee has no right to sue for damages for wrongful dismissal but must accept the pay. The main authority for this is *Collier* v *Sunday Referee* (1940) where Mr Justice Asquith said: 'If I pay my cook her wages she cannot complain if I take all my meals out.'

There are some exceptions at common law. For example, a salesperson who is paid by commission must be allowed to work in order to earn that commission and if he is not his employer is in breach of contract and can be sued for damages. This is also the case with actors and actresses because they need to keep a public image which requires occasional public performances.

However, in *William Hill Organisation Ltd* v *Tucker* (1998) the Court of Appeal decided that there could be a duty to provide work beyond the traditional bases for it, i.e. publicity-based careers and commission-based remuneration. The case would appear to extend the common law duty to provide work (in this case during a long six-month notice period) to all skilled workers who may need work to preserve and enhance their skills. If in such a situation an employer wishes to pay the employee but not allow him to work out the notice, there must be a specific provision in the contract to that effect. Otherwise, the employer may be in breach of contract which would allow the employee to leave at once so that the employer loses the advantage of delaying the employee's competition straightaway, which these long notice periods are designed to postpone.

Employee's property

An employer has in fact no duty to protect his employee's property.

Deyong v *Shenburn* (1946)

The claimant entered into a contract of employment with the defendant under which the claimant was to act the dame in a pantomime for three weeks. Rehearsals took place at a theatre and on the second day the claimant had stolen from his dressing room his overcoat as well as two shawls and a pair of shoes forming part of his theatrical equipment. In the county court the judge found that the defendant had been negligent in failing to provide a lock on the dressing room door and having no one at the stage door during the morning of the particular rehearsal day to prevent the entry of unauthorised persons. However, the county court judge decided that the defendant was under no duty to protect the clothing. The claimant appealed to the Court of Appeal which also decided that the defendant was not liable. The Court of Appeal accepted that if there was an accident at work caused by the employer's negligence, then in an action for personal injury the employee could also include damage to his clothing if there had been any. In addition, if in such an accident the employee's clothes were, say, torn off his back but he suffered no personal injury, then it would seem that he could be entitled to recover damages in respect of the loss of his clothes. However, outside of this an employer has no duty to protect the property of his employee.

Comment. This decision was also applied in the later case of *Edwards v West Herts Group Hospital Management Committee* (1957) where the claimant, a resident house physician at the defendants' hospital, had some articles of clothing and personal effects stolen from his bedroom at the hostel where he was required to live. He brought an action for breach of an implied duty under his contract of employment to protect his property. His action was dismissed in the county court and his appeal to the Court of Appeal was also dismissed on the basis that there was no such contractual duty in respect of property.

Employee's indemnity

An employer is bound to indemnify (that is, make good) any expenses, losses and liabilities incurred by an employee while carrying out his duties.

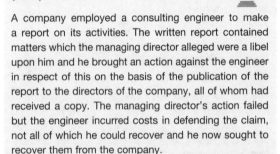

Re Famatina Development Corporation Ltd (1914)

A company employed a consulting engineer to make a report on its activities. The written report contained matters which the managing director alleged were a libel upon him and he brought an action against the engineer in respect of this on the basis of the publication of the report to the directors of the company, all of whom had received a copy. The managing director's action failed but the engineer incurred costs in defending the claim, not all of which he could recover and he now sought to recover them from the company.

The Court of Appeal decided that the comments made in the report were within the scope of the engineer's employment. His terms of engagement required him to report fully and frankly and in the circumstances he was entitled to the indemnity.

Comment. There is no duty to indemnify an employee against liability for his own negligence. Thus, if by negligence an employee injures a third party in the course of employment and the third party sues the employee, the employer is not required to indemnify the employee and, indeed, if the employer is sued as vicariously liable (see later in this chapter) he has a right to an indemnity against the employee. This was decided in *Lister v Romford Ice and Cold Storage Ltd* (1957), though the action is unlikely to be brought because it upsets industrial relations.

Trade union matters – recognition

Employers were free to decide for themselves whether they wished to recognise trade unions regardless of the wishes of their employees, and irrespective of the level of union membership among their workers. Under the provisions of the Employment Relations Act 1999, which are in force, employers will have to recognise trade unions where a majority of those voting in a ballot and at least 40 per cent of those eligible to vote are in favour of recognition. Organisations employing fewer than 21 workers will be exempt. However, in those organisations where more than 50 per cent of the workers are members of the union, there will be automatic recognition on the grounds that there is a manifest demonstration that the employees wish to be represented by the union for the purposes of collective bargaining. The Employment Relations Act 1999 gives protection against dismissal for those campaigning on behalf of recognition and unions will be allowed reasonable access to the workforce to seek their support and to inform employees about ballots. Those who employ less than 21 workers are exempt.

The compulsory recognition provisions give trade unions the right to negotiate on matters relating to pay, hours of work and holidays. Union recognition also gives the union, through its representatives, the right to be consulted on redundancies and on a transfer of business and to accompany a worker at a grievance or disciplinary hearing. In addition, the employer must respond to requests for information about the business which the union needs for collective bargaining.

However, whether or not there is a recognised union, the Trade Union and Labour Relations (Consolidation) Act 1992 gives employees the right to belong or not to belong to a trade union and whether or not that or any other union is recognised by the employer, individuals are given some basic protection against being penalised because they are or are not or have been members of a trade union. These are set out below.

Trade union matters – employment protection

Under the Trade Union and Labour Relations (Consolidation) Act 1992 employers have a duty not to take action against employees, including dismissal and selection for redundancy, just because they are members of, or take part in at an appropriate time the activities of, a trade union which is independent of the employer. According to the decision in *Post Office v Union of Post Office Workers* (1974), this includes activities on the employer's premises. Under the provisions of s 152 of the 1992 Act dismissal for failure to join a trade union is always automatically unfair even if there is a closed shop situation within the industry concerned. This provision greatly weakens the maintenance by trade unions of closed shops.

If action is taken against employees, they may complain to a tribunal which can award money compensation or make an order saying what the trade union rights of the employee are so that the employer can grant them in the future. If the employee has been dismissed, the unfair dismissal remedies apply.

In addition, s 137 of the 1992 Act gives job seekers a right not to be refused employment or the services of an employment agency on the grounds that they are or are not trade union members. Any individual who believes that he or she has been unlawfully refused employment or the services of an employment agency because of union or non-union membership can complain to a tribunal within three months of refusal. If the case is made out, the tribunal can award compensation.

The compensation will generally be paid by the employer or employment agency concerned but in cases where a trade union is joined as a party and the tribunal decides that the unlawful refusal resulted from pressure applied by the union where the employee refused to join the union it may order the union to pay some or all of the compensation. The tribunal can also recommend that the prospective employer or employment agency should take action to remedy the adverse effect of their unlawful action on the complainant.

In *Harrison* v *Kent County Council* (1995) it was held that an employer's refusal to employ an applicant because of his previous activities in another post could amount to an unlawful refusal of employment on grounds of union membership.

Time off work without pay

Under the ERA 1996 employees have a right to time off work in certain circumstances. Sometimes they are also entitled to pay, as in the case of trade union officials and of redundant employees who are looking for work or wanting to arrange training for another job. These and other cases have already been looked at as part of the law relating to pay. However, there are other cases in which employees are entitled to time off but the employer is not under a duty to pay wages or salary for it. These are as follows:

1 Trade union activities. An employee who is a member of an independent trade union *which the employer recognises* is entitled to *reasonable* time off for trade union

activities. The employee is not entitled to pay unless he is a trade union official and the time off is taken under provisions previously considered. The Advisory, Conciliation and Arbitration Service (ACAS), a statutory body set up by the Employment Protection Act 1975 to promote, for example, the improvement of industrial relations, has published a *Code of Practice 3* which gives guidance on the time off which an employer should allow (the latest version came into effect in January 2010). *Paid time off* for *union officials* for union duties has already been considered.

2 Public duties. Employers also have a duty to allow employees who hold certain public positions and offices reasonable time off to carry out the duties which go along with them. Details are given in the ERA 1996 which covers such offices as magistrate, member of a local authority, member of an employment tribunal, and member of certain health and education authorities. There has more recently been an extension made by statutory instrument to cover members of boards of visitors and visiting committees for prisons, remand centres and young offender institutions.

Complaints in regard to failure to give time off under 1 and 2 above may be taken to an employment tribunal. In general the complaint must be made within three months of the date when the failure to give time off occurred. An employment tribunal may make an order declaring the rights of the employee so that these can be observed by the employer and may also award money compensation to be paid by the employer where there is injury to the employee, e.g. hurt feelings.

3 Family emergency. We have already considered this particular time off at p 487 ○.

Testimonials and references

There is no law which requires an employer to give a reference or testimonial to an employee or to answer questions or enquiries which a prospective employer may ask him. This was decided in *Carroll* v *Bird* (1800). An exception occurs where a reference is required by a regulatory body, such as the Financial Services Authority as part of its duty to ensure that financial services are handled only by authorised and competent persons.

However, if an employer does give a reference or testimonial, either orally or in writing, which is false, he commits a criminal offence under the Servants' Characters Act 1792. The employer may also be liable in civil law to pay damages to certain persons as follows:

1 To a subsequent employer, who suffers loss because of a false statement **known** to the former employer to be untrue (*Foster* v *Charles* (1830)), or made **negligently** without reasonable grounds for believing the statement to be true, because it was decided in *Lawton* v *BOC Transhield Ltd* (1987) that an employer who gives another employer a reference concerning an employee owes a duty of care in negligence to the recipient employer. It should be noted that if words of disclaimer such as 'This reference is given in good faith. No responsibility is accepted for any errors or omissions which it contains or for any loss or damage resulting from reliance on it' are used they will have to satisfy the test of 'reasonableness' under the Unfair Contract Terms Act 1977. A court might think such a clause reasonable in regard to a reference given to an employee expressing a view upon his ability to do a type of job which he had not done before.

The Rehabilitation of Offenders Act 1974 is also relevant here. The provisions of the Act are an attempt to give effect to the principle that when a person convicted of crime has been successfully living it down and has avoided further crime, his efforts at rehabilitation should not be prejudiced by the unwarranted disclosure of the earlier conviction.

The Act therefore prevents any liability arising from failure by an employee to disclose what is called a spent conviction to a prospective employer. For example, the Act removes the need to disclose convictions **resulting in a fine** recorded more than five years before the date of the reference or testimonial.

Sentences of imprisonment for life or of imprisonment for a term exceeding 30 months are not capable of rehabilitation. The rehabilitation period for a prison sentence exceeding six months but not exceeding 30 months is 10 years, and for a term not exceeding six months it is seven years or, as we have seen, if the sentence was a fine, it is five years.

If an employer does refer to a spent conviction in a testimonial or reference the employee may sue him for **libel** in the case of a written testimonial or reference, or **slander** where the testimonial or reference is spoken. The defence of justification, i.e. that the statement that there was a conviction is true, will be a defence for the employer only if he can show that he acted without malice.

While discussing the 1974 Act it is worth noting that it makes provision for questions by employers relating to a person's previous convictions to be treated as not applying to spent convictions.

The Act also provides that a spent conviction or any failure to disclose a spent conviction shall not be a proper ground for dismissing or excluding a person from any office, profession, or occupation, or employment, or for prejudicing him in any way in any occupation or employment.

However, the Rehabilitation of Offenders Act 1974 (Exceptions) (Amendment) Order 1986 (SI 1986/1249) allows those who employ persons who will have contact with those under 18 to ask, for example, questions designed to reveal even spent convictions, particularly any with a sexual connotation.

Certain employees are excluded from the 1974 Act and their convictions can be disclosed. Included in the exceptions are doctors, chartered and certified accountants, insurance company managers and building society officers (see SI 1975/1023 and SI 1986/2268).

2 To the former employee, for libel or slander if things have been stated in a testimonial or reference which damages the employee's reputation. However, the employer has the defence of qualified privilege, as it is called, so that he can speak his mind about the employee and so in order to get damages the employee would have to prove that the employer made the statement out of malice, as where there was evidence that the employer had a history of unreasonable bad treatment of the employee and knew that what he said or wrote was untrue. It is also possible, however, for the employee to sue the employer in negligence and there is then no defence of qualified privilege available to the employer, and the defence can be bypassed. The following case gives an illustration.

Spring v Guardian Assurance plc (1994)

Mr Spring failed to get three jobs for which he applied because of a bad reference given to him by the defendant employer. It stated that while he had been employed by the defendants as an insurance sales manager he had not managed the sales team fairly, and among other things had kept the best leads (i.e. client contacts) to himself. The person who prepared the reference on behalf of the company did so on the basis of internal memoranda though she was not malicious in any way. However, the judge found that there was a duty of care and that the claimant could base his case in negligence. There should have been a more rigorous check on the memoranda and it had been negligent not to do this. The statements made about Mr Spring were not in the view of the judge always justified and it was no defence to an action in negligence that the person preparing the reference may have honestly believed them.

This decision of the High Court was eventually affirmed by the House of Lords in 1994.

Given then that there is a claim in negligence for a breach of duty by the employer, what is the employer's duty of care? It was held in *Bartholomew* v *Hackney London Borough Council* (1999) that the duty imposed upon the employer is to ensure that the reference is fair, just and reasonable and that the employer should take all reasonable care to ensure that there is no misstatement. This duty applies, said the court in *Bartholomew*, even if the factual statements in the reference are correct. The overall impression must be fair.

In this connection, the Employment Appeal Tribunal has ruled that an employer was in fundamental breach of contract justifying a successful claim of constructive dismissal by revealing to a prospective employer in a reference complaints about the applicant which had not been disclosed to her. This blocked her progress in the financial services sector.

TSB Bank plc v *Harris* (2000)

H was a savings and investment adviser with the TSB. She received a final written warning following an incident in which she forged a client's initials on a corrected form entry. A number of unconnected complaints were made against her. In accordance with standard practice in the industry, these complaints were investigated without her knowledge. She applied for another job and told her prospective employer about the forgery. However, TSB supplied a reference in which it stated that 17 complaints had been made against her, four of which had been valid, and eight of which were still to be investigated. H was not offered the job. She resigned and claimed unfair constructive dismissal. The Employment Appeal Tribunal held that she had been constructively dismissed and that the dismissal was unfair. The fact that H had had no opportunity to refute the complaints was capable of being a fundamental breach of the implied term of trust and confidence.

If TSB supplied a reference, it had to be fair and reasonable. The fact that the procedure for investigating complaints was the standard one in the financial

services industry did not justify the misleading nature of the reference. Bald accuracy was not necessarily enough to make a reference reasonable. TSB could have ensured that H was not taken by surprise by the allegations being revealed for the first time in the arena of her application for another job. The fact that she had intended to leave in any case did not alter the fact that when she actually left she had no other job to go to.

Comment. If employers give references, they must ensure that they are not only truthful and accurate but also fair and reasonable. It is also worth noting that under the Data Protection Act 1998 an employee may be able to apply to the new employer for a copy of the reference.

3 What constitutes a satisfactory reference? If an employer offers a job 'subject to satisfactory references' which are then taken up, who decides whether or not the references are satisfactory? In *Wishart* v *National Association of Citizens' Advice Bureaux* (1990) the Court of Appeal said it was a matter for the potential employer. So, if the potential employer does not think the reference is satisfactory, it is not. **The test is a subjective one** but presumably the employer must be reasonable and not regard a perfectly good reference as unsatisfactory in order to get out of the contract made subject to the reference condition. It is better in any case not to make an offer of any kind until references are to hand.

4 Defacing references. Finally, an employee who maliciously defaces his own reference or testimonial commits a criminal offence under the Servants' Characters Act 1792.

References and discrimination

The Sex Discrimination Act 1975 (Amendment) Regulations 2003 (SI 2003/1657) insert into the 1975 Act s 20A that prohibits discrimination after the end of an employment (or partnership) relationship if the act is closely related to the relationship, e.g. unreasonable refusal to give a reference. The Race Relations Act 1976 (Amendment) Regulations 2003 (SI 2003/1626) deal in similar fashion with race discrimination cases as do the Religion and Belief (SI 2003/1660), Sexual Orientation (SI 2003/1661) and Age (SI 2006/1031) Regulations. Disability cases are covered by the Disability Discrimination Act 1995 (Amendment) Regulations 2003 (SI 2003/1673).

These can now be seen in the Equality Act 2010 – see s 108 of the Act.

References and data protection

The Information Commissioner has issued a good practice note on the giving and receiving of references. It is available at www.ico.gov.uk.
    The main points are as follows.

- The employer giving the reference is protected by Sch 7 to the Data Protection Act 1998. A reference given for the purposes of the education, training or employment of the data subject is 'exempt information' and need not be disclosed by the reference-giver to the person concerned. The recipient of the reference will, however, hold personal data on the relevant individual and must consider any request for a copy under the usual data protection rules on subject access. The subject of the reference is, however, only entitled to information about himself or herself and not information about other people including their opinions.
- The employer should not withhold information already known to the person concerned. Employment dates and absence records will be known to the person concerned and should be provided. Information relating to performance may also have been discussed with the subject of the reference as part of an appraisal system. These disclosures could be made even where a reference is marked 'in confidence'.
- Where it is not clear whether the subject of the reference knows about certain parts of the information the Commissioner advises that the receiving employer should contact the reference-giver and ask whether he or she objects to the information provided in the reference being given to the subject and, if so, why.

Non-contractual duties of the employer

Before leaving the contractual duties of the employer, it should be noted that he has other duties in regard to the health, safety and welfare of his employees. These are based mainly on the common law of tort and statutes such as the Health and Safety at Work etc. Act 1974. These duties will be considered later.

It is, however, appropriate at this point to deal with legislation concerning the monitoring of workplace communications.

Employee surveillance

The Telecommunications (Lawful Business Practice) (Interception of Communications) Regulations 2000 (SI 2000/2699) came into force in October 2000. They provide employers with lawful consent access to their employees' use of email and other communications in order to establish whether the use is related to business. In addition, the employer is enabled to record all communications without obtaining the consent of the employee for the following purposes: (1) to establish the existence of facts relevant to the business as by keeping records of transactions and other communications in situations where it is desirable to know the specific facts of the conversation; (2) to ascertain compliance with regulatory or self-regulatory practices or procedures applying to the business; (3) to demonstrate or ascertain standards that are or ought to be achieved by persons using the telecoms system, such as monitoring for quality control and/or staff training; (4) to prevent or detect crime; (5) to investigate and detect unauthorised use of the employer's telecoms systems; (6) to ensure the effective operation of the system as by monitoring for viruses or other matters that threaten the system.

Monitoring, but not recording, may also take place without consent in the following situations: (a) to determine whether or not the communications are relevant to the business as by checking email accounts to access business communications in staff absence; and (b) in regard to communications that are to a confidential, anonymous counselling or support helpline.

Businesses that wish to rely on the above exceptions are required to make all reasonable efforts to tell those who use their telecoms system that their communications might be intercepted. This applies only to the employer's own staff.

Note. The regulations are a significant relaxation of the prohibitions contained in the Regulation of Investigatory Powers Act 2000 and are made under a provision in the Act that allows the Secretary of State to side-step the general requirement of consent in the case of conduct where it is felt legitimate to dispense with consent.

Involvement of the Information Commissioner

The Information Commissioner has issued a *Practice Code* on employee monitoring. The main feature is to require employers to carry out an 'impact assessment' to ensure that monitoring of employees' communications takes place only in accordance with needs. Monitoring must be justified by ensuring that the benefits to the organisation outweigh any detriment to the employees concerned. The code does not support covert monitoring, which should be rare, but might be used for the prevention or detection of crime given that it has been authorised at the highest management level, and where there is a risk that the purpose would be frustrated by informing the employee.

Given the rather vague nature of the law and the code, employers will find that it is more efficient to have a compliant company surveillance policy and communicate it effectively to the employees.

Human rights

There is some input from Art 8 of the Convention on Human Rights. This gives a right of privacy that covers correspondence and the workplace. The case of *Halford v United Kingdom* (1997) is relevant. The European Court of Human Rights found that interception of Ms Halford's calls to her lawyer relating to a dispute with her employer, a police authority, from her office was a breach of her rights under Art 8.

Duties of an employee

To use reasonable skill and care in the work

The **common law** provides that an employee who claims to have a particular skill or skills but shows himself to be incompetent may be dismissed without notice. His employer can also raise the matter of the incompetence of the employee if the employer is sued under **statute law**, i.e. the ERA 1996 for unfair dismissal.

The common law also requires unskilled employees to take reasonable care in carrying out the job. However, they may be dismissed only if there is a serious breach of this implied term of the contract.

To carry out lawful and reasonable instructions

The law implies a term into a contract of employment which requires the employee to obey the lawful and reasonable instructions of his employer. However, an employee is not bound to carry out illegal acts. In *Gregory v Ford* (1951) one of the decisions of the court was that an employee could not be required to drive a vehicle which was not insured so as to satisfy the law set out in what is now the Road Traffic Act 1988. If the employee does refuse, he is not in breach of his contract.

The duty to give faithful service (or the duty of fidelity)

This is an implied term of a contract of employment. Certain activities of employees are regarded by the law as breaches of the duty to give faithful service. Thus, as we have seen, an employee who while employed copies the names and addresses of his employer's customers for use after leaving the employment can be prevented from using the information (*Robb v Green* (1895)).

However, the implied term relating to fidelity does not apply once the contract of employment has come to an end. Therefore, a former employee cannot be prevented under this implied term from encouraging customers of his former employer to do business with him, though he can be prevented from using actual lists of customers which he made while still employed. If an employer (A) wants to stop an employee (B) from trying to win over his, A's, **customers**, then the contract of employment between A and B must contain an **express** clause in restraint of trade preventing this. Such a clause must, as we have seen, be reasonable in time and area (see also Chapter 7 ⊙).

A former employee can, however, be prevented by the court from using his former employer's trade **secrets** or **confidential information** without a clause in the contract about restraint of trade.

However, as we have seen, the ruling of the Court of Appeal in *Pocton Industries Ltd v Michael Ikem Horton* (2000) stresses the importance to employers of putting **express terms** into their contracts of employment to control the use and disclosure of confidential information after the employment contract ends. The courts seem to prefer the contractual approach to the rather vague concept of the implied term. The contract can give more specific guidance to the court as to what is to be protected.

Confidential information

It is an implied term of a contract of service that the employee must not disclose **trade secrets**, e.g. a special way of making glass as in *Forster & Sons Ltd v Suggett* (1918), or **confidential information** acquired during employment. There is strictly no need for an express clause in the contract.

However, the use by an employee of knowledge of trade secrets and information cannot be prevented if it is just part of the total job experience. An employee cannot be prevented from using what he could not help but learn from doing the job.

Printers & Finishers v Holloway (No 2) (1964)

The claimants brought an action against Holloway, their former works manager, and others, including Vita-tex Ltd, into whose employment Holloway had subsequently entered. They claimed an injunction against Holloway and the other defendants, based, as regards Holloway, on an alleged breach of an implied term in his contract of service with the claimants that he should not disclose or make improper use of confidential information relating to the claimants' trade secrets. Holloway's contract did not contain an express covenant relating to non-disclosure of trade secrets.

The claimants were flock printers and had built up their own fund of 'know-how' in this field. The action against Vita-tex arose because Holloway had, on one occasion, taken a Mr James, who was an employee of Vita-tex Ltd, round the claimants' factory. Mr James' visit took place in the evening and followed a chance meeting between himself and Holloway. However, the plant was working and James did see a number of processes. It also appeared that Holloway had, during his employment, made copies of certain of the claimants' documentary material and had taken these copies away with him when he left their employment. The claimants wanted an injunction to prevent the use or disclosure of the material contained in the copies of documents made by Holloway.

The court held that the claimants were entitled to an injunction against Holloway so far as the documentary material was concerned, although there was no express term in his contract regarding non-disclosure of secrets.

However, the court would not grant an injunction restraining Holloway from putting at the disposal of Vita-tex Ltd his memory of particular features of the claimants' plant and processes. He was under no express contract not to do so and the court would not extend its jurisdiction to restrain breaches of confidence in this instance. Holloway's knowledge of the claimants' trade secrets was not readily separable from his general knowledge of flock printing.

An injunction was granted restraining Vita-tex Ltd from making use of the information acquired by Mr James on his visit.

It is worth noting that the above principles may not be applied where there is an *express* restraint of trade in the contract. In *SBJ Stevenson Ltd v Mandy* (1999) the High Court stated that whether information is confidential should be assessed by its *nature* and not by the way in which it has been *acquired*. It was unacceptable,

said the court, that an employee who has entered into a restrictive covenant as to confidentiality and soliciting of customers should be allowed to use information learned as part of doing the job even if at the time he acquired it he had no intention to misuse it.

The High Court's approach appears to be right. If not, nearly all express confidentiality restraints would be unenforceable. The High Court in *Mandy* was dealing with the insurance broking industry, which is highly competitive.

Before leaving the topic of confidentiality, three further points should be noted.

1 Setting up a competing business. If an employee leaves without giving the employer proper notice in order to set up a competing business or work for a competitor, the employer may be able to get an injunction to prevent the employee from acting in this way. The action is most useful where the employee has a contract requiring a long period of notice. Suppose that a senior manager in a business is employed under a contract which requires 12 months' notice and that the manager deals with the affairs of two important clients or customers. He or she resigns giving only one month's notice in order to set up in business and take the work of the two major clients or customers. There are no post-employment restraints of trade in the contract. In these circumstances it may be possible for the employer to get an injunction to prevent the setting up of the new business for 12 months. This principle was established in *Evening Standard Co Ltd v Henderson* (1987), though it is, of course, a relevant consideration in the employer's favour if he is prepared to pay the employee during the notice period even though he does not return to work.

The principle is sometimes referred to as 'garden leave' since the employee cannot go back to work and cannot work for another employer so he may prefer to tend his garden to pass the time!

It is necessary now to consider the 'garden leave' cases in the light of the Court of Appeal decision in *William Hill Organisation v Tucker* (1998) where the ruling was that if the court considered that the employee should be allowed to work out his notice even though he was not in the traditional categories, e.g. commission workers, then an injunction would not be granted unless there was an express term in the contract allowing the employer to pay but specifically to refuse to allow the employee to work.

2 Confidentiality in reverse. It is also of interest to note that while it is normal for employers to bring claims against employees to prevent them from using confidential information obtained in the employment, confidentiality works both ways. Thus, in *Dalgleish v Lothian and Borders Police Board* (1991) the Lothian Council asked the Board for details of the names and addresses of its employees so that the Council could identify community charge defaulters. The court granted the employees an injunction to prevent this. The information was confidential between employer and employee. As more and more people become concerned about data protection, this case shines a welcome light on the employee's right of privacy and the employer's duty not to infringe it by wrongful disclosure.

3 Whistleblowing. When discussing an employee's duty of confidentiality, mention should be made of the provisions of the Public Interest Disclosure Act 1998. The Act protects workers from being dismissed or penalised for disclosing information about the organisation in which they work that they reasonably believe exposes financial malpractice, miscarriages of justice, dangers to health and safety, and dangers to the environment. Disclosure may be made to an employer, but where the disclosure relates to the employer or there is danger of victimisation, it may be made, for example, to a regulator such as the Financial Services Authority for City frauds. Whistleblowers who are dismissed or otherwise victimised may complain to an employment tribunal.

A number of successful claims under the Public Interest Disclosure Act 1998 have been made (see e.g. *Fernandes* v *Netcom Consultants (UK) Ltd* (2000)). Mr Fernandes, the claimant, is an accountant and was employed by Netcom Consultants, a telecoms consultancy, as finance officer. Netcom is a subsidiary of the US XSource Corporation. As part of his job, Mr Fernandes checked expenses claims, including those of his boss Steven Woodhouse. It appeared that Mr Woodhouse failed to provide receipts to back up his claims and Mr Fernandes reported this matter to the US parent company. Despite making requests for supporting documents, Mr Woodhouse 'fobbed him off' with explanations but did not produce receipts. Mr Fernandes sent a fax to an official of the US company making clear his concerns but was instructed to destroy his copy of the fax and told, 'You must look after your butt.' Later Mr Woodhouse's expenses rose steeply but were still not backed by receipts. The company's cash flow was causing concern and Mr Fernandes complained by letter to the US parent company. He was later sacked from his £70,000-a-year post after being told by XSource that he had lost the respect of the US parent for not acting sooner! Mr Woodhouse remained in employment, but after investigation was asked to resign. Mr Fernandes complained to an employment tribunal in Reading and was found to be protected by the 1998 Act and, therefore, automatically unfairly dismissed. The tribunal said that the US company had made a clear attempt to intimidate and pressurise Mr Fernandes to resign to keep the matter quiet. Mr Fernandes' award was £290,000.

Even in the absence of legislation, it may still be a breach of contract for an employer to dismiss an employee for making or attempting to make disclosures of fraud. An employment tribunal has made an award of damages for breach of contract to a salesman who attempted to alert his employer to an alleged fraud in the organisation. He reported the matter to his managing director and was dismissed. He could not claim unfair dismissal because he did not have the required service, but was awarded damages for breach of contract (see *Re Richard Jordan* (1997)).

The Employment Appeal Tribunal has ruled that an employee's misconduct cannot amount to a public interest disclosure under the Public Interest Disclosure Act 1998, even if it is linked to the disclosure and is intended to show that the employee's concerns are reasonable.

Bolton School v Evans (2006)

An employee of the school hacked into its computer system to demonstrate security flaws and told his employer. The EAT ruled that hacking into the system could not amount to a protected disclosure. The legislation protected disclosure but not other conduct on the part of the employee, even though it was connected with the disclosure. The law did not protect an employee who committed misconduct in the hope of finding evidence to support his or her allegations.

Thus, when the employer disciplined the employee for misconduct, it did not subject him to a detriment for making a protected disclosure. Furthermore, the employee was not automatically unfairly dismissed when he resigned in response and made allegations of unfair dismissal.

The employment contract and shop workers

The Sunday Trading Act 1994, which came into force on 26 August 1994, repealed previous restrictions on Sunday trading. Recognising the impact of this on shop workers, Sch 4 to the Act provided them with new and important rights. These rights, which are now contained in the ERA 1996 (Part IV), are:

- not to be dismissed or made redundant for refusing to work on Sunday; and
- not to suffer a detriment for the same reason.

These rights extend to all shop workers in England and Wales if they are asked to do shop work on a Sunday. They are not available to Sunday-only workers.

The ERA 1996 defines a shop worker as an employee who is required or may be required by contract to work in or about a shop on a day when the shop is open to serve customers.

However, the worker need not actually serve customers and the provisions extend beyond sales assistants and check-out operators to clerical workers doing work related to the shop, managers and supervisors, cleaners, storepersons, shelf fillers, lift attendants and security staff. Even those employed by outside contractors (but not self-employed) could be covered as also could van drivers based at the store who deliver goods to customers.

A shop is defined as including any premises where any retail trade or business is carried on. This does not include the sale of meals, refreshments, or intoxicating liquor for consumption on the premises, e.g. public houses, cafés and restaurants, nor places preparing meals or refreshments to order for immediate consumption off the premises, e.g. take-aways.

The ERA 1996 defines two categories of shop workers:

- Protected shop workers, i.e. those employed as such when the Act came into force, and those taking up employment afterwards whose contracts do not require Sunday working.
- Opted-out shop workers, i.e. those who are employed after commencement of the Act under contracts which require them to work on Sundays but who opt out of this by giving three months' notice to the employer (see below).

Protected workers will have the rights immediately regardless as to whether they have previously agreed to a contract requiring them to work on a Sunday. No procedures are involved. They can simply decide they no longer wish to work on Sundays.

Protected workers are able to give up their right to refuse to work on Sundays but only if:

- the employer is given a written 'opting-in notice' which must be signed and dated and state expressly that they do not object to Sunday working or actually wish to work Sundays; and
- they then enter into an express agreement with the employer to work Sundays or on a particular Sunday.

Opted-out workers, i.e. those engaged after commencement of the Act or who have opted in to Sunday working, have the right to opt out. To do this they must give the employer a signed and dated written notice stating that they object to Sunday work. They then have to serve a three-month notice period. During this time they are still obliged to do Sunday work and if they refuse will lose statutory protection under the Schedule. However, they cannot be dismissed or made to suffer some other detriment merely because they have given an opting-out notice. After the period of three months has expired, the worker has a right not to do Sunday work.

The ERA 1996 provides that dismissal or redundancy of protected and opted-out workers will be regarded as unfair dismissal if the reason or principal reason was that the worker(s) concerned refused or proposed to refuse to work on Sundays.

The ERA also gives protected and opted-out workers the right not to be subjected to any other detriment, e.g. non-payment of seniority bonuses, for refusing to work on a Sunday. Under the ERA the rights set out above apply regardless of age, length of service or hours of work.

Employer's explanatory statement

The ERA 1996 provides that employers are required to give every shop worker who enters into a contractual agreement to work on Sundays after the new Act comes into force a written explanatory statement setting out their right to opt out. If an employer does not issue such a statement within two months of the worker entering into such a contractual agreement, the opt-out period is reduced from three months to one.

The ERA gives a prescribed form of statement to be given to employees (see Figure 16.2).

STATUTORY RIGHTS IN RELATION TO SUNDAY SHOP WORK

You have become employed as a shop worker and are or can be required under your contract of employment to do the Sunday work your contract provides for.

However, if you wish, you can give a notice, as described in the next paragraph, to your employer and you will then have the right not to work in or about a shop which is open once three months have passed from the date on which you gave the notice.

Your notice must –

> be in writing;
> be signed and dated by you;
> say that you object to Sunday working.

For three months after you give the notice, your employer can still require you to do all the Sunday work your contract provides for. After the three-month period has ended, you have the right to complain to an employment tribunal if, because of your refusal to work on Sundays on which the shop is open, your employer –

> dismisses you, or
> does something else detrimental to you, for example failing to promote you.

Once you have the rights described, you can surrender them only by giving your employer a further notice, signed and dated by you, saying that you wish to work on a Sunday or that you do not object to Sunday working and then agreeing with your employer to work on Sundays or on a particular Sunday.

Figure 16.2 Prescribed form of statement re Sunday shop work

Source: See, for example, http://www.direct.gov.uk/en/Employment/Employees/WorkingHoursAndTimeOff/DG_10028516

Other important provisions of the ERA are as follows:

- provisions under which an employer is not obliged to compensate the employee for loss of Sunday work, either in terms of extra hours or remuneration;
- provisions ensuring that an agreement between a shop worker and his or her employer cannot generally exclude the provisions of the ERA;
- provisions under which the dismissal of an employee for asserting a statutory right contained in the ERA is to be regarded as being automatically unfair.

The Deregulation and Contracting Out Act 1994 amended the Betting, Gaming and Lotteries Act 1963 to allow betting offices and bookmaking establishments to do business on Sundays. Workers are protected against unfair dismissal or victimisation if they object to working on Sunday. The provisions are largely the same as those set out above and are also contained in the ERA 1996. They apply to workers regardless of age, hours of work or length of service.

Vicarious liability: transfer of control

We have already considered, when describing the relationship between employer and employee, how such a relationship can come into being for the limited purpose of liability when a person A who is in general terms the employee of B may be regarded for the purposes of vicarious liability as being in the 'employment' of C. Consideration has been given to the latest movement in this area, which is, in appropriate circumstances, to find joint vicarious liability, as in the ruling of the Court of Appeal in *Viasystems Ltd* v *Thermal Transfer (Northern) Ltd* (2005). What follows is a description of the general law relating to vicarious liability.

Vicarious liability

Because of this principle of the law an employer is liable for damage caused to another person by his employee, **while the employee was carrying out his work** (or while he was in the course of employment, as it is called). The principle applies whether the injury was to an outsider or to a fellow employee (see further below). The employer is liable even though he was not in any way at fault and this rule, which seems at first sight to be unfair to the employer, is based upon **law** and **policy**.

So far as the law is concerned, employer and employee are regarded as **associated parties** in the business in which both are engaged. If the amount of work increases so that the owner of a business cannot do it all with his own hands, he must employ other hands and is in law responsible for the damage done by those hands as he would be for damage done by his own.

The point of policy is to provide the injured person with a defendant who is likely to be able to pay any damages which the court may award. An employer and the business generally profit from the employee's work and it is perhaps not entirely unreasonable that the employer should compensate those who are injured by the employee. The employer will normally insure against the risk of liability and of course the cost of that insurance is represented in the price at which the goods or services of the business are sold. Thus, in the end, the injured person is compensated by those members of the public who buy the goods or services.

It is worth noting here that under the Employers' Liability (Compulsory Insurance) Act 1969 an employer **must insure** himself against liability for bodily injury or disease sustained by employees and arising out of and in the course of their employment in Great Britain and so in effect in respect of injuries caused by his employees to fellow employees, but insurance is **not compulsory** (though highly advisable) in respect of injuries to outsiders.

Finally, it should be noted that the employee who actually caused the injury is always liable personally along with the employer, but of course the prime defendant is the employer because he has either insurance or other funds which the employee probably does not have.

The course of employment

Whether an employee was or was not acting in the course of employment when he brought about the injury for which the person injured wants to make the employer liable is a matter for the court to decide in each case. The decision is sometimes a difficult one to make and we may all from time to time disagree with a decision made by a judge in a particular case.

However, the following analysis of the cases gives some idea of the way in which the courts have dealt with this most important aspect of employers' liability.

1 Acts outside the contractual duties. If the employee is engaged on a private matter personal to him, the employer will not be liable for injuries caused by the employee during this time.

Britt v *Galmoye & Nevill* (1928)

Nevill was employed by Galmoye as a van driver. Nevill wanted to take a friend to the theatre after he had finished work and Galmoye lent Nevill his private motor car for this purpose. Nevill, by negligence, injured Britt and Britt's action against Galmoye was based upon vicarious liability so that it was necessary to deal with the matter in course of employment. The court decided that as the journey was not on Galmoye's business and Galmoye was not in control, he was not liable for Nevill's act.

Comment.

(i) Britt's case is a rather obvious example of an act outside the contract of service. However, sometimes the court is called upon to make a more difficult decision. In particular it should be noted that an employee does not make his employer liable by doing some act which is of benefit to the employer during the course of what is basically an outside activity. For example, in *Rayner* v *Mitchell* (1877) a van man employed by a brewer took, without permission, a van from his employer's stables in order to deliver a child's coffin at the home of a relative. While he was returning the van to the stables he picked up some empty beer barrels and was afterwards involved in an accident which injured Rayner. Rayner sued the van man's employer and it was held that the employer was not liable. The journey itself was unauthorised and was not converted into an authorised journey merely because the employee performed some small act for the benefit of his employer during the course of it.

(ii) In *Trotman* v *North Yorkshire County Council* (1999) the Court of Appeal held that acts of sexual misconduct by a deputy headmaster on male pupils while on a school trip abroad was a personal act and an independent course of conduct that was outside the scope of his employment (but see below).

(iii) In more recent times there has been a significant move by the courts towards greater employer liability in what might be called the 'acts personal to the employee' cases. In *Lister* v *Hesley Hall Ltd* (2001) the claimants were boys at a school for children with emotional difficulties. It was owned and managed by the defendant company. The company employed a warden and housekeeper to look after the claimants. He systematically abused them. They brought claims for personal injury against the company as vicariously liable for the acts of the warden. The case reached the House of Lords on Appeal. Their Lordships were faced by a defence that in essence stated that the warden in abusing the claimants was not acting in the course of his employment but was, in abusing the claimants, doing acts personal to himself. The abuse was no part of his employment. The employment merely gave him the *opportunity* to abuse the claimants. The House of Lords did not accept this defence. Whatever may be the grounds for this *fact* decision, it must be regarded as an essential background to the case that the employers were better able to pay any damages awarded to the claimants. Nevertheless, it would now seem to be the law that even though the act is not within the ordinary course of employment and where the employment merely gives the employee an *opportunity to commit the tortious act* the employer may nevertheless be held liable for it. A previous decision by the Court of Appeal in *Trotman v North Yorkshire County Council* (1999) that acts of sexual abuse were beyond the scope of employment so that the employer was not liable was overruled by the House of Lords in the *Lister* case.

(iv) The decision of the Court of Appeal in *Fennelly v Connex South Eastern Ltd* (2001) further liberalises the attitude of the courts to what can be regarded as within the scope of employment.

The facts of the case occurred at Bromley South railway station. Mr Fennelly had already shown his ticket to an inspector and refused to show it again to another inspector, a Mr Sparrow. There was an altercation that ended with Mr Sparrow assaulting Mr Fennelly by putting a headlock on him and dragging him down a few steps on the station stairway. On being sued as vicariously liable for the assault, Mr Sparrow's employer Connex was held not liable because the trial judge said that Mr Sparrow had become angry and 'was pursuing his own ends'. The Court of Appeal did not agree and found Connex liable. The judgment says that the High Court, from which the appeal was made, had taken too narrow a view of the facts. What had occurred would not have done so without Mr Sparrow's power given by his employers to inspect tickets while he was on his employer's premises. The downside of decisions like this is that the business employer, who is normally insured against these risks, has to pay higher insurance premiums. They are not helpful to the consumer either since the employer's insurance costs are normally passed on to the consumer by way of increased prices for the goods and/or services. The third party benefits, of course, but ultimately at the consumer's expense.

(v) A further and later example is to be found in the ruling of the Court of Appeal in *Mattis v Pollock (t/a Flamingo's Nightclub)* (2004). In that case the defendant ran a nightclub and employed a doorman. The defendant knew that the doorman was prepared to use physical force when carrying out his duties. The claimant became involved in an altercation with the doorman. Afterwards the doorman went home and armed himself with a knife. He returned to the vicinity of the nightclub intending to take revenge for the injuries he had received earlier. He attacked the claimant with the knife. The claimant's spinal cord was severed and he was rendered a paraplegic. The claimant sued the defendant as owner of the nightclub and so vicariously liable for the damage caused by the injuries.

The Court of Appeal ruled that the defendant was vicariously liable because:

- The doorman had been encouraged by the defendant to carry out his duties in an aggressive and intimidatory manner. This had included manhandling the customers.
- The stabbing represented the end of an incident that had started in the club. It could not in any fair or just sense be treated in isolation from the earlier events. It was not a separate and distinct incident.
- At the moment of the stabbing, the responsibility for the acts of the aggressive doorman that rested with the defendant had not been extinguished and so the defendant was vicariously liable.

2 Unauthorised ways of performing the contractual duties. The employer may be liable in spite of the fact that the employee was acting improperly if the act was, even so, part of his contractual duties.

Century Insurance Co v Northern Ireland Road Transport Board (1942)

The driver of a petrol tanker was engaged in transferring petrol to an underground tank when he lit a cigarette and threw the match to the floor. This caused a fire and an explosion which did great damage, and the question of the liability of the Board, his employer, for that damage arose. The court decided that the employer was liable for the driver's negligence. His negligence was not independent of the contract of service but was a negligent way of discharging his actual duties under that contract of service.

3 Acts which the employer has forbidden the employee to do. Just because an employer has told his employee not to do a particular act does not always excuse the employer from vicarious liability if the employee causes damage when doing the forbidden act. There are two sorts of cases, as follows:

(a) *Where the act itself is forbidden.*

Joseph Rand Ltd v Craig (1919)

The defendants' employees were taking rubbish from a site and depositing it on the defendants' dump. They were working on a bonus scheme related to the number of loads per day which they dumped. The defendants had strictly forbidden their employees to tip the rubbish elsewhere than on the authorised dump. However, some of the employees deposited their loads on the claimants' property which was nearer. The defendants were sued on the basis that they were vicariously liable in trespass, the claimants arguing that the employees had general authority to cart and tip rubbish. The court decided that the defendants were not liable. The employees were employed to cart the rubbish from one definite place to another definite place. Shooting the rubbish on to the claimants' premises was a totally wrongful act not directly arising out of the duties that they were employed to perform.

Comment. A contrast is provided by *Rose v Plenty* (1976). Leslie Rose, aged 13, liked helping Mr Plenty, a milkman, to deliver the milk. Cooperative Retail Services Ltd, who employed Mr Plenty, expressly forbade their milkmen to take boys on their floats or to get boys to help them deliver the milk. On one occasion, while helping Mr Plenty, Leslie was sitting in the front of the float when his leg caught under the wheel. The accident was caused partly by Mr Plenty's negligence. The court decided that Mr Plenty had been acting in the course of his employment so that his employers were liable to compensate Leslie Rose for his injuries. There is really quite a difference in the facts of this case and those in *Rand*. Leslie Rose's presence on the milk float was connected with the delivery of the milk which was a reason connected with the employment and this seems to be why the court decided as it did.

(b) *Where the employer's instruction relates only to the way in which the contractual duty is to be done.* Obviously, perhaps, an employer cannot avoid liability by saying to his employees: 'Do your job in such a way as not to injure anyone.'

Limpus v London General Omnibus Co (1862)

The claimant's bus was overturned when the driver of the defendants' bus drove across it so as to be first at a bus stop to take all the passengers who were waiting. The defendants' driver admitted that the act was intentional and arose out of bad feeling between the two drivers. The defendants had issued strict instructions to their drivers that they were not to obstruct other omnibuses. The court decided that the defendants were liable. Their driver was acting within the scope of his employment at the time of the collision, and it did not matter that the defendants had expressly forbidden him to act as he did.

4 Employee's fraudulent acts. At first the courts would not make an employer liable for the fraudulent acts of his employee. Gradually, however, they began to accept that the employer could be liable, first in cases where the employee's fraud was committed for the employer's benefit, and later even in cases where the fraud was carried out by the employee entirely for his own ends, as the following case shows.

Lloyd v Grace, Smith & Co (1912)

Smith was a Liverpool solicitor and Lloyd was a widow who owned two properties at Ellesmere Port and had also lent money on mortgage. She was not satisfied with the income from these investments and she went to see Smith's managing clerk, Sandles, for advice. He told her to sell the properties and call in the mortgages, and reinvest the proceeds. At his request she signed two deeds which, unknown to her, transferred the properties and the mortgage to him. Sandles then mortgaged the properties and transferred the other mortgages for money and paid a private debt with the proceeds. The court decided that the firm of solicitors was vicariously liable for Sandles' fraudulent acts. An employer could be vicariously liable for a tort committed by an employee entirely for his own ends.

Comment.
(i) This decision seems to contain at least some public policy and to be based on the principle that since someone must be the loser by reason of the fraud of the employee, it is more reasonable that the employer who engages and puts trust and confidence in the fraudulent employee should be the loser rather than an outsider.

(ii) Where the basis of a particular decision is public policy then circumstances can alter cases. When, as distinct from a 'consumer' situation as seen in the above case, the scenario is business the court may reach the conclusion that the act is within the course of employment but the fraud is not so that the employer is not liable for it. This was the attitude taken by the Court of Appeal in *Generale Bank Nederland NV v Export Credits Guarantee Department* (1997) where an employee of the Department had assisted in a fraudulent operation to obtain export guarantees which caused loss to the bank. The Department was not liable.

5 Employee's criminal acts. An employer may even be vicariously liable for a criminal act by his employee. The criminal act may be regarded as in the course of employment so that the employer will be liable at civil law for any loss or damage caused by the employee's criminal act.

Morris v C W Martin & Sons Ltd (1965)

The claimant sent a mink stole to a furrier for the purpose of cleaning. With the claimant's consent the furrier gave it to the defendants to clean. While it was in the possession of the defendants the fur was stolen by a person called Morrisey, who had been employed by the defendants for a few weeks only, though they had no grounds to suspect that he was dishonest. The claimant sued the defendants for damages for the tort of conversion. The county court judge held that the act of Morrisey, who had removed the stole by wrapping it around his body, was beyond the scope of his employment.

The Court of Appeal, however, decided that the defendants were liable to the claimant because Morrisey had been entrusted with the stole in the course of his employment.

Comment.

(i) The above rule applies only in circumstances where the employee is entrusted with, or put in charge of, the goods by his employer.

The mere fact that the employee's employment gives him the opportunity to steal goods is not enough. Thus, in *Leesh River Tea Co v British India Steam Navigation Co* (1966) a person employed to unload tea from a ship stole a brass cover plate from the hold of the ship while he was unloading the tea and the court decided that he was not acting in the course of his employment on the grounds that his job had nothing to do with the cover plate.

Perhaps if the plate had been stolen by someone who was sent to clean it, then that person would have been acting within the course of employment and his employer might well have been liable.

(ii) The fraudulent or criminal act must be committed as part of the employment, that is as an act within the scope of employment. In *Heasmans v Clarity Cleaning* (1987) the Court of Appeal decided that the defendants were not liable when their employee, who was sent to the claimant's premises to clean phones, made unauthorised calls on them to the value of £1,400. He was employed to *clean* phones not to *use* them.

6 Corporations and the *ultra vires rule*. Where the employer is a corporation there are further difficulties as regards the corporation's vicarious liability, because the act which the employee does when he causes injury may be beyond the corporation's powers, or *ultra vires*, i.e. beyond the scope of what its constitution says it can do, though little if anything would be beyond the scope of a company which had adopted the 'one line objects clause' approach as a general commercial company (see further, Chapter 6 ○). This constitution may, as we have seen, be a statute or a charter, as with a professional body, such as the Institute of Chartered Secretaries and Administrators, or the objects clause of the memorandum in the case of a registered company. It is necessary, therefore, to distinguish between those acts of employees which are within the company's powers (*intra vires*) and outside its powers (*ultra vires*).

(a) *Intra vires activities.* If an employee of a corporation injures someone by negligence while acting in the course of his employment in an *intra vires* activity, then the corporation is liable. Although it has been said that any wrongful act committed on behalf of a corporation must be *ultra vires* since the corporation has no authority in its constitution to commit wrongful acts, this view has not been accepted by the courts. Therefore, a corporation can have liability in law without capacity in law.

A corporation is liable, therefore, under the rule of vicarious liability, for injuries caused by its employees on *intra vires* activities. Thus, a bus company which is, obviously, authorised by its memorandum to run buses, will be liable if an employee injures a pedestrian while driving a bus along its routes.

(b) *Ultra vires activities.* A corporation will not be liable if one of its employees gets involved in an act which is *ultra vires* the corporation unless he has **express authority** from management to do the act.

Poulton v London & South Western Railway Co (1867)

The claimant was arrested by a station master for non-payment of carriage in respect of his horse. The defendants, who were the employers of the station master, had power to detain passengers for non-payment of their own fare, but for no other reason. The court decided that since there was no express authorisation of the arrest by the defendants, the station master was acting outside the scope of his employment and the defendants were not liable for the wrongful arrest.

Comment.

(i) A contrast is provided by *Campbell v Paddington Borough Council* (1911). The members of the Council had passed a resolution authorising the erection of a stand in Burwood Place, London, in order that members of the Council could view the funeral procession of King Edward VII passing along the Edgware Road. The claimant, who had premises in Burwood Place, often let them so that people could view public processions passing along the Edgware Road. The Council's stand obstructed the view of the funeral procession from the claimant's house and she could not let the premises for that purpose. The court decided that the Council was liable. The fact that the erection of the stand was probably *ultra vires*, since there was no specific power in the Council's charter to put one up, did not matter. There had been authorisation by the Council resolution.

(ii) So far as registered companies are concerned, the Companies Act 1989 made amendments to the Companies Act 1985 (see now Companies Act 2006) under which a company may alter its objects by special resolution, or be registered with objects, which state merely that it is to carry on business as a general commercial company so that it may carry on any trade or business whatsoever. The company also has power to do all such things as are incidental or conducive to that end without listing those powers.

Such a company will have effectively opted out of the *ultra vires* rule so that its employees are likely always to be engaged on *intra vires* activities so long as they are within the scope of their employment. The company will of course continue to escape liability where the employee is doing something he is not employed to do, as in *Heasmans v Clarity Cleaning* (1987) (above).

In addition, companies formed under the Companies Act 2006 need not state their objects on registration. They may do so voluntarily in the articles (not the memorandum as before) and so for business or commercial companies the matter of *ultra vires* does not arise.

The old principles of *ultra vires* will continue to apply to charter and statutory companies.

Employer's defences

There are three main defences which an employer may have if he is sued under the rule of vicarious liability. These are set out below:

1 An exclusion clause in a contract or notice. Because of the Unfair Contract Terms Act 1977, an employer, like other people, cannot exclude or reduce his liability for **death or bodily injury** caused by his own negligence or that of his employees. As regards other types of damage, such as damage to property, an exemption clause in a contract or a notice will apply to exclude or reduce the liability, but only if the court thinks that it is **reasonable** that this should happen.

Thus, in the case of a dry-cleaning contract, if by the negligence of employees cleaning material is not properly removed so that the owner of the clothing contracts a skin disease, to which he is not especially susceptible, no exclusion clause in the contract for cleaning or in a notice in the shop can remove or restrict the employer's liability for this bodily harm.

However, if the clothing is, by reason of an employee's negligence, merely damaged and there is no resulting physical injury, then an exclusion clause or notice might operate to remove or restrict the liability of the employer if the judge thought it was reasonable for it to do so in the circumstances.

Although the Act gives no criteria for what is reasonable and it is a matter to be decided by the judge in each case, it would be generally true to say that the device of an exclusion clause in a contract or notice has lost a lot of its force as an employer's defence (see further, Chapter 9 ◯).

As regards the position of the employee where the employer has taken an exemption clause in the contract, e.g. for damage to the other party's property while in the course of transit, then although such a clause may be effective to exempt the employer, it has not protected the employee who is not in privity of contract with the third party. Reference should now be made to the Contracts (Rights of Third Parties) Act 1999 under which the parties to the contract, i.e. the employer and the third party, may, if they wish, extend the exemption clause to the employee or the court may infer that this has been done unless the original parties have expressly excluded third party (i.e. the employee's) rights.

2 Voluntary assumption of risk. This defence is also referred to as *volenti non fit injuria* (to one who is willing no harm is done). This defence is most often tried in employment cases when employees sue their employers for injuries received at work. We will have a look at these cases later in this chapter. However, the defence is available to an employer when an outsider sues him on the basis of vicarious liability for injury caused by his employees.

Cutler v United Dairies (London) Ltd **(1923)**

The defendants' employee left the defendants' horse and van, two wheels only being properly chained, while he delivered milk. The horse, being startled by the noise coming from a river steamer, bolted down the road and into a meadow. It stopped in the meadow and was followed there by the employee who, being in an excited state, began to shout for help. The claimant, who had seen all of this, went to the employee's assistance and tried to hold the horse's head. The horse lunged and the claimant was injured. The claimant sued the defendants alleging negligence because apparently the horse was given to bolting and should not have been used on a milk round at all.

The court decided that in the circumstances the claimant voluntarily and freely assumed the risk. This was not an attempt to stop a runaway horse so that there was no sense of urgency to require the claimant to act as he did. He therefore knew of the risk and had had time to consider it and by implication must have agreed to incur it.

Comment. A different situation arises in what are known as the rescue cases. In these the claimant is injured while trying to save life or property which has been put in danger by the defendant's negligence. If the intervention is a reasonable thing to do for the saving of life or property, then this does not constitute an assumption of risk, nor does the defence of contributory negligence (see below) apply. Cutler, of course, was not effecting a rescue.

---

3 Contributory negligence. Sometimes when an injury occurs the person injured and the person causing the injury have both been negligent. In such a situation liability can be divided between the person injured and the person causing the injury.

The person injured can still claim damages but under the Law Reform (Contributory Negligence) Act 1945 they will be reduced according to how much the court thinks he was to blame. Thus, if the court thinks that A who has been injured by B's negligence is entitled to £1,000 but is 60 per cent to blame for the injury, it will deduct £600 from A's damages so that he will get only £400.

Again, this defence is most often used where an employee is suing his employer for injuries received at work and the employer claims that the employee was partly to blame and his damages should be reduced. This situation has yet to be looked at. However, an employer, A, who was sued as vicariously liable for injuries caused by employee B to a person who was not an employee, C, could, in the right circumstances, claim that the damages given to C should be reduced because of C's contributory negligence.

Employer's liability for injuries to his employees

In addition to the duties of an employer under the contract of service with which we have been dealing so far, an employee who is injured at work by a negligent act will want to sue his employer for damages. Under the Employers' Liability (Compulsory Insurance) Act 1969 an employer **must** insure himself in respect of liability for injuries caused to his employee where these arise from a negligent act.

These employee claims are brought on the basis of negligence by the employer and, because of the decision of the House of Lords in *Wilsons and Clyde Coal Co v English* (1938), the employer's duties towards his employees, i.e. the duty to take care which he owes them, can be set out under the headings which appear below.

Safe plant, appliances and premises

An employer has a duty to provide and maintain suitable plant, appliances and premises.

Lovell v Blundells and Crompton & Co Ltd (1944)

Lovell was told by the defendants, who were his employers, to carry out an overhaul of a ship's boiler tubes. He could not reach some of the tubes so he got some planks for himself and from them he made up his own staging. The planks were unsound and collapsed, injuring Lovell. The defendants had not provided any form of staging, nor had they laid down any system of working.

The court decided that the employers were liable in negligence. They had failed to supply plant in a situation where there was an obvious requirement for it.

Comment. Having supplied plant, an employer will be liable if the employee is injured by it by reason of the employer's failure to inspect and maintain it and remedy defects. Thus, in *Baker* v *James Bros and Sons Ltd* (1921) Baker, who was a commercial traveller employed by the defendant, had to travel in a particular district taking orders and for this purpose the defendant supplied him with a car. The starting gear was defective and Baker complained to the defendants several times about this but nothing was done. On one occasion when Baker was out taking orders he was badly injured while trying to start the car with the starting handle. The court decided that Baker was entitled to damages. His employers had failed to maintain the car as they should. In the circumstances Baker could not be regarded as having consented to run the risk of injury, nor could he be regarded as guilty of contributory negligence.

The Employer's Liability (Defective Equipment) Act 1969 puts liability on an employer who provides defective equipment to an employee which causes that employee injury. The employer's liability is strict, which means that he is liable even though he was not himself negligent, as where the injury was caused by the negligence of the organisation which made the equipment. However, this does not affect the employer's right to claim that the injury was caused by the contributory negligence of the employee. Where the defect in the equipment is the fault of the manufacturer, the employer, having been sued for damages by the employee, can himself sue the manufacturer to recover from him any damages awarded to the employee. The employee can also sue the manufacturer direct if he chooses to do so.

Safe system of work

An employer is required to set up a safe way of working. It is also the duty of an employer to enforce the safe system once having set it up. Thus, where an employee may suffer damage to his eyes by flying sparks, as in welding, the employer must provide goggles or a face guard and introduce a system of supervision to ensure, as far as he can, that the protective equipment is being used by the relevant workforce.

Sometimes the duty on the employer is a high one. For example, it was held in *Crouch* v *British Rail Engineering Ltd* (1988) that where the work which an employee does puts him **regularly** at risk of damage to the eyes then it is not enough to provide goggles from a central store at the workplace. Goggles must be given to the employee and form part of his tool kit which he carries with him. He should not be required to go and fetch goggles from the store each time the job he is doing requires him to protect his eyes by using goggles. His employer was held liable for damages because the employee, a maintenance engineer, was not given goggles 'into his hand'. His damages were not reduced because according to the court there was no contributory negligence (see below).

Problems of causation

One of the major developments in the liability of employers for injury to their employees came in the landmark ruling of the House of Lords in *Fairchild* v *Glenhaven Funeral Services Ltd* (2002). The House of Lords ruled that where a claimant has contracted a disease from exposure to asbestos over a period of time during which he has had several employers, all of whom may have in some degree exposed him to asbestos, the claimant may claim against any one of them for the full amount of the damage, leaving the employer who has paid to seek a contribution from the other employers who may have been involved and settle the amount of contribution on the basis of what is decided to be the culpability of each of them. This greatly simplifies the matter for the claimant, who might otherwise have difficulty in establishing which employers were liable and to what extent. However, the House of Lords did not follow *Fairchild* in a later case where a differently constituted House took the view that it was fairer that each employer should be liable only for his share of the damage (see *Barker* v *Saint Gobain Pipelines plc* (2006)).

The ruling in *Fairchild* was restored by s 3 of the Compensation Act 2006.

Employer's defences

1 Contributory negligence. Contributory negligence is available as a defence to an employer in a claim brought against him by an employee who says he has been injured because of his employer's negligence.

Cakebread v *Hopping Brothers (Whetstone) Ltd* (1947)

The employers of the claimant, who was engaged in a woodworking factory, had failed to see that the guard on a circular saw was properly adjusted and the claimant, who worked the saw, was injured as a result. However, it appeared that the claimant did not like working the machine with the guard properly adjusted and he had arranged with the foreman that the saw should be operated with an improperly adjusted guard. The court decided that the employer was in breach of his duty of care, but also that the claimant had failed to exercise the care of a prudent employee for his own safety and reduced his damages by 50 per cent.

2 Assumption of risk by the employee. This is unlikely to provide the employer with a successful defence these days since it is now the law that just because an employee **knows** of the risk he cannot for that reason be regarded as having **consented** to it.

Smith v *Baker & Sons* (1891)

Smith was employed by Baker & Sons to drill holes in some rock in a railway cutting. A crane, operated by fellow employees, often swung heavy stones over Smith's head while he was working on the rock face. Both Smith and his employers realised that there was a risk that the stones might fall, but the crane was nevertheless operated without any warning being given at the moment that it began to swing the stones over Smith's head. Smith was injured by a stone which fell from the crane because of the negligent strapping of the load.

The court decided that Smith had not voluntarily undertaken the risk of his employers' negligence and that his knowledge of the danger did not prevent him recovering damages.

Fatal accidents

If, as a result of the employer's negligence, an employee is killed in the course of his employment the personal representatives of the deceased have a claim on behalf of the estate under the Law Reform (Miscellaneous Provisions) Act 1934. In addition, under the Fatal Accidents Act 1976 certain dependant relatives, e.g. husband or wife and children, are entitled to claim in a personal capacity if they were dependent on the deceased for their living expenses.

The connection between physical and psychological injury and death was considered by the House of Lords in *Corr* v *IBC Vehicles* (2008). In this case, the employee was seriously injured at work. As a result of his injuries he suffered from post traumatic stress disorder. He became depressed and, six years after the accident, he committed suicide. Prior to his death, he commenced proceedings against IBC Vehicles for his physical and psychological injuries. His wife was substituted as claimant after his death. The employer accepted that the accident involved a breach of the duty owed – the duty to take reasonable care not to cause him both physical and psychological injury. The dispute centred on whether a claim under the Fatal Accidents Act was possible given that the employee took his own life.

The House of Lords held that the employer owed Corr a duty not to cause him physical and psychological injury. Further, it held that he would not have committed suicide but for this injury. Depression was a foreseeable consequence of the injury and this illness impaired his capacity to make reasoned and informed judgements about his future. Accordingly, a claim for damages for Corr's death, under the Fatal Accidents Act, was possible because the deceased's was not unreasonable.

Health and safety at work

Health and safety regulations

The general principles of health and safety and enforcement procedures and offences are contained in the Health and Safety at Work etc. Act 1974. That Act also establishes the Health and Safety Commission and the Health and Safety Executive (these two organisations merged in 2008). The central core of provisions relating to health and safety at work are now to be found in sets of regulations which came into force at the beginning of

1993. They apply to work activity generally and, like the health and safety provisions which we have had since the Health and Safety at Work Act 1974 was passed into law, the regulations place duties on employers to protect their employees and in some cases others, e.g. members of the public who may be harmed by the work being carried out.

Self-employed persons also have duties under the regulations to protect themselves and others who might be affected by the work being done, and although we talk about 'employers' in this section of the book, remember the expression also includes the self-employed.

The regulations implement EC Directives on health and safety at work. They were made under Art 118A of the Treaty of Rome which was added for this purpose. There is one set of regulations for each directive.

The duties in the regulations are not absolutely new but they clarify and state more explicitly what the law is. Those who have followed previous health and safety law should not find the new rules unfamiliar. However, there are some new aspects, i.e. management of health and safety, manual handling of loads and the use of display screens. The regulations are considered below.

Management of Health and Safety at Work Regulations 1999 (SI 1999/3242)

The latest version of these regulations came into force on 29 December 1999. They set out the general duties of employers in regard to the management of health and safety as follows:

- Every employer is required to assess the risks to the health and safety of his employees and record the significant findings of the risk assessment together with means by which the employer controls them.
- Employers must make arrangements to implement health and safety measures to deal with the risks identified and put these into written form where there are five or more employees. A *written* risk assessment is not required if there are fewer than five employees.
- Competent safety advisers must be appointed to deal with the implementation of health and safety measures. These persons may come from within the organisation or from outside, and may recommend a health surveillance of employees if thought appropriate.
- Procedures must be put in place to deal with health and safety emergencies.

- Employees must be informed about arrangements for health and safety and be given adequate training. They must also be sufficiently competent at their jobs to avoid risk. Employers must give health and safety information to temporary workers.
- There must be cooperation with other employers sharing the same workplace.

The regulations also place duties on employees to follow health and safety instructions and report danger, and employers must consult employees' safety representatives and provide facilities for them.

There is an approved code of practice to accompany the 1999 regulations.

Young people and new and expectant mothers

The regulations include provisions relating to what should be done to protect the health and safety at work of new and expectant mothers and young persons. A new or expectant mother is defined as an employee who is pregnant or who has given birth within the previous six months or who is breastfeeding. A young person means any person who has not attained the age of 18. The definition of 'child' where that word appears means a person who is not over compulsory school age. The key changes are as follows:

Young persons

- the main regulations as outlined above do not apply fully to young persons who are involved in occasional or short-term work on domestic service in a private household or a family business where the work is not harmful, dangerous or damaging to young people;
- there are provisions requiring employers to give certain information to the parents of a child they intend to employ, e.g. regarding the risks to health and safety identified by a risk assessment and the preventive and protective measures to be taken;
- there are additional requirements in regard to the risk assessment process in the case of young persons which must take account of, e.g., inexperience and immaturity.

New and expectant mothers

- a regulation is added requiring assessment and avoidance of risks to health and safety from any processes or working conditions or physical, chemical or biological agents;

- there is a regulation regarding night work under which the employer is required to operate a suspension from work at night upon receipt of a certificate from a medical practitioner or midwife that night work should not be undertaken for a specified period;

- a regulation requires employers to pay particular attention in any risk assessment to the health and safety of new and expectant mothers.

Where it is not possible to take steps to avoid any risk, the woman should be suspended from work. Where it is necessary for her health and safety, a new or expectant mother should be removed from night work.

Finally, although the main regulations are enforced under health and safety inspectorate arrangements breach of any duty imposed by them did not of itself confer a right of action in any civil proceedings. However, the Management of Health and Safety at Work and Fire Precautions (Workplace) (Amendment) Regulations 2003 (SI 2003/2457) allow employees to bring civil claims for breach of the regulations against their employers. The changes made create a significant impact. For example, employees with work-related stress or other personal injuries have now an additional claim for damages for breach of statutory duty in addition to any negligence or contractual claims. Employers also have a right to claim at civil law against employees for loss caused by the employee's breach of health and safety duties placed on him or her.

Workplace (Health, Safety and Welfare) Regulations 1992 (SI 1992/3004)

These regulations tidy up and make more clear requirements formerly contained in statutes such as the Factories Act 1961 and the Offices, Shops and Railway Premises Act 1963. The regulations apply to all places of work, subject to some exceptions such as construction sites and fishing boats.

It is not necessary in a book of this nature to set out all the provisions in detail but in broad terms there are general requirements in four areas:

1 The working environment. These include provisions relating to temperature, and effective provision must be made for securing and maintaining a reasonable temperature in rooms where persons are employed other than for short periods. If the work being done does not involve serious physical effort, a temperature of not less than 16° C (60.8° F) after the first hour is reasonable. Incidentally, although we have included the Fahrenheit

temperature, there are now in force regulations implementing an EC Directive which require all legislation and other materials, such as guidance notes concerning health and safety, to be in metric units of measurement. A thermometer must be provided in a conspicuous place on each floor of the premises. There are some temperature exceptions such as rooms in which goods are stored which would deteriorate at 16° C. However, employees who work in such rooms must be provided with convenient, accessible and effective means of warming themselves.

As regards ventilation, every room in which persons are employed must be adequately ventilated and supplied with fresh or artificially purified air. There must also be suitable, sufficient lighting – either natural or artificial – in all parts of the premises. In addition, rooms in which people work must not be overcrowded.

2 Safety. Floors, passages and stairs must be of sound construction, properly maintained and kept free from obstruction and slippery substances. Handrails must be provided on stairways, and where a stairway is open on both sides there must be two handrails and both sides must be guarded to prevent persons slipping between the rails and the steps. All openings in floors must be fenced, except where the nature of the work makes fencing impracticable.

3 Facilities. Suitable and sufficient toilets must be provided. These must be kept clean and be properly maintained, lit and ventilated. Where there are male and female employees, separate toilets must be provided for each sex. Suitable and sufficient washing facilities must also be provided. This includes a supply of clean running hot and cold (or warm) water, soap and clean towels or other suitable means of drying.

The number of persons at work is to be taken as the likely maximum number in the workplace at any one time. Where men and women are employed, the calculation should be carried out separately for each sex.

An adequate supply of wholesome drinking water must be made available. If the supply is not piped, it must be contained in suitable vessels and must be renewed daily. If water is supplied other than by jet, a supply of disposable drinking vessels must be available, and if washable non-disposable vessels are used there must be a supply of clean water in which to rinse them.

Suitable and sufficient provision must be made for clothing which is not worn at work, and so far as is reasonably practicable arrangements must be made for drying the clothing.

Where reasonable opportunities exist for sitting during working hours, suitable sitting facilities must be made available, and those who sit to do their work must be provided with a seat together with a footrest if, for example, an employee is short-legged and cannot support his or her feet comfortably without one.

4 Housekeeping. All premises, furniture, furnishings and fittings must be kept clean and properly maintained and suitable drainage of the premises must be provided. It should be noted that other people connected with the workplace are involved, so that the owner of a building leased to one or more employers or self-employed people must ensure that requirements falling within his control are satisfied, as where the owner provides jointly used toilet facilities.

Health and Safety (Display Screen Equipment) Regulations 1992 (SI 1992/2792)

These regulations do not replace former legislation. They cover for the first time a new area of activity. The risks involved with work on display screens are not high but can lead to muscular problems, eye fatigue and mental stress.

The regulations apply where there are one or more employees who habitually use display screen equipment as a significant part of daily work. The employer's duties are to:

(a) assess display screen equipment workstations and reduce any risks which are discovered;

(b) ensure that workstations satisfy minimum requirements in terms of the display screen itself, the keyboard, desk and chair, working environment and task design and software;

(c) plan work on display screen equipment so that the user has breaks or changes of activity;

(d) provide information and training for display equipment users.

Users are also entitled to eye and eyesight tests and to special spectacles where normal ones cannot be used.

Provision and Use of Work Equipment Regulations 1998 (SI 1998/2306)

These regulations tidy up and bring together the law relating to equipment used at work. Instead of legislation relating to particular types of equipment in different industries, e.g. the Factories Act 1961 fencing provisions, the regulations place general duties on employers and list minimum requirements for work equipment to deal with selected hazards, regardless of the type of industry.

'Work equipment' is broadly defined to include everything from a hand tool, through all kinds of machines to a complete plant such as a refinery.

Safety in 'use' includes safety in starting, stopping, installing, dismantling, programming, setting, transporting, maintaining, servicing and cleaning. Specific requirements include the guarding of dangerous parts of machinery and replace previous provisions on this.

Manual Handling Operations Regulations 1992 (SI 1992/2793)

These apply to any manual handling operation which may cause injury at work. They cover not only the lifting of loads but also lowering, pushing, pulling, carrying or moving them, whether by hand or other bodily force.

An amendment made in 2002 specifies factors to be taken into account in determining whether operations involve risk, particularly of back injury, to workers.

Personal Protective Equipment at Work (PPE) Regulations 1992 (SI 1992/2966)

These regulations set out the principles to be followed in selecting, providing, maintaining and using PPE. They include protective clothing such as eye, foot and head protection, safety harnesses, life jackets and high-visibility clothing. The regulations cover maintenance, cleaning and replacement, storage, proper use and training information, and instructions on use given to employees.

Directors' reports

Under the Health and Safety at Work etc. Act 1974 the Secretary of State may make regulations under which the annual reports of company directors must contain information regarding arrangements in force during the year relating to the health, safety and welfare of employees. At the time of writing, no such regulations have been made.

Duties of employers and the self-employed to persons who are not their employees – generally

It is the duty of every employer to carry on his business in such a way as to make sure, so far as is reasonably practicable, that persons who are **not** his employees but who might be affected by the conduct of the business are not exposed to risks to their health or safety. This duty is placed also on self-employed persons.

A wide variety of people is covered, including customers in a shop, people who occupy the premises next door, and even members of the public who pass the workplace. It is a criminal offence for which the person at fault can be prosecuted, whether any one is injured or not, to run a business **negligently** or to create a **nuisance**.

Thus, if a customer in a shop trips over a trailing wire left by a maintenance man, there is the possibility of an action by the customer for damages for negligence, and the possibility, also, of a criminal prosecution. In a similar way, excess noise or vibration from premises on which the business is conducted may result in an action by a person who occupies premises next door for nuisance and there is also the possibility of a criminal prosecution.

R v Mara (1986)

This provides an illustration of the above provisions. In that case it was alleged that the director of a company was in breach of his duty, where machinery belonging to his cleaning and maintenance company was left at a store which his company was under contract to clean, and the cleaning company agreed that employees of the store could use the machinery for part of the cleaning, and one of the employees of the store was electrocuted because of a fault in the cable of one of the machines. The Court of Appeal held that the director concerned was in breach of his duty and dismissed his appeal from Warwick Crown Court where he had been fined £200.

The legal point was one of construction of the relevant provisions of the 1974 Act. Mr Mara claimed that when the electrocution took place his company was not conducting its undertaking at all; the only undertaking being conducted was that of the store whose employees were using the machine to clean their own premises.

The Court of Appeal did not accept this. Mr Mara's company had, as its undertaking, the provision of cleaning services. It appeared from the facts that the way it chose to carry out that undertaking, in this case, was to do the cleaning and also leave machines and other equipment on the store's premises with permission for employees of the store to use them and with the knowledge that they would in fact use them. The unsafe cable

formed part of the equipment. The failure to remove or replace the cable was a clear breach by Mr Mara's company of its duty both to its own employees and also to the employees of the store.

Comment. The case shows the wide ambit of the relevant law. The liability of a director for offences by the company is set out in the 1974 Act which provides that where an offence is committed by a body corporate then its officers, e.g. directors and secretary, are also liable if the offence was committed with their consent or connivance. There is also a civil claim for damages for this kind of breach. The above case was concerned solely with the criminal offence.

It should also be noted that the courts are allowed to impose fines of up to £20,000 for breaches of the relevant legislation. Furthermore, the Company Directors Disqualification Act 1986 applies if there is a prosecution of a director on indictment in the Crown Court (see Chapter 6 ○). A director who is convicted of an indictable offence may be disqualified by the court, and this was done in *R v Chapman* (1992) at Lewes Crown Court where a director was convicted of an indictable offence under Health and Safety legislation arising out of the running of a dangerous quarry. He was fined £5,000 and disqualified from being a company director for two years (the maximum period is 15 years).

Duties of employers and the self-employed to non-employees – premises

Certain duties are imposed upon employers and the self-employed in regard to people who are not employees but who come on to their business (not domestic) premises. The duty is to make sure, so far as is reasonably practicable, that the premises and the means of getting in and out of them, and any plant or substance on the premises, are safe and without risk to health. These duties also apply to a landlord who is letting business premises. Failure to comply with these duties may lead to prosecution.

Once again, a wide variety of people is covered, such as window-cleaners and painters, the employees of contractors maintaining lifts or installing central heating. The actual employer owes the duties of an employer to these people also, and must, for example, set up a safe system of working. However, the occupier of the premises owes the duties we have been looking at in regard to injuries received from defects in the premises or plant or a substance on them. Obviously, the occupier can assume that the employees of contractors will take proper steps, as trained people, to avoid the risks which are usually associated with the job.

Duties in regard to harmful emissions in the atmosphere

The Health and Safety at Work etc. Act 1974 allows the Trade and Industry Secretary to control by regulations the emission into the atmosphere from premises of noxious or offensive substances and for making harmless and inoffensive such substances as may be emitted. The provisions are concerned only with air pollution. Other forms of pollution, such as the discharge of effluent into rivers, are not controlled by them.

The main regulations made so far under this head are entitled the Control of Substances Hazardous to Health Regulations 2002 (SI 2002/2677).

General duties of those who make, import or supply articles of equipment or substances, or who erect or install equipment

This part of the 1974 Act creates the following duties:

1 To ensure, so far as is reasonably practicable, that the article, e.g. a machine, is so designed and constructed as to be safe and without risks to health when properly used or, in the case of a substance, e.g. cyanide, is safe and without risk to health when properly used.

2 To carry out or arrange for the carrying out of such testing and examination as may be necessary for the performance of the duty laid down in 1 above.

3 To take such steps as may be necessary to make sure that there is available as regards the use of the article or substance at work adequate information about the use for which it is designed or made and has been tested, and about any conditions necessary to make sure that when the article or substance is put to that use it will be safe and without risk to health.

All forms of supply are included and this part of the 1974 Act covers the supplying by way of sale, leasing, hire or hire-purchase.

As regards the installation and erection of equipment, the 1974 Act provides that it is the duty of any person who erects or installs any article for use at work in any premises where the article is to be used by people at work

to make sure, as far as is reasonably practicable, that nothing about the way in which it is erected or installed makes it unsafe or a risk to health when properly used.

Under amendments made by the Consumer Protection Act 1987 the above general duties are extended to those who supply any article of fairground equipment.

Research, examination and testing

This part of the 1974 Act makes it the duty of any person who undertakes the design or manufacture of an article for use at work or the manufacture of a substance for use at work to carry out or arrange for the carrying out of any necessary research with a view to the discovery, and, so far as is reasonably practicable, the elimination or minimisation of any risks to health or safety to which the design, article or substance may give rise.

There is no need to repeat any testing, examination or research which has been done by someone else if it is reasonable to rely on the results of another's testing, examination or research. For example, those who lease goods are not required to go again through the manufacturer's testing, examination and research programmes.

If you design, manufacture, import or supply an article to someone else's specification or request, the Act says that if you have a **written undertaking** as part of the documentation of the contract from that person to take specified steps sufficient to ensure, so far as is reasonably practicable, that the article will be safe and without risk to health when properly used, then the written undertaking will relieve the designer, manufacturer, importer or supplier of liability to such an extent as is reasonable having regard to the terms of the undertaking.

General duties of employees at work

It is the duty of every employee while at work:

1 To take reasonable care for the health and safety of himself and of other persons who may be affected by his acts or omissions at work.

2 As regards any duty or requirement put upon his employer or any other person by the relevant Acts of Parliament to cooperate with him so far as is necessary to enable that duty or requirement to be carried out or complied with. Therefore, if the employer is required to provide his workers with goggles, the workers have a duty to wear them.

Furthermore, the 1974 Act provides that no person shall intentionally or recklessly interfere with or misuse anything provided in the interests of health, safety or welfare, e.g. remove a safety guard from a machine. To do so is an offence for which the employee can be prosecuted.

These are useful sections which could enable an employer to enforce his safety policies. Some workers are reluctant to use safety equipment, such as machine guards, because they feel it slows them down or prevents the most efficient operation of the machine in terms of its production. If the employee's wages depend, because of the system of payment, upon his production, then it is even more difficult to gain his acceptance of safety devices which might affect production.

In this connection it should be noted that an employee's consent to a dangerous practice, or his willing participation in it, is no defence for an employer who is prosecuted under the Act.

Duty not to charge employees for things done or provided by the employer by law

The 1974 Act states that no employer shall levy or permit to be levied on any employee of his any charge in respect of anything done or provided by the employer as a result of the provisions of an Act of Parliament or statutory instrument. This would apply, for example, to personal protective clothing which an employer was required to provide by law. For example, in workplaces where there is a noise hazard from a woodworking machine, ear protectors must be provided and the employee must not be charged for them. The employee, in turn, must treat them properly and not misuse them.

The statutory duties and civil liability

As we have already noted, civil liability has been extended to cover breaches of health and safety legislation (see further, p 516 ○).

However, the ordinary action for negligence at common law remains available. If there is an action by an employee at common law, say for injuries received at work by what he alleges to be the employer's negligence, the employee can plead that the employer has been convicted under the Act and where this is so the employee's claim is near certain to succeed but will not inevitably do so. Therefore, where the employer has infringed the

Act and this has caused injury to the employee, the Act is a relevant part of establishing the employee's case for damages at civil law.

Offences and civil claims for accidents at work are more likely to arise in a factory than in an office. However, the following are examples of accidents which can occur and medical conditions which can arise in an office environment:

(a) injury in a fire caused by a discarded cigarette or by an overloaded or defective electrical system;
(b) a fall or other injury caused by a defect in the premises, such as a dangerous and badly lit staircase;
(c) an electric shock caused by badly fitted or defective electrical equipment;
(d) injury caused by a defect in or careless use of equipment, such as a guillotine or stapler;
(e) a medical condition caused by defective or ill-designed chairs supplied to employees, particularly secretaries;
(f) eye strain and other conditions caused by exposure to VDU screens.

Many of the claims brought broadly under headings (e) and (f) above have been in regard to what is called repetitive strain injury.

It is also necessary to note the case of *Walker* v *Northumberland County Council* (1994) where damages, eventually settled out of court at £175,000, were awarded to Mr Walker when he suffered psychiatric damage because he was overworked by his employer. The employer was in breach of his duty to provide a safe system of work for the employee and was therefore liable in negligence for not doing so.

Claims under the above headings could now also be framed as breaches of statutory duty, which is normally easier to prove than common law negligence.

Claims for workplace stress have become quite common since the *Walker* case. A major development favourable to the employer occurred in the House of Lords ruling in *Hatton* v *Sutherland* (2002), the most important aspect being that an employer is normally entitled to assume that the employee can stand the normal pressures of the particular job **unless he or she knows of some particular vulnerability or problem**. So an employee who, as it were, suffered in silence would apparently be at risk of losing a claim.

The House of Lords took a different view in *Barber* v *Somerset County Council* (2004), stating that employers must be proactive in the matter of workplace stress. Their

Lordships placed the onus on the employer to develop a knowledge of occupational stress and keep up to date with effective precautions that can be taken to alleviate it. This ruling, which represents the current law, is of course much more favourable to an employee's claim.

Stress claims acquired a new jurisdiction in *Majrowski* **v** *Guy's and St Thomas's NHS Trust* (2005), where a successful claim for damages was brought by the claimant under the Protection from Harassment Act 1997. The stress was caused to the claimant by, among other things, the setting of unreasonable job targets and bullying by hospital managers. Interestingly enough, the employer was held vicariously liable, there being no proceedings against the manager. Claims under the 1997 Act can be brought for up to six years (not three as in common law claims) and there is no requirement of foreseeability of damage by the employer. The Act does not apply to a situation of harassment on one occasion.

Civil claims – strict liability

Some areas of health and safety legislation have always allowed civil actions to be framed around breach of statutory duty and in some cases liability is strict, which means that an employer can be liable even in the absence of negligence on his or her part. An example of such legislation relates to the provision of equipment to employees as the following case shows.

Stark v *Post Office* (2000)

The Court of Appeal ruled that where the employer's equipment caused personal injury to an employee a claim by that employee for damages against the employer can succeed even though the employer has not been negligent in terms, for example, of its maintenance. Mr Stark was a postman. The Post Office provided him with a bicycle. During the course of his employment he was riding the bicycle when the front wheel locked, sending him over the handlebars and causing him serious injuries. It was accepted that the bicycle had been maintained and that the defendants were not negligent. Even so, the court found that the employer was liable to Mr Stark since there is strict liability under health and safety legislation.

Comment. Despite the fact that the Post Office had a safe system of maintenance and repair, the claimant suceeded. A reasonable system for maintenance may no longer be an adequate defence. Employers faced with health and safety incidents should take note of the implications of this ruling.

Smoking in the workplace – generally

It is also arguable that at common law an employer is at fault in requiring employees to work in an atmosphere containing heavy concentrations of cigarette or cigar smoke, although it may be possible to call medical evidence to challenge the existence or degree of the risks involved in 'passive smoking'. In fact, in *Bland* **v** *Stockport Metropolitan Borough Council* (1993), a woman who had been exposed to passive smoking from 1979 to 1990 when her employer implemented a no-smoking policy, received £15,000 damages for injury to her health, including, in particular, chronic bronchitis and sinusitis. There is, of course, a statutory duty now the new regulations apply. Certainly there is no implied contractual right to smoke at work and if an employee leaves because he or she is not allowed to smoke, there is no constructive dismissal (see *Dryden* **v** *Greater Glasgow Health Board* (1992)); and it may well be that a dismissal for infringement of a no-smoking rule properly communicated and agreed with staff would not be unfair.

More recently the Employment Appeal Tribunal has decided that the secretary in a solicitor's office who left because of discomfort caused at the workplace by colleagues who smoked was constructively dismissed (see *Waltons and Morse* **v** *Dorrington* (1997)). In previous passive smoking cases the complainant has suffered physical injury. However, in this case, the EAT, after ruling that it is an implied term in all employment contracts that the employer will provide and continue to monitor, as far as is reasonably practicable, a working environment which is reasonably suitable for employees to carry out their duties, then went on to comment that the right of an employee not to be required to sit in a smoky atmosphere affects the welfare of employees at work, even though employees who complain cannot necessarily prove that there has been any health and safety risk to them. It would appear that discomfort is enough.

Smoking in the workplace

HSE is not responsible for enforcing the legislation. It works with local authority officers both in raising employers' awareness of their responsibilities and in encouraging employers and employees to comply with the new legislation above.

Smoking in the workplace – legislative duties

Relevant legislation includes the following:

- *The Health and Safety at Work etc. Act 1974.* Exposure to environmental tobacco smoke (ETS) is a health hazard, and by exposing non-smokers to ETS, the employer could be in breach of the Act.
- *Management of Health and Safety at Work Regulations 1999 (as amended).* These impose specific requirements to make risk assessments in regard to health, safety and welfare at work of all employees. Given the evidence of the risks involved in exposure to ETS, this should be included as a risk and appropriate measures taken to deal with the risk.
- *Workplace (Health, Safety and Welfare) Regulations 1992.* Under these regulations where rest areas are provided arrangements must be made to ensure that non-smokers can use them without the discomfort of ETS.
- *Employment Rights Act 1996.* This provides for a general duty on the employer to protect employees from risks. Non-smokers who are subjected to ETS where the employer will not do anything about it could resign and claim constructive dismissal.

A workplace smoking ban

The government has issued and consulted on the Smoke-free (Premises and Enforcement) Regulations 2006 (SI 2006/3368). These ban smoking in enclosed public places, including most workplaces, on 1 July in England. The Welsh ban came into force on 2 April 2007. The regulations give definitions of 'enclosed' and 'substantially enclosed' premises, together with requirements for displaying no-smoking signs in smoke-free premises and duties to prevent smoking in smoke-free vehicles, enforcement by local authorities and the form of penalty notices for offences.

As regards penalties, employees caught smoking in regulated areas after the regulations are in force will face a fixed penalty of £50. Those who pay within 15 days will have the fine reduced to £30, but those who fail to pay could face a fine of up to £200 and a criminal record. Company cars must also be non-smoking if they are likely to be used by more than one person, unless the car is a convertible and the roof is open.

Drink and drugs in the workplace

Because of the duties of care placed upon them by statute and common law, employers must take reasonable steps to ensure that their workers are not under the influence of drink or drugs where it would create a risk

to the health and safety of others if the workers' performance was impaired in this way. Employees who are under the influence of drink or drugs – or who fail to report fellow workers who are – may also be in breach of their own common law or statutory duties of care.

Except for these rather general duties, there is little specific regulation in regard to drink and drugs in the workplace, though there is some regulation in regard to railways.

Abusive fellow workers – a health and safety risk

The decision of the EAT in *Harvest Press Ltd* v *McCaffrey* (1999) provides an unexpected application of s 100(1)(d) of the Employment Rights Act 1996. This states that it is automatically unfair to dismiss an employee who has left his work because circumstances of danger of a serious nature appear imminent, which one normally associates with a health and safety risk. The EAT ruled that an employment tribunal's decision that the dismissal of McCaffrey after he left his work in the middle of a shift because of the abusive behaviour of a fellow worker was automatically unfair within s 100(1)(d). The subsection had a wide scope and was without limitation and could cover any danger howsoever arising.

The Health and Safety Commission and the Health and Safety Executive

The 1974 Act establishes the the Health and Safety Commission and the Health and Safety Executive and describes their powers. The Department for Work and Pensions announced in 2008 that these two bodies would be merged to form a single regulatory body: the Health and Safety Executive.

Corporate killing

It has proved difficult successfully to prosecute companies and their officers for manslaughter, even though it has been clear that there have been management failures in safety matters resulting in a death or deaths. The problem under the present law is that prosecutions for corporate manslaughter can be brought only where a company through the controlling mind of one of its agents carries out an act that fulfils the requirements of the crime of manslaughter. It is necessary to identify the agent in order to carry the crime back to the company, and in all of the major disasters brought about by a failure of a company-supplied service – as in a ferry or train disaster – the effective acts of carelessness are diffused throughout the company's structure.

In *A-G's Reference (No 2 of 1999)* (2000) the Court of Appeal affirmed the principle, in regard to a finding of corporate manslaughter by gross negligence, that a corporation cannot be convicted unless there is evidence that establishes the guilt of an *identified human individual* for the same crime.

One of the few convictions is to be found in *R v OLL* (1994), a prosecution heard at Winchester Crown Court in 1994, where the managing director of an activity centre was sentenced to three years' imprisonment for manslaughter following the deaths of four teenagers in the Lyme Bay canoe disaster. Here there was no difficulty in establishing the controlling mind because the company was a 'one-man band'.

Corporate Manslaughter and Corporate Homicide Act 2007

This Act came into force on 6 April 2008. It introduces a new offence where there has been a gross organisational failing in the management of health and safety which has had fatal consequences.

The Act sets out a new offence for convicting an organisation where a gross failure in the way activities were managed or organised results in a person's death. This will apply to a wide range of organisations across the public and private sectors. In England and Wales and Northern Ireland, the new offence will be called corporate manslaughter. It will be called corporate homicide in Scotland.

Previously, a company could only have been convicted of corporate manslaughter if there is enough evidence to find a single senior person guilty. This approach did not reflect the reality of modern corporate life. Under this new approach, courts will look at management systems and practices across the organisation, providing a more effective means for prosecuting the worst corporate failures to manage health and safety properly. Companies found guilty of corporate manslaughter will be subject to an unlimited fine. The court will also be able to impose a remedial order to take specified steps to remedy the breach within a specified period.

The Working Time Regulations (WTR)

The Working Time Regulations (SI 1998/1833) came into force on 1 October 1998. They enact the European Working Time Directive (93/104). From that date there are detailed rules which govern hours of work and entitlement to paid holidays, as set out in general terms below:

- A maximum 48-hour working week, averaged over 17 weeks.
- At least 5.6 weeks' annual holiday entitlement (from April 2009).
- A daily rest period of at least 11 consecutive hours in 24 hours.
- A weekly rest period of at least 24 hours in each seven-day period. This may be averaged over a two-week period, i.e. a worker is entitled to 48 hours' rest in 14 days or to two periods of 24 hours' rest in 14 days. The days off for weekly rest are in addition to paid annual leave.
- An in-work rest break of 20 minutes for those working more than six hours a day. This should not be taken at either the start or the end of a working day and should not overlap with a worker's daily rest period. Rest breaks are not in addition to lunch breaks.
- The normal hours of night workers should not exceed eight hours for each 24 hours.

The Court of Appeal has ruled that periods of downtime during which the worker is still at the disposal of the employer do not count as rest breaks. A worker must be free to use the time as he or she pleases. (See *Gallagher v Alpha Catering Services Ltd* (2005), where the workers drove food out to aircraft. Periods of downtime between aircraft landing were not rest breaks.)

It should also be noted that although employers must ensure that their workers can take leave, they are not forced to see that they actually do. However, a ruling by the European Court of Justice in *European Commission v United Kingdom* (2006) is to the effect that UK regulations are defective in not enforcing rest breaks. The UK government is currently considering what steps to take, since the UK Working Time Regulations are out of line with the EU Working Time Directive in this respect.

Who is a worker?

Generally speaking, a worker is a person employed under a contract of service, but the majority of agency workers will be included as will trainees who are engaged on work experience. The regulations also apply in part to domestic employees though the working time limits do not apply but they are entitled to the rest breaks, rest periods and paid annual leave. Those who are genuinely self-employed are not covered.

What is working time?

Working time is defined by the Working Time Regulations (WTR) as when a worker is working at his employer's disposal and carrying out his duty or activities. *Training time* is included but, according to guidance, time when a worker is 'on call' but is otherwise free to pursue his own activities or is sleeping would not be working time. On-call time where the worker is restricted to the workplace is working time. Lunch breaks spent at leisure would not be working time, but working lunches and working breakfasts would be. Travelling to and from a place of work is unlikely to be working time. The regulations usefully allow workers or their representatives and employers to make agreements to add to the definition of working time.

Must a worker actually work?

In *Kigass Aero Components v Brown* (2002) the Employment Appeal Tribunal ruled that an employee who had been off work for a considerable time with a long-standing back injury was entitled, under the 1998 regulations, to be paid the statutory holiday pay due to him, although his entitlement had accumulated while he was not working. It appeared from this decision that so long as workers are on the payroll, they can build up holiday-pay entitlement, even though they are not actually at work.

In *Inland Revenue Commissioners v Ainsworth* (2005) the Court of Appeal ruled that *Kigass* was wrongly decided. A worker on long-term sick leave was not entitled under the WTR to four weeks' annual leave in a year when he had not been able to work so that a claim for holiday pay must also fail. *Kigass* was overruled.

The 48-hour week

The law does not say that employees cannot work more than 48 hours in any one week. The 48-hour limit is averaged over a 'reference period' which will generally be a 17-week rolling period, in the absence of any other agreement. This gives a certain amount of flexibility for businesses to cope with surges in demand, so long as the average over the whole reference period is not exceeded.

The reference period may be increased to 26 weeks if the worker is a special case, as in hospital work, or where there is a foreseeable surge of activity as in agriculture, tourism and postal services. The reference period can be increased to 52 weeks by a workforce agreement (see below) or by individual agreement with the employer (see below).

A High Court judge has ruled that all contracts of employment should be read as providing that an employee should not work more than an average of 48 hours in any week during the 17-week working time reference period, unless the relevant employee has opted out in writing. The judge also ruled that if the average hours are equalled or exceeded during the reference period, an employee may refuse to work *at all* during the remainder of the period until the working hours come down to the required level. (See *Barber v RJB Mining (UK) Ltd* (1999).)

Mr Justice Gage gave his ruling in a case brought by five members of the pit deputies' union NACODS against RJB Mining, their employer. They had all been required to carry on working, although they had all worked in excess of 816 hours in the 17-week reference period. The judge also granted them an injunction (breach of which by the employer could lead to sanctions of contempt of court) to the effect that they could refuse to work any more during a 17-week reference period where the 48-hour average had been equalled or exceeded. The decision could present a number of employers with major problems, particularly in terms of staff in key areas. They could face the prospect of a number of workers being able to refuse to do any more work until their hours came down to the required level.

Paid annual leave

The entitlement is to 5.6 weeks (28 days) of paid leave. This is not additional to contractual entitlements so that taking contractual paid leave in a particular leave year counts against the worker's entitlement under the regulations. In the absence of any agreement, the employer can require a worker to take all or any of the leave at specified times, subject to giving the worker notice of at least twice the period of the leave to be taken. The worker is also required to give notice to the employer of the wish to take leave. The notice period must again be at least twice the period of leave to be taken.

Hill v Chapell (2003)

Miss Hill gave in her resignation after taking 15 days' holiday in six months of the leave year. The employer contended that he could recover a sum equivalent to five days of overpaid holiday. However, the EAT refused the claim. The Working Time Regulations do not allow credit to the employer for any leave taken and paid for in excess of the accrued entitlement in the absence of a contract that provides to the contrary. There was no agreement covering Miss Hill's employment.

Comment.

(i) This is an aspect of the WTR that should be considered by employers when making employment contracts. It is often convenient to allow leave to be taken in advance of entitlement and where there is no resignation there will not be a problem. However, contractual arrangements should cover the possibility of resignation and allow the employer to recover the excess.

(ii) It should also be noted that if a worker's employment ends, he or she has a right to be paid for leave accrued but not taken. This applies even where an employee is fairly dismissed (see **Witley and District Men's Club v Mackay**) (2001) where the dismissal was for dishonesty!

(iii) *Leave does not accrue on a pro rata basis after the first year* and all this means is that the worker is not obliged to wait until holiday has accrued before being allowed to take it. Nevertheless, problems such as those seen in the *Hill* case will still arise because entitlement may have been exceeded on leaving. Contractual arrangements for recovery of the excess payment by the employer are the answer to this problem, as they are in the first year of employment.

The leave entitlement under the regulations is not in addition to bank holidays because there is no statutory right to paid leave on bank and public holidays. There are eight annual bank and public holidays in most parts of the UK and currently employers are allowed to include these in the minimum annual entitlement.

Paying a rolled-up rate

It will be appreciated that calculating the various paid leave entitlements of a workforce is a time-consuming job for the employer and some have resorted to paying a rolled-up rate including a proportion of holiday pay with the weekly or monthly basic pay. The Court of Appeal ruled in *Blackburn* v *Gridquest (t/a Select*

Employment) (2002) that rolled-up pay will not be effective unless the employee concerned agrees to it and that in the payment holiday pay is stripped out so that the employee can see what is holiday pay and what is basic pay. Failure to do this has resulted, as it did in the *Gridquest* case, in the employer being successfully sued for failing to pay for annual leave, with the result that the employer paid twice!

After the expenditure of much time and money in litigation the Court of Appeal gave definitive guidelines on rolled-up pay in *Marshalls Clay Products Ltd* v *Caulfield* (2003). The guidelines were:

- the rolled-up holiday pay must be incorporated clearly into the contract of employment and expressly agreed with the worker;
- the percentage or amount of holiday pay must be clearly identified in the contract and preferably also on the payslip;
- it must be a true addition to the contractual rate of pay;
- records of holiday must be kept and reasonably practicable steps must be taken to require workers to take their holidays before the expiry of the relevant holiday year.

The above arrangements gave the employer considerable calculation advantages in a shift operation.

However, in a number of conjoined appeals from the Court of Appeal on the subject of rolled-up holiday pay the ECJ ruled that for the future it was unlawful. Where before the ruling an employer has operated a system of rolled-up pay and the payments have been made in a transparent and comprehensible manner these payments can be set off against any future annual leave payments made at the time of taking leave. An employer must not, however, proceed with further rolled-up pay payments. (See *Robinson-Steele* v *RD Retail Services Ltd*; *Clarke* v *Frank Staddon Ltd*; *Caulfield* v *Hanson Clay Products Ltd* (2006). By the time of the ECJ ruling Hanson had acquired Marshalls Clay.)

Length of night work

Night work is presumed to be work between 11 pm and 6 am, unless otherwise defined by agreement.

Excluded sectors

The regulations, other than those parts which apply to young workers (see below), do not currently apply to workers who are employed in the following sectors:

- air transport;
- rail;
- road transport;
- sea transport;
- inland waterway and lake transport;
- sea fishing;
- other work at sea, e.g. offshore work in the oil and gas industry.

The Working Time (Amendment) Regulations 2003 (SI 2003/1684) deal with the above-mentioned excluded categories and amend the main regulations as they are applied to the relevant categories. The main provisions of the regulations are as follows:

- In the case of workers in the armed forces or emergency services, where their activities conflict with the 1998 regulations, crew members on board civil aircraft and doctors in training, the following provisions are disapplied:
  - weekly working time and night work limits, the daily, weekly and in-work rest periods, the entitlement to paid annual leave, the right to a health assessment if a night worker and pattern of work protection for certain categories of worker. A 48-hour time limit for doctors in training will be phased in over a period ending on 31 July 2009.
- Regulation 8 inserts a 52-week reference period for workers employed in offshore work.
- The 1998 regulations are disapplied in their entirety in the case of seafarers, workers on board seagoing fishing vessels and workers on certain ships and hovercraft on inland waterways.

The original regulations did not apply to the activities of doctors in training but the 48-hour week now applies to trainee doctors since August 2009 (SI 2009/1567).

Road Transport (Working Time) Regulations 2005

These regulations (SI 2005/639) came into force on 4 April 2005 in order to implement the Road Transport (Working Time) Directive into UK law. They give working time protection for all mobile workers (in general drivers and crew travelling in vehicles that are subject to tachograph requirements) such as goods vehicles over 3.5 tonnes, coaches and inter-urban bus services. The regulations cover mobile workers in the haulage industry and those who work for companies with their own transport section and agency drivers. They do not apply to self-employed drivers working for a number of clients.

The detail of the regulations is beyond the scope of this introductory text.

Police

The main regulations are applied to the police by reason of the Working Time Regulations 1998 (Amendment) Order 2005 (SI 2005/2241), effective from 1 September 2005.

Derogations

Employees whose working time is not measured or predetermined were exempt from the provisions relating to the 48-hour week, daily and weekly rest periods, rest breaks and limits on night work but not the holiday provisions. Examples given in the WTR included 'managing executives or other persons with autonomous decision making powers, family workers and ministers of religion'.

The above derogations were removed by the Working Time (Amendment) Regulations 2006 (SI 2006/99), effective from 6 April 2006. It appears that some organisations had used the derogations to pressurise junior workers to work in some cases limitless unpaid overtime. Derogations allowing this are now removed.

Collective and workforce agreements

The regulations allow employers to modify or exclude the rules relating to night work, daily and weekly rest periods and rest breaks and extend the reference period in relation to the 48-hour week – *but not the 48-hour week itself* – by way of agreement as follows:

- A collective agreement between an independent trade union and the employer (or an employers' association).
- A workforce agreement with representatives of the relevant workforce *or if there are 20 workers or fewer the agreement may be with a majority of the workforce which obviates the need to elect worker representatives.* As regards worker representatives, these may be representatives elected for other purposes, e.g. health and safety consultation.
- Individuals may also choose to agree with their employer to work in excess of the 48-hour weekly time limit. *This is all that an individual agreement can cover.*
- In addition, a workforce agreement may apply to the whole of the workforce or to a group of workers within it.

These agreements can only last for a maximum of five years.

Records: weekly working time

An employer must keep adequate records to show that he has complied with the weekly working time limit. The records must be kept for two years. It is up to the employer to determine what records must be kept. Pay records may adequately demonstrate a worker's working hours.

Similar provisions apply in regard to records showing that the limits on night work are being complied with. Records need not be kept in regard to rest periods and in-work rest breaks nor in regard to paid annual leave.

Compensatory rest

Employers who make use of the derogations or who enter into collective or workforce agreements must provide an equivalent period of rest or, if this is not possible, give appropriate health and safety protection. Thus the regulations allow, through agreement, flexibility in the way its rights are delivered, but they do not allow those rights to be totally avoided.

Health and safety assessments

An employer must offer a free health assessment to any worker who is to become a night worker. Employers must also give night workers the opportunity to have further assessments at regular intervals.

Young (or adolescent) workers

The regulations also apply rights to persons over the minimum school-leaving age but under 18. These are set out below:

- *weekly working hours*: adult and young workers are treated the same;
- *night work limit*: adult and young workers are treated the same;
- *health assessments for night workers*: adolescent workers are entitled to a health and capacity assessment if they work during the period 10 pm to 6 am. Such an assessment for an adolescent worker differs in that it considers issues like physique, maturity and experience and takes into account the competence to undertake the night work that has been assigned;
- *daily rest*: for young workers this is 12 hours' consecutive rest between each working day;

- *weekly rest*: for young workers the general requirement is two days off per week;
- *in-work rest breaks*: for young workers the general provision is 30 minutes if the working day is longer than $4^{1}/_{2}$ hours;
- *paid annual leave*: adult and young workers are treated the same.

Young Workers Directive

The above-mentioned provisions of the WTR were made under a UK opt-out from the Young Workers Directive (94/33/EC). Government regulations have now amended the WTR 1998. Young workers (those over the minimum school leaving age but under 18) are not allowed to work more than 40 hours per week. In addition, working time is limited to eight hours in any one day. Night working is prohibited between 10 pm and 6 am or 11 pm and 7 am. There are some exceptions, such as hospitals and hotel catering work (but not in restaurants or bars).

Young workers in the seafaring and seafishing industries and the armed forces are excluded from the provisions.

The regulations are entitled Working Time (Amendment) Regulations 2002 (SI 2002/3128).

Other young workers rules

The Children (Protection at Work) (No 2) Regulations 2000 (SI 2000/2548), reg 2 limits the number of hours a child of school age can work – in any week during which he or she is required to attend school – to 12. This could lead to problems in small businesses, such as newsagents.

The Protection of Children Act 1999 makes changes to the law with the object of creating a framework for identifying people who are unsuitable for work with children and to compel, or in some cases to allow, employers to access a single point for checking the names of people they propose to employ in a post involving the care of children. This will involve permitting checks against criminal records and two lists of people considered unsuitable for work with children. The Department of Health and the Department for Work and Pensions will maintain the lists to be made via the Criminal Records Bureau, which has come into operation under Part V of the Police Act 1997.

Other relevant provisions appear in Part II of the Criminal Justice and Court Services Act 2000 where a court has made a 'disqualification order' against a person convicted of an offence against a child. Those who knowingly employ such persons in work with children commit a criminal offence.

Enforcement and remedies

The weekly working time limit, the night work limit and health assessments for night workers are enforced by the Health and Safety Executive or local authority environmental health officers. The usual criminal penalties for breach of the health and safety law apply. In addition, workers who are not allowed to exercise their rights under the regulations or who are dismissed or subjected to a detriment – whether a pay cut, demotion or disciplinary action – for doing so will be entitled to present a complaint to an employment tribunal. In view of the abolition on the ceiling of awards for unfair dismissal, in these cases employment tribunal claims could be much more expensive than health and safety fines.

Discrimination and the Equality Act 2010

Those involved

In the material which follows we shall refer only to 'discrimination'. The reader can take it that this word will refer to discrimination in all the areas covered by discrimination law. There will be sometimes a special mention of disability discrimination because here there are special features, such as the types of disability covered and the need so far as disabled people are concerned for the employer to make adjustments to enable a disabled person to do the job at least as far as is practicable. There are no such adjustment provisions in the other areas of discrimination law.

The areas of discrimination covered by UK discrimination law are set out below:

- *Sex discrimination and marital discrimination*, which is discrimination mostly against women, though men are covered by the law, and discrimination against a person because the person is married.
- *Race discrimination*, which is discrimination on the grounds of race, colour, nationality or ethnic or national origins.
- *Sexual orientation*, which is discrimination on the grounds that a person is gay, heterosexual or bisexual.
- *Religion or belief*, which is discrimination on grounds involving religion, religious belief or similar

philosophical belief. Atheism may fall within the definition but political beliefs will not. In deciding whether discrimination law should be applied, tribunals will most likely look at factors such as collective worship, a clear belief system and/or a profound belief affecting a person's way of life or view of the world.

- *Transsexuality*, being discrimination against persons who have gender dysphoria and wish to live and work in their adopted sex.
- *Disability*, being discrimination against a person on the grounds of his or her disability.
- *Age discrimination*, which is discrimination on the ground of being too old or too young for a particular appointment and, in the case of age, too old to go on working.

Although we consider here discrimination in employment, these discrimination laws apply also to engagement in a *partnership* business or profession.

It is worth noting here the Equality Act 2006. The Act provides for the establishment of a Commission for Equality and Human Rights. The Commission took over the responsibilities of the Commission for Racial Equality, the Disability Rights Commission and the Equal Opportunities Commission and became operative in 2007.

Equality Act 2010

First announced in June 2008, introduced in the House of Commons on 8 April, the Equality Act 2010 received Royal Assent on 8 April 2010 and is regarded as 'the most significant piece of equality legislation for years' by the Equality and Human Rights Commission. Discrimination legislation has existed for over 40 years. However, the body of law in this area had developed inconsistencies in approach. The Act is intended to reduce 'nine major pieces of legislation, and around 100 statutory instruments into a single Act, making the law more accessible and easier to understand, so that everyone can be clear on their rights and responsibilities' and 'promote fairness and equality of opportunity; tackle disadvantage and discrimination'. In other words, the purpose of the Act is to introduce a single legal framework providing clearer law.

The current laws are mainly contained in the following legislation:

- The Equal Pay Act 1970.
- The Sex Discrimination Act 1975.

- The Race Relations Act 1976.
- The Disability Discrimination Act 1995.
- The Employment Equality (Religion or Belief) Regulations 2003.
- The Employment Equality (Sexual Orientation) Regulations 2003.
- The Employment Equality (Age) Regulations 2006.
- The Equality Act 2006, Part 2.
- The Equality Act (Sexual Orientation) Regulations 2007.

The Act brings together and reinstates the enactments listed above but not all the sections would appear precisely as in the original Acts. The intention is to harmonise existing provisions to give a single approach where appropriate. Most of the existing legislation will be repealed. As stated above, the Equality Act 2006 Part 2 will remain in force (as amended by the Equality Act 2010) where it relates to the constitution and operation of the Equality and Human Rights Commission.

The Act is also intended to strengthen the law in a number of areas. As highlighted in the Preamble to the Act, it:

- places a new duty on certain public bodies to consider socio-economic disadvantage when making strategic decisions about how to exercise their functions;
- extends the circumstances in which a person is protected against discrimination, harassment or victimisation because of a protected characteristic;
- extends the circumstances in which a person is protected against discrimination by allowing people to make a claim if they are directly discriminated against because of a combination of two relevant protected characteristics;
- creates a duty on listed public bodies when carrying out their functions and on other persons when carrying out public functions to have due regard when carrying out their functions to: the need to eliminate conduct which the Act prohibits; the need to advance equality of opportunity between persons who share a relevant protected characteristic and those who do not; and the need to foster good relations between people who share a relevant protected characteristic and people who do not. The practical effect is that listed public bodies will have to consider how their policies, programmes and service delivery will affect people with the protected characteristics;

- allows an employer or service provider or other organisation to take positive action so as to enable existing or potential employees or customers to overcome or minimise a disadvantage arising from a protected characteristic;
- extends the permission for political parties to use women-only shortlists for election candidates to 2030;
- enables an employment tribunal to make a recommendation to a respondent who has lost a discrimination claim to take certain steps to remedy matters not just for the benefit of the individual claimant (who may have already left the organisation concerned) but also the wider workforce;
- amends family property law to remove discriminatory provisions and provides additional statutory property rights for civil partners in England and Wales;
- amends the Civil Partnership Act 2004 to remove the prohibition on civil partnerships being registered in religious premises.

The provisions in the Equality Act will come into force at different times. The core provisions of the Act commenced in October 2010. It is envisaged that provisions concerning public sector equality duty and age protection outside the workplace will start to apply in 2011 and 2012.

For our purpose, it is important to note the key concepts on which the Act is based, including definitions of 'protected characteristics'. These can be found under Part 2 of the Act (and see, e.g., Explanatory notes to the Act):

- The characteristics which are protected (age, disability, gender reassignment, marriage and civil partnership, pregnancy and maternity, race, religion or belief, sex and sexual orientation);
- The definitions of direct discrimination, discrimination arising from disability, indirect discrimination, harassment and victimisation.

These concepts of the 'protected characteristics' were set out under s 4, namely the following:

- age;
- disability;
- gender reassignment;
- marriage and civil partnership;
- pregnancy and maternity;
- race;

- religion or belief;
- sex;
- sexual orientation.

Definitions of the above characteristics can be found in ss 5–12.

These key concepts are clarified in the subsequent parts of the Equality Act 2010 and how these characteristics are to be protected from direct or indirect discrimination, harassment and victimisation.

Types of discrimination

There are two forms of discrimination, as follows:

1 Direct discrimination – the statutory definition can now be found in s 13 of the Equality Act 2010. This occurs where an employer or prospective employer treats a person less favourably than another because of a 'protected characteristic', as where an employer refuses, on discriminatory grounds, to grant a suitably qualified person an interview for a job. In addition, the segregation of workers once in employment on discriminatory grounds is also unlawful direct discrimination.

Examples are provided by the following cases.

Coleman v Skyrail Oceanic Ltd (1981)

The claimant, Coleman, who was a female booking clerk for Skyrail, a travel agency, was dismissed after she married an employee of a rival agency. Skyrail feared that there might be leaks of information about charter flights and had assumed that her dismissal was not unreasonable since the husband was the breadwinner. The Employment Appeal Tribunal decided that the dismissal was reasonable on the basis that the husband was the breadwinner. However, there was an appeal to the Court of Appeal which decided that those provisions of the Sex Discrimination Act which dealt with direct discrimination and dismissal on grounds of sex had been infringed. The assumptions that husbands were breadwinners and wives were not were based on sex and were discriminatory. The claimant's injury to her feelings was compensated by an award of £100 damages.

Comment. The claimant was also held to be unfairly dismissed having received no warning that she would be dismissed on marriage. The additional and discriminatory reason regarding the breadwinner cost the employer a further £100.

Johnson v Timber Tailors (Midlands) (1978)

When the claimant, a black Jamaican, applied for a job with the defendants as a wood machinist the defendants' works manager told him that he would be contacted in a couple of days to let him know whether or not he had been successful. Mr Johnson was not contacted and, after a number of unsuccessful attempts to get in touch with the works manager, was told that the vacancy had been filled. Another advertisement for wood machinists appeared in the paper on the same night as Mr Johnson was told that the vacancy had been filled. Nevertheless, Mr Johnson applied again for the job and was told that the vacancy was filled. About a week later he applied again and was again told that the job had been filled although a further advertisement had appeared for the job on that day. An employment tribunal decided that the evidence established that Mr Johnson had been discriminated against on the grounds of race.

Bloomberg Financial Markets v Cumandala (2000)

C applied for a post in Madrid but the company did not offer him the job because he wanted to return to London every weekend to see his wife. C was black and of Angolan nationality. He claimed marital and race discrimination. The EAT ruled that there was no marital discrimination. The employer simply felt that C could not give the necessary commitment to the job given the weekly commuting. The employer would have taken the same view if, for example, C had been a keen football fan and had wished to commute every weekend in the season to see his favourite team. However, in appointing a white person, the view had been expressed that he would 'fit in better'. The EAT ruled that there had, in consequence, been unlawful race discrimination in that aspect of the employment.

Comment. Shorter-distance commuting may result in a successful claim for marital discrimination in the case where an applicant wants to see his family at weekends.

2 Indirect discrimination – as where an employer has applied requirements or conditions to a job but the ability of some persons to comply because of sex, disability, marital status or race is considerably smaller and cannot be justified. The statutory definition can now be found in s 19 of the Equality Act 2010.

Examples are provided by the following cases.

Price v The Civil Service Commission (1977)

The Civil Service required candidates for the position of executive officer to be between 17½ and 28 years. Belinda Price complained that this age bar constituted indirect sex discrimination against women because women between those ages were more likely than men to be temporarily out of the labour market having children or caring for children at home. The Employment Appeal Tribunal decided that the age bar was indirect discrimination against women. The court held that the words 'can comply' in the legislation must not be construed narrowly. It could be said that any female applicant could comply with the condition in the sense that she was not obliged to marry or have children, or to look after them – indeed, she might find someone else to look after them or, as a last resort, put them into care. If the legislation was construed in that way it was no doubt right to say that any female applicant could comply with the condition. However, in the view of the court, to construe the legislation in that way appeared to be wholly out of sympathy with the spirit and intention of the Act. A person should not be deemed to be able to do something merely because it was theoretically possible; it was necessary to decide whether it was possible for a person to do so in practice as distinct from theory.

Bohon-Mitchell v Council of Legal Education (1978)

The claimant, an overseas student, complained of discrimination in regard to a requirement of the defendants that a student would have to undergo a 21-month course, as opposed to a diploma of one year, to complete the academic stage of training for the Bar where he did not have a UK or Irish Republic university degree. This rule was regarded by an industrial tribunal to be discriminatory because the proportion of persons not from the UK or Irish Republic who could comply was considerably smaller than persons from the UK or Irish Republic who could and the rule was not justifiable on other grounds. The claimant satisfied the tribunal that there had been indirect discrimination.

Comment. The other side of the coin is illustrated by **Panesar v Nestlé Co Ltd** (1980) where an orthodox Sikh, who naturally wore a beard which was required by his religion, applied for a job in the defendants' chocolate factory. He was refused employment because the defendants applied a strict rule under which no beards or excessively long hair were allowed on the grounds of

hygiene. The claimant made a complaint of indirect discrimination but the defendants said that the rule was justified. The Court of Appeal decided that as the defendants had supported their rule with scientific evidence there was in fact no discrimination.

Equal pay

The Equal Pay Act 1970 (EPA 1970) implied a term called an equality clause into contracts of service. This clause means that a man or a woman must be given contractual terms not less favourable than those given to an employee of the opposite sex, i.e. the comparator, when they are each employed:

1 **on like work,** in the same employment (but not necessarily in the same kind of job); or
2 **on work rated as equivalent** in the same employment, e.g. by a job evaluation scheme; or
3 **on work which is in terms of demands made on the worker,** under such headings as effort, skill and decision-making, of **equal value** to that of a worker in the same employment.

The relevant provisions can now be found in Part 5 of the Equality Act 2010 and s 66 of the Act is designed to replicate the effect of definitions contained in the EPA 1970.

The clauses are not necessarily identical and the Act retained the 'dual system of sex discrimination law' as highlighted in the Parliamentary research paper. As regards the relationship between the EPA 1970 and the Sex Discrimination Act (SDA) 1975, these two Acts do not overlap. Complaints of discrimination in regard to pay and other non-monetary matters governed by the contract of employment, such as hours of work, are dealt with under the Equal Pay Act and complaints of discrimination in regard, for example, to access to jobs are dealt with under the Sex Discrimination Act. A complaint to an employment tribunal need not be based from the beginning on one Act or the other. A tribunal is empowered to make a decision under whichever Act turns out to be relevant when all the facts are before it. The EPA 1970 covers not only matters concerning wages and salaries, but also other terms in the contract of service, such as sick pay, holiday pay and unequal working hours. Other forms of sex discrimination in employment, such as discrimination in recruitment techniques, are covered by the SDA 1975. In addition, unlike the SDA 1975, a woman must find an actual man with whom she can be compared. It is not enough to ask a tribunal to imply that her pay and conditions are worse than a man's would have been. Under s 79, for comparison, the Equality Act 2010 sets out the circumstances in which employees and others are taken to be comparators for the purposes.

Some illustrative cases under the Equal Pay Act

We will consider some of the cases that were decided under the Equal Pay Act below:

1 If a woman is engaged in the same or broadly similar work as a man and both work for the same or an associated employer (see below), the woman is entitled to the same rate of pay and other terms of employment as the man.

The comparison was usually made with a previous holder of the same job. In *Macarthys Ltd* v *Smith* (1979) the EAT decided that Mrs Smith, a stockroom manageress, was entitled to pay which was equal to that of a previous manager of the stockroom, a Mr McCullough. However, the EAT did say that tribunals must be cautious in making such comparisons unless the interval between the two employments is reasonably short and there have not been changes in economic circumstances.

The Equality Act 2010 introduced a new section, s 64, on 'relevant types of work'. The intention (as can be seen in the explanatory notes) is that this section should be combined with s 79 which provides the reference on the 'comparators'. The Act provides for the treatment of the claimant to be compared with a comparator, either of any actual or a hypothetical person – the comparator under s 79 – who does not have the same protected characteristics as the claimant.

In the light of the *Macarthys Ltd* v *Smith* decision, section 64(2) has been included to ensure that the effect of the existing case law will be maintained, in other words, while the comparator need not be someone who is employed at the same time as the person making a claim under these provisions, he or she could be a predecessor in the job.

In *Hallam Diocese Trustee* v *Connaughton* (1996) the EAT decided that an employment tribunal could hear a claim for equal pay under Art 119 of the Treaty of Rome where the applicant relied for arrears of pay on the salary of a man appointed *after* her resignation. A claim under the EPA requires employment *at the same time* but Art 119 is of direct application, as it was in the *Macarthys* case.

The term 'broadly similar work' under the Equal Pay Act meant that although there may be some differences between the work of the man and the woman, these would not be of sufficient practical importance to give rise to what the EPA calls a 'material difference'. Thus, in a case where women clean offices and toilets and men also clean offices but also clean urinals, the fact that the men clean urinals would be a difference but not a 'material difference', so that the women would be entitled to the same pay as the men. Section 65 of the Equality Act provides the definition of 'equal work' which provides the guidance on work is to be compared.

The following case, decided under the Equal Pay Act, illustrates a material difference.

Capper Pass v *Lawton* (1976)

A female cook who worked a 40-hour week preparing lunches for the directors of Capper was paid a lower rate than two male assistant chefs who worked a 45-hour week preparing some 350 meals a day in Capper's works canteen. The female cook claimed that by reason of the EPA 1970 (as amended) she should be paid at the same rate as the assistant chefs since she was employed on work of a broadly similar nature.

It was held by the EAT that if the work done by a female applicant was of a broadly similar nature to that done by a male colleague it should be regarded as being like work for the purposes of the EPA 1970 unless there were some practical differences of detail between the two types of job. In this case the EAT decided that the work done by the female cook was broadly similar to the work of the assistant chefs and that the differences of detail were not of practical importance in relation to the terms and conditions of employment. Therefore, the female cook was entitled to be paid at the same rate as her male colleagues.

Comment. An interesting contrast is provided by ***Navy, Army and Airforce Institutes*** v ***Varley*** (1977). Miss Varley worked as a Grade E clerical worker in the accounts office of NAAFI in Nottingham. NAAFI conceded that her work was like that of a Grade E male clerical worker employed in NAAFI's London office. However, the Grade E workers in Nottingham worked a 37-hour week, while the male Grade E clerical workers in the London office worked a 36½-hour week. Miss Varley applied to an employment tribunal under the EPA 1970 for a declaration that she was less favourably treated as regards hours worked than the male clerical workers in London and that her contract term as to hours should be altered so as to reduce it to 36½ hours a week. The employment tribunal granted that declaration but NAAFI appealed to the EAT which held that the variation in hours was genuinely due to a material difference other than the difference of sex. It was due to a real difference in that the male employees worked in London where there was a custom to work shorter hours. Accordingly, NAAFI's appeal was allowed and Miss Varley was held not to be entitled to the declaration. The judge said that the variation between her contract and the men's contracts was due really to the fact that she worked in Nottingham and they worked in London.

Another common example of a sensible material difference occurs where, for example, employee A is 21 and employee B is a long-serving employee of 50, and there is a system of service increments, then it is reasonable to pay B more than A though both are employed on like work. Obviously, however, it is not enough to say that because at the present time men are on average paid more than women this is a material difference justifying paying a woman less in a particular job. This was decided in *Clay Cross (Quarry Services) Ltd v Fletcher* (1979).

It is also a material difference when the men work nights and the women do not (*Thomas v National Coal Board* (1987)).

Those applying for equal pay may choose only one comparator, as the following case illustrates.

Degnan v Redcar and Cleveland Borough Council (2005)

The Court of Appeal has ruled that applicants for equal pay can choose only one comparator. Where the employer's remuneration package contains different elements for different jobs the applicant can pick the comparator with the terms most advantageous to him or her. They are not, however, entitled to 'cherry-pick' elements from the various remuneration terms in the employer's package.

Some female employees claimed equal pay with male gardeners, refuse workers and road workers. The same basic rate was applied to those workers. Equal value of the work of the claimants was accepted. It appeared that the gardeners got a fixed bonus, the refuse workers got a lower bonus, but a higher attendance allowance, while the road workers got a lower bonus and a lower attendance allowance. These were therefore all aspects of the employer's remuneration package.

The applicants' claim was for the higher bonus by comparison with the gardeners and the higher attendance allowance of the refuse workers. The point of contention was that no one male comparator could qualify for both of these, with the result that if the claim was successful the claimants would be earning more than any male comparator on the grounds of 'equal' pay. The difficulty for the employer was that the ECJ ruled in *Barber v Guardian Royal Exchange Assurance Group* (1990) that equal pay entails equality in each component of remuneration.

The Court of Appeal, looking again at the case law, ruled that while all the benefits were part of the employer's remuneration package, the applicants could choose only one comparator. This could be the comparator with the terms most advantageous to them. They were not, however, entitled in law to take elements from the remuneration terms. Only those of one comparator of their choosing were available in an equal pay claim.

2 If the job which the woman does has been given the same value as a man's job under a job evaluation scheme, then the woman is entitled to the same rate of pay and other terms of employment as a man. On the other hand, an employer will have a complete answer to a claim for equal pay if the jobs of the woman and the male comparator have been given different ratings under a job evaluation scheme, provided that the scheme has been carried out objectively and analytically, preferably by specialist consultants, and that the scheme itself is not directly or indirectly discriminatory, as where, for example, it overvalues traditional male skills and attributes, such as greater physical strength.

3 Equal value. If the job which a woman does in terms of the demands made upon her, for instance under such headings as effort, skill and decision-making, is of equal value to that of a man in the same employment, then the woman is entitled to the same pay and other contractual terms as the man, as she is if her work has been graded as of higher value (*Murphy v Bord Telecom Eireann* (1988)). It might be thought that in such a case she should be paid more but at least the law can ensure equal pay for her.

The point about the 'equal value' ground is that it is available even if the jobs are totally dissimilar, so that a woman secretary may name a male accounts clerk as a comparator.

A complaint may be made to a tribunal on the grounds of equal value even if the two jobs have been regarded as unequal in a job evaluation study. However, there must be reasonable grounds to show that the study was itself discriminatory on the grounds of sex.

When a complaint about equal value is made, the tribunal can (but is not obliged to) commission a report from an expert on the matter of value. The report of the expert goes to the tribunal and copies go to the parties. Although the report will obviously be extremely important in the decision which the tribunal makes, it is not in any way bound by it and can disregard it.

It was once thought that in claims for equal pay the tribunal must look not merely at pay, but also at fringe benefits.

In *Hayward* v *Cammell Laird Shipbuilders Ltd* (1986) a qualified canteen cook, Miss Julie Hayward, who had convinced a tribunal that she was of equal value with male painters, joiners and thermal heating engineers and therefore entitled to equal pay, was told by the Employment Appeal Tribunal that she could not isolate the term about pay. The EAT asked the Tribunal to look at the case again. Although Miss Hayward's pay was not equal, her employers claimed that she had better sickness benefit than the men and also paid meal breaks and extra holidays which they did not have. So it might be possible to say that she was, looked at overall, treated as well. However, Julie Hayward won her appeal in the House of Lords. It was held that her claim to equal pay for work of equal value was justified even though she had better fringe benefits. Her employers were not entitled to compare her total package but should instead consider her basic pay. The decision should ensure that miscellaneous benefits are not seen as 'pay' and will not be used to keep wages down in future.

It is also interesting to note that in *Pickstone* v *Freemans plc* (1986) the Employment Appeal Tribunal decided that a woman could not bring a claim that her work was of equal value to that done by a man employed by the same firm in a different job because men were employed in the same job as her own on the same rates of pay and terms.

On the facts of the case this meant that the woman could not claim that her work as a warehouse packer was of equal value to that of a checker warehouse operative merely because she worked on the same terms with other male warehouse packers. The decision was eventually overruled by the House of Lords which decided that a woman is not debarred from making a claim for parity of pay with a male comparator in a different job merely because a man is doing the same job as herself for the same pay. The decision effectively kills off the device of employing a 'token man' with the women employees as a way of defeating equal pay claims, as by employing one or two low-paid men in a predominantly female area of work.

Associated employers

Comparison of contracts of service for equality purposes is usually made with people who work at the same place. However, comparison can be made with people who work at different places so long as the employer is the same or is an associated employer. As regards an associated employer, this would be the case with a group of companies. Thus, if H plc has two subsidiaries, A Ltd and B Ltd, workers in A Ltd could compare themselves with workers in B Ltd, and workers in B Ltd with those in A Ltd, and workers in A Ltd and B Ltd could compare themselves with workers in H plc. Workers in H plc could, of course, compare themselves with workers in A Ltd and B Ltd.

Also important in these days, where outsourcing of public services is common, workers employed by a private contractor can compare themselves with other persons still employed by a local authority, as the House of Lords decided in *Ratcliffe* v *North Yorkshire County Council* (1995). This ruling may put off some private contractors who might have tendered for council services, intending to do the job more cheaply by cutting wages.

Reference to an employment tribunal

Part 9, Chapter 3 of the Act sets out the types of claims under the Act the employment tribunals have jurisdiction to hear. The effect of a successful claim is twofold. For the future, the complainant has a contractual entitlement to the higher rate of pay or other contract term enjoyed by the comparator. The tribunal can also award compensation in respect of the disparity to date or make an appropriate recommendation.

The Employment Tribunals (Constitution and Rules of Procedure) (Amendment) Regulations 2004 (SI 2004/2351)

These regulations contain at Sch 6 the Employment Tribunals (Equal Value) Rules of Procedure which give employment tribunals powers to insist on the early exchange of relevant information, facilitate the fact-finding process and penalise parties who do not comply with tribunal directions.

Of particular importance are powers under which employers can be ordered to grant access to their premises to an expert where one has been appointed by the tribunal or the claimant or their representative where no expert has been appointed in order to question certain employees, e.g. alleged comparators.

Time limits for claims

Section 123 provides that the claims must be brought to the tribunals within three months of the alleged conduct taking place. The tribunals, however, have the discretion to grant permission for a claim to be brought after the set time limits. The test set under s 123 is what is 'just and equitable'.

For instance, this may be extended where the claimant has worked under, say, a series of fixed-term contracts forming a stable employment relationship, each contract being for unequal pay; then the six-month limit runs from the end of the last of such contracts. The period may also be extended where the employer has deliberately concealed the possibility of a claim. Here time runs from when the claimant discovered the facts or could with reasonable diligence have discovered them. Where the claimant was under a disability in terms of bringing the claim, as where the claimant was a minor at the time, the period runs from the end of the disability, i.e. from reaching 18.

The House of Lords ruled in *Powerhouse Retail Ltd* v *Burroughs* (2006) that, where an employee's employment has been transferred under TUPE 2006, the time for making a claim in respect of employment with the previous employer runs from the date of the transfer, not the eventual end of the employment with the transferee employer.

Community law

It is important to note that any gaps or exceptions in UK legislation can be overcome by resort to Community law. Article 141 of the Treaty of Rome is relevant since it establishes the principle that men and women are entitled to equal pay for work of equal value.

As we have seen in *Macarthys Ltd* v *Smith* (1979), it was decided that where a man who leaves his employment is replaced by a woman who receives a lower rate of pay the woman cannot make a claim under UK legislation based on the former male employee's pay, but she can do so under Article 141 (and note also the decision in *Hallam Diocese Trustee* v *Connaughton* (1996)).

An important consequence of the applicability of Art 141 is to be found in the field of pensions, redundancy and severance and termination payments. UK legislation contains exceptions for all these matters but Art 141 overrides this and follows from the decision of the European Court in *Barber* v *Guardian Royal Exchange Assurance Group* (1990). The effect of this decision is that pension, redundancy, severance and termination payments are treated as pay for the purposes of Art 141 and there must not be an inequality on the grounds of sex in relation to the payments made.

The Pensions Act 1995 deals with the main provisions relating to equality in pensions law, and in broad terms provides equal treatment for men and women in regard to the terms and conditions on which they become members of the scheme and their rights once members. The Act will be repealed by the Equality Act 2010 and the equal treatment will be covered in s 67 of the 2010 Act.

In recruitment and selection of employees

Recruitment and offers of employment

As in previous legislation, s 33 of the Equality Act 2010 makes it unlawful for a person in relation to an employment by him at a place in England, Wales or Scotland and on British ships, aircraft and hovercraft to discriminate against men or women on the above stated grounds:

- in the arrangements made for the purpose of deciding who should be offered the job; or
- in the terms on which the job is offered; or
- by refusing or deliberately omitting to offer the job.

The Equality Act 2010 introduced a new provision – under s 60, an employer must not ask about an applicant's health or disability until the applicant has been offered a job. The questions can only be asked, as provided under the legislation, to find out, for instance, if a job applicant would be able to participate in an assessment to test his or her suitability for the work or that the information can be used to provide reasonable adjustments to enable the applicant to participate in the interview/recruitment process.

'Arrangements' is a wide expression covering a range of recruitment techniques, e.g. asking an employment agency to send only white applicants, or male applicants.

Discrimination by employment agencies themselves is also covered.

As regards the terms of the contract of employment, it is unlawful to discriminate against an employee on the grounds listed above in terms of the employment which is given to him or the terms of access to opportunities for promotion, transfer or training, or to any other benefit, facilities or services, or subjecting him to any other detriment. Thus, it is unlawful to discriminate in regard to matters such as privileged loans, and mortgages by banks and building societies, and discounts on holidays given to employees of travel firms.

A person who takes on workers supplied by a third party, rather than employing them himself or herself, is obliged by the Act not to discriminate in the treatment of them or in the work they are allowed to do. This means that temporary staff supplied by an agency are covered by the anti-discrimination provisions.

Exceptions

Section 69 of the Equality Act provides a defence for material factor. The sex equality section will apply normally but not if the employer can show that the difference in the contractual terms is due to a material factor which is relevant and significant.

Under the previous legislation, there are some circumstances in which it is lawful to discriminate such as when there are genuine occupational qualifications or requirements. So far as sex discrimination is concerned, an employer may confine a job to a man where male sex is a 'genuine occupational qualification' (GOQ) for a particular job. This could arise, for example, for reasons of physiology, as in modelling male clothes, or authenticity in entertainment, as where a part calls for an actor and not an actress. Sometimes a man will be required for reasons of decency or privacy, such as an attendant in a men's lavatory. Sometimes, too, where the job involves work outside the United Kingdom in a country whose laws and customs would make it difficult for a woman to carry out the job, being a male may be a GOQ. As regards marital status, it may be reasonable to discriminate in favour of a man or a woman where the job is one of two held by a married couple, as where a woman is a housekeeper living in with her husband who is employed as a gardener.

There are, of course, some situations where female sex would be a GOQ for a certain type of job, as the following case illustrates.

Sisley v Britannia Security Systems (1983)

The defendants employed women to work in a security control station. The claimant, a man, applied for a vacant job but was refused employment. It appeared that the women worked 12-hour shifts with rest periods and that beds were provided for their use during such breaks. The women undressed to their underwear during these rest breaks. The claimant complained that by advertising for women the defendants were contravening the Sex Discrimination Act 1975. The defendants pleaded genuine occupational qualification, i.e. that women were required because the removal of the uniform during rest periods was incidental to the employment.

The Employment Appeal Tribunal accepted that defence. The defence of preservation of decency was, in the circumstances, a good one. It was reasonably incidental to the women's work that they should remove their clothing during rest periods.

Comment. However, s 27(4) of the 1975 Act imposes a duty on employers to take reasonable steps to avoid relying on the GOQ exceptions. Thus, in *Etam plc v Rowan* (1989) Steven Rowan applied for a vacancy as a sales assistant in Etam's shop in Glasgow which sold only women's and girls' clothing. He was not considered for the post because of his sex and complained to an employment tribunal. There was later an appeal by the employer to the Employment Appeal Tribunal (EAT). The EAT affirmed the employment tribunal's award of £500 to Mr Rowan. He had been discriminated against on the grounds of sex. The EAT found that he would have been able quite adequately to carry out the bulk of the job of sales assistant. Such parts as he could not carry out, such as attendance on women in fitting rooms for the purpose of measuring or otherwise assisting them, could easily have been done by other female sales assistants without causing any difficulty or inconvenience to the employer. It is also worth noting that in *Wylie v Dee & Co (Menswear) Ltd* (1978) a woman was refused employment in a men's tailoring establishment in which the rest of the staff were men because it was considered inappropriate for her to measure the inside legs of male customers. An employment tribunal decided that she had been discriminated against because those measurements could have been carried out by other male employees.

A further illustrative example from case law is provided by *Lasertop Ltd v Webster* (1997) which also reveals a gap in discrimination law. In that case a man's complaint of sex discrimination, made when he applied for an appointment as a sales staff/trainee manager at a women's health club and was told that only female staff would be employed, failed. The employer was entitled to rely on the defence that being a woman was a 'GOQ' for the post in order to preserve decency and/or privacy. The EAT ruled that it could not be said that the holding of the post, with duties that would involve showing prospective members around the premises, could be undertaken without inconvenience if the post-holder was a man.

A major point of interest in the case relates to the contention that a GOQ could not be applied because the relevant aspects of the job, i.e. those involving decency or privacy such as showing new members around saunas and changing rooms, could have been carried out by female staff. This argument failed because the business was recruiting for start-up staff at the particular branch and *at the time of refusal of the post* there were no female staff actually in employment there. Section 7(4) of the SDA 1975 states that the GOQ defence does not apply where the employer 'already has' (male) (female) employees capable of carrying out the GOQ duties. There would appear to be a gap in discrimination law in the sense that if the branch had been in operation the GOQ reference may not have applied, leaving the male applicant discriminated against.

Positive action

Part 11, Chapter 2 of the Equality Act 2010 provides that the Act does not prohibit the use of positive action measures to alleviate disadvantage experienced by people who share protected characteristics. It is to encourage their representation in relation to particular activities, and meet their particular needs.

The tests suggested by the Equality and Human Rights Commission is that positive action will be allowed if it is to:

- be related to the level of disadvantage that exists;
- not be simply for the purposes of favouring one group of people over another where there is no disadvantage or under-representation in the workforce.

Discrimination once in employment

As we have seen, discrimination on the grounds of sex, race, disability, sexual orientation, religion and belief, transsexuality and age are unlawful. As regards employees, it is unlawful to discriminate as regards opportunities for promotion, training or transfer to other positions or in the provision of benefits, facilities or services or by selection for redundancy or dismissal.

In addition to the direct discrimination and indirect discrimination as highlighted above, the Equality Act 2010 has also included victimisation and harassment under 'Other prohibited conducts' (ss 26–27).

Direct and indirect discrimination bear the same definitions in the employment context as they do in recruitment. Victimisation and harassment are normally found, if at all, once employment has commenced and require treatment in this section of the text.

In direct and indirect discrimination a genuine occupational qualification or requirement if acceptable to the tribunal can be a defence for the employer. In the case of disability discrimination, however, the employer is required, where possible, to make reasonable adjustments to overcome individual difficulties with the job.

Some general illustrative case law under the previous legislation

The concept of discrimination is wider than the relationship of employer and employee under a contract of service or apprenticeship. It includes employment 'under a contract personally to execute any work or labour' and no period of service is required before a claim can be brought. Rights are also given to partners in all partnerships.

An example of the broad nature of discrimination law is provided by *Harrods Ltd* v *Remick*; *Harrods Ltd* v *Seely*; *Elmi* v *Harrods* (1996). In that case the three complainants were dismissed by their employers from 'shops within a shop' at Harrods because Harrods said they were in breach of the Harrods' dress code: for example, in Mrs Seely's case the wearing of a nose stud. Although their contract of employment was not with Harrods, that store was liable for sex discrimination when their employers dismissed them because Harrods threatened to withdraw the 'shop within a shop' concession. They were 'doing work for Harrods' and were ultimately under Harrods' control, in view of the power to withdraw the concession.

The matter of the liability of the employer for the discriminatory acts of third parties who are not employees arose in *Burton* v *De Vere Hotels Ltd* (1997).

The EAT ruled that an employer could be regarded as having subjected employees to harassment, in this case racial harassment, by allowing a third party to inflict racial abuse on them in circumstances in which he could have prevented the harassment or reduced the amount of it. The complainants were two black women who were employed as waitresses at a Round Table function at a hotel in Derby and were subjected to racially offensive remarks by Mr Bernard Manning, a guest speaker, for example about the sexual organs of black men and their sexual abilities. The employer did not withdraw them from the room at once as he should have done and was liable.

The House of Lords discredited this ruling in *MacDonald v A-G for Scotland; Pearce v Governing Body of Mayfield School* (2003). In *MacDonald* and *Pearce* the claims were brought for discrimination against homosexual people but it is the last part of their Lordships' ruling in those cases that has most significance. Although the matter did not arise directly and the decision is not technically binding, the House of Lords stated that an employer would no longer be liable for failing to protect his or her employees from the acts of third parties, such as Mr Manning, for whose acts the employer is not vicariously liable, unless that failure is in itself less favourable treatment on discriminatory grounds. It appeared that the manager would not have withdrawn white waitresses from a situation involving sex discrimination. In fact, he said in evidence that the matter of withdrawing the waitresses never occurred to him. So the employer is liable only for *his own discrimination* in this situation as where he or she leaves employees in a discriminatory situation because he or she in effect wishes to see them embarrassed or does not care whether they are.

An employer is liable for the acts of his employees 'in the course of employment'. Employers have tried to defend themselves by saying that their employees were not employed to discriminate but in *Jones v Tower Boot Co Ltd* (1997) the Court of Appeal rejected this defence saying a purposive interpretation must be put on 'in course of employment' for discrimination purposes. The case involved the harassment of a 16-year-old black youth who was called 'Baboon', 'Chimp' and 'Monkey' and was branded with a hot screwdriver. An employer has a defence where he or she can show that best endeavours were used to prevent the conduct. That was not the case in *Jones*. All reasonable steps to prevent the abuse were not used.

Victimisation in employment

Under discrimination legislation it is unlawful to treat a person less favourably than another because that person asserts rights under anti-discriminatory legislation or is or has helped another to do so. Damages can be awarded where victimisation has occurred. An example is to be found in *Cornelius v Manpower Services Commission*

(1986) where the Commission refused to consider C for a permanent post for which she had applied because one of the references which she supplied indicated that she was involved in an unresolved sexual harassment case.

Harassment: generally

Most complaints of harassment have involved sexual harassment, though *Jones v Tower Boot Co Ltd* (1997) provides a particularly bad situation of racial harassment.

There is now a separate head of liability for harassment in regard to race, disability, sexual orientation, religion or belief and age. It is no longer an aspect of detriment as it has been for many years. The definition, which results from the new regulations in these areas, described earlier in this chapter, is defined as follows.

> Harassment occurs where on grounds of sex, race or ethnic or national origins or sexual orientation or religion or belief or age or for a reason which relates to a disabled person's disability – A engages in **unwanted conduct** which has the purpose or effect of (a) **violating B's dignity**; or (b) **creating an intimidating, hostile, degrading, humiliating or offensive environment** for B. The conduct is deemed to have the required effect if having regard to all the circumstances including in particular the **perception of B** it should reasonably be considered as having that effect [author's emphasis].

Obviously, tribunals will be concerned to interpret this definition but it is likely that many of the cases on 'detriment' will fit the new definition.

Sexual harassment

So far as sexual harassment is concerned, the relevant provision under the Equality Act 2010 can be found under ss 26(2) and 26(3):

- unwanted conduct related to the sex of a person occurs with the purpose or effect of violating the dignity of that person; and
- any form of unwanted, non-verbal or physical conduct of a sexual nature occurs with the purpose or effect of violating the dignity of a person, in particular, when creating an intimidatory, hostile, degrading, humiliating or offensive environment.

Harassment and case law

There are numerous cases of mainly sexual harassment. Most of these provide different *fact* situations of such harassment and cannot, because of their number, be reproduced here. However, a leading case containing guidance from the EAT that can be applied in other cases even under the new definition of harassment is *Driskel* v *Peninsular Business Services Ltd* (2000). Mrs Driskel was an adviceline consultant with Peninsular. She claimed that she had been sexually harassed by the head of her department. She alleged that she had been subject to sexual banter and comments and that at an interview for promotion he had suggested that she wear a short skirt and a see-through blouse showing plenty of cleavage. This advice was not accepted. She then refused to return to work unless the head of department was moved elsewhere. She was then dismissed and made a claim to an employment tribunal. Her claim was rejected because the incidents looked at *in isolation* were not enough. She appealed and the EAT substituted a finding of sexual harassment and in doing so stated:

- the tribunal should have looked at the *total or overall effect* of the acts complained of;
- a woman's failure to complain at times throughout the conduct should not necessarily be taken as significant;
- sexual 'banter' between heterosexual men cannot be equated with, so as to excuse, similar comments towards a woman.

Harassment: other legislation

When harassment is intended and studied the Criminal Justice and Public Order Act 1994 creates a criminal offence of intentional harassment. It appears as s 4A inserted into the Public Order Act 1986. The penalty on conviction by magistrates is imprisonment for up to six months and/or a fine of up to £5,000.

It is clear from the wording of s 4A that harassment in the workplace is covered. This means that employees who are harassed at work are able to report the matter to the police.

The Protection from Harassment Act 1997 is also relevant. The Act is very wide ranging and covers discriminatory harassment and bullying at work. It is also possible to bring civil proceedings against offenders under the Act. (See *Majrowski* v *Guy's and St Thomas's NHS Trust* (2005).)

An ACAS code of practice

ACAS has issued a code of practice to assist employers in complying with the regulations on sexual orientation and religion and belief. It can be accessed at: www.acas.org.uk.

Sexual orientation

The following matters arise.

1 In recruitment. When advertising, employers should avoid unnecessary job criteria that could prevent persons applying because of their sexual orientation. During the interviewing process the employer should avoid questions regarding marital status and children.

2 Vetting. It may be that the employer has, because of the nature of the work, e.g. work with children, followed the vetting process through the Criminal Records Bureau, and where this shows relevant offences, then exclusion of a particular candidate would not be unlawful. Furthermore, sexual offences do not become spent under the Rehabilitation of Offenders Act 1974 and should be disclosed. However, where a criminal record bears no relationship to the job and does not affect skills or competence, exclusion may be unlawful.

3 Genuine occupational requirement. As we have seen, it may sometimes be lawful to treat a gay person differently as where the work is in an area such as the Middle East where homosexuality is illegal and may lead to proceedings against gay men, lesbian women and bisexuals. The regulations also allow difference in treatment where the work is for the purposes of organised religion.

4 Fitting in. Employers should not engage in stereotyping and make assumptions as to whether a person would fit into the organisation.

5 Harassment. Taunting by workers about the actual or perceived sexual orientation of a fellow worker or those associated with him or her are illegal. Staff should be informed that the organisation will not allow such behaviour.

In all cases employers should look at and revise as necessary their equal opportunities policy.

Comment. In *Reaney* v *Hereford Diocesan Board of Finance* (2007), Reaney, a gay man, applied for a job as a diocesan youth officer. The issue of homosexuality was discussed during his interview. In the light of the Church's position on this issue, he was asked whether he intended to remain celibate for the duration of the post. He declared that this was his intention. The applicant was the preferred candidate for the job. However, the Bishop was not prepared to accept this assurance and he was not appointed. The employment tribunal decided that while the genuine occupational requirement was relevant to the case, the Bishop's decision to reject Reaney's assurance was unreasonable and therefore it found that Reaney had been the victim of discrimination.

Religion and belief

The following matters arise.

1 In recruitment. Advice should be given to applicants as to the requirements of the job so that they can ascertain whether there could be a clash with their religion or belief, e.g. late Friday night working could conflict with those of Muslim or Jewish faith.

When interviewing, employers should avoid questions relating to an applicant's religion or belief.

2 Genuine occupational requirement. As we have seen, the employer may have an ethos based upon a particular religion or belief such as a denominational school. If the employer can show that a particular religion or belief is a requirement of the job then a GOR may be applied.

3 Dress requirements. These must be justified by health and safety or sound business reasons. Flexibility is the key in other situations where staff can dress according to their religion or beliefs and still meet the requirements of the organisation. Thus the wearing of neck beads should be allowed unless there is a health or safety requirement.

4 Holiday leave. Certain workers may wish to take accrued annual leave at specific times to celebrate festivals, spiritual observance or bereavement. This should be allowed subject to genuine business requirements. Enforced holiday periods, e.g. Christmas closure for all staff, may have to be evaluated to avoid allegations of indirect discrimination.

5 Dietary requirements. Employers must be sensitive to any special dietary requirements of staff who have religious or belief convictions in terms of food. Staff canteens and corporate events should be monitored. Where food is brought to the workplace, separate storage and heating facilities may have to be considered.

6 Prayer, meditation and rest periods. Subject to it causing problems for other workers, employers should agree to a request to make available a quiet place for the above. It may be necessary to consider storage of ceremonial equipment. Permitted rest periods under working time provisions may be required by some staff to fit a religious obligation to pray at certain times of the day.

7 Changing facilities and showers. Some staff may because of religion or belief feel unable to undress with others present. A private area may be a requirement for this and showering purposes. To insist on same-sex changing and shower facilities may be indirect discrimination.

8 Staff discussion. There is no harm in sensible discussion about religion and belief but offensive behaviour should be prevented. Staff should be told that there must be no harassment for which they and the employer could be liable.

Comment. The recent case of *Lillian Ladele* v *Islington Borough Council* (2008) illustrates the difficulty of resolving conflicting rights in the context of claims of discrimination. Ladele, a registrar of births, marriages and deaths, was required to provide registration services for civil partnerships, which had recently been introduced. The Council argued that it had a legal duty to offer such a service to same-sex couples. Ladele did not wish to be involved in the provision of this particular service because it conflicted with her Christian faith. The Council claimed that her position discriminated against gay people while she counter-claimed that she was the victim of religious discrimination. Ladele instituted legal proceedings. The employment tribunal upheld her claim. Upon Council's appeal, the Employment Appeal Tribunal reversed the Tribunal decision on the ground that the prohibition of discrimination by the Equality Act (Sexual Orientation) Regulations 2007 took precedence over any right which a person would otherwise have by virtue of his/her religious belief or faith to practice discrimination on the ground of sexual orientation. The ETA's decision was affirmed by the Court of Appeal.

Disability discrimination

What is disability?

Section 6 of the Equality Act 2010, as it appeared in the Disability Discrimination Act 1995, defines a disabled person as a person who has a physical or mental impairment which has a substantial and long-term adverse effect on his or her ability to carry out normal day-to-day activities. Schedule 1 and regulations that will be made under the Act will further define what constitutes a disability. For instance, Schedule 1 provides provision on determination of a disability and provides definition of a 'long term effect'. A new provision has also been provided under the 2010 Act that it is discrimination to treat a disabled person unfavourably not because of the person's disability itself but because of something arising from, or in consequence of, his or her disability, such as the need to take a period of disability-related absence.

Some general illustrative case law under the previous legislation

A variety of conditions can be brought under the general definition of physical and mental impairment. In *O'Neill* v *Symm & Co Ltd* (1998) the EAT accepted that chronic fatigue syndrome (ME) fell within the definition. The EAT has also accepted that employees who were suffering from depression were disabled persons under the Act (see *Kapadia* v *Lambeth London Borough Council* (2000)). It is clear from the above decisions that employers should be especially cautious before they dismiss employees on the grounds of ill-health since the condition may be regarded as a 'disability' for the purposes of the 1995 Act. Medical reports should be obtained and the employer should consult with the employee to see whether any adjustments can be made in the work situation such as a transfer to a new post or by providing additional training or making modifications in the workplace or equipment. It is the need to take these steps that distinguishes dismissal for an unsatisfactory sickness record (which may be fair) from a disability dismissal leading to a claim for uncapped damages. In this connection, the Court of Appeal has rejected the idea that in a disability dismissal there can be a comparison between the treatment of a disabled person and a person suffering from long-term sickness (see *Clark* v *TDG Ltd (t/a Novacold)* (1999)).

Impairment of long-term effect

Schedule 1 applies and states that impairment is of long-term effect if it has lasted for 12 months, or is likely so to last, or is likely to last for life. A severe disfigurement is included. The effect on normal day-to-day activities is dealt with by a list in para 4 of Sch 1 which includes mobility, manual dexterity, physical coordination and lack of ability to lift or speak, see, hear, remember, concentrate, learn or understand or to perceive the risk of physical danger. Also included are those who have a progressive condition such as HIV from the time of diagnosis. Persons who were on the register of disabled persons kept under s 6 of the Disabled Persons (Employment) Act 1944 when the relevant provisions came into force are deemed disabled.

Employees who are within the definition

It is unlawful for an employer to discriminate against a disabled employee:

- in the terms of employment and the opportunities for promotion, transfer, training or other benefits or by refusing the same;
- by dismissal or any other disadvantage.

An important case that questions the existing scope of disability discrimination is *Coleman* v *Attridge Law* (2008). Sharon Coleman, the primary carer for her disabled son, claimed that she had been treated less favourably than other employees with children as a result of her association with a disabled person. In particular, she alleged that the employer refused to allow her the same flexible working arrangements that were granted to employees with non-disabled children. She instituted a claim for constructive dismissal. Coleman sought to rely on the Disability Discrimination Act and EC Directive 2000/78. The Directive established a general framework for equality of treatment in situations of employment and occupation. The complainant argued that the Directive extended protection from discrimination to individuals who are not themselves disabled but are the victims of discrimination by association. Accordingly, the Disability Discrimination Act should be interpreted in conformity with the Directive.

The employment tribunal referred the question of the proper construction of the Directive to the European Court of Justice. The question was addressed by an Opinion by the Advocate-General in January 2008. The Opinion stated that:

> It is not necessary for someone who is the object of discrimination to have been mistreated on account of 'her disability'. It is enough if she was mistreated on account of 'disability'. Thus, one can be a victim of unlawful discrimination on the ground of disability under the Directive without being disabled oneself . . . Therefore, if Ms Coleman can prove that she was treated less favourably because of her son's disability she should be able to rely on the Directive.

This is a potentially ground-breaking interpretation of the Directive, which would require the Disability Discrimination Act to be revised in order to reflect this interpretation. It should be noted that the Advocate-General's Opinion is not binding. Nevertheless, it may influence the ECJ's decision when it considers the case.

If the Court endorses this interpretation it will have profound consequences for the scope of disability discrimination in the UK.

As regards insurance benefits, where an employer makes arrangements for employees with an insurance company for matters such as private health insurance, the insurance company will under s 18 act unlawfully if it treats a disabled person in a way which would be an act of discrimination if done by the insurance company to a member of the public generally. This covers refusal to insure and the levying of higher premiums unless justified as it may be if there are reasonable grounds for supposing that the disabled person represents a higher than normal risk.

Employer's defence

The question is whether the decision can be objectively justified. Schedule 9 to the Act provides a general exception to what would otherwise be unlawful direct discrimination in relation to work. This allows employer discrimination if, but only if, the reason is both material to the circumstances of the case and substantial. Thus, less favourable treatment may be *justified* if the employer believes on reasonable grounds that the nature of the disability substantially affects the disabled person's ability to perform the required task. The burden of proof will be on the person who is seeking to justify the exception.

In previous cases, the factor of reasonableness was related to practicability in terms of how useful the adjustments would be and the cost and the ability of the organisation to meet them. The value of the employee, which includes training, skill and service, is also a relevant factor. Thus a high cost adjustment might be required as reasonable for a long-serving managing director but not for a temporary cleaner.

In this regard, an employment tribunal accepted the defence of justification in *Kelly* v *Hampshire Constabulary* (1997). The claimant suffered from cerebral palsy and so needed help in various ways including eating and using the toilet. The employers offered him employment on the basis that they would try to make the necessary arrangements to accommodate him. The employers were later able to satisfy a tribunal that, although they had made every effort to do this, it was impossible for them to accommodate him and because of this they were held not to have discriminated when the employment did not continue.

It is, or course, important that the employer be aware of the disability. See *O'Neill* v *Symm & Co Ltd* (1998), where the employers were not liable for the dismissal of an accounts clerk suffering from ME because they had not been aware of the nature of her illness and so could not have treated her less favourably than an employee who did not have this disability. The dismissal was for the amount of sick leave taken and non-production of a doctor's certificate, which the contract of employment required. In addition, the employers had not infringed the requirement of the Act to take all reasonable steps to find out about the disability since in the circumstances of the case there was nothing to put the employers on inquiry. Where, however, the employer is aware of facts which put him on inquiry, the matter may be different.

H J Heinz v Kenrick (2000)

K was dismissed after a long period of sickness absence. His employers knew of his symptoms and that ME was a disability within the scope of the DDA 1995. They did not know, however, the exact nature of the reason behind his absence when they dismissed him. The EAT did not follow its earlier decision in *O'Neill* and in fact doubted it. The employers' lack of precise knowledge as to absence was no defence and K's dismissal was unlawful as a dismissal based on disability discrimination.

Comment. The result of this case in terms of employers is that where an employee has been absent for sickness for a reasonable amount of time and it appears that this will continue, it is prudent for the employer to start asking more questions about the reasons for that absence. Failure to do so could result in a disability claim where there is no cap on compensation by reason of the employer's own inaction or lack of knowledge.

Duty to make adjustments

Part 13 and Schedule 21 deal with reasonable adjustments in relation to premises.

It is important to understand that the employer is only required to make adjustments if possible in terms of the job that the disabled person is employed to do. The duty does not extend to offering different types of employment contracts within the organisation and without competition from other applicants. In other words, if, after taking reasonable adjustments into account, the applicant would not be the best person for the position he or she applied for, this would not affect the recruitment decision.

This can also be seen in previous case law. In *Archibald v Fife Council* (2004) Ms Archibald was a road sweeper. She had an accident and became unable to walk. The employer allowed her to apply for other posts within the organisation which were sedentary but it allowed others to apply and Ms Archibald was unsuccessful. She was later dismissed on the ground of incapacity and claimed discriminatory dismissal. She lost her claim before an employment tribunal and the EAT. The Scottish Court of Session also refused an appeal. It was, of course, impossible to adjust and modify Ms Archibald's contract as a road sweeper because it is an irreducible minimum requirement that a road sweeper under Ms Archibald's type of contract should be able to walk. Given that no adjustment can be made, the employer has no further duty to provide alternative employment, said the court.

Appeal Note. The House of Lords reversed the above decision and ruled that where an employee has become disabled and is in danger of losing the employment because of inability to perform the manual tasks required but is capable of doing other jobs within the organisation the employer is under a duty under the DDA 1995, s 6 to take reasonable steps to prevent that disadvantage. These may, depending on the circumstances, extend to arranging a transfer to a sedentary post at a higher grade without requiring the worker to compete with other applicants. The case was remitted to the employment tribunal for reconsideration.

Constructive dismissal

In *Catherall* v *Michelin Tyre* (2003) the EAT disagreed with earlier rulings of the EAT and stated that dismissal under the DDA 1995 included constructive dismissal. The Disability Discrimination Act 1995 (Amendment) Regulations 2003 support this statement by introducing a provision into the 1995 Act that dismissal includes the termination of a person's employment by the giving of notice in circumstances such that he or she is entitled to terminate it without notice by reason of the employer's conduct (see reg 5, inserting s 4(5)(b)). This regulation operated from 1 October 2004.

Enforcement

As state above, complaints are to be presented to an employment tribunal. The claim must be brought within three months of the act complained of and the tribunal may take any of the following steps as it considers just and equitable:

- make a declaration of the rights of the complainant as a basis for these to be adopted by the employer;
- order monetary compensation with no limit;
- recommend steps to be taken by the employer within a specified period to obviate or reduce the adverse effects of which the employee complains.

The services of ACAS can also be invoked with a view to settlement without a tribunal hearing.

There is no cap upon the compensation which may be awarded for disability discrimination. In *Kirk* v *British Sugar plc* (1998) a partially sighted employee who was able to prove that his defective eyesight was the dominant factor in his selection for redundancy was awarded £100,000. The scores he achieved in his assessment were influenced by his disability and were not an objective assessment based upon his past work performance. The tribunal accepted that a partially sighted person would have greater difficulties in obtaining employment and based the award on the finding that he would not get alternative employment for the rest of his working life of 15 years, less 20 per cent to take account of the risk that had he stayed on his eyesight might have deteriorated to the point where he could not continue.

Employers should note that the number of cases involving disability discrimination is increasing. In this area, as in so much of modern labour law, employers need to be aware of their duties and to be proactive in respect of them.

The Equality and Human Rights Commission has issued guidance for employers on how to avoid discrimination, covering a whole range of situations. A link will be provided at the end of this chapter.

Termination of the contract of employment

Unfair dismissal – generally

Before a person can ask an employment tribunal to consider a claim that another has unfairly dismissed him or her it is once again essential to establish that the relationship of employer and employee exists between them. In this connection the ERA provides that an employee is a person who works under a contract of service or apprenticeship, written or oral, express or implied.

An example of a case where a person failed in an unfair dismissal claim because he was unable to show that he was an employee is given below.

Massey v Crown Life Insurance Co (1978)

Mr Massey was employed by Crown Life as the manager of their Ilford branch from 1971 to 1973, the company paying him wages and deducting tax. In 1973, on the advice of his accountant, Mr Massey registered a business name of J R Massey and Associates and with that new name entered into an agreement with Crown Life under which he carried out the same duties as before but as a self-employed person. The Inland Revenue were content that he should change to be taxed under Schedule D as a self-employed person. His employment was terminated and he claimed to have been unfairly dismissed. The Court of Appeal decided that being self-employed he could not be unfairly dismissed.

Unfair dismissal – excluded categories

Employees above retiring age were excluded but are no longer by reason of the Employment Equality (Age) Regulations 2006. Examples of excluded categories include: dismissal in circumstances in which the employee failed to make use of the statutory grievance procedure; and dismissals where the employee has entered into a valid compromise agreement.

As regards the period of employment, the general unfair dismissal provisions do not apply to the dismissal of an employee from any employment if the employee, whether full time or part time, has not completed one year's continuous employment ending with the effective date of termination of employment unless the dismissal is automatically unfair. Such dismissals are actionable regardless of service or hours worked. There are exceptions in the case, for example, of maternity dismissals, health and safety dismissals and dismissals for asserting statutory rights, e.g. asking for written particulars. These dismissals are automatically unfair and are not service-based.

Persons who ordinarily worked outside Great Britain were formerly excluded. However, s 32(3) of the Employment Relations Act 1999 repealed the relevant provision of the Employment Rights Act 1996, but unfortunately put nothing in its place. The position now is that if the worker's contract is for work in the UK but the worker is posted abroad, UK remedies apply, but where the contract is for work abroad, UK remedies may not apply. However, in *Lawson* v *Serco* (2006) the House of Lords ruled that the claimant, who was employed to work on Ascension Island as distinct from being posted there, could pursue a claim for unfair dismissal under UK employment law. Mr Lawson was a civilian working at a UK airforce base which was described by the House of Lords as sufficient of a UK enclave to allow the claim.

Certain other categories are excluded by the ERA, e.g. members of the police force and those taking unofficial industrial action. The Employment Relations Act 1999 provides that a worker who is dismissed by reason of taking official and legal industrial action will be able to claim unfair dismissal, provided that the dismissal takes place within the first 12 weeks of the action beginning with the day on which the employee took part in industrial action. Thus, in a long period of official industrial action, these rules of dismissal protection would not apply.

Members of the armed forces are now covered by the unfair dismissal provisions of the ERA, provided that they have first availed themselves of services redress procedures (ERA 1996, s 192).

It should also be noted that s 9 of the Employment Tribunals Act 1996 contains provisions to test the strength of the case of each party before a full hearing proceeds. Pre-hearing reviews are introduced at which the chairman of the tribunal may sit alone without the two lay assessors. The chairman may, at his discretion and following an application by one of the parties, or of his own motion, require a deposit of up to £500 from the other party as a condition of proceeding further if it is considered that his or her case has no reasonable prospect of success, or that to pursue it would be frivolous, vexatious or otherwise unreasonable. Chairmen of employment tribunals are referred to as 'judges' since 1 December 2007.

There are other points worth noting following the attempts to reduce the number of applications to tribunals set out in the Employment Act 2002. Section 22 contains a provision allowing awards of costs and expenses against representatives such as lawyers instead of the parties. This is designed to deal with vexatious claims or inappropriate behaviour. It could mean that a representative could not recover his fees from his client and may have to pay the other party's costs. The expression 'representatives' does not include those who do not charge for their services. The section also provides that if a party has acted unreasonably, the tribunal may order that party to make a payment to the other in regard to the time that other has spent in preparing his case (usually this will be the employer in respect of time spent on the defence). Under s 24 tribunals have a power to postpone the fixing of a time and place for a hearing in order for the proceedings to be settled through conciliation by the Advisory, Conciliation and Arbitration Service: the *power* of ACAS to conciliate returns after the period for conciliation set by a tribunal during which time ACAS has a *duty* to conciliate.

Dismissal – meaning of

An employee cannot claim unfair dismissal unless there has first been a dismissal recognised by law. We may consider the matter under the following headings.

Actual dismissal

This does not normally give rise to problems since most employees recognise the words of an actual dismissal, whether given orally or in writing.

A letter arranging a disciplinary meeting appears in Figure 16.3 and a letter to follow that meeting is set out in Figure 16.4.

Constructive dismissal

This occurs where it is the employee who leaves the job but is compelled to do so by the conduct of the employer. In general terms, the employer's conduct must be a fundamental breach so that it can be regarded as a repudiation of the contract. Thus, if a male employer were to sexually harass a female employee, then this would be a fundamental breach entitling her to leave and sue for her loss on the basis of constructive dismissal.

It would also occur if the employer unilaterally changed the terms and conditions of the employment contract as by unilaterally reducing wages under the contract (see *Rigby* v *Ferodo* (1987)). Furthermore, the EAT decided in *Whitbread plc (t/a Thresher)* v *Gullyes* (1994) that an employee who resigned from a management position because her employer did not give her proper support – because, among other things, the most experienced staff were transferred out of her branch without consultation – was constructively dismissed.

Fixed-term contracts

When a fixed-term contract expires and is not renewed, there is a dismissal. Under the provisions of the Employment Relations Act 1999, the ERA 1996 is amended so that an employee can no longer waive his or her right to claim unfair dismissal where a contract for one year or more is not renewed. It used to be possible to forgo the right to claim a redundancy payment at the end of a fixed-term contract that was of at least two years' duration. This is no longer possible by reason of the Fixed-term Employees (Prevention of Less Favourable Treatment) Regulations 2002 (SI 2002/2034).

Dear   Date

I am writing to tell you that .... [insert organisation name] is considering dismissing OR taking disciplinary action [insert proposed action] against you.

This action is being considered with regard to the following circumstances:

You are invited to attend a disciplinary meeting in .... at .... am/pm which is to be held in .... where this will be discussed.

You are entitled, if you wish, to be accompanied by another work colleague or your trade union representative.

Yours sincerely

Signed Manager

Figure 16.3 Letter to be sent by the employer, setting out the reasons for the proposed dismissal or action short of dismissal and arranging the meeting (for statutory procedure)

Source: http://www.acas.org.uk/index.aspx?articleid=920

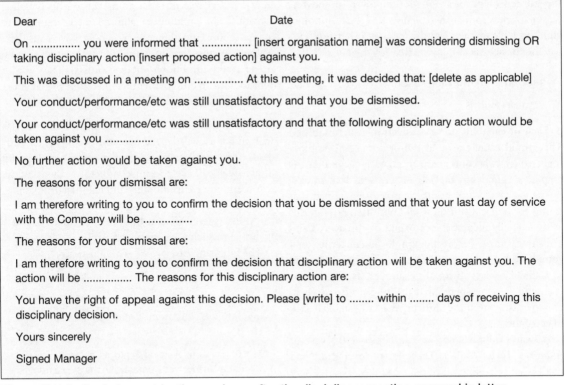

Dear   Date

On .... you were informed that .... [insert organisation name] was considering dismissing OR taking disciplinary action [insert proposed action] against you.

This was discussed in a meeting on .... At this meeting, it was decided that: [delete as applicable]

Your conduct/performance/etc was still unsatisfactory and that you be dismissed.

Your conduct/performance/etc was still unsatisfactory and that the following disciplinary action would be taken against you ....

No further action would be taken against you.

The reasons for your dismissal are:

I am therefore writing to you to confirm the decision that you be dismissed and that your last day of service with the Company will be ....

The reasons for your dismissal are:

I am therefore writing to you to confirm the decision that disciplinary action will be taken against you. The action will be .... The reasons for this disciplinary action are:

You have the right of appeal against this decision. Please [write] to .... within .... days of receiving this disciplinary decision.

Yours sincerely

Signed Manager

Figure 16.4 Letter to be sent by the employer after the disciplinary meeting arranged in letter (for statutory procedure)

Source: http://www.acas.org.uk/index.aspx?articleid=920

Dismissal – grounds for

If an employer is going to escape liability for unfair dismissal, he or she must show that they acted *reasonably* and, indeed, the ERA 1996, s 92 requires the employer to give their reasons for dismissal to the employee in writing.

It should be remembered that the question of whether a dismissal is fair or not is a matter of *fact* for the particular tribunal hearing the case, and one cannot predict with absolute accuracy what a particular tribunal will do on the facts of a particular case. Basically, when all is said and done, the ultimate question for a tribunal is – 'was the dismissal fair and reasonable' in fact?

A problem that has arisen in this connection is whether the tribunal in looking at reasonable employer responses can decide the issue on the basis of what it thinks is reasonable or unreasonable or whether the tribunal must decide the matter by considering the range of reasonable responses employers might make.

The matter was resolved by the Court of Appeal in *Post Office* v *Foley; HSBC Bank* v *Madden* (2001) where the court ruled that tribunals were not to approach the matter of reasonableness or unreasonableness of a dismissal by reference to their own judgment of what would have been done if they had been the employer. Thus, a tribunal should conclude that a dismissal is fair if it is within the range of reasonable responses an employer might make, even though the tribunal would not have regarded the response of a particular employer as reasonable. It should be noted that the test refers to 'reasonable' responses so that a perverse or objectively unreasonable response would not be acceptable.

Section 98 of the ERA 1996 includes in the test of reasonableness required in determining whether a dismissal was fair, the 'size and administrative resources of the employer's undertaking'. This was included as a result of fear that the unfair dismissal laws were placing undue burdens on small employers and causing them not to engage new workers. Earlier legislation also removed the burden of proof from the employer in showing reasonableness so that there is now no 'presumption of guilt' on the employer and the tribunal is left to decide whether or not the employer acted reasonably.

Reasons justifying dismissal

These are as follows.

1 Lack of capability or qualifications: unsuitability. This would usually arise at the beginning of employment where it becomes clear at an early stage that the employee cannot do the job in terms of lack of skill or mental or physical health. It may be imagined that claims for unfair dismissal would not often arise in this area: generally incompetence would be discovered and a dismissal made before the employee concerned had completed the necessary one year's service to be entitled to claim. However, there are examples, as seen below. It should be remembered that the longer a person is in employment, the more difficult it is to establish lack of capability.

By way of illustration, we can consider the case of *Alidair* v *Taylor* (1977). The pilot of an aircraft had made a faulty landing which damaged the aircraft. There was a board of inquiry which found that the faulty landing was due to a lack of flying knowledge on the part of the pilot, who was dismissed from his employment. It was decided that the employee had not been unfairly dismissed, the tribunal taking the view that where, as in this case, one failure to reach a high degree of skill could have serious consequences, an instant dismissal could be justified.

However, it was decided in *British Sulphur* v *Lawrie* (1987) that the dismissal of an employee who was alleged to be unwilling or incompetent to do a particular job could still be unfair if the employee was not provided with adequate training.

As regards qualifications, this could occur where a new employee does not have the qualifications claimed or fails to get a qualification which was a condition of employment, as in the case of legal and accounting trainees who fail to complete their examinations. It should also be noted that the Court of Appeal decided in *Nottinghamshire County Council* v *P* (1992) that even though an employee had to be dismissed from an employment for which he had become unsuitable, it could still be unfair dismissal if the employer failed to make a reasonable investigation of possible alternative employment. P was an assistant groundsman at a girls' school and had pleaded guilty to a charge of indecent assault on his daughter. Obviously, he could not be allowed to continue to work at the school, but the council should have considered alternative employment within the authority. Failure to do so could amount to unfair dismissal. The case was sent back to an employment tribunal to see what efforts the council had made if any.

2 Misconduct. This is always a difficult matter to deal with and much will depend upon the circumstances of the case. However, incompetence and neglect are relevant, as are disobedience and misconduct, e.g. by assaulting fellow employees. Immorality and habitual drunkenness could also be brought under this heading and so, it seems, can dress where this can be shown to affect adversely the way in which the contract of service is performed.

The following case provides an illustration.

> **Boychuk v H J Symons (Holdings) Ltd (1977)**
>
> Miss B was employed by S Ltd as an accounts clerk, but her duties involved contact with the public from time to time. Miss B insisted on wearing badges which proclaimed the fact that she was a lesbian and from May 1976 she wore one or other of the following: (a) a lesbian symbol consisting of two circles with crosses (indicating women) joined together; (b) badges with the legends: 'Gays against fascism' and 'Gay power'; (c) a badge with the legend: 'Gay switchboard' with a telephone number on it and the words: 'Information service for homosexual men and women'; (d) a badge with the word 'Dyke', indicating to the initiated that she was a lesbian.
>
> These were eventually superseded by a white badge with the words 'Lesbians ignite' written in large letters on it. Nothing much had happened in regard to the wearing of the earlier badges, but when she began wearing the 'Lesbians ignite' badge, there were discussions about it between her and her employer. She was told that she must remove it – which she was not willing to do – and that if she did not she would be dismissed. She would not remove the badge and was dismissed on 16 August 1976 and then made a claim for compensation for unfair dismissal.
>
> No complaint was made regarding the manner of her dismissal in terms, e.g., of proper warning. The straight question was whether her employers were entitled to dismiss her because she insisted on wearing the badge. An employment tribunal had decided that in all the circumstances the dismissal was fair because it was

within an employer's discretion to instruct an employee not to wear a particular badge or symbol which could cause offence to customers and fellow employees. Miss B appealed to the Employment Appeal Tribunal which dismissed her appeal and said that her dismissal was fair. The court said that there was no question of Miss B having been dismissed because she was a lesbian or because of anything to do with her private life or private behaviour. Such a case would be entirely different and raise different questions. This was only a case where she had been dismissed because of her conduct at work. That, the court said, must be clearly understood.

Comment.

(i) The decision does not mean that an employer by a foolish or unreasonable judgement of what could be expected to be offensive could impose some unreasonable restriction on an employee. However, the decision does mean that a reasonable employer, who is, after all, ultimately responsible for the interests of the business, is allowed to decide what, upon reflection or mature consideration, could be offensive to customers and fellow employees, and he need not wait to see whether the business would in fact be damaged before he takes steps in the matter.

(ii) In *Kowalski* v *The Berkeley Hotel* (1985) the EAT decided that the dismissal of a pastrycook for fighting at work was fair though it was the first time he had done it. Also, on the issue of conduct, the EAT decided in *Marshall* v *Industrial Systems and Control Ltd* (1992) that a company acted reasonably in dismissing its managing director after discovering that along with another manager he was planning to set up a business competing with the company and to take on the business of its best customer and that active steps had been taken to achieve this. It should be noted that an employee does not breach the duty of loyalty merely by forming an intention to compete at some future date (*Laughton* v *Bapp Industrial Supplies Ltd* (1986)). As regards smoking at work, it was decided in *Dryden* v *Greater Glasgow Health Board* (1992) that employees have no implied contractual right to smoke at work. If, as in Ms Dryden's case, the employee leaves because he or she is not allowed to smoke, there is no constructive dismissal. The employer in this case had offered counselling but without success.

Crime inside employment will normally justify a dismissal on the ground of misconduct. For example, the EAT has decided that an employee was dismissed fairly on the ground of theft from the employer, even though the employer could not specifically prove loss of stock but had only a reasonable belief in the employee's guilt. No specific stock loss could be proved but the employee had been seen by a security guard loading boxes into his car at night at the employer's warehouse (see *Francis* v *Boots the Chemist Ltd* (1998)).

Dismissal on the ground of theft may also be fair even though what is stolen is of little value. Thus, in *Tesco Stores Ltd* v *Khalid* (2001) the employee was dismissed for misappropriation of cigarettes from a petrol station where he worked. His dismissal was held to be fair even though the cigarettes were from damaged stock due for return to the manufacturer. Dismissal was within the range of reasonable responses of an employer.

Crime outside employment raises more difficult issues and generally speaking the employer will have to show damage to his organisation. Thus, in *Post Office* v *Liddiard* (2001) a Post Office employee was involved in football violence in France. His dismissal for this reason was held to be unfair. It might be different, of course, where an accountant has been convicted of dishonesty as treasurer of a local charity for which he or she works part time and voluntarily, or where a teacher has been convicted of offences involving violence in his or her non-work environment.

An employee's use of drugs or alcohol outside the workplace is unlikely to amount to a fair reason for dismissal, nor will the mere fact that an employee did not reveal that he or she used drugs or alcohol when interviewed for a post. However, use of drugs or excessive drinking may constitute a fair reason for dismissal where the employer believes on reasonable grounds that it makes the employee *unsuitable for the position held*. An employer who wishes to dismiss employees for drink or drug misconduct should have a drink and drugs policy and make it part of the employee's contract.

3 **Redundancy.** Genuine redundancy is a defence. Where a person is redundant, his employer cannot be expected to continue the employment, although there are safeguards in the matter of *unfair selection for redundancy*. Examples are selection because of pregnancy or trade union membership or activities or for asserting statutory rights or on health and safety matters as by selection of health and safety representatives.

4 **Dismissals which are union-related.** These are known as the '*section 152 reasons*'. They are set out in the Trade Union and Labour Relations (Consolidation) Act 1992, s 152. An employee will be regarded as automatically

unfairly dismissed so that no particular period of service or hours worked is required if the principal reason for the dismissal was that he was, or proposed to become, a member of a trade union which was independent of the employer; that he had taken part or proposed to take part in the activities of such a union at an appropriate time, i.e. outside working hours or within working hours with the consent of the employer; that he was not a member of any trade union or of a particular one or had refused or proposed to refuse to become or remain a member. Under the relevant provisions of the Trade Union and Labour Relations (Consolidation) Act 1992 all closed-shop dismissals are now automatically unfair.

Dismissal will also be automatically unfair if the employee is selected for redundancy on any of the above 'trade union' grounds. Furthermore, the Court of Appeal decided in *Fitzpatrick* v *British Railways Board* (1992) that a dismissal for trade union activities in a previous employment was automatically unfair.

It is also worth noting at this point that under s 146 of the Trade Union and Labour Relations (Consolidation) Act 1992 an employee has a right not to have action taken against him short of dismissal, such as victimisation in terms of not being offered overtime, where this is related to union membership or activities. There is, however, a provision in the 1992 Act under which protection against victimisation continues but does not prevent an employer, acting reasonably, from implementing a decision to negotiate personally with his employees and not through a union and to offer inducements such as increased pay to those who sign personal contracts, while denying these benefits to those who do not sign.

5 Statutory restriction placed on employer or employee. If, for example, the employer's business was found to be dangerous and was closed down under Act of Parliament or ministerial order, the employees would not be unfairly dismissed. Furthermore, a lorry driver who was banned from driving for 12 months could be dismissed fairly.

6 Some other substantial reason. An employer may on a wide variety of grounds which are not specified by legislation satisfy an employment tribunal that a dismissal was fair and reasonable.

Crime and suspicion of crime may be brought under this heading, as well as misconduct, though if dismissal is based on suspicion of crime, the suspicion must be reasonable and in all cases the employee must be told

that dismissal is contemplated and in the light of this information be allowed to give explanations and make representations against dismissal.

Where an employee has been charged with theft from the employer and is awaiting trial, the best course of action is to suspend rather than dismiss him, pending the verdict. Investigations which the employer must make, as part of establishing a fair dismissal, could be regarded as an interference with the course of justice. It is best, therefore, not to make them, but to suspend the employee. The case of *Wadley* v *Eager Electrical* (1986) should be noted. In that case husband and wife worked for the same company. The wife was convicted for stealing £2,000 from the company while employed as a shop assistant. The husband was a service engineer with the company. Husband and wife were dismissed and it was held that the husband's dismissal was unfair. He was a good employee of 17 years' standing and no misconduct had been made out against him.

The matter of fair or unfair dismissal depends also upon the terms of the contract. If the difficulty is that a particular employee is refusing to do work which involves him, say, spending nights away from home, then his dismissal is likely to be regarded as fair if there is an *express term* in his contract requiring this. Of course, the nature of the job may require it, as in the case of a long-distance lorry driver where such a term would be implied, if not expressed.

Employees who are in breach of contract are likely to be regarded as fairly dismissed. However, this is not an invariable rule. Thus a long-distance lorry driver who refused to take on a particular trip because his wife was ill and he had to look after the children would be unfairly dismissed (if dismissal took place) even though he was, strictly speaking, in breach of his contract.

Dismissal could also be for a substantial reason where a breakdown of relationships either within the office or with a customer have made an employee's position untenable. The following example illustrates the possibilities.

In a small office there are two order clerks working closely together. They are very good friends. One of them sets up home with the other's wife. They are no longer on speaking terms and cannot work together. The employer has no other office to which one of them could be transferred.

There may be no alternative to dismissal. If no solution can be found in discussion with the workers, one should be dismissed on the basis of length of service and other factors that would be relevant if one of them was being selected for redundancy.

In *Cobley* v *Forward Technology Industries plc* (2003) the Court of Appeal ruled that the chief executive of a public listed company was not unfairly dismissed when the shareholders removed him from his office as a director by a resolution in general meeting. This effected his dismissal as CEO because his contract said that he could not continue as CEO unless he was also a director of the company. His dismissal was, ruled the court, for 'some other substantial reason' under the Employment Rights Act 1996 and that made the dismissal fair. The removal followed a successful hostile takeover of the company and the case shows that business reorganisations such as this can be brought under the heading of 'some other substantial reason'. The new owners clearly cannot be expected to retain the former board members.

Grievance and disciplinary procedures

1 The Employment Act 2002 in s 29 and Sch 2 provides statutory dismissal, disciplinary procedures and grievance procedures. These have already been considered. Section 30 makes it an implied term of every contract of employment that the statutory procedures are to apply and employers and employees cannot contract out of them. Provided these procedures are followed in a reasonable manner, their fairness will not normally be questioned by the courts, and the major case on the requirement for fair procedures – the House of Lords' ruling in *Polkey* v *A E Dayton Services Ltd* (1987) – will have no application.

However, it may not always be necessary to consult, as where the employer has reasonably taken the view, having thought about it, that the exceptional circumstances of a particular case make it, for example, undesirable. Thus in *Eclipse Blinds* v *Wright* (1992) Mrs Wright was dismissed because of poor health. The employer had received a medical report with her consent. It revealed that she was much more seriously ill than she had thought and, rather than upset her in a consultation process, the personnel officer wrote her a letter in sympathetic terms ending her employment on the grounds of incapability. The court decided that she had not been unfairly dismissed even though there was no proper consultation.

2 Where conduct is the main reason the employer must show, on a balance of probabilities, that at the time of the dismissal he believed the employee was guilty of misconduct and that in all the circumstances of the case it was reasonable for him to dismiss.

3 During the disciplinary hearings and the appeal process, the employer must have been fair to the employee. In particular, the employee must have been heard and allowed to put his case properly or, if he was not at a certain stage of the procedures, this must have been corrected before dismissal.

Under reforms made to disciplinary hearings by the Employment Relations Act 1999, an employee has a *right* to be accompanied at such hearings by a trade union representative or a fellow employee. This applies even if an employer does not recognise trade unions. As a result, hearings are likely to become more adversarial and formal, and so lengthier. Legal advice should perhaps now be sought by employers in the hearings, bearing in mind that a combined basic and compensatory award could exceed £63,000.

Employee's contributory fault

This can reduce the compensation payable to the employee by such percentage as the tribunal thinks fit. Suppose an employee is often late for work and one morning his employer, who can stand it no more, sacks him. The dismissal is likely to be unfair in view of the lack of warning but a tribunal would very probably reduce the worker's compensation to take account of the facts.

Principles of natural justice also apply; it is necessary to let the worker state his case before a decision to dismiss is taken. Furthermore, reasonable enquiry must be made to find out the truth of the matter before reaching a decision. Failure to do this will tend to make the dismissal unfair.

Unacceptable reasons for dismissal

These are as follows.

1 Dismissal in connection with trade unions. This has already been considered.

2 Unfair selection for redundancy. An employee dismissed for redundancy may complain that he has been unfairly dismissed if he is of the opinion that he has been unfairly selected for redundancy, as where the employer has selected him because he is a member of a trade union or takes part in trade union activities, or where the employer has disregarded redundancy selection arrangements based, for example, on 'last in, first out'.

Ideally, all employers should have proper redundancy agreements on the lines set out in the Department of Work and Pensions booklet, *Dealing with Redundancies*.

However, even though there is in existence an agreed redundancy procedure, the employer may defend himself by showing a 'special reason' for departing from that procedure, e.g. because the person selected for redundancy lacks the skill and versatility of a junior employee who is retained.

There is, since the decision of the Employment Appeal Tribunal in *Williams* v *Compair Maxam* (1982), an overall standard of fairness also in redundancy arrangements. The standards laid down in the case require the giving of maximum notice; consultation with unions, if any; the taking of the views of more than one person as to who should be dismissed; a requirement to follow any laid down procedure, e.g. last in, first out; and finally, an effort to find the employees concerned alternative employment within the organisation. However, the EAT stated in *Meikle* v *McPhail* (*Charleston Arms*) (1983) that these guidelines would be applied less rigidly to the smaller business. The statutory provisions relating to consultation on redundancy are considered later in this chapter.

3 Industrial action. The position in this context has already been considered.

4 Dismissals in connection with pregnancy and childbirth and parental and adoption and paternity leave. The relevant law has already been considered.

5 Pressure on employer to dismiss unfairly. It is no defence for an employer to say that pressure was put upon him to dismiss an employee unfairly. So, if other workers put pressure on an employer to dismiss a non-union member so as, for example, to obtain a closed shop, the employer will have no defence to a claim for compensation for the dismissal if he gives in to that pressure. If an employer alleges that he was pressurised into dismissing an employee and that pressure was brought on him by a trade union or other person by the calling, organising, procuring or financing of industrial action, including a strike, or by the threat of such things, and the reason for the pressure was that the employee was not a member of the trade union, then the employer can join the trade union or other person as a party to the proceedings if he is sued by the dismissed worker for unfair dismissal. If the tribunal awards compensation, it can order that a person joined as a party to the

proceedings should pay such amount of it as is just and equitable, and if necessary this can be a complete indemnity so that the employer will recover all the damages awarded against him from the union.

6 Transfer of business. The Transfer of Undertakings (Protection of Employment) Regulations 2006 apply. Under the regulations if a business or part of it is transferred and an employee is dismissed because of this, the dismissal will be treated as automatically unfair. However, the person concerned is not entitled to the extra compensation given to other cases of automatically unfair dismissal.

If the old employer dismissed before transfer, or the new employer dismissed after the transfer, either will have a defence if he can prove that the dismissal was for 'economic, technical or organisational' reasons requiring a change in the workforce and that the dismissal was reasonable in all the circumstances of the case.

The following case is relevant.

Meikle v *McPhail (Charleston Arms)* (1983)

After contracting to take over a public house and its employees, the new management decided that economies were essential and dismissed the barmaid. She complained to an employment tribunal on the grounds of unfair dismissal. Her case was based upon the fact that the 1981 regulations state that a dismissal is to be treated as unfair if the transfer of a business or a reason connected with it is the reason or principal reason for the dismissal. The pub's new management defended the claim under another provision in the 1981 regulations which states that a dismissal following a transfer of business is not to be regarded as automatically unfair where there was, as in this case, an economic reason for making changes in the workforce. If there is such a reason, unfairness must be established on grounds other than the mere transfer of the business.

The EAT decided that the reason for dismissal was an economic one under the regulations and that the management had acted reasonably in the circumstances so that the barmaid's claim failed.

Comment. It should be noted that in *Gateway Hotels Ltd* v *Stewart* (1988) the EAT decided that on a transfer of business dismissal of employees of the business transferred prior to the transfer at the insistence of the purchaser of the business is not an 'economic' reason within the regulations so that the dismissals are unfair.

7 Health and safety dismissals and detriments.
Designated or acknowledged health and safety representatives must not be subjected to detriments, for example loss of overtime, for carrying out health and safety activities in the workplace. Dismissal for these reasons is automatically unfair which means that there is no service requirement. These provisions also apply to ordinary employees, regardless of service, who leave or refuse to return to the workplace because of a health hazard reasonably thought to exist. The same is true under the Health and Safety (Consultation with Employees) Regulations 1996 (SI 1996/1513) where the dismissal is of a worker safety representative elected to take part in the health and safety consultation process where there is no recognised union.

8 Dismissal for asserting statutory right. This protects employees regardless of service against dismissal for trying to enforce employment rights under the EPA that can be brought before a tribunal. Dismissal will be unfair even if the worker does not in fact have the right provided he has acted in good faith.

9 Dismissal for performing the duties of a member-nominated trustee of an occupational pension scheme.

10 Dismissal for performing the duties of an employee representative in redundancy consultation or putting up for election to be one.

Automatically unfair dismissals

Having noted some of these in various parts of the text, it may be useful to bring them together in a list, remembering that dismissals of this kind do not require any particular period of service with the employer.

The reasons which make a dismissal automatically unfair can briefly be listed as follows:

- trade union membership or activities;
- not belonging to a trade union or particular union;
- pregnancy and dismissals in connection with parental and adoption and paternity leave;
- selection for redundancy on any of the above grounds;
- the transfer of the undertaking or a reason connected with it (unless there is an ETO: economic, technical or organisational reason) (it should, however, be noted at this point that the one-year qualifying period does not apply where the complaint is based on dismissal

for one of the automatically unfair reasons, though if the dismissal related to the transfer of an undertaking the one-year qualifying period does apply);

- asserting a statutory employment right under the ERA 1996, s 104;
- in health and safety cases involving union safety representatives and now including being an employee safety representative or putting up for election to be one;
- performing the duties of a member-nominated trustee under the Pensions Act 1995;
- being an employee representative in redundancy consultation or putting up for election to be one (ERA 1996, s 103);
- refusing (in certain circumstances) to do shop or betting work on a Sunday;
- exercising rights under the Working Time Regulations including rights as an employee representative in connection with the workforce agreements (s 101(A), ERA 1996, as inserted by the regulations);
- asserting rights under the National Minimum Wage Act 1998 (s 104(A), ERA 1996, as inserted by the NMWA 1998);
- asserting rights to time off for study and training under s 63A of the ERA 1996, as inserted by the Teaching and Higher Education Act 1998;
- dismissals of employees because they exercised or tried to exercise the right to be accompanied at a disciplinary and grievance hearing or because they accompanied a fellow worker at such a hearing;
- whistleblowing – protection of whistleblowers is provided by the Public Interest Disclosure Act 1998.

Unfair dismissal and frustration of contract

In cases appearing before employment tribunals, there is a certain interplay between the common law rules of frustration of contract (see Chapter 7 ○) and the statutory provisions relating to unfair dismissal. At common law, a contract of service is frustrated by incapacity, e.g. sickness, if that incapacity makes the contract substantially impossible of performance at a particularly vital time, or by a term of imprisonment. If a contract has been so frustrated, then a complaint of unfair dismissal is not available because the contract has been discharged on other grounds, i.e. by frustration. Thus termination of a contract of service by frustration prevents a claim for unfair dismissal.

It is, of course, necessary now in terms of sickness/incapacity for the employer to be alert to the rules about disability discrimination, particularly where an adjustment to working conditions might enable an employee or recruit to do the job satisfactorily.

Remedies for unfair dismissal

These are as follows.

Conciliation

An employment tribunal will not hear a complaint until a conciliation officer has had a chance to see whether he can help, provided that he or she has been *requested* so to do by a party to the potential complaint. A copy of the complaint made to the employment tribunal will in such a situation be sent to a conciliation officer of the Advisory, Conciliation and Arbitration Service (ACAS) and, if he is unable to settle the complaint, nothing said by the employer or employee during the process of conciliation will be admissible in evidence before the tribunal.

The reference of cases to a conciliation officer has led to the settlement of some one-third of them before the tribunal hearing but the parties do not have to become involved in this procedure.

ACAS arbitration and compromise agreements

The following provisions of the Employment Rights (Dispute Resolution) Act 1998 should be noted.

Part II of the Act contains provisions to allow parties to opt for their dispute to be resolved by independent binding arbitration and gives ACAS powers to pay for and provide an arbitration service for claims of unfair dismissal and unlawful discrimination.

Part II also contains provisions making changes to the law relating to compromise agreements. Currently, the parties to an individual employment rights dispute may conclude that dispute by reaching, for example, a financial settlement. For such an agreement to be binding, the parties must have settled after an ACAS-appointed conciliation officer has taken action, or, alternatively, the terms of the settlement must be contained in a private compromise agreement. Formerly, a compromise agreement that had not involved ACAS had to be made in circumstances where the employee had received independent legal advice from a qualified lawyer.

The 1998 Act changes this to advice from any independent adviser, provided that advice is covered by an insurance policy or an indemnity provision for members of a profession or professional body (ss 9 and 10). This will allow trade unions, advice agencies and others – in addition to lawyers – to give relevant advice.

Other provisions of Part II allow ACAS-appointed conciliation officers to conciliate in claims relating to statutory redundancy payments where before they had no duty to conciliate, as they have in almost all other individual employment rights disputes (s 11).

There are also provisions that clarify, streamline and make more flexible current legislation under which employers and employer-recognised trade unions can, by making a dismissal procedures agreement, opt out of the statutory rules on unfair dismissals (s 12).

Other remedies

An employee who has been dismissed may:

- seek reinstatement or re-engagement; or
- claim compensation.

The power to order reinstatement or re-engagement is discretionary and in practice is rarely exercised. However, reinstatement means taken back by the employer on exactly the same terms and seniority as before; re-engagement is being taken back but on different terms.

Calculation of compensation

Before proceeding further with a study of the calculations, it should be noted that the basic award is based on *gross* pay, but the compensatory award is based on *net* pay, as the sample calculations show. It should also be noted that the cap of £63,000 on unfair dismissal compensatory awards is removed for staff who are unfairly dismissed for blowing the whistle on illegal practices or over health and safety matters and who are protected against such dismissal by the Public Interest Disclosure Act 1998. There is, therefore, no ceiling on such awards. It was feared that some senior executives might have been deterred from whistleblowing about, e.g., legal irregularities in their companies' operation since they would have the most salary to lose.

The compensation for unfair dismissal is in four parts, as follows.

1 The basic award (maximum: £9,900 for those with 20 years' service or more). This award is computed as a redundancy payment (see p 552 before reading on). Contributory fault of the employee is taken into account.

Example

Fred, a 35-year-old van driver employed for 10 years earning £400 per week (take home £350) is unfairly dismissed. He did his best to get a comparable job but did not in fact obtain one until two weeks after the tribunal hearing. Fred had a history of lateness for work and his contributory fault is assessed at 25 per cent.

Fred's basic award: Fred is in the category over 22 years of age but under 41 years of age for redundancy which allows one week's pay for every year of service up to a maximum of £330 per week.

10 × £330	£3,300
Less: 25%	£825
	£2,475 = basic award

If Fred's dismissal had been automatically unfair, for example for union membership, the minimum award would be £4,400. This may be reduced for contributory fault.

2 Compensatory award (maximum: £63,000). This consists of:

- estimated loss of wages, net of tax and other deductions to the date of the hearing less any money earned between the date of dismissal and the hearing;
- estimated future losses;
- loss of any benefits such as pension rights and expenses;
- loss of statutory rights. It is rare to get an award under this heading but it can be given for loss of minimum notice entitlement. For example, Fred has been continuously employed for 10 years. He was entitled to 10 weeks' notice, which he did not get. He now has a new job but it will take him time to build up that entitlement again. A tribunal can award something for this. Once again, contributory fault is taken into account.

Fred's compensatory award:

Note. For the avoidance of doubt, the compensatory award is based on actual *net* earnings with no cap.

		£
The loss up to the hearing	10 × £350	3,500
Loss up to time of getting new job	2 × £350	700
		4,200
Less: 25%		1,050
		3,150

Loss of statutory rights:		
a nominal figure of	£100	
Less: 25%	£25	75
		3,225

Fred's total award is therefore:	£
Basic	2,475
Compensatory	3,225
	5,700

If Fred has lost anything else, such as the use of the firm's van at weekends and/or pension rights, these would be added to the compensatory award subject to 25 per cent discount for contributory fault.

Those on higher salaries may very well reach the maximum of £63,000, but this will be likely only in cases of higher-ranking executives.

3 Additional award. This is available in addition to the above where an employer fails to comply with an order for reinstatement or re-engagement unless it was not practicable for him to do so. The amount of the additional award is an amount of not less than 26 weeks' nor more than 52 weeks' pay, subject to a weekly maximum of £330, in other words £8,580 minimum and £17,160 maximum.

Any unemployment or supplementary benefits received by the employee are deducted from any award made by a tribunal. However, the employer must pay the amount(s) in question direct to the DSS.

As regards *ex gratia* payments, the general principle is that if the employer has made an *ex gratia* payment to the complainant in connection with the dismissal, credit will be given for this payment in fixing the amount of compensation if and only if the dismissal is in the context of being unfairly chosen for redundancy. This results from the provisions of s 122 of the ERA 1996, as interpreted in *Boorman* v *Allmakes Ltd* (1995). If the dismissal is not in that context the employee keeps the *ex gratia* payment in addition to any compensation.

4 Time limits. A claim for compensation against an employer for unfair dismissal must reach the tribunal within three months of the date of termination of employment. A worker can claim while working out his notice, but no award can be made until employment ends.

A tribunal can hear a claim after three months if the employee can prove that:

- it was not reasonably practicable for him to claim within three months;
- he did so as soon as he could in the circumstances.

Unfair dismissal: damages for injury to feelings

For many years the position regarding injury to feelings damages in unfair dismissal cases was clear. The judgment of the President of what was then the Industrial Relations Court in *Norton Tool Co* v *Tewson* (1973) applied and was to the effect that no such damages were available. Loss in unfair dismissal claims was restricted to direct economic loss.

However, in *Johnson* v *Unisys Ltd* (2001) Lord Hoffmann in remarks not essential to his judgment, i.e. *obiter*, took the view that there was no reason why damages for injured feelings should not be awarded.

Since then some tribunals have gone along with Lord Hoffmann's remarks and made awards for injured feelings while others have refused to do so and have stood by the decision in *Norton Tool*.

An appeal in *Dunnachie* reached the Court of Appeal (see *Dunnachie* v *Kingston-Upon-Hull City Council* (2004). The Court of Appeal ruled: (1) that *Norton Tool* was wrongly decided and should no longer be followed; (2) that s 123 of the ERA 1996, which deals with the compensatory award in unfair dismissal cases, was wide enough to cover non-economic loss, but (3) tribunals should only compensate for 'a real injury' to self-respect. However, an award of £10,000 to Mr Dunnachie was within a reasonable band in what was a case involving extreme workplace bullying, which was not redressed by management.

The Court of Appeal then invited an appeal to the House of Lords. Their Lordships ruled that an employee claiming unfair dismissal cannot recover compensation for non-economic loss. Such a claim is not within s 123 of the ERA 1996 (see *Dunnachie* v *Kingston-Upon-Hull City Council* (2004)).

Discriminatory dismissal

In addition to legislation relating to unfair dismissal generally, discrimination legislation deals with complaints to employment tribunals for dismissal on the grounds of discrimination. The nature and scope of these provisions have already been considered and it is only necessary to add here that there are provisions in the ERA 1996 which prevent double compensation being paid, once under discrimination legislation, and once under the general unfair dismissal provisions of the ERA.

Redundancy

The ERA 1996 gives an employee a right to compensation by way of a redundancy payment if he is dismissed because of a redundancy.

Meaning of redundancy

Under the ERA 1996 redundancy is *presumed* to occur where the services of employees are dispensed with because the employer ceases or intends to cease carrying on business, or to carry on business at the place where the employee was employed, or does not require so many employees to do work of a certain kind. Employees who have been laid off or kept on short time without pay for four consecutive weeks (or for six weeks in a period of 13 weeks) are entitled to end their employment and to seek a redundancy payment if there is no reasonable prospect that normal working will be resumed.

Bumped redundancies

After a number of conflicting judicial decisions on this issue the matter has been largely resolved by the ruling of the House of Lords in *Murray* v *Foyle Meats Ltd* (1999). The ruling affirms that 'bumped' redundancies are acceptable. The problem occurs where an employee is made redundant while carrying out job A because of a diminution of work in job A, even though he can under his contract be employed on other work and has from time to time been so employed. Nevertheless, if there is a diminution in work leading to a diminution in the requirement for employees *generally*, the employer has a choice and can apply, e.g., a first-in first-out principle of redundancy and regard as redundant those doing job A or someone else within the group for which work has diminished, regardless of what their contract says or what they are doing or able to do. The contract and function tests are inappropriate, said the House of Lords. The Lord Chancellor said that for employees to be regarded as redundant two things had to be shown:

- that there is a state of affairs in the employer's business which meets the statutory definition of redundancy, e.g. less work; and
- that the employee's dismissal is wholly or mainly *attributable* to that state of affairs.

Thus employer A makes widgets. There is a loss of orders and a diminution in the requirements of production. Therefore, anyone dismissed by reason of the general reduction in orders is to be regarded as redundant. The contract and function tests need not be applied if the dismissal is *attributable* to the loss of orders.

In addition, a redundancy may be 'bumped'. Thus, if Jones is to be dismissed because the employer no longer needs anyone to do his job, the employer may, instead of dismissing Jones, give him Green's job and dismiss Green, e.g. on a first-in last-out basis. Under *Murray* Green may well be found to have been dismissed on the ground of redundancy (rather than unfair dismissal) although he has been 'bumped' out of his job by Jones.

It should be noted, however, that although the House of Lords put it in terms that Green's dismissal was attributable to redundancy, it does seem that his dismissal arises not so much out of the redundancy situation but rather out of the way it was *managed*. The employer saves money by not being sued for unfair dismissal where compensation can be higher.

Eligibility

In general terms, all those employed under a contract of service as employees are entitled to redundancy pay, including a person employed by his or her spouse. Furthermore, a volunteer for redundancy is not debarred from claiming. The right to a redundancy payment is no longer lost at age 65, by reason of the Age Regulations. However, certain persons are excluded by statute or circumstances. The main categories are listed below:

1 A domestic servant in a private household who is a close relative of the employer. The definition of 'close relative' for this purpose is father, mother, grandfather, grandmother, stepfather, stepmother, son, daughter, grandson, granddaughter, stepson, stepdaughter, brother, sister, half-brother, or half-sister.

2 An employee who has not completed at least two years of continuous service. Alternate week working does not break continuity (*Colley* v *Corkindale t/a Corker's Lounge Bar* (1996)). These provisions remain unchanged under amendments made by the Unfair Dismissal and Statement of Reasons for Dismissal (Variation of Qualifying Period) Order 1999 (SI 1999/1436), which apply only to claims for unfair dismissal:

3 An employee who is dismissed for misconduct will lose the right to a redundancy payment. Thus, if we look back at the circumstances in the *Boychuk* and *Kowalski* cases, we can note that, although these cases were brought for unfair dismissal, they would also have been situations in which the employees concerned would have lost the right to a redundancy payment because it would be held that the dismissal was not for redundancy. In such cases, therefore, the only issue will be the possibility of unfair dismissal.

4 An employee who accepts an offer of suitable alternative employment with his employer is not entitled to a redundancy payment. Where a new offer is made, there is a trial period of four weeks following the making of the offer, during which the employer or the employee may end the contract while retaining all rights and liabilities under redundancy legislation.

An employee who unreasonably refuses an offer of alternative employment is not entitled to a redundancy payment, as illustrated in the following case.

Fuller v *Stephanie Bowman* (1977)

F was employed as a secretary at SB's premises which were situated in Mayfair. These premises attracted a very high rent and rates so SB moved its offices to Soho. These premises were situated over a sex shop and F refused the offer of renewed employment at the same salary and she later brought a claim before an employment tribunal for a redundancy payment. The tribunal decided that the question of unreasonableness was a matter of fact for the tribunal and F's refusal to work over the sex shop was unreasonable so that she was not entitled to a redundancy payment.

Comment.

(i) It should be noted that in **North East Coast Ship Repairers v Secretary of State for Employment** (1978) the Employment Appeal Tribunal decided that an apprentice who, having completed the period of his apprenticeship, finds that the firm cannot provide him with work, is not entitled to redundancy payment. This case has relevance for trainees and others completing contracts in order to obtain relevant practical experience.

(ii) In *Elliot* v *Richard Stump Ltd* (1987) the EAT decided that a redundant employee who is offered alternative employment by an employer who refuses to accept a trial period is unfairly dismissed. In *Cambridge and District Co-operative Society Ltd* v *Ruse* (1993) the EAT held that it was reasonable for an employee to refuse alternative work if the new job involved what he reasonably believed to be a loss of status. In that case the manager of a Co-op mobile butcher's shop was offered a post in the butchers' section of a Co-op supermarket, which he refused to accept because he was under another manager, which he felt, quite reasonably, involved a loss of status. He was successful in his claim for a redundancy payment.

(iii) In *Fisher* v *Hoopoe Finance Ltd* (2005) the EAT ruled that offers of alternative employment are ineffective unless information is given regarding wages or salary of the post(s) involved. Mr Fisher was employed by Hoopoe as a new business manager. He was later made redundant and as a consequence brought a claim for unfair dismissal on the basis that Hoopoe had failed to take sufficient and appropriate steps to bring the possibility of suitable alternative employment to his notice. He also alleged that Hoopoe had promised him a new role or to retain his existing role.

The tribunal dismissed his claim and he appealed to the EAT, which ruled that:

- As regards the promise to offer a new role or to retain the existing one, the tribunal had accepted the evidence of Hoopoe's witnesses that the promise was not made and not raised by Mr Fisher at any stage before his dismissal. The EAT found that there was clear evidence that Mr Fisher had raised the matter of the promise before his dismissal and that the tribunal's reasons for preferring the Hoopoe witnesses' evidence were fallacious and amounted to an error in law.
- As regards the offer of alternative employment, the tribunal had misdirected itself in regard to this. Mr Fisher was given a list of alternative roles but none of the written correspondence between the parties gave details as to financial prospects, including the fact that one of the posts, i.e. field-based sales account manager, carried a similar annual salary. There was no evidence as to why this information was not available.
- The decision of the tribunal did not give written reasons, so it did not comply with rule 30(6) of Sch 1 to the Employment Tribunals (Constitution and Rules of Procedure) Regulations 2004 (SI 2004/1861) on written reasons for a judgment and relevant case law. The tribunal's decision consequently amounted to an error in law.

Mr Fisher's appeal was allowed and his claim was remitted back for hearing by a freshly constituted tribunal. This ruling is a reminder to employers to give as much information as they can about suitable alternative employment, including, preferably, written notification as to remuneration. Basically, sufficient information must be given to allow the employee to decide whether to accept or reject the new employment.

As regards time limits, the employee must make a written claim to the employer or to an employment tribunal within six months from the end of the employment. If the employee does not do this, an employment tribunal may extend the time for a further six months, making 12 months in all, but not longer, from the actual date of termination of the employment, provided that it can be shown that it is just and equitable having regard to the reasons put forward by the employee for late application and to all relevant circumstances.

Amount of redundancy payment

It is necessary to ascertain the amount of a week's pay. This amount is whichever is the smaller of the following amounts:

- the employee's weekly wage; or
- the sum of (currently) £330.

The redundancy payment then consists of the total of the following amounts:

- half a week's pay for each complete year during the relevant period for which the employee was aged 21 *and under*;
- one week's pay for each complete year during the relevant period for which the employee was aged between 22 and 40;
- one and a half weeks' pay for each complete year during the relevant period for which the employee was aged 41 or more.

Under the age discrimination regulations the two-year qualifying period remains as does the age-related multiplier and the maximum of 20 years' service taken into account but there is no lower age of 18 to commence the calculation and the upper age limit of 65 is removed. Service under age 18 will now count. The former reduction by one-twelfth where the employee is over 64 is also removed.

Example

A man of 52 who is made redundant having been continuously employed for 18 years and earning £280 per week as gross salary at the time of his redundancy would be entitled to a redundancy payment as follows:

34 to 41 years = 7 years at one week's pay	= 7 weeks
41 to 52 years = 11 years at one and a half weeks' pay	= 16½ weeks
	23½ weeks

It follows, therefore, that the redundancy payment would be 23½ weeks × **£330** = £7,755.

Consider also the case of an employee aged 62 dismissed on the ground of redundancy: he had been continuously employed for 30 years; his gross weekly wage was more than £330. His redundancy payment will be based on his last 20 years of service and he will be entitled to the current maximum of **£9,900** (20 × 1½ × £330 = £9,900).

Complaints by employees in respect of the right to a redundancy payment or questions as to its amount may, as we have seen, be made to an employment tribunal, which will make a declaration as to the employee's rights which form the basis on which payment can be recovered from the employer.

Procedure for handling redundancies

Any agreed formula must be followed, for example last in, first out. Selection procedures may also be based on poor work performance or attendance record and there is no requirement on the employer to find out reasons for this (*Dooley* v *Leyland Vehicles Ltd* (1986)). If there is no agreed procedure, the employer must decide after considering the pros and cons in each case. It should be noted that the dismissal may well be unfair if some reasonable system of selection is not followed. In this connection the EAT decided in *Rogers* v *Vosper Thorneycroft (UK) Ltd* (1988) that 'last in, first out' is a relevant system, but merely asking for volunteers is not. There must be some criteria, though calling for volunteers is acceptable as a preliminary step in the matter of eventual selection. The decision was affirmed by the Court of Appeal.

Everyone should as far as possible be allowed to express their views, for example through elected representatives, if any. Every attempt should be made to relocate a redundant worker. Failure to do so can result in a finding of unfair dismissal – unless, of course, there

was no chance of finding suitable alternative work. Fairness in the search for alternative work involves looking at other companies within a group (EAT decision in *Euroguard Ltd* v *Rycroft* (1993)).

Selecting, say, a white, single, young woman or a West Indian single man to go, rather than a married white man with two children and a mortgage might appear to be humane. However, unless the decision is made on the basis of competence, experience, reliability, and so on, the dismissal is likely to be unfair and also a breach of discrimination legislation.

Consultation over collective redundancies

The Collective Redundancies and Transfer of Undertakings (Protection of Employment) (Amendment) Regulations 1995 (SI 1995/2587) and 1999 (SI 1999/1925) apply. The regulations substantially amend s 188 of the Trade Union and Labour Relations (Consolidation) Act 1992 (TULR(C)A 1992) as follows:

■ The obligation to consult about redundancies now arises where the employer is proposing to dismiss as redundant 20 or more employees at one establishment within a period of 90 days or less. This change has removed the need to consult from some 96 per cent of UK businesses.

■ Where consultation is required, the employer must consult all those who are 'appropriate representatives'.

■ Appropriate representatives of employees are:
 – employee representatives elected by them; or
 – if an independent trade union is recognised by the employer, representatives of the union.

Where the employees elect representatives and belong to a recognised union, the employer has a choice of whether to consult the union representatives or the elected representatives. It should be noted that the regulations extend the requirement to consult to non-union workplaces. They further provide that:

■ Employee representatives may be elected by the employees for the specific purpose of consultation or may be members of an existing works council or joint consultative committee. In all cases the employee representatives must be employed by the employer and not be outsiders. No method of election is stipulated in the regulations which means that *ad hoc* procedures as and when a redundancy situation is to arise are acceptable.

- Consultation must begin 'in good time' as distinct from the 'earliest opportunity' as was formerly required and, in any case:
- Where the employer is proposing to dismiss 100 or more employees at one establishment within 90 days or less, consultation must begin 90 days before the first dismissals take effect. In cases involving less than 100 but at least 20 employees, consultation must begin 30 days before that date.
- Appropriate representatives must be given access to employees who are to be or may be made redundant and facilities, e.g. a telephone and office, must be made available to them.

The employer's other obligation is to notify BIS of proposed redundancies. The obligation is to give written notice to BIS:

- at least 90 days before any notice dismissal has been issued in the case of 100 or more redundancies;
- at least 30 days before any notice dismissal has been issued in the case of 20 or more redundancies.

The BIS has issued new regulations on notifying collective redundancies. The Collective Redundancies (Amendment) Regulations 2006 (SI 2006/2387) amend s 193 of the TULR(C)A 1992 to make it clear that employees must notify the Secretary of State at least 30 or 90 days (depending on the number of redundancies) before any *notice of dismissal* has been issued rather than before the first of the redundancies takes place. The employees thus get the full consultation period plus pay for the notice period plus any redundancy package.

The employer must give a copy of the notice to the relevant appropriate representatives.

If there are special circumstances which make it not reasonably practicable for the employer to comply with the requirements, he must do everything that is reasonably practicable. If the special circumstances prevent the full required notice being given, the employer must give as much notice as possible. Failure to comply with the above BIS requirements means that the employer can be prosecuted and fined.

Complaints about failure to consult can be made to an employment tribunal by any employee who has been or might be dismissed as redundant or by a recognised trade union or by any employee representative. The tribunal may make a *protective award* requiring the

employer to pay remuneration for up to 90 days where 90 days' minimum notice should have been given, or up to 30 days in any other case in which consultation was required.

Consultation was firmed up by legislation in 1993 which inserted new provisions into the TULR(C)A 1992, under which consultation must cover specific areas as follows: (a) the reason for the redundancy proposals; (b) the numbers and description of employees to be dismissed; (c) the method of selection for redundancy; (d) the procedure and timing of dismissals; and (e) the method of calculating any non-statutory redundancy payments, i.e. payments extra to the basic requirement. Consultation must also include a consideration of ways to avoid the redundancies and/or to reduce the number to be dismissed and to mitigate the consequences of the dismissals which do take place.

If a company is in the hands of an insolvency practitioner that practitioner must also follow the above procedures, though there may be special circumstances, such as the immediate collapse of the company, which make this impossible.

General standards of fairness for redundancy were laid down by the EAT in *Williams* v *Compair Maxam* (1982). These were the giving of maximum notice; consultation with unions, if any; the taking of the views of more than one person as to who should be dismissed; the requirement to follow any laid down procedure, e.g. last in, first out; and, finally, an effort to find the employees concerned alternative employment within the organisation. It should be noted that in *Meikle* v *McPhail* (*Charleston Arms*) (1983) the EAT stated that these guidelines would be applied less rigidly to the smaller business.

As we have seen, when a worker is to be made redundant, the ACAS code of practice and the decision in *Williams* v *Compair Maxam* (1982) (above) both stress the importance of consultation. An employer that does not act properly will no longer be able to say that, since subsequent events justified redundancy, as where the firm was insolvent, there was no point in consultation. An employer that fails to consult may face the more costly claim of unfair dismissal rather than redundancy. However, the law does not lay down that there must *always* be consultation, as the *Eclipse Blinds* case shows, but in most cases the law will require it.

Individual consultation may be required where the numbers are less than 20 and even where the numbers have been more, there has been consultation with representatives (*Mugford* v *Midland Bank plc* (1997)). The case states that a tribunal will at least listen to an allegation of unfairness by an individual even where the usual methods of consultation have been carried out.

It should also be noted:

- that consultation must cover employees who have volunteered for redundancy; and
- although consultation does not have to end in agreement, it must always be carried out.

It is, perhaps rather obviously, direct discrimination not to consult an employee about redundancy because she is on maternity leave and presumably also those who are on parental or adoption leave (see *McGuigan* v *T & G Baynes* (1999)).

Redundancy and other consultation requirements

The BIS has published a new guidance document on redundancy consultation and notification. The document also explains how the rather long-standing obligations contained in Part IV of the TULR(C)A 1992 (see above) fit in with the new duties of consultation under the Information and Consultation of Employees Regulations 2004 (SI 2004/3426) (ICE), which came into force for the larger companies on 6 April 2005.

As an answer to the question, 'Is there a minimum period for consultation?' the guidance states that '*the employer must begin the process of consultation in good time and complete the process before any redundancy notices are issued*' (BIS emphasis). The guidance refers to a decision of the ECJ in *Junk* v *Kühnel* (2005). This case dealt with redundancy in Germany and in fact the 1992 Act does not impose such an obligation. However, the BIS statement could well be relied upon in tribunals by those seeking to obtain a purposive judgment of the 1992 Act, i.e. the Act may not say this, but this was its purpose and intention.

The ICE Regulations require consultation and information to be undertaken or given to employees on an ongoing basis about issues affecting the business in which they work. From 6 April 2005 the regulations have applied to employers with at least 150 employees. From 6 April 2007 they will apply to undertakings employing at least 100 employees, and from 6 April 2008 to those with at least 50 employees.

The guidance states that the ICE Regulations are in addition to the 1992 Act provisions and makes the following points:

- An employer who proposes to make collective redundancies must comply with the 1992 Act, even though he has established separate consultation arrangements under the ICE Regulations. Thus, if a trade union is recognised in regard to employees affected by proposed collective redundancies, the employer must consult with representatives of that union, even where there is a separate group of employees put in place as a result of consultation requirements under the ICE Regulations.
- Where there is a separate group of employee representatives set up under the ICE Regulations, the employer will only be required to consult that group if he has agreed to do so as part of a 'negotiated agreement' under the ICE Regulations.
- An employer who is subject to the standard information and consultation provisions in the ICE Regulations need not consult employees under those provisions if notification is made to those representatives on each occasion, that the 1992 Act consultation duties have been triggered and that consultation will take place under the 1992 Act.

The role of ACAS

ACAS has now taken on redundancy pay entitlement as an issue on which it has a duty to conciliate. The Employment Rights (Dispute Resolution) Act 1998 confers a duty on ACAS to conciliate if a person puts in an application to an employment tribunal concerning entitlement to redundancy pay.

Collective agreements on redundancy

The Secretary of State may, on the application of the employer and the unions involved, make an order modifying the requirements of redundancy pay legislation if he is satisfied that there is a collective agreement which makes satisfactory alternative arrangements for dealing with redundancy. The provisions of the agreement must be 'on the whole at least as favourable' as the statutory provisions, and must include, in particular, arrangements allowing an employee to go to an independent arbitration or to make a complaint to an employment tribunal.

Other methods of termination of the contract of service

Having considered the termination of the contract by unfair or discriminatory dismissal or redundancy, we must now turn to other ways in which the contract of service may be brought to an end. These are set out below.

By notice

A contract of service can be brought to an end by either party giving notice to the other, although, where the employer gives notice, even in accordance with the contract of service or under the statutory provisions of the ERA 1996, he may still face a claim for unfair dismissal or a redundancy payment.

The most important practical aspect is the length of notice to be given by the parties, in particular the employer. The ERA 1996 contains statutory provisions in regard to *minimum* periods of notice and the only relevance of the express provisions of a particular contract of service on the matter is that a contract may provide for longer periods of notice than does the ERA. Under the ERA an employee is entitled to one week's notice after employment for one month or more; after two years' service the minimum entitlement is increased to two weeks, and for each year of service after that it is increased by one week up to a maximum of 12 weeks' notice after 12 years' service.

An employee, once he has been employed for one month or more, must give his employer one week's notice and the period of one week's notice applies for the duration of the contract so far as the employee is concerned, no matter how long he has served the employer. It should be noted that, so far as oral notice is concerned, it does not begin on the day it is given but on the following day. This means, for example, that in the case of oral notice seven days' notice means seven days exclusive of the day on which the notice is given (see *West* v *Kneels Ltd* (1986) below). There appears to be no particular ruling on written notice and so it may be that one could give notice starting from the date of the letter if the letter was served on the employee (or employer) on that day. However, it would seem preferable to commence the notice from the day after service of the letter.

West v *Kneels Ltd* (1986)

Julie West claimed that her employers had dismissed her unfairly. An employment tribunal decided that the claim failed because she had not been employed for the necessary qualifying period. This was true if the week's notice commenced on the day it was given. If it started the next day she would qualify. Mr Justice Popplewell decided that it accorded with good industrial practice that in the case of oral notice seven days' notice meant seven days exclusive of the day on which the notice was served. This meant that Julie West had in fact been employed for the necessary qualifying period.

Breach of the provisions relating to minimum periods of notice do not involve an employer in any penalty, but the rights conferred by the ERA 1996 will be taken into account in assessing the employer's liability for breach of contract. Thus an employer who has dismissed his employee without due notice is generally liable for the wages due to the employee for the appropriate period of notice at the contract rate.

It should be noted that the ERA 1996 provisions regarding minimum periods of notice do not affect the common law rights of an employer to dismiss an employee at once without notice for misconduct, e.g. disobedience, neglect, drunkenness or dishonesty. An example is to be found in *Connor* v *Kwik Fit Insurance Services Ltd* (1997), where the managing director of an insurance company, who had falsely declared when signing a professional indemnity insurance form that he had not been involved with any company that had been wound up, was guilty of gross misconduct and could be summarily dismissed.

In practice, a contract of service is often terminated by a payment instead of notice and this is allowed by the ERA 1996.

In these days when there is a great need for skilled personnel, it is tempting for employees to break their contracts by leaving at short notice to go to other jobs. However, in *Evening Standard Co Ltd* v *Henderson* (1987) the employer, Evening Standard, was granted an injunction to restrain an employee from working for a rival during his contractual notice period of 12 months as long as the employer agreed (which he did) to provide him with remuneration and other contractual benefits until the proper notice period would have run out, or, alternatively, let him stay at work until the proper notice period had expired.

By agreement

As in any other contract, the parties to a contract of employment may end the contract by agreement. Thus, if employer and employee agree to new terms and conditions on, for example, a promotion of the employee, the old agreement is discharged and a new one takes over.

An employee could agree to be 'bought off' by his employer under an agreement to discharge the existing contract of service. In this connection it should be noted that discharge of a contract of service by agreement is not a 'dismissal' for the purposes, for example, of an unfair dismissal claim, but should a claim for unfair dismissal be brought by an employee who has been 'bought off', the tribunal concerned will want to see evidence of a genuine and fair agreement by employer and employee and may allow a claim of unfair dismissal if the discharging agreement is one-sided and biased in favour of the employer.

By passage of time

In the case of a fixed-term contract, as where an employee is engaged for, say, three years, the contract will terminate at the end of the three years, though there may be provisions for notice within that period.

By frustration

A contract of service can, as we have already seen, be discharged by frustration which could be incapacity, such as illness. However, other events can bring about the discharge of a contract of service by frustration, e.g. a term of imprisonment. Thus, in *Hare* v *Murphy Bros* (1974) Hare was a foreman employed by Murphy Bros. He was sentenced to 12 months' imprisonment for unlawful wounding and could not, obviously, carry out his employment. The court held that his contract was frustrated.

Furthermore, death of either employer or employee will discharge the contract by frustration from the date of the death so that, for example, the personal representatives of the employer are not required to continue with the contract. However, the estate has a claim for wages or salary due at the date of death.

Under the ERA 1996 claims for unfair dismissal arising before the employer's death survive and may be brought after the death of the employer against his estate.

Furthermore, the death of a human employer is usually regarded as a 'dismissal' for redundancy purposes and the employee may make a claim against the employer's estate.

If the employee is re-engaged or the personal representatives renew his contract within eight weeks of the employer's death, the employee is not regarded as having been dismissed. Where an offer of renewal or re-engagement is refused on reasonable grounds by the employee, then he is entitled to a redundancy payment. If he unreasonably refuses to renew his contract or accept a suitable offer of re-engagement he is not entitled to such a payment.

Ordinary partnership dissolution

A person who is employed by an ordinary partnership which is dissolved is regarded as dismissed on dissolution of the firm. Under the ERA 1996 this is regarded as having occurred because of redundancy.

The dismissal is also regarded as wrongful at common law and there may be a claim by the employee for damages but these will be nominal only if the partnership business continues and the continuing partners offer new employment on the old terms (*Brace* v *Calder* (1895)).

A partnership is dissolved whenever one partner dies or becomes bankrupt or leaves the firm for any reason, e.g. retirement. However, the business usually continues under a provision in the partnership articles but there is nevertheless a technical dissolution.

Of course, if a firm or sole trader sells the business as a going concern, employees are transferred to the new employer automatically under the Transfer of Undertakings (Protection of Employment) Regulations 2006.

Limited liability partnerships: administration and liquidation

The rules set out above for the ordinary partnership do not apply to limited liability partnerships under the Limited Liability Partnerships Act 2000 and regulations made under it. Such a partnership is a separate legal person from its members, and the insolvency structures applying to it in terms of the appointment of an administrator and of a liquidator mirror the corporate legal rules set out below.

Appointment of an administrator – corporate rehabilitation

The object of administration orders is *primarily* to allow a company to be put on a profitable basis if possible, or at least disposed of more profitably than would be the case if other forms of insolvency proceedings, such as liquidation, were used. On the appointment of an administrator, the company's executive and other directors are not dismissed but their powers of management are exercisable only if the administrator consents. He also has power to dismiss and appoint directors.

Since an administrator is made an agent of the company by the court under the administration order, employees are not automatically dismissed. In addition, an administrator who wishes to trade with the company and for that purpose to retain employees may adopt their contracts of employment. Such adoption is automatic. This does not mean that he and his firm will become employers in the true sense. However, if, when the administrator finishes his work and leaves the company, there are outstanding, e.g., any wages or salaries of retained employees, they must be paid before the administrator is entitled to his fees and expenses. The effect of adoption is not, therefore, to make an administrator personally liable for wages or salary, but adoption may affect their fees and expenses. This provision is to correct a possible unfairness which existed under the previous law before the coming into force of the present insolvency provisions which are contained in the Insolvency Act 1986 (as amended by the Insolvency Act 2000). In earlier times an administrator would have been able to take the services of an employee of the company for a short period of time and then say 'your contract is with the company: the company is insolvent and I do not intend to pay you'. Thus the employee might work without any right to pay. As we have seen under the provisions of the current law, if an administrator allows an employee of the company to contribute his services, he is deemed to have adopted the contract and the employee must be paid before the insolvency practitioner is entitled to his fees and expenses.

If, of course, an administrator dismisses an employee, that employee can make a claim for a redundancy payment.

It is worth noting that the above provisions of the Insolvency Act 1986 relating to adoption of employment contracts gave insolvency practitioners an incentive to opt out of the liability and statements made in the High Court in *Re Withall and Conquest and Specialised Moldings Ltd* (1987) to the effect that a form of letter sent to employees during the first 14 days of an administration or administrative receivership disclaiming adoption would work to the extent that during an administration or receivership remuneration including holiday pay and contributions to occupational pension schemes would be paid, as was the practice anyway where the insolvency practitioner traded on, but no more. The major concern of insolvency practitioners was to get rid of the potential liability to make payments in lieu of notice. If trading fails an insolvency practitioner is rarely able to give employees notice and in the case of senior employees the notice period may be three months or more and since such employees are usually on high salaries the potential burden is considerable. However, in *Powdrill v Watson* (1994) the Court of Appeal held that the letter was of no effect and that after the requisite 14 days employment contracts were adopted including liability to pay in lieu of notice. In order to sustain the administration and receivership procedures which would have otherwise collapsed, leaving liquidation as the only insolvency procedure, the government rushed through Parliament the Insolvency Act 1994 which confirms that contracts are adopted but restricts the liability of the insolvency practitioner to certain 'qualifying liabilities'. Only these liabilities will be payable in priority to other claims such as the holder of a floating charge and preferential creditors and the fees and expenses of the insolvency practitioner. The qualifying liabilities are wages or salaries including sickness and holiday pay and contributions to occupational pension schemes. Payments in lieu of notice are not included. The liabilities concerned must have been incurred after the adoption of the contract. Other employment liabilities will remain but will be treated as unsecured claims against the company and may not be paid in view of the insolvency unless the insolvency practitioner can trade out of trouble.

Demise of the administrative receiver

Where a company had borrowed money and given security for the loan by charging its assets under a debenture, the debenture holders could if, for example, they were not paid interest on the loan, appoint a receiver and manager, later referred to as an administrative receiver. The most common appointment was by a bank in respect of an overdraft or loan facility to a company.

There is no point in dealing with the effect of the appointment of an administrative receiver on contracts of employment since under the Insolvency Act 1986 these appointments can no longer be made except in very specialised areas beyond the scope of this text. Those, such as banks and other secured creditors, can now only appoint administrators or liquidators.

Company liquidation

The possibilities are as follows:

1 A compulsory winding-up. Here the court orders the winding-up of the company, usually on the petition of a creditor because it cannot pay his debt. The making of a compulsory winding-up order by the court may have the following effects according to the circumstances of the case:

(a) Where the company's business ceases, the winding-up order will operate as a wrongful dismissal of employees.

(b) Where the liquidator continues the business, as where he allows employees to continue with work in progress in order to make complete and more saleable products, he may be regarded as an agent of the company so that the employment continues. Alternatively, the court may regard the appointment of the liquidator as a giving of notice to the employee who then works out that notice under the liquidator. It is, however, the better view that employees may, if they so choose, regard themselves as dismissed because the company has ceased to employ them, the new contract being with the liquidator. In practice, if the liquidator continues to use the services of the employees and pays them, the Department of Work and Pensions treats the redundancy of the employees as occurring at the time of their eventual dismissal by the liquidator.

2 A voluntary winding-up. This commences on the resolution of the members and if the company's business ceases there is a dismissal of employees. If the company's business continues, the position would appear to be as set out in 1(b) above.

Bankruptcy

The bankruptcy of an employer, such as a sole trader, or indeed of the employee, does not automatically discharge the contract of service, though it will if there is a term to that effect in the agreement. Thus, the employment can continue, though in practical terms it may

be impossible to pay employees' wages, and in this case they will be discharged and will be able to make a claim for a redundancy payment, as well as one in the bankruptcy for wages accrued, in regard to which they have a preferential claim in the bankruptcy.

A trustee in bankruptcy cannot insist that an employee continue in service because the contract is one of a personal nature. The bankruptcy of an employee will not normally affect the contract of service unless there is a term to that effect in the contract. Company directors provide a special case since the articles of most companies provide for termination of the office on becoming bankrupt.

Wrongful and summary dismissal at common law

The claim at common law for wrongful dismissal is based on a general principle of the law of contract, i.e. wrongful repudiation of the contract of service by the employer.

The common law action has, of course, been largely taken over by the statutory provisions relating to unfair dismissal and a common law claim is only likely to be brought by an employee who has a fixed-term contract at a high salary. Thus a company director who has a fixed-term contract for, say, three years at a salary of £150,000 per annum might, if wrongfully dismissed, find it more profitable in terms of damages obtainable to sue at common law for breach of contract, though the employer may be able to resist the claim where the employee was guilty, for example, of misconduct, disobedience or immorality.

This may well change since there is now no monetary cap at all where dismissal is because the employee has blown the whistle on his employer and reports, e.g., a health and safety infringement within the organisation to the Health and Safety Executive or a suspected fraud to a City of London regulator, such as the Financial Services Authority.

In other cases where the contract of service is not for a fixed term, there is no claim for damages at common law, provided that the employer gives proper notice or pays wages instead of notice, though in such a case the employee has, at least potentially, a claim for unfair dismissal which he could pursue. Again, the employer may resist a claim for unfair dismissal on the basis of misconduct, disobedience or immorality. We have already given some consideration to these matters in the context of statutory unfair dismissal.

Under powers given by s 3 of the Employment Tribunals Act 1996, employment tribunals can hear cases of wrongful dismissal, though there is a cap of £25,000 (i.e. *less* than the statutory claim for unfair dismissal) on the damages that can be awarded. Claims for higher sums must be made in the county court or High Court.

Wrongful dismissal and unfair dismissal: effect of damages cap

What is the position where a tribunal hears a case for wrongful dismissal and, while accepting that the claimant's loss is greater, makes an award of £25,000 being governed by its cap? Can the claimant then proceed with a claim in a county court or the High Court for the balance between the capped award and the actual loss?

The Court of Appeal dealt with this situation in the following case.

Fraser v HLMAD Ltd (2007)

F appealed against an order striking out his claim form and dismissing his wrongful dismissal claim in the High Court against HLMAD Ltd. F's dismissal was effected by insolvency practitioners of HLMAD Ltd. F claimed unfair dismissal and wrongful dismissal before a tribunal. In his claim initiating proceedings in the tribunal he stated that he reserved the right to pursue an action in the High Court for damages for wrongful dismissal in excess of £25,000, the tribunal maximum. F later began an action in the High Court for wrongful dismissal but did not withdraw the tribunal claim. The tribunal went on to rule in F's favour on the unfair dismissal and the wrongful dismissal claims, capping the damages on the latter claim to £25,000, even though it found that F had suffered a greater loss.

F's claim in the High Court was struck out and this was upheld by the Court of Appeal.

The civil procedure rule of merger applied. The effect of a judgment for the claimant absorbs any claim that was the subject of the action into the judgment so that the claimant's rights are then confined to enforcing the judgment. The claim for the excess over £25,000 was not a separate cause of action, since this could not be split into two causes of action: one for damage up to £25,000, and another for the balance. A claimant who expected to recover more than £25,000 for wrongful dismissal should bring that claim in the county court or High Court. The merger of the claim into the judgment of the tribunal was not prevented by the express statement made in the tribunal claim form that F reserved his right to bring High Court proceedings for the excess of £25,000.

The wrongful dismissal claim

Some of the main reasons for preferring a wrongful dismissal claim are as follows:

- An employee who is dismissed may not have completed the one year's service required for an unfair dismissal claim. This bar does not apply to wrongful dismissal claims.
- The time limit – i.e. three months – for bringing claims of unfair dismissal may have expired. The period for wrongful dismissal, which is a common law claim in the county court or High Court, is six years from dismissal. However, the three-month period applies to wrongful dismissal claims before an employment tribunal, unless the tribunal decides that it was not 'reasonably practicable' for the complaint to be presented during that period.
- Awards for unfair dismissal may be reduced substantially by a sum representing the fault of the employees – e.g. late arrival at work. Damages for wrongful dismissal are not subject to a deduction for contributory fault.
- The damages for wrongful dismissal in the case, e.g., of a highly paid person could still well exceed the maximum amount of compensation available for unfair dismissal – where the compensatory award is currently a maximum of £63,000.

When does wrongful dismissal occur?

The main situations of wrongful dismissal are as follows:

- where the contract is of indefinite duration but terminable by notice, the termination of the contract without notice or with shorter notice than that to which the employee is entitled, and, of course, summary dismissal without any notice at all;
- in the case of a fixed-term contract, termination before the fixed term expires;
- in the case of a contract to carry out a specific task, termination before the task is completed;
- where the employer dismisses the employee on disciplinary grounds but does not follow a procedure laid down in the contract;
- selection for redundancy in breach of a procedure set out in the contract.

When dismissal is justified

Various forms of misconduct will justify a dismissal. As we have seen in *Connor v Kwik Fit Insurance Services Ltd*

(1997), the managing director of an insurance company, who had falsely declared when signing a professional indemnity insurance form that he had not been involved with any company that had been wound up, failed in a claim for wrongful dismissal. Again, in *Blayney* v *Colne Liberal Club* (1995) a bar steward's claim for wrongful dismissal failed. He had been summarily dismissed for failure to hand over the bar takings to his employer or to put them in the safe and hand over the safe keys.

Rights and remedies on dismissal

These are as follows.

Written statement of reasons for dismissal

At common law an employer is not required to give his employee any reasons for dismissal. However, the ERA 1996 provides that where an employee is dismissed, with or without notice, or by failure to renew a contract for a fixed term, he must be provided by his employer on request, within 14 days of that request, with a written statement giving particulars of the reasons for his dismissal. This provision applies only to employees who have been continuously employed full or part time for a period of one year (ERA 1996, s 92), though there is no service requirement in pregnancy dismissals. All women, regardless of service or hours worked, have a right to written reasons for dismissal if dismissed while pregnant or during the statutory maternity leave period and regardless of whether the woman requests it or not. The written statement is admissible in evidence in any proceedings relating to the dismissal and if an employer refuses to give a written statement the employee may complain to an employment tribunal. If the tribunal upholds the complaint, it may make a declaration as to what it finds the employer's reasons were for dismissing the employee and must make an award of two weeks' pay without limit as to amount to the employee.

Employer's insolvency

If the employer is bankrupt or dies insolvent, or where the employer is a company and is in liquidation, the unpaid wages of an employee have under Sch 6 to the Insolvency Act 1986 priority as to payment but only to a

maximum of £800 (taken by insolvency practitioners to be the *gross* wage) and limited to services rendered during the period of four months before the commencement of the insolvency. Any balance over £800 or four months ranks as an ordinary debt. Also preferential is accrued holiday remuneration payable to an employee on the termination of his employment before or because of the insolvency.

The Schedule adds to the above preferential debts by including in the list sums owed in respect of statutory guarantee payments, payments during statutory time off for trade union duties, antenatal care and to look for work, remuneration on suspension for medical grounds, or remuneration under a protective award given because of failure to consult properly on redundancy. Statutory Sick Pay, Statutory Maternity Pay, parental leave and adoption leave pay are also preferential.

It should also be noted that under the ERA 1996 an employee may, in the case of his employer's insolvency, make a claim on the National Insurance Fund rather than relying on the preferential payments procedure set out above. The relevant insolvency practitioner, e.g. a liquidator, will *normally* calculate what is due and obtain authorisation through BIS. In so far as any part of this payment is preferential, the rights and remedies of the employees concerned are transferred to the BIS, which becomes preferential in respect of them.

The limits of the employee's claim on the National Insurance Fund are as follows:

- arrears of pay for a period not exceeding eight weeks with a maximum of £290 per week;
- holiday pay with a limit of six weeks and a financial limit of £290 per week;
- payments instead of notice at a rate not exceeding £290 per week;
- payments outstanding in regard to an award by an employment tribunal of compensation for unfair dismissal;
- reimbursement of any fee or premium paid by an apprentice or articled clerk.

There is no qualifying period before an employee becomes eligible and virtually all people in employment are entitled and the amount of £290 refers to the employee's *gross* wage.

It should be noted that claims on the National Insurance Fund were, in the past, not admitted unless the relevant insolvency practitioner gave the BIS a state-ment of the amount due, though this could payments made if there was likely to be an unreasonable delay in providing the statement. Chapter VI of the ERA 1996 now provides that the DTI (now BIS) may make payments without a statement if it is satisfied that adequate evidence of the amounts due has been made available. Nevertheless, the relevant insolvency practitioner will normally provide a statement.

Damages for wrongful dismissal

An award of damages is the most usual remedy for wrongful dismissal. The period by reference to which damages will be calculated is either:

- in the case of a contract of indefinite duration, the period between the date of wrongful dismissal and the earliest date on which the employer could lawfully have terminated the contract – generally the date required by the period of notice set out in the contract. If no such period is expressed in the contract, the court will imply a 'reasonable' period or the minimum period laid down in s 86 of the Employment Rights Act 1996, whichever is the longer; *or*
- if the employee was employed under a fixed-term contract, the damages period will in general be the unexpired remainder of the fixed term, unless the employer could terminate the contract by notice before the fixed term expired, in which case the damages period will be the period of that notice.

Case law has laid down 'reasonable' periods of notice in the absence of specific provision in the contract. These vary from three months for a company director (*James v Kent & Co Ltd* (1950)) to one week for a hairdresser's assistant (*Marulsens* v *Leon* (1919)) – though, according to length of service, the ERA 1996 periods, which may be longer in the latter case, could apply.

Heads of damage

No damages can be recovered for the manner of dismissal – e.g. for hurt feelings – nor for the fact that the dis~~al~~ may make it more difficult to get another job.

~~...er,~~ a claim may be made for loss of pension
~~...tion~~ rights and other fringe benefits such
~~...~~t only to the extent that it was made

otherwise damages will be reduced by the sum that could reasonably have been earned from new employment or self-employment during the damages period. The court will take into account the nature of any reference given to the employee and the difficulty a dismissed employee may have in finding other suitable work.

Where there is a contractual provision that allows the employer to summarily dismiss the employee on making a payment in lieu of notice but he fails to pay it, that sum, when claimed, is in the nature of liquidated (or agreed) damages and is not subject to mitigation. It is payable, therefore, without deduction even where the ex-employee goes straight into another job (see *Cerberus Software Ltd* v *Rowley* (1999)).

Damages are compensatory

If the employee had worked during the damages period, he would have received net, not gross, pay. Thus, under the common law rule set out in *BTC* v *Gourley* (1955) the court will deduct from the gross award a notional sum to represent income tax. Under the Income Tax (Earnings and Pensions) Act 2003 the first £30,000 of the net award is tax-free. If the net award exceeds that sum, the balance will be taxed again in the ex-employee's hands. Therefore, the court will add a sum to the non-exempt balance to ensure that after payment of tax on the sum awarded, the ex-employee is left with an appropriate net sum (see *Shove* v *Downs Surgical plc* (1984)).

Example

Fred, a managing director on a gross salary of £120,000 a year and with a contract giving him the right to receive six months' notice, is dismissed without notice. His net pay is calculated at £80,000 so he is awarded £40,000 for failure to give him notice. The first £30,000 of this sum is tax free but £10,000 will be taxed again as income for the year in which the damages are received, at his highest rate (currently 40 per cent). If Fred's tax liability on the £10,000 is estimated to be £4,000, the award will be £44,000, so that, after payment of that tax, Fred ends up with £40,000.

The equitable remedy of specific performance and injunction

A decree of specific performance is, as we have seen, an order of the court and constitutes an express instruction to a party to a contract to perform the actual obligations which he undertook under its terms. If the person who is subject to the order fails to comply with it, he is in contempt of court and potentially liable to be fined or imprisoned until he complies with the order and thus purges his contempt. For all practical purposes the remedy is not given to enforce performance of a contract of service, largely because the court cannot supervise that its order is being carried out. A judge would have to attend the place of work on a regular basis to see that the parties were implementing the contract.

An injunction is, as we have seen, an order of the court whereby an individual is required to refrain from the further doing of the act complained of. Again, a person who is subject to such an order and fails to comply with it is in contempt of court and the consequences set out above follow from the contempt. An injunction may be used to prevent many wrongful acts, e.g. the torts of trespass and nuisance, but in the context of contract the remedy has been granted to enforce a negative stipulation in a contract in a situation where it would be unjust to confine the claimant to damages. An injunction has been used as an indirect method of enforcing a contract for personal services, but a clear negative stipulation is required. Reference should be made to *Warner Brothers v Nelson* (1936) in Chapter 7 as an illustration of the application of the negative stipulation rule and the developments in it in more recent times ◗.

In this connection it should also be noted that s 236 of the Trade Union and Labour Relations (Consolidation) Act 1992 provides that no court shall by way of specific performance or an injunction compel an *employee* to do any work or attend any place for the doing of any work.

Thus although, as the *Warner Bros* case illustrates, an injunction was potentially available to enforce compliance with a contract of employment, the prohibition in s 236 (above) prevents a court from issuing a decree of specific performance or an injunction *against an employee*. The section would not affect the use at least of an injunction where the contract was for services and not employment, as would be the case between a boxer and his manager though even there the courts are reluctant to make the order (see *Warren v Mendy* (1989)).

Employee's breach of contract

An employer may sue his employees for damages for breach of the contract of service by the employee. Such claims are potentially available, for example, for damage to the employer's property, as where machinery is damaged by negligent operation, as was the case in *Baster v London and County Printing Works* (1899), or for refusal to work resulting in damage by lost production, as was the case in *National Coal Board v Galley* (1958). Such claims are rare and impractical because of the fact that the employee will not, in most cases, be able to meet the claim, and also, perhaps more importantly, because they lead to industrial unrest. In these circumstances we do not pursue the matter further here.

Actions by employers against their employees are, of course, not uncommon in the area of contracts in restraint of trade and for breach of the duty of confidentiality. These matters were considered in Chapter 7 to which reference should be made ◗.

Self-test questions/activities

1 How is the relationship of employer and worker established?

2 In connection with the provisions for maternity leave and statutory maternity pay:
   (a) What is the maximum leave entitlement?
   (b) What is the amount of maternity pay?
   (c) For how long must the claimant have been continuously employed?

3 Des and Eric are both employed by a bus company. Des is a bus driver and Eric a conductor. Eric has always nursed an ambition to be a driver and Des has, on occasion, let Eric drive a bus around the depot before other employees turned up for work. Last week, while Eric was having a drive around the yard, he struck Des who was riding his motor bike around the yard at 60 mph. Discuss the liability of Eric and the bus company in regard to the injuries suffered by Des.

4 Monty signalled to a van driver of Python Ltd to stop and asked him to take him to the Grotty Towers Hotel. The hotel was some five miles away from the

route which the driver would usually take in the course of his duties, but he nevertheless agreed to give Monty a lift to the hotel. When the driver had deviated a quarter of a mile from his authorised route, he carelessly collided with another vehicle and Monty was injured. As company secretary of Python Ltd, you have received a letter from a firm of solicitors representing Monty threatening legal action against Python Ltd. Your managing director asks you to draft a memorandum for him on the legal aspects of the case. Draft the memorandum.

5 You have recently been appointed the company secretary of Foundry Ltd. The following problems emerge at the first board meeting.

   (a) The members of the board are concerned as to whether they are taking appropriate steps to communicate with the employees as to how the company is fulfilling its obligations under health and safety legislation. You are asked to write an explanatory memorandum for the next board meeting as to the legal requirements and indicate the steps which the company should be taking.

   (b) It appears that Foundry Ltd employs 100 women and 50 men in an area where there is a large number of immigrant families. The managing director appears to have paid little or no attention to sex, race and equal pay legislation. The board, which is concerned about this, asks for an explanatory memorandum, again, for the next board meeting, summarising the main provisions of the relevant legislation and setting out procedures which the company should adopt to ensure that the law is complied with.

6 John is one of the employees of a firm in which you are a partner. He suffers badly from arthritis. He has been employed for 10 years. However, he has had a number of absences of two to three weeks' duration over the past three years. John is employed as a shop assistant and the manager of the shop has just informed you that John has now been off work for eight weeks with arthritis and is still not fit to come back to work. The manager wants to write to John telling him that he is dismissed. Prepare a note for your next partnership meeting as to the legal position if John is dismissed.

7 Alan worked for 10 years for Pleasant Ltd. It was taken over 18 months ago by Aggressive Ltd and Alan continued in his job. He has found the management of Aggressive Ltd to be very difficult and domineering. Amongst other things, the management has asked him to work in the stores issuing and accounting for equipment issued to Aggressive's employees. Alan feels that he has not been trained to do this and has given in his notice. Advise him as to his rights.

8 The company of which you are secretary makes components for cars. Business has fallen off lately and the board has decided that it will have to dismiss 120 employees during the next five weeks. Write an explanatory memorandum to the board regarding any legal requirements there may be in terms of:

   (a) notification of the redundancies;
   (b) selection of employees for redundancy;
   (c) amounts of compensation that may be involved;
   (d) the consultation requirements.

Specimen examination questions

1 (a) Explain by reference to case law how the courts make the distinction between a contract of service and a contract for services. What is the importance of this distinction?

   (b) Fred is employed by Dan's Garage. John, a customer, fills up with petrol and goes to pay. Because of a mechanical fault there is a difference between the value of the sale shown by the pump and that shown by the terminal which Fred is using. Fred insists that the pump is wrong and that the value of the sale is £5 more than the pump is showing. There is an argument and suddenly Fred gives John a punch which breaks his nose. John is now claiming against Dan on the basis that he is liable for the damage resulting from the assault.
   Explain the legal position to Dan.

2 Jane has recently taken up employment as an accounts clerk at Bodge Builders' warehouse. She is the only female employee at the premises. Jane has complained to Joe the foreman that she is constantly being subjected to remarks by some of the male employees comparing her physique and sexual attractiveness unfavourably with a large number of female pin-ups which the men have posted conspicuously in various parts of the warehouse that can be seen from Jane's office. Advise the management in terms of liability.

3 Tom and Harry are shop assistants and short of cash. They decide to borrow from the till. Tom leaves a note in the till and replaces the money the following day. Harry neither leaves a note nor does he replace the money. The employer has discovered what has happened and wishes to dismiss Tom and Harry but does not wish to incur liability. Advise the employer.

Website references

http://www.acas.org.uk/index.aspx?articleid=2174 ACAS (Advisory, Conciliation and Arbitration Service) website provides guidance on disciplinary and grievance procedures.

http://www.bis.gov.uk/policies/ employment-matters/rights For guidance on employment rights, see Department for Business, Innovation and Skills website.

http://www.equalityhumanrights.com/ advice-and-guidance/guidance-equality-act-2010/ equality-act-2010-guidance Equality and Human Rights Commission Guidance on recruitment.

http://www.cipd.co.uk Also useful in the above area, the Chartered Institute of Personnel and Development.

http://www.direct.gov.uk/en/Employment/Employees/ Pay/index.htm For guidance on the National Minimum Wage.

http://www.lowpay.gov.uk The Low Pay Commission.

http://www.ico.gov.uk The Information Commissioner's Office is an independent supervisory authority that reports directly to Parliament. See the following link for their guidance on how the Data Protection Act applies to employment: http://www.ico.gov.uk/upload/ documents/library/data_protection/practical_application/ references_v1.0_final.pdf.

http://www.equalityhumanrights.com On equal pay and equality in employment generally, the Commission for Equality and Human Rights.

Visit **www.mylawchamber.co.uk/richesallen** to access study support resources including answers to questions in this chapter and legal updates, all linked to the **Pearson eText** version of **Keenan and Riches' Business Law** which you can **search**, **highlight** and **personalise** with your **own notes** and **bookmarks**.

Use **Case Navigator** to read in full some of the key cases referenced in this chapter with commentary and questions:

Fairchild v *Glenhaven Funeral Services Ltd* (2002)
Barber v *Somerset County Council* (2004)
Post Office v *Foley; HSBC Bank* v *Madden* (2001)
Johnson v *Unisys Ltd* (2001)

Index